New Teaching Solutions

Teacher Wraparound Edition

- Classroom Strategies
- Individualized Assessment
- Study Skills and Standardized Test-Taking Practice

Digital Solutions

- TeacherWorks™ Plus CD
- Presentation Plus! CD
- Interactive Student Edition CD

Teacher Support

- Using Graphic Organizers
- Unit Thematic Projects
- Integrating Reading and Mathematics

Welcome to Glencoe Online

Log on to the *Business and Personal Law* Online Learning Center at glencoe.com

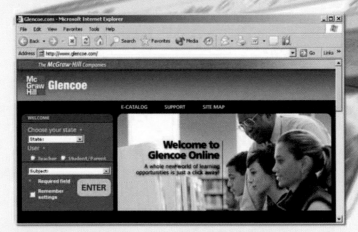

Learn Anytime, Anywhere

- Podcasts
- Study-to-Go™

Succeed Online

- Homework Hints
- Self-Check Quizzes

Study Independently

- Test Preparation
- WebQuest Internet Projects

Teacher Wraparound Edition

Glencoe
Business and Personal Law
Real-World Connections

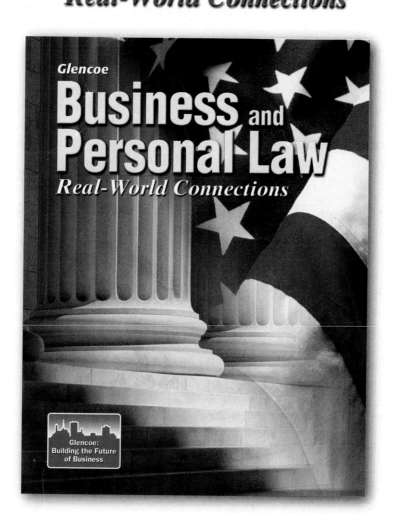

Glencoe
Business and Personal Law
Real-World Connections

Glencoe: Building the Future of Business

Teacher Manual

Gordon W. Brown, J. D.
Member of the Massachusetts Bar
Professor Emeritus of Law
North Shore Community College
Beverly, Massachusetts

Paul A. Sukys, J. D.
Member of the Ohio Bar
Professor of Law and Legal Studies
North Central State College
Mansfield, Ohio

 Glencoe

New York, New York   Columbus, Ohio   Chicago, Illinois   Woodland Hills, California

Our Partners at McGraw-Hill

STANDARD &POOR'S

Standard & Poor's is the world's leading provider of independent investment research, indexes, and ratings. The investment data and analysis provided by *Standard and Poor's* are used around the world by financial decision-makers to help create growth and manage wealth. *Standard & Poor's* publishes the S&P 1200, the premier global equity performance benchmark; the S&P 500, the premier U.S. financial-market index; and credit ratings on more than 220,000 securities and funds worldwide.

BusinessWeek

BusinessWeek is the leading global resource for ground-breaking business news and news analysis that offers essential insight into the real world of business. *BusinessWeek* is the world's most widely read business magazine, with more than 8 million readers each week, including online and television viewers.

 Glencoe

The **McGraw·Hill** Companies

Send all inquiries to:
Glencoe/McGraw-Hill
21600 Oxnard Street, Suite 500
Woodland Hills, CA 91367

ISBN: 978-0-07-874369-6   (Student Edition)
MHID: 0-07-874369-9   (Student Edition)
ISBN: 978-0-07-874370-2   (Teacher Wraparound Edition)
MHID: 0-07-874370-2   (Teacher Wraparound Edition)

1 2 3 4 5 6 7 8 9   027/043   12 11 10 09 08 07

Meet Our Authors

Gordon W. Brown has taught at the high school and the college level for 38 years. He attended Suffolk University Law School, Boston, MA, at night for four years, while teaching during the day. After law school, he became a member of the Massachusetts Bar. In 1998, Mr. Brown was awarded the Outstanding Educator Award from his alma mater, Salem State College. In addition to this text, Mr. Brown is the co-author of *Business Law with UCC Applications*, *Legal Terminology*, and *Administration of Wills, Trusts, and Estates*.

Paul A. Sukys is professor of philosophy, law, and legal studies in the Business and Education Division of North Central State College in Mansfield, OH. In addition to teaching business law courses at North Central State College, he specializes in teaching interdisciplinary courses such as, The Legal and Ethical Aspect of Health Care.
    He is co-author of *Business Law with UCC Applications*. He was chairperson of the Business Law Committee in the development of the National Standards for Business Education established by the National Business Education Association (NBEA).

Business and Career Education Industry Advisory Board

Peggy Bradfield
Vons, A Safeway Co.
Burbank, CA

Andy Chaves
Marriott International Inc.
Washington, DC

Mike De Fabio
Otis Spunkmeyer
Torrance, CA

Brian Dunn
JD Power & Associates
Westlake Village, CA

Donna Farrugia
Carrie Nebens
Robert Half International
Westlake Village, CA

Mark Hatch
Ohio Association of Public
  School Employees
Columbus, OH

Mike Kulis
Sherwin Williams Co.
Cleveland, OH

Dr. David M. Mitchell
Johnson & Wales University
Providence, RI

Debbie Moreton
JCPenney
Dallas, TX

Joyce Winterton
USA Today
McLean, VA

Educational Reviewers

We wish to acknowledge the contributions of the following reviewers:

Barbara Beadle
Program Specialist, Business
Indiana

Katherine Bullard
Middleton High School
Tampa, FL

Cheryl Cooper
Southeast Career Center
Columbus, OH

Joy Davis
Delaware Area Career Center
Delaware, OH

Linda Gallo
Sickles High School
Tampa, FL

Karol Gotte
Largo High School
Largo, FL

Brian Gray
Myers Park High School
Charlotte, NC

Colleen Hunt
Iowa State Department of Education
State Business Education Department

John Husinka
East Bay High School
Gibsonton, FL

Vivian King
Independence High School
Columbus, OH

Connie Meek
CCSD
Coordinator, Business Education
Nevada

Elaine Metcalf
Chairperson/Career & Tech Education
   Facilitator
Missouri

Vanessa Moorhead
Alonso High School
Tampa, FL

Jennifer Morley
Blake High School
Tampa, FL

Barb Motley

Deanna Peck
David W. Butler High School
Matthews, NC

Terri Phillips
H. B. Pant High School
Tampa, FL

Janet Richards
Riverview High School
Riverview, FL

Josephine Rumore
Tampa Bay Tech High School
Tampa, FL

Natalie Schaublin
Westerville North High School
Westerville, OH

Michelle See
East Mecklenburg High School
Charlotte, NC

Rebecca Seher
ROP District
Long Beach, CA

Julie Smith
Southeast Career Center
Columbus, OH

Jaclyn Soles
East Bay High School
Tampa, FL

Glenn Stamm
Osceola High School
Seminole, FL

JoeAnn Streeter
Supervisor, Business Technology
Tampa, FL

Eileen Wascisin
Lynden High School
Lynden, WA

Liz Watt
North Education Center High School
Columbus, OH

Legal Reviewer:

Mark Mathiasen, J.D., Esq.,
Middleton, ID

Contributing Writers:

Jane A. Brown
Groveland, MS

Donna Lee Sirkis, MBA, MAEd,
CMS-Myers Park High School, Charlotte, NC

We wish to acknowledge the National Business Education Association for the development of national business law standards which this book was developed to meet. We also thank the National Council of Teachers of English, the National Council of Teachers of Mathematics, and the National Council for the Social Studies for allowing the use of their national standards in this textbook.

Teacher Wraparound Edition
Table of Contents

CONNECT
students TO THE **COMMUNITY,**

Units

The 21 chapters in *Business and Personal Law* are organized into seven units, each with its own theme. The unit opening content previews activities and themes in the chapters ahead.

Thematic Project Preview This activity launches a capstone project that students can work on throughout the unit. Use this preview to stimulate research and design strategies to complete the project.

Web Quest This feature dovetails with the unit's topic, giving students a hint at how to start their research.

Standard & Poor's leads the unit with a question and answer session on a pressing financial question. This is also an opportunity to expand the discussion to the unit's forthcoming chapters and to ask students to conduct some research online.

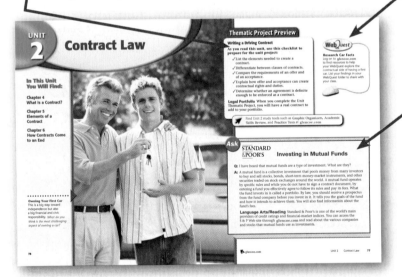

real COMPANIES, and real CAREERS.

Careers in Law
This feature provides students with inside access to the world of business law. Read an interview with a law professional, and discover the skills training needed to fulfill the position.

The Writing Connection Allow students to sharpen their research and writing skills, two key factors needed in all of academics. They will also incorporate the Writing Tips and Essay Test Strategies for standardized testing and collegiate entrance exams.

The **Thematic Project** applies concepts students have learned and turns them into a valuable portfolio project that will show their diversity of interests.

Landmark Cases are extensive extracts of real court cases. They cover legal issues that are explained in the unit.

Chapters

Each chapter of *Business and Personal Law* contains two sections. Each section outlines major legal concepts, and gives students tools for reading, studying, and comprehension.

BusinessWeek News Understanding law relies on concept application of the cases. Law is also about the real world. These excerpts from *BusinessWeek* introduce students to a real business situation with important legal implications.

Flex Your Reading A good reader is a careful reader who learns and practices the cues of active reading skills. Students follow the advice in the opening of the chapter and partake in an exercise to practice a particular facet of strengthening their reading skills as they pertain to law.

Chapter Photo This tidbit and query offers insight into the chapter's contents.

Chapter Review and Assessment

Use end-of-chapter activities to assess learning and to reach goals. The chapter Review and Assessment is a practical way to check students' understanding of the concepts and prepare for tests.

Review The Section Summaries, Vocabulary Review, Key Points Review, Standardized Test Practice, Apply and Debate, Case Practice Study, Ethics Application, and Internet Application offer students the opportunity to review and refine their knowledge of law and academics.

Practice The Standardized Test Practice and Test-Taking Tip are designed to address the practical aspects of taking standardized tests.

Academic Activities This feature helps students build and enhance their vocabulary skills.

Application Activities Thinking, writing, technology, analytical, and ethics activities provide opportunities to assess skills and apply content to varied real-world situations.

Sections

Each section begins with a Reading Guide to preview the section's content.

Graphic Organizer A graphic organizer gives a visual tool to help students organize and remember new content. These are downloadable from the *Business and Personal Law* Online Learning Center.

Pre-reading Pedagogy
What You'll Learn and Why It's Important are pre-reading guides and strategies to prompt students to focus their reading in the section.

Academic Standards
Academic standards are integrated into the text content.

SECTION **4.1**

Agreements and Contracts

What You'll Learn

- ◆ Explain the nature and importance of contracts.
- ◆ Identify the elements of a valid contract.
- ◆ Analyze the different classes of contracts.
- ◆ Differentiate between express and implied, unilateral and bilateral, and oral and written contracts.

Why It's Important

Knowing the elements and characteristics of a contract will help you determine whether an agreement is valid or not.

Academic Standards

Reading and completing the activities in this section will help you practice the following academic standards:

Math (NCTM CS2 3) Recognize and apply mathematics in contexts outside of mathematics. Solve problems that arise in mathematics and in other contexts.

English Language Arts (NCTE 6) Apply knowledge of language structure, language conventions, media techniques, figurative language, and genre to create, critique, and discuss print and non-print texts.

Reading Guide

Before You Read

Connect If you have ever agreed to conditions to enter a Web site, you have made a contract. What are some contracts you have made lately?

Focus on Ideas

For a contract to be valid, it must meet several requirements and have certain characteristics.

Take Notes

Create a graph like the one shown and use it to take notes as you read this section. Go to glencoe.com to find graphic organizers and tips on how to improve your note-taking skills.

offer

Contracts

The Six Components of a Contract

Key Terms

You will learn these legal words and expressions in this chapter. You can also find these terms in *Black's Law Dictionary* or in an online legal dictionary.

- contract
- offer
- acceptance
- genuine agreement
- express contract
- implied contract
- bilateral contract
- unilateral contract

Academic Vocabulary

You will find these words in your readings and in your tests. Look them up in a dictionary and familiarize yourself with them.

- determine
- assume
- require

80   Unit 2   Contract Law

glencoe.com

Reading Strategies

The reading strategies are offered on a gradual level throughout the section to provide a steady knowledge-based model of think-remember-connect.

As You Read This margin feature provides a cue to connect background knowledge to what students will read.

Reading Check Reading Check allows students to take a quick inventory of their comprehension.

After You Read Students answer a section review question that helps reinforce key legal concepts.

Student Edition Preview

Features

The features in each chapter help students see the relevance between concepts learned in the classroom and the real world.

WebQuest
Research Car Facts

A teen driver-family agreement is a form of contract. Log on to **glencoe.com** to find WebQuest resources, research key issues, and continue your WebQuest project.

List your findings in your WebQuest folder to share with your class.

WebQuest

Students will practice their technology and research skills by completing the WebQuest activities on the *Business and Personal Law* Online Learning Center.

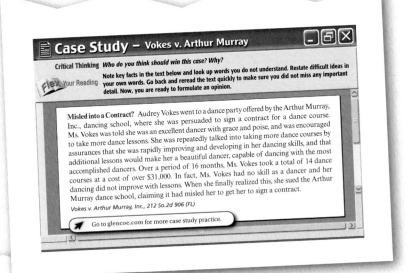

Case Study – Vokes v. Arthur Murray

Critical Thinking *Who do you think should win this case? Why?*

Flex Your Reading — Note key facts in the text below and look up words you do not understand. Restate difficult ideas in your own words. Go back and reread the text quickly to make sure you did not miss any important detail. Now, you are ready to formulate an opinion.

Misled into a Contract? Audrey Vokes went to a dance party offered by the Arthur Murray, Inc., dancing school, where she was persuaded to sign a contract for a dance course. Ms. Vokes was told she was an excellent dancer with grace and poise, and was encouraged to take more dance lessons. She was repeatedly talked into taking more dance courses by assurances that she was rapidly improving and developing in her dancing skills, and that additional lessons would make her a beautiful dancer, capable of dancing with the most accomplished dancers. Over a period of 16 months, Ms. Vokes took a total of 14 dance courses at a cost of over $31,000. In fact, Ms. Vokes had no skill as a dancer and her dancing did not improve with lessons. When she finally realized this, she sued the Arthur Murray dance school, claiming it had misled her to get her to sign a contract.

Vokes v. Arthur Murray, Inc., 212 So.2d 906 (FL)

Go to glencoe.com for more case study practice.

Case Study

The Case Study is an excerpt from a famous legal case which poses a critical thinking question for content enrichment. Send students to the Online Learning Center through **glencoe.com** for more case study practice.

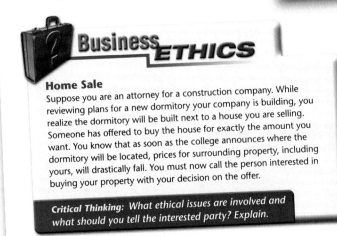

Business ETHICS
Home Sale

Suppose you are an attorney for a construction company. While reviewing plans for a new dormitory your company is building, you realize the dormitory will be built next to a house you are selling. Someone has offered to buy the house for exactly the amount you want. You know that as soon as the college announces where the dormitory will be located, prices for surrounding property, including yours, will drastically fall. You must now call the person interested in buying your property with your decision on the offer.

Critical Thinking: What ethical issues are involved and what should you tell the interested party? Explain.

Business Ethics

Business Ethics presents dynamics conversations that stem from ethical dilemmas and how these intersect with legal issues.

Legal Talk and Vocabulary Builder

These sidebar features analyze how words are built around roots. They require students to practice different parts of speech. Encourage students to build sentences using the acquired words.

Legal Talk

Bilateral: *adj* Affecting two sides or parties. From Latin *bilateralis; bi* = two + *latus* = side: having two sides.

Unilateral: *adj* Done or undertaken by one person or party. From Latin *unus* = one + *latus* = side: having one side.

Vocabulary Builder List and define five words that begin with the prefix *bi* or with the prefix *uni*.

Look It Up! Check definitions in *Black's Law Dictionary* or an online glossary. For direct links, go to **glencoe.com** to find more vocabulary resources.

Vocabulary Builder

❶ On a sheet of paper, use each of these terms in a sentence.

Key Terms

- contract
- offer
- acceptance
- genuine agreement
- express contract
- implied contract
- bilateral contract
- unilateral contract
- invitations to negotiate
- mirror image rule
- counteroffer
- revocation
- rejection

Academic Vocabulary

- determine
- assume
- require
- definite
- specify
- impose

Go to **glencoe.com** to play a game and improve your legal vocabulary.

CYBERLAW

American Airlines, Inc. v. FareChase, Inc.
Case No. 067-194022-02 (Texas, 67th Dist., Mar. 8, 2003).

FareChase, Inc., is a search engine whose customers are travel agencies. Its software scours—or scrapes—the Web sites of airlines, hotels, and car rental agencies to find the best rates. In February, 2003, American Airlines (AA) won an injunction against FareChase, alleging that FareChase scraped AA's site and took information without its permission. AA also claimed that FareChase violated the law of "trespass to chattels"—or interfering with someone's ownership of goods. Even though AA's Web site, AA.com, is a public site, its home page contains a statement restricting the use of the information on its site.

Ruling and Resolution

FareChase appealed the ruling on the grounds that the statement on AA's home page used a shrinkwrap or browsewrap agreement, which unfairly limits the use of facts. AA eventually settled with FareChase. According to the settlement, AA agreed to let FareChase search its site with some restrictions.

Critical Thinking Did FareChase have any type of contract with American Airlines? Do you thin[k] that FareChase did need a contract allowing the search of a public Web site? Why or why not?

Cyblerlaw

Students familiarize themselves with the ever-expanding world of cyberlaw with the study of real-world cases. These cases are briefly described, and then students engage in critical thinking that asks them to blend learned content and their own theories to arrive at an ingenious answer.

Global Law

International business requires knowledge of business relationships, policies, and etiquette within these working relationships. This activity provides insight into various legal practices in the United States that have global implications. Critical thinking activity requires students to summarize and identify the issue.

Global Law

Entering Contracts in China

In the United States, a signed contract means that all parties know who will do what, with what level of quality, and by what deadline. Once the contract is signed, the parties move on to fulfill the contract, knowing that everyone will do their part. These rules do not exist in China. When people sign a contract there, they simply agree that they want to do business with one another, that the goals of the contract are desirable, and that the terms of the contract are reasonable. However, everyone knows that activities do not always happen as planned.

Camille Schuster, a consultant, speaker, and professor of marketing, international negotiations, and consumer-centered business practices, gives these guidelines for conducting business and managing contracts in China:

❶ Maintain frequent, regular communication.

❷ Asking "yes" or "no" questions will not generate useful information. You will be spared embarrassment, you will feel reassured, and you will know nothing. Instead of asking your Chinese contact if the production deadline will be met, try

asking about significant events in the production process during the past week or month, or to describe recent activities of members of the production team.

❸ Meet face-to-face. This is a relationship culture that requires personal, one-to-one commitment.

❹ Represent all levels. Chinese culture is hierarchical and communication serves to preserve harmony. Problems are not freely discussed with superiors. Your team needs to include people at different levels of the hierarchy so that quality-control managers talk with other quality-control managers, and line engineers talk with other line engineers.

Across Cultures: The Importance of *Guanxi*

Guanxi (*gwan-shee*) means relationships. In the Chinese business world, personal connections are the basis for most business deals and contracts. It is very common for employees from one company to visit the residence of acquaintances from other organizations and bring gifts.

Critical Thinking: *What key contractual components are not included in Chinese contracts?*

Student Edition Preview

Assessment

Business and Personal Law features end-of-section and end-of-chapter review and assessment. Varied assessments enable you and your students to evaluate understanding.

Section Assessment

Each section ends with review and academic questions.

Assess comprehension with **Self Check** questions. Link the content to academics with the **Academic Connection** questions.

Chapter Review and Assessment

The chapter Review and Assessment contains a variety of review tools, activities, and assessment questions.

Summary The summaries restate the main concepts of each section.

Key Points Review Before proceeding through the book, use this portion to reinforce key contents.

Standardized Test Practice These activities provide an opportunity to sharpen students' test-taking skills. The activities also include a valuable Test-Taking Tip.

Vocabulary Builder Review the vocabulary taught in the chapter.

Apply and Debate Activate debating skills with partners. The activity requires communication skills, critical thinking, and reasoning.

Case Study Practice Take a real-world case and decipher the legalities of its outcome.

Chapter 4 Review and Assessment

Apply and Debate

Read the following scenarios. Get together with other students in pairs or groups of three and take a position on each scenario. Debate your position in class with students taking the opposite position or prepare a written argument justifying your position.

⑪ Twin Pines
The Galaxy Research Center e-mailed an offer to the owners of Twin Pines, a farm in rural Arkansas. The e-mail message stated: "Please consider this our offer to purchase between 9,000 and 11,000 acres of your 15,000-acre tract of farmland near Twin Pines, Arkansas. Our offering price is between $15,000 and $19,000 per acre. Respond ASAP."
You Debate | *Is this e-mail message a legally effective offer? Why or why not?*

⑫ Homecoming
Connie Adler agreed to go to the homecoming dance with Fred Wolfe. Later, Steve McNamara, the captain of the football team, asked Connie to be his date for homecoming. Connie broke her date with Fred to go to the dance with Steve.
You Debate | *Does Fred have a legal claim against Connie? Why or why not?*

⑬ Pocket Calculator
Bob Goodman made a verbal agreement to buy a pocket calculator from Howard Hermann for $35. When Hermann delivered the calculator, Goodman refused to accept it, stating that he was not bound by his verbal agreement.
You Debate | *Was Goodman correct? Why or why not?*

⑭ Waterbeds
Home Furniture Company advertised its waterbeds in a local newspaper. The newspaper mistakenly advertised the beds for $49 instead of $249.
You Debate | *Must Home Furniture sell the beds at the advertised price? Defend your position by citing which legal principle is involved and how it applies.*

⑮ Revocation
Victor Archer mailed an offer to Sally Miles. Sally mailed a properly addressed and stamped letter of acceptance ten minutes before she received a revocation from Victor.
You Debate | *Was the revocation effective? Defend your position by citing which legal principle is involved and how it applies.*

96 Unit 2 Contract Law

Chapter 4 Review and Assessment

Case Study Practice – Heiman v. Parrish

⑯ Is an Agreement a Contract? In August of 1994, Jerod Heiman purchased a $9,033 diamond engagement ring. He then asked Heather Parrish to marry him. She said yes and took the ring. About a year later, in October 1995, Mr. Heiman broke off the engagement. Mr. Heiman asked Ms. Parrish to return the ring to him, but she refused. Mr. Heiman then sued her to retrieve the ring.
Ms. Parrish argued to the court that an engagement ring is a part of a contract between two parties to get married at a later date. She argued that Mr. Heiman broke off the engagement, breached the contract, and could not recover the ring.
Mr. Heiman argued that the proposal and engagement were not a binding contract but rather a statement that the parties would get married. The ring was a conditional gift to Ms. Parrish, which Ms. Parrish could keep if the two got married. Since the two did not get married, Mr. Heiman had a right to recover the ring.
Source: Heiman v. Parrish, 942 P.2d 631 (Kan. 1997)

Practice Was there a contract between Mr. Heiman and Ms. Parrish?

⑰ Ethics Application

Reward or Not? Suppose you posted a reward notice that read, "Reward: $50 for the return of my lost iPod." Someone who did not know about the reward offer found your iPod and returned it to you.
◆ Would it be legal not to pay the reward money to the person who returned your iPod? Explain.
◆ Would it be ethical not to pay the reward money? Explain.

⑱ Internet Application

Find out About Contracts A youth group to which you belong plans to build a teen activity center. You and other members of the group are in charge of researching what the key contractual issues would be between the youth group and a contractor and how to go about writing a contract draft.

Go to glencoe.com to access the Web site sponsored by QuickForm Contracts and follow the instructions for the drafting of a hypothetical contract.

Reading Connection
Outside Reading Go to glencoe.com for a list of reading suggestions about contracts.

glencoe.com

Chapter 4 What Is a Contract? **97**

Internet Application Use the Internet to download contents for practicing and drafting legal documents.

Ethics Application A hypothetical scenario requires contemplation and ethical reasoning to support a position on the issue.

Choose PROVEN teaching solutions

Units

Units begin with well-organized, easy-to-reference pages preceding each unit of the student text.

Unit Objectives
This guide outlines the chapters' objectives for easy review before getting started on the unit.

Reading and Writing Support
This grid showcases the unit's topics and appropriate reading and writing strategies.

Unit Overview
Introduce the unit with a review of the chapters' summaries. Out of Time? helps you adjust to varied scheduling issues.

5-Minute Launch
Immerse the students into the unit's contents by engaging them in a quick hands-on activity.

for EFFECTIVE results.

Career Decisions This checklist provides some determining factors students might consider when contemplating a career choice.

Research Technology Extend the conversation of a career in law with a tidbit related to technology. Then, offer students the opportunity to further their knowledge on research technology by engaging in the activity.

Writing Connection Activities Build and strengthen writing skills with these activities.

Assignments Use this in conjunction with The Writing Connection to prepare students with pre-writing strategies.

Universal Access Consult these strategies to reach all students in the classroom.

Time Management Rubric To direct students' focus on a large assignment, share these strategies with them as they determine and develop their project's needs.

Winning the Case Extend the Landmark Case discussions by posing another angle to the situation.

Chapters

Chapters in *Business and Personal Law* are organized around the major legal issues that face businesspeople and consumers. Each chapter has two sections, each with an individual lesson plan.

Introduce the Chapter Introduce the chapter with a brief summary of its contents and main ideas. Building Background provides suggestions for accessing prior knowledge. Follow up with answer to the *BusinessWeek* News feature.

Practice the Concept Select from one of the three diverse and conceptual activities to begin forming a foundation for the forthcoming chapter's content.

Reading Strategy This feature offers extension probes to aid in an enriched discussion.

Classroom Resources All print and technology resources that accompany the chapter are listed in this box, enabling complete lesson preparation.

Using Visuals Answer and discuss the ideas presented in the photo leading the chapter. Direct students to demonstrate their visual literacy by connecting their own experiences with the photo's implied message.

Chapter Review and Assessment

Summary by Sections Assist students with their study time by focusing their attention with this tidbit.

Vocabulary Builder The comprehension of legalese is incredibly important for students to wholly understand a concept. These key term activities are extensions of the content discussed in the chapter.

Study Skills for Success and **Standardized Test Practice** Use Study Skills for Success to review and share the study tips with students to maximize their opportunity for success in coursework. Extend their preparation for high-stakes testing with Strategies for Standardized Test Practice.

Apply and Debate, Case Study, Ethics Application, Internet Application Answers Answer suggestions begin here and continue onto the next spread to accompany the questions that appear in the student edition.

Sections

Each chapter has two sections with its own six-part Glencoe Classroom Management Plan. Each lesson features teaching suggestions, background information, point-of-use teaching strategies, leveled activities for differentiated instruction, and answer keys. Bracketed letters on the reduced student edition pages correspond to teaching strategies in the Teacher Wraparound Edition, showing exactly where to use the teaching strategy and activities.

FOCUS

A **Bell-Ringer Activity** begins the lesson, then **Preteaching** activities assure that all students have the same background and preparation.

TEACH

This part of the lesson provides suggestions, discussions, reading activities, guided practices, answer keys, and development of concepts for the majority of the section.

D Develop Concepts

Use this optional activity to further develop learned content with this discussion probe.

S Skills Practice

Connect with each style of learner in the classroom by assigning leveled activities.

ASSESS

Review the various opportunities presented in the section that enabled students to learn. Evaluate their effectiveness and supplement accordingly.

RETEACH

Independent writing practice, reading strategies, and enrichment activities are provided to reinforce lesson content. The variety of activities in RETEACH allows students to assimilate their knowledge using varied learning styles.

W Writing Support
Consult these activities for writing development opportunities.

U Universal Access
These are strategies to reach all students in the classroom.

C Critical Thinking
Questions are designed to help students apply and extend what they have learned.

ASSESS

Re-evaluate student comprehension with varied assignments. Answers to the After You Read section review are provided. Direct students to the Online Learning Center for a Practice Test covering the content of the section.

CLOSE

Provides a culminating activity designed to use new knowledge in an independent assignment. The CLOSE activity helps students make the connection between what they read and its meaning and application to the real world.

EXPLORE *teaching* SOLUTIONS

Print Resources

Student Activity Workbook with Academic Integration

The Student Activity Workbook with Academic Integration includes a variety of activities for each chapter in the text.

- Note Taking
- Academics
  - English/Language Arts
  - Mathematics
  - Science
  - Social Studies
- Study Skills
- Test Prep
- Test Taking
- Content Vocabulary
- Academic Vocabulary

Student Activity Workbook with Academic Integration Teacher Annotated Edition

The Teacher Annotated Edition of the Student Activity Workbook includes annotated answers to all of the student activities.

for PLANNING and instructional SUPPORT.

Technology Solutions

TeacherWorks™ Plus

TeacherWorks Plus gives you instant access to a variety of useful program resources in one easy-to-use CD. The software provides a calendar format for you to plan lessons, manage daily activities, access textbook materials, and utilize Internet resources. TeacherWorks Plus includes built-in lesson plans that can be customized to meet your individual classroom needs. It also includes links to printable program resources:

Resources

- Teacher Wraparound Edition
- Student Activity Workbook with Academic Integration Teacher Annotated Edition

Teacher Materials

- Lesson Plans
- National and State Standards Correlations
- Note-Taking Graphic Organizers
- Chapter Outlines
- Chapter Summaries
- Enrichment Activities Masters
- Supplemental Cases
- Internet Connection Student Activities Masters
- Blackline Masters for Student Edition Figures and Supplemental Figures
- Ethics and Business Law Activities
- Competitive Events and Test-Taking Prep
- Reproducible Chapter Tests

Program Resources

Interactive Student Edition

The Interactive Student Edition CD includes the complete text of the student edition, formatted like the hardbound book, in a PDF format, viewable through Adobe Acrobat Reader®. With Glencoe's Interactive Student Edition, you can search through a multitude of materials quickly, and click on the hotlinks to locate documents correlated to the Student Edition.

ExamView Assessment Suite

Streamline assessment from start to finish with the ExamView Assessment Suite CD. This Suite (including the Test Generator and Test Manager) is a comprehensive solution for creating, administering, and scoring tests. It provides an accurate and exhaustive source of test items for a wide variety of examination styles. It also contains thousands of test questions organized by chapter and unit. This easy-to-use software will help you to quickly create customized chapter, unit, midterm, and final assessments.

Use ExamView Test Generator to:
- Create a paper test in fewer than five minutes.
- Print multiple versions of the same test.
- Enter your own questions.
- Develop tests using state and national standards.
- Prepare an online test, study guide, and worksheet.
- Upload tests to WebCT and Blackboard.

Use ExamView Test Manager to:
- Create a class roster.
- Automatically score a paper test using a scanner.
- Administer and score an online test.
- Prepare a variety of useful class and student reports.

Presentation Plus!

The *Business and Personal Law* Presentation Plus! CD provides PowerPoint® presentations that enable teachers to present dynamic lessons for every section in *Business and Personal Law*. It also includes chapter assessment presentations that can be used with TurningPoint.

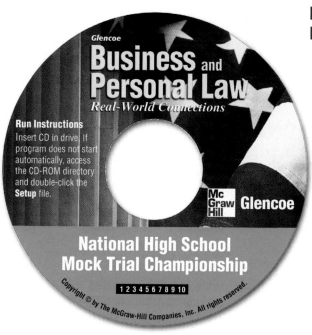

National High School Mock Trial Championship

Conduct a realistic, hands-on experience of the litigation process with the **National Mock Trial Championship DVD** and accompanying booklet. Students role-play as attorneys, jurors, witnesses, and other parties in order to practice argumentation in favor of a case. Through the examination of evidence, legal documents, statement of facts, juror instructions, witness statements, exhibits, trial procedures, rules, verdict, and other forms, students utilize their communication skills, critical thinking, ethics, and reasoning.

Program Resources

Digital Resources

Online Learning Center

The *Business and Personal Law* Online Learning Center provides resources to enrich and enhance learning.

Glencoe's Study-to-Go is online content that students can download onto their PDAs, giving them a portable version of textbook-related materials.

Glencoe's Teaching Today Web site provides teaching tips, free downloadable materials, in-depth articles, and a host of other features.

Online Student Edition

The Online Student Edition is an interactive version of the textbook. It offers the same content as the printed text, as well as multimedia-enhanced content.

Teach BUSINESS LAW and ACADEMICS at the same time.

Scope and Sequence

These charts provide an overview of the academic standards covered in *Business and Personal Law*.

National Council of Teachers of Mathematics Standards for Grades 9-12	
Number and Operation	
NCTM NOS 2 Understand the meanings of operations and how they relate to one another.	pp. 47, 239, 425
NCTM NOS 2a Judge the effects of such operations as multiplication, division, and computing powers and roots on the magnitude of quantities.	pp. 193, 371
Algebra	
NCTM AS 4 Analyze change in various contexts.	p. 65
Measurement	
NCTM MS 2b Understand and use formulas for the area, surface area, and volume of geometric figures, including cones, spheres, and cylinders.	p. 206
Data Analysis and Probability Standard	
NCTM DAPS 2 Select and use appropriate statistical methods to analyze data.	p. 27
Problem Solving	
NCTM PSS 1 Build new mathematical knowledge through problem solving.	pp. 275, 315
NCTM PSS 2 Solve problems that arise in mathematics and in other contexts.	pp. 114, 123, 301
NCTM PSS 3 Apply and adapt a variety of appropriate strategies to solve problems.	p. 257
Communication	
NCTM CS1 2 Communicate the mathematical thinking coherently and clearly to peers, teachers, and others.	p. 389
Connections	
NCTM CS2 1 Recognize and use connections among mathematical ideas.	p. 147
NCTM CS2 3 Recognize and apply mathematics in contexts outside of mathematics.	pp. 86, 139, 167, 451, 471

Scope and Sequence

National Council of Teachers of English Standards for English Language Arts	
NCTE 1 Read a wide range of print and non-print text to build an understanding of texts; to acquire new information; to respond to the needs and demands of society and the workplace; and for personal fulfillment.	pp. 12, 37, 46, 55, 89, 92, 110, 142, 145, 174, 183, 184, 208, 235, 237, 252, 267, 272, 294, 309, 313, 329, 380, 404, 406, 424, 441, 442
NCTE 2 Develop an understanding of the multi-dimensional human experience genres of literature from various time periods.	p. 98
NCTE 3 Apply a wide range of strategies to comprehend, interpret, evaluate, and appreciate texts.	pp. 4, 20, 31, 32, 42, 51, 52, 64, 69, 78, 84, 97, 98, 102, 127, 128, 138, 151, 160, 164, 179, 180, 189, 198, 209, 215, 224, 228, 243, 244, 249, 259, 262, 271, 279, 288, 298, 305, 306, 318, 319, 323, 324, 334, 345, 354, 360, 365, 375, 376, 388, 393, 394, 399, 411, 412, 423, 429, 438, 450, 455, 456, 467, 475
NCTE 4 Adjust use of spoken, written, and visual language to communicate effectively with a variety of audiences and for different purposes.	pp. 10, 26, 28, 93, 128, 233, 341, 472, 479
NCTE 6 Apply knowledge of language structure and conventions, media techniques, figurative language, and genre to create, critique, and discuss print and non-print texts.	pp. 6, 15, 18, 26, 28, 34, 37, 46, 48, 54, 58, 60, 66, 80, 81, 85, 87, 88, 94, 100, 105, 115, 124, 130, 140, 144, 148, 162, 166, 168, 176, 182, 187, 188, 190, 194, 200, 202, 206, 212, 226, 234, 236, 240, 246, 250, 251, 255, 258, 264, 266, 270, 276, 290, 292, 296, 302, 308, 312, 316, 320, 326, 332, 339, 342, 356, 366, 367, 372, 378, 379, 384, 390, 396, 399, 401, 408, 414, 416, 419, 426, 440, 443, 446, 452, 458, 465, 469
NCTE 7 Conduct research on issues and interests by generating ideas and questions, and by posing problems.	pp. 298, 329, 383, 466
NCTE 8 Use a variety of technological and information resources to gather and synthesize information and to create and communicate knowledge.	pp. 59, 133, 295, 415
NCTE 9 Develop an understanding of diversity of and respect in language use, patterns, and dialects across cultures, ethnic groups, geographic regions, and social roles.	p. 34, 37, 41, 45, 55, 92, 110, 145, 174, 183, 208, 237, 252, 272, 294, 309, 329, 380, 404, 424, 442, 459
NCTE 10 Students whose first language is not English make use of their first language to develop competency in English language arts and to develop an understanding of content across the curriculum.	pp. 6, 15, 28, 34, 37, 46, 48, 54, 58, 60, 66, 80, 81, 85, 87, 88, 94, 100, 105, 115, 124, 130, 140, 144, 148, 162, 166, 168, 176, 182, 188, 190, 194, 200, 202, 206, 212, 226, 234, 236, 240, 246, 251, 255, 258, 264, 266, 270, 276, 290, 292, 296, 302, 308, 312, 316, 320, 326, 332, 339, 342, 356, 366, 367, 372, 378, 379, 384, 390, 396, 399, 401, 408, 414, 416, 419, 426, 440, 443, 446, 452, 458, 465, 469, 472
NCTE 11 Participate as knowledgeable, reflective, creative, and critical members of a variety of literacy communities.	pp. 396
NCTE 12 Use spoken, written, and visual language to accomplish their own purposes.	pp. 14, 40, 41, 45, 48, 175, 205, 445

National Council for the Social Studies

NCSS 1 Study culture and cultural diversity.	pp. 233, 464
NCSS 2 Demonstrate understanding of how and why human beings view themselves the way they do over time.	pp. 14, 102, 110. 175, 249, 331
NCSS 3 Study people, places, and environments.	pp. 189, 205, 269, 407
NCSS 4 Study individual developments and identity.	p. 450
NCSS 5 Social studies programs should include experiences that provide of the study of interactions among individuals, groups, and institutions.	pp. 40, 59, 237, 252, 294, 318, 363, 380
NCSS 6 Study how people create and change structures of power, authority, and governance.	pp. 280, 209, 334, 388
NCSS 7 Study how people organize for the production, distribution, and consumption of goods and services.	pp. 164, 360, 363
NCSS 8 Study relationships among science, technology, and society.	p. 424
NCSS 9 Study global connections and interdependence.	pp. 272, 309, 313, 418
NCSS 10 Demonstrate understanding of why experiences shape ideals, principles, and practices in society.	pp. 20, 61, 442

21st Century Skills

Learning Skills	
Information and Communication Skills	**Information and Media Literacy Skills** Analyzing, accessing, managing, integrating, evaluating, and creating information in a variety of forms and media; understanding the role of media in society **Communication Skills** Understanding, managing, and creating effective oral, written, and multimedia communication in a variety of forms and contexts
Thinking and Problem-Solving Skills	**Critical Thinking and Systems Thinking** Exercising sound reasoning in understanding and making complex choices; understanding the interconnections among systems **Problem Identification, Formulation, and Solution** Ability to frame, analyze, and solve problems **Creativity and Intellectual Curiosity** Developing, implementing, and communicating new ideas to others; staying open and responsive to new and diverse perspectives
Interpersonal and Self-Directional Skills	**Interpersonal and Collaborative Skills** Demonstrating teamwork and leadership; adapting to varied roles and responsibilities; working productively with others; exercising empathy; respecting diverse perspectives **Self-Direction** Monitoring one's own understanding and learning needs; locating appropriate resources; transferring learning from one domain to another **Accountability and Adaptability** Exercising personal responsibility and flexibility in personal, workplace, and community contexts; setting and meeting high standards and goals for oneself and others; tolerating ambiguity **Social Responsibility** Acting responsibly with the interests of the larger community in mind; demonstrating ethical behavior in personal, workplace, and community contexts

SOURCE: Partnership for 21st Century Skills

National Standards

National Business Education Standards

I. Basics of Law

A. Ethics and the Law
I.A.1. Identify consequences of unethical and illegal contact.
I.A.2. Describe how to develop an ethical and legal lifestyle.
I.A.3. List the most common sources of the law.
I.A.4. Explain the way social forces may sometimes conflict.

B. Sources of Law
I.B.1. Describe the powers and limitations of the federal government as stated in the Constitution.
I.B.2 Identify the basic freedoms guaranteed by the Bill of Rights and describe several key constitutional amendments beyond the Bill of Rights.
I.B.3. Compare and contrast the national constitution with state, territory, and province constitutions.
I.B.4. Determine how courts make law and explain the role of precedent in the legal system.

C. Structure of the Courts
I.C.1. Differentiate between cases that belong within the jurisdiction of the federal and state, territory, and province court systems.
I.C.2. Compare the role of juvenile court with the role of other courts within a state, territory, or province.
I.C.3. Explain the role of the national and state, territory, and province appellate courts.
I.C.4. Differentiate between the roles of the U.S. Supreme Court and state, territory, and province supreme courts.
I.C.5. Differentiate between the rules of the International Law Commission, the U.N. Commission on International Trade Law, and the World Trade Organization.

D. Classification of Procedural Law
I.D.1. Define litigation.
I.D.2. Define alternate dispute resolution (ADR).
I.D.3. Explain the advantages and disadvantages of arbitration, mediation, and conciliation.
I.D.4. Compare and contrast the steps in a civil law suit with the steps in a criminal prosecution.
I.D.5. List and explain the steps in criminal and civil trials.
I.D.6. Describe the appellate process in criminal and civil cases.
I.D.7. Define the statute of limitations.

E. Classification of Substantive Law
I.E.1. Define different types of business crime (e.g., arson, forgery, and embezzlement).
I.E.2. Determine several defenses to criminal acts (e.g., insanity defense and self-defense).
I.E.3. Distinguish between a tort and a crime. law and the remedies available in tort law.
I.E.4. Differentiate between and give examples of negligence and intentional torts.
I.E.5. Explain the concepts of the reasonable person test and proximate cause.
I.E.6. Explain the concept of strict liability and describe circumstances under which it is imposed.
I.E.7.Describe the penalties available in criminal

II. Contract Law, Law of Sales, and Consumer Law

A. Contract Law
II.A.1. Differentiate between classes of contracts (e.g., bilateral and unilateral, express and implied, and oral and written).
II.A.2. Explain how offer and acceptance can create contractual rights and duties.
II.A.3. Determine whether or not an agreement is definite enough to be enforced as a contract.
II.A.4. Differentiate between the ways that assent can be undermined (e.g., fraud, nondisclosure, misrepresentation, mistake, duress, and undue influence).
II.A.5. Define and distinguish between different types of consideration and list the exceptions to the requirements of consideration.
II.A.6. Explain a minor's right to avoid a contract.
II.A.7. Identify categories of people who lack contractual capacity.
II.A.8. Describe the concept of unconscionability and compare it to legality.
II.A.9. List the essential information that should be included in writing under the statute of frauds.
II.A.10. Explain the parole evidence rule.
II.A.11. Describe the various rules applied to the interpretation of contracts.
II.A.12. Describe the various rules applied to contracts involving third parties.
II.A.13. List the ways a contract can be discharged.
II.A.14. Describe breach of contract and the remedies available when a contract is breached.
II.A.15. Discuss the impact of the laws of different countries on contractual transactions.

B. Law of Sales
II.B.1. Distinguish between a sale of goods and other transactions relating to goods.
II.B.2. Describe the Uniform Commercial Code (UCC).
II.B.3. Explain why the UCC has been adopted by individual states.
II.B.4. Describe the Uniform Computer Information Transactions Act (UCITA), the Uniform Electronic Transactions Act, the Electronic Signatures in Global and National Commerce Act, and the Millennium Digital Commerce Act.
II.B.5. Discuss the issue of taxation and e-commerce

C. Consumer Law
II.C.1. Identify legislation that regulates consumer credit and electronic credit transactions (e.g., Fair Credit Reporting Act, Fair Credit Billing Act, Equal Opportunity Act, Fair Credit Collection Practices Act, and Consumer Credit Protection Act).
II.C.2. Discuss consumer protection legislation (e.g., Federal Trade Commission, Consumer Product Safety Act, and Consumer Leasing Act).

III. Agency and Employment

A. Agency
III.A.1. Distinguish between an agent and individuals such as independent contractors, real estate brokers, bailees, and trustees.
III.A.2. Distinguish between a general power of attorney, a durable power of attorney, and a limited power of attorney.
III.A.3. Explain the different types of agents.
III.A.4. Define ratification and its elements.
III.A.5 Explain the concept of vicarious liability.

B. Employment
III.B.1. Explain the relationship of Title VII of the Civil Rights Act to employment.
III.B.2. Explain the difference between disparate treatment and disparate impact in discrimination cases.
III.B.3.Explain the Civil Rights Act of 1991.III.B.4. Determine what questions can and cannot be asked during an employment review.
II.B.5. Demonstrate an understanding of the basis on which employees or applicants may be asked to take tests (e.g., aptitude, psychological, polygraph, and drug tests).
IIII.B.6. Identify legislation that regulates employee rights (e.g., Americans with Disabilities Act, Age Discrimination in Employment Act, Family and Medical Leave Act, and Older Workers Benefit Protection Act).

III.B.7. Identify legislation that regulates employment conditions (e.g. Fair Labor Standards Act, Immigration Reform and Control Act, and Occupational Safety and Health Act).

III.B.8. Identify legislation that guarantees worker benefits (e.g., unemployment insurance, pension protection, workers' compensation, and Social Security legislation).

III.B.9. Describe the collective bargaining process.

III.B.10. Identify legislation that regulates union activities (e.g., National Labor Relations Act, Taft-Hartley Act, and Lundrum-Griffin Act).

IV. Business Organizations

A. Sole Proprietorships and Partnerships

IV.A.1. Outline the legal procedures for forming and running a sole proprietorship.

IV.A.2. Describe legislation that affects partnerships (e.g., Uniform Partnership Act and Revised Uniform Partnership Act).

IV.A.3. Explain the property rights involved in partnerships (e.g., tenancy in partnership and sharing of profits).

IV.A.4. Discuss other partnership rights (e.g., right to manage, right to reimburse, right to inspect the books, and right to an account).

IV.A.5. Identify how a partnership may be dissolved by the acts of the partners, operation of the law, and order of the court.

IV.A.6. Determine, after a dissolution, whether a partnership would continue or terminate through a winding up.

IV.A.7. Explain the winding up of partnership affairs and distribution of partnership assets after dissolution.

IV.A.8. Distinguish between a limited partnership and a general partnership.

IV.A.9. Describe how the Revised Uniform Limited Partnership Act affects limited partnerships.

IV.A.10. Explain the rights and duties of limited partners and general partners in a limited partnership.

IV.A.11. Explain the distribution of assets after the dissolution of a limited partnership.

IV.A.12. Differentiate between other partnership-type business organizations (e.g., joint ventures, limited partnership associations, and registered partnerships having limited liability).

B. Corporations

IV.B.1. Differentiate between types of corporations (e.g., profit, nonprofit, domestic, foreign, and alien corporations).

IV.B.2. Explain the steps involved in forming a corporation.

IV.B.3. Explain the circumstances under which courts may disregard the corporate entity and "pierce the corporate veil."

IV.B.4. Describe the functions of the board of directors and officers of a corporation with regard to control of corporate affairs.

IV.B.5. Differentiate between common and preferred stock.

IV.B.6. Identify shareholder rights (e.g., right to receive dividends, right to vote, right to inspect the books) and preemptive rights.

IV.B.7. Explain the nature of the shareholders' liability.

IV.B.8. Describe when promoters, directors, and officers are liable to the corporation, shareholders, and third persons.

IV.B.9. Differentiate between types of corporate expansion (e.g., mergers, consolidations, and conglomerates).

IV.B.10. Identify federal, state, territory, and province statutes that regulate corporations.

IV.B.11. Describe the ways corporate existence may be terminated.

C. Limited Liability Companies

IV.C.1. Define a limited liability company.

IV.C.2. Explain the steps in forming a limited liability company.

IV.C.3. Explain the advantages and disadvantages of doing business as a limited liability company.

IV.C.4. Explain the nature of management responsibilities in a limited liability company.

IV.C.5. Describe the effects of the tax code on limited liability companies.

V. Property Law

A. Personal Property

V.A.1. List different methods by which property is acquired.

V.A.2. Identify the forms of co-ownership of personal property.

V.A.3. Explain how a bailment is created and describe the standard of care different bailees are required to exercise over bailed property.

V.A.4. Distinguish between an ordinary bailment and a special bailment.

V.A.5. Define intellectual property and list types of intellectual property.

V.A.6. Identify a common carrier's liability for loss or damage to goods.

B. Real Property

V.B.1. Distinguish among liens, licenses, and easements and explain the differences.

V.B.2. List the major estates in land and describe the major features of each.

V.B.3. List and describe the forms of co-ownership of real property.

V.B.4. Illustrate the method of transferring title (deeding) to real property.

V.B.5. Describe the kinds of rental relationships that landlords and tenants may create.

VI. Commercial Paper, Insurance, Secured Transactions, Bankruptcy

A. Commercial Paper

VI.A.1. Explain the importance and function of commercial paper.

VI.A.2. Demonstrate an understanding of the concept of negotiability and distinguish it from assignability.

VI.A.3. Identify and explain the essential elements of a negotiable instrument.

VI.A.4. Describe the different types of negotiable instruments and different types of endorsements.

VI.A.5. Explain the contractual relationship between a bank and its customers.

VI.A.6. Describe stop-payment orders.

VI.A.7. Describe the legal effect of forgeries and material alterations.

B. Insurance

VI.B.1. Define insurance and differentiate between requirements for an insurable interest for property insurance and those needed for life insurance.

VI.B.2. Compare and contrast the different types of life insurance (e.g., ordinary, limited payment, endowment, and term).

VI.B.3. Compare and contrast the different types of property insurance (e.g., automobile, homeowner's, and marine).

VI.B.4. Explain some of the differences in health insurance coverages.

C. Secured Transactions

VI.C.1. Describe a secured transaction and explain the requirements for creating a valid security interest.

VI.C.2. Define the major types of collateral.

D. Bankruptcy

VI.D.1. Describe and discuss the various aspects of bankruptcy (e.g., Chapter 7–Liquidation, Chapter 11–Reorganization, and Chapter 13–Reorganization of Debts).

VI.D.2. Compare the differences between voluntary bankruptcy and involuntary bankruptcy cases.

VI.D.3 Explain the procedure for the administration of the debtor's estate.

VII. Computer Law

A. Basics of Computer Law

VII.A.1. Define the key terms involved in computer law.

VIII. Environmental Law and Energy Regulation

A. Environmental Law

VIII.A.1. Describe the various federal statutes (e.g., National Environmental Policy Act, Clean Air Act, Clean Water Act, and Toxic Substance Control Act) that impact the environment.

VIII.A.2. Describe the various state statutes that impact the environment.

VIII.A.3. Describe the various international initiatives that influence environmental regulations.

B. Energy Regulation

VIII.B.1. Describe the various federal agencies (e.g., Department of Energy, Energy Regulatory Commission, and Nuclear Regulatory Commission) that impact energy regulation and conservation.

VIII.B.2. Describe the various state statutes that impact energy regulations and conversation.

IX. Domestic Relations Law

A. Marriage and Its Legal Consequences

IX.A.1. Identify the issues and concerns that might be included in a prenuptial agreement.

IX.A.2. Distinguish between common law and ceremonial marriages.

IX.A.3. Identify the types of marriages that are prohibited by law.

B. Divorce and Its Legal Consequences

IX.B.1. Describe the law as it relates to the distribution of property in a divorce.

IX.B.2. Explain the law of domestic relations as it relates to child custody.

IX.B.3. Outline the law of domestic relations as it relates to child support.

X. Wills and Trusts

A. Wills

X.A.1. Define testamentary capacity and testamentary intent.

X.A.2. Identify the requirements necessary for a valid will.

X.A.3. Distinguish between signing, attesting, and publishing a will.

X.A.4. Explain how a will may be modified or revoked.

X.A.5. Distinguish between the protection given to spouses and to children under the law of wills.

X.A.6. Explain what happens to a decedent's estate when a person dies without a will.

B. Trusts

X.B.1. Identify the key characteristics of trusts.

X.B.2. Explain the advantages and disadvantages of establishing a trust.

X.B.3. Differentiate between the various types of trusts (e.g., charitable, private, spendthrift, revocable, and irrevocable trusts).

Make your *TEACHING* *FLEXIBLE*

90 Day

and **adaptable** *to* *ANY* *SCHEDULE.*

180 Day

Class Periods

Unit 1   What Is Law?
Chapter 1   The Law and the Courts.................8
Chapter 2   Criminal Law..............................8
Chapter 3   Tort Law 7
Unit 1   Careers in Law, The Writing Connection,
            Thematic Project, and
            Landmark Case...........................2

Unit 2   Contract Law
Chapter 4   What Is a Contract? 9
Chapter 5   Elements of a Contract.................9
Chapter 6   How Contracts Come to an End......7
Unit 2   Careers in Law, The Writing Connection,
            Thematic Project, and
            Landmark Case...........................2

Unit 3   Consumer Law
Chapter 7   Consumer Law and Contracts.........8
Chapter 8   Personal Property........................7
Chapter 9   Renting or Owning a Home.............7
Unit 3   Careers in Law, The Writing Connection,
            Thematic Project, and
            Landmark Case...........................2

Unit 4   Your Money and the Law
Chapter 10 Banking and Negotiable
                  Instruments................................9
Chapter 11 Credit and Debt 7
Chapter 12 Credit Protection and Bankruptcy....9
Unit 4   Careers in Law, The Writing Connection,
            Thematic Project, and
            Landmark Case...........................2

Class Periods

Unit 5 The Law and the Workplace
Chapter 13 Agency and Employment.................7
Chapter 14 Agency Authority and Termination ...7
Chapter 15 Employment Law.........................9
Unit 5   Careers in Law, The Writing Connection,
            Thematic Project, and
            Landmark Case...........................2

Unit 6   Starting a Business
Chapter 16 Forms of Business 9
Chapter 17 Operating a Corporation...............8
Chapter 18 Business and Regulations 7
Chapter 19 Cyberlaw and E-Commerce............7
Unit 6   Careers in Law, The Writing Connection,
            Thematic Project, and
            Landmark Case...........................2

Unit 7   Family Law
Chapter 20 Marriage and Divorce 7
Chapter 21 Insurance and Estate Planning.....10
Unit 7   Careers in Law, The Writing
                  Connection, Thematic Project, and
                  Landmark Case...........................2

INTEGRATE *academics*
and *workplace* SKILLS

● **NBEA National Business Law Standards**
Each chapter interleaf highlights the sections' content in relation to meeting the National Business Education Association standards.

● **Skills and Competencies** Each chapter interleaf includes a chart on the 21st Century Skills, Foundation Skills, and Workplace Competencies so that the students will develop these areas as they study the chapter.

● **NCLB Academic Standards** Each chapter interleaf includes a chart outlining where features and activities meet specific No Child Left Behind standards.

into the APPLIED LEARNING classroom.

No Child Left Behind

Brackets on the reduced student edition pages correspond to activities that help students practice and improve their abilities in Mathematics, English Language Arts, and Social Studies.

Academic Standards English Language Arts, Social Studies, and Mathematics are listed in the Academic Standards at the beginning of each section and correlate to the section's content.

Academic Connection
Academic Connection in the Section Assessment reviews are correlated to English Language Arts, and Mathematics or Social Studies standards.

RAISE the BAR and help STUDENTS clear it.

Academic Integration

Academic skills are crucial for success both inside and outside the classroom. In addition to traditional academic skills, your students will need communication skills, interpersonal skills, and strong technology skills in order to compete in the workplace. Basic skills will support your students in completing the tasks that their jobs and lives will demand.

The No Child Left Behind Act

The No Child Left Behind Act of 2001 emphasizes student achievement in basic academic subjects. It introduces strict accountability measures for schools in the form of standardized testing. No Child Left Behind names the following academic subjects:

- English
- Reading/Language Arts
- Mathematics
- Science
- World Languages
- Civics and Government
- Economics
- Art
- History
- Geography

The Importance of Integrating Academics into the Curriculum

In a recent survey of high school graduates—many of whom had gone directly to work rather than into postsecondary education—more than half the respondents said their high schools should have placed more emphasis on the basic academic skills.

By explicitly integrating academic skills into the business curriculum, you can make students more aware of the connections between schoolwork and the real world.

Integrated learning offers the following additional benefits to students:

- It provides real-world learning and thus establishes patterns of lifelong learning.
- It improves the academic achievement of all students—including those who will begin their careers directly after high school, those who will go on to postsecondary education or training, and those who will obtain four-year college degrees and beyond.
- It supports students in making realistic career and educational goals.

Academics in the Business Curriculum

Integrate academic skills into the classroom as a regular part of your classroom activities. For example, by having students read class assignments and texts, write letters and reports, give presentations, and perform mathematics exercises, you are helping them improve their academic skills. Make expectations clear. For example, if you ask your students to prepare a written report, explain that grammar, and spelling will also be evaluated. Stress that clear writing, accuracy, and attention to detail are skills that students will need for success in school and at work.

To integrate academics into your business course, you must incorporate principles from other subjects in a way that students can understand either on a concrete level or on metaphoric terms.

Deliver *EFFICIENT* INSTRUCTION to all students.

Accountability

A consequential result of the No Child Left Behind Act, and the reauthorization of the Perkins Act through 2012, is that more states require testing for graduation at the secondary level. Accountability measures new to the Perkins reauthorization bill include:

- Academic proficiency as measured by the state criteria developed under NCLB;
- Graduation rates as defined by NCLB;
- Number of students to continue to postsecondary education;
- Number of students to complete state or industry certification or licensure; and
- Student achievement on assignments aligned with industry standards.

Connection to Relevance

With the mandatory requirements for proven test scores and graduation numbers, how can we assure that our students are learning? Most educators agree it is by connecting the relevance of education to life.

ACTE president Bob Scarborough says the Perkins reauthorization "ensures we are providing all students with an education that will help them succeed in the workplace and in life." William Daggett writes in *Achieving Academic Excellence through Rigor and Relevance*:

"What is important is that students enter the global economy with the ability to apply what they learned in school to a variety of ever-changing situations that they couldn't foresee before graduating.

The Rigor/Relevance Framework, developed at the International Center for Leadership in Education, illustrates leveled learning processes that enable students to perform high-level thinking. The learning process defines student performance in four sequential categories: acquisition, application, assimilation, and adaptation."

Applications

Studies show that students understand and retain knowledge when they experience or apply it to relevant situations. The authors of *Business and Personal Law* are dedicated to meet the challenge. Every chapter in *Business and Personal Law* is filled with ways to engage students in experiential learning and apply this knowledge to their lives.

Features designed to help students find the relevance in content include:

- Careers in Law
- Unit Thematic Project
- Ask Standard & Poor's
- *BusinessWeek* News
- Global Law
- Business Ethics
- Ethics Application
- Cyberlaw
- Case Studies
- Landmark Cases

The content and teaching strategies in *Business and Personal Law* are designed to help applied learning students acclimate into the real world and to prepare them for high-skill, high-wage, and high-demand professions.

Gather *the* TOOLS *you'll* need *to*

Universal Access

by Douglas Fisher, Ph.D.

Today's classroom includes students from many backgrounds with a variety of learning styles, strengths, and challenges. As teachers, we face the challenge of helping all of our students reach their educational potential. With careful planning, you can address the needs of all students in you classroom. The basis for this planning is universal access. When classrooms are planned with universal access in mind, fewer students require specific accommodations.

Universal Design

Universal design was first conceived as an architectural design concept when business people, engineers, and architects began making adjustments to allow for physical access to buildings. The idea was to plan the environment in advance to ensure that everyone had access. As a result, the environment would not have to be changed later for people with physical disabilities, people pushing strollers, workers who had injuries, or others for whom the environment would be difficult to negotiate. The Center for Universal Design www.design.ncsu.edu/cud defines Universal Design as: The design of products and environments to be usable by all people, to the greatest extent possible, without the need for adaptation or specialized design.

Universal Design and Access in Education

Researchers, teachers, and parents have expanded the development of built-in adaptations and inclusive accommodations from architectural space to the educational experience, especially in the area of curriculum.

In 1998, the National Center to Improve the Tools of Educators, with the partnership of the Center for Applied Special Technology, proposed an expanded definition of universal design focused on education: In terms of learning, universal design means the design of instructional materials and activities that allows learning goals to be achievable by individuals with wide differences in their abilities to see, hear, speak, move, read, write, understand English, attend, organize, engage, and remember.

Universal design and access, as they apply to education and schooling, suggest the following:

- **Inclusive Classroom Participation**—Curricula should be designed with all students and their needs in mind. The Glencoe/McGraw-Hill texts and materials are designed to accommodate a wide range of students. For example, understanding that English learners and students who struggle with reading will be using this textbook, vocabulary is specifically taught and reinforced. Teacher-support materials provide multiple instructional methods to meet the needs of the students in the class. The text is written to identify the main idea for all learners. Activating prior knowledge an identifying connections between what students know and think about are made within the text.

- **Maximum Text Readability**—In universally designed classrooms that provide access for all students, texts

REACH EVERY student.

use direct language, clear noun-verb agreements, and clear construct-based wording. In addition to these factors, Business and Personal Law uses embedded definitions for key terms and academic vocabulary, provides for specific instruction in reading skills, uses a number of visual representations, and includes note-taking guides.

- **Adaptable and Accommodating**—The content in this textbook can be easily translated, read aloud, or otherwise changed to meet the needs of students in the classroom. The section and end-of-chapter assessments provide students with multiple ways to demonstrate their content knowledge and activities to help them see the connection between course study and the real world.

Differentiated Instruction

To differentiate instruction, teachers must appreciate student differences in background knowledge and current reading, writing, and English language skills. They must also consider student learning styles and preferences, interests, and needs, so they can react accordingly. There are a number of general guidelines for differentiating instruction in the classroom to reach all students, including:

- **Link Assessment with Instruction**—Assessments should occur before, during, and after instruction to ensure that the curriculum is aligned with what students do and do not know. Using assessments in this way allows you to plan instruction for whole groups, small groups, and individual students. Backward planning, where you

establish the assessment before you begin instruction is also important.

- **Clarify Key Concepts and Generalizations**—Students need to know what concepts are essential and how this information can be used in their future learning. In addition, students need to develop a sense of the Big Ideas—ideas that transcend time and place.

- **Emphasize Critical and Creative Thinking**—The content, process and classroom should require students to think about what they are learning. While some students may require support, additional motivation, varied tasks, materials, or equipment, the overall focus on critical and creative thinking allows all students to participate in the lesson.

- **Include Teacher- and Student-Selected Tasks**—A differentiated classroom includes both teacher- and student-selected tasks and activities. At some points in the day or lesson, the teacher must provide instruction and assign learning activities. In other parts of the lesson, students should be provided with choices in how they engage with the content. A balance of guided and chosen activities increases motivation, engagement, and learning.

Support for Individual Students

The vast majority of students will thrive in a universal access classroom that is focused on differentiated instruction. However, wise teachers recognize that no single option will work for all students and that there may be students who require unique systems of support to be successful.

Tips for Instruction

The following tips for instruction can support your efforts to help all students reach their maximum potential:

- Survey students to discover their individual differences. Use interest inventories to learn their unique talents so you can encourage contributions in the classroom.
- Be a model for respecting others. Adolescents crave social acceptance. Students with learning differences are especially sensitive to correction and criticism, particularly when it comes from a teacher. Your behavior will set the tone for how students treat one another.
- Expand opportunities for success. Provide a variety of instructional activities that reinforce skills and concepts.
- Establish measurable objectives and decide how you can best help students who meet them.
- Celebrate successes and make note of and praise "work in progress."
- Keep it simple. Point out problem areas if doing so can help a student effect change. Avoid overwhelming students with too many goals at one time.
- Assign cooperative group projects that challenge all students to contribute in solving a problem or creating a product.

Students with Learning Disabilities

- Provide support and structure. Clearly specify rules, assignments, and responsibilities.
- Practice skills frequently. Use games and drills to help maintain student interest.
- Incorporate many modalities into the learning process. Provide opportunities

to hear, speak, write, read, and act out important concepts and information.
- Link new skills and concepts to those that have already been mastered.
- If possible, allow students to record answers on audiotape.
- Allow extra time to complete assessments and assignments.
- Let students demonstrate proficiency with alternative presentations, including oral reports, role plays, art projects, and musical presentations.
- Provide outlines, notes, or tape recordings of lecture materials.
- Pair students with peer helpers, and provide class time for pair interaction.

Students with Behavioral Challenges

- Provide a structured environment with clear-cut schedules, rules, seat assignments, and safety procedures.
- Reinforce appropriate behavior and model it for students.
- Cue distracted students back to the task using verbal signals and teacher supervision.
- Set goals that can be achieved in the short term. Work for long-term improvement in the big areas.

Students with Physical Challenges

- Openly discuss any uncertainties you have about when to offer aid with the student.
- Ask family members or therapists and students what special devices or procedures are needed and whether any special safety precautions need to be taken.
- Welcome students with physical challenges into all activities, including field trips, special events, and projects.
- Provide information about needed support to class members and adults.

Students with Visual Impairments

- Facilitate independence. Modify assignments as needed.
- Teach classmates how and when to serve as visual guides.
- Limit unnecessary noise in the classroom if it distracts students with visual impairments.
- Provide tactile models whenever possible.
- Foster a spirit of inclusion. Describe people and events as they occur in the classroom. Remind classmates that students with visual impairments cannot interpret gestures and other forms of nonverbal communication.
- Provide taped lectures and reading assignments for use outside the classroom.
- Team students with a sighted peer for written work.
- Seat students where they can see your lip movements easily and where they can avoid any visual distractions.
- Avoid standing with your back to the window or to a light source.
- Use an overhead projector so you can maintain eye contact while writing notes for students.
- Write all assignments on the board, or hand out written instructions.
- If the student has a manual interpreter, allow both the student and interpreter to select the most favorable seating arrangements.
- Teach students to look directly at each other when they speak.

English Language Learners

- Remember, a student's ability to speak English does not reflect his or her academic abilities.
- Try to incorporate the student's cultural experience into your instruction. The help of a bilingual aid may be effective.
- Avoid any references in your instruction that could be construed as cultural stereotypes.
- Preteach important vocabulary and concepts.
- Encourage students to preview text before they begin reading, noting headings.
- Remind students to use graphic organizers, photographs, and maps take advantage of the information contained in these visuals.
- Use realia and photographs whenever possible to build background knowledge and understanding.

Gifted Students

- Make arrangements for students to take selected subjects early and to work on independent projects.
- Ask "what if" questions to develop high-level thinking skills. Establish an environment safe for risk-taking in your classroom.
- Emphasize concepts, theories, ideas, relationships, and generalizations about the content.
- Promote interest in the past by inviting students to make connections to the present.
- Let students express themselves in alternate ways such as through creative writing, acting, debates, simulations, drawing, or music.
- Provide students with a catalog of helpful resources, listing such things as agencies that provide free and inexpensive materials, appropriate community services and programs, and community experts who might be called upon to speak to your students.
- Assign extension projects that allow students to solve real-life problems related to their communities.

Empower *your* students *with the*

How Can I Motivate Students to Read?

As a teacher, your role is to help students make personal connections in order to understand "Why do I need to learn this?" Emphasize that reading is not only a necessity for work and for life; it can also bring enjoyment and enlightenment.

Ask your students, "What role does reading play in your life?" You can open this discussion by modeling examples: I love historical biographies; I read menus and order meals in Spanish; I read magazines and the Internet to stay up-to-date on my favorite sports teams.

Improving or fine-tuning reading skills will help your students:

- *Improve grades*
- *Read faster and more efficiently*
- *Improve their study skills*
- *Remember more information accurately*
- *Improve their writing*

The Reading Process

Good reading skills build on one another, overlap, and spiral in much the same way that a winding staircase goes around and around while leading readers to a higher place. The Reading Skills Handbook is designed to help your students find and use the tools to use before, during, and after reading.

Reading Strategies

- *Identify, understand, and learn new words*
- *Understand why you read*
- *Take a quick look at the whole text*
- *Try to predict what you are about to read*
- *Take breaks during reading and ask questions about the text*
- *Take notes*
- *Keep thinking about what will come next*
- *Summarize*

Vocabulary Development

Word identification and vocabulary skills are the building blocks of the reading and writing. By learning to use a variety of strategies to build word skills and vocabulary, your students will become stronger readers.

READING SKILLS *they will use* *in the* REAL WORLD.

Use Context to Determine Meaning

The best way for your students to expand and extend vocabulary is to read widely, listen carefully, and participate in a rich variety of discussions. When reading independently, students can often figure out the meanings of new words by looking at their context, the other words, and sentences that surround them.

Predict a Possible Meaning

Another way to determine the meaning of a word is to take the word apart. If a reader understands the meaning of the base, or root, part of a word, and knows the meanings of key syllables added either to the beginning or end of the base word, it becomes easy to figure out what the word means.

Word Origin   Since Latin, Greek, and Anglo-Saxon roots are the basis for much of our English vocabulary, having some background in one of these languages can be a useful vocabulary tool. For example, *astronomy* comes from the Greek root *astro*, which means "relating to the stars." *Stellar* also has a meaning referring to stars, but its origin is Latin. Knowing root words in other languages can help readers determine meanings, derivations, and spellings in English.

Prefixes and Suffixes   A prefix is a word part that can be added to the beginning of a word. For example, the prefix *semi* means "half" or "partial," so *semicircle* means "half a circle." A suffix is a word part that can be added to the end of a word. Adding a suffix often changes a word from one part of speech to another.

Using Dictionaries   A dictionary provides the meaning or meanings of a word. Look at the sample dictionary entry in the student edition Reading Skills Handbook to see what other information it provides.

Thesauruses and Specialized Reference Books   A thesaurus provides synonyms and often antonyms. It is a useful tool to use to expand vocabulary. Remind students to check the exact definition of the listed words in a dictionary before using a thesaurus. Specialized dictionaries such the *Barron's Dictionary of Business Terms* or *Black's Law Dictionary* list terms and expressions not commonly included in a general dictionary. See glencoe.com for direct links to online dictionaries.

Glossaries   Many textbooks and technical works contain condensed dictionaries that provide an alphabetical listing of words used in the text and their specific definitions.

Recognize Word Meanings across Subjects   Words often have different meanings when used for different purposes. The word *product* may mean one thing in math and another in science. For example:

Math *After you multiply the two numbers, explain how you arrived at the product.*

Science *One product of photosynthesis is oxygen.*

Economics *The Gross National Product is the total dollar value of goods and services produced by a nation.*

Help Students Understand What They Read

Reading comprehension means understanding—deriving meaning from—what has been read. Using a variety of strategies can help improve comprehension and make reading more interesting and more fun.

Read for a Reason

To get the greatest benefit from reading, teach students to establish a purpose for their reading. In school, some of the reasons for reading include:

- To learn and understand new information
- To find specific information
- To review before a test
- To complete an assignment
- To prepare (research) before you write

As reading skills improve, you will notice that your students apply different strategies to fit the different purposes for reading. For example, a person reading for entertainment may read quickly, but reading to gather information or follow directions might require reading more slowly, taking notes, constructing a graphic organizer, or rereading sections of text.

Draw on Personal Background

Drawing on personal background, or activating prior knowledge, helps students connect their culture and experiences to their reading. Before introducing a new topic, you may want to encourage students to ask:

- What have I heard or read about this topic?
- Do I have any personal experience relating to this topic?

You can also set common background knowledge with discussion before reading. For example, to prepare students to read *A Farewell to Arms*, you might lead a discussion about these common background themes:

- World War I
- Italy (You might ask a student to show Italy on a map)
- Other Ernest Hemingway titles
- the Nobel Prize in literature

Having this historical background will help to set the scene for students as they read.

Using a KWL Chart A KWL chart is a good device for organizing information gathered before, during, and after reading. In the first column, students list what they already know, then list what they want to know in the middle column. They use the third column to review and assess what they learned. You or your students can add more columns to record places where they found information and places where they can look for more information.

K (What I already know)	W (What I want to know)	L (What I have learned)

Adjust Your Reading Speed Reading speed is a key factor in how well students understand what they read. Reading speed can vary depending on the purpose for reading.

Scanning *means running one's eyes quickly over the material to look for words or phrases. Readers scan to find a specific piece of information.*

Skimming *means reading a passage quickly to find its main idea or get an overview. Skim a passage as a preview to determine what the material is about.*

Reading for detail *involves careful reading while paying attention to text structure and monitoring understanding. Readers read for detail to learn concepts, follow complicated directions, or prepare to analyze a text.*

Techniques to Help Students Understand and Remember What They Read

Preview

Previewing strategies help students begin at a visual level, then drill down to evaluate, predict, draw conclusions, and use contextual clues about what they will read.

Previewing Strategies

Read the title, headings, and subheadings of the selection.
Look at the illustrations and notice how the text is organized.
Scan the selection. Glance at the whole thing.
Skim the passage for an overview.
Decide what the main idea might be.
Predict what a selection will be about.

Predict

As students read, they take educated guesses about story events and outcomes. They make predictions before and during reading. This helps them focus their attention on the text and that focus improves understanding.

Determine the Main Idea

When students look for the main idea, they are looking for the most important statement in a text. Depending on what kind of text they read, the main idea can be located at the very beginning (news stories in newspaper or a magazine) or at the end (scientific research document).

Encourage students to ask these questions to determine the main idea:

- What is each sentence about?
- Is there one sentence that is more important than all the others?
- What idea do the details support or point out?

Keep track of the text's structure (see below). Looking at headers and content structure will give students important clues about the main idea.

Taking Notes

Cornell Note-Taking System: There are many methods for note taking. The Cornell Note-Taking System is a well-known method that can help students organize what they read. To the right is a note-taking activity based on the Cornell Note-Taking System.

Graphic organizers: Using a graphic organizer to retell content in a visual representation will help students remember and retain content. Encourage students to make charts or diagrams to organize what they have read. Some good examples are:

Venn diagrams: A Venn diagram is a good way to organize information in a compare-and-contrast text structure. The outer portions of the circles show how two characters, ideas, or items contrast, or are different, and the overlapping part compares two things, or shows how they are similar.

Flow charts: Students can a track sequence of events or cause and effect on a flow chart. Demonstrate how to arrange ideas or events in their logical, sequential order. Then draw arrows between ideas to indicate how one idea or event flows into another.

Go to **glencoe.com** for more information about note taking and additional study tools.

Visualize

Encourage students to try to form a mental picture of scenes, characters, and events as they read. This helps them to use the details and descriptions the author gives readers. If students can visualize what they read, they will become more interested and will remember the information better.

Question

Tell students to ask questions about the text while they read. Encourage them to ask about the importance of the sentences they read, how the sentences relate to one another, whether they understand what they just read, and what they think is going to come next.

Clarify

Encourage students to try these techniques when they don't understand meaning (through questioning):

What Students Should Do When They Do Not Understand

- ◆ Reread confusing parts of the text.
- ◆ Diagram (chart) relationships between chunks of text, ideas, and sentences.
- ◆ Look up unfamiliar words.
- ◆ Separate the text out of one's self. Pretend to tell it to someone else.
- ◆ Read the passage once more.

Review

Make sure students take time to stop and review what they have read. Use note-taking outlines or any other graphic organizers, charts, or visual aids.

Monitor Your Comprehension

Teach students to continue to check their understanding using the following two strategies:

Summarize   Pause and state the main ideas of the text and the key supporting details. Try to answer the following questions: Who? What? When? Where? Why? and How?

Paraphrase   Pause, close the book, and try to retell what they have just read in their own words. It helps students to retell, or paraphrase reading, into their own words.

Understanding Text Structure

Good writers do not just put together sentences and paragraphs, they organize their writing with a specific purpose in mind. That organization is called *text structure*. When students understand and follow the structure of a text, it is easier to remember the information they read. There are many ways text may be structured.

Each type of structure usually makes use of some specific words. Teach students to watch for these signal words: They will help them follow the text's organization (remind them to use these techniques as they write).

Comparison and Contrast

This structure shows similarities and differences between people, things, and ideas. This is often used to demonstrate that things that seem alike are really different, or vice versa.

Signal words: *similarly, more, less, on the one hand / on the other hand, in contrast, but, however*

Cause and Effect

Writers use the cause-and-effect structure to explore the reasons for something happening and to examine the results or consequences of events.

Signal words: *so, because, as a result, therefore, for the following reasons*

Problem and Solution

When writers organize text around the question how, they state a problem and suggest solutions.

Signal words: *how, help, problem, obstruction, overcome, difficulty, need, attempt, have to, must*

Sequence

Sequencing tells readers in which order to consider thoughts or facts. Examples of sequencing are:

Chronological order refers to the order in which events take place.

Signal words: *first, next, then, finally*

Spatial order describes the organization of things in space (e.g., to describe a room).

Signal words: *above, below, behind, next to*

Order of importance lists things or thoughts from the most important to the least important (or the other way around).

Signal words: *principal, central, main, important, fundamental*

Thinking about Reading

It is important for students to think about what they are reading to get the most information from a text, to understand the consequences of what the text says, to remember the content, and to form their own opinions about what they read.

Interpret

Interpreting involves asking, "What is the writer really saying?" and then using what students already know to answer the question.

Infer

Writers do not always state exactly everything they want readers to understand. They sometimes imply certain information by providing clues and details. An **inference** involves using reasoning and experience to develop the idea, based on what an author implies or suggests. What is most important when drawing inferences is to be sure that readers have accurately based their guesses on supporting details from the text. If students cannot point to a place in the selection to help back up an inference, encourage them to rethink that guess.

Draw Conclusions

A conclusion is a general statement a reader can make and explain using reasoning or supporting details from a text.

Analyze

To understand persuasive nonfiction (a text that lists facts and opinions to arrive at a conclusion), readers must analyze statements and examples to see if they support the main idea. To understand an informational text, students need to keep track of how the ideas are organized to find the main points.

> **Hint:** *Have students use graphic organizers and note-taking charts.*

Distinguish Facts and Opinions

This is one of the most important reading skills students can learn. A fact is a statement that can be proven. An opinion is what the writer believes. A writer may support opinions with facts, but an opinion cannot be proven. For example:

> **Fact:** *California produces fruit and other agricultural products.*

> **Opinion:** *California produces the best fruit and agricultural products.*

Evaluate

Remind students that to rely on accurate information, they will need to consider who wrote it and why. Where did the writer get information? Is the information one-sided? Can readers verify the information?

Reading for Research

To guide students in reading actively to research a topic, encourage them to follow these directions:
- generate an interesting, relevant, and researchable question
- categorize that information
- evaluate the information
- organize information in a new way for a specific audience
- draw conclusions about the original research question

Link ACADEMIC vocabulary

What Is Academic English?
by Robin Scarcella, Ph.D.

Academic English is the language commonly used in business and education. It is the language used in academics, business, and courts of law. It is the type of English used in professional books, including textbooks, and it contains specific linguistic features that are associated with all disciplines. Proficiency in reading and using academic English is strongly related to long-term success in all parts of life.

What Is Academic Vocabulary?

By the time children have completed elementary school, they must have acquired the knowledge needed to understand academic vocabulary. How many words should they acquire to be able to access their textbooks? A basic 2,000-word vocabulary of high-frequency words makes up 87% of the words. Three percent of the remaining words are technical words. The remaining 2% are low-frequency words. There may be as many as 123,000 low-frequency words in academic texts.

Why Should Students Learn Academic Vocabulary?

English language learners who have mastered a basic 2,000-word vocabulary are ready to acquire the majority of general words found in their texts and on standardized tests.

Knowledge of academic words, combined with continued acquisition of general words, can significantly boost an English learner's comprehension level of academic texts. English learners who learn and practice these words before they graduate from high school are likely to be able to master academic material with more confidence and speed. They waste less time and effort in guessing words than those students who know only the basic 2,000 words that characterize general conversation.

Academic Vocabulary and Academic English in the Business Classroom

Teachers can provide their students with rich samples of academic vocabulary and help students understand and attend to the academic English of their text.

To develop academic English, students must have already acquired a large amount of basic proficiency in the grammar of everyday English.

Academic English should be taught within contexts that make sense. Academic English arises not only from a knowledge of linguistic code and cognition but also from social practices in which academic English is used to accomplish

to BUSINESS content.

communicative goals. The acquisition of academic vocabulary and grammar is necessary to advance the development of academic English.

Tips for Teaching Academic Vocabulary

- **Expose Students to Academic Vocabulary**—Students learn academic vocabulary through use and in reading content. You do not need to call attention to all academic words students are learning because they will acquire them subconsciously.

- **Do Not Correct Students' Mistakes When Using the Vocabulary Words**—All vocabulary understanding and spelling errors are developmental and will disappear once the student reads more.

- **Help Students Decode the Words Themselves**—Once they learn the alphabet, they should be able to decode words. Decoding each word they do not recognize will help them more than trying to focus on sentence structure. Once they can recognize words, they can read "authentic" texts.

- **Do Not Ignore the English Learner in This Process**—They can learn academic vocabulary before they are completely fluent in spoken English.

- **Helping Students Build Academic Vocabulary Leads to Broader Learning**—Students who have mastered the basic academic vocabulary are ready to continue acquiring words from the rest of the vocabulary groups. Use the Internet to find lists of appropriate vocabulary word lists.

There are a number of guidelines that teachers can follow when teaching academic English and vocabulary:

Guidelines for Teaching Academic Vocabulary

1. Use direct and planned instruction.
2. Employ models that have increasingly difficult language.
3. Focus attention to form by pointing out linguistic features of words.
4. Provide practice opportunities.
5. Motivate student interest and self-confidence.
6. Provide instructional feedback.
7. Use assessment tools on a regular basis.

Generate *the* BEST

Assessment

In response to the growing demand for accountability in the classroom, educators must use multiple assessment measures to accurately gauge student performance. In addition to quizzes, tests, essay exams, and standardized tests, assessment today incorporates a variety of performance-based measurements and portfolio opportunities.

Performance assessment activities provide hands-on approaches to learning concepts. Through activities students are able to actually experience these concepts rather than just reading and listening about them. These types of activities also help students become aware of diverse audiences for their work. Performance assessment tasks are based on what is most essential in the curriculum and what is interesting to the student.

Performance-Based Assessments

One good way to present a performance assessment is in the form of an open-ended question.

- Journals—Students write from the perspective of a businessperson or a consumer of a particular historical era.
- Letters—Students write a letter from one businessperson to another or to a family member or another audience.
- Position Paper or Editorial—Students explain a controversial issue and present their own opinions and recommendations, supported with strong evidence and convincing reasons.
- Newspaper—Students write stories from the perspective of a business reporter.

- Biographies and Autobiographies—Students write about business leaders either from the third person point of view (biography) or from the first person (autobiography).
- Creative Stories—Students integrate business events into a piece of fiction.
- Poems and Songs—Students follow the conventions of a particular type of song or poem as they tell about a business event or person.
- Research Reports—Students synthesize information from a variety of sources into a well-developed research report.

Oral Presentations

Oral presentations allow students to demonstrate their business literacy in front of an audience.

- Simulations—Students hold simulations of actual events, such as a role play in a business scenario.
- Debates—Students debate two or more sides of a business policy or issue.
- Interview—Students conduct a mock interview of a business leader or worker.
- Oral Reports—Students present the results of research in a lively oral report, often accompanied by visuals.
- Skits and Plays—Students use business events as the basis for a play or skit.

Visual Presentations

Visual presentations allow students to demonstrate their understanding in a variety of visual formats. Visual presentations can be either group or individual projects.

- Model—Students make a model to represent a business process.

performance *FROM YOUR* students.

- Museum Exhibit—Students create a rich display of materials around a topic. Typical displays might include models, illustrations, photographs, videos, writings, and presentation software.
- Graph or Chart—Students analyze and represent data in a line graph, bar graph, table, or other chart format.
- Drawing—Students represent a business event or period through illustration.
- Posters and Murals—Posters and murals may include maps, time lines, diagrams, illustrations, photographs, and written explanations that reflect students' understanding of business information.
- Quilt—Students sew or draw a design for a patchwork quilt that shows a variety of perspectives, events, or issues related to a key topic.
- Videotapes—Students film a video to show a simulation of a business event.
- Multimedia Presentation or Slide Show— Students create a computer-generated multimedia presentation containing business information and analysis.

How Are Performance Assessments Scored?

There are a variety of means used to evaluate performance tasks. Some or all of the following methods may be used.

- Scoring Rubrics—A scoring rubric is a set of guidelines for assessing the quality of a process and/or product. It sets out criteria used to distinguish acceptable responses from unacceptable ones, generally on a scale from excellent to poor. Rubrics may be used as guidelines as the students prepare their products. They are also commonly used for peer-to-peer assessment or self-assessment.
- Models of Excellent Work—Teacher-selected models of excellent work illustrate expectations and help students set goals for their own projects.
- Student Self-Assessment—Common methods of self-assessment include ranking work in relation to the model, using a scoring rubric, and writing their own goals and then evaluating how well they have met these goals.
- Peer or Audience Assessment—Many of the performance tasks target an audience other than the classroom teacher. If possible, the audience of peers should give students feedback. Have the class create rubrics for specific projects.
- Observation—As students carry out tasks, you may want to formally observe them at work. Develop a checklist and identify all the specific behaviors and understandings you expect students to demonstrate. Then observe students as they carry out performance tasks and check off behaviors as you observe them.
- Interviews—As a form of ongoing assessment, you may want to conduct interviews with students, asking them to analyze, explain, and assess their participation in performance tasks. When projects take place over an extended period of time, you can hold periodic interviews as well as exit interviews. In this way the interview process allows you to gauge the status of the project and to guide the students' efforts along the way.

PREPARE your STUDENTS WELL,

Test-Prep Strategies

Students can follow the steps below to prepare for the standardized assessments they are required to take.

- Read About the Test—Students can familiarize themselves with the format, the types of questions, and the amount of time they will have to complete the test. It is very important for students to budget their time during test taking.

- Review the Content—Consistent study will help students build knowledge and understanding. If there are specific objectives or standards that are tested, help students review facts or skills.

- Practice—Provide practice, ideally with real tests, to build students' familiarity with the content, format, and timing of the real exam. Students should practice all the types of questions they will encounter on the test.

- Pace—Students should pace themselves differently depending on how the test is administered. As students practice, they should try to increase the number of questions they can answer correctly. If students have trouble with an item, they should mark it and come back to it later.

- Analyze Practice Results—Help students improve test-taking performance by analyzing their test-taking strengths and weaknesses. Help students identify what kinds of questions they found the most difficult. Look for patterns in errors and tailor instruction to review the appropriate test-taking skills or content.

Test-Taking Strategies

It's not enough for students to learn facts and concepts—they must be able to show what they know in a variety of test-taking situations.

Objective Tests

Apply the following strategies to help students do their best on objective tests.

Multiple-Choice Questions

- Students should read the directions carefully to understand what answer the test requires—the best answer or the right answer.

- Advise students to watch for negative words in the questions, such as *not*, *except*, *unless*, and *never*.

- Students should try to mentally answer the question before reading the choices.

- Students should read all the answer choices and eliminate those that are obviously wrong.

True/False Questions

- It is important that students read the entire question before answering. For an answer to be true, the entire statement must be true. If one part of a statement is false, the answer should be marked false.

- Remind students to watch for words such as *all*, *never*, *every*, and *always*. Statements containing these words are often false.

Matching Questions

- Students should read through both lists before they mark any answers.

- Unless an answer can be used more than once, students should cross out each choice as they use it.

- Using what they know about grammar can help students find the right answer. For instance, when matching a word with its definition, the definition is often the same part of speech (noun, verb, adjective, and so forth) as the word.

and you will IMPROVE their PERFORMANCE.

Essay Tests

Help students use these strategies on essay tests.

Read the Question

The key to writing successful essay responses lies in reading and interpreting questions correctly. Teach students to identify and underline key words in the questions that will help them understand what the question asks.

Plan and Write the Essay

Once students understand the question, they should follow the writing process to develop their answer. Encourage students to follow the steps below to plan and write their essays.

1. Map out an answer. Make lists, webs, or an outline to plan the response.
2. Decide on an order in which to present the main points.
3. Write an opening statement that directly responds to the essay question.
4. Write the essay. Expand on the opening statement. Support key points with specific facts, details, and reasons.
5. Write a closing statement that brings the main points together.
6. Proofread to check for spelling, grammar, and punctuation.

Writing Strategies	
Analyze	To analyze means to systematically and critically examine all parts of an issue or event.
Classify or Categorize	To classify or categorize means to put people, things, or ideas into groups, based on a common set of characteristics.
Compare and Contrast	To compare is to show how things are similar, or alike. To contrast is to show how things are different.
Describe	To describe means to present a sketch or impression. Rich details, especially details that appeal to the senses, flesh out a description.
Discuss	To discuss means to systematically write about all sides of an issue or event.
Evaluate	To evaluate means to make a judgment and support it with evidence.
Explain	To explain means to clarify or make plain.
Illustrate	To illustrate means to provide examples or to show with a picture or other graphic.
Infer	To infer means to read between the lines or to use knowledge and experience to draw conclusions, make a generalization, or form a prediction.
Justify	To justify means to prove or to support a position with specific facts and reasons.
Predict	To predict means to tell what will happen in the future, based on an understanding of prior events and behaviors.
State	To state means to briefly and concisely present information.
Summarize	To summarize means to give a brief overview of the main points of an issue or event.
Trace	To trace means to present the steps or stages in a process or event in sequential or chronological order.

BASE *your* teaching ON BEST PRACTICES,

Critical Thinking

One of the factors that determine workplace success is a person's ability to deal with the varied demands of the fast-paced business world. This requires insightful decision making, creative problem solving, and interactions with diverse groups necessary to achieve success.

The Value of Critical Thinking

Critical thinking is the process of reasonably or logically deciding what to do or believe. it involves the ability to:

- Compare and contrast
- Solve problems
- Make decisions
- Analyze and evaluate
- Synthesize and transfer knowledge
- Engage in metacognition

Critical thinking skills are important to help students::

- investigate their own problem-solving mechanisms,
- find creative resolutions,
- compare and contrast what they know with unknowns, and
- make decisions about their own learning while making them aware of their learning processes.

Cognitive Development

All learning requires thinking. Benjamin Bloom's Taxonomy of the Cognitive Domain is probably the most widely recognized schema of levels of thinking. Each of Bloom's six cognitive categories lists various thinking skills and indicates the types of behavior students are expected to perform to fulfill specific learning goals. See chart below.

CATEGORY	GOAL	EXPECTED STUDENT RESPONSE	APPROPRIATE QUESTIONS/PROMPTS
Knowledge	Identify and recall of information	Define, recognize, recall, identify, label, show, collect, understand, examine	Who...? What...? When...? Where...? How...? Describe....
Comprehension	Organize and select facts and ideas	Translate, interpret, explain, describe, summarize, extrapolate	Retell in your own words.... What is the main idea of...?
Application	Use facts, rules, and principles	Apply, solve, show, experiment, predict	How is...an example of...? How is...related to...?
Analysis	Separate a whole into component parts	Connect, relate, differentiate, classify, arrange, check, group, distinguish, organize, categorize, detect, compare, infer	Classify...according to.... How does... compare/ contrast with...?
Synthesis	Combine ideas to form a new whole	Produce, propose, design, construct, combine, formulate, compose, plan, hypothesize	What would you predict/infer from...? What might happen if you combined...with...?
Evaluation	Develop opinions, judgments, or decisions	Appraise, judge, criticize, decide	What do you think about...? Prioritize....

and your STUDENTS WILL BENEFIT.

Cooperative Learning

Studies show that students learn faster and retain more information when they are actively involved in the learning process. Cooperative learning is one method that gets students actively involved in learning and at the same time allows for peer teaching.

Using Cooperative Learning

Your business course provides many opportunities for students to learn and apply the skills necessary for positive interpersonal relationships. Through the use of cooperative learning, you can offer a structured method of teaching team-building, collaborative social skills, and team decision making while teaching basic concepts— essential skills for the workplace.

Cooperative Learning in this Text

In *Business and Personal Law*, students and teachers have a variety of materials to assist with cooperative learning activities. Many of the features and section and chapter assessment activities can be completed in a cooperative learning environment.

The Benefits of Cooperative Learning

- Cooperative learning emphasizes working toward group goals rather than the traditional emphasis on individual competition and achievement.
- Students discover that not only must they learn the material themselves, but they are also responsible for helping everyone in the group learn the material.
- Cooperative learning increases academic achievement and develops essential social skills.
- Students learn valuable problem-solving, team-building, and creativity skills that transfer to real-world occupations and work environments.
- People who help each other and work together toward a common goal generally begin to feel more positive about themselves and each other.
- Students have the opportunity to perceive other students as colleagues rather than competitors. As a result, they recognize the value of helping others rather than working competitively.

School-to-Career

A major goal set by the No Child Left Behind Act and the Perkins Act, reauthorized through 2012, is to prepare students to succeed in the constantly changing work world. *Business and Personal Law* successfully integrates work skills preparation with course content and academics. Each chapter in this Teacher Wraparound Edition is preceded by a 21st Century Skills and Workplace Competencies correlations chart that previews the essential skills to be developed in chapter content and activities. Using the charts as guidelines, you can target the needs of your class and the needs of students as individuals to prepare them all for high-skill, high-wage, and high-demand professions.

School-to-career programs are important developments in providing students a sense of relevance in their learning. These programs assume different forms in order to meet the needs of different communities, schools, and students.

Benefits of School-to-Career Programs

All school-to-career programs provide these benefits to students:

- An improved understanding of self
- An appreciation of the relevance of school learning to "real life," and
- A clearer vision of a productive future and how to make that vision a reality
- Familiarity with a wide range of career options
- Increased motivation to stay in and to succeed in school.

An effective school-to-career program involves a close relationship between schools and local businesses. This relationship can result in benefits to schools and to businesses alike, as well as to parents and the community.

PURPOSES OF SCHOOL-TO-CAREER PROGRAMS
• To facilitate the creation of a universal, high-quality school-to-career transition system to enable students to identify and pursue paths to progressively more rewarding roles in the workplace
• To utilize workplaces as learning environments in the educational process by making employers and educators joint partners in providing opportunities for students to participate in high-quality, work-based learning
• To promote the formation of partnerships dedicated to linking the worlds of school and work among secondary schools and private and public employers, labor organizations, government, community-based organizations, parents, students, state and local educational agencies, and training and human services agencies
• To increase knowledge and improve student skills by integrating academic and occupational learning and building links between secondary and postsecondary educational institutions
• To motivate all students to stay in or return to school and strive to continue their education in postsecondary institutions
• To expose students to a broad array of career opportunities and facilitate the selection of major areas of study, based on individual interests, goals, and abilities.

Technology

Technology affects how all people work, interact, and live. Technology will affect your students in the work world. For example, they may keep records using a computer, advertise on the Internet, or telecommute. It will also affect your students as consumers. An increasing number of people buy products on the Web. It is critical that your students become familiar and comfortable with technology now in order to prepare for successful careers.

Activities

Business and Personal Law helps you integrate technology into your teaching with technology-based activities:

- Ask Standard & Poor's follow-up asks students to access the S&P Web site to improve their financial literacy.
- The unit feature Thematic Project suggests additional graphical tools and aids available online at glencoe.com to sharpen their knowledge on the legal content.
- The chapter opening Flex Your Reading provides a link to the OLC for students to download the printable graphic organizer for each section.
- The feature WebQuest provides a research activity through the OLC at glencoe.com.
- Use Internet Application to extend knowledge on a law topic by researching it via the Internet.
- The *Business and Personal Law* Online Learning Center (OLC) through glencoe.com provides assessment and other extension activities to assist students in finding answers and to further research the topic or find a project.
- Reading Connection links the student to the OLC for outside reading suggestions for each chapter.

- The OLC also provides podcasts with chapter summaries and quizzes.

Using the Internet Effectively

There are steps you can take to use the Internet effectively in the classroom:

- Look for sites that are created by the government or universities (their URLs typically end in .gov or .edu). These are reliable sites with factual integrity and stability.
- Find out who created the site. If the purpose and creator of the Web site are unclear, its content may be unreliable.
- Use multiple search engines when you are looking for information on a topic. This will help you find as many of the pertinent sites as possible.
- Use search words or key words effectively. Use unique key words to get specific results.
- Use quotation marks to refine your search. If you want to search for business law, your search will return results for both "business" and "law." To find specific sources of information on the concept of business law, use quotations around the two words: "business law."
- Use the Find or Ctrl+F keys to search the text of a site for a specific key word. This function allows you to quickly find the key word within context and determine whether the site is relevant to your search.
- If you have looked through at least 30 sites and you have not found what you are looking for, then start a new search with different search words or phrases.
- Combine your Internet research with traditional research methods. Ask librarians and experts for information and sources. Use books and magazines.

Ethics

Helping students learn about ethical behavior and how to consider the effects of a decision before it is made are important life skills for your students preparing for the business world.

The Benefits of Integrating Ethics

The goal of teaching ethical decision-making skills is not to teach values. It is to help students clarify their ethical beliefs and learn how to evaluate ethical situations. Make your classroom a risk-free environment in which students can discuss issues and make ethical decisions. Students need to learn how to evaluate their actions and to ask questions such as, "Will I be proud of myself if I take this action?" and "Would I want others to know about my actions?"

The Ethical Decision Model

Your students will learn to analyze ethical situations better if they have a model to use in deliberating the issues that helps them to understand how a decision can affect others. Several decision models exist, but the basic steps for an ethical decision model are as follows:

1. Determine the ethical issue.
2. Identify the actions for handling the situation.
3. Identify the people affected by the situation.
4. Analyze how the situation affects the people involved.
5. Decide which of the actions to take.

Classroom Strategies

The application activities presented in the features Business Ethics and Ethics Application provide real-world situations posing legal and ethical conundrums. Both features can be catalysts for lively classroom discussion. In addition, you might lead discussions about topical ethics issues or have students bring in newspaper or magazine articles that suggest ethical dilemmas. Have students analyze the situations in class and, perhaps, write short reports on their analyses and conclusions. Some formats, such as learning groups, role plays, and debates, are particularly well suited to teaching students about of ethics.

Classroom Cooperative Learning Groups

Small groups of students are especially well suited to discuss cases and share their ideas about ethical issues. Divide students into groups of four or five. Observe groups and encourage all students to participate. Allow each group to reach its own conclusions, and then ask a member of each group to share their ideas with the class.

Classroom Role Plays and Debates

Have your students role-play ethical situations, using their own ideas about how to respond to a given situation. Discuss class responses to the role play, guiding students in using the ethical decision model. Set up debate teams to present different sides of an ethical issue.

Home Sale

Suppose you are an attorney for a construction company. While reviewing plans for a new dormitory your company is building, you realize the dormitory will be built next to a house you are selling. Someone has offered to buy the house for exactly the amount you want. You know that as soon as the college announces where the dormitory will be located, prices for surrounding property, including yours, will drastically fall. You must now call the person interested in buying your property with your decision on the offer.

Critical Thinking: What ethical issues are involved and what should you tell the interested party? Explain.

Diversity

Business and Personal Law is designed to help students recognize and discuss issues of cultural diversity. During class activities, you may also find it appropriate to integrate questions related to cultural diversity. For example, you might expand a class discussion by asking:

- Would your response change if the client did not speak the same language as you speak? If so, how?
- Would you treat your client differently if his or her ethnic background were different from yours?
- Would your decision change if your coworker were a male or female? From your own ethnic background? From a different background? Why?

Integrating Cultural Diversity

As future legal professionals, your students will be faced with a diverse world in which people of many different cultures are both workers and consumers. Cultural knowledge may be the difference between success and failure in conducting business in the global economy. For students to become productive workers and responsible citizens, they must be open to cultural differences.

As students learn about skills needed to be successful, they should keep in mind the wide diversity of the people they are likely to encounter in every aspect of their working and personal lives. In the classroom and in one-on-one conferences, you can help your students consider the diversity of the U.S. population, not only in terms of ethnicity, but also in terms of customs, attitudes, religious beliefs, language backgrounds, and physical capabilities. High school students need to understand that ability and success are not related to skin color or gender.

Multicultural Education

Multicultural education incorporates the idea that all students—regardless of their gender and social class, and their ethnic, racial, or cultural characteristics—should have an equal opportunity to learn in school. Learning about other cultures concurrently with their own culture helps students recognize similarities and appreciate differences, without perceiving inferiority or superiority of one or the other. To foster cultural awareness:

- Recognize that all students are unique, possessing special talents and abilities.
- Promote uniqueness and diversity as positive traits.
- Know, appreciate, and respect the cultural backgrounds of your students.
- Use authentic situations to provide cultural learning and understanding.
- Make sure people of all cultures are represented fairly and accurately.
- Make sure that historical information is accurate and nondiscriminatory.
- Make sure that materials do not include stereotypical roles.
- Make sure there is gender equity.
- Welcome family and community involvement.
- Use current news stories or advertisements to call students' attention to cultural differences that influence the marketing of products.

Our Partners at McGraw-Hill

STANDARD &POOR'S

Standard & Poor's is the world's leading provider of independent investment research, indexes, and ratings. The investment data and analysis provided by *Standard and Poor's* are used around the world by financial decision-makers to help create growth and manage wealth. *Standard & Poor's* publishes the S&P 1200, the premier global equity performance benchmark; the S&P 500, the premier U.S. financial-market index; and credit ratings on more than 220,000 securities and funds worldwide.

BusinessWeek

BusinessWeek is the leading global resource for ground-breaking business news and news analysis that offers essential insight into the real world of business. *BusinessWeek* is the world's most widely read business magazine, with more than 8 million readers each week, including online and television viewers.

Our Business Alliances

National Business Education Association

The National Business Education Association (NBEA) is the nation's largest professional organization devoted exclusively to serving individuals and groups engaged in instruction, administration, research, and dissemination of information for and about business.

National Mock Trial Championships

The National High School Mock Trial Championship was created to provide a competitive event for high school teams in which to demonstrate their skills and knowledge in courtroom procedures and application of law.

Future Business Leaders of America (FBLA)

Future Business Leaders of America is a not-for-profit education association of students preparing for careers in business and business-related fields.

Business Professionals of America (BPA)

Business Professionals of America is a student organization promoting leadership, citizenship, academic, and technology skills for students at the secondary and postsecondary level.

Treasure Hunt

Business and Personal Law: Real-World Connections contains practical information about the U.S. legal system. The trick is to know where to look to access all the information in this book. If you go on the treasure hunt with your teacher, you will discover how this textbook is organized and how to get the most out of your reading and study time. Let's Start!

1 How many units and chapters does this textbook have?

7 units and 21 chapters

2 What of the textbook will help you practice your essay-writing skills?

the Writing Connection activity at the end of each unit

3 Where can you find out about the rights of minors?

Chapter 6 pages 97 through 99

4 What are the three book features that give you real court case examples?

Case studies in every chapter, Case Study Practice in every Chapter Review and Assessment, and Landmark Case at the end of each unit

5 Where can you learn about your rights and duties when you rent an apartment?

in Chapter 9, pages 186 and 187

6 Where can you find out about business laws in foreign countries?

in the Global Law feature that appears in each chapter

7 What academic skill will you practice in Chapter 4, Section 4.1

math: using fractions and decimals

8 What is the URL that takes you to the *Business and Personal Law* Online Learning Center?

glencoe.com

Table of Contents

Table of Contents

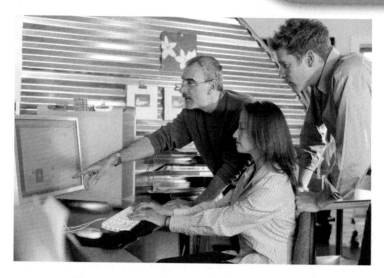

Table of Contents

Table of Contents

Table of Contents

Table of Contents

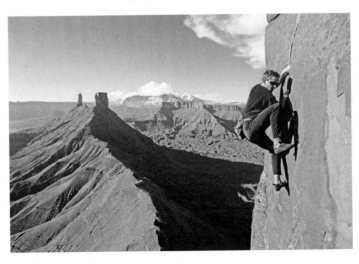

Welcome To...

Business and Personal Law

Study online at glencoe.com

Follow these steps to access the textbook resources available to you at the *Business and Personal Law* Online Learning Center: Practice tests, word games, extra case studies, and more.

Step 1
Go to glencoe.com

Step 2
Select your state from the pull-down menu

Step 3
Select Student/Parent

Step 4
Select Business Administration

Step 5
Click ENTER

Step 6
Select Business and Personal Law

Step 7
Click Student Center to access student resources

Review key terms with Vocabulary Builder Flashcards and Word Puzzles.

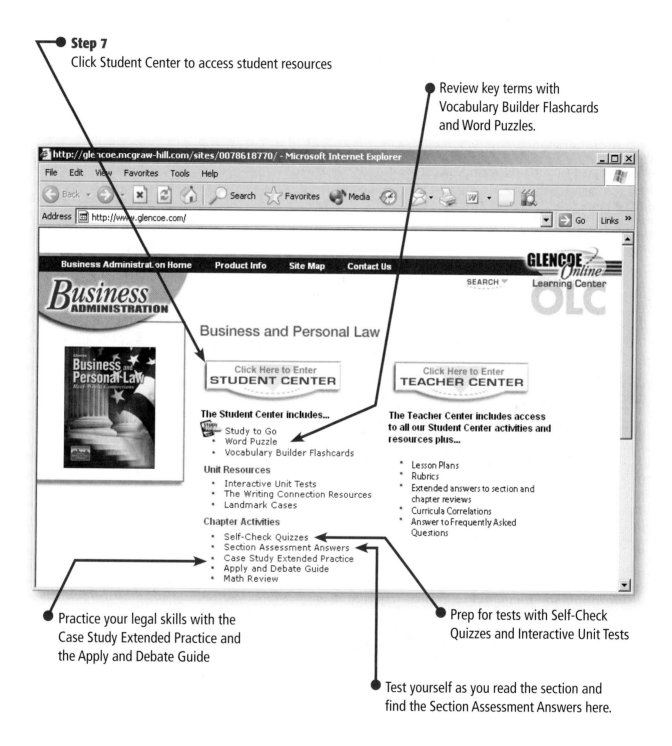

Practice your legal skills with the Case Study Extended Practice and the Apply and Debate Guide

Prep for tests with Self-Check Quizzes and Interactive Unit Tests

Test yourself as you read the section and find the Section Assessment Answers here.

Open the units:
What will you learn about law?

Law relates to life, everyday and everywhere, whether you are the CEO of a large company or a high school student applying for a first job. Here is how you can use this textbook to study law.

Thematic Project Preview launches a capstone project that you can work on throughout the unit, as you study the chapters. With this preview, you can start thinking about research and strategies you will need to complete the project.

Web Quest fits in with the topic of the unit project and gives you a hint and some help with getting your research started. You will find WebQuest follow-up tips throughout the chapters.

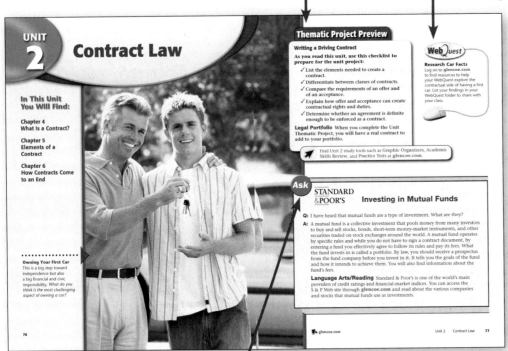

Standard & Poor's is a leading publisher of financial research and analysis. All units begin with a feature that answers a basic financial question. This is also an opportunity for you to read more about the topic online

Close the units:
Discover the world of law practice.

Careers in Law Have you thought of a career in the legal field? This page gives you several ways to ponder the possibilities: Read an interview with a law professional, and discover which skills, training, courses would give you the most useful background. Find out even more with the online Legal Career Guide!

The Writing Connection helps you sharpen your writing skills and get ready for essay tests.

Landmark Cases are extensive excerpts of real court cases. The cases have been selected for key decisions on issues covered in the unit. They cover legal issues that are explained in the unit. Follow the steps outlined for you and you will get more comfortable reading long legal documents.

Thematic Project lets you apply what you have learned throughout the unit and turn it all into a valuable portfolio project that will show what you can do. An evaluation rubric and step-by-step instructions are there to guide you.

Open the chapters:
What is this all about?

Each chapter of *Business and Personal Law* contains two sections and the content outlines major legal concepts while giving you tools to help you read, study, and understand.

BusinessWeek News Understanding law relies on concept applications and cases. Law is also about the real world. These excerpts from *BusinessWeek* introduce you to a real business situation that has some legal implications.

Look at the Photo! It gives you a hint about the whole chapter.

Close the chapters: Make sure you know and understand the concepts.

Use end-of-chapter activities to assess your learning and reach your goals.

First, Read the Section Summaries! This is a quick way to review the main concepts explained in the chapter.

Then, Answer the Key Points Questions! Try and answer all the questions without looking back at the summaries or at the chapter. Note what you don't know and find the answers in the summaries and in the chapter.

Standardized Test Practice Take this opportunity to read a real-world text and exercise your critical reading skills.

Vocabulary Builder Review and practice all the key terms. Don't forget to practice the academic terms! They will help you improve your reading and writing skills.

Applications Make sure you truly understand what you have read and learned: Apply it! First, with mini-scenarios, then step up to Case Practice and consider a real court case. Finally, brainstorm Ethics Applications and Internet Applications.

Start a section with study tools and goals.

Each section starts with a Reading Guide and a list of objectives. Follow the steps to efficient reading and studying.

Connect Think of an answer to this question so you can develop an idea of what the section is about

Graphic Organizer Use this idea to organize your study notes on this section. Go to glencoe.com to find the same figure in a large format.

Focus This sentence zeroes in on the main idea in the section.

Objectives and Standards Preview the main concepts and the academic standards that are applied in this section.

Key Terms Preview all the key terms in the section

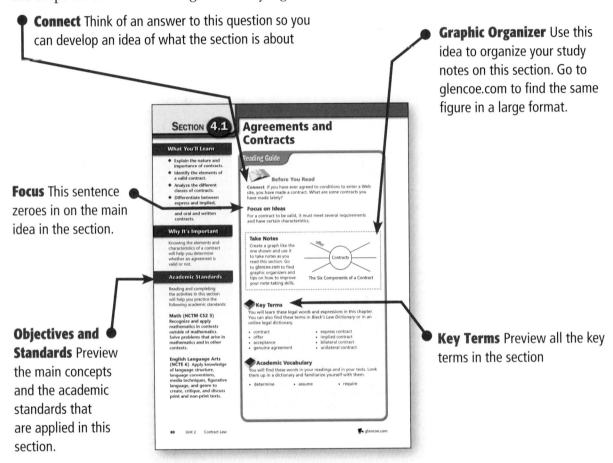

End a section with self-assessment.

Assessing what you have learned is part of the learning process. Review and check your understanding, apply this new knowledge and get ready for tests.

Section Assessments Check your understanding and your recall of the main concepts by answering three self-check questions. Find the answers at glencoe.com

Critical Thinking Use this question to determine if you can apply what you have learned.

Study law with real cases: Step out of the classroom and into the world.

Studying law is about learning concepts and rules. It is also about understanding how the rules apply in real life. *Business and Personal Law* shows you how the law works with real court cases in every chapter and unit.

Preview the Cases

Global law: Real-world connections.

If you were a businessperson working for global company, how would the laws of other countries affect your business transactions and your behavior? Find out with Global Law features!

Global Law

Entering Contracts in China

In the United States, a signed contract means that all parties know who will do what, with what level of quality, and by what deadline. Once the contract is signed, the parties move on to fulfill the contract, knowing that everyone will do their part. These rules do not exist in China. When people sign a contract there, they simply agree that they want to do business with one another, that the goals of the contract are desirable, and that the terms of the contract are reasonable. However, everyone knows that activities do not always happen as planned.

Camille Schuster, a consultant, speaker, and professor of marketing, international negotiations, and consumer-centered business practices, gives these guidelines for conducting business and managing contracts in China:

1 Maintain frequent, regular communication.

2 Asking "yes" or "no" questions will not generate useful information. You will be spared embarrassment, you will feel reassured, and you will know nothing. Instead of asking your Chinese contact if the production deadline will be met, try

asking about significant events in the production process during the past week or month, or to describe recent activities of members of the production team.

3 Meet face-to-face. This is a relationship culture that requires personal, one-to-one commitment.

4 Represent all levels. Chinese culture is hierarchical and communication serves to preserve harmony. Problems are not freely discussed with superiors. Your team needs to include people at different levels of the hierarchy so that quality-control managers talk with other quality-control managers, and line engineers talk with other line engineers.

Across Cultures: The Importance of *Guanxi*

Guanxi *(gwan-shee)* means relationships. In the Chinese business world, personal connections are the basis for most business deals and contracts. It is very common for employees from one company to visit the residence of acquaintances from other organizations and bring gifts.

Critical Thinking: *What key contractual components are not included in Chinese contracts?*

Across Cultures gives you meaningful cross-cultural information that would help you, should you ever have business dealings in the featured country.

Think Critically! Apply your cross-cultural and legal knowledge and develop an informed answer to this question.

Learn About Law in Global Law

Learn about ethics in law and business through practice.

Practice analyzing facts and situations in order to make ethical decisions.

Business Ethics encourages you to think critically about a business situation.

Business ETHICS

Home Sale

Suppose you are an attorney for a construction company. While reviewing plans for a new dormitory your company is building, you realize the dormitory will be built next to a house you are selling. Someone has offered to buy the house for exactly the amount you want. You know that as soon as the college announces where the dormitory will be located, prices for surrounding property, including yours, will drastically fall. You must now call the person interested in buying your property with your decision on the offer.

Critical Thinking: What ethical issues are involved and what should you tell the interested party? Explain.

⑰ Ethics ←?→ Application

Reward or Not? Suppose you posted a reward notice that read, "Reward: $50 for the return of my lost iPod." Someone who did not know about the reward offer found your iPod and returned it to you.

◆ Would it be legal not to pay the reward money to the person who returned your iPod? Explain.
◆ Would it be ethically not to pay the reward money? Explain.

Ethics Application puts you in a decision-making position where ethics play an important role.

Study with visuals: Pictures can help you understand key concepts.

Use the visuals in *Business and Personal Law* to analyze, understand, and remember key legal concepts.

Photos and Images Relate the concepts in the text to real life through illustrations. Read the captions and answer the caption questions to make the connection.

Figures Review content and visualize how concepts relate to each other.

Develop your vocabulary skills.

Legal Talk

Legal Talk Analyze how words are built around roots, practice thinking of words with the same root in different parts of speech. Finally, use these new words in sentences.

Bilateral: *adj* Affecting two sides or parties. From Latin *bilateralis; bi = two + latus =* side: having two sides.

Unilateral: *adj* Done or undertaken by one person or party. One-sided. From Latin *unus = one + latus =* side: having one side.

Vocabulary Builder List and define five words that begin with the prefix bi or with the prefix uni.

Look it up! Check definitions in the *Black's Law Dictionary* or an online glossary. For direct links, go to **glencoe.com** to find more vocabulary resources.

Vocabulary Builder At the end of each chapter, recap and recall the legal key terms. At the same time, review the academic words to boost your reading and writing skills.

 Vocabulary Builder

❶ On a sheet of paper, use each of these terms in a sentence.

Key Terms

- contract
- offer
- acceptance
- genuine agreement
- express contract
- implied contract
- bilateral contract
- unilateral contract
- invitations to negotiate
- mirror image rule
- counteroffer
- revocation
- rejection

Academic Vocabulary

- determine
- assume
- require
- definite
- specify
- impose

Go to **glencoe.com** to play a game and improve your legal vocabulary.

Play and Practice Go to the *Business and Personal Law* Online Learning Center for crossword puzzles and for vocabulary flash cards.

Apply your writing skills: Practice different writing styles.

Writing Connection Essay-writing skills are an important key to success in class, on tests, and in life after high school.

Practice All Essay Styles The Writing Connection gives you tips and techniques for persuasive writing, personal essays, and expository writing.

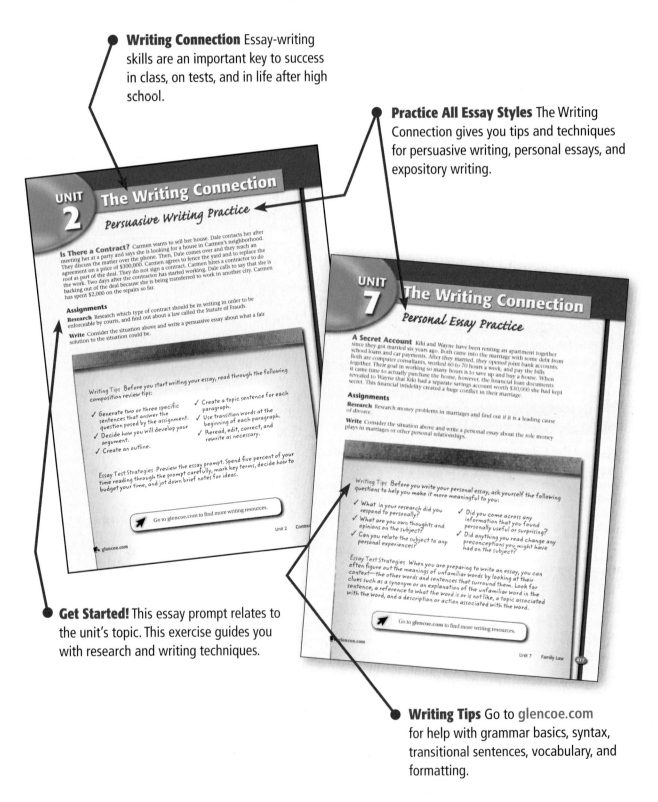

UNIT 2

The Writing Connection
Persuasive Writing Practice

Is There a Contract? Carmen wants to sell her house. Dale contacts her after meeting her at a party and says she is looking for a house in Carmen's neighborhood. They discuss the matter over the phone. Then, Dale comes over and they reach an agreement on a price of $300,000. Carmen agrees to fence the yard and to replace the roof as part of the deal. They do not sign a contract. Carmen hires a contractor to do the work. Two days after the contractor has started working, Dale calls to say that she is backing out of the deal because she is being transferred to work in another city. Carmen has spent $2,000 on the repairs so far.

Assignments

Research Research which type of contract should be in writing in order to be enforceable by courts, and find out about a law called the Statute of Frauds.

Write Consider the situation above and write a persuasive essay about what a fair solution to the situation could be.

Writing Tips Before you start writing your essay, read through the following composition review tips:

✓ Generate two or three specific sentences that answer the question posed by the assignment.
✓ Decide how you will develop your argument.
✓ Create an outline.
✓ Create a topic sentence for each paragraph.
✓ Use transition words at the beginning of each paragraph.
✓ Reread, edit, correct, and rewrite as necessary.

Essay Test Strategies Preview the essay prompt. Spend five percent of your time reading through the prompt carefully, mark key terms, decide how to budget your time, and jot down brief notes for ideas.

Go to glencoe.com to find more writing resources.

Unit 2   Contrac

glencoe.com

UNIT 7

The Writing Connection
Personal Essay Practice

A Secret Account Kiki and Wayne have been renting an apartment together since they got married six years ago. Both came into the marriage with some debt from school loans and car payments. After they married, they opened joint bank accounts. Both are computer consultants, worked 60 to 70 hours a week, and pay the bills together. Their goal in working so many hours is to save up and buy a house. When it came time to actually purchase the house, however, the financial loan documents revealed to Wayne that Kiki had a separate savings account worth $30,000 she had kept secret. This financial infidelity created a huge conflict in their marriage.

Assignments

Research Research money problems in marriages and find out if it is a leading cause of divorce.

Write Consider the situation above and write a personal essay about the role money plays in marriages or other personal relationships.

Writing Tips Before you write your personal essay, ask yourself the following questions to help you make it more meaningful to you:

✓ What in your research did you respond to personally?
✓ What are you own thoughts and opinions on the subject?
✓ Can you relate the subject to any personal experiences?
✓ Did you come across any information that you found personally useful or surprising?
✓ Did anything you read change any preconceptions you might have had on the subject?

Essay Test Strategies When you are preparing to write an essay, you can often figure out the meanings of unfamiliar words by looking at their context—the other words and sentences that surround them. Look for clues such as a synonym or an explanation of the unfamiliar word in the sentence, a reference to what the word is or is not like, a topic associated with the word, and a description or action associated with the word.

Go to glencoe.com to find more writing resources.

glencoe.com

Unit 7   Family Law   177

Get Started! This essay prompt relates to the unit's topic. This exercise guides you with research and writing techniques.

Writing Tips Go to glencoe.com for help with grammar basics, syntax, transitional sentences, vocabulary, and formatting.

Apply what you have learned:
Develop a research project.

Compete and Learn! There are several student organizations that put together local and national competitions with a focus on business law. This is a great way to challenge yourself, build credentials for your résumé, and have fun. Go to **glencoe.com** for direct links.

Set Goals and Organize! This rubric shows you how your teacher will grade your work, and gives you a lineup of goals to strive for as you develop your project.

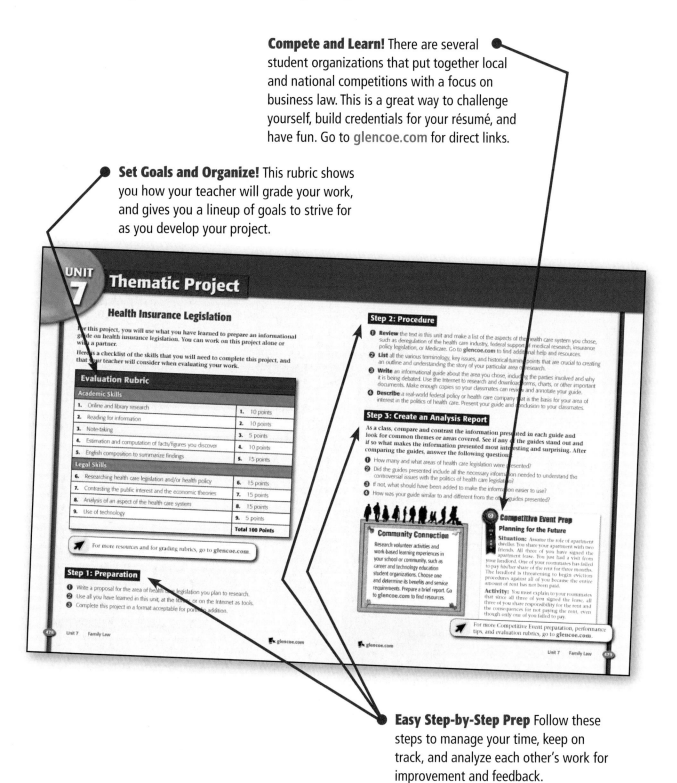

Easy Step-by-Step Prep Follow these steps to manage your time, keep on track, and analyze each other's work for improvement and feedback.

Use reading strategies to study effectively.

The Reading Guide
Take a few minutes to read this: it will connect you to the text.

Reading Checks Use these self-help tools to make sure you understand what the text is about.

How a Contract Begins

SECTION 4.2

Reading Guide

Before You Read

Connect Businesses make offers to potential customers using a variety of methods. What are some ways you have received offers?

Focus on Ideas
A contract begins with a clear offer, which can be either accepted, changed, or terminated.

Take Notes
Create a graph like the one shown and use it to take notes as you read this section. Go to glencoe.com for tips on how to improve your note-taking skills.

Key Terms
You will learn these legal words. You can also find these terms in an online legal dictionary.
- invitations to negotiate
- mirror image rule
- counteroffer

Academic Vocabulary
You will find these words in your reading and tests. Look them up in a dictionary and familiarize yourself with them.
- definite
- specify

What You'll Learn
- Explain the requirements of a valid offer.
- Recognize the requirements of an acceptance.
- Distinguish the differences between an offer, an invitation to negotiate, an acceptance, and a counteroffer.
- Explain how offers are terminated.

Why It's Important
You need to know when an offer has been made and accepted for a contract to go into effect.

Burglary
Burglary, under common law, is breaking and entering into a house at night to commit a felony. State laws have expanded the definition of burglary to include daytime breaking and entering, breaking and entering places other than homes, and breaking and entering to commit a misdemeanor. If any part of the definition of burglary cannot be proven, the defendant cannot be found guilty.

Larceny
Larceny is the unlawful taking of someone's personal property with the intent to keep the property away from that person. In some states, larceny is called theft. Petty larceny, a misdemeanor, is stealing property of a small monetary value. The individual states usually set that value between $300 and $1,000. Grand larceny, a felony, is stealing property valued at more than a state's limit for petty larceny.

Robbery
Robbery is the wrongful taking of someone's property by threatening violence or using violence. The penalty for robbery is greater than the penalty for larceny.

Vandalism
Vandalism is willful or malicious damage to property. It is also called **malicious mischief or criminal damage.** To be guilty of vandalism, a person does not have to be the one who actually does the damage. Anyone who supports vandalism by being a lookout, for example, can also be charged.

Crimes Involving Business
Could you be charged with shoplifting before you actually leave a store with unpaid merchandise?

Crimes involving business are also called white collar crimes. Business crimes include embezzlement, shoplifting, fraud, money laundering, arson, and forgery.

Embezzlement
Embezzlement is the wrongful taking of property by someone lawfully entrusted with possession and control of that property. Embezzlement is often committed by an agent or employee of a business who has the power to write checks and to withdraw funds from the firm's bank accounts.

Vandalism To be guilty of vandalism you do not have to be the person who actually did the damage. *Is graffiti considered a form of vandalism?*

Reading Check
Explain What is the difference between murder and manslaughter, and what is the difference between robbery and burglary?

44 Unit 1 What Is Law?

What Are Ethics and Morality?
Do you think choosing between right and wrong always involves rules?

Determining the difference between right and wrong can be difficult. People use different methods to decide on the right thing to do in any given situation. **Morality involves the values that govern a group's ideas about right and wrong. Ethics refers to the rules used to determine the difference between right and wrong.** In this book, the words *ethics* and *morality* will be used for both ideas.

What Does Ethics Come From?
Using ethical rules will help you deal with big and small moral questions.

The Greatest Good One way to decide about right and wrong is to apply the greatest good idea. This examines whether the action will cause the greatest good for the greatest number of people. The more good that results, the more right the action. It is used incorrectly when people think only of their own good, or if a person sees only the good created for a small group.

The Golden Rule The Golden Rule says, "Do unto others as you would have them do unto you." Many people prefer this rule because it works in many situations. The heart of the Golden Rule is **empathy.** Empathy means putting yourself in another person's position. One way to test whether an action is right or wrong under the Golden Rule is to ask, "Would I want to be treated this way?" If your answer is no, then the action breaks the Golden Rule.

Real-World Ethics Real-world ethics says that there are moral rules that most people know instinctively, without thinking. For example, lying is wrong. However, real-world ethics says that there are rare times when a person might have to lie. For example, it might be **permissible** to lie to save somebody's life. This does not mean what you have done is right. It means that what you have done is less wrong. If you lie to save a life, you know that the lie is still wrong, but you also know that it is less wrong than saying something that leads to someone's death.

Hammurabi's Code One of the earliest written set of laws is the Code of Hammurabi, which was carved in stone. *Who was Hammurabi and how long ago was his code of law written?*

As You Read
Predict How do you know you are making the right ethical decision?

Vocabulary You can find vocabulary definitions in the **Key Terms** glossary and Academic Vocabulary glossary in the back of this book.

After You Read
Summarize List the components of a legal contract.

Chapter 1 The Law and the Courts 7

Ms. Chen would then owe the finder the reward.

Oral or Written Contracts
An oral contract is created by word of mouth and comes into existence when two or more people form a contract by speaking to each other. One person usually offers to do something, and the other party agrees to do something else in return. Most contracts are oral contracts of this nature.

Sometimes, however, it is desirable to put contracts in writing. A written contract assures that both parties know the exact terms of the contract and also provides proof that the agreement was made. A law, the Statute of Frauds, requires that certain contracts must be in writing to be enforceable.

SECTION 4.1 ASSESSMENT

Self Check
1. What are the differences among valid, void, and voidable contracts?
2. What are the differences between express and implied contracts?
3. What is a unilateral contract?

Academic Connection

Mathematics You recently borrowed $500 from a friend. You signed a contract that requires you to pay back one third of the loan every month for three months. How much will you

have to pay back each of the first two months? How much will you have to pay back the third month?

THEORY Number and Operations: Using Fractions, Decimals, and Rounding To figure out 1/3 of $500, divide 500 by 3 and round to the nearest cent. Remember to round numbers of 5 or more up and numbers less than 5 down. For example, $2.224 rounds to $2.22 and $2.226 rounds to $2.23. To get the payment for the third month, subtract the

amounts for the first two months from 500.

For more math practice, go to the Math Appendix.

Critical Thinking

Reward: Lost Backpack You lost your backpack and posted a $20 reward for it. If someone who did not know about the backpack returned the backpack, would you be legally obligated to pay the reward?

Go to **glencoe.com** to check your answers.

86 Unit 2 Contract Law

XXX

Characteristics of a Contract

Now that you know about the different elements of a contract, can you think of different types of contracts?

Contracts can be created in different ways and can **assume** diverse forms. A contract can be described by any of the following characteristics:

- Valid, void, voidable, or unenforceable
- Express or implied
- Bilateral or unilateral
- Oral or written

Look at these questions! What do you think? What would you do? These questions prompt you to develop an opinion before you read. This will help you focus and understand.

Flex Your Reading Just like you flex a muscle to make it stronger, this feature encourages you to be aware of what specific skills you need for a reading activity.

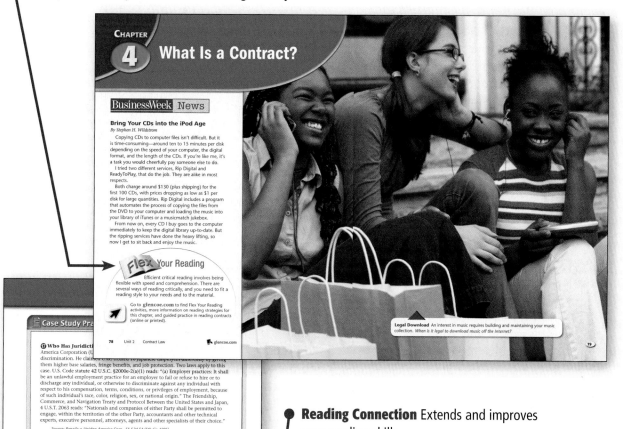

Reading Connection Extends and improves your reading skills.

▶ Reading: What's in It for You?

What role does reading play in your life? The possibilities are countless. Are you on a sports team? Perhaps you like to read about the latest news and statistics in your sport or find out about new training techniques. Are you looking for a part-time job? You might be looking for advice about résumé writing, interview techniques, or information about a company. Are you enrolled in an English class, an algebra class, or a business class? Then, your assignments require a lot of reading.

Improving or Fine-Tuning Your Reading Skills Will:

- ◆ Improve your grades
- ◆ Allow you to read faster and more efficiently
- ◆ Improve your study skills
- ◆ Help you remember more information accurately
- ◆ Improve your writing

▶ The Reading Process

Good reading skills build on one another, overlap, and spiral around in much the same way that a winding staircase goes around and around while leading you to a higher place. This handbook is designed to help you find and use the tools you will need **before, during,** and **after** reading.

Strategies You Can Use

- ◆ Identify, understand, and learn new words
- ◆ Understand why you read
- ◆ Take a quick look at the whole text
- ◆ Try to predict what you are about to read

- ◆ Take breaks while you read and ask yourself questions about the text
- ◆ Take notes
- ◆ Keep thinking about what will come next
- ◆ Summarize

▶ Vocabulary Development

Word identification and vocabulary skills are the building blocks of the reading and the writing process. By learning to use a variety of strategies to build your word skills and vocabulary, you will become a stronger reader.

Use Context to Determine Meaning

The best way to expand your vocabulary is to read widely, listen carefully, and participate in a rich variety of discussions. When reading on your own, though, you can often figure out the meanings of new words by looking at the **context; look at** the other words and sentences that surround them.

Tips for Using Context

Look for clues such as:

A synonym or an explanation of the unknown word in the sentence:
  *Elise's shop specialized in **millinery**, or **hats for women.***

A reference to what the word is or is not like:
  *An **archaeologist,** like a **historian,** deals with the past.*

A general topic associated with the word:
  *The **cooking** teacher discussed the best way to **braise** meat.*

A description or action associated with the word:
  *He used the **hoe** to **dig up** the garden.*

Predict a Possible Meaning

Another way to determine the meaning of a word is to take the word apart. If you understand the meaning of the **base,** or **root** part of a word, and also know the meanings of key syllables added either to the beginning or end of the base word, you can usually figure out what the word means.

Word Origins Since Latin, Greek, and Anglo-Saxon roots are the basis for much of our English vocabulary, having some background in languages can be a useful vocabulary tool. For example, *astronomy* comes from the Greek root *astro,* which means "relating to the stars." The word *stellar* also refers to stars, but its origin is Latin. Knowing basic root words can help you determine meanings, derivations, and spellings in English.

Prefixes and Suffixes A prefix is a word part that can be added to the beginning of a word. For example, the prefix *semi* means "half" or "partial," so *semicircle* means "half a circle." A suffix is a word part that can be added to the end of a word. Adding a suffix often changes a word from one part of speech to another.

Using Dictionaries A dictionary provides the meaning or meanings of a word. Look at the sample dictionary entry on the next page to see what other information it provides.

Thesauruses and Specialized Reference Books A thesaurus provides synonyms and often antonyms. It is a useful tool to expand your vocabulary. Remember to check the exact definition of the listed words in a dictionary before you use a thesaurus. Specialized dictionaries such as *Barron's Dictionary of Business Terms* or *Black's Law Dictionary* list terms and expressions that are not commonly included in a general dictionary. You can also use online dictionaries.
See **glencoe.com** for direct links.

Glossaries Many textbooks and technical works contain condensed dictionaries that provide an alphabetical listing of words used in the text and their specific definitions.

Dictionary Entry

Forms of
the word

Numbered
definitions

Usage label

Part of
speech

Example
of use

help (help) **helped** or (archaic) **holp**, **helped** or (archaic) **hol-pen**, **help-ing**. *v.t.* **1.** to provide with support, as in the performance of a task; be of service to: *He helped his brother paint the room.* ▲ also used elliptically with a preposition or adverb: *He helped the old woman up the stairs.* **2.** to enable (someone or something) to accomplish a goal or achieve a desired effect: *The coach's advice helped the team to win.* **3.** to provide with sustenance or relief, as in time of need or distress; succor: *The Red Cross helped the flood victims.* **4.** to promote or contribute to; further. *The medication helped his recovery.* **5.** to be useful or profitable to; be of advantage to: *It might help you if you read the book.* **6.** to improve or remedy: *Nothing really helped his sinus condition.* **7.** to prevent; stop: *I can't help his rudeness.* **8.** to refrain from; avoid: *I couldn't help smiling when I heard the story.* **9.** to wait on or serve (often with to): *The clerk helped us. The hostess helped him to the dessert.* **10. cannot help but.** *Informal* cannot but. **11. so help me (God).** oath of affirmation. **12. to help oneself to.** to take or appropriate: *The thief helped himself to all the jewels.* —*v.i.* to provide support, as in the performance of a task; be of service. —*n.* **1.** act of providing support, service, or sustenance. **2.** source of support, service, or sustenance. **3.** person or group of persons hired to work for another or others. **4.** means of improving, remedying, or preventing. [Old English *helpan* to aid, succor, benefit.] **Syn.** *v.t.* **1.** Help, aid, assist mean to support in a useful way. Help is the most common word and means to give support in response to a known or expressed need or for a definite purpose: *Everyone helped to make the school fair a success.* **Aid** means to give relief in times of distress or difficulty: *It is the duty of rich nations to aid the poor.* **Assist** means to serve another person in the performance of his task in a secondary capacity: *The secretary assists the officer by taking care of his corresponding.*

Idioms

Origin
(etymology)

Synonyms

Recognize Word Meanings across Subjects Have you learned a new word in one class and then noticed it in your readings for other subjects? The word might not mean exactly the same thing in each class, but you can use the meaning you already know to help you understand what it means in another subject area. For example:

Math *After you multiply the two numbers, explain how you arrived at the* **product***.*

Science *One* **product** *of photosynthesis is oxygen.*

Economics *The Gross National* **Product** *is the total dollar value of goods and services produced by a nation.*

▶ Understanding What You Read

Reading comprehension means understanding—deriving meaning from—what you have read. Using a variety of strategies can help you improve your comprehension and make reading more interesting and more fun.

Read for a Reason

To get the greatest benefit from what you read, you should **establish a purpose for reading.** In school, you have many reasons for reading. Some of them are:

- To learn and understand new information
- To find specific information
- To review before a test
- To complete an assignment
- To prepare (research) before you write

As your reading skills improve, you will notice that you apply different strategies to fit the different purposes for reading. For example, if you are reading for entertainment, you might read quickly, but if you read to gather information or follow directions, you might read more slowly, take notes, construct a graphic organizer, or reread sections of text.

Draw on Personal Background

Drawing on personal background may also be called activating prior knowledge. Before you start reading a text, ask yourself questions like these:

- What have I heard or read about this topic?
- Do I have any personal experience relating to this topic?

Using a KWL Chart A KWL chart is a good device for organizing information you gather before, during, and after reading. In the first column, list what you already **know,** then list what you **want** to know in the middle column. Use the third column when you review and you assess what you **learned.** You can also add more columns to record places where you found information and places where you can look for more information.

K (What I already know)	W (What I want to know)	L (What I have learned)

Adjust Your Reading Speed Your reading speed is a key factor in how well you understand what you are reading. You will need to adjust your speed depending on your reading purpose.

Scanning *means running your eyes quickly over the material to look for words or phrases. Scan when you need a specific piece of information.*

Skimming means reading a passage quickly to find its main idea or to get an overview. Skim a text when you preview to determine what the material is about.

Reading for detail involves careful reading while paying attention to text structure and monitoring your understanding. Read for detail when you are learning concepts, following complicated directions, or preparing to analyze a text.

▶ Techniques to Understand and Remember What You Read

Preview

Before beginning a selection, it's helpful to **preview** what you are about to read.

> ### Previewing Strategies
>
> **Read** the title, headings, and subheadings of the selection.
> **Look** at the illustrations and notice how the text is organized.
> **Skim** the selection: Take a glance at the whole thing
> **Decide** what the main idea might be.
> **Predict** what a selection will be about.

Predict

Have you ever read a mystery, decided who committed the crime, and then changed your mind as more clues were revealed? You were adjusting your predictions. Did you smile when you found out you guessed the murderer? You were verifying your predictions.

As you read, take educated guesses about story events and outcomes; that is, **make predictions** before and during reading. This will help you focus your attention on the text and it will improve your understanding.

Determine the Main Idea

When you look for the **main idea**, you are looking for the most important statement in a text. Depending on what kind of text you are reading, the main idea can be located at the very beginning (news stories in newspaper or a magazine) or at the end (scientific research document). Ask yourself:

- What is each sentence about?
- Is there one sentence that is more important than all the others?
- What idea do details support or point out?

Take Notes

Cornell Note-Taking System: There are many methods for note taking. The **Cornell note-taking system** is a well-known method that can help you organize what you read. To the right is a note-taking chart based on the Cornell note-taking system.

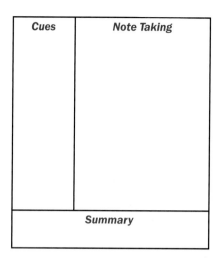

Graphic organizers: Using a graphic organizer to retell content in a visual representation will help you remember and retain content. You might make a **chart** or **diagram** to organize what you have read. Here are some examples of graphic organizers:

Venn diagrams: When mapping out a comparison-and-contrast text structure, you can use a Venn diagram. The outer portions of the circles will show how two characters, ideas, or items are different. The overlapping part will compare two things, or show how they are similar.

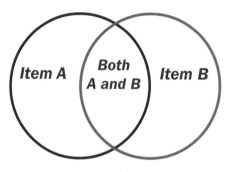

Flow charts: To help you track the sequence of events, or cause and effect, use a flow chart. Arrange ideas or events in their logical, sequential order. Then draw arrows between your ideas to indicate how one idea or event flows into another.

Go to **glencoe.com** for more information about note taking and more study tools.

Visualize

Try to form a mental picture of scenes, characters, and events as you read. Use the details and descriptions the author gives you. If you can **visualize** what you read, it will be more interesting and you will remember it better.

Question

Ask yourself questions about the text while you read. Ask yourself about the importance of the sentences, how they relate to one another, if you understand what you just read, and what you think is going to come next.

Clarify

If you feel you do not understand meaning (through questioning), try these techniques:

> **What to Do When You Do not Understand**
>
> ◆ Reread confusing parts of the text.
> ◆ Diagram (chart) relationships between chunks of text, ideas, and sentences.
> ◆ Look up unfamiliar words.
> ◆ Talk out the text to yourself.
> ◆ Read the passage once more.

Review

Take time to stop and review what you have read. Use your note-taking tools (graphic organizers or Cornell notes charts). Also, review and consider your KWL chart.

Monitor Your Comprehension

Continue to check your understanding by using the following two strategies:

Summarize   Pause and tell yourself the main ideas of the text and the key supporting details. Try to answer the following questions: Who? What? When? Where? Why? How?

Paraphrase   Pause, close the book, and try to retell what you have just read in your own words. It might help to pretend you are explaining the text to someone who has not read it and does not know the material.

▶ Understanding Text Structure

Good writers do not just put together sentences and paragraphs, they organize their writing with a specific purpose in mind. That organization is called text structure. When you understand and follow the structure of a text, it is easier to remember the information you are reading. There are many ways text may be structured. Watch for these **signal words**: They will help you follow the text's organization (also, remember to use these techniques when you write).

Compare and Contrast

This structure shows similarities and differences between people, things, and ideas. This is often used to demonstrate that things that seem alike are really different, or vice versa.

Signal words: *similarly, more, less, on the one hand / on the other hand, in contrast, but, however*

Cause and Effect

Writers used the cause and effect structure to explore the reasons for something happening and to examine the results or consequences of events.

> **Signal words:** *so, because, as a result, therefore, for the following reasons*

Problem and Solution

When they organize text around the question "how?" writers state a problem and suggest solutions.

> **Signal words:** *how, help, problem, obstruction, overcome, difficulty, need, attempt, have to, must*

Sequence

Sequencing tells you in which order to consider thoughts or facts. Examples of sequencing are:

Chronological order refers to the order in which events take place.

> **Signal words:** *first, next, then, finally*

Spatial order describes the organization of things in space (to describe a room, for example).

> **Signal words:** *above, below, behind, next to*

Order of importance lists things or thoughts from the most important to the least important (or the other way around).

> **Signal words:** *principal, central, main, important, fundamental*

▶ Reading for Meaning

It is important to think about what you are reading to get the most information out of a text, to understand the consequences of what the text says, to remember the content, and to form your own opinion about what the content means.

Interpret

Interpreting is asking yourself, "What is the writer really saying?" and then using what you already know to answer that question.

Infer

Writers do not always state exactly everything they want you to understand. By providing clues and details, they sometimes imply certain information. An **inference** involves using your reason and experience to develop the idea on your own, based on what an author implies or suggests. What is most important when drawing inferences is to be sure that you have accurately based your guesses on supporting details from the text. If you cannot point to a place in the selection to help back up your inference, you may need to rethink your guess.

Draw Conclusions

A conclusion is a general statement you can make and explain with reasoning, or with supporting details from a text. If you read a story describing a sport where five players bounce a ball and throw it through a high hoop, you may conclude that the sport is basketball.

Analyze

To understand persuasive nonfiction (a text that discusses facts and opinions to arrive at a conclusion), you need to analyze statements and examples to see if they support the main idea. To understand an informational text (a text, such as a textbook, that gives you information, not opinions), you need to keep track of how the ideas are organized to find the main points.

> **Hint:** *Use your graphic organizers and notes charts.*

Distinguish Facts and Opinions

This is one of the most important reading skills you can learn. A fact is a statement that can be proven. An opinion is what the writer believes. A writer may support opinions with facts, but an opinion cannot be proven. For example:

> **Fact:** *California produces fruit and other agricultural products.*

> **Opinion:** *California produces the best fruit and other agricultural products.*

Evaluate

Would you take seriously an article on nuclear fission if you knew it was written by a comedian? If you need to rely on accurate information, you need to find out who wrote what you are reading and why. Where did the writer get information? Is the information one-sided? Can you verify the information?

▶ Reading for Research

You will need to **read actively** in order to research a topic. You might also need to generate an interesting, relevant, and researchable **question** on your own and locate appropriate print and nonprint information from a wide variety of sources. Then, you will need to **categorize** that information, evaluate it, and **organize** it in a new way in order to produce a research project for a specific audience. Finally, **draw conclusions** about your original research question. These conclusions may lead you to other areas for further inquiry.

Locate Appropriate Print and Nonprint Information

In your research, try to use a variety of sources. Different sources present information in different ways, and your research project will be more interesting and balanced when you read from a variety of sources.

Textbooks Textbooks include any book used as a basis for instruction or a source of information.

Book Indices and bibliographies A bibliography is an alphabetical listing of books. A book index lists a variety of topics or resources.

Periodicals Magazines and journals are issued at regular intervals, such as weekly or monthly. One way to locate information in magazines is to use the *Readers' Guide to Periodical Literature*. This guide is available in print form in most libraries.

Technical Manuals A manual is a guide or handbook intended to give instruction on how to perform a task or operate something. A vehicle owner's manual might give information on how to operate and service a car.

Reference Books Reference books include encyclopedias and almanacs, and are used to locate specific pieces of information.

Electronic Encyclopedias, Databases, and the Internet There are many ways to locate extensive information using your computer. Infotrac, for instance, acts as an online readers guide. CD encyclopedias can provide easy access to all subjects.

Organize and Convert Information

As you gather information from different sources, taking careful notes, you will need to think about how to **synthesize** the information, that is, convert it into a unified whole, as well as how to change it into a form your audience will easily understand and that will meet your assignment guidelines.

1. First, ask yourself what you want your audience to know.
2. Then, think about a pattern of organization, a structure that will best show your main ideas. You might ask yourself the following questions:
   - When comparing items or ideas, what graphic aids can I use?
   - When showing the reasons something happened and the effects of certain actions, what text structure would be best?
   - How can I briefly and clearly show important information to my audience?
   - Would an illustration or even a cartoon help to make a certain point?

Unit Objectives

Chapter	Section	Objectives
Chapter 1	**1.1**	• **Explain** how ethical decisions are made. • **Identify** the different ethical character traits. • **Describe** how the law relates to ethics. • **Explain** the importance of the law. • **Identify** the parts of the Constitution. • **Explain** the components of common law. • **Explain** the purposes of statutory law. • **Identify** the ways that the courts make law.
	1.2	• **Define** jurisdiction. • **Describe** the structure of the federal court system. • **Explain** the role of the United States Supreme Court. • **Determine** the common structure of most state court systems. • **Identify** alternative dispute resolution techniques. • **Differentiate** between civil and criminal cases. • **Describe** the steps in a civil lawsuit. • **Explain** the rights of criminal defendants. • **List** the steps in a criminal prosecution.
Chapter 2	**2.1**	• **Explain** the differences between categories of crime. • **Distinguish** federal from state criminal law. • **Describe** the elements of a crime. • **Determine** several defenses to criminal acts. • **Explain** the differences between penalties for committing felonies and misdemeanors.
	2.2	• **Describe** the different categories of crime. • **Identify** several special crimes that involve the use of motor vehicles. • **Define** different types of business crimes, such as arson, forgery, and embezzlement.
Chapter 3	**3.1**	• **Distinguish** between a tort and a crime. • **Differentiate** between and give examples of negligence and intentional torts. • **Explain** a person's rights and duties in relation to tort law. • **Describe** remedies available in tort law. • **List** the main intentional torts against people and property.
	3.2	• **Define** negligence. • **Explain** the concepts of the reasonable person test and proximate cause. • **Explain** the concept of strict liability. • **Compare and contrast** negligence, strict liability, and proximate cause.

Understanding Brackets, Letters, and Ability Levels in the Teacher Wraparound Edition

Brackets Brackets on the reduced student edition page correspond to teaching strategies and activities in the Teacher Wraparound Edition. As you teach the lesson, the brackets show you exactly where to use the teaching strategies and activities.

Letters The letters on the reduced student edition page identify the type of strategy or activity. See the key below to learn about the different types of strategies and activities.

Ability Levels Teaching strategies that appear throughout the chapters have been identified by one of three codes to give you an idea of their suitability for students of varying learning styles and abilities.

Resources Key program resources are listed in each chapter. Icons indicate the format of resources.

KEY TO LETTERS

R **Reading Strategy** activities help you teach reading skills and vocabulary.

C **Critical Thinking** strategies help students apply and extend what they have learned.

S **Skills Practice** strategies help students practice historical analysis and geographical skills.

W **Writing Support** activities provide writing opportunities to help students comprehend the text.

D **Develop Concepts** activities use various strategies to help teachers gauge and plan for students' concept development.

U **Universal Access** activities provide differentiated instruction for English language learners and suggestions for teaching various types of learners.

NCLB **No Child Left Behind** activities help students practice and improve their abilities in academic subjects.

KEY TO ABILITY LEVELS

L1 strategies should be within the ability range of all students. Often full class participation is required.

L2 strategies are for average to above-average students or for small groups. Some teacher direction is necessary.

L3 strategies are designed for students able and willing to work independently. Minimal teacher direction is necessary.

KEY TO RESOURCE ICONS

📁 Print Material

💿 CD/DVD

🖥 Internet

TeacherWorks™
All-In-One Planner and Resource Center

Teacher Wraparound Edition

Student Activity Workbook with Academic Integration Teacher Annotated Edition

For the Unit:
Lesson Plans
National and State Standards Correlations

For the Chapters:
Lessons Plans
Note-Taking Graphic Organizers
Chapter Outlines
Chapter Summaries
Enrichment Activities Masters

Supplemental Cases
Internet Connection Student Activities Masters
Blackline Masters for Student Edition Figures and Supplemental Figures
Ethics and Business Law Activities
Competitive Events Test-Taking Prep
Reproducible Chapter Tests

@ Link to the *Business and Personal Law* **Online Learning Center** with Podcasts through glencoe.com.

Real-World Applications

Demonstrate Case Resolutions

Case Study

Learning Objective

- Understand the role of the U.S. Supreme Court (p. 20).
- Understand the impact of a negative influence on a jury (p. 42).
- Identify the elements of negligence (p. 64).

Case Study Practice

- Understand the concept of jurisdiction (p. 31).
- Explain the concept of valid consent (p. 51).
- Understand the concepts of strict liability and negligence (p. 69).

Landmark Case

- Understand the differences between federal and state law (pp. 74–75).

Apply Business Law Concepts

BusinessWeek News

Learning Objective

- Understand how the law relates to ethics and cybercrime (p. 4).
- Understand categories of crime (p. 32).
- Understand tort law (p. 52).

Global Law

- Identify international sources of law (p. 12).
- Explain the International Criminal Court (p. 37).
- Differentiate between tort law in Mexico and the U.S. (p. 55).

Business ETHICS

- Explain ethical decisions (p. 9).
- Understand the concept of negligence (p. 61).

Ethics Application

- Apply an ethical decision-making process (p. 31).
- Apply an ethical decision-making process (p. 51).
- Understand the ethical duty to disclose (p. 69).

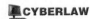

CYBERLAW

- Understand state criminal law (p. 46).

Teach Financial Literacy

Ask STANDARD &POOR'S

Learning Objective

- Understand the ethical and legal issues related to investing (p. 3).

Bring Project-Based Learning into the Law Classroom

Unit Thematic Project

Small Claims Suits

- **Introduce Concepts**
  A small claim suit is filed when the debt or damage does not normally exceed $7,500 exclusive of interest and costs.
- **Explore Concepts**
  Read the Thematic Project Preview and the WebQuest activity (p. 3).
  Ask students to think about the information they need to gather to prepare a case as they study Chapters 1, 2, and 3.
- **Apply Concepts**
  Research agencies that can help with small claims problems and court forms needed for filing, outline the case key points (pp. 72 and 73).

Extend Content

Reading Connection

Using American Bar Association (ABA) Resources

- Direct students to pages 31, 51, and 69 in the Student Edition.
- Ask them to use glencoe.com to find links to ABA resource documents.
- Students should browse and select one document for each chapter.
- See pages 31, 51, 69, and 75 in this edition for specific instructions.

Reading and Writing Support

Feature or Activity	Topic	Reading Strategy	Writing Strategy
STANDARD &POOR'S	Investing money	Reading a primary source document	
Thematic Project Preview	Small claims court		Researching and taking notes
BusinessWeek	Readings about cybercrime (Ch. 1), corporate fraud (Ch. 2), and liability (Ch. 3)	Reading for detail Developing flexibility in reading speed	
Section Reading Guide	Before-reading activities and tools	Connect students' lives with content Focus on the main idea	Using a graphic organizer to take notes
As You Read	During-reading tool	Predict content Determine what students already know	
Reading Check	During-reading tool	Self-check understanding of content	
After You Read	After-reading tool	Summarize section content	Writing and organizing a list of key concepts
Standardized Test Practice	Senate Document 105-14 (Ch. 1) Department of Motor Vehicles (Ch. 2) National Highway Traffic Safety Administration (Ch. 3)	Reading a primary source document Practicing critical reading skills	
Reading Connection	American Bar Association online resources	Reading a primary source document Extending and applying content Reading for knowledge Developing critical reading skills. Developing flexibility of reading speed	Taking notes Summarizing
The Writing Connection	Expository writing		Creating outlines, topic sentences, editing
Unit Thematic Project	Writing a guide for small claims court	Using resources notes to support writing effort	Creating outlines, writing drafts, editing
Landmark Case	Federal versus state law case	Developing critical reading skills	Summarizing

Unit Overview

Main) Idea

Unit 1 introduces the fundamentals of the U.S. legal system, including the basics of law, such as criminal, civil, and tort law. In addition, the court system is examined, which is a foundation for forthcoming chapters.

00:00 OUT OF TIME?

If class time is too short to cover the chapters thoroughly, have students:

- Write down the vocabulary terms and their definitions.
- Read What You'll Learn and Why It's Important at the beginning of each section.
- Go to the *Business and Personal Law* Online Learning Center at glencoe.com and download the free Study-to-Go content to their cell phones or PDAs.

▶ **USING VISUALS ....**

Separation of Powers
Answer The legislative branch consists of the U.S. Congress and has the power to enact laws.

UNIT 1 What Is Law?

In This Unit You Will Find:

Chapter 1
The Law and the Courts

Chapter 2
Criminal Law

Chapter 3
Tort Law

• • • • • • • • • • • • • • • • •

Separation of Powers
There are three branches of the U.S. government: the executive, the judicial, and the legislative. The executive branch is headed by the President and has the power to carry out the law. The judicial branch consists of the courts and has the power to interpret the law. *What is the legislative branch?*

2

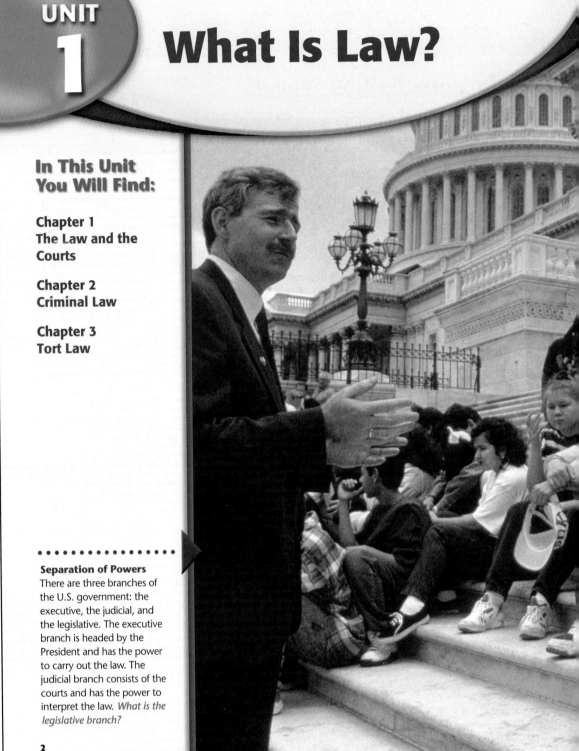

Unit Thematic Project Preview

W Writing Support

In Washington state, a district county court awarded a free-speech group damages in a small-claims suit against a company for using unsolicited e-mail to deceptively send its marketing message. Washington is one of a few states with anti-spam laws.

Critical Thinking Ask students to find spam e-mails or ads and analyze the advertisement's language. They should decipher persuasive writing techniques. (Word choice, emotional appeal, hyperbole, irony, etc.)

Thematic Project Preview

Small Claims Suits

As you read this unit, use this checklist to prepare for the unit project:

✓ List terms and concepts commonly used in small claims court.

✓ Determine what type of preparation is needed for a small claims case.

✓ Evaluate whether the facts are sufficient enough to make a decision in the small claims case you create.

Legal Portfolio When you complete the Unit Thematic Project, you will have a guide for filing an action in your state's small claims court to add to your portfolio.

 Web**Quest**

Small Claims
Small claims courts handle cases where a claim's value normally does not exceed $7,500 (although the amount can vary from state-to-state). Log on to **glencoe.com** to get a list of agencies that can help you with any small claims problems. List your findings in your WebQuest folder to share with your class.

 Find Unit 1 study tools such as **Graphic Organizers, Academic Skills Review,** and **Practice Tests** at **glencoe.com**.

 Ask

STANDARD &POOR'S   Invest Your Money Wisely

Q: What is a typical investment scam, and what can I do to avoid it?

A: A common way investors lose money is through penny stock scams. Penny stocks are highly risky stocks that sell for under one dollar. In a penny stock scam, a scammer buys a large amount of cheap stock in a worthless company. The scammer then drums up interest in the stock with hot tips spread by word of mouth and over the Internet. As people buy up the stock, thinking they are getting in on a great deal, it drives up demand for the stock—and the price. By the time investors discover the stock is worthless and demand dries up, the scammer has sold all the stock at a tidy profit. Consider the source of a stock tip, treat every tip with doubt, and resist peer pressure. Most importantly, do not get greedy. Always heed the old saying, "If it sounds too good to be true, it probably is." Thoroughly investigate investment opportunities you are considering. Conduct research or consult with an investment professional.

R **Language Arts/Reading** Standard & Poor's is one of the world's main providers of credit ratings and financial-market indices. Go to **glencoe.com** and read more about investment.

 glencoe.com

Unit 1   What Is Law?   **3**

 Ask

STANDARD &POOR'S

R **Reading Strategy**
Language Arts/Reading Direct students to explore S&P's resources on investments.

Math Activity If you buy 100 shares of a $3 stock and you sell this stock after it grows to $5 per share, what will be your total gross proceeds, and what is your net capital gain?
($5 \times 100 = 500$; $(5 - 3) \times 100 = 200 net capital gain)

5-minute ➤ **Launch**

KWL Chart Have students make a list of any criminal justice system dramas or stories they have seen on television such as network news agencies, fictional prime-time dramas, or documentaries. Next, ask them to skim Unit 1 and notice the headers, figures, and photos. Using a KWL chart for their responses, have them indicate their knowledge level of the law based on their media experiences.

Building Law Background
Ask students these questions to activate prior knowledge:

Chapter 1
Why are laws needed to govern a country? (To reflect and promote the values of its society. Laws are intended to protect the welfare, safety, and diverse interests of individuals and society in general.)

Chapter 2
What do you think are the "hot button" current issues in criminal law in your state? (Incarceration, death penalty, homeland terrorism, transborder crime, etc.)

Chapter 3
Can a civil lawsuit also have elements of a criminal action? (Perhaps, in the case of wire and mail fraud, or other federal offenses.)

Plan Your Lesson Section by Section

NBEA	NATIONAL BUSINESS LAW STANDARDS
Section 1.1	• **Identify** consequences of unethical and illegal contact. • **Describe** how to develop an ethical and legal lifestyle. • **List** the most common sources of the law. • **Explain** the way social forces may sometimes conflict. • **Describe** the powers and limitations of the federal government as stated in the Constitution. • **Identify** the basic freedoms guaranteed by the Bill of Rights and describe several key constitutional amendments beyond the Bill of Rights. • **Compare** and contrast the national constitution with state, territory, and province constitutions. • **Determine** how courts make law and explain the role of precedent in the legal system.
Section 1.2	• **Differentiate** between cases that belong within the jurisdiction of the federal and state, territory, and province court systems. • **Compare** the role of juvenile court with the role of other courts within a state, territory, or province. • **Explain** the role of the national and state, territory, and province appellate courts. • **Differentiate** between the roles of the U.S. Supreme Court and state, territory, and province supreme courts. • **Define** litigation. • **Define** alternate dispute resolution (ADR). • **Explain** the advantages and disadvantages of arbitration, mediation, and conciliation. • **Compare** and contrast the steps in a civil lawsuit with the steps in a criminal prosecution. • **List** and explain the steps in criminal and civil trials. • **Describe** the appellate process in criminal and civil cases. • **Define** the statute of limitations.

NCLB	ACADEMIC STANDARDS	Activity/Feature
	English Language Arts: NCTE 3 Apply a wide range of strategies to comprehend, interpret, evaluate, and appreciate texts.	*BusinessWeek* News, Case Study, Case Study Practice
	English Language Arts: NCTE 6 Apply knowledge of language structure, language conventions, media techniques, figurative language, and genre to create, critique, and discuss print and non-print texts.	Legal Talk, ad copy, Key Terms, and Academic Vocabulary
	Social Studies: NCSS 2 Study the way human beings view themselves in and over time.	Section 1.1 Assessment
	Mathematics: NCTM DAPS 2 Select and use appropriate statistical methods to analyze data.	Section 1.2 Assessment
	English Language Arts: NCTE 12 Use spoken, written, and visual language to accomplish your own purposes.	Global Law
	English Language Arts: NCTE 10 Students whose first language is not English make use of their first language to develop competency in the English language arts and to develop understanding of content across the curriculum.	Key Terms, Academic Vocabulary, Legal Talk, Vocabulary Builder
	English Language Arts: NCTE 1 Read a wide range of print and non-print texts to build an understanding of texts; to acquire new information; to respond to the needs and demands of society and the workplace; and for personal fulfillment.	Global Law, Cyberlaw
	Social Studies: NCSS 10 Study the ideals, principles, and practices of citizenship in a democratic republic.	Case Study

Connect Your Business Law Classroom to the World of Work

This chart shows the 21st Century Skills, foundation skills, and workplace competencies that students develop as they work in this chapter.

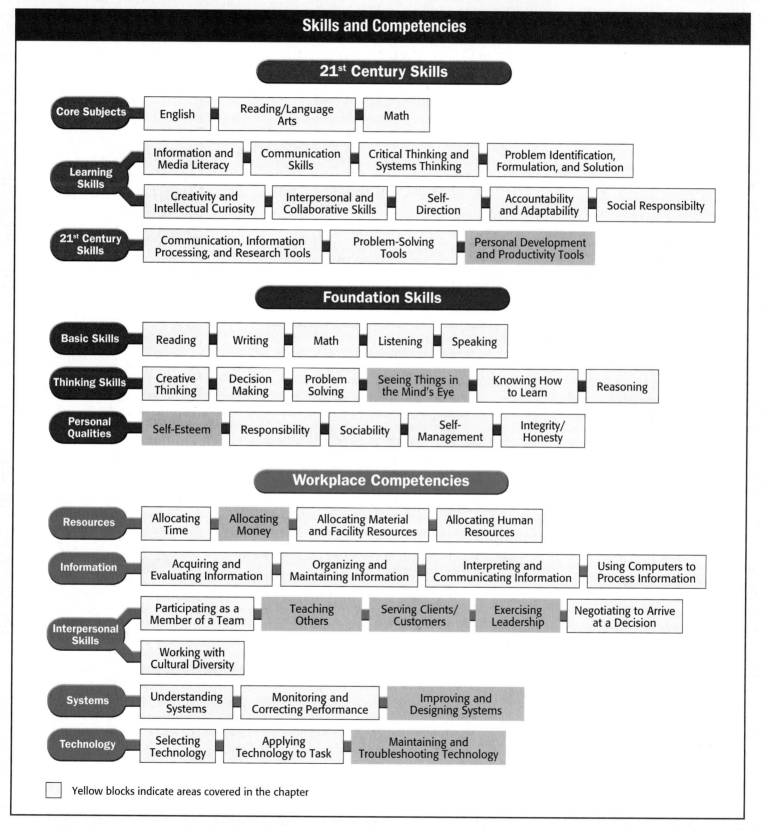

Skills and Competencies

21st Century Skills

Core Subjects: English | Reading/Language Arts | Math

Learning Skills: Information and Media Literacy | Communication Skills | Critical Thinking and Systems Thinking | Problem Identification, Formulation, and Solution | Creativity and Intellectual Curiosity | Interpersonal and Collaborative Skills | Self-Direction | Accountability and Adaptability | Social Responsibilty

21st Century Skills: Communication, Information Processing, and Research Tools | Problem-Solving Tools | Personal Development and Productivity Tools

Foundation Skills

Basic Skills: Reading | Writing | Math | Listening | Speaking

Thinking Skills: Creative Thinking | Decision Making | Problem Solving | Seeing Things in the Mind's Eye | Knowing How to Learn | Reasoning

Personal Qualities: Self-Esteem | Responsibility | Sociability | Self-Management | Integrity/Honesty

Workplace Competencies

Resources: Allocating Time | Allocating Money | Allocating Material and Facility Resources | Allocating Human Resources

Information: Acquiring and Evaluating Information | Organizing and Maintaining Information | Interpreting and Communicating Information | Using Computers to Process Information

Interpersonal Skills: Participating as a Member of a Team | Teaching Others | Serving Clients/Customers | Exercising Leadership | Negotiating to Arrive at a Decision | Working with Cultural Diversity

Systems: Understanding Systems | Monitoring and Correcting Performance | Improving and Designing Systems

Technology: Selecting Technology | Applying Technology to Task | Maintaining and Troubleshooting Technology

Yellow blocks indicate areas covered in the chapter

1 The Law and the Courts

Introduce the Chapter

The Law and the Courts

Chapter 1 explains the process of ethical decision making and expands into a study of how ethics and law differ. Students will study the primary sources of U.S. law and gain insight into how the legal system works.

Building Background

Introduce the topic of ethics by asking students to examine why doing the right thing feels good. Ask them to discuss the influences in society that help citizens act in appropriate and considerate ways (morals of parents, religion, peer pressure, laws)

BusinessWeek News

Explain to students that spam is any unsolicited e-mail sent in bulk. Tell students that the CAN-SPAM Act of 2003 requires that unsolicited commercial e-mail messages be labeled, and it prohibits the use of deceptive subject lines and false headers in such messages.

R Reading Strategy

Your Reading

Ask students about their experience reading e-mails and online documents. Do they know how to make sure that an e-mail or an attachment is from a reliable source? How do they decide if an online document is factually accurate?

BusinessWeek News

Another Spammer Flames Out
By Elizabeth Woyke

One of the world's biggest spammers may face time in the slammer. On June 30, federal authorities arrested Christopher Smith (aka "Rizler") of Burnsville, Minn., after he stepped off a plane in Minneapolis. Smith, 25, was returning from the Dominican Republic, where he went in May after an FBI raid seized $4.2 million in assets, including a fleet of luxury cars.

Experts call Smith one of the ten most prolific spammers. Gregg Mastoras of software firm Sophos says Smith sent more than 1 billion e-mail pitches for things like fake college degrees and hair-growth products, eventually building a chain of Web sites staffed by an 85-person office. The Feds allege that Smith kept operating from overseas under an alias, making $18 million this year alone selling medications without proper prescriptions or a medical license. He's charged with criminal contempt of a court order and could face up to six months in jail.

 Flex Your Reading

Efficient critical reading involves being flexible with speed and comprehension. There are several ways of reading critically, and you need to fit a reading style to your needs and to the material.

Go to **glencoe.com** for Flex Your Reading activities, more information on reading strategies for this chapter, and for guided practice in reading legal documents.

4 Unit 1 What Is Law?   🡒 glencoe.com

Classroom Resources

- Student Edition
- Teacher Wraparound Edition
- Student Activity Workbook with Academic Integration (SE/TAE)
- TeacherWorks™ Plus! CD
- *ExamView® Assessment Suite* CD
- *Presentation Plus!* CD

- National Mock Trial Championship DVD
- Online Learning Center with Podcasts at glencoe.com
- Study-to-Go™ at glencoe.com
- Online Student Edition
- Interactive Student Edition

Trial by Jury A defendant has a right to be tried before either a judge or a jury. *What are the steps in a jury trial?*

5

SECTION 1.1 **The Foundations of Law**

FOCUS

Bell Ringer Activity

Write this open-ended sentence on the board and ask students to complete it and expand on it with supporting ideas.

• If our country did not have a legal system, it would _____.

Preteaching

Key Terms

Read the definitions and ask students to create a sentence using each term.

Academic Vocabulary

Explain that developing vocabulary is key to academic success. An effective method to develop vocabulary is to study how words are formed.

• **empathy** Noun, from the Greek *empathos*, *em* + *pathos* (feelings, emotion). Means to be sensitive to the feelings and experience of another.

• **permissible** Adjective, from the Latin *permittere*, *per* (through) + *mittere* (to let go). Means allowable.

• **prevalent** Adjective, from the Latin *praevalere* (to be stronger). Means widely existing.

Activity Ask students to give a noun, an adjective, a verb, or an adverb form that comes from each word.

 Connects to academic content

6

What You'll Learn

◆ Explain how ethical decisions are made.
◆ Identify the different ethical character traits.
◆ Describe how the law relates to ethics.
◆ Explain the importance of the law.
◆ Identify the parts of the Constitution.
◆ Explain the components of common law.
◆ Explain the purposes of statutory law.
◆ Identify the ways that the courts make law.

Why It's Important

Knowing where laws come from will help you understand your own legal rights and responsibilities.

Academic Standards

Reading and completing the activities in this section will help you practice the following academic standards:

Social Studies (NCSS 2) Study the ways human beings view themselves in and over time.

English Language Arts (NCTE 12) Use spoken, written, and visual language to accomplish your own purposes.

Reading Guide

Before You Read

Connect Have you ever been tempted to cheat on an exam? If you have, you have faced an ethical decision.

Focus on Ideas

The law is a set of rules developed over centuries from many different sources. It develops as society changes.

Take Notes

Create a graph like the one shown and use it to take notes as you read this section. Go to **glencoe.com** to find graphic organizers and tips on how to improve your note-taking skills.

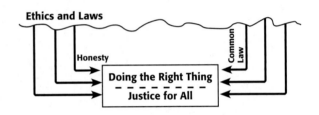

Ethics and Laws

Honesty

Common Law

Doing the Right Thing
Justice for All

Key Terms

You will learn these legal words and expressions in this chapter. You can also find these terms in *Black's Law Dictionary* or in an online legal dictionary.

• morality
• ethics
• justice
• law

• constitution
• common law
• statute
• administrative law

Academic Vocabulary

You will find these words in your readings and in your tests. Look them up in a dictionary and familiarize yourself with them.

• empathy
• permissible
• prevalent

glencoe.com

R Reading Strategy

Read for Knowledge

1. **Survey** or preread the chapter.
2. **Question** or formulate questions before you read.
3. **Recite** or read your questions, answers, and notes out loud.
4. **Review** or reread your notes.

Note-Taking Basics

• Listen attentively
• Have note-taking materials ready
• Skim through the lesson material
• Write down key words and ideas
• Anticipate what comes next
• Review notes soon after taking them

What Are Ethics and Morality?

Do you think choosing between right and wrong always involves rules?

Determining the difference between right and wrong can be difficult. People use different methods to decide on the right thing to do in any given situation. **Morality involves the values that govern a group's ideas about right and wrong. Ethics refers to the rules used to determine the difference between right and wrong.** In this book, the words *ethics* and *morality* will be used for both ideas.

What Does Ethics Come From?

Using ethical rules will help you deal with big and small moral questions.

The Greatest Good One way to decide about right and wrong is to apply the greatest good idea. This examines whether the action will cause the greatest good for the greatest number of people. The more good that results, the more right the action. It is used incorrectly when people think only of their own good, or if a person sees only the good created for a small group.

The Golden Rule The Golden Rule says, "Do unto others as you would have them do unto you." Many people prefer this rule because it works in many situations. The heart of the Golden Rule is **empathy.** Empathy means putting yourself in another person's position. One way to test whether an action is right or wrong under the Golden Rule is to ask, "Would I want to be treated this way?" If your answer is no, then the action breaks the Golden Rule.

Real-World Ethics Real-world ethics says that there are moral rules that most people know instinctively, without thinking. For example, lying is wrong. However, real-world ethics says that there are rare times when a person might have to lie. For example, it might be **permissible** to lie to save somebody's life. This does not mean what you have done is right. It means that what you have done is less wrong. If you lie to save a life, you know that the lie is still wrong, but you also know that it is less wrong than saying something that leads to someone's death.

Hammurabi's Code One of the earliest written set of laws is the Code of Hammurabi, which was carved in stone. *Who was Hammurabi and how long ago was his code of law written?*

As You Read

Predict How do you know you are making the right ethical decision?

Vocabulary You can find vocabulary definitions in the **Key Terms** glossary and **Academic Vocabulary** glossary in the back of this book.

1.1 SECTION

TEACH
Discussion Starter

Class Discussion
Write the following question on the board: What constitutes ethical behavior? Ask students to brainstorm answers and write them on the board. Ask them to consider behaviors, character traits, and actions. Revisit all answers after studying this section.

As You Read

Predict Students' answers will likely focus on concepts such as values, and being mindful of others' well-being and rights. Ask students if they know what the Golden Rule is and where it comes from.

D Develop Concepts

Ethical Decisions Outline the following elements that play a role in ethical decision making:

- The greatest good
- The Golden Rule
- Real-world ethics
- Character traits

Ask students to comment on which element guides their decision making most frequently.

▲ USING VISUALS

Hammurabi's Code **Answer** Hammurabi was the sixth king of Babylon. His code of about 300 laws was created in 1780 B.C., and set rules and punishments if rules of conduct were broken. The innocent-until-proven-guilty idea comes from this document. Here are some examples:

- If a robber is caught while stealing, he will be killed.
- If someone is in debt, and cannot pay, he can sell himself, his wife, his son, and his daughter into labor; after three years they shall be set free.

TEACH (cont.)

D Develop Concepts

Ethical Versus Legal Conflicts Ask students to think of actions that might be considered unethical but are not illegal. Have them consider why individuals might do something unethical but would avoid doing something illegal. (no legal consequences to an unethical action)

Extending the Content

Ethics and Business

Explain to students that the concepts of integrity and confidentiality play an important role in business. Ask students to investigate the ethical rules that apply to professionals such as accountants and lawyers. Have students write a one-page report on the code of ethics that governs a profession or business activity such as marketing.

Guided Practice

Ethical Character Traits

Write the following traits on the board:

- Honesty
- Justice
- Compassion
- Integrity

Have students volunteer fictional situations in which these traits are demonstrated.

Reading Check

Explain *Is an ethical decision always the correct legal decision?*

Ethical Character Traits

In difficult cases where moral rules and legal guidelines do not help, specific character traits become a compass you can use. For example, think of a situation in which you have to decide whether to tell the truth, knowing that the truth will get you and others into trouble.

Honesty Honesty is a character trait of someone who is truthful in dealings with others.

Justice **Justice means treating people fairly and equally.** That means everyone, not just relatives and friends. A just person will see that everyone gets his or her fair share.

Compassion Compassion means caring about other people and the situation they are in. Compassionate people understand other people's mistakes and motivations.

Integrity Integrity is a willingness and determination to do the right thing. People with integrity stand up for their convictions, even when many people are against them.

The Relationship between Ethics and Law

What does the law have to do with right and wrong?

D If people used ethics all the time to guide their behavior, there would be no need for law. In the real world, people sometimes do the wrong thing. This happens even when they know better. In order to develop and live both an ethical and a legal lifestyle, you must follow the law and incorporate ethics into your life.

Why Is Law Necessary?

Ethics tell you what you ought to do. However, people do not always do what they are supposed to, so governments create laws. **Law is a system of rules of conduct established by a country's government to maintain stability and justice according to the values that are relevant to that country.** The law defines the legal rights and responsibilities of the people. Under the different types of laws, the government can require certain actions, or it can forbid others. Laws create specific responsibilities for people. In the United States, the law is a way to enforce the rights and duties of everyone through the police, the courts, the legislature, and regulatory agencies. It is everyone's responsibility to obey the law.

The law has the power to punish people for acting illegally. Consider the contrast between a dishonest but legal business transaction and one that is both dishonest and illegal. If you tell a friend that you have no money to lend him when, in fact you have a lot of money and could easily lend him what he needs, your action is perfectly legal. However, no matter which ethical theory you use, you will have to admit that you have lied, which is clearly dishonest. The law cannot force you to tell the truth in this

---

Reading Check

Explain Sometimes an ethical decision may not always be the correct legal decision. Students' answers should reflect an understanding of real-world ethics. While law is based on ethics, in extreme situations one might have to choose the lesser of two evils.

situation. On the other hand, if you steal money to lend to your friend, you have done something that is both dishonest and illegal. The law can clearly punish you for stealing.

Many new laws are created as a response to a person's or a company's unethical practices. For example, in the late 1990s some American corporations lied about their finances before they went bankrupt and many people lost money they had invested in the corporations on the stock market. As a result, the U.S. Congress established a new set of laws that made corporations more accountable to the public.

Ethical and Legal Conflicts

Ethics and the law affect each other. Changes in ethical standards can help us make new laws, or get rid of old laws. Changes in the law can help people adjust their ideas on morality. The conflict between social forces has led to such changes in the United States. For example, desegregation laws have changed the way many people act toward one another.

The Five Main Sources of the Law

What document is the basis of all U.S. laws?

In general, law in the United States today comes from five main sources.

Constitutional Law

A constitution is a country's formal document that spells out the principles by which its government operates. In our country, the most basic law is the U.S. Constitution.

The Constitution of the United States The United States Constitution describes the three branches of the U.S. government and their roles. It sets up the limits within which the federal and state

Home Sale

Suppose you are an attorney for a construction company. While reviewing plans for a new dormitory your company is building, you realize the dormitory will be built next to a house you are selling. Someone has offered to buy the house for exactly the amount you want. You know that as soon as the college announces where the dormitory will be located, prices for surrounding property, including yours, will drastically fall. You must now call the person interested in buying your property with your decision on the offer.

Critical Thinking: What ethical issues are involved and what should you tell the interested party? Explain.

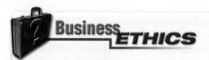

Answer In this situation, you, as the attorney, should probably decline the offer without giving the reason. If you happen to know when the college will be announcing the location, you may tell the buyer that you need until that date to make a decision. You also should not take any other offers until after the location is made public. That way, the playing field is leveled, and you no longer have an unfair advantage. The ethical rules of attorneys require them not to take advantage of unequal situations such as this.

TEACH *(cont.)*

W Writing Support

Ethics, Law, and Personal Beliefs Some people, called pacifists, do not believe it is ever ethical to fight in a war. Yet U.S. law prescribes that all male citizens must register for the military draft when they turn 18. Have students write a short report on the government's legal perspective and the pacifist's ethical perspective. Ask them to consider the relationship here between laws and ethics.

D Develop Concepts

Constitutional Law Remind students that the U.S. Constitution defines the fundamental rights of citizens. Ask students to describe what they think is meant when a law or a government action is described as unconstitutional. (Students should demonstrate an understanding that the action violates the provisions of the U.S. Constitution.)

Guided Practice

Law as a Response to Unethical Practices

Have students describe instances in which they have been affected by the unethical practices of a company. (failing to stand by return policies or sale prices) Emphasize that laws provide a means of enforcing the rights and duties of a society and its members.

9

TEACH (cont.)

D Develop Concepts

Amendments to the Constitution Emphasize to students that several of the amendments made to the Constitution will have a direct impact on their lives. Tell students that the Twenty-Sixth Amendment lowered the voting age to 18 years of age. Tell female students that the Nineteenth Amendment gave women the right to vote, while the Sixteenth Amendment imposed income taxes.

Legal Talk

(precede, precedence, preceding;

integral, integer, integration)

Ask students to practice their academic and legal vocabulary with the electronic flashcards available at the *Business and Personal Law* Online Learning Center through glencoe.com.

Guided Practice

Mock Trial

The Twenty-Sixth Amendment gives 18-year-old Americans the right to vote. Have students form three teams. Ask one team to defend the amendment and another to rebuke it. Allow the third team to decide whether or not it should be passed based on the strength of both teams' arguments and rebuttals.

Legal Talk

Precedent: *n* An earlier occurrence. From Latin *praecedere:* prior in time.

Integrity: *n* Firm adherence to a code of moral or artistic values, the quality of being undivided. From Latin *integritas:* entire.

Vocabulary Builder List three words that have the same origin as precedent and three words that have the same origin as integrity. Define and name parts of speech for each word.

Look It Up! Check definitions in *Black's Law Dictionary* or an online glossary. For direct links, go to **glencoe.com** to find more vocabulary resources.

---

governments may pass laws. The Constitution also sets down the rights of the people. The Constitution was created upon a basic value system the Founding Fathers felt was appropriate to all Americans.

Article I sets up the legislative branch of government: the Congress, which is responsible for passing laws for the country. Article II creates the executive branch. The executive branch includes the President and all of the different departments within the government, such as the State Department and the Department of Defense. The executive branch is responsible for ensuring that the laws passed by Congress are upheld and followed. Finally, Article III describes the judiciary branch of government, which is responsible for interpreting the laws passed by Congress and adjudicating criminal cases in federal matters and disputes between parties.

These initial three Articles form a system of checks and balances, so that one branch is not more powerful than another. No one branch has the sole authority to pass laws, enforce laws, and adjudicate laws. These responsibilities are divided among the three branches.

Article IV requires each state to give full faith and credit to the laws of all other states. This means that each state must accept the laws of all the other states. This Article is especially important to American businesses. For example, since many companies do business in more than one state, it would be difficult if one state decided to stop recognizing the business laws of another state. Article V tells how laws may be added to the Constitution—by creating amendments.

Article VI contains the supremacy clause. This clause states that the U.S. Constitution and the laws of the United States are the highest laws in the country. Article VII, the last article, explains how to approve the Constitution. This event took place in 1787.

The Constitution now has 27 amendments. The first ten amendments were approved in 1791. They are called the Bill of Rights. They limit the powers of the government. The basic goal of the Bill of Rights is to protect our individual rights and freedoms. For example, the First Amendment protects some very important rights, such as freedom of speech, religion, assembly, and freedom of the press. No law may be passed by Congress, or any state, that would limit these individual rights and freedoms. Other important amendments include the 13th Amendment, which abolished slavery in the U.S.; the 19th Amendment, which gave women the right to vote; and the 26th Amendment, which lowered the voting age to 18 years of age.

State Constitutions Each state has its own constitution. State constitutions are not the same as the United States Constitution. Although state constitutions usually include a number of similarities, such as three branches of government and the protection of certain basic rights, state constitutions are often longer and more detailed than the United States Constitution.

Extending the Content

Changes in the Law

The Fourteenth Amendment provides that no state shall "deprive any person of liberty, or property, without due process of law; nor deny to any person within its jurisdiction the equal protection of laws." This is known as the equal protection clause. As a major principle of justice, this amendment requires equal treatment of all people under the law. The Fourteenth Amendment requires state governments to give their citizens the same rights that the federal government must give to U.S. citizens under the Fifth Amendment. In 1982, the U.S. Supreme Court held that the single-sex admission policy of the Mississippi University for Women School of Nursing (a state school) violated the equal protection clause of the Fourteenth Amendment when it denied admission to Joe Hogan solely because of gender. The court said that the school policy continued the stereotype of nursing as a woman's job. Hogan was ultimately admitted to the school of nursing.

Common Law

In the early days of England's history, the king tried to centralize the English court system. Judges traveled around the country deciding cases. Because there was no written law, judges made decisions based on the customs and traditions of the people. Judges shared their decisions with one another so that the same laws would be applied everywhere in the country. This practice formed the basis of common law.

The common law is a set of laws made by the courts which provide a series of consistent rules that later courts must follow. The early American colonists came from England, so it was natural for them to use the common law of England in their new land.

Eventually, these court decisions were written down and a body of cases developed. Judges could then refer to past cases when making their decisions. These past cases came to be known as precedent. A precedent is a past case that a court follows when making a present decision.

The process of relying on past court cases is called stare decisis. This means "let the decision stand." English common law is not used today as much as it was in the past. However, parts of the common law are still used in some states.

Statutes and the Civil Law System

The origin of civil law can be traced back to the Roman Empire during the 6th century when Emperor Justinian I called for the collection of all the different laws created by previous Roman emperors. This is the basis of the civil law system that is **prevalent** in Europe and the state of Louisiana.

Unlike common law, civil law is law based on statutes, rather than court decisions. **A statute is a law passed by a government body that has been made for the purpose of creating laws.** A government body that has been set up to pass statutes is called a legislature. A statute can declare the law on an issue. Statutes may also order people to do something. For example, a statute might say people have to pay taxes or wear seat belts. Other statutes say that people cannot do something. This is what a criminal statute does when it says murder is a crime.

A statute is created when legislature passes a proposed law, or bill. After the bill is passed, it is sent to the President or the

Law at the State Level
State legislatures and state courts play an important role in the U.S. legal system. Legislatures vote on statutes and create laws. State courts review and interpret statutes and also create case law. *Where is your state's supreme court located? Where is your state legislature located?*

TEACH (cont.)

D Develop Concepts

Statutes Remind students that statutes are laws. Statutes can be passed by Congress or by a state legislature. Ask students what must happen before a law goes into effect. (must be signed by the president or by the governor of the appropriate state)

S Skills Practice

Have students work in pairs to research common law and complete the following activities.

Describe Write a brief report on common law. **L1**

Explain What is *stare decisis* and how is it used? (the process of relying on past court cases. Judges should follow binding precedents set by an equal or higher court, when trying a case.) **L2**

Analyze Name some advantages and disadvantages of using *stare decisis.* (Advantages: legislature can change case law by statute; following precedents makes decisions "predictable." Disadvantages: it preserves wrongly decided cases; allowing unelected judges to make law, it is considered undemocratic.) **L3**

▲ USING VISUALS

Law at the State Level   Answer Answers will vary depending on where students are located. Ask students who have lived in another state if they know the answers for their former home states.

Activity Ask students to write a paragraph on why they think laws might differ between states. For example, the minimum driving age in North Dakota is 14½ years, while in Indiana it is 16 years and 1 month. (For this particular example, the laws might differ due to socioeconomic reasons, climate, and driving conditions. Students should consider the culture, industry, and populations of different states as they examine this question.)

TEACH (cont.)

W Writing Support

Federal Statutes Remind students that the U.S. Congress has the authority to enact laws that deal with spending, taxing, and borrowing money. Congress also is allowed to regulate commerce among the states and on the Internet. Have students write a brief opinion about whether the federal government should be involved in interstate commerce or if that should be handled by the states themselves.

Extending the Content

State Constitutions

Ask your students to obtain a copy of your state's constitution. The school library or the Internet are among the places where your students might find this information. Have students skim the major sections of the document and describe the portions that are of the most interest to them. (Most state constitutions contain sections on education, taxation, voting, powers of government, and impeachment.)

Governor, depending on whether it is a federal law or a state law, to sign the bill into law. A law does not go into effect until the President or Governor signs it.

Federal Statutes Laws that are passed by the U.S. Congress and signed by the president are called federal statutes. The United States Congress is a legislature. It has the job of making statutes under the powers given to the federal government by the Constitution. These powers include such things as the power to spend, tax, and borrow money.

W **Commerce Clause** One important clause is the commerce clause. The commerce clause gives Congress the power to make laws pertaining to interstate commerce, or commerce between the states. Congress has used this clause to pass laws that affect American businesses on various topics such as civil rights and interstate trucking.

Global Law

International Sources of Law

Countries throughout the world have many sources of law: national constitutions, religious texts, court-created case law, and voter-initiated propositions. Even within the United States, diversity abounds. Louisiana, for example, uses a code-based legal system inherited from the French tradition, whereas most other states follow a case law system that originates in England.

European systems of law were adopted by many countries around the world. France and the United Kingdom were very influential. The United States created a legal system that incorporates parts of both French and British law.

The United States has four primary sources of law:

1. The U.S. Constitution
2. International treaties
3. Statutes passed by the U.S. Congress
4. Case law created by the U.S. Supreme Court

France, on the other hand, has three sources of law with no case law:

1. The French Constitution
2. International treaties
3. The *Code civil des français,* or French Civil Code

Finally, the United Kingdom also has only three sources of law, with no constitution:

1. International treaties
2. Statutes passed through the Houses of Parliament
3. Case law created by the House of Lords in its holdings

Across Cultures: What's a lawyer called in England?

In England lawyers are divided into two categories based on the legal work that they do. Barristers engage in trial work and often prepare trial briefs, and solicitors handle office work. Barristers count on solicitors to provide them trial work because they are not allowed to do it on their own.

Critical Thinking: *What are the advantages (or disadvantages) of having a supreme court that can create law? What about a constitution?*

Global Law

International Sources of Law

Answer The advantages include judicial expediency: if a higher court has already ruled on one issue, it is easier for lower courts to follow those decisions. The disadvantages include reliance on a system in which unelected officials are responsible for creating or removing laws. A constitution provides a supreme law for the land and may give supreme courts an authority to make final rulings. The disadvantage is that the constitution may cease to be applicable in certain ways as a society changes.

As noted earlier, the U.S. Constitution is the supreme law of the land. This means that Congress cannot pass laws that conflict with the U.S. Constitution, including the Bill of Rights. The Supreme Court may declare any statute that does go against the Constitution to be unconstitutional. This means that the statute is invalid.

State Statutes Each state also has its own legislature. Like Congress, the state legislatures cannot pass statutes that conflict with the U.S. Constitution or their own constitutions.

> **Example** Lawmakers in Massachusetts wanted to have a graduated income tax that would very much be like the federal income tax. A graduated tax requires people with larger income to pay a higher tax rate than people with smaller incomes. Such a tax could not be passed because the Massachusetts constitution requires all people to be taxed at an equal percentage rate.

As a way of lessening confusion and creating similar statutes in all the states, there are many different uniform codes. One of the best known examples is the Uniform Commercial Code, or UCC. Every state has passed a version of the UCC, which means that statutes relating to commerce are essentially the same in all the states, and people do not have to worry about knowing 50 different sets of law with regard to business transactions.

Ordinances Most local governments, like cities and towns, have the power to create laws that affect their citizens. These laws are known as ordinances and can apply to topics such as parking fines and noxious weed control.

Court Decisions

Most people are surprised to learn that courts make law. Court-made law is often called case law, court decisions, and judge-made law. Courts make law in three ways: through the common law tradition, by interpreting statutes, and by judicial review.

Creating Laws Decisions tmade by the highest court of a state are the law of that state. These decisions must be followed by other courts in that state. These decisions continue to be law until they are changed by statute or a new court decision.

Interpreting Laws A second type of court decision involves interpreting statutes. When a statute is confusing, the court must figure out what the statute means. A judge cannot interpret a statute unless the statute is part of a case.

Judicial Review The courts can also decide whether laws conflict with the Constitution. Any laws or government actions that conflict with the Constitution are unconstitutional. The Supreme Court of the United States has the last word on whether a statute conflicts with the Constitution.

ASSESS

Quiz

Ask students to answer the following questions:

1. **Why is law different from ethics?** (Law creates specific and enforceable responsibilities. Ethical considerations may guide behaviors but are not enforceable.)

2. **What is the Golden Rule?** (Do unto others as you would have them do unto you.)

3. **What are the five primary sources of the law in the United States?** (constitutional law, common law, statutes and civil law system, court decisions, administrative regulations)

RETEACH

Guided Practice

Amendments to the Constitution

Ask students to choose an amendment to the Constitution that has been passed since the Bill of Rights was written. Have them write a short report about the people who proposed the amendment, what opposition it faced, and how it came to pass.

> STUDY TO GO
> Have students go to the *Business and Personal Law* Online Learning Center through glencoe.com to download free Study-to-Go content to their cell phones or PDAs.

Independent Practice

Sources of Law

Ask students to reflect on the fact that our laws come from different sources. Explain that common law, statutory law, and agency regulations are all sources of law. Have them discuss why there are so many sources of law.

Ask for suggestions on why our system has such diversity. (Answers will vary but should include some understanding of the practical limitations of legislatures. Students may also mention the need to preserve regularity and predictability in the law by being consistent with past court decisions unless there is a good reason to overturn them.)

RETEACH *(cont.)*

After You Read

Summarize
constitutional law,
common law, statutes
and the civil law system,
court decisions, and
administrative regulations

ASSESS

Self-Assessment

Have students go to the
Business and Personal Law
Online Learning Center
through **glencoe.com** to take
the Section 1.1 Practice Test.

CLOSE

Culminating Activity

Sources of Law

Match the following
activities with one of
these: (1) administrative
agency, (2) court, or (3) city
ordinance.

- Govern cable company (1)
- Define parking fines (3)
- Decide whether state
  statute conflicts with U.S.
  Constitution (2)

Administrative Regulations

The legislature must regulate many activities. This is true of Congress and of the state legislatures. However, legislators do not have knowledge in every field. They also do not have the time to do everything that they are charged with doing. For these reasons, legislatures will give the power to regulate certain activities to an administrative agency. For example, the Federal Communications Commission (FCC) has the power to regulate radio, television, and cable companies.

Administrative agencies are departments of government that are formed to carry out certain laws. These agencies can make and enforce rules directly related to the area of responsibility given to them by the legislature. **Administrative law is the body of rules created by government agencies.**

Administrative agencies have a lot of power. However, there are checks and balances that keep them from becoming too powerful. The legislature that created an agency has the power to end the agency or to change its power. A final decision by an agency can be reviewed by the courts.

International Law

Although not a major source of law in the United States, international law can be equally important. International treaties signed by the United States and other countries are held to the same level as federal statutes. Like a federal statute, everyone in the U.S. must follow any treaty that the U.S. has signed.

In addition to treaties, there are international agreements between countries, such as trade agreements, that are not binding on the countries, but provide recommendations for how countries should interact within the international community.

After You Read

Summarize What are the five main sources of the law?

SECTION 1.1 ASSESSMENT

Self Check

1. What is the difference between morality and ethics?

2. Why is the law necessary?

3. What are the possible purposes of a statute?

N C L B

Academic Connection

Social Studies The Bill of Rights clearly spells out the immunities for the individual citizen. Why do you think the writers of the Bill of Rights were so concerned with this?

English Language Arts Using the Bill of Rights as a guide, write a bill of rights addressing student rights to a free education.

Critical Thinking

Software Downloading Suppose that your best friend had a way to hack into your math teacher's computer so that he could download the answers to your next test. Your friend offers to give you the answers for five dollars. Would you go along with your friend's tempting offer? Why or why not? What ethical rule would you use to make this decision?

 Go to **glencoe.com** to check your answers.

 glencoe.com

SECTION 1.1 ASSESSMENT

Self Check

1. Morality involves the values regarding right and wrong. Ethics are a way to figure out what those values should be.

2. to maintain stability and justice

3. to create law

Academic Connection

Social Studies
Students should discuss the importance of giving citizens fair treatment and the restriction/prevention of abuse of power by the federal government.

English Language Arts
Answers should reflect knowledge of the Bill of Rights (see Appendix).

Critical Thinking

Urge students to give a yes-or-no answer and support it with an ethical rule.

N C L B Activities correlated to the academic standards on page 6

The Court System and Trial Procedures

Reading Guide

Before You Read

Connect If a 16-year-old gets into legal trouble, does the case always go to a juvenile court?

Focus on Ideas

There are many different levels of the court system to deal with different types of legal problems.

Take Notes

Create a graph like the one shown and use it to take notes as you read this section. Go to glencoe.com to find graphic organizers and tips on how to improve your note-taking skills.

Litigation

1. Filing a Complaint _____
2. _____
3. _____
4. _____

Key Terms

You will learn these legal words and expressions in this chapter. You can also find these terms in *Black's Law Dictionary* or in an online legal dictionary.

- jurisdiction
- appellate court
- alternative dispute resolution (ADR)
- arrest
- bail
- arraignment
- detention hearing

Academic Vocabulary

You will find these words in your readings and in your tests. Look them up in a dictionary and familiarize yourself with them.

- informal
- mediator
- jeopardy

What You'll Learn

- ◆ Define jurisdiction.
- ◆ Describe the structure of the federal court system.
- ◆ Explain the role of the United States Supreme Court.
- ◆ Determine the common structure of most state court systems.
- ◆ Identify alternative dispute resolution techniques.
- ◆ Differentiate between civil and criminal cases.
- ◆ Describe the steps in a civil lawsuit.
- ◆ Explain the rights of criminal defendants.
- ◆ List the steps in a criminal prosecution.

Why It's Important

Learning about the structure of the U.S. court systems will help you understand how the U.S. legal system works.

Academic Standards

Reading and completing the activities in this section will help you practice the following academic standards:

N C L B

Social Studies (NCSS 10) Study the ideals, principles, and practices of citizenship in a democratic republic.

Math (NCTM DAPS 2) Select and use appropriate statistical methods to analyze data.

FOCUS

Bell Ringer Activity

Ask students to name the kind of court that a teenager might have to appear in if he or she commits an offense. (juvenile court) Have them discuss why such a court was created. (deals with minors under age 18 and hands down decisions appropriate to their age and level of understanding)

Preteaching

Key Terms

Read the definitions and ask students to create a sentence using each term.

Academic Vocabulary

Explain that developing vocabulary is key to academic success. An efficient method to develop vocabulary is to study how words are formed.

- **informal** Adjective, from the Latin *informar*, in + *formare* (to shape). Means not formal, unofficial.
- **mediator** Noun, from the Latin *mediare* (to be in the middle). Means one who reconciles differences.
- **jeopardy** Noun, from the Latin *iocus* (game) + *partire* (to part). Means a defendant's risk of conviction.

Activity Ask students to give a noun, an adjective, a verb, or an adverb form that comes from each word.

N C L B Connects to academic content

R Reading Strategy

Read for Knowledge

1. **Survey** or preread the chapter.
2. **Question** or formulate questions before you read.
3. **Recite** or read your questions, answers, and notes out loud.
4. **Review** or reread your notes.

Note-Taking Basics

- Listen attentively
- Have note-taking materials ready
- Skim through the lesson material
- Write down key words and ideas
- Anticipate what comes next
- Review notes soon after taking them

TEACH

Discussion Starter

Class Discussion

Ask students to recall a court case that appeared in local or national news recently. Have them recall the court in which the case was tried (federal, state, district, appeals, etc.). Inform them that this section will provide information on the various types of courts and the cases they hear.

D Develop Concepts

The Federal Court System
Explain to students that different courts have the power to hear different types of cases. Draw the three tiers of federal courts on the board: U.S. district courts, U.S. courts of appeals, and the U.S. Supreme Court. For each type of court, ask students to suggest what happens in that court. (District court—original jurisdiction over most federal civil and criminal cases. Courts of appeals—hear appeals from lower courts. U.S. Supreme Court—hears appeals on chosen cases.)

As You Read

Predict No. Not all cases go to court. Litigation is avoided by means of compromise, mediation, or arbitration.

As You Read

Predict Do all cases get resolved in court?

The Supreme Court The highest court in the land is the U.S. Supreme Court. Supreme Court justices have vast legal experience as lawyers and judges. *Who was the first African-American appointed to the Supreme Court?*

A Dual Court System

Are all the U.S. courts of justice the same no matter where you live?

The United States have two major court systems: federal and state. Federal courts hear cases involving federal subjects. They also hear cases involving citizens from different states or from another country. According to the U.S. Constitution, powers not specifically granted to the federal government are reserved for the states. So states have their own courts with their own rules.

The Federal Court System

Jurisdiction is a court's power to hear a case and to make a judgment. Federal courts have jurisdiction over certain types of cases. These cases include:

1. Actions in which the United States or one state is a party, except those actions between a state and its citizens
2. Cases that raise a federal question, such as interpreting the Constitution
3. Cases, which involve citizens of different states and in which the amount of money in dispute exceeds $75,000
4. Admiralty cases, or those pertaining to the sea
5. Patent and copyright cases
6. Bankruptcy cases

Federal courts are arranged in three tiers. The first tier is the U.S. district court. Each state has at least one district court; many have more. The second tier consists of the U.S. courts of appeals and the highest tier is the U.S. Supreme Court (see **Figure 1.1,** page 17).

District Courts District courts have original jurisdiction over most federal civil and criminal cases. Original jurisdiction means that a court has the power to hear a case for the first time. Most federal cases begin in one of the U.S. district courts.

Courts of Appeals U.S. courts of appeals are the appellate courts of the federal system. An appeal is a request to a higher court to reverse a lower court's decision. **An appellate court is a court that hears appeals and reviews cases from the lower courts.**

In the federal system, the courts of appeals are intermediate courts. An intermediate court is one that is between lower courts and the highest court of a system and has appellate jurisdiction. Appellate jurisdiction is the power to hear an appeal from a lower court.

D

▲ USING VISUALS

➡ **The Supreme Court** Answer The first African-American to serve on the Supreme Court was Thurgood Marshall, who served from 1967 to 1991.

Ask students who was the first woman to serve on the Supreme Court. (Sandra Day O'Connor was appointed in 1981.)

Activity Have students examine the makeup of the Supreme Court. Ask them to express any opinions they may have about the age, race, or gender of the justices.

Figure 1.1 Court Systems in the United States

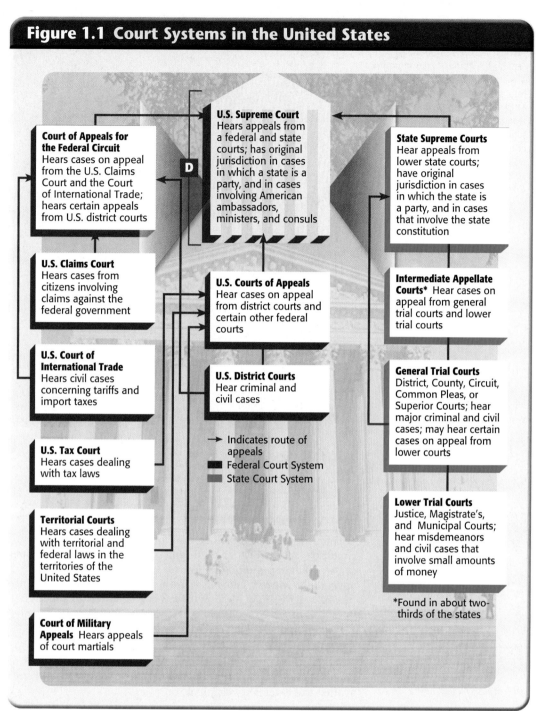

Court of Appeals for the Federal Circuit Hears cases on appeal from the U.S. Claims Court and the Court of International Trade; hears certain appeals from U.S. district courts

U.S. Claims Court Hears cases from citizens involving claims against the federal government

U.S. Court of International Trade Hears civil cases concerning tariffs and import taxes

U.S. Tax Court Hears cases dealing with tax laws

Territorial Courts Hears cases dealing with territorial and federal laws in the territories of the United States

Court of Military Appeals Hears appeals of court martials

U.S. Supreme Court Hears appeals from a federal and state courts; has original jurisdiction in cases in which a state is a party, and in cases involving American ambassadors, ministers, and consuls

U.S. Courts of Appeals Hear cases on appeal from district courts and certain other federal courts

U.S. District Courts Hear criminal and civil cases

→ Indicates route of appeals
■ Federal Court System
■ State Court System

State Supreme Courts Hear appeals from lower state courts; have original jurisdiction in cases in which the state is a party, and in cases that involve the state constitution

Intermediate Appellate Courts* Hear cases on appeal from general trial courts and lower trial courts

General Trial Courts District, County, Circuit, Common Pleas, or Superior Courts; hear major criminal and civil cases; may hear certain cases on appeal from lower courts

Lower Trial Courts Justice, Magistrate's, and Municipal Courts; hear misdemeanors and civil cases that involve small amounts of money

*Found in about two-thirds of the states

The courts in the United States are divided into federal and state systems. *In which court system would a criminal trial be heard?*

▲ USING VISUALS

➡ Who Gets to Be a Supreme Court Justice? Answer Answers will vary. Students may suggest that the challenging part of studying law is the procedures of the court, the education required to become an attorney, or the evolving nature of law. Direct students to the American Bar Association Web site's Student Resources page, where they can find a wealth of information about studying law.

TEACH (cont.)

D Develop Concepts

Supreme Court Remind students that United States Supreme Court justices serve for life. Bring library materials about the United States Supreme Court to class. Ask students to find the names of the current United States Supreme Court justices. (Ginsburg, Souter, Thomas, Breyer, Scalia, Stevens, Kennedy, Roberts, Alito)

Extending the Content

Special U.S. Courts

Ask students to research the types of special courts that exist in the United States. Ask the students to name the special courts that have nationwide jurisdiction. (U.S. Court of International Trade and U.S. Court of Federal Claims)

Guided Practice

Types of Courts

Tell students that William Bell, who lives in Texas, is involved in a lawsuit with an individual from Florida in a dispute over $150,000. Ask students if the case can be heard in a federal court or a state court. (The case can be heard in either federal or state court. It can be heard in federal court because the case is between two persons from different states and the amount in question is more than $75,000. It can also be heard in an appropriate state court, if filed in the state where the defendant resides or owns property.)

TEACH (cont.)

U Universal Access

Visual/Spatial Learners
Ask students to create diagrams showing the relationship between state and federal court systems. Explain that they may use Figure 1.1 as a starting point, but must change it in ways that make the distinctions more apparent. For example, they might change the diagram to a flowchart, use a software program to create it electronically, or add photos or captions. Ask students to display and explain their charts to the class.

Guided Practice

Court Systems

Emphasize that the court systems in other countries may operate very differently from the court system in the United States. Explain that nearly all criminal trials in Mexico are tried by a judge without a jury. In India, the Supreme Court implemented a policy that compensates victims of violence suffered while in police custody. Ask for volunteers from other countries to offer information on their country's court and legal system.

➡ **Who gets to be a Supreme Court Justice?** A diverse student body representing the country's demographics is the goal of many colleges that train future lawyers, judges, and justices. Many private companies, such as Honda, also foster diversity in law schools and colleges and use their efforts as promotion. *What do you think the most challenging part of studying law and becoming a lawyer is?*

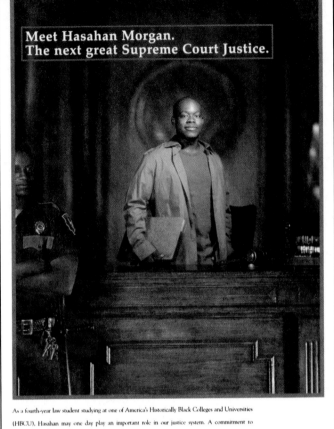

Meet Hasahan Morgan. The next great Supreme Court Justice.

As a fourth-year law student studying at one of America's Historically Black Colleges and Universities (HBCU), Hasahan may one day play an important role in our justice system. A commitment to developing future leaders is why Honda sponsors HBCU programs such as the Honda Campus All-Star Challenge and Honda Battle of the Bands. Because of the important work done by these great educational institutions, young people like Hasahan will make important contributions to our laws and society.

For information about America's Historically Black Colleges and Universities visit hbcu-central.com or honda.com. © 2005 American Honda Motor Co., Inc.

The United States is divided into thirteen judicial circuits. Each circuit has several district courts and one court of appeals. A panel of three judges is responsible for rendering decisions in most appeals. No witnesses are heard, no evidence is presented, and no jury is present. Only questions of law can be raised on appeal, not questions of fact. Appellate courts only determine whether the lower court correctly applied the law in the case.

Special U.S. Courts Congress has set up several special federal courts. These courts have jurisdiction in certain kinds of cases. These cases include lawsuits that are brought by citizens against the federal government.

Supreme Court The United States Supreme Court is the highest court in the country. It consists of the Chief Justice of the United States and eight associate justices.

▲ USING VISUALS

➡ **Figure 1.1 Court Systems in the United States** Answer Both systems hear criminal cases.
Activity Ask students to imagine that they are involved a dispute with the IRS. Which court will hear the initial case? (U.S. tax court)
Which court will hear the appeal? (U.S. court of appeals)

The President chooses the justices with the consent of the Senate. Like all federal judges, the justices who sit on the United States Supreme Court serve for life. The Court's main job is to hear appeals. The Court decides which appellate cases it will hear. This requires a vote of at least four of its nine justices. The Supreme Court will hear cases that affect a wide range of people and those that involve the Constitution. A case is also likely to reach the Supreme Court when several lower courts have faced the issue, but have disagreed on how to resolve it. The Supreme Court has original jurisdiction in all cases that involve ambassadors, consuls, and other public ministers. It also has original jurisdiction in cases that involve a state.

State Court Systems

Each state has its own court system. However, the general pattern is the same in all states.

Local Trial Courts Local courts are courts of limited jurisdiction. Limited jurisdiction means that a court handles minor matters. Such cases might involve disputes over small amounts of money which are heard in small-claims courts. Minor cases are also heard by traffic, police, or mayor's courts.

General Trial Courts In most states, each county has one general trial court, also called a court of general jurisdiction. Courts with general jurisdiction handle criminal and civil cases.

Juvenile Courts Juvenile courts deal with juvenile offenders and with children who need the protection of the state. These courts deal with children up until the age of majority, which is 18 in most states. They have special jurisdiction over delinquent, unruly, abused, and neglected children.

Procedures in juvenile courts differ from those in other courts. Most juvenile matters are sealed, meaning that unlike other court proceedings, they are not open to the general public. This is to protect the privacy of the minor. Hearings are often more **informal** than in other courts of law. Young people who appear before a juvenile court have no right to a trial by jury and no right to be released on bail. However, the Supreme Court has held that there must be proof beyond a reasonable doubt to convict a child as an adult.

Intermediate Appellate Courts Some states have intermediate appellate courts that hear appeals. Appeals may be made to a state intermediate court when the parties believe they did not have a fair trial in the lower court. They may also appeal to the intermediate court if the judge did not interpret the law correctly. State appellate courts hear appeals only on questions of law. No witnesses testify. Appeals judges hear arguments from attorneys. They also study the documents and records in the case.

State Supreme Courts The highest court in most states is the supreme court. A state's highest court decides matters of law appealed from lower courts. Supreme courts do not hold a second trial.

Vocabulary You can find vocabulary definitions in the **Key Terms** glossary and **Academic Vocabulary** glossary in the back of this book.

Role Play

When a U.S. district judge determined that Microsoft had violated the Sherman Antitrust Act and had to be broken up, the Seattle-based company's lawyers decided to take it to the next level. Microsoft's lawyers questioned the objectivity of the trial judge. Ask students to research and role play the high-tech giant's lawyers' appeal to take its case to the Supreme Court. Specifically they might address why they believe the higher court would be more qualified to determine the outcome of the case than the lower court. (The case with the federal government was later settled, and the company remained intact.)

TEACH (cont.)

D Develop Concepts

Local Trial Courts Ask students to describe what the term *limited jurisdiction* means. (handles minor matters) Explain that traffic disputes or disputes over small amounts of money might be heard in a local trial court.

Extending the Content

Trial Research

Have students work in pairs to research a recent trial. The trial can be a local, national, civil, or criminal case. Ask students to cover the following items in their report:

- Was the trial criminal or civil?
- What court was the case originally heard in?
- Who were the parties involved?
- What were the charges or the dispute?
- What was the verdict?

U Universal Access

Visual Impairment Explain to students that each county has its own unique system of local and general trial courts. Students with visual impairments can learn from assignments that do not include a large amount of written work. Have students call the local county clerk or magistrate's office to ask questions about the system. Ask students to share their findings orally with the class.

TEACH (cont.)

D Develop Concepts

Trial Procedure Ask students to imagine that they are founding a new social system. Have them consider what kind of legal system they would develop and the trial procedures they would adopt. In what ways would these procedures be the same or different from the procedures they are learning in this chapter? In a written report, have them explain the reasons for their system, and discuss why it is the same as or different from our system in the United States.

Guided Practice

Civil Trial Procedure

Discuss the ways in which people settle disputes other than litigation. Have three students role-play an arbitration in which two students disagree on whether they should go to a movie or play sports after school. (Arbitrator should hear both sides of the argument and make a ruling.)

They do not look at the facts in the case. Instead, they decide whether the lower court made a mistake in interpreting or applying the law. At times, cases that have been decided by a state supreme court may be appealed to the United States Supreme Court.

Civil Trial Procedure

Suppose you are suing your neighbor for damaging your property. Will your case appear in the court as a criminal case?

The law can be divided into two very simple categories: substantive law and procedural law. Substantive law tells us what the law is. There are many different classifications of substantive law ranging from criminal law to business law, family law to bankruptcy law. Most of this book is devoted to substantive law.

Procedural law tells us how the law works. The two major divisions in this area of the law are civil procedure and criminal procedure. Criminal procedure and civil procedure are very different from one another.

The government brings criminal cases to court for offenses against the public. Criminal law is enacted to protect the public from harm. In contrast, individuals who believe they have been injured bring civil cases. Civil law is enacted to govern

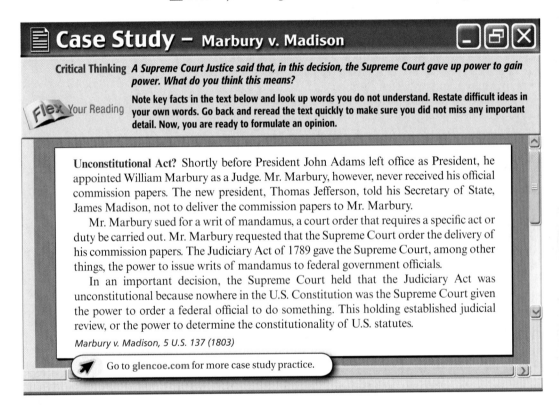

Case Study – Marbury v. Madison

Critical Thinking *A Supreme Court Justice said that, in this decision, the Supreme Court gave up power to gain power. What do you think this means?*

Flex Your Reading Note key facts in the text below and look up words you do not understand. Restate difficult ideas in your own words. Go back and reread the text quickly to make sure you did not miss any important detail. Now, you are ready to formulate an opinion.

Unconstitutional Act? Shortly before President John Adams left office as President, he appointed William Marbury as a Judge. Mr. Marbury, however, never received his official commission papers. The new president, Thomas Jefferson, told his Secretary of State, James Madison, not to deliver the commission papers to Mr. Marbury.

Mr. Marbury sued for a writ of mandamus, a court order that requires a specific act or duty be carried out. Mr. Marbury requested that the Supreme Court order the delivery of his commission papers. The Judiciary Act of 1789 gave the Supreme Court, among other things, the power to issue writs of mandamus to federal government officials.

In an important decision, the Supreme Court held that the Judiciary Act was unconstitutional because nowhere in the U.S. Constitution was the Supreme Court given the power to order a federal official to do something. This holding established judicial review, or the power to determine the constitutionality of U.S. statutes.

Marbury v. Madison, 5 U.S. 137 (1803)

Go to **glencoe.com** for more case study practice.

Case Study

Marbury v. Madison

Answer Prior to the decision, the U.S. Supreme Court had the power to command federal officials to act in a certain way. The U.S. Supreme Court gave up that power in order to gain the power of judicial review. By declaring a law unconstitutional, the U.S. Supreme Court took it upon itself to determine whether laws passed by an elected Congress were within the bounds of the Constitution. The power to order an official to act could be beneficial if judges or justices need to ensure that their decisions are carried out. But, in the broad scheme of things, it is more beneficial to protect the public from laws that are contrary to what the founders envisioned.

the relationships between two individual parties, and does not normally involve the government. The injured person begins a lawsuit by filing a complaint with the court. Another name for bringing a civil lawsuit is litigation.

There are many advantages to litigation. One advantage is that, since litigation has a long history in our legal system, the courts have had a chance to develop rules that make the process as fair as possible. However, there are disadvantages too. For instance, when an individual brings a civil case to an attorney, the lawyer investigates the case. This investigation can be costly and time consuming. Unlike in criminal cases, a person in a civil lawsuit is not guaranteed or provided an attorney. Many people choose to represent themselves in court, and they are expected to follow the same specific rules that attorneys follow during litigation.

Important Civil Statutes

There are many reasons for civil litigation. For example, if someone is hit by a car and dies, the victim's family may sue the driver of the car for wrongful death. The family may get money to compensate for the pain of losing their loved one.

Survival statutes are written to ensure that when a plaintiff dies, a representative for the deceased can continue the case, or bring a new case on the deceased's behalf. Statutes of limitation are passed to provide time limits for when a plaintiff may sue a defendant. For example, the statute of limitation for bringing a wrongful death claim may be three years. In the above example, that means that the family of the victim has three years to begin a suit against the driver for their loss. There are different time limits for each separate claim.

Alternative Dispute Resolution

To cut costs and to save time, people have begun to explore substitutes for lawsuits. **Alternative dispute resolution (ADR) occurs when parties try to resolve disagreements outside of the usual court system.** Some ADR techniques are mediation, arbitration, conciliation, and negotiation.

Mediation Mediation occurs when parties to a dispute invite a **mediator** to help them solve the problem. This can be done voluntarily, or as required by a court. A mediator tries to persuade the parties to compromise. A major advantage to mediation is that the final decision remains in the hands of the parties. A disadvantage is that, if carried out too quickly, mediation can highlight the disagreement between the parties rather than the points of agreement.

Arbitration Sometimes, the parties give the power to settle their dispute to a third party. This process is called arbitration. The person who is hired to settle the case is the arbitrator. An advantage to arbitration is that it often results in a fair solution because the decision is in the hands of an independent, objective third party. A disadvantage is that the final decision does not remain in the hands of the people who have a dispute.

Chapter 1   The Law and the Courts   **21**

Reading Check

Enumerate Federal courts include the district, appeals, and special courts. The U.S. Supreme Court is the highest court in the nation. State courts include local trial courts, general trial courts, juvenile courts, and state appellate courts.

Reading Check

Enumerate List the different types of federal courts and state courts.

TEACH (cont.)

D Develop Concepts

Alternatives to Litigation
Tell students that some in our society believe that U.S. citizens are too quick to resort to a lawsuit when involved in a dispute. Ask students to describe instances in which they or their families have experienced disagreements with others. Ask the following questions:

- How was the disagreement handled?
- Did the parties seek the advice of a third party?
- What final course of action was chosen?
- Was the outcome agreeable to all involved?

Emphasize to students that citizens have access to alternatives to litigation when involved in a dispute.

Guided Practice

Alternative Dispute Resolution

Tell students that there is an important difference between mediation and arbitration. Ask a volunteer to describe that difference. (In arbitration, a third party determines a decision. In mediation, the ultimate decision is still left in the hands of the parties in dispute.) Have students role-play a mediation in which a mediator helps two students settle a dispute over which weekend concert they should attend.

TEACH *(cont.)*

Guided Practice

D Develop Concepts

Pleadings Ask students to explain the purpose of pleadings. (Answers should include a statement to the effect that the issues that the trial is to address must be clearly documented before the trial can begin.)

Guided Practice

Discovery

Have students contact a trial attorney to learn more about the various methods for discovery. Have them inquire about instances in which each might be used. Ask students to prepare a brief presentation of their findings.

Role Play
Steps in a Jury Trial
List the steps in a jury trial on the board. Ask for volunteers from the class to role-play the steps in the trial as you discuss them in class. Alternately, you may wish to use a well-known trial like the O. J. Simpson trial to illustrate each step. (jury selection; arguments and evidence; instructions to the jury; verdict and judgment; execution of judgment)

Conciliation Conciliation is similar to mediation and arbitration. In conciliation, however, the intermediary, who is generally referred to as the conciliator, does not bring the parties together in a face-to-face conversation. Instead, the conciliator shuttles back and forth between the parties seeking a consensus. An advantage to conciliation is that the parties are kept apart from one another. This reduces the possibility of an angry confrontation. A disadvantage is that conciliation takes more time because the conciliator must meet separately with everyone involved.

Negotiation In negotiation, each party appoints a spokesperson to represent him or her in the reconciliation process. The negotiators then meet to hammer out an agreement. Negotiation is just one step closer to litigation, which involves an actual lawsuit. An advantage to negotiation is that it permits the parties to determine the relative merits of their arguments without going to court. A disadvantage is that often negotiation simply leads to litigation, thus adding an extra step to an already long process.

Civil Case Procedures
How do court trials start?

 Civil litigation begins with pleadings: formal papers filed with the court by the plaintiff and defendant. The plaintiff is the person bringing the lawsuit. The defendant is the person who the lawsuit is against. The complaint expresses the plaintiff's claims against the defendant. The answer is the defendant's official response to the claims in the complaint.

Methods of discovery are used to bring facts out before trial. They include depositions, interrogatories, requests for documents and other evidence, physical and mental examinations, and requests for admission. If a case cannot be settled at that point, the court clerk places the case on the calendar, or court docket, for trial.

Pretrial Hearing Before the trial takes place, a pretrial hearing occurs. This hearing is an informal meeting before a judge. Sometimes, people settle the case at the pretrial hearing. If they do not settle the case, then they try to simplify things so the trial can run smoothly.

Jury Duty People are summoned at random for jury duty. *How many people sit on a jury?*

Steps in a Trial
When a case is filed, the parties must decide whether they want a jury trial or a court trial. With a court trial, there is no jury, and a judge makes all the decisions. If a jury trial is requested, then the trial begins by choosing the jury members. The trial then moves to opening statements. After the opening statements, the evidence is

22   Unit 1   What Is Law?

▲ USING VISUALS

Jury Duty **Answer** twelve for felony and major civil cases; as few as six for misdemeanor or minor civil cases

Activity Ask students if they know somebody who has served on a jury. If they have, ask them to interview that person about the experience and to share their findings with the class. Suggest the following questions for the interview: How was the process of jury selection handled? Once selected, how many days did you serve on the jury? Were you paid for your service? What was the verdict?

introduced. When there is no more evidence to show, the closing arguments begin. Then, the judge gives the jury its instructions. The jury then decides the case and brings a verdict. The verdict is followed by a judgment.

Selecting the Jury The judge calls the court to order. Then the judge has a jury drawn from a group of people who have been called to serve. The jury must determine the facts of the case. The jury also applies the law to those facts. The lawyers question each juror to predict whether a juror will be fair or unfair. The lawyers consider the juror's background, education, experience, relationships, attitudes, and employment.

"No, you can't choose dare—only truth."

Arguments and Evidence After jury members are chosen, the lawyers make opening statements. The opening statements explain what the lawyers intend to prove. The plaintiff's lawyer goes first. The defendant's lawyer goes next, or waits to give an opening statement until after the plaintiff's evidence has been presented.

The plaintiff's lawyer presents all of the plaintiff's evidence. Witnesses testify at this time, including expert witnesses. Expert witnesses give authoritative opinions on evidence in the case.

The defense lawyer has the chance to cross-examine the plaintiff's witnesses. The cross-examination is supposed to test the truth of a witness's statements. It might also bring out evidence that was not brought out on direct examination. When the plaintiff's lawyer is done, the defendant's lawyer presents evidence. The plaintiff's lawyer may then cross-examine. When both lawyers are done, they rest their cases.

The plaintiff's lawyer is the first to give a closing argument. This is followed by the defense lawyer. Each lawyer gives a summary of the evidence and suggests reasons why the judge or jury should find in favor of their client.

Instructions to the Jury The judge must explain the law to the jury. This is a process called jury instruction. Lawyers from both sides may suggest instructions.

Verdict and Judgment Jury members go to the jury room to talk about the case. After discussing the case, the jury will decide who has won the suit. This decision is called the verdict. States may allow a less than unanimous decision by jurors to agree on a verdict. Following the jury's verdict, the court issues a judgment. The judgment is the court's determination of liability in the case, or who is responsible for what. If there is no jury, the judge issues findings of fact, which are similar to a jury verdict, and then conclusions of law and a judgment.

The Witness Stand A witness testifies under oath at a trial (a deposition may be used in a trial if the witness is not available). The plaintiff or the defendant may be witnesses. Witnesses testify about what they have seen, heard, or experienced, or about the signing of a document such as a contract or a will. *What is the most important responsibility of a witness?*

Chapter 1   The Law and the Courts   **23**

TEACH (cont.)

C Critical Thinking

Jury Selection Ask students why the selection of a jury is an important step in the trial process. (Jurors' education, relationships, attitudes, and employment may have a bearing on their view of the proceedings and evidence.) Explain that lawyers use a procedure called *voir dire* to choose jurors. *Voir dire* means "to speak the truth"; it helps determine the prospective jurors' qualifications for jury service.

Guided Practice

Evidence

Ask for volunteers to list what items might be used as evidence in a trial. (documents, photos, testimony, recordings, witnesses) Have students contact local trial attorneys or court personnel, or perform research on the Web to find out what specific rules of evidence must be followed in one of your local courts of law. Instruct students to bring copies of some of the rules to class. Ask students to analyze what the rules mean and why they were drafted.

D Develop Concepts

Verdict and Judgment Ask students to describe the difference between a verdict and judgment. (A verdict is a decision on who has won the lawsuit. A judgment is the court's determination of liability in the case.) Explain that if a jury cannot agree on a verdict, the judge may declare a "hung" jury, declare a mistrial, and order a new trial.

▲ USING VISUALS

➡ **The Witness Stand** **Answer** Witnesses must answer questions truthfully. Expert witnesses give authoritative opinions on evidence in the case. Other witnesses testify as to what they saw or heard in regard to the case.

TEACH (cont.)

C Critical Thinking

Appeal Process Ask students why parties are permitted to appeal the judgment of the court. (mistakes made or incorrect decisions entered by judge at lower court level)

S Skills Practice

Have students create an outline of this section using the headings and ask them to answer the following questions.

List List the steps in a jury trial. (selecting the jury, opening statements, introduction to evidence, closing arguments, instructions to the jury, verdict, and judgment) **L1**

Describe What are the steps in a criminal trial procedure? (arrest of the defendant, the arraignment, the trial, and sentencing) **L2**

Compare How do the remedies provided in a civil trial compare to the sentences given in a criminal trial? (In both cases money may be paid—in civil cases as a payment of damages and in criminal trials as fines. In civil cases an equitable remedy may be required but in criminal cases sentences include imprisonment and the death penalty.) **L3**

Lawyers and Clients Court decisions may be appealed. In appeals cases, lawyers prepare to make their arguments to an appellate court. *What is the main difference between an appeal case and a trial?*

Remedies When a defendant is found liable in a civil trial, the plaintiff is granted a remedy. Courts provide two types of remedies. One type is the payment of money. The other type requires some other action by the defendant. The plaintiff may want the defendant to keep a promise in a contract. This is called specific performance. Sometimes the plaintiff wants the defendant to stop doing something. In that case, the plaintiff seeks an injunction.

Execution of Judgment After the trial, the judgment of the court must be carried out. A judgment is enforced when the judge issues an execution order. The judge might order the sheriff to take some of the property that belongs to the losing party. The sheriff would then sell the property at an auction. The sheriff must use the money made at the auction to pay the winning party.

The Appeal Process

The parties are permitted to appeal the judgment of the court. The appeals process is different from trial. An appeal can only be based on a legal mistake by the judge. This is why attorneys object to certain procedures and to certain decisions made by the judge at the lower court level. There is no retrial at the appellate level. The lawyers argue their case before the appellate court, which then can affirm, reverse, or remand the case back to the lower court. **C**

Criminal Trial Procedure

What happens when the police arrest a criminal suspect?

An arrest occurs when a person is legally deprived of his or her freedom. Criminal cases often start when the defendant is arrested. Defendants have a right to due process of law, or fair treatment according to established legal principles. The law requires a court hearing right away. This is supposed to protect the defendant's rights. The trial is planned for later to give both lawyers time to prepare their cases. The rules in criminal procedure must be followed exactly. In contrast, in a civil case, procedure can often be altered or changed by the agreement of the parties and judge. This is to protect the rights of the defendant. **S**

Rights of the Defendant

The Supreme Court, in a case called Miranda v. Arizona, decided that people must be informed of their constitutional rights when they are arrested. The Miranda warnings require the police to tell people what crimes they are being arrested for. The police must also tell people they arrest that they have the right to a lawyer. If a defendant cannot afford a lawyer, the court must appoint one at no cost. The police must also tell people they arrest that they have the right to not say anything and that anything they do say can be used against them in court.

▲ USING VISUALS

Lawyers and Clients **Answer** An appeal case is based on a legal mistake in the judgment of the court in the course of a trial. No new evidence is admitted during an appeal; a retrial does not occur.

Activity Have students research a recent trial in which an appeal was filed for the defendant. If students use the Internet for research, suggest that they use the terms *appeal* and *case*. Ask them to describe the arguments on which the appeal was filed.

A police officer may arrest a person at any time if the officer has a warrant. A police officer may arrest a person without a warrant if the officer believes the person has committed or is committing a crime in the officer's presence.

Bail A person who has been arrested can sometimes be released on bail. **Bail is money or other property that is left with the court to assure that a person who has been arrested, but released, will return to trial.** A judge determines bail.

Search and Seizure A police officer may search a person, car, house, or other building only if permission is given or if the officer has a search warrant. The search must only be the area mentioned in the warrant. An officer may conduct a limited search, or frisk, if the officer believes a person is carrying a weapon. When the search is over, the person must either be released or arrested. Persons who have been arrested may be searched without a warrant.

The Arraignment

The suspect is brought before the court as soon as possible after an arrest. At this brief hearing, the criminal defendant is informed of the complaint. The defendant is also made aware of his or her rights. At this time, the judge may find a reason to dismiss the complaint. The judge might also decide that there is probable cause that a crime was committed.

Grand Jury Depending upon the jurisdiction, the prosecuting lawyer either prepares an information or presents the case to the grand jury. An information is a set of formal charges drawn up by the prosecuting attorney. A grand jury is a jury made up of citizens who must decide whether there is enough evidence to justify accusing a person of a crime. A grand jury conducts its hearings in private to determine whether someone must stand trial. If jurors decide a crime has been committed, they issue an indictment, or written accusation charging the individual. This does not mean that the named person is guilty but that the grand jury believes there is a possibility the person is guilty.

Following the indictment, the accused is brought to court for arraignment. **An arraignment is a formal hearing during which the defendant is read the indictment or information and is asked to plead guilty or not guilty.** The accused is informed of his or her rights. If the person pleads guilty, the judge may then impose the sentence. If the person pleads not guilty, the case goes on to trial. A defendant may also plead guilty pursuant to a plea agreement. This is an agreement between the government and the defendant. Trial can be difficult, so the government may offer to change the charges to a crime with a lesser sentence if the defendant will plead guilty without a trial.

The Trial

If the defendant requests a jury trial, the jury members must be selected. Otherwise, the case is tried before the judge, which rarely

TEACH *(cont.)*

Independent Practice

Search and Seizure

Ask students to describe the instances when and reasons for which a police officer is allowed to search a person, house, car, or building. (Using a warrant; if permission is given; if officer believes a weapon is being carried. If arrest is made in a car, search can be performed. School officials may search students without a warrant.)

Extending the Content

Search and Seizure

The Fourth Amendment to the U.S. Constitution protects the right to privacy and the right to protection from arbitrary government actions. It protects the right of our persons and effects to be secure from unreasonable searches and seizures by the government. Any authorization for search and seizure, whether from statute or the common law, must comply with this amendment. Even if the search is legally authorized, it must be carried out in a reasonable manner or it may still violate the Constitution.

Guided Practice

Court Cases

Ask groups of students to write the clerks' offices or public information offices of several courts in your area to obtain the most recent statistics on cases filed in that court. Explain that some states also provide online records of court cases. Have each group analyze the information provided and issue a report on their particular court.

The Arraignment

Have students describe the goals of the arraignment in their own words. Ask them to describe the actions that would immediately follow the arraignment.

TEACH (cont.)

Legal Talk

(disappoint, discourage)

Ask students to practice their academic and legal vocabulary with the electronic flashcards available at the *Business and Personal Law* Online Learning Center through glencoe.com.

ASSESS

Quiz

Ask students to answer the following questions:

1. What does jurisdiction mean? (power and authority given to a court to hear a case and make a judgment)

2. Are judges able to sentence convicted individuals using any reasonable punishment? (No. The law provides certain sentencing guidelines and penalties.)

3. What is the purpose of discovery? (to find all relevant facts important to the case)

RETEACH

Guided Practice

Trial Process

Have students recall the purpose of the arraignment. (defendant informed of complaint and made aware of his or her rights)

Ask students to describe what happens in the actual jury trial. (opening statements, evidence, closing statements, judge's instructions to the jury verdict, and judgment)

26

Legal Talk

Disposition: *n* Final arrangement or settlement. From Latin *dis* = apart + *ponere* = to arrange.

Adjudicatory: *adj* Relates to a judge's decision or sentence. From Latin *adjudicare,* to judge.

Vocabulary Builder List and define two words that begin with the prefix *dis.*

Look It Up! Check definitions in *Black's Law Dictionary* or an online glossary. For direct links, go to **glencoe.com** to find more vocabulary resources.

happens in criminal trials. The actual trial is similar to a civil trial. The lawyers make opening statements. They introduce evidence. The trial ends with each lawyer's closing statement. The closing statements are followed by the judge's instructions to the jury.

In a criminal case with a jury, the verdict must be unanimous. When a jury cannot unanimously agree, it is called a hung jury and a mistrial is called. A new trial may be held at the option of the prosecution. If the verdict is not guilty, the defendant is released. If the defendant is guilty, the judge imposes a sentence in the form of a fine, imprisonment, or both. In a criminal matter, if the defendant is guilty, that means that beyond all reasonable doubt, the defendant is the person who did the crime. In addition, for every crime, there is an element of intent, which means the defendant must have intended to break the law. A person who is found not guilty cannot be tried twice for the same crime in the same court. This is the principle of double **jeopardy** which is defined in the Fifth Amendment of the U. S. Constitution.

Sentencing

After a person has been convicted of a crime, the court will sentence that individual. This means the judge decides the punishment. The law provides certain sentencing guidelines and penalties. The penalties could include fines, imprisonment, and even death.

Fines A fine is the payment of money as a penalty for committing a crime. Fines are levied against a defendant when the crime is minor. However, fines can also be attached to more serious penalties, such as imprisonment.

Imprisonment States deal with imprisonment in different ways. In some states, the judge may hand down an indefinite sentence. This means that the judge orders a minimum and maximum amount of time that the convicted criminal may spend in prison, such as five to ten years. Other states make the judge state the exact period of time a criminal will spend in prison. Some states have made mandatory sentences for certain crimes which cannot be changed for any reason.

The Death Penalty Our Constitution says death penalty laws must include guidelines to ensure fair treatment. The U.S. Supreme Court has held that a jury, not a judge, must now decide whether a defendant deserves the death penalty. The United States Supreme Court has ruled that criminal defendants under 18 years of age and those who are mentally incompetent cannot be sentenced to death.

Disposition of Juvenile Cases

Cases involving juvenile offenders are handled by the juvenile court. As a first step, the judge usually holds a detention hearing. **A detention hearing is a court session during which the judge tries to learn whether there are good reasons to keep the accused in custody.** The court's probation department or a

 glencoe.com

Independent Practice

Court Systems

Write the following cases on the board.

1. Bankruptcy

2. Violation of a curfew by a teen

3. Abandonment of duty by a naval officer

Ask students to name the court in which the case will likely be tried. (1. U.S. district court; 2. State juvenile court; 3. U.S. military court)

Extending the Content

Assign students to research teen courts and write a brief report explaining how these courts function and what type of cases they handle. (Teen courts, also known as youth or peer courts, are prevention and intervention programs that handle relatively minor crimes. Usually, first-time juvenile offenders are sentenced by their peers.) Ask students whether they would consider participating in a teen court.

child welfare agency investigates the minor's background and home life. The judge might dismiss the charges after hearing the results of the investigation.

Adjudicatory Hearings If the charges are not dismissed, the judge conducts an adjudicatory hearing. This is the informal hearing of the case by the court. The judge may question the young person and the parents, listen to witnesses, or seek advice from the probation officer. After a hearing, the judge may decide the outcome of the case in one of three ways.

- The judge may allow the offender to return home on probation for a period of time, under the supervision of a probation officer.
- The judge may place the offender in an agency or foster home. The natural parents will then be required to pay what they can toward the offender's support.
- The judge may commit the offender to a training or reform school.

The judge can also order the juvenile offender to pay for the damages with money, work, or both. The parents of the offender may have to repay the victim. Sentences for youthful offenders are set with rehabilitation in mind. They are generally limited to probation under court supervision, confinement for not more than three years in a reformative institution, or another course of action designed to help, rather than to punish.

After You Read

Summarize List differences and similarities between civil and criminal court procedures?

SECTION 1.2 ASSESSMENT

Self Check

1. What is the difference between a civil and a criminal case?
2. What is the role of the United States Supreme Court?
3. Under what conditions can a police officer search a person?

Academic Connection

Mathematics Create a table listing which of the 13 original colonies were represented in the 39 signatures to the U.S. Constitution. Calculate the percent that figure represents of the total participants.

THEORY **Number and Operations: Using Fractions, Decimals, and Rounding.** To figure out the problem, take the number for each category and divide by the total. For example, $8 \div 39 = .205$. Then change the decimal to a percent by moving the decimal to the right two spaces and adding a percent sign. Round numbers of 5 or more up and numbers less than 5 down. For example, .2045 rounds to 20.5% and .2044 rounds to 20.4%.

 Math For more math practice, go to the Math Appendix.

Critical Thinking

Search and Seizure
Suppose that the principal of your school has decided that all students will be searched when they enter the school building in the morning and when they leave in the afternoon. Write a legal argument that you could present to the principal when you ask him or her to reconsider the new search policy.

 Go to **glencoe.com** to check your answers.

1.2 SECTION

RETEACH (cont.)

After You Read

Summarize One main difference is that procedure rules must be followed strictly in criminal trials whereas they can be changed by common agreement in a civil case.

ASSESS

Self-Assessment

Have students go to the *Business and Personal Law* Online Learning Center through **glencoe.com** to take the Section 1.2 Practice Test.

CLOSE

Culminating Activity

Jury Trial
Ask students to make a chart depicting the sequence of steps in a jury trial. (selection of jury, opening statements, evidence introduced, closing arguments, instructions to jury, jury decides case, verdict, judgment)

SECTION 1.2 ASSESSMENT

Self Check

1. civil case begins with pleadings; criminal case begins with arrest of defendant
2. hears appeals from federal and state courts
3. with the person's permission, with a search warrant, or if the person has been arrested

Academic Connection

Mathematics
DE 6.4%; PA 16.1%; MA 8.9%; NH 5.4%; RI 3.6%; NY 7.1%; GA 5.4%; VA 12.5%; NC 5.4%; SC 7.1%; NJ 8.9%; CT 7.1%; MD 7.1%

Critical Thinking

Students should refer to basic civil rights as outlined by the Constitution. This should be weighed against the principal's responsibility to keep the school safe.

 Activity correlated to the Mathematics standard on page 15

Summary by Sections

Ask students to read the summaries one key point at a time. Then, ask them to work in groups to create two examples to illustrate each key point.

Vocabulary Builder

Cooperative Learning

1. Have students work in groups to prepare their sentences. Ask the groups to exchange their sentences and assess each other's sentences.

Vocabulary Development

- Ask students to use a dictionary or to go online to look up the etymology of each key term listed.
- Then, ask students to list several words derived from the same root or origin. For example, *contract* has the same root as *contractual* or *contractually*.

Chapter 1 Review and Assessment

Summary

Section 1.1 The Foundations of Law

- ◆ Ethical decisions can be made by applying the greatest good principle, or by following the Golden Rule.
- ◆ Four ethical character traits are: honesty, justice, compassion, and integrity.
- ◆ Ethics may be subjective. Laws provide an objective standard of behavior.
- ◆ The U.S. Constitution, which consists of seven articles and 27 amendments, enumerates the fundamental rights of citizens, names the functions of the three branches of government, and creates a system of checks and balances.
- ◆ Common law is a set of laws that provide rules for courts of justice. It is the basis of the U.S. legal system. Statutory law is the body of laws derived from statutes.
- ◆ Legislatures form regulatory agencies, which have a wide range of powers to create, enforce, and adjudicate rules and procedures.

Section 1.2 The Court System and Trial Procedures

- ◆ Jurisdiction is the power and authority given a court to hear a case and make a judgment.
- ◆ Federal courts are arranged in three levels: U.S. district courts, U.S. courts of appeals, and the Supreme Court of the United States.
- ◆ State court systems consist of local trial courts, courts of general jurisdiction, appellate, and supreme courts.
- ◆ Mediation, arbitration, conciliation, and negotiation are examples of reactive Alternate Dispute Resolution (ADR).
- ◆ In civil court, the plaintiff sues the defendant for a remedy. In a criminal proceeding, the district attorney prosecutes on behalf of the government.
- ◆ The steps in a civil trial are: jury selection, opening statements, evidence, closing arguments, instructions to the jury, the jury verdict, and the court's judgment.

Vocabulary Builder

❶ On a sheet of paper, use each of these terms in a sentence.

Key Terms

- morality
- ethics
- justice
- law
- constitution

- common law
- statute
- administrative law
- jurisdiction
- appellate court

- alternative dispute resolution (ADR)
- arrest
- bail
- arraignment
- detention hearing

Academic Vocabulary

- empathy
- permissible

- prevalent
- informal

- mediator
- jeopardy

Go to **glencoe.com** to play a game and improve your legal vocabulary.

Study Skills for Success

Prepare Your Students for Studying

Tell students that they can improve their ability to understand and remember material from their courses by learning and practicing study skills. Remind students to:

- **Get motivated!** Motivation must come from within. To motivate yourself, think of ways in which what you learn now will fit into your long-term personal and professional goals.
- **Get organized!** Make studying part of your daily routine, not something you do at the last minute.
- **Concentrate!** Study in an environment that is as free of distractions as possible.

Key Points Review

Answer the following questions. Refer to the chapter for additional reinforcement.

2 What are the four ethical character traits?

3 What are the parts of the U.S. Constitution?

4 What is common law?

5 How do the courts make laws? What is the structure of the federal court system?

6 What is the common structure of most state court systems?

7 What are some alternative dispute resolution techniques?

8 What are the steps in a civil lawsuit?

9 What rights does a criminal defendant have?

10 What are the steps in a criminal prosecution?

Standardized Test Practice

11 Read this excerpt of Senate Document 105-14 entitled "How Our Laws Are Made" and complete questions 1 and 2.

"Laws may be initiated in either chamber of Congress, the House of Representatives or the Senate. For this example, we will track a bill introduced in the House of Representatives.

When a representative has an idea for a new law, s/he becomes the sponsor of that bill and introduces it by giving it to the clerk of the House or by placing it in a box, called the hopper. The clerk assigns a legislative number to the bill, with H.R. for bills introduced in the House of Representatives and S. for bills introduced in the Senate. The Government Printing Office (GPO) then prints the bill and distributes copies to each representative."

1. The first step for a new law is

Ⓐ Get a sponsor

Ⓑ Create an idea

Ⓒ Give it to the House

Ⓓ Call the hopper

2. Laws can be initiated through

Ⓐ House of Representatives or Senate

Ⓑ Government Printing Office or House of Representatives

Ⓒ House of Representatives or President

Ⓓ President, Senate, or House of Representatives

 Test-Taking Strategies Make sure you read all the answer choices, identify choices that are obviously wrong, and choose from answers that remain.

Standardized Test Practice

11. B and A

 ## Strategies for Standardized Test Prep Success

Whether your students have a standardized test coming up in a few days or a few weeks, these last-minute test-prep tips and strategies will help them relax and do their best.

- **Test Format** Help students become familiar with the format of the test by practicing with test items that imitate the actual test items as closely as possible.

- **Test Timing** Have your students take timed practice tests so that they become comfortable with the length, design, and timing of the actual test.

Review and Assessment

Key Points Review

2. honesty, justice, compassion, integrity

3. seven articles and 27 amendments

4. originates from England and can be applied to interpret statutory law

5. through the common law tradition, by interpreting statutes, and by deciding issues of constitutionality; for the structure of the federal court system, see Figure 1.1

6. in tiers, from lowest to highest: local trial courts, general trial courts, intermediate appellate courts, and state supreme courts

7. mediation, arbitration, conciliation, and negotiation

8. pleadings (complaint and answer), discovery, attempts to settle; if no settlement, pretrial hearing, trial (jury selection, evidence and arguments, verdict), judgment, execution of judgment, then appeal

9. Miranda rights: right to know what crimes are alleged to have been committed; right to an attorney (at no cost, if necessary); the right to remain silent

10. arrest, arraignment; if guilty plea, sentencing; if not guilty plea, trial (jury selection, evidence and arguments, unanimous verdict); based on the verdict, either release or sentencing

Apply and Debate

Students should use chapter content to arrive at conclusions. Possible legal resolutions are listed below:

12. If an ethical duty exists, it can be determined by applying one of the ethical rules.

13. No. Law and ethics create different responsibilities for people. Students should also contrast unethical behavior with illegal behavior under the law.

14. No. The First Amendment to the U.S. Constitution and rulings on the First Amendment have limited the rights of students while at school.

15. Students should weigh the idea of a safer society with the costs and time of going to trial.

16. The police officer's action raises the question of whether entrapment occurred, which Manik can use as a defense in a trial.

C Critical Thinking

Jury Selection Give students the following scenario: Danielle is involved in a civil case and has requested a jury trial. She believes that the jury will contain individuals of her age, who will understand her case and rule in her favor.

C Read the following scenarios. Get together with other students in pairs or groups of three and take a position on each scenario. Debate your position in class with students taking the opposite position or prepare a written argument justifying your position.

12 Lost Wallet

As you walked down the street you found a wallet full of money on the ground. You placed an ad in the lost and found section of the local paper. After a month of running the ad no one has responded to it.

You Debate — *Is it your ethical duty to find the rightful owner?*

13 Eyewitness

Alex witnessed a mugging on his way home but did not stop to get involved. Other witnesses saw Alex leaving the area. Later Alex saw on TV that the police were asking for witnesses to the mugging to come forward and give a statement.

You Debate — *Can the law force Alex to give a statement?*

14 Free Speech

Rini is running for student council and has placed flyers on all the cars and inside the campus buildings. The principal suspended her for doing this without school's permission. Rini argued she is entitled to free speech under the First Amendment.

You Debate — *Does free speech extend to flyers posted for a student election?*

15 Plea Bargaining

Roberto is an accountant charged with stealing company funds from Haven's Landscaping. The district attorney offered Roberto a deal of one year in prison if he would plead guilty to the crime. Roberto accepted the deal.

You Debate — *Should punishment for a crime be lessened in exchange for the defendant pleading guilty without the expense of a trial?*

16 Entrapment

Manik has always been an upstanding citizen. A man came in to Manik's used electronics store and offered to sell him flat-screen TVs at an extremely low price. Manik did not question the low sales price. When Manik paid the man for the goods, he discovered that the man was an undercover police officer, who charged Manik with purchasing stolen goods.

You Debate — *Can Manik argue that the charge was entrapment?*

Debate Practice

- How will Danielle's trial begin? (choosing jury members)

- What responsibility does the jury have in the case? (to hear and understand the facts of the case, interpret the law, render a verdict)

- Will Danielle's attorney be able to select jurors that will be sympathetic to Danielle? (Her attorney can attempt to select jurors whose background, education, and experience are similar to Danielle, but this is not guaranteed.)

Case Study Practice– Papaila v. Uniden America Corp.

17 Who Has Juridiction? Theodore Papaila, an American employee of Uniden America Corporation (UAC), a subsidiary of a Japanese company, sued UAC for racial discrimination. He claimed UAC treated 16 Japanese employees differently by giving them higher base salaries, fringe benefits, and job protection. Two laws apply to this case. U.S. Code statute 42 U.S.C. §2000e-2(a)(1) reads: "(a) Employer practices: It shall be an unlawful employment practice for an employer to fail or refuse to hire or to discharge any individual, or otherwise to discriminate against any individual with respect to his compensation, terms, conditions, or privileges of employment, because of such individual's race, color, religion, sex, or national origin." The Friendship, Commerce, and Navigation Treaty and Protocol Between the United States and Japan, 4 U.S.T. 2063 reads: "Nationals and companies of either Party shall be permitted to engage, within the territories of the other Party, accountants and other technical experts, executive personnel, attorneys, agents and other specialists of their choice."

Source: Papaila v. Uniden America Corp., 51 F.3d 54 (5th Cir. 1995)

Practice Which law should apply to this case? What are the ethical implications?

18 Ethics ←?→ Application

Guilty by Silence? As you enter the classroom, you see another student named Jonathan copying down the answers to today's test from the teacher's desk.

◆ What would be the ethical decision to make regarding this situation?

19 Internet Application

Learn How to File a Complaint In your neighborhood, the sidewalks are not handicap accessible, which prevents your wheelchair-bound grandmother from using them. You have contacted the city manager's office but have had no luck in getting them changed.

 Go to **glencoe.com** to access the Americans with Disabilities Act Mediation Program Web link to learn how to file a complaint. Outline the steps to share with your class.

Reading Connection

Outside Reading Go to **glencoe.com** for a list of reading suggestions about ethics and the court system.

 glencoe.com

Case Study Practice

17. The treaty between Japan and the United States was the prevailing law, since the employees were Japanese nationals. Uniden had a right to treat its Japanese employees differently than its American employees if those employees were executive or professional in nature. Ethically speaking, students should consider whether this is still a good treaty for the United States. It was signed in 1953.

Chapter

Review and Assessment

←?→ Ethics Application

18. Possible suggestions could include asking Jonathan to tell the teacher he saw the test answers or informing the teacher after class what you witnessed. Acting ethically is not always an easy choice.

Internet Application

19. An ADA complaint should contain the contact information of the party discriminated against, the name of the organization that has discriminated, a description of the act or acts of discrimination, the date or dates of the discriminatory acts, the name or names of the individuals who you believe discriminated, and any other important information.

R Reading Strategy

Reading Connection

American Bar Association Resources

Go to the *Business and Personal Law* Online Learning Center through glencoe.com to find links for further readings that relate to this chapter. Ask students to read, review, and summarize the documents. Advise students to keep their reviews and summaries to use as reference material for their Unit Thematic Project on pages 72–73.

Plan Your Lesson Section by Section

NBEA	NATIONAL BUSINESS LAW STANDARDS
Section 2.1	• **Determine** several defenses to criminal acts (e.g., insanity defense and self-defense). • **Describe** the penalties available in criminal law and the remedies available in tort law.
Section 2.2	• **Define** different types of business crime (e.g., arson, forgery, and embezzlement). • **Describe** the penalties available in criminal law and the remedies available in tort law.

NCLB — ACADEMIC STANDARDS	Activity/Feature
English Language Arts: NCTE 3 Apply a wide range of strategies to comprehend, interpret, evaluate, and appreciate texts.	*BusinessWeek* News, Case Study, Case Study Practice
English Language Arts: NCTE 9 Develop an understanding of and respect for diversity in language use, patterns, and dialects across cultures, ethnic groups, geographic regions, and social roles.	Global Law
English Language Arts: NCTE 6 Apply knowledge of language structure, language conventions, media techniques, figurative language, and genre to create, critique, and discuss print and non-print texts.	Legal Talk, ad copy, Key Terms, and Academic Vocabulary
Social Studies: NCSS 5 Study interactions among individuals, groups, and institutions.	Section 2.1 Assessment
English Language Arts: NCTE 12 Use spoken, written, and visual language to accomplish your own purposes.	Section 2.1 Assessment
Mathematics: NCTM NOS 2 Understand meanings of operations and how they relate to one another.	Section 2.2 Assessment
English Language Arts: NCTE 10 Students whose first language is not English make use of their first language to develop competency in the English language arts and to develop understanding of content across the curriculum.	Key Terms, Academic Vocabulary, Legal Talk, Vocabulary Builder
English Language Arts: NCTE 1 Read a wide range of print and non-print texts to build an understanding of texts; to acquire new information; to respond to the needs and demands of society and the workplace; and for personal fulfillment.	Global Law, Cyberlaw
Social Studies: NCSS 10 Study the ideals, principles, and practices of citizenship in a democratic republic.	Global Law, Cyberlaw

Connect Your Business Law Classroom to the World of Work

This chart shows the 21st Century Skills, foundation skills, and workplace competencies that students develop as they work in this chapter.

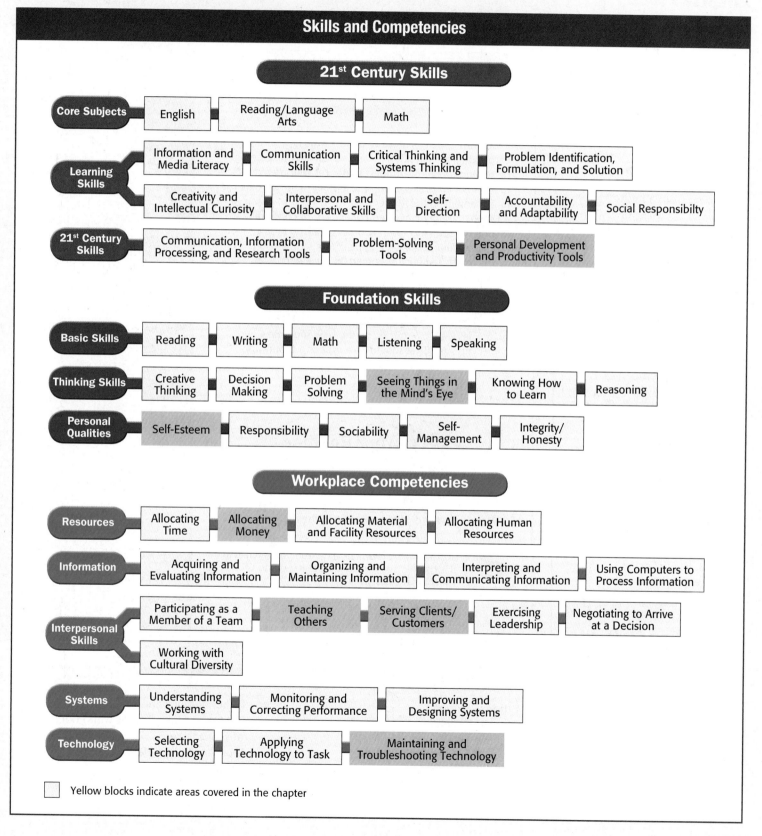

Skills and Competencies

21st Century Skills

Core Subjects
- English
- Reading/Language Arts
- Math

Learning Skills
- Information and Media Literacy
- Communication Skills
- Critical Thinking and Systems Thinking
- Problem Identification, Formulation, and Solution
- Creativity and Intellectual Curiosity
- Interpersonal and Collaborative Skills
- Self-Direction
- Accountability and Adaptability
- Social Responsibilty

21st Century Skills
- Communication, Information Processing, and Research Tools
- Problem-Solving Tools
- Personal Development and Productivity Tools

Foundation Skills

Basic Skills
- Reading
- Writing
- Math
- Listening
- Speaking

Thinking Skills
- Creative Thinking
- Decision Making
- Problem Solving
- Seeing Things in the Mind's Eye
- Knowing How to Learn
- Reasoning

Personal Qualities
- Self-Esteem
- Responsibility
- Sociability
- Self-Management
- Integrity/Honesty

Workplace Competencies

Resources
- Allocating Time
- Allocating Money
- Allocating Material and Facility Resources
- Allocating Human Resources

Information
- Acquiring and Evaluating Information
- Organizing and Maintaining Information
- Interpreting and Communicating Information
- Using Computers to Process Information

Interpersonal Skills
- Participating as a Member of a Team
- Teaching Others
- Serving Clients/Customers
- Exercising Leadership
- Negotiating to Arrive at a Decision
- Working with Cultural Diversity

Systems
- Understanding Systems
- Monitoring and Correcting Performance
- Improving and Designing Systems

Technology
- Selecting Technology
- Applying Technology to Task
- Maintaining and Troubleshooting Technology

☐ Yellow blocks indicate areas covered in the chapter

Introduce the Chapter

Criminal Law
Criminal law is a body of laws that deal with crime and the punishment of criminal offenses. Chapter 2 introduces the criminal law system in the United States and outlines classifications and types of crimes.

Building Background
Introduce the topic of crime by reading from a local newspaper, focusing on articles about theft, murder, or traffic violations. Point out the varying degrees of severity of the crimes.

BusinessWeek News

Executives such as Bernard Ebbers are held responsible for the financial statements issued by their companies. Tell students that the Sarbanes-Oxley Act of 2002 is a federal law passed in response to a number of major corporate and accounting scandals involving prominent companies in the United States. Explain that the CEO and CFO must certify that the company's financial statements fairly represent, in all material respects, the financial condition and results of company operations.

R Reading Strategy

 Your Reading

Tell students that a speeding ticket contains critical legal information. Late fees, court fees, and appeal process procedures are usually outlined to help citizens pay their fine or contest the infraction.

Criminal Law

BusinessWeek News

Bernard Ebbers: Stiff Sentence
By Mike France

Bernard Ebbers orchestrated one of the largest corporate frauds in history—and now it looks like he'll be serving one of the longest sentences ever meted out to a former chief executive. U.S. District Judge Barbara Jones sentenced the former CEO to 25 years in prison. A Manhattan jury convicted Ebbers, 63, of conspiracy, securities fraud, and seven counts of making false regulatory filings. Ebbers is appealing his conviction.

The tough sentence stemmed, in large part, from the estimated $2 billion in investor losses prosecutors attributed to Ebbers' fraud. Judges can still take this into account in determining punishment for white-collar felons, even though the federal sentencing guidelines were overturned by the U.S. Supreme Court earlier this year. That should be a sobering thought for other execs facing criminal trials in coming months.

Flex Your Reading

Efficient critical reading involves being flexible with speed and comprehension. There are several ways of reading critically, and you need to fit a reading style to your needs and to the material.

Go to **glencoe.com** for Flex Your Reading activities, more information on reading strategies for this chapter, and guided practice in reading about criminal law cases.

 Classroom Resources

- Student Edition
- Teacher Wraparound Edition
- Student Activity Workbook with Academic Integration (SE/TAE)
- TeacherWorks™ Plus! CD
- *ExamView® Assessment Suite* CD
- *Presentation Plus!* CD

- National Mock Trial Championship DVD
- Online Learning Center with Podcasts at glencoe.com
- Study-to-Go™ at glencoe.com
- Online Student Edition
- Interactive Student Edition

Crime Scene The elements of a crime are the criminal act and the required state mind. *What is the state of mind required of a person to be guilty of murder?*

33

Practice the Concept

Criminal Law
Ask students to consider television programs that focus on criminal investigations or prosecutions. Have them discuss the types of crimes committed, court proceedings, and punishments related to specific crimes.

Key Terms Movies or television programs that feature crimes and criminal law use terms such as *felony, misdemeanor, plaintiff,* and *defendant.* Because the law is specific in its description of forbidden activities, legal experts are often hired to act as consultants for these productions. While some crime programs may glamorize crime and criminal law, tell students that they can also serve to raise public awareness about how evidence is gathered and how the legal system works.

The Fine Print When a person is charged with a crime, there is a chain of legal documents that are drafted, including the police report, a brief, indictment, and the court docket. Each of these documents presents information on the circumstances, events, and other supporting evidence for substantiating or dismissing the charge. The preparer of each document must pay special attention to the accuracy of such information. Serious errors in some of these documents could cause a court case to be dismissed.

▲ USING VISUALS

Felonies and Misdemeanors Answer Answers will vary, but students will likely suggest monetary fines and jail time. Community service is also an option in some misdemeanor convictions. Tell students that the specific penalties often depend on the facts of the case and the state in which the case is presented. In some cases, the court may require counseling or probation for the offender.

FOCUS

Bell Ringer Activity

Read the pertinent details from one newspaper article to the class that features a recent crime. Have students discuss the kind of penalty or punishment they believe would be appropriate for the crime. Then discuss the actual penalty or punishment described in the article.

Preteaching

Key Terms

Read the definitions and ask students to create a sentence using each term.

Academic Vocabulary

Explain that developing vocabulary is key to academic success. An efficient method to develop vocabulary is to study how words are formed.

- **intent** Noun, from the Latin *intentus* (attention). Means purpose.
- **motive** Noun, from the Latin *motus* (move). Means that which inwardly moves a person a certain way.
- **impulse** Noun, from the Latin *impellere* (to drive). Means stimulus in the mind arising from some feeling.

Activity Ask students to give a noun, an adjective, or an adverb form that comes from each word.

 Connects to academic content

What You'll Learn

- ◆ Explain the differences between categories of crime.
- ◆ Distinguish federal from state criminal law.
- ◆ Describe the elements of a crime.
- ◆ Determine several defenses to criminal acts.
- ◆ Explain the differences between penalties for committing felonies and misdemeanors.

Why It's Important

Knowing the elements of a crime and the defenses to crimes will help you if you are ever accused of a crime or the victim of a crime.

Academic Standards

Reading and completing the activities in this section will help you practice the following academic standards:

Social Studies (NCSS 5) Study interactions among individuals, groups, and institutions.

English Language Arts (NCTE 12) Use spoken, written, and visual language to accomplish your own purposes.

Crimes and Criminal Justice

Reading Guide

Before You Read

Connect You have may seen trials on television and in movies. In real life, what does a prosecutor have to prove to convict someone of a crime?

Focus on Ideas

There are different categories of crimes based on their level of seriousness.

Take Notes

Create a graph like the one shown and use it to take notes as you read this section. Go to **glencoe.com** to find graphic organizers and tips on how to improve your note-taking skills.

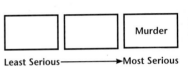

Least Serious ——————→ Most Serious

Classifications of Crimes

Key Terms

You will learn these legal words and expressions in this chapter. You can also find these terms in *Black's Law Dictionary* or in an online legal dictionary.

- crime
- defendant
- plaintiff
- prosecutor

- felony
- misdemeanor
- infraction

Academic Vocabulary

You will find these words in your readings and in your tests. Look them up in a dictionary and familiarize yourself with them.

- intent
- motive
- impulse

glencoe.com

 Reading Strategy

Read for Knowledge

1. **Survey** or preread the chapter.
2. **Question** or formulate questions before you read.
3. **Recite** or read your questions, answers, and notes out loud.
4. **Review** or reread your notes.

Note-Taking Basics

- Listen attentively.
- Have note-taking materials ready.
- Skim through the assignment topic in advance.
- Write down key words and ideas.
- Anticipate what comes next.
- Review notes soon after taking them.

Classifications of Crimes

What types of crimes can you go to jail for?

A crime is an offense committed against the public good, or society. U.S. criminal law is very specific and the penalties for most criminal offenses are very serious. A person who is convicted of a crime can be fined, imprisoned, or sometimes even sentenced to death. The Constitution of the United States limits how the government can deal with people who have been accused of a crime to protect the innocent from unjust accusations or imprisonment.

A defendant is a person who is accused of a crime. The state or the federal government, representing the public, is the plaintiff. **A plaintiff is the party that accuses a person of a crime. The prosecutor is the government official who brings the case against the defendant.** In some states, the prosecutor is called a district attorney. The prosecutor represents the people, or the public, in a criminal case.

Felonies

A felony is a major crime. A person who commits a felony may be punished by a fine, or by imprisonment in a penitentiary, or both. Murder and robbery are examples of felonies. The most serious felony is murder. In some states, murder is punishable by death. Felonies may also be called high misdemeanors. People convicted of a felony may also be liable for a civil penalty awarded to the victim or the victim's family. For example, a rape victim may be able to sue the defendant to recover the costs of medical bills and counseling.

Misdemeanors

A misdemeanor is a less serious crime. A person who commits such a crime can also be punished by a fine, by jail time, or both. However, the maximum amount of time in jail is usually less than a year. Also, if a defendant gets jail time, it is usually served in a smaller, county jail, rather than in a state penitentiary. Driving an automobile without a license is an example of a misdemeanor.

Infractions

Both felonies and misdemeanors are punishable with imprisonment. **An infraction is a minor offense that is usually punishable with a fine and not with jail time.** Some states refer to these as minor misdemeanors, while others call them petty crimes. Minor traffic violations, such as speeding tickets, are considered infractions.

As You Read

Predict What is the difference between a serious crime and a petty crime?

Criminal Cases Serious crimes are prosecuted in courts and rely on physical evidence and testimonies of witnesses and experts. *Is a misdemeanor a crime?*

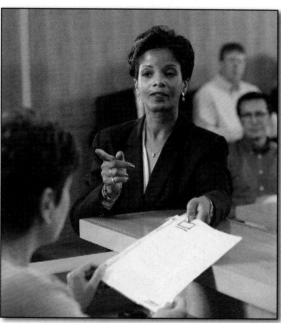

2.1 SECTION

TEACH

Discussion Starter

Class Discussion
Ask students to discuss the types of crimes they consider to be the most severe. Then have them list crimes they believe less serious. Introduce the terms *misdemeanor, felony,* and *infraction.*

As You Read

Predict Help students understand the difference between petty crimes and serious crimes by making sure they understand the meaning of the word *petty.* Tell them that petty means of small importance or secondary in rank. (The goal of predicting content is to encourage students to make guesses and focus their attention on the topic. Tell students that felonies such as murder and robbery are major crimes. Misdemeanors such as driving without a license are less serious, but still can be punished by jail time, a fine, or both.)

D Develop Concepts

Classifications of Crimes
Illustrate the differences between felonies, misdemeanors, and infractions by listing examples of each on the board. (Felony: murder and rape. Misdemeanor: petty theft. Infraction: traffic offenses.)

▲ USING VISUALS

Criminal Cases A misdemeanor is a crime. It is less serious than a felony, but it can still carry a jail sentence.

Activity Ask students to list other offenses that would be considered misdemeanors. (public intoxication, vandalism, disorderly conduct, trespassing) Next, ask students to list crimes that would be classified as felonies. (murder, rape, aggravated battery, arson, drug possession, burglary)

TEACH (cont.)

D Develop Concepts

Criminal Acts Ask students to list some of the rules of their school. (must attend class, must not bring guns to school, must abide by the dress code) Emphasize that criminal law, in the same way, sometimes describes conduct that is forbidden (murder) or indicates conduct that is expected (paying taxes).

C Critical Thinking

Elements of a Crime Ask students whether they think a person who robs a bank does so by accident or intends to do so. Tell them that the act of robbing a bank requires intent on the part of the criminal. Explain that the two elements that make up a crime are the criminal act itself and the required state of mind.

Guided Practice

Federal and State Agencies

Explain that agencies such as the FBI and ATF are federal agencies, but not all federal agencies have police forces. Ask students to name a few state or local agencies that enforce the law. (highway patrol, city police, county sheriff)

Criminal Law in the U.S. Legal System

Are all criminal law courts federal courts?

The American legal system is actually made up of two court systems: federal and state. The federal court system deals with laws on a national level. In addition, each state has its own court system. Both the federal and state courts have the power to make and enforce criminal laws. However, the powers of each are different.

Federal Criminal Law

The Constitution limits the powers of the federal government. For example, the federal government cannot make criminal laws. However, there are exceptions to this rule. For example, the federal government can make laws against counterfeiting money because money is printed by the federal government.

The federal government also has a police force. This police force is called the Federal Bureau of Investigation (FBI). The power to create this police force comes from a special clause in the Constitution known as the Commerce Clause. The Commerce Clause says that the U.S. Congress can regulate interstate commerce, or business that crosses state lines. This includes criminal activities that cross state lines. For this reason, federal criminal law usually involves commerce among the states.

State Criminal Law

Each state government has the built-in power to make criminal laws. That power is called the state's police power. Many states have criminal laws that are just like the criminal laws in other states. Still, the definitions and names of certain crimes are not exactly the same in every state. For example, a crime that is called theft in one state may be called stealing in another.

⬇ **Evidence** During the investigation of a crime, police collect as much evidence as possible. This evidence may be used in court to prove or disprove a defense to a crime. *What type of evidence might help prove self-defense?*

Elements of a Crime

Can you be convicted of a crime if the state cannot prove you had a motive?

A crime is made up of two elements. The first element is the criminal act. The second element is the required state of mind.

Criminal Act

Criminal laws must describe the specific conduct that the law forbids. For example, the definition of theft is stealing another person's property, while the definition of robbery is stealing another person's property through violence or the threat of violence. Some criminal laws make not doing something a crime. For example, not paying taxes that are owed is a crime.

Global Law

The International Criminal Court

The International Criminal Court (ICC) is an independent criminal court located in The Hague, Netherlands. It was created by treaty on July 1, 2002, 60 days after the final ratification of the treaty by 60 countries. The original treaty was signed by 120 countries, although only 60 had to ratify the treaty for it to go into effect. It is the first permanent, treaty-based international criminal court established to promote the international rule of law and ensure that the worst international crimes are prosecuted. It was created to be a complement to national criminal jurisdictions. The jurisdiction of the ICC is defined as follows:

1. The jurisdiction of the Court shall be limited to the most serious crimes of concern to the international community as a whole. The Court has jurisdiction in accordance with this Statute with respect to the following crimes:

   (a) The crime of genocide
   (b) Crimes against humanity
   (c) War crimes
   (d) The crime of aggression

Since its implementation on July 1, 2002, the ICC has taken three cases under consideration. Those three cases come from alleged violations in the Democratic Republic of Congo, the Republic of Uganda, and the Darfur region of Sudan. Five warrants for arrest have been issued in the Republic of Uganda case against commanders of a rebel group alleged to have committed numerous crimes against civilians in Uganda.

> **Across Cultures: Equality on the Court**
>
> The International Criminal Court is trying to be the first court founded on equality. Under the founding documents, the ICC must try to have an equal number of male and female judges and attorneys. Furthermore, there cannot be more than one judge from any country and each geographic region must be equally represented.

Critical Thinking *The United States has decided not to join the International Criminal Court, arguing that by joining the ICC the U.S. would allow its citizens to be prosecuted by an international organization that may not offer the same protections that the U.S. offers. Is this a good reason, or should the U.S. join the ICC?*

A criminal act must be voluntary; it cannot be a person's condition. For example, it is not a crime to be an alcoholic. This is because alcoholism is a condition, not an act. However, the government may create laws that make it a crime to operate a vehicle while under the influence of alcohol.

Required State of Mind

The second element of a crime is the required state of mind. The law defining murder forbids the intentional taking of a person's life. The required mental state is **intent**. The law defining involuntary manslaughter forbids the negligent taking of somebody's life. The required mental state is negligence. In both laws the criminal act is taking a person's life. In the law against murder, the mental state is intent, meaning the defendant must have intended to take another person's life. In the law against involuntary manslaughter, the mental state is negligence, meaning the defendant was negligent or careless, and because of this negligence, another person died.

Vocabulary You can find vocabulary definitions in the **Key Terms** glossary and **Academic Vocabulary** glossary in the back of this book.

Chapter 2   Criminal Law   **37**

Global Law

The International Criminal Court

Answer Answers will vary. The United States is one of the few Western nations that are not a party to the ICC. Most, if not all, of the United States's allies in Europe are signatories to the ICC. By not joining the ICC, the United States is maintaining its autonomy. However, it is also creating divisions among the international powers as to who has the authority to punish individuals who commit heinous acts against others.

TEACH (cont.)

D Develop Concepts

Required State of Mind
Write the following offenses on the board:

- Murder
- Involuntary manslaughter

Ask students what they think the required state of mind is for these acts. (Murder – intent; Involuntary manslaughter – negligence)

Guided Practice

Analyze the News

Bring to class several weeks' worth of local and national newspapers. Organize students into groups and ask them to read and summarize crime stories. Then, ask each group to classify each crime and list actual or possible defenses to each crime.

Extending the Content

Criminal State of Mind

In addition to a criminal act, a required state of mind is the second element that is necessary to establish a crime. An understanding of psychology is required to properly identify and understand the mind-state of an accused criminal. Have students develop lists of psychology-related legal professions by conducting searches on the Internet, interviews with legal workers, or talks with guidance counselors.

38

TEACH *(cont.)*

Writing Support

Persuasive Writing Ask students to imagine that they are defense attorneys for a client accused of murder. Ask them to draft an opening statement to be read in court that uses a defense of insanity. Ask volunteers to read their statements. *(Statements should include an understanding that the defendant should not be held responsible for his or her actions because the person did not know what he or she was doing.)*

✓ Reading Check

Enumerate defendant, attorney, victim, witness, plaintiff, prosecutor, judge, jury

---

ASSESS

Independent Practice

Elements of a Crime
Outline the following scenario to students. The police stopped a car that was weaving in traffic. The driver was intoxicated. It was later determined that she was in a program for alcoholics. Ask students whether the woman can be prosecuted for a crime. *(Yes. It is a crime to operate a car under the influence regardless of whether the defendant was an alcoholic.)*

✓ Reading Check

Enumerate *Name the different people who play a role in a trial.*

Motive

In detective movies and television shows there is often a heavy emphasis on proving a defendant's **motive**. In reality, motive plays no part in proving that a person committed a crime. All that is needed is to prove that a defendant committed an act with the required state of mind. The motive does not matter. Motive only helps to explain why a defendant did what he or she did.

Defenses to Crimes

What are some reasons for pleading not guilty in a criminal case?

In any legal proceeding, civil or criminal, defendants have several possible defenses they may use to try and explain their actions. The main defenses for defendants in criminal cases, as shown in **Figure 2.1,** include insanity, entrapment, self-defense, and defense of family members.

Insanity

U.S. law says that people cannot be held responsible for their actions if they do not know what they are doing. This means that insanity can be a defense to criminal conduct.

The oldest legal test of insanity is called the M'Naghten Rule. This rule goes back to an 1843 English case. A man named Daniel M'Naghten was acquitted of killing the Prime Minister's secretary

---

Figure 2.1 Defenses to Crimes

Entrapment is when a law enforcement official tricks someone into committing a crime he or she would otherwise not have committed.

An **insanity** defense requires that the person did not know the difference between right and wrong when he or she committed the crime.

⬆ In a criminal case, the defense tries to show that the prosecution failed to prove the required elements of the crime. *What element of a crime does the insanity defense seek to eliminate?*

▲ USING VISUALS

➡ **Figure 2.1 Defenses to Crimes Answer** The insanity defense seeks to eliminate the required state of mind.

Activity Ask students to research the psychological aspects of the state-of-mind concept and develop lists of psychology-related legal professions.

because he was insane and did not know what he was doing. Under this rule, a defendant must have a mental disease so serious that he or she does not know the difference between right and wrong when he or she commits the crime.

Another test used by some states is the irresistible **impulse** test. Under this rule, the defendant must have a mental disease that makes telling the difference between right and wrong impossible or makes the defendant unable to stop him- or herself from committing the crime.

The American Law Institute (ALI) has a more modern test for insanity. Under the ALI rule, the defendant must have a mental disease so serious that he or she lacks substantial capacity either to appreciate the criminality of his or her conduct or to conform his conduct to the requirements of law.

People who are found not guilty by reason of insanity do not go free. They must go to a mental institution to receive psychiatric treatment. These people are released only when they are found to be sane.

Entrapment

If a police officer talks a person into committing a crime, the person may have a defense. This defense is called entrapment. Entrapment means that a person was talked into or tricked by a police officer into committing a crime he or she would not otherwise have committed.

WebQuest

Scholarship Scams
Each year the Federal Trade Commission (FTC) lists scams directed toward high school students looking for college scholarships. Log on to **glencoe.com** to begin your WebQuest project and to find links that will help you search for types of scholarship scams.

List three scams you find and how to avoid them in your WebQuest folder to share with your class.

People can claim **self-defense** when they believe they were in imminent danger and had no choice but to use force to protect themselves.

With **defense of family members**, a person can use force to protect family members who are in danger of being hurt or killed.

WebQuest

Research Tips Instruct students to go to the **ftc.gov** site and use the Search box at the top of the page to find resources on scholarship scams. Tell students to use search terms such as *scholarship fraud* or *scholarship scams.*

2.1 SECTION

RETEACH
Guided Practice

Defenses to Crimes
Ask students to think of situations in which entrapment might be used as a defense and explain what would be necessary to prove entrapment in each case.

C Critical Thinking

Impulse and Insanity Ask students to discuss the difference between tests for impulse and those for insanity. (Insanity means having a mental disease so serious that the person does not know the difference between right and wrong when committing the crime. The irresistible impulse test looks to determine whether the defendant has a mental disease that makes telling the difference between right and wrong impossible or makes the defendant unable to stop him- or herself from committing the crime.)

STUDY TO GO Have students go to the *Business and Personal Law* Online Learning Center through **glencoe.com** to download free Study-to-Go content to their cell phones or PDAs.

RETEACH (cont.)

After You Read

Summarize The four main defenses to a crime are insanity, entrapment, self-defense, and defense of family.

ASSESS

Self-Assessment

Have students go to *the Business and Personal Law Online Learning Center* through glencoe.com to take the Section 2.1 Practice Test.

CLOSE

Culminating Activity

Criminal Defense and Crime

Ask students to role-play the defense attorney representing a man who set fire to the storage facility of a competitor. Ask students to think of defense arguments.

Self-Defense

There are situations when people believe they are in danger of being hurt or killed. In such cases, they may use force to protect themselves. This is known as self-defense. In some states, the person using self-defense must try to run away first. Running away is not necessary if the person is in his or her own home. People cannot use self-defense in court if they started the confrontation or if they continued to use force even after the danger was gone.

Defense of Family Members

Sometimes, someone believes a family member is in danger of being hurt or killed. In such cases, the person may use force to protect the family member. This defense is called defense of family members. As in the case of self-defense, the rescuer must have a good reason to believe the victim was in danger of severe bodily injury or death.

People cannot use this defense if the crime occurs after the threat of harm has passed. For example, a parent cannot go after someone who hurt his or her child if that person has left the area and is no longer capable of hurting the child.

After You Read

Summarize Name and define the four main defenses to a crime.

SECTION 2.1 ASSESSMENT

Self Check

1. Where did the federal government get the power to create the Federal Bureau of Investigation (FBI)?

2. What is the oldest insanity test used in the United States and what does that test say?

3. What does the defense of entrapment involve?

Academic Connection

Social Studies The law of the land in the United States is based on the Constitution, which gave the federal government certain powers, and the Bill of Rights (passed in 1791), which amended the Constitution to protect the rights of individuals. How does the federal government keep up with changing values in American society? Give a couple of examples.

English Language Arts Amendments to the Constitution have to be carefully worded to address a specific right and to avoid misinterpretation. Write a 28th Amendment to the Constitution guaranteeing a specific right you think everyone should have.

Critical Thinking

When Does Self-Defense Become a Crime? Sam and Wade are walking home after school when they are attacked by two gang members. Sam and Wade overpower their attackers. Sam knocks his attacker to the ground and sits on him until the police arrive, but Wade keeps hitting his attacker in the head even after he is lying on the ground unconscious. Can Sam claim self-defense? Can Wade? Explain.

 Go to **glencoe.com** to check your answers.

glencoe.com

SECTION 2.1 ASSESSMENT

Self Check
1. Commerce Clause in the Constitution
2. M'Naughten Rule; defendant must have mental illness that removes the knowledge of right and wrong
3. a person was talked or tricked into committing a crime that might not otherwise have been committed

Academic Connection
Social Studies
adding amendments to the Constitution

English Language Arts
Suggest that students use the text of an existing amendment as a guideline.

Critical Thinking
They can claim self-defense because they did not initiate the fight and had the right to protect themselves. Wade cannot claim self-defense for his actions after the attacker was lying unconscious since danger was no longer imminent.

NCLB Activity correlated to the academic standards on page 34

Types of Crimes

Reading Guide

Before You Read

Connect Crimes can affect both people and property. Can you name crimes that directly involve people as victims?

Focus on Ideas

Every criminal law must use specific language to describe the conduct that is forbidden by that law.

Take Notes

Create a graph like the one shown and use it to take notes as you read this section. Go to glencoe.com to find graphic organizers and tips on how to improve your note-taking skills.

Crimes Against Business

Shoplifting

Key Terms

You will learn these legal words and expressions in this chapter. You can also find these terms in *Black's Law Dictionary* or in an online legal dictionary.

- murder
- manslaughter
- battery
- assault
- burglary
- larceny
- robbery
- vandalism

Academic Vocabulary

You will find these words in your readings and in your tests. Look them up in a dictionary and familiarize yourself with them.

- domestic
- malicious
- contempt

What You'll Learn

- ◆ Describe the different categories of crime.
- ◆ Identify several special crimes that involve the use of motor vehicles.
- ◆ Define different types of business crimes, such as arson, forgery, and embezzlement.

Why It's Important

Knowing how to distinguish among various crimes will help you understand criminal liability.

Academic Standards

Reading and completing the activities in this section will help you practice the following academic standards:

Social Studies (NCSS 10) Study the ideals, principles, and practices of citizenship in a democratic republic.

Math (NCTM NOS 2) Understand meanings of operations and how they relate to one another.

R Reading Strategy

Read for Knowledge

1. **Survey** or preread the chapter.
2. **Question** or formulate questions before you read.
3. **Recite** or read your questions, answers, and notes out loud.
4. **Review** or reread your notes.

Note-Taking Basics

- Listen attentively.
- Have note-taking materials ready.
- Skim through the assignment topic in advance.
- Write down key words and ideas.
- Anticipate what comes next.
- Review notes soon after taking them.

FOCUS

Bell Ringer Activity

Tell students that some countries do not allow citizens to own guns in order to prevent an increase in violent crimes. Have students discuss the pros and cons of gun ownership and how they think it relates to crime.

Preteaching

Key Terms

Read the definitions and ask students to create a sentence using each term.

Academic Vocabulary

Explain that developing vocabulary is key to academic success. An efficient method to develop vocabulary is to study how words are formed.

- **domestic** Adjective, from the Latin *domesticus* (belonging to household). Means relating to the home.
- **malicious** Adjective, from the Latin *maliciosus* (full of malice). Means showing ill will.
- **contempt** Noun, from the Latin *contemptus* (scorn). Means disdain for someone or something.

Activity Ask students to give a noun, an adjective, or an adverb form that comes from each word.

NCLB Connects to academic content

TEACH

Discussion Starter

Class Discussion
Write the terms manslaughter, murder, burglary, and embezzlement on the board. Ask students to define these terms in their own words. Have them pair the words in terms of whether the crimes are against people or property. Tell students that this section will cover the major crimes against people and property, as well as crimes related to businesses, the government, and society.

As You Read

Predict Discuss with students the crimes they have read about in the newspaper or seen on television. Ask them who or what was the victim of the crime. (crimes against people, property, business, government, or society)

C Critical Thinking

Murder or Manslaughter?
While driving 85 miles an hour in a 65-mile-per-hour zone, Mitchell Perry accidently struck and killed a child who was crossing the street. Did Mitchell commit second-degree murder? First, ask students for their verdict. Then, ask them to name the legal principle they are applying to reach their verdict. (Mitchell Perry committed involuntary manslaughter because he killed another person during the commission of an unlawful or reckless act.)

42

As You Read

Predict Name one or more categories of crimes.

Crimes against People

What could you be charged with if you killed someone by accident?

Crimes can be categorized into crimes against people, property, business, government, society, and crimes involving motor vehicles. Common crimes against people include murder, manslaughter, assault, battery, kidnapping, and domestic violence.

Murder

Murder is the intentional killing of another person. First-degree murder involves one or more of the following circumstances: killing after making a detailed plan to kill; killing in an especially vicious way, such as by torture; and killing while committing another serious crime. If none of these conditions apply, the crime may be second-degree murder. The distinction between first-degree murder and second-degree murder is important because a person convicted of first-degree murder can receive the death penalty in some states.

Manslaughter

Manslaughter is killing another person without intending to do so. Manslaughter is either voluntary or involuntary. Voluntary manslaughter happens when someone kills a person while in a state of great distress and without a prior plan to kill. Involuntary manslaughter occurs when someone kills another person accidentally while committing an unlawful or reckless act.

Assault and Battery

Battery is the unlawful touching of another person. It involves the forceful use, however slight, of a person's hand, of a weapon, or other instrument against another person.

Case Study – Deck v. Missouri

Critical Thinking *Do you believe the jury was negatively influenced? Why or why not?*

Flex Your Reading Note key facts in the text below and look up words you do not understand. Restate difficult ideas in your own words. Go back and reread the text quickly to make sure you did not miss any important detail. Now, you are ready to formulate an opinion.

A Bad Impression When Carman Deck appeared before the jury to be sentenced after a murder conviction, he was in chains and shackles. The jury sentenced him to death. Deck later appealed his sentenced arguing that the chains and shackles had negatively influenced the jury.

Deck v. Missouri, 544 U.S. 622

 Go to glencoe.com for more case study practice.

42   Unit 1   What Is Law?

glencoe.com

Case Study

Deck v. Missouri

Answer Answers will vary. However, according to the United States Supreme Court, the U.S. Constitution prohibits the use of visible chains and shackles on a defendant during trial except in cases of court security because it prejudices the jury. The judge in this case made no determination that chains and shackles were necessary for security reasons. The jury should not have been placed in a position where it might be prejudiced when deciding on a death sentence.

Battery may be committed by ordering a dog to attack a person or even kissing someone who does not want to be kissed. **An assault is an attempt to commit a battery.** Waving a baseball bat at someone is assault. Hitting the person with the baseball bat is battery. Simple assault and battery are misdemeanors. Aggravated assault and battery are felonies. To be aggravated, the crime must be committed with a deadly weapon, or with the intent to commit murder, rape, or robbery.

Traffic Laws Young drivers do not get any special treatment when they violate traffic laws. *Can you get a ticket if you did not know you were driving past curfew hours?*

Kidnapping

Kidnapping is the unlawful removal or restraint of a person against his or her will. Most state laws distinguish between simple kidnapping and more serious offenses, such as child stealing and kidnapping for ransom.

Sex Offenses

The crime of rape involves one person forcing another to have sexual intercourse. The law applies to both men and women. Statutory rape involves having sexual intercourse with a minor, with or without force. A minor can be prosecuted for having sex with another minor. Sexual assault by a friend or a date is a sexual offense, called date rape or acquaintance rape.

Domestic Violence

Any reckless form of physical or mental harm in a family or household is **domestic** violence. Domestic violence laws protect children, spouses, and other family members from neglect, mental abuse, or physical abuse by another member of the family or household. Children are protected by child endangerment and child abuse laws. Abused spouses may request a court order to stop an abusing spouse from coming near them.

Vocabulary You can find vocabulary definitions in the **Key Terms** glossary and **Academic Vocabulary** glossary in the back of this book.

Crimes against Property

If someone breaks into a house and takes $2,000 worth of computer equipment, which crime was committed?

The most common crimes against property include burglary, robbery, arson, larceny, and vandalism. Crimes against property can be felonies or misdemeanors.

TEACH (cont.)

D Develop Concepts

Crimes against Property
Write the following common crimes on the chalkboard: burglary, robbery, arson, larceny, and vandalism. Ask students if they have or if someone they know has been the target of any of these crimes.

Extending the Content

Crime Prevention

Ask students if they are aware of any organizations that seek to prevent crime. Suggest that they use the Internet to research programs, campaigns, or neighborhood organizations that help keep crime under control. (National Crime Prevention Council, Neighborhood Watch programs, National Night Out)

Extending the Content

Domestic Violence

Emphasize that the courts consider domestic violence a serious crime. Ask a representative from your county's social services department to speak on the topic of your state's statutes governing domestic violence.

▲ USING VISUALS

Traffic Laws Answer Driving a vehicle is a privilege, and drivers are required to know and understand all applicable driving laws. A driver can be given a ticket for violating driving past curfew laws, even though the driver claims not to have known about the curfew.

Activity Ask students if they know what the laws are concerning seat belts in your state. Tell students that only about half of the states have a primary seat-belt enforcement law, which allows law enforcement officers to stop a car for noncompliance with seat-belt laws. Most states have secondary laws that mean that officials can only issue seat-belt violations if they stop motorists for other infractions. Have students research the seat-belt law in your state.

TEACH (cont.)

D Develop Concepts

Larceny Tell students to imagine that Richard asks John if he can borrow a binder for class. John agrees and tells Richard to look in his locker. Richard finds John's iPod and stuffs it in his backpack with the intent of keeping it. Ask students how this crime would be categorized. (larceny or petty theft)

Guided Practice

Burglary and Vandalism

Divide the class into two groups. Have the groups research the punishments for burglary and vandalism in your state and the states surrounding it. In a class discussion, compare the punishments for the two crimes in the different states.

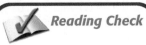

Reading Check

Explain Murder is intentional, while manslaughter is unintentional. Robbery involves the threat or use of violence, while burglary does not.

⬆ **Vandalism** To be guilty of vandalism you do not have to be the person who actually did the damage. *Is graffiti considered a form of vandalism?*

Reading Check

Explain *What is the difference between murder and manslaughter, and what is the difference between robbery and burglary?*

Burglary

Burglary, under common law, is breaking and entering into a house at night to commit a felony. State laws have expanded the definition of burglary to include daytime breaking and entering, breaking and entering places other than homes, and breaking and entering to commit a misdemeanor. If any part of the definition of burglary cannot be proven, the defendant cannot be found guilty.

Larceny

Larceny is the unlawful taking of someone's personal property with the intent to keep the property away from that person. In some states, larceny is called theft. Petty larceny, a misdemeanor, is stealing property of a small monetary value. The individual states usually set that value between $300 and $1,000. Grand larceny, a felony, is stealing property valued at more than a state's limit for petty larceny.

D

Robbery

Robbery is the wrongful taking of someone's property by threatening violence or using violence. The penalty for robbery is greater than the penalty for larceny.

Vandalism

Vandalism is willful or malicious damage to property. It is also called **malicious** mischief or criminal damage. To be guilty of vandalism, a person does not have to be the one who actually does the damage. Anyone who supports vandalism by being a lookout, for example, can also be charged.

Crimes Involving Business

Could you be charged with shoplifting before you actually leave a store with unpaid merchandise?

Crimes involving business are also called white collar crimes. Business crimes include embezzlement, shoplifting, fraud, money laundering, arson, and forgery.

Embezzlement

Embezzlement is the wrongful taking of property by someone lawfully entrusted with possession and control of that property. Embezzlement is often committed by an agent or employee of a business who has the power to write checks and to withdraw funds from the firm's bank accounts.

▲ USING VISUALS

➡ **Vandalism Answer** The act of committing graffiti is considered a form of vandalism. Inform students that someone who acts as a lookout while graffiti is being done can also be charged with the crime.

Activity Ask students to imagine that they have just helped build a new community center for their neighborhood. They helped paint and decorate the exterior of the building for a grand opening celebration. Tell them that the night before the celebration, someone painted the sides of the building with names and symbols. Have students discuss how they would feel about this.

Shoplifting

Shoplifting is stealing goods from a store. Shoplifting costs American consumers billions of dollars each year because prices of goods are raised to make up the loss. In some cases, people may be charged with shoplifting just for hiding merchandise in their pants or stuffing them under a baggy sweatshirt, even before they leave the store.

Fraud

Fraud is when a person or a business engages in some form of deception to obtain money or property. Fraud undermines the very foundation of the business world. Some types of fraud are federal offenses. Using the United States Postal Service to commit fraud is referred to as mail fraud. Using the telephone or other forms of electronic communication, such as the Internet, to commit fraud is called wire fraud.

Money Laundering

When criminals obtain large amounts of money illegally, they need to hide the money. They often do this by putting the money into legal businesses to launder it, as one would clean laundry to remove the dirt. The federal government has passed laws to prosecute anyone involved in money laundering even if they did not steal the money themselves.

Arson

Sometimes, business owners who find themselves on the verge of bankruptcy will destroy their own property to collect the insurance on it. They commit arson. Under common law rules, arson is defined as the willful and malicious burning of someone else's house. Today, most states define arson as the burning of any building.

Forgery

Forgery is placing a false signature on a check or other document with the intent to deceive someone in order to deprive that person of his or her property. It is a felony subject to a fine and imprisonment. Forgery does not require that the property actually change hands. Once the false signature is placed on the check, the signer has committed forgery.

Crimes against the Government

Is it a crime if you ignore an order to appear in court?

Crimes that involve direct offenses against the government itself include treason, perjury, obstruction of justice, contempt of court, and bribery.

Treason

Treason is defined in Article III, Section 3 of the United States Constitution as waging war against the United States, or giving aid and comfort to the enemies of the United States. Treason is the only crime that is mentioned by name in the U.S. Constitution.

Legal Talk

Embezzlement: *n* The crime of fraudulently appropriating money or property for one's own use. From Anglo-French *embesiller* = to make away with.

Allegedly: *adv* From Middle English *allegen* = to submit as justification; to assert without proof.

Vocabulary Builder The suffix *-ment* comes from the Latin root *-mentum*, and means the result of an action. List three words that end with *-ment* and define them.

Look It Up! Check definitions in *Black's Law Dictionary* or an online glossary. For direct links, go to **glencoe.com** to find more vocabulary resources.

 glencoe.com

TEACH (cont.)

Guided Practice

Treason in the Constitution

Ask students to read Article III, section 3, of the U.S. Constitution and answer the following questions:

1. What is required to convict a person of treason? (two eyewitnesses or a confession by the accused) **L1**

2. What does treason against the United States consist of? (levying war against the United States, adhering to the nation's enemies aid and comfort) **L2**

3. What does the word *attainder* mean in the last sentence? (1. extinction of the civil rights and capacities of a person upon sentence of death or outlawry, usually after a convinction of treason; 2. dishonor) **L3**

Legal Talk

(entrapment: being talked or tricked into committing a crime; allotment: a portion that is given; involvement: the state of being involved; entertainment: the product of an entertaining action; contentment: a state of being content)

Ask students to practice their academic and legal vocabulary with the electronic flashcards available at the *Business and Personal Law* Online Learning Center through **glencoe.com**.

ASSESS

Quiz

Ask students the following questions:

1. What is the difference between assault and battery? (Battery is the unlawful touching of another person, including using a weapon or other instrument. Assault is an attempt to commit a battery.)

2. What are examples of crimes against property? (burglary, larceny, robbery, vandalism)

3. What is bribery? (giving money or property to a public official in exchange for a favor from that official)

RETEACH

Independent Practice

Ethics and Social Views

Ask students to select one of the crimes discussed in this section. Then have them write a one- to two-page paper in which they relate ethical and social attitudes to changes in the law. You may suggest that they use the Internet, library, or other resource to trace the development of the law over time.

Guided Practice

Robbery and Larceny

Divide the class into groups. Have the groups research the punishments for robbery and larceny in your state and the states surrounding it. You may also select other crimes of particular interest to your students. In a class discussion, compare the punishments for the two crimes in the different states. Have students discuss why they think the punishments differ (if they do).

Review Key Terms

Encourage students to access the *Business and Personal Law* Online Learning Center through glencoe.com and use the electronic flashcards to review the key terms.

CYBERLAW

Commonwealth v. Jaynes
65 Va. Cir. 355 (2004)

Jeremy Jaynes was charged by the Commonwealth of Virginia with violating a Virginia law governing the transmission of unsolicited bulk e-mail (spam). In a period of three days, Mr. Jaynes allegedly sent millions of spam e-mails to America Online (AOL) addresses using false or forged e-mail transmission or routing information. Mr. Jaynes had used fake e-mail addresses and falsified the transmission information, making it appear that the e-mails had originated in the country of Belize, not the United States.

Ruling and Resolution
Mr. Jaynes argued that the law disallowing him from sending spam e-mail was unconstitutional because it violated his right to free speech under the First Amendment of the U.S. Constitution. The Virginia court held, though, that the law prohibited e-mails using false or forged information, but did not prohibit people from sending bulk e-mails using a valid e-mail address from a valid computer.

Critical Thinking Do you think Mr. Jaynes has a right to send his e-mails to anyone from any e-mail address? If not, what do you think Mr. Jaynes's penalty should be?

Perjury, Obstruction of Justice, and Contempt of Court

Perjury, obstruction of justice, and **contempt** of court all involve offenses that undermine the administration of the courts. Perjury occurs when a person lies under oath during a court process or an administrative procedure. Generally, the lie must involve a fact that is material to the proceeding.

Obstruction of justice occurs when an individual does something that hinders the ability of the court to move forward in a judicial proceeding. It might involve suppressing evidence or shielding someone from arrest. Contempt of court occurs when an individual ignores a court order or shows a lack of proper respect for the integrity of the court.

Bribery

Bribery is giving money or property to a public official in exchange for a favor from that official. Both the person offering the bribe and the public official accepting the bribe are guilty of bribery. For instance, if a company executive offers a bribe to the chairperson of a government planning board in exchange for a vote approving his or her company's bid, that executive is guilty of paying a bribe. If the chairperson actually takes the bribe, he or she is guilty of accepting a bribe.

It is against the law to pay a bribe, to offer a bribe, or to accept a bribe. It is also against the law to ask for a bribe when none has been offered. This crime is called bribery solicitation.

CYBERLAW

Commonwealth v. Jaynes

Answer Answers will vary. No one can argue that legitimate companies should be prohibited from sending bulk e-mails to their customers or potential customers. However, a problem arises when people send unsolicited e-mail from false e-mail addresses that cannot be tracked. Mr. Jaynes was ultimately convicted under the Virginia law and sentenced to nine years in jail for his spamming.

Crimes Against Society

Can you be prosecuted for using racist language?

All criminal law statutes involve offenses against society. Some deserve special attention because they prohibit behavior that endangers the public peace.

Disorderly Conduct and Rioting

Disorderly conduct is an activity that threatens to disrupt the social order, to imperil public safety, or to jeopardize the health of the public at large. Rioting is an activity that generally requires a gathering of at least three individuals who threaten to harm people or to damage property, or who violently commit one or the other of those offenses.

Motor Vehicle Violations

Do you have a right to a driver's license?

A license to drive a motor vehicle is a privilege, not a right. If drivers abuse that privilege, they may lose it. All drivers who ignore traffic laws are treated the same. Young drivers do not get a break when they speed, drive recklessly, or run red lights. They may be tried in traffic court and they can be fined. They can also have their licenses suspended or taken away permanently. Many states outlaw drag racing and joyriding. Drag racing is racing two vehicles side by side or timing vehicles that separately run a prearranged course. Joyriding is taking a vehicle without the owner's permission. In both cases, everybody who joins in is liable.

After You Read

Summarize Give two examples of crimes in each category.

SECTION 2.2 ASSESSMENT

Self Check

1. What is the only crime specifically named in the U.S. Constitution?

2. What are the different ways an anti-bribery statute can be violated?

3. What are white collar crimes?

Academic Connection

Mathematics In the United States, there was an estimated 56,146 felony cases filed in the state courts of the 75 largest counties during May 2002.

About a fourth of these felony defendants were charged with a violent offense, usually assault (12.7%) or robbery (5.4%). Those charged with murder (0.8%) or rape (1.8%) accounted for a small percentage of defendants overall. About three-fourths of defendants were charged with a nonviolent felony. The most frequently charged nonviolent offenses were drug trafficking (17.1%), other drug offenses (18.6%), theft (8.8%), and burglary (8.1%). Create a table showing this information in numerical versus percent form.

 For more math practice, go to the Math Appendix.

THEORY Number and Operations: Using Fractions, Decimals, and Rounding. Figure out the total number for each percent given. For example: 56,146 × .127 (12.7%) = 7,130.5 assaults. Remember to round numbers of 5 or more up and numbers less than 5 down. For example, .542 rounds to .5.

Go to **glencoe.com** to check your answers.

glencoe.com

2.2 SECTION

RETEACH (cont.)

 After You Read

Summarize against people—murder, assault; against property—arson, burglary; against business—fraud, forgery; against government—treason, bribery

ASSESS

Self-Assessment

Have students go to the *Business and Personal Law* Online Learning Center through **glencoe.com** to take the Section 2.2 Practice Test.

CLOSE

Culminating Activity

Classifying a Crime
Tell students that Rachael worked at a local grocery store for three years. During that time, she took a candy bar and a drink for her lunch break every day without paying for them. What crime is she probably guilty of? (embezzlement)

SECTION 2.2 ASSESSMENT

Self Check

1. treason

2. by offering a bribe, by accepting a bribe, or by asking for a bribe

3. crimes committed either against or by a business, including embezzlement, shoplifting, fraud, money laundering, arson, and forgery

Academic Connection

Mathematics

Classification	Percent	Number of Cases
Felony	**25%**	**14,037**
Assault	12.7%	7,131
Robbery	5.4%	3,032
Rape	1.8%	1,011
Murder	0.8%	449
Other	4.3%	2,414

Nonviolent Felony	75%	42,110
Other Drug Offenses	18.6%	10,443
Drug Trafficking	17.1%	9,601
Theft	8.8%	4,941
Burglary	8.1%	4,548
Other	22.4%	12,577

NCLB Activity correlated to the Mathematics standard on page 41

Summary by Sections

Ask students to read the summaries one key point at a time. Then, ask them to work in groups to create two examples to illustrate each key point.

Vocabulary Builder

Cooperative Learning

1. Have students work in groups to prepare their sentences. Ask the groups to exchange their sentences and assess each other's sentences.

Vocabulary Development

- Ask students to use a dictionary or to go online to look up the etymology of each key term listed.

- Then, ask students to list several words derived from the same root or origin. For example, *contract* has the same root as *contractual* or *contractually*.

Chapter 2 Review and Assessment

Summary

Section 2.1 Crimes and Criminal Justice

- A crime is an act against the public good. Crimes are divided into felonies or misdemeanors. A felony is a major crime punishable by imprisonment or death. A less serious crime is called a misdemeanor.

- An infraction is a minor offense punishable by a fine.

- Both federal and state courts can make and enforce criminal laws.

- A crime is defined by two elements: the criminal act and the required state of mind.

- Criminal defendants can use the following defenses: insanity, entrapment, self-defense, and defense of family members.

Section 2.2 Types of Crimes

- Crimes against people include murder, manslaughter, assault, battery, kidnapping, sex offenses, and domestic violence.

- Crimes against property include burglary, larceny, embezzlement, robbery, arson, vandalism, and shoplifting.

- Business crimes include embezzlement, shoplifting, fraud, money laundering, arson, and forgery.

- Crimes against the government include treason, perjury, obstruction of justice, contempt of court, and bribery.

- Crimes against society include statutes that involve disorderly conduct, and statutes that prohibit rioting.

Vocabulary Builder

 On a sheet of paper, use each of these terms in a sentence.

Key Terms

- crime
- defendant
- plaintiff
- prosecutor
- felony
- misdemeanor
- infraction
- murder
- manslaughter
- battery
- assault
- burglary
- larceny
- robbery
- vandalism

Academic Vocabulary

- intent
- motive
- impulse
- domestic
- malicious
- contempt

Go to **glencoe.com** to play a game and improve your legal vocabulary.

Study Skills for Success

Prepare Your Students for Studying

Tell students that they can improve their ability to understand and remember material from their courses by learning and practicing study skills. Remind students to:

- **Get motivated!** Motivation must come from within. To motivate yourself, think of ways in which what you learn now will fit into your long-term personal and professional goals.

- **Get organized!** Make studying part of your daily routine, not something you do at the last minute.

- **Concentrate!** Study in an environment that is as free of distractions as possible.

Key Points Review

Answer the following questions. Refer to the chapter for additional reinforcement.

2 What are the differences between a felony and a misdemeanor?

3 What are the elements of a crime?

4 What are the defenses to a crime?

5 What are the major crimes that can be committed against people?

6 What are the major crimes that can be committed against property?

7 What crimes can be committed directly against the government?

8 What crimes can be committed against society?

9 What are two crimes that involve the use of motor vehicles?

Standardized Test Practice

10 Read the following information provided by the Department of Motor Vehicles (DMV) and complete questions 1 and 2

All states offer courses in defensive driving through the DMV. Passing a defensive driving course can often reduce the cost of your auto insurance. However, the key reason to take defensive driving should be to improve your driving skills. Some basic concepts of defensive driving include the following guidelines. Slow down, especially during inclement weather conditions or at night. Do not follow too closely. Concentrate on your driving at all times. Never drive if you are impaired by lack of sleep or are under the influence. Check your mirrors frequently. Assume that drivers will run through stop signs or red lights at intersections and be prepared to react. Keep a watchful eye on pedestrians and pets along the roadside. Incorporating these defensive driving tips into your everyday driving technique will help you become a better driver.

1. Defensive driving teaches drivers that

Ⓐ pedestrians do not walk on the sidewalk

Ⓑ they should assume some drivers may run a stop sign

Ⓒ accidents are caused by following too closely

Ⓓ there are more accidents when it rains

2. What are three of the recommendations given for defensive driving?

Ⓐ Do not follow closely, keep pets in a carrier, and be prepared to react.

Ⓑ Slow down, watch for pedestrians, and watch for intersections.

Ⓒ Concentrate, check mirrors frequently, and watch for pedestrians.

Ⓓ Slow down, keep radio volume low, and watch for pets.

Test-Taking Strategies If you are preparing for a multiple-choice test, find out whether points are deducted for each wrong answer.

Chapter 2

Review and Assessment

Key Points Review

2. Serious crimes are called felonies. They can lead to imprisonment for more than a year and very high fines. Less serious crimes are called misdemeanors. Fines are much lower than for felonies, and sentences are usually less than a year.

3. the criminal act and the required mental state

4. insanity, entrapment, self-defense, and defense of others

5. murder, manslaughter, assault, battery, kidnapping, sex offenses, and domestic violence

6. burglary, robbery, arson, larceny, and embezzlement

7. treason, perjury, obstruction of justice, contempt of court, and bribery

8. disorderly conduct and rioting

9. drag racing and joyriding

Standardized Test Practice

10. B and B

Strategies for Standardized Test Prep Success

Whether your students have a standardized test coming up in a few days or a few weeks, these last-minute test-prep tips and strategies will help them relax and do their best.

- **Test Format** Help students become familiar with the format of the test by practicing with test items that imitate the actual test items as closely as possible.

- **Test Timing** Have students take timed practice tests so that they become comfortable with the length, design, and timing of the actual test.

Apply and Debate

Students should use chapter content to arrive at conclusions. The legal resolutions are listed below.

11. Yes. Self-defense can be used if an imminent life-and-death danger exists.

12. Felony. Isabel could have endangered the lives of others by burning a dwelling, even though she quickly changed her mind.

13. Yes. Unauthorized access to a home and taking personal items would probably be considered burglary.

14. Probably. Double jeopardy attaches when a person is found not guilty of a crime, but only attaches to that specific charge. Given the additional evidence and the fact that Lois was not tried for the crime of stealing, it is probable that a judge would allow her to be tried for stealing, as long as the statute of limitations has not run out.

15. Maybe. The actions by John and his friends constituted felony vandalism, and, if old enough, such as if they are in high school, they could be tried as adults for such actions. However, if John and his friends are young enough and/or if the school district agrees, then they could probably be tried in juvenile court on a charge of mischief.

50

C Apply and Debate

11. Self-Defense

While cooking dinner, Jack and Rick got into a fight over Jack's girlfriend. Rick picked up a vase to hit Jack, so Jack grabbed a knife from the counter and stabbed Rick.

You Debate *Can Jack's actions be considered self-defense?*

12. Felony or Misdemeanor

Isabel intended to burn her house down when she set fire to it. As the house started to burn, however, she changed her mind and used a hose to put it out. Isabel is arrested and charged with arson.

You Debate *Should Isabel's crime be classified as a felony or a misdemeanor since she changed her mind and did less than $500 damage to her property?*

13. Burglary

Yolanda went over to a friend's house to visit. When she arrived, her friend was not home, but had left the door unlocked. Yolanda went inside the house and took a laptop before returning home.

You Debate *Should this be considered burglary since the house was left unlocked?*

14. Double Jeopardy

Lois was charged with embezzling money from her employer. She was tried in court before a jury who found her innocent of the crime. After the trial, the police found additional evidence clearly showing Lois was guilty of the crime.

You Debate *Since Lois cannot be charged with embezzlement again, can she be charged with stealing?*

15. Mischief or Vandalism

On Halloween night, John and several friends decided to pull some pranks at their school and damaged some of the classrooms. The next morning, school security officers reviewed the security videotapes to see who had done the damage. They arrested the students for vandalism.

You Debate *Since John and his friends are under the age of 18, was their Halloween behavior mischief?*

C Critical Thinking

Vandals or Not? Before a championship basketball game at Fairview High School, several students from a visiting team's school decided to break into Fairview's gymnasium to damage the equipment and spray-paint the walls. Sara and Jamal only agreed to be lookouts, because they thought they would not be held responsible if their friends got caught.

Debate Practice

- Are Sara and Jamal correct? (No. All those who participate in vandalism, including lookouts, are responsible.)

- What is the legal principle that would be used in their case? (criminal liability)

- Why do people commit acts of vandalism? (Students' opinions may differ; vandalism can be the result of substance abuse, anger, peer pressure, or thrill seeking.)

Case Study Practice– State v. Ham
⎕ 🗗 ✖

16 Who Has Valid Consent? Andrew Ham was 19 and lived with his mother in a two-bedroom apartment. In February, Andrew entered into an informal agreement with his mother to pay rent for his bedroom, which he shared with a younger brother. He paid the rent for February and March, but failed to pay rent in April. Since he did not pay the rent, Mrs. Ham told Andrew that he would have to move out. Prior to moving out, the police began to investigate Andrew in connection with a burglary. The police went to the Hams' apartment and asked Mrs. Ham whether they could search Andrew's bedroom, even though the police did not have a warrant to perform the search. Mrs. Ham consented. While searching the bedroom, the police found the stolen property in Andrew's closet.

Source: State v. Ham, 744 P.2d 133 (Id. Ct. App. 1987)

Practice Can Andrew's mother provide consent to the police to search Andrew's room? Does it make a difference whether Andrew paid rent to his mother?

⑰ Ethics ←?→ Application

Responsible Party You have been invited to a Friday night party with a group of your friends. Your family says it is okay for you to go as long as there is adult supervision and no underage drinking. When you arrive, you see that there are no adults present and a lot of the partygoers are drinking alcohol.

◆ Do you call your family to let them know what is happening at the party?

⑱ Internet Application

Identity Theft Susan finds out that she is the victim of identity theft. Several charge cards have been opened and used in her name without her knowledge. These financial companies are now demanding payment from Susan.

 Go to **glencoe.com** to access the Federal Trade Commission's Web site on identity theft. Then list the steps to take when you are a victim of identity theft.

> **R** 📖 **Reading Connection**
> **Outside Reading** Go to **glencoe.com** for a list of reading suggestions about criminal offenses.

Review and Assessment

←?→ Ethics Application

17. Lead a class discussion about who is responsible when a minor buys and drinks alcohol: the minor, the family, or both? Explain to students what the responsibilities of a minor are in the eyes of the law.

💻 Internet Application

18. FTC recommends: 1) placing a "Fraud Alert" on your credit reports by notifying one or all of the three credit reporting companies to prevent additional accounts from being opened without your knowledge; 2) closing any accounts that have been fraudulently opened or tampered with. Start by calling the credit companies, and following up in writing; 3) filing a police report with your local law enforcement; and 4) reporting the theft to the FTC.

R Reading Strategy

Reading Connection

American Bar Association Resources

Go to the *Business and Personal Law* Online Learning Center through glencoe.com to find links for further readings that relate to this chapter. Ask students to read, review, and summarize the documents. Advise students to keep their reviews and summaries to use as reference material for their Unit Thematic Project on pages 72–73.

📄 Case Study Practice

16. The Idaho Court of Appeals held that Andrew's mother could give valid consent. The test to apply is whether Andrew had exclusive right to the room and had a reasonable expectation of privacy within the room. In this case, Andrew shared the room with a younger brother, and his mother could enter the room at any time. It is not relevant whether or not Andrew paid rent to his mother for the room. For the argument to be successful, Andrew's mother would not have been able to enter the room at any time, and Andrew would have had to believe only he was entitled to be in the room.

Plan Your Lesson Section by Section

NBEA	NATIONAL BUSINESS LAW STANDARDS
Section 3.1	• **Distinguish** between a tort and a crime. • **Differentiate** between and give examples of negligence and intentional torts. • **Describe** the penalties available in criminal law and the remedies available in tort law.
Section 3.2	• **Explain** the concepts of the reasonable person test and proximate cause. • **Explain** the concept of strict liability and describe circumstances under which it is imposed.

NCLB	ACADEMIC STANDARDS	Activity/Feature
English Language Arts: NCTE 3 Apply a wide range of strategies to comprehend, interpret, evaluate, and appreciate texts.		*BusinessWeek* News, Case Study, Case Study Practice
English Language Arts: NCTE 9 Develop an understanding of and respect for diversity in language use, patterns, and dialects across cultures, ethnic groups, geographic regions, and social roles.		Global Law
English Language Arts: NCTE 6 Apply knowledge of language structure, language conventions, media techniques, figurative language, and genre to create, critique, and discuss print and non-print texts.		Legal Talk, ad copy, Key Terms, and Academic Vocabulary
Social Studies: NCSS 5 Study the interaction among individuals, groups, and institutions.		Section 3.1 Assessment
English Language Arts: NCTE 8 Use a variety of technological and information resources to gather and synthesize information and to create and communicate knowledge.		Section 3.1 Assessment
Mathematics: NCTM AS4 Analyze changes in various contexts.		Section 3.2 Assessment
English Language Arts: NCTE 10 Students whose first language is not English make use of their first language to develop competency in the English language arts and to develop understanding of content across the curriculum.		Key Terms, Academic Vocabulary, Legal Talk, Vocabulary Builder
English Language Arts: NCTE 1 Read a wide range of print and non-print texts to build an understanding of texts; to acquire new information; to respond to the needs and demands of society and the workplace; and for personal fulfillment.		Global Law, Cyberlaw
Social Studies: NCSS 10 Study the ideals, principles, and practices of citizenship in a democratic republic.		Business Ethics

Connect Your Business Law Classroom to the World of Work

This chart shows the 21st Century Skills, foundation skills, and workplace competencies that students develop as they work in this chapter.

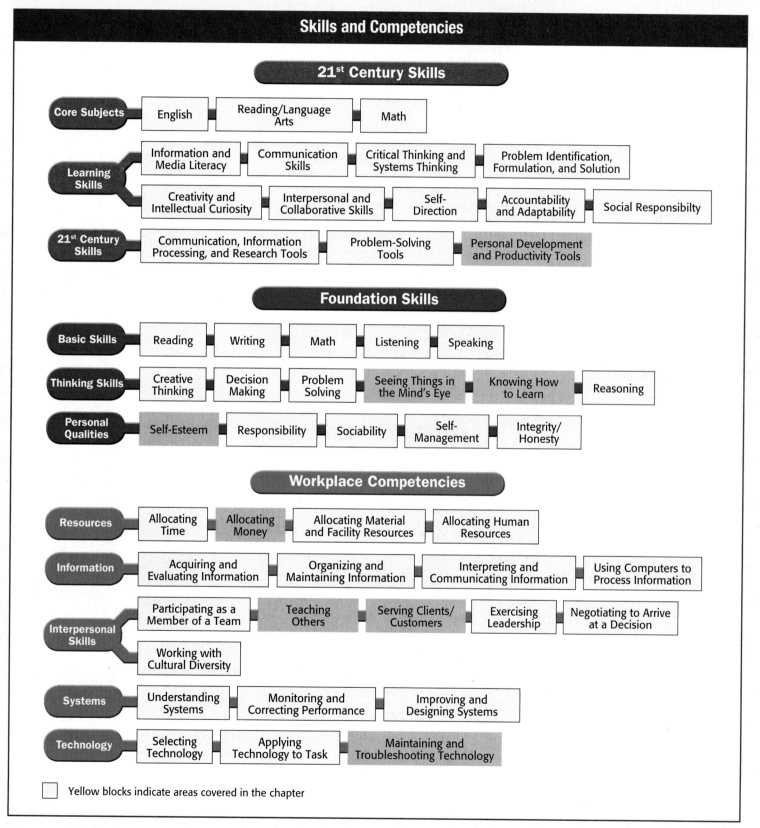

Skills and Competencies

21st Century Skills

Core Subjects: English | Reading/Language Arts | Math

Learning Skills: Information and Media Literacy | Communication Skills | Critical Thinking and Systems Thinking | Problem Identification, Formulation, and Solution | Creativity and Intellectual Curiosity | Interpersonal and Collaborative Skills | Self-Direction | Accountability and Adaptability | Social Responsibilty

21st Century Skills: Communication, Information Processing, and Research Tools | Problem-Solving Tools | Personal Development and Productivity Tools

Foundation Skills

Basic Skills: Reading | Writing | Math | Listening | Speaking

Thinking Skills: Creative Thinking | Decision Making | Problem Solving | Seeing Things in the Mind's Eye | Knowing How to Learn | Reasoning

Personal Qualities: Self-Esteem | Responsibility | Sociability | Self-Management | Integrity/Honesty

Workplace Competencies

Resources: Allocating Time | Allocating Money | Allocating Material and Facility Resources | Allocating Human Resources

Information: Acquiring and Evaluating Information | Organizing and Maintaining Information | Interpreting and Communicating Information | Using Computers to Process Information

Interpersonal Skills: Participating as a Member of a Team | Teaching Others | Serving Clients/Customers | Exercising Leadership | Negotiating to Arrive at a Decision | Working with Cultural Diversity

Systems: Understanding Systems | Monitoring and Correcting Performance | Improving and Designing Systems

Technology: Selecting Technology | Applying Technology to Task | Maintaining and Troubleshooting Technology

☐ Yellow blocks indicate areas covered in the chapter

CHAPTER
3 Tort Law

Introduce the Chapter

Tort Law
Tort law is based on the rights of the individual. Chapter 3 introduces intentional and unintentional torts against persons and property, along with the concepts of liability, negligence, and risk.

Building Background
Explain to students that if one person interferes with the rights of another person, a tort is involved. Ask students to consider rights of theirs that they would not want another person to interfere with.

BusinessWeek News

Explain to students that companies such as N&M Inc. have been blamed for "stacking the deck" on one side of health-based lawsuits. Pulmonary Testing Services ceased doing business in the mid-1990s after asbestos manufacturer Owens Corning accused the company of rigging testing procedures to ensure positive findings.

R Reading Strategy

Flex Your Reading

Tell students to first take stock of the overall chapter length and the time they have to read the material. Often, this practice will give the reader an idea of how quickly the material needs to be covered, balancing reading speed with comprehension.

CHAPTER 3 Tort Law

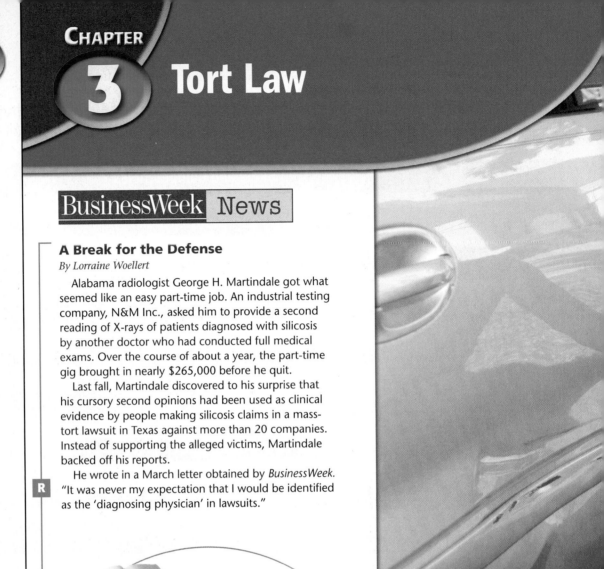

BusinessWeek News

A Break for the Defense
By Lorraine Woellert

Alabama radiologist George H. Martindale got what seemed like an easy part-time job. An industrial testing company, N&M Inc., asked him to provide a second reading of X-rays of patients diagnosed with silicosis by another doctor who had conducted full medical exams. Over the course of about a year, the part-time gig brought in nearly $265,000 before he quit.

Last fall, Martindale discovered to his surprise that his cursory second opinions had been used as clinical evidence by people making silicosis claims in a mass-tort lawsuit in Texas against more than 20 companies. Instead of supporting the alleged victims, Martindale backed off his reports.

R He wrote in a March letter obtained by *BusinessWeek.* "It was never my expectation that I would be identified as the 'diagnosing physician' in lawsuits."

Flex Your Reading

Efficient critical reading involves being flexible with speed and comprehension. There are several ways of reading critically, and you need to fit a reading style to your needs and to the material.

Go to **glencoe.com** for Flex Your Reading activities, more information on reading strategies for this chapter, and guided practice in reading about civil law cases.

Classroom Resources

- Student Edition
- Teacher Wraparound Edition
- Student Activity Workbook with Academic Integration (SE/TAE)
- TeacherWorks™ Plus! CD
- *ExamView® Assessment Suite* CD
- *Presentation Plus!* CD

- National Mock Trial Championship DVD
- Online Learning Center with Podcasts at glencoe.com
- Study-to-Go™ at glencoe.com
- Online Student Edition
- Interactive Student Edition

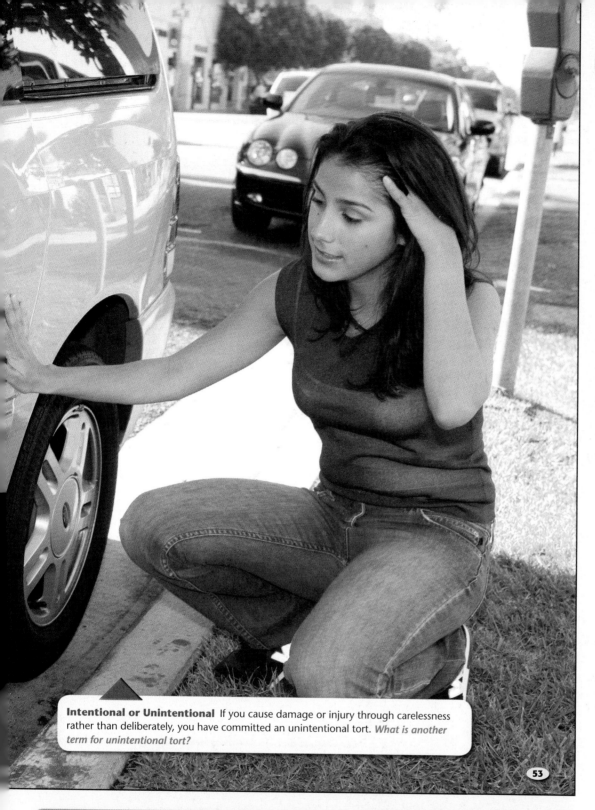

Intentional or Unintentional If you cause damage or injury through carelessness rather than deliberately, you have committed an unintentional tort. *What is another term for unintentional tort?*

53

3 CHAPTER

Practice the Concept

Torts
Ask students to consider why a simple act of carelessness might result in a legal action. Have them discuss the types of carelessness they have witnessed that could cause harm to a person or property.

Key Terms Tell students that the word *tort* comes from the Latin term *torquere*, which means "twisted" or "wrong." Explain that a "wrong" might be committed intentionally or unintentionally by a person. The person who has been wronged has the right to seek compensation for injuries or damage. The law of torts seeks to restore the injured person to the position he or she was in before the tort was committed, commonly called being "made whole."

Legal Basics Tort law cases are common in our society and are often highly publicized by the media. Tort lawsuits are often controversial because they deal with intangible harms such as pain and suffering, and attempt to allocate responsibility between consumers and manufacturers for product-related problems.

▲ USING VISUALS

Intentional or Unintentional Answer Another term for an unintentional tort is *negligence*. Tell students that negligence is the failure to exercise the degree of care that a reasonable person would have exercised. Inform students that unintentional torts are the most common type of tort. Have students suggest reasons why unintentional torts are more common than intentional torts. (Carelessness or negligence might increase in a stressed or busy society.) Tell students they will learn about negligence in Section 2 of this chapter.

Definition of a Tort

FOCUS

Bell Ringer Activity

Ask students whether they have ever been wrongly accused of behaving with prejudice, cheating, or lying. Have them discuss whether the accusation harmed their reputations. Indicate that this type of tort will be covered in this section.

Preteaching

Key Terms

Read the definitions and ask students to create a sentence using each term.

Academic Vocabulary

Explain that developing vocabulary is key to academic success. An efficient method to develop vocabulary is to study how words are formed.

- **compensate** Verb, from the Latin *compensare*, *com* + *pensare* (to weigh). Means to counterbalance.

- **confidential** Adjective, from the Latin *confidere*, *com* + *fidere* (to trust). Means private, secret.

- **distress** Noun, from the Latin *distringere* (to hinder). Means seizure and detention.

Activity Ask students to give a noun, an adjective, or an adverb form that comes from each word.

 Connects to academic content

What You'll Learn

- ◆ Distinguish between a tort and a crime.
- ◆ Differentiate between and give examples of negligence and intentional torts.
- ◆ Explain a person's rights and duties in relation to tort law.
- ◆ Describe remedies available in tort law.
- ◆ List the main intentional torts against people and property.

Why It's Important

Knowing the difference between a tort and a crime will help you understand what your legal options are if you ever feel you have been victimized.

Academic Standards

Reading and completing the activities in this section will help you practice the following academic standards:

Social Studies (NCSS 5) Study interactions among individuals, groups, and institutions.

English Language Arts (NCTE 8) Use a variety of technological and information resources to gather and synthesize information and to create and communicate knowledge.

Reading Guide

Before You Read

Connect Has anyone ever intentionally embarrassed you, scared you, or victimized you? Did you think that there was any legal action you could take?

Focus on Ideas

A tort is not a crime against society. A tort is a wrong one person commits against another person.

Take Notes

Create a graph like the one shown and use it to take notes as you read this section. Go to glencoe.com to find graphic organizers and tips on how to improve your note-taking skills.

```
                    Intentional Torts

   Against Persons                  Against Property

       Assault
```

 ### Key Terms

You will learn these legal words and expressions in this chapter. You can also find these terms in *Black's Law Dictionary* or in an online legal dictionary.

- tort
- tortfeasor
- intentional tort

 ### Academic Vocabulary

You will find these words in your readings and in your tests. Look them up in a dictionary and familiarize yourself with them.

- compensate
- confidential
- distress

glencoe.com

R Reading Strategy

Read for Knowledge

1. **Survey** or preread the chapter.
2. **Question** or formulate questions before you read.
3. **Recite** or read your questions, answers, and notes out loud.
4. **Review** or reread your notes.

Note-Taking Basics
- Listen attentively
- Have note-taking materials ready
- Skim through the lesson material
- Write down key words and ideas
- Anticipate what comes next
- Review notes soon after taking them

The Nature of Tort Law

If someone assaults you, is it a crime against you or against society?

D

Tort law is based on the idea that everyone in our society has certain rights. For example, the right to walk around freely without being falsely arrested, the right to privacy, or the right to one's good name and reputation. Along with having certain rights, everyone has the duty to respect the rights of others. The purpose of tort law is to enforce those rights and duties.

What Is a Tort?

In law, **a tort is a private wrong committed by one person against another. A tortfeasor is a person who commits a tort.** A person who commits a tort interferes with another person's rights. There are three elements to any tort: (1) the possession of certain rights by an innocent party; (2) a violation of those rights by the tortfeasor; and (3) a resulting injury that somehow hurts the person whose rights were violated. The person injured is usually called the victim, the innocent party, or the plaintiff in a lawsuit. The tortfeasor is the defendant in a lawsuit.

As You Read

Predict Name actions that can violate someone's rights.

Global Law

Tort Law in Mexico

Tort law in Mexico differs quite a bit from U.S. tort law. In the United States, if someone is injured in an accident, it is not uncommon for the victim to sue the person who caused the accident. In Mexico, however, such a procedure is less likely to occur.

Mexican culture, not the law, holds that a person who causes an accident should help pay for any costs incurred by the victim, including medical expenses and expenses to replace damaged property. The Mexican Federal Labor Act provides the calculation of lost wages so that the victim can be compensated for those as well. Mexican law does not provide for the recovery of punitive damages or compensation for pain and suffering. Although Mexican culture provides for the non-litigious resolution of most tort claims, there are two pieces of legislation that provide for tort claims in court.

Mexican Tort Legislation

1 The Mexican Civil Code

The Civil Code provides for tort claims arising out of contractual liability between two parties. It further has a section that covers objective liability, which is similar to strict liability in the United States.

2 The Mexican Federal Labor Act

The Federal Labor Act was passed by the Mexican Legislature in part to cover personal injury cases arising from accidents that occur while on the job.

Across Cultures: Historic Legal System

When Spain conquered Mexico in the 1500s, the Spanish found that the indigenous peoples had created a legal system that was so effective the Spanish maintained it for more than 300 years. When Mexico gained its independence, it created a new system.

Critical Thinking: *Should the Mexican Legislature change its laws to allow punitive damages or compensation for pain and suffering?*

Global Law

Tort Law in Mexico

Answer Answers will vary based on students' views. Provide students the following information on the United States' laws to help students decide whether the Mexican system should change. Punitive damages awards in the United States have become very large in the last few years, and there is now an effort to limit those awards. Many states have already limited the amount a plaintiff can recover, and it is a constant topic of review before Congress. In the United States, punitive damages awards are subject to the limitations imposed by the due process of law clauses of the Fifth and Fourteenth Amendments to the United States Constitution.

TEACH

Discussion Starter

Class Discussion
Ask students to list the personal rights that we all possess as citizens of the United States. Explain that a basic understanding of these rights will help in the study of tort law. (Students may mention personal and property security, religious freedom, reasonable working conditions, and personal privacy.)

D Develop Concepts

The Nature of Tort Law
Have students describe the rights they possess when they go about their daily activities in their communities. Explain that the purpose of tort law is to ensure that these rights are respected. (right to exist without being harassed or harmed, right to privacy, right to one's good reputation)

As You Read

Predict Have students list the kinds of intentional harm that one person might inflict on another. Then ask students to describe situations in which someone interferes with or damages property. (The goal of predicting content is to encourage students to make guesses and focus their attention on the topic. Assault and battery, deceit, defamation, trespassing, invasion of privacy, and emotional distress are actions that violate someone's rights.)

TEACH (cont.)

S Skills Practice

Define Ask students to describe the defining difference between a crime and a tort. (A tort is a private wrong; a crime is a public wrong.) **L1**

Explain Have students think of a tort that might also be a crime. Ask them to describe why that particular tort is a threat to society also. (A person uses a gun to rob a home. Crime—robbery; Tort—tresspassing and conversion. The gun and breaking and entering pose a threat to society.) **L2**

Conclude Ask students to write a paragraph describing why a victim is entitled to damages. (compensates the innocent for lost property, pain and suffering, or lost wages, depending on the circumstances) **L3**

Reading Check

Connect Intentional torts include assault and battery, false imprisonment, defamation, and invasion of privacy.

Vocabulary You can find vocabulary definitions in the **Key Terms** glossary and **Academic Vocabulary** glossary in the back of this book.

The Difference between Criminal Law and Tort Law

Torts are different from crimes. A crime is a wrong committed against the public good. A tort is a wrong committed against a particular person or property. A tort is considered a civil or private wrong rather than a criminal wrong. However, sometimes a tort is also a crime. For example, an assault is both a tort and a crime because it not only hurts an individual, but poses a threat to all members of society. Slander is a tort but not a crime because it hurts only an individual and does not threaten society in general.

S **Penalties in Criminal Law** The purpose of criminal law is to protect society from criminal offenders by punishing them. The penalties for most criminal offenses are very serious.

Remedies in Tort Law The purpose of tort law is to **compensate** the victim for injuries caused by the tortfeasor. Remedies in tort law usually consist of the court making the tortfeasor pay a fair amount of money—called damages—to the injured party. Damages can be awarded for pain and suffering, to pay medical expenses, to replace (or repair) damaged property, or to pay for lost wages. The court might also award punitive damages to punish a tortfeasor for especially serious acts.

Intentional Torts against Persons

Can you sue someone for telling lies about you?

Intentional torts are, most of the time, actions that deliberately hurt, embarrass, or scare people. Some intentional torts are much more serious than others. The most common intentional torts against people are assault, battery, false imprisonment, defamation, invasion of privacy, and the intentional infliction of emotional distress (see **Figure 3.1**).

Assault and Battery

Assault and battery are two separate torts. They can be committed together or by themselves. A person commits an assault by threatening to harm an innocent person. For example, if someone pulls a knife on you, you have been assaulted even if you manage to escape. The assault occurs as soon as you are afraid of immediate harm to your body.

Battery involves the unlawful, unwanted touching of another person. A battery is committed even if the physical contact is not harmful. Battery can also be touching something closely associated with a person's body, such as a backpack or cap, that causes them harm. For example, if you pull the chair out from under someone before the person sits down, you have committed a battery.

False Imprisonment

People have a right to move around freely. If somebody interferes with this right, then that person has committed false imprisonment. For example, security guards in a store must have

Reading Check

Connect *What are two examples of intentional torts?*

ASSESS

Quiz

Ask students to answer the following questions:

1. What is the difference between a crime and a tort? (A crime is a public offense. A tort is a private offense against an individual or that person's property.)

2. Name two intentional torts against a person. (assault and battery, false imprisonment, defamation, invasion of privacy)

3. Name the three elements to a tort. (possession of certain rights by innocent party; violation of rights by tortfeasor; resulting injury)

Figure 3.1 Intentional Torts against Persons

Assault and Battery An assault occurs as soon as a person is afraid of immediate harm, even if the person is not physically touched. Battery is the unlawful touching of another person, even if the physical contact does not cause injury.

Prying into Other People's Lives Invasion of privacy is interfering with a person's right to be left alone and to be free from unwanted publicity. This includes using a person's name or likeness without the person's permission.

The Right to Move about Freely To detain someone without reasonable cause is called false imprisonment.

Defamation Telling lies about someone damages that person's reputation. Libel includes lies that are printed or broadcast.

A person who commits a tort interferes with another person's rights and can be sued for damages by that person. This figure shows four main types of torts. *What is a fifth main tort and what does it require?*

TEACH *(cont.)*

C Critical Thinking

Tort or Crime? Emphasize that a wrongful act may be both a tort and a crime. An act of this sort is subject to two separate legal actions: criminal prosecution by the state and a civil suit by the injured individual. Ask students to suggest why they think two forms of legal actions are appropriate. (Government protects society under criminal law and assigns punishment. Individuals are awarded compensation for their losses or injuries.)

W Writing Support

Intentional Torts Ask students to select one intentional tort shown in Figure 3.1 and write a fictional account of the wrongdoing. Students may shape their accounts in the form of a news article. Ask volunteers to share their accounts with the class.

▲ USING VISUALS

➡ **Figure 3.1 Intentional Torts Against Persons** The fifth tort is intentional infliction of emotional distress. It is caused by extreme and outrageous conduct meant to cause distress in the victim.

Activity Have students share any personal experiences they have had with any of the five torts.

TEACH (cont.)

Independent Practice

Intentional Torts Against Persons

Ask students to create a crossword puzzle using the names of the intentional torts against persons. Remind them to prepare three elements for the puzzle: the blank crossword puzzle grid, the "Down" and "Across" clues, and the solution puzzle grid.

 Legal Talk

(malpractice: improper practice; malfeasance: misconduct; malformation: deformity)

Ask students to practice their academic and legal vocabulary with the electronic flashcards available at the *Business and Personal Law* Online Learning Center through glencoe.com.

RETEACH

 STUDY TO GO Have students go to the *Business and Personal Law* Online Learning Center through glencoe.com to download free Study-to-Go content to their cell phones or PDAs.

Legal Talk

Actual malice: *nominal phrase* Libel made with reckless disregard for the truth. From Latin *actus* = act + *malitia* = ill will, spite: action made with the desire to harm.

Remedy: *n* From Latin *re* + *mederi* = to heal. A medicine that cures a disease. Also, the legal means to recover a right or redress a wrong.

Vocabulary Builder In Latin, *malus* or *mal* means bad. Look up three words in the dictionary that begin with the prefix *mal* and define them.

Look It Up! Check definitions in *Black's Law Dictionary* or an online glossary. For direct links, go to glencoe.com to find more vocabulary resources.

---

reasonable grounds to suspect shoplifting before they stop a customer. They must also hold the person in a reasonable way and only for a reasonable time.

Defamation

Defamation occurs when somebody lies about another person in a way that hurts the innocent person's reputation. There are two types of defamation: libel and slander.

Libel consists of lies about a person in written, printed, or recorded form, including television shows, magazine stories, Web sites, and e-mails. Slander consists of verbal or spoken lies that damage a person's reputation.

Movie stars, famous athletes, and politicians have a hard time winning libel suits because the Supreme Court ruled that public figures must prove that lies about them are told with actual malice. Actual malice means that the person who published the lie knew it was a lie and published it anyway. Actual malice could also mean that the person who published the lie thought it was true but did a poor job checking out the facts.

Invasion of Privacy

Invasion of privacy is interfering with a person's right to be left alone. This includes the right to be free from unwanted publicity. It also means that people must stay out of your private matters.

People who use **confidential** records in their jobs, such as doctors, nurses, lawyers, teachers, and counselors, have to be extremely careful with those records. A nurse may talk to another nurse about a patient if both nurses are taking care of that patient. The same nurse, however, cannot let outsiders see the patient's records or talk about them to outside people. It is also an invasion of privacy for somebody to use your photograph, likeness, or name without your permission for advertising, publicity, or marketing purposes.

Intentional Infliction of Emotional Distress

Someone can cause great emotional or mental **distress** to another person, even if there is no intent to cause physical harm. For example, one person might falsely convince another person that a close family member has died. In the past, the victim had no recourse to remedy. Today, you can sue for intentional infliction of emotional distress. The distress, however, must be caused by extreme and outrageous conduct.

Intentional Torts Against Property

Can you sue someone for borrowing something and not returning it?

Some intentional torts are actions that affect property. The most common intentional torts against property are trespass, conversion, nuisance, and disparagement.

glencoe.com

Review Key Terms

Encourage students to access the *Business and Personal Law* Online Learning Center through glencoe.com and use the electronic flashcards to review the key terms.

Trespass

A trespass is interfering with somebody's real property. Real property is land. It also includes things built on the land, such as a storage shed, and things that are attached to the land permanently, such as a house or a tree. It can even include whatever might be under the property, such as minerals and oil.

Conversion

Conversion is interfering with a person's right to personal property. Suppose you lend a friend your cell phone. If your friend never returns it, your friend has converted your property to his or her own and interfered with your right of ownership.

Nuisance

Nuisance is anything that interferes with the enjoyment of property. Loud music at night, foul odors, or fumes coming from a nearby house are nuisances. If a nuisance affects only one person or household, it is a private nuisance. If it affects a lot of people, such as an entire neighborhood, it is a public nuisance.

Disparagement

Disparagement consists of lies about objects. The lies can be about quality or ownership. For example, if you try to sell your used car, which is in excellent condition, to a friend and someone claims your car is defective, that person has committed disparagement. In court, you must prove that you actually lost money as a result of the lie.

After You Read

Summarize List the main differences between crimes and torts.

SECTION **3.1** ASSESSMENT

Self Check

1. Is it possible for a wrongful act to be both a crime and a tort? Explain.

2. What is the definition of an intentional tort? Give an example.

3. What are the three elements of any tort?

Academic Connection

Social Studies The National Highway Traffic Safety Administration (NHTSA), under the U.S. Department of Transportation, was established by the Highway Safety Act of 1970 to carry out safety programs under the National Traffic and Motor Vehicle Safety Act of 1966 and the Highway Safety Act of 1966. Why do you think this agency was formed?

English Language Arts
Go to **glencoe.com** and visit the NHTSA Web site to read what programs and benefits are available to consumers. Prepare an informational flyer to share with your class on the information you discover.

Critical Thinking

The Actual Malice Test
Suppose you wrote an article for the school newspaper accusing the mayor of your town of corruption. The accusation turns out to be totally false. Can the mayor sue you, and possibly your school, for defamation? If so, will the suit be based on slander or libel? Will the actual malice test be applied by the court? Why or why not?

 Go to **glencoe.com** to check your answers.

glencoe.com

SECTION **3.1** ASSESSMENT

Self Check
1. Yes. An assault, for example, is both because it hurts an individual and also poses a threat to society.
2. actions that hurt, embarrass, or scare people; assault
3. possession of rights by innocent party, violation of those rights, resulting injury

Academic Connection
Social Studies
Answers will vary. Students may discuss the need for safety standards.

English Language Arts
Answers will vary.

Critical Thinking
The mayor could file a libel suit, because the defamation was in writing. The court will probably apply the actual malice test because the mayor is a public figure.

N C L B Activity correlated to the academic standards on page 54

FOCUS

 Bell Ringer Activity

Tell students that the janitor of the school applied an extra coat of wax on the floors. A student slips and falls on the slippery floor, injuring his or her back. Have students decide whether this is a case of negligence. Introduce the idea of duty of care and the reasonable person test.

Preteaching

Key Terms
Read the definitions and ask students to create a sentence using each term.

Academic Vocabulary
Explain that developing vocabulary is key to academic success. An efficient method to develop vocabulary is to study how words are formed.

- **reasonable** Adjective, from the Latin *ratio* (reason, calculation). Means rational, fair.
- **objective** Adjective, from the Latin *objectivus* (relating to an object). Means realistic, impartial.
- **foreseeable** Adjective, from *fore* (before) + *see*. Means reasonably anticipated.

Activity Ask students to give a noun, an adjective, or an adverb form that comes from each word.

N C L B Connects to academic content

60

What You'll Learn

- ◆ Define negligence.
- ◆ Explain the concepts of the reasonable person test and proximate cause.
- ◆ Explain the concept of strict liability.
- ◆ Compare and contrast negligence, strict liability, and proximate cause.

Why It's Important

Understanding what negligence is will help you if you are ever the victim of an accident or the cause of an accident.

Academic Standards

Reading and completing the activities in this section will help you practice the following academic standards:

N C L B **Social Studies (NCSS 10)** Study the ideals, principles, and practices of citizenship in a democratic republic.

Math (NCTM AS 4) Analyze change in various contexts.

Reading Guide

 Before You Read

Connect List all the careless things that you think you did during the past few months. Could the examples on your list have caused injury to another person or damage to property?

Focus on Ideas
Negligence involves a certain level of carelessness that people must avoid or they could suffer legal consequences.

Take Notes
Create a graph like the one shown and use it to take notes as you read this section. Go to **glencoe.com** to find graphic organizers and tips on how to improve your note-taking skills.

Duty of Care

Elements of Negligence

 Key Terms
You will learn these legal words and expressions in this chapter. You can also find these terms in *Black's Law Dictionary* or in an online legal dictionary.

- negligence
- proximate cause
- contributory negligence
- comparative negligence
- assumption of risk
- strict liability

Academic Vocabulary
You will find these words in your readings and in your tests. Look them up in a dictionary and familiarize yourself with them.

- reasonable
- objective
- foreseeable

glencoe.com

R **Reading Strategy**

Read for Knowledge

1. **Survey** or preread the chapter.
2. **Question** or formulate questions before you read.
3. **Recite** or read your questions, answers, and notes out loud.
4. **Review** or reread your notes.

Note-Taking Basics
- Listen attentively
- Have note-taking materials ready
- Skim through the lesson material
- Write down key words and ideas
- Anticipate what comes next
- Review notes soon after taking them

Negligence

Can you be sued if you hurt someone by accident?

Negligence is a tort that results when one person carelessly injures another. It is an accidental tort. It is also the tort that occurs most often. In contrast to an intentional tort, it requires no actual intent by the tortfeasor. Negligence is being less careful than a **reasonable** person should be in the same situation. Negligence can occur in an automobile accident, in the meltdown of a nuclear power plant, or when someone slips on the ice.

Elements of Negligence

The law has tough standards for negligence. To succeed in a tort suit for negligence, the plaintiff must prove all of the following elements:

- The defendant owed the plaintiff a duty of care.
- The defendant breached that duty by being careless.
- The defendant's carelessness was the proximate cause of harm.
- The plaintiff was really hurt by the defendant's carelessness.

Remember, you have to prove all the elements. Fail to prove just one and you will not receive remedy from a defendant.

Duty of Care The law of torts is grounded in the concept of rights. Because every person has certain rights in our society, all of us have a duty to not violate these rights. This concept of duty is extremely important in negligence lawsuits. When plaintiffs cannot prove that the defendants owed a duty of care—the obligation to use a reasonable standard of care to prevent injury to others—the judge will throw out the case.

Breach of Duty You breach, or break, your duty to another person when you fail to use reasonable care in dealing with

As You Read

Predict Can you be sued for negligence even if no harm was caused?

Vocabulary You can find vocabulary definitions in the **Key Terms** glossary and **Academic Vocabulary** glossary in the back of this book.

Defective Cars

Suppose you are an attorney for a car manufacturer. A company engineer informs you that one in 1,000 of the company's new cars may suffer from a transmission failure if it idles too long at a stoplight. Your company has sold 50,000 of the new cars so far. To recall the cars would cost the company $5 million. It could cost a lot less to settle the 50 potential lawsuits that might result because of the defective cars.

Critical Thinking: What is your advice to the company?

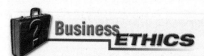

Answer The advice would depend on two things: the potential monetary loss from the 50 potential lawsuits, and the potential loss of public goodwill for the company. A recall not only costs money but tells the public that a company's product is faulty, which could lead to a loss in sales. The recall, however, avoids potential lawsuits and can boost the company's reputation for safety. If the company can settle each case for $10,000, then it can settle for a total of $500,000, or 10 percent of the cost of a recall. You might also take into account that the particular problem does not pose a serious danger.

3.2 SECTION

TEACH

Discussion Starter

Class Discussion

Ask students to describe circumstances in which they may have unintentionally caused an accident or an injury to another person or to property. Explain that careless behavior is known as *negligence* and that this section will cover the legal issues surrounding negligence.

As You Read

Predict Ask students to think of situations in which negligence might be a factor, yet no harm was done. (If no injury or damage occurred, there can be no negligence.)

Extending the Content

Duty of Care

Tell students that professionals are often held to a higher standard of duty of care than those who are not. Have students research the kind of duty of care expected from a health care professional. (possess medical knowledge and skills necessary to treat the patient, exercise care in the application of that knowledge, use reasonable medical judgment)

TEACH (cont.)

D Develop Concepts

Proximate Cause To help students understand proximate cause, discuss the term in parts. Explain that *proximate* means very near or immediate and *cause* means the producer of a result. Thus, proximate cause means the immediate producer of a result. Ask students to identify one proximate cause for obesity. (overeating)

W Writing Support

Reasonable Person Test Ask students to imagine that a woman is hosting a birthday party for friends at her swimming pool. Have them write a paragraph discussing the precautions that a reasonable person would take regarding this event. (Answers should demonstrate an understanding that a reasonable person would consider how likely the event is to cause injury, how serious any injuries might be, and the actions to be taken to avoid the injuries.)

Proximate Cause Proximate cause involves a negligent act that could lead to an injury or accident. *What do courts use to determine if proximate cause exists?*

that person. Just how careful do you have to be? To determine whether certain conduct is negligent, the law has developed a standard called the reasonable person test. The reasonable person test is an **objective** test. It does not change because the injured party changes.

According to the reasonable person test, you have to be as careful as a reasonable person would be in the same situation. A reasonable person considers how likely a certain act is to cause harm, how serious the harm would be, and the burden involved in avoiding the harm. For example, suppose the walkway leading to your home has some cracks in it that could cause someone to trip and fall. The likelihood that someone will trip is small and the harm would probably not be serious. The cost of replacing the walkway could be substantial compared to how unlikely it is to cause an accident. However, it would be reasonable to patch the worst cracks or post a warning sign to avoid the harm.

Proximate Cause It is not enough to show that a defendant's actions were unreasonable. The action or behavior must also be the proximate cause of the injury. **Proximate cause, also called legal cause, exists when the link between the negligent conduct and the injury is strong enough to be recognized by the law.** Without proximate cause, there would be no injury.

To determine if proximate cause exists, courts use the foreseeability test. The court asks whether the injury to the victim was **foreseeable** at the time of the negligent conduct. If the injury to the victim was foreseeable, then proximate cause exists, and the defendant is liable for negligence.

▲ USING VISUALS

Proximate Cause **Answer** Explain that proximate cause, also called legal cause, exists when the link between the negligent conduct and the injury is strong enough to be recognized by the law. Courts use the foreseeability test to determine if proximate cause exists. The court asks whether the injury to the victim could have been foreseen at the time of the negligent conduct. If it was foreseeable, the defendant is liable for negligence.

Actual Harm If a victim was not actually harmed, there can be no negligence. The victim must suffer an injury, have property destroyed, or lose a lot of money. Without actual harm, even the biggest mistake will not result in negligence.

Defenses to Negligence

You can defend yourself in a negligence suit by eliminating one of the four elements. For example, you could argue that you owed no duty to the plaintiff. You could also claim that you were as careful as a reasonable person would have been in the same situation. You could also state that your actions did not cause the victim's injury. Finally, you could try to prove that the victim was not really injured in the way that he or she claims.

A defendant who cannot get rid of at least one of these elements could be in serious trouble. However, that defendant is still not necessarily liable. There are three other defenses that a defendant could use against negligence.

Contributory Negligence **Contributory negligence is a defense against negligence whenever the defendant can show that the victim did something that helped cause his or her own injuries.** If the defendant can prove this, then the plaintiff loses the lawsuit. It does not matter how small the victim's negligence was. Many states no longer follow this doctrine. This is because it is unfair to plaintiffs who may have been only very slightly negligent. These states use another standard called comparative negligence.

Comparative Negligence **Comparative negligence is a defense against negligence which is raised when the carelessness of each party is compared to the carelessness of the other party.** The amount of money plaintiffs can receive in damages is reduced by the percent of their carelessness. Comparative negligence actually protects plaintiffs. This is because plaintiffs can still collect damages even if they were careless.

There is a condition, however, called the 50 percent rule. Most states use the 50 percent rule. According to the 50 percent rule, the plaintiff is allowed to receive some damages if the plaintiff's negligence is less than the defendant's. If the plaintiff's negligence is more than half, however, the plaintiff gets nothing.

Assumption of Risk **Assumption of risk is a defense against negligence that is raised when the plaintiff knew of the risk involved and still took the chance of being injured.** People who are injured while participating in extreme sports may also be unable to bring lawsuits for negligence. This is because they assume the risk involved with a dangerous sport. If you jump out of an airplane that is in good condition, you have assumed a risk of injury, even with the parachute on your back. The same is true if you bungee jump, skateboard, or windsurf.

Reading Check

Analyze How does negligence relate to proximate cause?

TEACH (cont.)

Extending the Content

Negligence
Tell students that in countries like Italy and Australia, cell phone use is prohibited while driving. Explain that some states have outlawed or are considering outlawing the use of cell phones while driving. Ask students to find out whether this is the case in the state in which they live.

Reading Check

Analyze Contributory negligence is a defense that shows that the victim did something that helped cause his or her own injuries.

C **Critical Thinking**

Assumption of Risk Ronda begged Marcus for a ride home from school, even though she knew he had been ticketed for speeding and reckless driving on several occasions. On the way home there was an accident, and Ronda's leg was broken. If she were to sue Marcus for negligence, do you think Marcus should claim assumption of risk as a defense? (To claim assumption of risk, Marcus must prove that Ronda knew of his reckless driving record and still took the chance of being injured.)

ASSESS

Independent Practice

Elements of Negligence

Mieko jogs in the city park every morning. In this park the sprinkler system is often left running during the night because of a bad timer. This morning, a stream of mud covers the path, and Mieko slips, falls, and sprains her ankle. She sues the city for negligence. Are the elements of negligence evident in this case? If so, what are they? If not, what is missing? (The city owes Mieko the duty of care; the city has probably committed a breach of duty by not exercising a degree of care necessary to keep the park safe.)

RETEACH

C Critical Thinking

Strict Liability Emphasize that the effect of the strict liability theory is to hold manufacturers and/or sellers liable, without question, for the safety of their products. It allows anyone injured because of a product defect to sue. Ask students if the injured party is required to prove negligence. (No.)

U Universal Access

Visual Impairment Students with visual impairments are constantly challenged because a large part of learning is visual. Plan for those challenges by giving detailed verbal descriptions of illustrations, photographs, charts, and procedures. Have a seeing student in the class describe the photographs in the chapter to any students who need help in this regard.

Independent Practice

Product Liability

Companies often issue product recalls when they discover product defects that may be potentially hazardous to consumers. Ask students to research recent product recalls using your school media center, newspapers, or the Internet. Have students share their findings with the class.

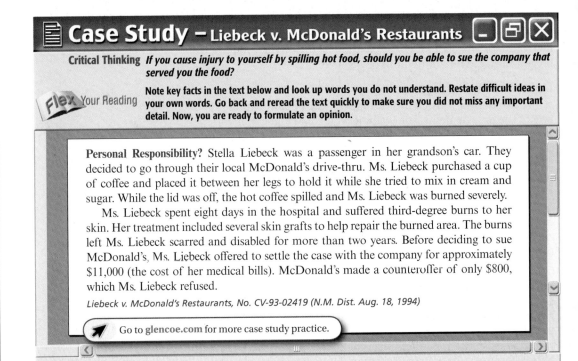

Case Study – Liebeck v. McDonald's Restaurants

Critical Thinking *If you cause injury to yourself by spilling hot food, should you be able to sue the company that served you the food?*

Flex Your Reading Note key facts in the text below and look up words you do not understand. Restate difficult ideas in your own words. Go back and reread the text quickly to make sure you did not miss any important detail. Now, you are ready to formulate an opinion.

Personal Responsibility? Stella Liebeck was a passenger in her grandson's car. They decided to go through their local McDonald's drive-thru. Ms. Liebeck purchased a cup of coffee and placed it between her legs to hold it while she tried to mix in cream and sugar. While the lid was off, the hot coffee spilled and Ms. Liebeck was burned severely.

Ms. Liebeck spent eight days in the hospital and suffered third-degree burns to her skin. Her treatment included several skin grafts to help repair the burned area. The burns left Ms. Liebeck scarred and disabled for more than two years. Before deciding to sue McDonald's, Ms. Liebeck offered to settle the case with the company for approximately $11,000 (the cost of her medical bills). McDonald's made a counteroffer of only $800, which Ms. Liebeck refused.

Liebeck v. McDonald's Restaurants, No. CV-93-02419 (N.M. Dist. Aug. 18, 1994)

Go to glencoe.com for more case study practice.

Strict Liability

Who is liable if you are injured by a faulty product?

C **Strict liability is a legal doctrine that says that some activities are so dangerous that liability will always follow any injury that results from those activities.** Some states call strict liability absolute liability. This rule applies only to ultrahazardous activities. These activities always involve a great risk to people and property. The risk is so great that no amount of care will eliminate it.

U Using explosives and keeping wild animals as pets are both in this category. If you keep a pet rattlesnake in a shoe box and it escapes and bites somebody, you are liable no matter how careful you were when you placed the rattler in the box.

Product Liability

Strict liability has been applied in product liability cases. When people are injured by defective products, both the firm that manufactured the products and the seller of the products are liable for injuries. Fault does not matter.

Limits to Product Liability

Product liability has limits. It does not apply if the seller of the defective product does not usually sell such items. For example, a corporation that auctions off some machinery after one of its

 glencoe.com

Case Study

Liebeck v. McDonald's Restaurants

Answer Answers will vary. At the end of the trial, the jury awarded Ms. Liebeck $160,000 in actual damages and $2.7 million in punitive damages. McDonald's served its coffee between 180 and 190 degrees. At 190 degrees, it takes less than three seconds for a third-degree burn to occur. In the decade prior to Ms. Liebeck's case, McDonald's had received over 700 reports of burns from its coffee, settling most of the cases at a cost of $500,000. McDonald's also acknowledged that it had never warned its customers that the coffee was extremely hot.

plants closes would not be liable for an injury caused by a defect in one of the machines. Product liability will also not apply if the only damage done by the product is damage to the product itself.

Tort Reform

If the injured party in a lawsuit dies, what happens to the lawsuit?

Some of the traditional rules of tort law are out of step with the real world. To solve this problem many state legislatures have passed new laws to reform tort law. Two such attempts involve survival statutes and wrongful death statutes.

Survival Statutes

In the past, under common law, when an injured person died, the right to sue also died. This meant that the defendant in a lawsuit was better off if the plaintiff died from injuries caused by the defendant. Most states now have survival statutes that say a lawsuit can continue even if both the plaintiff and the defendant die.

Wrongful Death Statutes

Also under common law, when an injured person died, the person's family forfeited, or gave up, the right to sue the party whose negligence caused the injury. This meant that, for example, a person who lost a spouse could not sue for damages even though he or she depended on the spouse's income for support. Wrongful death statutes now prevent this injustice and allow the relatives to bring a lawsuit even if the victim has died.

After You Read

Summarize Name the four elements of negligence.

After You Read

Summarize duty of care, breach of duty, proximate cause, and actual harm

ASSESS

Self-Assessment

Have students go to the *Business and Personal Law* Online Learning Center through glencoe.com to take the Section 3.2 Practice Test.

CLOSE

Culminating Activity

Strict Liability

Remind students that companies may not always be liable for injuries in negligence lawsuits. Ask students to explain situations to which this applies. (all elements of negligence have not been proved; contributory negligence; comparative negligence; plaintiff knew of the risks)

SECTION 3.2 ASSESSMENT

Self Check

1. What does duty of care mean?

2. What does breach of duty mean?

3. What types of activities are involved in strict liability?

Academic Connection

Mathematics The projected tort-related costs in product liability lawsuits for each American citizen in 2005 was $1,000. In 1950 it was $12 per citizen. What percent change does the 2005 figure represent over the figure from 1950?

THEORY **Number and Operations:** To calculate the percent change, divide the amount of change by the base figure. In this problem, the amount of change is the amount in 2005 minus the amount in 1950, and the base figure is the amount in 1950.

Critical Thinking

Bad Brakes Suppose that you are driving to work after school and your brakes fail. All that happens is you glide to a stop in the parking lot. However, on two more occasions your brakes fail. You cannot afford to pay for repair costs yet so you decide to take your chances. Applying your knowledge of negligence, explain whether you could be held liable.

 Go to **glencoe.com** to check your answers.

SECTION 3.2 ASSESSMENT

Self Check

1. the obligation to use a reasonable standard of care to prevent injury to others

2. broken duty to another person

3. ultrahazardous activities, such as using explosives and keeping wild animals, in which the risk is so great that no amount of care will eliminate it

Academic Connection

Mathematics
82.33%

Critical Thinking
The action fails the reasonable person test. By knowingly driving a car with faulty brakes, you are risking causing an accident for which you, as the driver, would be liable.

 Activity correlated to the Mathematics standard on page 60

Summary by Sections

Ask students to read the summaries one key point at a time. Then, ask them to work in groups to create two examples to illustrate each key point.

Vocabulary Builder

Cooperative Learning

1. Have students work in groups to prepare their sentences. Ask the groups to exchange their sentences and assess each other's sentences.

Vocabulary Development

- Ask students to use a dictionary or to go online to look up the etymology of each key term listed.
- Then, ask students to list several words derived from the same root or origin. For example, *contract* has the same root as *contractual* or *contractually*.

Chapter 3 Review and Assessment

Summary

Section 3.1 Definition of a Tort

- A tort is a private wrong committed by one person against another. A tortfeasor is a person who commits a tort. A person who commits a tort interferes with another person's rights.
- The law of torts is grounded in rights. Under tort law, all people are entitled to certain rights simply because they are members of our society.
- The law imposes a duty on all of us to respect the rights of others.
- The major intentional torts that can be committed against people are assault, battery, false imprisonment, defamation, invasion of privacy, and intentional infliction of emotional distress.
- The major intentional torts against property are trespass, conversion, nuisance, and disparagement.

Section 3.2 Negligence and Liability

- Negligence is an accidental or unintentional tort. It is the tort that occurs most often.
- Negligence is the failure to exercise the degree of care that a reasonable person would have exercised.
- A suit for negligence must prove four elements: duty of care, breach of duty, proximate cause, and actual harm.
- People can defend themselves against negligence by eliminating one of the four elements. If the defendant cannot eliminate one of the elements, he or she may still be able to use contributory negligence, comparative negligence, or assumption of risk as a defense.
- According to the doctrine of strict liability, those who engage in ultrahazardous activities will be held liable for any injury or damage that occurs because of that activity, regardless of intent or care.

 Vocabulary Builder

1 On a sheet of paper, use each of these terms in a sentence.

Key Terms

- tort
- tortfeasor
- intentional tort
- negligence
- proximate cause
- contributory negligence
- comparative negligence
- assumption of risk
- strict liability

Academic Vocabulary

- compensate
- confidential
- distress
- reasonable
- objective
- foreseeable

 Go to **glencoe.com** to play a game and improve your legal vocabulary.

 Study Skills for Success

Prepare Your Students for Studying

Tell students that they can improve their ability to understand and remember material from their courses by learning and practicing study skills. Remind students to:

- **Get motivated!** Motivation must come from within. To motivate yourself, think of ways in which what you learn now will fit into your long-term personal and professional goals.
- **Get organized!** Make studying part of your daily routine, not something you do at the last minute.
- **Concentrate!** Study in an environment that is as free of distractions as possible.

Key Points Review

Answer the following questions. Refer to the chapter for additional reinforcement.

2 What are the three elements of a tort?

3 What is the difference between a crime and a tort?

4 What is the difference between libel and slander?

5 What are the main intentional torts against people?

6 What are the main intentional torts against property?

7 What is negligence?

8 What are the elements of negligence?

9 What are the major defenses to negligence?

10 What is strict liability?

Standardized Test Practice

11 Read the following information about the National Highway Traffic Safety Administration (NHTSA) and complete questions 1 and 2.

The NHTSA is responsible for reducing deaths, injuries, and economic losses resulting from motor vehicle crashes. This is accomplished by setting and enforcing safety performance standards for motor vehicles and motor vehicle equipment, and through grants to state and local governments to enable them to conduct effective local highway safety programs.

The NHTSA investigates safety defects in motor vehicles, sets and enforces fuel economy standards, helps states and local communities reduce the threat of drunk drivers, promotes the use of safety belts, child safety seats, and air bags, investigates odometer fraud, establishes and enforces vehicle anti-theft regulations, and provides consumer information on motor vehicle safety topics. (*Information excerpted from the NHTSA Web site.*)

1. How does the NHTSA accomplish reducing deaths, injuries and economic losses from vehicle crashes?

Ⓐ educational grants and incentives for drivers

Ⓑ building new interstate highways and rest stops

Ⓒ reducing the cost of GPS tracking systems

Ⓓ setting and enforcing safety performance standards

2. The purpose of NHTSA investigating motor vehicle safety defects is to

Ⓐ build less expensive cars to increase new car sales

Ⓑ install anti-theft devices to prevent vehicles from being stolen

Ⓒ mandate child safety seats and air bag standards

Ⓓ advertise employment possibilities at the NHTSA

Test-Taking Strategies Try to include time at the end of the test to review your test before turning it in.

Chapter 3   Tort Law   **67**

Chapter **3**

Review and Assessment

Key Points Review

2. possession of certain rights by an innocent party; violation of rights by the tortfeasor; and resulting injury that hurts the person whose rights were violated

3. A crime is an offense against society. A tort is a wrong committed against a person.

4. Libel is written, printed, or recorded defamation; slander consists of verbal or spoken defamation.

5. assault and battery, false imprisonment, defamation, invasion of privacy, and the intentional infliction of emotional distress

6. trespass, conversion, nuisance, and disparagement

7. a tort that results when one person carelessly injures another (an accidental tort)

8. duty of care, breach of duty, proximate cause, and actual harm

9. eliminating one or more of the four elements, or proving contributory negligence, comparative negligence, or assumption of risk

10. legal doctrine that states that some actions are so extremely dangerous that liability will automatically attach to any injury that results from those activities

---

Standardized Test Practice

11. D and C

 Strategies for Standardized Test Prep Success

Whether your students have a standardized test coming up in a few days or a few weeks, these last-minute test-prep tips and strategies will help them relax and do their best.

- **Test Format** Help students become familiar with the format of the test by practicing with test items that imitate the actual test items as closely as possible.

- **Test Timing** Have your students take timed practice tests so that they become comfortable with the length, design, and timing of the actual test.

Chapter 3

Review and Assessment

Apply and Debate

Students should use chapter content to arrive at conclusions. The legal resolutions are listed below:

12. Yes, loud music is a nuisance. Students may also make a distinction between private and public nuisance.

13. Yes. Even if Donna left the checkbook out in the open, Matthew did more than just glance at it.

14. Assault, if Megan was really afraid of imminent harm to her physical person.

15. Libel, especially if the statements were lies. The teacher may sue but if the teacher is a "public figure," libel would require a showing of actual malice.

16. If Leslie sues the resort for negligence, the resort can use the defense of assumption of risk, since snowboarding is a dangerous sport.

C Critical Thinking

What Defense Can Be Used? Danny invited his friends over to his house for a pool party. Jared, one of Danny's friends, while clowning around jumped from the side of the diving board, grazing his head on the edge of the pool. Later that night, Jared's mother took her son to the emergency room because he was feeling nauseous and had a severe headache. She threatened to sue Danny and his parents for negligence.

68

Apply and Debate

C Read the following scenarios. Get together with other students in pairs or groups of three and take a position on each scenario. Debate your position in class with students taking the opposite position or prepare a written argument justifying your position.

12 Disturbing the Peace

To celebrate Kama's sixteenth birthday, 42 friends and family members gave her a surprise party. As the party went into the evening hours, her next door neighbors complained about the noise and the cars parked on the street.

You Debate   Under the tort of nuisance doctrine, are the neighbors justified in their complaint?

13 Invasion of Privacy

Donna and Matthew share an office. Donna was balancing her checkbook when she was called away from her desk. Matthew saw the checkbook on her desk and went through it while she was away.

You Debate   Did Matthew's actions constitute invasion of privacy?

14 Assault and Battery

Tania and Megan were arguing over which one of them should be homecoming queen. Tania told Megan that if she won the race she would cause her severe bodily injury. Megan told her parents of the threat and they contacted the police.

You Debate   Did Tania commit assault or battery or should the statement not be taken seriously because of the context in which it was said?

15 Defamation of Character

Aisha wrote an unfavorable article about one of her teachers for her high school newspaper. She did not talk to the teacher to get the teacher's side of the story. As a result of the article, the teacher was put on suspension pending an investigation.

You Debate   Is Aisha's article slander or libel and can the teacher do anything about it?

16 Assumption of Risk

Leslie went snowboarding with a group of friends at a local resort. As she slid down the mountain, she hit a trail marker sign, flipped off her board, and broke her leg.

You Debate   Can Leslie sue the resort for placing a sign where users might run into it and be injured?

Debate Practice

- Are all the elements of negligence present in this case? (No. Duty of care was taken, and no carelessness occurred on the part of Danny or his parents.)

- What defense could Danny and his parents use in the case of a lawsuit? (Contributory negligence or assumption of risk. Since Jared was clowning around and jumped off the side of the diving board, his actions contributed to the injury. Contributory negligence might be used as a defense. As a high school student, Jared should understand the dangers involved in and around water. The assumption of risk defense might also be used.)

Case Study Practice – Kolarik v. Cory International Corp. ▭▭☒

⑰ Who Is Liable? Douglas Kolarik bought a jar of pitted olives. When he bit into one of the olives, Mr. Kolarik broke a tooth on a piece of olive pit or some other hard object in the olive. He sued the olive company on grounds of strict liability and negligence. Under the theory of strict liability, Mr. Kolarik claimed the jar of olives had left the processing plant in a defective condition and that the defect was dangerous to any consumer. Mr. Kolarik further claimed that he had used the olives in an ordinary manner and that if the olives had left the processing plant without defects, his injury would not have occurred. Mr. Kolarik also argued that the olive company was negligent in failing to remove all pits or hard objects from the olives or preventing them from entering the olives as they were processed. Prior to trial, the olive company moved to dismiss the case, arguing it was not liable for stray pits left in olives.

Source: Kolarik v. Cory Int'l Corp., LACV063821 (Ia. Dist. Ct. March 31, 2004)

Practice Should the court dismiss this case? Why or why not?

⑱ Ethics ←?→ Application

Duty to Disclose After listing your car for sale, you are sent a notice regarding a mechanical recall on your vehicle. This afternoon you have an interested buyer coming to look at the car. After seeing and test driving the car, the buyer makes you an immediate offer to pay what you are asking.

◆ What would be the ethical way to handle this situation?

⑲ Internet Application

Anti-bullying Laws Suppose you are being constantly harassed in and out of school by another student. You have complained about the harassment to the bully, to the school, and to your family, who contacted the bully's family and told them about problem. Still, the bully continues to harass you.

Go to **glencoe.com** to find out about federal and state anti-bullying laws and what you can do legally to protect yourself.

R **Reading Connection**
Outside Reading Go to **glencoe.com** for a list of reading suggestions about tort law.

←?→ Ethics Application

18. You are not legally required to disclose the problem because you are a private seller; only dealerships are required to do so under National Highway and Safety Commission regulations. However, it is ethical to inform the buyer of the recall and what actions are required to correct the defect. Since most recalls are covered by the manufacturer, there most likely would be no cost involved in correcting the problem.

💻 Internet Application

19. Students should use search words such as *anti-bullying, bullying,* and *law.* They should find out about bill H.R. 4776, the Federal Anti-bullying Bill introduced on July 7, 2004.

R Reading Strategy

Reading Connection

American Bar Association Resources

Go to the *Business and Personal Law* Online Learning Center through glencoe.com to find links for further readings that relate to this chapter. Ask students to read, review, and summarize the documents. Advise students to keep their reviews and summaries to use as reference material for their Unit Thematic Project on pages 72–73.

Case Study Practice

17. Yes. Normally this case would have been dismissed, but the trial court in Iowa chose not to dismiss it. Although it is a general principle of tort law that one cannot usually sue over natural foreign objects found in food, in this case the court found that it was unclear what role the olive-processing company played in the actual processing of the olives. Normally, if you find a piece of pit in a can of peaches, for example, you cannot sue the processors for injury because it is almost impossible to remove all pieces of pits, and it would be prohibitively costly if manufacturers had to guarantee a 100 percent absence of pits.

UNIT 1

Careers in Law

Introduce Career Planning

Bell Ringer Activity

Give students the opportunity to brainstorm and put together a list of possible ways of contacting a future employer. Have them indicate how they might initially contact an employer.

Career Decisions

Self-Assessment Checklist

Use this checklist to help students determine their career path:

✓ Think about things you are good at
✓ Write down your interests
✓ Think about the lifestyle you want
✓ Write down your aptitudes and abilities
✓ Consider your personality
✓ Determine your learning style
✓ List some careers that might match these characteristics

Résumé Builder

Answer These elements comprise first and lasting impressions. People are more likely to complete business transactions with those who project confidence and intelligence.

Denise M. Howell
Counsel, Appellate Group
Publisher, BagandBaggage.com

What do you do at work?

"My specialty is appellate practice and procedure, which means I have devoted a good deal of time and study to the art of presenting cases to appellate tribunals, which differ greatly from the trial courts. Half the fun of being a litigator of any kind is the freedom it affords you to be a generalist (regarding subject matter). It's a rare case where I'm not learning about some area of the law with which I was not already very familiar. That said, my personal and professional interests mostly intersect in the ever-changing area of technology and intellectual property law."

What skills are most important to you?

"Effective and efficient information gathering and research techniques are especially important. It's also important to have the ability to analyze and tie sources together into a persuasive presentation."

What training do you recommend?

"The best training for appellate practitioners is to spend lots of time with other appellate practitioners, and let them shred your work—over and over again. It can be demoralizing, but it's effective. Whatever your area of legal expertise or interest, I recommend looking into the world of legal weblogs, or blogs. At the minimum, you will likely find free and informative writing by legal professionals who keep meticulously current on developments in your field. You might also find you have something to contribute to the discussion and analysis."

What is your key to success?

"Steve Jobs told Stanford's 2005 graduating class that it is best not to let many consecutive days pass by if you dislike what you are doing. Instead, change the course, select another option, move on, and find your passion. If you find that passion, you'll project the positive attitude, professional behavior, and personal responsibility so necessary for professional success."

Résumé Builder

Academic Skills

- Strong ability to investigate and conduct research
- Analyze information gathered into meaningful pieces

Education and Training

Collegiate focus will vary based on the specialty of work chosen. The following high school and college courses will help develop the necessary background knowledge:

- English Language Arts
- Social Studies
- U.S. Government
- Introduction to Law (in high school)
- Basic law courses (in college)
- Business, contracts, and consumer law

Critical Thinking

How can appropriate business attire, respect for confidentiality, and ethical behavior help you to project a professional image?

 Go to **glencoe.com** to find legal careers resources.

 glencoe.com

Research Technology

Specialized technology is available for a variety of law-related tasks. For example, LexisNexis and Westlaw are two competing electronic databases that attorneys and other legal professionals use to conduct research. These services give users access to online legal information, including the text of court decisions and legislation, the content of public records, and many legal articles.

Activity Ask students to access the American Bar Association's Web site through glencoe.com and read about technology uses in legal professions.

Expository Writing Practice

What Happened, and What Is the Crime? Henry, a 78-year-old man, makes a right-hand turn onto a street temporarily closed because of the farmer's market, where hundreds of people mingle and buy produce and other goods. His car runs over the orange pylons and makeshift gates closing off the street. He continues to drive, allegedly accelerating through the market, injuring dozens of people and instantly killing six before his car runs into a vendor's tent and stops. Bystanders pull Henry from his car and proceed to shout at him. He seems dazed and confused at all the commotion. Police arrive at the scene, interview witnesses, and cover the bodies, as paramedics tend to the injured. The police take Henry into custody for questioning.

Assignments

Research Research what particular charges might be filed against Henry. Determine your state's rules for crimes against people.

Write Imagine you are a public defender assigned to the case, and there is still much unknown about what exactly happened. Consider the situation above and write an expository essay analyzing how and what you need to find out from Henry regarding his character and the day at the market. Describe in detail the information you know and the information you need to gather in order to create a picture of the day and the man.

Writing Tips Before you start writing your essay, read through the following composition review tips:

✓ Determine and define your audience.

✓ Define your purpose.

✓ Explain your main idea in a clear thesis statement.

✓ List facts as supporting details.

✓ Focus on cause-effect relationships between facts.

Essay Test Strategies The word expository is a derivative of the word expose, which means to make known or explain. Expository writing explains and informs. Make sure you can explain your position clearly and support it with facts.

Go to **glencoe.com** to find more writing resources.

The Writing Connection

W Writing Support

Objectives

Write a brief expository essay outlining the type of charges that may be filed and also by analyzing the situation.

Essay Rubric

Evaluate students' writing according to the following criteria:

- The essay clearly expands its purpose. **(6 points)**
- The essay shows critical thinking through the use of questions and facts. **(6 points)**
- The organization is clear and effective. **(5 points)**
- The essay uses appropriate language with accuracy. **(4 points)**
- Syntax, grammar, and spelling are error-free. **(4 points)**

Total: 25 points

C Critical Thinking

Separating Parts Ask students to consider closely their critical-thinking process while writing the essay by exploring connections they make. By slowing down the process of composition they can identify the strengths and weaknesses of pieces of evidence.

Culminating Activity

Ask students to work in groups to give each other feedback on their first drafts.

Assignments

After assigning the topic, discuss with the class a general list of crimes against people in your state that might be applicable in this situation. Refrain from coming to any conclusions but arrange this as more of an information-gathering and sharing session for students to understand the possible charges.

While writing their essays, students need to synthesize the information they have gathered regarding this case, combining all the pieces effectively into a persuasive written document.

Thematic Project

FOCUS

Bell Ringer Activity

Ask students to write down all the elements needed to file a small claims suit. Also have them list what does not qualify as a small claims suit. The aim is to list from memory, in a short period of time, all they have learned thus far regarding small claims.

TEACH

Workshop Overview

The objective of this workshop is to familiarize students with the process of filing an action in a small claims court.

Social Studies

Ask students to research another country's court system equivalent of the United States' small claims courts. They can provide a timeline or overview of major events starting from the 1900s until today. Ask them to share their findings in class and discuss the strengths and weaknesses of both court systems.

Small Claims Suits

For this project, you will use what you have learned to prepare a checklist and a guide for filing an action in one of your state's small claims courts.

Here is a checklist of the skills that you will need to complete this project and that your teacher will consider when evaluating your work.

Evaluation Rubric	
Academic Skills	
1. Online and library research	**1.** 10 points
2. Reading for information	**2.** 10 points
3. Note-taking	**3.** 5 points
4. Essay structure and outline	**4.** 10 points
5. Grammar, spelling, and transitional and topic sentences	**5.** 10 points
Legal Skills	
6. Research of small court procedures	**6.** 15 points
7. Requirements of a plaintiff and defendant in small claims cases	**7.** 15 points
8. Analysis of the essential procedural information	**8.** 20 points
9. Use of technology	**9.** 5 points
	Total 100 Points

Go to **glencoe.com** for more resources and for grading rubrics.

Step 1: Preparation

1 Create a vocabulary reference guide of terminology used in small claims court.
2 Use all you have learned in this unit, at the library, or on the Internet as tools.
3 Complete this project in a format acceptable for a portfolio addition.

Time Management Rubric

Have students evaluate their usage of time by rating the skills below on a scale of "poor" to "apprentice" to "proficient."

- Organization (materials, files, data)
- Leadership (self-disciplined, motivated)
- Attention to detail (conscientious, efficient)

- Communication (technique, effectiveness)
- Problem solving (identifies, investigates, devises, evaluates)
- Critical thinking (defines, concludes, examines, constructs, supports, assesses)

Step 2: Procedure

❶ **Review** the text in this unit and make a list of the terminology with definitions.

❷ **List** the following sub-categories: 1) small claims court; 2) what you cannot do in small claims court; 3) do you need a lawyer; 4) costs involved in filing a suit in small claims court; 5) small claims court terminology; and 6) small claims checklist.

❸ **Write** a guide using the categories above to use for gathering information to present a case in small claims. Use the Internet to download a copy of your state's small claims filing form. Make enough copies of your guide and checklist so your classmates can review and annotate your information.

❹ **Describe** a scenario that would require you to file a suit in small claims court using your guide as a reference. Present the facts to support your case to your class and have them act as the judge in determining if the information would be sufficient to make a decision in the case.

Step 3: Create an Analysis Report

As a class, compare the checklists and guides that are presented. Create a spreadsheet to list and summarize the best ideas of the projects presented. In reviewing your classmates' checklists and guides, answer the following questions:

❶ How many subcategories and items were presented in the checklists?

❷ Did all of the guides include all the necessary elements to file a suit?

❸ If not, how does the absence of the element(s) affect the validity of a suit?

❹ How was your guide similar to and different from the other guides presented?

Community Connection

Find information on small claims cases in your state or county. Also, find out from your district court administrator if there is a dispute resolution center in your area and what its jurisdiction is. Prepare an oral presentation to report your findings to your classmates. Go to **glencoe.com** to find resources.

Competitive Event Prep
Knowing about the Law

Situation Assume the role of an experienced employee at a deli counter that is a favored spot for nearby office workers to pick up lunch. Employees of the deli are allowed a 30 percent discount on the sandwiches and salads that they purchase for themselves. This discount does not extend to persons other than the employee. A new employee has been purchasing two sandwiches each day, then passing one of the sandwiches to a friend who eats lunch with the employee.

Activity You are to explain to the new employee (event judge) that this behavior is a violation of the employee discount privilege.

For more Competitive Event preparation, performance tips, and evaluation rubrics, go to **glencoe.com**.

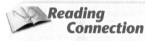

TEACH (cont.)
Extending the Content
Cases of Interest

Ask students to use the Internet to find a small claims case that is interesting to them. They should explain their reasons for selecting it and present any surprising findings.

 Reading Connection

American Bar Association Resources

Ask students to go back to their ABA readings, notes, and summaries. Direct them to apply any relevant ABA content to review and revise their outline and first draft.

ASSESS
Evaluation

Discuss the evaluation rubric with the students. Ask them to analyze their notes and offer suggestions on how to organize their notes and thoughts better.

CLOSE
Culminating Activity
Reflection

Ask students to reflect on their notes with the newly acquired advice in mind, to determine the current strengths and weaknesses of their note-taking ability.

S Skills Practice
Collecting Debt

James won his small claims case against Rosario and expects her to pay up immediately. He assumes the court will force her to pay the fine within ten days. However, after 30 days he is surprised not to have heard from Rosario and that the court has not forced her to pay off her debt. What is the plaintiff in a small claims judgment to do? At what point (if any) is the debt considered not collectible? Ask students to create a list of legal and fair methods for collecting a debt.

FOCUS

Why It's Important

- The ruling is a landmark expansion of the responsibility of cigarette manufacturers.

- This case affirms that tobacco companies are now more vulnerable to litigation brought by and on behalf of injured consumers.

TEACH

Preteaching

Flex Your Reading

This text is a long excerpt from a key case where U.S. consumer protection law was applied.

Preread Skim the text, look at headings and the first few sentences of every section.

C Critical Thinking

Framers of Tort Law Ask students if it is right for warning labels on cigarette packages to preclude any claims based on failure to warn. Many consumers feel that tobacco companies do everything they can, including conspiring and committing fraud, to keep information regarding smoke-related hazards from the public. Should tobacco companies be held responsible for a portion of the significant healthcare costs that are caused by cigarette smoking?

74

Cipollone v. Liggett Group, Inc.
United States Supreme Court 505 U.S. 504 (1992)

Read Critically As you read the case, ask yourself the following questions:

1. Why did the jury deny Rose Cipollone's claim for compensation?
2. What defense did the cigarette manufacturers raise in this case?
3. What is the effect of the supremacy clause in the U.S. Constitution?
4. When does federal law preempt state law?

Assignment When you are done, write a short summary of the situation. Include the court's decision and a couple of sentences about why or how the court reached its decision.

Facts **Health Problems from Cigarettes** After 42 years of smoking, Rose Cipollone died of lung cancer. During the last 15 years of her life, cigarette packages contained the following label: "WARNING: THE SURGEON GENERAL HAS DETERMINED THAT CIGARETTE SMOKING IS DANGEROUS TO YOUR HEALTH."

Rose and her husband brought suit in federal court against three cigarette manufacturers. They blamed the cigarette makers for Rose's cancer and sought compensation based upon New Jersey tort law.

Manufacturer's Response The manufacturers argued they were not liable for state law tort claims arising before 1966. They further argued that the Federal Cigarette Labeling and Advertising Act of 1965 and the Public Health Cigarette Smoking Act of 1969 preempted such claims.

Jury Verdict Rose died before trial. The jury ruled in favor of the manufacturers, stating that Rose had voluntarily assumed the risks of smoking. However, the jury did award Rose's husband $400,000 as compensation for his losses, holding that Liggett, a cigarette manufacturer, had breached its express warranties that smoking was not hazardous. Both sides appealed.

Opinion **Congressional Actions** In 1965, Congress passed the Federal Cigarette Labeling and Advertising Act, which required cigarette packages to contain the following label: "CAUTION: CIGARETTE SMOKING MAY BE HAZARDOUS TO YOUR HEALTH." Congress later passed the Public Health Cigarette Smoking Act of 1969, which required a stronger label to be placed on cigarette packages: "WARNING: THE SURGEON GENERAL HAS DETERMINED THAT CIGARETTE SMOKING IS DANGEROUS TO YOUR HEALTH."

The Petitioner's Complaint The petitioner's complaint alleged that the cigarette makers were responsible for Rose's illness on the following grounds:

Landmark Case Questions

R Reading Strategy

Answers

1. The jury determined that she was not entitled to compensation, because she had "voluntarily" assumed the risk of smoking.

2. The cigarette manufacturers asserted that federal laws preempted New Jersey's tort laws.

3. Under the supremacy clause, if a state law conflicts with a federal law, the federal law supersedes the state law.

4. When it is "the clear and manifest purpose of Congress."

- **Design Defect** The cigarette manufacturers did not use a safer alternative design, and the dangers created by cigarettes outweighed their social value.
- **Failure to Warn** There was no adequate warning about the health dangers of cigarettes, and manufacturers were negligent when "they tested, researched, sold, promoted, and advertised" cigarette products.
- **Express Warranty** The cigarette makers expressly warranted that their cigarettes did not pose serious health dangers.
- **Fraudulent Misrepresentations** The cigarette manufacturers tried to negate federal health warning labels and ignored scientific evidence demonstrating the hazards of smoking.
- **Conspiracy to Defraud** The cigarette makers tried to deny scientific evidence about the hazards of smoking.

The Defendant's Reply The cigarette manufacturers replied that federal laws preempt New Jersey's tort laws.

According to the supremacy clause of the U.S. Constitution, if a state law conflicts with a federal law, the federal law overrules the state law.

The petitioner claimed that state tort law should apply in this case because, unlike the 1969 Act, state tort claims for damages do not impose "requirement[s] or prohibition[s]" by statutes or regulations. Instead, the petitioner seeks compensation based upon prior court decisions (common law).

The Relationship of Federal and State Law In its opinion, the Court rejected the petitioner's argument. It held that state common law tort actions are based on the existence of a legal duty, which imposes "requirements and prohibitions."

The Court also cited an earlier case in which it said "[state] regulation can be effectively exerted through an award of damages as through some form of preventative relief. The obligation to pay

compensation can be, indeed is designed to be, a potent method of governing conduct and controlling policy."

Consequently, the Court rejected the petitioner's claim that common law tort claims brought by individuals do not constitute matters of state law, and therefore ruled that federal law could overrule them.

After clarifying the applicable law, the Court examined each of the petitioner's claims to determine if it was preempted by the federal law. To determine whether a state law is preempted, the Court said that it must look to the intent of Congress. It ruled that federal law does not preempt state law unless it is "the clear and manifest purpose of Congress" that a federal law supersedes a state law.

Holding The Court's Decision

The Court held that the 1965 Act did not preempt state tort claims because Congress did not intend that result. The Court further held that, although the 1969 Act preempted state claims based on failure to warn, it did not preempt claims based upon express warranty, intentional fraud and misrepresentation, or conspiracy.

TRIAL PREP

The National High School Mock Trial Association organizes competitions at the local, regional, and national levels where teams of high school or college students prepare and argue fictional legal cases before practicing attorneys and judges. Mock Trial team members are each assigned a role as either an attorney or witness. Each team must develop a courtroom strategy, legal arguments, and a presentation style.

Go to **glencoe.com** to find guided activities about case strategy and presentation.

glencoe.com

ASSESS

Independent Practice

Recent Tobacco Lawsuits
Ask students to research recent lawsuits that involved tobacco companies. They should analyze how the ruling compares to the findings in this particular landmark case. Have them critically consider how the outcome affects society, business, consumers, and so on. They should prepare a brief paper outlining their findings.

CLOSE

Understand the Decision

What would the consequences have been if the tobacco company had won the case? (Other tobacco companies would have been able to use compliance with the federal labeling statute as a protective cloak while continuing their prior policies regarding the manufacture and sale of tobacco against the public. The view of caveat emptor (that any product is acceptable as long as no one is misled as to the nature of the product or the harm it might cause) corrupts the very principles of tort law—making injured people "whole" again.)

Winning the Case

Drawing Comparisons

If the students were to litigate a case based on smoking-related injuries, they could make comparisons using the following:

(a) A consumer who chose a convertible top on a car when a steel top was available is not barred from claiming that the soft top was defective in design.

(b) Despite FDA approval, a jury believes testimony that a drug's dangerous characteristics outweigh its benefits, and concludes that no reasonable manufacturer would market it. While tobacco is not the only product capable of causing damage when used as directed, it may well be the only product that cannot be used safely and that has no apparent substantial utility.

75

Unit Objectives

Chapter	Section	Objectives
Chapter 4	4.1	• **Explain** the nature and importance of contracts • **Identify** the elements of a valid contract. • **Analyze** the different classes of contract. • **Differentiate** between express and implied contracts, unilateral and bilateral contracts, and oral and written contracts.
	4.2	• **Explain** the requirements of a valid offer. • **Recognize** the requirements of an acceptance. • **Distinguish** between an offer, an invitation to negotiate, an acceptance, and a counteroffer. • **Explain** how offers are terminated.
Chapter 5	5.1	• **Assess** contractual capacity. • **Explain** the Statute of Frauds and the parol evidence rule. • **List** minors' contractual rights and responsibilities. • **Define** legality and illegality.
	5.2	• **Analyze** the requirements for valid consideration. • **Define** the different types of consideration. • **List** exceptions to the requirements of consideration. • **Compare** unconscionability and illegality.
Chapter 6	6.1	• **Explain** how and when contracts can be discharged. • **Analyze** the concept of performance. • **Describe** the rules that apply to transfer of rights and duties. • **Understand** the difference between delegation and assignment.
	6.2	• **Define** breach of contract. • **Explain** what remedies are available when a contract is breached. • **Differentiate** among the ways contracts can be undermined (fraud, non-disclosure, misrepresentation, mistake, duress, and undue influence).

Understanding Brackets, Letters, and Ability Levels in the Teacher Wraparound Edition

Brackets Brackets on the reduced student edition page correspond to teaching strategies and activities in the Teacher Wraparound Edition. As you teach the lesson, the brackets show you exactly where to use the teaching strategies and activities.

Letters The letters on the reduced student edition page identify the type of strategy or activity. See the key below to learn about the different types of strategies and activities.

Ability Levels Teaching strategies that appear throughout the chapters have been identified by one of three codes to give you an idea of their suitability for students of varying learning styles and abilities.

Resources Key program resources are listed in each chapter. Icons indicate the format of resources.

KEY TO LETTERS

R **Reading Strategy** activities help you teach reading skills and vocabulary.

C **Critical Thinking** strategies help students apply and extend what they have learned.

S **Skills Practice** strategies help students practice historical analysis and geographical skills.

W **Writing Support** activities provide writing opportunities to help students comprehend the text.

D **Develop Concepts** activities use various strategies to help teachers gauge and plan for students' concept development.

U **Universal Access** activities provide differentiated instruction for English language learners and suggestions for teaching various types of learners.

NCLB **No Child Left Behind** activities help students practice and improve their abilities in academic subjects.

KEY TO ABILITY LEVELS

L1 strategies should be within the ability range of all students. Often full class participation is required.

L2 strategies are for average to above-average students or for small groups. Some teacher direction is necessary.

L3 strategies are designed for students able and willing to work independently. Minimal teacher direction is necessary.

KEY TO RESOURCE ICONS

📁 Print Material

💿 CD/DVD

🖲 Internet

Teacher Wraparound Edition

Student Activity Workbook with Academic Integration Teacher Annotated Edition

For the Unit:
Lesson Plans
National and State Standards Correlations

For the Chapters:
Lessons Plans
Note-Taking Graphic Organizers
Chapter Outlines
Chapter Summaries
Enrichment Activities Masters

Supplemental Cases
Internet Connection Student Activities Masters
Blackline Masters for Student Edition Figures and
   Supplemental Figures
Ethics and Business Law Activities
Competitive Events Test-Taking Prep
Reproducible Chapter Tests

 Link to the ***Business and Personal Law* Online Learning Center** with Podcasts through glencoe.com.

Real-World Applications

Demonstrate Case Resolutions

Learning Objective

- Explain the validity of contracts (p. 84).
- Identify voidable contracts (p. 102).
- Describe impossibility of performance (p. 133).

- List elements of a valid contract (p. 97).
- Identify the characteristics of valid agreements (p. 127).
- Describe valid offers (p. 151).

- Explain interpretations of contract terms (p. 156).

Apply Business Law Concepts

Learning Objective

- Understand online contracts (p. 78).
- Identify illegal sales (p. 98).
- Explain when a contract is void (p. 128).

- Understand Chinese business laws (p. 92).
- Explain oral contracts and fraud in Canadian contractual law (p. 107).
- Recognize the concepts of remedy and breach in Japan (p. 145).

- Apply the concept of consideration (p. 117).

- Practice making ethical decisions (pp. 97, 127, 151).

CYBERLAW

- Differentiate between public and proprietary information on the Internet (p. 89).
- Understand how contracts may change (p. 143).

Teach Financial Literacy

Learning Objective

- Understand financial contract terms and compute real revenue and fund fees (p. 77).

Bring Project-Based Learning into the Law Classroom

Writing a Driving Contract

- **Introduce Concepts**
  Contracts are official, legally enforceable agreements. Contracts imply negotiation.
- **Explore Concepts**
  Read the Thematic Project Preview and the WebQuest activity (p. 77).

  Ask students to think about creating ground rules for new drivers as they study Chapters 4, 5, and 6.
- **Apply Concepts**
  Research contract forms, make estimation of costs, formulate contract terms (pp. 154 and 155).

Extend Content

Using American Bar Association (ABA) Resources

- Direct students to pages 97, 127, and 151 in the Student Edition.
- Ask them to use glencoe.com to find links to ABA resource documents.
- Students should browse and select one document for each chapter.
- See pages 97, 127, 151, and 155 in this edition for specific instructions.

Reading and Writing Support

Feature or Activity	Topic	Reading Strategy	Writing Strategy
STANDARD &POOR'S	Mutual funds	Reading a primary source document	
Unit Thematic Preview	Writing a contract		Researching and taking notes
BusinessWeek	Reading a Web contract document	Reading for detail Developing flexibility in reading speed	
Section Reading Guide	Before-reading activities and tools	Connect students' lives with content Focus on the main idea	Using a graphic organizer to take notes
As You Read	During-reading tool	Predict content Determine what students already know	
Reading Check	During-reading tool	Self-check understanding of content	
After You Read	After-reading tool	Summarize section content	Writing and organizing a list of key concepts
Standardized Test Practice	UCC Code	Reading a primary source document Practicing critical reading skills	
Reading Connection	American Bar Association online resources	Reading a primary source document Extending and applying content Reading for knowledge Developing critical reading skills. Developing flexibility of reading speed	Taking notes Summarizing
The Writing Connection	Persuasive essay		Creating outlines, topic sentences, editing
Unit Thematic Project	Writing a contract	Using resources notes to support writing effort	Creating outlines, writing drafts, editing
Landmark Case	Contractual law case	Developing critical reading skills	Summarizing

Unit Overview

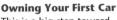

Unit 2 introduces and develops the concept of the contract. This concept is the foundation of business law, and will provide a frame of reference for students throughout this textbook (the units on consumer law, on marriage and divorce, on insurance, and so on, will refer to contractual terms and forms of contracts).

⏱ 00:00 OUT OF TIME?

If class time is too short to cover the chapters thoroughly, have students:

- Write down the vocabulary terms and their definitions.
- Read What You'll Learn and Why It's Important at the beginning of each section.
- Go to the *Business and Personal Law* Online Learning Center at glencoe.com to download the free Study-to-Go content to their cell phones or PDAs.

▶ USING VISUALS ....

Owning Your First Car
Answer Answers may vary, but should include financing a car and obtaining insurance, both of which entail signing and honoring contracts, as well as obeying traffic laws.

UNIT 2 Contract Law

In This Unit You Will Find:

Chapter 4
What Is a Contract?

Chapter 5
Elements of a Contract

Chapter 6
How Contracts Come to an End

• • • • • • • • • • • • • • • • • •

Owning Your First Car
This is a big step toward independence but also a big financial and civic responsibility. *What do you think is the most challenging aspect of owning a car?*

Unit Thematic Project Preview

W Writing Support

Many states have adopted the Uniform Electronic Transactions Act (UETA). According to UETA, contracts can be signed electronically and have the same legal status as contracts signed by hand.

Critical Thinking What are some the problems that can occur with electronic contracts? (Contracts could be forged or altered with no obvious signs; sent to old, rarely checked, or incorrect e-mail addresses; accidentally lost or deleted; or signed by an unauthorized third party.)

Thematic Project Preview

Writing a Driving Contract

As you read this unit, use this checklist to prepare for the unit project:

✓ List the elements needed to create a contract.

✓ Differentiate between classes of contracts.

✓ Compare the requirements of an offer and of an acceptance.

✓ Explain how offer and acceptance can create contractual rights and duties.

✓ Determine whether an agreement is definite enough to be enforced as a contract.

Legal Portfolio When you complete the Unit Thematic Project, you will have a real contract to add to your portfolio.

Find Unit 2 study tools such as **Graphic Organizers, Academic Skills Review,** and **Practice Tests** at **glencoe.com**.

WebQuest

Research Car Facts
Log on to **glencoe.com** to find resources to help your WebQuest explore the contractual side of having a first car. List your findings in your WebQuest folder to share with your class.

W

Ask

STANDARD &POOR'S

Investing in Mutual Funds

Q: I have heard that mutual funds are a type of investment. What are they?

A: A mutual fund is a collective investment that pools money from many investors to buy and sell stocks, bonds, short-term money-market instruments, and other securities traded on stock exchanges around the world. A mutual fund operates by specific rules and while you do not have to sign a contract document, by entering a fund you effectively agree to follow its rules and pay its fees. What the fund invests in is called a portfolio. By law, you should receive a prospectus from the fund company before you invest in it. It tells you the goals of the fund and how it intends to achieve them. You will also find information about the fund's fees.

R **Language Arts/Reading** Standard & Poor's is one of the world's main providers of credit ratings and financial-market indices. You can access the S & P Web site through **glencoe.com** and read about the various companies and stocks that mutual funds use as investments.

 glencoe.com

Ask

STANDARD &POOR'S

R Reading Strategy

Language Arts/Reading Direct students to explore S&P's resources on mutual funds.

Math Activity Operating fees (expense ratio) cover the cost of maintaining a fund.

They can exceed earnings: Your $10,000 mutual fund earned $300 last year. The expense ratio consisted of a 2% investment advisory fee, a 1% administrative fee, and a 1% distribution fee. How much did you earn? (The amount in the fund, including the earnings, is $10,300. 2% + 1% + 1% = 4% × $10,300 = $412 expense ratio. You lost $112.)

5-minute ⟩ Launch

KWL Chart Have students make a list of what they know about contracts. Next, ask them to skim Unit 2 and notice the headers, the figures, and photos. Ask students what questions came up and have them list what they now want to know about contracts. Discuss the lists and create a KWL chart with their responses. After completing the unit, revisit the chart and reassess their knowledge by asking them what they learned about contracts.

Building Law Background

Ask students these questions to activate prior knowledge:

Chapter 4
What do you think makes a contract different from an ordinary agreement? (A contract is an agreement that is enforceable by law.)

Chapter 5
What are emancipated minors, and are they responsible for the contracts they make? (Emancipated minors are minors who are no longer under the control of their parents, and they are responsible for the contracts they make.)

Chapter 6
Do you think you can cancel a signed contract? (Specific reasons such as impossibility of performance, death or illness, or illegal alteration, etc. must be cited and proven in order to cancel a contract.)

Plan Your Lesson Section by Section

NBEA	NATIONAL BUSINESS LAW STANDARDS
Section 4.1	• **Differentiate** between classes of contracts (e.g., bilateral and unilateral, express and implied, and oral and written).
Section 4.2	• **Explain** how offer and acceptance can create contractual rights and duties. • **Determine** whether an agreement is definite enough to be enforced as a contract. • **Discuss** the impact of the laws of different countries on business contracts.

NCLB	ACADEMIC STANDARDS	Activity/Feature
English Language Arts: NCTE 3 Apply a wide range of strategies to comprehend, interpret, evaluate, and appreciate texts.		*BusinessWeek* News Case Study Case Study Practice
English Language Arts: NCTE 9 Develop an understanding of and respect for diversity in language use, patterns, and dialects across cultures, ethnic groups, geographic regions, and social roles.		Global Law
English Language Arts: NCTE 6 Apply knowledge of language structure, language conventions, media techniques, figurative language, and genre to create, critique, and discuss print and non-print texts.		Legal Talk, ad copy, Key Terms and Academic Vocabulary
Mathematics: NCTM CS2 3 Recognize and apply mathematics in contexts outside of mathematics.		Section 4.1 Assessment
English Language Arts: NCTE 5 Employ a wide range of strategies to write and use different writing process elements appropriately to communicate with different audiences for a variety of purposes.		Section 4.2 Assessment
English Language Arts: NCTE 10 Students whose first language is not English make use of their first language to develop competency in the English language arts and to develop understanding of content across the curriculum.		Key Terms, Academic Vocabulary Legal Talk Vocabulary Builder
English Language Arts: NCTE 1 Read a wide range of print and non-print texts to build an understanding of texts; to acquire new information; to respond to the needs and demands of society and the workplace; and for personal fulfillment.		Global Law Cyberlaw

Connect Your Business Law Classroom to the World of Work

This chart shows the 21st Century Skills, foundation skills, and workplace competencies that students develop as they work in this chapter.

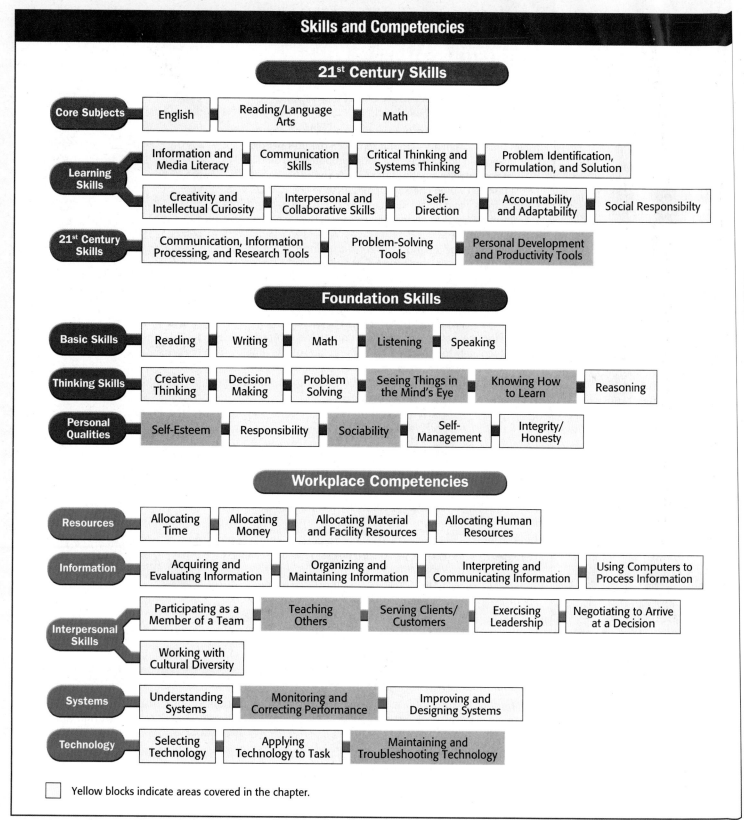

Skills and Competencies

21st Century Skills

Core Subjects
- English
- Reading/Language Arts
- Math

Learning Skills
- Information and Media Literacy
- Communication Skills
- Critical Thinking and Systems Thinking
- Problem Identification, Formulation, and Solution
- Creativity and Intellectual Curiosity
- Interpersonal and Collaborative Skills
- Self-Direction
- Accountability and Adaptability
- Social Responsibilty

21st Century Skills
- Communication, Information Processing, and Research Tools
- Problem-Solving Tools
- Personal Development and Productivity Tools

Foundation Skills

Basic Skills
- Reading
- Writing
- Math
- Listening
- Speaking

Thinking Skills
- Creative Thinking
- Decision Making
- Problem Solving
- Seeing Things in the Mind's Eye
- Knowing How to Learn
- Reasoning

Personal Qualities
- Self-Esteem
- Responsibility
- Sociability
- Self-Management
- Integrity/Honesty

Workplace Competencies

Resources
- Allocating Time
- Allocating Money
- Allocating Material and Facility Resources
- Allocating Human Resources

Information
- Acquiring and Evaluating Information
- Organizing and Maintaining Information
- Interpreting and Communicating Information
- Using Computers to Process Information

Interpersonal Skills
- Participating as a Member of a Team
- Teaching Others
- Serving Clients/Customers
- Exercising Leadership
- Negotiating to Arrive at a Decision
- Working with Cultural Diversity

Systems
- Understanding Systems
- Monitoring and Correcting Performance
- Improving and Designing Systems

Technology
- Selecting Technology
- Applying Technology to Task
- Maintaining and Troubleshooting Technology

☐ Yellow blocks indicate areas covered in the chapter.

CHAPTER 4

What Is a Contract?
Contract law forms the foundation for all other areas of business law. Chapter 4 explains the nature, elements, and requirements of a contract.

Building Background
Introduce the general concept of contracts by bringing in different types of contracts: credit card offers received in the mail, or sales receipts. Contracts do not always have to be in writing. Give examples of oral agreements.

BusinessWeek News

Tell students that one of the most common types of contracts is a ticket to a movie, concert, or sporting event. Contract terms and conditions are often listed on the ticket. A typical condition states that you may not resell the ticket at a price greater that its face value (commonly called scalping). Explain to students the meaning of these terms and conditions and how they relate to contract law.

R Reading Strategy

Flex Your Reading

Ask students to read some contract samples you have brought to class. Ask them what the most challenging part of reading such documents is. List their opinions on the board and ask them to brainstorm strategies to overcome these challenges.

CHAPTER 4 What Is a Contract?

BusinessWeek News

Bring Your CDs into the iPod Age
By Stephen H. Wildstrom

Copying CDs to computer files isn't difficult. But it is time-consuming—around ten to 15 minutes per disk depending on the speed of your computer, the digital format, and the length of the CDs. If you're like me, it's a task you would cheerfully pay someone else to do.

I tried two different services, Rip Digital and ReadyToPlay, that do the job. They are alike in most respects.

Both charge around $130 (plus shipping) for the first 100 CDs, with prices dropping as low as $1 per disk for large quantities. Rip Digital includes a program that automates the process of copying the files from the DVD to your computer and loading the music into your library of iTunes or a musicmatch jukebox.

R From now on, every CD I buy goes to the computer immediately to keep the digital library up-to-date. But the ripping services have done the heavy lifting, so now I get to sit back and enjoy the music.

Flex Your Reading

Efficient critical reading involves being flexible with speed and comprehension. There are several ways of reading critically, and you need to fit a reading style to your needs and to the material.

Go to **glencoe.com** to find Flex Your Reading activities, more information on reading strategies for this chapter, and guided practice in reading contracts (online or printed).

 Classroom Resources

- Student Edition
- Teacher Wraparound Edition
- Student Activity Workbook with Academic Integration (SE/TAE)
- TeacherWorks™ Plus! CD
- *ExamView®* Assessment Suite CD
- *Presentation Plus!* CD

- National Mock Trial Championship DVD
- Online Learning Center with Podcasts at glencoe.com
- Study-to-Go™ at glencoe.com
- Online Student Edition
- Interactive Student Edition

Practice the Concept

Contracts

Bring in credit card offers and applications. Go over a typical offer or application with students. Compare the offers with the actual terms and conditions and locate important information such as:

Key Terms Tell students to be wary of expressions such as "0% introductory rate," "free," "earn," and "no annual fee." These are often meant to create the impression that the card does not come with any interest charges, costs, or fees. Point out that "introductory" means the 0 percent interest rate is temporary and the rate might go up to 17 or 18 percent after six months. To find the actual fees and rates, students should look for expressions such as "regular APR," "transaction fee," "late fee," and "cash advance APR." Also explain terms such as *default* and *variable*.

The Fine Print Most important, students should be instructed to always read the fine print, both literally and figuratively. The fine print, which usually contains the real costs of credit, is often found buried in footnotes or within long paragraphs at the end of a credit card agreement to discourage people from reading it. The same card that offers a 0 percent introductory APR might have a default APR of 31.49 percent if the student makes a late payment.

Legal Download An interest in music requires building and maintaining your music collection. *When is it legal to download music off the Internet?*

79

▲ USING VISUALS

Legal Download **Answer** Read the photo caption to students. Explain that many students do not know when they are illegally downloading music off the Internet, or engaging in music piracy. Illegally downloading music violates copyright laws and costs not only music companies money, but deprives the artists who created the music of some income. Ask students to discuss the legality, costs, ethics, and illegal music downloads from the points of view of artist, music executive, and music pirate.

SECTION 4.1

FOCUS

Bell Ringer Activity

Write this statement on the board and have the students complete it:

When I access a music download service on the Internet, I have to read a document called a _____ and check a box that says that I _____ the terms of the agreement.

(contract and accept)

Preteaching

Key Terms
Read the definitions and ask students to create a sentence using each term.

Academic Vocabulary
Explain that developing vocabulary is key to academic success. An efficient method to develop vocabulary is to study how words are formed.

- **determine** Verb, from the Latin *de* (off) + *terminare* (to mark the end or boundary). Means to decide or to discover.

- **assume** Verb, from the Latin *assumere, ad + sumere* (to take). Means to receive, to undertake, or to suppose.

- **require** Verb, from the Latin *re + quaerere* (to seek or to ask). Means to impose or to demand.

Activity Ask students to give a noun, an adjective, or an adverb form that comes from each word.

 Connects to academic content

What You'll Learn

- ◆ Explain the nature and importance of contracts.
- ◆ Identify the elements of a valid contract.
- ◆ Analyze the different classes of contracts.
- ◆ Differentiate between express and implied, unilateral and bilateral, and oral and written contracts.

Why It's Important

Knowing the elements and characteristics of a contract will help you determine whether an agreement is valid or not.

Academic Standards

Reading and completing the activities in this section will help you practice the following academic standards:

Math (NCTM CS2 3) Recognize and apply mathematics in contexts outside of mathematics. Solve problems that arise in mathematics and in other contexts.

English Language Arts (NCTE 6) Apply knowledge of language structure, language conventions, media techniques, figurative language, and genre to create, critique, and discuss print and non-print texts.

Agreements and Contracts

Reading Guide

Before You Read

Connect If you have ever agreed to conditions to enter a Web site, you have made a contract. What are some contracts you have made lately?

Focus on Ideas
For a contract to be valid, it must meet several requirements and have certain characteristics.

Take Notes
Create a graph like the one shown and use it to take notes as you read this section. Go to glencoe.com to find graphic organizers and tips on how to improve your note-taking skills.

The Six Components of a Contract

Key Terms
You will learn these legal words and expressions in this chapter. You can also find these terms in *Black's Law Dictionary* or in an online legal dictionary.

- contract
- offer
- acceptance
- genuine agreement
- express contract
- implied contract
- bilateral contract
- unilateral contract

Academic Vocabulary

You will find these words in your readings and in your tests. Look them up in a dictionary and familiarize yourself with them.

- determine
- assume
- require

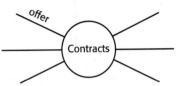 glencoe.com

---

R Reading Strategy

Read for Knowledge

1. **Survey** or preread the chapter.
2. **Question** or formulate questions before you read.
3. **Recite** or read your questions, answers and notes out loud.
4. **Review** or reread your notes.

Note-Taking Basics
- Listen attentively
- Have note-taking materials ready
- Skim through the lesson material
- Write down key words and ideas
- Anticipate what comes next
- Review notes soon after taking them

Understanding Contract Law

Do you think a contract always is a written document that needs to be signed?

If you bought your first car last year or sold your old video games at a garage sale, you might know that these activities involve contracts. Many common daily activities also involve contracts, from buying a fast food meal to filling your car with gas. Most people think a contract is a long, printed, formal document that they sign when buying a vehicle, selling their house, or purchasing insurance. Such formal documents represent only a small fraction of the contracts that you will make in your lifetime. The truth is that you create a contract any time you agree to exchange things of value.

As You Read

Predict Does a contract have to be in writing to be valid?

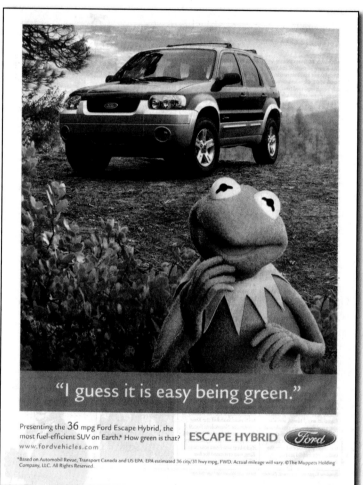

"I guess it is easy being green."

Presenting the 36 mpg Ford Escape Hybrid, the most fuel-efficient SUV on Earth.* How green is that? www.fordvehicles.com

ESCAPE HYBRID *Ford*

*Based on Automobil Revue, Transport Canada and US EPA. EPA estimated 36 city/31 hwy mpg, FWD. Actual mileage will vary. ©The Muppets Holding Company, LLC. All Rights Reserved.

Contracts Are Everywhere Contractual agreements are not always obvious, but they are everywhere in our lives. *Do you think Ford's claim of 36 miles per gallon gas consumption is a contract? Why or why not? When you have finished reading and studying this chapter, look at this ad again. Would you change your original answer? Explain how and why?*

TEACH

Discussion Starter

Class Discussion
Following through on a promise is an important underlying assumption in a contract between people and businesses. Explain to students that certain key elements must exist for a contract to be legally binding. Ask students to suggest which type of elements they think must exist between parties so that the contract is binding.

As You Read

Predict Ask students to brainstorm whether contracts are always in writing. Ask them to think of daily life examples (such as buying gas). (The goal of predicting content is to encourage students to make guesses and focus their attention on the topic. Do tell them at the end of this process that in this section they will learn that contracts do not have to be in writing to be valid.)

▲ Using Visuals

Contracts Are Everywhere Answer Some students might think that the claim of 36 miles per gallon is a contractual promise on the part of Ford Motors. However, this does not constitute a contract: there is no formal offer, or acceptance, or genuine agreement between parties. Use this ad to explore the concept of parties agreeing to certain terms. Stress the idea of acceptance and the idea of genuine agreement. You can use this ad again later on in this chapter when the concept of implied contracts is introduced.

SECTION 4.1

TEACH (cont.)

D Develop Concepts

Social Agreements
Illustrate the difference between a contract and a social agreement by saying, "I promise to take you all out to dinner this weekend. You can order anything you want, and I will pay for it." After the reaction from the class subsides, say, "I forgot, I have to go out of town this weekend. I won't be able to do it." Discuss whether a contract had taken place. (No. Consideration is missing from this agreement.)

S Skills Practice

List Using the scenario above, ask students to make a list of all the implied terms of the promise. (They can order whatever they want and dinner will not cost them anything. The teacher will pay. This will take place this weekend.) **L1**

Explain Have students write a paragraph explaining why they think they could force the teacher to take them out to dinner. (Explanations will vary, but most will include the very specific terms of the promise.) **L2**

Classify Use this scenario to introduce the six components of a legal contract. All elements must be present for a contract to be legally binding. Write each element on the board. Ask students to consider the scenario. List under each part a situation that represents a component or have an X if the component is missing. **L3**

82

Research Car Facts
A teen driver-family agreement is a form of contract. Log on to **glencoe.com** to find WebQuest resources, research key issues, and continue your WebQuest project.

List your findings in your WebQuest folder to share with your class.

Vocabulary You can find vocabulary definitions in the **Key Terms** glossary and **Academic Vocabulary** glossary in the back of this book.

The Nature of a Contract

Are all agreements you make contracts?

A contract is any agreement enforceable by law. You should never enter into a contract without understanding the legal responsibilities involved. Not all agreements are contracts. An informal promise to take out the trash is not a contract. In contrast, an ad in a newspaper offering a reward for a lost skateboard is a type of contract. If someone answers the ad and returns the skateboard, the person who placed the ad will owe the person who returned the skateboard what was promised as a reward in the ad.

The Three Theories of Contract Law

The legal responsibilities associated with contracts are based on what the parties involved do and say to one another. In the past, courts asked whether the parties to a contract exchanged things of equal value. This was called the equity theory of contract law. As industrial capitalism developed, the courts focused on the exercise of each party's will: they asked whether the parties really had agreed to the terms of an agreement. This was called the will theory of contract law. But, it was still very difficult to **determine** what the parties were thinking as they had entered into an agreement. The courts tried to determine if the parties had reached a meeting of the minds and, gradually, this led to a search for elements that consistently appeared in genuine agreements. The courts focused on the form of agreements. This became known as the formalist theory of contract law.

The Elements of a Contract

The six elements of a contract, as shown in **Figure 4.1,** are offer, acceptance, genuine agreement, consideration, capacity, and legality. To be legally complete, a contract must include all six elements. Notice that the list does not include anything written. Not all contracts have to be in writing to be enforceable.

An offer is a proposal by one party to another intended to create a legally binding agreement. An acceptance is the second party's unqualified willingness to go along with the first party's proposal. A genuine agreement means that an agreement is true and genuine: a valid offer is met by a valid acceptance. Circumstances such as fraud, misrepresentation, mistake, undue influence, and economic duress can destroy the genuineness of an agreement. The fourth element, capacity, is the legal ability to enter a contract. The law generally assumes that anyone entering a contract has the capacity, but this assumption can be disputed. The fifth element, consideration, is the exchange of things of value. In an offer to let someone borrow a car, there is no consideration in the agreement if nothing is offered in return. People cannot enter into contracts that include illegal acts. Legality, the sixth element, means that the contract does not entail violating any laws.

82   Unit 2   Contract Law

 glencoe.com

Research Tip Access the *Business and Personal Law* Online Learning Center through glencoe.com and print a couple examples of the resources available. Make sure students understand how to use them in their research project.

Figure 4.1 Elements of a Contract

Capacity The law presumes that anyone entering a contract has the legal capacity to do so. Minors are generally excused from contractual responsibility, as are mentally impaired people and individuals under the influence of drugs or alcohol.

Consideration Consideration is the thing of value promised to one party in a contract in exchange for something else of value promised by the other party. The mutual exchange binds the parties together.

Legality Parties are not allowed to enforce contracts that involve illegal acts. Some illegal contracts involve agreements to commit a crime or a tort. Others involve activities made illegal by statutory law.

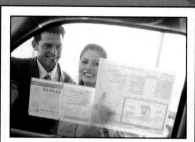

Offer A proposal made by one party (the offeror) to another party (the offeree) indicating a willingness to contract.

Acceptance The agreement of the offeree to be bound by the terms of the offer.

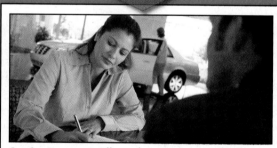

Genuine Agreement Offer and acceptance go together to create genuine agreement or a meeting of the minds. Agreement can be destroyed by fraud, misrepresentation, mistake, duress, or undue influence.

An agreement is not a contract unless it contains the six elements of contracts.
Of the six elements, which is the most crucial to setting up a valid contract?

TEACH *(cont.)*

D Develop Concepts

Elements of a Contract
Write the following items on the board:

- Capacity
- Consideration
- Legality
- Offer
- Acceptance
- Genuine agreement

Have volunteers call out an explanation of each element of a contract. (Capacity is the legal ability to enter into contract. Consideration is something of value promised in exchange for something of value. Legality means contract does not contain illegal acts. Offer is proposal to contract. Acceptance is agreement to terms of offer. Genuine agreement means meeting of the minds.)

U Universal Access

Visual Impairment Students with visual impairments are constantly challenged because a large part of traditional learning is visual. Plan for these challenges by giving detailed verbal descriptions of illustrations, photographs, charts, and procedures. Have course outlines prepared in an alternative format, such as Braille, enlarged print, or audio recording.

USING VISUALS

Figure 4.1 Elements of a Contract Answer The best answer is "consideration" because the other elements can be present in an ordinary noncontractual agreement. One person may offer to drive another person to work one morning and the other might accept. Such an arrangement would have offer, acceptance, and agreement, yet it would not be a contract. If the offeror had a driver's license, owned his car to which he had proper access, and had the appropriate mental capacity to make such an offer, the agreement would also have capacity and legality, but would still not be a contract. Only when some sort of payment (monetary or not) or promise of payment flows from the passenger to the driver (consideration) would it be contract.

TEACH (cont.)

Guided Practice

Characteristics of a Contract

Explain to students that a contract may assume different forms. Ask ten students to assume responsibility for describing these ten types of contracts to the class:

Valid, void, voidable, unenforceable, express, implied, bilateral, unilateral, oral, and written.

Remind students that they can research the meaning of these terms in the section or in the glossary of their textbook.

Reading Check

Enumerate A contract needs six elements to be complete: offer, acceptance, genuine agreement, consideration, capacity, and legality.

Reading Check

Enumerate *How many elements does a contract need to be complete?*

Characteristics of a Contract

Now that you know about the different elements of a contract, can you think of different types of contracts?

Contracts can be created in different ways and can **assume** diverse forms. A contract can be described by any of the following characteristics:

- Valid, void, voidable, or unenforceable
- Express or implied
- Bilateral or unilateral
- Oral or written

Any contract can have characteristics from one or more of these four groups. That is, a contract can be valid, express, bilateral, and written. Let's take a closer look at what these characteristics indicate about a contract.

Valid, Void, Voidable, or Unenforceable Contracts

The word valid means legally good, thus a valid contract is one that is legally binding. On the other hand, a contract that is void has no legal effect. An agreement that is missing one of the previously discussed elements would be void, such as any agreement to do something illegal.

When a party to a contract is able to void or cancel a contract for some legal reason, it is a voidable contract. It is not void in

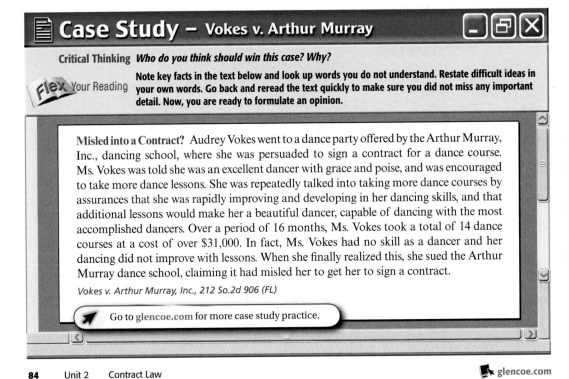

Case Study – Vokes v. Arthur Murray

Critical Thinking *Who do you think should win this case? Why?*

Flex Your Reading Note key facts in the text below and look up words you do not understand. Restate difficult ideas in your own words. Go back and reread the text quickly to make sure you did not miss any important detail. Now, you are ready to formulate an opinion.

Misled into a Contract? Audrey Vokes went to a dance party offered by the Arthur Murray, Inc., dancing school, where she was persuaded to sign a contract for a dance course. Ms. Vokes was told she was an excellent dancer with grace and poise, and was encouraged to take more dance lessons. She was repeatedly talked into taking more dance courses by assurances that she was rapidly improving and developing in her dancing skills, and that additional lessons would make her a beautiful dancer, capable of dancing with the most accomplished dancers. Over a period of 16 months, Ms. Vokes took a total of 14 dance courses at a cost of over $31,000. In fact, Ms. Vokes had no skill as a dancer and her dancing did not improve with lessons. When she finally realized this, she sued the Arthur Murray dance school, claiming it had misled her to get her to sign a contract.

Vokes v. Arthur Murray, Inc., 212 So.2d 906 (FL)

Go to **glencoe.com** for more case study practice.

glencoe.com

Case Study

Vokes v. Arthur Murray

Answer The customer should win this case because her agreement with the dance school includes necessary components of a legally binding implied contract.

Activity Ask students to brainstorm examples of implied contracts. For example, when someone buys gas at a self-service pump, the customer's actions indicated a willingness to pay for the gas.

itself but may be voided by one or more of the parties. A contract between two minors could be voidable by either of them because minors have the right to get out of contracts (see Chapter 5).

An unenforceable contract is one the court will not uphold, generally because of some rule of law, such as the statute of limitations. If you wait too long to bring a lawsuit for breach of contract, the statute of limitations may have run its course, making the contract unenforceable.

Express or Implied Contracts

An express contract is a contract statement that may be oral or written. An implied contract is a contract that comes about from the actions of the parties. People often enter into implied contracts without exchanging a single word.

> **Example** Herb Schneider went to a self-service gas station that requires payment before the attendant will turn on the pumps. He handed the attendant $10, returned to his car, pumped $10 worth of gas into his tank, and drove off. Neither party spoke a single word, yet an implied contract arose from their actions.

Bilateral or Unilateral Contracts

Another characteristic of a contract to consider is whether it is bilateral or unilateral. See **Figure 4.2** for a visual representation of bilateral and unilateral contracts. A **bilateral contract is a contract that contains two promises.** One party promises to do something in exchange for the other's promise to do something else. Most contracts are created this way.

A unilateral contract is a contract that contains a promise by only one person to do something, if and when the other party performs some act. If your friend

Legal Talk

Bilateral: *adj* Affecting two sides or parties. From Latin *bilateralis; bi* = two + *latus* = side: having two sides.

Unilateral: *adj* Done or undertaken by one person or party. From Latin *unus* = one + *latus* = side: having one side.

Vocabulary Builder List and define five words that begin with the prefix *bi* or with the prefix *uni*.

Look It Up! Check definitions in *Black's Law Dictionary* or an online glossary. For direct links, go to glencoe.com to find more vocabulary resources.

Figure 4.2 How Parties Reach Agreement

Unilateral Contract

Offer
Promise by offerer
↓
Agreement
↓
Acceptance
Act performed by offeree at offeror's request

Bilateral Contract

Offer
Promise by offerer
↓
Agreement
↓
Acceptance
Promise made by offeree at offeror's request

A contract may be unilateral or bilateral. *In which type of contract do both parties, the offeror and the offeree, make promises?*

glencoe.com

▲ USING VISUALS

⮕ Figure 4.2 How Parties Reach Agreement Answer In a bilateral contract, both parties make promises.

Activity Ask students to read the content of this figure and give examples of bilateral and unilateral contracts. A classic example of a unilateral contract is a reward advertisement placed on a bulletin board or in a newspaper. Explain to students that when they read an ad offering a reward for a lost item, a contract does not yet exist. The contract only comes into existence when the lost item is returned to the rightful owner. If the finder has no knowledge of the ad, the owner owes nothing to the finder.

TEACH (cont.)

Legal Talk

(bicycle; bicentennial, bifocal, bicultural, bilingual unify, uniform, unicorn, unique, univocal)

Ask students to practice their academic and legal vocabulary with the electronic flashcards available at the *Business and Personal Law* Online Learning Center through glencoe.com.

ASSESS

Independent Practice

Elements of a Contract

Tell students that Autoworld posted an ad for a Corolla with 72,000 miles on its Web site. Jody sends an e-mail to the business and says she will buy the car at the advertised price. When she arrives, she notices that the car has 78,000 miles on it. Ask students to describe which element of a contract is missing. (genuine agreement due to misrepresentation of the mileage)

RETEACH

Have students go to the *Business and Personal Law* Online Learning Center through glencoe.com to download free *Study-to-Go* content to their cell phones or PDAs.

RETEACH (cont.)

After You Read

Summarize offer, acceptance, genuine agreement, consideration, capacity, and legality

ASSESS

Self-Assessment

Have students go to the *Business and Personal Law* Online Learning Center through **glencoe.com** to take the Section 4.1 Practice Test.

CLOSE

Culminating Activity

Elements of a Contract

Your friend, Arkadi, has begun teaching contract law classes. Write a paragraph to explain the six elements of a contract in a way that will help Arkadi create his course outline. Include information on historical development of contract law.

---

says, "I'll sell you my DVD player for $150 if you give me the cash before noon tomorrow," he or she will not be **required** to keep the promise unless you hand over the cash before noon on the following day.

A reward offer is one of the most common instances of a unilateral contract. The acceptance of the reward offer must precisely comply with the offer.

> **Example** Anne Chen placed an ad in the local newspaper offering a reward for the return of her lost laptop computer. Ms. Chen's offer of a reward alone did not create a contract. The contract would come into existence only when someone returns the laptop. Ms. Chen would then owe the finder the reward.

Oral or Written Contracts

An oral contract is created by word of mouth and comes into existence when two or more people form a contract by speaking to each other. One person usually offers to do something, and the other party agrees to do something else in return. Most contracts are oral contracts of this nature.

Sometimes, however, it is desirable to put contracts in writing. A written contract assures that both parties know the exact terms of the contract and also provides proof that the agreement was made. A law, the Statute of Frauds, requires that certain contracts must be in writing to be enforceable.

After You Read

Summarize List the components of a legal contract.

SECTION 4.1 ASSESSMENT

Self Check

1. What are the differences among valid, void, and voidable contracts?
2. What are the differences between express and implied contracts?
3. What is a unilateral contract?

Academic Connection

Mathematics You recently borrowed $500 from a friend. You signed a contract that requires you to pay back one third of the loan every month for three months. How much will you have to pay back each of the first two months? How much will you have to pay back the third month?

> **THEORY** **Number and Operations: Using Fractions, Decimals, and Rounding** To figure out 1/3 of $500, divide 500 by 3 and round to the nearest cent. Remember to round numbers of 5 or more up and numbers less than 5 down. For example, $2.224 rounds to $2.22 and $2.226 rounds to $2.23. To get the payment for the third month, subtract the amounts for the first two months from 500.

 For more math practice, go to the Math Appendix.

Critical Thinking

Reward: Lost Backpack You lost your backpack and posted a $20 reward for it. If someone who did not know about the reward returned the backpack, would you be legally obligated to pay the reward?

Go to **glencoe.com** to check your answers.

SECTION 4.1 ASSESSMENT

Self Check

1. A valid contract is one that is legally binding. One that is void has no legal effect. A voidable contract is one that may be voided by one or more parties if the party so chooses.
2. An express contract involves words while an implied contract does not.
3. A unilateral contract is a one-sided contract in which one party makes a promise in exchange for an act.

Academic Connection

Mathematics
First and second month: $166.67; third month: $166.66

Critical Thinking

There is no legally binding obligation to pay a reward if the person who brings back the item is not aware of the reward offer.

NCLB Activity correlated to the Mathematics standard on page 80

How a Contract Begins

Reading Guide

Before You Read

Connect Businesses make offers to potential customers using a variety of methods. What are some ways you have received offers?

Focus on Ideas

A contract begins with a clear offer, which can be either accepted, changed, or terminated.

Take Notes

Create a graph like the one shown and use it to take notes as you read this section. Go to glencoe.com for tips on how to improve your note-taking skills.

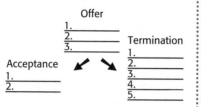

Offer
1. _____
2. _____
3. _____

Acceptance
1. _____
2. _____

Termination
1. _____
2. _____
3. _____
4. _____
5. _____

Key Terms

You will learn these legal words and expressions in this chapter. You can also find these terms in *Black's Law Dictionary* or in an online legal dictionary.

- invitations to negotiate
- mirror image rule
- counteroffer
- revocation
- rejection

Academic Vocabulary

You will find these words in your readings and in your tests. Look them up in a dictionary and familiarize yourself with them.

- definite
- specify
- impose

What You'll Learn

- ◆ Explain the requirements of a valid offer.
- ◆ Recognize the requirements of an acceptance.
- ◆ Distinguish the differences between an offer, an invitation to negotiate, an acceptance, and a counteroffer.
- ◆ Explain how offers are terminated.

Why It's Important

You need to know when an offer has been made and accepted for a contract to go into effect.

Academic Standards

Reading and completing the activities in this section will help you practice the following academic standards:

N C L B

English Language Arts (NCTE 9) Develop an understanding of and respect for diversity in language use, patterns, and dialects across cultures, ethnic groups, geographic regions, and social roles.

English Language Arts (NCTE 6) Apply knowledge of language structure, language conventions, media techniques, figurative language, and genre to create, critique, and discuss print and non-print texts.

R Reading Strategy

Read for Knowledge

1. **Survey** or preread the chapter.
2. **Question** or formulate questions before you read.
3. **Recite** or read your questions, answers and notes out loud.
4. **Review** or reread your notes.

Note-Taking Basics

- Listen attentively
- Have note-taking materials ready
- Skim through the lesson material
- Write down key words and ideas.
- Anticipate what comes next
- Review notes soon after taking them

FOCUS

Bell Ringer Activity

Ask students to take five minutes to brainstorm answers, and write each answer on the board. Tell students they will revisit these answers after studying this section.

Preteaching

Key Terms

Read the definitions and ask students to create a sentence using each term.

Academic Vocabulary

Explain that developing vocabulary is key to academic success.

- **definite** Adjective, from the Latin *de* + *finire* (to limit or to end). Means having distinct limits, with no uncertainty.
- **specify** Verb, from the Latin *specificare* (to name). Means to state in detail.
- **impose** Verb, from the Latin *in* + *ponere* (to put). Means to establish or apply by authority; or to take advantage of something or somebody.

Activity Ask students to give a verb, an adjective, or an adverb form that comes from each word.

 N C L B Connects to academic content

TEACH

Discussion Starter

Evaluate Intent

Describe the following situation to your students: Janine and Sedrick were joking about how difficult it was to get back in college after the summer break. Janine said she wished she were back at home and would sell all her books to the first person who gave her $100. Sedrick pulled out $100 and offered it to Janine for her books. Ask students if Janine should be required to sell her books to Sedrick. Lead a class discussion about serious intent.

As You Read

Predict As students read, they will learn that offers to enter into a contract are different from invitations to deal. Advertisements in newspapers are treated as invitations to negotiate. (The goal of predicting content is to encourage students to make guesses and focus their attention on the topic.)

C Critical Thinking

Invitation to Negotiate
Invitations to negotiate are often confused with genuine offers. Ask students if a price tag on a sale item is an offer or an invitation to negotiate. Lead a class discussion and then explain to the class that price tags, signs in store windows and on counters, and prices marked on merchandise are invitations to negotiate.

88

As You Read

Predict Are most advertisements in newspapers and magazines offers to enter into a contract?

Requirements of an Offer

How do you know if an offer is real?

The six elements of a contract form the heart of contract law. Understanding the elements of offer and acceptance is necessary before moving on to other matters, such as which contracts must be in writing, how contract rights are transferred, how contracts end, and what happens when one party breaches a contract. **An offer is a proposal by one party to another party to enter into a legally binding agreement.** The person making the offer is the offeror, and the person who receives the offer is the offeree. An offer has three basic requirements. It must be:

- made seriously
- definite and certain
- communicated to the offeree

Serious Intent

An offer must be made with the intention of entering into a legal obligation. An offer made in the heat of anger or as a joke would not meet this requirement. For example, a friend complaining about her unreliable car might say, "Give me five dollars and it's yours." This statement may sound like an offer, but your friend cannot be forced to sell her car for five dollars.

Often an invitation to negotiate is confused with an offer. **Invitations to negotiate are invitations to deal, trade, or make an offer.** Sellers usually have limited merchandise to sell and cannot possibly sell an advertised product to everyone who sees an ad. For this reason, most advertisements in newspapers, magazines, and catalogs are not treated as offers but as invitations to negotiate. If customers say they would like to buy an advertised item, they are actually making an offer to buy the item at the advertised price. The storeowner is free to accept or reject the offer. There are exceptions to this rule.

Invitation to Negotiate or Contract? This ad promotes summer sales for different goods. The sale promotion is for selected products only and is time specific. *Is this ad an invitation to negotiate or a contract? Explain your answer.*

88 Unit 2 Contract Law

▲ USING VISUALS

Invitation to Negotiate or Contract? **Answer** The REI ad is a contract because it is very definite (for example it applies only to specific dates). If an ad did not specify an end date to an offer or specific contract, it would be an invitation to negotiate.

The courts consider some advertisements as offers when they contain specific promises, use phrases such as "first come, first served," or limit the number of items that will be sold. In such cases, under the terms of the advertisement, the number of people who can buy the product becomes limited, making the advertisement an offer rather than an invitation to negotiate.

Price tags, signs in store windows and on counters, and prices marked on merchandise are treated as invitations to negotiate rather than as offers.

Definiteness and Certainty

An offer must be **definite** and certain to be enforceable. A landlord of an apartment with faulty plumbing might agree to pay a share of the cost if the tenant fixes the plumbing, but the court would not enforce the contract because it was not possible to determine what the parties meant by a share.

Communication to the Offeree

Offers may be made by telephone, letter, telegram, fax, e-mail, or by any other method that communicates the offer to the offeree.

Vocabulary You can find vocabulary definitions in the **Key Terms** glossary and **Academic Vocabulary** glossary in the back of this book.

Requirements of an Acceptance

How can you tell if an offer has been accepted?

The second element of a legally binding contract is acceptance of the offer by the offeree. As in the case of an offer, certain basic requirements must be met: the acceptance must be unconditional and must follow the rules regarding the method of acceptance.

American Airlines, Inc. v. FareChase, Inc.

Case No. 067-194022-02 (Texas, 67th Dist., Mar. 8, 2003).

FareChase, Inc., is a search engine whose customers are travel agencies. Its software scours—or scrapes—the Web sites of airlines, hotels, and car rental agencies to find the best rates. In February, 2003, American Airlines (AA) won an injunction against FareChase, alleging that FareChase scraped AA's site and took information without its permission. AA also claimed that FareChase violated the law of "trespass to chattels"—or interfering with someone's ownership of goods. Even though AA's Web site, AA.com, is a public site, its home page contains a statement restricting the use of the information on its site.

Ruling and Resolution
FareChase appealed the ruling on the grounds that the statement on AA's home page used a shrinkwrap or browsewrap agreement, which unfairly limits the use of facts. AA eventually settled with FareChase. According to the settlement, AA agreed to let FareChase search its site with some restrictions.

Critical Thinking Did FareChase have any type of contract with American Airlines? Do you think that FareChase did need a contract allowing the search of a public Web site? Why or why not?

Chapter 4   What Is a Contract?   **89**

American Airlines, Inc. v. FareChase, Inc.

Answer FareChase, Inc. had no contract, implied or express, with American Airlines, Inc. The search engine company did need a contractual agreement with American Airlines because it was using the company's proprietary information.

TEACH (cont.)

D Develop Concepts

Requirements of an Offer
Describe the three basic requirements of an offer: serious intent, definiteness and certainty, and communication to the offeree. Ask students to write down an offer that does not meet all three requirements on a sheet of paper. Have students exchange papers and ask the recipients of the offers to explain why they are not valid offers.

C Critical Thinking

Serious Intent Ask students why serious intent is a basic requirement of an offer. What would happen if it were not? (Answers may vary but should mention that without serious intent, offers would be made unintentionally and the offerees would have an unfair advantage.)

TEACH *(cont.)*

D Develop Concepts

The Mirror Image Rule
Ask the students to imagine that they want to purchase a house, but they cannot afford the price at which the house is listed. Ask them what would happen if they decided they wanted this house so badly that they signed a sales agreement even though they knew the price was beyond their means. Explain that on real estate and service contracts the acceptance must repeat the exact terms that are used in the offer.

Role Play
Art Clifford sent a letter to Marge and Norm Grayson offering to buy their home for $250,000. The Graysons, who had advertised their house at $280,000, wrote in reply, "We accept your offer. However, we would like the price set at $265,000."

Ask the students if they think this situation represents an unconditional acceptance. (The Graysons did not really accept Art Clifford's offer. Instead, they made a counteroffer, which Art is free to accept or reject. He may also choose to make a counteroffer of his own, agreeing to buy the home for an amount somewhere between $250,000 and $265,000. Then the initiative to accept or reject would fall back to the Graysons. This process would continue until the terms of the offer and the acceptance mirror each other.)

Unconditional Acceptance

The acceptance must not change the terms of the original offer in any way according to the mirror image rule. **The mirror image rule means that the terms stated in the acceptance must exactly mirror or match the terms of the offer.** Any change in the terms of the offer means the offeree has not really accepted the offer but has made a counteroffer. **A counteroffer is a response to an offer in which the terms of the original offer are changed.** In that case, the original offeror is not obligated to go along, and no contract results. Instead, the offeror becomes an offeree and may accept or reject the counteroffer.

Contracts for the sale of goods are exceptions to the mirror image rule. These exceptions include contracts for personal property such as clothing, furniture, food, motor vehicles, appliances, and other items. The primary exceptions are created by the Uniform Commercial Code (UCC), which is a set of statutes that covers the law of sales as well as other areas of commercial law. It was drafted to make trade among the states easier and has been adopted with minor variations by 49 states. Only Louisiana has not adopted all of its provisions.

Methods of Acceptance

The time at which an acceptance takes place is important because that is when the contract comes into existence. When the parties are dealing face-to-face or on the telephone, no special problem exists. One party speaks, and the other listens and communicates the offer or the acceptance.

Special rules, however, govern acceptances that take place when the parties are separated by a distance and must communicate by letters, telegrams, or fax. According to common law, an acceptance that must be sent over long distances is effective when it is sent. Any method of communication that has been expressly or impliedly endorsed by the offeror would qualify. Common law also says that an acceptance is implied when the offeree accepts by the same or a faster means than that used by the offeror.

The authorization of an acceptance can also be implied by any reasonable means, including past practices between the parties, the usual method in the trade, or the customary means in comparable transactions. Naturally, the offeree must correctly address the acceptance so that it is delivered to the right place. If the address is faulty, the acceptance is not complete until delivery has been made to the offeror. It is also possible for the offeror to **specify** the time by which the acceptance must be received to be effective.

This rule applies to contracts for real estate and services. For sale-of-goods contracts under the UCC, the acceptance takes place when it is sent, as long as the method of communication is reasonable. Consequently, the acceptance of a mailed offer for goods would be effective when it is sent electronically, via fax, or through an overnight carrier. If the offeror states in the offer what method the offeree must use to accept, that method must be followed.

Reading Check

Explain *What are the characteristics of an offer?*

✓ Reading Check

Explain Students should recall the three characteristics: serious intent, definiteness and certainty, and communication to the offeree.

ASSESS

Quiz
Ask students the following questions:

1. Who or what is an offeror? (the person making the offer)

2. Who or what is an offeree? (the person receiving the offer)

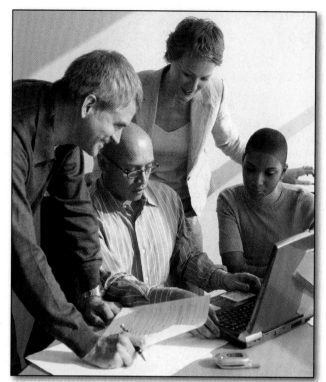

Sometimes, an offer specifies that it must be accepted by an action. In these cases, the action must take place before there is an acceptance. The offeror cannot **impose** silence on the offeree as the means of acceptance unless he or she has previously agreed to this condition or has allowed silence to signal acceptance in the past. In contrast, if the offeror has established silence as the means of acceptance, then he or she will have to live by that condition if the offeree accepts by remaining silent.

Termination of an Offer

Can you change your mind and withdraw an offer?

Even though an offer has been properly communicated to the offeree, it may be terminated. This termination may occur in any of five ways: revocation, rejection, counteroffer, expiration of time, and death or insanity.

Revocation

Revocation is the taking back of an offer by the offeror. The offeror has a change of mind or circumstances and decides to withdraw the offer before it has been accepted. Two important rules govern revocation: an offer can be revoked any time before it is accepted, and a revocation becomes effective when it is received by or communicated to the offeree.

Chapter 4   What Is a Contract?   **91**

Long Distance Acceptance Problems may arise when the acceptance of a contract must travel over long distances. *How can people make certain that an acceptance is valid and effective when it must travel to a distant location?*

RETEACH

Independent Practice

Offers and Invitations to Negotiate

Have students clip several advertisements from newspapers and divide them into groups: Offers and invitations to negotiate. Divide the class into groups and have each group present their ads and explain why each belongs in one category or another.

Case Study Practice

Offer or Invitation?
Read the following scenario to the students and then ask them if it constitutes a genuine offer or an invitation to negotiate:

An advertisement in the newspaper read: "Lava lamps, $49.98." James Darling went to the store the next day and said, "I would like to buy a lava lamp." The salesperson apologized and said the lamps had sold out within an hour after the store opened.

(This is merely an invitation to come in and make an offer.)

▲ USING VISUALS

Long Distance Acceptance **Answer** Students answer should reflect that one way to make certain that an acceptance is valid and effective when it is sent rather than when it is received is to operate face to face or on the telephone. It is best to send the acceptance by a properly authorized method.

RETEACH (cont.)

Guided Practice

Review

Remind students of their answers to each Discussion Starter question from the text. Post these answers again and review them with the class. Which answers were correct? Which answers were wrong? Each time determine why the answers were wrong and what the correct answer would be and why.

Review Key Terms

Encourage students to access the *Business and Personal Law* Online learning Center through **glencoe.com** and use the electronic flashcards to review the key terms.

Independent Practice

Sales Contracts in Other Countries

Assign students to research the laws regulating sales contracts in another country of their choice. Ask them to find out if that country has adopted laws similar to the special rules for sales contracts discussed in this chapter. Have students write a short paragraph summarizing their findings and ask them to be ready to share their research with the class.

Global Law

Entering Contracts in China

In the United States, a signed contract means that all parties know who will do what, with what level of quality, and by what deadline. Once the contract is signed, the parties move on to fulfill the contract, knowing that everyone will do their part. These rules do not exist in China. When people sign a contract there, they simply agree that they want to do business with one another, that the goals of the contract are desirable, and that the terms of the contract are reasonable. However, everyone knows that activities do not always happen as planned.

Camille Schuster, a consultant, speaker, and professor of marketing, international negotiations, and consumer-centered business practices, gives these guidelines for conducting business and managing contracts in China:

1 Maintain frequent, regular communication.

2 Asking "yes" or "no" questions will not generate useful information. You will be spared embarrassment, you will feel reassured, and you will know nothing. Instead of asking your Chinese contact if the production deadline will be met, try asking about significant events in the production process during the past week or month, or to describe recent activities of members of the production team.

3 Meet face-to-face. This is a relationship culture that requires personal, one-to-one commitment.

4 Represent all levels. Chinese culture is hierarchical and communication serves to preserve harmony. Problems are not freely discussed with superiors. Your team needs to include people at different levels of the hierarchy so that quality-control managers talk with other quality-control managers, and line engineers talk with other line engineers.

Across Cultures: The Importance of *Guanxi*

Guanxi *(gwan-shee)* means relationships. In the Chinese business world, personal connections are the basis for most business deals and contracts. It is very common for employees from one company to visit the residence of acquaintances from other organizations and bring gifts.

Critical Thinking: *What key contractual components are not included in Chinese contracts?*

Rejection

Rejection is a refusal of an offer by the offeree that brings the offer to an end. For example, if someone says to you, "I'll sell you my camera for $150," and you say, "I don't want it," then the offer has come to an end.

Counteroffer

A counteroffer ends the first offer. If someone says to you, "I'll sell you my camera for $50," and you say, "I'll give you $35 for it," no contract comes into existence unless the original offeror accepts your new offer. If you later say, "Okay, I'll give you $50 for the camera," you will be making a new offer, which the original offeror may accept or reject.

Expiration of Time

If the offeror sets a time limit for the acceptance of the offer, it must be honored. Assume that Bradley has offered to sell Franz his motorcycle for $1,745. Bradley tells Franz the offer will remain

---

Global Law

Entering Contracts in China

Answer Definiteness and certainty are missing components of the offer. Unconditional acceptance is also missing. There are issues related to abiding to the mirror image rule.

Activity Ask students to access the International Law section of the American Bar Association through **glencoe.com** and select one of the Web-based research guides. Ask the students to prepare a short review of their selected resource.

open until noon of the following day. To create the contract, Franz must accept within that time period.

If no time for acceptance is stated in the offer, it must be accepted within a reasonable time. Otherwise, no contract exists. What is a reasonable time depends on the circumstances. For example, a reasonable time to accept an offer for purchasing a truckload of ripe tomatoes would be different from a reasonable time to accept an offer for purchasing a house.

When an offeree pays money or other consideration to an offeror to hold an offer open for an agreed period of time, an option contract comes into existence. An option is a binding promise to hold an offer open for a specified period of time. It offers to the holder of the option the exclusive right to accept the offer within the agreed time, subject to the terms of the option. For example, you might offer a seller $50 to hold an offer open for two days. Such a contract is legally binding. For an entire contract to be completed, the option must be exercised by the person holding the option. This requires an absolute, unconditional, unqualified acceptance exactly according to the terms of the option.

Death or Insanity

If the offeror dies or becomes insane before the offer is accepted, the offer comes to an end. Although death ends an offer, it does not end a contract, except for contracts related to personal services.

After You Read

Summarize List the key requirements of an offer and of an acceptance.

RETEACH (cont.)

After You Read

Summarize An offer requires intent, certainty, and communication to the offeree. An acceptance must not change the terms of the offer.

ASSESS

Self-Assessment

Have students go to the *Business and Personal Law* Online Learning Center through glencoe.com to take the Section 4.2 Practice Test.

CLOSE

Culminating Activity

Negotiating a Contract

Ask one student to make an offer to another student to sell a product or a service. Ask the other student to make a counteroffer. Ask the two to make offers and counteroffers until there is an offer and an acceptance.

SECTION 4.2 ASSESSMENT

Self Check

1. What are the requirements of an offer?
2. What are the requirements of an acceptance?
3. When is an offer terminated?

Academic Connection

English Language Arts
Now that you have learned why contracts are so important in business life, imagine that you work as an executive manager for a company that outsources the manufacturing of electrical components to a company in China. Make sure you read the Global Law feature on page 92 and research contractual and communication issues between U.S. and Chinese businesses. Draft an e-mail memo addressed to the five mid-level production and marketing managers who have been asked to travel to China next month to make sure component production is going according to plan. Outline specific instructions and general advice on how to handle potential problems during the upcoming trip. Make sure your e-mail follows appropriate memo format.

Critical Thinking

Identifying an Offer
Why is it important to be able to distinguish between an offer and an invitation to negotiate?

 Go to **glencoe.com** to check your answers.

SECTION 4.2 ASSESSMENT

Self Check

1. serious intent, clear and definite terms, and communication to the offeree
2. unconditional and must follow the rules regarding the method of acceptance
3. upon revocation by the offeror, on rejection by the offeree, when a counter-offer is made, after the expiration of a set period of time, and/or the death or insanity of the offeror

Academic Connection

English Language Arts
Memos should include suggestions on how to watch out for missing contract elements and how to palliate those lackings.

Critical Thinking

Answers should include that an offer is part of a legally binding contractual agreement; invitation is not binding.

 Activity correlated to the English Language Arts standards on page 87

Summary by Sections

Ask students to read the summaries one key point at a time. Then, ask them to work in groups to create two examples to illustrate each key point.

Vocabulary Builder

Cooperative Learning

1. Have students work in groups to prepare their sentences. Ask the groups to exchange their sentences and assess each other's sentences.

Vocabulary Development

- Ask students to use a dictionary or to go online to look up the etymology of each key term listed.
- Then, ask students to list several words derived from the same root or origin. For example, *contract* has the same root as *contractual* or *contractually*.

Chapter 4 Review and Assessment

Summary

Section 4.1 Agreements and Contracts

- A contract is any agreement enforceable by law. The six elements of a contract are: offer, acceptance, genuine agreement, consideration, capacity, and legality.
- Valid contracts are legally binding. A void contract has no legal effect because at least one element is missing. A contract may be voided by one of the parties because of a defect.
- An express contract is stated in words. It may be written or oral. An implied contract is implied from the actions of the parties.
- Bilateral contracts are formed by promises that parties make to each other. A unilateral contract contains one party's promise that it will fulfill if and when the other party performs an act.
- Oral contracts are created when a party verbalizes a promise and the other party responds with a spoken promise. A written contract contains the promises in writing.

Section 4.2 How a Contract Begins

- An offer is a proposal by one party to another party to enter a contract. An offer must be (1) seriously intended, (2) definite and certain, and (3) communicated to the offeree.
- An invitation to negotiate may look like an offer, but it is not. Any such invitation cannot be made into an offer by agreeing to the terms of the invitation.
- An acceptance must meet two requirements: (1) it must be unconditional; and (2) it must follow the rules regarding the method of acceptance. Unconditional acceptances do not seek to change the terms of the original offer in any way.
- An offer must be accepted without change to its terms. If an offeree changes the terms of an offer, this is not an acceptance, but a counteroffer which the original offeree then may choose to accept or reject.
- An offer is terminated by revocation, rejection, counteroffer, expiration of time, death, or insanity.

Vocabulary Builder

❶ On a sheet of paper, use each of these terms in a sentence.

Key Terms

- contract
- offer
- acceptance
- genuine agreement
- express contract

- implied contract
- bilateral contract
- unilateral contract
- invitations to negotiate

- mirror image rule
- counteroffer
- revocation
- rejection

Academic Vocabulary

- determine
- assume

- require
- definite

- specify
- impose

Go to **glencoe.com** to play a game and improve your legal vocabulary.

 glencoe.com

Study Skills for Success

Prepare your Students for Studying

Tell students that they can improve their ability to understand and remember material from their courses by learning and practicing study skills. Remind students to:

- **Get motivated!** Motivation must come from within. To motivate yourself, think of ways in which what you learn now will fit into your long-term personal and professional goals.
- **Get organized!** Make studying part of your daily routine, not something you do at the last minute.
- **Concentrate!** Study in an environment that is as free of distractions as possible.

Key Points Review

Answer the following questions. Refer to the chapter for additional reinforcement.

2 Describe the formalist theory of contract law.

3 Explain the elements of legal contracts.

4 What are the exceptions to the mirror image rule?

5 When an acceptance is sent over a long distance, when does it become effective?

6 Under what circumstances is a contract voidable?

7 Why is it desirable to put some contracts in writing?

8 What two rules govern the revocation of contracts?

9 Explain the differences between bilateral and unilateral contracts.

Standardized Test Practice

10 Read this excerpt of the Uniform Commercial Code (UCC) and complete questions 1 and 2.

§ 1-103. Construction of UCC to Promote its Purposes and Policies: Applicability of Supplemental Principles of Law.

The UCC must be liberally construed and applied to promote its underlying purposes and policies, which are: (1) to simplify, clarify, and modernize the law governing commercial transactions; (2) to permit the continued expansion of commercial practices through custom, usage, and agreement of the parties; and (3) to make uniform the law among the various jurisdictions.

§ 1-105. Severability.

If any provision or clause of the UCC or its application to any person or circumstance is held invalid, the invalidity does not affect other provisions or applications of the UCC which can be given effect without the invalid provision or application, and to this end the provisions of the UCC are severable.

1. The purpose of the UCC is to

Ⓐ simplify criminal law

Ⓑ simplify and bring up-to-date the law that rules commercial transactions

Ⓒ create different rules for different jurisdictions

Ⓓ none of the above

2. The UCC section 1-105 on severability means that

Ⓐ if one section of the UCC does not apply to a case, all sections of the UCC are invalid

Ⓑ if a UCC provision does not apply, it can be severed and other provisions remain valid

Ⓒ no provision or clause can ever be severed, or set aside, from the UCC

Ⓓ all of the above

 Test-Taking Strategies Read the stem of the statement carefully, then read each of the answer options all the way through.

Key Points Review

2. Relies on the form of an agreement, examining the parties' actions and words to see if certain fixed elements existed. If they existed, the court would hold that a contract existed.

3. Elements of a legal contract are offer, acceptance, consideration, capacity, legality, and genuine agreement.

4. contracts for the sale of good and contracts for personal property such as furniture, clothing, foodstuff, motor vehicles, appliances, etc.

5. As long as acceptance is sent by authorized method of communication, it is effective upon sending.

6. if one party is a minor

7. to know the exact terms and provide proof of the agreement

8. An offer can be revoked at any time before accepted; a revocation becomes effective when received or communicated to the offeree.

9. Bilateral contracts are formed by promises between each party. Unilateral contracts contain one party's promise to fulfill certain terms if the other party performs an act.

Standardized Test Practice

10. B and B

Strategies for Test-Taking Success

Whether your students have a standardized test coming up in a few days or a few weeks, these last-minute test-prep tips and strategies will help them relax and do their best.

- **Test Format** Help students become familiar with the format of the test by practicing with test items that imitate the actual test items as closely as possible.

- **Test Timing** Have your students take timed practice tests so that they become comfortable with the length, design, and timing of the actual test.

Apply and Debate

Students should use chapter content to arrive at conclusions. The legal resolutions are listed below:

11. The e-mail is not legally an effective offer because the terms are too vague.

12. No. This was a moral or a social obligation. There was no consideration, so no valid contract existed.

13. No. An oral agreement involving a small amount of money is enforceable if it meets all other requirements of a valid contract.

14. No. Advertisements, as a rule, are considered invitations to negotiate rather than offers.

15. No. If an offer is accepted in the same manner of communication as was made, the contract is binding as soon as acceptance is met.

C Critical Thinking

Is There a Contract?
Tell students the following scenario: Tara and Victor had a deal. Each week, Victor cleans Tara's house. In return Tara pays Victor $50. For the past few weeks, however, Victor missed a few things. He forgot to dust the living room one week; another time he forgot to clean the oven. Tara was not happy and she deducted $10 from his fee. Victor argued Tara should not have deducted from his fee because they had a contract and his forgetfulness concerned minor things. Tara disagreed.

96

 Apply and Debate

Read the following scenarios. Get together with other students in pairs or groups of three and take a position on each scenario. Debate your position in class with students taking the opposite position or prepare a written argument justifying your position.

11 Twin Pines
The Galaxy Research Center e-mailed an offer to the owners of Twin Pines, a farm in rural Arkansas. The e-mail message stated: "Please consider this our offer to purchase between 9,000 and 11,000 acres of your 15,000-acre tract of farmland near Twin Pines, Arkansas. Our offering price is between $15,000 and $19,000 per acre. Respond ASAP."

You Debate | *Is this e-mail message a legally effective offer? Why or why not?*

12 Homecoming
Connie Adler agreed to go to the homecoming dance with Fred Wolfe. Later, Steve McNamara, the captain of the football team, asked Connie to be his date for homecoming. Connie broke her date with Fred to go to the dance with Steve.

You Debate | *Does Fred have a legal claim against Connie? Why or why not?*

13 Pocket Calculator
Bob Goodman made a verbal agreement to buy a pocket calculator from Howard Hermann for $35. When Hermann delivered the calculator, Goodman refused to accept it, stating that he was not bound by his verbal agreement.

You Debate | *Was Goodman correct? Why or why not?*

14 Waterbeds
Home Furniture Company advertised its waterbeds in a local newspaper. The newspaper mistakenly advertised the beds for $49 instead of $249.

You Debate | *Must Home Furniture sell the beds at the advertised price? Defend your position by citing which legal principle is involved and how it applies.*

15 Revocation
Victor Archer mailed an offer to Sally Miles. Sally mailed a properly addressed and stamped letter of acceptance ten minutes before she received a revocation from Victor.

You Debate | *Was the revocation effective? Defend your position by citing which legal principle is involved and how it applies.*

Debate Practice

- Do Tara and Victor have a valid contract? (No, communication to offeree and unconditional acceptance are missing.)

- Is it voidable (Yes. Key elements are missing.)

- What should happen if Victor forgets to do a few things? (Terms of the agreements should be negotiated.)

- If you were Tara, what would you do? (Tara and Victor should revise their arrangements and make sure that they agree on all terms and that the format of their agreement fulfills all contractual requirements.)

Case Study Practice – Heiman v. Parrish

16 **Is an Agreement a Contract?** In August of 1994, Jerod Heiman purchased a $9,033 diamond engagement ring. He then asked Heather Parrish to marry him. She said yes and took the ring. About a year later, in October 1995, Mr. Heiman broke off the engagement. Mr. Heiman asked Ms. Parrish to return the ring to him, but she refused. Mr. Heiman then sued her to retrieve the ring.

Ms. Parrish argued to the court that an engagement ring is a part of a contract between two parties to get married at a later date. She argued that Mr. Heiman broke off the engagement, breached the contract, and could not recover the ring.

Mr. Heiman argued that the proposal and engagement were not a binding contract but rather a statement that the parties would get married. The ring was a conditional gift to Ms. Parrish, which Ms. Parrish could keep if the two got married. Since the two did not get married, Mr. Heiman had a right to recover the ring.

Source: Heiman v. Parrish, 942 P.2d 631 (Kan. 1997)

Practice Was there a contract between Mr. Heiman and Ms. Parrish?

17 Ethics ←?→ Application

Reward or Not? Suppose you posted a reward notice that read, "Reward: $50 for the return of my lost iPod." Someone who did not know about the reward offer found your iPod and returned it to you.

◆ Would it be legal not to pay the reward money to the person who returned your iPod? Explain.

◆ Would it be ethical not to pay the reward money? Explain.

18 Internet Application

Find out About Contracts A youth group to which you belong plans to build a teen activity center. You and other members of the group are in charge of researching what the key contractual issues would be between the youth group and a contractor and how to go about writing a contract draft.

Go to **glencoe.com** to access the Web site sponsored by QuickForm Contracts and follow the instructions for the drafting of a hypothetical contract.

R **Reading Connection**
Outside Reading Go to **glencoe.com** for a list of reading suggestions about contracts.

 glencoe.com

Chapter 4   What Is a Contract?   **97**

←?→ Ethics Application

17. In the case of rewards and offers for the return of lost items, a contract comes into existence only when the lost item is returned to its owner. If the finder has no knowledge of the offer, the owner is not legally bound to give the reward. Answers about the ethical side of this question will vary but many students might argue that it would be ethical to pay the reward.

Internet Application

18. Make sure students remember all the necessary components of a contract and their definitions. Ask students to list all the components and to use that list as a rubric to check their work.

R Reading Strategy

Reading Connection

American Bar Association Resources

Go to the *Business and Personal Law* Online Learning Center through glencoe.com to find links for further readings that relate to this chapter. Ask students to read, review, and summarize the documents. Advise students to keep their reviews and summaries to use as reference material for their Unit Thematic project on pages 154–155.

Case Study Practice

16. The Kansas Supreme Court found there was no contract when gifts (such as engagement rings) are given in contemplation of marriage. Review the six components of a contract: offer, acceptance, genuine agreement, consideration, capacity, and legality. While a marriage constitutes a legal and binding contract, an engagement does not. There is no communication to the offeree of the circumstances under which the ring would be returned. There is no unconditional acceptance on the part of the offeree and therefore, there is no genuine agreement.

Plan Your Lesson Section by Section

NBEA	NATIONAL BUSINESS LAW STANDARDS
Section 5.1	• **Identify** categories of people who lack contractual capacity. • **Explain** the parole evidence rule. • **Explain** a minor's right to avoid a contract.
Section 5.2	• **Define** and distinguish between different types of consideration and list the exceptions to the requirements of consideration. • **List** the essential information that should be included in writing under the statute of frauds. • **Describe** the concept of unconscionability and compare it to legality.

NCLB	ACADEMIC STANDARDS	Activity/Feature
English Language Arts: NCTE 3 Apply a wide range of strategies to comprehend, interpret, evaluate, and appreciate texts.		*BusinessWeek* News, Case Study, Case Study Practice
English Language Arts: NCTE 9 Develop an understanding of and respect for diversity in language use, patterns, and dialects across cultures, ethnic groups, geographic regions, and social roles.		Global Law
English Language Arts: NCTE 6 Apply knowledge of language structure, language conventions, media techniques, figurative language, and genre to create, critique, and discuss print and non-print texts.		Legal Talk, ad copy, Key Terms, and Academic Vocabulary
Mathematics: NCTM PSS 2 Solve problems that arise in mathematics and in other contexts.		Section 5.1 Assessment, Section 5.2 Assessment
English Language Arts NCTE 2 Read a wide range of literature from many periods in many genres to build an understanding of the many dimensions of the human experience.		*BusinessWeek* News
English Language Arts: NCTE 10 Students whose first language is not English make use of their first language to develop competency in the English language arts and to develop understanding of content across the curriculum.		Key Terms, Academic Vocabulary, Legal Talk, Vocabulary Builder
English Language Arts: NCTE 1 Read a wide range of print and non-print texts to build an understanding of texts; to acquire new information; to respond to the needs and demands of society and the workplace; and for personal fulfillment.		Global Law
Social Studies: NCSS 2 Study the ways human beings view themselves in and over time.		Case Study, Global Law

Connect Your Business Law Classroom to the World of Work

This chart shows the 21st Century Skills, foundation skills, and workplace competencies that students develop as they work in this chapter.

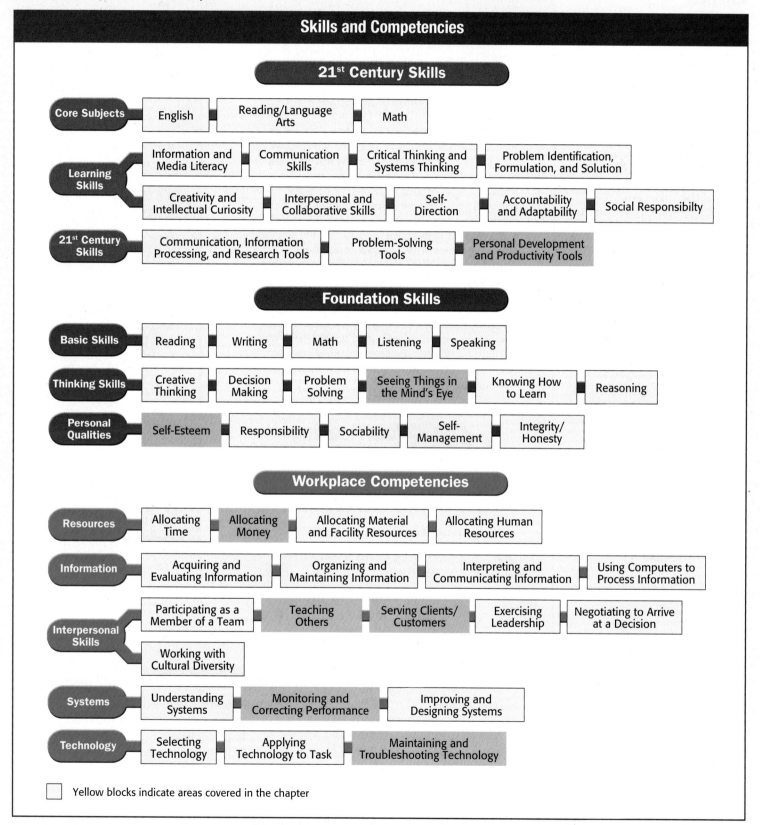

Skills and Competencies

21st Century Skills

Core Subjects
- English
- Reading/Language Arts
- Math

Learning Skills
- Information and Media Literacy
- Communication Skills
- Critical Thinking and Systems Thinking
- Problem Identification, Formulation, and Solution
- Creativity and Intellectual Curiosity
- Interpersonal and Collaborative Skills
- Self-Direction
- Accountability and Adaptability
- Social Responsibilty

21st Century Skills
- Communication, Information Processing, and Research Tools
- Problem-Solving Tools
- Personal Development and Productivity Tools

Foundation Skills

Basic Skills
- Reading
- Writing
- Math
- Listening
- Speaking

Thinking Skills
- Creative Thinking
- Decision Making
- Problem Solving
- Seeing Things in the Mind's Eye
- Knowing How to Learn
- Reasoning

Personal Qualities
- Self-Esteem
- Responsibility
- Sociability
- Self-Management
- Integrity/Honesty

Workplace Competencies

Resources
- Allocating Time
- Allocating Money
- Allocating Material and Facility Resources
- Allocating Human Resources

Information
- Acquiring and Evaluating Information
- Organizing and Maintaining Information
- Interpreting and Communicating Information
- Using Computers to Process Information

Interpersonal Skills
- Participating as a Member of a Team
- Teaching Others
- Serving Clients/Customers
- Exercising Leadership
- Negotiating to Arrive at a Decision
- Working with Cultural Diversity

Systems
- Understanding Systems
- Monitoring and Correcting Performance
- Improving and Designing Systems

Technology
- Selecting Technology
- Applying Technology to Task
- Maintaining and Troubleshooting Technology

Yellow blocks indicate areas covered in the chapter

Introduce the Chapter

Elements of a Contract
Contract law can be one of the most difficult areas of law to grasp. In this chapter, students will study the issues of capacity, legality, and consideration—all necessary elements to a binding contract.

Building Background
Ask students to raise their hands if they have ever signed a contract. Have them identify any contract-related legal protections available to minors that they are aware of. Tell them that minors are treated differently than legal adults in this regard.

BusinessWeek News

The Association of American Publishers (AAP) considers the protection of intellectual property in all media among its highest priorities. Tell students that it is estimated that American publishers lost over 500 million dollars last year due to copyright piracy.

Reading Strategy

Flex Your Reading

Reading printed documents is not the only form of reading required today. Reading materials online requires different skills. It is far easier to miss important details when scanning electronic versions of text. Students should also be aware that reading electronic documents is more tiring to the eyes.

BusinessWeek News

Harry Potter and the Cyberpirates
By Mira Serrill-Robins

Sales of *Harry Potter and the Half-Blood Prince,* the sixth book in J.K. Rowling's series, are scorching: More than 8.9 million copies moved in the first 24 hours of publication in the U.S. and Britain. But those are just the legal copies. Pirated electronic versions also are hot, with copying more frenzied than for any of the previous five Potter books. About 15,000 text and audio versions were downloaded during the first three days of release, says Web market-research firm BigChampagne. That's a remarkable pace for books, which aren't as popular with e-pirates as music or movies. Moreover, in this case, pirates had to scan 672 pages. BigChampagne found numerous links, including several attached to files using the free BitTorrent file-sharing program. One site turned up 258 items when the term *Harry Potter* was searched. Rowling, who hasn't OK'd electronic versions of her books, may have to conjure an anti copying spell.

Flex Your Reading

Efficient critical reading involves being flexible with speed and comprehension. There are several ways of reading critically, and you need to fit a reading style to your needs and to the material.

Go to **glencoe.com** for Flex Your Reading activities, more information on reading strategies for this chapter, and guided practice in reading contracts.

 glencoe.com

Classroom Resources

- Student Edition
- Teacher Wraparound Edition
- Student Activity Workbook with Academic Integration (SE/TAE)
- TeacherWorks™ Plus! CD
- *ExamView® Assessment Suite* CD
- *Presentation Plus!* CD

- National Mock Trial Championship DVD
- Online Learning Center with Podcasts at glencoe.com
- Study-to-Go™ at glencoe.com
- Online Student Edition
- Interactive Student Edition

Minors and Contracts Suppose you need to purchase a cell phone. *If you are under 18, can you sign an agreement, such as a wireless phone contract?*

99

Practice the Concept

Contracts

Ask students how often they think contracts come into play in daily life. List activities such as purchases of merchandise, posting an ad for a garage sale, or arrangements for services like haircuts or construction projects. Emphasize that contracts are a part of almost every facet of life, and that it is therefore important to understand what makes a contract legal.

Key Terms Many contract disputes involve a disagreement between the parties about what terms in the contract require each party to do or not do. Therefore, many rules of contract law relate to the interpretation of terms of a contract that are vague or ambiguous. Tell students that it is important to fully understand the terms of a contract before signing it.

The Fine Print Ask students to consider any contracts they may have entered into, such as video rental contracts or subscriptions to magazines. Contracts contain critical details in the "fine print." While many people sign contracts without reading the tiny print at the bottom of the contract, important information is given there.

▲ USING VISUALS

Minors and Contracts Answer Many states allow minors to sign a contract under certain circumstances, although minors have the ability to disallow some contracts if they change their mind. Companies are often hesitant to sign contracts with minors, since minors can disallow their contracts. Tell students that they will learn more later about the limitations and protections that apply to minors in the area of contracts.

FOCUS

 Bell Ringer Activity

Have students imagine that they have just won *American Idol*. Ask them if they think they would have the legal ability to sign a deal with a record label. (Use the discussion to introduce ideas of capacity and minority.)

Preteaching

Key Terms
Read the definitions and ask students to create a sentence using each term.

Academic Vocabulary

Explain that developing vocabulary is key to academic success. An efficient method to develop vocabulary is to study how words are formed.

- **assumption** Noun, from the Latin *assumptio* (adoption). Means the act of taking to or upon oneself.

- **usury** Noun, from the Latin *usura* (use). Means lending money and charging interest at an illegally high rate.

- **dispensing** Verb, from the Latin *dispensare* (to dispense). Means dealing out in parts.

Activity Ask students to give a noun, a verb, an adjective, or an adverb form that comes from each word.

 Connects to academic content

What You'll Learn

- ◆ Assess contractual capacity.
- ◆ Explain the statute of frauds and the parol evidence rule.
- ◆ List minors' contractual rights and responsibilities.
- ◆ Define legality and illegality.

Why It's Important

Understanding legality and capacity will enable you to assess and interpret contracts correctly.

Academic Standards

Reading and completing the activities in this section will help you practice the following academic standards:

N C L B

Social Studies (NCSS 2) Study the ways human beings view themselves in and over time.

Math (NCTM PSS2) Solve problems that arise in mathematics and in other contexts.

Reading Guide

Before You Read

Connect Does everybody have the same right to enter into any type of contract?

Focus on Ideas

Specific rules govern who can enter into contracts and whether a contract is legal, valid, or void.

 Take Notes

Create a graph like the one shown and use it to take notes as you read this section. Go to **glencoe.com** to find graphic organizers and tips on how to improve your note-taking skills.

Contractual Rights and Duties of Minors

Duties

Rights

 Key Terms

You will learn these legal words and expressions in this chapter. You can also find these terms in *Black's Law Dictionary* or in an online legal dictionary.

- capacity
- minor
- majority
- emancipated
- disaffirm
- ratification
- public policy
- Statute of Frauds

Academic Vocabulary

You will find these words in your readings and in your tests. Look them up in a dictionary and familiarize yourself with them.

- assumption
- usury
- dispensing

R

 glencoe.com

R ## Reading Strategy

Read for Knowledge

1. **Survey** or preread the chapter.
2. **Question** or formulate questions before you read.
3. **Recite** or read your questions, answers, and notes out loud.
4. **Review** or reread your notes.

Note-Taking Basics
- Listen attentively
- Have note-taking materials ready
- Skim through the lesson material
- Write down key words and ideas
- Anticipate what comes next
- Review notes soon after taking them

Requirements of Capacity

Can you think of some people who might not be able to enter into contracts?

For a contract to be valid, offer, acceptance, genuine agreement, capacity, legality, and consideration are required. Whenever people negotiate the terms of a contract, they assume that everyone has the power or capacity to do so. **Capacity is the legal ability to enter into a contract.** The **assumption** that another person has the capacity to contract is called rebuttable presumption. The law allows some people to say after the fact that they did not have the capacity to enter into a contract.

Contractual Capacity Rules and Limitations

According to the law, several types of people may have the right to disaffirm a contract: minors, people with mental impairments, and people under the influence of drugs or alcohol.

People with Mental Impairments People with mental impairments can argue that they cannot be bound by contract. A mental impairment could be an injury. It could be a physical problem that someone has had from birth. It could also be a psychological problem that was recently diagnosed. The law only says that if a person had a mental problem when he or she entered a contract, then that person may not be bound to the contract. The mental problem must have made it impossible for the person to understand what was going on when the contract was made. The law requires doctors, not lawyers or judges, to determine if someone is mentally impaired.

As You Read

Predict Can minors cancel contracts to which they have agreed?

 Contracts and Minors
Minors have rights and duties when it comes to contracts. They may, for example, change their minds and terminate a contract they have entered. However, they must be truthful about their age when making agreements. *How does this apply to buying movie tickets?*

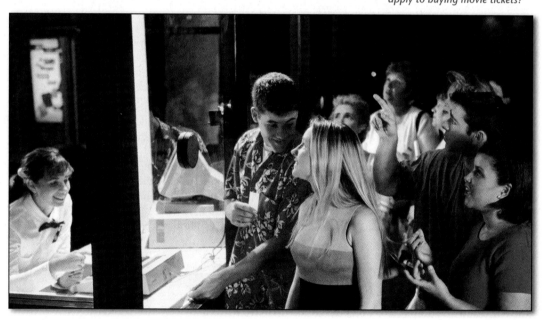

TEACH (cont.)

D Develop Concepts

Capacity Limitations
Remind students that *capacity* is the legal ability to enter into a contract. A party lacks capacity to contract if he or she does not have a full understanding of his or her rights and is lacking the mental capacity to understand the nature, purpose, and legal effect of the contract. Capacity-to-contract issues generally involve minors and mentally impaired and intoxicated persons.

Guided Practice

Mental Capacity

Ask students whether they think a severely depressed person has the capacity to contract. (Some students may believe that capacity is not hindered and that the person is still capable of making decisions. Others will suggest that the state of depression will impact their ability to make sound judgments.) Explain that such cases are not black and white. The degree to which an illness impacts the ability to make sound decisions is sometimes subjective and must be determined by a doctor.

Sometimes, people have a mental problem that is so severe they cannot take care of themselves. If the court decides that is the case, it will appoint a guardian for that person. The mentally impaired person's contracts are then declared void. This means that the person cannot make any contracts at all.

It is also possible that a contract made by a person with a mental impairment is perfectly valid. If the person was not suffering from the impairment when the contract was made or, if suffering from the impairment, the person still knew what he or she was doing at the time, then the contract is valid.

Minors Most of the time, minors are able to enter into and honor contracts. The law allows minors to get out of contracts. It considers them too inexperienced, immature, unknowledgeable, or naive to be permitted to enter into contracts without some sort of protection. If a minor does decide to get out of a contract, most adults choose not to fight it. To make contracts, there are a number of rules that minors must follow. Adults can also protect themselves from deceitful minors by refusing to enter into contracts with minors, unless parents also enter the contract. This approach is generally used for very expensive items such as cars. It protects the adult by obligating the parents if the minor tries to escape the contract. **A minor is a person who has not yet reached the age of adulthood.** Sometimes we say that a person who is still not an adult is in his or her minority. A person who has reached the age of adulthood is said to have reached his or her majority.

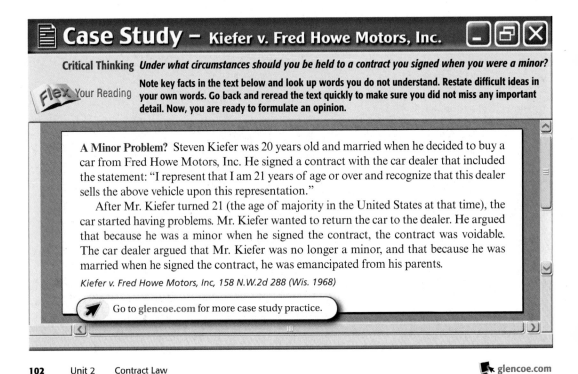

Case Study – Kiefer v. Fred Howe Motors, Inc.

Critical Thinking *Under what circumstances should you be held to a contract you signed when you were a minor?*

Flex Your Reading Note key facts in the text below and look up words you do not understand. Restate difficult ideas in your own words. Go back and reread the text quickly to make sure you did not miss any important detail. Now, you are ready to formulate an opinion.

A Minor Problem? Steven Kiefer was 20 years old and married when he decided to buy a car from Fred Howe Motors, Inc. He signed a contract with the car dealer that included the statement: "I represent that I am 21 years of age or over and recognize that this dealer sells the above vehicle upon this representation."

After Mr. Kiefer turned 21 (the age of majority in the United States at that time), the car started having problems. Mr. Kiefer wanted to return the car to the dealer. He argued that because he was a minor when he signed the contract, the contract was voidable. The car dealer argued that Mr. Kiefer was no longer a minor, and that because he was married when he signed the contract, he was emancipated from his parents.

Kiefer v. Fred Howe Motors, Inc, 158 N.W.2d 288 (Wis. 1968)

Go to **glencoe.com** for more case study practice.

Case Study

Kiefer v. Fred Howe Motors, Inc.

Answer The court held that the age of majority was 21 and, regardless of the circumstances, the contract was signed by a minor and thus voidable. The federal government has since lowered the age of majority to 18. As a rule, the law considers minors too immature to enter into contracts and normally will not be held to any contract signed. Minors can enter into contracts with a guardian's signature. However, it should also be noted that minors who misrepresent their age are committing fraud.

The age of majority is 18 in most states. Many states have made the drinking age 21, the age at which someone may legally purchase or consume alcohol. In most states, however, the age at which a person can legally purchase tobacco products is 18.

In the eyes of the law, people reach a particular age at the beginning of the day before their birthday. The law does not deal in fractions of days. One second after the clock strikes midnight means that the entire new day has been counted by the law. On your eighteenth birthday, you are legally considered eighteen and one day old.

An emancipated minor is one who is no longer under the legal control of his or her parents. Emancipated minors are responsible for their own contracts. Minors are automatically emancipated when they get married or set up their own households. Minors may also seek a court's permission for emancipation by suing for emancipation.

Minors who claim to be adults are committing fraud. In some states, when minors lie about their age and then insist on getting out of a contract, the other parties may sue for fraud. All five elements of fraud (see Chapter 6) must be proven for such a lawsuit to succeed. Other states still follow a much older rule that says minors cannot be sued for fraud, even if they lie about their age. These states still see it as a criminal offense when minors lie about their age to get age-restricted products, such as cigarettes and alcohol.

Intoxicated Persons People who are under the influence of drugs or alcohol can sometimes get out of a contract. Persons claiming intoxication must have been so impaired that they did not know what they were doing when they entered the contract. This decision is made by a judge or a jury.

Other Limits on Capacity In a few states, convicts have a limited capacity to contract. Aliens, citizens of other countries living in the United States, may also have limited contractual capacity. In wartime, foreign-born people identified as enemy aliens may be denied certain legal capacities.

The law makes exceptions when contracts involve necessaries such as food, clothing, shelter, medical care, and other things a person needs to live. It is up to a judge or a jury to decide whether a particular item is necessary.

Rights and Duties of Minors

Contracts made by minors are voidable by the minor. This means that minors have the right to disaffirm, or avoid their contracts if they choose. **To disaffirm a contract means to show the intent not to live up to the contract.** This intent can be shown by action or by statement. Minors can disaffirm contracts even when they have used poor judgment.

Returning Goods Minors who still have the goods they purchased when they disaffirm sales contracts must return those goods within a reasonable time. What reasonable time is, is decided by a judge or jury.

Chapter 5   Elements of a Contract   **103**

TEACH (cont.)

D Develop Concepts

Age of Majority Ask students what it will mean when they "reach their age of majority." (reaching the age of adulthood: 18 in most states) Explain that for legal purposes, a person reaches a particular age at the beginning of the day before his or her birthday.

Guided Practice

Emancipation

Ask for a volunteer from the class to read the definition of *emancipation* from the dictionary. (freeing someone from the control of another) Have students list conditions under which a minor might be emancipated from his or her parents. (set up his or her own household, get married, suing for emancipation)

Independent Practice

Misrepresentation of Age

Tell students that a minor has lied about his age to an adult for the purpose of buying alcohol or cigarettes. Ask students how they think the law sees this action. (Some states see this as a criminal offense. Some states may allow the seller to sue the minor for fraud if all five elements of fraud can be shown.)

Extending the Content

Capacity Limitations for Workers from Other Countries

The worldwide surge in technology has created a need for workers in the high-tech field. Companies now often recruit workers from other countries on the H-1B visa program.

These workers are hired on for lower wages than would be paid to U.S. individuals. Ask students what benefits or detriments they see to hiring skilled workers from other countries. (Answers may include the benefits of lower wage expenses to the companies, but disadvantages may include the loss of jobs for U.S. workers.)

TEACH (cont.)

D Develop Concepts

Disaffirming Contracts
Explain to students that disaffirming a contract has various implications for a minor.

- Returning Merchandise: If the minor still has the merchandise, he or she must return it when disaffirming the contract.

- Disaffirming Whole Contracts: Minors must disaffirm all or none of a contract they have entered into. They may not be selective about what they choose to change.

- Disaffirming Contracts Made with Other Minors: When two minors contract, both have the right to disaffirm.

Reading Check

Enumerate Ask students to reflect on driving laws and local ordinances that might make a contract void. (Individuals should be aware of statutes regarding the age of maturity, citizenship, and mental capacity.)

Guided Practice

Ratification

Ask students to explain how contracts are commonly agreed to. (in writing, by actions, or by spoken words) Explain that a minor can decide to ratify a contract after becoming an adult. Once this is done, the contractual rights he or she had as a minor are gone.

104

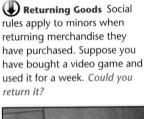

Reading Check

Enumerate *What statutes that affect capacity should you be aware of when entering a contract?*

The more perishable the goods, the less time will be considered reasonable. The minor can give back the goods by actually handing the goods over to the other party or by making an offer to do so. In some states an amount can be deducted for damaged, dirty, tattered, and torn items that the minor returns. Young people can also disaffirm a contract after becoming an adult. They must do this within a reasonable amount of time. Sometimes, even minors who no longer have the goods can get out of their agreements.

Disaffirming Contracts Minors cannot pick and choose the parts of the contract they want to keep and those they want to disaffirm. When two minors make a contract with each other, both of them can get out of the contract. Minors are, therefore, at risk when they enter a contract with another minor.

D If an adult discovers that the other party is a minor, the adult has no right to get out of the contract for that reason alone. Sometimes, people buy goods from somebody who bought the goods from a minor. If the minor then decides to get out of the original contract, the ownership rights of the innocent third party are protected. This rule applies only to goods, not to land.

Ratification of a Minor's Contracts **Ratification is the act of agreeing to go along with a contract that could have been avoided.** A person can ratify a contract by words or actions. The words can be spoken or written. A minor can ratify a contract after becoming an adult. Once this is done, all the contractual privileges that the person had as a minor are gone. If a minor makes a payment that is due under a contract after becoming an adult, that minor has ratified the contract.

Returning Goods Social rules apply to minors when returning merchandise they have purchased. Suppose you have bought a video game and used it for a week. *Could you return it?*

Exceptions to the General Rule The law may use exceptions to the rule that lets minors get out of their contracts. For example, minors must pay the fair value of the necessaries. Some states will hold minors to contracts for things required by law, such as car insurance. Some states give limited capacity to minors who own businesses. Other states say that married minors are adults. Others treat an apartment rental agreement as a contract for a necessary. Minors also cannot get out of military enlistment agreements.

Minors as Drivers Driving is a privilege, not a right. As a privilege, it must be earned, and then kept under conditions of good behavior. Many states will not permit minors to earn a license until they reach the age of 16.

▲ USING VISUALS

Returning Goods **Answer** Minors must return merchandise they bought and have in their possession when they disaffirm the contract. If the minor cannot return the merchandise, then he or she must pay the reasonable value of the merchandise. Upon return of merchandise, all consideration received from the minor must be returned. Two legal theories are applicable in this case: the "infancy doctrine" protects minors from their own lack of judgment, and the "benefit rule" holds that return of the full purchase price is subject to a deduction for the minor's use of the merchandise when the contract is disaffirmed.

Minors must also meet certain minimum requirements before earning a license. The requirements generally include a written test to qualify for a temporary driving permit, a driver's education course, and a final examination that consists of a road test and a vision exam. A minor with a driver's license generally has the same rights and responsibilities as an adult driver.

Minors as Students Students in a school setting may be searched if school officials have reason to suspect the law or a school rule has been broken. While adult speakers and writers are granted freedom in how they can express themselves in speech or in print, students may be restrained from printing certain matters in a school-sponsored newspaper.

The Rights and Duties of Parents and Guardians

Parents have certain rights under the law. They have the right to discipline their children and to manage their children's property. Adoptive parents have the same rights. Neither natural nor adoptive parents can abuse those rights.

The law protects children from abusive parents under the *parens patriae* doctrine. This doctrine holds that the state can act as a child's parent when natural or adoptive parents cannot or will not perform their parental duties.

The law also states that both natural and adoptive parents have the duty to provide their children with necessaries. If minors are forced to purchase the necessaries on their own, the parents will be liable for that contract. If a minor becomes emancipated, parental duties come to an end.

In their wills, parents may name guardians for their minor children. Two types of guardians can be appointed by the parents. Guardians of the child will act as the parents would act in relation to the child. Property guardians will handle the child's property. This right ends when the child reaches the age of majority.

Legality

Is a contract valid if one of its terms breaks the law?

Illegality can destroy an otherwise valid contract. It can also expose people who agree to the contract to potential charges of criminal conduct and other legal consequences. While most laws are widely known and understood, there are many laws against doing things that are not so obvious, such as having a yard sale without a license. These laws create what is called a hidden dimension of illegality.

Effect of Illegality

In general, a court will not help any party to an illegal contract. Instead, it will leave the parties where they put themselves. Neither party can enforce the agreement. Neither party can get help from the court. An exception is made when the parties are not equally at fault. In such cases, the court may help people who are less at fault in getting back any money or property they may have lost.

Legal Talk

Illegal: *adj* Against the law. From Latin *il* = not + *leg*, *lex* = law: not lawful.
In pari delicto: Latin adverbial phrase = in equal fault.

Vocabulary Builder *Il, im, in,* or *ir* at the beginning of a word (that is, as a prefix) often means not. List five words that begin with these prefixes and define them using the word not. For example, improper = not proper.

Look It Up! Check definitions in *Black's Law Dictionary* or an online glossary. For direct links, go to **glencoe.com** to find more vocabulary resources.

TEACH *(cont.)*

D Develop Concepts

Rights of Parents and Guardians Ask students to describe the rights that they think parents have in regard to their children. (discipline, manage children's property) Explain that the law protects children from abuse under the *parens patriae* doctrine. Have students list the types of duties expected of parents by law. (to provide necessaries)

C Critical Thinking

Minors as Drivers Ask students whether they think driving is a right or a privilege. (privilege) Have students describe the requirements to earn a driver's license and to keep it. (age 16, depending on the state, pass written test, driving course, vision exam, road test)

Legal Talk

(*illegible*, not legible; *illegitimate*, not legitimate; *immaterial*, not important; *impossible*, not possible; *irrelevant*, not relevant)

Ask students to practice their academic and legal vocabulary with the electronic flash cards available at the *Business and Personal Law* Online Learning Center through glencoe.com.

U Universal Access

Bodily/Kinesthetic Learners Students who learn by hands-on methods will benefit from the role play of legal situations. Create index cards with various roles for your students to play. Examples include: a minor who has contracted with an insurance agent to purchase insurance; insurance agent; a minor who has lied about his or her age to rent an apartment; an apartment manager; the judge who will hear the disputes between the insurance agent, the apartment manager, and the minors involved. Guide students through the situations by asking questions such as "Can this contract be voided?" "Can the adults in these situations sue for fraud?"

TEACH (cont.)

Guided Practice

Divisible Contracts

Tell students that Jimmy Connor, a truck driver, agreed to drive nonstop from Vermont to Arizona to deliver a shipment. Regulations prohibit drivers from driving more than eight hours without a layover and rest. Jimmy's nonstop trip would take more than eight hours. Ask students whether this contract can be divided into a legal segment. (Yes. The main purpose of the agreement, to deliver the goods, is legal, and can be separated from the illegal part. Jimmy should be paid for delivering the goods because that part of the contract is valid.)

C Critical Thinking

Usury Explain that the term refers to charging more than the legal rate of interest for "using" money. Ask students why some lenders may attempt to charge more than the rate of legal interest to some individuals. (Individuals who are in need of money may not be able to secure loans from reputable lenders, so they seek out less-than-reputable sources.)

Illegality in Entire Agreement Sometimes, a contract cannot be divided into separate promises and different acts. If a contract cannot be divided, then anything illegal within the contract makes the entire contract illegal. The whole contract is, therefore, void. This is true even if sections of the agreement are legal.

***In Pari Delicto* and Divisible Contracts** If certain promises and actions in a contract can be performed by themselves, the contract is divisible. The courts may enforce parts of the agreement that are legal and cancel the parts that are not.

The parties are said to be in pari delicto (in equal fault) if they both know that the agreement is illegal. In that case, the court will not help either party. On the other hand, if one party is not aware of the illegality and had no intent to break the law, then the parties are not in pari delicto. The courts may grant relief to the innocent party.

Agreements That Break Statutes

State legislatures pass laws that make some agreements illegal because they violate the state's civil or criminal statutes, **usury** statutes, gambling statutes, licensing statutes, or Sunday statutes.

Civil and Criminal Statutes Agreements that require one party to commit a tort or a crime are illegal. Common torts are slander, libel, and fraud. Crimes include burglary, larceny, murder, and arson. An agreement is illegal if it is made to interfere with or to violate the rights of another person. Agreements to protect one party from the consequences of the torts or the crimes he or she has committed are also illegal.

Usury Statutes A contract to buy stolen goods or commit arson is obviously illegal. Usury, however, is an example of an activity that has the hidden dimension of illegality. Interest is the fee a borrower pays to a lender for using money. Usury is charging more than the maximum legal interest rate. Each state has a statute that sets a maximum interest rate that lenders can charge for loans. Charging whatever you want for interest is not only unfair, it is also illegal.

The Truth in Lending Act is one step the federal government has taken to make consumers aware of the cost of borrowing money. Under this law, the lender must clearly report the annual percentage rate (APR) to the borrower. Before you sign any loan agreement or credit card, look for the true rate of interest (APR).

Gambling Statutes Gambling statutes fall within the hidden dimension of illegality: Playing cards, betting on sports events, or entering an office pool for money may seem harmless, but they are illegal in many states. If you win money gambling but have trouble collecting, the court will not enforce the debt, and may consider you to be in violation of the law.

Today, many types of regulated gambling are legal. A state may legalize one form of gambling and outlaw others. One form of gambling might be legal in one state but not in another.

106 Unit 2 Contract Law

Guided Practice

Gambling Statutes

Tell students to imagine that they entered a football pool with friends. The organizer of the pool refused to pay the winner. Ask students if they think a court would enforce the debt. (In most states, the court will not enforce an illegal contract, and players may be considered in violation of the law.)

Extending the Content

State Statutes

Ask students to perform research on statutes for your state. Have them select one statute or code of particular interest to them and prepare a summary of its purpose. (Most states have statutes regarding alcohol, labor, education, and utilities.)

Giveaway games by stores or businesses for promotion are legal as long as you are not required to buy a ticket or product to participate. Betting at racetracks is allowed in New York, Illinois, California, Massachusetts, Ohio, and some other states. Lotteries, other than those run by the state government, are still illegal in many places. Many states have set up their own state-run lotteries to raise money.

Sunday Statutes In early colonial days, some American colonies passed special Sunday statutes, also called blue laws, that made agreements made on a Sunday void. An offer made on a day other than Sunday, but accepted on a Sunday, is void. If an offer is made on a Sunday but accepted on another day, the contract is valid because acceptance marks the creation of the contract. If an agreement is made on a Sunday, but a date other than Sunday is placed on the agreement, the contract is void. States that still observe Sunday laws often apply the same restrictions to legal holidays.

Licensing Statutes All states have statutes that require a license to do certain jobs. A license is a legal document that grants permission from the government to do a certain job. Licenses protect people from dealing with unqualified persons. Trade and professional people such as nurses, doctors, lawyers, funeral directors, barbers, and plumbers must be licensed. An agreement made with an unlicensed person working in such jobs is illegal. Some state statutes require licenses simply to raise money. Any person who pays the fee gets a license. A law requiring a vendor's (seller's) license is designed to raise revenue for the local government that issues the license. In these cases, agreements made with unlicensed people are valid. However, the unlicensed person might be fined.

Special Statutes Doctors and most people in medical professions have to obtain and display a license to practice medicine. *What is the purpose of licensing medical personnel?*

TEACH (cont.)

Extending the Content

Latin Legal Terms

Explain to students that Latin is often still used in the legal system today. Have students look up the following Latin terms using an online Latin dictionary:

- *Non Compos Mentis* (not sound in mind)
- *In Curia* (in open court)
- *Bona Fide* (in good faith)

Guided Practice

Licensing Statutes

Tell students that Carl Williams, a handyman, agreed to construct a patio for Cindy Troy. He is required to pay a $50 fee to the city for a construction permit but he fails to apply for the permit. After the job is finished, Cindy learns that Carl did not secure the permit, and she refuses to pay him for the job. Ask students whether Cindy is justified in her refusal to pay. (No. Under the licensing statutes, she must pay Carl for the job. The $50 fee is a revenue fee for the city. Carl may be fined for failure to pay the fee.)

▲ USING VISUALS

Special Statutes Answer A license authorizes a professional to work through the issuance of a legal permit or formal permission from a constituted authority. Licensing is a required governmental process that protects the public from potential harm caused by individuals who are practicing their profession without official authorization. Medical personnel are at higher risk of causing harm to the public, as they interact directly with the health and safety of the public, and the consequences of a potential error can be very serious.

Activity Ask students to research which trades or professions require licensing in your state.

TEACH (cont.)

D Develop Concepts

Restraint of Trade Discuss with students what they think *restraint of trade* means. Then have a volunteer find its definition in the text. (limitation on the full exercise of doing business with others) Point out that the law tries to protect the rights of persons to do business freely in a competitive market. If persons enter into contracts that take away these rights, the law will restore the rights to them.

W Writing Support

Public Policy Ask students to identify the kinds of regulatory powers that belong to the federal and state governments. (health, safety, welfare of the public and public morals) Ask students to write one paragraph on why this public policy benefits society as a whole.

Guided Practice

Restrictive Covenant

Explain to students that when a business is sold to another person, the buyer is also purchasing the seller's goodwill and customer base. The seller will often agree not to open a competing business within a certain area for a period of time. Ask students if they think a court would enforce this agreement. (Yes. Restrictive covenants should include a reasonable geographic area and time frame.)

Agreements Contrary to Public Policy

W Not all illegal agreements break statutes. Some agreements are illegal because they break public policy. The power to regulate the public's health, safety, welfare, and morals belongs to the government. The states have this power because they have governmental authority. The federal government has this power because of the U.S. Constitution. **Public policy is a legal principle that holds that nobody should be allowed to do something that harms the public.** Public policy allows the courts to get involved to protect the public welfare when other laws do not.

Agreements That Unreasonably Restrain Trade

D The law protects the right to make a living. If a contract takes away this right, the law will label the contract void. Restraint of trade agreements take away somebody's ability to do business with others. Three types of contracts circumvent this rule: agreements not to compete, agreements to fix prices, and agreements to defeat competitive bidding.

Agreements Not to Compete

When someone buys a business, that person also buys the seller's goodwill not to compete. One way to ensure goodwill is to add a restrictive covenant to a sales contract. A restrictive covenant not to compete is an agreement in which the seller promises not to open a business that competes with the buyer within a certain area for a period of time.

⤓ Bidding for Public Works Contracts It is illegal for contractors to engage in any type of price fixing when bidding for public works contracts. *Why does this rule protect the public?*

▲ USING VISUALS

➔ Bidding for Public Works Contracts **Answer** Price fixing occurs when competitors agree on certain price ranges within which to set their prices. Price fixing discourages competition and raises prices. Competitors who seek to fix prices may be prosecuted by state or federal agencies under the Sherman Act and antitrust laws.

Activity Ask students to research methods of price fixing. (Selling at a common price, buying raw material from the suppliers at a certain "maximum" price, offering standard credit terms to purchasers, and establishing uniform costs are some of the methods.)

A court will uphold this agreement, which keeps it out of the hidden dimension of illegality if it is reasonable in time, location, and type of business. If the restraint is unreasonable considering the nature of the business sold, then the restraint is illegal. Promises not to compete are also found in employment contracts. Employees agree not to work at similar jobs for a period of time after they leave this employment. Such contracts are enforced only as needed to protect the former employer.

Agreements for Price Fixing In the United States, some laws have been created to protect competition. Price fixing is when competitors agree to set prices within certain ranges. In some cases, competitors agree to sell a particular product or service at an agreed price. In other cases, manufacturers dictate the price at which retailers must sell a product. Price fixing hurts competition and keeps prices artificially high. Because they are contrary to public policy, the courts will not uphold price-fixing agreements. In fact, competitors who seek to fix prices may be prosecuted by state or federal agencies.

Agreements to Defeat Competitive Bidding A bid is an offer to buy or sell goods or services at a stated price. Laws often require governments to construct public works or buy goods and services through competitive bidding. In this process, competitors submit bids for a project, and the the lowest qualified bid wins the contract. If competitors agree not to bid lower than a certain price, then they are not bidding competitively. The agreements and the contracts are not enforceable.

Agreements to Obstruct Justice A contract that gets in the way of the **dispensing** of justice is illegal. Such contracts include protecting someone from arrest, encouraging lawsuits, giving false testimony, or bribing a juror. It also includes an agreement to pay a non-expert to testify at a trial. It could also include an agreement to take money to stop a legal action against a person who has committed a crime.

Agreements Inducing Breach of Duty or Fraud Many persons hold positions of trust and have a responsibility for the well-being of others. Your representative in Congress, your state senator, and all other public officials hold positions of trust. They owe a duty to work for the best interest of the public. Any contract that tries to influence these people for private gain is unenforceable. This rule also applies to private persons who are in positions of trust.

Agreements to Give Up the Right to Litigate or Arbitrate Contracts may include clauses that limit the ability of the parties to bring a lawsuit or to arbitrate a claim. Sometimes, such clauses are valid. However, they might be offered on a take-it-or-leave-it basis by the party with the most power. The clause must be fair. If it is not, the court might say it is unconscionable and strike it down as illegal.

TEACH (cont.)

C Critical Thinking

Price Fixing Tell students to imagine that Whitehall Ski Rental Company and SlopeZone Ski Rental Company are located in the Denver area. They have agreed to price their services at the same rates so that one company does not offer more competitive prices than the other. This way customers can choose either company based on other criteria but not on price. Ask students if this pricing agreement is legal and if it can be enforced. (No. Price-fixing agreements are not enforceable because they are contrary to public policy.)

Guided Practice

Obstruction of Justice

Ask students if they have ever heard the phrase "obstruction of justice" on a television show or in a newscast. If so, have them describe what they think the phrase means. (hiding key evidence from police, withholding knowledge of a crime or suspects, keeping police from solving a crime) Explain that any contract that causes obstruction of the justice system is illegal.

Extending the Content

Breach of Duty

Explain to students that any contract that tries to influence public officials or private citizens in a position of trust to use their position for private gain is unenforceable. Ask students to research whether any local or state officials (e.g., city council or state representatives, judges, county commissioners) have been associated with cases involving breach of duty.

U Universal Access

Language Deficiencies If students do not understand the concept of an agreement to defeat competitive bidding, have them role-play the positions of a government department and competing vendors. Have the "vendors" agree not to bid less than a certain price. Then identify how the department and the public interest would lose out.

TEACH (cont.)

C Critical Thinking

Interfering with Marriage
Remind students that a contract that interferes with good family relationships is illegal. Ask students to discuss whether they think a prenuptial agreement might interfere with a good family relationship. Explain that a prenuptial is an agreement that outlines what each party is or is not entitled to if the marriage were to fail. (Courts generally uphold such contracts.)

Guided Practice

Statute of Frauds

Emphasize that certain types of contracts must be in writing. These contracts are governed by the Statute of Frauds. Ask students why certain contracts must be in writing. (clarifies an agreement for both parties and for the court, especially in situations dealing with large sums of money or detailed transactions)

Extending the Content

Standard Contracts

Ask for volunteers to interview attorneys, real estate agents, or insurance agents about the standard printed contracts they use. If possible, have students bring a blank copy of such agreements to class. They may be able to download certain contracts from the Internet.

110

C Agreements Interfering with Marriage Contracts that discourage, damage, or destroy good family relationships are illegal. For instance, if Mr. Popson promises to give his daughter, Angela, $100,000 if she never gets married, the contract is void.

The Statute of Frauds

What happens if you want to make changes to a contract after you agreed to its terms?

In the past, under common law rule, a person accused of breaking a contract could not testify about it in court. Instead, only people who were not parties to the contract could testify. This encouraged bribery. To prevent this, the English Parliament passed a law in 1677 that required certain contracts to be in writing in order to be enforceable. The law was called An Act for the Prevention of Frauds and Perjuries.

Global Law

Contract Differences in Canada

The United States and Canada have a legal tradition based upon English common law. Many of their legal principles, including those dealing with contracts, are similar. Some differences have occurred since the two countries gained their independence from England. Two major differences relate to entering into noncommercial oral contracts and the elements of proving fraud in a contract dispute.

Oral Contracts

In the United States, oral contracts are considered as valid as written contracts for almost everything except the sale of real estate.

In Canada, however, there is a presumption that people do not enter into oral contracts for non-business, religious, or charitable reasons. This includes entering into contracts with family members and friends.

This is demonstrated in a case in which a Canadian court held that an agreement entered into by friends to share a set of season hockey tickets was not a valid oral contract because it was not for business reasons.

Fraud

Another contract law difference between the United States and Canada relates to fraud. In the United States, the parties must prove that the victim suffered an actual loss from the fraud in order to recover losses. In Canada, a loss is not required to recover damages against the perpetrator of the fraud. This can be especially advantageous when the victim wishes to rescind or cancel a contract before harm occurs.

Across Cultures: Quebec's Legal System

Most Canadian provinces have a common law system. However, Quebec has a civil code system inherited from the French; so does the state of Louisiana in the United States.

Critical Thinking *Would an oral agreement between neighbors for splitting the cost of a fence be considered a valid oral contract in Canada? In the United States?*

Global Law

Contract Differences in Canada

Answer In Canada it is possible that a contract between neighbors would not be enforceable. The Canadian courts are not eager to recognize oral contracts between parties that are presumed to be social friends. There is a presumption that friends enter into agreements all the time without expecting to be bound by the arrangements. However, in the United States, there is more of a presumption that if the parties agreed to terms such as splitting the cost of a fence, and one party acted upon that assumption, then a valid oral contract would exist.

Today, most states in the United States now have a Statute of Frauds. **A Statute of Frauds is a state law that requires that certain contracts be in writing.** This is so there is evidence that (1) the contact exists, and that (2) it has certain definitive terms.

Elements of a Written Contract

A written contract can be a letter, a sales slip, an invoice, or several words placed on a check. There are some specific requirements. The written contract must, for example, identify the place, date, parties, subject matter, price and terms, and intent of the parties. It should also contain the signature of the party who may be charged.

Interpretation of Contracts and Clashing Terms It may be necessary to make changes to a contract in handwriting because it is too inconvenient to print a whole new contract. The court will enforce handwritten terms. The court assumes that the handwritten changes were placed in writing after the contract was printed and represent the final intent of the parties. According to the law: (1) handwriting prevails over typewriting, preprinting, or word processing; (2) typewriting or word processing prevails over preprinting. The court will honor the amount on a check that is written in words.

When a written contract is filled with confusing language, the court will lean against the party who actually wrote the contract. Words, phrases, and sentences should be clear and unambiguous.

Contracts That Must Be in Writing

The Statute of Frauds adds a requirement to the six elements of a valid contract: offer, acceptance, genuine agreement, capacity, consideration, and legality. Certain contracts must be in writing to be enforceable. Be aware that the Statute of Frauds applies only to executory contracts (contracts that have not been fully performed).

Contracts to Pay Somebody Else's Debt A contract to pay someone else's debts must be in writing to be enforceable. The debtor still owes the money; the person promising to cover the debt does so only if the debtor fails to pay.

Contracts to Pay Debts of a Person Who Has Died When a person dies, somebody has to pay that person's debts and divide up the rest of his or her property among any remaining relatives. Executors and administrators handle such matters. The law says that executors and administrators are not personally responsible for the debts.

Often, executors are close relatives of the deceased. They may feel responsible for the deceased's debts when the estate runs out of money and agree to pay them. Later, the executor might have second thoughts about having made such a promise. To protect someone in such a vulnerable position, the law requires that such an agreement be in writing.

TEACH *(cont.)*

Guided Practice

Clashing Terms

To reinforce how courts evaluate contradictory terms, ask students to explain why handwritten terms prevail over typewritten terms and why amounts written in words prevail over amounts written in figures. (court assumes that handwriting was added to a printed contract after it was prepared; amounts written in figures are easily miswritten or mistyped, while amounts written in words are assumed less likely to contain errors)

S Skills Practice

Have students research England in 1677 and answer the following questions.

List Who ruled England in 1677? (Charles II) **L1**

Describe What was occurring in English politics at the time? (the restoration of the monarchy) **L2**

Explain Why might this have been a good time for the establishment of the Act for the Prevention of Frauds and Perjuries? (The period was marked by an advance in colonization and trade.) **L3**

U Universal Access

Visual/Spatial Learning Ask students to collect types of contracts such as magazine subscription offers, book club ads, and rental applications. Then have them make a chart that lists the components of each contract. (e.g., name, address, date, and purpose). Ask students to identify ways in which the contracts are similar and different. Ask students to present reports detailing their findings.

R Reading Strategy

Contracts That Must Be in Writing Have a volunteer from the class read aloud all contract elements listed in the section "Contracts That Must Be in Writing." Ask the other students to record each type on separate 5" × 7" index cards. Have them write brief notes on each element as they are discussed in class. Tell students that each state defines the types of contracts that must be in writing.

TEACH (cont.)

Guided Practice

Marriage

Jennifer and Carl want to get married, so they enter into a contract stating that they will get married in the future. Ask whether this contract is enforceable. (not enforceable by present-day law) Jennifer and Carl eventually have a wedding where they exchange vows and enter into a marriage. Ask students whether a contract exists. (Yes. Consideration given is the promise to marry.)

ASSESS

Independent Practice

Ask students to answer the following questions:

1. For legal purposes, how is the age of majority determined? (when an individual reaches a particular age, 18 or 21, at the beginning of the day before his or her birthday)

2. Is it possible for a person with a mental impairment to enter into a valid contract? (Yes. If the person was not suffering from the impairment when the contract was made, or still knew what he or she was doing.)

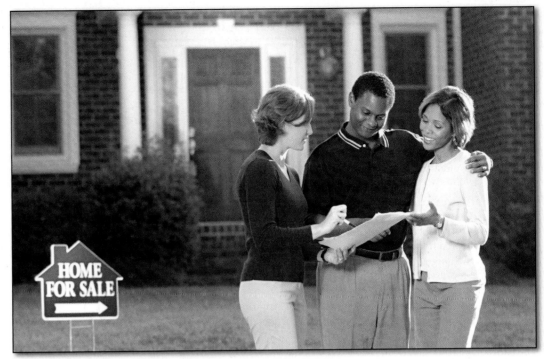

Real Estate Contracts Contracts that involve real estate sales must be in writing. *What is the exception to this rule?*

Contracts Requiring More than a Year to Perform

Any contract that cannot be performed within one year must be in writing to be enforceable. The year begins to run when the contract is made, not when the performance is to start. Agreements in which the amount of time involved is uncertain do not have to be in writing.

Contracts in Consideration of Marriage

When two persons agree to marry, they enter into a contract. The promises they make to each other are consideration for the contract. Agreements to marry have never required a written contract. Under present-day law, an agreement between two people to marry is not enforceable. Either party can break the agreement. If one person agrees to marry another person for a third person's promise of money or property, the agreement must be in writing. A promise to adopt a child from a former marriage or to care for another relative in return for a promise of marriage must be in writing to be enforceable.

Contracts for the Sale of Goods

Although the Uniform Commercial Code (UCC) lists many exceptions to this rule, a contract for the sale of goods for $500 or more must be in writing.

▲ USING VISUALS

Real Estate Contracts **Answer** An exception to the requirement of real estate contracts being in writing in order to be enforceable is *equitable estoppel*. Under the equitable estoppel rule, a court will not grant a judgment or other legal relief to a party who has not acted fairly; for example, by having made false representations or concealing material facts from the other party.

Activity Ask students to research and name other major types of estoppel. (estoppel by record, estoppel by deed, reliance-based estoppels, estoppel by representation of fact, promissory estoppel, proprietary estoppel, estoppel by delay)

Goods are movable items such as furniture, books, computers, PDAs, cultivated crops, clothing, vehicles, and MP3 players.

According to the UCC, a written agreement is valid if it indicates that a contract for sale has been made between the parties. The written agreement must also be signed by the party being sued. The UCC does not require that all the terms of the contract be in writing.

Contracts to Sell Real Property Contracts for the sale of real property must be in writing to be enforceable. Real property is land and anything permanently attached to the land. One important contract for real property you might enter into is the contract to buy or sell a home. The contract of sale, sometimes called a purchase and sale agreement, consists of an offer that is made by the buyer and accepted by the seller.

One major exception to the requirement that a contract for the sale of real property be in writing is called equitable estoppel. According to equitable estoppel, a party cannot claim the Statute of Frauds if the other party did something extreme, such as making excess improvements to the property, because of what the other party promised.

Special Rules for the Interpretation of Contracts

It is crucial to understand which contracts must be in writing to be enforceable in a court of law. There are also special rules for the interpretation of written contracts. These rules include the parol evidence rule and the best evidence rule.

The Parol Evidence Rule A written contract should contain everything that was agreed upon between the parties so that neither party can go to court and claim a contract is incorrect or fails to show the parties' real intentions.

This long-established rule is called the parol evidence rule. Parol means word of mouth; evidence, in this instance, means anything presented as proof in a trial. The parol evidence rule says that evidence of oral statements made before signing a written agreement cannot be presented in court to change or add to the terms of that written agreement. The court presumes that a written contract contains all of the terms and provisions intended by the parties.

There are exceptions to this general rule. Parol evidence may be introduced to explain some point that is not clear in a written agreement. It may be used to show that certain terms were incorrectly placed in the written contract. It also may be presented to prove that one party was tricked by another.

The Best Evidence Rule This rule requires that the original written agreement (rather than a copy) be used as evidence in court. The rule means a court does not want to look at photocopies or faxed copies of a written agreement. Copying a contract can make it easier for a dishonest person to hide alterations to the original. For this reason, when a contract is reduced to writing, each party receives an original version of the contract.

Independent Practice

Anatomy of a Contract

Ask students to create a contract for an imaginary business. For example, it could be a health club membership application, a disclaimer for a rock-climbing gym, or a membership agreement at a local video rental store. Encourage students to find examples of the type of contract they are creating and ensure that they use proper and precise language and a sensible layout. (Review the documents for elements that would make a contract valid. Discuss any omissions from the contracts your students have created.)

RETEACH
Guided Practice

Importance of Written Contracts

Stress the importance of capturing all details in writing in an agreement between two parties. Tell students that a woman was told by a car dealership that she would receive free oil changes for the first year after buying her new car. This fact was not contained in her bill of sale on the new car. Ask students whether she will be able to enforce the verbal statement made about oil changes. (No. The parol evidence rule will prevent her from relating the statement in court.)

Extending the Content

Limitations on Contracts

Have students consider all the ways in which contracts are limited. Some of these include capacity, legality, and public policy. Ask students to interpret the underlying reason why these items limit contractual agreements. (all seek to protect the parties to a contract and the public at large)

STUDY TO GO Have students go to the *Business and Personal Law* Online Learning Center through glencoe.com to download free Study-to-Go content to their cell phones or PDAs.

RETEACH (cont.)

After You Read

Summarize contractual capacity, legality of contract, whether the contract violates any local statutes, and whether any contradictory language exists

ASSESS

Self-Assessment

Have students go to the *Business and Personal Law* Online Learning Center through glencoe.com to take the Section 5.1 Practice Test.

CLOSE

Culminating Activity

Capacity to Contract

Tell students that Ralph purchased a car from a used car dealership on the day before his 18th birthday. On his 18th birthday, he decides to disaffirm the contract. Ask students if he can do so. (For legal purposes, Ralph is considered to be of majority age on the day before his birthday. He cannot disaffirm the contract.)

Duplicate originals are original versions of a contract that are signed by and provided to all of the parties to a contract.

Real-World Rules When you are asked to sign an order blank, sales slip, or other printed form, such documents may contain small print on the front or reverse side. The words are often difficult to read, and the language may be hard to understand. Often, the small print is not written in your favor. Follow these guidelines before you sign:

- Read the entire text of the document before you sign it.
- If you do not understand something or do not agree to it, cross it out before you sign. Do not be shy about having the other party initial the change too. The change is meaningless unless the other party has initialed it.
- Do not be afraid to make changes on a printed or word-processed form. If any extra-added promises are made to you, write them in.
- If a contract is for something major, such as the purchase of a house or car, and contains a lot of legal language—or legalese—you do not understand, have a lawyer review it before you sign.
- Refuse to sign a written contract if you do not agree with everything contained in the writing.

After You Read

Summarize What should you consider when you are evaluating a contract?

SECTION 5.1 ASSESSMENT

Self Check

1. What rights does a minor have in relation to contracts?
2. What happens when a minor becomes emancipated?
3. How are minors protected under the parens patriae doctrine?

Academic Connection

Mathematics As a part of your sales contract with Wilson Sporting Goods Company, you are entitled to a trade discount. The invoice is for $1,454.00

with the terms 6/15/n30, which means that if your bill is paid within 15 days of receipt you receive a 6% discount. If you take the full 30 days to pay, no discount applies. Calculate the discount and the amount due for the invoice.

THEORY **Number and Operations: Use Fractions, Decimals, and Rounding** To solve this problem use the following formulas:

$$\frac{\text{Cash}}{\text{Discount}} = \frac{\text{Net}}{\text{Price}} \times \frac{\text{Cash-}}{\text{Discount Rate}}$$

$$\frac{\text{Cash}}{\text{Price}} = \frac{\text{Net}}{\text{Price}} - \frac{\text{Cash}}{\text{Discount}}$$

 For more math practice, go to the Math Appendix.

Critical Thinking

Contracts between Minors Suppose that you have purchased an MP3 player from a classmate. Can that classmate change his mind, ask you to return the player, and offer you a refund? Explain.

Go to **glencoe.com** to check your answers.

glencoe.com

SECTION 5.1 ASSESSMENT

Self Check

1. ability to void contracts
2. Emancipated minors are responsible for their own contracts.
3. protects minors from abuse; state can act as a child's parents when natural parents cannot or will not perform their parental duties

Academic Connection

Mathematics
Cash Discount: $87.24
Amount Due: $1,366.76

Critical Thinking

When two minors enter a contract, either has the right to disaffirm the contract.

One minor cannot force the other to continue honoring the contract.

 Activity correlated to the Mathematics standard on page 100

Consideration

Reading Guide

Before You Read

Connect If you agree to sell your MP3 player to your best friend for $50, what do you gain and what do you lose? What does your friend gain and lose?

Focus on Ideas

Consideration is a kind of exchange and it is a key element of a valid contract.

Take Notes

Create a graph like the one shown and use it to take notes as you read this section. Go to glencoe.com to find graphic organizers and tips on how to improve your note-taking skills.

Consideration Definition: _____

Requirement
Requirement
Requirement
Requirement

Key Terms

You will learn these legal words and expressions in this chapter. You can also find these terms in *Black's Law Dictionary* or in an online legal dictionary.

- consideration
- forbearance
- unconscionable contract
- adhesion contract
- accord and satisfaction
- promissory estoppel

Academic Vocabulary

You will find these words in your readings and in your tests. Look them up in a dictionary and familiarize yourself with them.

- contain
- indicating
- obligation

What You'll Learn

- ◆ Analyze the requirements for valid consideration.
- ◆ Define the different types of consideration.
- ◆ List exceptions to the requirements of consideration.
- ◆ Compare unconscionability and illegality.

Why It's Important

Understanding the concept of consideration will help you make sure that contracts you enter into are valid.

Academic Standards

Reading and completing the activities in this section will help you practice the following academic standards:

English Language Arts (NCTE 3) Apply a wide range of strategies to comprehend, interpret, evaluate, and appreciate texts.

Math (NCTM PSS 2) Solve problems that arise in mathematics and in other contexts.

R Reading Strategy

Read for Knowledge

1. **Survey** or preread the chapter.
2. **Question** or formulate questions before you read.
3. **Recite** or read your questions, answers, and notes out loud.
4. **Review** or reread your notes.

Note-Taking Basics

- Listen attentively
- Have note-taking materials ready
- Skim through the lesson material
- Write down key words and ideas
- Anticipate what comes next
- Review notes soon after taking them

FOCUS

Bell Ringer Activity

Ask students to call out their understanding of the term *consideration*. ("careful thought" or "regard.") Ask students to reflect on a meaning in the legal context. (exchange of benefits and detriments by contracting parties)

Preteaching

Key Terms

Read the definitions and ask students to create a sentence using each term.

Academic Vocabulary

Explain that developing vocabulary is key to academic success. An efficient method to develop vocabulary is to study how words are formed.

- **contain** Verb, from the Latin *continere, com* (together) + *tenere* (to hold). Means to hold together or enclose.
- **indicating** Verb, from the Latin *indicare, in-* + *dicare*, (to proclaim). Means pointing out.
- **obligation** Noun, from the Latin *obligare* (to bind). Means a promise or contract.

Activity Ask students to give a noun, a verb, an adjective, or an adverb form that comes from each word.

NCLB Connects to academic content

TEACH

Discussion Starter

Class Discussion

Explain consideration by saying, "I'll pay you $30 if you agree to walk my dog every day this week." Have one student agree to walk the dog. Ask the class what the benefits are for both parties. (Student gains $30; teacher freed of the chore) Ask the class what the detriment is for each party. (Student gives up free time; teacher gives up $30.) Explain to students that *consideration* is the exchange of benefits and detriments by parties to a contract. Tell students that this section will help them understand the legal concept of consideration.

 As You Read

Predict Ask students to venture an answer to this question and record it in their notebooks. Have them review their answer when they read the applicable answer in their text. (Yes. The exchange or the promise to exchange something of value is what binds the parties together.)

As You Read

Predict Does a contract have to include an exchange to be valid?

Vocabulary You can find vocabulary definitions in the **Key Terms** glossary and **Academic Vocabulary** glossary in the back of this book.

Consideration Consideration is an exchange of benefits and detriments by the parties to an agreement. *Is consideration necessary to make a contract legally binding?*

The Legal Concept of Consideration

Is ordering a taco at a street stand consideration?

Consideration is the exchange of benefits and detriments by the parties to a contract. A benefit is something that a party receives in the agreement. A detriment is something a party gives up in the agreement (see **Figure 5.1**). There are three types of detriments:

- Giving up something that you have the right to keep
- Doing something that you have the right not to do
- Not doing something that you have the legal right to do

The last type of detriment listed is also called forbearance. **Forbearance is not doing what you have the right to do.**

Requirements for Valid Consideration

The parties must bargain with each other if there is to be a contract. Each side in the agreement must give up something and get something in exchange. The exchange or the promise to exchange something of value is what binds the parties together. A date for Friday night or a promise to pick up a friend before school are not contracts because neither one **contains** consideration.

The Characteristics of Consideration

There are three characteristics of consideration:

- Consideration must involve a bargained-for exchange.
- Consideration must involve something of value.
- The benefits and detriments that make up consideration must be legal.

Figure 5.1 Consideration

Benefit: The right to receive the money.

Promisor

"I'll sell you my car for $3,500."

Legal Detriment: The promise to give up the $3,500.

Promisee

"I'll buy it for that price."

Joseph Duffey
1122 Reeling Way
Flatwood, MO

PAY

THE BIG BANK
ANYPLACE, USA

Promisee

Legal Detriment: The promise to give up the car.

Promisor

Benefit: The right to receive the car.

▲ USING VISUALS

Figure 5.1 Consideration Answer Yes. In most cases, consideration is necessary to make an agreement legally binding.

Activity Have students research cases involving disputes over consideration. Ask them to select one case and explain to the class how it involves consideration. Encourage class discussion of the cases.

Business ETHICS

Cheap Computers

Suppose you work for a computer manufacturer. You have two outdated personal computers at home you want to replace. You work out an arrangement with a fellow employee, who is a salesperson for the company, to get a great deal on two new computers. A contract is drawn up where you will buy the computers from the company for $5 each, even though each computer retails for $1,500.

Critical Thinking: *Is there consideration in the contract? Should you sign the contract?*

Bargained-for Exchange A contract involves a bargained-for exchange when a promise is made in return for another promise. It also occurs when an act is exchanged for an act or a promise not to act. Bargaining means that a party will lose something if the other party does not come through as promised. Conversely, both parties gain something when the promises are kept or the acts are performed.

Something of Value Something of value to one person may be worthless to another. The law is not concerned with the value of consideration and does not set value in a contract. All that matters is that the parties agree freely on the value and the price, and that consideration be present and the parties agree to it.

The only time a court might look at the value of consideration is if it thinks that the consideration offered is so far from what it should be that it is grossly unfair. This type of contract is said to be unconscionable. **An unconscionable contract is an agreement in which the consideration is so out of line with the actual value of the subject matter and so unfair that it shocks the court's conscience.**

Two additional conditions must be present for a contract to be unconscionable:

- There must be uneven power between the parties.
- The party with all the power tells the other party to take it or leave it.

This is called an adhesion contract. **An adhesion contract is a take-it-or-leave-it offer made by a party who holds most of the power in a bargaining session.** When the courts are faced with this type of situation, they will do one of three things:

- Refuse to enforce the entire contract.
- Enforce the contract without the unconscionable clause (if possible).
- Limit the enforcement of that clause.

TEACH (cont.)

D Develop Concepts

Value Tell students the courts are not generally concerned with the value at which two parties agree to exchange something. Ask students if they can think of a situation in which the court might take issue with the value of an exchange. (when consideration is so out of line with the actual value of the subject matter that one party is taking advantage of the other) Explain that this is called an *unconscionable contract.*

Guided Practice

Characteristics of Consideration

Write the three characteristics of consideration on the board:

- Promises involving the concept of a bargained-for exchange
- Something of value involved
- Benefits and detriments promised must be legal

Ask students to think of an example of an agreement that contains each of these elements. (Suggest ideas like purchasing a car or contracting for a lawn service.)

Business ETHICS

Answer Yes, there is consideration. The amount of consideration is not an issue. If both parties have the capacity to contract, it does not matter that one side is getting a better deal than the other when determining the validity of a contract. However, there are definitely other factors to consider. Fraud may be an issue, especially if the salesperson is not authorized to sell a computer at such a ridiculously low price.

TEACH *(cont.)*

D Develop Concepts

A Promise Not to Sue Tell students to imagine that a man slips and falls down in a grocery store aisle. After making sure the person has no injuries, the manager of the store asks the person to sign a release promising that he will not sue the store. The man will receive free groceries for a month in return. Ask students to identify the benefit to both parties. (Store is gaining assurance that no suit will be filed; man gains free groceries for a month.)

Extending the Content

Unconscionability

Common law judges only make exceptions to the standard about the adequacy of consideration when they encounter a situation that they believe is unconscionable. One famous exception, demonstrating judicial intervention, is the case of Schnell v. Nell, an 1861 agreement in which a man promised to pay $600 in return for the loan of one penny.

Reading Check

Enumerate money as consideration; property and services as consideration; a promise not to sue

---

Reading Check

Enumerate *List three common types of consideration.*

Legality and Unconscionability The law requires that the consideration that passes from one party to another be legal. If the consideration is illegal, the contract is void. For example, someone cannot give up something, such as a stolen bicycle, that he or she does not own. Illegality is not the same as unconscionability. Consideration may be legal, as when money is paid for an item, but unconscionable because the amount paid is so unfair that it shocks the conscience of the court.

Types of Consideration

If you agree to sell your laptop to a classmate, what do you think consideration could be?

There are very few limits on what consideration can be: it is what two parties agree it should be. Courts see some everyday things as consideration: money, property, services, promises not to sue, and promises made to a charity (see **Figure 5.2**).

Money as Consideration

Often, one party offers money in exchange for the other party's property or services. Sometimes, when costs get out of hand, the government might step in and control prices. There are also a few laws, like the Federal Fair Labor Standards Act, which sets a minimum wage for workers, that dictates the amount that can be offered in certain contracts.

Property and Services as Consideration

Service as consideration is part of a contract with some workers; for example, when your family hires a gardener to take care of the lawn or a plumber to fix a leaky pipe or when you buy the services of the hair stylist who cuts your hair. Property is also consideration. This is the type of agreement you enter whenever you go to the mall to buy CDs. Contracts for the purchase of a new house are another example. Property is consideration in barter agreements, such as when when you trade video games with your friends.

A Promise Not to Sue

D Giving up the right to sue is a type of forbearance. Lawsuits are often settled when one party agrees not to sue the other party. The other party promises to pay a set amount of money in return. A signed agreement not to sue is called a release. This practice is so common that many insurance companies have preprinted forms that they use to settle cases before they even get filed.

Charitable Pledges

Charities depend on money from businesses and individuals. This has led the courts to uphold donation promises as if they were contracts, although there often is no consideration in the agreement. Courts uphold these pledges because charities provide services to society.

S Skills Practice

List Ask students to think of instances in which they have made an exchange of items of value. Have them list the types of consideration commonly used. (money, property, services, promises not to do something, promises to donate to charity) **L1**

Illustrate Ask students to think of an example in which property is used as consideration in a contract. (purchase of merchandise, contract to buy house, trade items of value) **L2**

Conclude Have students discuss why a barter arrangement has consideration. (Two individuals agree to trade goods of value.) **L3**

Figure 5.2 Types of Consideration

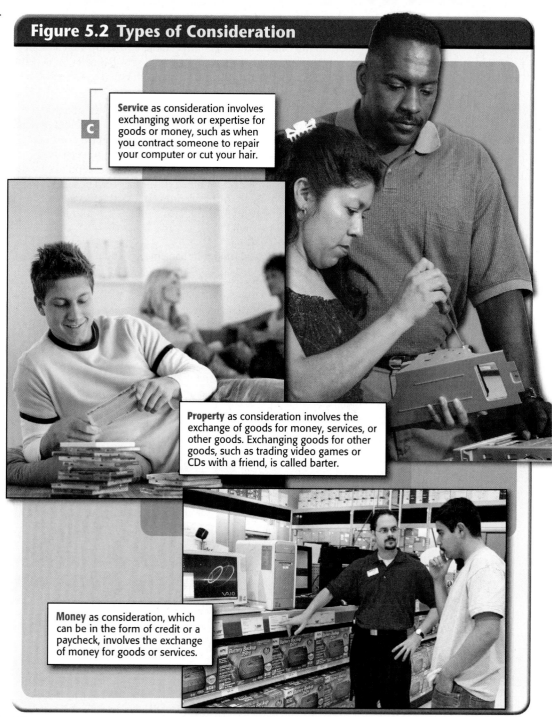

C **Service** as consideration involves exchanging work or expertise for goods or money, such as when you contract someone to repair your computer or cut your hair.

Property as consideration involves the exchange of goods for money, services, or other goods. Exchanging goods for other goods, such as trading video games or CDs with a friend, is called barter.

Money as consideration, which can be in the form of credit or a paycheck, involves the exchange of money for goods or services.

Money, property, and services are the most common forms of consideration in a contract. *What are two other forms of consideration?*

Chapter 5   Elements of a Contract   **119**

D Develop Concepts

Types of Consideration
Ask students to think of contracts that they or their families have been involved in. Have them volunteer the type of consideration given or received in each contract. (consideration may have been money, property, or services) Explain that lesser-known types of consideration include a promise not to sue or a charitable pledge.

C Critical Thinking

Services as Consideration
Ask students if the following scenario contains valid consideration: Janet agrees to babysit for Brenda's children on the first Saturday of each month. Brenda will drive Janet's child to school every Friday. (The two women have entered into an agreement that uses services as consideration.)

U Universal Access

English Language Learners
For English language learners, using visuals in the text is a good opportunity to reinforce concepts. Have students look at the photos on this page and speculate on what events are taking place. Explain what consideration there is in each situation.

▲ USING VISUALS

➡ **Figure 5.2 Types of Consideration** Answer Two other forms of consideration are promises not to do something and promises to donate money to a charity.

Activity Ask students to create a fictitious situation in which a binding agreement is made between two individuals. Have them identify the consideration offered and describe what is being exchanged. (Students' situations should describe detriments and benefits to both parties.)

TEACH *(cont.)*

D Develop Concepts

Disputed Amounts Explain to students that accord and satisfaction is a legal way to settle a dispute about the amount owed in a contract. Tell students to imagine that a woman purchased a television set from a store. She thought the television was on sale. The store later billed her for the full amount of $3,000. She cannot pay the amount in full. The two parties agree that the woman can pay $2,000 to settle the debt. Ask students to identify the accord and the satisfaction parts of this new agreement. (Accord: acceptance of the new amount by the creditor. Satisfaction: the agreed-to settlement as contained in the accord.)

ASSESS

Quiz

1. How is a dispute settled by accord and satisfaction? (Creditor accepts a payment that is less than the amount due as full payment.)

2. Why do the courts enforce charitable pledges as if they were contracts? (Charities depend on contributions for financial stability.)

3. Why is a promise not to sue in exchange for something of value considered one form of consideration? (One person giving up the right to sue is forbearance; the other party is giving up something of value for that promise.)

120

Problems with Consideration

Sometimes, the parties to a contract disagree on how much money is due. There is a way out of such disagreements. The solution depends on whether there really is a genuine disagreement as to the amount that is owed.

D **Disputed Amounts** If there is a genuine issue as to the amount owed, the parties can use accord and satisfaction to settle the argument. **Accord and satisfaction is a legal way to settle contractual disputes by which one party agrees to accept less than the amount due as full payment.** The acceptance by the creditor of less than what was billed is the accord. The agreed-to settlement as contained in the accord is the satisfaction. The dispute must be real and in good faith. Finally, the amount involved cannot be trivial.

> **Example:** Alison and Jeremy Brisbane made a contract with the Port Clinton Construction Company to put siding on their house in Lakeside, Ohio. The company charged $50 per hour for a job that lasted 200 hours. The final bill for labor was $11,250. When they looked at the bill, the Brisbanes saw that they had been charged an hour per day for travel time from the company's home base to their house. The Brisbanes thought it unfair for them to be charged for travel time. They deducted $1,250 from the bill (25 travel hours at $50 per hour). They sent a check for $10,000 to the company. On the check, they wrote, "In full payment for the siding placed on our summer home at 206 Jasmine, Lakeside, Ohio." When Port Clinton Construction cashed the check, they accepted the lesser amount as full payment.

Amount Due Disagreement A contractor and a homeowner might not agree on an amount due in exchange for work performed. *In what case could accord and satisfaction not be used to settle the issue?*

USING VISUALS

Amount Due Disagreement **Answer** *Accord and satisfaction* is applied in resolving disputes that are real, not trivial, and pursued in good faith. The contractor and homeowner could not use accord and satisfaction if the amount in dispute is trivial, not really in dispute (such as if one party is bargaining for a better payment), or if one of the parties is not acting in good faith (the homeowner offers to pay $5,000 for a $50,000 job). Rule 8 of the Federal Rules of Civil Procedure gives *accord and satisfaction* as a defense in civil cases. A leading case on the exception of accord and satisfaction is the 1884 case of Foakes v. Beer from the British House of Lords.

Undisputed Amounts If the parties have agreed to a set amount of money in the contract, then accord and satisfaction does not apply. This is true even if the party who owes the money finds out that the product was on sale for a lesser amount somewhere else.

Exceptions to the Requirements of Consideration

Some agreements are valid even without consideration. Specific rules vary from state to state, but some agreements always fall into this group.

Promises Under Seal A seal is a mark or an impression placed on a written contract **indicating** that it is a formal agreement. Most states today do not require a seal. Those that do generally allow the word seal on the letters, L.S., or the phrase *locus sigilli* (place of the seal) after the signature. Contracts for goods do not require a seal. Some contracts for land do need a seal.

Promises After Discharge in Bankruptcy Sometimes, people who have had their debts discharged in bankruptcy court promise to pay the debts anyway. A court hearing is required when such promises are made. In the hearing, the debtor is told about the legal consequences of making such a promise. Some states do not require any consideration for this promise. The promise is supported by contractual intent. Some states say the promise must be in writing.

Debts Ended by the Statute of Limitations A statute of limitations sets up the time limit for suing somebody. Different states have different time limits. Such variations can run from three to ten years. The same state may also have different time limits for different types of contracts. For instance, the statute of limitations may set one time limit for oral contracts and a different one for written contracts. A time limit for a contract for goods may be different from a contract for the sale of real property.

Promises Enforced by Promissory Estoppel If someone making a promise should have reasonably expected the other person to rely on the promise, and the other person did rely on the promise and suffered a loss, the innocent party can use promissory estoppel to make the other party compensate him or her for the loss. The doctrine stops one party (the estoppel part) from denying that they made a promise that hurt the second party (the promissory part). **Promissory estoppel is the principle that a promise made without consideration may nonetheless be enforced to prevent injustice.** The following elements must be present:

- The promise was made about the innocent party's action (or lack of action).
- The innocent party gave no consideration in exchange for that promise.

RETEACH
Extending the Content

Consideration
Have students use the Internet or the library to research cases involving disputes over consideration. Ask them to select one case and report to the class on how it involves consideration. Encourage class discussion of the cases.

Guided Practice

Statute of Limitations
Ask students if they have ever wanted to take legal action against someone who failed to keep a promise or fulfill an agreement. Ask them if they think there is a time limit on when this action must take place. (Yes. The statute of limitations sets up the time limit for suing somebody. Some states set this limit at periods as long as ten years.)

Independent Practice

Barter

Have each student think of a good or service he or she could barter with other students. Divide the class in half and have one half remain seated while the other half makes a list of items for which they could barter. Then have students complete the following activities.

Describe Have students explain what service or goods they bartered. **L1**

Explain Have students explain whether or not they were able to barter for necessaries with their goods or services. **L2**

Analyze Have students explain how consideration is part of a bartered agreement. (By exchanging goods and services, you are exchanging things of value.) **L3**

RETEACH (cont.)

Role Play

Bargained-For Exchange
Ask students to form pairs and work together to create a scenario in which a bargained-for exchange is agreed upon. Have each pair present their scenario to the class. (agreements must include a promise made in return for another promise, an act, or a promise not to act; requires that a party will be injured if the other party does not keep his or her promise)

U Universal Access

Gifted Learners Challenge the gifted learners in your class by asking them to research a recent contract law dispute online. Have them outline the case, detailing the types of consideration used, what the dispute involved, and how the case was settled. Ask volunteers to share their findings with the class.

Review Key Terms

Encourage students to access the *Business and Personal Law* Online Learning Center through glencoe.com and use the electronic flashcards to review the key terms.

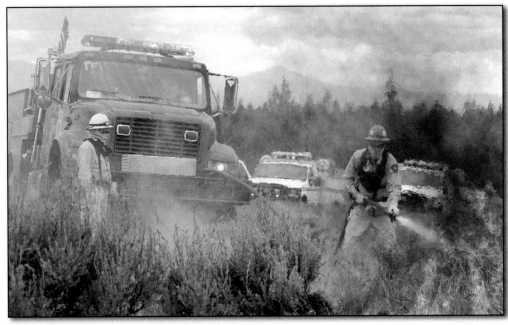

Preexisting Duty
Preexisting duties cannot be made consideration in a new contract. *Why does the law prevent preexisting duties from being consideration in new contracts?*

- The innocent party relied on the promise and did something that changed his or her position in a major way (such as sold a car, moved out of an apartment, sold a house, or took a vacation).
- Injustice can be avoided only by enforcing the promise and making up for the loss.

Option Sometimes one person will pay another person money to keep an offer open for a set period of time. This is called an option. When the contract involves goods, the offer can be held open without the money payment. This is called a firm offer. A firm offer requires a written offer stating the period of time during which the offer will stay open. The time cannot go beyond three months. The person making the written offer must be a merchant who deals in the types of goods involved on an everyday basis.

Agreements Without Consideration

Some agreements and promises seem to include consideration, but in reality they do not, and what passes for consideration is actually not enforceable by law.

Illusory Promises For a contract to be real, all the parties must be required to do something. Sometimes, a contract seems to require something when it really does not. For example, this happens when a restaurant agrees to buy all the apples it needs for the summer from a particular farmer. The promise seems real, but since the restaurant can simply say it did not need any apples that summer, the promise is not real. This is an illusory promise.

▲ USING VISUALS

Preexisting Duty Answer The law prohibits preexisting duties from being offered as consideration in a new contract because one party is already required to act under the preexisting duty and, therefore, would not be giving up anything new to qualify as consideration in another contract. For example, a police officer who promises to provide security protection to homeowners for a fee is making an empty promise. The police officer is already required by law to provide such services, so such an arrangement is not enforceable.

Activity The nature of duty has been a common topic for philosophers from Confucius to Plato to Bentham. Give students examples of the views of several thinkers from the past and have them discuss where they think obligations should lie.

Future Gifts and Legacies A person's promise to give a gift to another person at some time in the future or to leave a legacy in a will cannot be enforced without consideration. This rule applies to promises of free services or to promise to lend somebody something.

Past Consideration The act of giving consideration must happen at the same time that the contract is made. Past consideration is something that was given or promised in the past that somebody tries to use again in a new contract. The courts do not accept past consideration. For example, suppose you help your older brother move into his college dormitory on Saturday. The next day, he promises to pay you $25 for helping. That promise is not binding because your consideration was given in the past.

Preexisting Duties The act of giving consideration requires a new promise for every new contract. A preexisting duty is an **obligation** that a person already has to do something and cannot be used again in a new contract. Suppose a person is already obligated to do something, such as mow the lawn every week. Then he or she cannot make it consideration in a new contract. If the courts allowed preexisting duties to bind a party in a new contract, they would be permitting one promise to do double duty.

Promise to Attend a Social Engagement All contracts are agreements, but not all agreements are contracts. A promise to take a friend to a concert would not be a legally binding agreement because the friend has given nothing in exchange for the promise: That agreement lacks consideration.

After You Read

Summarize What are contractual situations in which consideration does not apply?

SECTION 5.2 ASSESSMENT

Self Check

1. What are the characteristics of consideration?

2. What is an unconscionable contract?

3. What is forbearance?

Academic Connection

Mathematics Mikiko Iwayama purchased a vacuum cleaner for $299.99. She lives in Wisconsin where the sales tax is 5%. What is the total amount that she will pay for the appliance? Does this purchase constitute a

contract? What is consideration in this case?

THEORY **Number and Operations: Computing Percentages** To solve this problem use the following formulas:

Sales Tax = Selling Price × Sales Tax Rate

Total Purchase Price = Selling Price + Sales Tax

 For more math practice, go to the Math Appendix.

Critical Thinking

Accord and Satisfaction Suppose that you make a contract to buy a skateboard for your friend, Hal. You then see the exact same skateboard on auction on eBay. You monitor the auction and discover that the winning bidder paid a lot less than you paid Hal. Can you use accord and satisfaction to pay the lesser amount for the skateboard? Explain.

 Go to **glencoe.com** to check your answers.

RETEACH (cont.)

After You Read

Summarize illusory promises, future gifts and legacies, past consideration

ASSESS

Self-Assessment

Have students go to the *Business and Personal Law* Online Learning Center through glencoe.com to take the Section 5.2 Practice Test.

CLOSE

Culminating Activity

Types of Agreements

Tell students that Rachael Smith made an agreement with the Main Street Chiropractic Clinic to perform any massages that the clinic's patients required. Ask students what type of agreement the clinic and Rachael have. (an illusory promise)

SECTION 5.2 ASSESSMENT

Self Check

1. must involve a bargained-for exchange, something of value, and the benefits and detriments must be legal

2. agreement in which consideration is out of line with value of subject matter and unfair

3. not doing what you have the right to do

Academic Connection

Mathematics
Total price: $314.99.
The purchase is a contract.
Consideration: $299.99

Critical Thinking

No. The agreement was made in good faith, and the amount in dispute is probably trivial.

 Activity correlated to the Mathematics standard on page 115

Chapter **5** Review and Assessment

Summary by Sections

Ask students to read the summaries one key point at a time. Then, ask them to work in groups to create two examples to illustrate each key point.

Vocabulary Builder

Cooperative Learning

1. Have students work in groups to prepare their sentences. Ask the groups to exchange their sentences and assess each other's sentences.

Vocabulary Development

- Ask students to use a dictionary or to go online to look up the etymology of each key term listed.

- Then, ask students to list several words derived from the same root or origin. For example, *contract* has the same root as *contractual* or *contractually.*

Summary

Section 5.1 Capacity and Legality

- Capacity is the legal ability to enter a contract.
- People who lack contractual capacity are: minors, people with mental impairment, and intoxicated persons.
- The law makes an exception when the contract involves necessaries. Necessaries are food, clothing, shelter, and medical care.
- Minors who decide to get out of their contracts can do so. A minor is a person who has not yet reached the age of adulthood.
- An emancipated minor is no longer under the control of his or her parents. Emancipated minors are responsible for their own contracts.
- Minors who claim to be adults are committing fraud.
- Minors must disaffirm an entire contract. They cannot pick and choose the parts of the contract they want to keep and those they want to disaffirm.
- Ratification is the act of agreeing to go along with a contract that could have been avoided.

Section 5.2 Consideration

- Consideration is the exchange of benefits and detriments by the parties to a contract. A benefit is something received in the agreement. A detriment is a loss.
- Consideration must involve a bargained-for exchange. It must involve something of value.
- Consideration includes money, property, and services. Other forms of consideration include promises not to sue and promises made to a charity.
- Accord and satisfaction is a legal way to settle contractual disputes by which one party agrees to accept less than the amount due as full payment.
- Agreements valid without consideration: promises under seal, promises after discharge in bankruptcy, debts ended by statute of limitations, promises enforced by promissory estoppel, and options.
- Agreements not valid without consideration: illusory promises, promise of future gifts or legacies, promises based on past consideration or on preexisting duties, and agreements to attend social engagements.

Vocabulary Builder

1 **On a sheet of paper, use each of these terms in a sentence.**

Key Terms

- capacity
- minor
- majority
- emancipated
- disaffirm

- ratification
- public policy
- Statute of Frauds
- consideration
- forbearance

- unconscionable contract
- adhesion contract
- accord and satisfaction
- promissory estoppel

Academic Vocabulary

- assumption
- usury

- dispensing
- contain

- indicating
- obligation

Go to **glencoe.com** to play a game and improve your legal vocabulary.

Study Skills for Success

Prepare Your Students for Studying

Tell students that they can improve their ability to understand and remember material from their courses by learning and practicing study skills. Remind students to:

- **Get motivated!** Motivation must come from within. To motivate yourself, think of ways in which what you learn now will fit into your long-term personal and professional goals.
- **Get organized!** Make studying part of your daily routine, not something you do at the last minute.
- **Concentrate!** Study in an environment that is as free of distractions as possible.

Key Points Review

Answer the following questions. Refer to the chapter for additional reinforcement.

2 Who determines whether a mental impairment compromised a person's ability to enter a contract?

3 What is the rule that determines if someone is so intoxicated that he or she cannot be held responsible for any contracts entered while in that state?

4 Can minors disaffirm part of a contract?

5 How can adults protect themselves from deceitful minors?

6 Why do the courts refuse to become involved trying to set the value of consideration?

7 Is it okay to agree to do something that might be considered illegal as consideration in a contract? Explain.

8 What ordinary things might be consideration in a contract?

Standardized Test Practice

9 Read the following information about the Census Bureau and complete questions 1 and 2.

The Census Bureau conducts many censuses and surveys. The most well known is the official population census of the United States, called the decennial census. It is conducted every ten years, most recently in April 2000. During each decennial census, the Census Bureau collects data from every household in the U.S. and its territories.

Besides the decennial census, the Census Bureau conducts nearly one hundred other surveys and censuses every year. By law, no one is permitted to reveal information from these censuses and surveys that could identify any person, household, or business. Individual records from each decennial census are made public 72 years after the census has been taken.

1. How often does the Census Bureau conduct censuses and surveys?

Ⓐ every eight years
Ⓑ every five years
Ⓒ every six years
Ⓓ every ten years

2. By law, what information cannot be revealed?

Ⓐ identify any person, business, or income records
Ⓑ identify any person, household, or business
Ⓒ identify any person, household, or individual record
Ⓓ identify any person, census taker, or business

 Test-Taking Strategies Read the stem of the question carefully, then read each of the possible answers all the way through.

Chapter 5   Elements of a Contract   **125**

Key Points Review

2. determined by doctors

3. Person must be so impaired that they did not know what they were doing when they entered the contract.

4. No. Minors must disaffirm the entire contract, not part of one.

5. Adults can either refuse to enter into contracts with minors, or can require minors' parents to be signatories on the contract.

6. Consideration varies between contracts, and its value can be anything the parties agree to. A court will only become involved if the value of consideration offered is grossly unfair to one of the parties—known as an *unconscionable contract*.

7. No. Consideration must be legal. If the consideration is illegal, then the contract is void.

8. property, promise not to sue, services

Standardized Test Practice

9. D and B

 Strategies for Standardized Test Prep Success

Whether your students have a standardized test coming up in a few days or a few weeks, these last-minute test-prep tips and strategies will help them relax and do their best.

• **Test Format** Help students become familiar with the format of the test by practicing with test items that imitate the actual test items as closely as possible.

• **Test Timing** Have your students take timed practice tests so that they become comfortable with the length, design, and timing of the actual test.

Apply and Debate

Students should use chapter content to arrive at conclusions. The legal resolutions are listed below:

10. Probably not. Kirsten must convince a judge that she would be better off emancipated. Just not getting along with her parents is probably not enough to achieve emancipation.

11. No. If Matthew freely entered into the contract for enlistment, then federal law prevents him from voiding the contract.

12. Yes. Under the theory of necessaries, emergency medical care given to a minor is a contract that cannot be voided just because the patient was a minor.

13. Maybe. Depending on how much Shawn has completed, he may benefit from the theory of substantial performance and could sue for breach of contract.

14. Probably not. Since Gayathri has not put any money down or put her option in writing, she probably cannot hold Malik to the option. Further, there cannot be a contract with no time limit to perform.

Apply and Debate

Read the following scenarios. Get together with other students in pairs or groups of three and take a position on each scenario. Debate your position in class with students taking the opposite position or prepare a written argument justifying your position.

10 **Emancipation**

Kirsten is 17 and a senior in high school. For the past six months, she has not been getting along with her parents and wants to move out on her own. Her parents reject this idea, so Kirsten decides to emancipate herself from her parents.

You Debate *In this situation, can Kirsten emancipate herself from her parents?*

11 **Rescinding a Contract**

Matthew is 17, a senior in high school, and in JROTC. A recruiter visits his school to recruit students for the navy. Matthew signs a contract to enlist without discussing it with his parents.

You Debate *Since Matthew is a minor and did not discuss this with his parents, can he rescind the contract?*

12 **Contract for Necessaries**

Jordan is 16. While mowing his grass, he seriously cut his hand. His neighbor took him to the emergency room where he was treated and released. Two weeks later, Jordan received a bill from the hospital for $575. Jordan refused to pay the bill.

You Debate *Since Jordan is a minor, can he still be held responsible for the hospital bill?*

13 **Consideration**

Shawn offered to paint Margaret's house in exchange for an old car she was selling for $4,000. Shawn failed to show up to finish painting the house or to contact Margaret. A week later, another person offered to purchase the car and Margaret sold it. The next day Shawn came by to finish painting the house and learned the car had been sold.

You Debate *Can Shawn sue Margaret for breach of contract?*

14 **Option**

Malik offered to sell his condo to Gayathri for $70,000. Gayathri said she did not have the money right now, but would like an option to buy it at a later date. Malik did not specify a time limit on the offer. A month later Malik had the opportunity to sell the condo for $70,000. Malik informed Gayathri, and she reminded Malik that she had an option with no time limit.

You Debate *Is Malik bound by this agreement with Gayathri?*

C Critical Thinking

Oral Agreements Kay Brandy works for Blooming Florist. Kay's doctor has recommended that she have surgery. The surgery will require her to take one month off work. Her boss says, "Don't worry, your job here is safe. When you're ready, just come back." When Kay returns one month later, she has been replaced and there is no job for her.

Debate Practice

- What legal theory might give Kay a cause of action against Blooming Florist? (doctrine of promissory estoppel)

- What circumstances must exist if Kay wishes to enforce the promise made by her boss? (Kay's position must have changed significantly in reliance on her boss's promise, and that promise must not have been fulfilled.)

Case Study Practice – Olsen v. Hawkins

⑮ A Case of Incompetence? Hobart Turner purchased a life insurance policy on his own life. He listed Marvin and Mercedes Olsen, his stepson and his stepson's wife, as the beneficiaries on his policy. Three years later, Mr. Turner changed the beneficiary to Charles Hawkins. Mr. Turner died two years later.

The Olsens sued Mr. Hawkins for the money, arguing that Mr. Turner was not competent to contractually change the beneficiary when he did because he was under the effects of alcoholism. There was no evidence that Mr. Turner was either drunk or insane at the time he changed the beneficiary, but he did suffer from chronic alcoholism. A jury agreed with the Olsens and held that Mr. Turner was incompetent when he changed the beneficiary to Mr. Hawkins because of his alcoholism.

Source: Olsen v. Hawkins, 408 P.2d 462 (Idaho 1965)

Practice Was the jury right in its findings?

⑯ Ethics ←?→ Application

Duty to Disclose? Shadonna typed up a simple agreement between Jonathan and herself for the sale of her computer equipment valued at $1000. When Jonathan read the agreement, he saw that Shadonna had made an error and typed the amount in at $100. Shadonna had already signed her name to the agreement without noticing the error, so Jonathan signed it then handed her $100.

◆ Is Jonathan required to point out the error in the amount to Shadonna before signing the contract?

⑰ Internet Application

Contractual Capacity of a Minor Diane is 16. She purchased a used car for cash in her name only. She now needs to purchase insurance in order to register her vehicle.

Log on to **glencoe.com** to access a car insurance Web site to determine the procedure for obtaining auto insurance as a minor. What limitations, if any, are in effect for the contractual transaction?

Reading Connection
Outside Reading Go to **glencoe.com** for a list of reading suggestions about contracts.

 glencoe.com

Case Study Practice

15. No. The Idaho Supreme Court held that simply being an alcoholic does not mean a person is incompetent to enter into a contract. Had Mr. Turner been drunk at the time he changed the beneficiaries, the situation may have been different. However, there was no evidence that Mr. Turner was drunk at the time he changed the beneficiaries, so the presumption was that he was competent to change the beneficiaries. Further, there had been no finding that he was insane by the jury; he had just been diagnosed as a chronic alcoholic, which did not mean that he was incompetent by reason of insanity.

Review and Assessment

←?→ Ethics Application

16. Legally, no. Since Jonathan did not generate the agreement, he does not have a legal duty to disclose the erroneous amount. However, depending on their personal relationship, Jonathan may want to disclose the error to prevent strife.

Internet Application

17. Minors will not be able to get car insurance on their own unless they have a valid driving license and their parents or guardians also enter into the contract. Parents or guardians can purchase insurance for their teens by adding them to their policy.

R Reading Strategy

Reading Connection

American Bar Association Resources

Go to the *Business and Personal Law* Online Learning Center through glencoe.com to find links for further readings that relate to this chapter. Ask students to read, review, and summarize the documents. Advise students to keep their reviews and summaries to use as reference material for their Unit Thematic Project on pages 154–155.

Plan Your Lesson Section by Section

NBEA	NATIONAL BUSINESS LAW STANDARDS
Section 6.1	• **Define** the statute of limitations. • **List** the ways a contract can be discharged. • **Explain** the various rules applied to contracts involving third parties.
Section 6.2	• **Describe** breach of contract and the remedies available when a contract is breached. • **Differentiate** between the ways that assent can be undermined (e.g., fraud, nondisclosure, misrepresentation, mistake, duress, and undue influence).

NCLB	ACADEMIC STANDARDS	Activity/Feature
English Language Arts: NCTE 3 Apply a wide range of strategies to comprehend, interpret, evaluate, and appreciate texts.		*BusinessWeek* News, Case Study, Case Study Practice
English Language Arts: NCTE 9 Develop an understanding of and respect for diversity in language use, patterns, and dialects across cultures, ethnic groups, geographic regions, and social roles.		Global Law
English Language Arts: NCTE 6 Apply knowledge of language structure, language conventions, media techniques, figurative language, and genre to create, critique, and discuss print and non-print texts.		Legal Talk, ad copy, Key Terms, and Academic Vocabulary
Mathematics: NCTM CS2 3 Recognize and apply mathematics in contexts outside of mathematics.		Section 6.1 Assessment
Mathematics: NCTM CS2 1 Recognize and use connections among mathematical ideas.		Section 6.2 Assessment
English Language Arts: NCTE 10 Students whose first language is not English make use of their first language to develop competency in the English language arts and to develop understanding of content across the curriculum.		Key Terms, Academic Vocabulary, Legal Talk, Vocabulary Builder
English Language Arts: NCTE 1 Read a wide range of print and non-print texts to build an understanding of texts; to acquire new information; to respond to the needs and demands of society and the workplace; and for personal fulfillment.		Global Law, Cyberlaw
English Language Arts: NCTE 8 Use a variety of technological and information resources to gather and synthesize information to create and communicate knowledge.		Case Study
English Language Arts: NCTE 4 Adjust the use of spoken, written, and visual language to communicate effectively with a variety of audiences and for different purposes.		*BusinessWeek* News, ad copy

Connect Your Business Law Classroom to the World of Work

This chart shows the 21st Century Skills, foundation skills, and workplace competencies that students develop as they work in this chapter.

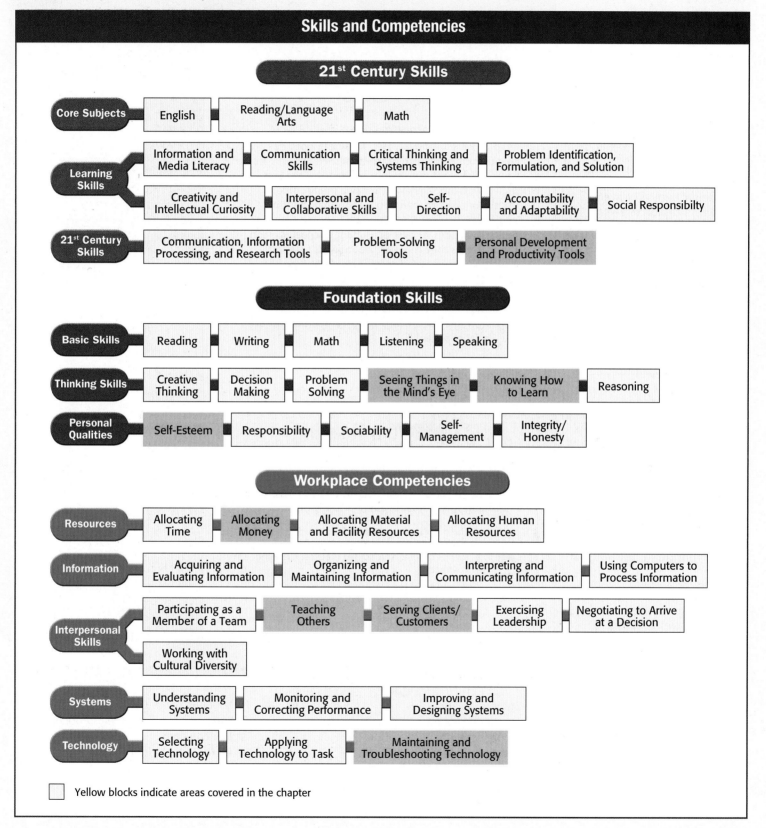

Skills and Competencies

21st Century Skills

Core Subjects
- English
- Reading/Language Arts
- Math

Learning Skills
- Information and Media Literacy
- Communication Skills
- Critical Thinking and Systems Thinking
- Problem Identification, Formulation, and Solution
- Creativity and Intellectual Curiosity
- Interpersonal and Collaborative Skills
- Self-Direction
- Accountability and Adaptability
- Social Responsibilty

21st Century Skills
- Communication, Information Processing, and Research Tools
- Problem-Solving Tools
- Personal Development and Productivity Tools

Foundation Skills

Basic Skills
- Reading
- Writing
- Math
- Listening
- Speaking

Thinking Skills
- Creative Thinking
- Decision Making
- Problem Solving
- Seeing Things in the Mind's Eye
- Knowing How to Learn
- Reasoning

Personal Qualities
- Self-Esteem
- Responsibility
- Sociability
- Self-Management
- Integrity/Honesty

Workplace Competencies

Resources
- Allocating Time
- Allocating Money
- Allocating Material and Facility Resources
- Allocating Human Resources

Information
- Acquiring and Evaluating Information
- Organizing and Maintaining Information
- Interpreting and Communicating Information
- Using Computers to Process Information

Interpersonal Skills
- Participating as a Member of a Team
- Teaching Others
- Serving Clients/Customers
- Exercising Leadership
- Negotiating to Arrive at a Decision
- Working with Cultural Diversity

Systems
- Understanding Systems
- Monitoring and Correcting Performance
- Improving and Designing Systems

Technology
- Selecting Technology
- Applying Technology to Task
- Maintaining and Troubleshooting Technology

Yellow blocks indicate areas covered in the chapter

CHAPTER 6

How Contracts Come to an End

BusinessWeek News

Cleaning Up at the Casino
By Eamon Javers

For years, the law firm Greenberg Traurig and its controversial lobbyist, Jack Abramoff, got huge checks from casino-rich Indian tribes. Now bucks are flowing the other way. In July, sources say, the firm settled with the Saginaw Chippewa Indian Tribe of Michigan for more than $10 million that the tribe says it was defrauded by Abramoff, who no longer works at the firm, and PR consultant Michael Scanlon. The tribe says they charged "outrageous fees" for work it has no record of receiving. A spokesman for Abramoff says he had no comment, and Scanlon couldn't be reached. An attorney says the tribe "will not disclose any details related to the agreement." A spokeswoman at the firm says: "Any settlement or talks are confidential."

Efficient critical reading involves being flexible with speed and comprehension. There are several ways of reading critically, and you need to fit a reading style to your needs and to the material.

Go to **glencoe.com** for Flex Your Reading activities, more information on reading strategies for this chapter, and guided practice in reading contracts.

Classroom Resources

- Student Edition
- Teacher Wraparound Edition
- Student Activity Workbook with Academic Integration (SE/TAE)
- TeacherWorks™ Plus! CD
- *ExamView®* Assessment Suite CD
- *Presentation Plus!* CD

- National Mock Trial Championship DVD
- Online Learning Center with Podcasts at glencoe.com
- Study-to-Go™ at glencoe.com
- Online Student Edition
- Interactive Student Edition

Delegation of Duties Contracts that require someone's personal skill and judgment cannot be delegated. *What are some types of jobs that cannot be delegated to someone else?*

Practice the Concept

Contracts and Delegation

Ask students if they have ever delegated a duty that they were supposed to do themselves. Have them consider school responsibilities, chores at home, or job duties. Explain that contracts often have clauses that address whether delegation is allowed.

Key Terms

Explain that when businesses or individuals write contracts, they must consider what the expectations are for the contract to be satisfied. In some cases, performance of duties may be delegated. The party who transfers the obligation to perform under the contract is called the delegator. The party who assumes the responsibility of performing this duty is called the delegatee. The party to whom this performance is owed is called the obligee.

The Fine Print

An assignment contract for a project can stipulate how the work should be performed and delivered, payment and invoicing procedures, and confidentiality clauses. Often, the assignee will not carefully and thoroughly read the contract to ensure that he or she agrees and abides by the terms of the contract. The assignee is not only jeopardizing his or her payment for the work due to potential breach of contract, but also risks losing future business with the assignor.

▲ USING VISUALS

Delegation of Duties Answer There are a variety of jobs that cannot be delegated to someone else because the personal skill, judgment, or talent of the contracting party is required. Singers, songwriters, architects, and celebrities, for instance, have special skills, fame, and experience that disallow delegation unless the contract says otherwise.

FOCUS

Transferring and Ending Contracts

Bell Ringer Activity

Ask students to recall instances in which they were not satisfied with the outcome of a contract. Ask if they were unhappy with the time frame in which the contract was completed or the fulfillment of the contract. Explain that, in order for a contract to be successfully discharged, certain conditions must be satisfied.

Reading Guide

Before You Read

Connect If you have signed a contract with someone or with a company, what are the ways this contract could end?

Focus on Ideas

Contracts may end because all rights and duties have been fulfilled or because the agreement has been broken.

What You'll Learn

◆ Explain how and when contracts can be discharged.
◆ Analyze the concept of performance.
◆ Describe the rules that apply to transfers of rights and duties.
◆ Understand the difference between delegation and assignment.

Why It's Important

Knowing when a contract ends is crucial for determining when the rights and duties of the parties terminate.

Academic Standards

Reading and completing the activities in this section will help you practice the following academic standards:

Math (NCTM CS2 3) Recognize and apply mathematics in contexts outside of mathematics.

English Language Arts (NCTE 8) Use a variety of technological and informa-tion resources to gather and synthesize information and to create and communi-cate knowledge.

Take Notes

Create a graph like the one shown and use it to take notes as you read this section. Go to glencoe.com to find graphic organizers and tips on how to improve your note-taking skills.

Components

 Key Terms

You will learn these legal words and expressions in this chapter. You can also find these terms in *Black's Law Dictionary* or in an online legal dictionary.

- substantial performance
- tender
- discharge by agreement
- impossibility of performance
- statute of limitations
- breach of contract
- assignment
- delegation

Academic Terms

You will find these words in your readings and in your tests. Look them up in a dictionary and familiarize yourself with them.

- substituted
- expire
- affected

Preteaching

Key Terms

Read the definitions and ask students to create a sentence using each term.

Academic Vocabulary

Explain that developing vocabulary is key to academic success. An efficient method to develop vocabulary is to study how words are formed.

- **substituted** Verb, from the Latin *substituere, sub* (under) + *statuere* (to cause to stand). Means replaced.

- **expire** Verb, from the Latin *expirare, ex* (out) + *spirare* (to breathe). Means to terminate.

- **affected** Verb, from the Latin *affectare* (to strive after, aim at). Means influenced.

Activity Ask students to give a noun, an adjective, or an adverb form that comes from each word.

R Reading Strategy

Read for Knowledge

1. **Survey** or preread the chapter.
2. **Question** or formulate questions before you read.
3. **Recite** or read your questions, answers, and notes out loud.
4. **Review** or reread your notes.

Note-Taking Basics

- Listen attentively
- Have note-taking materials ready
- Skim through the lesson material
- Write down key words and ideas
- Anticipate what comes next
- Review notes soon after taking them

Ending a Contract

If you sign a contract with a personal trainer, and the trainer has an accident and cannot work with you, is your contract still valid?

A contract is discharged when it comes to an end. The parties to a contract may enforce their rights and must perform their duties, according to the terms of the contract, up to the time of discharge. The law tells us when contracts can end so that people will know when their rights and duties conclude. Contracts can be discharged in two ways:

- by performance
- by agreement

Discharge by Performance

D Most contracts are discharged by performance. Performance is a series of activities that fulfills the purpose of a contract. As long as all the terms of the contract have been followed properly and completely, the contract has been discharged. Complete performance represents a stage in the contract at which all the terms have been carried out properly.

Time for Performance The time for completing performance may be important to one or both of the parties. If the time for performance is not stated in a contract and there is a question of performance, the court will say that all duties under the contract must be completed in a reasonable time.

Reasonableness is determined by what is suitable, fair, and proper to the goal of the contract. A reasonable time for selling tomatoes, for instance, is not the same as a reasonable time for selling a house.

 Time Is of the Essence A reasonable amount of time to sell produce is not the same as a reasonable amount of time to sell a car. *What are some types of goods or services in which time is of the essence in delivering or selling them?*

As You Read

Predict Think of three reasons why a contract would end.

TEACH

Discussion Starter

Class Discussion
Obtain samples of release forms and other legal documents that are used to discharge contracts. These might include a general release, a release of a mechanic's lien, or a release from a judgment lien. Pass to students and have them describe passages from the documents in their own words. (consideration amount, property released, name of parties, and lienholder)

D Develop Concepts

Discharge by Performance
Explain that contracts often require performance by both parties. Ask students if they contracted to have their car detailed, what kind of basic performance might be required of both parties? (cleaned car, performed within the time frame promised, payment given)

As You Read

Predict Have students volunteer ideas on how a contract might legally end. (ending by performance, by agreement of parties, and by expiration of the contract due to impossibility of performance or by operation of law)

▲ USING VISUALS

Time Is of the Essence Answer Answers will vary but may include retail sales contracts associated with holidays or perishable items, tickets for entertainment events or hotel reservations on a specific date, real-time stock purchases, and courier or overnight shipping services.

Activity Ask students to speculate whether there is an increase or decrease in the need for time-sensitive goods and services. Have students support their positions. (increased need, as there is a higher demand for online consumer sales, online business-to-business transactions, and use of wireless technology)

TEACH (cont.)

D Develop Concepts

Satisfactory Performance
Ask students to explain the difference between the expressions *in a satisfactory manner* and *to the other's satisfaction.* (Reasonable person test is used to measure whether a contract was performed in a satisfactory manner. If the contract stipulates "to the other's satisfaction," the other party must be satisfied with the performance before it is considered completed.)

C Critical Thinking

Substantial Performance
Ask students to imagine that Green Landscaping Co. was contracted to lay sod and install shrubbery for a golf course. The contract stipulates completion of the job before the next pro tournament. The landscaper completes all of the sod and 95 percent of the shrubbery by the tournament date. Ask students whether the golf course can withhold payment for the job. (No. Payment should be made, though the golf course might deduct the cost of the shrubbery not yet planted.)

If the parties state a time limit in the contract, the court may still give them more time if asked to do so by one of the parties. To avoid any kind of misunderstanding about time, the time limit should be included in the contract along with the words *time is of the essence.*

Satisfactory Performance The law requires that contractual services be done in a satisfactory manner. Sometimes, a contract says nothing about satisfaction; at other times, a contract may say that the work must be done in a satisfactory manner. In both situations, when one party believes the job is unsatisfactory, the dispute may end up in court.

In a lawsuit, the court uses the reasonable person test to measure whether the contract was performed in a satisfactory manner. This means the court asks whether a reasonable person would believe that the job was completed in a satisfactory manner. The jury generally gives the answer to this question. If there is no jury, the judge gives the answer. Occasionally one party will agree to perform services to the other party's satisfaction. In such a case, the other party must be satisfied to be held to the contract.

Substantial Performance Both parties must fully perform their duties for a contract to end by complete performance. Someone who has not fully performed his or her duties cannot, in most cases, win a lawsuit against the other party for money owed or for other damages.

An exception to this rule is known as the doctrine of substantial performance. **Substantial performance is a situation in which a party has, in good faith, completed the major requirements of a contract, leaving only a few minor details unfinished.** The court will allow that person to recover the amount agreed upon under the contract, minus the cost of completing the job. However, the court will allow recovery only if it can determine that it would be unfair to deny that recovery. The doctrine of substantial performance is often applied to construction contracts.

Tender of Performance A party can fulfill the terms of a contract by performing an act or by paying money. **A tender is an offer to do what you have agreed to do under a contract.** It is important to make tender even if you know the other party will not perform his or her part of the contract. In some states, making tender is necessary to test the other party's willingness and ability to perform. If neither party has made tender, then neither party can bring a lawsuit against the other.

If a person who must perform an act makes a tender of performance and that tender is rejected, that person is excused from fulfilling the contract. This principle does not apply to debts. An offer to pay a certain amount to fulfill a contract is a tender of payment. If a person makes a tender of payment and is rejected, that person is not excused from the debt. He or she is only excused from paying further interest on the amount of debt included in the tender of payment.

Guided Practice

Substantial and Satisfactory Performance

Sometimes small deviations occur in long and involved contracts. Ask students what happens if there is a slight deviation from the original terms of the contract. (Courts will generally permit the person who substantially performed to recover the amount agreed to, minus the cost of fixing the deviation.) Then ask students to consider a situation in which one person agrees to perform services for another "to the other's satisfaction." If a party is dissatisfied with the services performed by the other party, can that party refuse to comply with the payment terms of the contract? (yes)

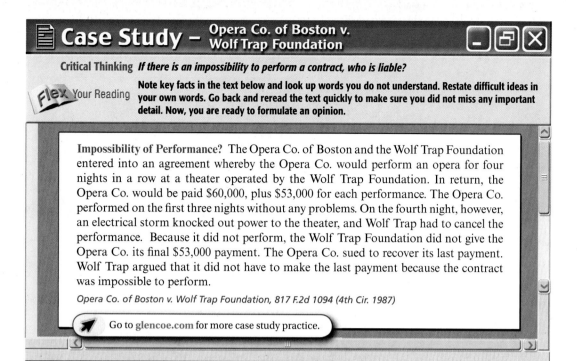

Case Study – Opera Co. of Boston v. Wolf Trap Foundation

Critical Thinking *If there is an impossibility to perform a contract, who is liable?*

Flex Your Reading Note key facts in the text below and look up words you do not understand. Restate difficult ideas in your own words. Go back and reread the text quickly to make sure you did not miss any important detail. Now, you are ready to formulate an opinion.

Impossibility of Performance? The Opera Co. of Boston and the Wolf Trap Foundation entered into an agreement whereby the Opera Co. would perform an opera for four nights in a row at a theater operated by the Wolf Trap Foundation. In return, the Opera Co. would be paid $60,000, plus $53,000 for each performance. The Opera Co. performed on the first three nights without any problems. On the fourth night, however, an electrical storm knocked out power to the theater, and Wolf Trap had to cancel the performance. Because it did not perform, the Wolf Trap Foundation did not give the Opera Co. its final $53,000 payment. The Opera Co. sued to recover its last payment. Wolf Trap argued that it did not have to make the last payment because the contract was impossible to perform.

Opera Co. of Boston v. Wolf Trap Foundation, 817 F.2d 1094 (4th Cir. 1987)

Go to **glencoe.com** for more case study practice.

The person offering to pay the required amount of money must offer legal tender. Under Federal Law, legal tender for debts, public charges, taxes, and dues is U.S. coins or currency.

Discharge by Agreement

Discharge by agreement means that people can end a contract by mutual agreement. This can be done by mutual release or by accord and satisfaction. A mutual release is an agreement between two parties to end a contract. Whatever the parties agree to do in the first place, they can later agree not to do. Otherwise, there would be no consideration for the promised release. A contract can also be discharged when one party agrees to accept a different performance from the other party. One contract is **substituted** for another. This is called accord and satisfaction. It is often used to settle an honest disagreement on an amount owed.

Involuntary Discharge

Some contracts are discharged involuntarily despite what the parties intend or what they actually do (see **Figure 6.1** on page 134). In these situations, the obligations under the contract may also **expire**. The two primary ways contracts are discharged in this way are:

- by impossibility of performance
- by operation of law

Vocabulary You can find vocabulary definitions in the **Key Terms** glossary and **Academic Vocabulary** glossary in the back of this book.

TEACH *(cont.)*

D Develop Concepts

Discharge by Agreement
Emphasize that contracts may be terminated by mutual agreement between the contract parties. Ask students to think of an example of such a situation. (A contractor signs a contract with Joe Blane to build his house. Joe is fired from his job the following week and decides he cannot afford the house. Both contractor and buyer decide to terminate the agreement.)

S Skills Practice

Define Ask students to define the act of accord and satisfaction. (One party agrees to accept a different performance from the other party.) **L1**

Illustrate Have students think of a situation in which a mutual release occurs. (Answers will vary but should demonstrate the understanding that the two parties to a contract can agree not to do what they originally contracted to do.) **L2**

Analyze Ask students to consider the safeguards parties might take when they decide to discharge a contract by agreement. (put the agreement to discharge the contract in writing so that there is no doubt that the contract responsibilities are no longer in force) **L3**

Case Study

Opera Co. of Boston v. Wolf Trap Foundation

Answer A foreseeability test is necessary to determine liability, if any. The Fourth Circuit held that the lower court failed to fully consider whether it was reasonable for Wolf Trap to foresee a potential loss of the power to the park. The reasonableness test includes things such as whether power losses were frequent in the area, what the likelihood of a power loss was during that contracted time period, and so forth. If the power loss was foreseeable, then Wolf Trap may be liable.

TEACH (cont.)

Guided Practice

Involuntary Discharge

Ask students to describe events or circumstances that might prevent two parties from completing a contract that they intended to complete. Emphasize that sometimes situations occur that are out of the parties' control. (death, illness, destruction of contract subject matter, illegality)

Role Play

Have two students take the part of the individuals in this scenario: Will hired Travis to repair a leak in his upstairs bathroom. Travis agrees but discovers that it cannot be fixed without hours of work that he had not anticipated and says that the contract must be discharged due to impossibility of performance. Will disagrees and expects Travis to perform. (Travis attempts to use the idea of impossibility of performance so that the contract can be discharged. Will can argue that the situation is not impossible, it is just an unexpected difficulty.)

Figure 6.1 Involuntary Discharge of a Contract

A contract cannot be completed if the subject matter of the contract, such as a piece of property, is destroyed through no fault of the parties to the contract.

The death or illness of a party to a contract may end the contract if it required the personal service of that person.

The law will discharge a contract if the Statute of Limitations for completing the contract runs out.

Despite what the parties intended to do, some contracts can be ended involuntarily for the reasons shown in the figure. *For what other reasons might an contract be ended involuntarily?*

134   Unit 2   Contract Law

▲ USING VISUALS

➡ **Figure 6.1 Involuntary Discharge of a Contract Answer** Contracts may also be ended involuntarily due to bankruptcy, illegality of performance (i.e., due to a new law), or wrongful alteration. Remind students that certain debts cannot be discharged under bankruptcy laws, therefore the contract still stands. Education loans, debts for taxes, and child support agreements are such debts.

Discharge by Impossibility of Performance

A contract that becomes legally impossible to perform generally may be discharged, and both parties may be released from the obligation. The courts allow a discharge for immmpossibility of performance. **Impossibility of performance may be allowed in case of death or illness that prevents the performance of a personal service contract; the destruction of the exact subject matter, or the means for performance; and illegality, or situations in which the performance of a contract becomes illegal.**

Death or Illness in a Personal Service Contract The death or illness of a party to a contract may be an excuse for nonperformance. This is true only if the contract requires the personal service of the person who has died or become ill.

Destruction of the Exact Subject Matter If the means or subject matter that is needed to perform the contract is destroyed through no fault of either party, the contract is discharged. The destruction must occur after the contract is entered, but before it is carried out.

Discharge by Operation of Law

At times, the best interests of society demand that a contract be terminated. Under these circumstances, the law declares contracts discharged by operation of law.

Wrongful Alteration One party's wrongful acts (such as altering or changing a contract) will discharge a contract by operation of law.

Statute of Limitations States laws specify how much time can pass before you can bring a legal action on a contract. These are called statutes of limitations. **A statute of limitations establishes a time limit for suing in a civil case, based on the date when the breach occurred or was discovered.** There are many special statutes of limitations in every state. To protect yourself fully in important business relationships, you should refer to the most recent statutes in your state. The statute of limitations for failure to perform contracts for the sale of goods is four years in most states. This means a legal action must be begun within four years after the contract is broken.

The parties may reduce the period of limitation to not less than one year by the original agreement. They may not, however, extend the period to more than the limit set by their state. However, a time-out is called when a creditor is a minor or is mentally ill. These situations stop the clock on the statute of limitations. In some states, people who are in prison suffer what is called civil death. They lose the right to vote, to make contracts, and to bring and defend against civil lawsuits. In these states, the statute of limitations on contracts often stops running while a person is in prison.

Reading Check

Analyze What are all the ways performance is looked at when determining if and how a contract may end?

TEACH (cont.)

D Develop Concepts

Civil Death Write the following sentence on the board: Brenda Carlson suffered a civil death when she was incarcerated for theft. Ask students to reflect on what the idea of the civil death means. (loss of right to vote, contract, bring and defend civil suits) Remind students that the statute of limitations on a contract often stops running while a person is in prison.

C Critical Thinking

Impossibility of Performance Tell students to imagine that the lead singer of a band was rushed to a hospital two hours before a scheduled concert. Ask whether the singer's illness discharges the band's contract to perform the concert. (If the contract requires the lead singer's presence, his illness can discharge the contract.)

Extending the Content

Personal Service Contract

Ask students to interview a family member or friend who has acted as the executor of an estate to find out if he or she was obligated to discharge a contract of the deceased. If possible, have students ask about the generalities of the contract and how the executor had the contract discharged.

Reading Check

Analyze When determining if and how a contract may end, these factors are important: time for performance, satisfactory performance, substantial performance, tender of performance, discharge by agreement, impossibility of performance, and/or discharge by operation of law.

TEACH (cont.)

D Develop Concepts

Breach of Contract Explain that when a contract is breached, the injured party has several choices. Write the following phrases on the board:

- acceptance of breach
- pursuit of money damages

Ask students if they have had experience with either situation.

Guided Practice

Exceptions to Discharging Contracts

Explain to students that while they have learned different ways that contracts can be discharged, some obligations cannot be released. Ask students if they can explain what bankruptcy involves. (People or businesses cannot pay debts, so some types of debts may be discharged.) List the types of debts that cannot be discharged:

- student loans
- taxes
- alimony
- child support

Ask students if they agree with these exceptions and why.

Transferring Duties Sometimes people have to shift some of their work to other qualified parties. *Can the duties of a physical trainer be transferred to another physical trainer?*

Debt and Statutes of Limitations In some instances, the debt may be renewed. If a debtor makes a partial payment or admits that the debt exists after the time period has passed, the debt is renewed for another time period set by the state statute. In New York and some other states, such a new promise must be in writing.

Bankruptcy Congress has the authority to pass bankruptcy laws that set procedures for discharging a debtor's obligations. These obligations still exist, but the debtor cannot be imprisoned for failure to pay. Certain debts cannot be discharged under bankruptcy laws. Education loans, for example, usually cannot be discharged during the first five years of the repayment period. In addition, debts for taxes, alimony, child support, and maintenance are not **affected** by a general discharge of debts in bankruptcy.

Breach of Contract

What can happen if a contract is not fulfilled?

A breach of contract is when a person fails to perform the duties spelled out by a contract. The effects of a breach vary depending on the case. When a breach of contract happens, one party is injured. The injuries are not physical, but that does not mean that they are not real. The injured party may demand justice. Many states permit the injured party to bring an action for damages at the time of breach (see page 145).

The Transfer of Contractual Rights and Duties

If you signed a contract with a personal trainer, can you be assigned another trainer without a new contract?

When people establish contracts, they receive rights (benefits) and acquire duties (detriments). Most of the time, people manage their own rights and duties. Sometimes, these rights and duties are moved to someone new. For example, some people give another person their right to receive money because they owe that person money they cannot pay otherwise. Other people take on more work than they can handle and have to shift some of their duties to other qualified parties. The law permits this sort of transfer, with a few exceptions.

▲ USING VISUALS

Transferring Duties Answer Unless the contract or agreement that the physical trainer has entered into states otherwise, the duties of a physical trainer can be transferred to another trainer.

Activity Ask how many of your students hold part-time jobs. Inquire whether any of them have ever asked a co-worker to cover their shift. Ask students to determine whether this constitutes transferring of duties. (This is essentially transferring of duties to another person. Since the other person worked the shift, they are entitled to the compensation for the work, or, in other words, they have been assigned the rights of receiving payment.)

Assignment and Transfer of Rights

An assignment is the transfer of a right under contract.
The general rule about assignments is that people can legally transfer contract rights as long as the contract does not specifically say they cannot. The party who transfers the rights is the assignor; the party who gets the rights is the assignee. The assignee is a third person who is not a party to the original contract.

> **Example** Anthony Cuomo entered into a contract with Cathy Michaud to rebuild the front steps of her house for $1,800. The carpenter was pleased to get the contract because he owed $1,800 to his landlord, David Brown. Before beginning work, Anthony assigned the right to receive payment for the work to his landlord. When payment was due, Cathy paid the $1,800 to David Brown directly.

How Rights May Be Assigned No consideration is necessary for an assignment to be valid. In most cases, the law does not even say how one party may assign a right to somebody else. However, it is best to put an assignment in writing because an oral assignment can be difficult to prove. Suppose that you owe money to a bank under a contract. Now suppose that the bank decides to assign the right to receive your money to another bank. Would you want to know about that change? Of course you would, and you would want the change in writing so that, when you send the money to the new bank, you know that you are doing the right thing.

What Rights May Be Assigned Most rights may be assigned unless the assignment changes the obligations of the other party to the contract in an important way. However, not all assignments are valid. For instance, the right to receive personal services usually cannot be assigned. An assignor can assign nothing more than the rights that he or she possesses. An assignee takes those rights, subject to other people's defenses.

> **Example** Suppose that when Anthony Cuomo, from the earlier example, assigned the right to receive the $1,800 to his landlord, Anthony then did a poor job. Cathy Michaud could raise the defense of a poor job if she were sued by the assignee, who wants to collect the $1,800.

Rights to the payment of money, such as wages, money owed on accounts, royalties on books, and rights to the delivery of goods are the most common types of rights that are assigned. After the assignment, the assignor no longer has an interest in the right that was assigned. This right now belongs exclusively to the assignee.

Generally, no special form is required to make an assignment. Any words that clearly indicate a person's intent are sufficient. This assignment may be made on a separate paper, or it may be written on the back of a written contract containing the rights to be assigned.

TEACH *(cont.)*

D Develop Concepts

Assignment Ask students what the term *assignment* means to them. (Students will probably define it as a task to be performed.) Explain that in the law it is a transfer of contractual rights. Ask students why they think the same term can be used for both a task and a transfer, and if necessary, point out that both have to do with giving—for example, giving someone a specific task is an assignment, and giving someone contractual rights is also an assignment.

Guided Practice

Transfer of Rights

Explain to students that, unless the contract states otherwise, they may legally transfer (assign) their rights under any contract to another party. Ask two members from the class to create a brief skit in which one party assigns his or her rights in a contract to the other.

ASSESS

Quiz

Ask students to answer the following questions:

1. How are most contracts discharged? (by performance)

2. What is substantial performance? (One party has completed the major requirements of a contract in good faith, leaving only a few minor details unfinished.)

3. Kevin's home was destroyed by a tornado one week before ABC Painting Co. was to repaint the home. Can this contract be enforced? (It can be discharged due to impossibility of performance, and destruction of subject matter.)

4. What is breach of contract? (When a person fails to perform the duties spelled out by a contract.)

RETEACH

Extending the Content

Ending a Contract

Have students each select one of the key terms from this section to research. Suggest they use a Web site or a dictionary of legal terms to find a comprehensive definition of their term. Ask students to write an example to illustrate its meaning. (*Substantial performance* might be illustrated as follows. A painter has been hired to paint an office building, complete the job in one week, and clean the area after completion. At the end of the week, he has painted the building, but has not yet removed his supplies and ladders. He has substantially completed the contract, so it would be unreasonable to deny him the payment.)

STUDY TO GO Have students go to the *Business and Personal Law* Online Learning Center through glencoe.com to download free Study-to-Go content to their cell phones or PDAs.

Review Key Terms

Encourage students to access the *Business and Personal Law* Online Learning Center through glencoe.com and use the electronic flashcards to review the key terms.

138

➡ **Third Parties** The make-up artist is putting finishing touches on a character from the movie *Judge Dredd*. Teachers, writers, and artists are selected to perform certain services because of their particular skills or talents. *In the context of rights, transfers of rights, and duties, do you think a chef you hired to oversee the catering of a dinner party could delegate the work to another cook?*

Delegation and Transfer of Duties

Delegation means transferring of a duty under a contract. A delegation should not be confused with an assignment. An assignment is a transfer of rights; a delegation is a transfer of duties. In a transfer of duties, a party to a contract trusts another person to do the job in his or her place.

> **Example** Ivan Remec, owner of the Eastern Print Shop, had overextended himself financially and could not meet all of his printing contracts. When the time came to print the monthly newsletter for the high school's Parent Teacher Association, he transferred his contract obligation to another printer who was not a party to the original contract. This was a legal form of subcontracting. However, if Ivan had told the PTA that he would personally do the printing, Ivan could not have delegated the task.

It is important to remember that the performance of an obligation may be delegated, but the responsibility for it may not. If both parties understand the situation, it is all right to hand over the duty of doing the work to someone else. This is a form of subcontracting that is common in business contracts. You may not delegate duties, however, in any of the following situations:

- A party agrees to perform the service personally.
- The contract calls for the exercise of personal skill and judgment.
- The contract itself prohibits delegation.

The offeror and the offeree may include in their contract a statement that the contract may not be assigned or delegated. In this case, both parties are restrained.

▲ USING VISUALS

➡ **Third Parties** **Answer** It is possible that the chef could delegate the work, depending on why you hired him or her. If the chef was hired to do the meal because you like the chef's food, then he or she probably could not delegate.

Activity Ask students to think of the types of persons they might hire for a service for which delegation would not be acceptable. (might include singers, bands, DJs, hair stylists, fashion designers)

If you have the right to delegate a contractual obligation and decide to do so, choose your third party carefully. As explained, you retain responsibility for any job duties that you subcontract or assign to a third party.

Novation You do not need the permission of the other party to assign contract rights or to delegate duties to a third person. If you do receive permission, and the other party agrees to deal with the assignee, the resulting contract is called a novation. A novation is an agreement whereby an original party to a contract is replaced by a new party. The other terms of the new contract generally remain the same as those in the original contract. To be effective, the change requires the consent of all of the parties involved.

Third Parties A contract is a binding agreement that establishes a relationship between the parties to the contract. This relationship between the parties is termed privity of contract. It determines who can sue whom over a question of performance required by a contract. Usually the parties to a contract have standing to sue.

A third person may sometimes enforce a contract when it is made specifically for that person's benefit. A person who is not a party to a contract but still benefits from the contract is called a third party beneficiary.

After You Read

Summarize List ways you could get out of a contract to sing at your school's football game.

RETEACH (cont.)

After You Read

Summarize Students may suggest that they might be able to get out of the obligation if they became sick, if the football game were canceled or the stadium were destroyed, or if the contract had been wrongfully altered.

ASSESS

Self-Assessment

Have students go to the *Business and Personal Law* Online Learning Center through glencoe.com to take the Section 6.1 Practice Test.

CLOSE

Culminating Activity

Involuntary Discharge

Tell students that Richard added a "0" after the date of June 3 in the contract to attempt to extend the date of completion. Ask students which method of involuntary discharge would be suitable in this case. (wrongful alteration)

SECTION **6.1** ASSESSMENT

Self Check

1. How can contracts be discharged by performance?

2. What situations permit a contractual discharge by impossibility of performance?

3. What situations permit a contractual discharge by operation of law?

Academic Connection

Mathematics Last week, Cynthia used a credit card to purchase a snowboard for $277.89. This week, she saw the same snowboard on sale online for $250.43. The sales tax in Cynthia's state is 8%. The online store is not based in her state and charges only for shipping. Shipping charges are 2% of the item's price. How much would Cynthia save if she could return her snowboard for a refund and order the one she saw online?

THEORY **Numbers and Operations: Calculating Percentages and Comparing Prices** Calculate 8% of $277.89 by multiplying the price by 0.08. Add the result to the price of the snowboard. Calculate shipping charges by multiplying 4250.43 by 0.02. Add the result to the price. Compare the two results to make a decision.

 For more math practice, go to the Math Appendix.

Critical Thinking

Discharged or Not? Debra agreed to work for Lupe for two years. At the end of two months, Debra went to Lupe and asked to be released from her contract. Lupe agreed. Was the contract discharged? Explain.

Go to **glencoe.com** to check your answers.

SECTION **6.1** ASSESSMENT

Self-Check

1. time for performance, satisfactory performance, substantial performance, tender of performance

2. death or illness, destruction of the exact subject matter or the means for performance, and illegality

3. wrongful alteration, statute of limitations, and bankruptcy

Academic Connection

Mathematics
$44.68 savings

Critical Thinking

Yes. Under the theory of mutual release, if both parties agree, then the contract ends.

N C L B Activity correlated to the Mathematics standard on page 130

FOCUS

🔔 **Bell Ringer Activity**

Outline the following situation to students. Ken plans to pay Bridget $20 per week to walk his dog daily while he is on vacation. Ask students to propose statement(s) Ken should add to this contract to identify what will happen if Bridget cannot meet the obligation. (reduction in fee, Bridget must arrange for another dogwalker)

Preteaching

Key Terms
Read the definitions and ask students to create a sentence using each term.

Academic Vocabulary
Explain that developing vocabulary is key to academic success. An efficient method to develop vocabulary is to study how words are formed.

- **intent** Noun, from the Latin *intentus* (lean toward). Means aim or purpose.

- **exaggerate** Verb, from the Latin *exaggeratus, ex* (thoroughly) + *aggerare* (heap up). Means to overstate.

- **mutual** Adjective, from the Latin *mutuus* (reciprocal). Means held in common.

Activity Ask students to give a noun, an adjective, or an adverb form that comes from each word.

 Connects to academic content

What You'll Learn

- ◆ Differentiate among the ways contracts can be undermined (fraud, non-disclosure, misrepresentation, mistake, duress, and undue influence).
- ◆ Explain what remedies are available when a contract is not fulfilled.

Why It's Important

Knowing the consequences of a breach of contract can help you prepare for the loss that follows and for deciding on possible recourse.

Academic Standards

Reading and completing the activities in this section will help you practice the following academic standards:

NCLB

English Language Arts (NCTE 4) Adjust the use of spoken, written, and visual language to communicate effectively with a variety of audiences and for different purposes.

Math (NCTM CS2 1) Recognize and use connections among mathematical ideas.

Voidable Contracts and Remedies

Reading Guide

Before You Read

Connect Have you ever been pressured into agreeing to do something you did not really want to do? Do you think you should have been able to get out of it?

Focus on Ideas
A contract can be breached either intentionally or unintentionally.

Take Notes
Create a graph like the one shown and use it to take notes as you read this section. Go to glencoe.com for tips on how to improve your note-taking skills.

📖 Key Terms
You will learn these legal words and expressions in this chapter. You can also find these terms in *Black's Law Dictionary* or in an online legal dictionary.

- fraud
- duress
- undue influence
- remedy
- damages
- punitive damages
- injunction

📖 Academic Terms
You will find these words in your readings and in your tests. Look them up in a dictionary and familiarize yourself with them.

- intent
- exaggerate
- mutual

 glencoe.com

R Reading Strategy

Read for Knowledge

1. **Survey** or preread the chapter.
2. **Question** or formulate questions before you read.
3. **Recite** or read your questions, answers, and notes out loud.
4. **Review** or reread your notes.

Note-Taking Basics
- Listen attentively
- Have note-taking materials ready
- Skim through the lesson material
- Write down key words and ideas
- Anticipate what comes next
- Review notes soon after taking them

Defective Agreements

If a contract appears to meet the requirements of offer, acceptance, agreement, consideration, capacity, and legality, what could still prevent the contract?

Sometimes, what seems to be a valid contract turns out to be nothing of the kind. In these cases, the agreement is defective. Several circumstances might lead to this situation: fraud, misrepresentation, mistake, duress, and undue influence.

Fraud

Fraud is a deliberate deception intended to serve an unfair and unlawful gain. If you figure out that the seller lied, then you may be able to get your money back. That means you may have to sue for money damages. Lying weakens the entire world of contracts, therefore the law will let the injured party get punitive damages. To win a lawsuit based on fraud, five elements must be shown:

- There must be a false representation of fact (a lie).
- The person who lied must know it was a lie.
- The lie must be made with the **intent** that it be relied on.
- The innocent party must reasonably rely on the lie.
- The innocent party must experience a loss.

As You Read

Predict What are some reasons why a contract may be voidable?

Vocabulary You can find vocabulary definitions in the **Key Terms** glossary and **Academic Vocabulary** glossary in the back of this book.

(1) **Victims of Fraud** Anybody can become a victim of fraud. *Why do unscrupulous telemarketers often target retired Americans for fraud?*

TEACH

Discussion Starter

Class Discussion

Ask students to recall all the elements that make a contract valid. Tell students that when the element of genuine agreement is no longer included, a contract becomes defective. Explain that this section will cover all the circumstances under which a contract becomes defective.

As You Read

Predict You may accept the breach, sue for money damages (and possibly punitive damages), and/or in some instances, request an equitable remedy, such as specific performance, or an injunction.

S Skills Practice

Have students research art fraud and complete the following activities:

List List sources for researching art fraud, including books, magazines, newspapers, or Web sites. **L1**

Describe Write a short report about art fraud in general or about a specific work of art that was discovered to be fake. **L2**

Practice Re-create a piece of art whose authenticity is or has been questioned. **L3**

▲ USING VISUALS

(→) **Victims of Fraud Answer** Retired people are more likely to have substantial savings and investments, to be at home to receive phone calls, and to listen respectfully to a sales pitch.

Activity Ask students to research and outline the financial and psychological effects of a fraud. (Financial effects: the majority lost money or property and a lesser percent suffered credit problems and health problems, and lost time off work. Psychological effects: self-doubt, shock, societal indifference, isolation, anger, resentment, frustration with criminal justice professionals, shame, embarrassment, fear for financial security, increased concern about personal safety and well-being.)

TEACH (cont.)

D Develop Concepts

False Representations
Place a cell phone on the table in front of the class. Tell students that the cell phone will never drop calls and is 100 percent reliable. Ask students to indicate what kinds of misrepresentations have been made. (never drops calls, 100 percent reliability) Explain to students that consumers might make decisions to buy the phone based on this representation. In a fraud case, the injured party must prove that he or she depended on the lie.

C Critical Thinking

False Representation Jeff purchased a used car from Quality Autos. The salesperson at the lot assured Jeff that his car had never been involved in an accident. While looking through his car's glove box a week after purchasing it, Jeff discovered repair receipts that indicated the car had been in a major accident. Can Jeff pursue a claim of false representation? (Yes. He would have to prove either that the salesperson knew of the car accident or that he made a reckless statement about the car's history and condition.)

CYBERLAW

BellSouth Communications System, LLC v. West
902 So.2d 653 (Ala. 2004)

BellSouth is an Internet Service Provider in Alabama, where Thomas West resides. In 2002, Mr. West signed up with BellSouth for Internet service. The advertised price was $15.95 per month. When Mr. West received his bill from BellSouth, he discovered he had been charged $19.85 for one month's service and a $15.00 set-up fee. Mr. West sued for breach of contract. BellSouth countered, arguing that the membership agreement that Mr. West had signed said that BellSouth could change any terms of the agreement (including the monthly fee) by posting notice on the Internet. Mr. West said he never saw the posting.

Ruling and Resolution
The Alabama Supreme Court held that BellSouth could not provide proof of when it had posted the change in fees on its Web site. Neither could BellSouth prove that Mr. West had accessed the Web site after the alleged change. Therefore, Mr. West was able to recover damages against BellSouth.

Critical Thinking Should companies be allowed to notify customers of changes to their contracts by posting notices on Web sites?

False Representation of Fact The law requires that the lie be about a material fact that is really important. It cannot be a promise of something that will happen in the future, and it cannot be just an opinion. The law allows sales people to **exaggerate** their claims just as long as the exaggerations are obviously a statement of the seller's opinion.

In the context of fraud, a lie is not just something false that is written or spoken. It can also be actions that the seller uses to cover up a defect or to hide some factual piece of evidence. If your friend, Phil, tells you that he is going to turn back the odometer of his '65 Mustang so he can get a better price for it, you should let him know that he is about to commit fraud. Sometimes people lie by inaction. This happens when they do not say something that they are supposed to say. This is called passive fraud, concealment, or nondisclosure.

Knowledge of the Lie To be responsible for the lie, the person telling the lie must know that it is a lie. The innocent party has to show this by giving evidence in court that the other person had actual knowledge that he or she was lying. Short of this, the innocent party might succeed in the lawsuit by showing that the other party told the lie recklessly. This means that the defrauding party told the lie without regard for the true story.

Lie Intended to Be Relied Upon To prove fraud, the innocent person must show that the liar told the lie knowing that the other party, would hear it, believe it, and act on it. In other words, he or she told the lie to tempt the other party into the false contract.

142 Unit 2 Contract Law

CYBERLAW

BellSouth Communications System, LLC, v. West

Answer Answers will vary. The courts have held that posting notices on Web sites is adequate notification to consumers that terms of contracts have changed. Some companies require customers to agree to notification by posting, but it is not required in most circumstances. It is presumed that customers keep themselves aware of such notices by regularly checking postings.

Lie Actually Relied Upon To prove fraud, the innocent party has to show that he or she depended on the lie. Sometimes the defrauding party lies, but the other party pays no attention to the lie. If that happens, there are no grounds for a lawsuit.

Resulting Loss You can be enticed into a contract by a lie that the other party knows is a lie, and you still might not be able to recover damages in court. This happens if the last element is missing. If the innocent party does not lose anything in the deal, there is no loss, and with no loss, there is no fraud.

Innocent Misrepresentation

Misrepresentation occurs when a person who is involved in contract negotiations says something that he or she believes to be true that turns out to be false. The law gives the innocent party the right to get out of the contract in this situation.

Mistake, Duress, and Undue Influence

Sometimes a person enters a contract with a mistaken idea of what is at stake. Later, when the mistaken person realizes that an error has been made, he or she tries to get out of the agreement. Is this possible? Sometimes the answer is yes, but more often it is no.

Unilateral Mistake

A unilateral mistake is an error on the part of one of the parties to the contract. Usually a person cannot get out of a contract just because of a mistake. The law wants people to pay attention to their business deals.

Mistake as to the Nature of the Agreement A mistake as to the nature of the agreement is one type of unilateral mistake. A unilateral mistake like this does not give anybody a way out of a contract. If you buy a DVD online and then find out that you have the exact same DVD on your shelf at home, you made a mistake. You will not be able to get out of the contract. People are bound to a contract even if they do not read it or are mistaken about what it says. Your signature shows that you agree to the terms whether you understood them or not. The rule applies even to those who cannot read English. People who cannot read English are expected to have someone who does understand the language read and explain the terms in the agreement.

Mistake as to Value A mistake as to value (about how much an object for sale is worth) is another type of unilateral mistake. It does not give anybody a way out of a contract.

⬇ **Unilateral Mistake** If you mistakenly buy a CD you already own, you cannot simply negate the contract. *What can you do to avoid this situation?*

Chapter 6   How Contracts Come to an End   **143**

W Writing Support

Innocent Misrepresentation Outline the following scenario to students. A salesman at a dealership routinely tells customers that a certain brand of truck is the most durable on the market. Tell students that the salesman later discovers that the brand has the worst record for durability. Ask students to write a paragraph on whether customers should be able to nullify their sales contracts. (innocent party can get out of the contract)

C Critical Thinking

Undue Influence Explain to students that an individual's free will may be disrupted by the undue influence of someone upon whom they depend. Ask them: Why is undue influence difficult to prove? (Answers should include that it is difficult to prove when the line has been crossed between mere influence and excessive pressure; evidence is scarce and difficult to obtain; and the dependent party may really believe that he or she is getting a great benefit from the independent party.)

▲ USING VISUALS

➡ **Unilateral Mistake** Answer When you buy an item and you need to return it to the store, ensure that the seller's contract includes a return policy before you buy.

Activity Most stores have a return policy. The return policy includes conditions regarding the return of a purchased product. Ask students to look up on the Internet the return policies of various stores and identify main points of a return policy. (Answers may include refunds or credit, exchanges, exceptions for open or damaged items, or issue of Returned Materials Authorization for the shipment of a returned item.)

TEACH (cont.)

Enumerate To prove that fraud has occurred, the following must be shown:

- False representation of fact (a lie)
- The person who lied must know that it was a lie
- The lie must be made with the intent that it be relied on
- The innocent party must reasonably rely on the lie
- The innocent party must experience a loss

Legal Talk

(hardness, severity, constraint)

Ask students to practice their academic and legal vocabulary with the electronic flashcards available at the *Business and Personal Law* Online Learning Center through glencoe.com.

Legal Talk

Duress: *n* Unlawful threat or coercion. From Latin *durus* = hard.

Punitive: *adj* Relating to punishment. From Latin *punitus* = punish.

Vocabulary Builder List and define three words that have a similar meaning to duress.

Look It Up! Check definitions in *Black's Law Dictionary* or an online glossary. For direct links, go to glencoe.com to find more vocabulary resources.

⬭ **Reading Check**
Enumerate *What is necessary to prove that fraud has occurred?*

Bilateral Mistake

A bilateral mistake is an error that is made on the part of both parties to the contract. This is also called **mutual** mistake. Often when the mistake is bilateral, either one of the parties can get out of the contract.

A bilateral mistake can be made as to the possibility of performance. This will get rid of the duty to perform. Suppose that you agree to pay your local bookstore owner $10 if he makes sure that you are the first person to buy the next Harry Potter novel. Now, suppose the author of the Harry Potter books says that she will never write another Harry Potter book—ever. Both you and the book dealer were mistaken as to the availability of a new Harry Potter book. The contract cannot be performed and the agreement is ended.

Suppose you believe you are buying the 2005 VHS version of *The Fantastic Four* feature film. When the tape arrives, you realize that the tape is actually the 1993 film. This is a bilateral mistake as to the subject matter. You were buying the 2005 version while the other party was selling the 1993 version. If the seller was selling one thing while the buyer was buying another, either party can void the contract.

Duress

Duress is the act of destroying somebody's free will by force, threat of force, or bodily harm. Agreements made under duress are either void or voidable.

Physical Duress When actual physical force is used to cause another person to enter a contract, the contract is void. When the threat of force is used, the contract is voidable. The threat can be against the person entering the contract or a family member of that person.

Economic Duress Economic duress is an act that threatens a person's income or business that makes that person enter a contract without real consent. To succeed in voiding a contract based on economic duress, the victim has to prove three things:

- The other party wrongfully placed them in a poor economic position.
- The victim had no choice other than to submit to the duress.
- Their submission to the duress was reasonable under the circumstances.

Undue Influence

Undue influence is an action or series of overly persuasive actions that make inappropriate use of one person's position of power over another person to create an agreement that is very favorable to the person with all the power. To succeed in voiding a contract based on undue influence, the victim has to prove three things:

- The existence of a caregiver-type relationship.
- The use of excessive pressure by the caregiver.
- A resulting contract that heavily favors the caregiver.

D

D Develop Concepts

Bilateral Mistake Distinguish between a unilateral and a bilateral mistake by pointing out that *uni* is a Latin prefix that means one, and *bi* is a Latin prefix that means two. Explain that if both parties in a contract make mistakes, either party can usually void the contract. Ask students to call out one or two reasons why people can get out of a contract due to a bilateral mistake. (obligation cannot be performed, subject matter of contract was not clear)

Guided Practice

Duress

Although students may be familiar with the idea that a person may be forced to do something by the threat of force or bodily harm, ask them to consider what economic duress might entail. (threat to a person's business or income that may cause that person to enter into a contract without real consent)

Remedies and Damages

What do you think you can do if someone has not fulfilled a contract you had agreed to?

When a contract is not fulfilled, the injured party has a choice of remedies. **A remedy is a legal means of enforcing a right or correcting a wrong.** If you are the injured party, you have three different options:

- You may accept the breach.
- You may sue for money damages.
- You may ask the court for an equitable remedy.

If one party breaches a contract, it is an excuse for the other party not to perform. For example, if someone failed to perform under a contract with you, you may simply accept the breach and consider the contract discharged. This is often the best choice, especially if no damages have been suffered.

Global Law

Remedies for Breach of Contract in Japan

The Japanese Civil Code was created in 1896. It was drafted by three private Japanese attorneys. Two of the drafters studied law in France, while the third had studied law in Germany. As a result, the Japanese Civil Code was influenced by both the French Code Napoléon and the German Civil Code. There are also traces of law from English and American sources. The drafters knew it would be almost impossible to base a system of laws on a Japanese common law created by judicial opinions since none existed.

Contract law was implemented in Japan for the first time under the Japanese Civil Code. The Japanese Civil Code includes some provisions that are unlike American contract law. Two major differences are the initial existence of the contract and remedies available for breach of contract.

Creation of Contract

In Japan, a contract comes into existence upon the sending of notice of acceptance. For example, if an offer is made via the mail and the recipient decides to accept the offer, the offer comes into existence the moment the acceptance is mailed. There is no chance to rescind the acceptance. Any rescission would constitute a breach.

Remedies for Breach

A remedy for breach of contract is only available if the contract was breached by the obligor, or the person required to perform under the contract. There are no remedies available if the obligee (the beneficiary of the contract) breaches.

> **Across Cultures: The Six Codes (六法 roppō)**
>
> In Japan, statutory law originates in the legislature, also called the National Diet of Japan. Under the current constitution, the Emperor may not veto or otherwise refuse to approve a law passed by the Diet.

Critical Thinking *Should the United States consider enacting statutory provisions similar to those in Japan?*

Global Law

Remedies for Breach of Contract in Japan

Answer Answers will vary. The ability to rescind an acceptance can be important at times, although it is less important today than it was in the past. Today, many offers are accepted almost immediately via telephone, Internet, or fax. The person making the offer can receive the acceptance instantaneously, so a delay would not exist in which the acceptance could be rescinded. Further, there is a legal theory in the United States that any person breaching a contract should be held responsible, regardless of whether it was the obligor or obligee who breached.

TEACH (cont.)

D Develop Concepts

Remedies Explain that when a contract is breached, the injured party has a choice of remedies. Ask students what they think of when they hear the word *remedy*. (Medicine to help an ailment will likely be mentioned.) Have students then infer a meaning for the word *remedy* in the context of a broken contract. (legal means of enforcing a right or correcting a wrong) Tell students that the injured party has three options:

- accept the breach
- sue for money damages
- ask court for an equitable remedy (in some cases)

Guided Practice

Accepting the Breach

Ask students if they have ever had a friend promise to take them to a concert or an event, only to have the friend fail to follow through. Ask students what actual damage has been suffered. (While missing the experience of the event could be considered a damage, no real damage was inflicted.)

ASSESS

Independent Practice

Fraud

Ask students to create a scenario in which a person makes a fraudulent representation to another individual. Emphasize that all five elements of fraud should be present. (lie, knowledge of lie, intent of lie to be relied on, lie relied on, resulting loss)

RETEACH

Guided Practice

Mistake

Ask students to write one or two sentences explaining why people cannot generally get out of a contract due to a unilateral mistake, but they can get out of a contract due to a bilateral mistake.

W Writing Support

Damages Divide students in teams of three or four. Have students research examples of court cases in which damages were awarded to the plaintiff. Ask teams to describe what types of damages were awarded and in what amount. Ask them how they think the amount was calculated and whether they think it is fair.

Figure 6.2 Damages

Type	Description
Actual Damages	An amount of money awarded for damages directly attributable to another party's breach of contract or tort; for example, physician's fees when one party wrongly injures another, and financial losses resulting from failure to deliver goods already contracted for.
Compensatory Damages	An award of an amount of money that compensates a plaintiff for the injuries suffered and nothing more.
Consequential Damages	Damage, loss, or injury (such as loss of profits) that does not flow directly and immediately from the act of the party but only from some of the consequences or results of the act.
Incidental Damages	Reasonable expenses that indirectly result from a breach of contract. They include expenses such as those incurred in stopping delivery of goods, transporting goods, and caring for goods that have been rightfully rejected by a buyer.
Liquidated Damages	An amount of anticipated damages, agreed to by both parties and contained in a contract, to be the basis of any award in the event of a breach of the contract.
Nominal Damages	Damages awarded by a court when a successful plaintiff has proven a legal injury but no actual resulting damages; six cents by common law, usually $1 today.
Punitive Damages	Damages in excess of losses suffered by the plaintiff awarded to the plaintiff as a measure of punishment for the defendant's wrongful act. Also called exemplary damages because they set an example of punishment awaiting other wrongdoers.
Speculative Damages	Damages not founded on fact but on the expectations that a party may have hoped for from a contract that has been breached; not allowed in any claim for money damages.

Suing for money damages is one remedy for breach of contract. *What is the objective of awarding damages to the injured party in a contract case?*

Damages

Damages are payment recovered in court by a person who has suffered an injury. (See **Figure 6.2.**) Damages awarded to recognize a breach of contract that did not cause loss often amount to less than one dollar. These damages are intended merely to recognize that a breach of contract has occurred. Your legal fees for pursuing and winning such a suit would likely far outweigh any damages you would receive.

Money Damages If you suffer a loss as the injured party, you may sue for money damages resulting from the breach of contract. The money damages should, by law, place you in the position you would have been in if the contract had been carried out. To recover damages, the injured party must make tender; that is, the injured party must offer to do what he or she agreed to do under the contract.

Punitive Damages or Rescission A plaintiff can also receive punitive damages in a lawsuit for fraud. **Punitive damages are money payments for damages that go beyond what the innocent party actually lost and that are designed to punish the wrongdoer.**

▲ USING VISUALS

Figure 6.2 Damages Answer The objective of damages in contract law is to place the injured party in as good a position as he or she would have been in had the contract been performed as originally promised.

Activity Point out that parties to a contract, rather than leaving the determination of damages to a court, may agree in advance what the damages will be in the event that one of them breaches the contract (known as liquidated damages). Ask students to think of a contract situation in which such liquidated damages would be important. (Answers will vary but may include a substantial loss of profits to either party.)

If the lawsuit is based on misrepresentation, the innocent party cannot receive punitive damages. The remedy available for innocent misrepresentation is rescission of the contract.

Equitable Remedies

The remedy of money damages is not always enough to repay an injured party for breach of contract. In these cases, the injured party may seek an equitable remedy. Two chief equitable remedies are specific performance and an injunction.

Specific Performance Specific performance asks the court to order the other party in a contract to do what he or she agreed to do. This remedy can only be used when money damages are not sufficient to give relief and when the subject matter of the contract is rare or unique. It would not be ordered in the case of contracts involving common goods or easily obtained services.

Injunction **An injunction is a court order that prevents a party from performing a specific act.** An injunction is only available in special circumstances, such as when money damages will be inadequate to compensate the injured party.

An injunction may be temporary or permanent. A temporary injunction is issued as a means of delaying further activity in any contested matter until the court determines whether a permanent injunction should be entered or the injunction should be removed entirely. One who disobeys an injunction does so under penalty of contempt of court.

After You Read

Summarize List all the possible remedies to a breach of contract.

SECTION **6.2** ASSESSMENT

Self Check

1. What are the elements of fraud?

2. What are the different remedies for fraud and misrepresentation?

3. What are the requirements of undue influence?

Academic Connection

Mathematics Veronica is considering a short-term commercial loan to expand her business. The amount of the loan would be $80,000 for sixty days at an interest rate of 10.5%. To see if this is a good deal, she will need to calculate the interest and the maturity value of her loan.

THEORY **Number and Operations: Calculating Interest** To solve this problem you will first need to calculate interest using the formula Interest = Principal × Rate × Time. Maturity value is calculated by adding the principal to the interest owed.

 For more math practice, go to the Math Appendix.

Critical Thinking

Lying Is Never Worth the Trouble Suppose you advertised your old laptop computer for sale for $200. Suppose further that you said it could handle floppy disks when you knew it could not. Suppose further that Jim, the president of the computer club, buys the laptop, sight unseen, relying only on your ad. Have you defrauded Jim whether or not he needs the laptop to handle floppy disks? Explain.

 Go to **glencoe.com** to check your answers.

After You Read

Summarize accepting the breach, suing for money and punitive damages, or requesting an equitable remedy

ASSESS

Self-Assessment

Have students go to the *Business and Personal Law* Online Learning Center through **glencoe.com** to take the Section 6.2 Practice Test.

CLOSE

Culminating Activity

Remedies

Tell students that the Prime Company was contracted to deliver 200 gallons of fruit to the J Jam Company. Prime delivered 150 gallons due to a planning mistake. Have students consider the kinds of remedies available to J Jam Company. (money damages, request that Prime find another company to deliver remaining 50 gallons)

SECTION **6.2** ASSESSMENT

Self Check

1. false representation (lie); person who lied must know it was a lie; lie made with intent that it be relied upon; reasonable reliance on the lie; loss is suffered

2. money damages, punitive damages, equitable remedies

3. caregiver relationship, use of excessive pressure, resulting contract that heavily favors caregiver

Academic Connection

Mathematics
Interest owed: $1,400
Maturity value: $81,400

Critical Thinking

Reliance on the statement about disk drive and actual loss by Jim might constitute fraud. Yet, due to the low price, it is unlikely there is a claim for fraud.

 Activity correlated to the Mathematics standard on page 140

Summary by Sections

Ask students to read the summaries one key point at a time. Then, ask them to work in groups to create two examples to illustrate each key point.

Vocabulary Builder

Cooperative Learning

1. Have students work in groups to prepare their sentences. Ask the groups to exchange their sentences and assess each other's sentences.

Vocabulary Development

- Ask students to use a dictionary or to go online to look up the etymology of each key term listed.
- Then, ask students to list several words derived from the same root or origin. For example, *contract* has the same root as *contractual* or *contractually*.

Chapter 6 Review and Assessment

Summary

Section 6.1 Transferring and Ending Contracts

◆ When contracts end, they are said to be discharged. The parties to the contract may enforce their rights and must perform their duties up to the time of discharge.

◆ When people perform contractual services, the law requires that those services be done in a satisfactory manner.

◆ Substantial performance is a situation in which a party has, in good faith, completed the major requirements of a contract, leaving only a few minor details unfinished.

◆ The courts allow a discharge for impossibility of performance, the destruction of the exact subject matter or the means for performance, and illegality.

◆ An assignment is the transfer of a right under a contract.

◆ A delegation is the handing over of a duty.

Section 6.2 Breaking a Contract

◆ When a contract is breached, the injured party has a choice of remedies. A remedy is a legal means of enforcing a right or correcting a wrong.

◆ Fraud is an unfair attempt to fool another person into buying something by lying to that person about a key characteristic of the thing that is up for sale.

◆ A unilateral mistake is an error on the part of one of the parties to the contract. A bilateral mistake is an error on the part of both parties to the contract.

◆ Duress is the act of destroying somebody's free will by force, threat of force, or bodily harm. Agreements made under duress are either void or voidable.

◆ Undue influence is an action or series of overly persuasive actions that make inappropriate use of one person's position of power over another person to create an agreement that is very favorable to the person with all the power.

Vocabulary Builder

1 On a sheet of paper, use each of these terms in a sentence.

Key Terms

- substantial performance
- tender
- discharge by agreement
- impossibility of performance
- statute of limitations
- breach of contract
- assignment
- delegation
- fraud
- duress
- undue influence
- remedy
- damages
- punitive damages
- injunction

Academic Vocabulary

- substituted
- expire
- affected
- intent
- exaggerate
- mutual

 Go to **glencoe.com** to play a game and improve your legal vocabulary.

Study Skills for Success

Prepare Your Students for Studying

Tell students that they can improve their ability to understand and remember material from their courses by learning and practicing study skills. Remind students to:

- **Get motivated!** Motivation must come from within. To motivate yourself, think of ways in which what you learn now will fit into your long-term personal and professional goals.
- **Get organized!** Make studying part of your daily routine, not something you do at the last minute.
- **Concentrate!** Study in an environment that is as free of distractions as possible.

Key Points Review

Answer the following questions. Refer to the chapter for additional reinforcement.

❷ Why will the courts allow an innocent party to collect damages in the case of fraud?

❸ What are punitive damages?

❹ What types of statements are not fraudulent, even though they might not be 100% accurate?

❺ Does fraud have to consist of words? Explain.

❻ What remedy is available in the case of misrepresentation?

❼ Is a person bound by the terms of an agreement that he or she failed to read? Explain.

Standardized Test Practice

❽ Read the following information about the general rule of law in construction and complete questions 1 and 2.

The general rule of law is that strict performance of the duties of a contract is a condition precedent to recovery on the contract. If that rule were applied to construction, it would mean that owners could refuse to pay for work that did not meet minor quality standards of the contract. For reasons of fairness, building contracts are an exception to the general rule.

In construction, there is the substantial performance doctrine, which says that if the performance nearly equals what was bargained for by the parties, then payment must be made. If the owner can use the work for the purpose that was intended, then the work will be deemed substantially complete, and the owner is obligated to make payment. However, it should be remembered that an owner is permitted to make a reasonable deduction for the cost of achieving full performance.

1. As a general rule, when must strict performance occur to recover on a contract?

Ⓐ before final payment is made
Ⓑ at the start of the construction job
Ⓒ at the conclusion of the job
Ⓓ prior to the contract

2. Why is strict performance defined differently in contracts dealing with construction?

Ⓐ to be fair to contractors
Ⓑ less contracts would be written
Ⓒ cost of construction would rise
Ⓓ owners would not be obligated to pay

 Test-taking Strategies Read the stem of each question carefully, then read each of the possible answers all the way through.

Key Points Review

2. because the innocent party relied on a lie to make decision and suffered actual loss

3. money payments that go beyond what was lost to punish the wrongdoer

4. innocent misrepresentation

5. No. Fraud can also occur through omission or silence, and through inaction.

6. innocent party can get out of contract

7. Yes. The law expects people to be careful when engaging in contracts.

Standardized Test Practice

8. D and A

Strategies for Standardized Test Prep Success

Whether your students have a standardized test coming up in a few days or a few weeks, these last-minute test-prep tips and strategies will help them relax and do their best.

- **Test Format** Help students become familiar with the format of the test by practicing with test items that imitate the actual test items as closely as possible.
- **Test Timing** Have your students take timed practice tests so that they become comfortable with the length, design, and timing of the actual test.

Review and Assessment

Apply and Debate

Students should use chapter content to arrive at conclusions. The legal resolutions are listed below:

9. Yes. Enola has misrepresented the history of the car.

10. No. Her offer did not have serious intent, nor did she agree to the amount to be charged for the task.

11. No. A caregiver relationship did not exist. Excessive pressure was not used. The buyer did not have to purchase at that price.

12. No. It would probably not be reasonable for Ray's Landscaping to submit to the duress even though it might lose the contracts for many homes in the development. Ray's has a choice whether or not to submit.

13. No. Consideration had not been given, so Sally should not be held to the agreement.

C Critical Thinking

Fraud The basement of Melanie Brown's house flooded every time it rained. When Roger Kellogg, a potential buyer, asked about water in the basement, Brown said that the basement was dry. Kellogg had an expert check the basement for dryness before he bought the home. After a heavy rain, Kellogg's basement in his new home flooded.

Apply and Debate

Read the following scenarios. Get together with other students in pairs or groups of three and take a position on each scenario. Debate your position in class with students taking the opposite position or prepare a written argument justifying your position.

9 False Representation

Enola was in a collision that caused over $5,000 in damage to her car. After she had it repaired, she sold the car for $8,500. The buyer asked Enola if the car had ever been in a major car accident. Enola said no because it had been completely fixed.

You Debate *Can Enola be accused of false representation?*

10 Implied Contract

While talking to a group of her friends at a picnic, Rosie said she would pay anything to get a tree cut down. The following day while she was at work, one of her friends cut the tree down and gave Rosie a $500 bill for doing the job.

You Debate *Is Rosie required to pay the bill because of her statement the day before?*

11 Undue Influence

Jules advertised his motorcycle in the paper for $2,000. Two people arrived at the same time, and both decided they wanted to buy it. One of them offered $2,500 for the motorcycle. The other said he could not afford that much, so Jules took the $2,500 offer. The next day the buyer accused Jules of undue influence for causing him to pay $500 more for the motorcycle than advertised.

You Debate *Did Jules use undue influence?*

12 Economic Duress

Mr. Sadri has had his lawn mowed by Ray's Landscaping for $25 a week for the past three years. Ray's Landscaping told Mr. Sadri that they were raising their fee to $30 a week. Mr. Sadri threatened Ray's Landscaping that if it did not keep the price at $25, he would tell his neighbors that Ray's had damaged his flower beds.

You Debate *Can Mr. Sadri be accused of duress?*

13 Breach of Contract

Sally offered to sell Paco her CD player for $20. Paco told her he would think about it and let her know later that day. Later, Paco told Sally that he would buy her CD player, but Sally told him she had changed her mind.

You Debate *Can Paco sue Sally for breach of contract?*

Debate Practice

- Did Brown commit fraud? (No. All elements of fraud must be met. Kellogg did not reasonably rely on Brown's false representation to make the home purchase, since he hired an expert to check for dryness.)

- Can Kellogg recover damages from Brown? (No. Kellogg cannot prove that the agreement he entered with Brown was defective on the premise that Brown defrauded him.)

Case Study Practice – Parker v. Twentieth Century Fox Film Corp.

⑭ What Is a Valid Offer? Shirley MacLaine Parker and Twentieth Century Fox signed a contract in which Ms. Parker would star in a movie entitled *Bloomer Girl* and she would receive guaranteed compensation of $750,000 for her performance. The studio decided not to make the movie and notified Ms. Parker of its decision.

To prevent any monetary damage to Ms. Parker, the studio offered her another role in a movie entitled *Big Country, Big Man*. The compensation for the new film would be identical with the compensation offered in the first contract. *Bloomer Girl*, however, was a musical to be filmed in California while *Big Country* was a Western set to shoot in Australia. Ms. Parker was given one week to consider the new offer, which she rejected.

Ms. Parker then sued Twentieth Century Fox for her guaranteed compensation of $750,000. Twentieth Century Fox argued that Ms. Parker failed to mitigate her damages by refusing to accept the second contract.

Source: Parker v. Twentieth Century Fox Film Corp, 474 P.2d 689 (Cal. 1970)

Practice Was Ms. Parker required to mitigate by accepting the second offer?

⑮ Ethics ←?→ Application

Compensation or Not? Lukas had contracted Wilson's Roofing to replace the roof on his home. Before they finished the job, Lukas suffered water damage to his carpet from a leak in the roof. To make up for the inconvenience, he decided to claim that his sofa and recliner had also been damaged by water. The company agreed to replace the items immediately and apologized for the mishap.

◆ Should Lukas be entitled to any compensation for his inconvenience resulting from the water damage to his carpet?

⑯ Internet Application

Yearbook Printing Whitney has a contract with a local printer for her school's yearbooks. When she picks up the yearbooks, she discovers they are filled with errors. The company refuses to reprint the yearbook. Whitney wants to bring a breach of contract suit against them. Research what her options are and which legal principles apply to her situation.

Go to **glencoe.com** to find links and access to reliable Web sites where you can research legal information. Locate and read relevant documents and draft a bullet-point list to advise Whitney on the strategy she could follow.

Reading Connection

Outside Reading Go to **glencoe.com** for a list of reading suggestions about contracts.

 glencoe.com

Review and Assessment

←?→ Ethics Application

15. Lukas is entitled to have his carpet repaired or replaced; however, compensation for his inconvenience would be for a court to decide.

Internet Application

16. Answers will vary. Students should consider the idea of satisfactory performance and whether a reasonable person would be satisfied with the printing job.

R Reading Strategy

Reading Connection

American Bar Association Resources

Go to the *Business and Personal Law* Online Learning Center through glencoe.com to find links for further readings that relate to this chapter. Ask students to read, review, and summarize the documents. Advise students to keep their reviews and summaries to use as reference material for their Unit Thematic Project on pages 154–155.

Case Study Practice

14. No. The California Supreme Court held that requirements to mitigate only pertain to substantially equivalent offers. The two movies offered were so different that the second movie was not an equivalent, but rather an inferior offer. People are not required to take inferior positions purely for reasons of mitigation.

Careers in Law

Introduce Career Planning

Bell Ringer Activity

Give students the career planning checklist, then ask them to write one or more paragraphs on preparing for a career. Have students use some of the academic vocabulary words from all the sections in this unit.

Career Decisions

Self-Assessment Checklist

Use this checklist to help students determine their career path:

✓ Think about things you are good at
✓ Write down your interests
✓ Think about the lifestyle you want
✓ Write down your aptitudes and abilities
✓ Consider your personality
✓ Determine your learning style
✓ List some careers that might match these characteristics

Résumé Builder

Answer Answers will vary but may include that the understanding of numerous perspectives allows the lawyer to predict possible problems and strategize against them.

UNIT 2 — Careers in Law

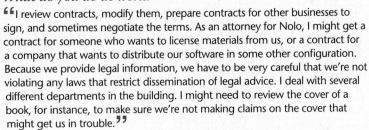

Richard Stim
Editor and General Counsel, Nolo Press

What do you do at work?
"I review contracts, modify them, prepare contracts for other businesses to sign, and sometimes negotiate the terms. As an attorney for Nolo, I might get a contract for someone who wants to license materials from us, or a contract for a company that wants to distribute our software in some other configuration. Because we provide legal information, we have to be very careful that we're not violating any laws that restrict dissemination of legal advice. I deal with several different departments in the building. I might need to review the cover of a book, for instance, to make sure we're not making claims on the cover that might get us in trouble."

What skills are most important to you?
"Organization is really important. Perspective is important too—you have to be able to see the agreement through the client's eyes, not just from a legal perspective. The ability to predict problems is pretty important, and another one would be the ability to resolve an impasse."

What training do you recommend?
"For contracts, it really helps to have some business experience, because the biggest problems lawyers have when doing contracts for business clients is that they view all potential disasters as being of equal importance. And that is not the case with most businesses—there is usually one main possible disaster that they are primarily concerned about. Having some business experience is really, really important."

What is your key to success?
"Lawyers are often worried about malpractice, and because they're so worried about it, it drives them to over-prescribe. And letting go of that is key, wherever you can learn that—and usually you learn that by being in business yourself. Also, if I have any success it's because I get to know the people and their business. It really helps to understand it, because in the end, it's never about the paper—it's always about the people."

Résumé Builder

Academic Skills
- Above average reading and writing skills
- Good speaking and debating skills

Education and Training
A bachelor's degree, a Juris Doctor degree, the bar exam in your state. The following high school and college courses will help develop the necessary background knowledge:

- English Language Arts
- Social Studies
- U.S. History
- U.S. Government
- Introduction to Law (in high school)
- Basic law courses (in college)
- Business, contracts, and consumer law

Critical Thinking
Why is it important for a lawyer to view a contract from the client's perspective, as well as from a legal perspective?

Go to **glencoe.com** to find legal careers resources.

glencoe.com

Research Technology

Specialized technology is available for a variety of law-related tasks. For example, LexisNexis and Westlaw are two competing electronic databases that attorneys and other legal professionals use to conduct research. These services give users access to online legal information, including the text of court decisions and legislation, the content of public records, and many legal articles.

Activity Ask students to access the American Bar Association's Web site through glencoe.com and read about technology uses in legal professions.

The Writing Connection

Persuasive Writing Practice

Is There a Contract? Carmen wants to sell her house. Dale contacts her after meeting her at a party and says she is looking for a house in Carmen's neighborhood. They discuss the matter over the phone. Then, Dale comes over and they reach an agreement on a price of $300,000. Carmen agrees to fence the yard and to replace the roof as part of the deal. They do not sign a contract. Carmen hires a contractor to do the work. Two days after the contractor has started working, Dale calls to say that she is backing out of the deal because she is being transferred to work in another city. Carmen has spent $2,000 on the repairs so far.

Assignments

Research Research which type of contract should be in writing in order to be enforceable by courts, and find out about a law called the Statute of Frauds.

Write Consider the situation above and write a persuasive essay about what a fair solution to the situation could be.

Writing Tips Before you start writing your essay, read through the following composition review tips:

✓ Generate two or three specific sentences that answer the question posed by the assignment.

✓ Decide how you will develop your argument.

✓ Create an outline.

✓ Create a topic sentence for each paragraph.

✓ Use transition words at the beginning of each paragraph.

✓ Reread, edit, correct, and rewrite as necessary.

Essay Test Strategies Preview the essay prompt. Spend five percent of your time reading through the prompt carefully, mark key terms, decide how to budget your time, and jot down brief notes for ideas.

Go to **glencoe.com** to find more writing resources.

 glencoe.com

Unit 2   Contract Law   153

The Writing Connection

W Writing Support

Objectives

To write a brief persuasive essay, take a position on an issue, and address a specific audience

Essay Rubric

Evaluate the students' writing according to the following criteria:

- The essay presents both supporting and opposing arguments **(6 points)**
- The essay precisely states an opinion **(6 points)**
- The organization is clear and effective **(5 points)**
- Supporting arguments are arranged in order of importance **(4 points)**
- Syntax, grammar, and spelling are error-free **(4 points)**

Total: 25 points

U Universal Access

English Language Learners

Essay Structure and Language Mechanics
Students acquiring English may have difficulty crafting an essay. Form work groups and use visuals to organize arguments and evidence.

Culminating Activity

Ask students to work in groups to give each other feedback on their first drafts.

Assignments

Do not let your students rush to start their writing assignments. After you have assigned the topic, indicate a target audience and a purpose, or ask the class to brainstorm various target audience and purpose possibilities. Next, ask students to list the important facts they want to convey in their essays and organize into an outline.

A writer needs to present strong evidence to persuade readers. That evidence may take various forms:

- First-hand observations
- Informed opinions
- Examples
- Reasons
- Facts
- Statistics

Thematic Project

FOCUS

🔔 Bell Ringer Activity

Ask students to form two relay teams. The object of the contest is to see which team can write the six elements of a contract on the board first. Each team member must write down one element and hand off the chalk/marker to the next student.

TEACH

Workshop Overview

The objective of this workshop is to familiarize students with business contracts, their elements, and their forms.

Mathematics

Your family bought your first car, but they expect you to pay for your own gas each week. You have a part-time job 6½ miles away that you drive to and from five days a week. You also drive another 40 miles each week for other activities. Your car gets 28 miles per gallon. The average cost of gas is $3.15 per gallon. How much will gas cost you each week? (Total miles driven per week: [6.5 × 2 × 5] + 40 = 105 Weekly cost of gas: [105 / 28] × $3.15 = $11.81)

Writing a Driving Contract

For this project, you will use what you have learned to prepare a written contract that lists issues and responsibilities associated with driving. You can work on this project alone or with a partner.

Here is a checklist of the skills that you will need to complete this project and that your teacher will consider when evaluating your work.

Evaluation Rubric	
Academic Skills	
1. Online and library research	1. 10 points
2. Reading for information	2. 10 points
3. Note-taking	3. 5 points
4. Estimation and computation of your car-related expenses	4. 10 points
5. English composition	5. 15 points
Legal Skills	
6. Research of possible contract forms	6. 15 points
7. Drafting the terms of the contract	7. 15 points
8. Analysis of the essential elements of the contract	8. 15 points
9. Use of technology	9. 5 points
	Total 100 points

 For more resources and for grading rubrics, go to **glencoe.com**

Step 1: Preparation

❶ Write a contract between yourself and a parent or a family member.

❷ Use all you have learned in this unit, at the library, or on the Internet as tools.

❸ Complete this project in a format acceptable for a portfolio addition.

 Time Management Rubric

Have students evaluate their usage of time by rating the skills below on a scale of "poor" to "apprentice" to "proficient."

1. Determine
- The length of presentation or paper
- Materials and resources you need
- The time allocated to the project
- The tasks to be completed

2. Develop
- A prioritized list of tasks
- A schedule
- A contract outline
- A first draft
- A final draft

Step 2: Procedure

❶ **Review** the text in this unit and make a list of the essential elements of a contract. Go to glencoe.com to find an appropriate contract form.

❷ **List** all the contractual terms you might include in your document. What will your obligations be? What will the other party's obligations be? How will these obligations be enforced?

❸ **Write** the contract based on your knowledge and research. Use the Internet to download a form for an agreement, or create a contract by using word-processing software. Make enough copies so your classmates can review and annotate your contract.

❹ **Describe** the real-life scenario that is the basis for your contract (the amount of driving you need or want to do, the insurance contract, who the car belongs to, the rules governing teen driving in your state, etc.) and present your contract to the class.

S Step 3: Create an Analysis Report

As a class, compare the contracts presented. Create a spreadsheet that describes the types of agreements created (for example, indicate whether the contracts are unilateral or bilateral) and the responsibilities involved. Make sure that you have also accounted for each of the elements required for a valid and enforceable contract. Look at the charts your classmates have created and answer the following questions:

❶ How many and what types of contracts were presented?

❷ Did all of the contracts presented include all the necessary elements?

❸ If not, how did the absence of the element(s) affect the contract(s)?

❹ How was your contract similar to and different from the other contracts presented?

Community Connection

Find statistics about teen driving offenses and accidents online. How do these facts relate to your contract project? Should teen driving offenses be handled in teen or youth courts? Prepare a brief research report to present in class. Go to **glencoe.com** to find resources.

Competitive Event Prep

Entering into Contracts

Situation Assume you are a sales associate for a cellular phone store. Besides selling cell phones, your store sells service contracts. You completed a sale to a teen-aged customer (event judge) for a phone and a contract. You checked the customer's identification and discovered that the customer is only 16 years old. Company policy states that any customer under 18 must have a parent or guardian sign the cell phone activation contract.

Activity Explain to your customer (event judge) that he or she is under the legal age to sign a contract and must bring a parent or guardian into the store to sign.

For more Competitive Event preparation, performance tips, and evaluation rubrics, go to **glencoe.com**.

glencoe.com

S Skills Practice

Contract Negotiations

Both parents and teen drivers need to decide what rules will govern the use of a teenager's first car. This process can be very much like contract negotiations. Have students go to glencoe.com for links to Web sites that offer information about teen driving issues. There are many ways teens can pay for their car that do not involve cash. Teens can agree to safety restrictions such as not driving other teens and not driving at night. Teens can also qualify for an insurance discount by maintaining a minimum B-average GPA.

TEACH (cont.)

Extending the Content

Research Contracts

Have students use the Internet or library to research the history of contracts. Ask students to present their research results.

Reading Connection

American Bar Association Resources

Ask students to go back to their ABA readings notes and summaries. Direct them to apply any relevant ABA content to review and revise their outline and first draft.

ASSESS

Evaluation

Introduce the students to the evaluation rubric. Explain each component. You may ask students to turn in their work in three stages (an outline, a first draft, a final draft).

CLOSE

Culminating Activity

Cooperative Learning

Ask students to bring in first drafts of their assignments and to work in groups to give each other feedback on their work.

FOCUS

Why It's Important

- The United States Supreme Court held that when there is ambiguity with a contract term, the term shall be interpreted in favor of the party who did not draft the document.

- This case affirms that all the provisions of a contract should be consistent with each other.

TEACH

Preteaching

 Your Reading

This text is a long excerpt from a key case where U.S. contract law was applied.

Preread Skim the text, look at headings and the first few sentences of every section.

U Universal Access

Stage the Case For English Language Learners, or students with visual impairments:

- Read the issues aloud. Explain any difficult word, such as *punitive, arbitrate, controversies, conflicting, provision,* and *prohibit.*

- Ask other students to read the case. Stop after each paragraph and ask students to summarize.

- Read the questions and the assignment aloud.

Mastrobuono v. Shearson Lehman Hutton, Inc.
United States Supreme Court 514 U.S. 52 (1995)

Read Critically As you read this case, ask yourself the following questions:

R
U

1. What type of contract is involved in this case?
2. Why did Shearson Lehman Hutton force the Mastrobuonos to participate in arbitration?
3. What does a court attempt to determine when it interprets a contract?

Assignment When you are done, write a short summary of the situation. Include the court's decision and a couple of sentences about why or how the court reached its decision.

Facts **Terms of the Contract** Antonio Mastrobuono and his wife started an investment account at Shearson Lehman Hutton, Inc. When they opened their account, the Mastrobuonos signed a contract provided by Shearson Lehman Hutton. The contract required that the parties arbitrate any disputes that might arise. The contract also contained a provision stating that it would be governed by New York state law. In an arbitration proceeding, the parties present their dispute to an impartial third person or panel and agree to abide by the arbitrator's lawful decision. Because arbitration is considered less time consuming and less costly than litigation, many contracts contain a provision in which the parties agree that disputes be resolved through arbitration.

Arbitration or Court? For a variety of reasons, the Mastrobuonos became dissatisfied with the investment services they received from Shearson Lehman Hutton. They closed their account and sued Shearson

Lehman Hutton, alleging that their account had been mismanaged. Because of the contract's arbitration provision, Shearson Lehman Hutton suspended the litigation and forced the Mastrobuonos to go before a three-member panel of arbitrators. The panel awarded the Mastrobuonos compensatory damages of $159,327 and punitive damages of $400,000. Compensatory damages are awarded to compensate an injured party for actual losses. Punitive damages may be awarded in limited circumstances to punish a person or company for wrongful conduct. Punitive damages are also awarded to prevent other companies from behaving in a similar unlawful or unethical manner. In many cases, the threat of suffering financial loss by way of punitive damages will discourage a company or individual from engaging in unscrupulous behavior. Shearson Lehman Hutton paid the compensatory damages but obtained a court order vacating the award for punitive damages because New York law permits only courts to award punitive damages.

? Landmark Case Questions

R Reading Strategy

Answers

1. a standard form written contract between Shearson Lehman Hutton, Inc. and its investment account customers, which was prepared by Shearson Lehman Hutton, Inc.

2. The contract between the parties contained a provision requiring that the parties arbitrate, rather than litigate, any dispute that may arise between them.

3. The court attempts to determine the intent of the parties at the time when they entered into the contract.

Opinion Different Interpretations

The Court observed that the contract between the parties in this case contained no express provision about punitive damages. Because the parties agreed to arbitrate a dispute, the Mastrobuonos claimed that the parties were bound by the arbitration panel's decision. Shearson Lehman Hutton argued that the contract limits the matters that may be arbitrated because the parties agreed that the contract would be governed by New York law, which only authorizes courts to award punitive damages. As a result of these differing views, the Court had to interpret the meaning of the contract.

Determining the Intent of the Parties

The Court said that when interpreting a contract, it must determine the intent of the parties at the time that they entered into the agreement. The original intent of the parties would be used to guide the court's decision. In this contract, the parties agreed that arbitration would be conducted in accordance with rules of the National Association of Security Dealers (NASD), which states that arbitrators may award "damages and other relief." The NASD manual further provides that "No agreement [between a member and a customer] shall include any condition which... limits the ability of a party to file any claim in arbitration or limits the ability of an arbitrator to make any award." However, the contract also states that it is governed by New York law, which permits only courts to award punitive damages. These conflicting provisions create an ambiguity in the contract.

Ambiguous Terms

Under common law, ambiguous terms in a contract are interpreted against the party that drafted the contract. Ambiguous terms can be understood in different ways. This view of ambiguity protects the party who did not prepare the contract. A party that had no input in drafting a contract cannot be blamed for that contract's ambiguities. As stated in the Restatement (Second) of Contracts § 206, Comment a (1979):

"Where one party chooses the terms of a contract, he is likely to provide more carefully for the protection of his own interests than for those of the other party. He is also more likely than the other party to have reason to know of uncertainties of meaning. Indeed, he may leave meaning deliberately obscure, intending to decide at a later date what meaning to assert. In cases of doubt, therefore, so long as other factors are not decisive, there is substantial reason for preferring the meaning of the other party."

Because Shearson Lehman Hutton prepared the contract for the Mastrobuonos' signatures, any ambiguity must be interpreted in favor of the Mastrobuonos.

Holding The Court's Decision

The contract between the parties is ambiguous. Under well-established rules of common law, ambiguities in a contract are construed against the party who wrote the contract. As a result, the arbitration panel's award of punitive damages was upheld.

TRIAL PREP

The National High School Mock Trial Association organizes competitions at the local, regional, and national levels where teams of high school or college students prepare and argue fictional legal cases before practicing attorneys and judges. Mock Trial team members are each assigned a role as either an attorney or witness. Each team must develop a courtroom strategy, legal arguments, and a presentation style.

Go to **glencoe.com** to find guided activities about case strategy and presentation.

Unit 2   Contract Law   **157**

Winning the Case

Determining Intent

In the Mastrobuonos' case, the plaintiffs were consumers who signed a standard agreement drafted by lawyers for a large company. In contrast, negotiations between companies involve lawyers for both (or multiple) parties. Imagine a situation in which the lawyer for one party initially drafts the agreement, and opposing counsel negotiates and redrafts several terms and provisions to represent his client's interests. If an ambiguity arises in this case, should the intent of the original drafting party be excluded merely because she or he initiated the drafting?

ASSESS
Role Play

Is It Right?

Divide the class into three groups: plaintiff, defendant, and the court.

Have the court consider arguments from defendant that to find in favor of plaintiff would be opening up too many possibilities for parties not to draft the contract to take unfair advantage of ambiguities. Plaintiff should counter that the parties that drafted the contract are often companies with a greater degree of bargaining strength and legal expertise.

CLOSE
Understand the Decision

Why did Shearson Lehman Hutton, Inc. not agree with the arbitration panel, given that it was the party that wanted the dispute to be resolved through arbitration? (Shearson Lehman Hutton, Inc. agreed to abide by the decision of the arbitration panel awarding compensatory damages of $159,327. However, it argued that the arbitration panel lacked the authority to award punitive damages of $400,000. New York State law allows only courts of law (not arbitrators) to award punitive damages. Because the contract states that it is governed by New York law, the arbitration panel had no authority to award the punitive damages.)

Unit Objectives

Chapter	Section	Objectives
Chapter 7	**7.1**	• **Explain** the Uniform Commercial Code. • **Compare** and contrast service contracts and contracts for the sale of goods. • **Explain** when title and risk of loss pass in a sale of goods. • **List** the remedies of the buyer and seller when a sales contract is breached.
	7.2	• **Distinguish** different types of consumer fraud. • **Describe** laws and agencies that protect consumers. • **Identify** various types of warranties. • **Describe** how warranties may be excluded or modified. • **Determine** where to get consumer protection assistance.
Chapter 8	**8.1**	• **Distinguish** between real property, personal property, and fixtures. • **Describe** the types of co-ownership of personal property. • **Explain** the concept of intellectual property. • **Give** examples of intellectual property. • **Define** the laws of patents, copyrights, and trademarks.
	8.2	• **Define** bailment. • **Explain** the different types of bailments. • **Discuss** the standard of care bailees must use. • **Define** a hotel keeper's liability. • **Identify** a common carrier's liability for loss or damaged goods.
Chapter 9	**9.1**	• **List** the different kinds of rental relationships. • **Explain** the rights and obligations of landlords and tenants. • **Identify** the conditions in which an eviction can occur. • **Determine** liability for landlords and tenants.
	9.2	• **Explain** the ways real property can be co-owned. • **Describe** how title to real property can be transferred. • **Explain** the function of warranty and quitclaim deeds. • **Define** and compare liens, licenses, and easements.

Understanding Brackets, Letters, and Ability Levels in the Teacher Wraparound Edition

Brackets Brackets on the reduced student edition page correspond to teaching strategies and activities in the Teacher Wraparound Edition. As you teach the lesson, the brackets show you exactly where to use the teaching strategies and activities.

Letters The letters on the reduced student edition page identify the type of strategy or activity. See the key below to learn about the different types of strategies and activities.

Ability Levels Teaching strategies that appear throughout the chapters have been identified by one of three codes to give you an idea of their suitability for students of varying learning styles and abilities.

Resources Key program resources are listed in each chapter. Icons indicate the format of resources.

KEY TO LETTERS

R **Reading Strategy** activities help you teach reading skills and vocabulary.

C **Critical Thinking** strategies help students apply and extend what they have learned.

S **Skills Practice** strategies help students practice historical analysis and geographical skills.

W **Writing Support** activities provide writing opportunities to help students comprehend the text.

D **Develop Concepts** activities use various strategies to help teachers gauge and plan for students' concept development.

U **Universal Access** activities provide differentiated instruction for English language learners, and suggestions for teaching various types of learners.

NCLB **No Child Left Behind** activities help students practice and improve their abilities in academic subjects.

KEY TO ABILITY LEVELS

L1 strategies should be within the ability range of all students. Often full class participation is required.

L2 strategies are for average to above-average students or for small groups. Some teacher direction is necessary.

L3 strategies are designed for students able and willing to work independently. Minimal teacher direction is necessary.

KEY TO RESOURCE ICONS

📁 Print Material

💿 CD/DVD

🖥 Internet

TeacherWorks™
All-In-One Planner and Resource Center

Teacher Wraparound Edition

Student Activity Workbook with Academic Integration Teacher Annotated Edition

For the Unit:
Lesson Plans
National and State Standards Correlations

For the Chapters:
Lessons Plans
Note-Taking Graphic Organizers
Chapter Outlines
Chapter Summaries
Enrichment Activities Masters

Supplemental Cases
Internet Connection Student Activities Masters
Blackline Masters for Student Edition Figures and
 Supplemental Figures
Ethics and Business Law Activities
Competitive Events Test-Taking Prep
Reproducible Chapter Tests

 Link to the ***Business and Personal Law* Online Learning Center** with Podcasts through **glencoe.com**.

Real-World Applications

Demonstrate Case Resolutions

Learning Objective

- Understand the application of the Uniform Commercial Code (p. 164).
- Apply the concept of bailment (p. 189).
- Explain the concept of eminent domain (p. 209).

- Describe the Uniform Commercial Code (p. 179).
- Explain trademark protection (p. 197).
- Understand the landlord-tenant relationship (p. 215).

- Explain federal warranty law (pp. 220–221).

Apply Business Law Concepts

Learning Objective

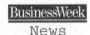

- Understand the Uniform Commercial Code and how it applies to buyers and sellers (p. 160).
- Explain intellectual property (p. 180).
- Explain transfer of title to real property (p. 198).

- Understand contracts and warranties in South Korean law (p. 174).
- Explain inheritance rights in property for women in Kenya (p. 183).
- Recognize property ownership rights in Cuba (p. 208).

- Understand the laws that protect consumers (p. 171).
- Understand the rights and obligations of landlords and tenants (p. 203).

- Understand the concept of a sale of goods (p. 179).
- Explain the standard of care bailees use for a mutual benefit bailment (p. 197).
- Identify the rights and obligations of tenants and landlords (p. 215).

- Explain the concept of trademark (p. 184).

Teach Financial Literacy

Learning Objective

- Differentiate between stocks and bonds (p. 159).

Bring Project-Based Learning into the Law Classroom

Product Safety and Recalls

- **Introduce Concepts**
  Government agencies protect consumers regarding the safety and recalls of products. These agencies provide support, guidance, and assistance to consumers about their rights and laws that protect them.

- **Explore Concepts**
  Read the Thematic Project Preview and the WebQuest activity (p. 159)

  Ask students to think about the information they need to collect to create a consumer awareness flyer as they study Chapters 7, 8, and 9.

- **Apply Concepts**
  Research government agencies that assist consumers, review safety and recall announcements for various products, study consumer rights (pp. 218 and 219).

Extend Content

Using American Bar Association (ABA) Resources

- Direct students to pages 179, 197, and 215 in the Student Edition.
- Ask them to use glencoe.com to find links to ABA resource documents.
- Students should browse and select one document for each chapter.
- See pages 179, 197, 215, and 221 in this edition for specific instructions.

Reading and Writing Support

Feature or Activity	Topic	Reading Strategy	Writing Strategy
STANDARD &POOR'S	Stocks and bonds	Reading a primary source document	
Thematic Project Preview	Product safety and recalls		Researching and taking notes
BusinessWeek	Readings about product return scams (Ch. 7), patent infringement (Ch. 8), and real-estate investments (Ch. 9)	Reading for detail. Developing flexibility in reading speed	
Section Reading Guide	Before-reading activities and tools	Connect students' lives with content Focus on the main idea	Using a graphic organizer to take notes
As You Read	During-reading tool	Predict content Determine what students already know	
Reading Check	During-reading tool	Self-check understanding of content	
After You Read	After-reading tool	Summarize section content	Writing and organizing a list of key concepts
Standardized Test Practice	Product warranty (Ch. 7) Bailment law for technology transfer (Ch. 8) Department of Housing and Urban Development (Ch. 9)	Reading a primary source document Practicing critical reading skills	
Reading Connection	American Bar Association online resources	Reading a primary source document Extending and applying content Reading for knowledge Developing critical reading skills. Developing flexibility of reading speed	Taking notes Summarizing
The Writing Connection	Persuasive writing		Creating outlines, topic sentences, editing
Unit Thematic Project	Product safety and recalls	Using resources notes to support writing effort	Creating outlines, writing drafts, editing
Landmark Case	Automobile warranty law case	Developing critical reading skills	Summarizing

UNIT 3 Consumer Law

Unit Overview

Main) Idea

Unit 3 describes the basic rules governing contracts for the sale of goods and the remedies available when such contracts are breached. It investigates the ways in which the law protects consumers (including with respect to personal property as well as renting or owning a home) from unfair and deceptive practices and can allocate liability.

00:00 OUT OF TIME?

If class time is too short to cover the chapters thoroughly, have students:

- Write down the vocabulary terms and their definitions.
- Read What You'll Learn and Why It's Important at the beginning of each section.
- Go to the *Business and Personal Law* Online Learning Center at **glencoe.com** and download the free Study-to-Go content to their cell phones or PDAs.

▶ **USING VISUALS ....**

Consumers Answer The consumers are restaurant customers; the goods are food items; and the services include the service provided by the waiter and, implicitly, the preparation of the food by the chef.

In This Unit You Will Find:

Chapter 7 Consumer Law and Contracts

Chapter 8 Personal Property

Chapter 9 Renting or Owning a Home

Consumers A consumer is anyone who buys or leases goods, real estate, or services. *Who are the consumers in this photo, and what goods and services are involved?*

158

Unit Thematic Project Preview

W Writing Support

The National Automobile Dealers Association estimates that Hurricane Katrina affected nearly 400,000 automobiles. The National Insurance Crime Bureau has a database of vehicles affected by the disaster. That database, however, is not completely comprehensive and only lists the vehicles brought to its attention.

Critical Thinking How might consumers find out if the vehicle they purchase has been water damaged? (If consumers want to find out the history of a vehicle, they can contact any agency that provides vehicle history reports.)

Thematic Project Preview

Product Safety and Recalls

As you read this unit, use this checklist to prepare for the unit project:

✓ List federal agencies that protect consumers.

✓ Differentiate among the types of federal agencies and community protection agencies.

✓ Find consumer action information.

✓ Explain how consumers can file a consumer complaint.

✓ Determine the average time to process a consumer complaint.

Legal Portfolio When you complete the Unit Thematic Project, create an informational flyer to add to your portfolio.

 Find Unit 3 study tools such as Graphic Organizers, Academic Skills Review, and Practice Tests at **glencoe.com**.

 WebQuest

Consumer Organizations
Log on to **glencoe.com** to explore the types of agencies that can help you when you have a problem with consumer rights and laws. List your findings in your WebQuest folder to share with your class.

W

Ask

STANDARD &POOR'S **Stocks and Bonds**

Q: I keep hearing about investing in stocks and bonds. What is the difference between them?

A: When you buy stock in a company, you are buying a share of ownership in it. When you buy a bond from the government or from a company, you are lending it money. Just as any other loan, a bond usually pays a specified amount of interest over time. The amount of money you make investing in bonds is the amount you collect in interest. The amount of money you make investing in stocks, on the other hand, is based on how well the company does. The better the company does, the more the value of its stock increases and the more money you make. If a company does poorly, however, the value of its stock decreases, and you can lose money on your investment.

R **Language Arts/Reading** Standard & Poor's is one of the world's main providers of credit ratings and financial-market indices. Go to **glencoe.com** and read more about investing in stocks and bonds.

Ask

STANDARD &POOR'S

R **Reading Strategy**

Language Arts/Reading Direct students to explore S&P's resources on stocks and bonds.

Math Activity To finance a major expansion program, Rover Inc. plans to

sell 300,000 shares of stock at $41.50 per share. The underwriting fee will be 6.5 percent of the value of the stock. Other expenses are estimated at $112,050. What net proceeds will Rover receive?

($41.50 × 300,000 = $12,450,000; costs: $809,250 ($12,450,000 × 6.5%) + $112,050 = $921,300; $12,450,000 − $921,300 = $11,528,700 net proceeds)

5-minute **Launch**

KWL Chart Have students create a KWL chart and insert their responses to the following questions in the appropriate column. Ask: What kinds of purchases do you make on a daily basis? What kind of big-ticket purchases would you like to make one day? What types of merchants are involved? Are the contracts oral, written, or both? What legal options, if any, do you have if you are not given what was promised? Once they have completed their charts, discuss these topics with the class. Point out in the unit where each topic will be covered.

Building Law Background

Ask students these questions to activate prior knowledge:

Chapter 7
What are the six elements of a contract? (offer, acceptance, genuine agreement, consideration, capacity, and legality)

Chapter 8
What is the definition of a consumer? (people who buy or lease goods, real estate, or services for personal, family, or household purposes)

Chapter 9
Bailment is the transfer of what kind of property and with what intent? (Personal property—someone transfers possession and control of personal property with the intent that the same property will be returned later.)

Plan Your Lesson Section by Section

NBEA	NATIONAL BUSINESS LAW STANDARDS
Section 7.1	• **Describe** the Uniform Commercial Code (UCC). • **Explain** why the UCC has been adopted by individual states.
Section 7.2	• **Discuss** consumer protection legislation (e.g., Federal Trade Commission, Consumer Product Safety Act, and Consumer Leasing Act). • **Describe** the various rules applied to the interpretation of contracts. • **Distinguish** between a sale of goods and other transactions relating to goods.

NCLB	ACADEMIC STANDARDS	Activity/Feature
English Language Arts: NCTE 3 Apply a wide range of strategies to comprehend, interpret, evaluate, and appreciate texts.		*BusinessWeek* News, Case Study, Case Study Practice
English Language Arts: NCTE 9 Develop an understanding of and respect for diversity in language use, patterns, and dialects across cultures, ethnic groups, geographic regions, and social roles.		Global Law
English Language Arts: NCTE 6 Apply knowledge of language structure, language conventions, media techniques, figurative language, and genre to create, critique, and discuss print and non-print texts.		Legal Talk, ad copy, Key Terms, and Academic Vocabulary
Mathematics: NCTM CS2 3 Recognize and apply mathematics in context outside of mathematics.		Section 7.1 Assessment
English Language Arts: NCTE 12 Use spoken, written, and visual language to accomplish your own purposes.		Section 7.2 Assessment
Social Studies: NCSS 2 Study the ways human beings view themselves in and over time.		Section 7.2 Assessment
English Language Arts: NCTE 10 Students whose first language is not English make use of their first language to develop competency in the English language arts and to develop understanding of content across the curriculum.		Key Terms, Academic Vocabulary, Legal Talk, Vocabulary Builder
English Language Arts: NCTE 1 Read a wide range of print and non-print texts to build an understanding of texts; to respond to the needs and demands of society and the workplace; and for personal fulfillment.		Global Law
Social Studies: NCSS 7 Study how people organize for the production, distribution, and consumption of goods and services.		Case Study

Connect Your Business Law Classroom to the World of Work

This chart shows the 21st Century Skills, foundation skills, and workplace competencies that students develop as they work in this chapter.

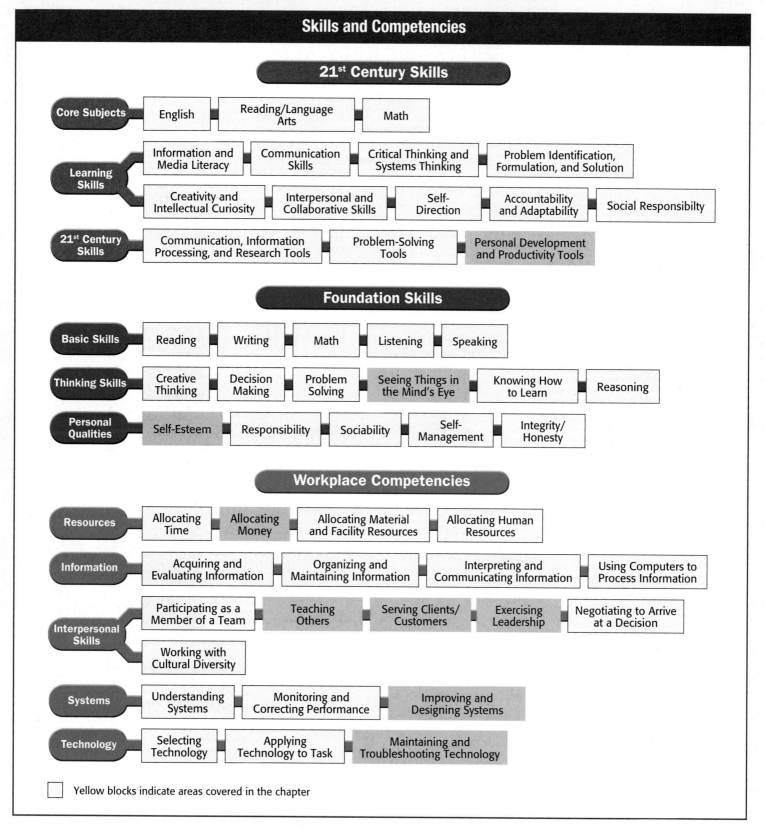

Skills and Competencies

21st Century Skills

Core Subjects: English | Reading/Language Arts | Math

Learning Skills: Information and Media Literacy | Communication Skills | Critical Thinking and Systems Thinking | Problem Identification, Formulation, and Solution | Creativity and Intellectual Curiosity | Interpersonal and Collaborative Skills | Self-Direction | Accountability and Adaptability | Social Responsibilty

21st Century Skills: Communication, Information Processing, and Research Tools | Problem-Solving Tools | Personal Development and Productivity Tools

Foundation Skills

Basic Skills: Reading | Writing | Math | Listening | Speaking

Thinking Skills: Creative Thinking | Decision Making | Problem Solving | Seeing Things in the Mind's Eye | Knowing How to Learn | Reasoning

Personal Qualities: Self-Esteem | Responsibility | Sociability | Self-Management | Integrity/Honesty

Workplace Competencies

Resources: Allocating Time | Allocating Money | Allocating Material and Facility Resources | Allocating Human Resources

Information: Acquiring and Evaluating Information | Organizing and Maintaining Information | Interpreting and Communicating Information | Using Computers to Process Information

Interpersonal Skills: Participating as a Member of a Team | Teaching Others | Serving Clients/Customers | Exercising Leadership | Negotiating to Arrive at a Decision | Working with Cultural Diversity

Systems: Understanding Systems | Monitoring and Correcting Performance | Improving and Designing Systems

Technology: Selecting Technology | Applying Technology to Task | Maintaining and Troubleshooting Technology

☐ Yellow blocks indicate areas covered in the chapter

CHAPTER 7
Consumer Law and Contracts

BusinessWeek News

Many Not-so-Happy Returns
By Elizabeth Woyke

Store-return swindles used to be simple: A customer buys a cocktail dress for a big soirée and returns it the next day, rumpled with the tags intact. But today's scams are far more sophisticated—and costly. The creativity of return artists is mind-boggling. E-tailers report that crooks buy differently priced but similar-looking DVD players online, then return the cheaper version as the expensive one after switching bar codes. Processing centers don't always check returned goods closely—in fact, Mark Hilinkski of software vendor The Return Exchange has even seen bricks returned in DVD boxes for refunds. In a tactic called "shoplisting," a thief pays maybe $10 for an unexpired receipt covering $500 of electronics or clothing, shoplifts the listed items, and returns them for a refund or gift card. The cards can be sold over the Net.

 Your Reading

Efficient critical reading involves being flexible with speed and comprehension. There are several ways of reading critically, and you need to fit a reading style to your needs and to the material.

Go to **glencoe.com** for Flex Your Reading activities, more information on reading strategies for this chapter, and guided practice in reading sales contracts.

160   Unit 3   Consumer Law   glencoe.com

Classroom Resources

- Student Edition
- Teacher Wraparound Edition
- Student Activity Workbook with Academic Integration (SE/TAE)
- TeacherWorks™ Plus! CD
- *ExamView® Assessment Suite* CD
- *Presentation Plus!* CD

- National Mock Trial Championship DVD
- Online Learning Center with Podcasts at glencoe.com
- Study-to-Go™ at glencoe.com
- Online Student Edition
- Interactive Student Edition

Practice the Concept

Consumer Protection
Tell students that one of the objectives of consumer protection laws is to protect buyers from dangerous products and fraudulent selling practices. Ask students to relay any personal experiences they may have had with an unsafe product or with false advertising.

Key Terms Emphasize to students that it is important to take time to read all the claims in an advertisement to protect against scams. For example, in an advertisement for a weight-loss product, phrases such as "lose weight more quickly than you ever imagined," or "works for everyone," or "no dieting ever required" contain red-flag qualifiers and terms that signal false claims.

The Fine Print When reading advertisements for products, tell students that it is critical to examine the fine print. The fine print lists exclusions, exceptions, date requirements, and qualifications for receiving the advertised product or price.

Product Guaranteed Always read a product warranty carefully to find out what it covers. *What does a limited warranty usually cover?*

161

▲ USING VISUALS

Product Guaranteed Answer Unlike a full warranty, which covers anything that goes wrong with a product, a limited warranty covers selective repairs, such as just parts or just labor. Limited warranties may also indicate specific time periods during which certain repairs may be made.

Activity Ask students to consider any recent purchases of electronics that they or their families may have made. Have them bring in the warranty brochure that came with the product and share it with the class.

FOCUS

Bell Ringer Activity

Ask students to work in groups of three or four to generate a list of various items bought and sold in the marketplace. Have them determine whether the sales contracts involved goods, services, or both. Ask them why they think laws are necessary for these types of transactions. (encourages fair and uniform treatment of consumers and sellers)

Preteaching

Key Terms

Read the definitions and ask students to create a sentence using each term.

Academic Vocabulary

Explain that developing vocabulary is key to academic success. An efficient method to develop vocabulary is to study how words are formed.

- **uniform** Adjective, from the Latin *uniformis* (having one form). Means consistent.

- **dominant** Adjective, from the Latin *dominans* (controlling). Means exercising the most control.

- **revoke** Verb, from the Latin *revocare* (to call back). Means to withdraw.

Activity Ask students to give a noun, an adjective, or an adverb form that comes from each word.

 Connects to academic content

162

What You'll Learn

- Explain the Uniform Commercial Code.
- Compare and contrast service contracts and contracts for the sale of goods.
- Explain when title and risk of loss pass in a sale of goods.
- List the remedies of the buyer and seller when a sales contract is breached.

Why It's Important

The more you know about the law of sales, the more you can protect your legal rights and your money when buying or selling goods.

Academic Standards

Reading and completing the activities in this section will help you practice the following academic standards:

Social Studies (NCSS 7) Study how people organize for the production, distribution, and consumption of goods and services.

Math (NCTM CS2 3) Recognize and apply mathematics in contexts outside of mathematics.

Reading Guide

Before You Read

Connect Some sales contracts you make are for goods, and some are for services. What are some examples of contracts you or someone you know made recently that included both goods and services?

Focus on Ideas

Sales contracts follow a special set of rules called the Uniform Commercial Code.

Take Notes

Create a graph like the one shown and use it to take notes as you read this section. Go to glencoe.com to find graphic organizers and tips on how to improve your note-taking skills.

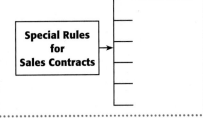

Key Terms

You will learn these legal words and expressions in this chapter. You can also find these terms in *Black's Law Dictionary* or in an online legal dictionary.

- Uniform Commercial Code (UCC)
- firm offer
- title
- bill of sale
- insurable interest
- voidable title
- risk of loss

Academic Vocabulary

You will find these words in your readings and in your tests. Look them up in a dictionary and familiarize yourself with them.

- uniform
- dominant
- revoke

glencoe.com

 Reading Strategy

Read for Knowledge

1. **Survey** or preread the chapter.
2. **Question** or formulate questions before you read.
3. **Recite** or read your questions, answers, and notes out loud.
4. **Review** or reread your notes.

Note-Taking Basics
- Listen attentively
- Have note-taking materials ready
- Skim through the lesson material
- Write down key words and ideas
- Anticipate what comes next
- Review notes soon after taking them

Sales of Goods

At what point do you become the legal owner of something you purchased?

General contract law governs contracts for such things as real estate, employment, and services. A subset of contract law is sales law, which governs the sale of goods. It does not apply to sales of real property (houses and land) or services (work performed by someone else).

Sales law was established through the customs and practices of businesspeople, merchants, and mariners, and has gone through many changes. As interstate commerce (trade that crosses state lines) developed, the need arose to make **uniform** the many commercial laws in effect among the states. The result was the development of the Uniform Commercial Code, which includes the sale and lease of goods. **The Uniform Commercial Code (UCC) is a collection of laws that governs various types of business transactions.** You apply the law of sales under the UCC whenever you have a contract for the sale of goods.

Goods are all things (other than money, stocks, and bonds) that are movable. Examples are your clothing, books, cell phone, food, car, and even the gas you put in the car. A sale is a contract in which ownership of goods is transferred from the seller to the buyer for a price. Thus, every time you buy or sell goods and transfer ownership of them, a sale occurs.

Leasing Goods

The sale-of-goods rules also apply to the leasing of goods, with a few exceptions. Thus, rentals for items such as a DVD player, tuxedo, computer, or car are governed by the UCC.

Contracts for Both Goods and Services

When a contract includes both goods and services, the **dominant** element determines the law that will apply. For example, if a business buys three new computers and has them installed, the sale of the goods—the computers—is dominant and the laws of the UCC apply. However, if the business has the computers serviced and some new hardware is installed, the service is dominant, so the common law of contracts applies instead.

Special Rules for Sales Contracts

A sales contract must contain the same elements as other contracts, but the UCC has relaxed some of the strict rules of contract law. The performance obligations of both parties are similar to general contract law and set forth in the UCC. The following special rules apply to contracts for the sale of goods.

As You Read

Predict How is a sales contract different from any other kind of contract?

Vocabulary You can find vocabulary definitions in the **Key Terms** glossary and the **Academic Vocabulary** glossary in the back of this book.

Uniform Commercial Code The UCC governs contracts for the sales of goods. *Why was the UCC created?*

Chapter 7   Consumer Law and Contracts   **163**

7.1 SECTION

TEACH
Discussion Starter

Class Discussion

Ask students to name some of the problems consumers encounter in the marketplace. Have them describe any personal experiences that may have involved misleading advertising, defective goods, or breach of contract.

As You Read

Predict Students should consider the laws that govern sales and the differences between sales transactions and other business transactions. Emphasize to students that the UCC relaxes some of the more rigid rules associated with general contract law and incorporates concepts such as good faith and methods of dealing. (A sales contract is governed by the UCC, rather than by general contract law.)

Extending the Content

Contracts in Practice

Have students interview local merchants who have been parties to sales contracts. Ask students to make these notes:

- Nature of the contracts
- What, if any, requirements had to be met before the contract was executed
- Problems with the contract, if any

Have students discuss their findings.

▲ USING VISUALS

Uniform Commercial Code **Answer** The UCC was created to standardize the laws for sales among the states.

Activity Tell students that Article 2 of the UCC covers the sales of goods. Ask students to find Article 2 of the UCC and transcribe the exact definition of *goods*. ("Goods" means all things (including specially manufactured goods) which are movable at the time of identification to the contract for sale other than the money in which the price is to be paid, investment securities (Article 8), and things in action.)

TEACH (cont.)

D Develop Concepts

Firm Offer Explain to students that merchants are held to a higher standard than nonmerchants due to their specialized knowledge and regular sale of merchandise. If a sporting goods store prepares a written promise to sell a kayak to a customer for a certain price, ask students if they think the store could revoke the offer. (No. The store must keep the offer open for the stated amount of time, or three months if not stated.)

W Writing Support

Ask students to define what it means to "act in good faith." Have students write a short paper about the importance of being honest with customers, the government, and even competitors. (Students' opinions will differ but most should recognize that people prefer to do business with people who are reliable, trustworthy, and straightforward.)

Extending the Content

Uniform Commercial Code

Have students find Article 2 of the Uniform Commercial Code online. Ask students which part of the article deals with general obligations and construction of contracts. (Part 3)

164

Methods of Dealing and Usage of Trade When you have dealt with another person before, the method you use to deal with them has special meaning. Similarly, any commonly used method of dealing in a particular area—or usage of trade—has special meaning. Unless you state otherwise, either an established method of dealing with someone or usage of trade may be used to supplement or qualify the terms of a sales contract.

W Good Faith Parties to a sales contract must treat each other fairly.

Offer and Acceptance of a Sales Contract You may make a sales contract in any manner that shows the parties have reached an agreement. It may be oral (with some exceptions) or in writing. You may accept an offer by any means and in any reasonable manner. However, the party making the offer may request a particular method to be used for the acceptance. A contract comes into existence when the acceptance is sent in a reasonable manner.

D Firm Offer The UCC holds merchants to a higher standard than nonmerchants. A merchant is a business or person who deals regularly in the sale of goods or who has a specialized knowledge of goods.

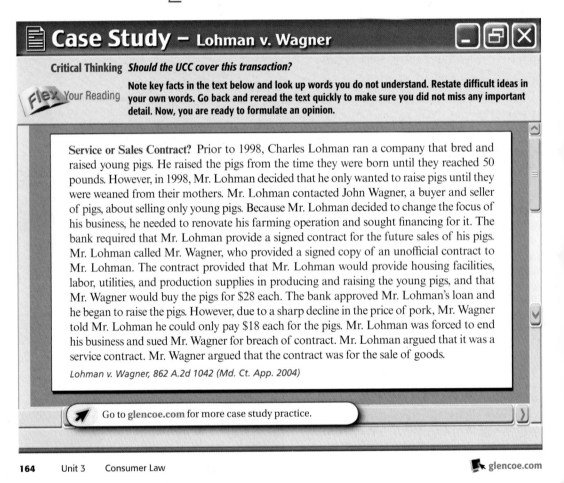

📄 Case Study – Lohman v. Wagner

Critical Thinking *Should the UCC cover this transaction?*

Flex Your Reading **Note key facts in the text below and look up words you do not understand. Restate difficult ideas in your own words. Go back and reread the text quickly to make sure you did not miss any important detail. Now, you are ready to formulate an opinion.**

Service or Sales Contract? Prior to 1998, Charles Lohman ran a company that bred and raised young pigs. He raised the pigs from the time they were born until they reached 50 pounds. However, in 1998, Mr. Lohman decided that he only wanted to raise pigs until they were weaned from their mothers. Mr. Lohman contacted John Wagner, a buyer and seller of pigs, about selling only young pigs. Because Mr. Lohman decided to change the focus of his business, he needed to renovate his farming operation and sought financing for it. The bank required that Mr. Lohman provide a signed contract for the future sales of his pigs. Mr. Lohman called Mr. Wagner, who provided a signed copy of an unofficial contract to Mr. Lohman. The contract provided that Mr. Lohman would provide housing facilities, labor, utilities, and production supplies in producing and raising the young pigs, and that Mr. Wagner would buy the pigs for $28 each. The bank approved Mr. Lohman's loan and he began to raise the pigs. However, due to a sharp decline in the price of pork, Mr. Wagner told Mr. Lohman he could only pay $18 each for the pigs. Mr. Lohman was forced to end his business and sued Mr. Wagner for breach of contract. Mr. Lohman argued that it was a service contract. Mr. Wagner argued that the contract was for the sale of goods.

Lohman v. Wagner, 862 A.2d 1042 (Md. Ct. App. 2004)

Go to **glencoe.com** for more case study practice.

📄 Case Study

Lohman v. Wagner

Answer Yes. Although the contract was written in such a way that it sounded like a service contract, the court looked at the contract as a whole and decided that it was for the sale of goods (pigs). The test is whether the thrust of the contract is for the sale of goods or the provision of services. This contract provided that Mr. Wagner would buy pigs from Mr. Lohman for $28 per pig. It was not a contract for Mr. Lohman to provide a service.

Although most rules under the UCC apply to both merchants and nonmerchants alike, some rules apply only to merchants. One such rule involves a firm offer.

A firm offer is a merchant's written promise to hold an offer open for the sale or lease of goods. No consideration is necessary when a merchant promises in writing to hold an offer open for the sale or lease of goods. A merchant cannot **revoke** a firm offer during the time stated in the offer or for a reasonable time if none is stated. However, no offer can stand for longer than three months.

Different or Additional Terms An acceptance may add different or additional terms. These terms are treated as proposals for additions to the contract if both parties are not merchants. If both parties are merchants, the changes become part of the contract unless they are major or the offeror objects. No consideration is necessary to modify—or change—a contract for the sale of goods. Modifications may be oral, unless the original agreement states that it must be modified in writing.

Statute of Limitations The statute of limitations for sales contracts is four years. However, the individual parties can reduce the time period to a minimum of one year, but may not extend it to longer than four years. The time limit begins to accrue when a breach occurs, regardless of whether the parties are aware the breach has occurred.

Form of Sales Contracts

If the price for goods is less than $500, an oral sales contract is enforceable. If the price is $500 or more, a sales contract must be in writing to be enforceable. This rule does not apply when:

- A written confirmation of an oral contract between two merchants is sent within a reasonable time, and no objection is made within ten days.
- The contract involves specially manufactured goods that cannot be resold easily.
- The buyer receives and accepts the goods or pays for them.
- The parties admit in court that they entered into an oral contract.

Title and Risk of Loss

When does right of ownership pass from seller to buyer?

The right of ownership to goods is known as title. People who own goods have title to them. **A bill of sale is formal evidence of ownership.** A bill of sale, however, only proves that you once had title, not that you still own the goods.

Insurable Interest

Insurable interest is a legal interest in the protection of property from injury, loss, or destruction. The buyer obtains an insurable interest when specific goods are identified as

Reading Check
Compare and Contrast
What is the longest an offer can stand on a sales contract?

TEACH (cont.)

▤ Case Study Practice

Specialty Manufactured Goods Have students imagine that Rockside Manufacturing has filled an order for a rock waterfall that was verbally ordered by a hotel for its pool area. If the hotel refused to take delivery of the waterfall and pay the invoice, does the manufacturer have recourse to enforce the contract? (Yes. Even though the contract was not in writing, this product cannot be easily resold to another buyer.) Explain to students that under certain conditions, contracts do not have to be in writing to be enforceable.

Guided Practice

Different or Additional Terms

Pose this question to students: Why does the addition of terms to the contract for the sale of goods not result in termination of an offer and introduction of a counteroffer as it does in a contract that is not for the sale of goods? (Answers should convey the idea that these additions are a form of negotiation.)

 Reading Check

Compare and Contrast Three months is the maximum because it allows the buyer a reasonable amount of time to act on the offer.

TEACH (cont.)

ASSESS

Quiz

Ask students to answer the following questions:

1. What is the statute of limitations for sales contracts? (four years, unless individual parties change the time period)

2. Does a bill of sale prove ownership? (No. It only proves that the holder once had title.)

RETEACH

Guided Practice

Damaged Goods

Remind students that they have remedies if they purchase items that are defective or are damaged. Ask them what they have done in the past with purchases that were damaged. (returned for replacement, returned for refund) Tell students that they can also refuse to accept delivery of damaged goods or make a claim for an adjustment to the price.

166

those in the contract. A seller retains insurable interest in goods when the seller retains title to the goods or has a security interest in the goods.

Voidable Title

Anyone who obtains property as a result of another's fraud, mistake, undue influence, or duress holds only voidable title to the goods. **Voidable title means title that may be voided (cancelled) if the injured party chooses to do so.** Voidable title is also received when goods are bought from or sold to a minor or a person who is mentally impaired. Anyone with voidable title to goods is able to transfer valid (good) title to others.

Passage of Title and Risk of Loss

Sometimes it is necessary to determine who has title to goods—the seller or the buyer. It is also necessary at times to determine who bears the risk of loss of goods. **Risk of loss is the responsibility for loss or damage to goods.** Title passes to the buyer when the seller does what is required under the contract to deliver the goods. No one can have title to goods that do not exist, such as crops that are not yet grown or items that are not yet made.

Shipment and Destination Contracts

A shipment contract is one in which the seller gives goods to a carrier for delivery to a buyer. A carrier is a transportation company. Both title and risk of loss pass to the buyer when the goods are given to the carrier.

Remedies for Breach of Sales Contract

What can you do if you receive damaged goods?

A breach of contract occurs when one party to a contract fails to perform the duties required by the contract. When this happens, there are things you can do as the buyer or the seller.

Seller's Remedies

Sometimes buyers refuse to accept goods that they ordered. They may also refuse to pay for them. When this happens, the seller may:

- Cancel the contract.
- Withhold delivery of goods.
- Stop delivery of any goods held by a carrier.
- Resell any goods that have been rightfully withheld, and bring a claim against the buyer for the difference between the agreed price and the resale price.
- If the goods cannot be resold, bring a claim against the buyer for the difference between the agreed price and the market price.
- Bring a claim against the buyer for the price of any goods that the buyer accepted.

📷 glencoe.com

U ## Universal Access

English Language Learners Students for whom English is a second language may have trouble distinguishing words with related meanings. For example, learning objectives may require students to identify, explain, or discuss. Inform students that identifying usually involves listing by category, explaining requires giving reasons in a complete form, and discussing requires giving pros and cons.

Buyer's Remedies

Sometimes sellers fail to deliver goods after agreeing to do so. They may also send incorrect, damaged, or defective goods. In these cases the buyer may:

- Cancel the contract.
- Bring a claim against the seller for the return of money that was paid.
- Bring a claim against the seller for the difference between the agreed price and the market price.
- Refuse to accept the goods if something is wrong with them. The buyer must notify the seller about this and give the seller time to correct the problem.
- Buy similar goods from someone else and bring a claim against the seller for the difference between the agreed price and the cost of the purchase.
- Give notice to the seller that the goods have been accepted, but that there is something wrong with them. If no adjustment is made, the buyer may bring a claim against the seller for breach of contract or warranty.
- Revoke the acceptance and return the goods if a serious defect was undetectable, or if the buyer was led to believe that the seller would fix the defect.

After You Read

Summarize Name the special rules that apply to sales contracts under the UCC.

SECTION 7.1 ASSESSMENT

Self Check

1. To what kinds of transactions does the law of sales apply?
2. When must sales contracts be in writing? What are the exceptions?
3. When do title and risk of loss pass from the seller to the buyer in a delivery contract?

Academic Connection

Mathematics Jonathan Asbil wants to purchase a used Ford Mustang, which is advertised for $9,800. It has an CD player/radio, air conditioning, power windows and locks, and manual transmission. It has a total of 84,000 miles driven on it. The used car guide indicates that the average value of the car is $7,375–$9,725 with a $125 subtraction for no automatic transmission. What average retail price should Jonathan keep in mind when he makes an offer for the car?

THEORY **Number and Operations:** To calculate the average retail value, you would first find the mid-range value. Find the difference between the high and low value and divide by two, then add to the low value. Then, subtract the $125 from the price for not having an automatic transmission.

 Math For more math practice, go to the Math Appendix.

Critical Thinking

Goods or Services? Darlene bought a pair of jeans from a clothing store. The jeans did not fit perfectly, so the store agreed to alter them for her. How can you determine whether to apply the law of sales?

 Go to **glencoe.com** to check your answers.

RETEACH (cont.)

After You Read

Summarize good faith, methods of dealing, usage of trade, offer and acceptance, firm offers, additional terms, statutes of limitations, and forms of sales contracts

ASSESS

Self-Assessment

Have students go to the *Business and Personal Law* Online Learning Center through glencoe.com to take the Section 7.1 Practice Test.

CLOSE

Culminating Activity

Seller's Remedies

Steady Software contracts in writing to buy several shipments of software from Source Inc. Midway through delivery, Steady refuses to pay for the goods. Ask students if Source can stop delivery of remaining shipments. (Yes, that is a viable remedy.)

SECTION 7.1 ASSESSMENT

Self Check

1. the sale and lease of goods
2. Must be in writing for the sale of goods for $500 or more. Exceptions: oral contracts between two merchants when a confirmation is sent in writing and no objection is made; oral contracts for specially manufactured goods; admissions in court; executed oral contracts.
3. When the seller does what is required under contract.

Academic Connection

Mathematics
$8,425 average retail price

Critical Thinking

When determining which law applies to a contract that contains both goods and services, you consider the dominant element of the transaction. In this case, the dominant element is Darlene's purchase of jeans at a clothing store.

 Activity correlated to the Mathematics standard on page 162

FOCUS

Bell Ringer Activity

Write the following sentence on the board: "Let the seller beware." Ask students to hypothesize the meaning of the sentence. (Manufacturers and sellers are held accountable for the products they produce and sell, and therefore must use care when selling and producing products.)

Preteaching

Key Terms

Read the definitions and ask students to create a sentence using each term.

Academic Vocabulary

Explain that developing vocabulary is key to academic success. An efficient method to develop vocabulary is to study how words are formed.

- **disclose** Verb, from the Latin *disclaudere, dis* (opposite of) + *claudere* (to close). Means to expose to view, to make known or public.

- **option** Noun, from the Latin *optare* (to choose). Means the power or right to choose.

- **exclude** Verb, from the Latin *excludere, ex* (out of) + *claudere* (to close). Means to prevent entrance, to bar from participation.

Activity Ask students to give a noun, an adjective, or an adverb form that comes from each word.

 Connects to academic content

SECTION 7.2 Consumer Protection

What You'll Learn

- ◆ Distinguish different types of consumer fraud.
- ◆ Describe laws and agencies that protect consumers.
- ◆ Identify various types of warranties.
- ◆ Describe how warranties may be excluded or modified.
- ◆ Determine where to get consumer protection assistance.

Why It's Important

Knowing about warranties and consumer protection laws will help you if you ever buy a faulty product.

Academic Standards

Reading and completing the activities in this section will help you practice the following academic standards:

Social Studies (NCSS 2) Study the ways human beings view themselves in and over time.

English Language Arts (NCTE 12) Use spoken, written, and visual language to accomplish your own purposes.

Reading Guide

  Before You Read

Connect What is the last thing you bought that has a warranty? How long is it for and what does it cover?

Focus on Ideas

A warranty is your personal guarantee that if a product does not work the way it should, you can get your money back or have it repaired or replaced.

Take Notes
Create a graph like the one shown and use it to take notes as you read this section. Go to glencoe.com to find graphic organizers and tips on how to improve your note-taking skills.

Types of Warranties — Express, Implied; Statement of Fact

  Key Terms

You will learn these legal words and expressions in this chapter. You can also find these terms in *Black's Law Dictionary* or in an online legal dictionary.

- warranty
- express warranty
- full warranty
- limited warranty
- implied warranty
- warranty of merchantability
- warranty of fitness for a particular purpose

Academic Vocabulary

You will find these words in your readings and in your tests. Look them up in a dictionary and familiarize yourself with them.

- disclose
- option
- exclude

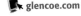 glencoe.com

---

R Reading Strategy

Read for Knowledge

1. **Survey** or preread the chapter.
2. **Question** or formulate questions before you read.
3. **Recite** or read your questions, answers, and notes out loud.
4. **Review** or reread your notes.

Note-Taking Basics

- Listen attentively
- Have note-taking materials ready
- Skim through the assignment topic in advance
- Write down key words and ideas
- Anticipate what comes next
- Review notes soon after taking them

Consumer Protection Laws

What is bait and switch?

Consumer protection laws apply to transactions between consumers and businesses. A consumer is someone who buys or leases goods, real estate, or services for personal, family, or household purposes. When you buy a new car from a car dealer, consumer protection laws can help you. When you buy a car from another consumer, however, you do not have the same protection. Nor do consumer protection laws protect you if you buy a product to use in your business.

The Federal Trade Commission (FTC) is the governmental agency that promotes free and fair trade competition. The Bureau of Consumer Protection safeguards consumers against unfair and deceptive practices.

Federal Consumer Protection Law

Both the federal and state governments have laws to protect the well-being of consumers in the marketplace.

Consumer Product Safety Act The federal Consumer Product Safety Act protects you from unreasonable risk of injury while using consumer products sold in interstate commerce. Manufacturers and sellers who place items on the market must test the quality and reliability (fitness) of all products before shipping. They must prove that the product has been tested and is safe.

Consumer Leasing Act The Consumer Leasing Act requires lease agreements to include certain terms of the lease, including the required number of lease payments and their dollar amounts. Leases must also include any penalties for not paying on time and whether there is a lump-sum payment due at the end of the lease.

State and Local Laws

The federal government has no control over intrastate commerce—the manufacturing and selling of goods within a state. For this reason many states have enacted their own product liability laws and have their own Department of Consumer Affairs.

Unfair and Deceptive Practices

An unfair and deceptive practice is an act that misleads consumers. Most states have enacted either the Uniform Deceptive Trade Practices Act or their own similar laws. In Texas, for example, the Texas Deceptive Trade Practices Act (DTPA) was enacted to protect consumers against false, misleading, and deceptive business and insurance practices, and breach of warranty.

Fraudulent Misrepresentation A fraudulent misrepresentation is any statement that deceives a buyer. A fraudulent misrepresentation occurs when a seller misstates or fails to **disclose** the facts about something that is important to the consumer. For example, it would be unlawful for a used car dealer to fail to inform a consumer that a car was damaged in a flood.

Vocabulary You can find vocabulary definitions in the **Key Terms** glossary and the Academic Vocabulary glossary in the back of this book.

Chapter 7   Consumer Law and Contracts   **169**

TEACH

Discussion Starter

Class Discussion
Bring several items that were purchased in a drugstore to class. Select items such as shampoo, hand lotion, or paper towels. Call attention to any claims made on the labels such as "boosts volume" or "most absorbent." Ask students whether these advertising claims would influence their buying habits.

As You Read

Connect What experiences have you had with faulty products or false advertising?

Connect Have students describe how they handled any experiences with faulty products. Ask students how they would determine whether federal or state product safety laws would apply to the product. (Students should demonstrate an understanding that federal product safety laws concern products sold in more than one state. For products sold or manufactured within one state, that state's product liability laws would apply.)

D Develop Concepts

Unfair and Deceptive Practices Review the definition of ethics with students. Ask them what consequences a business might suffer if it engages in unethical and deceptive practices. (compromised brand or image, tarnished reputation, loss of business, failed consumer confidence, and lawsuits)

Extending the Content

Reporting Requirements
Companies that distribute consumer products subject to the provisions of the Federal Hazardous Substances Act (FHSA), Flammable Fabrics Act (FFA), and Poison Prevention Packaging Act (PPPA) must also comply with the Consumer Product Safety Act. If a company has knowledge of product safety issues, the company is required to report this information to the U.S. Consumer Product Safety Commission within five days. Ask students why such expediency might be required. (Consumer safety is at risk; recalls might be necessary.)

TEACH (cont.)

D Develop Concepts

FTC Trade Regulation
Ask students if they have ever joined a CD club in which the club sends a selection of their choice if the member does nothing. Have students call out the types of information that the seller (club) must legally provide to the buyer. (buying requirements, how to cancel membership, how to refuse the selection of the month, how to get credit for returning a selection, how postage is charged, how forms and announcements are received)

C Critical Thinking

Cooling-off Rule Ask students to describe the rules that apply to a sale made at a location other than the seller's permanent business location. (Seller should inform buyer of right to cancel, and give the buyer a cancellation form and a copy of the contract or receipt.)

Reading Check

Analyze Negative options are those that require the buyer to notify the seller when he or she does not want a product that will be otherwise automatically sent without specific notification to the contrary.

Reading Check

Analyze How is a negative option negative?

Bait and Switch Advertising In bait and switch advertising, a store advertises bargains that do not really exist to lure customers in hopes that they will buy something more expensive. This practice is illegal because the advertiser is trying to sell a different product than the one advertised.

FTC Trade Regulation Rules

D The FTC has established trade regulation rules for interstate commerce to correct wrongdoing in the marketplace.

Negative Option Rule When you subscribe to a magazine, book club, CD club, or other plan that sends products regularly, the negative **option** rule applies. The business sends you a description of its current selection. If you do not want the selection, you must tell the seller not to send it. If you do not respond, the seller sends you the selection automatically. Under the negative option rule, sellers must legally tell you how many selections you must buy, if any, how to notify the seller when you do not want the selection, and when you can get credit for the return of a selection. They must also tell you how often you will receive announcements and forms, and how and when you can cancel your membership.

The Cooling-off Rule The cooling-off rule gives you three business days to cancel a transaction made away from a seller's regular place of business, such as a hotel, a restaurant, a fair, or your home. The rule applies to purchases of $25 or more. The seller must inform you of your right to cancel at the time the sale takes place. The seller must also give you a cancellation form and a copy of your contract or receipt. If you cancel, within 10 days the seller must cancel and return any papers you signed, refund your money, tell you whether any product left with you will be picked up, and return any trade-in. The cooling-off rule does not apply to contracts for real estate, insurance, securities, or emergency home repairs.

Telemarketing Sales Rule The Telemarketing Sales Rule protects you from abusive people who try to sell you products by phone. The Do Not Call Registry helps to reduce the number of unwanted calls you receive. Under the Telemarketing Sales Rule, it is illegal for telemarketers to call you if you have asked not to be called. Calling times are restricted to the hours between 8 a.m. and 9 p.m. Before beginning their sales pitch, telemarketers must inform you that they are making a sales call and identify the company that they represent. Telemarketers must tell you the total cost of the products or services offered and any restrictions that apply. It is also illegal for telemarketers to make false statements about their goods or services.

Shopping by Mail, Phone, Fax, or Internet The FTC has established rules to protect you when ordering goods by mail, telephone, fax, and the Internet. Sellers must ship goods within the time they promise in their catalogs or advertisements. If no time is stated, sellers must ship goods within 30 days after receiving an order. You have the right to cancel orders and get your money

Telemarketers It is illegal for telemarketers to call you without your permission. *Where should you report telemarketers who persist in calling you?*

▲ USING VISUALS

Telemarketers **Answer** People should call their state Attorney General's office.

Activity Inform students that the Consumer and Governmental Affairs Bureau of the Federal Communications Commission (FCC) has issued a publication called Unwanted Telephone Marketing Calls, which is posted on the FCC site. Ask students to review the document and report on the law created to protect consumers against telemarketing calls. (The Telephone Consumer Protection Act (TCPA) of 1991 was created to grant consumers certain rights to defend themselves against unsolicited telemarketing calls and the use of automated and prerecorded messages.)

Business ETHICS

Online Sales

You run a small bookstore that is expanding its Internet business. You know that Yolanda Price is due to release her new book next month, and everyone will want to buy it. You decide to advertise the book cheaper than your local rivals. On the Web site, you state that if people pre-order the book from your company, you will deliver the book "as soon as possible after it is published," even though you know that your supplier will deliver the book to you one week after it delivers the book to the bigger bookstores.

Critical Thinking: Should you change your claim on the Web site?

back if time limits are not met. Sellers must notify you of any delay in shipment and give you a postcard or other free means of responding to the delay. When buyers are notified of a delay in a shipment of goods, they may either cancel the order and get their money back or agree to a new shipping date.

Warranties

What can I do if I buy something and it breaks down a month later?

A warranty is a guarantee, usually by a seller to a buyer, that a product will perform as promised. Warranty law gives consumers a great deal of protection. This protection is an important benefit in sales contracts.

Express Warranties

An express warranty is an oral or a written statement, promise, or other representation about the quality of a product. There are three ways an express warranty can be made: by a statement of fact or a promise by the seller; by a description of the goods; or by the use of a sample or model (see **Figure 7.1** on page 172).

Statement of Fact or Promise An express warranty is created when a private party or a merchant sells goods and makes a statement of fact or a promise about the goods to the buyer. The use of formal words, such as *warranty* or *guarantee*, is not necessary. Express warranties are often found in sales brochures, circulars, and advertisements.

To be useful, a warranty must be stated in precise and understandable terms. Statements such as "This product is guaranteed" are not enough to give you protection. You need to know exactly what the seller will do for you in the event that a problem arises.

Chapter 7   Consumer Law and Contracts   **171**

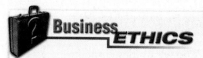

Business ETHICS

Online Sales Answer The FTC has regulations that require companies to send products ordered over the Internet in the time provided on the Web site. If no specific time is listed, then sellers must send the product within 30 days after receiving the order. The advertisement in question does not list a specific time period, so your company would be required to send the product within 30 days of receiving an order.

TEACH *(cont.)*

D Develop Concepts

Warranties Explain that a warranty is a promise, statement, or other representation that a thing has certain qualities. Then ask students if they think warranties help improve product quality. (Since manufacturers must repair any broken or ineffective products under a warranty, they are likely to make a better quality product.) Lead students to understand that manufacturers and sellers offer warranties as incentives to buy their products.

Guided Practice

Express Warranties

Point out that an express warranty can be expressed or stated in one of three ways: statement of fact, description of goods, or by use of a sample or model. Ask students to discuss their experiences with each type of express warranty.

C Critical Thinking

Product Packaging Ask students to discuss why they think the designs and labeling that go on product packages are so important. (Since photos and labels are considered a description or sample of the goods, these are express warranties.)

TEACH (cont.)

Guided Practice

Express Warranties

Emphasize that formal words such as *warranty* and *guarantee* do not have to be used to create an express warranty; even using those words does not mean a warranty is created. If the seller's language is a statement of fact or a promise about the goods and is part of the transaction, an express warranty is created. Have students role-play the sale of their notebooks or folders to one another. Ask the selling student to make a few statements about his or her notebook or folder, then ask whether an express warranty has been made to the buyer.

Extending the Content

Better Business Bureau

Have students perform online research to find out what kinds of complaints the Better Business Bureau receives on products that failed to satisfy implied warranties. Ask them to describe how the bureau handles such complaints.

Figure 7.1 Express Warranties

An express warranty can be an oral statement or promise a seller makes to a buyer.

An express warranty can be a description of a product in an advertisement or on the box the product comes in.

An express warranty can be in the form of an actual sample of the product.

Express warranties are oral or written guarantees about how a product will perform. *Is it necessary to include the word* warranty *or* guarantee *in a warranty?*

172   Unit 3   Consumer Law

▲ Using Visuals

Figure 7.1 Express Warranties Answer No. Since some warranties come in the form of a sample or model, the word *warranty* or *guarantee* does not necessarily have to be present. Other types of warranties are those of a written or oral nature. A description of the goods can also act as a warranty.

Description or Sample of the Goods Any description or sample of the goods that is part of a transaction also creates an express warranty, such as in an advertisement or even the box the item comes in. The seller warrants that the goods will be the same as the description or sample.

Advertising Express Warranties Advertisements stating that a product is warranted must tell you how to get a copy of the warranty before you buy the product. Advertisers who warrant products for a lifetime must fully explain the terms of their promises.

Magnuson-Moss Warranty Act Under the Magnuson-Moss Warranty Act, a written warranty on goods in interstate commerce costing more than $10 must disclose whether it is full or limited. **A full warranty is an assurance that a defective product will be repaired or replaced without charge within a reasonable time. A limited warranty is any written warranty that does not meet the requirements of a full warranty.** Some limited warranties will cover parts, but not labor. Others cover a product only as long as it is owned by the original buyer.

Implied Warranties

An implied warranty is a guarantee of quality imposed by law. It comes automatically rather than verbally or in writing. There are three types of implied warranties: warranty of merchantability, warranty of fitness for a particular purpose, and usage of trade.

Merchantability **A warranty of merchantability is an implied warranty that goods are fit for the ordinary purpose for which the goods are sold.** Unless excluded, this warranty is given whenever a merchant sells goods. Retailers, wholesalers, and manufacturers imply this warranty in every sale. To be merchantable, goods must pass without objection in the trade under the contract description. They must be fit for the ordinary purposes for which the goods are used. They must also be adequately contained, packaged, and labeled, and conform to any promises or statements made on the container or label. Items that courts have held to be non-merchantable include a boat motor that produced excessive amounts of black smoke, applesauce that was inedible because of poor taste and smell, and food containing pieces of glass.

Fitness for a Particular Purpose **A warranty of fitness for a particular purpose is an implied warranty that goods will be fit for a specific use.** It comes about when the seller knows the purpose for which the goods are needed, such as a truck to haul heavy equipment. The seller warrants by implication that the goods will be fit for the purpose for which they are to be used. This warranty exists whether the seller is a merchant or a private party.

Better Business Bureau
In purchasing goods or services, warranties are important to insure your investment. Log on to **glencoe.com** to begin your WebQuest project. Visit the Better Business Bureau mediation program to see what services are available to consumers in your state. Then review the types of recourse you have available under your state's law.

List your findings in your WebQuest folder to share with your class.

TEACH (cont.)
Guided Practice

Complaint Letter
Relay the following scenario to students: Ed decided to purchase a new DVD player from an online merchant. He was promised Model AR1 for $89.95 plus shipping and handling costs. When the DVD player arrived, it was model AR13, and his credit card was charged for $189.50. Ask students to write a complaint letter to the Better Business Bureau. Have students exchange letters to analyze the potential effectiveness of their correspondence.

ASSESS

Independent Practice

Compare
Ask students to compare an express warranty to an implied warranty. (Express makes specific promises regarding the quality of product, while implied is a guarantee of quality imposed by law.)

Better Business Bureau Answer After students find resources on mediation services, ask them to draft a sample letter that a consumer might send to a retailer with which he or she has a complaint.

RETEACH

Guided Practice

Consumer Protection

Ask students to discuss why consumer protection laws are important to our society. (helps keep sellers more honest and motivates buyers to continue making purchases)

STUDY TO GO Have students go to the *Business and Personal Law* Online Learning Center through glencoe.com to download free Study-to-Go content to their cell phones or PDAs.

Independent Practice

Warranties for Services

Implied warranties do not cover contracts for services. Ask students to write a brief paragraph describing why they think services are not included in this consumer protection. (Expectation of certain services varies widely and cannot be generalized.)

Review Key Terms

Encourage students to access the *Business and Personal Law* Online Learning Center through glencoe.com and use the electronic flashcards to review the key terms.

Global Law

Contracts and Warranties in South Korea

The South Korean legal system is very similar to the civil code systems found in Europe. However, after World War II, in 1948, South Korea adopted a constitution that was similar to the United States Constitution, although the civil code is still the primary source of law. Contract and warranty law stems from the South Korean Civil Code. There are some unique features in South Korean law.

There is no consideration for a contract. The concept of consideration is not present in South Korean contracting. Rather, there are 14 different types of contracts laid out in the Civil Code and the requirements for each type.

There is no Statute of Frauds. There is no law requiring specific contracts to be in writing, such as contracts for the sale of land. However, there is a definite preference in the courts for contracts to be done in writing.

In the case of breach, South Korea has a deposit clause. Any money that has been deposited in contemplation of a contract can be considered liquidated damages. That is, if a party puts down money to buy a house and then decides not to buy the house, that party can breach the contract by giving up the money. Alternatively, if the seller decides not to sell and breaches the contract, then that party must only pay twice the amount of the deposit.

There are specific warranty statutes. As in the U.S., sellers are liable for express warranties. The Korean Civil Code, again, is explicit on what qualifies as a warranty. However, a seller's liability depends upon whether the seller is aware of the defect. There are only limited situations where a seller is liable for unknown defects.

Across Cultures: Trials in South Korea

One major difference between U.S. and South Korean trials is that there is no jury in South Korea. Rather, a court comprised of one or three judges hears the case and makes a decision.

Critical Thinking: *Should manufacturers only be liable for known defects, as in South Korea, or should there be strict liability, as in the U.S.?*

Warranty of Title

In all sales, the seller warrants that the title being given to the buyer is good and that the transfer is lawful. This is called the warranty of title. It is a guarantee that the goods have no liens, or claims by others. If you buy stolen goods, the real owner has the right to the return of the goods. You may recover your loss from the seller, who breached the warranty of title.

Exclusion of Warranties

To **exclude** the warranty of merchantability, the word *merchantability* must be mentioned specifically. If the exclusion is in writing, the word must be written prominently. The warranty of title may not be excluded.

In some states, implied warranties can also be excluded or modified by the words *as is* and *with all faults*. Having buyers examine goods before the sale is another way to exclude or modify warranties. Under federal law, implied warranties cannot be excluded when an express warranty is given to a consumer.

Global Law

Contracts and Warranties in South Korea

Answer Answers will vary. There is an argument that a manufacturer should only be liable for known defects, because if a defect is unknown, a manufacturer has no reason to prevent the item from entering the market. However, if the manufacturer bears no responsibility and someone gets hurt, the victim would have no recourse. This is the thought behind the U.S. system of strict liability. There is an incentive for the manufacturer to do everything in its power to ensure that the product is safe; otherwise it will be liable for any damages.

Responsibilities of Consumers

Warranties are designed to protect you as a consumer. As a consumer, however, you also have certain responsibilities. You have a responsibility to use a product safely and as it is intended to be used. If a product comes with information, such as a warranty, you have a responsibility to read that information. To succeed in a claim for breach of warranty, you have a duty to notify the seller within a reasonable time after you discover the defect. Failure to do so will prevent you from recovering damages.

Consumer Protection Assistance

Where can I go if I feel I have been cheated by a business?

Many state and local governments have offices of consumer affairs to educate consumers and help protect them against fraud. The federal Consumer Product Safety Commission establishes safety standards for consumer products. It has the power to recall unsafe products and to impose fines on violators. The local business community also polices itself to protect consumers from questionable practices.

If a consumer feels wronged, the consumer should first try to contact the business involved. If that does not work, then the consumer can contact the Better Business Bureau (BBB). The BBB is a private agency that hears consumer complaints at the local and state levels. The BBB's mission is to promote highly ethical relationships between businesses and the public through voluntary self-regulation, consumer and business education, and service excellence. The BBB, however, does not have the power to enforce laws or recommend one business over another.

After You Read

Summarize Name the different types of warranties.

SECTION 7.2 ASSESSMENT

Self Check

1. What is the cooling-off rule?
2. What are the three ways an express warranty can be made?
3. What is the warranty of title?

Academic Connection

Social Studies In 1962, President John F. Kennedy presented to the American public what he called the Consumer Bill of Rights. The bill said that every person has four basic consumer rights. Over the years, three more rights were added. Look up these rights in the library or on the Internet and list them in your notebook.

English Language Arts Write a letter to your state's attorney general to find out what rights you have in your state when you purchase a defective car. Make sure to use proper business letter format.

Critical Thinking

Bait and Switch Bait and switch is an old gimmick unethical businesses use to lure people into a store and then get them to spend more money than they intended. Why do you think they call it bait and switch?

 Go to **glencoe.com** to check your answers.

RETEACH (cont.)

After You Read

Summarize express, implied, title

ASSESS

Self-Assessment

Have students go to the *Business and Personal Law* Online Learning Center through glencoe.com to take the Section 7.2 Practice Test.

CLOSE

Culminating Activity

Warranty of Title

Randall purchased a camera from his friend Zach, which included a warranty of title. He tells his mother that this warranty will cover any defects he discovers in the camera for 90 days. Ask students to indicate whether this is true. (No. Coverage of product quality or performance is not included in a warranty of title.)

SECTION 7.2 ASSESSMENT

Self Check

1. gives buyer three business days to cancel contracts made away from seller's regular place of business
2. by a statement of fact, by a description of the goods, and by presenting a sample
3. guarantee that title being given is good and transfer is lawful

Academic Connection

Social Studies
Right to be informed; to choose; to safety; to be heard. Rights added later were right to have problems corrected; to consumer education; to service.

English Language Arts
Letters may vary. Provide a sample of a correct letter format.

Critical Thinking

The bait is like a worm on a hook intended to lure buyers into a store. The switch consists of talking people into buying a more expensive item than the advertised item.

NCLB Activities correlated to the academic standards on page 168

175

Summary by Sections

Ask students to read the summaries one key point at a time. Then, ask them to work in groups to create two examples to illustrate each key point.

Vocabulary Builder

Cooperative Learning

1. Have students work in groups to prepare their sentences. Ask the groups to exchange their sentences and assess each other's sentences.

Vocabulary Development

- Ask students to use a dictionary or to go online to look up the etymology of each key term listed.
- Then, ask students to list several words derived from the same root or origin. For example, *contract* has the same root as *contractual* or *contractually*.

Chapter **7** Review and Assessment

Summary

Section 7.1 Sales Contracts

- The sale of goods is governed by sales law under the Uniform Commercial Code (UCC). The sale of services and real property is governed by general contract law.
- When a contract includes both goods and services, the dominant element of the contract determines whether it is a contract for goods or a contract for services.
- Title to goods is passed from a seller to a buyer when the seller does what is required under the contract to deliver the goods. The risk of loss is born by the party responsible for loss or damage to goods.
- Most contracts for the sale of goods of $500 or more must be in writing to be enforceable.
- There are several remedies both buyers and sellers may seek if a sales contract is breached.

Section 7.2 Consumer Protection

- The Federal Trade Commission (FTC) was created to promote free and fair trade competition. The Bureau of Consumer Protection safeguards consumers against unfair and deceptive practices. The Consumer Product Safety Act protects consumers from unsafe goods.
- An express warranty is an oral or written statement about the quality, ability, or performance of a product. An implied warranty is a guarantee of quality imposed by law.
- A full warranty promises to fix or replace a defective product at no extra charge within a reasonable time. A limited warranty covers only specific costs, such as parts but not labor.
- Consumer protection can be obtained from state and local consumer protection agencies, such as the Consumer Product Safety Commission and the Better Business Bureau.

 Vocabulary Builder

❶ On a sheet of paper, use each of these terms in a sentence.

Key Terms

- Uniform Commercial Code (UCC)
- firm offer
- title
- bill of sale

- insurable interest
- voidable title
- risk of loss
- warranty
- express warranty

- full warranty
- limited warranty
- implied warranty
- warranty of merchantability
- warranty of fitness for a particular purpose

Academic Vocabulary

- uniform
- dominant

- revoke
- disclose

- option
- exclude

 Go to **glencoe.com** to play a game and improve your legal vocabulary.

 Study Skills for Success

Prepare Your Students for Studying

Tell students that they can improve their ability to understand and remember material from their courses by learning and practicing study skills. Remind students to:

- **Get motivated!** Motivation must come from within. To motivate yourself, think of ways in which what you learn now will fit into your long-term personal and professional goals.
- **Get organized!** Make studying part of your daily routine, not something you do at the last minute.
- **Concentrate!** Study in an environment that is as free of distractions as possible.

Key Points Review

Answer the following questions. Refer to the chapter for additional reinforcement.

2 How are contracts for the sales of goods different from contracts for services or real property?

3 What are a seller's remedies when a buyer breaches a sales contract?

4 What are a buyer's remedies when a seller breaches a sales contract?

5 When do title and risk of loss pass from the seller to the buyer in a sale of goods?

6 What types of transactions do consumer protection laws cover and not cover?

7 What are the three types of implied warranties?

8 What are ways that warranties can be excluded or modified?

9 What organizations, businesses, and government agencies can consumers go to for assistance?

Standardized Test Practice

10 Read the following excerpt from a product warranty and complete questions 1 and 2.

The company will provide parts to replace defective parts without charge for one year from the date of the original retail purchase. Certain parts are excluded from this warranty. The company will provide the labor without charge for a period of one year from the date of the original retail purchase.

This warranty only covers failures due to defects in material or workmanship which occur during normal use. It does not cover damage which occurs in shipment, or failure or damage which results from accident, misuse, abuse, mishandling, misapplication, alteration, faulty installation, improper maintenance, commercial use such as for hotel or office use, or damage which results from fire, flood, or other natural disaster.

1. What does the warranty cover for the first year?

A parts only
B labor only
C labor and all parts
D labor and certain parts

2. Which type of damage is covered by the warranty?

A damage due to a natural disaster
B faulty installation
C defects in workmanship
D damage that occurs in shipment

Test-Taking Strategies Skip difficult questions until all other questions are answered. Keep a record of the unanswered items to return to, if time permits, on a scrap piece of paper.

---

2. Sales of goods: governed by the law of sales under the UCC. Services or real property: governed by general contract law.

3. cancel contract; withhold delivery; stop delivery of goods held by carrier; or bring claim against buyer for the price of any goods the buyer accepted

4. cancel contract; bring claim for the return of money paid; bring claim for difference between agreed price and market price; refuse to accept goods; bring claim against the seller for breach of contract or warranty; or revoke the acceptance and return the goods

5. when seller does what is required under the contract to deliver goods

6. apply to purchases made for personal, family, or household use; do not apply to transactions between consumers or businesses, or purchases made for business uses

7. warranty of merchantability, of fitness for a particular purpose, and usage of trade

8. Implied warranties can be excluded or modified by the words *as is* and *with all faults*.

9. Examples: consumer affairs offices, state fraud offices, Federal Consumer Product Safety Commission, or Better Business Bureau.

 Standardized Test Practice

10. D and C

Strategies for Standardized Test Prep Success

Whether your students have a standardized test coming up in a few days or a few weeks, this last-minute test-prep tip will help them relax and do their best.

- **Test Format** Help students become familiar with the format of the test by practicing with test items that imitate the actual test items as closely as possible.

- **Test Timing** Have your students take timed practice tests so that they become comfortable with the length, design, and timing of the actual test.

Apply and Debate

Students should use chapter content to arrive at conclusions.

11. Probably not. When a contract is between two merchants, terms can be modified without notice, as long as the changes are not major.

12. Probably not. If Mattie's order contract states a specific delivery schedule, then she can reject the shipment as nonconforming.

13. Yes. Since the clerk is an agent of the store, the DVD player can be returned.

14. No. The Magnuson-Moss Warranty Act only applies when the merchant gives a written warranty on a product selling for more than $10.

15. Yes. The store advertised a low-cost computer, but then attempts to sell a higher-priced model.

C Critical Thinking

Buyer's Remedies Brenda ordered two dozen tricycles for her day care center. When they arrive, half of them are damaged. Brenda will not accept the delivery from the delivery company and plans to place her order with another company.

 Apply and Debate

C Read the following scenarios. Get together with other students in pairs or groups of three and take a position on each scenario. Debate your position in class with students taking the opposite position or prepare a written argument justifying your position.

⑪ Firm Offer

Nathan's Burgers has bought its hamburger buns from a local bakery for a set price for the past five years based on an oral agreement. Recently, Nathan picked up his order and discovered that the cost for hamburger buns had increased ten percent.

You Debate *Is the bakery required to notify Nathan prior to the price increase?*

⑫ Bulk Transfer

Mattie places an order with a moving company to deliver new fall fashions to her clothing shop in stages. The next day, she discovers that all of the merchandise has been delivered in bulk with a bill to be paid in full in ten days.

You Debate *Is Mattie required to accept the merchandise and pay the bill in full?*

⑬ Express Warranty

You buy the floor model of a DVD player at half price. The sales clerk tells you it can be returned for a full refund if it is faulty. At home you discover it is missing the cables and remote, so you return to the store for a refund. Above the service desk is a sign stating, "All floor models are sold as is and cannot be returned."

You Debate *Are you entitled to a refund?*

⑭ Full Warranty

Maria buys a set of tools at a trade show from a dealer who owns a store in the same town. When Maria uses the tools for the first time, one of them breaks. She goes to the merchant's local store for a refund. The merchant tells Maria she is not entitled to a refund since the sale was made at the trade show and not the store.

You Debate *Does the Magnuson-Moss Warranty Act apply to this situation?*

⑮ Bait and Switch?

You find an ad for a great deal on a computer at a local store. When you get to the store, the clerk tells you they are out of stock and shows you another computer that is more expensive.

You Debate *Is this a case of bait and switch?*

Debate Practice

- Is Brenda justified in refusing the shipment? (Yes. Damaged goods do not have to be accepted.)

- The seller expects Brenda to accept and pay for the half of the order that was not damaged. Is the seller justified in this expectation? (No. Since the seller will be able to resell goods to another buyer, Brenda does not have to accept delivery and pay for the tricycles.)

Case Study Practice– Princess Cruises, Inc. v. General Electric Co.

16 **Which Type of Contract Applies?** Princess Cruises (Princess) owns and operates the SS Sky Princess. In December of 1994, Princess requested that General Electric (GE) perform routine servicing and repair on the ship and provide any parts necessary.

GE noted rust on the rotor and removed it. However, good metal was also removed, which caused the rotor to become unbalanced. Even though GE attempted to correct the imbalance, the imbalance caused damage to the ship. Princess sued GE for damages. The case went to trial and the court instructed the jury on applying UCC protections, since repair parts were included in the contract. The jury awarded Princess $4,577,743 in damages. GE appealed the case, arguing that the trial court erroneously instructed the jury on principles from the UCC, since the contract was primarily for providing a service rather than for the sale of goods.

Source: Princess Cruises, Inc. v. General Electric Co., 143 F.3d 828 (4th Cir. 1998)

Practice Did the judge correctly use UCC principles, since the contract included the sale of repair parts?

17 Ethics ←?→ Application

Keep the Customer Satisfied You sell sprinkler systems to farmers. Your old customers have never signed a contract with you because most of your sprinkler systems sell for $400, and the UCC only requires written contracts for sales above $500. Your newest sprinkler system sells for $525. Some of your old customers want the new system, but want to keep the arrangement informal and not sign a contract.

◆ What can you do to keep your old customers happy?

18 Internet Application

Research Consumer Information Christina wanted to purchase a used vehicle for under $6,000. Before deciding which make and model she should buy, she researched information on recalls, average maintenance costs, and reliability.

 Go to **glencoe.com** to access the Web site sponsored by the Consumer Protection Agency Safety Commission and research various makes and models of vehicles to see what types of recall information you can find on them. Then look at the form for filing a consumer product incident report.

Reading Connection

Outside Reading Go to **glencoe.com** for reading suggestions about consumer protection.

 glencoe.com

←?→ Ethics Application

17. forego having customers sign contracts, or lower price of sprinkler systems to under $500

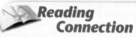 Internet Application

18. The consumer product incident report can be used to report an injury or death involving consumer products, or to report an unsafe product. Students should understand that the form will require information about the incident as well as the product brand name, manufacturer, serial number, and date the product was purchased.

R Reading Strategy

Reading Connection

American Bar Association Resources

Go to the *Business and Personal Law* Online Learning Center through glencoe.com to find links for further readings that relate to this chapter. Ask students to read, review, and summarize the documents. Advise students to keep their reviews and summaries to use as reference material for their Unit Thematic Project on pages 218–219.

Case Study Practice

16. No. The 4th Circuit Court of Appeals held that even though the contract included the sale of any necessary repair parts, the main thrust of the contract was for GE to provide service on the ship, not to sell Princess goods. The standard for invoking the protections of the UCC is not the fact that the sale of goods is included in a service contract. Rather, the court must look at what is the predominant factor in the contract, and in this case, that was the service, not the sale of goods.

Plan Your Lesson Section by Section

NBEA	NATIONAL BUSINESS LAW STANDARDS
Section 8.1	• **Identify** the forms of co-ownership of personal property. • **Define** intellectual property and list types of intellectual property.
Section 8.2	• **Explain** how a bailment is created and describe the standard of care different bailees are required to exercise over bailed property. • **Distinguish** between an ordinary bailment and a special bailment. • **Identify** a common carrier's liability for loss or damage to goods.

NCLB	ACADEMIC STANDARDS	Activity/Feature
English Language Arts: NCTE 3 Apply a wide range of strategies to comprehend, interpret, evaluate, and appreciate texts.		*BusinessWeek* News, Case Study, Case Study Practice
English Language Arts: NCTE 9 Develop an understanding of and respect for diversity in language use, patterns, and dialects across cultures, ethnic groups, geographic regions, and social roles.		Global Law
English Language Arts: NCTE 6 Apply knowledge of language structure, language conventions, media techniques, figurative language, and genre to create, critique, and discuss print and non-print texts.		Legal Talk, ad copy, Key Terms, and Academic Vocabulary, Section 8.1 Assessment
Social Studies: NCSS 8 Study relationships among science, technology, and society.		Section 8.1 Assessment
Mathematics: NCTM NOS 2a Judge the effects of such operations as multiplication, division, and computing powers and roots on the magnitude of quantities.		Section 8.2 Assessment
English Language Arts: NCTE 10 Students whose first language is not English make use of their first language to develop competency in the English language arts and to develop understanding of content across the curriculum.		Key Terms, Academic Vocabulary, Legal Talk, Vocabulary Builder
English Language Arts: NCTE 1 Read a wide range of print and non-print texts to build an understanding of texts; to acquire new information; to respond to the needs and demands of society and the workplace; and for personal fulfillment.		Global Law, Cyberlaw
Social Studies: NCSS 3 Study people, places, and environments.		Case Study

Connect Your Business Law Classroom to the World of Work

This chart shows the 21st Century Skills, foundation skills, and workplace competencies that students develop as they work in this chapter.

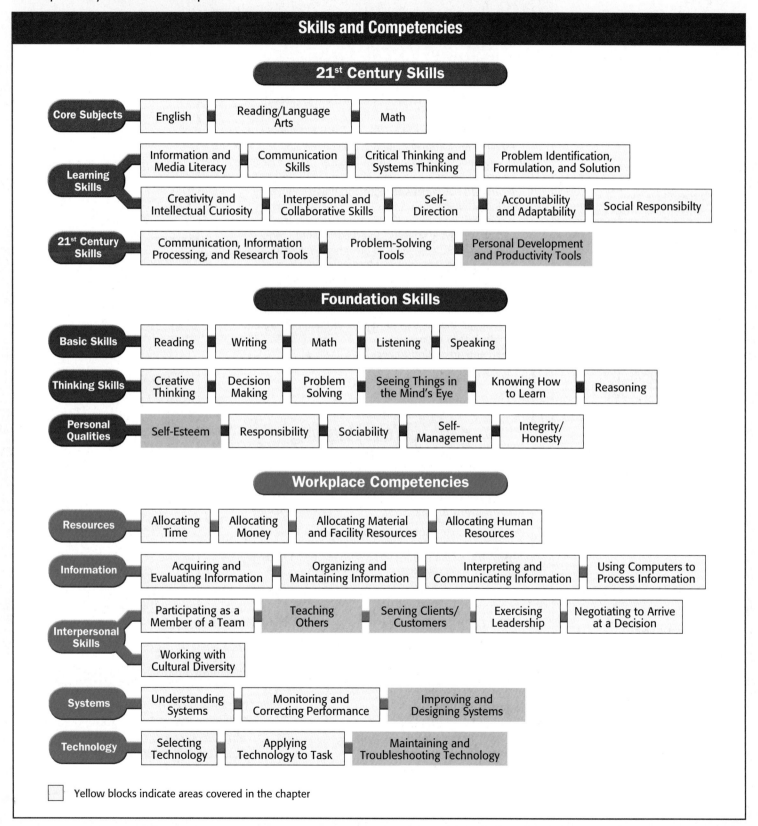

Skills and Competencies

21st Century Skills

Core Subjects
- English
- Reading/Language Arts
- Math

Learning Skills
- Information and Media Literacy
- Communication Skills
- Critical Thinking and Systems Thinking
- Problem Identification, Formulation, and Solution
- Creativity and Intellectual Curiosity
- Interpersonal and Collaborative Skills
- Self-Direction
- Accountability and Adaptability
- Social Responsibilty

21st Century Skills
- Communication, Information Processing, and Research Tools
- Problem-Solving Tools
- Personal Development and Productivity Tools

Foundation Skills

Basic Skills
- Reading
- Writing
- Math
- Listening
- Speaking

Thinking Skills
- Creative Thinking
- Decision Making
- Problem Solving
- Seeing Things in the Mind's Eye
- Knowing How to Learn
- Reasoning

Personal Qualities
- Self-Esteem
- Responsibility
- Sociability
- Self-Management
- Integrity/Honesty

Workplace Competencies

Resources
- Allocating Time
- Allocating Money
- Allocating Material and Facility Resources
- Allocating Human Resources

Information
- Acquiring and Evaluating Information
- Organizing and Maintaining Information
- Interpreting and Communicating Information
- Using Computers to Process Information

Interpersonal Skills
- Participating as a Member of a Team
- Teaching Others
- Serving Clients/Customers
- Exercising Leadership
- Negotiating to Arrive at a Decision
- Working with Cultural Diversity

Systems
- Understanding Systems
- Monitoring and Correcting Performance
- Improving and Designing Systems

Technology
- Selecting Technology
- Applying Technology to Task
- Maintaining and Troubleshooting Technology

Yellow blocks indicate areas covered in the chapter

CHAPTER 8 Personal Property

Introduce the Chapter

Personal Property
In Chapter 8, students will learn about the rights and responsibilities associated with personal property. The law of patents, trademarks, and copyrights is highlighted, along with the study of bailments.

Building Background
Have students raise their hands if they have ever downloaded music from the Internet or borrowed a piece of software from a friend. Ask students if they know that these kinds of property are usually protected under copyrights or patents.

NTP succeeded in protecting its patents through its litigation against Research in Motion. Under the $612.5 million settlement, RIM was granted the right to keep running its BlackBerry business. The settlement came just after the patent office issued its second rejection of NTP's patents, probably resulting in a smaller settlement amount than analysts had initially predicted.

 Reading Strategy

Flex Your Reading

Tell students that references to rights to intellectual property, such as trademarks or copyrights, are easy to overlook, yet are important. Before using software, downloading music, or copying materials that were created by others, students should look for copyright and trademark symbols like these: ©, ®, ™.

180

 News

Nasty Thorns in the BlackBerry Patch
By Roger O. Crockett

Things are looking dicey for Research in Motion Ltd., maker of the cultish BlackBerry e-mail device. On Nov. 9, U.S. District Court Judge James Spencer made it clear he was growing increasingly impatient with the protracted battle between RIM and tiny tech investor NTP Inc., which alleges that RIM's wireless e-mail technology infringes on several of its patents. He also said he was "very unlikely" to accede to RIM's request that he postpone the case to give the U.S. Patent & Trademark office a chance to weigh in: "I've spent enough of my life and time on NTP and RIM."

With Spencer pushing to wrap things up, a settlement seems increasingly likely. And it could be a great deal higher than the $450 million RIM and NTP agreed to before talks collapsed in June. Some analysts say RIM could end up cutting a check for $1 billion.

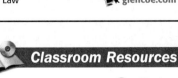 **Flex Your Reading**

Efficient critical reading involves being flexible with speed and comprehension. There are several ways of reading critically, and you need to fit a reading style to your needs and to the material.

Go to **glencoe.com** for Flex Your Reading activities, more information on reading strategies for this chapter, and guided practice in reading sales contracts.

 Classroom Resources

- Student Edition
- Teacher Wraparound Edition
- Student Activity Workbook with Academic Integration (SE/TAE)
- TeacherWorks™ Plus! CD
- *ExamView*® Assessment Suite CD
- *Presentation Plus!* CD

- National Mock Trial Championship DVD
- Online Learning Center with Podcasts at glencoe.com
- Study-to-Go™ at glencoe.com
- Online Student Edition
- Interactive Student Edition

Practice the Concept

Personal Property
Ask students to think of different types of property that belong to them. Have them envision items in their homes and their cars. Ask if they might be working on ideas or projects (such as a Web site or a business venture) that they would consider belonging to them. Have students discuss the measures they take to protect their property.

Key Terms Write on the board the items that students list in the activity above. Categorize each of the items listed as tangible personal property and intangible personal property. Use these examples to introduce the idea of intellectual property.

Legal Basics Explain that issues often arise between individuals or companies surrounding real property and intangible property. Properties might be stolen, borrowed, lost, or abandoned, and the law can help resolve these situations.

Intellectual Property Patents, trademarks, and copyrights protect one's creative ideas from being stolen. *What are some examples of intellectual property?*

181

▲ USING VISUALS

Intellectual Property Answer Examples of intellectual property include patents, copyrights, trademarks, logos, inventions, and works of art. Intellectual property is an original work fixed in a tangible medium of expression.

SECTION **8.1**

Types of Property

FOCUS

Bell Ringer Activity

Before students arrive for class, place several "lost" or "forgotten" items on different desks throughout the classroom (cell phone, book, jacket). Ask students whether they felt an obligation to find the owner of each item. Have students discuss whether they think there are legal issues to consider when they find property that does not belong to them.

Preteaching

Key Terms

Read the definitions and ask students to create a sentence using each term.

Academic Vocabulary

Explain that developing vocabulary is key to academic success. An efficient method to develop vocabulary is to study how words are formed.

- **tangible** Adjective, from the Latin *tangere* (to touch). Means that which may be touched.
- **exclusive** Adjective, from the Latin *exclusivus* (keep out). Means to hinder.
- **downloading** Verb, from *down* + *load* (carry). Means transferring files from a host computer.

Activity Ask students to give a noun, an adjective, or an adverb form that comes from each word.

 Connects to academic content

182

What You'll Learn

- ◆ Distinguish between real property, personal property, and fixtures.
- ◆ Describe the different types of co-ownership of personal property.
- ◆ Explain the concept of intellectual property.
- ◆ Give examples of intellectual property.
- ◆ Define the laws of patents, copyrights, and trademarks.

Why It's Important

Knowing the law about personal property will help you protect your possessions.

Academic Standards

Reading and completing the activities in this section will help you practice the following academic standards:

Social Studies (NCSS 8) Study relationships among science, technology, and society.

English Language Arts (NCTE 6) Apply knowledge of language structure, language conventions, media techniques, figurative language, and genre to create, critique, and discuss print and non-print texts.

Reading Guide

Before You Read

Connect Intellectual property can be anything you created, discovered, or designed. Name some things you have done that could be considered intellectual property.

Focus on Ideas

There are different ways to protect the ownership rights to different types of intellectual property.

Take Notes

Create a graph like the one shown and use it to take notes as you read this section. Go to **glencoe.com** to find graphic organizers and tips on how to improve your note-taking skills.

Patent	Copyright	Trademark
music player	novel	slogan
Examples		

Intellectual Property Protection

Key Terms

You will learn these legal words and expressions in this chapter. You can also find these terms in *Black's Law Dictionary* or in an online legal dictionary.

- personal property
- intellectual property
- patent
- copyright
- trademark

Academic Vocabulary

You will find these words in your readings and in your tests. Look them up in a dictionary and familiarize yourself with them.

- tangible
- exclusive
- downloading

182   Unit 3   Consumer Law

glencoe.com

R Reading Strategy

Read for Knowledge

1. **Survey** or preread the chapter.
2. **Question** or formulate questions before you read.
3. **Recite** or read your questions, answers, and notes out loud.
4. **Review** or reread your notes.

Note-Taking Basics

- Listen attentively
- Have note-taking materials ready
- Skim through the lesson material
- Write down key words and ideas
- Anticipate what comes next
- Review notes soon after taking them

Personal Property

Can you keep something you find on the street?

Personal property is everything, other than real property, that can be owned. Real property is land and anything connected to it, including buildings, the earth below, and the air above. Items of property permanently attached to real property, such as built-in stoves and kitchen cabinets, are called fixtures and are considered real property. **Tangible** personal property is property that has substance and can be touched, such as CD players, vehicles, and food. Intangible personal property, is property that has no substance and cannot be touched, such as patents, copyrights, and trademarks. If someone owes you money, the right to receive the money is intangible personal property. It is necessary to distinguish between real and personal property because the law that applies to each may be different.

As You Read

Predict What is the difference between personal property and real property?

Vocabulary You can find vocabulary definitions in the **Key Terms** glossary and the **Academic Vocabulary** glossary in the back of this book.

Global Law

Inheritance Rights in Property for Women in Kenya

Women in the United States are granted the same rights in property as their male counterparts. However, that is not the case in the country of Kenya. Although the Kenyan Constitution outlaws discrimination on the basis of sex, there are numerous exemptions that provide for a system that seemingly discriminates against women.

The Kenyan Constitution permits discrimination in matters pertaining to adoption, marriage, divorce, burial, distribution of property upon death, or other matters of personal law.

One such act that discriminates against women is The Law of Succession Act of 1981, which affects the distribution of property after someone dies. The law states:

1 Both male and female inherit equally if there is no surviving spouse.

2 However, if a spouse survives, the spouse inherits all the movable property in the house but can only live in the house and does not own it. If the spouse chooses to sell the house, court permission must be granted. Further, if the surviving spouse is a woman and she remarries, she loses all interest in the property when she remarries. If the surviving spouse is a man, he can remarry and his interest does not terminate.

3 If someone dies and does not have either a spouse or children, the estate passes first to the deceased's father and then, if the father is dead, to the mother.

4 Finally, the Act was amended in 1990 to exempt Muslim families from the provisions. Muslims in Kenya are subject only to Islamic laws, which provide that a son generally inherits double the share of a daughter. Also, if there are children and a wife, the wife only gets one-eighth of the estate.

Across Cultures: Source of Law in Kenya

Although Kenya has a constitution and statutory law, customary law (primarily unwritten) from each of the different regions is also valid law in those regions. The authorities must consider customary law to the extent it does not conflict with the constitution.

Critical Thinking: *Should different ethnic groups be able to follow their own laws, even though they are members of a larger country?*

Global Law

Inheritance Rights in Property for Women in Kenya

Answer Answers will vary. In Kenya, for example, there are five different laws for marriages. There are civil, Christian, Muslim, Hindu, and customary marriages, each with its own set of statutes. One could argue that each group has a common goal and can effectively govern itself. The United States is not exempt from this proposition. Native American groups in the United States are considered sovereign nations and can pass and enforce their own laws.

TEACH

Discussion Starter

Class Discussion

Have students tell of any circumstances in which they found a lost item that belonged to another person. Ask if there was a reward offered, or if they were compensated in any way for returning the item. Tell students that disputes over lost property are generally governed by local law.

As You Read

Predict Help students understand the difference between real property and personal property by giving examples of each. (Real property is land and anything connected to it, such as a house, the earth below, and the airspace above. Personal property is anything owned that is not real property.)

D Develop Concepts

Tangible Versus Intangible Personal Property Help students understand the difference between tangible personal property and intangible personal property by explaining that one is a *right* rather than a physical object. The right represents something of value rather than being of value itself. Ask students which type of personal property represents a right. (intangible)

TEACH (cont.)

Guided Practice

Co-ownership of Personal Property

Tell students that Joe and Brenda own a condo as joint tenants. Ask students what could happen with the condo if Joe were to die. (Joe's share passes to Brenda.) Ask students how this would differ if the two owned the property as tenants in common. (Joe's share would pass to Joe's heirs.) Explain that this distinction would be important when two people decide how they will share ownership of property.

 Critical Thinking

Misplaced Property Explain to students that if they find a cell phone on a table at a restaurant, it would be considered misplaced rather than lost. Ask students to suggest what should be done with the cell phone if found. (Leave it with the restaurant management or owner.)

> ✓ *Reading Check*
>
> **Explain** No. The stolen item belongs to its original owner, who can always regain prossession.

Most property is acquired by:
- purchase
- gift
- inheritance

Co-ownership of Personal Property

When two or more people own personal property as tenants in common, each owner's share passes to his or her heirs upon death. If, instead, they own it as joint tenants, each owner's share passes to the surviving joint tenants upon death. Nine states recognize community property. This is property (except a gift or inheritance) that is acquired by the personal efforts of either spouse during marriage. It belongs to both spouses equally.

Lost, Misplaced, and Abandoned Property

If you find a watch, you have a legal duty to try to find the true owner. If you cannot find the owner, you may be able to keep the watch after following local requirements. Local laws may require you to advertise for the true owner or to deposit the article at the police station while the owner is being sought.

C If property is found on the counter of a store, at a table in a restaurant, or on a chair in a washroom, it is considered misplaced rather than lost. The owner may recall where it was left and return for it. If you find an article in such a place, you should leave it with the proprietor. Abandoned property is property that has been discarded by the owner without the intent to reclaim it. With exceptions, anyone who finds abandoned property may keep it.

CYBERLAW

Venetian Casino Resort, LLC v. VenetianGold.com
380 F.Supp.2d 737 (E.D. Va. 2005)

The Venetian Casino Resort is a prominent Las Vegas casino known for its elaborate Venetian-style architecture. The Resort has trademarked numerous names, including, "Venetian," "The Venetian," and "The Venetian Resort Hotel Casino." After those names were trademarked, Vincent Coyle launched an international gambling Web site using the name VenetianGold.com. He also registered Web site names such as VenetianGoldCasino.com, VenetianCasinoVegas.com, and VeniceGoldCasino.com, all of which took users to the gambling Web site. The Venetian Casino Resort then sued VenetianGold.com under the Anti-Cybersquatting Consumer Protection Act.

Ruling and Resolution
The U.S. District Court in Virginia held that the Venetian Casino Resort in Las Vegas was a distinct trademark and that VenetianGold.com had tried to profit from using similar names on its Web sites. Therefore, Mr. Coyle's company must cease using Web site names that were similar and include the term "Venetian," along with similar-themed words.

Critical Thinking If users realize that the Web site is not actually the Las Vegas resort, then should Mr. Coyle be able to use similar names?

184 Unit 3 Consumer Law

CYBERLAW

Venetian Casino Resort, LLC v. VenetianGold.com

Answer Answers will vary. The court pointed to the fact that the Venetian Casino Resort had spent $13.5 million in 2000 and 2001 advertising the resort in numerous publications around the United States. The court reasoned that VenetianGold.com was able to profit, at least partially, from that advertising by having a similar name. There are numerous cases in which companies have tried to protect their names on the Internet.

Stolen Personal Property

A person has no title to goods that are stolen and cannot give good title to anyone else. An innocent purchaser who acquires a stolen item in good faith is obliged to return it to the owner. Title to stolen goods never leaves the owner, who can always regain possession.

Gifts of Personal Property

A gift of personal property is completed when three requirements are met:

- The donor (gift-giver) must intend to make the gift.
- The gift must be delivered.
- The donee (gift-receiver) must accept the gift.

Once all three requirements are met, the gift cannot be taken back by the original owner.

 Gifts Like a contract, offer and acceptance are required for a gift to be complete. *How does a gift differ most from a contract?*

Intellectual Property

Can you patent a peanut butter and jelly sandwich?

Intellectual property is an original work fixed in a tangible medium of expression. Examples of intellectual property include inventions, works of art, software, and logos (see **Figure 8.1** on page 186). Intellectual property law has become even more important with the increase of computers and technology. Due to high research and development costs, technology companies want to ensure that their products are protected from other companies. Patents, copyrights, and trademarks assure that the rightful owners of intellectual property will have **exclusive** rights to their creations.

Patents

A patent is a grant giving an inventor the exclusive right to make, use, or sell an invention for a period set by Congress. The period is generally 20 years. To be patented, a device must be useful and consist of a new principle or idea. It also must not be obvious to people with ordinary skill in the field. For example, in 1999, the Smucker's Company obtained a patent on Uncrustables—frozen, crustless peanut butter and jelly pockets. Later, the company sought to expand its patent, arguing that the sealed edge was one of a kind. In 2005, the court held against the expansion, saying that the crimped edges on Uncrustables are similar to ravioli or pie crust. The patent office said it would reexamine the original patent given to Smucker's.

> ✓ *Reading Check*
>
> **Explain** *Can you keep something you bought that you later find out was stolen?*

8.1 SECTION

TEACH (cont.)

C Critical Thinking

Intellectual Property
Explain that a claim to intellectual property, such as a patent or trademark, ensures that the owner retains rights to his or her creation. Ask students what might happen if individuals did not have the right to their intellectual property. (Motivation to create could be impaired.)

Guided Practice

Patents and Copyrights

Have students discuss the similarities between patents and copyrights. (Patents and copyrights both give the owner exclusive right to use or sell their creations.) Explain that copyrighted works are protected for the life of the author plus 70 years, while patents are generally only granted for 20 years but may be extended.

ASSESS

Quiz

1. What type of property has no substance and cannot be touched? (intangible personal property)

2. What are three examples of intangible personal property? (patents, copyrights, trademarks)

▲ USING VISUALS

➲ **Gifts** **Answer** A gift is given without getting something in return, so it lacks consideration, which is a key element to a contractual relationship.

Activity Gifts can be classified into two categories: *causa mortis* or *inter vivos*. Ask students to look up the two Latin terms and describe what each means. (*Causa mortis* or *donation mortis causa* means "gift caused by death" and is a type of gift that is made during the life of the donor but is only delivered upon his or her death. *Inter vivos*, which means during the life of the donor, is the gift which is delivered immediately.)

RETEACH

Guided Practice

Gifts of Personal Property

Tell students that Rachael promised to give Claire her inline skates after her skating lesson. Rachael left the skates on Claire's front porch while Claire was finishing up her tutoring session. Ask students if the three requirements of a gift of personal property have been met. (Rachael intended to make the gift and the gift was delivered, but Claire never actually accepted the gift. Therefore the requirements have not been met.)

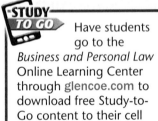

STUDY TO GO Have students go to the *Business and Personal Law* Online Learning Center through glencoe.com to download free Study-to-Go content to their cell phones or PDAs.

U Universal Access

Visual/Spatial Learners

Students who have difficulty retaining what they read may find that they learn easier from diagrams or figures. Explain that figures can convey major portions of content that also appears in paragraph form. Many learners respond favorably to information organized into brief, columnar formats.

Figure 8.1 Intellectual Property Rights

Logos Photos Inventions Songs Fonts

The Apple Computer Corporation owns numerous patent, copyright, and trademark rights. *What types of intellectual property protection are used to cover the different items in the figure?*

▲ USING VISUALS

Figure 8.1 Intellectual Property Rights **Answer** Inventions are protected by patents; photos, songs, and fonts are protected by copyright; and logos are protected by trademarks.

Activity Ask students to research the federal government organization responsible for the examination and registration of intellectual property. Have the students visit the appropriate government Web site and look up more information on intellectual property. (The United States Patent and Trademark Office, a Department of Commerce federal agency, is responsible for the examination and issue of patents and registration of trademarks.)

Copyrights

A copyright is a right granted to an author, composer, photographer, or artist to exclusively publish and sell an artistic or literary work. Copyrighted works are protected for the life of the author plus 70 years. In addition to printed items, computer software, graphic arts, architectural designs, motion pictures, and sound recording may be copyrighted. **Downloading** someone else's music from the Internet without paying a fee violates copyright law.

Under the fair use doctrine, copyrighted material may be reproduced without permission in certain cases. Copying is allowed for literary criticism, news reporting, teaching, school reports, and other research. The amount and use of the material must be reasonable and not harmful to the copyright owner.

Trademarks

A trademark is a distinctive mark, symbol, or slogan used by a business to identify and distinguish its goods from products sold by others. It may consist of a word, name, symbol, or other device. Owners of trademarks have the exclusive right to use the particular word, name, or symbol that they have adopted as their trademark. A trademark continues for ten years and may be renewed for additional ten-year periods. The ® symbol indicates that a trademark is legally registered.

After You Read

Summarize What are the three most common ways property is acquired?

SECTION 8.1 ASSESSMENT

Self Check

1. Give two examples of tangible personal property and one example of intangible personal property.

2. What are the three requirements of a completed gift?

3. When is copying allowed without permission?

Academic Connection

Social Studies Copyright law goes back to the invention of the printing press. The first copyright law enacted in the U.S. is the Copyright Act of 1790. Since then, there have been major and minor revisions to the act in 1831, 1865, 1870, 1909, 1912, and 1976. Go to the library or on the Internet to look up the Copyright Act and why it was changed each time. Create a time line describing the changes.

English Language Arts Suppose you lost or misplaced a valuable item of personal property. Write an ad to be posted in a newspaper and around your neighborhood describing the item and offering a reward for its return.

Be sure to use proper sentence structure and check your work for grammatical, punctuation, and spelling errors.

Critical Thinking

Give and Take When you admire your friend's portable CD player, your friend replies, "I've got another one just like it that you can have. I'll give it to you at school tomorrow." Two days later, you learn that your friend gave the player to someone else. Was the player a gift to you?

Go to **glencoe.com** to check your answers.

RETEACH (cont.)

After You Read

Summarize Property is most often acquired by buying it, by receiving it as a gift, or by inheriting it.

ASSESS

Self-Assessment

Have students go to the *Business and Personal Law* Online Learning Center through glencoe.com to take the Section 8.1 Practice Test.

CLOSE

Culminating Activity

Copyrights

Tell students that Paul made copies of several copyrighted poems he found online. He plans to use the copies for a literary criticism report for a class assignment. Ask students whether Paul has violated copyright law. Have students explain why or why not. (No. Fair use doctrine allows use for school reports and other research.)

SECTION 8.1 ASSESSMENT

Self Check
1. tangible: clothing, books intangible: money owed to you
2. (1) Donor intends to make gift, (2) gift must be delivered, and (3) donee must accept.
3. literary criticism, news reporting, teaching, school reports

Academic Connection
Social Studies
1831, copyright length extended and musical composition added; 1865, photographs added; 1870, works of art added; 1912, motion pictures added; 1976, revised for new technology and to protect computer software

English Language Arts
Answers will vary.

Critical Thinking
No, since the requirements were not met.

NCLB Activity correlated to the academic standards on page 182

187

FOCUS

Bell Ringer Activity

Ask students to describe the contexts in which they have heard the term *bail* used. Explain that many shows depict situations in which individuals in jail leave an amount of money or property with the court to ensure that they will return to stand trial.

Preteaching

Key Terms

Read the definitions and ask students to create a sentence using each term.

Academic Vocabulary

Explain that developing vocabulary is key to academic success. An efficient method to develop vocabulary is to study how words are formed.

- **standard** Noun, from the Latin *extendere* (unit of measure). Means rule.
- **benefit** Noun, from the Latin *benefactum* (good deed). Means advantage.
- **register** Verb, from the Latin *regerrere* (to collect). Means to record.

Activity Ask students to give a noun, an adjective, or an adverb form that comes from each word.

Connects to academic content

What You'll Learn

- ◆ Define bailment.
- ◆ Explain the different types of bailments.
- ◆ Discuss the standard of care bailees must use.
- ◆ Define a hotel keeper's liability.
- ◆ Identify a common carrier's liability for loss or damaged goods.

Why It's Important

Knowing the law of bailment will help you understand your rights when you let someone hold your property for you.

Academic Standards

Reading and completing the activities in this section will help you practice the following academic standards:

Social Studies (NCSS 3) Study people, places, and environments.

Math (NCTM NOS 2a) Judge the effects of such operations as multiplication, division, and computing powers and roots on the magnitudes of quantities.

Reading Guide

Before You Read

Connect A bailment is created whenever you let someone else keep something you own temporarily. Name some times when you had to do this in public.

Focus on Ideas

Different types of bailments require different standards of care.

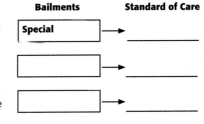

Take Notes	Bailments	Standard of Care
Create a graph like the one shown and use it to take notes as you read this section. Go to glencoe.com to find graphic organizers and tips on how to improve your note-taking skills.	Special → _____
	→ _____
	→ _____

Key Terms

You will learn these legal words and expressions in this chapter. You can also find these terms in *Black's Law Dictionary* or in an online legal dictionary.

- bailment
- special bailment
- gratuitous bailment
- mutual benefit bailment
- carrier
- common carrier

Academic Vocabulary

You will find these words in your readings and in your tests. Look them up in a dictionary and familiarize yourself with them.

- standard
- benefit
- register

glencoe.com

R Reading Strategy

Read for Knowledge

1. **Survey** or preread the chapter.
2. **Question** or formulate questions before you read.
3. **Recite** or read your questions, answers, and notes out loud.
4. **Review** or reread your notes.

Note-Taking Basics

- Listen attentively
- Have note-taking materials ready
- Skim through the lesson material
- Write down key words and ideas
- Anticipate what comes next
- Review notes soon after taking them

Bailments

Is leaving your laptop at a repair shop considered a bailment?

You may have rented movies at a video store, left your car at a shop to be repaired, or dropped clothes off at the cleaners. These were all bailments. **A bailment is the transfer of possession and control of personal property to another with the intent that the same property will be returned later.** The person who transfers the property is the bailor. The person to whom the property is transferred is the bailee.

In a bailment, there is no intent to pass title to property. The bailee has an obligation to return the same property to the bailor. The bailee also has a responsibility to exercise a certain **standard** of care of the property. The standard of care depends on who receives the most **benefit** from the bailment. There are three types of bailments, each with a different standard of care.

Types of Bailments

A special bailment is a bailment for the sole benefit of the bailee. If you borrow a friend's laptop, with nothing offered in return, you alone benefit from bailment. This type of

As You Read

Predict What is a tortious bailee?

Vocabulary You can find vocabulary definitions in the **Key Terms** glossary and the **Academic Vocabulary** glossary in the back of this book.

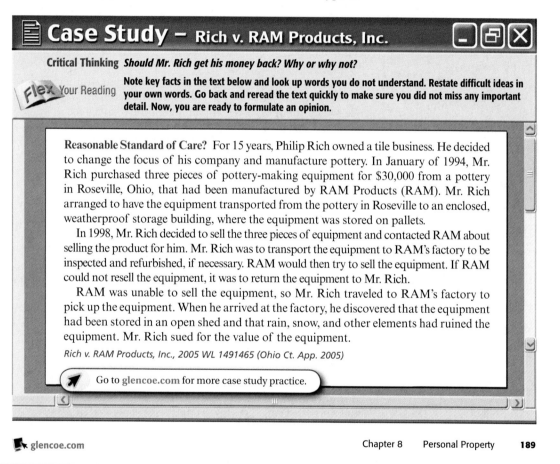

📄 Case Study – Rich v. RAM Products, Inc. ▢▢✕

Critical Thinking *Should Mr. Rich get his money back? Why or why not?*

Flex Your Reading Note key facts in the text below and look up words you do not understand. Restate difficult ideas in your own words. Go back and reread the text quickly to make sure you did not miss any important detail. Now, you are ready to formulate an opinion.

Reasonable Standard of Care? For 15 years, Philip Rich owned a tile business. He decided to change the focus of his company and manufacture pottery. In January of 1994, Mr. Rich purchased three pieces of pottery-making equipment for $30,000 from a pottery in Roseville, Ohio, that had been manufactured by RAM Products (RAM). Mr. Rich arranged to have the equipment transported from the pottery in Roseville to an enclosed, weatherproof storage building, where the equipment was stored on pallets.

In 1998, Mr. Rich decided to sell the three pieces of equipment and contacted RAM about selling the product for him. Mr. Rich was to transport the equipment to RAM's factory to be inspected and refurbished, if necessary. RAM would then try to sell the equipment. If RAM could not resell the equipment, it was to return the equipment to Mr. Rich.

RAM was unable to sell the equipment, so Mr. Rich traveled to RAM's factory to pick up the equipment. When he arrived at the factory, he discovered that the equipment had been stored in an open shed and that rain, snow, and other elements had ruined the equipment. Mr. Rich sued for the value of the equipment.

Rich v. RAM Products, Inc., 2005 WL 1491465 (Ohio Ct. App. 2005)

➤ Go to **glencoe.com** for more case study practice.

📘 glencoe.com

Class Discussion
Ask how many students have ever borrowed a friend's car or computer. Explain that this action constituted a bailment because control and possession of the car or computer is transferred, and the property is expected to be returned.

D Develop Concepts

Bailments Explain that the transfer of personal property gives rise to specific rights and duties on the part of the bailor and bailee. Ask what rights and duties would be involved if one person borrowed a friend's laptop for the day. (Bailee must return the laptop after using it, take care of laptop, use for only the specified time period.)

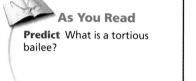

As You Read

Predict A *tortious bailee* is one who maintains control of property wrongfully, either by wrongfully keeping lost or stolen property, or by continuing to control property after a bailment has ended.

📄 Case Study

Rich v. RAM Products, Inc.

Answer Yes. The Ohio Court of Appeals held that under the law of bailments, the bailor (Mr. Rich) has a right to retrieve his property in the same condition in which it had been delivered previously. When Mr. Rich had delivered the equipment to RAM, it was valued at the $30,000 purchase price from four years prior. When the property was returned, it had been damaged and was then worth only $5,000, so under bailment law, Mr. Rich was entitled to recover the $25,000 in damages.

TEACH *(cont.)*

 D Develop Concepts

Benefits of Bailments Tell students that when transfers of property occur, the benefits to the parties can vary. Ask students to imagine that they have borrowed a snowboard from a friend in exchange for lending their motorcycle for the weekend. Have students discuss the benefits to each party. (use of snowboard, use of motorcycle) What responsibility does each party bear? (reasonable care)

Guided Practice

Types of Bailments

Emphasize that the law of bailments affects almost everyone on a daily basis. Have students think of two bailments in which they have participated and explain why they were bailments. (Type of bailment will depend on who benefited from the exchange.)

Legal Talk

(signpost, signal, signature)

Ask students to practice their academic and legal vocabulary with the electronic flashcards available at the *Business and Personal Law* Online Learning Center through glencoe.com.

---

bailment requires great care. That means you, as the bailee, are liable for any kind of damage to the laptop while it is in your possession.

A gratuitous bailment is a bailment for the sole benefit of the bailor. This type of bailment might occur if a friend asks you to hold something, like a watch, while he or she goes swimming. Since your friend, as the bailor, receives the sole benefit of the bailment, you are required to use only slight care and can only be held liable for gross negligence. If the watch is scratched or stolen, you are not liable.

A mutual benefit bailment is a bailment in which both the bailor and the bailee receive benefits. This type of bailment might occur if you leave your car at a garage to be repaired. You, as the bailor, will have your car repaired, and the mechanic, as the bailee, will receive payment for the service. This type of bailment requires reasonable care, or the amount of care a reasonable person would use.

D

Sale-on-Consignment and Sale-on-Approval A consignment is a type of mutual benefit bailment. The consignor entrusts goods to the consignee for the purpose of selling them. If the goods are sold, the consignee, known as a factor, will forward the proceeds, minus a fee, to the consignor. If the goods are not sold, they are returned to the consignor. When goods are sold on approval, they remain the property of the seller until the buyer approves them.

Tortious Bailees Bailees have the right to use another person's property only for the purpose for which the bailment was created. Use for another purpose or for a longer time than agreed upon is a wrongful act.

A tortious bailee is someone who holds property wrongfully. This includes someone who keeps someone else's lost property or knowingly possesses stolen property. One who refuses to return property at the termination of a bailment is also a tortious bailee. Tortious bailees are responsible for all damage to property in their possession.

Burden of Proof Sometimes items are damaged, lost, or stolen when they are in the possession of a bailee. The bailor is not in a position to know what caused the loss. If a bailor brings suit for damages, courts shift the burden of proof to the one who is in the best position to know what happened—the bailee. As a result, the burden is on the bailee to prove a lack of negligence.

Special Bailments

What can you do if an airline loses your luggage?

Certain types of bailees have special obligations in addition to the duties imposed on all bailees. These include hotel keepers and common carriers.

 Legal Talk

Consignment: *n* Giving goods to a dealer to sell for the owner. From Latin *com* = with + *sign* = mark or seal + *ment* = act of: to transfer authority to.

Lien: *n* A charge upon real or personal property for the satisfaction of some debt or duty. From Latin *ligare:* to bind.

Vocabulary Builder The root word *sign* means mark, seal, or symbol. Name words that contain *sign* and explain their meaning.

Look It Up! Check definitions in *Black's Law Dictionary* or an online glossary. For direct links, go to **glencoe. com** to find more vocabulary resources.

 glencoe.com

Extending the Content

Burden of Proof

There are three different burdens of proof in the United States: preponderance of the evidence; beyond a reasonable doubt; and clear and convincing evidence. The burden of proof of preponderance of the evidence requires that a judgment is based on the likelihood that evidence admitted is true and convincing. The burden of proof of beyond a reasonable doubt requires that there is no doubt, which would make a reasonable person hesitate to make a decision. Clear and convincing evidence, as a burden of proof, requires less than "beyond a reasonable doubt" yet more than "a preponderance of the evidence," in that it requires the evidence must be substantially more likely than not to be true.

Hotel Keepers

A hotel keeper is the operator of a hotel, motel, or inn that regularly offers rooms to the public for a price. If rooms are available, a hotel keeper must accept all people who are not dangerous to the health, welfare, or safety of others and who are able to pay for their lodging. Moreover, the Civil Rights Act makes it a crime for hotel keepers to refuse a room to anyone on the grounds of race, creed, color, gender, or national origin.

Hotels and motels must provide a minimum standard of comfort, safety, and sanitation. Minimum standards include heat and ventilation, clean beds, and reasonably quiet surroundings. Guests are guaranteed the right of privacy.

With exceptions, hotel keepers are held by law to be insurers of their guests' property. In the event of loss, the hotel keeper may be held liable, regardless of the amount of care exercised.

Hotel keepers are not liable as insurers in the following cases:

- losses caused by a guest's own negligence
- losses to the guest's property due to acts of God (events such as earthquakes, floods, or cyclones) or due to acts of the public enemy (such as terrorists or wartime enemies)
- loss of property because of accidental fire in which no negligence may be attributed to the hotel keeper

Hotel Keeper's Lien and Credit Card Blocking Hotel keepers have a lien on their guests' property. If a guest cannot pay, the hotel keeper may hold the guest's property as security for payment at some later time.

Credit card blocking is a method used by hotels to secure payment for a room. Under this system, guests are asked for a credit card number when they **register**. The hotel contacts the card company with the estimated cost of the bill. If the card company approves the transaction, the guest's available line of credit is reduced by the estimated amount. This procedure is known as a block. The final actual charge for the room will replace the block within a day or two after the guest checks out.

Common Carriers

A carrier is a business that transports persons, goods, or both. A common carrier is a carrier that is compensated for providing transportation to the general public.

 Hotel Keepers Hotel keepers cannot turn away anyone who is not a danger to others if a room is available. *What can hotel keepers do to ensure guests pay their bills?*

 Reading Check

Analyze Why is the burden of proof on the bailee rather than the bailor when property is damaged, lost, or stolen?

▲ USING VISUALS

Hotel Keepers Answer Hotel keepers might collect payment in advance or use credit card blocking to ensure that guests pay their bills. In addition, hotel keepers may hold a guest's property as security for payment at some later time.

TEACH (cont.)

Guided Practice

Hotel Keepers

- Have students describe the general standards expected by hotel guests. (clean, private, and safe accommodations) **L1**

- Ask students to describe ways in which hotels help keep guests and their belongings safe. (security guards, safes, locks) **L2**

- Have students suggest circumstances under which the hotel keeper might not be held liable in case of loss. (Guest is negligent in keeping property safe. Natural disasters such as floods or earthquakes cause damage. Accidents such as fires cause damage.) **L3**

Extending the Content

Reasonable Care

Have students discuss how someone might try to prove that they had exercised reasonable care when they were in possession of another person's property. (testimony of witness, documentation of actions)

Reading Check

Analyze Since the bailor is not in a position to know what happened when property is damaged, lost, or stolen, because he or she is not in possession of the property, the bailee carries the burden of proof.

ASSESS

Quiz

1. If Brandon borrows Kelly's guitar, who is the bailor? (Kelly)

2. Who has the burden of proof in a bailment lawsuit? (bailee)

3. What are a carrier and a common carrier? (A carrier is a business that transports persons, goods, or both, and a common carrier provides transportation to the general public.)

RETEACH

Guided Practice

Passengers' Baggage

A carrier is an insurer of all luggage that is checked through the baggage desk. However, a carrier is not responsible for items that you keep at your seat or in overhead compartments. Ask students if they agree with this exception to the responsibility of passenger's baggage. Have students with opposing views argue for their opinion in front of the class and take a vote to see if your class agrees with this rule.

Review Key Terms

Encourage students to access the *Business and Personal Law* Online Learning Center through glencoe.com and use the electronic flashcards to review the key terms.

➡ **Common Carriers** Federal regulations require the screening of airline passengers and property. *What happens to passengers who do not consent to being screened?*

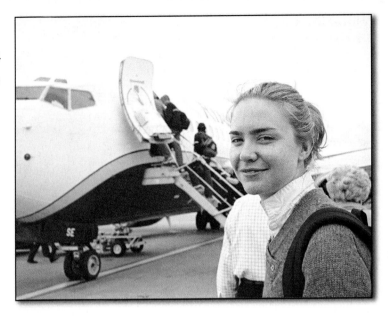

As with hotels, common carriers cannot turn away people who ask for their services.

Common Carriers of Goods Common carriers are liable for damages to all goods they ship, regardless of whether they are negligent. However, carriers are not liable when damages occur as a result of acts of God, the public enemy, public authorities, the shipper, and the **inherent** nature of the goods.

With these exceptions, common carriers must accept all goods offered to them for shipment. However, common carriers:

- are not required to accept goods they are not equipped to carry
- may refuse goods that are inherently dangerous
- may refuse goods that they do not haul
- may refuse goods that are improperly packaged
- may refuse goods that are not delivered at the proper place and time

Common carriers will not be excused from liability for losses because of strikes, mob violence, fire, and similar causes. Labor unions are required to give notice of impending strikes weeks in advance of the strike dates to allow carriers to reject shipments that might be damaged by delays during a strike.

Carriers have a lien on all goods shipped for the amount of the shipping charges due. Should the shipper and the party receiving the goods fail to pay the charges, the carrier may sell the goods at public sale.

192   Unit 3   Consumer Law

▲ **USING VISUALS**

➡ **Common Carriers** **Answer** Passengers who do not consent to screening must be refused transportation. Ask students to explain the purpose of this rule. (protection of other passengers)

Activity Have students consider how security measures for airline passengers have changed over the past few years. (additional screening of carry-on items, banning of liquids or gels aboard flights, limited use of electronic devices in flight, new X-ray technologies, required IDs)

Common Carriers of Passengers Carriers are responsible for protecting passengers. They are not responsible, however, if injuries are unforeseeable or unpreventable. Federal regulations require the screening of airline passengers and property. Passengers who do not consent to the screening must be refused transportation.

Bumped Airline Passengers When an airline flight is overbooked, the airline is responsible for accommodating passengers. The airline must ask for volunteers to give up their seats for seats on the next available flight. If there are not enough volunteers, other passengers may be denied a seat. Passengers who are bumped may be entitled to compensation plus the money back for their tickets.

Baggage Carriers are obligated to accept a reasonable amount of passengers' baggage. Luggage kept at one's seat does not count toward the weight limits permitted each passenger. You may ship excess baggage by paying additional fees. Dangerous weapons, explosives, destructive items, and those that are a potential threat are not allowed.

Federal rules place limits on the liability of airlines for lost luggage. Within the U.S., the maximum liability is $2,500 per passenger. Excess valuation may be declared on certain types of articles. Some carriers assume no liability for fragile, valuable, or perishable articles.

After You Read

Summarize What are the different standards of care required by bailees for the different types of bailments?

RETEACH (cont.)

After You Read

Summarize A special bailment requires great care, a gratuitous bailment requires slight care, and a mutual benefit bailment requires reasonable care.

ASSESS

Self-Assessment

Have students go to the *Business and Personal Law* Online Learning Center through glencoe.com to take the Section 8.2 Practice Test.

CLOSE

Culminating Activity

Bailments

Tell students that Jennifer took her prom dress to a consignment shop to put it up for sale. Ask students what type of bailment Jennifer is participating in. (mutual benefit) What kind of care is required by the bailee? (reasonable care)

SECTION 8.2 ASSESSMENT

Self Check

1. What is the difference between a bailor and a bailee?

2. What is credit card blocking?

3. What do federal regulations require when passengers do not consent to a screening?

Academic Connection

Mathematics Duo Corporation manufactures home security monitors. It needs to rent storage space to warehouse its monitors. Each monitor is packaged in a carton measuring 2 feet long, 1.5 feet wide, and 2 feet high. How many cubic feet of space does Duo Corporation need to store 800 monitors?

 For more math practice, go to the Math Appendix.

THEORY **Number and Operations: Using Fractions, Decimals, and Rounding** To solve this problem you will need to find the volume per item first. This is done by doing the following: length × width × height = volume per item. Next you will need to find the storage space, which is calculated by volume per item × number of items.

Critical Thinking

Living Bailments The agricultural class at your school raises small animals, such as hamsters and rabbits. Every weekend several students take the animals home to feed them. Is this a bailment? If so, what kind?

 Go to **glencoe.com** to check your answers.

SECTION 8.2 ASSESSMENT

Self Check

1. Bailor is the person who transfers a property. Bailee is the person to whom the property is transferred.

2. a method used by hotels to secure payment for a room by the use of a credit card number

3. The passengers must be refused transportation.

Academic Connection

Mathematics
4,800 cu. ft.

Critical Thinking

Yes. Some will argue that it is a bailment for the sole benefit of the school, because it is having its animals cared for at no charge. Others will argue that it is a mutual benefit bailment because students benefit from enjoying the animals.

 Activity correlated to the Mathematics standard on page 188

Summary by Sections

Ask students to read the summaries one key point at a time. Then, ask them to work in groups to create two examples to illustrate each key point.

Vocabulary Builder

Cooperative Learning

1. Have students work in groups to prepare their sentences. Ask the groups to exchange their sentences and assess each other's sentences.

Vocabulary Development

- Ask students to use a dictionary or to go online to look up the etymology of each key term listed.
- Then, ask students to list several words derived from the same root or origin. For example, *contract* has the same root as *contractual* or *contractually*.

Chapter 8 Review and Assessment

Summary

Section 8.1 Types of Property

- Personal property is everything, other than real property, that can be owned.
- Real property is land and anything connected to it, including buildings.
- Most property is acquired by purchase, as a gift, or by inheritance.
- Forms of co-ownership of personal property include tenants in common, joint tenants, and community property.
- A gift of personal property is completed when the donor intends to give the gift, it is delivered, and the donee accepts the gift.
- Intellectual property is an original work fixed in a tangible medium of expression, such as an invention, a work of art, or a logo.
- Intellectual property is protected by patents, copyrights, and trademarks.

Section 8.2 Bailments

- A bailment is the transfer of possession and control of personal property to another with the intent that the property will be returned later.
- The main types of bailments are: special bailment for the sole benefit of the bailee; gratuitous bailment for the sole benefit of the bailor; and mutual benefit bailment in which both the bailor and the bailee receive benefits.
- Hotel keepers are held by law to be insurers of their guests' property. In the event of loss, a hotel keeper may be held liable, regardless of the amount of care exercised.
- Common carriers are liable for damages to all goods they ship, regardless of whether they are negligent.
- Common carriers are responsible for protecting passengers.

Vocabulary Builder

1 On a sheet of paper, use each of these terms in a sentence.

Key Terms

- personal property
- intellectual property
- patent
- copyright

- trademark
- bailment
- special bailment
- gratuitous bailment

- mutual benefit bailment
- carrier
- common carrier

Academic Vocabulary

- tangible
- exclusive

- downloading
- standard

- benefit
- register

> Go to **glencoe.com** to play a game and improve your legal vocabulary.

Study Skills for Success

Prepare Your Students for Studying

Tell students that they can improve their ability to understand and remember material from their courses by learning and practicing study skills. Remind students to:

- **Get motivated!** Motivation must come from within. To motivate yourself, think of ways in which what you learn now will fit into your long-term personal and professional goals.
- **Get organized!** Make studying part of your daily routine, not something you do at the last minute.
- **Concentrate!** Study in an environment that is as free of distractions as possible.

Key Points Review

Answer the following questions. Refer to the chapter for additional reinforcement.

2 What is the difference between personal property, real property, and fixtures?

3 What are some of the types of personal property?

4 What are some methods of acquiring ownership of personal property?

5 What are the different forms of co-ownership of personal property?

6 What is intellectual property and what are some types of intellectual property?

7 How is a bailment created?

8 What are the principal types of bailments?

9 What are some of the responsibilities of common carriers?

Standardized Test Practice

10 Read the following information about the use of bailment law to transfer technology and then answer questions 1 and 2.

In the 1980s, biotechnology companies solved the problem of transferring tangible material through use of the ancient legal tool of bailment, where possession, but not title, of tangible personal property is transferred for a limited purpose and duration. Then universities started utilizing bailment to transfer new technology as well. Bailment is a useful technology transfer tool in two particular situations. One case arises out of the explosive growth of biotechnology over the last two decades, and the other case is a mechanism to accomplish technology transfer through the use of tangible research products generally. In many instances over the past two decades, the traditional patent system has not been able to provide practical or cost-effective protection for a biotechnology invention, if any protection was available.

1. How did biotechnology companies solve the problem of material transfer?

Ⓐ Stopped new technology transfer

Ⓑ Transferred for limited purpose or duration

Ⓒ Required formal licensing

Ⓓ Utilized bailment laws

2. What have traditional patent systems not been able to provide?

Ⓐ Laws that have evolved in patents

Ⓑ National laboratories run by universities

Ⓒ Practical or cost-effective protection

Ⓓ Tangible research products

Test-Taking Strategies If you find yourself taking too long to answer a question, skip it and go back to it later.

Chapter 8

Review and Assessment

Key Points Review

2. Real property: land and anything permanently attached to it. Personal property: everything that can be owned other than real property. Fixtures: items permanently attached to real property.

3. Tangible: CD players, vehicles, food Intangible: patents, copyrights, trademarks

4. purchase, gift, inheritance

5. tenants in common, joint tenants, and community property

6. An original work fixed in a tangible medium of expression. Examples: inventions, works of art, software, and logos

7. It is created when someone transfers possession and control of personal property to another with the intent that the same property will be returned later.

8. bailment for the sole benefit of the bailor, bailment for the sole benefit of the bailee, and mutual benefit bailment

9. They provide transportation to the general public; cannot turn away people who ask for their services.

Standardized Test Practice

10. D and C

 Strategies for Standardized Test Prep Success

Whether your students have a standardized test coming up in a few days or a few weeks, this last-minute test-prep tip will help them relax and do their best.

- **Test Format** Help students become familiar with the format of the test by practicing with test items that imitate the actual test items as closely as possible.

- **Test Timing** Have your students take timed practice tests so that they become comfortable with the length, design, and timing of the actual test.

Apply and Debate

Students should use chapter content to arrive at conclusions. The legal resolutions are listed below.

11. Neither the domain name nor the logo is protected without a trademark. However, the domain name may be protected by contract or federal law simply by having been purchased.

12. Probably not. In order to use copyrighted material without permission, it must be done for a research or educational purpose.

13. Probably not. No permission is necessary from the players since the game would be a public, non-artistic event. Only the school would have intellectual property rights to the video. It is presumed that the club is part of the school and could use the video without express permission from the school.

14. Yes, there was a bailment. However, because it was a gratuitous bailment, the friend is only liable for gross negligence and would not be liable for the damage in this situation.

15. Yes, there was a mutual-benefit bailment. The water park is obligated to Jonathan to use reasonable care when in possession of his items.

Apply and Debate

C Read the following scenarios. Get together with other students in pairs or groups of three and take a position on each scenario. Debate your position in class with students taking the opposite position or prepare a written argument justifying your position.

⑪ Trademarks

Jana is a junior in high school. She designed a Web site to promote her small business and purchased a domain name and logo, but did not trademark them.

You Debate *Is Jana's business protected from another company using her domain name and logo?*

⑫ Copyrights

The Myers High School literary club wants to sell a book of students' poems for $12. It will include quotes from famous authors and a credit line for each quote.

You Debate *Can the literary club legally use copyrighted material without the owner's permission or paying a royalty fee?*

⑬ Non-Profit

The Ellis High School Business Club plans to sell buttons featuring players' photos. To create the photos, the club members used video clips from previous games without asking the players' permission. The Business Club is a nonprofit club and the video clips were created by the school to use for promoting school sports.

You Debate *Is the club in violation of intellectual property laws since it did not create or own the video clips and did not receive permission?*

⑭ Bailment

Joycelyn's friend agreed to keep Jocelyn's iPod in her purse since it was beginning to rain. When she gave the iPod back to Joycelyn, they discovered a pen had leaked ink all over the iPod and damaged it. Joycelyn said her friend did not take proper care of the iPod and should replace it.

You Debate *Was there a bailment between Joycelyn and her friend and, if so, is the friend liable for the damages?*

⑮ Mutual-Benefit Bailments

Jonathan rented a key-locker for $3.00 at a waterpark. When he went back to the locker, he found it open and his things were missing.

You Debate *Was there a mutual-benefit bailment present? If so, what did the water park owe Jonathan?*

C Critical Thinking

Liability of Hotel Keeper You and your family take a trip and stay in a hotel. Before you go out for the day, you notice that your sink is leaking and call the front desk to have it repaired. When you return, a camera, cash, and a watch are missing. Your sink has been repaired.

Debate Practice

• What liability do you think the hotel bears? (Students may suggest that the hotel is not liable since the guests should not have left valuables in the room while repairs were being performed. Hotel may be liable since the valuables were items that they would normally have on their person.)

Case Study Practice – Vigil v. Walt Disney Co.

⑯ Who Owns the Trademark? In 1992, the Walt Disney Company (Disney) released the movie *The Mighty Ducks*, the story of a fictional hockey team. Disney later acquired the rights to a real hockey team, naming it the Mighty Ducks. The logo for both consists of a hockey mask shaped like a duck's bill and crossed hockey sticks.

Mark Vigil argued that he created the logo Disney used and that he owned the intellectual property rights to it. Disney introduced evidence to the court that it had applied to register the logo as a trademark with the U.S. Patent and Trademark Office (PTO) on June 7, 1993. The logo was officially registered on April 26, 1994.

Mr. Vigil argued that Disney did not enter its logo until September 18, 1993, and that he had filed disclosure documents with the PTO on June 8, 1993. Disclosure documents are not applications for a trademark or patent, but rather give notice to the PTO that a specific design or invention may later be trademarked or patented.

Source: Vigil v. Walt Disney Co., 1995 WL 621832 (N.D. Cal. 1995)

Practice Does Mr. Vigil have a right to the Mighty Ducks logo?

⑰ Ethics ←?→ Application

Duty of Care? Fernando asked Nikki to store his computer at her house while he was away for the summer. Fernando never made any comments about whether Nikki could use it. Nikki used the computer every day to do her schoolwork. She was very careful with the computer, but eventually the keyboard stopped working properly.

◆ Should Nikki have to replace the keyboard?

⑱ Internet Application

Copyright Protection Matthew has created a new Web site that allows users to search the Internet quickly and easily. Before Matthew uploads his site, he wants to get it copyrighted to protect his idea.

Go to **glencoe.com** to access the Web site sponsored by the U.S. Copyright Office. Write a brief summary of what rights Matthew has under Circular 66— Copyright Registration of Online Works.

Reading Connection

Outside Reading Go to **glencoe.com** for a list of reading suggestions about intellectual property rights.

 glencoe.com

←?→ Ethics Application

17. Ethically Nikki should offer to replace the keyboard since it stopped working while she was using it.

💻 Internet Application

18. Students should convey an understanding that the rights of this copyright extend only to the copyrightable content of the work as registered with the U.S. Copyright Office. The application for registration should exclude any material that has been previously registered or published or that is in the public domain. Any revisions to the site must be registered separately.

R Reading Strategy

Reading Connection

American Bar Association Resources

Go to the *Business and Personal Law* Online Learning Center through glencoe.com to find links for further readings that relate to this chapter. Ask students to read, review, and summarize the documents. Advise students to keep their reviews and summaries to use as reference material for their Unit Thematic Project on pages 218–219.

📄 Case Study Practice

16. No. Under the Federal Lanham Act, trademarks are protected from the date of application as long as the trademark enters the stream of commerce within six months of the application. Although Disney did not enter the logo into the stream of commerce until September of 1993, it was within six months of the June 7, 1993, filing. Mr. Vigil was unable to provide to the court any documentation from the PTO that he had filed for protection prior to June 8, 1993.

Plan Your Lesson Section by Section

NBEA	NATIONAL BUSINESS LAW STANDARDS
Section 9.1	• **Describe** the kinds of rental relationships that landlords and tenants may create.
Section 9.2	• **List** different methods by which property is acquired. • **List** and describe the forms of co-ownership of real property. • **Illustrate** the method of transferring title (deeding) to real property. • **Distinguish** among liens, licenses, and easements and explain the differences. • **List** the major estates in land and describe the major features of each.

NCLB	ACADEMIC STANDARDS	Activity/Feature
English Language Arts: NCTE 3 Apply a wide range of strategies to comprehend, interpret, evaluate, and appreciate texts.		*BusinessWeek* News, Case Study, Case Study Practice
English Language Arts: NCTE 9 Develop an understanding of and respect for diversity in language use, patterns, and dialects across cultures, ethnic groups, geographic regions, and social roles.		Global Law
English Language Arts: NCTE 6 Apply knowledge of language structure, language conventions, media techniques, figurative language, and genre to create, critique, and discuss print and non-print texts.		Legal Talk, ad copy, Key Terms, and Academic Vocabulary
Social Studies: NCSS 3 Study people, places, and environments.		Section 9.1 Assessment
English Language Arts: NCTE 12 Use spoken, written, and visual language to accomplish your own purposes.		Section 9.1 Assessment
Mathematics: NCTM MS 2 Apply appropriate techniques, tools, and formulas to determine measurements.		Section 9.2 Assessment
English Language Arts: NCTE 10 Students whose first language is not English make use of their first language to develop competency in the English language arts and to develop understanding of content across the curriculum.		Key Terms, Academic Vocabulary, Legal Talk, Vocabulary Builder
English Language Arts: NCTE 1 Read a wide range of print and non-print texts to build an understanding of texts; to respond to the needs and demands of society and the workplace; and for personal fulfillment.		Global Law
Social Studies: NCSS 6 Study how people create and change structures of power, authority, and governance.		Global Law, Case Study

Connect Your Business Law Classroom to the World of Work

This chart shows the 21st Century Skills, foundation skills, and workplace competencies that students develop as they work in this chapter.

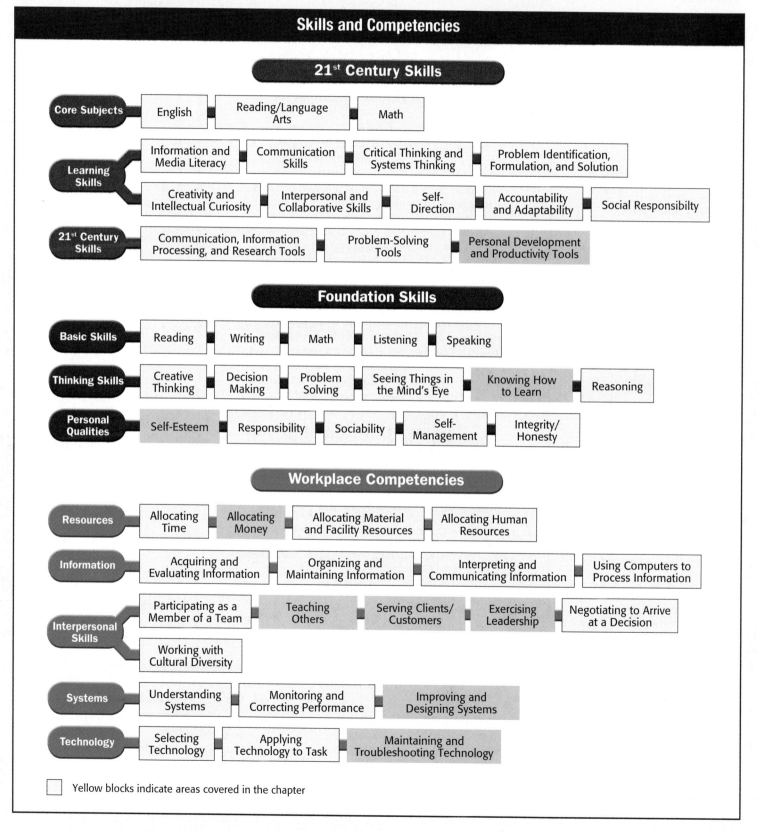

Skills and Competencies

21st Century Skills

Core Subjects
English | Reading/Language Arts | Math

Learning Skills
Information and Media Literacy | Communication Skills | Critical Thinking and Systems Thinking | Problem Identification, Formulation, and Solution

Creativity and Intellectual Curiosity | Interpersonal and Collaborative Skills | Self-Direction | Accountability and Adaptability | Social Responsibilty

21st Century Skills
Communication, Information Processing, and Research Tools | Problem-Solving Tools | Personal Development and Productivity Tools

Foundation Skills

Basic Skills
Reading | Writing | Math | Listening | Speaking

Thinking Skills
Creative Thinking | Decision Making | Problem Solving | Seeing Things in the Mind's Eye | Knowing How to Learn | Reasoning

Personal Qualities
Self-Esteem | Responsibility | Sociability | Self-Management | Integrity/Honesty

Workplace Competencies

Resources
Allocating Time | Allocating Money | Allocating Material and Facility Resources | Allocating Human Resources

Information
Acquiring and Evaluating Information | Organizing and Maintaining Information | Interpreting and Communicating Information | Using Computers to Process Information

Interpersonal Skills
Participating as a Member of a Team | Teaching Others | Serving Clients/Customers | Exercising Leadership | Negotiating to Arrive at a Decision

Working with Cultural Diversity

Systems
Understanding Systems | Monitoring and Correcting Performance | Improving and Designing Systems

Technology
Selecting Technology | Applying Technology to Task | Maintaining and Troubleshooting Technology

☐ Yellow blocks indicate areas covered in the chapter

Introduce the Chapter

Renting or Owning a Home
Renting or buying a home is often an exciting event in life. Students will learn about the rights of landlords and tenants in various kinds of tenancies in this chapter. In addition, Chapter 9 distinguishes types of co-ownership and deeds involved in home ownership.

Building Background
Bring the classified section of your local newspaper to class. Ask for volunteers to read ads for apartments for rent and houses for sale. Explain to students that signing a lease for an apartment or buying a home carries responsibilities that will be discussed in this chapter.

BusinessWeek News
Tell students that lenders may give 100 percent financing to people with very good credit scores, since they are likely to repay the loan. This means that individuals like Thompson who are interested in house flipping may not have to use any of their own money for house buying. Instead, personal cash can be used for repairs and cosmetic fixes.

R Reading Strategy

Your Reading

Encourage students to anticipate what they will learn in this chapter. Have them list three ideas that they infer from the photo and the chapter title. Suggest that they write down two questions about these topics.

Renting or Owning a Home

BusinessWeek News

Piggy Bank—Or House of Cards?

By Peter Coy

Multitalented Joaquin L. Thompson of Mableton, Ga., is a baker, a nurse for an insurance company, and now, a successful real estate Investor. On Aug. 3, he made $14,500 by flipping a house he owned for only 53 days. A small Atlanta bank financed his entire purchase price. All Thompson put up was $1,200 in earnest money that went into escrow. Not bad: In less than two months, Thompson walked away with a 1,100 percent gain on the money he started with.

More and more homebuyers are discovering that in a bull market, acquiring assets with other people's money is the path to riches. The danger is that if prices begin to fall, people who have stretched to buy houses with 100% financing will be under water on their mortgages and at risk of default if they have to sell. "I always tell people, look at the worst scenario," says James R. Gillespie, chief executive of Coldwell Banker Real Estate Corp. But many buyers ignore the warning.

Flex Your Reading

Efficient critical reading involves being flexible with speed and comprehension. There are several ways of reading critically, and you need to fit a reading style to your needs and to the material.

Go to **glencoe.com** for Flex Your Reading activities, more information on reading strategies for this chapter, and guided practice in reading about home ownership.

Classroom Resources

- Student Edition
- Teacher Wraparound Edition
- Student Activity Workbook with Academic Integration (SE/TAE)
- TeacherWorks™ Plus! CD
- *ExamView*® *Assessment Suite* CD
- *Presentation Plus!* CD

- National Mock Trial Championship DVD
- Online Learning Center with Podcasts at glencoe.com
- Study-to-Go™ at glencoe.com
- Online Student Edition
- Interactive Student Edition

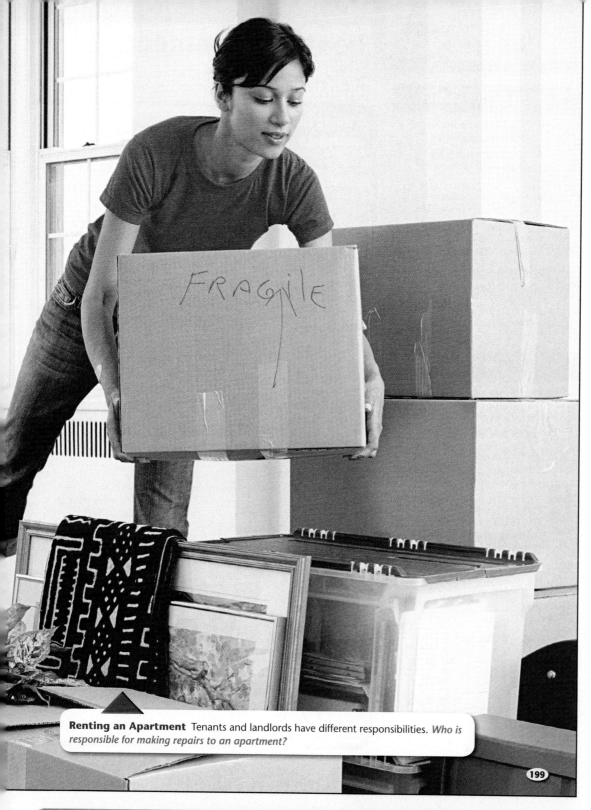

Renting an Apartment Tenants and landlords have different responsibilities. *Who is responsible for making repairs to an apartment?*

199

Practice the Concept

Renting a Home
Ask students to share what they already know about renting a house or an apartment. Encourage students who have been through the rental process with their families to offer details about lease terms, landlord and tenant responsibilities, deposits, and lease agreements.

Key Terms Tell students that the key to understanding a lease agreement is to understand the terms contained in the document. Introduce a few important terms by writing this sentence on the board. Ask students to infer its meaning.

• The lessor risked eviction unless he could convince his friend to sign a sublease on the apartment. (lease holder will be made to leave apartment unless friend takes on obligations of the apartment)

The Fine Print The details of a lease agreement or a deed document should never be overlooked. Additional clauses to a basic lease may cover the policy on pets, on the consequences of late rental payments, on alterations to the property, on renter's insurance, or on services paid for by the landlord. Renters should always carefully read each section of their lease before signing on the dotted line.

▲ USING VISUALS

Renting an Apartment **Answer** Unless otherwise stipulated in the lease agreement, the landlord is generally responsible for repairs to the apartment that fall under general maintenance. For example, if the air conditioner is broken, the landlord should have the unit fixed as soon as possible. Tell students if the landlord does not maintain the property after notification of a problem, the tenant may pay rent to the court instead of to the landlord until the problem is resolved. Each state provides guidelines for the rights of tenants and landlords.

FOCUS

Bell Ringer Activity

Bring in floor plan brochures for rental apartments in your community. Pass them around the class and have students discuss the pros and cons of each apartment. Call students' attention to any lease terms, amenities, or restrictions.

Preteaching

Key Terms

Read the definitions and ask students to create a sentence using each term.

Academic Vocabulary

Explain that developing vocabulary is key to academic success. An efficient method to develop vocabulary is to study how words are formed.

- **vacate** Verb, from the Latin *vacare* (to be empty). Means to leave, give up.
- **assign** Verb, from the Latin *assignare* (to mark out). Means to transfer.
- **provision** Noun, from the Latin *providere* (to provide). Means supplementary conditions.

Activity Ask students to give a noun, an adjective, or an adverb form that comes from each word.

 Connects to academic content

What You'll Learn

- List the different kinds of rental relationships.
- Explain the rights and obligations of landlords and tenants.
- Identify the conditions in which an eviction can occur.
- Determine liability for landlords and tenants.

Why It's Important

You need to know your rights and responsibilities as a tenant if you rent or lease property.

Academic Standards

Reading and completing the activities in this section will help you practice the following academic standards:

Social Studies (NCSS 3) Study people, places, and environments.

English Language Arts (NCTE 12) Use spoken, written, and visual language to accomplish your own purposes.

Reading Guide

Before You Read

Connect You may want to rent your own apartment some day. What would your responsibilities as a tenant be?

Focus on Ideas

Rental agreements are contracts about real property that create rights and responsibilities.

Take Notes

Create a graph like the one shown and use it to take notes as you read this section. Go to glencoe.com to find graphic organizers and tips on how to improve your note-taking skills.

Key Terms

You will learn these legal words and expressions in this chapter. You can also find these terms in *Black's Law Dictionary* or in an online legal dictionary.

- lease
- lessee
- lessor
- tenancy
- sublease
- fixtures
- eviction

Academic Vocabulary

You will find these words in your readings and in your tests. Look them up in a dictionary and familiarize yourself with them.

- vacate
- assign
- provision

glencoe.com

R Reading Strategy

Read for Knowledge

1. **Survey** or preread the chapter.
2. **Question** or formulate questions before you read.
3. **Recite** or read your questions, answers, and notes out loud.
4. **Review** or reread your notes.

Note-Taking Basics

- Listen attentively
- Have note-taking materials ready
- Skim through the lesson material
- Write down key words and ideas
- Anticipate what comes next
- Review notes soon after taking them

The Landlord-Tenant Relationship

How do you become a landlord or tenant?

If you rent real property, such as an apartment or house, you are a tenant. If you own real property and rent it to someone else, you are a landlord. **A lease is the contract between a tenant and a landlord. In a lease, the lessee is the tenant, and the lessor is the landlord.**

Types of Tenancies

Tenants own an interest in the real estate they lease called a leasehold estate or tenancy. The types of tenancies are tenancy for years, periodic tenancy, tenancy at will, and tenancy at sufferance.

Tenancy for Years A tenancy for years is the right to occupy property for a definite or fixed period of time. It may be for one week, six months, one year, five years, 99 years, or any other period of time, as long as the time period is definite. A tenancy for 100 years or more has the effect of transferring absolute ownership to the tenant. Some states require every tenancy for years to be in writing. Others require it to be in writing only if it exceeds a year.

Periodic Tenancy A periodic tenancy is a tenancy that continues for successive, fixed periods of time. A periodic tenancy may be from year to year, month to month, or week to week.

As You Read

Predict How far in advance do you have to notify a landlord if you plan to move?

Discrimination Landlords cannot legally refuse to rent to anyone because of their race, color, or national origin. *What laws require landlords to refrain from discrimination?*

▲ USING VISUALS

➡ Discrimination Answer The federal Civil Rights Act and various state laws prohibit discrimination in renting property based on race, religion, color, national origin, age, gender, ancestry, or marital status.

Activity Ask students to recall other areas of life in which people must refrain from discriminatory practices. (employment, enrollment in college or other activities, armed forces enlistment, health care, access to public facilities)

9.1 SECTION

TEACH

Discussion Starter

Class Discussion

Tell students that Will signs a one-year lease on an apartment. The following week, he learns that his company is transferring him to another city. Ask students to discuss what options Will has in regard to his lease. (If allowed in lease agreement, Will may be able to sublet or assign the lease. Otherwise, he may have to break the lease agreement.) Tell students that they will learn more about lease agreements in this section.

D Develop Concepts

Lease Explain that a lease is a contract between a landlord and a tenant, and is governed by contract rules. Therefore, a court must find all the elements of a valid contract in order to enforce a lease agreement. Ask students whether they would be the lessor or the lessee if they were to rent an apartment. (lessee)

As You Read

Predict Ask students to scan the headings of the section and tag the heading under which they think the answer to this question will be provided. (The required notice for termination of tenancy varies by state, though most leases require at least a 30 days' notice.)

SECTION 9.1

TEACH (cont.)

D Develop Concepts

Tenancy Point out that when you rent you are paying the owner of the property a fee for using it in somewhat the same way as if it were yours. Your rights are much more limited than they would be if you owned the property. Your legal status depends on the lease that you agree upon with the landlord. Ask students what kinds of limitations might apply to the use of someone's property. (term of living on the property, painting or changing the property, pets)

Legal Talk

(convene, convenient, convention)

Ask students to practice their academic and legal vocabulary with the electronic flashcards available at the *Business and Personal Law* Online Learning Center through **glencoe.com**.

Legal Talk

Covenant: *n* A binding written agreement between parties to perform or refrain from performing an action. From Latin *convenire* = to come together, to agree: an agreement.

Sufferance: *n* Sanction or permission implied or given by failure to prohibit. From Latin *sufferre* = to suffer: suffering or tolerance.

Vocabulary Builder *Convenire* is a Latin term that means to meet or to agree. List three words that use this Latin root and define them.

Look It Up! Check definitions in *Black's Law Dictionary* or an online glossary. For direct links, go to **glencoe.com** to find more vocabulary resources.

Vocabulary You can find vocabulary definitions in the **Key Terms** glossary and the **Academic Vocabulary** glossary in the back of this book.

Either party may terminate this tenancy by giving advance notice to the other party. If such notice is not given, the tenancy continues for the same period of time. State laws establish the required notice.

Tenancy at Will A tenancy at will is an interest in real property that continues for an indefinite period of time. No writing is necessary to create this tenancy. It ends when the landlord or tenant gives the notice required by law. In most states, the required notice is 30 days.

Tenancy at Sufferance A tenancy at sufferance occurs when a tenant does not leave the premises when the tenancy expires. Tenants at sufferance, also called holdover tenants, are wrongdoers. They no longer have legal rights in the property. They are not entitled to notice to **vacate** and must pay rent for the illegal occupancy.

The Lease Agreement

A written agreement between a lessor and a lessee is called a lease. The lease creates the landlord-tenant relationship. It provides the tenant with exclusive possession and control of the real property of the landlord. The general rules of contract law apply to this form of agreement.

Terms in a Lease The terms of a lease, known as covenants, set forth the rights and duties of the landlord and the tenant. Tenants' basic rights are possession and continued occupancy, free from intrusion or annoyance. Landlords' basic rights are rent and possession of the property in good condition at the term's end.

Security Deposit In addition to the first month's rent, landlords often require a security deposit and the last month's rent at the beginning of a tenancy. The security deposit often equals one month's rent. Some states limit the amount of a security deposit and require interest to be paid on it.

Assignment and Subletting An assignment of a lease occurs when you transfer the remaining period of time in a lease to someone else. **A sublease is the transfer of part of the term of a lease, but not the remainder of it, to someone else.** If a landlord does not want a tenant to **assign** or sublet the property, a covenant in the lease must say that. Otherwise, a tenant may either assign or sublet the property to someone else. Nevertheless, the original tenant is responsible to the landlord for the rent.

Option to Renew Many leases contain a **provision** allowing renters the option to renew the lease for one or more additional periods. This provision gives renters the right to a new lease, under the same terms, for an additional period. To exercise an option, a lessee must notify the lessor on or before the date set forth in the lease.

 glencoe.com

Role Play

Ask for two volunteers from the class to role-play a scenario in which a college student visits an apartment that he or she wishes to rent. Have one student play the role of college student and the other student play the role of the landlord showing the apartment. Before the role play begins, have both students make notes on what they want to discuss with the other party regarding the apartment and the lease. (Students may discuss topics such as lease term, deposit, rental amount, pets, noise, and repairs.)

Responsibilities of Landlord and Tenant

What are your duties as a tenant or as a landlord of a rental property?

Both landlords and tenants have legal obligations when property is rented.

The Landlord's Duties and Obligations

Landlords have specific responsibilities imposed by law, in addition to those found in a lease. These duties include refraining from discrimination in renting property, maintaining the premises, and providing peaceful possession.

Refrain from Discrimination The federal Civil Rights Act and various state laws place special emphasis on human rights. It is against the law to refuse to rent property to any person because of race, religion, color, national origin, gender, age, ancestry, or marital status.

Maintain the Premises Rental property offered for dwelling purposes must be fit for human habitation. This means that it must be relatively clean, properly heated, furnished with utilities, and safe. In some states, if the landlord does not maintain the premises, you can pay rent to the court instead of the landlord until problems are resolved. In other states, after notifying the landlord, you can correct problems at your own expense and deduct the amount you spent from the rent.

Transfer Peaceful Possession Tenants are entitled to the exclusive peaceful possession and quiet enjoyment of the premises. Quiet enjoyment is the right to use and enjoy property without interference.

Trade Fixtures

You own a jewelry business that is looking at leasing a new storefront on Main Street. The current occupier of the property, Ace Company, runs a pawn shop. When Ace originally moved into the property, there were no enclosed glass cases on the premises, so Ace purchased a number of glass cases to house its products. You know that Ace can remove the cases, but you also know that it will be expensive to install new cases, if Ace takes them. You are pretty sure that Ace believes the trade fixtures must remain after it vacates the property.

Critical Thinking: *Should you tell Ace that it can legally remove the cases?*

Reading Check

State *What can you do if your landlord fails to maintain the premises properly?*

TEACH *(cont.)*

D Develop Concepts

Landlord Responsibilities
Ask students to brainstorm ideas for responsibilities that landlords have when renting property. (keep property maintained, no discrimination, allow tenant to use property as intended)

C Critical Thinking

Peaceful Possession
Emphasize that tenants are entitled to peaceful possession of the property. This means that they should be free from interference from the landlord. Ask students to describe some ways in which the landlord might disturb the tenants. (knocking on the door to check the premises unannounced, continuous construction or changes to the property)

Reading Check

State If the landlord fails to maintain the premises as promised in the lease, the lessee can pay rent to the court instead of the landlord until the problems are resolved. Lessee may also correct problems at his or her expense and deduct the cost from the rent.

Business ETHICS

Answer Students' answers will vary. The landlord is under no legal obligation to inform Ace of its rights. Tenants are presumed to understand their rights when it comes to trade fixtures. However, as a courtesy, the landlord might wish to make the company aware of its rights. If Ace later found that the cases could have been removed, the landlord's reputation may be harmed. The perceived goodwill of any company is based on how it conducts its business.

ASSESS

Independent Practice

Discrimination or Property Rights?

Outline the following scenario to students. Randy prefers renting his property to single women because he feels they make better tenants and take better care of the premises. He only advertises in hair salons. When men call, he tells them that the property has already been rented. Ask students whether this is a legal right of the owner. (No. The landlord is discriminating based on gender.)

RETEACH

STUDY TO GO Have students go to the *Business and Personal Law* Online Learning Center through glencoe.com to download free Study-to-Go content to their cell phones or PDAs.

Guided Practice

List Ask students to name at least three types of tenancies. (tenancy for years, periodic tenancy, tenancy at will, or tenancy at sufferance) **L1**

Differentiate Ask students to describe the difference between a tenancy for years and a tenancy at will. (for years: definite period of time; at will: indefinite period) **L2**

Analyze If a tenant is on a month-to-month lease, what type of tenancy is this? (periodic tenancy) **L3**

Fixtures Fixtures become part of the property and belong to the landlord, even when installed by the tenant. *What are some examples of fixtures?*

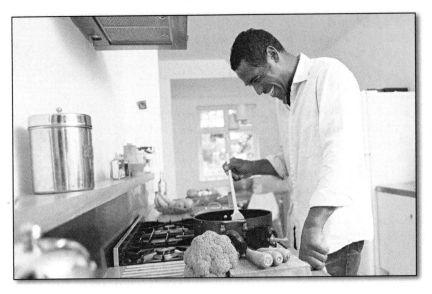

The Tenant's Duties and Obligations

Tenants have the duties of paying rent, abiding by the terms of the lease, avoiding waste, and returning fixtures.

Abide by the Terms of the Lease As a tenant, you have the duty to pay rent to the landlord when it is due. You must also observe the valid restrictions contained in the lease. Failure to abide by the restrictions gives the landlord the right to seek eviction.

Avoid Waste Tenants have a duty to avoid waste; that is, damaging or destroying the property. Waste is damage to premises that significantly decreases a property's value. You must return the premises to the landlord in as good a condition as when you moved in, except for reasonable wear and tear.

Return Fixtures The tenant must turn over to the landlord all fixtures in the premises at the end of the tenancy. **Fixtures are items of personal property attached in such a way that they become real property.** They include built-in stoves, kitchen cabinets, and ceiling light fixtures. Unless otherwise agreed, fixtures are part of the real property and belong to the landlord, even when installed by the tenant.

In determining whether an item is a fixture, courts consider the following questions:

- Has there been a temporary or permanent installation of the personal property?
- Can the fixture be removed without damaging the building?
- What was the intent of the parties at the time the attachment was made?

Trade fixtures are fixtures attached to business property that are needed to carry on the business. For example, if you leased a storefront for a small mending business, you might install sewing

▲ USING VISUALS

Fixtures Answer Cabinets, light fixtures, stoves, built-in microwaves, in-ground pools, and attached hot tubs are considered fixtures that must stay with the property when the tenant leaves.

Activity Tell students that a tenant wishes to improve the landscaping of his or her dwelling. The landlord agrees to pay for flowers and shrubbery if the tenant performs the labor to plant everything. Ask students to determine whether the new landscaping would be considered a fixture that stays with the property. (Yes. Since the landlord paid for the items and since removing them would damage the property, they would be considered fixtures.)

machines, shelves, and special lights. When you leave, you could take these items with you. Contrary to the general rule, trade fixtures remain the property of the tenant.

Eviction

Can a landlord force you to move out of your apartment?

An eviction occurs when a landlord deprives a tenant of the possession of the premises. You can be evicted for not paying rent, staying after the lease expires, damaging the premises, and violating provisions in the lease.

It is illegal in every state for landlords to use force to evict tenants. Landlords must first obtain a court order. The court appoints an officer to carry out the eviction.

A constructive eviction occurs when a landlord breaches a duty under a lease. This may occur if the landlord deprives you of heat, electricity, or some other service called for by the lease. When a constructive eviction occurs, you may consider the lease terminated, leave the premises, and stop paying rent.

Tort Liability

When someone is injured on rented or leased property, both the landlord and the tenant may be liable. Whoever is in control of the area where the injury occurs determines liability. Landlords can be held liable for injuries caused by defects in common areas, such as hallways or stairways. Tenants can be held liable for injuries caused by defects in private areas within the leased property.

After You Read

Summarize What are the most basic rights of landlords and tenants?

SECTION 9.1 ASSESSMENT

Self Check

1. What is a lease?
2. What is the difference between a tenancy for years and a tenancy at will?
3. How must an eviction be carried out?

Academic Connection

Social Studies Most laws that affect the tenant-landlord relationship are governed by state and federal statutes. Go on the Internet, visit the local library, or get a copy of a rental agreement to find out what the rights of renters are in your area. In class, discuss what you think are the most important things renters should know.

English Language Arts Put yourself in the place of a landlord. You own an apartment building with units you want to rent. Write up a list of basic conditions you expect your tenants to meet.

Critical Thinking

Injury Liability You rent an apartment in a building that has a swimming pool. You have a group of friends over for a swimming party. One of them slips on the wet pavement next to the pool and is injured. Who is liable for the injury? Why?

 Go to **glencoe.com** to check your answers.

RETEACH (cont.)

After You Read

Summarize Tenant: abide by lease, avoid waste, return fixtures; Landlord: no discrimination, maintain premises, allow for peaceful possession.

ASSESS

Self-Assessment

Have students go to the *Business and Personal Law* Online Learning Center through **glencoe.com** to take the Section 9.1 Practice Test.

CLOSE

Culminating Activity

Tenancy

Tell students that Jill wants to sign a lease in which she is allowed to rent an apartment for one year. Ask what kind of lease Jill is seeking. (tenancy for years) Tell students that Rick's lease has just ended, but that he has not yet moved out of the property. Ask what kind of tenancy is occurring. (tenancy at sufferance)

SECTION 9.1 ASSESSMENT

Self Check

1. contract between a tenant and a landlord
2. tenancy for years: definite period of time; tenancy at will: indefinite time period
3. Landlord must obtain a court order; court appoints officer to carry out eviction.

Academic Connection

Social Studies
Answers will vary. Lease obligations should be read carefully in a lease agreement.

English Language Arts
Answers should include conditions like paying rent on time, avoiding waste, and keeping the property in good condition.

Critical Thinking

Landlord may be liable because the injury occurred in a common area over which the landlord had control.

 Activities correlated to the academic standards on page 200

FOCUS

🔔 Bell Ringer Activity

Ask students to create a drawing of the home they hope to own one day. Have students add a description underneath the drawing that explains the size, location, and approximate price of the home.

Preteaching

Key Terms

Read the definitions and ask students to create a sentence using each term.

Academic Vocabulary

Explain that developing vocabulary is key to academic success. An efficient method to develop vocabulary is to study how words are formed.

- **permission** Noun, from the Latin *permittere* (to allow). Means formal consent.

- **spouse** Noun, from the Latin *sponsus* (bridegroom). Means one's husband or wife.

- **consent** Noun, from the Latin *consentire, com* (together) + *sentire* (to feel). Means permission.

Activity Ask students to give a verb, an adjective, or an adverb form that comes from each word.

N C L B Connects to academic content

206

What You'll Learn

◆ Explain the ways real property can be co-owned.

◆ Describe how title to real property can be transferred.

◆ Explain the function of warranty and quitclaim deeds.

◆ Define and compare liens, licenses, and easements.

Why It's Important

You need to know your rights and responsibilities as a homeowner when you buy real property.

Academic Standards

Reading and completing the activities in this section will help you practice the following academic standards:

N C L B

Social Studies (NCSS 6) Study how people create and change structures of power, authority, and governance.

Math (NCTM MS 2) Understand meanings of operations and how they relate to one another.

Reading Guide

Before You Read

Connect You might want to buy your own home some day. What are the advantages and disadvantages of owning a home?

Focus on Ideas

Ownership of a home or other real property is shown through legal documents called title and deed.

Take Notes

Create a graph like the one shown and use it to take notes as you read this section. Go to **glencoe.com** to find graphic organizers and tips on how to improve your note-taking skills.

Types of Deeds			
General Warranties	**Special Warranties**	**Bargain and sale**	**Quitclaim**
Contains express warranties that title to property is good			

Key Terms

You will learn these legal words and expressions in this chapter. You can also find these terms in *Black's Law Dictionary* or in an online legal dictionary.

- real property
- estate
- deed
- eminent domain
- lien
- license
- easement

Academic Vocabulary

You will find these words in your readings and in your tests. Look them up in a dictionary and familiarize yourself with them.

- permission
- spouse
- consent

R Reading Strategy

Read for Knowledge

1. **Survey** or preread the chapter.
2. **Question** or formulate questions before you read.
3. **Recite** or read your questions, answers, and notes out loud.
4. **Review** or reread your notes.

Note-Taking Basics

- Listen attentively
- Have note-taking materials ready
- Skim through the lesson material
- Write down key words and ideas
- Anticipate what comes next
- Review notes soon after taking them

The Nature of Real Property

What do you really own when you own real property?

Real property is the ground and everything permanently attached to it. It includes buildings, fences, and trees on the surface; and soil, rocks, and minerals under the surface. Landowners own the airspace as high as they can effectively use. Some courts have applied the same rule to how deep one owns property underground. The federal government owns the navigable airspace, where air traffic occurs.

Estate is the interest or right that a person has in real property. A leasehold estate consists of one of the tenancies discussed in the previous section and is evidenced by a lease. A freehold estate is an estate in which the holder owns the land for life or forever. Anyone having a freehold estate may transfer the interest to another by sale, gift, will, or by dying without a will. There are two types of freehold estates. A fee simple estate is an estate in which the owner owns the property outright with the exclusive right to use it or dispose of it freely. Most real property is owned this way. A life estate is an estate in which the owner owns real property for the length of the owner's life or for the life of another.

Taking Ownership

How can you show or prove that you own a piece of property?

Ownership of property comes about by deed, inheritance, or law. Title can be taken in your name alone or with someone else as a co-owner.

Co-ownership

The principal forms of co-ownership are tenancy in common, joint tenancy, community property, tenancy by the entirety, and tenancy in partnership. All co-owners, or co-tenants, own an undivided interest in the entire property.

Tenancy in common is a type of co-ownership with each owner's share going to his or her heirs upon death. An owner may deed away his or her interest without **permission** of the other owners.

Joint tenancy is a type of co-ownership with each owner's share going to the surviving co-owners upon death. An owner may deed away ownership interest without permission of the other owners.

Community property is property acquired by the efforts of either **spouse** during marriage. By law, it belongs to both spouses equally. A gift or an inheritance does not become part of community property. Only nine states recognize community property.

Tenancy by the entirety is property held by a husband and wife, who have an equal right to the property. Each spouse owns the entire property, which neither can transfer without the other's **consent**. When one spouse dies, the survivor owns the property outright.

As You Read

Predict If you cannot repay someone to whom you owe a lot of money, can that person take your home away from you?

Vocabulary You can find vocabulary definitions in the **Key Terms** glossary and the **Academic Vocabulary** glossary in the back of this book.

TEACH

Discussion Starter

Class Discussion
Explain that a variety of factors affect one's decision to buy a home or not. Individuals must consider what they can afford, location, job stability, and what type of home they are interested in. Studying the concepts of this section can better prepare students for these decisions.

D Develop Concepts

Co-ownership Ask students if they have ever owned anything jointly with another person. (Answers will vary but might include electronics or CDs.) Explain that when people own property together and each person's share of the property goes to his or her heirs upon death, the tenancy is called a tenancy in common.

As You Read

Predict Tell students to skim the headings in the section. List students' answers to this question on the board. Refer back to these answers when the section is finished. (Property may be taken away from the owner, but only if a lien must be placed on the property.)

Extending the Content

Timeshare Ownership

Tell students that a timeshare is a form of shared property ownership, commonly in vacation or condominium property. Several owners have rights to use the property for a specified period each year. As in all deeded properties, recording fees are charged to the purchasing party and paid to the county in which the deed is being drawn up. Ask students to explain why someone might be interested in purchasing interest in a timeshare. (resort-style property without resort prices, property amenities, less expensive than owning a vacation home)

TEACH (cont.)

D Develop Concepts

Deeds Write the following types of deeds on the board: general warranty deed, special warranty deed, bargain and sale deed, and quitclaim deed. Tell students that the primary difference between these types of deeds is the level of protection given to the person who takes the ownership or the one buying the property. Ask students which type of deed gives the buyer the most protection. (general warranty deed)

Guided Practice

Parties to a Deed

Tell students that two terms identify the parties to a deed: *grantor* and *grantee*. Ask them to define the role of each party. (The grantor is the person transferring ownership. The grantee is the person receiving ownership.)

Extending the Content

Types of Deeds

Ask students to call a real estate agent and inquire about the types of deeds commonly transferred in property transactions. Have them ask for examples of any unusual agreements that they have encountered.

Ownership of real property by partners is called a tenancy in partnership. Partners have the right to use the property only for partnership purposes. When a partner dies, the heirs inherit an interest in the partnership but not the specific real property.

Transfer of Ownership

Most real property is transferred by a written deed. A deed is not the same as a lease. **A deed is a written instrument that transfers title of ownership of property.** A lease transfers only possession of property. The person transferring ownership is the grantor. The person given ownership is the grantee. Title is transferred when the deed is signed and delivered. The are four main types of deeds.

A general warranty deed contains express warranties that title to the property is good. The warranties are the personal promises of the grantor that if title is discovered to be faulty, the grantor will make up for any loss suffered by the grantee. This is the most desirable form of deed because it gives the grantee the most protection.

A special warranty deed contains express warranties that no defect arose in the title during the time that the grantor owned the property. Unlike a general warranty deed, no warranties are made as to defects arising before the grantor owned the property.

A bargain and sale deed transfers title to property without giving warranties. A bargain and sale deed requires consideration to be valid. As a result, it cannot be used to make a gift of real property.

Global Law

Property Ownership in Cuba

Cuba became an independent sovereign nation in 1898. Since then property ownership rights in that country have changed.

Agricultural Reform

In 1959, Fidel Castro became the nation's leader and undertook property reform. One of the first reforms limited land ownership to about 165 acres per person or corporation. The Cuban government recognized 66 acres as the bare minimum amount of land a person needed to live on, so every rural person was guaranteed that amount, for free. This meant that 229,000 people became landowners.

Urban Reform

In Cuba's cities, property ownership was also reformed. The government took control of all rental property and set up a payment plan so that the inhabitants would eventually own their homes. Following further reforms, by 2004, 90% of all Cuban adults held title to their homes.

Across Cultures: Trade Embargo

The United States has had an embargo, which is a ban on trade, against Cuba since 1962. It is illegal to buy Cuban products in the U.S., and travel between the U.S. and Cuba is restricted.

Critical Thinking: *Are there benefits to a system of property ownership such as Cuba's?*

Global Law

Property Ownership in Cuba

Answer Answers will vary. Students may state that the accessibility of home ownership is greater in Cuba, since renting property is prohibited. The absence of interest payments also makes home ownership easier for Cubans. Tell students that, as in companies from foreign countries are buying property in Cuba, although U.S. companies are prohibited from doing so. Tell students that, as in Cuba, the U.S. government owns a large percentage of land within its borders, especially in the western half of the country. The U.S. Department of the Interior is responsible for maintaining and managing U.S. public lands.

Case Study – Kelo v. City of New London, CT

Critical Thinking *Can a government use eminent domain to give property to private interests?*

Flex Your Reading **Note key facts in the text below and look up words you do not understand. Restate difficult ideas in your own words. Go back and reread the text quickly to make sure you did not miss any important detail. Now, you are ready to formulate an opinion.**

In the Interests of the Public? In 2000, the city of New London, Connecticut, approved a plan to revive the city's economy. In contrast to the rest of the state, New London was economically depressed. The city of New London had the New London Development Corporation (NLDC) devise a plan for economic development.

The NLDC chose an area of the city known as Fort Trumbull for the revival. The land comprised 115 acres of privately owned land as well as 32 acres of public land.

The city of New London was able to purchase most of the privately owned land. However, a few owners declined to sell their land. The city then exercised its power of eminent domain, claiming that the land was needed to create jobs, bring in tax money, and help build downtown New London.

The Plaintiffs argued that, since the city was going to turn the land over to private developers, the eminent domain action was a "taking," contrary to the Fifth Amendment of the United States Constitution, and was not for a "public use."

Kelo v. City of New London, Connecticut, 545 U.S. ___ , 125 S.Ct. 2655 (2005)

Go to **glencoe.com** for more case study practice.

A quitclaim deed transfers whatever interest the grantor has in the property, but it does not warrant that the grantor has any interest. It merely releases the grantor's rights to the property.

Limitations on Property Use

There are limitations on property use you should know about when you become a homeowner. These limits may affect how you build on your land, and how you can use your property. (See **Figure 9.1** on page 210.)

Communities have zoning laws that limit the way property may be used in specified areas. One area, for example, might be zoned for single-family houses only, another for multifamily dwellings, and another for business, industry, or farming. Zoning laws might also regulate how tall or how large a building may be.

Eminent domain is the right of the government to take private land for a public purpose. Usually, governments take private land for such things as public buildings, highways, and schools. In 2005, the Supreme Court held that the government could take private property to promote private economic development.

Reading Check

Infer *Why would communities want to create different zones for different types of property use?*

glencoe.com

Chapter 9   Renting or Owning a Home   **209**

Case Study

Kelo v. City of New London, CT

Yes. The U.S. Supreme Court held that government entities could exercise their power of eminent domain over property, even if the property was to be used by private organizations. The proposed use must be such (serving to create jobs and tax revenue) that the general public should benefit from the ultimate development of the land. Some states have since passed legislation that prevents their individual governments from exercising eminent domain on behalf of private interests; however, state laws do not prevent the federal government from exercising its power of eminent domain.

9.2 SECTION

TEACH (cont.)

Guided Practice

Quitclaim Deed

Give students the following scenario. Reba purchased a house and learned that the previous owner had deeded to a neighbor the right to park an RV on the back of the property. Reba did not want the RV parked on her property. Ask students what kind of deed could be used to end the neighbor's rights. (quitclaim deed with small amount of consideration given in return)

U Universal Access

Kinesthetic Learning Have students construct model versions of their homes or a relative's home. They can use materials such as clay, building blocks, or cardboard. Ask students to present their homes as if they were real estate agents describing features, price, and type of deed involved. (Students should demonstrate an understanding of what warranty their deed offers.)

Reading Check

Infer Zones are created so that different types of property do not interfere with each other. For example, factories cannot be placed in a residential neighborhood, and private residences cannot be placed in a commercial district.

209

ASSESS

Quiz

Ask students to answer the following questions:

1. Under which type of ownership does a surviving co-owner receive a deceased co-owner's share of the property? (joint tenancy)

2. Which type of deed transfers title without giving warranties? (bargain and sale)

3. What is the person transferring ownership of title called? (grantor)

RETEACH

C Critical Thinking

Eminent Domain Ask students if they think that government should have the right to take private land, even with compensation to its owners, for public use. Have them discuss this issue from the perspective of the government, then from the perspective of the property owner. (Answers will vary. The government sometimes requires land for roads or other development for the good of the public at large, though some property owners may not wish to sell property that has been in their family for generations, at any price.)

Review Key Terms

Encourage students to access the *Business and Personal Law* Online Learning Center through glencoe.com and use the electronic flashcards to review the key terms.

210

Figure 9.1 Limitations on Property Use

Zoning laws restrict how property can be used in specified areas. For example, an area might be zoned for single-family houses or for business properties only.

Adverse possession occurs when someone has had open possession of a property for so long, usually over 20 years, that they have a right to claim ownership of it.

Eminent domain is the right of the government to take land from a private owner to use for the public good. The private owner, however, must be paid a fair amount for the property.

Homeowners face some limitations on how they can use their property. *Under eminent domain, can the government take private property to use for private development? Why or why not?*

210   Unit 3   Consumer Law

▲ USING VISUALS

➡ **Figure 9.1 Limitations on Property Use** Yes. Under the U.S. Supreme Court, government entities can exercise their power of eminent domain over property to acquire private land for private use. Numerous state legislatures have passed legislation to prevent their individual governments from exercising eminent domain for private interests. However, the federal government may still exercise its power of eminent domain over property. The term *eminent domain* is used primarily in the United States, where the term was derived from a legal treatise written by the Dutch jurist Hugo Grotius in 1625 (the term he used was *dominium eminens*).

Ownership of real property can be lost by adverse possession. This occurs when someone who does not own a property occupies it for a period set by state law—often 20 years. The possession must be open, not secretive, with a claim that is done rightfully.

Property use can also be limited by liens, licenses, or easements. To finance the cost of buying a house or other real property, the buyer will usually take out a mortgage. A mortgage is a type of loan in which the borrower pledges the property to the lender in the form of a lien. **A lien is a legal claim against another person's property as security for a debt or loan to ensure it will be repaid.** The lien is released when the debt is repaid. If the debt is not repaid, the lender has the right to take the property (or foreclose on it) and sell it to collect the amount owed.

Property that is foreclosed may have more than one lien on it. In that case, the lienholder with a perfected lien has priority over one with an unperfected lien. A lien is perfected when the lienholder files an official statement with a government office or actually possesses the property. If none of the lienholders has a perfected lien, whoever filed the first lien has priority. If all of the lienholders have a perfected lien, whoever files to collect first has priority.

A license is a temporary, revocable right to the limited use of another's land. The right to use the land can be taken away at any time by the owner of the land.

An easement is an irrevocable right to the limited use of another's land. It might be a right to cross someone else's property at a particular place, such as a driveway, or the right to use it for a particular purpose, such as extending wires or laying pipes. Once established, an easement cannot be terminated without the consent of the owner of the right.

After You Read

Summarize What are the different types of limitations on the use of property?

After You Read

zoning laws, eminent domain, adverse possession, liens, licenses, easements

ASSESS

Self-Assessment

Have students go to the *Business and Personal Law* Online Learning Center through glencoe.com to take the Section 9.2 Practice Test.

CLOSE

Culminating Activity

Tenancy

Outline the following situation to students. Joanne and Kevin Wu, a married couple, decide to buy a house. They want to choose a type of co-ownership that will allow the surviving spouse, after the other spouse's death, to inherit the house. Which type of co-ownership should they choose? (tenancy by entirety)

SECTION **9.2** ASSESSMENT

Self Check

1. What is an estate?

2. What is the major difference between co-owning property as tenants in common and as joint tenants?

3. What is a lien?

Academic Connection

Mathematics Samantha and Fernando are buying a new home for $175,000.

A 15% down payment is required. What is the amount of the mortgage loan needed to finance the purchase?

THEORY **Number and Operations:** To find the down payment, multiply the cost of the house by the percent of the down payment. To find the mortgage loan amount, subtract the down payment from the selling price.

 For more math practice, go to the Math Appendix.

Critical Thinking

Lending Criteria If you were planning to borrow money to buy a home, why would your employment history be important to a lender?

Go to **glencoe.com** to check your answers.

glencoe.com

SECTION **9.2** ASSESSMENT

Self Check

1. a right to or an interest in real property

2. tenancy in common: deceased's share goes to his or her heirs; joint tenancy: deceased's share goes to surviving co-owners

3. legal claim against another person's property as security

Academic Connection

Mathematics
$148,750

Critical Thinking
Stability, reliability, and dependability on a job can indicate how reliable a person will be when repaying a loan.

Activities correlated to the Mathematics standard on page 206

Summary by Sections

Ask students to read the summaries one key point at a time. Then, ask them to work in groups to create two examples to illustrate each key point.

Vocabulary Builder

Cooperative Learning

1. Have students work in groups to prepare their sentences. Ask the groups to exchange their sentences and assess each other's sentences.

Vocabulary Development

- Ask students to use a dictionary or to go online to look up the etymology of each key term listed.
- Then, ask students to list several words derived from the same root or origin. For example, *contract* has the same root as *contractual* or *contractually*.

Summary

Section 9.1 Rental Agreements

- The tenant is the lessee; the landlord is the lessor.
- The types of tenancies are tenancy for years, periodic tenancy, tenancy at will, and tenancy at sufferance.
- Landlords must avoid discrimination, transfer peaceful possession, and maintain the premises. Tenants must pay rent on time, observe lease restrictions, avoid waste, and return fixtures.
- A landlord can evict a tenant for not paying rent, damaging the premises, or violating provisions in the lease. A constructive eviction occurs when a landlord breaches a duty under a lease.
- Landlords are liable for injuries that occur in common areas. Tenants can be held liable for injuries that occur in private areas.

Section 9.2 Buying a Home

- The two major types of estates are leasehold estates and freehold estates. The two types of freehold estates are fee simple estates and life estates.
- The principal forms of co-ownership are tenancy in common, joint tenancy, community property, tenancy by the entirety, and tenancy in partnership.
- Property may be transferred by sale, gift, will, or by dying without a will.
- The four main types of deeds are general warranty deed, special warranty deed, bargain and sale deed, and quitclaim deed.
- Property use can be limited by liens, licenses, or easements.

Vocabulary Builder

1 On a sheet of paper, use each of these terms in a sentence.

Key Terms

- lease
- lessee
- lessor
- tenancy
- sublease

- fixtures
- eviction
- real property
- estate
- deed

- eminent domain
- lien
- license
- easement

Academic Vocabulary

- vacate
- assign

- provision
- permission

- spouse
- consent

Go to **glencoe.com** to play a game and improve your legal vocabulary.

Study Skills for Success

Prepare Your Students for Studying

Tell students that they can improve their ability to understand and remember material from their courses by learning and practicing study skills. Remind students to:

- **Get motivated!** Motivation must come from within. To motivate yourself, think of ways in which what you learn now will fit into your long-term personal and professional goals.
- **Get organized!** Make studying part of your daily routine, not something you do at the last minute.
- **Concentrate!** Study in an environment that is as free of distractions as possible.

Key Points Review

Answer the following questions. Refer to the chapter for additional reinforcement.

2 What is the difference between a lease and a deed?

3 What are the different types of tenancy for rental property?

4 What are the rights and responsibilities of landlords and tenants toward each other?

5 What are the rights of landlords regarding eviction?

6 What is the difference between a fee simple estate and a life estate?

7 What are the different forms of co-ownership of real property?

8 What are the different ways real property can be transferred, or deeded?

9 What are the differences between a lien, a license, and an easement?

Standardized Test Practice

10 Read the following information about the Department of Housing and Urban Development and complete questions 1 and 2.

The Department of Housing and Urban Development (HUD) enforces the Fair Housing Act and the other federal laws that prohibit discrimination and the intimidation of people in their homes, apartment buildings, and condominium developments—and nearly all housing transactions, including the rental and sale of housing and the provision of mortgage loans.

Equal access to rental-housing and home-ownership opportunities is the cornerstone of this nation's federal housing policy. Landlords who refuse to rent or sell homes to people based on race, color, national origin, religion, sex, familial status, or disability are violating federal law, and HUD will vigorously pursue them.

1. Landlords can refuse to rent or sell homes based on:

A race, color, or national origin

B familial status, disability, or education

C work history, religion, or familial status

D none of the above

2. The above passage can best be summarized as:

A rights under the Department of Housing and Urban Development

B how to rent or purchase a home in the United States

C landlords can't refuse to rent or sell their properties

D housing discrimination is only illegal if you get caught

Test-Taking Strategies Do not cram the night before a test. Plan to get a full eight hours of sleep.

---

2. A deed transfers title of ownership. A lease transfers possession.

3. tenancy for years, periodic tenancy, tenancy at will, and tenancy at sufferance

4. Landlords: avoid discrimination, transfer peaceful possession, maintain the premises. Tenants: pay rent on time, observe lease restrictions, avoid waste, return fixtures.

5. can evict a tenant for not paying rent, staying after the lease expires, damaging the premises, and violating provisions in the lease

6. Fee simple estate: owner owns real property outright with the exclusive right to use it or dispose of it freely. Life estate: owner owns real property for the length of the owner's life or for the life of another person.

7. tenancy in common, in partnership, by the entirety; joint tenancy, community property

8. general warranty, special warranty, bargain and sale, quitclaim

9. Lien: legal claim against another's property as security for a debt. License: temporary and revocable right to the limited use of another's land. Easement: irrevocable right to the limited use of another's land.

Standardized Test Practice

10. D and A

Strategies for Standardized Test Prep Success

Whether your students have a standardized test coming up in a few days or a few weeks, these last-minute test-prep tips and strategies will help them relax and do their best.

- **Test Format** Help students become familiar with the format of the test by practicing with test items that imitate the actual test items as closely as possible.

- **Test Timing** Have your students take timed practice tests so that they become comfortable with the length, design, and timing of the actual test.

Review and Assessment

 Apply and Debate

Students should use chapter content to arrive at conclusions. The legal resolutions are listed below:

11. No. Property owners cannot restrict the air space above their property. The federal government owns all navigable air space.

12. This would probably not qualify as discrimination. Under the Federal Civil Rights Act, children and/or pets are not protected.

13. No. If Sally has a tenancy for years with six months left, then she has a right to live there for those remaining six months.

14. Management is responsible for Emilo's actual injuries, because it is responsible for the upkeep of the common areas. However, it is unlikely that punitive damages will be awarded because management was only recently given notice of the defect.

15. An apartment complex may have great disparity between rental rates. There are no specific laws that prohibit complexes from having "rental specials." It could be discriminatory, though, if special prices are given to certain groups.

 Apply and Debate

Read the following scenarios. Get together with other students in pairs or groups of three and take a position on each scenario. Debate your position in class with students taking the opposite position or prepare a written argument justifying your position.

⑪ Air-Space Ownership

Jacques purchased a house 15 years ago in a large development. A local airport is proposing an alternative flight path directly over his house. Jacques is petitioning the rezoning court for an injunction to prevent the change.

You Debate — *Can property owners restrict the use of air-space above their property?*

⑫ Discrimination

The Butlers are in their thirties with two young girls. They apply for an apartment. Two weeks later, they have heard nothing, but continue to see it advertised. The Butlers discover that most of the residents are over 50, with no children.

You Debate — *If the Butlers met all requirements for rental, could their application be rejected on an unwritten rule of no children or pets?*

⑬ Lease Agreement

Sally rents a condo. Her lease does not expire for six months. A two-month notice is required for any change to the terms of the lease. The owners inform Sally that she must vacate the condo in two months, before her lease is up.

You Debate — *Does the two month clause regarding changes of "terms" in the lease allow the condo owner to force Sally to vacate before her current lease is up?*

⑭ Apartment Complex Liability

Chen and Emilo share a third-floor apartment. Chen notices one of the stair treads is loose and reports this to the management office. Later, Emilo falls on the stairs and breaks his leg.

You Debate — *Who is responsible for Emilo's medical bills and lost wages? Could punitive damages be awarded?*

⑮ Rental Rates

Paolo signed a lease two months ago for $700 a month. Now the apartment complex rents the same-size apartment for $350–$600 a month.

You Debate — *Can an apartment complex charge such a varying amount under the clause of rental specials or could this be a way to discriminate?*

C Critical Thinking

What Defense Can Be Used? Kala signed a one-year lease on an apartment with central air and heat. She moved in on the first of January and found that the heater was not working. She called the landlord daily to fix the broken heater. By February 1, the heater had still not been repaired. Kala moved out to find another place to live.

Debate Practice

- Does Kala have the right to stop paying rent? (Yes. The lease was for an apartment with central air and heat. The landlord is required to provide a heated apartment.)

- Can Kala consider the lease terminated, even if the landlord fixes the heater on February 15? (If a court rules that a constructive eviction has occurred, Kala can consider the lease terminated.)

Case Study Practice– Reeves v. Rodgers

⑯ What Is a Tenant at Sufferance? Roy and Mary Reeves, along with their daughter, Sandra Jean Rodgers, bought a number of residential properties in Oregon and Arizona over a period of fifteen years. In 1994, Mr. and Mrs. Reeves bought a home in Hillsboro, Oregon. Although Ms. Rodgers had helped to buy other properties, she did not contribute any money to buy the Hillsboro home.

In the fall of 2001, Ms. Rodgers moved into the Hillsboro home. The Reeves alleged that Ms. Rodgers had an oral agreement with them that she would pay $895.00 per month in rent to help cover the expenses of the property. After moving in, however, Ms. Rodgers failed to make monthly rent payments. Mr. and Mrs. Reeves then sued Ms. Rodgers, alleging that Ms. Rodgers was a tenant at sufferance of the property and that upon giving notice, the Reeves could evict Ms. Rodgers.

Ms. Rodgers alleged that there was no rental agreement between the parties. She claimed that she had some ownership in the property because she had transferred some of her ownership rights to her parents from the other houses that they owned together.

Source: Reeves v. Rodgers, 129 P.3d 721 (Ore. Ct. App. 2006)

Practice Can Mr. and Mrs. Reeves evict their daughter, Ms. Rodgers?

⑰ Ethics ←?→ Application

Cat and Mouse Raul lives in an apartment building with a lease that forbids owning pets. The apartment building had a mouse problem until a stray cat showed up and scared the mice away. To keep the cat around so the mice will not come back, Raul started feeding the cat.
◆ Does Raul have an ethical obligation to report the cat to the landlord as a pet?

⑱ Internet Application

Subleasing an Apartment Monique and Josh have an opportunity to work in France for six months. However, the lease on their apartment does not expire for nine months. To be able to afford going, they need to sublease their apartment.

 Go to **glencoe.com** to research your state's statutes on subleasing and prepare a general sublease agreement that Monique and Josh could use. Compare your agreement with classmates for similarities and differences.

R 〉 **Reading Connection**

Outside Reading Go to **glencoe.com** for a list of reading suggestions about real property rights.

Review and Assessment

←?→ Ethics Application

17. Once Raul starts feeding the cat it technically becomes a pet, and he could be evicted for violating the terms of the lease. Raul should report the cat's presence to the landlord and explain the circumstances regarding the mice.

Internet Application

18. Answers will vary by state. In Texas, for example, tenants may not sublet without the consent of the landlord.

R Reading Strategy

〉 **Reading Connection**

American Bar Association Resources

Go to the *Business and Personal Law* Online Learning Center through **glencoe.com** to find links for further readings that relate to this chapter. Ask students to read, review, and summarize the documents. Advise students to keep their reviews and summaries to use as reference material for their Unit Thematic Project on pages 218–219.

🗎 Case Study Practice

16. No. The Oregon Court of Appeals held that in order for a tenancy at sufferance to occur, and thus the ability to evict the tenant to exist, there must originally be a rental agreement between the parties that had already expired by its own terms. This was not the case here, because the rental agreement between the parents and Sandra was an open-ended rental agreement. It could not expire by its own terms.

Careers in Law

Introduce Career Planning

Bell Ringer Activity

Solicit students' personal experiences in negotiating for something they wanted. Select one scenario to discuss in detail as a class. Students should consider the positions each party took. Did either side have to give something up to reach agreement?

Career Decisions

Self-Assessment Checklist

Use this checklist to help students determine their career path:

✓ Think about things you are good at

✓ Write down your interests

✓ Think about the lifestyle you want

✓ Write down your aptitudes and abilities

✓ Consider your personality

✓ Determine your learning style

✓ List some careers that might match these characteristics

Résumé Builder

Answer networking, real-world experience, career planning, obtaining school credits/requirements, polishing skills, and honing decision-making skills

216

Dino Tsibouris
Attorney, Mallory & Tsibouris Co., LPA

What do you do at work?
"I am responsible for negotiating software licenses and data processing agreements when a company hires another company to host Web sites, perform data processing services, or perform electronic payments.

I also help companies comply with all of the laws and regulations that require personal and financial information to be held and processed privately and securely.

We represent banks, insurance companies, and government agencies as they offer new services over the Internet."

What skills are most important to you?
"My writing skills. A lawyer must be able to draft documents and agreements in a concise and understandable style. I try to draft my agreements in a manner that allows the reader to understand the terms of a transaction using a minimum of legal jargon if possible. Clearly written agreements are more enforceable in court. I also have to be able to communicate clearly with my clients. Communication isn't just about talking to the client or opposing party; it's about listening carefully."

What kind of training do you recommend?
"I majored in business administration, with an emphasis in finance. I represent a number of financial institutions, so my undergraduate training has helped me better understand how to create solutions for their business-specific needs. Developing a work-related network through social contacts is important. If you have the opportunity to obtain a clerkship or internship in your desired area of practice before graduation, you can gain practical experience and professional relationships—as well as a possible job."

What is your key to success?
"I have to stay current on changing legal trends and new laws that may affect my clients. I also participate in presentations through the bar associations and professional organizations."

Résumé Builder

Academic Skills
- Strong writing skills
- Good communication skills (attentive listener)

Education and Training
A bachelor's degree of business administration, finance, accounting, or other areas specific to the attorney's specific industry. The following high school and collegiate courses will help develop the necessary background knowledge:

- Business, contracts, and consumer law
- Business law courses
- Communication courses
- E-commerce
- English Language Arts (composition and rhetoric in particular)
- Mathematics for business
- U.S. government

Critical Thinking
List the benefits of social contacts, clerkships, and internships.

 Go to **glencoe.com** to find legal careers resources.

 glencoe.com

 # Research Technology

Specialized technology is available for a variety of law-related tasks. For example, LexisNexis and Westlaw are two competing electronic databases that attorneys and other legal professionals use to conduct research. These services give users access to online legal information, including the text of court decisions and legislation, the content of public records, and many legal articles.

Activity Ask students to access the American Bar Association's Web site through **glencoe.com** and read about technology uses in legal professions.

The Writing Connection

Persuasive Writing Practice

Who Pays? Four college friends, all 20, rent a three-bedroom apartment on the top floor of a small building. Everyone has her own bedroom except Amie and Caitlin, who share a bedroom; hence they each pay about $260 less than Claire and Jasmine. One night water started leaking from the light fixture in Amie and Caitlin's bedroom. Soon the leak turned into a gush, pouring water into their bedroom. Within minutes the ceiling fell in their bedroom and practically everything in the room was soaked and covered in wet drywall. Firemen shut off the water and investigated the leak. The landlord arrived and said to the girls, "Wow, I hope one of you has renter's insurance." For one month after the incident, Amie and Caitlin lived in a hotel since their portion of the apartment was uninhabitable.

Assignments

W
R

Research Research what a renter's rights are in such a situation. Also research who pays for the damages if the tenants do not have renter's insurance but are still considered dependents under their parents' homeowners' insurance policy.

Write Consider the situation above and write a persuasive essay about what a fair solution could be.

Writing Tips Before you start writing your essay, read through the following writing tips:

✓ Organize logical arguments to support your position and support them with evidence.

✓ Make sure the evidence you use is up-to-date, unbiased, and verifiable.

✓ Use different types of evidence: firsthand observation, informed opinions (double-check your sources), facts, or statistics.

✓ Avoid generalizations and oversimplification.

Essay Test Strategies Beyond describing the issue and state of your opinion, be sure to convince others of your viewpoint. Review your outline to detect flaws in logic.

Go to **glencoe.com** to find more writing resources.

glencoe.com

Unit 3   Consumer Law   **217**

The Writing Connection

W Writing Support

Objectives
Write a brief persuasive essay outlining a fair solution for the renters.

Essay Rubric
Evaluate students' writing according to the following criteria:

- The essay presents both supporting and opposing evidence. **(6 points)**
- The essay precisely states an opinion. **(6 points)**
- The organization is clear and effective. **(5 points)**
- Supporting arguments are arranged in order of importance. **(4 points)**
- Syntax, grammar, and spelling are error-free. **(4 points)**

Total: 25 points

R Reading Strategy

Comparing-Contrasting
Students who write a persuasive essay might organize their information into four paragraphs. Each paragraph opens with transitional cues, such as "first," "next," "last," and "in conclusion."

Culminating Activity

Ask students to work in groups to give each other feedback on their first drafts.

Assignments

Before students start drawing a conclusion on a fair solution, ask them to think about a few questions that might help frame their answer:

- Who should pay for the damages? The hotel expenses?
- Who should pay for Amie and Caitlin's portion of the rent and utilities for the month they do not get to live in the apartment?

Students need to provide reasoned support for their conclusions. When proposing a solution they should be sure to restate their opinion clearly and show evidence backing up that solution.

Thematic Project

FOCUS

Bell Ringer Activity

What happens when a product is not safe, yet the appointed industry and government officials cannot locate the exact cause of a problem? Do they tell consumers to avoid the product altogether? Discuss any current or recent instances in which a product's safety placed consumers in possible danger.

TEACH

Workshop Overview

The objective of this workshop is to familiarize students with the types of federal agencies that offer support, guidance, and help to consumers regarding product safety.

Language Arts

Ask students to recall from their studies of American history the consequences for consumers of laissez-faire policies during the industrial era. Discuss the meaning of *caveat emptor*, and ask students to what extent this is an adequate means of protecting consumers. They might debate the appropriate balance between promoting a market economy and the need to protect consumers.

Product Safety and Recalls

For this project, you will use what you have learned about the types of federal agencies that offer support, guidance, and help to consumers regarding product safety and recalls. You can work on this project alone or with a partner.

Here is a checklist of the skills that you will need to complete this project. Your teacher will consider these skills when evaluating your work.

Evaluation Rubric

Academic Skills

1.	Online and library research	1.	10 points
2.	Reading for information	2.	10 points
3.	Note-taking	3.	5 points
4.	Estimation and computation of facts/figures you discover	4.	10 points
5.	English composition to summarize findings	5.	15 points

Legal Skills

6.	Research of governmental consumer protection agencies	6.	15 points
7.	Ability to translate code enforcement in a method to explain concept	7.	15 points
8.	Analysis of essential statistical information	8.	15 points
9.	Use of technology	9.	5 points
			Total 100 Points

 For more resources and for grading rubrics, go to **glencoe.com**.

Step 1: Preparation

❶ Create a vocabulary reference guide of terminology consumers will need to know in understanding procedures used for recalls.

❷ Use all you have learned in this unit, at the library, or on the Internet as tools.

❸ Complete this project in a format acceptable for a portfolio addition.

Time Management Rubric

Have students evaluate their usage of time by rating the skills below on a scale of "poor" to "apprentice" to "proficient."

1. Reading Skills
- Uses prior knowledge
- Distinguishes fact from opinion
- Evaluates
- Interprets

- Questions
- Understands cause and effect

2. Writing Traits
- Organization of ideas
- Creative and effective presentation of ideas
- Fluency and variety of sentences
- Correct use of terminology

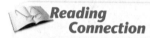
Step 2: Procedure

❶ **Review** the text in this unit and make a list of consumer protection agencies that are sponsored by the government. Go to **glencoe.com** to find an appropriate contract form.

❷ **List** all the terms a consumer might see in understanding their rights and that you will include in your informational flyer. What information is important to include in your flyer? How will you organize your research to present a concise product? Where can consumers go for additional guidance and help?

❸ **Write** an outline based on your knowledge and research to use in creating your informational flyer. Use the Internet to download frequently asked questions for the area you will be covering. Make enough copies of your outline, so your classmates can review and annotate the information you plan on presenting for completeness and understanding.

❹ **Describe** a real-life scenario that a consumer could resolve by using the information you have created, and present your flyer to the class.

Step 3: Create an Analysis Report

As a class, compare the informational flyers presented. List the governmental agencies available to consumers and explain their span of control. Look at the outlines your classmates have created and answer the following questions:

❶ How many and what types of agencies were presented?

❷ Did all of the outlines presented include all the necessary elements to give guidance to a consumer in search of help?

❸ If not, how does the absence of the element(s) affect the ability for a consumer to solve his or her problem/situation?

❹ How was your outline similar to and different from the other outlines presented?

Community Connection

Find recall statistics for a product that you used in your project. How would researching product recalls help your purchase decisions? Does a manufacturer recall when problems occur? Prepare a brief report on how to request a product recall. Go to **glencoe.com** to find resources.

Competitive Event Prep

Understanding Consumer Law

Situation Assume the role of a high school business law student. Your friend is ready to buy first car. The salesperson recommends buying an extended warranty that would take effect after the manufacturer's warranty expires. Your friend is unclear about what warranties do and do not offer. Your friend also has a specific budget for this purchase. Your friend asks you for advice about the extended warranty.

Activity Explain the pros and cons of warranties. Make a recommendation about purchasing an extended warranty.

 For more Competitive Event preparation, performance tips, and evaluation rubrics, go to **glencoe.com**.

C ### Critical Thinking
Making Generalizations

As a class, discuss the government's role in consumerism as presented in this chapter as well as from the students' own experiences. Have students make generalizations about government protection. Write these generalizations on the board. Allow students to refine and change their generalizations as the discussion progresses.

S ### Skills Practice
Research

Invite interested students to learn more about the beginning of a government protection agency. Suggest they work in pairs to research its history, purpose, and funding. Then they can create a trivia game on the subject that can be played in class.

TEACH *(cont.)*
Extending the Content
Consumer Protection

Ask students to use the Internet to find a consumer protection watchdog, organization, or weblog that is interesting to them. They should explain their reason for selecting it and present any surprising findings.

Reading Connection
American Bar Association Resources

Ask students to go back to their ABA readings, notes, and summaries. Direct them to apply any relevant ABA content to review and revise their outline and first draft.

ASSESS
Evaluation

Make sure students review the evaluation rubric. They should be able to speak with fluency on one agency that fits in this category.

CLOSE
Culminating Activity
Cooperative Learning

Invite students to create a display that showcases the various government agencies and how they work to protect consumers.

FOCUS

Why It's Important

- The court's decision held that vertical privity was no longer required in breaches of implied warranties of merchantability in Indiana.

- The case affirms that when a consumer purchases a car, and is told it is under a manufacturer's warranty, the consumer can reasonably believe that the manufacturer, not the dealer, will solve any relevant problems that arise.

TEACH

Preteaching

Your Reading

This text is a long excerpt from a key case where U.S. warranty law was applied.

Preread Skim the text, look at headings and the first few sentences of every section.

U Universal Access

Creating a Table Have students create a table showing the key terms used in this case. For example, they might include *warranty, overturn, vertical privity, privity of contract, merchantability, breach of express warranty,* and so on. They should write the definitions of each and indicate how they pertain to the case.

220

UNIT 3 Landmark Case

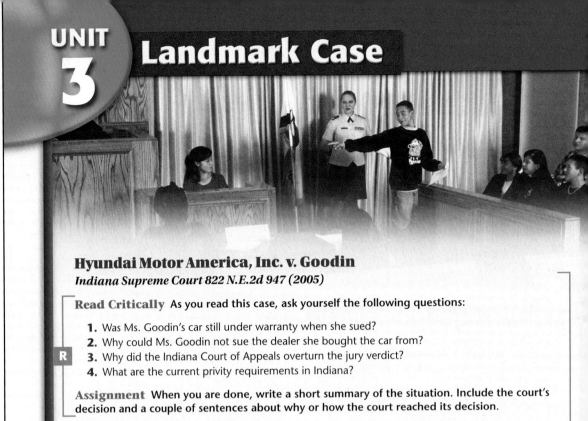

Hyundai Motor America, Inc. v. Goodin
Indiana Supreme Court 822 N.E.2d 947 (2005)

R **Read Critically** As you read this case, ask yourself the following questions:

1. Was Ms. Goodin's car still under warranty when she sued?
2. Why could Ms. Goodin not sue the dealer she bought the car from?
3. Why did the Indiana Court of Appeals overturn the jury verdict?
4. What are the current privity requirements in Indiana?

Assignment When you are done, write a short summary of the situation. Include the court's decision and a couple of sentences about why or how the court reached its decision.

Facts **Automobile Purchase** On
November 18, 2000, Sandra Goodin test drove a Hyundai Sonata at AutoChoice Hyundai in Evansville, Indiana. The car only had 19 miles on the odometer, but when Ms. Goodin drove the car and applied the brakes, she experienced a "shimmy, shake, pulsating type feel." The dealer told Ms. Goodin that it was caused by flat spots on the tires due to extended inactivity and offered to have the tires rotated and inspected. After that, Ms. Goodin purchased the vehicle for $22,710.00.

Automobile Warranty The vehicle that Ms. Goodin purchased came with 3 limited warranties from Hyundai Motor America: 1 year/12,000 miles on "wear items"; 5 years/ 60,000 miles "bumper to bumper"; and 10 years/100,000 miles on the powertrain. The brakes were covered under the 5 years/ 60,000 mile warranty; however, only if the repair work, or replacement, was done by an authorized Hyundai dealer. Further, separate

from Hyundai's warranty papers, the dealer, AutoChoice, included wording on its own sale papers that stated:

All warrantaies, if any, by a manufacturer or supplier other than dealer are theirs, not dealer's and only such manufacturer or other supplier shall be liable for performance under such warranties, unless dealer furnishes buyer with a separate written warranty mde by dealer on its own behalf. Dealer hereby disclaims all warranties, express or implied, including any implied warranties of merchantability or fitness for a particular purpose, on all goods and services sold by dealer.

U

Jury Verdict In the year following Ms. Goodin's purchase, she took the car to a Hyundai dealer at least seven times to have the brakes looked at. During those visits, numerous repairs were done, but the brakes continued to sound and act improperly. Ms. Goodin said that she experienced problems with her brakes about 70 percent of the time.

? Landmark Case Questions

R Reading Strategy

Answers

1. No. The warranty was only good for the first 60,000 miles driven.

2. The dealer specifically disclaimed all express and implied warranties.

3. Ms. Goodin did not have vertical privity with Hyundai, and therefore could not sue Hyundai directly.

4. Vertical privity is no longer required in actions for breach of an implied warranty of merchantability.

Ms. Goodin had driven the car for two years and put 77,600 miles on it. Ms. Goodin was still frustrated by the brakes and decided to sue Hyundai and request a refund for breach of an express warranty, or breach of an implied warranty of merchantability. After a jury trial, the jury returned a verdict for Hyundai on the claim for breach of express warranty, but for Ms. Goodin on the breach of an implied war-ranty of merchantability. Hyundai appealed.

Opinion Indiana Court of Appeals

Proceedings Hyundai appealed the verdict of the jury on the grounds that Ms. Goodin lacked vertical privity with Hyundai and could not bring a claim for breach of an implied warranty against them. Hyundai argued that Ms. Goodin could sue the dealer that she purchased the vehicle from, AutoChoice, but could not sue the actual car manufacturer. The Indiana Court of Appeals agreed with Hyundai and reversed the jury verdict for Ms. Goodin. Ms. Goodin then appealed to the Indiana Supreme Court.

Federal Warranty Law Ms. Goodin's original case was brought under the Federal Magnuson-Moss Warranty Act. Although it is a federal law, the act looks to state law to determine the source of any express or implied warranty. The Indiana Court of Appeals held that Indiana case law required vertical privity between Ms. Goodin and Hyundai, that is, there must be a contract between Hyundai and Ms. Goodin. In this case, there was a contract between Ms. Goodin and AutoChoice, but not between Ms. Goodin and Hyundai.

Origin of Privity Privity of contract is a concept American courts adopted from England. It limits the tort relief for breach of warranties by requiring parties to have some sort of contractual relationship. Ms. Goodin argued that traditional vertical privity was not required between herself and Hyundai because Hyundai provided an express warranty under the Magnuson-Moss Warranty Act, and as such, an implied warranty can also exist without any requisite vertical privity.

 glencoe.com

Further, Ms. Goodin argued that AutoChoice's disclaimer did not allow her to sue them, and she could only sue Hyundai.

Privity in Indiana The state of privity requirements evolved over the years in most states. Originally, privity requirements were quite stringent, but as consumer protection issues have become more developed, courts have lessened the privity requirements. In Indiana, the state legislature passed a Product Liability Act in 1999 that no longer required vertical privity in order to assert a products liability claim against a manufacturer.

Before the passage of the act, the Uniform Commercial Code allowed breach of warranty claims to be initiated by family members or guests of persons who actually purchased the product. They do not have to have privity with the manufacturer. However, neither of these provisions applied directly to Ms. Goodin's situation.

Holding The Court's Decision The Court held that vertical privity was no longer required in breaches of implied warranties of merchantability in the state of Indiana. Consumer expectations are such that when they buy a car and are told it is under war-ranty by the manufacturer, consumers believe they can obtain recourse from the manufacturer, not the dealer.

TRIAL PREP

The National High School Mock Trial Association organizes competitions at the local, regional, and national levels where teams of high school or college students prepare and argue fictional legal cases before practicing attorneys and judges. Mock Trial team members are each assigned a role as either an attorney or witness. Each team must develop a courtroom strategy, legal arguments, and presentation style.

Go to **glencoe.com** to find guided activities about case strategy and presentation.

Winning the Case

Requirements for Privity

In the past, the requirement for privity of contract has prevented many cases from proceeding to litigation. The theory of privity stems from the fact that a contract cannot exist where the element of consideration has never passed between the parties. In this case, Ms. Goodin never gave or received consideration from Hyundai. She purchased her car from the dealer, not the company. What would have happened if Ms. Goodin had financed the car directly through one of Hyundai's subsidiary loan companies? Would Ms. Goodin then have had privity with Hyundai?

ASSESS

Independent Practice

Writing a Letter

Have students take the role of Sandra Goodin who had issues with her Hyundai. Have students write a formal business letter to the manufacturer outlining the issues with the vehicle and expectations based on the car's warranty. The letter should explain the purpose, suggest solutions, and ask for the manufacturer's input with regard to solving the problem.

CLOSE

Understand the Decision

Since Ms. Goodin brought her case under the federal Magnuson-Moss Warranty Act, why was this case not brought in Federal Court under federal jurisdiction? (The Magnuson-Moss Warranty Act provides for a federal right of action to enforce a written or implied warranty where the victim claims that the warrantor failed to comply with a warranty. However, there are no federal laws about what constitutes a valid express or implied warranty, so that must be determined in state courts or by applying applicable state law. Since state law must be determined, it is preferable to bring such action in a state court, where judges are more familiar with the relevant law.)

Unit Objectives

Chapter	Section	Objectives
Chapter 10	**10.1**	• **Describe** the function of negotiable instruments. • **Identify** the different types of negotiable instruments. • **List** the essential elements of negotiable instruments. • **Differentiate** between a draft, a note, and a certificate of deposit.
	10.2	• **Explain** the contractual relationship between a bank and its customers. • **Distinguish** stop-payment orders, forgeries, and material alterations. • **Differentiate** between types of checks. • **Define** electronic fund transfer.
Chapter 11	**11.1**	• **Define** the main types of credit. • **Explain** what a secured transaction is. • **Describe** how a security interest is created. • **Identify** the main types of collateral.
	11.2	• **Define** finance charge and annual percentage rate. • **Describe** the advantages to using a credit card. • **Determine** how to obtain student loans. • **Recognize** the warning signs of debt problems.
Chapter 12	**12.1**	• **Define** repossession and garnishment. • **Describe** the federal laws that regulate consumer credit. • **Discuss** your rights under the Consumer Credit Protection Act, the Fair Credit Reporting Act, and the Fair Credit Billing Act. • **Explain** the purpose of the Equal Credit Opportunity Act and the Fair Credit Collection Practices Act.
	12.2	• **Identify** and discuss alternatives to bankruptcy. • **Distinguish** between the different types of bankruptcy. • **Explain** the differences between voluntary and involuntary bankruptcy. • **Identify** debts which cannot be discharged by bankruptcy.

Understanding Brackets, Letters, and Ability Levels in the Teacher Wraparound Edition

Brackets Brackets on the reduced student edition page correspond to teaching strategies and activities in the Teacher Wraparound Edition. As you teach the lesson, the brackets show you exactly where to use the teaching strategies and activities.

Letters The letters on the reduced student edition page identify the type of strategy or activity. See the key below to learn about the different types of strategies and activities.

Ability Levels Teaching strategies that appear throughout the chapters have been identified by one of three codes to give you an idea of their suitability for students of varying learning styles and abilities.

Resources Key program resources are listed in each chapter. Icons indicate the format of resources.

KEY TO LETTERS

R **Reading Strategy** activities help you teach reading skills and vocabulary.

C **Critical Thinking** strategies help students apply and extend what they have learned.

S **Skills Practice** strategies help students practice historical analysis and geographical skills.

W **Writing Support** activities provide writing opportunities to help students comprehend the text.

D **Develop Concepts** activities use various strategies to help teachers gauge and plan for students' concept development.

U **Universal Access** activities provide differentiated instruction for English language learners, and suggestions for teaching various types of learners.

NCLB **No Child Left Behind** activities help students practice and improve their abilities in academic subjects.

KEY TO ABILITY LEVELS

L1 strategies should be within the ability range of all students. Often full class participation is required.

L2 strategies are for average to above-average students or for small groups. Some teacher direction is necessary.

L3 strategies are designed for students able and willing to work independently. Minimal teacher direction is necessary.

KEY TO RESOURCE ICONS

🗀 Print Material

💿 CD/DVD

🖱 Internet

TeacherWorks™
All-In-One Planner and Resource Center

Teacher Wraparound Edition

Student Activity Workbook with Academic Integration
Teacher Annotated Edition

For the Unit:
Lesson Plans
National and State Standards Correlations

For the Chapters:
Lessons Plans
Note-Taking Graphic Organizers
Chapter Outlines
Chapter Summaries
Enrichment Activities Masters

Supplemental Cases
Internet Connection Student Activities Masters
Blackline Masters for Student Edition Figures and
   Supplemental Figures
Ethics and Business Law Activities
Competitive Events Test-Taking Prep
Reproducible Chapter Tests

 Link to the **Business and Personal Law** Online **Learning Center** with Podcasts through glencoe.com.

Real-World Applications

Demonstrate Case Resolutions

Learning Objective

- Explain and apply the Federal Credit Union Act (p. 228).
- Understand the advantages to using a credit card (p. 249).
- Describe the bankruptcy law rules (p. 271).

- Explain the elements of a negotiable instrument (p. 243).
- Understand the laws as they apply to credit (p. 261).
- Explain bankruptcy as it pertains to student loans (p. 279).

- Describe federal laws regarding consumer credit (pp. 284–285).

Apply Business Law Concepts

Learning Objective

- Understand the contractual relationship between a bank and its customers (p. 224).
- Describe what businesses are doing to combat electronic security breaches (p. 244).
- Understand the bankruptcy laws and when they apply (p. 262).

- Understand banking in Switzerland (p. 237).
- Explain the German lemon law (p. 252).
- Identify the conditions under which a debtor can be declared bankrupt in Chile (p. 272)

- Understand secured transactions (p. 247).

- Describe the contractual relationship between a bank and its customers (p. 243).
- Apply an ethical decision to a situation (p. 261).
- Describe the concept of bankruptcy (p. 279).

CYBERLAW

- Explain electronic fund transfers (p. 235).
- Understand the Racketeer Influenced and Corrupt Organizations Act (RICO) and the Federal Wire Act (p. 267).

Teach Financial Literacy

Learning Objective

- Understand how to obtain a student loan (p. 223).

Bring Project-Based Learning into the Law Classroom

Correcting a Credit Report Error

- **Introduce Concepts**
  Credit is the arrangement through which a person may receive cash, goods, or services immediately, and pay for them in the future. Credit reporting agencies rate credit activity and provide credit reports.

- **Explore Concepts**
  Read the Thematic Project Preview and the WebQuest activity (p. 223)

  Ask students to think about the structure and content of their credit report dispute letter as they study Chapters 10, 11, and 12.

- **Apply Concepts**
  Research credit reporting agencies and credit rating calculation, explain how credit disputes are resolved, and substantiate the claim for error (pp. 282 and 283).

Extend Content

Reading Connection

Using American Bar Association (ABA) Resources

- Direct students to pages 243, 261, and 279 in the Student Edition.
- Ask them to use glencoe.com to find links to ABA resource documents.
- Students should browse and select one document for each chapter.
- See pages 243, 261, 279, and 285 in this edition for specific instructions.

Reading and Writing Support

Feature or Activity	Topic	Reading Strategy	Writing Strategy
STANDARD &POOR'S	Student loans	Reading a primary source document	
Thematic Project Preview	Correcting a credit report error		Researching and taking notes
BusinessWeek	Readings about banking laws (Ch. 10), credit card fraud (Ch. 11), and bankruptcy law (Ch. 12)	Reading for detail Developing flexibility in reading speed	
Section Reading Guide	Before-reading activities and tools	Connect students' lives with content Focus on the main idea	Using a graphic organizer to take notes
As You Read	During-reading tool	Predict content Determine what students already know	
Reading Check	During-reading tool	Self-check understanding of content	
After You Read	After-reading tool	Summarize section content	Writing and organizing a list of key concepts
Standardized Test Practice	Uniform Commercial Code (Ch. 10) Federal Reserve Board (Ch. 11) Credit card terms and conditions (Ch. 12)	Reading a primary source document Practicing critical reading skills	
Reading Connection	American Bar Association online resources	Reading a primary source document Extending and applying content Reading for knowledge	Taking notes Summarizing
The Writing Connection	Persuasive writing		Creating outlines, topic sentences, editing
Unit Thematic Project	Correcting a credit report error	Using resources notes to support writing effort	Creating outlines, writing drafts, editing
Landmark Case	Consumer credit law case	Developing critical reading skills	Summarizing

Unit Overview

 Main)) Idea

Unit 4 describes in detail the two kinds of negotiable instruments (notes and drafts), financing with credit (credit cards, student loans), and federal laws that regulate consumer credit.

00:00 OUT OF TIME?

If class time is too short to cover the chapters thoroughly, have students:

- Write down the vocabulary terms and their definitions.
- Read What You'll Learn and Why It's Important at the beginning of each section.
- Go to the *Business and Personal Law* Online Learning Center at glencoe.com and guide students to download the free Study-to-Go content to their cell phones or PDAs.

▶ USING VISUALS ....

Methods of Payment
Answer Answers include credit cards, such as Visa and MasterCard, charge cards for department stores, such as Macy's and Sears, ATM cards, gas cards, and smart cards.

UNIT 4 Your Money and the Law

In This Unit You Will Find:

**Chapter 10
Banking and Negotiable Instruments**

**Chapter 11
Credit and Debt**

**Chapter 12
Credit Protection and Bankruptcy**

Methods of Payment
In the age of e-commerce virtually all purchase and credit transactions can now be done electronically. *What are some types of cards you can use to make a purchase?*

222

Unit Thematic Project Preview

W Writing Support

In the event that personal information has been lost or stolen, the Federal Trade Commission advises closing financial accounts, contacting any of the three nationwide consumer-reporting agencies to place an initial fraud alert, and replacing government-issued identification cards such as a driver's license.

Critical Thinking How might identity thieves get hold of personal information? (stealing records from businesses, the mail, purses or wallets, from credit card information using a "skimming" device, from change of address forms, etc.)

Thematic Project Preview

Correcting a Credit Report Error

As you read this unit, use this checklist to prepare for the unit project:

✓ List the three major credit reporting bureaus.

✓ Define the five main components used to calculate credit rating.

✓ Explain ways of repairing a low credit rating.

✓ Explain what information is needed to resolve a credit dispute.

✓ Determine the appropriate tone and style for a credit report dispute letter.

Legal Portfolio When you complete the Unit Thematic project, you will have a sample letter for reporting a credit dispute to add to your portfolio.

WebQuest

W

Credit Rating
A good credit rating is crucial to your financial health and purchasing power. Log on to **glencoe.com** to find out how to establish, maintain, and protect a good credit rating. List your findings in your WebQuest folder to share with your class.

Find Unit 4 study tools such as **Graphic Organizers, Academic Skills Review,** and **Practice Tests** at **glencoe.com**.

Ask

STANDARD &POOR'S

Paying for a College Education

Q: I cannot pay for college on my own and will need to apply for financial aid. What is the best way to go about this?

A: To apply for financial aid from almost every public and private college and university in the U.S., you need to fill out the Free Application for Federal Student Aid (FAFSA). You can get the application from your guidance counselor at school or online. At many colleges and universities, the FAFSA is the only form you need to fill out. After you submit the form, the Department of Education determines your expected family contribution (EFC), which is based on your family's income and assets. Once you have been accepted to a school, you might be offered a financial aid package. This often includes a combination of loans and scholarships and possibly work-study arrangements.

R **Language Arts/Reading** Standard & Poor's is one of the world's main providers of credit ratings and financial-market indices. Go to **glencoe.com** and read more about paying and saving for college.

Unit 4　　Your Money and the Law　　**223**

5-minute **Launch**

KWL Chart Have students make a list of what they know about credit. Next, ask them to skim Unit 4 and notice the headers, the figures, and the photos. Ask students what questions came up and have them list what they now want to know about credit. Discuss the lists and create a KWL chart with their responses. After completing the unit, revisit the chart and reassess their knowledge by asking them what they have learned about credit.

Building Law Background

Ask students these questions to activate prior knowledge:

Chapter 10
What forms of payment are available other than a cash transaction? (bartering, credit, check, electronic banking, etc.)

Chapter 11
Describe credit and some of its possible problems. (Credit is an arrangement through which you may receive cash, goods, and services now and pay for them in the future; overspending, high interest rates, bankruptcy, etc.)

Chapter 12
Give some tips on how not to be defrauded when using a credit card online. (Do not give the number out online unless the latest security protocols are in place, read the fine print, shop around, do not pay fees up front to get a credit card, use credit wisely, etc.)

Ask

STANDARD &POOR'S

 Reading Strategy

Language Arts/Reading Direct students to explore S&P's resources on paying for higher education.

Math Activity The State College president and its board have been discussing a tuition hike over a five-year period. Currently, tuition is $8,500 a year. They propose a 5 percent increase each year. Determine the tuition amount for each of the next five years.
(Year 1 $8,925;
Year 2 $9,371.25;
Year 3 $9,839.81;
Year 4 $10,331.80;
Year 5 $10,848.39)

Plan Your Lesson Section by Section

NBEA	NATIONAL BUSINESS LAW STANDARDS
Section 10.1	• **Explain** the importance and function of commercial paper. • **Demonstrate** an understanding of the concept of negotiability and distinguish it from assignability. • **Describe** the different types of negotiable instruments and different types of endorsements. • **Identify** and explain the essential elements of a negotiable instrument.
Section 10.2	• **Explain** the contractual relationship between a bank and its customers. • **Describe** stop-payment orders. • **Describe** the legal effect of forgeries and material alterations.

NCLB	ACADEMIC STANDARDS	Activity/Feature
English Language Arts: NCTE 3 Apply a wide range of strategies to comprehend, interpret, evaluate, and appreciate texts.		*BusinessWeek* News, Case Study, Case Study Practice
English Language Arts: NCTE 9 Develop an understanding of and respect for diversity in language use, patterns, and dialects across cultures, ethnic groups, geographic regions, and social roles.		Global Law
English Language Arts: NCTE 6 Apply knowledge of language structure, language conventions, media techniques, figurative language, and genre to create, critique, and discuss print and non-print texts.		Legal Talk, ad copy, Key Terms, and Academic Vocabulary
Social Studies: NCSS 1 Study culture and cultural diversity.		Section 10.1 Assessment
English Language Arts: NCTE 4 Adjust the use of spoken, written, and visual language to communicate effectively with a variety of audiences and for different purposes.		Section 10.1 Assessment
Mathematics: NCTM NOS 2 Understand meanings of operations and how they relate to one another.		Section 10.2 Assessment
English Language Arts: NCTE 10 Students whose first language is not English make use of their first language to develop competency in the English language arts and to develop understanding of content across the curriculum.		Key Terms, Academic Vocabulary, Legal Talk, Vocabulary Builder
English Language Arts: NCTE 1 Read a wide range of print and non-print texts to build an understanding of texts; to acquire new information; to respond to the needs and demands of society and the workplace; and for personal fulfillment.		Global Law, Cyberlaw
Social Studies: NCSS 5 Study interactions among individuals, groups, and institutions.		Global Law, Cyberlaw

Connect Your Business Law Classroom to the World of Work

This chart shows the 21st Century Skills, foundation skills, and workplace competencies that students develop as they work in this chapter.

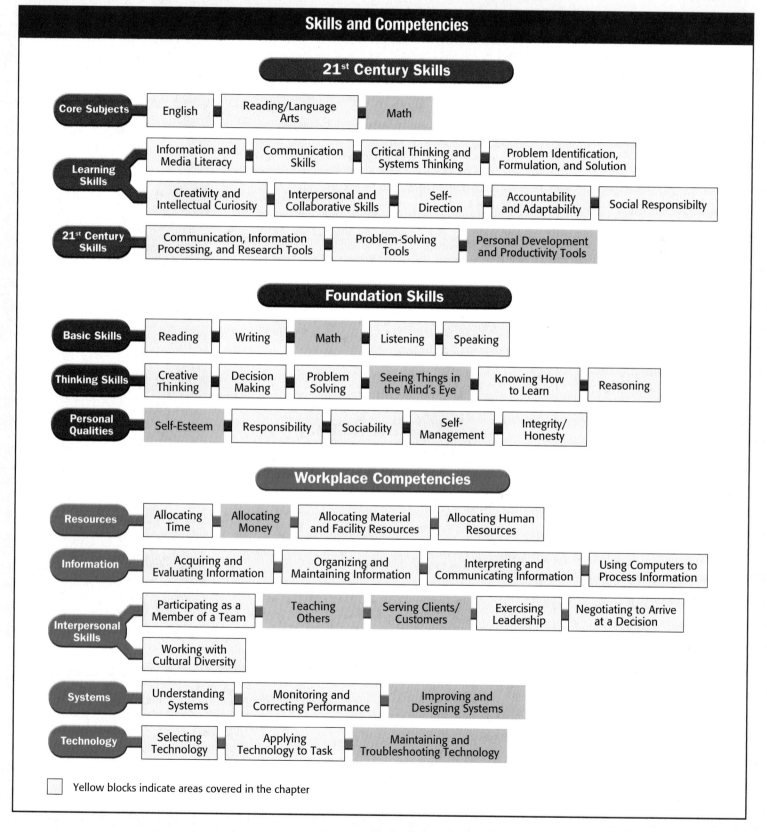

Skills and Competencies

21st Century Skills

Core Subjects
- English
- Reading/Language Arts
- Math

Learning Skills
- Information and Media Literacy
- Communication Skills
- Critical Thinking and Systems Thinking
- Problem Identification, Formulation, and Solution
- Creativity and Intellectual Curiosity
- Interpersonal and Collaborative Skills
- Self-Direction
- Accountability and Adaptability
- Social Responsibilty

21st Century Skills
- Communication, Information Processing, and Research Tools
- Problem-Solving Tools
- Personal Development and Productivity Tools

Foundation Skills

Basic Skills
- Reading
- Writing
- Math
- Listening
- Speaking

Thinking Skills
- Creative Thinking
- Decision Making
- Problem Solving
- Seeing Things in the Mind's Eye
- Knowing How to Learn
- Reasoning

Personal Qualities
- Self-Esteem
- Responsibility
- Sociability
- Self-Management
- Integrity/Honesty

Workplace Competencies

Resources
- Allocating Time
- Allocating Money
- Allocating Material and Facility Resources
- Allocating Human Resources

Information
- Acquiring and Evaluating Information
- Organizing and Maintaining Information
- Interpreting and Communicating Information
- Using Computers to Process Information

Interpersonal Skills
- Participating as a Member of a Team
- Teaching Others
- Serving Clients/Customers
- Exercising Leadership
- Negotiating to Arrive at a Decision
- Working with Cultural Diversity

Systems
- Understanding Systems
- Monitoring and Correcting Performance
- Improving and Designing Systems

Technology
- Selecting Technology
- Applying Technology to Task
- Maintaining and Troubleshooting Technology

Yellow blocks indicate areas covered in the chapter

CHAPTER
10

Banking and Negotiable Instruments

Introduce the Chapter

Banking and Negotiable Instruments

Chapter 10 outlines the various kinds of negotiable instruments and explains how they are used. The requirements of negotiability, the methods of transfer, and the use of a checking account are discussed.

Building Background

Ask if any students in the class have checking accounts. Have a volunteer describe how a check is written. Explain that a check is one type of negotiable instrument. Tell students that they will learn about other forms of negotiable instruments in this chapter.

BusinessWeek News

Newman's ability to turn around a sinking ship was greatly needed at SDB. Newman was shocked to find that branch loan officers did not generate regular reports detailing which loans were being paid off and which were not. The loan officers rarely secured approval from headquarters when granting loans. Bad loans accounted for 11 percent of the bank's loan book.

R Reading Strategy

Flex Your Reading

Stress to students that negotiable instruments are a part of daily life. If students encounter ideas that they find challenging, suggest that they read these sections aloud when studying at home.

BusinessWeek News

The Great Bank Overhaul

By Brian Bremner

When Frank Newman paid a visit to Shenzhen Mayor Xu Zongheng in early June, it wasn't just to exchange pleasantries. Newman will soon be chairman of Shenzhen Development Bank (SDB), the first foreigner ever to hold such a post, and he needed Mayor Xu's help. The private bank, which is 18 percent owned by Newman's other employer, Fort Worth-based private-equity firm Newbridge Capital Group, is loaded with bad debt. Newman was there to explain his restructuring plan to the mayor and seek his help in collecting from some local deadbeats. Having seen an ornamental sword in the office of Shenzhen Vice-Mayor Chen Yingchun a week earlier, Newman said to Xu only half-jokingly, "Maybe you can use that sword on these guys." Xu smiled and assured Newman that "we will use the sword of the law."

Flex Your Reading

Efficient critical reading involves being flexible with speed and comprehension. There are several ways of reading critically, and you need to fit a reading style to your needs and to the material.

Go to **glencoe.com** for Flex Your Reading activities, more information on reading strategies for this chapter, and guided practice in reading about negotiable instruments.

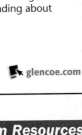

Classroom Resources

- Student Edition
- Teacher Wraparound Edition
- Student Activity Workbook with Academic Integration (SE/TAE)
- TeacherWorks™ Plus! CD
- *ExamView® Assessment Suite* CD
- *Presentation Plus!* CD

- National Mock Trial Championship DVD
- Online Learning Center with Podcasts at glencoe.com
- Study-to-Go™ at glencoe.com
- Online Student Edition
- Interactive Student Edition

Negotiable Instruments
Write the following terms on the board:

- checks
- notes
- certificates of deposit
- stocks
- bonds

Ask students to suggest what all these items have in common. (written, give rights to the holder that may be transferred) Explain that these instruments represent monetary value that can be retained or transferred by the holder. Tell students that certain U.S. laws govern how these instruments may be issued and transferred.

Key Terms Tell students that when bankers or financial experts talk about negotiable instruments they will use a variety of terms that may be new to students. For example, an application for a bank account might include terms such as *payee, drawer, draft,* or *indorsement.* Understanding each term is key to managing personal finances.

The Fine Print Explain that a negotiable instrument contains language that is critical to its validity. Emphasize to students that if they are involved in a transaction in which they receive an instrument such as a check, they should review it carefully. Is the check signed? Is it dated? Does the amount in figures match the amount in words? These are all issues that will be discussed in the chapter.

For Deposit Only If your check is lost or stolen, it could be cashed by someone else. *What can you do to make sure your check can only be used to deposit in your bank account?*

(225)

▲ USING VISUALS

For Deposit Only **Answer** A special restrictive indorsement limits the use of an instrument such as a check. Writing "For Deposit Only" on the back of the check and signing it means that it must first be deposited into the indorser's bank account before it can be negotiated further. If the check contains only a blank indorsement or a signature alone, anyone can cash the check.

FOCUS

SECTION 10.1 Using Negotiable Instruments

Bell Ringer Activity

Bring in samples of negotiable instruments and distribute to students as they enter the classroom. Ask them to describe the elements found on each instrument. (promise from one person to pay a certain amount to another person)

Preteaching

Key Terms
Read the definitions and ask students to create a sentence using each term.

Academic Vocabulary
Explain that developing vocabulary is key to academic success. An efficient method to develop vocabulary is to study how words are formed.

- **advantage** Noun, from the Latin *abante* (before). Means a state favorable to success.
- **signature** Noun, from the Latin *signare* (to mark). Means one's own name written in one's own hand.
- **unconditional** Adjective, from the Latin *un-* (not) + *condicere* (to agree). Means without limitations.

Activity Ask students to give a noun, a verb, an adjective, or an adverb form that comes from each word.

Connects to academic content

226

SECTION 10.1 Using Negotiable Instruments

What You'll Learn

- ◆ Describe the function of negotiable instruments.
- ◆ Identify the different types of negotiable instruments.
- ◆ List the essential elements of negotiable instruments.
- ◆ Differentiate between a draft, a note, and a certificate of deposit.

Why It's Important

If you ever get a certificate of deposit or borrow money to buy a car, you need to know about the law of negotiable instruments.

Academic Standards

Reading and completing the activities in this section will help you practice the following academic standards:

Social Studies (NCSS 1) Study culture and cultural diversity.

English Language Arts (NCTE 4) Adjust the use of spoken, written, and visual language to communicate effectively with a variety of audiences and for different purposes.

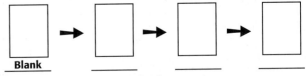
Reading Guide

Before You Read

Connect Have you ever received a paper that could be exchanged for cash? If so, you have some idea of what a negotiable instrument is.

Focus on Ideas

A negotiable instrument is a written promise or order by one person to pay another.

Take Notes

Create a graph like the one shown and use it to take notes as you read this section. Go to **glencoe.com** to find graphic organizers and tips on how to improve your note-taking skills.

Blank	→		→		→	

Types of Indorsements

 Key Terms

You will learn these legal words and expressions in this chapter. You can also find these terms in *Black's Law Dictionary* or in an online legal dictionary.

- negotiable instrument
- note
- maker
- payee
- draft
- drawer
- drawee
- negotiation
- holder
- assignment
- indorsement
- holder in due course

 Academic Vocabulary

You will find these words in your readings and in your tests. Look them up in a dictionary and familiarize yourself with them.

- advantage
- signature
- unconditional

 glencoe.com

 Reading Strategy

Read for Knowledge

1. **Survey** or preread the chapter.
2. **Question** or formulate questions before you read.
3. **Recite** or read your questions, answers, and notes out loud.
4. **Review** or reread your notes.

Note-Taking Basics
- Listen attentively
- Have note-taking materials ready
- Skim through the lesson material
- Write down key words and ideas
- Anticipate what comes next
- Review notes soon after taking them

Types of Negotiable Instruments

How can you guarantee payment when you have no cash or credit card?

People often need to conduct business without carrying around large sums of money, or to buy items they can pay for later. Negotiable instruments were created to meet these needs.

A negotiable instrument, also known as commercial paper, is a written document giving legal rights that may be passed to others by indorsement or delivery. A negotiable instrument is a type of contract. However, the laws of negotiable instruments are governed by the Uniform Commercial Code (see Chapter 7) rather than general contract law. There are two basic kinds of negotiable instruments: notes (including certificates of deposit, stocks, and bonds) and drafts (including checks and bills of sale). Negotiable instruments can be obtained from places such as banks, credit unions, and other types of financial institutions.

Notes

A note (often called a promissory note) is a written promise to pay money. A maker is a person who promises to pay money in a note. A payee is a person in a note to whom the promise to pay is made. Two or more persons who sign a note are known as comakers. An **advantage** of using a note is that it can be negotiated (transferred) to other people easily.

A demand note is a note that is payable at the time the payee demands payment. In contrast, a time note is a note that is payable at a future date. An installment note is a note that is paid in a series of payments. People often sign this type of note when they borrow money to buy a car or a house.

A certificate of deposit (CD) is a note issued by a bank that earns interest over time. CDs are written for specific time periods, such as six months, one year, two years, and five years. The interest on a CD is higher than the interest on a savings account because the depositor cannot withdraw the money before the due date. Banks pay higher interest for longer-term CDs.

Drafts

A note is a promise to pay money. **A draft is an order to a third party to pay money. A drawer is a person who orders money to be paid in a draft. A drawee is person one to whom an order is given to pay money in a draft.**

Although ordered to pay money, drawees are not required to do so unless they agree. Drawees agree to pay a draft by writing the word *accepted* on the document and signing their name. A drawee that has done this is called an acceptor and must pay the draft. The person to whom the draft is paid is called the payee.

A sight draft is a draft that is payable when it is given to the drawee for payment. A time draft is a draft that is not payable until a particular period of time has passed.

As You Read

Predict How many types of negotiable instruments can you list?

Vocabulary You can find vocabulary definitions in the **Key Terms** glossary and the **Academic Vocabulary** glossary in the back of this book.

TEACH

Discussion Starter

Class Discussion

Ask students to describe the ways in which people pay for their purchases. (cash, check, credit cards, debit cards) Explain that negotiable instruments help individuals transact business in efficient ways.

D Develop Concepts

Negotiable Instruments Have students imagine they live in a country in which paper money and negotiable instruments have no value. Everything must be purchased with precious metals such as silver or gold. Ask students to contrast this process with the negotiable instruments we use today. (cumbersome and difficult using precious metals versus ease of using paper documents)

As You Read

Predict Ask students to scan the headings in this section. (notes and drafts)

Extending the Content

Negotiable Instruments

Explain to students that *negotiable* means "capable of being negotiated." Have students use a comprehensive dictionary or an online etymological dictionary to research the etymology of *negotiate* and report their findings to the class. (derived from the Latin *negotiatus*, meaning to trade). Ask students to list items or circumstances that might have to be negotiated. (contracts, pathways, an arrangement, a dance step, a financial instrument)

TEACH (cont.)

D Develop Concepts

Drafting Instruments Tell students that Mark promised to pay Jennifer $500 in 90 days. Inform them that Mark needs to put this promise in a negotiable instrument. Ask students to brainstorm the items that the instrument needs to contain. (signed by Mark, no conditions on promise, amount of $500, date of payment, payable to Jennifer)

U Universal Access

Kinesthetic Learners Ask students to create two instruments. One instrument should be negotiable and one nonnegotiable. Ask students to exchange instruments to see if they can determine which one is negotiable. Remind students to be sure that all essential elements are included in the negotiable instrument.

Letters of credit are a special type of draft used in international business. Banks issue letters of credit on behalf of buyers, agreeing to pay sellers money when specific conditions are met. The bank accepts liability for the payment of the money involved in the transaction. The seller is guaranteed payment even if the buyer changes his or her mind. However, if the bank pays, the buyer is still liable for payments to the bank.

Drafting Instruments
What makes an instrument negotiable?

To be negotiable, negotiable instruments must have several elements.

Written Instrument

The promise, or order, to pay must be in writing. It can be printed, typed, or handwritten in pen or pencil. A negotiable instrument written in pencil is, however, an invitation for forgery or alteration.

Case Study – National Credit Union v. First National Bank

Critical Thinking *Can the federal government restrict credit union membership qualifications?*

 Your Reading Note key facts in the text below and look up words you do not understand. Restate difficult ideas in your own words. Go back and reread the text quickly to make sure you did not miss any important detail. Now, you are ready to formulate an opinion.

Open Membership? Congress passed the Federal Credit Union Act (FCUA) in 1934 during the Great Depression. The Act provided for the creation of certain federal credit unions. The credit unions were allowed to provide banking services to a select group of members as determined by the credit union's individual charter. Section 109 of the Act specifically stated:

Federal credit union membership shall be limited to groups having a common bond of occupation or association, or to groups within a well-defined neighborhood, community, or rural district.

In 1982, the National Credit Union Administration (NCUA) allowed for multiple unrelated employer groups to become members of credit unions. As a result of the change, AT&T Family Federal Credit Union (AT&T FFCU) opened its membership to local persons unrelated to AT&T. Ultimately, only 35 percent of its members were actual AT&T employees. First National Bank & Trust Company then sued the NCUA, arguing that the FCUA did not provide for open membership to credit unions and that AT&T FFCU cannot open its membership to unrelated persons.

Nat'l Credit Union Admin. v. First Nat'l Bank & Trust Co., 522 U.S. 479 (1998)

Go to **glencoe.com** for more case study practice.

Case Study

National Credit Union v. First National Bank

Answer Yes. The United States Supreme Court held that the FCUA was a valid act and Congress's intent was clear—credit union membership must be limited to only those persons with a common bond of employment or association. Although there is an argument that Congress is restricting commerce by limiting membership, it must be recognized that credit unions are not independent private commercial organizations, but are chartered by the government and are member-run. The FCUA cannot be considered a limitation on credit unions, since it allows any person who shares the common bond to join.

Signature of Maker or Drawer Banks keep signature cards on file to verify the signature on a check. *What are other ways a signature can be verified?*

Signature of Maker or Drawer

D

A negotiable instrument must be signed. The maker must sign a note, and the drawer must sign a draft. A **signature** may be any mark placed on the instrument with the intent to be a signature. The signature on a check, however, should match the signature card on file with the bank. The signature card is a record of an account holder's signature that the bank uses to verify it.

Unconditional Promise or Order

C

The promise in a note, or the order in a draft, must be **unconditional**. If either is qualified in any way, the instrument is not negotiable.

Fixed Sum of Money

A negotiable instrument must be payable in a fixed sum of money. This can be in U.S. dollars or the currency of a foreign country.

U

Payable on Demand or at a Definite Time

Negotiable instruments must be payable on demand. Instruments that state they are payable "on demand" or "on sight" are called demand paper. Instruments must also be payable at a definite time. For instance, a check payable when a person marries or reaches a certain age is not negotiable because the time of payment is not definite.

Payable to Order or Bearer

Except for checks, negotiable instruments must be payable to order or to bearer. The words *to the order of* and *to bearer* are called the words of negotiability. The maker or drawer may write "Pay to the order of Jane Doe," "Pay to Jane Doe or order," or "Pay to Jane Doe or her assigns."

Chapter 10   Banking and Negotiable Instruments   **229**

10.1 SECTION

TEACH (cont.)

D Develop Concepts

Maker or Drawer Tell students that Chris agreed to lend Brad $100. Brad agreed to repay the money in one month and to draw up a note to reflect this transaction. Ask students to identify the maker and the payee of this instrument. (Chris—payee; Brad—maker)

C Critical Thinking

Unconditional Promise Tell students that Foley promised to pay his brother $1,000 on December 31 if he had the extra money. He agreed to put the promise in writing and sign it. Ask students whether the document would be negotiable. (No. The promise is conditional, so it is not negotiable.)

U Universal Access

Visual/Spatial Learners Ask students to draw a picture of a check from a checking account with all the elements needed for it to be a negotiable instrument. They can use their own name as the payee and a fictitious name as the drawer. (include signature, amount, bank name, date, payable to name)

▲ USING VISUALS

Signature of Maker or Drawer Answer A signature on a check can also be verified with an official signed document, such as a driver's license or passport.

Activity Many stores and online businesses use electronic signature devices or digital signatures for customer ease and convenience. Ask students to research how electronic and digital signatures work, and have them prepare a report outlining the advantages and disadvantages of using electronic or digital signatures for verification of a customer's identification.

TEACH *(cont.)*

D Develop Concepts

Assignment Ask students what they think of when they hear the word *assignment.* (school papers or homework, chores at home) Explain that *assignment* in the sense of a negotiable instrument means that your rights under a contract are transferred to someone else. Tell students that the person who assigns an instrument is the *assignor* and the person who receives the assignment is the *assignee.*

C Critical Thinking

Dates Tell students that Frank failed to write the date on a check he issued to his landlord. When his landlord received the check, she argued that the check was not negotiable. Ask students if this is correct. Why or why not? (No. The date on which the check was received is considered to be the date of issue, if the date was omitted.)

Reading Check

Enumerate Negotiable instruments must be written, signed, unconditional, payable in a fixed sum of money, payable on demand or at a definite time, and payable to order or bearer.

230

Reading Check

Enumerate *What are the main characteristics of negotiable instruments?*

Dates and Controlling Words

When the date is omitted, the date on which the instrument is received is considered the date of issue. A check can also be post-dated, or written with a later date on it than the date it is signed.

Sometimes, due to an error or alteration, the words or figures on a negotiable instrument do not match each other. In that case, words control, or win out, over figures. Terms that are typed control terms that are printed, and terms that are handwritten control typed and printed terms.

Transferring Negotiable Instruments

What is the right way to sign a negotiable instrument?

When an instrument is signed by the maker or drawer and given to another person, the instrument is issued. When that person gives it to a third party, the instrument is transferred. The transfer can be done by assignment or by negotiation. **Negotiation is the transfer of an agreement in such a way that the transferee becomes a holder. A holder is a person who possesses a negotiable instrument payable to "the order of" the person holding it or to "bearer."** You are a holder when you receive a check made out in your name. Negotiability is the ability of an instrument to be transferred in a way that the transferee becomes a holder.

Figure 10.1 Types of Indorsements

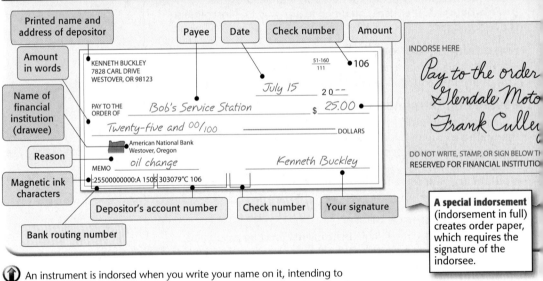

An instrument is indorsed when you write your name on it, intending to transfer ownership to another. The type of indorsement depends on how much information you include. *Why should you avoid using a blank indorsement?*

230   Unit 4   Your Money and the Law

USING VISUALS

➡ **Figure 10.1 Types of Indorsements** Answer Blank indorsements allow for an instrument to be cashed by anyone holding the check. It is best to avoid this type of indorsement because the instrument can be cashed by anyone if it is stolen or lost. The blank indorsement should only be used in limited situations such as at the teller's window. Explain to students that a check should be indorsed on the back, near the trailing edge. This is directly behind the "Pay to the order of "area. Explain that the middle area of the back of a check is reserved for the depository bank indorsement.

Instruments that do not meet the requirements of negotiability cannot be negotiated, but they can be assigned. **An assignment is the transfer of your rights under a contract to someone else.** Assignability is the ability of an instrument to be transferred to someone else without the transferee becoming a holder.

The person who assigns an instrument is the assignor. The person who receives the assignment is the assignee. Instruments are assigned when a person whose indorsement is required transfers the instrument without indorsing it.

Indorsements

An indorsement is the act of placing one's signature on an instrument, usually on the back, to transfer it to another. The person who writes the indorsement is called the indorser, and the person to whom the instrument is transferred is the indorsee. Indorsements may be written in ink, typed, or stamped with a rubber stamp. They are usually placed on the back of the instrument. There are four types of indorsements (see **Figure 10.1**).

Blank Indorsement A blank indorsement consists of a signature alone on the instrument. By signing an instrument in this way, you are saying in effect, "This instrument may be paid to anyone." An instrument indorsed in blank becomes bearer paper and may be transferred by delivery alone. If it is lost or stolen, someone else can cash it.

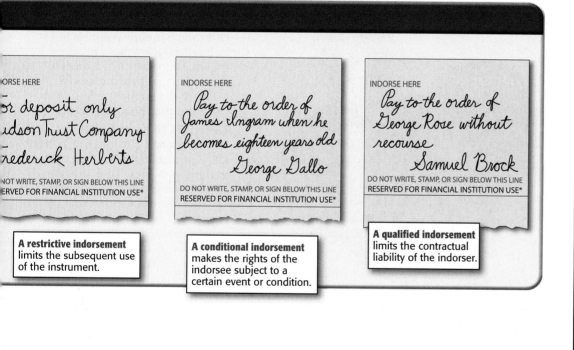

INDORSE HERE
r deposit only
udson Trust Company
rederick Herberts
NOT WRITE, STAMP, OR SIGN BELOW THIS LINE
ERVED FOR FINANCIAL INSTITUTION USE*

INDORSE HERE
Pay to the order of
James Ingram when he
becomes eighteen years old
George Gallo
DO NOT WRITE, STAMP, OR SIGN BELOW THIS LINE
RESERVED FOR FINANCIAL INSTITUTION USE*

INDORSE HERE
Pay to the order of
George Rose without
recourse
Samuel Brock
DO NOT WRITE, STAMP, OR SIGN BELOW THIS LINE
RESERVED FOR FINANCIAL INSTITUTION USE*

A restrictive indorsement limits the subsequent use of the instrument.

A conditional indorsement makes the rights of the indorsee subject to a certain event or condition.

A qualified indorsement limits the contractual liability of the indorser.

TEACH *(cont.)*

R Reading Strategy

Endorse vs. Indorse Ask students to look up the terms *endorsement* and *indorsement* in the dictionary. Have a volunteer read the differing definitions. (endorsement—approval or sanction; indorsement—placing of one's signature)

W Writing Support

Indorsements Ask students to call a local bank to inquire about the form of indorsements the bank accepts and what each one means. Have students prepare a brief memo explaining the results of their conversation.

Guided Practice

Indorsements

Have students who have checking accounts discuss which indorsement they typically use when they deposit checks into their accounts or when cashing checks. (Answers will vary.) Explain that the restrictive indorsement "For Deposit Only" means that the individual cannot receive a portion of the check as cash.

Extending the Content

Two-Party Check Indorsements

Explain to students that on some occasions a person may receive a check, then want to sign it over to another person. For example, Joe may receive a check from his mother for $50. He owes Steve $50. Ask students how Joe can use the check to pay Steve. (Joe can simply sign the check on the back and give it to Steve. This blank indorsement is technically sufficient for Steve to cash the check. However, in practice, for fraud prevention, banks may be less willing to accept a check from Steve that is not made payable to him. A special indorsement such as "Pay to the order of Steve" will prevent anyone else from cashing the check and raise fewer questions about fraud.)

ASSESS

Quiz

Ask students to answer the following questions:

1. What kind of indorsement includes "pay to the order of…"? (special)

2. What kind of indorsement consists of the signature alone on the instrument? (blank)

3. What is the person who promises to pay money in a note called? (maker)

RETEACH

STUDY TO GO Have students go to the *Business and Personal Law* Online Learning Center through glencoe.com to download free Study-to-Go content to their cell phones or PDAs.

Guided Practice

Negotiation

Have students review the information on the negotiation of order paper and the negotiation of bearer paper, and complete the following activities.

Describe Write two sentences that explain the difference between order paper and bearer paper. **L1**

Illustrate Make a sample check that reflects either negotiated order paper or negotiated bearer paper. **L2**

Demonstrate Have students perform a role play in pairs that demonstrates the negotiation of both order paper and bearer paper. **L3**

232

Special Indorsement A special indorsement is an indorsement with the words *pay to* or *pay to the order of*. This is followed by the name of the transferee and signed by the indorser. It is also called an indorsement in full. When indorsed this way, the instrument remains an order instrument and must be indorsed by the indorsee before negotiating it further.

Restrictive Indorsement A restrictive indorsement is an indorsement in which words have been added that limit the use of an instrument. Before it can be further transferred, an instrument must be used as stated in the indorsement. For example, when a check is indorsed "for deposit only," that amount of money must be added to the indorser's bank account before it can be negotiated further. Retail stores often stamp checks "for deposit only" when they are received. This provides protection in the event the checks are stolen.

Qualified Indorsement A qualified indorsement is an indorsement that limits the liability of the indorser. The words *without recourse,* for example, mean the indorser is not liable if the maker or drawer does not pay.

Holder in Due Course

A holder in due course is a holder who takes an instrument for value, in good faith, and without notice that the instrument is defective. To be a holder in due course, you must first be a holder. You must also give value for an instrument, which means you give the consideration that was agreed upon, such as payment of a debt. You must take the instrument in good faith, which means to do it fairly and honestly. You must also be unaware of anything wrong with the instrument, such as a claim to the instrument by someone else, evidence of alteration or forgery, or the instrument being overdue.

Defenses to Negotiable Instruments Holders in due course take instruments free from all claims to them by anyone. They also take instruments free from all personal defenses of anyone with whom they have not dealt. They are only subject to real defenses.

Personal, or limited, defenses are defenses that can be used against a holder, but not a holder in due course. The most common personal defenses are breach of contract, lack of consideration, fraud in the inducement, lack of delivery, and payment.

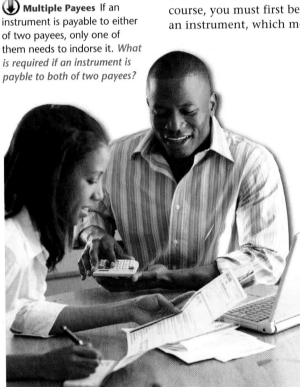

Multiple Payees If an instrument is payable to either of two payees, only one of them needs to indorse it. *What is required if an instrument is payble to both of two payees?*

232   Unit 4   Your Money and the Law

▲ USING VISUALS

➡ Multiple Payees **Answer** If an instrument is payable to two or more payees, all payees must indorse it.

Activity Regulation CC has issued check indorsement standards that specify where the indorsement must be placed on the check. Ask students to research Regulation CC and look up the standard stating where on the check the indorsement would be placed. Have students draw a check and mark the indorsement area. (the first one-and-one-half inches from the trailing edge of the back of the check directly behind "pay to the order of").

Real, or universal, defenses are defenses that can be used against everyone, even holders in due course. No one is required to pay an instrument when there is a real defense. Real defenses include mental incompetence, illegality, duress, bankruptcy, unauthorized signature, and alteration.

Liability

No person is liable on an instrument unless that person's signature appears on it. A signature can be written by an authorized agent. Parties to negotiable instruments have different liability.

The following (formerly known as primary parties) are absolutely liable to pay:

- the maker of a note
- the issuer of a cashier's check or other draft in which the drawer and drawee are the same person
- the acceptor of a draft

When there are two or more makers on a note, all have absolute liability. Very often, one of the comakers is the person who borrowed the money. The other serves as a surety—a person who promises to pay another's debt whether or not the other defaults.

Discharge of Negotiable Instruments

Obligations of parties to pay negotiable instruments are discharged by payment, by agreement, by the debtor becoming the holder after maturity, and by the intentional cancellation of the instrument by the holder. Indorsers are discharged when anyone entitled to enforcement extends the due date, or agrees to modify the instrument.

After You Read

Summarize How can you transfer negotiable instruments?

SECTION 10.1 ASSESSMENT

Self Check

1. What is the difference between a note and a draft?

2. What qualifies as a signature on a note or draft?

3. What is an indorsement?

Academic Connection

Social Studies The use of metal for money can be traced back over 4,000 years. The first coins were made of electrum, a natural mixture of silver and gold. They were crude lumps of metal bearing a primitive mark that certified its weight or fineness. Beads, shells, and even leather were also used to create money. Go on the Internet or to the library to look up what other cultures have used as a form of money or currency and make a short list of them.

English Language Arts Get together in teams with other students in your class.

Using props, drawings, or other visual means of communication, describe what each of the key terms in this section refer to and how they relate to each other.

Critical Thinking

Negotiable Instruments Why do you think a person who writes a negotiable instrument in pencil would be responsible for any loss due to negligence?

Go to **glencoe.com** to check your answers.

SECTION 10.1 ASSESSMENT

Self Check

1. A note is a promise to pay money; a draft is an order to a third party to pay money.

2. A signature may be any mark placed on the instrument with the intent to be a signature. The signature on a check, however, should match the signature card on file with the bank.

3. An indorsement is the act of placing one's signature on an instrument, usually on the back, to transfer it to another.

Academic Connection

Social Studies

Answers will vary. Examples include cattle or livestock in Africa, whale teeth in Fiji.

Language Arts

Presentations will vary.

Critical Thinking

A check written with a pencil could be easily forged or altered.

Activities correlated to the academic standards on page 226

233

10.1 SECTION

RETEACH (cont.)

After You Read

Summarize by assignment or by negotiation

ASSESS

Self-Assessment

Have students go to the *Business and Personal Law* Online Learning Center through **glencoe.com** to take the Section 10.1 Practice Test.

CLOSE

Culminating Activity

Negotiable Instruments

Ask students to match each situation listed with a note, a CD, or a draft.

1. Marg gave Merchants Bank $1,500 to be held for two years at a 5 percent interest rate. (CD)

2. Jill borrowed $3,000 to be repaid in six months with no interest. (note)

3. Alan directed his bank to pay MT Salons $300. (draft)

FOCUS

Bell Ringer Activity

Write a fictitious signature on the board. Ask students to attempt to forge that signature on a sheet of paper. Explain that forgery is a crime subject to a fine and imprisonment.

Preteaching

Key Terms

Read the definitions and ask students to create a sentence using each term.

Academic Vocabulary

Explain that developing vocabulary is key to academic success. An efficient method to develop vocabulary is to study how words are formed.

- **schedule** Noun, from the Latin *scida* (a papyrus strip). Means printed timetable.
- **reconcile** Verb, from the Latin *reconciliare*, *re-* (again) + *conciliare* (to make friendly). Means to bring together again.
- **substitute** Noun, from the Latin *substituere*, *sub* (in place of) + *statuere* (to cause to stand). Means one that takes the place of another.

Activity Ask students to give a noun, a verb, an adjective, or an adverb form that comes from each word.

 Connects to academic content

234

What You'll Learn

- ◆ Explain the contractual relationship between a bank and its customers.
- ◆ Distinguish stop-payment orders, forgeries, and material alterations.
- ◆ Differentiate between types of checks.
- ◆ Define electronic fund transfer.

Why It's Important

You need to know what your legal rights and duties are when you open a checking account.

Academic Standards

Reading and completing the activities in this section will help you practice the following academic standards:

Math (NCTM NOS 2) Understand meanings of operations and how they relate to one another.

Social Studies (NCSS 5) Study interactions among individuals, groups, and institutions.

Reading Guide

 Before You Read

Connect Take a note card or cut out a piece of paper and sign your name on it. Now give it to the teacher. You have just created a signature card.

Focus on Ideas

Checks are the most common type of negotiable instrument.

Take Notes

Create a graph like the one shown and use it to take notes as you read this section. Go to **glencoe.com** to find graphic organizers and tips on how to improve your note-taking skills.

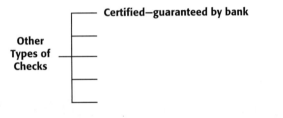

Other Types of Checks — Certified—guaranteed by bank

 Key Terms

You will learn these legal words and expressions in this chapter. You can also find these terms in *Black's Law Dictionary* or in an online legal dictionary.

- forgery
- electronic fund transfer (EFT)

Academic Vocabulary

You will find these words in your readings and in your tests. Look them up in a dictionary and familiarize yourself with them.

- schedule
- reconcile
- substitute

R Reading Strategy

Read for Knowledge

1. **Survey** or preread the chapter.
2. **Question** or formulate questions before you read.
3. **Recite** or read your questions, answers, and notes out loud.
4. **Review** or reread your notes.

Note-Taking Basics

- Listen attentively
- Have note-taking materials ready
- Skim through the lesson material
- Write down key words and ideas
- Anticipate what comes next
- Review notes soon after taking them

Checking Accounts

How does a checking account work?

The check is the most common type of negotiable instrument. The parties to a check are the same as the parties to a draft. The person who writes the check is the drawer. The bank that is ordered to pay the money is the drawee. The one to whom the check is payable is the payee.

To open a checking account, you deposit money in a bank and sign a signature card. A signature card is a record of your signature the banks uses to verify your identity.

A checking account creates a contractual relationship between a bank and a customer. When you write a check, you order your bank to pay someone money from your checking account. The bank agrees to pay money out, up to the amount you have deposited when you write a check. People to whom you write checks can cash them or deposit them in their own bank. Their bank then collects the money from your bank, which takes it out of your account. If your bank refuses to cash your check when sufficient funds are on deposit, it would be a breach of the bank's contract.

A bank may refuse to pay a stale check, which is a check that is more than six months old. A bank may also refuse to pay a check if it is submitted ten days after the death of the drawer.

As You Read

Predict Is it a crime if you write a check and do not have enough money in your checking account to cover it?

CYBERLAW

Hospicomm, Inc. v. Fleet Bank, N.A.
338 F.Supp.2d 578 (E.D. Penn. 2004)

Hospicomm, Inc. provides data processing and other management services to health care providers. In 2002, Hospicomm began to provide services to Hamilton Continuing Care Center. On Hamilton's behalf, Hospicomm opened several bank accounts with Fleet Bank. Access to those bank accounts was limited to those persons who were authorized signatories on the account. In 2003, Hospicomm ended the employment of Guillermo Martinez. It was discovered that Mr. Martinez, without authorization, had obtained an ATM card for the Fleet Bank accounts over the Internet and had withdrawn $148,000 from the accounts. Hospicomm sued Fleet Bank for negligence in giving Mr. Martinez an unauthorized ATM card and allowing the unauthorized ATM withdrawals.

Ruling and Resolution
The Federal District Court held that Hospicomm could not sue Fleet for negligence since the relationship between Hospicomm and Fleet was based in contract. Further, the Court held that the UCC does not apply because ATM transactions are not considered banking deposits or collections.

Critical Thinking Should the UCC be updated to cover electronic transactions such as ATM usage?

CYBERLAW

Hospicomm, Inc. v. Fleet Bank, N.A.
Answer Students' opinions will vary. Rather than update the UCC, it appears that Congress and other legislative bodies have chosen to enact separate laws. For example, the Electronic Fund Transfer Act was passed by Congress to provide some rights and liability distinctions to ATM and other electronic transactions. As the banking world moves toward a paperless system, government will most definitely need to update banking laws that have been in effect since before computers were invented.

TEACH

Discussion Starter

Class Discussion

Checking Accounts Ask how many students have checking accounts by a show of hands. Have volunteers explain the process of opening the account. Ask them to list the types of decisions they had to make when they opened the account. (type of checking account, type of checks, services such as online banking, paper or electronic statements) Remind them that a check is the most common type of negotiable instrument.

As You Read

Predict Tell students to state an opinion on this question and offer a reason for their answer. Refer back to students' answers when the section is finished. (It is a crime to deliberately write a bad check.)

Extending the Content

Federal Reserve
Have students research the Federal Reserve System, which is the central banking system of the United States. Ask students to describe the role of the Federal Reserve as it relates to banking institutions and the applicable rules established by the Federal Reserve on bank accounts.

TEACH (cont.)

Critical Thinking

Availability of Funds Tell students that Cheryl made a deposit of $1,000 into her account on Monday in Arizona. The check was from her grandmother in Florida. Ask students whether they think the funds will be available immediately for Cheryl. (Maybe not. Depending on how new Cheryl's account is and her bank's specific availability of funds policy, the bank may place a hold on the check since it is from another state.) Tell students that banks have set schedules under which they make funds available after checks are deposited.

Extending the Content

Check 21 Act

Ask students to research how the Check 21 Act has impacted banks and their customers. Tell students to use the Internet and use the search term "Check 21 Act." (Answers will vary, but students should understand that the Act allows for faster processing of checks. Items listed on a checking account statement may look different from one another. Fees may be charged if a customer wants cancelled checks returned. The banking industry now operates under a more efficient and less costly check-processing system.)

236

 Legal Talk

Forge: *v* To imitate falsely with intent to defraud. From Latin *fabrica* = workshop.

Certified: *adj* Officially endorsed or attested to. From Latin *certus* = certain + *facere* = to do: to make certain.

Vocabulary Builder The Latin root *facere* means to do, to make, or to form. List and define three words that have *facere* as a root.

Look it up! Check definitions in *Black's Law Dictionary* or an online glossary. For direct links, go to **glencoe.com** to find more vocabulary resources.

Vocabulary You can find vocabulary definitions in the **Key Terms** glossary and the **Academic Vocabulary** glossary in the back of this book.

Reading Check

Interpret Why do you think a bad check is also called a bounced or rubber check?

Availability of Funds

Under federal law, banks must make funds available to you according to a set **schedule**. Exceptions are made for new accounts, accounts that are often overdrawn, and suspicious deposits. Some state laws require even shorter time periods for banks to make funds available.

Balancing Your Checkbook

Whenever you write a check, you should record it in your check register, a checkbook log of all your checking transactions. Every month you should receive a statement of the bank's record of all your transactions, called a bank statement. You should balance—or **reconcile**—your bank statement soon after receiving it. Carefully compare the check register balance with the bank statement balance to be sure they agree. Do not forget to account for outstanding checks. Outstanding checks are checks you have written that have not yet been returned to the bank for payment.

The Check 21 Act

Physically moving paper checks throughout the country can take time and increase the possibility of checks getting lost or mishandled. Congress enacted the Check 21 Act (named after the 21st Century) which allows electronic processing to clear checks quickly and safely. An instrument called a **substitute** check is used. A substitute check is a paper copy of both sides of an original check. Check 21 also allows for an electronic signature to replace an original signature on the substitute check. It is processed just like the original check. Bank customers no longer have the right to have their original canceled checks returned to them.

Writing Checks

You should take care to write checks so they cannot be changed easily. You are responsible for altered checks only if your negligence contributed to the alteration. Sign your name in ink. Sign it the same way it appears on the bank signature card, such as with a middle initial. Never sign a blank check. Never cross out or change a check once it has been written. If you make a mistake when writing a check, shred it and write a new one.

Stopping Payment of a Check

Sometimes you want to cancel a check you have already written but has not yet been paid. You can put a stop on the check by requesting a stop-payment order from your bank. An oral stop-payment order is binding on the bank for 14 calendar days, unless the order is confirmed in writing within that period. A written stop-payment order is effective for six months, unless it is renewed in writing. If the bank pays the check anyway, it is liable for any loss you suffer as a result. If you stop payment on a check given in payment of an amount actually owed, you still owe the amount of the debt.

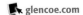 glencoe.com

---

Reading Check

Interpret When the bank rejects the check due to insufficient funds, it bounces back to the drawer as if it were made of rubber.

Legal Talk

(quantify, gratify, affect)

Ask students to practice their academic and legal vocabulary with the electronic flashcards available at the *Business and Personal Law* Online Learning Center through **glencoe.com**.

Bad Checks

A bad check, also called a bounced check or rubber check, is a check you draw on an account in which you do not have enough funds. Unless it is accidental, writing a check on an account with insufficient funds is a crime.

Forgeries and Material Alterations

Suppose a large amount of money disappears from your checking account. You discover someone has stolen one of your checks and faked your signature on it or changed the amount on a check you wrote to a much larger amount. This is called forgery. **Forgery is the fraudulent making or material alteration of a writing.** A forged check is one that is signed by someone other than the drawer without authority. A material alteration occurs when someone changes a check you wrote, such as adding an extra "0" to the amount. Forgery is a crime subject to a fine and imprisonment. It is the bank's duty to know the signatures of its depositors.

Global Law

Banking in Switzerland

Since 1685, Swiss banks have provided services to their clients that range from ordinary checking accounts to large numbered accounts. Swiss banks also provide services such as offering stocks and bonds for sale.

Secrecy

One of the most famous aspects of Swiss banks is their attention to secrecy.

As in most countries around the world, banks are prohibited from giving out any information about their clients. Swiss banking law was amended in 1934, one year after Adolph Hitler became Chancellor of Germany, to create criminal penalties for any bank employee who divulges information about a client's account.

The penalties include six months in jail and/or a fine of 50,000 Swiss Francs (approximately $39,000). There are only four reasons why a bank may give secret information about a client to another party:

1 a criminal investigation (national or international)

2 an investigation by financial market authorities

3 bankruptcy proceedings

4 some civil proceedings (such as inheritance and divorce cases)

Secret numbered accounts enjoy the same protections as named accounts. The main distinction is that only a few select people in the bank know the names associated with the accounts. In other words, there are really no anonymous bank accounts in Switzerland. Someone always knows who owns the money.

Across Cultures: Lingua Franca

Switzerland has four official languages: French, German, Italian, and the native language of Romansh. However, the language used to conduct business internationally, or the lingua franca, is English.

Critical Thinking *Why do you think Switzerland passed such strict banking laws when it did?*

TEACH (cont.)

Extending the Content

Bad Checks

Ask for volunteers to survey local businesses to find out if they charge a penalty fee for a bad check, and if so, the amount of the fee. Have them inquire how the business asks the customer to take care of the bad check. Have students report their findings to the class. (Answers will vary. Businesses may charge fees ranging from $15 to $25 and may ask customers to return to the business to cover their bad check with cash.)

Case Study Practice

Material Alterations
Tell students that Patricia wrote a check to her dry cleaner for $35.50. When the check is paid, the bank pays $85.50. The "3" had been changed to an "8." Ask students whether this is considered a crime. (yes) Ask students to describe what they think will happen in this case. (Since Patricia was not negligent, the bank must bear the loss. The bank could seek repayment from the dry cleaner.)

Global Law

Banking in Switzerland

Answer By 1934 the Nazi government had already begun confiscating the property of Jews, and many German Jews held bank accounts with Swiss banks. The strict banking laws were created to protect the accounts of German Jews and to prevent bank employees from cooperating with Nazi officials. Tell students that the Right to Financial Privacy Act governs how the financial records of consumers are protected. It provides customers the right to expect that their financial activities will have a reasonable amount of privacy from federal government scrutiny.

Electronic Banking With electronic banking, you can withdraw or deposit money, or check your account balance 24 hours a day. *Can a debit card be used the same as a credit card?*

If a bank pays a forged check and the drawer was not negligent, the bank must bear the loss. The bank must also bear the loss if a check is changed from its original amount to a higher amount.

Knowingly giving a forged instrument to someone else is a criminal offense called uttering. You are guilty of this crime even if you did not personally commit the act of forgery. If one of your checks is forged, you must notify your bank within a reasonable time. Otherwise, the bank is relieved of liability.

Other Types of Checks

If you do not have a regular checking account or need to use a check for a special purpose, such as a gift or to write checks in a foreign country, you can purchase other types of checks from banks and other financial institutions. These other types of checks include:

- certified checks, which are checks guaranteed by a bank
- cashier's checks, which are checks drawn by a bank upon itself
- bank drafts, which are drawn by a bank against funds the bank has on deposit with another bank
- money orders, which are drafts that substitute for checks and may be purchased from places such as banks and post offices
- traveler's checks, which are like cashier's checks in that the financial institution that issues them is both the drawer and the drawee

Electronic Banking

Can you pay for things using your checking account without writing a check?

Computer technology and the Internet have greatly reduced the need to use paper and increased the speed of banking transactions. **Electronic fund transfer (EFT) is a computerized system for transferring funds electronically rather than by writing check.** With electronic banking, or e-banking, you can access your bank account on a computer or by using a debit card. A debit card, also called an ATM card or a check card, is a bank card that takes money from your own bank account, as if writing a check.

238   Unit 4   Your Money and the Law

EFT is safe, secure, and less expensive than paper check payments. When you purchase a product online using EFT, you can pay for it by having money transferred from your checking account to the checking account of the seller. You can also use EFT to pay routine bills online.

To regulate this means of banking, the federal government enacted the Electronic Fund Transfer Act (EFTA). Under the EFTA you can:

- purchase merchandise at a store with your debit card
- withdraw money from your bank at an automated teller machine (ATM) 24 hours a day
- authorize your employer to deposit your earnings directly into your bank account
- authorize direct withdrawals from your account to pay bills automatically
- make payments from your bank by telephone
- use your computer to view your account balances and pay bills electronically
- have your paper check changed to an e-check (electronic check) so that it can be processed instantly

If your debit card is lost or stolen, you must notify the bank within two business days after learning that the card is missing. You will then lose no more than $50 if someone else uses your card. If you do not notify the bank within two business days and your card is used, you can lose as much as $500, or even more if 60 days have passed.

After You Read

Summarize Who are the different parties to a check?

ASSESS

Self-Assessment

Have students go to the *Business and Personal Law* Online Learning Center through glencoe.com to take the Section 10.2 Practice Test.

CLOSE

Culminating Activity

Checks

Tell students that Julian wrote a $50 check payable to Chris, but she lost the check before she could cash it. Ask students what Julian should consider before he writes another check. (He should place a stop-payment on the check. He might ask Chris to pay the fee that he will be charged for placing a stop-payment order.)

SECTION 10.2 ASSESSMENT

Self Check

1. How do you open a checking account?

2. Summarize the process of balancing your checkbook.

3. What should you take care to do when writing a check?

Academic Connection

Mathematics Aisha Brewer's checking account has a balance of $523.45. She has a check for $435.62 and a check for $65.98. She would like to receive $40 in cash and deposit the rest of the money in her checking account. What is Aisha's total deposit and what will her new checking account balance be?

THEORY **Number and Operations:** To calculate the amount of the deposit, first add the total amount of the items to be deposited and then subtract the amount of cash to be received. Next, to obtain the new checking account balance, take the current balance and add the amount of the net deposit.

For more math practice, go to the Math Appendix.

Critical Thinking

Stop-payment Order Why might you want to stop payment on a check?

Go to **glencoe.com** to check your answers.

Self Check

1. Deposit money in the bank and sign a signature card.

2. Compare the check register balance with the bank statement balance to make sure they agree.

3. Sign your name in ink the way it appears on the signature card. Never sign a blank check or change a check.

Academic Connection

Mathematics
Deposit: $461.60;
Account balance: $985.05

Critical Thinking

Check seems to be lost in the mail or the check has been stolen.

 Activity correlated to Mathematics standards on page 234

Summary by Sections

Ask students to read the summaries one key point at a time. Then, ask them to work in groups to create two examples to illustrate each key point.

Vocabulary Builder

Cooperative Learning

1. Have students work in groups to prepare their sentences. Ask the groups to exchange their sentences and assess each other's sentences.

Vocabulary Development

- Ask students to use a dictionary or to go online to look up the etymology of each key term listed.
- Then, ask students to list several words derived from the same root or origin. For example, *contract* has the same root as *contractual* or *contractually*.

Summary

Section 10.1 Using Negotiable Instruments

- There are two basic kinds of negotiable instruments—notes and drafts. A note is a promise to pay money. A draft is an order to a third party to pay money.
- To be negotiable, an instrument must be in writing, signed by the maker or drawer, and contain an unconditional promise or order to pay.
- An instrument must be made out for a fixed amount of money, payable on demand or at a definite time.
- The four types of indorsements are blank indorsements, special indorsements, restrictive indorsements, and qualified indorsements.
- A holder in due course must take an instrument for value, in good faith, and without notice that the instrument is defective.

Section 10.2 Banking Basics

- The check is the most common type of negotiable instrument. The parties to a check are the same as the parties to a draft.
- When you write a check, you order your bank to pay someone money from your checking account. If your bank refuses to cash your check when sufficient funds are on deposit, it would be a breach of the bank's contract.
- You can put a stop on the check by requesting a stop-order payment from your bank.
- A forged check is one that is signed by someone other than the drawer without authority. A material alteration occurs when someone changes a check you wrote.
- Electronic fund transfer (EFT) is a computerized system for transferring funds electronically rather than by writing check.

Vocabulary Builder

❶ **On a sheet of paper, use each of these terms in a sentence.**

Key Terms

- negotiable instrument
- note
- maker
- payee
- draft
- drawer
- drawee
- negotiation
- holder
- assignment
- indorsement
- holder in due course
- forgery
- electronic fund transfer (EFT)

Academic Vocabulary

- advantage
- signature
- unconditional
- schedule
- reconcile
- substitute

> Go to **glencoe.com** to play a game and improve your legal vocabulary.

Study Skills for Success

Prepare Your Students for Studying

Tell students that they can improve their ability to understand and remember material from their courses by learning and practicing study skills. Remind students to:

- **Get motivated!** Motivation must come from within. To motivate yourself, think of ways in which what you learn now will fit into your long-term personal and professional goals.
- **Get organized!** Make studying part of your daily routine, not something you do at the last minute.
- **Concentrate!** Study in an environment that is as free of distractions as possible.

10 Chapter

Review and Assessment

Key Points Review

Answer the following questions. Refer to the chapter for additional reinforcement.

2 What are the different types of negotiable instruments?

3 Who are the parties to each kind of negotiable instrument?

4 What are the elements of negotiable instruments?

5 What are the different types of indorsements?

6 What are the requirements to be a holder in due course?

7 What is a stop-payment order, and what are the different types?

8 What are the legal responsibilities for forgeries and material alterations?

9 What are electronic fund transfers?

Standardized Test Practice

10 Read the following excerpt from the Uniform Commercial Code (UCC) and complete problems 1 and 2.

§ 3-104. NEGOTIABLE INSTRUMENT.

(e) An instrument is a "note" if it is a promise and is a "draft" if it is an order. If an instrument could be a note or a draft, a person may treat it as either.

(f) "Check" means (i) a draft, other than a documentary draft, payable on demand and drawn on a bank or (ii) a cashier's check or teller's check.

(g) "Cashier's check" means a draft with respect to which the drawer and drawee are the same bank or branches of the same bank.

(h) "Teller's check" means a draft drawn by a bank (i) on another bank, or (ii) payable at or through a bank.

(i) "Traveler's check" means an instrument that (i) is payable on demand, (ii) is drawn on or payable at or through a bank, (iii) is designated by the term "traveler's check" or by a substantially similar term, and (iv) requires, as a condition to payment, a countersignature by a person whose specimen signature appears on the instrument.

1. If an instrument could be a note or a draft

A it must be treated as a note

B it must be treated as a draft

C it may be treated as either

D it must be treated as neither

2. Which of the following is *not* true about a traveler's check?

A It is payable on demand.

B It is drawn on or payable at or through a bank.

C It is a type of draft.

D It is a type of note.

Test-Taking Strategies Before a test or exam, break study sessions into manageable time segments and meaningful units.

Key Points Review

2. notes, including CDs, stocks, and bonds; drafts, including checks and bills of sale

3. note: maker, payee; draft: drawer, drawee, payee

4. in writing; signed by the maker or drawer; contain unconditional promise to pay; fixed amount of money; payable on demand or at a definite time; payable to order or to bearer

5. blank, special, restrictive, qualified

6. be a holder, give value, take an instrument in good faith, and take an instrument without notice

7. a request to stop payment on a check; may be oral or written

8. If bank pays a forged check and the drawer was not negligent, the bank must bear the loss. The drawer is responsible only if the drawer's negligence contributed to the alteration or forgery. If the drawer knows a check is forged, he or she must notify the bank within a reasonable amount of time or the bank will be relieved of liability.

9. transferring funds electronically without the presence of a physical negotiable instrument

Standardized Test Practice

10. C and D

Strategies for Standardized Test Prep Success

Whether your students have a standardized test coming up in a few days or a few weeks, these last-minute test-prep tips and strategies will help them relax and do their best.

- **Test Format** Help students become familiar with the format of the test by practicing with test items that imitate the actual test items as closely as possible.

- **Test Timing** Have your students take timed practice tests so that they become comfortable with the length, design, and timing of the actual test.

Students should use chapter content to arrive at conclusions. The legal resolutions are listed below:

11. Alan is correct. The ink color on a check does not matter.

12. Yes. Smita's bank can be required to credit her account for the erroneously deducted $900. When there is a dispute as to the amount of a check, it is the written amount, not the numerical amount, that controls.

13. Maybe. The bank may be responsible for not checking the date. In practice, most banks have contracts with customers that give them permission to process checks automatically regardless of the date.

14. Yes. Macy has given her mechanic a written instrument that is signed, dated, and contains an order to pay a fixed amount of money. However, in real practice, it is doubtful that Macy's bank would pay on this document.

15. No. Robin is not liable. If a forgery occurs through no fault of the customer, the bank must suffer the loss for having paid on checks that were forged.

242

Read the following scenarios. Get together with other students in pairs or groups of three and take a position on each scenario. Debate your position in class with students taking the opposite position or prepare a written argument justifying your position.

⑪ Checks

Alan filled out a check in red ink to pay for a new suit. The cashier said the bank would not cash the check and refused to accept it. Alan disagreed.

You Debate   *Who is correct, Alan or the cashier?*

⑫ Check Dispute

Smita paid $100 for textbooks at the college bookstore by check. She incorrectly wrote the number $1,000.00 on the check rather than $100.00. She correctly wrote the words "one hundred and no cents." When Smita received her bank statement, she saw the check had been cashed for $1,000 and not $100. She notified the bookstore of the error, but the bookstore refused to refund the $900 over-payment.

You Debate   *Can Smita require the bank to credit her account for $900?*

⑬ Overdrawn

Harriet post-dated a check to Xander and asked him not to cash it until Friday. That same day Xander took the check to the bank, which cashed it. When Harriet looked at her account balance a couple days later, she discovered she was overdrawn.

You Debate   *Is the bank responsible for not checking the date, and should it have refused the check?*

⑭ Negotiability

Macy took her car in for repairs. When she arrived at the garage to pick it up, she realized she did not have her checkbook. Macy drew a picture of a check made out to the mechanic with the name of her bank, account number, date, and signature for payment.

You Debate   *Is Macy's drawing of a check a negotiable instrument?*

⑮ Forged Checks

Robin hired a cleaning company to shampoo her carpets. A couple days later, she discovered some of her checks were missing. When she notified the bank, she learned that several checks had been forged and cashed.

You Debate   *Is Robin liable for the amount of the money taken from her account?*

242   Unit 4   Your Money and the Law

C Critical Thinking

Negotiable or Not? Kyle works at Audio Globe. He accepted a check from a customer for $52.33 payable to Audio Globe. Later, Kyle noticed that the figures and words for the amount of the check did not match. Also, the check was written in pencil.

Debate Practice

- Is the check negotiable? Why or why not? (Yes, the check is legally negotiable. However, in practice, the bank probably would not honor a check written in pencil, especially if the figures and words do not correspond, because it can easily be forged and/or fraudulent.)

- What should Kyle do now? (Students may suggest that Kyle should ask the customer for a replacement check that is properly written.)

Case Study Practice – Leavings v. Mills

16 What Is a Negotiable Instrument? In 1984, John and Evelyn Leavings contracted with Solar Marketing to have a heating system installed in their home. The Leavings signed a note with Solar Marketing to make 120 monthly payments in the amount of $146.82 each. Solar Marketing then placed a lien on the Leavings's property.

Solar Marketing assigned the note and lien to Briercroft Service Corporation (BSC). BSC, in turn, assigned the note and lien to Briercroft Savings Association (BSA). After numerous problems with the system, the Leavings stopped making payments. BSC sent a letter in 1989 advising the Leavings that their note was in default. The Leavings's attorney responded to BSC. BSC did not pursue demands for payment any further.

In 1997, after Mr. Leavings had died, Mrs. Leavings received a letter from a Mr. James Mills. The letter stated that Mrs. Leavings's installment contract had fully matured and she must pay $21,196 immediately or Mr. Mills would foreclose on her property. Mrs. Leavings argued that Mr. Mills could not foreclose on the property because the contract was not payable "to bearer" or "to order" and thus was not a negotiable instrument.

Source: Leavings v. Mills, 175 S.W.3d 301 (Tx. Ct. App. 2004)

Practice Is the retail installment contract a negotiable instrument?

17 Ethics ←?→ Application

Who Is Responsible? Deborah goes to the bank to cash her payroll check for $160. At the bank, the teller accidentally gives Deborah $180. Deborah instantly notices the error but puts the money into her wallet and leaves the bank.

◆ Is not telling the bank teller that she gave you too much money the same as stealing?

18 Internet Application

Research CDs Aida's company gave her a $4,000 bonus. She wants to put the money in a safe investment. After looking at several options, she decides to invest the money in a certificate of deposit (CD).

Go to **glencoe.com** to access the Web site sponsored by the Federal Deposit and Insurance Corporation (FDIC) to learn about tips for investing in CDs. Summarize the information into a table to present to your class.

Reading Connection

Outside Reading Go to **glencoe.com** for a list of outside reading suggestions about certificates of deposit and other types of negotiable instruments.

 glencoe.com

Chapter 10 Banking and Negotiable Instruments **243**

←?→ Ethics Application

17. Deborah is not relieved of any legal or ethical responsibility just because it was the teller's mistake and she did not actively take the money but merely remained silent about the error. To not do or say something can be as unethical as saying or doing something unethical. Deborah knew she was not entitled to the money and that it rightfully belonged to the bank.

Internet Application

18. Suggest that students use the search box provided at the FDIC home page. When buying a CD, the investor should find out when it matures and whether it has any call features, confirm the interest rate, research penalties for early withdrawal, and find out how interest will be paid.

R Reading Strategy

Reading Connection

American Bar Association Resources

Go to the *Business and Personal Law* Online Learning Center through glencoe.com to find links for further readings that relate to this chapter. Ask students to read, review, and summarize the documents. Advise students to keep their reviews and summaries to use as reference material for their Unit Thematic Project on pages 282–283.

 Case Study Practice

16. No. The Texas Court of Appeals held that since the retail installment contract did not contain the words "to bearer" or "to order" it was not a negotiable instrument. Mr. Mills could not initiate foreclosure proceedings against the property. Further in its decision, the Court held that Mr. Mills must provide satisfactory evidence and/or testimony that he was the legitimate holder of the note. However, just because Mr. Mills could not initiate foreclosure proceedings did not mean he could not seek payment on the note, if he was, in fact, the legal holder of the note.

Plan Your Lesson Section by Section

NBEA	NATIONAL BUSINESS LAW STANDARDS
Section 11.1	• **Describe** a secured transaction, and explain the requirements for a valid security interest. • **Define** the major types of collateral. • **Explain** the contractual relationship between a bank and its customers.
Section 11.2	• **Describe** the Uniform Commercial Code (UCC). • **Describe** breach of contract and the remedies available when a contract is breached.

NCLB	ACADEMIC STANDARDS	Activity/Feature
English Language Arts: NCTE 3 Apply a wide range of strategies to comprehend, interpret, evaluate, and appreciate texts.		*BusinessWeek* News, Case Study, Case Study Practice
English Language Arts: NCTE 9 Develop an understanding of and respect for diversity in language use, patterns, and dialects across cultures, ethnic groups, geographic regions, and social roles.		Global Law
English Language Arts: NCTE 6 Apply knowledge of language structure, language conventions, media techniques, figurative language, and genre to create, critique, and discuss print and non-print texts.		Legal Talk, ad copy, Key Terms, and Academic Vocabulary
English Language Arts: NCTE 6 Apply knowledge of language structure, language conventions, media techniques, figurative language, and genre to create, critique, and discuss print and non-print texts.		Section 11.1 Assessment
Mathematics: NCTM PSS 3 Apply and adapt a variety of appropriate strategies to solve problems.		Section 11.2 Assessment
English Language Arts: NCTE 10 Students whose first language is not English make use of their first language to develop competency in the English language arts and to develop understanding of content across the curriculum.		Key Terms, Academic Vocabulary, Legal Talk, Vocabulary Builder
English Language Arts: NCTE 1 Read a wide range of print and non-print texts to build an understanding of texts; to acquire new information; to respond to the needs and demands of society and the workplace; and for personal fulfillment.		Global Law, Cyberlaw
Social Studies: NCSS 2 Study the ways human beings view themselves in and over time.		Case Study
Social Studies: NCSS 5 Study interactions among individuals, groups, and institutions.		Global Law

Connect Your Business Law Classroom to the World of Work

This chart shows the 21st Century Skills, foundation skills, and workplace competencies that students develop as they work in this chapter.

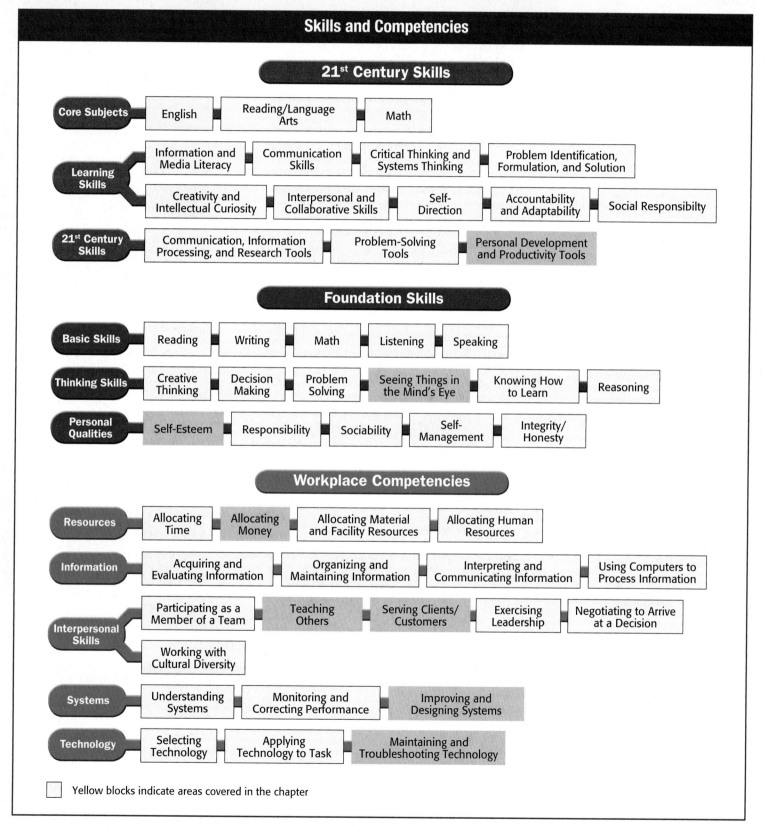

Skills and Competencies

21st Century Skills

Core Subjects
- English
- Reading/Language Arts
- Math

Learning Skills
- Information and Media Literacy
- Communication Skills
- Critical Thinking and Systems Thinking
- Problem Identification, Formulation, and Solution
- Creativity and Intellectual Curiosity
- Interpersonal and Collaborative Skills
- Self-Direction
- Accountability and Adaptability
- Social Responsibilty

21st Century Skills
- Communication, Information Processing, and Research Tools
- Problem-Solving Tools
- Personal Development and Productivity Tools

Foundation Skills

Basic Skills
- Reading
- Writing
- Math
- Listening
- Speaking

Thinking Skills
- Creative Thinking
- Decision Making
- Problem Solving
- Seeing Things in the Mind's Eye
- Knowing How to Learn
- Reasoning

Personal Qualities
- Self-Esteem
- Responsibility
- Sociability
- Self-Management
- Integrity/Honesty

Workplace Competencies

Resources
- Allocating Time
- Allocating Money
- Allocating Material and Facility Resources
- Allocating Human Resources

Information
- Acquiring and Evaluating Information
- Organizing and Maintaining Information
- Interpreting and Communicating Information
- Using Computers to Process Information

Interpersonal Skills
- Participating as a Member of a Team
- Teaching Others
- Serving Clients/Customers
- Exercising Leadership
- Negotiating to Arrive at a Decision
- Working with Cultural Diversity

Systems
- Understanding Systems
- Monitoring and Correcting Performance
- Improving and Designing Systems

Technology
- Selecting Technology
- Applying Technology to Task
- Maintaining and Troubleshooting Technology

Yellow blocks indicate areas covered in the chapter

CHAPTER 11 Credit and Debt

Introduce the Chapter

Credit and Debt
Chapter 11 identifies various forms of credit and discusses borrowing money. It explains the use of credit cards, and how student and car loans operate.

Building Background
Bring a sample of a credit card application to class. Go over the items required on the form with the class. Ask if any students currently use credit cards and, if so, if they have ever had problems with overspending when using them. Explain that the average U.S. household carries approximately $18,700 in credit card and auto loan debt.

BusinessWeek News

Discuss with students how Internet fraud hurts small business. Explain that fraudulent purchases cost a business the price of inventory and shipping charges, and also requires it to repay the true credit card holder's cost for the transaction. Prices are raised to cover these costs.

 R Reading Strategy

 Your Reading

As a class, discuss reading strategies, such as writing an outline, taking notes, and reading heads beforehand. Have students talk about which approach works best for them.

BusinessWeek News

Swiping Back at Credit-Card Fraud
By Robert Berner and Adrienne Carter

Every other week, it seems, another bank, credit-card company, or data-processing outfit announces a security breach of personal financial data. With criminals freely trading card numbers, Social Security numbers, and mothers' maiden names, you might think credit-card fraud was going through the roof.

In the past couple of years, however, bigger e-tailers such as Amazon.com Inc. and eBay Inc. have gotten more aggressive, adding staffers to combat fraud and sophisticated technology to screen for it. In addition, they have shared information on the problem and worked more closely with credit-card associations, banks, and agencies such as the FBI. That has prompted fraudsters to switch to smaller retailers, who can't afford those defenses and who don't work closely together. "So much for the Internet leveling the playing field," says Avivah Litan, an analyst at research firm Gartner Inc.

Flex Your Reading

Efficient critical reading involves being flexible with speed and comprehension. There are several ways of reading critically, and you need to fit a reading style to your needs and to the material.

Go to **glencoe.com** for Flex Your Reading activities, more information about reading strategies for this chapter, and guided practice in reading about credit.

Classroom Resources

- Student Edition
- Teacher Wraparound Edition
- Student Activity Workbook with Academic Integration (SE/TAE)
- TeacherWorks™ Plus! CD
- *ExamView®* Assessment Suite CD
- *Presentation Plus!* CD

- National Mock Trial Championship DVD
- Online Learning Center with Podcasts at glencoe.com
- Study-to-Go™ at glencoe.com
- Online Student Edition
- Interactive Student Edition

Buying on Credit Some purchases are too expensive to pay for in cash and you need to use credit. *What is the maximum percentage of your monthly income that should go to making credit payments, according to financial experts?*

245

Buying on Credit Some purchases are too expensive to pay for in cash and you need to use credit. *What is the maximum percentage of your monthly income that should go to making credit payments, according to financial experts?*

245

11 CHAPTER

Practice the Concept

Credit
Ask students to recall locations at which credit cards are offered to consumers. Examples may include gas stations, department stores, and sporting events. Incentives might include a free tank of gasoline, discounts on initial purchases, free shipping, or team T-shirts. Discuss with students why credit card companies go to such lengths to acquire new customers.

Key Terms Suggest to students that checks, certificates of deposit, and loans are identical in concept to credit cards. Each involves getting something now and paying for it later. Ask students to look for examples of credit being offered in newspaper ads, looking for words such as *interest*, *principal*, and *penalties*. Convey to students that wise consumers understand the details of credit before taking advantage of it.

Legal Basics Tell students that although credit can be costly, it can also be used responsibly. Ask students for their opinions on how credit can be used wisely. After students have finished studying the chapter, have them revisit their opinions.

▲ USING VISUALS

Buying on Credit **Answer** Financial experts perform a debt analysis to compare the difference between your monthly income and the monthly amount you spend to maintain your debt (e.g., minimum payments on credit cards, car payments). This is called a debt-to-income ratio. If you have a low debt-to-income ratio and you apply for credit, you are viewed as a good candidate, with a better capacity to repay your debt. A debt-to-income ratio less than 20 percent is considered "very good." If you manage to spend less than 20 percent of your monthly income on debt, then you are probably able to save part of your income and either increase your savings or use all or part of these savings to repay any outstanding debt.

FOCUS

Bell Ringer Activity

Write this open-ended statement on the board and ask students to complete it and explain their thoughts: Credit is a _____ for consumers. (Answers will vary, but may include "tool" or "trap.")

Preteaching

Key Terms

Read the definitions and ask students to create a sentence using each term.

Academic Vocabulary

Explain that developing vocabulary is key to academic success. An efficient method to develop vocabulary is to study how words are formed.

- **assets** Noun, from the Latin *ad* (to) + *satis* (enough). Means the property that a person owns.
- **acquired** Verb, from the Latin *acquirere* (to seek). Means gained by one's efforts or actions.
- **effective** Adjective, from the Latin *efficere* (to accomplish). Means having an effect or producing a result.

Activity Ask students to give a noun, an adjective, or an adverb form that comes from each word.

N C L B Connects to academic content

What You'll Learn

- ◆ Define the main types of credit.
- ◆ Explain what a secured transaction is.
- ◆ Describe how a security interest is created.
- ◆ Identify the main types of collateral.

Why It's Important

You need to know what your legal obligations are when you borrow money or obtain credit.

Academic Standards

Reading and completing the activities in this section will help you practice the following academic standards:

N C L B

Social Studies (NCSS 2) Study the ways human beings view themselves in and over time.

English Language Arts (NCTE 6) Apply knowledge of language structure, language conventions, media techniques, figurative language, and genre to create, critique, and discuss print and non-print texts.

 Reading Guide

 Before You Read

Connect Have you ever used a credit card or borrowed money to buy something you could not afford?

Focus on Ideas

To borrow money or buy on credit, you need to own something of value.

Take Notes

Create a graph like the one shown and use it to take notes as you read this section. Go to glencoe.com to find graphic organizers and tips on how to improve your note-taking skills.

Key Terms

You will learn these legal words and expressions in this chapter. You can also find these terms in *Black's Law Dictionary* or in an online legal dictionary.

- credit
- creditor
- debtor
- interest
- secured loan
- collateral
- security interest
- default

 Academic Vocabulary

You will find these words in your readings and in your tests. Look them up in a dictionary and familiarize yourself with them.

- assets
- acquired
- effective

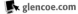 glencoe.com

R

R Reading Strategy

Read for Knowledge

1. **Survey** or preread the chapter.
2. **Question** or formulate questions before you read.
3. **Recite** or read your questions, answers, and notes out loud.
4. **Review** or reread your notes.

Note-Taking Basics

- Listen attentively
- Have note-taking materials ready
- Skim through the lesson material
- Write down key words and ideas
- Anticipate what comes next
- Review notes soon after taking them

Credit

What is a possible financial solution if you really need to buy something and you do not have enough money?

Credit is an arrangement in which you receive cash, goods, or services now and pay in the future. The creditor is the party who sells the goods on credit or lends the money. The debtor is the party who buys the goods on credit or borrows the money. Interest is a fee creditors charge for lending money or extending credit.

The amount of interest you pay depends on the amount of the loan or purchase, the length of time it takes to pay back the money, and the interest rate. The longer you take to pay off a loan and the larger the amount of the loan, the more you have to pay in interest.

Open-End Credit

Open-end credit is credit that can be increased by the debtor by continuing to purchase goods or services on credit, up to a certain limit. You are given a line of credit—a maximum amount of money available to you. Credit cards issued by a bank, such as Visa and MasterCard, and charge cards for a particular store, such as Macy's and Target, are examples of open-end credit.

Closed-End Credit

Closed-end credit is credit given for a specific amount of money, which cannot be increased by making additional purchases. Buying a vehicle, a house, a refrigerator, or a couch for a fixed amount and paying for it in monthly installments is an example of closed-end credit.

Business ETHICS

Necessary Guarantors and Sureties

You are the owner of a local major appliance store that sits on the border of two states. As normal practice, you allow your customers to buy items on credit, while retaining a security interest in the appliance. However, through your personal experience, you feel that residents from your neighboring state are more likely to default on their loans than the residents in your own state. After talking to fellow business owners, you discover that one option would be to require buyers from the neighboring state to have a guarantor or a surety when they sign a credit agreement with you.

> *Critical Thinking: Should you require buyers from a neighboring state to have a guarantor or surety?*

As You Read

Predict What can happen if you are unable to repay a loan?

TEACH

Discussion Starter

Class Discussion

Tell students to imagine that a friend would like to borrow money from them. Ask them what questions they might ask before they agreed to loan the money. (How much money is needed? When will it be repaid? Is the friend trusted to repay the money? What will happen if the money is not repaid?)

As You Read

Predict Explain that failure to repay a loan is a serious matter. Have students consider what might happen if the loan was secured by property. (Loans secured by property, as collateral, allow the lender to repossess the property.)

Guided Practice

Types of Credit

Explain that if a lender grants a flexible amount of money, up to a certain limit, this is known as open-end credit. If credit is given for a specific amount of money, it is called closed-end credit. Ask students to give examples of both. (open-ended: credit card; closed-end: loan)

Necessary Guarantors and Sureties *Answer* Answers will vary. It is doubtful that it would be illegal for you to require a guarantor or a surety for the out-of-state buyers. However, there is a public opinion issue at play here. You could be labeled as a store that is unfriendly to out-of-state buyers and you could lose business. You could also lose business due to the fact that it could be difficult for people to obtain a guarantor or a surety, and they would not be able to take advantage of your credit agreement or make purchases at your store.

TEACH (cont.)

D Develop Concepts

Obtaining Credit When lenders decide whether to issue credit, they look at an applicant's assets. Assets are the personal and real property, tangible and intangible, owned by someone. Ask students to discuss what can be categorized as assets. (Answers will vary but may include savings, investments, and major possessions such as cars, condos, or houses.)

Guided Practice

Are the Credit Rules Fair?

Ask students to debate the fairness of credit. Is it fair for people who have a lot of money to get credit easily while people with less money have difficulty getting it? Divide the class in half, and have each side alternate between defending and criticizing the credit system. Afterward, ask students what steps might be taken to improve the system. (Answers may include education and more services to help people in debt.)

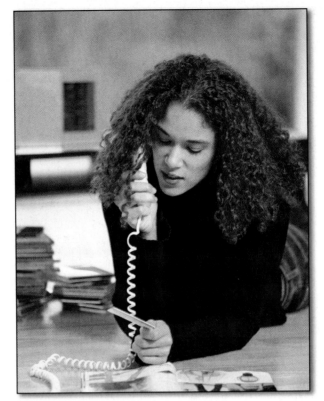

🕐 **Credit Score** Once you start using credit cards, paying bills, and borrowing money, credit reporting agencies collect financial information on you and assign you a credit score. *Why is your credit score important?*

Vocabulary You can find vocabulary definitions in the **Key Terms** glossary and **Academic Vocabulary** glossary in the back of this book.

Obtaining Credit

If you borrow money, how can the creditor be sure the money is not lost?

To obtain credit or a loan, you need to fill out an application from a store, bank, or other financial institution. Lenders will usually check into your credit history, your income, and your **assets**, to determine if you are a good credit risk. Lenders also need security—a way of getting their money back in case the borrower does not pay.

D

Secured Transactions

A secured loan is a loan which is backed up by property that the creditor can take if the loan is not repaid. Collateral is the property that is offered as a security interest. A security interest is a creditor's right to use collateral to recover a debt. Main types of collateral are consumer goods, fixtures, equipment, inventory, and farm products.

A security can be created by the creditor possessing the collateral. It can also be created by the debtor signing a security agreement that identifies the collateral. The lender who holds the security interest is called the secured party.

If a debtor defaults, the secured party may take the collateral and sell it at a public auction or private sale. **Default is failure to make timely payments on a loan.** Different types of collateral have different laws with regard to default. There are more conditions when a debtor defaults on something as major as a home loan than when a debtor defaults on a car loan.

An unsecured loan does not require any collateral. However, because the risk is much greater to the creditor, the interest on an unsecured is usually much higher than on a secured loan. Unsecured loans are usually available only to well-established businesses or customers.

Attachment of Security Interest A security interest is said to attach when it is legally enforceable by the secured party. Attachment occurs when:

- The debtor owns the collateral.
- The secured party transfers something of value, such as money or goods, to the debtor.
- The secured party either takes possession of the collateral or signs a security agreement.

▲ USING VISUALS

➡️ **Credit Score** **Answer** Credit scores impact a person's ability to secure loans, rent apartments, and acquire credit cards. Examples of situations that require good credit include borrowing money to buy a vehicle or a piece of real estate.

Activity Ask students to find advertisements that offer to help individuals with bad credit mend their scores. Have students describe what the process entails.

Security agreements may contain provisions that include future advances of credit. Future advances of credit allow the debtor to get additional credit in the future that is secured by the same collateral, such as a house.

In a transaction for the sale of goods, the security interest attaches to the actual individual goods. In contrast, when the security interest is on inventory, which are all the things you own, the security interest attaches to the inventory as a whole, including new inventory that comes and goes from a business. The inventory is what is called after-acquired property, since the property was **acquired** after the credit agreement was entered into.

Reading Check

Interpret What is secure about a secured loan?

> **Example** Good Health Grocers bought ten cases of a special health food from a wholesaler on credit. The security agreement signed by the grocer contained a clause covering all future goods the grocer bought. In this way, all replacement goods were covered by the original security agreement as the grocer's inventory was continuously sold and restocked.

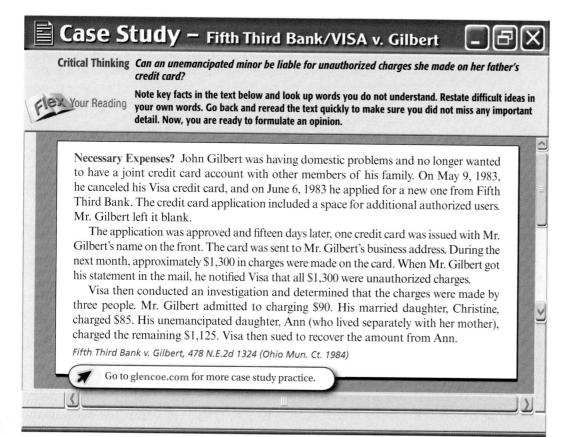

Case Study – Fifth Third Bank/VISA v. Gilbert

Critical Thinking *Can an unemancipated minor be liable for unauthorized charges she made on her father's credit card?*

Flex Your Reading Note key facts in the text below and look up words you do not understand. Restate difficult ideas in your own words. Go back and reread the text quickly to make sure you did not miss any important detail. Now, you are ready to formulate an opinion.

Necessary Expenses? John Gilbert was having domestic problems and no longer wanted to have a joint credit card account with other members of his family. On May 9, 1983, he canceled his Visa credit card, and on June 6, 1983 he applied for a new one from Fifth Third Bank. The credit card application included a space for additional authorized users. Mr. Gilbert left it blank.

The application was approved and fifteen days later, one credit card was issued with Mr. Gilbert's name on the front. The card was sent to Mr. Gilbert's business address. During the next month, approximately $1,300 in charges were made on the card. When Mr. Gilbert got his statement in the mail, he notified Visa that all $1,300 were unauthorized charges.

Visa then conducted an investigation and determined that the charges were made by three people. Mr. Gilbert admitted to charging $90. His married daughter, Christine, charged $85. His unemancipated daughter, Ann (who lived separately with her mother), charged the remaining $1,125. Visa then sued to recover the amount from Ann.

Fifth Third Bank v. Gilbert, 478 N.E.2d 1324 (Ohio Mun. Ct. 1984)

Go to glencoe.com for more case study practice.

Case Study

Fifth Third Bank/VISA v. Gilbert

Answer Yes. The Ohio Municipal Court held that Ann was liable to VISA for the charges. The court rejected the argument that because Ann was a minor she should not be held liable. For that argument to be valid, Ann must have tried to return the merchandise, which she did not. Further, the court held that Mr. Gilbert was not liable for the debt because Ann had not made the purchases out of necessity. The "necessary doctrine" allows a minor to bind his or her parents if the minor is entering into the contract due to necessity.

11.1 SECTION

TEACH (cont.)

 Reading Check

Interpret In a secured loan, *secure* means that if the loan is not repaid, the lender can take the collateral to recover or offset the debt.

ASSESS

Quiz

Ask students to answer "true" or "false" to these questions:

1. Security agreements cannot contain provisions for future advances of credit. (F)
2. A secured interest is a creditor's right to use collateral to recover a debt. (T)

RETEACH

Guided Practice

Collateral

Have students list examples of collateral that can be offered as security interest to secure a loan. (consumer goods, fixtures, equipment, inventory, and real estate)

STUDY TO GO Have students go to the *Business and Personal Law* Online Learning Center through glencoe.com to download free *Study-to-Go* content to their cell phones or PDAs.

RETEACH (cont.)

After You Read

Summarize creditor and debtor

ASSESS

Self-Assessment

Have students go to the *Business and Personal Law* Online Learning Center through **glencoe.com** to take the Section 11.1 Practice Test.

CLOSE

Culminating Activity

Repossession

Ty Carmen has fallen behind on his monthly car payment. One night, his car is repossessed. Is the repossession legal? (Yes. Since Ty is not paying on the loan, the lender has the right to take the car.)

Perfection of Security Interest When a security interest attaches, it is **effective** only between the debtor and creditor. To be effective against the claims of any other creditors, a creditor must perfect the interest. A security interest is perfected when the secured party has done everything that the law requires to give the secured party a greater claim than anyone else has.

A security interest can be perfected in three ways:

- attachment alone for consumer goods bought in a store
- filing a financial statement in a public office for most other items
- possession of the collateral (such as with a pawn shop)

> **Example** When Jane bought a truck, the dealer took a security interest in the vehicle. To protect the dealer's rights in the vehicle, notice of the security interest would be written on the back of Jane's certificate of title to the truck.

Guarantors and Sureties

A loan can be protected by having another party stand behind the loan to guarantee it will be repaid. There are two types of parties who can guarantee a loan: guarantors and sureties. A guarantor, sometimes referred to as a secondary party, agrees to pay off a debt only if the debtor defaults. A surety, sometimes called a primary party, agrees to pay off a debt outright, just as the debtor would have.

There are certain defenses guarantors and sureties can use when called upon to pay back a loan. These include that the debtor has already paid back or released the debt, their own minority, insanity, or bankruptcy.

After You Read

Summarize Who are the various parties to credit?

SECTION 11.1 ASSESSMENT

Self Check

1. Give some examples of open-end credit and closed-end credit.

2. What are the main types of collateral?

3. What are future advances of credit?

Academic Connection

English Language Arts The history of credit and banking goes back at least 4,000 years to ancient Egypt. The Egyptians used a type of banking called the giro system, in which grain was deposited in state-run storehouses and could be used to pay off debts. In medieval Italy, loans and other banking transactions were conducted in large open areas where each merchant would work from a bench, or *banco*, which is where we get the word *bank* from.

Go on the Internet or to a library and look up how these first banks worked and write a brief description of them.

Critical Thinking

Credit and Debit How is a credit card different from a debit card?

 Go to **glencoe.com** to check your answers.

SECTION 11.1 ASSESSMENT

Self Check

1. Open-end credit: credit cards issued by banks or department store charge cards. Closed-end credit: vehicle, house, or furniture loans.

2. consumer goods, fixtures, equipment, inventory, farm products, and real estate

3. They allow debtors to get additional credit that is secured by the same collateral, such as a house.

Academic Connection

English Language Arts
Reports should discuss how the development of banks and money systems allows people to take more specialized jobs in a society.

Critical Thinking

Credit cards allow users to borrow money up to a specific limit to make purchases. Debit cards draw money immediately from the cardholder's bank account.

 Activity correlated to the English Language Arts standard on page 246

Credit and You

Reading Guide

Before You Read

Connect Do you have a department store charge card? If so, you are familiar with having credit.

Focus on Ideas

Credit cards, charge cards, car loans, and student loans are types of credit.

Take Notes

Create a graph like the one shown and use it to take notes as you read this section. Go to glencoe.com to find graphic organizers and tips on how to improve your note-taking skills.

Advantages of Credit	Disadvantages of Credit
Finance Large Purchases	_____
_____	_____
_____	_____
_____	_____
_____	_____

Key Terms

You will learn these legal words and expressions in this chapter. You can also find these terms in *Black's Law Dictionary* or in an online legal dictionary.

- finance charge
- annual percentage rate (APR)

Academic Vocabulary

You will find these words in your readings and in your tests. Look them up in a dictionary and familiarize yourself with them.

- involved
- unauthorized
- subsidized

What You'll Learn

- ◆ Define finance charge and annual percentage rate.
- ◆ Describe the advantages of using a credit card.
- ◆ Determine how to obtain student loans.
- ◆ Recognize the warning signs of debt problems.

Why It's Important

There are things you need to know if you want to finance a car, get a credit card, or take out a student loan.

Academic Standards

Reading and completing the activities in this section will help you practice the following academic standards:

NCLB

Social Studies (NCSS 5) Study interactions among individuals, groups, and institutions.

Math (NCTM PSS 3) Apply and adapt a variety of appropriate strategies to solve problems.

R Reading Strategy

Read for Knowledge

1. **Survey** or preread the chapter.
2. **Question** or formulate questions before you read.
3. **Recite** or read your questions, answers, and notes out loud.
4. **Review** or reread your notes.

Note-Taking Basics

- Listen attentively
- Have note-taking materials ready
- Skim through the lesson material
- Write down key words and ideas
- Anticipate what comes next
- Review notes soon after taking them

11.2 SECTION

FOCUS

Bell Ringer Activity

Bring in car brochures from a local dealership. Pass these around the class. Ask students to estimate the sticker price of each car. Then distribute loan applications to the class. Ask students which items from the application they believe are most important to a lender. (income, job)

Preteaching

Key Terms

Read the definitions and ask students to create a sentence using each term.

Academic Vocabulary

Explain that developing vocabulary is key to academic success. An efficient method to develop vocabulary is to study how words are formed.

- **involved** Verb, from the Latin *volvere* (to roll). Means related or included.
- **unauthorized** Adjective, from the Latin *un-* (not) + *auctor* (author). Means lacking official approval.
- **subsidized** Verb, from the Latin *subsidium* (auxiliary forces). Means supported or aided.

Activity Ask students to give a noun, an adjective, and an adverb form that comes from each word.

NCLB Connects to academic content

TEACH

Discussion Starter

Class Discussion

Ask students to talk about a car they would like to buy. After they discuss topics such as power, handling, and style, steer the conversation toward price and payments. Remind them that if they cannot pay cash, they will have to borrow money and pay interest on the loan.

As You Read

Predict APR is the annual percentage rate, or the true interest rate, of a loan.

D Develop Concepts

Buying a Vehicle Tell students that if they want to buy a car, they must first find out how much they can afford to spend. Ask students how they might determine this. (contrast savings and monthly earnings with living expenses and amount of existing debt)

As You Read
Predict What is an APR?

Financing Your Future

What are some things you might need and that might cause you to borrow a large amount of money?

You will need to use credit to finance many things from short-term goals, such as buying a computer, to long-term goals, such as buying a house (see **Figure 11.1**). To build up credit for long-term goals, you need to set priorities, start with small purchases, and stay within your credit limit and income.

Buying a Vehicle

What can you do if you cannot afford to buy a car with cash?

You will probably buy many automobiles in your life. The law that applies to these purchases comes from several different sources. Because cars are considered goods, the Uniform Commercial Code (UCC) applies to their sale. If you buy a car for personal purposes, both federal and state consumer protection laws apply. In addition, if you finance the car, special laws regulate credit.

If you want to buy a car, you should first find out how much you can afford. This depends on your savings, monthly earnings, living expenses, and the amount of your debt.

Financing a Vehicle

When buying a car, you can save money by paying cash because car loans require you to pay interest. Offering to pay cash also puts you in a better position to negotiate a lower price. If you need to borrow money, you can save by shopping around. Federal law requires lenders to disclose the finance charge and annual percentage rate (APR) to borrowers. **The finance charge is the cost of the loan in dollars and cents. The annual percentage rate (APR) is the true interest rate of the loan.**

Before you sign any documents, you should know the following information:

- the exact price you are paying for the vehicle
- the amount you are financing
- the finance charge
- the APR
- the number and amount of payments
- the total sales price (the sum of the monthly payments plus the down payment)

Dealers sometimes offer very low financing rates for specific models but may not negotiate. They also may require a large down payment. As a result, it is sometimes better to pay higher financing charges on a car with a lower price or to buy a car that requires a smaller down payment.

W Writing Support

How to Buy a Car Inform students that car buyers are faced with a vast range of options and decisions. Have them explore various Web sites that address car-buying issues, and then write a step-by-step manual for the first-time buyer. Remind students to include information about financing the car. Encourage them to be specific and comprehensive.

Figure 11.1 Financing Future Goals

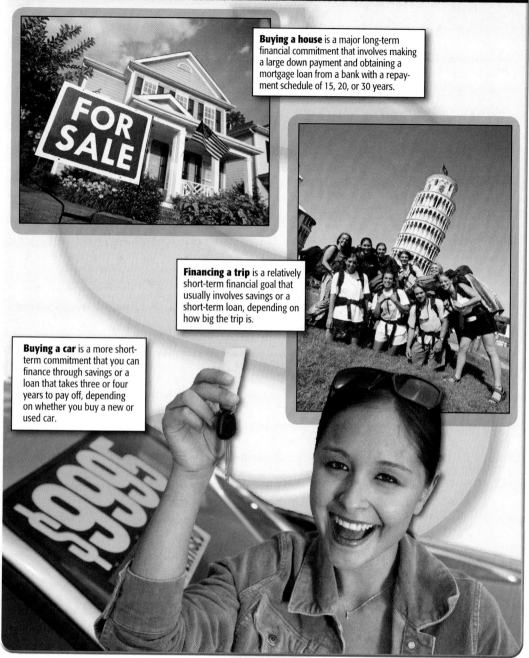

Buying a house is a major long-term financial commitment that involves making a large down payment and obtaining a mortgage loan from a bank with a repayment schedule of 15, 20, or 30 years.

Financing a trip is a relatively short-term financial goal that usually involves savings or a short-term loan, depending on how big the trip is.

Buying a car is a more short-term commitment that you can finance through savings or a loan that takes three or four years to pay off, depending on whether you buy a new or used car.

Your future goals might involve long-term or short-term financial commitments. *What are some immediate financial goals you have?*

Chapter 11   Credit and Debt   **253**

11.2 SECTION

TEACH (cont.)

Independent Practice

Disputed Purchases

Ask students what advantage using a credit card has over paying cash if there is later a dispute over the item purchased. (If the item purchased is unsatisfactory, the buyer can notify the credit card company and ask that the amount be put on hold. The card issuer will attempt to resolve the problem and inform you of the results.)

Guided Practice

Stolen Credit Cards

Tell students to imagine that they have just lost their wallet and all its contents, including a VISA credit card issued by First Main Bank of Sarasota, Florida. Inform students that card issuers provide a telephone number to report stolen cards. Have students write a follow-up letter to the company. Remind them to include all pertinent data in the letter. After students' letters are prepared, ask them to exchange and evaluate each other's letters.

▲ USING VISUALS

➡ Figure 11.1 Financing Future Goals Answer Answers will vary, but students may discuss financial goals such as saving money to buy a car, to pay for higher education, or to get an apartment when they graduate from high school.

Activity Have students discuss their medium- and long-term goals. Ask them to explain their strategies for addressing each of these goals.

TEACH (cont.)

D Develop Concepts

Defective Vehicles Explain that consumer law protects buyers against "lemons," or vehicles that continually have mechanical problems. Ask students what kinds of remedies are available to the buyer. (have the car fixed by the seller, have seller pay to have it fixed, return car to seller and receive a refund) Emphasize that the seller must be proven liable on grounds of a breach of warranty.

R Reading Strategy

Make a Chart Ask students to draw a table with two columns. In one column, have them list the benefits of using credit cards. In the other column, have them show the costs of using credit cards. Suggest to students that such a chart can help them organize their thoughts, but not necessarily determine the value of credit cards.

Extending the Content

Using Credit Cards Wisely

Have students use the Internet or library to find articles on managing credit card debt, and then report their findings to the class.

254

Global Law

German Lemon Law

As a member of the European Union, Germany was recently directed to change its laws on the sales of tangible property, including the sales of vehicles, to better protect the consumer. Previously, dealers of automobiles could provide little or no warranty as to the condition of used vehicles it sold. Now the consumer has the benefit of Germany's own lemon law.

1 All German dealers must warrant used cars for a minimum of one year. Unfortunately, this applies only to dealerships and does not apply to private sales of used cars.

2 The dealer is responsible for any defect determined to have been present at the time of sale. There is no protection for damage done during normal wear and tear on a vehicle. For example, worn brake pads are probably not warranted. The determination is normally done by an independent third-party appraiser.

3 The claim must be filed within one year of the purchase of the vehicle. There is no additional time period for the filing of claims. Claims can only be filed during the one-year period.

4 The European Union directive applies to all mobile property. A European Union directive that required member states to pass statutes providing for consumer protection also applies to other sales of goods. Therefore, not only is there a one-year warranty on cars, but on other items such as televisions and motor homes.

> **Across Cultures: European Union Protections**
> Although this example details the German law, the European Union directive applies to all member countries of the European Union. Those countries must also pass similar warranty laws for their citizens.

Critical Thinking: *What are the benefits and detriments of having a mandatory one-year warranty on all goods?*

Defective Vehicles

Some cars continually have mechanical problems. The seller may be liable on any of the following grounds:

D
- breach of an express warranty, if a guarantee was made and not kept
- breach of warranty of merchantability, if the seller was a dealer and the car was not fit to drive
- fraud or breach of an express warranty, if the seller made any statements about the car that were not true
- breach of the state consumer protection law, if the vehicle was for non-business use

Using Credit Cards

What are some of the costs of using credit?

R When you use a credit card, you are borrowing money. The interest rate and late-payment fees can be very high unless you pay your bill by the due date. You can go deeply into debt, even bankrupt, if you do not use your credit card carefully. In order to make a wise decision when purchasing on credit, you must consider all the fees and costs **involved**.

Global Law

German Lemon Law

Answer Answers will vary. The benefits of having a mandatory one-year warranty on all goods may include better experiences for consumers and an improvement of products to reduce repair and replacement costs. Detriments may include higher prices to cover the costs, and that people may choose to purchase items from other countries because they cost less there.

> **Example** Tim charged many items on his credit card, up to its $2,000 limit. Each month he pays $40 on the account, the minimum required by the card issuer. The interest rate is 19 percent. If Tim maintains the same payment rate, it will take him 33 years to erase the debt. He will pay $7,000 in interest on the $2,000 that he borrowed to make his purchases. Tim could save a lot of money by doubling his monthly payments and making every effort to bring the account balance down to zero as soon as possible.

Reading Check

Explain Is it better to pay cash for electronic goods or buy them on credit?

There is an advantage to using a credit card if you have a dispute involving a purchase. You do not have to pay the bill for the disputed item. Instead, notify the credit card issuer by telephone immediately. The issuer must put the disputed amount on hold and send you a form to fill out explaining the dispute. The card issuer will attempt to resolve the dispute and inform you of the results. If the problem is not corrected and the credit card issuer brings suit, you may use as a defense the fact that unsatisfactory goods or services were received.

Another advantage of using a credit card arises if the card is stolen. You may have to pay up to $50 of **unauthorized** charges made before you notify the credit card issuer of the loss. You are not, however, responsible for charges made after the issuer has been notified.

> **Example** Tara lost her credit card but did not notify the card issuer for a week. Meanwhile, someone who found the card had charged a purchase of $175 with it. Tara will have to pay $50 toward this unauthorized purchase. If she had notified the card issuer before the illegal purchase happened, however, she would not have had to pay anything.

Student Loans

What can you do if you cannot afford to pay for college?

Education costs are on the rise and do not seem to be slowing down. For most people, going to college requires careful planning in order to pay the costs of tuition and basic living expenses.

A common way of financing your education is through student loans. There are two types of student loans, government loans and private loans.

Government Student Loans

The Federal Government is an enormous student loan lender. Under the Direct Loan Program, money is lent to students based on need. When a student applies to college, he or she fills out a FAFSA, or Free Application for Federal Student Aid. This application asks detailed information about the student and his or her family. The government then makes a determination about how much money it can loan the student. The figure is also based on the amount necessary to attend a specific college.

Legal Talk

Dispute: *v* To question the truth and validity. From Latin *disputare* = to examine.

Resolve: *v* To find a solution; to solve. From Latin *resolvere* = to untie.

Vocabulary Builder Look up the words *dispute* and *resolve* in the dictionary. Break them down into and define their root words.

Look It Up! Check definitions in *Black's Law Dictionary* or an online glossary. For direct links, go to glencoe.com to find more vocabulary resources.

TEACH (cont.)

C Critical Thinking

Student Loans Ask students the following question: Why does the U.S. government lend money to students and offer ways to forgive loans, such as AmeriCorps and the Peace Corps? (Answers will vary, but students may agree that a more educated population is good for society and the economy. Students may also recognize a benefit to domestic and foreign communities by forgiving student loans when students work for social organizations.)

Reading Check

Explain It depends on the circumstances. Credit card companies typically offer their users protection against faulty purchases but may also charge interest.

Legal Talk

(Dispute is derived from the Latin *dis* (apart) and *putare* (to think), and means to argue about. Resolve is derived from the Latin *re* (backward) and *solvere* (loosen), and means to untie or free.

Ask students to practice their academic and legal vocabulary with the electronic flashcards available at the *Business and Personal Law* Online Learning Center through glencoe.com.

---

glencoe.com

ASSESS

Quiz

Ask students to answer the following questions:

1. Why does buying a car with cash save you money? (because car loans require you to pay interest)

2. What are the costs associated with using a credit card? (interest, late payment fees, annual fees)

3. What does the government's Direct Loan Program base lending upon, and how does one apply for it? (It is need-based and is applied for via a Free Application for Federal Student Aid (FAFSA).)

RETEACH

Independent Practice

Benefits of Credit

Ask: "How does credit benefit both the buyer and the seller? (Students should recognize that buyers are allowed to pay for the things they need over a period of time, and sellers may make a sale whether the customer has cash or not.)

Extending the Content

Credit Abroad

Ask students if they and their families have ever traveled abroad. Have them explain how they made purchases there. Explain that using a credit card can be the best option when traveling. While ATMs and currency exchange services may charge fees or inflated exchange rates, a credit card will automatically pay the exact amount in the local currency. Recently, however, some credit cards have begun charging fees for international transactions, making them less advantageous. Students must remember, though, that any savings with a credit card are only effective if the consumer pays the credit card bill on time and in full.

Review Key Terms

Encourage students to access the *Business and Personal Law* Online Learning Center through glencoe.com and use the electronic flashcards to review the key terms.

256

Figure 11.2 Ways to Build and Protect Your Credit

☑ Open a checking or savings account, or both.
☑ Apply for a local department store credit card.
☑ Take out a small loan from your bank.
☑ Make payments on time.

Be aware that a creditor must:

1. Evaluate all applicants on the same basis.
2. Consider income from part-time employment.
3. Consider the payment history of all joint accounts, if this accurately reflects your credit history.
4. Disregard information on accounts if you can prove that it does not affect your ability or willingness to repay.

Be aware that a creditor cannot:

1. Refuse you individual credit in your own name if you are creditworthy.
2. Require your spouse to cosign a loan. Any creditworthy person can be your cosigner if one is required.
3. Ask about your family plans or assume that your income will be interrupted to have children.
4. Consider whether you have a telephone listing in your name.

Firm Foundation If you want a good credit rating, you must prove you can use credit wisely. *Why is it a good idea to apply for a local department store credit card or a small loan from your bank?*

Within the Direct Loan Program, there are two types of government loans, **subsidized** and unsubsidized. If you receive a subsidized loan, the government pays the interest on the loan while you are in school. However, with an unsubsidized loan, the student remains responsible for the interest that accrues on the loan while in school. Under both loans, the student will pay interest on the loan after graduation. For more information visit the U.S. Department of Education Web site.

Private Student Loans

Private student loans are similar to other consumer loans. They are offered by banks across the country. The amount of money offered is based on the cost of tuition at your specific school. The interest rate on private loans is usually higher than on government loans, and students are responsible for the interest that accrues, even while the student is in school. Private education loans are also available to parents who want to take out loans to pay for their children's education.

Student Loan Repayment

Student loans in most circumstances must be repaid. There are a few exceptions. Student loans can be discharged in bankruptcy, but only in cases of extreme hardship. The government will discharge some or all of a student loan debt for students who enter special job programs after they graduate. These programs, such as AmeriCorps

---

▲ USING VISUALS

Figure 11.2 Ways to Build and Protect Your Credit **Answer** Students may suggest that applying for a local department store credit card, using it wisely, and making payments on time is one way to build good credit. Taking a small loan from your bank and paying it off on time builds good credit as well.

Activity Have students bring in applications for credit cards and loans. Discuss how they can help build or ruin one's credit, depending on their use.

and the Peace Corps, usually require students to work in the health, education, or public safety field in an underdeveloped community for a certain period of time.

Warning Signs of Debt Problems

How can you tell if you have credit problems?

It is important to use credit wisely to build a good credit rating and to avoid getting heavily into debt early in life (see **Figure 11.2**). Here are some of the warning signs you should watch out for that you may be in financial trouble:

- You make only the minimum monthly payment on credit cards or have trouble paying even that much. The total balance on your credit cards increases every month.
- You miss loan payments or often pay late.
- You receive second or third payment due notices from creditors.
- You borrow money to pay off old debts.
- You exceed the credit limits on your credit cards.
- You have been denied credit because of a bad credit rating.

If you experience two or more of these warning signs, it is time to rethink your financial priorities.

After You Read

Summarize Identify the advantages and disadvantages of using credit.

SECTION 11.2 ASSESSMENT

Self Check

1. On what grounds can a seller be liable for selling a defective vehicle?

2. What can you do if you have a dispute involving a purchase on a credit card?

3. What is the difference between a subsidized and an unsubsidized student loan?

Academic Connection

Mathematics You want to buy a used car from a dealer for $8,400. The dealer requires a 20% down payment and you will have to finance the rest with a car loan. Use two different methods to figure out how much you will have to finance.

THEORY Problem **Solving: Use a Variety of Appropriate Strategies to Solve Problems** One method is to multiply the percent of the down payment from the total cost to find out the amount of the down payment. Then subtract the amount of the down payment from the total cost. Another method is to subtract the percent of the down payment from 100% to find out the

percent of the amount you will have to finance, then multiply that by the total cost of the car.

 For more math practice, go to the Math Appendix.

Critical Thinking

Disadvantages of Credit Advantages of using credit are that it is convenient, you can pay for expensive items over time, and it contributes to the growth of the economy. What are some of the disadvantages of using credit?

 Go to **glencoe.com** to check your answers.

After You Read

Summarize Advantages include not having to carry large amounts of cash or having to pay for an item if there is a dispute over the purchase. Disadvantages include paying a high interest rate unless you pay the debt on time and in full.

ASSESS

Self-Assessment

Have students go to the *Business and Personal Law* Online Learning Center through **glencoe.com** to take the Section 11.2 Practice Test.

CLOSE

Culminating Activity

Safety

Ask students to think of measures they should take to prevent unauthorized use of their credit cards. (Answers may include shredding bills and making online purchases on secured sites.)

SECTION 11.2 ASSESSMENT

Self Check

1. breach of an express warranty or warranty of merchantability, fraud or breach of an express warranty, breach of state consumer protection law

2. Notify the credit card company to put the disputed amount on hold.

3. While in school, government pays the interest on a subsidized student loan. Student pays interest on an unsubsidized student loan while in school.

Academic Connection

Mathematics
$6,720

Critical Thinking

paying high interest rates if you do not pay your bills on time and in full; going into debt quickly

 Activity correlated to the Mathematics standard on page 251

Chapter 11 Review and Assessment

Summary by Sections

Ask students to read the summaries one key point at a time. Then, ask them to work in groups to create two examples to illustrate each key point.

Vocabulary Builder

Cooperative Learning

1. Have students work in groups to prepare their sentences. Ask the groups to exchange their sentences and assess each other's sentences.

Vocabulary Development

- Ask students to use a dictionary or to go online to look up the etymology of each key term listed.

- Then, ask students to list several words derived from the same root or origin. For example, *contract* has the same root as *contractual* or *contractually*.

Summary

Section 11.1 Understanding Credit

- ◆ Open-end credit is credit that can be increased by continuing to purchase goods or services on credit. Closed-end credit is credit given for a specific amount of money.

- ◆ A secured loan is a loan which is backed up by property, called collateral, that the creditor can take if the loan is not repaid.

- ◆ A security interest is created by the creditor possessing the collateral for a loan, or by the debtor signing a security agreement that identifies the collateral.

- ◆ The main types of collateral are consumer goods, fixtures, equipment, inventory, and farm products.

Section 11.2 Credit and You

- ◆ Before you sign any documents to buy a vehicle, you should know the exact price you are paying, the amount you are financing, the finance charge, the APR, the number and amount of payments, and the total sales price.

- ◆ When you use a credit card, you are borrowing money. You can go deeply into debt, even bankrupt, if you do not use your credit card carefully.

- ◆ There are both government and private loans available to students. To apply for government student loans, students fill out a FAFSA, or Free Application for Federal Student Aid.

Vocabulary Builder

❶ **On a sheet of paper, use each of these terms in a sentence.**

Key Terms

- credit
- creditor
- debtor
- interest
- secured loan
- collateral
- security interest
- default
- finance charge
- annual percentage rate (APR)

Academic Vocabulary

- assets
- acquired
- effective
- involved
- unauthorized
- subsidized

 Go to **glencoe.com** to play a game and improve your legal vocabulary.

 ## Study Skills for Success

Prepare Your Students for Studying

Tell students that they can improve their ability to understand and remember material from their courses by learning and practicing study skills. Remind students to:

- **Get motivated!** Motivation must come from within. To motivate yourself, think of ways in which what you learn now will fit into your long-term personal and professional goals.

- **Get organized!** Make studying part of your daily routine, not something you do at the last minute.

- **Concentrate!** Study in an environment that is as free of distractions as possible.

Key Points Review

Answer the following questions. Refer to the chapter for additional reinforcement.

❷ What is the difference between open-end credit and closed-end credit?

❸ What is a secured loan?

❹ What are the three ways a security interest is attached?

❺ What is the difference between a guarantor and a surety?

❻ What are the six things you need to know before you sign a document to buy a vehicle?

❼ What are a finance charge and an APR?

❽ What are some advantages to using a credit card?

❾ What are the different types of government loans available to students?

Standardized Test Practice

❿ Read the following excerpt from the Federal Reserve Board on how to use your credit card and complete questions 1 and 2.

The first step in choosing a credit card is thinking about how you will use it.

- If you expect to always pay your monthly bill in full (and other features such as frequent flyer miles don't interest you) your best choice may be a card that has no annual fee and offers a longer grace period.

- If you sometimes carry over a balance from month to month, you may be more interested in a card that carries a lower interest rate (stated as an annual percentage rate, or APR).

- If you expect to use your card to get cash advances, you'll want to look for a card that carries a lower APR and lower fees on cash advances. Some cards charge a higher APR for cash advances than for purchases.

1. When you choose a credit card, you should be more concerned about

Ⓐ the credit card features

Ⓑ who the credit card issuer is

Ⓒ what the credit limit is

Ⓓ what the interest rate is

2. If you expect to pay your credit card bill in full every month, you should choose a credit card that offers a

Ⓐ lower fee for purchases

Ⓑ lower cash advance fee

Ⓒ longer grace period

Ⓓ lower interest rate

Test-Taking Strategies Formulate your own answer before reading the options when answering multiple-choice questions.

---

11 Chapter

Review and Assessment

Key Points Review

2. Open-end credit can be increased by the debtor. Closed-end credit is for a specific amount of money.

3. a loan backed by collateral that the creditor can take if the loan is not repaid

4. Debtor owns the collateral; secured party transfers something of value to debtor; or secured party takes possession of the collateral or signs a security agreement.

5. A guarantor agrees to pay off a debt only if the debtor defaults. A surety agrees to pay off a debt outright regardless of whether the debtor defaults.

6. the price being paid; the amount being financed; the finance charge; APR; the number and amount of payments; and the total sales price

7. The finance charge is the cost of the loan. The APR is the true interest rate.

8. not having to pay for a disputed item, gaining extended warranties, getting a true exchange rate when doing business in another currency

9. subsidized and unsubsidized student loans

Standardized Test Practice

10. D and C

⚠ Strategies for Standardized Test Prep Success

Whether your students have a standardized test coming up in a few days or a few weeks, these last-minute test-prep tips and strategies will help them relax and do their best.

- **Test Format** Help students become familiar with the format of the test by practicing with test items that imitate the actual test items as closely as possible.

- **Test Timing** Have your students take timed practice tests so that they become comfortable with the length, design, and timing of the actual test.

Apply and Debate

 Apply and Debate

Students should use chapter content to arrive at conclusions. The legal resolutions are listed below:

11. Yes. Since the loan company has a security interest on the computer, when Wilson purchased the computer, he also purchased the security interest. He may have a claim against Jana, but the loan company can still repossess the computer.

12. Probably not. Since the problems are minor, it is doubtful the lemon laws would apply here. The lemon laws were created for major defects, not for minor, repairable defects.

13. Maybe. He can probably get out of the credit card agreement but will probably still be responsible for some of the charges that were necessaries and for returning items purchased with the credit card.

14. Probably not. If he has already maxed out a credit card, it is doubtful he will be able to get another card with a lower interest rate and lower payments.

15. A student loan. Student loan interest rates are usually lower than those of credit cards. Levar will also be able to defer payments on his student loans until after he has graduated.

Read the following scenarios. Get together with other students in pairs or groups of three and take a position on each scenario. Debate your position in class with students taking the opposite position or prepare a written argument justifying your position.

⑪ **Collateral**

Wilson purchased a used computer from Jana for $400. He did not know that Jana had purchased the computer through a loan company and had not been making her payments on time. The loan company decided to repossess the computer.

You Debate — *Can the loan company repossess the computer from Wilson?*

⑫ **Lemon Laws**

Tomas purchased a new car from a local dealer. Within two months he began to have several minor mechanical problems. Although the repairs were not major, Tomas felt that since there were so many of them, the car fell under the lemon law.

You Debate — *Is Tomas entitled to get his money back for the car?*

⑬ **Credit Cards**

Quinton, a seventeen-year-old college freshman, was offered a credit card and accepted. He quickly ran up charges until he was unable to afford the payments. Just prior to his eighteenth birthday he attempted to get out of his contract with the credit card company because he was a minor when he received the credit card.

You Debate — *Can Quinton get out of his debt with the credit card company?*

⑭ **Credit Limit**

Travis has reached the limit on his credit card and cannot make the monthly payments. He receives an offer in the mail for another credit card and is considering getting the other card to pay off some of the debt on his current card.

You Debate — *Should Travis use the second card to pay off some of the first card?*

⑮ **Student Loans**

Levar was accepted to the college of his choice but did not qualify for a grant or scholarship. He makes money working a part-time job, but not enough to pay for all his expenses. He can cover the rest by taking out a student loan, which he will have to pay back later, or by using his credit card, which he can pay off on a monthly basis.

You Debate — *Is Levar better off taking out a student loan or using his credit card?*

C Critical Thinking

Warning Signs of Debt Problems Ask students: What are some warning signs of a debt problem? (Answers will vary, but may include sending only the minimum required payment per month, using one credit card to pay off another, and giving up hope on paying off debts.)

Debate Practice

- Who does a debt problem hurt more, the debtor or the lender? (Students may either sympathize with a consumer's problems or note that money is rightfully owed the lender.)

- Whose responsibility should it be to teach consumers to spend responsibly? (Answers will vary, but may include parents and schools.)

Case Study Practice – Patzka v. Viterbo College

⑯ **The Price of Credit** Mariann Patzka was enrolled at Viterbo College in Wisconsin. She incurred debt in the amount of $3,530.16 during her first semester. At that time, Ms. Patzka was not informed of any fees she could be charged if she did not pay in full by the first day of classes. Interest charges came to $2,253.55, making the total amount due $5,783.71. Ms. Patzka paid $1,510.00 to Viterbo College, but still owed $4,274.16.

Viterbo College assigned the debt to a collection agency, Security Credit. Prior to doing so, the College assessed Ms. Patzka a collection fee of 33% ($1,410.47), making the total amount due $5,684.63. Ms. Patzka made payments to Security Credit in the amount of $4,284.63. Ms. Patzka now argues that she does not owe the remaining $1,400 because her account was an open-end credit account and she was never informed of the potential charges and fees when credit was extended as required under the Federal Fair Debt Collection Practices Act.

Source: Patzka v. Viterbo College, 917 F.Supp.654 (W.D. Wis. 1996)

Practice Does Ms. Patzka need to pay the remaining $1,400?

⑰ Ethics Application

Breach of Trust? Arjang's parents gave him a credit card to use for textbooks, supplies, and in case of an emergency. When he was short of cash, he used the credit card to buy a new computer game at the campus bookstore. Since the purchase would show up as computer software, his parents would assume the purchase was a required school supply and he would not have to ask their permission.

◆ Was Arjang's purchase of the computer game without his parent's permission ethical? Why or why not?

⑱ Internet Application

Find out about Student Loans You do not have the money to pay for college tuition and books. You need to apply for a federal student loan. You have many options of student loans to choose from, so you must research what the right student loan for you is and prepare the student application.

Go to **glencoe.com** to access the Web site sponsored by Nellie Mae, select the right loan for you, download a blank application, and fill it out.

 Reading Connection

Outside Reading Go to **glencoe.com** for a list of reading suggestions on student loans.

 glencoe.com

Chapter 11   Credit and Debt   **261**

11 Chapter

Review and Assessment

←?→ Ethics Application

17. Answers will vary, but many students will recognize that without his parents' permission, Arjang's actions were not ethical. To further the discussion, ask students to discuss what Arjang's parents might do if they found out that he had charged the computer game without their permission.

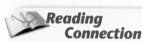 **Internet Application**

18. Loans and applications will vary, but should be filled out as clearly and completely as possible.

R Reading Strategy

Reading Connection

American Bar Association Resources

Go to the *Business and Personal Law* Online Learning Center through **glencoe.com** to find links for further readings that relate to this chapter. Ask students to read, review, and summarize the documents. Advise students to keep their reviews and summaries to use as reference material for their Unit Thematic Project on pages 282–283.

Case Study Practice

16. No. The Federal District Court in Wisconsin held that the college account was an open-end credit account under the regulations of the Federal Fair Debt Collection Practices Act. Under that act, debtors are required to receive a copy of the schedule of interest rates and fees associated with the account. In this case, Ms. Patzka did not receive notice of the interest rate and/or additional fees. Therefore, because Ms. Patzka did not receive notice, she was not liable for paying any fees or interest on the account and received a refund in the amount of $2,264.02.

Plan Your Lesson Section by Section

NBEA	NATIONAL BUSINESS LAW STANDARDS
Section 12.1	• **Identify** legislation that regulates consumer credit and electronic credit transactions (e.g., Fair Credit Reporting Act, Fair Credit Billing Act, Equal Opportunity Act, Fair Credit Collection Practices Act, and Consumer Credit Protection Act). • **Describe** a secured transaction and explain the requirements for creating a valid security interest.
Section 12.2	• **Describe** and discuss the various aspects of bankruptcy (e.g., Chapter 7—Liquidation, Chapter 11—Reorganization, and Chapter 13—Reorganization of Debts). • **Compare** the differences between voluntary bankruptcy and involuntary bankruptcy cases. • **Explain** the procedure for the administration of the debtor's estate.

NCLB	ACADEMIC STANDARDS	Activity/Feature
English Language Arts: NCTE 3 Apply a wide range of strategies to comprehend, interpret, evaluate, and appreciate texts.		*BusinessWeek* News, Case Study, Case Study Practice
English Language Arts: NCTE 9 Develop an understanding of and respect for diversity in language use, patterns, and dialects across cultures, ethnic groups, geographic regions, and social roles.		Global Law
English Language Arts: NCTE 6 Apply knowledge of language structure, language conventions, media techniques, figurative language, and genre to create, critique, and discuss print and non-print texts.		Legal Talk, ad copy, Key Terms, and Academic Vocabulary
Social Studies: NCSS 2 Study the ways human beings view themselves in and over time.		Section 12.1 Assessment
Mathematics: NCTM PSS 1 Build new mathematical knowledge through problem solving.		Section 12.2 Assessment
English Language Arts: NCTE 10 Students whose first language is not English make use of their first language to develop competency in the English language arts and to develop understanding of content across the curriculum.		Key Terms, Academic Vocabulary, Legal Talk, Vocabulary Builder
English Language Arts: NCTE 1 Read a wide range of print and non-print texts to build an understanding of texts; to acquire new information; to respond to the needs and demands of society and the workplace; and for personal fulfillment.		Global Law, Cyberlaw
Social Studies: NCSS 9 Study global connections and interdependence.		Global Law

Connect Your Business Law Classroom to the World of Work

This chart shows the 21st Century Skills, foundation skills, and workplace competencies that students develop as they work in this chapter.

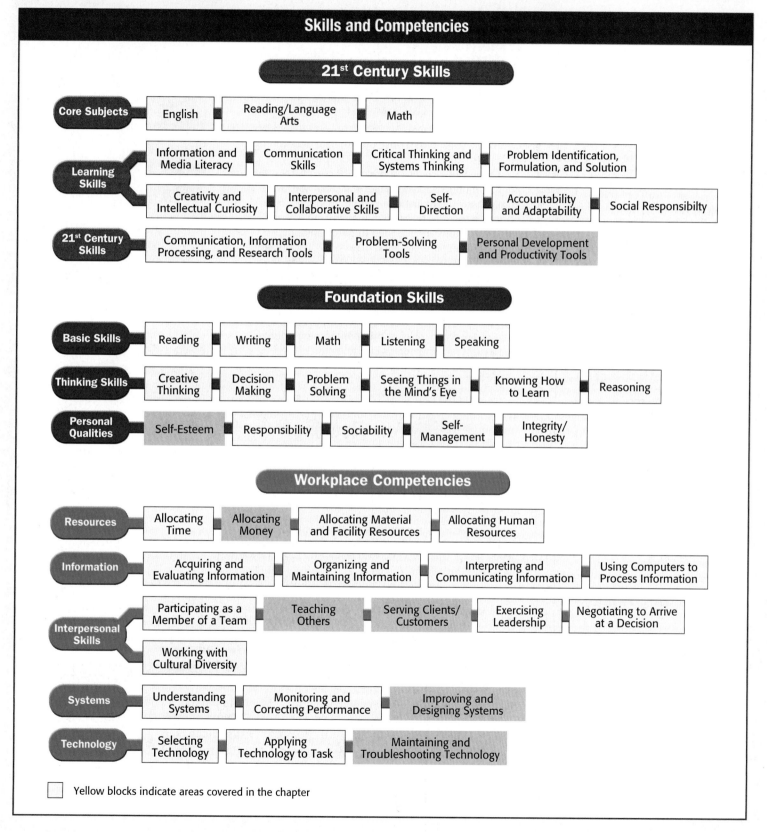

Skills and Competencies

21st Century Skills

Core Subjects
- English
- Reading/Language Arts
- Math

Learning Skills
- Information and Media Literacy
- Communication Skills
- Critical Thinking and Systems Thinking
- Problem Identification, Formulation, and Solution
- Creativity and Intellectual Curiosity
- Interpersonal and Collaborative Skills
- Self-Direction
- Accountability and Adaptability
- Social Responsibilty

21st Century Skills
- Communication, Information Processing, and Research Tools
- Problem-Solving Tools
- Personal Development and Productivity Tools

Foundation Skills

Basic Skills
- Reading
- Writing
- Math
- Listening
- Speaking

Thinking Skills
- Creative Thinking
- Decision Making
- Problem Solving
- Seeing Things in the Mind's Eye
- Knowing How to Learn
- Reasoning

Personal Qualities
- Self-Esteem
- Responsibility
- Sociability
- Self-Management
- Integrity/Honesty

Workplace Competencies

Resources
- Allocating Time
- Allocating Money
- Allocating Material and Facility Resources
- Allocating Human Resources

Information
- Acquiring and Evaluating Information
- Organizing and Maintaining Information
- Interpreting and Communicating Information
- Using Computers to Process Information

Interpersonal Skills
- Participating as a Member of a Team
- Teaching Others
- Serving Clients/Customers
- Exercising Leadership
- Negotiating to Arrive at a Decision
- Working with Cultural Diversity

Systems
- Understanding Systems
- Monitoring and Correcting Performance
- Improving and Designing Systems

Technology
- Selecting Technology
- Applying Technology to Task
- Maintaining and Troubleshooting Technology

☐ Yellow blocks indicate areas covered in the chapter

Introduce the Chapter

Credit Protection and Bankruptcy

In Chapter 12 students will learn about how excessive debt can impact individuals and businesses. They will study the primary laws that offer protection to creditors, and how bankruptcy can be used as a method to discharge or reorganize financial obligations.

Building Background

Ask if students have ever had a debt they were not able to repay. Have them discuss what they did to rectify the situation. Explain that many people can get caught up in the ease of using credit cards, and then not be able to pay back the money.

BusinessWeek News

Tell students that a recent study by Global Insight says that rising interest rates and inflation combined with slower income growth and housing value appreciation are the main reasons that the rate of bankruptcy filings will increase. Nevada, Maryland, New Jersey, Virginia, and Utah will experience the most significant increases.

 Reading Strategy

Your Reading

Tell students to first take stock of the overall chapter length and consider the time allocated to read the material. Often, this practice will give the reader an idea of how quickly the material needs to be covered, balancing reading speed with comprehension.

262

CHAPTER 12 Credit Protection and Bankruptcy

BusinessWeek News

A Business Rife with Bad Guys

By Amy Borrus

The new bankruptcy law imposes two requirements on anyone seeking to reduce or eliminate debt through the courts. To file for Chapter 7 or Chapter 13, you must have had a credit-counseling briefing within the prior six months. Once you file, you can't walk away from debts without first completing an instructional course on personal financial management.

The provisions are intended to curb bankruptcies by helping people work out a plan to pay back what they owe and better manage their finances. But the rules will send hundreds of thousands of people into a minefield where legitimate counseling agencies do business alongside unsavory players. "In this industry the good players are the exception, not the rule," says Eric Friedman, chief of the Montgomery County, Maryland, Consumer Affairs Division.

 Your Reading

Efficient critical reading involves being flexible with speed and comprehension. There are several ways of reading critically, and you need to fit a reading style to your needs and to the material.

Go to **glencoe.com** for Flex Your Reading activities, more information on reading strategies for this chapter, and guided practice in reading about bankruptcy laws.

Classroom Resources

- Student Edition
- Teacher Wraparound Edition
- Student Activity Workbook with Academic Integration (SE/TAE)
- TeacherWorks™ Plus! CD
- *ExamView*® *Assessment Suite* CD
- *Presentation Plus!* CD

- National Mock Trial Championship DVD
- Online Learning Center with Podcasts at glencoe.com
- Study-to-Go™ at glencoe.com
- Online Student Edition
- Interactive Student Edition

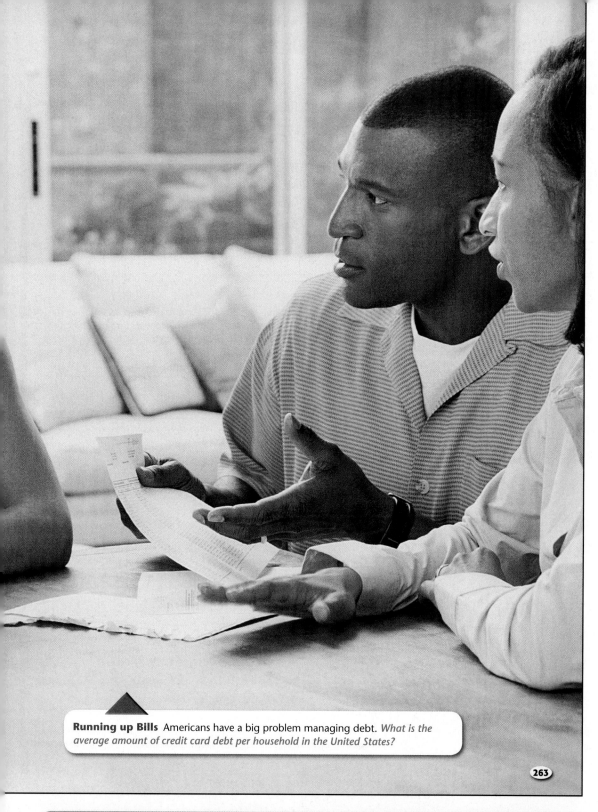

Running up Bills Americans have a big problem managing debt. *What is the average amount of credit card debt per household in the United States?*

(263)

Practice the Concept

Credit
Explain that using credit wisely can be a great benefit to individuals and businesses. Over 80 percent of U.S. households have at least one credit card. One obvious advantage to using credit in the form of credit cards is the ease of use. It is much simpler to swipe a credit card for a purchase instead of keeping up with cash or writing a check. In addition, some people who use credit cards utilize the monthly statement to track their spending.

Key Terms Stress to students that the use of credit can be risky. When consumers begin to experience debt problems, their credit rating suffers, and eventually they may have problems paying their obligations. Explain that when evaluating credit reports, terms like *sub-prime* scores, *credit risk*, or *lien* may surface. Generally, a credit rating below 620 is considered *sub-prime*, and this debtor may be considered to be a *credit risk* from the lender's perspective.

The Fine Print Explain to students that when evaluating credit options, it is important to review *all* fine print on the application. Emphasize that applicants should first understand a loan's annual percentage rate, transaction fees, late fee charges, and annual fees before signing to accept the loan.

▲ USING VISUALS

Running up Bills **Answer** The average amount of credit card debt per household in the United States is about $8,000.

Activity Have students use the Internet, your school's media center, or your local library to find articles on debt management and have them report their findings to the class.

FOCUS

Bell Ringer Activity

Write the following sentence on the board: "Money spent with a credit card is not like real money." Ask students to comment on this sentence. (Students should conclude that while money spent from a credit card may not *seem* like real money to many individuals, it must be repaid with *real* money.)

Preteaching

Key Terms

Read the definitions and ask students to create a sentence using each term.

Academic Vocabulary

Explain that developing vocabulary is key to academic success. An efficient method to develop vocabulary is to study how words are formed.

- **dominant** Adjective, from the Latin *dominari* (to master). Means controlling or prevailing over all others.
- **exceed** Verb, from the Latin *excedere* (to go beyond). Means to be greater than.
- **impersonate** Verb, from the Latin *in* + *personare* (to bear the character of). Means to assume or act the character of.

Activity Ask students to give a noun, an adjective, or an adverb form that comes from each word.

Connects to academic content

What You'll Learn

- ◆ Define repossession and garnishment.
- ◆ Describe the federal laws that regulate consumer credit.
- ◆ Discuss your rights under the Consumer Credit Protection Act, the Fair Credit Reporting Act, and the Fair Credit Billing Act.
- ◆ Explain the purpose of the Equal Credit Opportunity Act and the Fair Credit Collection Practices Act.

Why It's Important

You need to know the laws that protect you from creditors when you borrow money or use credit.

Academic Standards

Reading and completing the activities in this section will help you practice the following academic standards:

Social Studies (NCSS 2) Study the ways human beings view themselves in and over time.

[NCLB] **English Language Arts (NCTE 6)** Apply knowledge of language structure, language conventions, media techniques, figurative language, and genre to create, critique, and discuss print and non-print texts.

Reading Guide

Before You Read

Connect Have you ever borrowed money from someone who tried to profit from your situation?

Focus on Ideas

The federal and state legal systems protect your rights as a credit user.

Take Notes

Create a graph like the one shown and use it to take notes as you read this section. Go to **glencoe.com** to find graphic organizers and tips on how to improve your note-taking skills.

Federal Laws Protecting Debtors

Consumer Credit Protection Act				

Key Terms

You will learn these legal words and expressions in this chapter. You can also find these terms in *Black's Law Dictionary* or in an online legal dictionary.

- repossession
- garnishment
- usury law
- Consumer Credit Protection Act
- Fair Credit Reporting Act
- Equal Credit Opportunity Act (ECOA)
- Fair Debt Collection Practices Act (FDCPA)
- Fair Credit Billing Act

Academic Vocabulary

You will find these words in your readings and in your tests. Look them up in a dictionary and familiarize yourself with them.

- dominant
- exceed
- impersonate

 glencoe.com

 Reading Strategy

Read for Knowledge

1. **Survey** or preread the chapter.
2. **Question** or formulate questions before you read.
3. **Recite** or read your questions, answers, and notes out loud.
4. **Review** or reread your notes.

Note-Taking Basics

- Listen attentively
- Have note-taking materials ready
- Skim through the lesson material
- Write down key words and ideas
- Anticipate what comes next
- Review notes soon after taking them

Laws Protecting Creditors

What can creditors do if you owe them money?

Historically, creditors have not needed special laws to protect them. They lend money or extend credit, and have the right to be paid back with interest. In their relations with debtors, creditors are the **dominant** parties. They are in a better position to control the terms of a transaction.

Repossession

When a debtor borrows money or uses credit to buy property such as a car or refrigerator, the creditor places a legal claim on the property called a lien. **Repossession is when a creditor reclaims property on which it has a lien if the debtor does not make payment.** Repossession must be done without causing a disturbance. If the debtor refuses to surrender the goods, legal process must be used to obtain them.

After repossessing goods, secured parties may keep them (with exceptions) or sell them. Sales may be public auctions or private sales. If the goods are consumer goods for which the debtor has paid 60 percent or more of the price, the secured party cannot keep them—they must be sold. The debtor must be notified and is entitled to receive any surplus of the sale after debts and expenses have been paid.

Garnishment of Wages

If a debtor defaults on a loan, creditors also have the right to garnish their wages. **Garnishment is the legal procedure through which a worker's earnings are withheld for payment of a debt.** Garnishment of a worker's wages cannot **exceed** 25 percent of weekly take-home pay, except for certain amounts of support payments and taxes.

As You Read

Predict Can a finance company take your car away from you for not making the monthly payments?

Vocabulary You can find vocabulary definitions in the **Key Terms** glossary and **Academic Vocabulary** glossary in the back of this book.

 Repossession Creditors have a right to repossess property when a debtor defaults on a loan. *What does a creditor need in order to claim property?*

12.1 SECTION

TEACH

Discussion Starter

Class Discussion
Tell students to imagine that the left half of the class loaned the right half of the class $1,000. The right half of the class has failed to make any payments on the debt. Ask what the right side of the class plans to do. (Use the discussion to introduce the protections available to debtors.)

D Develop Concepts

Repossession of Goods
Explain that a creditor who holds a lien on property has the right to repossess it if the debtor does not make the payments on the loan. Ask students what they think the creditor can do with the property once repossessed. (keep property if the debtor has paid less than 60 percent of the value; or sell property) Inform students that sale of the goods may be public or private.

As You Read

Predict Ask students to scan the section for the topic of repossession and read the sentence defining the term. (If payment is not made on property on which the creditor has a lien, the debtor may repossess it.)

▲ USING VISUALS

Repossession Answer In order to repossess property, the creditor must hold a lien on the property. Explain that repossession usually occurs only after several attempts to collect on the loan itself. The act of repossession and resale can be a costly event for the creditor, even though the property is recovered. Tell students that if the creditor sells the property, the debtor must be notified and is entitled to receive any surplus of the sale after the debts and expenses have been paid.

TEACH (cont.)

D Develop Concepts

Consumer Credit Protection Act Write the phrase "truth in lending" on the board. Ask students to venture ideas as to the meaning of the phrase. *(honest representation of terms of lending money)* Tell students that the Consumer Credit Protection Act, also known as the Truth in Lending Law, is a federal law that requires creditors (lenders) to inform consumers of the costs and terms of credit.

Reading Check

Analyze Lenders rely on credit reports to find out if individuals are a good credit risk, so debtors should ensure the report only contains accurate information.

Legal Talk

(encircle: to form a circle around; enclose: to close in; enlist: to enter a list; enroll: to register in something; entrap: to lure into a compromising act)

Ask students to practice their academic and legal vocabulary with the electronic flashcards available at the *Business and Personal Law* Online Learning Center through glencoe.com.

266

Legal Talk

Entitle: *v* To furnish with a right or claim to something. From Latin *intitulare;* in = provide with + *titulus* = title: to give a name or title to.

Discriminate: *v* To make distinctions on the basis of class or category without regard to individual merit; show preference or prejudice. From Latin *discriminare* = to distinguish between.

Vocabulary Builder List and define five words that begin with the prefix *en*, where *en* has the meaning of "to be in something."

Look It Up! Check definitions in *Black's Law Dictionary* or an online glossary. For direct links, go to **glencoe.com** to find more vocabulary resources.

Reading Check

Analyze *Why is it important to find out what is in your credit report?*

Laws Protecting Debtors

What rights do you have when you borrow money or use credit?

To protect consumers, both the federal and state governments regulate the credit industry. Most states, for example, have set a maximum amount that can be charged for interest. **A usury law is a law restricting the amount of interest that can be charged.** Other laws created by the federal government to protect debtors include the Consumer Credit Protection Act, the Fair Credit Reporting Act, the Equal Credit Opportunity Act, the Fair Credit Collection Practices Act, and the Fair Credit Billing Act.

Consumer Credit Protection Act

The Consumer Credit Protection Act, also known as the Truth in Lending Law, is a federal law that requires creditors to inform consumers of the costs and terms of credit. Creditors must tell you both the finance charge and the annual percentage rate (APR) of a loan. With this information you can compare the costs of loans from different lenders.

D

> **Example** When shopping for a truck, Carmen asked each dealer she visited what the APR would be to finance the purchase. The first dealer said 7.9 percent, another dealer quoted 8.2 percent, and her bank said that it would be 12 percent. Carmen went back to the first dealer, confident that she had found the best deal when shopping around for credit.

U

Fair Credit Reporting Act

The Fair Credit Reporting Act is a federal law that grants people the right to know what is contained in their credit reports. You have the right to know all personal information that is in a credit reporting agency's files and the sources of that information.

The three national credit reporting agencies in the United States are:

- Equifax
- Trans Union
- Experian

Under recent federal legislation, every person has a right to receive one copy of their credit report for free every year from each of the three credit reporting agencies. To find out more, visit the government's official Web site about annual credit reports.

You also have the right to be told the name of anyone who received a copy of your credit report in the past year (and in the past two years if the credit report relates to a job application). You may correct errors in the report. If the credit reporting agency retains information that you believe is inaccurate, your version of the facts must be inserted in the file.

U Universal Access

Visual/Spatial Learners Help students learn the names and purposes of the federal laws covered in this section by asking them to create a visual depiction of each showing how it helps consumers. Encourage students to use photos, digital artwork, clip art, or original art in their presentations.

CYBERLAW

In re MasterCard International, Inc., et al.
132 F.Supp.2d 468 (E.D. La. 2001)

Larry Thompson and Lawrence Bradley filed a class action lawsuit against various banking companies and Internet gambling sites. They argued that the companies had entered into agreements that were illegal under the Racketeer Influenced and Corrupt Organizations Act (RICO) and the Federal Wire Act. Thompson and Bradley argued that Internet gambling is illegal in the United States and that because credit card companies such as MasterCard and Visa allowed customers to use their credit cards to buy gambling chips on foreign Internet gambling Web sites, the American banks were committing illegal racketeering activities. The foreign Web sites included graphics of the MasterCard and Visa logos on their sites. Thompson and Bradley argued that they were charged outrageous fees by MasterCard and Visa when they used their credit cards on these gambling sites.

Ruling and Resolution
The Federal District Court in Louisiana held that the RICO Act did not apply to this case. Although Internet gambling may be illegal in the U.S., the Web sites were all foreign and the Federal Wire Act only prohibits Internet gambling on sporting events, not on other types of gambling. Therefore, the banks could not be sued under the RICO Act.

Critical Thinking Should the Federal Wire Act be amended to prohibit all Internet gambling?

Equal Credit Opportunity Act

The Equal Credit Opportunity Act (ECOA) makes it illegal for banks and businesses to discriminate against credit applicants on the basis of their gender, race, marital status, national origin, religion, age, or because they get public assistance income. There are only three reasons a creditor may deny credit: low income; large current debts; and a poor record of making payments in the past. If you are denied credit, under the ECOA you have the right to know why (see **Figure 12.1** on page 268). If it is due to information in your credit report, you have a right to receive a copy of the report for free. If you find inaccurate or incomplete information in the report, you have the right to dispute it and have it corrected.

Fair Debt Collection Practices Act

The Fair Debt Collection Practices Act (FDCPA) prohibits certain practices by debt collectors. The FDCPA makes it illegal for debt collectors to threaten debtors with violence, use obscene language, or contact consumers by telephone at inconvenient times or places. Debt collectors are not allowed to **impersonate** government officials or attorneys, obtain information under false pretenses, or collect more than is legally owed. They must identify themselves, tell why they are calling you, and cannot tell anyone else about the debt.

Chapter 12   Credit Protection and Bankruptcy   **267**

CYBERLAW

In re MasterCard International, Inc., et al.

Answer Answers will vary. The government is trying to control many international online activities that may be illegal in the United States but are legal in other countries. A number of Internet gambling sites are based in Caribbean nations as a way to evade U.S. gambling laws, but there is nothing to prevent U.S. citizens from accessing those Web sites. Any U.S. legislation that attempts to prohibit Internet gambling on these sites would be hard to enforce.

ASSESS

Independent Practice

Protection of Consumers

Rachael applied for a credit card but was turned down due to a poor credit score. She had no idea what could possibly have affected her score negatively. Under what law can Rachael find out what is contained in her credit report? (The Fair Credit Reporting Act deals with unfavorable credit reports.)

RETEACH

Guided Practice

Fair Debt Collection Practices Act

Ask students to imagine that they have fallen behind on their car payments. The loan company has hired a collection agency to pursue payment on the loan. The representative from the collection agency calls every night at 10 P.M. and makes rather threatening remarks. Have students write a letter of complaint to the loan company about the practices of the collection agency. Ask them to reference the appropriate federal law when outlining their rights.

STUDY TO GO Have students go to the *Business and Personal Law* Online Learning Center through glencoe.com to download free Study-to-Go content to their cell phones or PDAs.

268

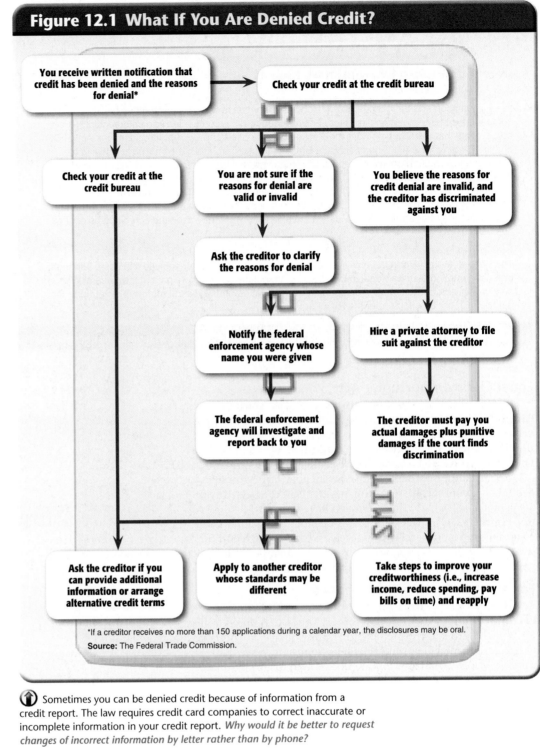

Figure 12.1 What If You Are Denied Credit?

You receive written notification that credit has been denied and the reasons for denial*

→ Check your credit at the credit bureau

Check your credit at the credit bureau

You are not sure if the reasons for denial are valid or invalid

You believe the reasons for credit denial are invalid, and the creditor has discriminated against you

Ask the creditor to clarify the reasons for denial

Notify the federal enforcement agency whose name you were given

Hire a private attorney to file suit against the creditor

The federal enforcement agency will investigate and report back to you

The creditor must pay you actual damages plus punitive damages if the court finds discrimination

Ask the creditor if you can provide additional information or arrange alternative credit terms

Apply to another creditor whose standards may be different

Take steps to improve your creditworthiness (i.e., increase income, reduce spending, pay bills on time) and reapply

*If a creditor receives no more than 150 applications during a calendar year, the disclosures may be oral.

Source: The Federal Trade Commission.

Sometimes you can be denied credit because of information from a credit report. The law requires credit card companies to correct inaccurate or incomplete information in your credit report. *Why would it be better to request changes of incorrect information by letter rather than by phone?*

▲ USING VISUALS

Figure 12.1 What If You Are Denied Credit? **Answer** Requesting changes of incorrect information would be better done in writing since this method would provide a paper trail of your attempts to correct inaccurate information. If requests are made by phone only, there is a risk that any record of the call will be lost or that your request will never be acted upon.

Fair Credit Billing Act

The Fair Credit Billing Act requires creditors to correct billing errors brought to their attention. When errors are made in bills sent by credit card companies and businesses that give credit, this law can help you. If you believe an error has been made, notify the creditor in writing within 60 days of the date of the statement. State your name, account number, the charge in question, and why you believe there is an error. The creditor must acknowledge your letter within 30 days. Also, the creditor must investigate and explain why the charge is correct or fix the mistake within 90 days. You do not have to pay the amount in dispute while waiting for an answer from the creditor, but you must pay all charges not in dispute. Creditors may not report you as being delinquent because of the disputed charge.

Credit Repair Organizations

Credit repair companies that promise they will fix your credit are not allowed to charge you until their services have been performed. They also must tell you about your legal rights. They must provide a written contract that details what services are to be performed, how long it will take, the total cost of the service, and any guarantees that are offered. The contract must also tell you that you have a three-day grace period to cancel the service at no charge.

After You Read

Summarize Name the federal laws that regulate consumer credit.

After You Read

Summarize Consumer Credit Protection Act, the Fair Credit Reporting Act, the Equal Credit Opportunity Act, the Fair Debt Collection Practices Act, and the Fair Credit Billing Act

ASSESS

Self-Assessment

Have students go to the *Business and Personal Law* Online Learning Center through **glencoe.com** to take the Section 12.1 Practice Test.

CLOSE

Culminating Activity

Debt Protection

Tell students to imagine that Will Gazaria has noticed two incorrect charges on his credit card statement. Which federal law gives Will 60 days to notify the creditor of the error? (Fair Credit Billing Act)

SECTION **12.1** ASSESSMENT

Self Check

1. What are two things creditors can do if a debtor defaults on a debt?

2. Under the Consumer Credit Protection Act, what must creditors tell consumers?

3. What are debt collectors prohibited from doing under the FDCPA?

Academic Connection

Social Studies Usury is lending money at an outrageous rate of interest. The practice of usury goes back at least four thousand years and originally meant simply charging interest. Even then, charging interest of any kind was considered immoral. It was prohibited by Chinese and Hindu law and frowned upon by the ancient Greeks. As the need to use credit to conduct business increased, however, the meaning of the word changed. It became acceptable for lenders to charge a reasonable rate of interest on loans so they could make a profit. In 1545, the British government set a maximum rate of interest that could be legally charged, and anything over that was considered usury. This practice was followed by most of the other European countries and later, the United States.

Research and write an outline on the historical development of usury or the attitude toward usury in different cultures.

Critical Thinking

Credit Protection Why do you think debtors need laws to protect them from creditors?

 Go to **glencoe.com** to check your answers.

SECTION **12.1** ASSESSMENT

Self Check

1. repossess property or garnish a worker's wages

2. the costs and terms of credit, including both the finance charge and APR of a loan

3. threatening debtors with violence, using obscene language, calling consumers at inconvenient times or places, impersonating government officials or attorneys, obtaining information under false pretenses, collecting more than is legally owed, or telling anyone else about the debt

Academic Connection

Social Studies

Reports will vary, but should include an organized discussion on usury.

Critical Thinking

to avoid unfair treatment by creditors

 Activity correlated to Social Studies standards on page 264

FOCUS

Bell Ringer Activity

Ask students to identify situations in which they might seek professional counseling. (emotional stress, work stress, legal difficulties, career planning, financial problems)

Preteaching

Key Terms

Read the definitions and ask students to create a sentence using each term.

Academic Vocabulary

Explain that developing vocabulary is key to academic success. An efficient method to develop vocabulary is to study how words are formed.

- **alternative** Adjective, from the Latin *alternus* (the other). Means offering a choice.

- **petition** Noun, from the Latin *petitionem* (a request). Means a formal written request.

- **discharge** Verb, from the Latin *discarricare*, *dis-* (do the opposite of) + *carricare* (load). Means to relieve of a charge or load.

Activity Ask students to give a noun, an adjective, or an adverb form that comes from each word.

 Connects to academic content

270

What You'll Learn

- ◆ Identify and discuss alternatives to bankruptcy.
- ◆ Distinguish between the different types of bankruptcy.
- ◆ Explain the difference between voluntary and involuntary bankruptcy.
- ◆ Identify debts which cannot be discharged by bankruptcy.

Why It's Important

You will need to know the laws about bankruptcy if you ever find yourself unable to pay off your debts.

Academic Standards

Reading and completing the activities in this section will help you practice the following academic standards:

Math (NCTM PSS 1)
Build new mathematical knowledge through problem solving.

Social Studies (NCSS 9)
Study global connections and interdependence.

Reading Guide

Before You Read

Connect Have you ever owed money and had no way of paying it back?

Focus on Ideas

Federal law provides the process for erasing your debts and restoring your credit.

Take Notes

Create a graph like the one shown and use it to take notes as you read this section. Go to glencoe.com to find graphic organizers and tips on how to improve your note-taking skills.

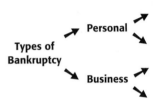

Key Terms

You will learn these legal words and expressions in this chapter. You can also find these terms in *Black's Law Dictionary* or in an online legal dictionary.

- bankruptcy
- voluntary bankruptcy
- involuntary bankruptcy
- Chapter 7 bankruptcy
- Chapter 11 bankruptcy
- Chapter 12 bankruptcy
- Chapter 13 bankruptcy

Academic Vocabulary

You will find these words in your readings and in your tests. Look them up in a dictionary and familiarize yourself with them.

- alternative
- petition
- discharge

270 Unit 4 Your Money and the Law

 glencoe.com

 Reading Strategy

Read for Knowledge

1. **Survey** or preread the chapter.
2. **Question** or formulate questions before you read.
3. **Recite** or read your questions, answers, and notes out loud.
4. **Review** or reread your notes.

Note-Taking Basics

- Listen attentively
- Have note-taking materials ready
- Skim through the lesson material
- Write down key words and ideas
- Anticipate what comes next
- Review notes soon after taking them

Bankruptcy

What can you do to avoid bankruptcy?

Sometimes people and businesses accumulate so much debt through no fault of their own that they can no longer afford to repay it. A business might suffer from a slump in the economy or be hit by a natural disaster. An individual might run up huge credit card debts because of a catastrophic illness and lack of medical insurance or simply by losing his or her job.

In the past, under old English law, people who could not pay their debts were put into debtor's prisons. The drafters of the U.S. Constitution opposed this treatment of debtors and gave Congress the authority to help people in this situation by enacting the bankruptcy law.

Bankruptcy is the legal process by which a debtor can make a fresh start through the sale of assets to pay off creditors. Certain bankruptcy proceedings allow a debtor to stay in business and use the revenue collected to pay his or her debt. Another purpose of bankruptcy law is to allow some debtors to free themselves from the debt they have accumulated, after their assets are distributed, even if their debts have not been paid in full.

D

As You Read

Predict Can you keep your business if you go bankrupt?

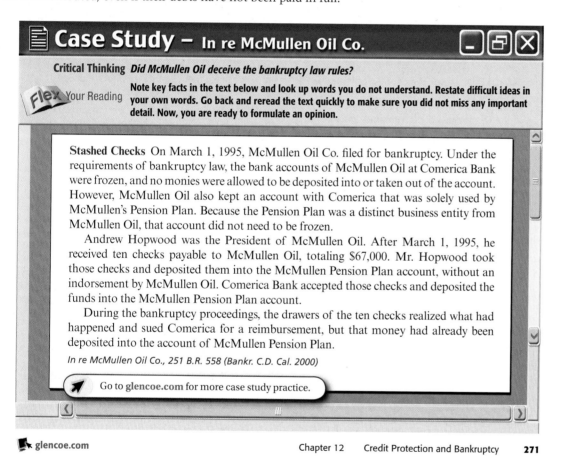

Case Study – In re McMullen Oil Co.

Critical Thinking *Did McMullen Oil deceive the bankruptcy law rules?*

Flex Your Reading Note key facts in the text below and look up words you do not understand. Restate difficult ideas in your own words. Go back and reread the text quickly to make sure you did not miss any important detail. Now, you are ready to formulate an opinion.

Stashed Checks On March 1, 1995, McMullen Oil Co. filed for bankruptcy. Under the requirements of bankruptcy law, the bank accounts of McMullen Oil at Comerica Bank were frozen, and no monies were allowed to be deposited into or taken out of the account. However, McMullen Oil also kept an account with Comerica that was solely used by McMullen's Pension Plan. Because the Pension Plan was a distinct business entity from McMullen Oil, that account did not need to be frozen.

Andrew Hopwood was the President of McMullen Oil. After March 1, 1995, he received ten checks payable to McMullen Oil, totaling $67,000. Mr. Hopwood took those checks and deposited them into the McMullen Pension Plan account, without an indorsement by McMullen Oil. Comerica Bank accepted those checks and deposited the funds into the McMullen Pension Plan account.

During the bankruptcy proceedings, the drawers of the ten checks realized what had happened and sued Comerica for a reimbursement, but that money had already been deposited into the account of McMullen Pension Plan.

In re McMullen Oil Co., 251 B.R. 558 (Bankr. C.D. Cal. 2000)

Go to **glencoe.com** for more case study practice.

glencoe.com

Case Study

In re McMullen Oil Co.

Answer Yes. During bankruptcy proceedings all monies coming into and leaving the company must be strictly monitored by the courts. McMullen Oil diverted $67,000 into other accounts. In addition, the United States Bankruptcy Court held that Comerica Bank could be held liable for accepting the checks without proper indorsement. Comerica Bank had allowed McMullen Oil's funds to be deposited to another business entity's account.

TEACH

Discussion Starter

Class Discussion

Explain to students that individuals often find themselves in tight financial situations, either due to illness, bad money management, or life circumstances beyond their control. Emphasize to students that all financial difficulties can be overcome by constructing a debt management plan or by seeking professional counseling.

D Develop Concepts

Bankruptcy Ask students if they have ever been in a situation in which they believed they needed a fresh start or a clean slate. (bad grades, poor work performance, difficult personal relationships) Explain that in many cases, bankruptcy gives debtors this opportunity. The bankruptcy laws that apply to individuals differ from those that apply to businesses.

As You Read

Predict Before students answer this question, tell them that there are various forms of bankruptcy. (Yes. Business bankruptcy laws are designed to let you reorganize your business or keep your family farm so you do not have to go out of business as a result of filing bankruptcy.)

TEACH (cont.)

Independent Practice

Avoiding Bankruptcy

Have students suggest ways in which they might change their lifestyle or their behavior if they were experiencing debt difficulties. (Answers will vary. Students may suggest that they would stop using credit cards or get counseling about what to do.) Tell students that consolidation loans are helpful to some consumers because they combine all debts into one loan with lower monthly payments.

Guided Practice

Society and Bankruptcy

Have students discuss whether they think that filing bankruptcy carries with it any social stigmas. Have students talk about the pros and cons of a decision to file bankruptcy. On TV, over the radio, and in junk mail, creditors offer ways for people in debt to combine their bills, reduce their monthly payments, and lower their interest rates. Have students research the problem of debt. How can it be lessened? Ask students to come up with ways to encourage people to use credit wisely through posters, advertisements, or commercials.

272

Avoiding Bankruptcy

If you are having trouble paying your bills, you should immediately stop using a credit card and switch to a debit card. As an **alternative** to bankruptcy, you can contact your creditors and work out an adjusted repayment plan. Another possible solution is to get a consolidation loan, which combines all your debts into one loan with lower payments. For example, you can combine monthly payments on credit cards, student loans, and a car into one lower monthly payment.

You can also contact a nonprofit financial counseling program. The Consumer Credit Counseling Service (CCCS) is a nonprofit organization affiliated with the National Foundation for Consumer Credit. Local branches of the CCCS provide debt-counseling services. Check the white pages of your telephone directory, the Internet, or call 1-800-388-2227. All information is kept confidential.

Vocabulary You can find vocabulary definitions in the **Key Terms** glossary and **Academic Vocabulary** glossary in the back of this book.

Global Law

Chilean Bankruptcy Law

Chile's original bankruptcy law was passed in 1931 and served the country for more than 50 years. In the 1980s the country decided to reform its bankruptcy laws. Chilean Law Number 18,175 of the Commercial Code went into effect in 1982.

The Chilean legal system follows the French civil system when it comes to bankruptcy. The bankruptcy laws apply to both businesses and individual persons. There are three specific conditions under which a debtor can be declared bankrupt.

1 Default: a qualified debtor is no longer making payments to its creditor

2 Pending Executions (Titulo Ejecutivo): a debtor has three or more outstanding contracts and can not pay at least two of them

3 Fugitive Debtor: a debtor leaves Chile as a fugitive

There are also two types of debtors in Chile: qualified and not qualified. A qualified debtor only applies to those debtors engaged in commercial, manufacturing, mining, or agricultural activities. Qualified debtors are allowed to begin bankruptcy proceedings on their own behalf. Not qualified

debtors can only have bankruptcy proceedings brought against them by their creditors. Individual persons are not qualified debtors.

Qualified debtors may also be subject to criminal proceedings to determine whether the debtor is claiming bankruptcy because of criminal or negligent acts. A qualified debtor has only 15 days to file for bankruptcy, once it becomes clear that it is bankrupt. Failure to file within 15 days is a criminal offense and the debtor is held criminally liable for the bankruptcy.

Once bankruptcy is determined, the debtor's assets are immediately liquidated so that creditors may be paid. However, some qualified debtors are allowed to continue to operate so that the entire business may be sold, rather than breaking up the business.

Across Cultures: Receipts

Whenever you buy something in Chile, you will always get a receipt. It is against the law in Chile to sell something and not give a receipt.

Critical Thinking *Is it fair that you can be declared bankrupt if you just stop paying your bills?*

Global Law

Chilean Bankruptcy Law

Answer Answers will vary. Only qualified debtors can have bankruptcy granted by default. The presumption is that if a company cannot pay its bills, it must have already exhausted all remedies. As far as individuals are concerned, their creditors must bring bankruptcy proceedings against them. Even then, the situation must be such that the individual owes multiple people and cannot make payments to at least two of those creditors. In the United States, the courts have more say in whether a debtor is granted bankruptcy, and a mere failure to pay bills would likely not be sufficient to grant it.

Filing for Bankruptcy

The moment a **petition** for bankruptcy is filed, an automatic stay goes into effect. An automatic stay is a postponement of collection proceedings against the debtor. Further efforts by creditors against the debtor to collect debts must stop immediately. Creditors, such as credit card companies and lenders of unsecured revolving loans, cannot bring suit for what is owed them. Debit cards can no longer be used because any money in the debtor's bank belongs automatically to the bankruptcy trustee. However, lawsuits involving evictions, divorces, and child custody and support proceedings may continue.

Personal Bankruptcy An individual might need to declare personal bankruptcy because of running up huge medical bills with no medical insurance. *What kinds of bankruptcy can an individual petition for?*

Types of Bankruptcy

What property are you allowed to keep if you declare bankruptcy?

Bankruptcy can be voluntary or involuntary. **Voluntary bankruptcy is when the debtor files for bankruptcy to eliminate or reduce the burden of debt. Involuntary bankruptcy is when creditors begin the proceeding instead of the debtor.** Three creditors must file the petition for bankruptcy if the debtor has 12 or more creditors. The combined debt owed to the three must exceed $11,625. A single creditor who is owed a debt of more than $11,625 can also file if the debtor has fewer than 12 creditors.

Bankruptcy law is federal statutory law contained in Title 11 of the United States Code. There are four main kinds of bankruptcy proceedings. They are named for the chapter of the federal Bankruptcy Code that describes them.

Chapter 7 Bankruptcy (Liquidation)

Chapter 7 bankruptcy, also called ordinary bankruptcy, is a type of bankruptcy which allows individual debtors to discharge all their debts and get a fresh start. With this form of bankruptcy, debtors must sell most of their property and pay their creditors from the proceeds. Debtors must also do the following:

- Get credit counseling from a nonprofit agency before filing for bankruptcy.
- Have a family income below the state's average family income. (If the income is greater, a debtor may be able to file Chapter 13 bankruptcy.)

Chapter 12   Credit Protection and Bankruptcy   **273**

TEACH (cont.)

Reading Check

Analyze Chapters 7 and 13 apply to individuals, and Chapters 11 and 12 apply to businesses.

ASSESS

Quiz

Ask students to answer the following questions:

1. To utilize Consumer Credit Counseling Services, does an individual have to be involved in bankruptcy proceedings? (no)

2. Which type of bankruptcy is intended for family farmers or fishing businesses? (Chapter 12)

3. Which type of bankruptcy helps a business reorganize its financial affairs? (Chapter 11)

RETEACH

Guided Practice

Exemptions

Remind students that as part of the fresh-start policy of the Bankruptcy Act, some assets may be retained by the debtor. Ask students if they agree with these exemptions. Have students with opposing views argue their opinion in front of the class. Then, take a vote to see if your class agrees or disagrees with the exemptions for bankruptcy.

274

Business Bankruptcy
A business might need to declare bankruptcy due to a natural disaster. *What should businesses do to avoid such problems?*

Reading Check

Analyze *Which types of bankruptcy apply to individuals and which types apply to businesses?*

- Provide a federal tax return for the most recent tax year.
- Complete a course in financial management after filing for bankruptcy.

As part of the fresh start policy of the Bankruptcy Act, some assets can be kept by the debtor. These so-called exemptions can be doubled for married couples filing jointly. Depending on your state law, you use either your own state exemptions or the federal ones.

Chapter 11 Bankruptcy (Reorganization)

Chapter 11 bankruptcy is a type of bankruptcy that allows businesses to reorganize their financial affairs and still remain in business. When a petition is filed, a reorganization plan for the business is developed. Once the plan is approved by a certain number of creditors and the court, it will go into operation. If the plan is successful, the business will continue. If not, it will be forced to close.

Chapter 12 Bankruptcy (Family Farmers)

Chapter 12 bankruptcy is a form of bankruptcy that lets family farmers, and fishing businesses, create a plan for debt repayment that allows them to keep their operations running. They must receive more than one-half of their total income from farming or fishing. Also, 50 percent of the debt must result from farm or fishing expenses.

Chapter 13 Bankruptcy (Repayment Plan)

Chapter 13 bankruptcy is a form of bankruptcy that permits individual debtors to reorganize their debts and develop repayment plans. During the period of repayment (three to five years) creditors may not continue collection activities. People who have too much income to file for Chapter 7 bankruptcy may file for Chapter 13. This can be done only if they can make debt repayments of $100 a month for five years. Debtors who wish to keep their car must pay the full loan amount on car loans.

Exceptions to Discharge

Some debts cannot be **discharged** by bankruptcy. That means you still have pay them even if you qualify for bankruptcy.

▲ USING VISUALS

Business Bankruptcy Answer Students will likely suggest that businesses should carry sufficient insurance to cover losses from natural disasters.

Activity Ask students to use the Internet or local library to research cases in which businesses have filed for bankruptcy protection. Ask them to prepare a report outlining the reason for the bankruptcy, the type of bankruptcy filed, and the outcome of the case. Suggest BankruptcyFinder.com as an online resource.

These include debts caused by the debtor's fraud, back taxes, and student loans that do not impose a hardship on the debtor.

Administration of the Debtor's Estate

Following a court hearing, a trustee will be appointed to sell the debtor's property, or estate, to obtain cash. The trustee then distributes the cash among the debtor's creditors according to a priority list. Secured debts are paid first, followed by administrative costs, wages, benefit plans, alimony and support, taxes, and unsecured debts.

Restoring Credit after Bankruptcy

Can you still get credit after you have declared bankruptcy?

A bankruptcy filing remains on a debtor's credit report for ten years and has a bad effect on obtaining a line of credit. However, most debtors who file bankruptcy already have a poor credit rating anyway, and bankruptcy gives them a chance to begin anew. Many of their debts become discharged, which improves their debt-to-income ratio—a factor that creditors look at carefully. The more time that elapses after the bankruptcy filing, the easier it is to reestablish credit.

After a bankruptcy, debtors must educate themselves on developing a budget, managing their money, and using credit and debit cards wisely to avoid accumulating debt again that they cannot resolve.

After You Read

Summarize What are the four main types of bankruptcy?

SECTION 12.2 ASSESSMENT

Self Check

1. What are some alternatives to bankruptcy?

2. What are the differences between voluntary and involuntary bankruptcy?

3. What is the difference between declaring Chapter 7 and Chapter 13 bankruptcy?

Academic Connection

Mathematics You applied for a loan. The lender tells you that you will get a better rate if your debt payments-to-income ratio is low. If your monthly income is $1,200 and your monthly debt payments total $180, what is your debt-payments-to-income ratio (DPR)?

 THEORY **Number and Operations:** To figure out a ratio, you need to use a fraction. To calculate the DPR ratio, divide the total debts by the total income. Convert the decimal outcome to a percentage by moving the decimal point two places to the right and adding a percent sign (%).

 For more math practice, go to the Math Appendix.

Critical Thinking

Debt Burden How much money do you think someone should owe before declaring bankruptcy?

 Go to **glencoe.com** to check your answers.

RETEACH (cont.)

After You Read

Summarize Chapter 7 (Liquidation), Chapter 11 (Reorganization), Chapter 12 (Family Farmers), and Chapter 13 (Repayment Plan)

ASSESS

Self-Assessment

Have students go to the *Business and Personal Law* Online Learning Center through glencoe.com to take the Section 12.2 Practice Test.

CLOSE

Culminating Activity

Bankruptcy

Ask students to list two reasons why someone might get into financial trouble. (poor money management, health problems with no health insurance) Have students describe the benefits and detriments of filing bankruptcy. (fresh start on an emotional and financial level; will experience difficulty securing credit afterward, social stigma)

SECTION 12.2 ASSESSMENT

Self Check

1. consolidation loans, payment plan with creditors, financial counseling

2. Voluntary bankruptcy—debtor files to eliminate or reduce burden of debt. Involuntary bankruptcy—creditors initiate bankruptcy proceedings against the debtor instead of the debtor him- or herself.

3. Chapter 7 discharges all (or most) debts. Chapter 13 reorganizes debts to get financial affairs in order.

Academic Connection

Mathematics
15%

Critical Thinking

Total amount of debt is not a factor. Bankruptcy is available to individuals or businesses that cannot pay their debts (regardless of amount) and seek relief through either discharge or reorganization.

Activity correlated to the Mathematics standard on page 270

Review and Assessment

Summary by Sections

Ask students to read the summaries one key point at a time. Then, ask them to work in groups to create two examples to illustrate each key point.

Vocabulary Builder

Cooperative Learning

1. Have students work in groups to prepare their sentences. Ask the groups to exchange their sentences and assess each other's sentences.

Vocabulary Development

- Ask students to use a dictionary or to go online to look up the etymology of each key term listed.
- Then, ask students to list several words derived from the same root or origin. For example, *contract* has the same root as *contractual* or *contractually*.

276

Summary

Section 12.1 Credit Protection Laws

- ◆ If a debtor fails to make payments, the creditor has a right to repossess property or garnish the person's wages.
- ◆ The Consumer Credit Protection Act requires creditors to inform consumers of the costs and terms of credit.
- ◆ The Fair Credit Reporting Act grants people the right to know what is contained in their credit reports.
- ◆ The Equal Credit Opportunity Act (ECOA) makes it illegal to discriminate against credit applicants.
- ◆ The Fair Debt Collection Practices Act (FDCPA) prohibits certain practices by debt collectors.
- ◆ The Fair Credit Billing Act requires creditors to correct billing errors brought to their attention.

Section 12.2 Bankruptcy Laws

- ◆ Bankruptcy can be voluntary or involuntary.
- ◆ Chapter 7 bankruptcy allows individual debtors to discharge all their debts and get a fresh start.
- ◆ Chapter 11 bankruptcy allows businesses to reorganize their financial affairs and still remain in business.
- ◆ Chapter 12 bankruptcy allows family farmers and fishing businesses to repay debts and still keep their operations running.
- ◆ Chapter 13 bankruptcy is a form of bankruptcy that permits individual debtors to develop repayment plans.
- ◆ Debts that cannot be discharged by bankruptcy include debts caused by fraud, back taxes, and student loans.

 Vocabulary Builder

❶ **On a sheet of paper, use each of these terms in a sentence.**

Key Terms

- repossession
- garnishment
- usury law
- Consumer Credit Protection Act
- Fair Credit Reporting Act

- Equal Credit Opportunity Act (ECOA)
- Fair Debt Collection Practices Act (FDCPA)
- Fair Credit Billing Act
- bankruptcy

- voluntary bankruptcy
- involuntary bankruptcy
- Chapter 7 bankruptcy
- Chapter 11 bankruptcy
- Chapter 12 bankruptcy
- Chapter 13 bankruptcy

Academic Vocabulary

- dominant
- exceed

- impersonate
- alternative

- petition
- discharge

 Go to **glencoe.com** to play a game and improve your legal vocabulary.

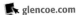
Study Skills for Success

Prepare Your Students for Studying

Tell students that they can improve their ability to understand and remember material from their courses by learning and practicing study skills. Remind students to:

- **Get motivated!** Motivation must come from within. To motivate yourself, think of ways in which what you learn now will fit into your long-term personal and professional goals.
- **Get organized!** Make studying part of your daily routine, not something you do at the last minute.
- **Concentrate!** Study in an environment that is as free of distractions as possible.

Key Points Review

Answer the following questions. Refer to the chapter for additional reinforcement.

2 What is garnishment and what is the most a creditor can garnish?

3 What rights does the Fair Credit Reporting Act give people?

4 What are the only three reasons a creditor may deny credit?

5 According to the Fair Credit Billing Act, what should you do if you believe an error has been made on a bill?

6 What are the differences between Chapters 7, 11, 12, and 13 bankruptcies?

7 Which types of bankruptcy are personal and which are business bankruptcies?

8 How is a debtor's property distributed upon bankruptcy?

9 Which debts are not extinguished by bankruptcy?

Standardized Test Practice

10 Read the following excerpt from the terms and conditions of a credit card and do problems 1 and 2.

Default Rate: All your APRs may increase if you default under any card agreement, if you fail to make a payment when due, you exceed your credit line, or you make a payment that is not honored. In these circumstances, we may automatically increase your interest rate on all balances to the default APR, which is equal to the prime rate plus 23.99% or up to 28.99%, whichever is greater.

Late Fee: We add a late fee to each billing period if you fail to pay by the due date. This fee is based on your account balance as of the payment due date. The late fee is: $15 on a balance up to $100, $29 on balances of $100 to $250, and $39 on balances over $250.

1. If you default under a card agreement, your interest rate can be automatically increased to:

Ⓐ the prime rate

Ⓑ 23.99%

Ⓒ the prime rate plus 23.99% or up to 28.99%, whichever is greater

Ⓓ the prime rate plus 23.99% or up to 28.99%, whichever is lower

2. You make a late payment on a balance of $234. You will be charged a late fee of:

Ⓐ $15

Ⓑ $29

Ⓒ $100

Ⓓ $39

 Test-Taking Strategies When trying to answer difficult questions, first eliminate answers you know are incorrect, then analyze the remaining answers.

---

2. legal procedure through which a worker's earnings are withheld for payment of a debt; cannot exceed 25 percent of weekly take-home pay, except for certain amounts of support payments and taxes

3. the right to know all personal information and sources in a consumer reporting agency's files; right to receive one copy of credit report free every year; right to be told the name of anyone who received a copy of your credit report in the past year

4. low income, large current debts, poor payment history

5. Notify the creditor in writing within 60 days of date of statement; include name, account number, the charge in question, and why you believe there is an error.

6. Chapter 7, discharge; Chapter 11, reorganization for businesses; Chapter 12, farming families; Chapter 13, reorganization for individuals.

7. Chapters 7 and 13 are for individuals; Chapters 11 and 12 are for businesses.

8. Trustee distributes cash from sale of property to creditors according to a priority list.

9. back taxes, student loans, and debts caused by debtor's fraud

---

Standardized Test Practice

10. C and B

 ## Strategies for Standardized Test Prep Success

Whether your students have a standardized test coming up in a few days or a few weeks, these last-minute test-prep tips and strategies will help them relax and do their best.

- **Test Format** Help students become familiar with the format of the test by practicing with test items that imitate the actual test items as closely as possible.

- **Test Timing** Have your students take timed practice tests so that they become comfortable with the length, design, and timing of the actual test.

Apply and Debate

Students should use chapter content to arrive at conclusions. The legal resolutions are listed below:

11. Yes, but only if that was the closing price of the auction. Since the bank held the lien on the car, they are allowed to repossess the car and sell it.

12. Yes. It is the responsibility of the lender to make the borrower aware of all the costs involved in his or her loan under the Consumer Credit Protection Act.

13. Yes. If no evidence could be found to show that the charge did not belong to Ned, he would be responsible for the charge.

14. No, not at the end of the initial meeting. Under federal law, Maria cannot be charged until after all services have been performed. At that point, Maria can be charged for the service as long as the company told her about her rights, that there is a three-day grace period to cancel the service at no charge, and provided a written contract with details and cost of the service.

15. Chapter 7 bankruptcy may be the best option if they have exhausted all other alternatives, such as establishing a payment plan or consolidation loans.

 Apply and Debate

C Read the following scenarios. Get together with other students in pairs or groups of three and take a position on each scenario. Debate your position in class with students taking the opposite position or prepare a written argument justifying your position.

⑪ **Repossession**

Tamara purchased a car for $5,000 down and a four-year loan with payments of $400 per month. During the last year of her loan, she lost her job and fell behind in her payments. The bank repossessed her car, leaving Tamara with nothing.

You Debate *Can the bank sell Tamara's car for below-market value to settle her loan?*

⑫ **Consumer Credit Protection Act**

Jason was reviewing the loan documents he had just signed with a lender, who had quoted him the lowest interest rate. He noticed that his loan was increased by $2,000, which is the cost of points he had to pay for the low interest rate. The lender had not explained this to him.

You Debate *Is the lender violating the Consumer Credit Protection Act by not disclosing the additional costs to Jason?*

⑬ **Fair Credit Billing Act**

When Ned received his credit card bill, he noticed a charge he had not made. He notified his credit card company by phone, then in writing. After an investigation, the company determined that Ned would be held responsible for the complete charge.

You Debate *If Ned did not make this charge, should he be required to pay for it even after the investigation?*

⑭ **Credit Repair Organizations**

Maria contacted a credit repair company to help her with her credit. At the end of her meeting, Maria was asked to pay $450 in administrative costs.

You Debate *Is Maria required by law to pay the fee to the credit repair company?*

⑮ **Chapter 7 Bankruptcy**

The Mundy family has not been able to pay their debts since Hurricane Katrina struck their home and business. They decided to file for Chapter 7 bankruptcy to get relief from their creditors.

You Debate *Is bankruptcy the best option for the Mundy's considering the circumstances?*

C **Critical Thinking**

Debt Problems Joseph and Danielle are newly married. Danielle was laid off and has been out of work for eight months. The couple has fallen behind on their student loans, car loans, and credit card bills. Joseph wants to file Chapter 7 bankruptcy and get rid of all these debts, but Danielle thinks it will ruin their credit forever.

Debate Practice

• Is Danielle correct that the couple's credit will be ruined forever? (Bankruptcy filing remains on a credit report for only ten years, but the filing does have a negative effect on obtaining credit during that time.)

• Can all their debts be discharged? (Generally student loans cannot be discharged. If the couple wishes to keep their car, they will have to retain that debt also.)

12 Chapter

Review and Assessment

17. It could be argued that Paul is still young, stands to make a lot of money in the future, and has an ethical responsibility to repay those who put him through college to secure his financial future. Paul could get credit counseling and arrange to make lower or later payments on his debts.

Internet Application

18. Changes in the bankruptcy law include a requirement for pre-filing credit counseling, post-filing financial education, and increased filing fees for individuals above a certain income level. A Chapter 7 discharge will be more difficult to receive without a means test to see if there is enough disposable income to fund a Chapter 13 filing instead.

R Reading Strategy

Reading Connection

American Bar Association Resources

Go to the *Business and Personal Law* Online Learning Center through glencoe.com to find links for further readings that relate to this chapter. Ask students to read, review, and summarize the documents. Advise students to keep their reviews and summaries to use as reference material for their Unit Thematic Project on pages 282–283.

Case Study Practice – Ardis v. Educational Management Corp.

16 Can Student Loans Be Discharged in Bankruptcy? In July 1991 Robert Ardis consolidated his student loans into one loan totaling $23,756. He made 14 payments totaling approximately $2,700 until August, 1994, when he stopped paying the loan. In April of 1995, his account went into default. Ten years later, in 2005, the amount, with interest, had increased to $70,600.

In 2005, Mr. Ardis sought to have his student loan debt discharged in bankruptcy. He had previously filed for bankruptcy in 1995 and 2003. Both times, the bankruptcy court declined to discharge his student loans. Mr. Ardis, a single father, worked as a teacher at an annual salary of $40,000 and did not anticipate any salary increases in the near future. His offer to pay a lump sum of $8,000 was rejected.

Student loan debt is not normally dischargeable in bankruptcy, but can be if the debtor demonstrates three things: 1) that the debtor could not maintain a minimal standard of living if forced to repay the loans; 2) that the debtor's financial situation is likely to persist into the future; and 3) the debtor has made good faith efforts to repay the loan.

Source: Ardis v. Educational Management Corp., 2006 WL 931563(D.S.C. 2006)

Practice Should Mr. Ardis's student loan debt be discharged?

17 Ethics ←?→ Application

Student Loans Paul graduated from college with a business degree owing $20,000 in credit cards and personal loans. Two years after graduating, he is not making enough money to keep up with his debts and is considering filing for bankruptcy.

◆ Would it be unethical for Paul to declare bankruptcy under these circumstances?

18 Internet Application

Preventing Abuse The Bankruptcy Abuse Prevention and Consumer Protection Act of 2005 created major changes in the bankruptcy system. Under the new law, people who want to file for Chapter 7 bankruptcy must meet certain requirements.

Go to **glencoe.com** to access the Web site FindLaw to read about the main changes in the bankruptcy law and write a brief description of them.

Reading Connection

Outside Reading Go to **glencoe.com** for a list of outside reading suggestions about credit and bankruptcy laws.

Case Study Practice

16. No. The Federal District Court in South Carolina held that, although an argument could be made that the first two conditions of the test—minimal standard of living and future earnings—apply to Mr. Ardis, the court could not find that he had made good-faith efforts to repay his loan. The fact that he had made no payments for ten years did not speak well for his good-faith efforts for repayment. Also, an offer of $8,000 for a $65,000 debt is not a reasonable offer of repayment.

Careers in Law

Introduce Career Planning

Bell Ringer Activity

When people dispute over an issue, they are arguing, debating, or questioning its validity. Ask students to think of examples that demonstrate disputes.

Career Decisions

Self-Assessment Checklist

Use this checklist to help students determine their career path:

✓ Think about things you are good at
✓ Write down your interests
✓ Think about the lifestyle you want
✓ Write down your aptitudes and abilities
✓ Consider your personality
✓ Determine your learning style
✓ List some careers that might match these characteristics

Résumé Builder

Answer A negotiator operating in a calm and collected manner when dealing with many personalities that are at odds in a tense situation will be negotiating from a position of strength.

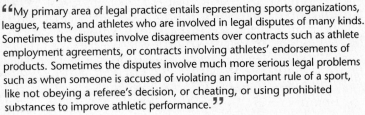

Ira A. Finkelstein
Attorney, Harnik & Finkelstein

What do you do at work?
"My primary area of legal practice entails representing sports organizations, leagues, teams, and athletes who are involved in legal disputes of many kinds. Sometimes the disputes involve disagreements over contracts such as athlete employment agreements, or contracts involving athletes' endorsements of products. Sometimes the disputes involve much more serious legal problems such as when someone is accused of violating an important rule of a sport, like not obeying a referee's decision, or cheating, or using prohibited substances to improve athletic performance."

What skills are most important to you?
"My ability to conduct a trial or hearing and, perhaps even more important, my ability to negotiate a settlement. Most sports disputes result in out-of-court settlements. It is also very important to me that I learn everything I can about the sport I am working with and the people who are involved in it."

What training do you recommend?
"Any good lawyer can become a good sports lawyer, because the basic legal skills and learning experiences are the same. However, lawyers who want to represent athletes or clubs in salary contract negotiations should have good training in employment negotiations. Since in so many sports the athletes are organized similar to labor unions, previous experience in labor relations law is a plus. I recommend that if you really love a particular sport, get involved at the local level of the sport initially to meet as many people as possible, and learn about all of the particular legal issues that the sport may involve."

What is your key to success?
"I believe in having a very close relationship of trust with my clients and demonstrating that I am interested in and care about their sports, businesses, and careers. I find it helpful that I constantly look for new challenges rather than doing the same kinds of legal work over and over."

Résumé Builder

Academic Skills
- Above average critical-thinking skills
- Good speaking and debating skills

Education and Training

A bachelor's degree in business administration, finance, sports and leisure science, or a basic legal background augmented with specific study of chosen industry or sport. The following high school and college courses will help develop the necessary background knowledge:

- Athletic administration (college)
- Athletic management (college)
- Business, contracts, and consumer law
- Business management
- English language arts (rhetoric and composition)
- Sports management (college)
- Sports marketing

Critical Thinking

Why does it benefit a negotiator to remain cool and calm while working on a deal?

Go to glencoe.com to find legal careers resources.

Research Technology

Specialized technology is available for a variety of law-related tasks. For example, LexisNexis and Westlaw are two competing electronic databases that attorneys and other legal professionals use to conduct research. These services give users access to online legal information, including the text of court decisions and legislation, the content of public records, and many legal articles.

Activity Ask students to access the American Bar Association's Web site through glencoe.com and read about technology uses in legal professions.

The Writing Connection

Persuasive Writing Practice

Is It Legal Even in a Changed World? After the events of September 11, 2001, Congress enacted the Uniting and Strengthening America by Providing Appropriate Tools Required to Intercept and Obstruct Terrorism Act of 2001, also known as the U.S. Patriot Act. The new crimes of domestic terrorism became credible threats to the Homeland Security. The White House states that the Act "has been vital to winning the War on Terror and protecting the American people." President George W. Bush stated in a speech that the Act allows intelligence and law enforcement officials to continue to share information by using tools against terrorists; the intent is to ensure the nation's security while safeguarding the civil liberties of the people.

Assignments

Research Research what makes the U.S. Patriot Act controversial legislation.

Write After considering the situation above and conducting research, write a persuasive essay about your stance on the constitutionality of the Act.

Writing Tips Before you start writing your essay, read through the following prewriting techniques:

✓ Read newspaper archives on your specific subject. Pay attention to the different angles of the editorials. How do you respond to the different issues raised?

✓ Reading editorials may give you ideas for developing evidence towards your position in the essay.

✓ Create a graphic organizer to help you organize and visually show the plan for your argument.

Essay Test Strategies Keep your audience and purpose in mind:

✓ Audience: peers, classmates, and teacher

✓ Purpose: present an opinion, acknowledge alternative viewpoints, and provide reasons for your opinion

 Go to **glencoe.com** to find more writing resources.

glencoe.com   Chapter 12   Credit and Debt   **281**

Assignments

When students start researching the U.S. Patriot Act, they may find some information on the way the government conducts surveillance on individuals' financial transactions and overall spending. This angle on the Act relates well to Unit 4.

If students are having a difficult time deciding their position on the Act, ask them to make a list of important rights upheld by the U.S. Constitution. Decide if the U.S. Patriot Act interferes with any of these rights. When they compare and contrast the facts, this might help crystallize their position.

The Writing Connection

W Writing Support

Objectives

Write a brief persuasive essay outlining a position on an issue.

Essay Rubric

Evaluate the students' writing according to the following criteria:

- The essay presents both supporting and opposing views. **(6 points)**
- The essay uses statement of fact to bolster position. **(6 points)**
- The essay demonstrates a voice that is affirmative and strong. **(5 points)**
- The essay employs semantic slanting when comparing ideas. **(4 points)**
- Syntax, grammar, and spelling are error-free. **(4 points)**

Total: 25 points

S Skills Practice

Analyze

Many nonprofit groups are concerned with discrimination. Have students analyze the Web sites of contrasting groups of an area of discrimination (e.g., gender, sexual orientation, race, religion, age, etc.).

Culminating Activity

Ask students to work in groups to give each other feedback on their first drafts.

FOCUS

Pose this scenario to students: they received the monthly statement of their department-store card activity, and they discovered that two of the transactions are listed in error. What are they to do?

TEACH

Workshop Overview

The objective of this workshop is to prepare a business letter disputing an error on a credit report.

Social Studies

Your monthly credit card statement shows a balance of $346.57. The statement shows an erroneous transaction in the amount of $146.82, and a finance charge of $44.19. You report the charge in question to the credit company but you still have to pay the remaining balance. Recalculate the finance charge and compute the new balance. ([44.19/346.57] × 100 = 12.75%; .1275 × [$346.57 − 146.82] = $25.47 new finance charge; New balance: $346.57 − 146.82 + 25.47 = $225.22)

Correcting a Credit Report Error

For this project, you will use what you have learned to prepare a business letter disputing an error you have discovered on your credit report. For this project, you will work individually.

Here is a checklist of the skills that you will need to complete this project. Your teacher will consider these skills when evaluating your work.

Evaluation Rubric	
Academic Skills	
1. Online and library research	**1.** 10 points
2. Reading for information	**2.** 10 points
3. Note-taking	**3.** 5 points
4. Estimation and computation of facts/figures	**4.** 10 points
5. English composition to summarize findings	**5.** 15 points
Legal Skills	
6. Research of consumer reporting and credit rights	**6.** 15 points
7. Methods of comparing the three main credit bureaus' reports	**7.** 15 points
8. Analysis of the essential statistical information	**8.** 15 points
9. Use of technology	**9.** 5 points
	Total 100 Points

 For more resources and for grading rubrics, go to **glencoe.com**.

Step 1: Preparation

❶ Write an outline of a business letter to dispute an error you have discovered on your credit report.

❷ Use all you have learned in this unit, at the library, or on the Internet as tools.

❸ Complete this project in a format acceptable for an addition to your portfolio.

 Time Management Rubric

Have students evaluate their usage of time by rating the skills below on a scale of "poor" to "apprentice" to "proficient."

- Defines priorities.
- Generates to-do list.
- Abides by weekly calendar.
- Lists goals.
- Tackles one action item on the to-do list at a time.

- Keeps agreement with self to complete a given item (lessens the feeling of being overwhelmed).
- Avoids distractions.
- Ignores mobile technology when concentrating on school assignment.
- Ignores urge to daydream.

Step 2: Procedure

❶ **Review** the text in this unit and make a list of essential tools to protect or repair your credit report. Go to **glencoe.com** to find additional resources for understanding credit reports based on the reporting agency.

❷ **List** all the credit terms you might use in your business letter. What are you disputing in the report? What remedy are you expecting from the reporting bureau? What proof can you offer that the information is incorrect? How long will you allow the agency to rectify the error?

❸ **Write** a standard business format letter, based on your knowledge and research, to one of the three credit report bureaus regarding a dispute on your credit report. Use the Internet to download a sample dispute letter, or create an original letter using word-processing software. Make enough copies of your letter to allow classmates to review and annotate.

❹ **Describe** the scenario that is the basis for your dispute business letter and present your contract to the class.

Step 3: Create an Analysis Report

As a class, compare the letters presented. Generate a list of common areas that all letters included and what information could make it easier to resolve the conflict.

❶ What formats of business letters were used to compose this assignment?

❷ Did the letters include all the necessary elements to resolve the conflict?

❸ If not, how does the absence of the element(s) affect the resolution?

❹ How was your letter similar to or different from the other business letters presented?

Community Connection

Find the information on the number of judicial courts, judgeships, and number of districts in the United States. What steps are required in filing a bankruptcy? How are jurors selected to stand on bankruptcy hearings? Are there any special requirements to being a juror in a judicial court? Go to **glencoe.com** to find resources.

Competitive Event Prep

Establishing Credit

Situation: Assume the role of a high school business law student who recently turned 18. Since turning 18, you have received a great many offers from several credit card companies. The offers vary in the interest rates charged and incentives such as airline frequent flier miles and points for free hotel stays. You have learned the importance of establishing credit and maintaining a good credit rating. You would like to begin to establish credit in your name by opening a credit card account.

Activity: You are to discuss with your parents your credit card options. Your discussion should include some selection criteria and other factors to consider when choosing a credit card.

For more Competitive Event preparation, performance tips, and evaluation rubrics, go to **glencoe.com**.

TEACH (cont.)

Extending the Content

Cases of Interest
Ask students to use the Internet to find some of the rules for using credit. They should share some of the more interesting tips found.

Reading Connection

American Bar Association Resources
Ask students to go back to their ABA readings, notes, and summaries. Direct them to apply any relevant ABA content to review and revise their outline and first draft.

ASSESS

Evaluation

Make sure students review the evaluation rubric. They should pay attention to their research on consumer reporting and credit rights.

CLOSE

Culminating Activity

Cooperative Learning
Ask students to research agencies that claim to repair bad credit. They should determine if these agencies are legitimate and helpful. They should also identify what the FTC stipulates about these agencies.

C Critical Thinking

Drawing Conclusions

An analysis of usage rates and trends by Nellie Mae (published May 2005) reported, "As students progress through school, credit card usage swells. Ninety-one percent of final-year students have a credit card compared to 42% of freshmen. Fifty-six percent of final-year students carry four or more cards while only 15% of freshmen carry that many. Final-year students carry an average balance of $2,864 while freshmen carry an average balance of $1,585." Based on these statistics, what conclusions can be drawn about young adults and their credit card usage?

FOCUS

Why It's Important

- The Supreme Court held that the Federal Reserve's Regulation Z is not defective, arbitrary, capricious, or contrary to the statute.

- Regulation Z excludes over-limit fees from the definition of "finance charge."

TEACH

Preteaching

Your Reading

This text is a long excerpt from a key case where U.S. administrative law was applied.

Preread Skim the text, look at headings and the first few sentences of every section.

U Universal Access

Differentiated Instruction Have students make journal entries about Americans' dependence on the use of credit as their form of purchasing power. Remind students that their experience is not limited to just their personal experiences, but information they read, hear, and witness. Instruct students to write an essay based on their journal entries.

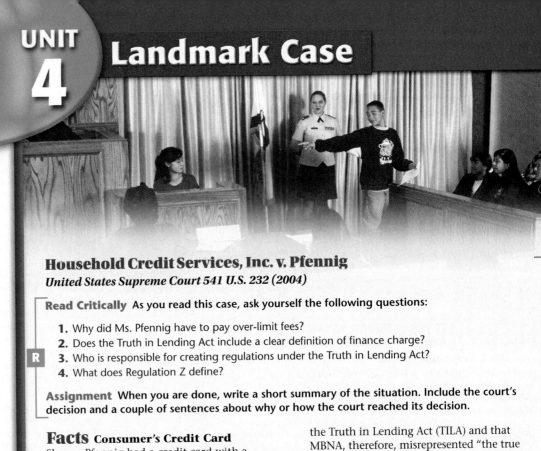

Household Credit Services, Inc. v. Pfennig
United States Supreme Court 541 U.S. 232 (2004)

Read Critically As you read this case, ask yourself the following questions:

1. Why did Ms. Pfennig have to pay over-limit fees?
2. Does the Truth in Lending Act include a clear definition of finance charge?
3. Who is responsible for creating regulations under the Truth in Lending Act?
4. What does Regulation Z define?

Assignment When you are done, write a short summary of the situation. Include the court's decision and a couple of sentences about why or how the court reached its decision.

Facts Consumer's Credit Card

Sharon Pfennig had a credit card with a limit of $2,000. She originally had the card issued by Household Credit Services, Inc. However, after she received the card, Household Credit Services, Inc. sold its credit card business to MBNA America Bank, N.A. Although she had a credit limit of $2,000, Ms. Pfennig was able to make charges on her credit card that caused her to exceed the limit. For every month that Ms. Pfennig exceeded her credit limit, she was charged an over-limit fee of $29.

Class Action Suit

On August 24, 1999, Ms. Pfennig filed a class action lawsuit against MBNA alleged on behalf of all consumers nationwide that they were charged or assessed over-limit fees on cards issued by MBNA. Ms. Pfennig alleged that MBNA allowed its customers to exceed its stated credit limits, thereby subjecting the customers to the over-limit fees. Ms. Pfennig further argued that the over-limit fees were "interest charges" under

the Truth in Lending Act (TILA) and that MBNA, therefore, misrepresented "the true cost of credit" to its customers.

The Truth in Lending Act

Congress passed the TILA as means to encourage the "informed use of credit" by American consumers. In order to achieve those ends, the TILA requires that creditors include adequate disclosure in their documentation to ensure that all the relevant credit terms are meaningfully disclosed. Congress also gave expansive power to the Federal Reserve Board to enact appropriate and extensive regulations to ensure that Congress's intent in passing the TILA was followed by creditors.

Under the specific legislation, TILA requires that:

The credit card statement must include the account's outstanding balance at the end of the billing period and the amount of any finance charge added to the account during the period, itemized to show the amounts, if any due to the

? Landmark Case Questions

R Reading Strategy

Answers

1. She exceeded her $2,000 credit limit.

2. No. That is why the Act provides authority for additional regulations to further clarify the law.

3. the Federal Reserve

4. the term "finance charge"

application of percentage rates and the amount, if any imposed as a minimum or fixed charge. 15 U.S.C. §1637(b)

A finance charge is an amount payable directly or indirectly by the person to whom the credit is extended, and imposed directly or indirectly by the creditor as an incident to the extension of credit. 15 U.S.C. §1605(a)

Regulation Z Under the TILA, Congress gave the Federal Reserve power to enact regulations that include "classifications, differentiations, or other provisions, and [to] provide for such adjustments and exceptions for any class of transactions, as in the judgment of the [Federal Reserve] are necessary or proper to effectuate the purposes of [the TILA], to prevent circumvention or evasion thereof, or to facilitate compliance therewith." Regulation Z is one of those more specific regulations that seeks to further define finance charge. Regulation Z specifically excludes some fees from the definition of finance charge.

Regulation Z excludes, among other things, the following:

1. *Application fees charged to all applicants for credit, whether or not credit is actually extended.*
2. *Charges for actual unanticipated late payment, for exceeding a credit limit, or for delinquency, default, or similar occurrence.*
3. *Charges imposed by a financial institution for paying items that overdraw an account, unless the payment of such items and the imposition of the charge were previously agreed upon in writing.*
4. *Fees charged for participation in a credit plan, whether assessed on an annual or other periodic basis.*
5. *Seller's points.*
6. *Interest forfeited as a result of an interest reduction required by law on a time deposit used as security for an extension of credit.*
7. *Certain fees related to real estate.*
8. *Discounts offered to induce payment for a purchase by cash, check, or other means, as provided in section 167(b) of the Act.*

 glencoe.com

Opinion **Court of Appeals** The Sixth Circuit Court of Appeals found that the TILA was ambiguous in its definition of finance charge. The Court reasoned that Ms. Pfennig only had to pay the over-limit fee because MBNA had chosen to extend her additional credit, thus allowing her to exceed her credit limit for a limited time. Therefore, the Court of Appeals held the MBNA might have violated the TILA and remanded the case to the Federal District Court.

Ambiguity Under the TILA, the definition of finance charge is ambiguous. Therefore, the Federal Reserve's regulation is binding on the courts, unless the regulation is "procedurally defective, arbitrary or capricious in substance, or manifestly contrary to the statute." The Supreme Court, thus, must determine whether Regulation Z falls under any of the above exclusions.

Holding **The Court's Decision** The Supreme Court held that the Federal Reserve's Regulation Z is not defective, arbitrary, capricious, or contrary to the statute. Therefore, because Regulation Z specifically excludes over-limit fees from the definition of finance charge, MBNA is not liable to Ms. Pfennig for failing to meaningfully disclose all finance charges under the TILA.

TRIAL PREP

The National High School Mock Trial Association organizes competitions at the local, regional, and national levels where teams of high school or college students prepare and argue fictional legal cases before practicing attorneys and judges. Mock Trial team members are each assigned a role as either an attorney or witness. Each team must develop a courtroom strategy, legal arguments, and a presentation style.

Go to **glencoe.com** to find guided activities about case strategy and presentation.

ASSESS

Guided Practice

Round Robin

Ask students to pair up to create a flashcard game on the unit's key terms. Once the cards have been created, they should take turns holding one up and recalling all the concepts that surrounded the topic. Encourage the partner to probe the other's memory to assist in the retrieval of information.

CLOSE

Understand the Decision

Class Action Lawsuits

Although this case was brought by Ms. Pfennig against her creditor, the case was actually a class action lawsuit. Class action lawsuits are brought as a way of providing relief to multiple parties wronged by the same person or entity. When a class is "certified" by this judge, it means that the case can proceed, and all potential members of the class need to determine if they wish to be part of the class. If you join a class, you give up your right to sue individually. What are the advantages to joining the class? (Sometimes there is "strength in numbers." Also, class action suits are generally less costly up-front to the complaining parties.)

Winning the Case

Drawing Comparisons

Have students research agency regulations in the Code of Federal Regulations (CFR). Why are agency regulations important? (Agency law is an important part of everyday life, but one that is not always understood. Although not exactly a federal "law," regulations hold almost the same weight and must be followed by citizens, just like a law. It would be very difficult for a law passed by Congress to be written so as to deal with every possible issue. That is why quite often laws allow specific agencies to write supplementary regulations to clarify and assist the law.)

Unit Objectives

Chapter	Section	Objectives
Chapter 13	**13.1**	• **Define** agency and explain the nature of an agency relationship. • **Explain** the difference between an agent and a principal. • **Distinguish** between an agent and an independent contractor. • **List** the ways agency relationships are created.
	13.2	• **Identify** the different types of agency authority. • **Explain** the difference between actual and apparent authority. • **Distinguish** between the different types of agents.
Chapter 14	**14.1**	• **Identify** the duties of agents to principals. • **Identify** the duties of principals to agents. • **Describe** the nature of contract liability in agency law. • **Explain** the doctrine of *respondeat superior* in relation to tort liability.
	14.2	• **Determine** when an agency relationship is terminated by operation of law. • **Explain** when an agency relationship is terminated by act of the parties. • **Identify** the individuals who are entitled to notice that an agency relationship has ended.
Chapter 15	**15.1**	• **Discuss** the employer-employee relationship. • **Define** employment-at-will. • **Name** the exceptions to employment-at-will. • **Explain** the collective bargaining process. • **Describe** the laws that regulate labor unions.
	15.2	• **Explain** how the law protects employee health and safety. • **Describe** the laws that guarantee fair wages and benefits. • **Identify** the laws that prohibit different forms of discrimination. • **Define** disparate treatment and disparate impact.

Understanding Brackets, Letters, and Ability Levels in the Teacher Wraparound Edition

Brackets Brackets on the reduced student edition page correspond to teaching strategies and activities in the Teacher Wraparound Edition. As you teach the lesson, the brackets show you exactly where to use the teaching strategies and activities.

Letters The letters on the reduced student edition page identify the type of strategy or activity. See the key below to learn about the different types of strategies and activities.

Ability Levels Teaching strategies that appear throughout the chapters have been identified by one of three codes to give you an idea of their suitability for students of varying learning styles and abilities.

Resources Key program resources are listed in each chapter. Icons indicate the format of resources.

KEY TO LETTERS

R **Reading Strategy** activities help you teach reading skills and vocabulary.

C **Critical Thinking** strategies help students apply and extend what they have learned.

S **Skills Practice** strategies help students practice historical analysis and geographical skills.

W **Writing Support** activities provide writing opportunities to help students comprehend the text.

D **Develop Concepts** activities use various strategies to help teachers gauge and plan for students' concept development.

U **Universal Access** activities provide differentiated instruction for English language learners, and suggestions for teaching various types of learners.

NCLB **No Child Left Behind** activities help students practice and improve their abilities in academic subjects.

KEY TO ABILITY LEVELS

L1 strategies should be within the ability range of all students. Often full class participation is required.

L2 strategies are for average to above-average students or for small groups. Some teacher direction is necessary.

L3 strategies are designed for students able and willing to work independently. Minimal teacher direction is necessary.

KEY TO RESOURCE ICONS

📁 Print Material

💿 CD/DVD

🖥 Internet

TeacherWorks™
All-In-One Planner and Resource Center

Teacher Wraparound Edition

Student Activity Workbook with Academic Integration Teacher Annotated Edition

For the Unit:
Lesson Plans
National and State Standards Correlations

For the Chapters:
Lessons Plans
Note-Taking Graphic Organizers
Chapter Outlines
Chapter Summaries
Enrichment Activities Masters

Supplemental Cases
Internet Connection Student Activities Masters
Blackline Masters for Student Edition Figures and Supplemental Figures
Ethics and Business Law Activities
Competitive Events Test-Taking Prep
Reproducible Chapter Tests

 Link to the **Business and Personal Law Online Learning Center** with Podcasts through **glencoe.com**.

Real-World Applications

Demonstrate Case Resolutions

Learning Objective

- Identify types of agent authority (p. 298).
- Understand how an agency relationship is terminated (p. 318).
- Explain how the law protects employee health and safety (p. 334).

- Differentiate between agents and principals (p. 305).
- Understand implied agency (p. 323).
- Explain laws that prohibit different forms of discrimination (p. 345).

- Describe laws that prohibit different forms of discrimination (pp. 350–351).

Apply Business Law Concepts

Learning Objective

News

- Understand agency relationships (p. 288).
- Understand the duties of agents to principals and principals to agents (p. 306).
- Explain labor unions in the United States (p. 324).

- Describe how to use a commercial agent in the United Arab Emirates to conduct business (p. 294).
- Understand the concept of using a commercial agent to do business in Israel (p. 309).
- Explain the collective bargaining laws in Poland (p. 329).

- Understand the concept of apparent authority (p. 299).
- Describe the laws that prohibit discrimination in employment (p. 340).

Ethics Application

- Recognize the concept of implied authority (p. 305).
- Apply ethics to the decision making process (p. 323).
- Apply ethics to the decision making process (345).

- Explain tort liability of principals (p. 313).

Teach Financial Literacy

Learning Objective

- Understand the purpose of saving for retirement (p. 287)

Bring Project-Based Learning into the Law Classroom

Employment Guide

- **Introduce Concepts**
  The relationship between an employer and an employee is governed by federal and state laws. The laws protect the rights and stipulate the responsibilities of both employees and employers.

- **Explore Concepts**
  Read the Thematic Project Preview and the WebQuest activity (p. 287)

  Ask students to keep track of the laws and legislation on employment as they study Chapters 13, 14, and 15.

- **Apply Concepts**
  Research employment forms, and federal and state laws, outline the rights and responsibilities of employees and employers, and document findings (pp. 348 and 349).

Extend Content

Reading Connection

Using American Bar Association (ABA) Resources

- Direct students to pages 305, 323, and 345 in the Student Edition.
- Ask them to use glencoe.com to find links to ABA resource documents.
- Students should browse and select one document for each chapter.
- See pages 305, 323, 345, and 351 in this edition for specific instructions.

Reading and Writing Support

Feature or Activity	Topic	Reading Strategy	Writing Strategy
STANDARD &POOR'S	Saving for retirement	Reading a primary source document	
Thematic Project Preview	Employment guide		Researching and taking notes
BusinessWeek	Readings about agency and employment (Ch. 13), agency relationships (Ch. 14), and labor unions (Ch. 15)	Reading for detail Developing flexibility in reading speed	
Section Reading Guide	Before-reading activities and tools	Connect students' lives with content Focus on the main idea	Using a graphic organizer to take notes
As You Read	During-reading tool	Predict content Determine what students already know	
Reading Check	During-reading tool	Self-check understanding of content	
After You Read	After-reading tool	Summarize section content	Writing and organizing a list of key concepts
Standardized Test Practice	IRS Publication 937 (Ch. 13) Carter v. Gugliuzzi case (Ch. 14) Occupational Health and Safety Act (Ch. 15)	Reading a primary source document Practicing critical reading skills	
Reading Connection	American Bar Association online resources	Reading a primary source document Extending and applying content Reading for knowledge Developing critical reading skills. Developing flexibility of reading speed	Taking notes Summarizing
The Writing Connection	Expository writing		Creating outlines, topic sentences, editing
Unit Thematic Project	Employment guide	Using resources notes to support writing effort	Creating outlines, writing drafts, editing
Landmark Case	Discrimination law case	Developing critical reading skills	Summarizing

Unit Overview

Main) Idea

Unit 5 explores issues relating to the agency relationship and examines the types of authority and agents. Employment agreements and employee rights are also investigated.

00:00 OUT OF TIME?

If class time is too short to cover the chapters thoroughly, have students:

- Write down the vocabulary terms and their definitions.
- Read What You'll Learn and Why It's Important at the beginning of each section.
- Go to the *Business and Personal Law* Online Learning Center at glencoe.com and download the free Study-to-Go content to their cell phones or PDAs.

▶ **USING VISUALS ....**

On the Job Answer
Answers include: health and safety protection; protection against wrongful discharge, discrimination, and harassment; and compensation in case of layoff, illness, or accident.

286

UNIT **5**

The Law and the Workplace

In This Unit You Will Find:

**Chapter 13
Agency and Employment**

**Chapter 14
Agency Authority and Termination**

**Chapter 15
Employment Law**

On the Job The federal government has passed a number of laws to protect employees. *What kinds of protection are workers guaranteed?*

286

Unit Thematic Project Preview

W Writing Support
Several federal agencies monitor places of employment, including in the construction and transportation industries.

Critical Thinking Why do you think it is necessary to watch industries such as those mentioned? (Employees' health, safety, and well-being are paramount in these industries. The Occupational Safety and Health Administration enforces health standards. Agencies other than the Department of Labor monitor the transportation industry.)

Employment Guide

As you read this unit, use this checklist to prepare for the unit project:

- ✓ List the laws, legislation, and acts governing employers and employees.
- ✓ Differentiate between federal and state labor laws.
- ✓ Compare advantages and disadvantages of each.
- ✓ Explain how laws protect employees as well as employers from possible litigation.
- ✓ Determine appropriate employment forms needed for employees to sign.

Legal Portfolio When you complete the Unit Thematic project, you will have created a guide of federal and your state's employment laws to add to your portfolio.

 Find Unit 5 study tools such as **Graphic Organizers**, **Academic Skills Review**, and **Practice Tests** at **glencoe.com**.

WebQuest

The Law at Work
In this project, you will explore your legal rights and responsibilities in the workplace. Log on to **glencoe.com** to review the types of laws and information available. Then, continue working on your WebQuest as you study Unit 5.

UNIT 5

5-minute > Launch

KWL Chart On the board, write this list summarizing the major areas of law overseen by the Department of Labor: wages and hours, workplace safety and health, employee benefits, unions, employee protection, Family and Medical Leave Act, plant closings and layoffs, and migrant and seasonal agricultural workers. Discuss the topics, and create a KWL chart with their responses. After completing the unit, revisit their responses and ask what they have learned about workplace law.

Building Law Background

Ask students these questions to activate prior knowledge:

Chapter 13
Specify what service a corporate recruiter, also known as a headhunter, might perform for a college graduate. (He or she works for an agency to aid in finding the graduate a corporate job.)

Chapter 14
Discuss what you remember as being true of most agency relationships. (Created by agreement, but not always contracts; follow the rules of contracts; created by operation of law if the party is reasonably believed to be an agent by the third party.)

Chapter 15
What duties does an agent owe to a principal? (obedience, good faith, loyalty, accounting of the principal's money handled by the agent, and the exercising of good judgment and skill in performing assigned work)

STANDARD &POOR'S   Saving for Your Retirement

Q: I am still in high school. Why should I think about saving for retirement now?

A: The fact is, retirement always seems far off and many people never start saving for it, even when they get close to retirement. The amount most people receive in Social Security benefits when they retire is usually not enough to live on comfortably. Many companies do not offer pension plans. So, it is wise to save money in a retirement account. The sooner you start, the better. Suppose that at the age of 35 you start putting $150 per month into a retirement account that pays an annual interest rate of 8 percent. By the time you retire at age 65, you will have about $225,000 in your account. Now suppose you start putting the same amount of money into the same account at age 25, ten years sooner. By the time you retire at age 65, you will have over $525,000 in the account, or more than $300,000 extra.

R **Language Arts/Reading** Standard & Poor's is one of the world's main providers of credit ratings and financial-market indices. Go to **glencoe.com** and read more about investing in retirement accounts.

STANDARD &POOR'S

R Reading Strategy

Language Arts/Reading Direct students to explore S&P's resources on retirement planning.

Math Activity The Pinters decide to invest some surplus cash in a $20,000 U.S.

Treasury bill for 120 days. The interest rate is 5 percent. The bank charges a service fee of $25 to obtain a Treasury bill. What is the cost of the Treasury bill? What is the yield for the Treasury bill?
($20,000 × 5% × 120/360 = $333.33;
$20,000 − $333.33 + $25 = $19,691.67 cost of Treasury bill;
$333.33 ÷ ($19,691.67 × 120/360) = 0.0507 or 5.1% yield for the Treasury bill)

Plan Your Lesson Section by Section

NBEA	NATIONAL BUSINESS LAW STANDARDS
Section 13.1	• **Distinguish** between an agent and individuals such as independent contractors, real estate brokers, bailees, and trustees. • **Define** ratification and its elements.
Section 13.2	• **Distinguish** between a general power of attorney, a durable power of attorney, and a limited power of attorney. • **Explain** the different types of agents.

NCLB	ACADEMIC STANDARDS	Activity/Feature
English Language Arts: NCTE 3 Apply a wide range of strategies to comprehend, interpret, evaluate, and appreciate texts.		*BusinessWeek* News, Case Study, Case Study Practice
English Language Arts: NCTE 9 Develop an understanding of and respect for diversity in language use, patterns, and dialects across cultures, ethnic groups, geographic regions, and social roles.		Global Law
English Language Arts: NCTE 6 Apply knowledge of language structure, language conventions, media techniques, figurative language, and genre to create, critique, and discuss print and non-print texts.		Legal Talk, ad copy, Key Terms, and Academic Vocabulary
English Language Arts: NCTE 8 Use a variety of technological and information resources to gather and synthesize information and to create and communicate knowledge.		Section 13.1 Assessment
Mathematics: NCTM PSS 2 Solve problems that arise in mathematics and in other contexts.		Section 13.2 Assessment
English Language Arts: NCTE 10 Students whose first language is not English make use of their first language to develop competency in the English language arts and to develop understanding of content across the curriculum.		Key Terms, Academic Vocabulary, Legal Talk, Vocabulary Builder
English Language Arts: NCTE 1 Read a wide range of print and non-print texts to build an understanding of texts; to acquire new information; to respond to the needs and demands of society and the workplace; and for personal fulfillment.		Global Law, Cyberlaw
Social Studies: NCSS 5 Study interactions among individuals, groups, and institutions.		Global Law
English Language Arts: NCTE 7 Conduct research on issues and interests by generating ideas and questions, and by posing problems.		Case Study

Connect Your Business Law Classroom to the World of Work

This chart shows the 21st Century Skills, foundation skills, and workplace competencies that students develop as they work in this chapter.

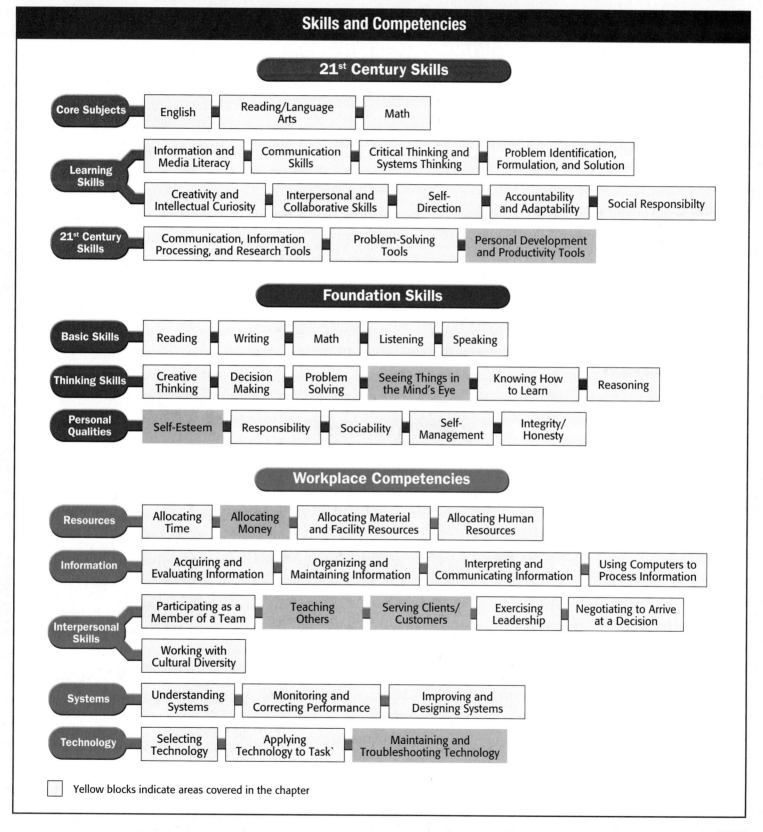

Skills and Competencies

21st Century Skills

Core Subjects
- English
- Reading/Language Arts
- Math

Learning Skills
- Information and Media Literacy
- Communication Skills
- Critical Thinking and Systems Thinking
- Problem Identification, Formulation, and Solution
- Creativity and Intellectual Curiosity
- Interpersonal and Collaborative Skills
- Self-Direction
- Accountability and Adaptability
- Social Responsibilty

21st Century Skills
- Communication, Information Processing, and Research Tools
- Problem-Solving Tools
- Personal Development and Productivity Tools

Foundation Skills

Basic Skills
- Reading
- Writing
- Math
- Listening
- Speaking

Thinking Skills
- Creative Thinking
- Decision Making
- Problem Solving
- Seeing Things in the Mind's Eye
- Knowing How to Learn
- Reasoning

Personal Qualities
- Self-Esteem
- Responsibility
- Sociability
- Self-Management
- Integrity/Honesty

Workplace Competencies

Resources
- Allocating Time
- Allocating Money
- Allocating Material and Facility Resources
- Allocating Human Resources

Information
- Acquiring and Evaluating Information
- Organizing and Maintaining Information
- Interpreting and Communicating Information
- Using Computers to Process Information

Interpersonal Skills
- Participating as a Member of a Team
- Teaching Others
- Serving Clients/Customers
- Exercising Leadership
- Negotiating to Arrive at a Decision
- Working with Cultural Diversity

Systems
- Understanding Systems
- Monitoring and Correcting Performance
- Improving and Designing Systems

Technology
- Selecting Technology
- Applying Technology to Task`
- Maintaining and Troubleshooting Technology

☐ Yellow blocks indicate areas covered in the chapter

Introduce the Chapter

Agency and Employment

Agency law is one of the foundations of employment law. Chapter 13 explains the nature of agency, how agency is created, and the types of authority and agents.

Building Background

Explain to students that many types of employees are considered agents representing their employer. Ask students to contrast, for example, the role and responsibilities of a manager in a department store with those of an independent plumber.

BusinessWeek News

Help students understand the three players in the article: the law firm, the former partner Lerach, and Lazar, who was a plaintiff filing lawsuits against companies. Discuss the suspicion raised by the fact that Lazar appears to have been paid by the law firm to file suits that the law firm handled. Explain to students how this situation shows a potential illegal use of an agent.

R Reading Strategy

Your Reading

Ask students to think about the different results obtained when they skim a text compared to when they read it closely. Have them draw conclusions about which method is most appropriate for them and in what circumstances.

288

BusinessWeek News

Suing Is Such Sweet Revenge

By Peter Burrows

Some in Silicon Valley can hardly contain their glee over the possibility of getting payback against the king of shareholder lawsuits. A federal probe involving the law firm Milberg Weiss Bershad & Schulman may ultimately pull in William Lerach, a onetime partner who left a year ago to start his own firm. No charges have been levied against Milberg Weiss or Lerach, but on June 23 Seymour Lazar, a plaintiff on multiple cases brought by the firm, was indicted by a grand jury.

The indictment, which does not mention Milberg Weiss or Lerach, alleges that Lazar was improperly paid for working with an undisclosed firm so it could quickly file suits. Many of the cases cited were brought in California courts, which were typically handled by Lerach's San Diego operation. Given Lerach's controversial reputation, many think he must be a key focus of the probe. Says one securities lawyer: "He's a high-profile guy, and he has made a lot of enemies."

Flex Your Reading

Efficient critical reading involves being flexible with speed and comprehension. There are several ways of reading critically, and you need to fit a reading style to your needs and to the material.

Go to **glencoe.com** for Flex Your Reading activities, more information on reading strategies for this chapter, and guided practice in reading about agency contracts.

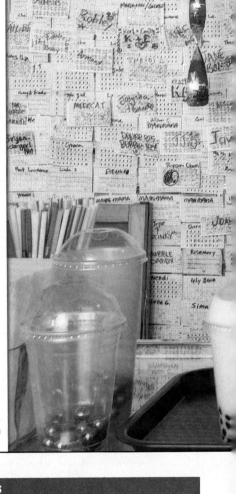

Classroom Resources

- Student Edition
- Teacher Wraparound Edition
- Student Activity Workbook with Academic Integration (SE/TAE)
- TeacherWorks™ Plus! CD
- *ExamView® Assessment Suite* CD
- *Presentation Plus!* CD

- National Mock Trial Championship DVD
- Online Learning Center with Podcasts at glencoe.com
- Study-to-Go™ at glencoe.com
- Online Student Edition
- Interactive Student Edition

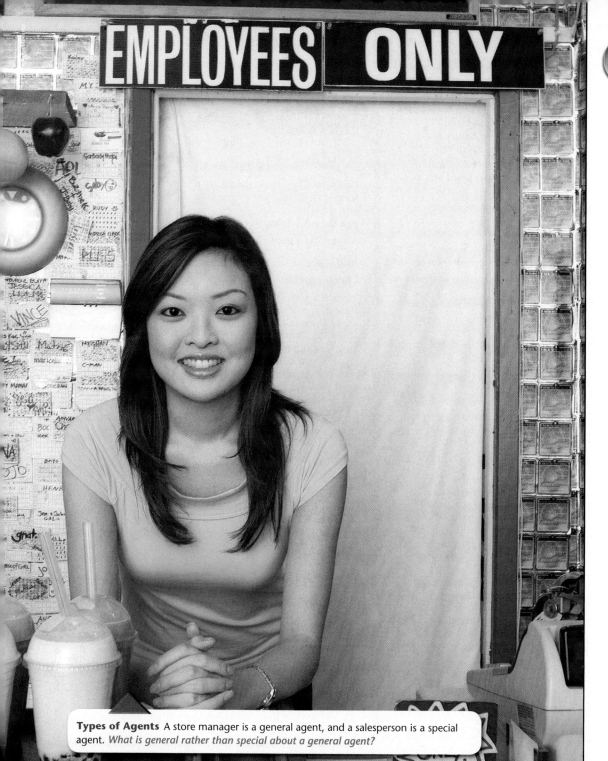

Types of Agents A store manager is a general agent, and a salesperson is a special agent. *What is general rather than special about a general agent?*

289

Practice the Concept

Being an Agent
Have students imagine that you can be their agent in selling their unwanted CDs and other items on eBay. Ask them to think of the terms they would wish to include in a contract for you to act as their agent. (your authority, price, and time limit)

Key Terms
Tell students that some agents are paid and some are not. An agent who works for free is called a *gratuitous agent*. The word *gratuitous* comes from the Latin *gratuitus* and means voluntary. Other meanings may include pleasing, beloved, agreeable, favorable, or thankful. The Latin root word also appears in such English words as *grace*, *disgrace*, *agree*, *grateful*, and *gratuity*.

Legal Basics
Of particular interest to students is the fact that, even as minors, they can be agents or principals. For example, if they invent something or write a song or book, they can hire an agent to represent them in the sale of their intellectual property. However, they need to be aware that their agent must tell any third party that he or she represents a minor who does not have contractual capacity and must obtain the third party's consent in order for the contract to hold.

▲ USING VISUALS

Types of Agents **Answer** Explain that store managers are general agents because they have broad authority to make decisions on behalf of the employer. For example, they can hire and fire employees, determine salaries, and order supplies and inventory. In contrast, salespeople have authority to do only specific tasks, such as working with customers and ringing up sales. They are thus considered special agents. Ask students if they can think of other work situations where one person is a general agent while others are special agents. (a manager in a shipping company compared to one of the delivery persons)

FOCUS

Bell Ringer Activity

Ask students to name types of agents they have had contact with or have seen on television or in the movies. (real estate agents, talent agents, sports agents, travel agents) Have students describe the functions that these agents perform.

Preteaching

Key Terms

Read the definitions and ask students to create a sentence using each term.

Academic Vocabulary

Explain that developing vocabulary is key to academic success. An efficient method to develop vocabulary is to study how words are formed.

- **genuine** Adjective, from the Latin *genuinus* (natural). Means actual, real, not counterfeit.

- **conduct** Verb, from the Latin *conducere* (to lead together). Means to manage, control, or direct the course of.

- **gratuitous** Adjective, from the Latin *gratuitus* (voluntary). Means free, without cost.

Activity Ask students to give a noun, an adjective, a verb, or an adverb form that comes from each word.

Connects to academic content

What You'll Learn

- ◆ Define agency and explain the nature of an agency relationship.
- ◆ Explain the difference between an agent and a principal.
- ◆ Distinguish between an agent and an independent contractor.
- ◆ List the ways agency relationships are created.

Why It's Important

You need to know your rights and responsibilities as an agent if you are ever hired to represent someone.

Academic Standards

Reading and completing the activities in this section will help you practice the following academic standards:

Social Studies (NCSS 5) Study interactions among individuals, groups, and institutions.

English Language Arts (NCTE 8) Use a variety of technological and information resources to gather and synthesize information and to create and communicate knowledge.

Reading Guide

Before You Read

Connect Name some situations in which you were paid to do specific tasks, such as running errands, in place of someone else.

Focus on Ideas

An agent is a person who represents someone else in business.

Take Notes
Create a graph like the one shown and use it to take notes as you read this section. Go to glencoe.com to find graphic organizers and tips on how to improve your note-taking skills.

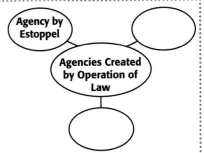

Key Terms

You will learn these legal words and expressions in this chapter. You can also find these terms in *Black's Law Dictionary* or in an online legal dictionary.

- agency
- principal
- agent
- third party
- independent contractor
- agency by estoppel

Academic Vocabulary

You will find these words in your readings and in your tests. Look them up in a dictionary and familiarize yourself with them.

- genuine
- conduct
- gratuitous

R Reading Strategy

Read for Knowledge

1. **Survey** or preread the chapter.
2. **Question** or formulate questions before you read.
3. **Recite** or read your questions, answers, and notes out loud.
4. **Review** or reread your notes.

Note-Taking Basics

- Listen attentively
- Have note-taking materials ready
- Skim through the lesson material
- Write down key words and ideas
- Anticipate what comes next
- Review notes soon after taking them

Understanding the Agency Relationship

How many people are involved in a work relationship?

The concept of agency is an important legal foundation in the work world. You can be in an agency relationship whether you work for a company or for yourself. **Agency refers to a type of working relationship in which one person represents another person in a business transaction with a third party.** The agency relationship involves three parties:

- **The principal is the person who authorizes someone to represent his or her interests.**
- **The agent is the person who has been authorized to do the work.**
- **The third party is the person with whom the agent does business on behalf of the principal.**

Agents can sign business deals, make contracts, and perform many other business tasks for the principal. An agency relationship underlies many employer-employee situations. The cashiers at a supermarket are agents for their store. Salespeople in a department store are agents. So is a literary agent representing an author to a publishing company. Whether a worker is actually called an agent does not matter. What counts in deciding if there is an agency relationship are the functions people play as principals, agents, or third parties.

Types of Work Relationships

Is a lawyer a type of agent?

Principal-Agent Relationship

The principal-agent relationship is a **genuine** agency relationship. The party who needs help is the principal; the party who provides help is the agent. Legally, agents are different from other types of representatives because agents can **conduct** business on behalf of a principal. When an agent acts for a principal, it is as if the principal has acted. Some agents, but not all, are employees. A real estate broker is an agent who represents a party in a contract involving the transfer of real property. Real estate brokers are agents, but they are not generally considered employees.

Not every job involves an agency relationship. There are other types of work relationships recognized by the law. The legal differences between these are especially important in determining which party has liability when there are errors, accidents, or contract disputes.

Proprietor-Independent Contractor Relationship

A proprietor is a person who hires someone to perform a task. **An independent contractor works for a proprietor to perform a particular task using his or her own tools and deciding the best way to do the job.** Proprietors and

---

TEACH

Discussion Starter

Class Discussion
Go over the roles of the principal, agent, and third party. Explain that what counts is the relationship among the individuals, not whether the word *agent* is used in the job title. Ask students whether they have ever acted in the capacity of an agent.

As You Read

Predict Have students predict, based on their own experiences, the types of tasks that agents of various types might do for a principal. (Answers will vary. Students might predict that an agent represents another person such as a sports agent. An agent can sign business deals, make contracts, and perform many business tasks for a principal.)

D Develop Concepts

Principal-Agent Relationship Explain when an agent acts for a principal, it is as if the principal has acted. Tell students that Jack asked Brian to sell his car while he was on vacation and Brian agreed. Ask students whether this is a principal-agent relationship. (Yes. Brian has been given the power to legally bind Jack to a sales contract.)

As You Read

Predict What does an agent do?

Vocabulary You can find vocabulary definitions in the **Key Terms** glossary and Academic Vocabulary glossary in the back of this book.

R Reading Strategy

Words with Two Functions Explain to students that many English words have multiple grammatical functions, such as being both a verb and a noun. For example, the text on this page utilizes the word *conduct*, which has both verb and noun meanings. Other examples on this page include *act*, *store*, *author*, *play*, and *transfer*. Write some sentences on the board contrasting the dual use of these words. Show students how the syntax and context of the sentence are key to knowing if a word is a verb or a noun.

TEACH (cont.)

D Develop Concepts

Independent Contractors
Review the difference between the principal-agent and proprietor-independent contractor relationship. Emphasize that agents are authorized to make decisions for the principal, while independent contractors have no authority to act on behalf of the proprietor. Ask students to give an example of a proprietor-independent contractor relationship.
(person hires a landscaper to perform landscaping services)

Legal Talk

(representative, delegate, proxy)

(employer, boss, supervisor)

Ask students to practice their academic and legal vocabulary with the electronic flashcards available at the *Business and Personal Law* Online Learning Center through glencoe.com.

C Critical Thinking

Distinguishing Differences
Tell students that an important skill in critical thinking is finding major differences between two items. Ask students to identify the difference between a principal and a proprietor.
(principal: person who authorizes someone to represent his or her interests; proprietor: person who hires an independent contractor to do a specific job without giving any authority)

Legal Talk

Agent: *n* One who is authorized to act in place of another. From Latin *agere* = to drive, lead, act, do.

Principal: *n* A person who has controlling authority. From Latin *principalis* = first in importance.

Vocabulary Builder Review the definitions above, and find three synonyms for the word *agent* and three synonyms for the word *principal.*

Look It Up! Check definitions in *Black's Law Dictionary* or an online glossary. For direct links, go to glencoe.com to find more vocabulary resources.

independent contractors can be either a single individual or an entire company. Plumbers, gardeners, electricians, accountants, lawyers, designers, architects, and s are often independent contractors.

The proprietor-independent contractor relationship is not legally the same as a principal-agent relationship. The proprietor has no control over the independent contractor. The independent contractor also cannot sign contracts or handle business transactions for the proprietor unless expressly authorized to do so, in which case the independent contractor can also be an agent for the proprietor.

Master-Servant Relationship

The terms *master* and *servant* are legal terms used to describe a type of work relationship. A master is a person who has the right to control the conduct of another person. The person who is performing the task for the master is a servant. Many employer-employee relationships are legally considered to be master-servant relationships when the employer has a high degree of control over the employee's time, place of work, tools and methods used, and output results. However, if a servant has authority to conduct business for the master, the servant can also be considered an agent for those tasks.

Bailees and Trustees

These are two special types of relationships that are discussed in depth elsewhere in this book. A bailee is a person who holds the personal property of another for a certain purpose (see Section 8.2). A trustee is an individual who manages a trust (see Section 21.2).

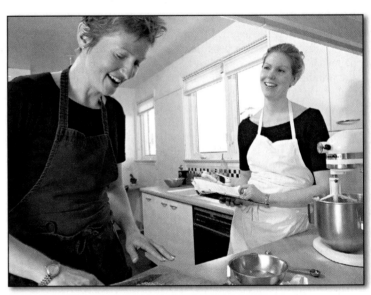

Independent Contractors
An independent contractor works for but is not an agent for a principal. *What makes an independent contractor independent, as opposed to an agent?*

▲ USING VISUALS

Independent Contractors **Answer** Explain that an independent contractor is independent because the proprietor has no control over his or her time, tools, or methods of working. For example, a proprietor cannot tell an independent plumber what time to show up, how to repair the sink, or what tools to use while doing the job. In contrast, a principal can tell an agent what terms he or she requires in a contract negotiated by the agent, what price to charge a third party, and exactly how a job should be done.

Creating an Agency Relationship

Can a minor be a principal or an agent?

Agency relationships are usually formed when a principal and an agent agree to the arrangement. Agreement makes the relationship consensual, meaning either party is free to terminate it at any time. However, if the arrangement involves the principal paying the agent, the agreement is contractual. Having a contract may prevent or limit one of the parties from terminating early, despite the consensual nature of the agreement.

The agency agreement can be oral or written. However, under the Equal Dignity Rule, if contracts made by the agent to third parties must be in writing, then the contract that creates the agency relationship must also be in writing.

Agreements Requiring Licensed Agents

Sometimes an agent represents a principal for free. This is called a **gratuitous** agent. The consensual arrangement in this case is not a contract and the agent can terminate at any time. While nearly anyone can act as a principal, all states regulate certain professions of agents. Lawyers, stock brokers, insurance agents, auctioneers, and real estate brokers must pass an examination and be licensed in their state before they can serve as agents.

Agreements Involving Minors

Even a minor can be a principal or an agent in a contractual agency agreement. However, because minors do not have contractual capacity, two situations can arise:

- A minor principal who has an adult agent—The agent may be liable if an injury, error, or breach of contract results unless the third party has been informed that the principal is a minor and the party still agrees to the contract.

- A minor agent representing an adult principal—A principal must uphold a contract made by a minor, unless it can be shown that the minor lacked capacity to understand the transaction.

Example Jason Bently, a 17-year old, invented a software game and hired Sam Lacey to represent him. Lacey sold the game to a small publisher but neglected to tell them that Bently was a minor. Bently did not like the contract and refused to accept it. Lacey is now liable for the $1,000 the company already spent in designing the packaging for the game.

Agencies Created by Operation of Law

In certain situations, an agency relationship may be created automatically by law even though the principal and agent did not consensually agree in advance.

Chapter 13   Agency and Employment   **293**

Reading Check

Explain When must a contract creating an agency relationship be in writing?

TEACH (cont.)

Guided Practice

Agency Agreements

Ask students to offer ideas on the difference between a verbal agency agreement and a written contract. (A verbal agreement is nonbinding, and either party can terminate at any time. A written contract is necessary when agents will be creating new contracts.)

 Writing Support

Sample Agency Contract Have students write a sample contract in which they hire someone to be their agent to sell an item, such as a used bicycle, on their behalf. Be sure students identify in the contract the names of the parties, the role each plays, the item to be sold, the price, the effective date of the contract, and the termination date.

Reading Check

Explain If the contracts made by the agent must be in writing, then the agency contract itself must also be in writing. The equal dignity rule governs this situation.

ASSESS

Quiz

Ask students to answer the following questions:

1. Can anyone be a principal? (Yes.)
2. Can anyone be an agent? (Yes. However, most states require certain professionals such as lawyers, real estate agents, stockbrokers, and insurance agents to be licensed prior to becoming an agent.)

3. What is an independent contractor? (a person who works for a proprietor to perform a particular task using his or her own tools and deciding the best way to do the job)

RETEACH

Guided Practice

Agencies Created by Operation of Law

Remind students that the agency relationship is usually created by an agreement. Ask them if they can think of any ways in which an agency relationship might be created by other means. Give them the following hints: (1) What if a government decides that a business must have an agent to represent it? (2) What if a principal inadvertently leads a third party to believe that someone is an agent for him or her? (3) What if an agent makes a wrong deal but the principal approves it? Discuss with students that these three situations create an agency by operation of law. (The first is agency by statute, the second is agency by estoppel, and the third is agency by ratification.)

STUDY TO GO Have students go to the *Business and Personal Law* Online Learning Center through glencoe.com to download free Study-to-Go content to their cell phones or PDAs.

Extending the Content

Agency Agreements

Have students bring to class a blank copy of a standard agreement between an agent and a buyer or seller. Have students compare their agreements with the rest of the class.

294

Global Law

Commercial Agents in the United Arab Emirates

When foreign companies wish to conduct business in the United Arab Emirates (UAE), there are two possible ways they can do this. First, the company can incorporate a new company in the UAE or open an office in the UAE. The second way to conduct business is by using a commercial agent.

If the foreign company chooses to tuse a commercial agent, it must follow the law as set forth in the UAE Commercial Agencies Law. There are six main requirements under the law:

1 The agents must be nationals (citizens) of the UAE or companies that are wholly-owned by UAE nationals.

2 Both the agent and the agency agreement must be registered with the UAE Ministry of Economy and Commerce.

3 An agent must be given its own territory that consists of at least one emirate (state) within the country.

4 Agents are normally paid for any sales that occur in their territory whether or not they made the sales themselves.

5 An agent can bar the products of the company with which he has a distribution agreement from being imported if the agent is not the exclusive importer and distributor for that company.

6 If the agent and agency agreement are properly registered, the agency relationship cannot be ended without just cause.

In the case that an agency relationship is ended without just cause, or if the foreign company fails to renew the agency relationship, then the agent is entitled to compensation. Further, the foreign company may not be able to appoint a replacement agent.

> **Across Cultures: UAE Courts**
>
> The UAE comprise seven independent emirates under a federal government. There is a federal court system, but it only has jurisdiction over five of the seven emirates. In each emirate there is a unique system of secular and Islamic courts.

Critical Thinking: *Does the UAE law benefit the agent in the UAE too much?*

Agency by Estoppel Sometimes a principal, through words or actions, may unintentionally lead a third party to believe that someone has authority to act as an agent on his or her behalf, when the person does not. **Agency by estoppel is when the principal's actions lead the third party to believe that the agent is working for the principal.** When estoppel occurs, the law prevents the principal from denying that the person was a nonagent. The principal is still liable for the agent's actions.

> **Example** Phil Tumbry told Terry Jankura to come to his jewelry store at 8 p.m. where someone would help her buy a ring on sale. However, Phil left his store early for a family emergency. He asked his acquaintance, Axel, to keep an eye on the store. Terry arrived at 8 p.m. and assumed that Axel was an employee. She picked out a ring and paid Axel $1,000. The next day, Phil called Terry and said her ring was not on sale and cost $500 more. Terry refused to pay it. She is within her rights because Phil created an agency by estoppel with Axel.

294 Unit 5 The Law and the Workplace

Global Law

Commercial Agents in the United Arab Emirates

Answer Answers will vary. The law provides a number of benefits to the agents within the UAE. However, one must contrast that with the fact that foreign companies are allowed to sell their products in the UAE without the expense of opening additional offices or establishing a separate UAE entity. The commercial agent may be a cost-saver to many foreign companies seeking to do business in the UAE. Further, it is the responsibility of a government to provide for its citizens, and this law does that, even if it appears to be to the detriment of foreign companies. The UAE has no responsibility to those foreign companies.

Agency by Ratification Sometimes a person performs a task he or she was not authorized by the principal to do, such as a stock clerk signing for a delivery. Sometimes an agent who has the authority to negotiate one type of contract oversteps that authority and negotiates another type of contract. In such cases, the principal for whom the agent claimed to act may either ignore the action or ratify it. An act is said to be ratified when a principal approves or accepts an agent's unauthorized act after the fact. The principal becomes bound as though the agent had authority to act. If the principal does not ratify the act, however, the would-be agent could be held liable to the third party.

To ratify the act, the principal must meet certain conditions. First, the principal must have the capacity to ratify and know all the facts. Second, the act to be ratified must be legal and done on behalf of the principal. Finally, the ratification must apply to the entire act of the agent, and ratification must occur before the third party withdraws.

Agency by Statute Sometimes a state legislature decides that certain situations justify automatic creation of an agency relationship by statute. For example, in many states the law requires corporations to appoint an agent within the state who can be served with a complaint and summons in case the corporation is sued. If the corporation's appointed agent leaves the state, the secretary of state automatically becomes its statutory agent of process. The state has a special interest to protect in this case: making certain that its citizens have a way to sue a corporation that has injured them.

After You Read

Summarize Name the ways in which an agency relationship can be created.

13.1 SECTION

RETEACH (cont.)

After You Read

Summarize An agency can be an oral or written agreement, or can be created by estoppel, by ratification, and by statute.

SECTION **13.1** ASSESSMENT

Self Check

1. What is agency and who are the parties in an agency relationship?

2. What is the difference between an agent and an independent contractor?

3. What is agency by ratification?

Academic Connection

English Language Arts
An independent contractor is a self-employed person

who provides a service to someone, but who is not controlled, supervised, or directed by that person. If you use the services of an independent contractor, you do not have to worry about collecting and paying that person's payroll taxes as you would an employee. Although the IRS has established 20 separate criteria to help employers distinguish between independent contractors and employees, the distinctions between one

type of worker and another can still be a puzzle. Go on the Internet or to the library and look up IRS Publication 937. Read the section called Employee or Independent Contractor?. Write a brief summary of your findings.

Critical Thinking

Representation What are some reasons why you might want to hire an agent to represent you?

 Go to **glencoe.com** to check your answers.

ASSESS

Self-Assessment

Have students go to the *Business and Personal Law* Online Learning Center through **glencoe.com** to take the Section 13.1 Practice Test.

CLOSE

Culminating Activity

Agency
Ask students to talk about the jobs they may want in the future and what type of employment relationship they may thus find themselves in. (Answers will vary. Students may be agents, principals, proprietors, independent contractors, masters, or slaves, depending on their profession and degree of control.)

SECTION **13.1** ASSESSMENT

Self Check

1. a relationship in which one person represents another person in a business transaction; agent, principal, and third party

2. An agent acts under the authority and on behalf of the principal. An independent contractor performs a particular task for a proprietor.

3. when a principal accepts or approves an unauthorized act by an agent after the fact

Academic Connection

English Language Arts
offers 20 criteria for distinguishing employees from independent contractors; classifies workers in various types of industries

Critical Thinking

when you lack the time, skills, or knowledge to accomplish the task yourself

Activity correlated to the English Language Arts standard on page 290

FOCUS

SECTION 13.2

Bell Ringer Activity

Ask students to think about the many types of authority they can give to an agent who represents them. Encourage them to come up with general concepts, such as oral authority, written authority, complete authority, and partial authority.

Preteaching

Key Terms

Read the definitions and ask students to create a sentence using each term.

Academic Vocabulary

Explain that developing vocabulary is key to academic success. An efficient method to develop vocabulary is to study how words are formed.

- **apparent** Adjective, from the Latin *apparere*, *ad* (adjacent to) + *parere*, (to show). Means clear or obvious.

- **incidental** Adjective, from the Latin *incidere*, *in* (on) + *cadere* (to fall or to happen). Means unpredictable or casual.

- **extent** Noun, from the Latin *extendere*, *ex* (out of) + *tendere* (to stretch). Means the degree to which something goes.

Activity Ask students to give a noun, an adjective, or an adverb form that comes from each word.

 Connects to academic content

Types of Authority and Agents

What You'll Learn

- ◆ Identify the different types of agency authority.
- ◆ Explain the difference between actual and apparent authority.
- ◆ Distinguish between the different types of agents.

Why It's Important

If you ever work as an agent, you need to know the extent of your authority and responsibility.

Academic Standards

Reading and completing the activities in this section will help you practice the following academic standards:

NCLB

Math (NCTM PSS 2) Solve problems that arise in mathematics and in other contexts.

English Language Arts (NCTE 7) Conduct research on issues and interests by generating ideas and questions, and by posing problems.

Reading Guide

 Before You Read

Connect Have you ever worked at a job where you were only allowed to perform specific tasks?

Focus on Ideas

Agents must act within the authority they receive from the principal.

Take Notes
Create a graph like the one shown and use it to take notes as you read this section. Go to glencoe.com to find graphic organizers and tips on how to improve your note-taking skills.

Types of Agency Authority — Actual

 Key Terms

You will learn these legal words and expressions in this chapter. You can also find these terms in *Black's Law Dictionary* or in an online legal dictionary.

- actual authority
- express authority
- power of attorney
- implied authority
- apparent authority
- general agent
- special agent
- subagent
- agent's agent

Academic Vocabulary

You will find these words in your readings and in your tests. Look them up in a dictionary and familiarize yourself with them.

- apparent
- incidental
- extent

 glencoe.com

R **Reading Strategy**

Read for Knowledge

1. **Survey** or preread the chapter.
2. **Question** or formulate questions before you read.
3. **Recite** or read your questions, answers, and notes out loud.
4. **Review** or reread your notes.

Note-Taking Basics
- Listen attentively
- Have note-taking materials ready
- Skim through the lesson material
- Write down key words and ideas
- Anticipate what comes next
- Review notes soon after taking them

Types of Agent Authority

If you are an agent, how much authority do you have to make decisions on you own?

Agents conduct business and make contracts on behalf of their principals. In order to know what they are allowed to do, agents must have authority from their principals. There are two types of authority: actual authority and **apparent** authority.

Actual Authority

Actual authority is the real power a principal gives to an agent. Actual authority may be specifically expressed in words or implied from the agreement.

Express Authority **Express authority comes from the orders, commands, or instructions a principal explicitly gives an agent.** The instructions may be oral or in writing. The wording of the instructions may be very general or very specific.

> **Example** Guinevere Kellogg was going away on a long business trip. She asked her friend Allen Eton to be her agent in selling her DVD collection. In a written document, Kellogg instructed Eton to accept no less than $2,000 in cash and to sell the collection to a person over the age of 18. These instructions made up Eton's express authority as the agent for Kellogg.

A power of attorney is any writing granting someone authority to act as an agent. The authority granted by a power of attorney comes in three forms:

- A general power of attorney gives the agent authority to act for the principal in a wide range of activities.
- A limited power of attorney gives the agent authority to deal only with the tasks named in the agreement.
- A durable power of attorney gives the agent the power to make health care decisions when the principal becomes incapacitated.

Powers of attorney end when the principal withdraws the authority or dies.

Implied Authority Writing down every single act that an agent is allowed to perform would make an agency agreement long and complicated. The law thus allows actual authority to be understood from the expressly stated terms of the principal. This is called implied authority.

As You Read

Predict What is the difference between actual and apparent authority?

Vocabulary You can find vocabulary definitions in the **Key Terms** glossary and **Academic Vocabulary** glossary in the back of this book.

 Implied Authority Authority may be implied that reasonably comes from the express authority. *What kind of authority might be reasonably implied this cashier does or does not have?*

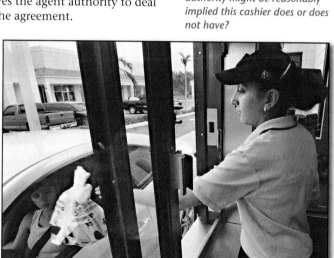

▲ USING VISUALS

Implied Authority **Answer** The cashier is an agent of the fast food establishment. Her implied authority probably includes taking orders, receiving cash or credit card payments, giving appropriate change or obtaining a credit card signature, answering questions about product selection, and giving the ordered food to the customer. The cashier would probably not have implied authority to accept foreign currency as payment, give food away for free or at a discount, order additional supplies (or food) for the restaurant, hire or fire an employee, or set the schedule for herself or fellow employees.

TEACH

Discussion Starter

Class Discussion
Clarifying the extent of authority is a necessary aspect of an agency agreement. Ask students to think of reasons why both the principal and agent need to be clear about authority. (One reason is to ensure that the business contracts and transactions the agent performs are in line with what the principal wants. Another is to determine who will be responsible in case there is an error, accident, or problem.)

As You Read

Predict Ask students to make an educated guess about the difference between actual and apparent authority. (Actual authority—implied or express—is the real power a principal gives to an agent. Apparent authority is authority that the third party believes an agent has, based on previous dealings.)

D Develop Concepts

Implied Authority Explain to students that the law recognizes a second type of actual authority beyond express authority. This is called *implied authority* and arises because it is usually impossible to write down every detail of authority in a contract. Thus, the law provides for additional authority that allows an agent to perform reasonable acts necessary to carry out express authority.

TEACH (cont.)

Reading Check

Infer The law recognizes apparent authority based on past dealings because the past sets a precedent for behavior. The law also recognizes agency by estoppel as a form of apparent authority because the principal has led a third party to believe that the agent has authority.

ASSESS

Case Study Practice

Authority
Travis has express authority to sell Abe's condo for no less than $250,000 while Abe is away on vacation. Abe learns that Travis has allowed prospective buyers to enter the property and have it inspected. Was Travis legally justified in these actions? (Yes. From the express authority given to Travis, he could assume an implied authority to take the steps necessary to secure a buyer.)

298

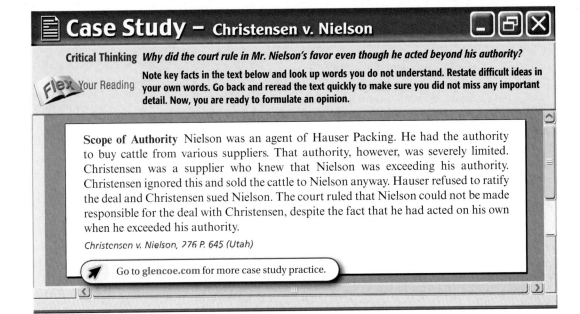

Case Study – Christensen v. Nielson

Critical Thinking Why did the court rule in Mr. Nielson's favor even though he acted beyond his authority?

Flex Your Reading Note key facts in the text below and look up words you do not understand. Restate difficult ideas in your own words. Go back and reread the text quickly to make sure you did not miss any important detail. Now, you are ready to formulate an opinion.

Scope of Authority Nielson was an agent of Hauser Packing. He had the authority to buy cattle from various suppliers. That authority, however, was severely limited. Christensen was a supplier who knew that Nielson was exceeding his authority. Christensen ignored this and sold the cattle to Nielson anyway. Hauser refused to ratify the deal and Christensen sued Nielson. The court ruled that Nielson could not be made responsible for the deal with Christensen, despite the fact that he had acted on his own when he exceeded his authority.

Christensen v. Nielson, 276 P. 645 (Utah)

Go to **glencoe.com** for more case study practice.

Implied authority is additional authority that allows an agent to perform reasonable acts necessary to carry out the express authority. In some states, implied authority is known as **incidental** authority.

> **Example** From the express authority Kellogg granted Eton in the previous example, it would be reasonably understood that Eton has the authority to allow potential buyers to inspect the collection and to play some of the DVDs. These instructions are not written down but are understood as reasonable actions the agent may take.

Sometimes an agent and a principal end up disagreeing about what powers can be implied from the express authority in an agreement. To resolve a dispute, the court says that implied authority must reasonably come from the express authority. In general, a court determines reasonableness by looking at the actions that other agents carry out in similar cases.

Reading Check

Infer For what reason do you think the law recognizes apparent authority?

Apparent Authority

Apparent authority is actually not authority that an agent has. **Apparent authority is authority that a third party believes an agent has while acting on behalf of the principal.** This belief can arise from the third party's previous dealings with the principal and agent in similar prior transactions. When apparent authority is based on previous dealings, it is known as customary authority. Apparent authority can also be created by law under agency by estoppel. If a principal gives the appearance

 glencoe.com

Case Study

Christensen v. Nielson

Answer The evidence that convinced the court to rule in Nielson's favor was that Christensen knew that Nielson was acting outside the scope of the responsibility granted to him by Hauser Packing.

Activity Role-play this case study. Have one student play Nielson, another student play Christensen, and a third student play the judge. Have Nielson and Christensen present their sides of the story to the judge. Allow the judge to ask questions. Then have the judge provide a verdict based on how the two parties argued the case.

to a third party that an agent has authority on his or her behalf, while in reality the agent does not, the principal can be required to uphold the contract.

Types of Agents

Can an agent hire another agent?

Agents can be distinguished from each other in two ways: on the **extent** of their authority to perform tasks for the principal or on their relationship to other agents (see **Figure 13.1** on page 300).

General Agent

A general agent is an agent who has authority to perform any act within the scope of a business. The manager of a department store, for instance, is a general agent. General agents are also called discretionary agents because they have the right to use their discretion, or judgment, in all matters involving the agency. General agents may decide to hire or fire employees, decide on salaries, purchase supplies, and add or dispose of stock.

Special Agent

A special agent, also called a limited agent, is an agent whose authority is restricted to accomplishing only a specific job or purpose. Many types of employees are considered limited agents. For example, the counter people at fast-food restaurants can take orders and collect money, but they cannot make purchases, sign for deliveries, or hire other employees.

Agents Who Relate to Other Agents

These terms are used to classify agents based on their relationship to other agents rather than to the principal.

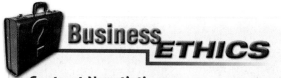

Contract Negotiations

You are a new attorney at the firm Smith, Jones, & Miller. On your second day of work, your boss tells you that you need to go to a negotiation meeting that your client, Large Corp., is having with another company, Small, Inc. When you arrive at the meeting, you realize that Small, Inc. is selling 400 cars to Large Corp. and that Small, Inc. wants $15,000 per car. You think that this is reasonable and agree to the contract. After you return to the office, you realize that Large Corp. only wanted to pay $14,000 per car and that you made a mistake.

Critical Thinking: *Did you have apparent authority?*

![Business ETHICS]

Answer Yes, you probably did. When your boss sent you to the meeting, he was indicating to Small, Inc. that you represented Large Corp. Unless you said something at the meeting about not having any authority, Small, Inc. can assume that an attorney who is signing contract documents has the authority to do so. It is your responsibility to ensure that parties do not infer authority from your action, if you do not have such authority. In this situation, you should have deferred action and consulted with either your boss or Large Corp. before signing an agreement that will cost Large Corp. an extra $400,000.

RETEACH (cont.)

C Critical Thinking

Types of Agents Ask students to identify the legal distinction between a subagent and an agent's agent. (The subagent is an agent who has been lawfully hired by another agent with the principal's knowledge. Thus, the principal is responsible for the subagent's activities. In contrast, an agent who hires another agent without the principal knowing about it has hired an agent's agent. The principal is not responsible for anything the agent's agent does.)

U Universal Access

Visual/Spatial Learners Ask students to create diagrams showing the nature of general versus special agent and subagent versus agent's agent. Invite students to present their charts to the class.

Role Play

Go around the room and tell students you want to hire them to do a task for you. Have each student respond with either "I know how to do that so I can be your agent," or "I don't know how to do that, so I will need to hire a subagent, okay?" Sample tasks to ask students about include: (1) sell your car; (2) buy a house for you; (3) go grocery shopping for you using your credit card; (4) sell tickets to a fundraiser you are involved in.

300

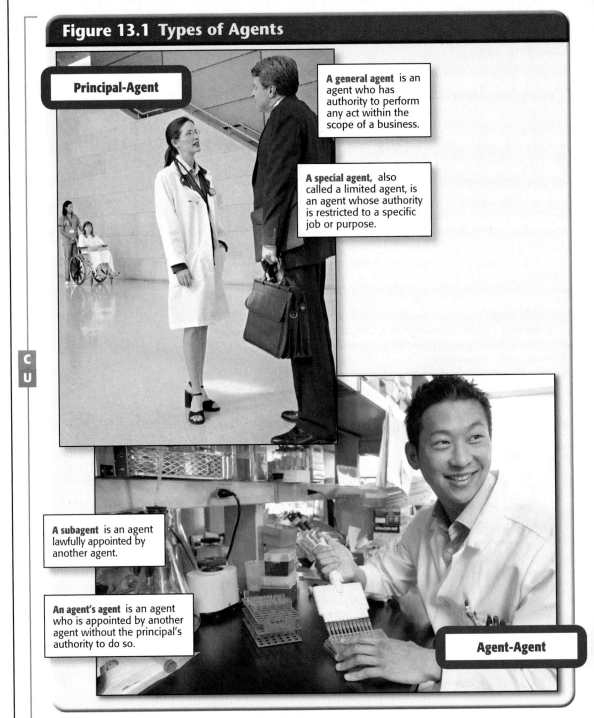

Figure 13.1 Types of Agents

Principal-Agent

A general agent is an agent who has authority to perform any act within the scope of a business.

A special agent, also called a limited agent, is an agent whose authority is restricted to a specific job or purpose.

A subagent is an agent lawfully appointed by another agent.

An agent's agent is an agent who is appointed by another agent without the principal's authority to do so.

Agent-Agent

An agent can be appointed by a principal or another agent. *How does an agent's agent relate to an agent in terms of the principal-agent relationship?*

300 Unit 5 The Law and the Workplace

▲ USING VISUALS

➡ **Figure 13.1 Types of Agents Answer** An agent's agent is an agent appointed by another agent without the principal's authority. In essence, the first agent becomes a principal in appointing the second agent to represent him or her. Be sure students understand that the principal who hired the first agent cannot be held responsible for the actions of the agent's agent, since he or she did not appoint the agent's agent.

Subagents A **subagent is an agent lawfully appointed by another agent.** For example, a principal may authorize an agent to appoint a subagent if the agent is too busy or faced with an emergency and needs someone to help or take over.

Agent's Agents An **agent's agent is an agent who is appointed by another agent without the principal's authority to do so.** The principal cannot be held liable for anything done by the agent's agent. In legal terms, the agent actually becomes the principal in relation to the agent's agent.

Coagents If the principal hires two or more agents, they are coagents. Coagents are subject to the authority of the principal unless the principal has authorized one agent to have power over others.

Agency Relationships and International Law

Are agency agreements made in the United States valid in other countries?

Agency law in this country is based on U.S. statutes and appellate decisions. However, agency law can differ in other countries. If you want to do business in other countries, it is therefore important to consult with a local attorney. Some countries may limit who may be an agent to citizens of those countries. The concepts of implied and apparent authority may also be different.

After You Read

Summarize Identify the different types of agents.

SECTION 13.2 ASSESSMENT

Self Check

1. What is the difference between express and implied authority?

2. What is a power of attorney?

3. What is the difference between a subagent and an agent's agent?

Academic Connection

Mathematics Marcus bought a house for $180,000. The real estate broker received a total fee of $8,100 on the amount of sale. According to the brokerage agreement, the real estate broker pays 2.5% out of the total fee to the real estate agent making the sale, and the broker keeps the remainder. What is the net broker fee in percentage form?

 THEORY **Problem Solving:** To figure out the net broker fee, you need to subtract the agent fee from the total broker fee. To figure out what percentage is the total broker fee, divide the total fee by the sales amount. To write the decimal as a percentage, move the decimal point two places to the right and add a percent sign.

Math For more math practice, go to the Math Appendix.

Critical Thinking

Agency and the Responsibilities of an Agent If you have ever worked for someone as a sales clerk, then you were involved in an agency relationship even if you did not know it at the time. What are some concerns that might face a person who has been given the responsibility to do business for somebody else?

Go to **glencoe.com** to check your answers.

After You Read

Summarize The different types of agents include general agent, special (limited) agent, subagent, agent's agent, and coagent.

ASSESS

Self-Assessment

Have students go to the *Business and Personal Law* Online Learning Center through **glencoe.com** to take the Section 13.2 Practice Test.

CLOSE

Culminating Activity

Hiring an Agent

Have students come to the front of the class in pairs. One will role play a principal hiring the other as an agent. Have the students engage in a conversation in which they carry on a dialogue about the nature of their relationship, the task at hand, the amount of authority being given, and the time frame.

SECTION 13.2 ASSESSMENT

Self Check

1. express authority explicitly gives an agent authority; implied authority allows an agent to perform reasonable acts necessary to carry out the express authority

2. a formal document granting someone authority to act as an agent

3. Subagent: lawfully appointed by another agent with principal's authorization; agent's agent: appointed by another agent without the principal's authority.

Academic Connection

Mathematics
2%

Critical Thinking
ability to carry out all duties; sufficient authority granted; the principal living up to his or her side of the deal; agent being held responsible for errors or accidents

 Activity correlated to the Mathematics standard on page 296

301

Summary by Sections

Ask students to read the summaries one key point at a time. Then, ask them to work in groups to create two examples to illustrate each key point.

Vocabulary Builder

Cooperative Learning

1. Have students work in groups to prepare their sentences. Ask the groups to exchange their sentences and assess each other's sentences.

Vocabulary Development

- Ask students to use a dictionary or to go online to look up the etymology of each key term listed.
- Then, ask students to list several words derived from the same root or origin. For example, *contract* has the same root as *contractual* or *contractually*.

302

Summary

Section 13.1 The Agency Relationship

- Agency is a relationship in which one person represents another person in a business transaction with a third party.
- A person hired to represent another person is the agent. The person who hires the agent is the principal. The person the principal and agent do business with is the third party.
- Agents can sign business deals, make contracts, and perform other business tasks for a principal.
- A proprietor-independent contractor relationship is different from a principal-agent relationship in that an independent contractor works for but is not under the control of a proprietor.
- Agency relationships are created by agreement or by operation of law.
- The law can create an agency relationship by estoppel, by ratification, or by statute.

Section 13.2 Types of Authority and Agents

- Actual authority is the real power a principal gives to an agent.
- Apparent authority is authority that a third party believes an agent has while acting on behalf of the principal.
- Express authority comes from the orders, commands, or instructions a principal explicitly gives an agent.
- Implied authority is additional authority that allows an agent to perform reasonable acts necessary to carry out the express authority.
- Power of attorney is a formal writing granting someone authority to act as an agent. Power of attorney can be general, limited, or durable.
- Different types of agents include general agents, special agents, subagents, agents' agents, and coagents.

Vocabulary Builder

❶ On a sheet of paper, use each of these terms in a sentence.

Key Terms

- agency
- principal
- agent
- third party
- independent contractor

- agency by estoppel
- actual authority
- express authority
- power of attorney
- implied authority

- apparent authority
- general agent
- special agent
- subagent
- agent's agent

Academic Vocabulary

- genuine
- conduct

- gratuitous
- apparent

- incidental
- extent

Go to **glencoe.com** to play a game and improve your legal vocabulary.

Study Skills for Success

Prepare Your Students for Studying

Tell students that they can improve their ability to understand and remember material from their courses by learning and practicing study skills. Remind students to:

- **Get motivated!** Motivation must come from within. To motivate yourself, think of ways in which what you learn now will fit into your long-term personal and professional goals.
- **Get organized!** Make studying part of your daily routine, not something you do at the last minute.
- **Concentrate!** Study in an environment that is as free of distractions as possible.

Key Points Review

Answer the following questions. Refer to the chapter for additional reinforcement.

2 How are agents different from other types of representatives?

3 What is the difference between the master-servant and proprietor-independent contractor relationship?

4 What is the difference between an agency created by agreement and one created by law?

5 What is agency by estoppel?

6 What is the difference between actual and apparent authority?

7 Distinguish the types of power of attorney.

8 What are the two ways agents can be distinguished from one another?

Standardized Test Practice

9 Read the following excerpts from IRS Publication 937 on the differences between employees and independent contractors, then complete problems 1 and 2.

Training. An employee may be trained to perform services in a particular manner. Independent contractors ordinarily use their own methods and receive no training from the purchasers of their services.

Set hours of work. An employee usually has set hours of work established by an employer. An independent contractor generally can set his or her own work hours.

Full time required. An employee may be required to work or be available full time. An independent contractor can work when, how, and for whom he or she chooses.

Payments. An employee is generally paid by the hour, week, or month. An independent contractor is usually paid by the job or on a straight commission.

Right to fire. An employee can be fired by an employer. An independent contractor cannot be fired so long as he or she meets the specifications of the contract.

1. What hours is an independent contractor required to work?

Ⓐ full time
Ⓑ hours established by an employer
Ⓒ hours he or she chooses
Ⓓ part time

2. Employees are generally paid

Ⓐ whatever they want
Ⓑ by the job
Ⓒ on a straight commission
Ⓓ by the hour, week, or month

Test-Taking Strategies Read test directions carefully and pay attention to details.

Standardized Test Practice

9. C and D

Strategies for Standardized Test Prep Success

Whether your students have a standardized test coming up in a few days or a few weeks, these last-minute test-prep tips and strategies will help them relax and do their best.

• **Test Format** Help students become familiar with the format of the test by practicing with test items that imitate the actual test items as closely as possible.

• **Test Timing** Have your students take timed practice tests so that they become comfortable with the length, design, and timing of the actual test.

Key Points Review

2. Agents can conduct business on behalf of a principal, while other representatives cannot.

3. A master controls the conduct of a servant. An independent contractor works for, but is not under the control of, a proprietor.

4. An agency by agreement involves the consent of the parties involved. An agency by operation of law happens automatically according to a law.

5. when the principal's actions lead the third party to believe that the agent is working for the principal

6. Actual authority is the real power a principal gives to an agent. Apparent authority is authority that a third party believes an agent has.

7. A general power of attorney allows the agent to act over a wide range of activities. A limited power of attorney deals only with specific tasks named in the agreement. A durable power of attorney allows the agent to make health-care decisions for the incapacitated principal.

8. based on the extent of their authority to perform tasks for the principal, and on their relationship to other agents

Review and Assessment

Apply and Debate

Students should use chapter content to arrive at conclusions. The legal resolutions are listed below:

10. Yes. Michael had implied authority to let the buyer delay the payment. Sheila told him to do "whatever it takes" to sell the snowmobile, and his action is reasonable.

11. No. The clerk told Kyle he was just a friend and asked him to wait. This is not an instance of agency by estoppel.

12. No. Ansar was not acting as an agent when he accepted the package. He did not purchase the item; he only attested to the delivery of the item.

13. No. Uma cannot tell the plumber how to repair the dishwasher, as long as the repair occurs.

14. Yes. The manager created an agency by ratification because he did not call the first customer and correct the mistaken price that Mark had given that customer.

Apply and Debate

Read the following scenarios. Get together with other students in pairs or groups of three and take a position on each scenario. Debate your position in class with students taking the opposite position or prepare a written argument justifying your position.

10 Snowmobile Sale

Sheila hired her friend Michael to sell her snowmobile, and to do "whatever it takes" to sell it for $1,000. He sold it, allowing the buyer pay in three months.

You Debate | *Did Michael have authority to let the buyer delay the payment?*

11 When Is a Clerk Not a Clerk?

Kyle went to a hardware store to purchase a saw. The clerk at the counter said he was a friend of the owner, who had gone to lunch, and asked Kyle to wait for the owner to return. But Kyle was in a hurry, so he paid and left. He tried to return the tool the next day, but the owner told him it was non-returnable.

You Debate | *Should Kyle be able to return the saw?*

12 Carpenter Signs for Package

Ansar, an independent carpenter, was building a cabinet at the Williams's home. Mrs. Williams left to pick up her child. The doorbell rang, so Ansar opened it and signed for a package delivery. Mrs. Williams returned and told him that she had cancelled that order and did not want the package.

You Debate | *Is Ansar responsible for paying for the goods?*

13 Independent Contractor

Uma hired an independent plumber to repair her dishwasher. The plumber repaired the motor and did not check any of the other parts. Uma felt the plumber should have checked all of the mechanical parts as a part of the repair service.

You Debate | *Does Uma have a right to tell the plumber how to repair the dishwasher?*

14 Sales Mistake

Mark was a new salesperson in an electronics store. He sold a TV to a customer and accidentally gave a 35% discount. His manager told him to be careful next time, but did not contact the customer to correct the sale. The next day, a friend of the original customer came in and wanted to buy the same TV with the same 35% discount.

You Debate | *Should the second customer be allowed to receive the same discount?*

C Critical Thinking

Garden Show Dilemma Jackson owned a flower nursery. A large flower convention was in town. Jackson could not attend, so he sent Pam, his assistant, and asked her to find some deals. Pam found a new species of roses and purchased 100 dozen. She returned to the nursery and told Jackson. However, when the roses were delivered, Jackson refused them. He told Pam that she had not been authorized to purchase 100 dozen roses.

Debate Practice

- Did Jackson authorize Pam to be his agent? (Yes. His communication to find deals made Pam believe she was his agent. He also created an agency by estoppel situation because the sellers believed Pam had the authority to purchase.)

- Can Jackson refuse the delivery? (No. By not cancelling the order when Pam told him, he ratified the purchase.)

Case Study Practice – Amedas, Inc. v. Brown

⑮ Independent Contractor or Agent? During the early 1980s, Craig Allen and his wife formed Amedas, Inc. to sell medical goods manufactured by Designs for Vision, Inc. (DVI). Mr. Allen contacted a former coworker, Edward Brown, about selling DVI goods for Amedas. Mr. Brown entered into a sales representative agreement with Amedas.

The agreement provided that Mr. Brown was to devote full time and to promote the best interests of Amedas. The agreement also stated that Mr. Brown was not allowed to represent any other company during the life of the agreement and that Mr. Brown would receive a ten percent commission for his sales.

In 1985, DVI told Mr. Allen that Amedas would no longer be able to sell DVI products. Mr. Brown had secretly been meeting with DVI about selling DVI on his own, and DVI decided to give him the exclusive sales contract. Amedas then sued Mr. Brown, claiming he violated his sales agreement. At issue before the court was whether Mr. Brown was an independent contractor or agent of Amedas.

Source: Amedas, Inc. v. Brown, 505 So.2d 1091 (Fla. Ct. App. 1987)

Practice Was Mr. Brown an agent of Amedas?

⑯ Ethics Application

Customer Freebies You work in a camera store. Your manager allows you to entice customers with two free add-ons to help make a sale. A customer of yours is ready to buy an expensive camera on which you will get a big commission. You offer a one-year warranty and batteries for free. The customer asks for a free carrying bag and you agree, just to make the sale.

◆ Is it ethical for you to offer more free items than you are allowed to make in order to make the sale? Explain.

⑰ Internet Application

Tax Preparers You have made enough money last year that you need to file an income tax return. You do not feel comfortable preparing your own tax return, so you are thinking of hiring a tax preparation agency to do it for you. You need to understand what your responsibilities will be and what the tax preparer's liability will be when you enter into such an agreement.

 Go to **glencoe.com** to access the Web site sponsored by the IRS on tax preparation. Draft a report stating the responsibilities that you and the tax preparer have.

 Reading Connection

Outside Reading Go to **glencoe.com** for a list of outside reading suggestions about agents.

 glencoe.com

Case Study Practice

15. No. The Florida District Court of Appeals held that Mr. Brown's contract was not an agency contract. Rather, it was a contract establishing Mr. Brown as an independent contractor. Under the contract, Mr. Brown's actions were not controlled by Amedas, and he was not paid a salary. Mr. Brown was able to set his own schedule and was paid by means of a 10 percent commission.

←?→ Ethics Application

16. Given that the store has specifically stated that its policy is to give two free add-ons, it is not ethical for you to decide on your own to give away extra add-ons to make a sale. You should ask the manager if you are allowed to make this decision yourself or must check with the manager each time.

Internet Application

17. You must provide the tax preparer with accurate and honest information about your income and deductions. The tax preparer must prepare your taxes without mistakes and sign the tax return. Point out that no matter who prepares the tax return, you are legally responsible for all the information it contains.

R Reading Strategy

Reading Connection

American Bar Association Resources

Go to the *Business and Personal Law* Online Learning Center through glencoe.com to find links for further readings that relate to this chapter. Ask students to read, review, and summarize the documents. Advise students to keep their reviews and summaries to use as reference material for their Unit Thematic Project on pages 348–349.

Plan Your Lesson Section by Section

NBEA	NATIONAL BUSINESS LAW STANDARDS
Section 14.1	• **Explain** the concept of vicarious liability. • **Distinguish** between an agent and individuals such as independent contractors, real estate brokers, bailees, and trustees.
Section 14.2	• **Explain** the procedure for the administration of the debtor's estate.

NCLB	ACADEMIC STANDARDS	Activity/Feature
	English Language Arts: NCTE 3 Apply a wide range of strategies to comprehend, interpret, evaluate, and appreciate texts.	*BusinessWeek* News, Case Study, Case Study Practice, Section 14.2 Assessment
	English Language Arts: NCTE 9 Develop an understanding of and respect for diversity in language use, patterns, and dialects across cultures, ethnic groups, geographic regions, and social roles.	Global Law
	English Language Arts: NCTE 6 Apply knowledge of language structure, language conventions, media techniques, figurative language, and genre to create, critique, and discuss print and non-print texts.	Legal Talk, ad copy, Key Terms, and Academic Vocabulary
	Mathematics: NCTM PSS 1 Build new mathematical knowledge through problem solving.	Section 14.1 Assessment
	English Language Arts: NCTE 10 Students whose first language is not English make use of their first language to develop competency in the English language arts and to develop understanding of content across the curriculum.	Key Terms, Academic Vocabulary, Legal Talk, Vocabulary Builder
	English Language Arts: NCTE 1 Students read a wide range of print and nonprint texts to build an understanding of texts; to acquire new information; to respond to the needs and demands of society and the workplace.	Global Law, Cyberlaw
	Social Studies: NCSS 9 Study global connections and interdependence.	Global Law, Cyberlaw
	Social Studies: NCSS 5 Study interaction among individuals, groups, and institutions.	Case Study

Connect Your Business Law Classroom to the World of Work

This chart shows the 21st Century Skills, foundation skills, and workplace competencies that students develop as they work in this chapter.

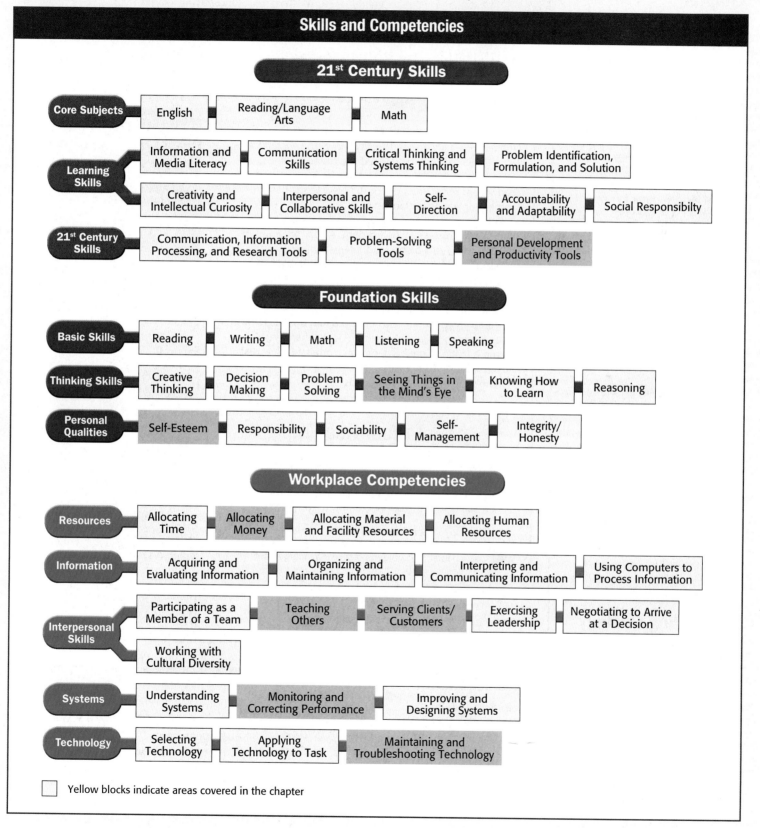

Skills and Competencies

21st Century Skills

Core Subjects: English · Reading/Language Arts · Math

Learning Skills: Information and Media Literacy · Communication Skills · Critical Thinking and Systems Thinking · Problem Identification, Formulation, and Solution · Creativity and Intellectual Curiosity · Interpersonal and Collaborative Skills · Self-Direction · Accountability and Adaptability · Social Responsibilty

21st Century Skills: Communication, Information Processing, and Research Tools · Problem-Solving Tools · Personal Development and Productivity Tools

Foundation Skills

Basic Skills: Reading · Writing · Math · Listening · Speaking

Thinking Skills: Creative Thinking · Decision Making · Problem Solving · Seeing Things in the Mind's Eye · Knowing How to Learn · Reasoning

Personal Qualities: Self-Esteem · Responsibility · Sociability · Self-Management · Integrity/Honesty

Workplace Competencies

Resources: Allocating Time · Allocating Money · Allocating Material and Facility Resources · Allocating Human Resources

Information: Acquiring and Evaluating Information · Organizing and Maintaining Information · Interpreting and Communicating Information · Using Computers to Process Information

Interpersonal Skills: Participating as a Member of a Team · Teaching Others · Serving Clients/Customers · Exercising Leadership · Negotiating to Arrive at a Decision · Working with Cultural Diversity

Systems: Understanding Systems · Monitoring and Correcting Performance · Improving and Designing Systems

Technology: Selecting Technology · Applying Technology to Task · Maintaining and Troubleshooting Technology

☐ Yellow blocks indicate areas covered in the chapter

Introduce the Chapter

Agency Authority and Termination

Chapter 14 explores the types of duties and responsibilities that belong to principals and agents. It also explains how agencies can be terminated.

Building Background

Ask students to role-play the following scenario. Juan asks Peter to act as his agent and sell his computer at no less than $150. Peter sells the computer to Carly for $180. Juan allows Peter to keep the extra $30 as his compensation for selling the computer. As a class, discuss the responsibilities of Juan and Peter in this relationship. (Use the discussion to introduce the concepts of compensation, duty, and good faith.)

BusinessWeek News

Inform students that duties of the agent to the principal include the following: obedience, good faith, loyalty, and to account and to perform his or her duties with judgment and skill. Ask them if Fields has satisfied these duties for Trump. (From Trump's perspective, the duties of good faith and loyalty have not been fulfilled.)

R Reading Strategy

Your Reading

Encourage students to think about why they like to read certain types of writing. Ask students to reread a favorite magazine article. Ask them to focus on what they like about the piece, including tone, word usage, and style.

306

---

14 Agency Authority and Termination

BusinessWeek News

Trump's Angry Apprentice

By Eamon Javers

Richard T. Fields could have been a real-life forerunner to Donald Trump's reality show, *The Apprentice*. From 1995 to 1999, he learned the casino business at The Donald's side as a consultant, and the pair had visions of expanding Trump's New Jersey-based gaming operation nationwide.

But this partnership has turned rockier than anything depicted in Trump's TV boardroom. A cozy relationship has given way to a blood feud, rife with allegations of dishonesty. Locked in an ongoing legal battle over a Florida casino project, Trump and Fields have filed dueling briefs that reveal the depth of their animosity. At stake: more than $1 billion.

R Trump charges that Fields betrayed him by snatching away a plan to build two casinos. (Fields) charges that Trump is trying to get his hands on a profitable deal that he passed up years ago.

Who's right in this war of words?

Flex Your Reading

Efficient critical reading involves being flexible with speed and comprehension. There are several ways of reading critically, and you need to fit a reading style to your needs and to the material.

 Go to **glencoe.com** for Flex Your Reading activities, more information on reading strategies for this chapter, and guided practice in reading about agency relationships.

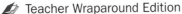
Classroom Resources

Student Edition
Teacher Wraparound Edition
Student Activity Workbook with Academic Integration (SE/TAE)
TeacherWorks™ Plus! CD
ExamView® *Assessment Suite* CD
Presentation Plus! CD

National Mock Trial Championship DVD
Online Learning Center with Podcasts at **glencoe.com**
Study-to-Go™ at **glencoe.com**
Online Student Edition
Interactive Student Edition

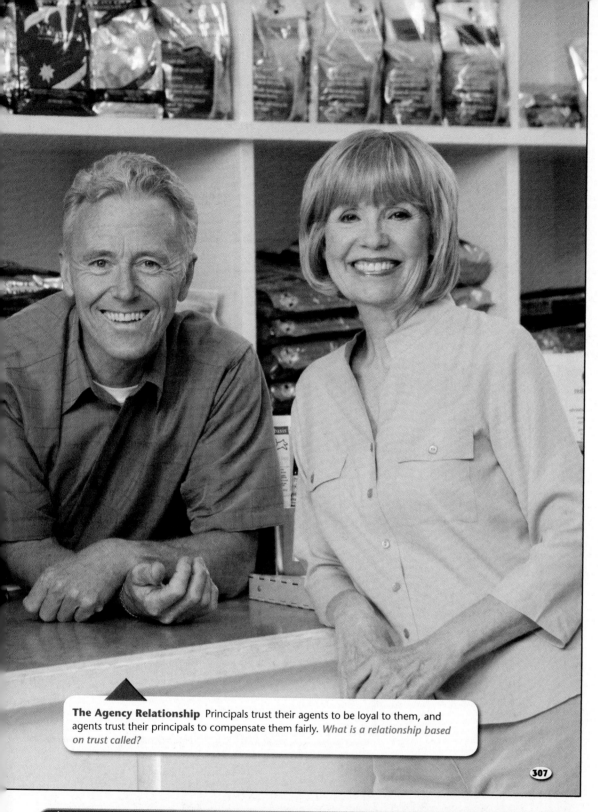

The Agency Relationship Principals trust their agents to be loyal to them, and agents trust their principals to compensate them fairly. *What is a relationship based on trust called?*

307

Practice the Concept

Agency
Ask students to imagine that they have been hired by the prom committee to buy 20 packages of streamers for no more than $1.50 per package. The committee will pay the students $10 to run this errand. Have students describe this task using the legal terms of *agency* that they learned in the previous chapter.

Key Terms Inform students that *express authority* is stated by a principal to his or her agent when the agency relationship is first created. As a class, review the agency given by the committee to them. What should they do if the store only has slightly faded streamers left over from the last holiday? What if the store sells a vastly superior streamer for a little more than $1.50? Inform students that *implied authority* is the understanding that an agent can make decisions on behalf of the principal even if they were never stated.

Legal Basics Suggest to students that the key to a successful relationship between principal and agent is an understanding of the extent of the agency and of each party's liability.

▲ **USING VISUALS**

The two-way relationship of trust created between a principal and an agent is called *fiduciary*. This relationship implies and necessitates great confidence and trust on the part of the principal and good faith on the part of the agent.

Activity Ask students to imagine that Roger has established a fiduciary relationship with Celeste. Roger has asked Celeste to sell his car for the best price she can get. Have students list duties they think Celeste should carry out to perform well under this fiduciary relationship. (Answers will vary but students may expect Celeste to act honestly, in good judgment, in accordance with Roger's wishes, in a loyal manner, and provide Roger with an accounting of the sale.)

FOCUS

SECTION 14.1

Duties and Liability in Agency Relationships

Bell Ringer Activity

Have students identify agency relationships that exist in their communities. Ask them to list the types of powers they think those agents have. (real estate agent has the power to locate a home for a buyer; attorney may have the power to execute a client's will)

Preteaching

Key Terms

Read the definitions and ask students to create a sentence using each term.

Academic Vocabulary

Explain that developing vocabulary is key to academic success. An efficient method to develop vocabulary is to study how words are formed.

- **loyal** Adjective, from the Latin *legalis* (law). Means faithful to the persons or ideals that one is under obligation to defend.

- **adhere** Verb, from the Latin *adhaerere*, *ad* (to) + *haerere* (to stick). Means to stay attached.

- **cooperation** Noun, from the Latin *cooperari*, *co* (together) + *operari* (to work). Means to work together.

Activity Ask students to give a noun, an adjective, or an adverb form that comes from each word.

N C L B Connects to academic content

What You'll Learn

- ◆ Identify the duties of agents to principals.
- ◆ Identify the duties of principals to agents.
- ◆ Describe the nature of contract liability in agency law.
- ◆ Explain the doctrine of *respondeat superior* in relation to tort liability.

Why It's Important

Understanding the duties and liability of agents and principals will help you in the world of work.

Academic Standards

Reading and completing the activities in this section will help you practice the following academic standards:

N C L B
- **Math (NCTM PSS 1)** Build new mathematical knowledge through problem solving.

- **Social Studies (NCSS 9)** Study global connections and interdependence.

Reading Guide

Before You Read

Connect Have you ever had to pay money out of your own pocket while running an errand for someone?

Focus on Ideas

Agency relationships are based on trust.

Take Notes

Create a graph like the one shown and use it to take notes as you read this section. Go to glencoe.com to find graphic organizers and tips on how to improve your note-taking skills.

Duties in Agency Relationships

Principal's Duties to Agent	Agent's Duties to Principal
	Obedience

 ### Key Terms

You will learn these legal words and expressions in this chapter. You can also find these terms in *Black's Law Dictionary* or in an online legal dictionary.

- fiduciary relationship
- double representation
- self-dealing
- compensation
- reimbursement
- indemnification
- respondeat superior
- nondelegable duty

Academic Vocabulary

You will find these words in your readings and in your tests. Look them up in a dictionary and familiarize yourself with them.

- loyal
- adhere
- cooperation

---

 glencoe.com

 R **Reading Strategy**

Read for Knowledge

1. **Survey** or preread the chapter.
2. **Question** or formulate questions before you read.
3. **Recite** or read your questions, answers, and notes out loud.
4. **Review** or reread your notes.

Note-Taking Basics

- Listen attentively
- Have note-taking materials ready
- Skim through the lesson material
- Write down key words and ideas
- Anticipate what comes next
- Review notes soon after taking them

Agent's Duties to the Principal

Suppose you are an employee in charge of a project. What are your duties?

Principals trust their agents with their business, property, money, and reputation. This is why an agency relationship is considered a fiduciary relationship. **A fiduciary relationship is a relationship based on trust.** The word comes from the Latin word for faith. A good way to remember this term is to think of the name people often give a faithful dog: Fido.

The law imposes five fiduciary duties that an agent owes a principal: obedience, good faith, loyalty, accounting, and judgment. If the agent does not uphold these duties or goes beyond them, the agent, not the principal, is liable for any resulting injury such as a lawsuit from a third party.

Obedience

Obedience means that the agent must obey all reasonable commands that lie within the scope of the agency agreement.

As You Read

Predict Does a principal have to pay you for any expenses or losses you incur while working as an agent?

TEACH

Discussion Starter

Class Discussion

Emphasize that all agents owe certain duties to their principals and all principals have certain responsibilities to their agents. Tell students that Julio Rodriguez, a star soccer player, has hired a sports agent. Ask students for examples of the responsibilities that the agent has to Julio. (secure a professional contract, handle endorsements of products, loyalty to Julio, honesty in his dealings) Ask students for examples of responsibilities that Julio has to the agent. (compensation for services, cooperation with agent's judgment)

As You Read

Predict Ask students to consider a situation in which they are asked by a friend to take a package to the post office and mail it. Have them discuss whether they should be reimbursed for gas and postage. (Inform students that agents have the right to reimbursement—the payment for money spent on behalf of the principal, and the right to indemnification—the right to payment for losses by the agent.)

Global Law

Doing Business in Israel

If a foreign company wants to market products in Israel, it can set up one of two different types of relationships with a party in Israel. Which one to choose depends on how much control the foreign company wants over its representative in Israel and how much liability it is willing to accept.

Commercial Agent

The first option is for the company to contract for a commercial agent in Israel. In Israel, an agent has the authority to act in the foreign company's name and bind the company to any contract the agent feels is proper. However, the agent is also required to follow any directives given by the foreign company.

Under Israel's Agency Act, the agent's obligations include:

1 Loyalty

2 Promotion of the interests of the foreign company

3 Not acting as an agent for competing companies

In return, the foreign company agrees to:

1 Provide just compensation to the agent

2 Insure the agent for any liabilities

Distributor

The second option is to contract with a distributor in Israel to market the products. A distributor is a lot like an independent contractor. The distributor in Israel buys the product from the foreign company and then resells the product in Israel under the distributor's own name. A distributor is responsible for promoting the product and getting liability insurance, but is not barred from selling competing products.

> **Across Cultures: Becoming a Citizen**
>
> The Israeli government has passed the Law of Return in Israel. The law allows any Jew, anywhere in the world, to become a citizen of Israel simply by moving there. Citizenship is automatically granted upon arrival in Israel.

Critical Thinking *Is the situation in Israel much different from the United States?*

Chapter 14   Agency Authority and Termination   **309**

Global Law

Doing Business in Israel

Answer No. The system of distributing products in the United States is very similar. A company in the United States may choose to operate its own chain of stores or may authorize a retailer to sell its products. For example, Apple maintains its own line of Apple Stores in select cities throughout the country that sell only Apple products. However, there are also numerous computer stores such as CompUSA that are authorized to sell Apple merchandise. These stores also sell competing computer products from makers such as IBM or Hewlett-Packard.

TEACH (cont.)

D Develop Concepts

Double Representation

Jack Jones works as the agent for Dee Campbell to sell her artwork to galleries. He also works for Dee's competitor to sell the competitor's work in the same places. Ask students to discuss if the agent can adequately serve both principals. (Probably not. One principal or the other may lose opportunities by having the competitor's artwork in the same locale; the agent benefits either way.)

S Skills Practice

Agent's Duties to the Principal

Have students review the five duties that an agent owes to the principal and complete the following activities:

List Close your textbook and list the five duties that an agent owes to the principal. (obedience, good faith, loyalty, accountability for money, and exercising good judgment and skill) **L1**

Describe Write two examples, one that describes one of the five duties being performed adequately and one that describes one of the five duties being performed inadequately. **L2**

Explain Write a scenario that describes a principal-agent relationship between two people and how the agent would perform all five duties adequately. **L3**

Even a gratuitous agent must follow instructions. If an agent disobeys instructions, he or she becomes liable to the principal for any resulting loss. However, an agent is not obligated to follow a principal's instructions to do anything illegal or immoral. For example, if a manager tells a salesperson to lie about a product's features, the agent may refuse to do so.

Good Faith

The duty of good faith means that the agent must deal honestly with other parties and have no intent to seek personal advantage. The agent must not commit fraud. Good faith also requires the agent to notify the principal of all matters that involve the agency.

Loyalty

Agents must be **loyal** to their principal. They must not work at the same time for one of their principal's competitors or for their own personal benefit. **Double representation is when an agent works simultaneously for two competing principals. Self-dealing is when agents make deals that benefit themselves rather than their principals.**

Duty to Account

An agent who handles money for the principal must keep a record and account for every cent. The agent must also keep the principal's money safe and separate from other people's money, including his or her own. This is done using trust accounts, which are separate banking accounts from the agent's personal or office accounts. If the agent mixes personal money with the principal's money and cannot figure out whose money is whose, the entire amount of money belongs to the principal.

Judgment

Agents must be skillful and use good judgment when working for the principal. However, agents are not perfect. Even the most well-informed agents make mistakes from time to time. For this reason, agents are not held liable for honest mistakes if they have performed to the best of their abilities.

Principal's Duties to the Agent

If you are an agent, what can you do if your principal does not pay you?

Principals also have obligations in dealing with their agents. These duties are compensation, reimbursement, indemnification, and cooperation. If a principal does not **adhere** to these duties, he or she may be liable to the agent or the third party.

Compensation

An agent has the right to receive compensation from a principal. **Compensation is fair payment for the job performed.** The principal must pay the compensation agreed to in the contract.

U Universal Access

Visual/Spatial Learner Museums often show artwork belonging to private collectors, other museums, or organized touring presentations. Ask students to describe the types of principals and agents that might be involved in such a situation. Have them identify the benefits and responsibilities for the lender and the museum in these cases. (responsibilities of museum—take care of artwork, compensate the lender; responsibilities of lender—deliver artwork as promised; benefit to museum—new art to offer to patrons; benefit to lender—prestige of having museum show art)

If no amount is stated, the principal must pay a reasonable amount, determined by checking the usual amount paid to other agents in the same line of work. The duty of compensation does not apply if the agent is a gratuitous agent who works for free.

Reimbursement and Indemnification

Agents have the right to reimbursement. **Reimbursement is payment for money spent by an agent on behalf of a principal.** Agents also have the right to indemnification. **Indemnification is payment for losses suffered by an agent because of a principal's instructions.**

Cooperation

The principal gives an agent the duty to perform certain tasks. The principal must not interfere with the performance of those tasks. This is called **cooperation**. If the principal makes the agent's job difficult or impossible, he or she has breached the duty of cooperation.

> **Example** Pam Phillips hired Jason Abrams and told him that he had exclusive rights to sell her company's video games online to all customers. But she said that to keep his job he had to sell $100,000 of product per quarter. Later, Abrams learned that Phillips had hired 15 other agents to sell the same video games online. This competition made it nearly impossible for Abrams to meet his quota. Abrams could argue successfully that Phillips had violated her duty to cooperate.

Reimbursement Agents have the right to be repaid for spending their own money on a principal's behalf. *What factors should be considered regarding whether the person in the photo should be reimbursed for gas money?*

Who Has Liability?

If you are a third party and something goes wrong with a deal you made, who do you take to court, the agent or the principal?

In business, mistakes happen, people disagree, and sometimes people are hurt in accidents. When such things happen, one party may experience a monetary, physical, or other loss and want compensation for the injury. Injury is any loss that a person experiences, not just physical harm. Who is liable for an injury depends on two questions:

- Are the parties in a principal-agent or proprietor-independent contractor relationship?
- Does the liability concern a contractual matter or a tort?

TEACH (cont.)

D Develop Concepts

Cooperation Sam Won hired Jack Johnson, a real estate agent, to find a rental property for his business. Sam wanted 2,500 square feet in a new strip shopping center with easy highway access at less than $18 per square foot. Jack found Sam 20 properties that met his guidelines, but Sam was not satisfied with any of them. Ask students whether Sam is cooperating in this agency agreement. (No. Sam is making it difficult if not impossible for Jack to complete his task. Cooperation is a responsibility of the principal.)

C Critical Thinking

Indemnification Explain that the word *indemnify* means to compensate for loss. Ask students to explain why they think a principal is responsible for indemnification in an agency relationship. (Without indemnification, the agent would be held responsible for losses incurred due to any misrepresentation, error, or oversight of the principal. This would open the agent up to unlimited potential losses.) Tell students that many contract agreements explicitly state that the agent cannot be held at fault for any claim, loss, or expense in connection with the affairs of the principal.

▲ USING VISUALS

➡ **Reimbursement Answer** Factors will vary, but may include whether the agent's entire tank of gas was used for the principal's behalf, whether the agent shopped for a reasonable price for fuel, why the highest grade is really necessary for the vehicle, and whether snacks and a car wash were really justified. Explain that when an agent is performing a duty for a principal, the agent is expected to exercise good faith with no intent to seek personal advantage.

TEACH (cont.)

W Writing Support

Agent's Liability to Third Parties Review the liability of agents. Then point out that there are two situations in which agents may be held responsible for contracts negotiated with a third party for the principal: when agents do not disclose the identity of the principal, or when agents wrongfully exceed their authority. Ask students to write explanations as to why these two situations would cause agents to be held responsible. (If principal is undisclosed, the third party has no choice but to hold the agent liable in case of breach of contract. If agent has negotiated an agreement beyond the scope of his or her authority, the third party holds the agent liable.)

Legal Talk

(inactive: not active; incomplete: not complete; inexperienced: not experienced; insoluble: not soluble; invisible: not visible)

Ask students to practice their academic and legal vocabulary with the electronic flashcards available at the *Business and Personal Law* Online Learning Center through glencoe.com.

Legal Talk

Indemnify: *v* To compensate for losses. From Latin *in-* = not + *damnum* = damage: undamaged.

Cooperation: *n* Common effort. From Latin *co-* = with + *operari* = to work: to work together.

Vocabulary Builder The Latin prefix *in-* usually means *not*. List and define five words in which *in-* is used this way. For example, indescribable means cannot be described.

Look It Up! Check definitions in *Black's Law Dictionary* or an online glossary. For direct links, go to glencoe.com to find more vocabulary resources.

The answer to the first question is important. However, the labels the parties use to describe themselves do not matter. Instead, the court considers numerous questions to determine the actual status of the relationship:

- Does the hiring person make available the tools for the worker?
- Is the worker paid hourly?
- Does the principal set the worker's hours?
- Is the worker employed only by the hiring person?
- Is the business of the worker the same as the business of the hiring person?
- Does the hiring person have the authority to hire or fire other workers?
- Does the hiring person supervise the tasks of the worker?
- Is little skill needed to do the worker's job?

The more questions with "yes" answers, the more likely it is a principal-agent relationship. If so, liability follows the rules that apply to principals and agents for contracts and torts. The more "no" answers, the more likely a proprietor-independent contractor relationship exists and liability follows the rules for this type of relationship.

Contractual Liability of Principals

When an agent makes a contract on behalf of a principal, it is just as if the principal had acted directly. The agent is said to "stand in the shoes of the principal." The law thus usually holds principals liable for proven injuries in contractual disputes.

Contractual Liability of Agents

Three situations can occur in which an agent becomes liable for an injury to a third party.

- The agent has made an agreement or performed tasks beyond his or her authority to do so.
- The principal is a minor or does not have the capacity to sign a contract, yet the agent has not disclosed this fact to the third party.
- The principal is undisclosed, and the third party cannot identify the principal.

The third situation often arises when a principal does not want to be identified, such as a celebrity principal. If a breach of contract occurs, the third party has no choice but to hold the agent liable or attempt to identify the principal to hold liable. However, the third party may not hold both of them liable.

Contractual Liability of Independent Contractors

In general, independent contractors are not agents because they are not authorized to make agreements or conduct business for the proprietor. However, if the contractor makes an agreement

 glencoe.com

C Critical Thinking

Commingling Funds Ask students, "Why do you think an agent should keep his or her money separate from money that belongs to the principal?" (Answers may vary, but students should recognize that if the correct distribution of the funds cannot be verified, the principal will be considered the rightful owner of all the funds.)

312

without the proprietor's authority, the contractor is liable. If the proprietor has authorized the contractor to act as his or her agent, the same contractual liability rules apply as in an agency relationship.

> **Example** Mister P., a famous rock star, hired a real estate agent to find him a home without revealing his identity. The agent found a house and told the seller that the buyer wanted to conceal his identity. After the contract was signed, however, Mister P. refused to buy the house. The seller can attempt to discover the identity of Mr. P. to sue him, or the seller can sue the agent. However, Mr. P. must indemnify the agent for any money paid out to satisfy the judgment since the agent acted on Mr. P.'s behalf.

Reading Check

Analyze Why is the principal usually responsible for contractual and tort liability?

Tort Liability of Principals

All people are responsible for their own torts. However, in legal terms, the law holds a person who hires another person responsible for the torts of the hired person if the torts are committed on the job. This is called vicarious liability. Vicarious liability is based on the principle of respondeat superior (see **Figure 14.1** on page 314). **Respondeat superior is a legal doctrine that holds that the master is responsible for the torts of his or her servants.** The law extends the master-servant relationship to the agent-principal relationship because the agent is acting on behalf of the principal. For example, a department store may be liable if a security guard falsely imprisons a suspected shoplifter.

CYBERLAW

Iceland Telecom, Ltd. v. Information Systems & Networks Corp.
268 F.Supp.2d 585 (D. Md. 2003)

Iceland Telecom entered into a contract with ISN Global Communications (Global) for Internet telecommunication services. Global ceased to exist as a company in 2001. Iceland Telecom then tried to sue Global's parent company, Information Systems & Networks Corp. (ISN), for breach of contract. A parent company is a company that owns or controls another company (called a subsidiary). Iceland Telecom argued that Global was an agent of ISN and that ISN could be held liable for Global's breach of contract. Iceland Telecom argued there was apparent authority between the two because Global had sent documents with ISN listed at the top and had told Iceland Telecom to contact ISN if there was a problem when Global's offices were closed.

Ruling and Resolution
The United States District Court in Maryland held that Global was not an agent of ISN. For apparent authority to exist, Iceland Telecom must prove that ISN, not Global, misled Iceland Telecom into believing that Global was its agent. This was not present in the facts of the case.

Critical Thinking Should parent companies be liable for the actions of their subsidiaries?

TEACH (cont.)

D Develop Concepts

Vicarious Liability Ask students if they have ever heard of the phrase "living vicariously through another person." Have them offer ideas on what the phrase means. (living through someone else's experiences) Explain that if an agent commits a tort while on the job, the principal is vicariously liable, or held liable, for that person's wrongdoing.

Reading Check

Analyze The law holds that the principal is usually responsible for the actions of the agent because of the doctrine of respondeat superior. That is, the master is responsible for the torts of his or her servants. However, under the law, parents are not usually considered masters of their children.

U Universal Access

Visual Learning Review with students the meaning of torts. Emphasize that all people are responsible for their conduct. However, in determining tort liability, certain relationships are controlling. Have students review the section on tort liability and draw a diagram that illustrates these relationships.

CYBERLAW

Iceland Telecom, Ltd., v. Information Systems & Networks Corp.
Answer Answers will vary. There are examples where subsidiaries are created to try and shield a parent company from liability, but those subsidiaries are actually 100 percent controlled by the parent company. Under the law, though, subsidiaries are distinct corporate entities with their own set of books and officers. Since they are separate entities, it may be wrong to hold a parent company liable for the subsidiary's actions.

ASSESS

Case Study Practice

Fulfilling Duties
Ask students to read the following scenario and answer the question: Dwane hired Cecelia, a seasoned investment analyst, to invest $200,000 of his retirement money in the best investment she could find. She invested the money in Brilliant Technologies, one of the best investment opportunities at the time. One week later, a hurricane hit the area and destroyed most of Brilliant's labs. The company's stock fell, and Dwane lost most of his investment. Can Cecelia be held liable for the loss? (No. Cecelia used her best judgment, and no one could have predicted the hurricane.)

RETEACH

STUDY TO GO Have students go to the *Business and Personal Law* Online Learning Center through glencoe.com to download free Study-to-Go content to their cell phones or PDAs.

Review Key Terms

Encourage students to access the *Business and Personal Law* Online Learning Center through glencoe.com and use the electronic flashcards to review the key terms.

314

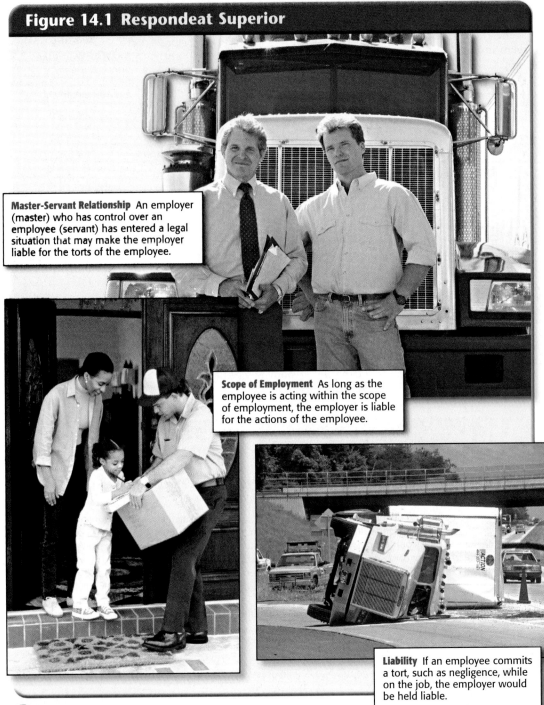

Figure 14.1 Respondeat Superior

Master-Servant Relationship An employer (master) who has control over an employee (servant) has entered a legal situation that may make the employer liable for the torts of the employee.

Scope of Employment As long as the employee is acting within the scope of employment, the employer is liable for the actions of the employee.

Liability If an employee commits a tort, such as negligence, while on the job, the employer would be held liable.

According to the doctrine of respondeat superior, a master is responsible for the torts of his or her servants. *What is the reasoning behind this?*

314   Unit 5   The Law and the Workplace

▲ USING VISUALS

Figure 14.1 Respondeat Superior **Answer** Masters have the right to control the physical conduct of their servants. They are, therefore, responsible when the servant injures a third party while the servant is on the job.

Activity Ask students to think of examples in which the master is responsible for a third party being injured on the job. (Answers may vary, but may include a publisher being responsible for a reporter's slanderous article or a club owner being responsible for a bouncer hurting a customer.)

A principal may escape vicarious liability if it can be shown that the agent was not acting within the scope of employment. For instance, the principal is not responsible for a delivery agent who has an accident while driving on personal business.

Tort Liability of Proprietors

A proprietor can sometimes be liable for the torts of an independent contractor. This is true if the proprietor's own actions lead to the injury. For example, a proprietor is liable if he or she is negligent when checking qualifications and hires someone who is incompetent. This is called negligent hiring. Another doctrine is called negligent retention. This arises when a proprietor fails to fire a contractor after learning that he or she is incompetent. In the meantime, the contractor injures someone. In these cases, the proprietor is held liable for his or her own negligence, not the actions of the independent contractor.

A proprietor can also be open to liability if a contractor has been hired to perform a task that involves a nondelegable duty. **A nondelegable duty is a duty that cannot be delegated, or transferred, to another party.** For example, a landlord has a nondelegable duty to maintain a building. The landlord can hire an independent contractor to do repairs, but cannot pass on the duty and is thus still liable if someone is injured due to poor maintenance.

After You Read

Summarize List the principal's duties to the agent.

SECTION 14.1 ASSESSMENT

Self Check

1. What is a fiduciary relationship?
2. What is the difference between reimbursement and indemnification?
3. What is the difference between negligent hiring and negligent retention?

Academic Connection

Mathematics Ann Finke is a real estate agent who sells real estate at a 7½% straight commission. Last week her sales totaled $180,000. What would her commission be? How much would it be if she earned 8%, and what is the difference between the two rates?

 THEORY **Number and Operations:** To find the amount of the commission you would use the following formula:

Total Sales × Commission Rate (remember to change the percent to a fraction) = Commission

 For more math practice, go to the Math Appendix.

Critical Thinking

When Do You Give In?
Suppose that your boss gave you $1,200 in cash and told you to buy a plasma screen television for his office.

Now, suppose that you found a discount plasma screen television at a store for $1,100. Can you keep the difference and use the extra $100 as your own pocket money? Why or why not?

 Go to **glencoe.com** to check your answers.

RETEACH (cont.)

After You Read

Summarize principal's duties—compensation, reimbursement, indemnification, cooperation

ASSESS

Self-Assessment

Have students go to the *Business and Personal Law* Online Learning Center through glencoe.com to take the Section 14.1 Practice Test.

CLOSE

Culminating Activity

Everyday Agency
Have students reenact three situations in the last week in which they acted as agents. Examples may include running errands for a parent, conducting business at work, or doing a favor for a friend. Have the class identify the type of agency and discuss the agency relationships.

SECTION 14.1 ASSESSMENT

Self Check

1. a relationship based on trust
2. reimbursement: repayment of money spent by agent on behalf of principal; indemnification: payment for losses suffered by agent due to principal's instructions
3. negligent hiring: proprietor fails to check qualifications; negligent retention: proprietor fails to fire a contractor after learning of incompetence

Academic Connection

Mathematics
Commission: $13,500; 8% commission: $14,400; Difference: $900

Critical Thinking

No. Agent must account for all funds belonging to the principal.

N C L B Activity correlated to the Mathematics standard on page 308

FOCUS

Bell Ringer Activity

Clip public notices from the newspaper relating to agency relationships and bring them to class. Lead a class discussion on the purposes of the notices and identify the agent, the principal, and third parties (if applicable).

Preteaching

Key Terms

Read the definitions and ask students to create a sentence using each term.

Academic Vocabulary

Explain that developing vocabulary is key to academic success. An efficient method to develop vocabulary is to study how words are formed.

- **benefit** Noun, from the Latin *bene factum* (favor). Means something that promotes well-being.

- **mutual** Adjective, from the Latin *mutuus* (lent, borrowed, akin to). Means directed by each toward the other or others.

- **irrevocable** Adjective, from the Latin *in* (not) and *revocabilis* (to recall or take back) and *facies* (the face, appearance). Means unalterable.

Activity Ask students to give a noun, a verb, an adjective, or an adverb form that comes from each word.

N C L B Connects to academic content

What You'll Learn

- ◆ Determine when an agency relationship is terminated by operation of law.
- ◆ Explain when an agency relationship is terminated by act of the parties.
- ◆ Identify the individuals who are entitled to notice that an agency relationship has ended.

Why It's Important

You need to know when an agency relationship ends so you know when your rights and duties end.

Academic Standards

Reading and completing the activities in this section will help you practice the following academic standards:

N C L B

English Language Arts (NCTE 3) Apply a wide range of strategies to comprehend, interpret, evaluate, and appreciate texts.

Social Studies (NCSS 5) Study interactions among individuals, groups, and institutions.

Reading Guide

Before You Read

Connect Suppose you are a writer, musician, or actor with an agent who has not found you work in months. How can you get out of your contract with the agent?

Focus on Ideas

Agency relationships come to an end because the parties end them on their own or because the law ends them.

Take Notes

Create a graph like the one shown and use it to take notes as you read this section. Go to glencoe.com to find graphic organizers and tips on how to improve your note-taking skills.

 Key Terms

You will learn these legal words and expressions in this chapter. You can also find these terms in *Black's Law Dictionary* or in an online legal dictionary.

- actual notice
- notice by publication

Academic Vocabulary

You will find these words in your readings and in your tests. Look them up in a dictionary and familiarize yourself with them.

- benefit
- mutual
- irrevocable

 glencoe.com

R Reading Strategy

Read for Knowledge

1. **Survey** or preread the chapter.
2. **Question** or formulate questions before you read.
3. **Recite** or read your questions, answers, and notes out loud.
4. **Review** or reread your notes.

Note-Taking Basics

- Listen attentively
- Have note-taking materials ready
- Skim through the lesson material
- Write down key words and ideas
- Anticipate what comes next
- Review notes soon after taking them

Ways to Terminate an Agency Relationship

If you were unhappy with an agent, how could you terminate your agreement?

If an agency is contractual, the usual rules that apply to ending contracts apply to ending agency relationships. Agency relationships can be terminated either by operation of law or by the acts of the parties.

Termination by Operation of Law

A major change can affect the parties involved in an agency relationship or alter its operation. When this happens, a court may say that the agency relationship has ended by operation of law.

The death of the agent or the principal will end the agency relationship.

The bankruptcy of the principal ends an agency. This is because it closes down all the principal's ordinary contracts. Bankruptcy also gives a trustee title to the principal's property for the **benefit** of creditors.

Bankruptcy of the agent sometimes ends the agency. This is true if the agent has used his or her own funds to do the principal's business. If not, there is no reason to terminate the agency because the agent may be able to continue doing business.

An agency can also end due to impossibility of performance. This happens if the necessary subject matter is destroyed. For example, if an agent is authorized to sell a boat for the principal, but the boat sinks in a storm, the loss of the boat terminates the agency. Performance can also become impossible if the agent or principal becomes incapacitated or ill.

D

As You Read

Predict Do agencies always end by agreement?

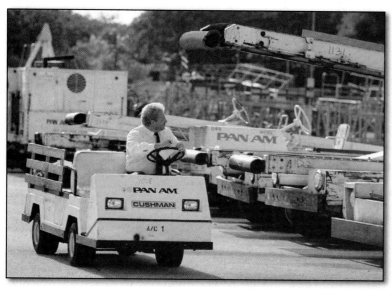

⬅ **Bankruptcy** An agency relationship is terminated by bankruptcy of the principal. *Does bankruptcy of the agent terminate an agency relationship?*

▲ USING VISUALS

⬅ **Bankruptcy Answer** Not necessarily. Students should understand that bankruptcy of the agent ends the agency only if the agent has used his or her own funds to do the principal's business. If not, then there is no reason to terminate the agency because the agent should be able to continue doing business.

14.2 SECTION

TEACH

Discussion Starter

Class Discussion
Explain to students that agency relationships are terminated by either an operation of law, such as bankruptcy or illegality, or by acts of the parties, such as mutual agreement or performance. As a class, think of examples for each case.

As You Read

Predict Ask students to make educated suggestions as to how agencies might terminate. Have them consider any unexpected occurrences that might terminate an agency agreement. (No. They may be terminated by impossibility of performance if the agent or principal dies; or by operation of law, such as bankruptcy or illegality.)

D Develop Concepts

Impossibility of Performance Ask students to brainstorm in teams of three or four students to come up with an agency relationship that was created but cannot be completed due to impossibility of performance. Have each team present their scenario to the class. Ask them to specifically identify how the contract has become impossible to perform.

317

✓ Reading Check

Discuss Principal and agent may establish end date or may mutually decide to end the arrangement for other reasons, such as disagreements between the parties or financial difficulties.

ASSESS

Quiz

Ask students the following true or false questions:

1. The death of a principal does not end an agency relationship. (false)

2. If the purpose of an agency becomes illegal, the agency is ended. (true)

3. Agency relationships can only end when the parties have fully carried out their duties. (false)

RETEACH

W Writing Support

Ways to Terminate an Agency Relationship Have students write one scenario describing a termination by operation of law and one scenario describing a termination by an act of the parties. Ensure that scenarios fully explain the agency agreement and the act or law that terminates the contract.

318

✓ Reading Check

Discuss Why might a principal and agent agree to end an agency before a task is completed?

The agency is ended if the agent's objective becomes illegal. If only part of the agent's activities becomes illegal, then only that part of the authority ends. The authority to perform the legal activities is still in effect.

Termination by Acts of the Parties

Most agency relationships end when the parties have fully carried out their duties. The relationship can also end by **mutual** consent. Certain acts by either party can also end the relationship.

An agency relationship ends through completion of performance if an agent accomplishes the specific result that the principal desired.

W The principal and the agent may end the agency by mutual agreement at a certain time. It could be a specific date or at any time they want. This can be binding even if the task is not done, as long as it is mutual.

The agent's withdrawal ends an agency. An agent may withdraw from the agency at any time. However, if the agency is terminated by the agent before the specified time in the agreement or causes a breach of contract, the principal can sue the agent for damages.

📄 Case Study – Morgan Associates, Inc. v. Midwest Mutual Insurance Co.

Critical Thinking *Does restricting an agent's business terminate an agency relationship?*

Flex Your Reading Note key facts in the text below and look up words you do not understand. Restate difficult ideas in your own words. Go back and reread the text quickly to make sure you did not miss any important detail. Now, you are ready to formulate an opinion.

Unfair Restrictions? Morgan Associates, Inc. (Morgan) was an insurance agency specializing in motorcycle and high-risk automobile insurance. It sold insurance on behalf of two companies, Colonial Insurance Co. of California (Colonial) and Midwest Mutual Insurance Co. (Midwest).

For years Morgan sold insurance for both companies without any problems. However, in early 1992, Colonial told Morgan that Morgan would no longer be able to write any new policies for Colonial until further notice. Colonial said that Morgan's clients were filing too many claims. Colonial told Morgan it could renew policies and Colonial would review the situation on a monthly basis.

In late 1992, Midwest also restricted Morgan's ability to write new policies for the same reason: its clients were filing too many claims. Morgan could renew current policies, and Midwest would continue the agency relationship in hopes that Morgan could improve its numbers.

Morgan then sued Colonial and Midwest, arguing that the two companies had constructively terminated the agency relationship contrary to Minnesota law by restricting Morgan's ability to write new policies.

Morgan Associates, Inc. v. Midwest Mutual Insurance Co., 519 N.W.2d 499 (Minn. Ct. App. 1994)

✈ Go to **glencoe.com** for more case study practice.

 glencoe.com

📄 Case Study

Morgan Associates, Inc., v. Midwest Mutual Insurance Co.

Answer No. The Minnesota Court of Appeals held that neither Midwest nor Colonial had terminated the agency relationship between their companies and Morgan. A mere restriction on the ability to write new policies did not amount to an impossibility of performance. Morgan was allowed to renew and service any current contracts it had with both companies. Further, both insurance companies expressed a desire to maintain a relationship with Morgan. There was no intent by Midwest or Colonial to permanently bar Morgan from writing new insurance policies; their intent was to encourage Morgan to become more profitable.

The agent's discharge can also end the agency. The principal may end the agency at any time by discharging, or firing, the agent. However, the principal may not be able to fire the agent if the agent has an interest in the subject matter of the agency. This is called **irrevocable** agency, meaning that the agency cannot be revoked until the agent is paid in full.

Giving Notice to Third Parties

If a third party has never heard of the agency relationship, the principal does not need to give notice. Otherwise, a principal must give notice to all third parties who have done business with the principal through the agent or who know of the agency relationship. A principal who does not notify third parties may be liable for future acts of the agent. The type of notice given to a third party depends on how business relations have been carried out. There are two types of notices:

- **Actual notice is formal notice given directly to a party, usually using certified mail with a receipt.** Actual notice is required when the third party has given credit to the principal through the agent.

- **Notice by publication is notice usually given by publishing a notice in a local newspaper.** When the third party has never given credit but has done a cash business with the agent, or knows that other persons have dealt with the principal only on a cash basis through the agent, notice by publication is sufficient.

After You Read

Summarize List the ways an agency relationship can be terminated by operation of law.

SECTION 14.2 ASSESSMENT

Self Check

1. What are the two ways an agency relationship can be terminated?

2. When is an agency relationship terminated by an act of the parties?

3. What parties are entitled to notice that an agency has ended?

Academic Connection

English Language Arts
Writers, musicians, actors, and athletes often hire talent agents to find jobs and negotiate contracts for

them. Assume you are an artist or athlete contracting an agent to represent you. Write up a set of conditions the agent has to meet or you can terminate the contract. For example, the agent has to find you work within a particular period of time.

Critical Thinking

Notice of Termination
Suppose you have just ended the agency relationship with your boss. Your job had been to buy stock on credit from a wide variety of suppliers,

including Freshwater Industries, Oppenheimer, Inc., and Harrisburg Supplies. You have also done a consistent cash business with Thompson Inc. and with Kennedy Industries. You also intended to call on Georgetown Ltd. the next day to buy some stock. Nobody at Georgetown has ever laid eyes on you. Who is entitled to actual notice, who is entitled to notice by publication, and who is not entitled to any notice?

 Go to **glencoe.com** to check your answers.

After You Read

Summarize death of the principal or agent, bankruptcy of the principal and sometimes of the agent, impossibility of performance, agent's objective becomes illegal

ASSESS

Self-Assessment

Have students go to the *Business and Personal Law* Online Learning Center through glencoe.com to take the Section 14.2 Practice Test.

CLOSE

Culminating Activity

Terminating Relationships

Tell students that Paul has an agreement to purchase hubcaps from Kelly. Recently Paul found out that Kelly steals the hubcaps that he supplies. Ask students whether Paul and Kelly still have an agency relationship. Why or why not? (No. The agent's objective is illegal.)

SECTION 14.2 ASSESSMENT

Self Check

1. by operation of law or by acts of the parties

2. when completed, by mutual assent, when agent withdraws or resigns, when the principal discharges the agent

3. third parties who have known of the agency relationship

Academic Connection

English Language Arts
Answers will vary. Conditions should be reasonable and attainable.

Critical Thinking

Actual notice: Freshwater Industries, Oppenheimer, Inc., and Harrisburg Supplies, Inc. Notice by publication:

Thompson, Inc., and Kennedy Industries. No notice: Georgetown, Ltd.

 Activity correlated to the English Language Arts standard on page 316

Chapter 14 Review and Assessment

Summary by Sections

Ask students to read the summaries one key point at a time. Then, ask them to work in groups to create two examples to illustrate each key point.

Vocabulary Builder

Cooperative Learning

1. Have students work in groups to prepare their sentences. Ask the groups to exchange their sentences and assess each other's sentences.

Vocabulary Development

- Ask students to use a dictionary or to go online to look up the etymology of each key term listed.

- Then, ask students to list several words derived from the same root or origin. For example, *contract* has the same root as *contractual* or *contractually*.

Summary

Section 14.1 Duties and Liability in Agency Relationships

- An agent's duties to a principal include obedience, good faith, loyalty, an accounting, and good judgment and skill.
- Agents are liable for fulfilling fiduciary duties.
- Principal's duties to an agent include compensation, reimbursement, indemnification, and cooperation.
- Respondeat superior is a legal doctrine that holds that a master is responsible for the torts of his or her servants.
- Negligent hiring occurs when a proprietor hires a person who is incompetent.
- Negligent retention occurs when a proprietor fails to fire a contractor after learning that he or she is incompetent.
- A nondelegable duty is a duty that cannot be delegated, or transferred, to another party.

Section 14.2 Termination of Agency Relationships

- Agency relationships can be terminated by operation of law or by the acts of the parties.
- Agency relationships can be ended by operation of law in the following circumstances: the death of the principal or the agent, bankruptcy, impossibility of performance, and illegality.
- Agency relationships can be ended by the acts of the parties in the following circumstances: completion of performance, mutual agreement, the agent's withdrawal, and the agent's discharge.
- Third parties who have done business with the principal through an agent or who knew of the agency relationship should receive a notice that it has ended.
- Actual notice is required when the third party has given credit to the principal through the agent.
- Notice by publication is sufficient when business has been done only by cash (not credit) between third parties and agents or principals.

Vocabulary Builder

1   On a sheet of paper, use each of these terms in a sentence.

Key Terms

- fiduciary relationship
- double representation
- self-dealing
- compensation
- reimbursement
- indemnification
- respondeat superior
- nondelegable duty
- actual notice
- notice by publication

Academic Vocabulary

- loyal
- adhere
- cooperation
- benefit
- mutual
- irrevocable

Go to **glencoe.com** to play a game and improve your legal vocabulary.

Study Skills for Success

Prepare Your Students for Studying

Tell students that they can improve their ability to understand and remember material from their courses by learning and practicing study skills. Remind students to:

- **Get motivated!** Motivation must come from within. To motivate yourself, think of ways in which what you learn now will fit into your long-term personal and professional goals.
- **Get organized!** Make studying part of your daily routine, not something you do at the last minute.
- **Concentrate!** Study in an environment that is as free of distractions as possible.

Key Points Review

Answer the following questions. Refer to the chapter for additional reinforcement.

2 What duties does an agent owe to the principal?

3 What are the three situations in which an agent becomes liable for an injury to a third party.

4 What is the doctrine of respondeat superior?

5 What is a nondelegable duty?

6 When is an agency relationship terminated by operation of law?

7 Does bankruptcy of the agent or the principal always end the agency relationship?

8 What might happen if the agency is terminated by the agent before the specified time in the agreement?

9 What two types of notices can a principal send a third party that an agency has ended?

Standardized Test Practice

10 Read the following excerpt from Carter v. Gugliuzzi (Vt. 1998) on an agent's duties to a principal and complete questions 1 and 2.

Ana Barreto and Flavia Gugliuzzi asked Ruth Bennett, a real estate agent who worked for Smith Bell Real Estate, to sell their house in Underhill, Vermont. Diana Carter, a California resident, visited the house as a potential buyer. Bennett worked under the supervision of David Crane, an officer of Smith Bell. Crane knew, but did not disclose to Bennett or Carter, the house was subject to frequent and severe winds, that a window had blown in years earlier, and that other houses in the area had suffered wind damage. Crane knew of this because he lived in the area. Carter bought the house. Several months later, high winds blew in a number of windows and damaged the property. Carter filed a suit in a Vermont state court against Smith Bell and others, alleging fraud. She argued in part that Crane's knowledge of the winds was imputable to Smith Bell. Smith Bell responded that Crane's knowledge was obtained outside the scope of employment.

1. Who is the injured party in this case?

Ⓐ Smith Bell Real Estate

Ⓑ Ruth Bennett

Ⓒ Diana Carter

Ⓓ David Crane

2. What is Smith Bell Real Estate's defense in this case?

Ⓐ Smith Bell did not know about the weather conditions in the area.

Ⓑ Smith Bell was not asked about the weather conditions.

Ⓒ Smith Bell did not have a legal obligation to disclose knowledge about the weather conditions.

Ⓓ The employee's knowledge about weather conditions was obtained outside the scope of employment.

Test-Taking Strategies When an essay question tells you to contrast, it is telling you to point out the differences between two or more things.

Key Points Review

2. obedience, good faith, loyalty, accounting, and good judgment

3. The agent has made an agreement or performed tasks beyond his or her authority to do so; the principal is a minor or does not have the capacity to sign a contract, yet the agent has not disclosed this fact to the third party; the principal is undisclosed, and the third party cannot identify the principal.

4. A master is responsible for the torts of his or her servants.

5. a duty that cannot be transferred to another party

6. at the death of the principal or agent, the bankruptcy of the principal, the bankruptcy of the agent if the agent deals with his or her own funds, by impossibility of performance, or if the agent's activities become illegal

7. Bankruptcy of the principal does but bankruptcy of the agent does not unless the agent used his or her own funds to do the principal's business.

8. The principal can sue the agent for damages.

9. actual notice and notice by publication

Standardized Test Practice

10. C and D

 ## Strategies for Standardized Test Prep Success

Whether your students have a standardized test coming up in a few days or a few weeks, these last-minute test-prep tips and strategies will help them relax and do their best.

- **Test Format** Help students become familiar with the format of the test by practicing with test items that imitate the actual test items as closely as possible.

- **Test Timing** Have your students take timed practice tests so that they become comfortable with the length, design, and timing of the actual test.

Apply and Debate

Students should use chapter content to arrive at conclusions. The legal resolutions are listed below:

11. Maybe. Since the other jewelry makers agreed to pay for gas and travel expenses, a hotel stay may be appropriate.

12. Yes. The public relations company, as an agent, must be loyal to their principal, Isaiah. Under the duty of loyalty, agents are not allowed to work at the same time for direct competitors.

13. Maybe. Under the theory of impossibility of performance, it is possible that Shinea could discharge Franklin and void the contract. If Franklin can still teach Shinea how to play tennis using his left arm, he may be able to retain his position.

14. Probably not. If the accident happened while Jorge was stopping to visit his friend, then it is doubtful his employer would be liable unless drivers are allowed to make nondelivery stops.

15. Probably not. As long as Andrews used good faith and good judgment, then he probably cannot be held liable for the losses. Federal law dictates that stockbrokers make their clients aware of the possibility of losses with stocks.

Apply and Debate

Read the following scenarios. Get together with other students in pairs or groups of three and take a position on each scenario. Debate your position in class with students taking the opposite position or prepare a written argument justifying your position.

11 Sharing Unexpected Expenses

Jackie, a jewelry artist, was attending a one-day fair in another city. She told two other jewelry makers that she would sell their work at the fair in exchange for a commission, but she wanted them to share her gas and travel expenses too. After the fair was over, Jackie was tired and decided to stay in a motel for $109.

You Debate Can Jackie ask the other artists to share in the cost of the hotel?

12 Multiple Clients

Isaiah hired a public relations company to promote his new business venture. Unknown to Isaiah, the company already represented one of his competitors, who asked not to be revealed.

You Debate Is the public relations company obligated to tell Isaiah that it also represents his competitor?

13 Tennis Pro with a Broken Arm

Shinea hired Franklin, a right-handed tennis pro, to teach at her tennis camp. Unfortunately, Franklin broke his right arm before the camp started. Frank insisted to Shinea that he could still teach tennis using his left arm.

You Debate Can Shinea discharge Frank because of his incapacitation to teach tennis?

14 Delivery Accident

Jorge is a senior in high school. He also works delivering pizzas using his personal car. While delivering a pizza one day, Jorge visited at a friend's house. While parking, he hit another car and damaged it. He continued to deliver the pizza.

You Debate Is the employer responsible for the damage Jorge caused the other car?

15 Stock Market Crash

Rena Pellas transferred $100,000 to her stockbroker, Bill Andrews. With Pellas's permission, Andrews invested the money in risky stocks. The portfolio soon rose to $140,000. However, the stock suddenly fell, and Andrews could not react fast enough to prevent his client from losing $50,000.

You Debate Can Andrews be held liable for Pellas's loss?

C Critical Thinking

Conflict of Interest You and Karl agree that he will act as your agent, promoting your services as a gardening specialist. Ms. Vincenza wants some landscaping done, but she insists that Karl do the work. Karl tells you that he will do the work and give you a portion of the money, but you feel this is not fair.

Debate Practice

• If Karl does the work, has he damaged the agency relationship? (Answers will vary. Students may believe that Karl is not upholding the duties of good faith, obedience, or loyalty.)

• Would you terminate your agency relationship with Karl? If so, how? (Answers will vary. Students who choose to terminate the relationship would do so by discharging the agent.)

Case Study Practice – Nationwide Mutual Insurance Co. v. Prioleau

⑯ **What Is Implied Agency?** On April 25, 1997, Julius Prioleau applied for auto insurance with Nationwide Mutual Insurance Company for himself and his wife, Paula. Ms. Prioleau was not with Mr. Prioleau at the time. While at the insurance agent's office, Mr. Prioleau declined to purchase additional uninsured and underinsured automobile coverage and signed a form stating his decision.

On February 3, 1998, Ms. Prioleau was involved in an automobile accident. She suffered bodily injuries in the accident and made a claim against the other driver. The other insurance company paid Ms. Prioleau the amount allowed under that driver's policy, but it did not cover all of her medical expenses. Ms. Prioleau then made a claim with Nationwide for underinsured motorist insurance. Nationwide claimed that she did not have underinsured coverage because her husband, acting as her agent, had declined it. Ms. Prioleau argued that she did not decline the coverage, and her husband could not make that decision for her.

Source: National Mutual Insurance Co. v. Prioleau, 597 S.E.2d 165 (S.C. Ct. App. 2004)

> **Practice** Was Julius Prioleau the agent of Paula Prioleau?

⑰ Ethics ←?→ Application

Hiring a Friend You are the manager of a clothing store. You must hire a new buyer who gets to go to New York and Paris to select inventory for your store. There are five candidates, including your friend. She has less experience than the others. However, since you know her, you believe she can learn the business quickly.

◆ Would it be ethical for you to hire your friend? Explain your reasons.

⑱ Internet Application

Small Claims Isaiah breeds AKC Yorkshire Terrier dogs. He asks Terra if she would sell his new litter of seven puppies at the rate of $600 per puppy. Terra sells all seven together for $600. Isaiah then threatens to sue her.

 Log on to **glencoe.com** to access the Web site Findlaw and search how to file a suit in small claims court or methods to reach an out-of-court settlement.

> ### 📖 Reading Connection
> **Outside Reading** Go to **glencoe.com** for a list of outside reading suggestions about liability in an agency relationship.

📄 Case Study Practice

16. Yes. The South Carolina Court of Appeals held that in South Carolina, the law of agency applies to the relationship between spouses. When looking at the situation, the court found that an implied agency existed between Mr. and Ms. Prioleau. Therefore, when Mr. Prioleau applied for insurance in his name and his wife's name, he was acting as her agent. By declining coverage, he was declining coverage for both himself and Ms. Prioleau.

 Chapter

Review and Assessment

←?→ Ethics Application

17. Answers will vary. Some students will suggest that except for experience, integrity, intelligence, and critical thinking skills may be just as important. If the friend has skills in these areas, hiring her would be allowable. Others may feel that experience is the only meaningful criterion; therefore, the friend would not be the ethical choice.

💻 Internet Application

18. To reach an out-of-court settlement for a small claims suit, the parties to the suit meet with a neutral third person who helps arrive at a solution. Mediation is now mandatory in some small claims courts. A small claims lawsuit is filed in the small claims court closest to the residence or headquarters of the party being sued.

Reading Strategy

> 📖 **Reading Connection**
>
> ***American Bar Association Resources***
>
> Go to the *Business and Personal Law* Online Learning Center through glencoe.com to find links for further readings that relate to this chapter. Ask students to read, review, and summarize the documents. Advise students to keep their reviews and summaries to use as reference material for their Unit Thematic Project on pages 348–349.

Plan Your Lesson Section by Section

NBEA	NATIONAL BUSINESS LAW STANDARDS
Section 15.1	• **Describe** the collective bargaining process. • **Identify** legislation that regulates union activities (e.g., National Labor Relations Act, Taft-Hartley Act, and Lundrum-Griffin Act).
Section 15.2	• **Explain** the relationship of Title VII of the Civil Rights Act to employment. • **Explain** the difference between disparate treatment and disparate impact in discrimination cases. • **Explain** the Civil Rights Act of 1991. • **Determine** what questions can and cannot be asked during an employment review. • **Demonstrate** an understanding of the basis on which employees or applicants may be asked to take tests (e.g., aptitude, psychological, polygraph, and drug tests). • **Identify** legislation that regulates employment conditions (e.g., Fair Labor Standards Act, Immigration Reform and Control Act, and Occupational Safety and Health Act). • **Identify** legislation that regulates employee rights (e.g., Americans with Disabilities Act, Age Discrimination in Employment Act, Family and Medical Leave Act, and Older Workers Benefit Protection Act). • **Identify** legislation that guarantees worker benefits (e.g., unemployment insurance, pension protection, workers' compensation, and Social Security legislation).

NCLB	ACADEMIC STANDARDS	Activity/Feature
English Language Arts: NCTE 3 Apply a wide range of strategies to comprehend, interpret, evaluate, and appreciate texts.		*BusinessWeek* News, Case Study, Case Study Practice
English Language Arts: NCTE 9 Develop an understanding of and respect for diversity in language use, patterns, and dialects across cultures, ethnic groups, geographic regions, and social roles.		Global Law
English Language Arts: NCTE 6 Apply knowledge of language structure, language conventions, media techniques, figurative language, and genre to create, critique, and discuss print and non-print texts.		Legal Talk, ad copy, Key Terms, and Academic Vocabulary
Social Studies: NCSS 2 Study the ways human beings view themselves in and over time.		Section 15.1 Assessment
English Language Arts: NCTE 4 Adjust the use of spoken, written, and visual language to communicate effectively with a variety of audiences and for different purposes.		Section 15.2 Assessment
English Language Arts: NCTE 10 Students whose first language is not English make use of their first language to develop competency in the English language arts and to develop understanding of content across the curriculum.		Key Terms, Academic Vocabulary, Legal Talk, Vocabulary Builder
English Language Arts: NCTE 1 Read a wide range of print and non-print texts to build an understanding of texts; to acquire new information; to respond to the needs and demands of society and the workplace; and for personal fulfillment.		Global Law
English Language Arts: NCTE 7 Conduct research on issues and interests by generating ideas and questions, and by posing problems.		Global Law
Social Studies: NCSS 6 Study how people create and change structures of power, authority, and governance.		Case Study

Connect Your Business Law Classroom to the World of Work

This chart shows the 21ˢᵗ Century Skills, foundation skills, and workplace competencies that students develop as they work in this chapter.

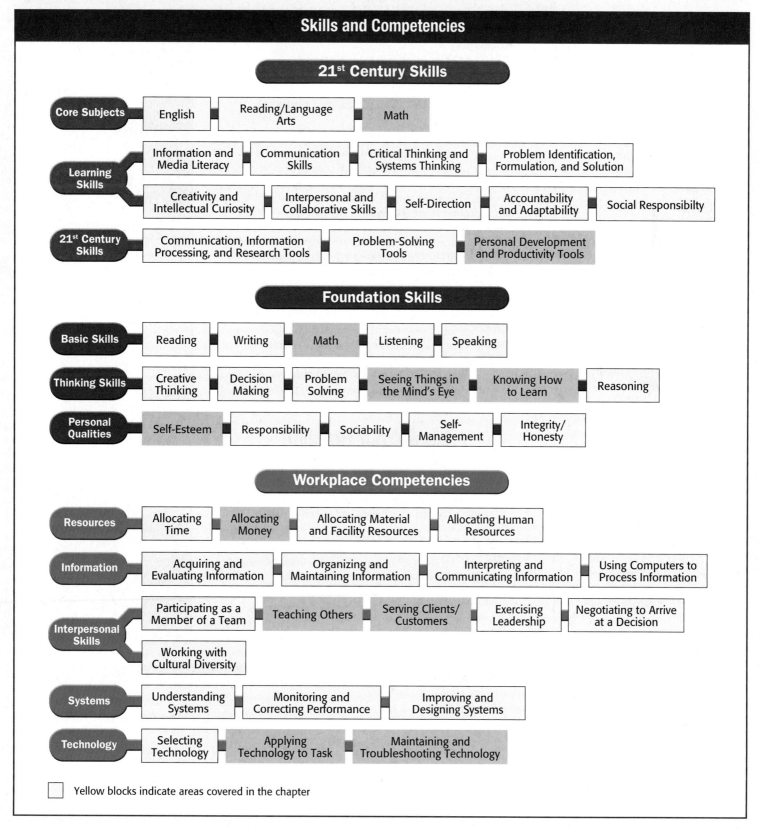

Skills and Competencies

21ˢᵗ Century Skills

Core Subjects
- English
- Reading/Language Arts
- Math

Learning Skills
- Information and Media Literacy
- Communication Skills
- Critical Thinking and Systems Thinking
- Problem Identification, Formulation, and Solution
- Creativity and Intellectual Curiosity
- Interpersonal and Collaborative Skills
- Self-Direction
- Accountability and Adaptability
- Social Responsibilty

21ˢᵗ Century Skills
- Communication, Information Processing, and Research Tools
- Problem-Solving Tools
- Personal Development and Productivity Tools

Foundation Skills

Basic Skills
- Reading
- Writing
- Math
- Listening
- Speaking

Thinking Skills
- Creative Thinking
- Decision Making
- Problem Solving
- Seeing Things in the Mind's Eye
- Knowing How to Learn
- Reasoning

Personal Qualities
- Self-Esteem
- Responsibility
- Sociability
- Self-Management
- Integrity/Honesty

Workplace Competencies

Resources
- Allocating Time
- Allocating Money
- Allocating Material and Facility Resources
- Allocating Human Resources

Information
- Acquiring and Evaluating Information
- Organizing and Maintaining Information
- Interpreting and Communicating Information
- Using Computers to Process Information

Interpersonal Skills
- Participating as a Member of a Team
- Teaching Others
- Serving Clients/Customers
- Exercising Leadership
- Negotiating to Arrive at a Decision
- Working with Cultural Diversity

Systems
- Understanding Systems
- Monitoring and Correcting Performance
- Improving and Designing Systems

Technology
- Selecting Technology
- Applying Technology to Task
- Maintaining and Troubleshooting Technology

☐ Yellow blocks indicate areas covered in the chapter

CHAPTER

15 Employment Law

Introduce the Chapter

Employment Law

Chapter 15 describes the employer-employee relationship and the rights and duties of each party. It also presents the major legislation that governs elements of employer-employee relationships such as fair wages, health and safety, and privacy.

Building Background

Explain to students that many laws govern employers and employees. Ask students to identify ways in which laws govern or protect employees. If necessary, prompt them by mentioning such areas as health, safety, discrimination, family leave, and privacy.

BusinessWeek News

Ask students if they are familiar with the concept of a union. Have them discuss stories or personal family experiences that involve unions. Explain that this article focuses on a problem that the largest union, the AFL-CIO, was having within its membership, because one faction disagreed with the leadership and wanted to split off to form its own federation. Tell students that the SEIU faction did eventually split off.

R Reading Strategy

Your Reading

Suggest to students that they use index cards for note taking on each of the employment statutes or laws presented in this chapter.

BusinessWeek News

This Would Be a Very Painful Divorce

By Aaron Bernstein

If organized labor goes through an ugly divorce, an outcome that seems to be gathering steam, expect divisive spats over everything from politics to money to new members. For now, AFL-CIO President John J. Sweeney has a majority of union leaders backing him for reelection at the federation's convention in late July. But dissident unions, which recently formed a group called Change to Win Coalition, are threatening to pull out of the AFL-CIO if the federation fails to undertake major reforms and reelects Sweeney.

In the past few months the possibility of a breakup has pushed antagonisms sky-high, and tensions will only worsen if anyone actually decamps. Even if the coalition, led by Service Employees International Union (SEIU) President Andy Stern, breaks off into a rival federation, both groups will have plenty of incentive to avoid open warfare. But it's also possible that the maneuvering could degenerate into tit-for-tat retaliation, causing nasty rifts.

Your Reading

Efficient critical reading involves being flexible with speed and comprehension. There are several ways of reading critically, and you need to fit a reading style to your needs and to the material.

 Go to **glencoe.com** for Flex Your Reading activities, more information on reading strategies for this chapter, and guided practice in reading about labor unions.

Classroom Resources

- Student Edition
- Teacher Wraparound Edition
- Student Activity Workbook with Academic Integration (SE/TAE)
- TeacherWorks™ Plus! CD
- *ExamView®* *Assessment Suite* CD
- *Presentation Plus!* CD

- National Mock Trial Championship DVD
- Online Learning Center with Podcasts at glencoe.com
- Study-to-Go™ at glencoe.com
- Online Student Edition
- Interactive Student Edition

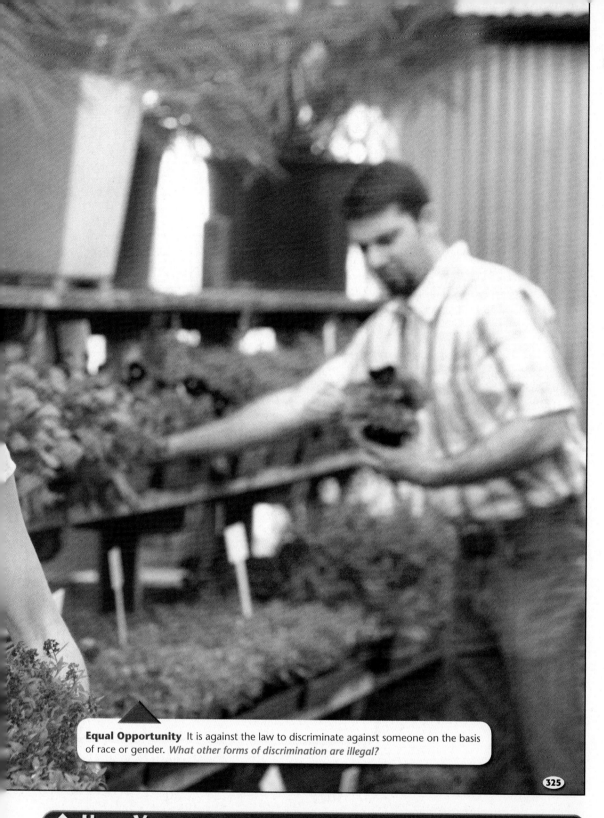

Equal Opportunity It is against the law to discriminate against someone on the basis of race or gender. *What other forms of discrimination are illegal?*

325

Equal Opportunity Answer It is illegal to discriminate based on age, religion, disability, or nationality. Tell students that discrimination is illegal in any aspect of employment, including hiring, firing, compensation, testing, retirement benefits, promotions, training, or use of company facilities.

Activity Tell students that job applications often contain language that mentions *equal opportunity*. Ask students to discuss what they believe this term means and how it relates to employment. (Equal opportunity means that all candidates have the same opportunities in employment based on their skills and experience, not based on their race, religion, gender, or color.)

Practice the Concept

Employment
Ask for students who have ever worked to volunteer to talk about their jobs. Let them discuss how they were hired, if they were given a contract, and what types of protections they were given regarding health and safety, privacy, and equal opportunity.

Key Terms Explain to students that one of the key terms in employment law is *employment-at-will*. Ask students to break the term down into its two parts (*employment* and *at-will*) and predict what each portion means. (Each party is free to end the employment relationship at any time.) Ask students to name what they think might be advantages and disadvantages of employment-at-will.

Legal Basics Explain that employment-at-will takes the place of a contract between a company and the employee. Most companies ask employees to sign an agreement acknowledging that they are employed-at-will. This is not the kind of contract that protects against employees being fired without good reason. Some types of employees do have contracts that protect them from being unreasonably fired or that grant them a severance pay package should they be terminated.

FOCUS

Bell Ringer Activity

Ask students whether they know someone who has been fired from a job. Have volunteers describe the conditions surrounding the termination. Use this discussion to introduce employment-at-will.

Preteaching

Key Terms

Read the definitions and ask students to create a sentence using each term.

Academic Vocabulary

Explain that developing vocabulary is key to academic success. An efficient method to develop vocabulary is to study how words are formed.

- **exception** Noun, from the Latin *exciper*, *ex* + *capere* (to take). Means a case that does not conform to a rule.
- **corruption** Noun, from the Latin *corrumpere* (to destroy). Means the act of becoming or being morally ruined; without honesty.
- **solicit** Verb, From the Latin *solicitare* (to disturb). Means to attract by persuasion.

Activity Ask students to give a noun, an adjective, or an adverb form that comes from each word.

 Connects to academic content

326

What You'll Learn

- ◆ Discuss the employer-employee relationship.
- ◆ Define employment-at-will.
- ◆ Name the exceptions to employment-at-will.
- ◆ Explain the collective bargaining process.
- ◆ Describe the laws that regulate labor unions.

Why It's Important

Understanding employment-at-will and wrongful discharge will help you protect your rights as an employee.

Academic Standards

Reading and completing the activities in this section will help you practice the following academic standards:

Social Studies (NCSS 2) Study the ways human beings view themselves in and over time.

English Language Arts (NCTE 7) Conduct research on issues and interests by generating ideas and questions, and by posing problems.

Reading Guide

Before You Read

Connect Has anyone in your family ever belonged to or dealt with a labor union?

Focus on Ideas

Employers and employees are free to end the employment relationship any time they choose.

Take Notes

Create a graph like the one shown and use it to take notes as you read this section. Go to **glencoe.com** to find graphic organizers and tips on how to improve your note-taking skills.

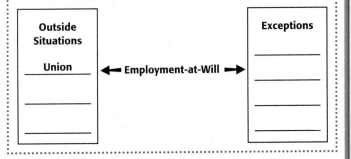

Key Terms

You will learn these legal words and expressions in this chapter. You can also find these terms in *Black's Law Dictionary* or in an online legal dictionary.

- employment-at-will
- union
- implied contract
- public policy tort
- implied covenant
- collective bargaining

Academic Vocabulary

You will find these words in your readings and in your tests. Look them up in a dictionary and familiarize yourself with them.

- exception
- corruption
- solicit

 glencoe.com

R Reading Strategy

Read for Knowledge

1. **Survey** or preread the chapter.
2. **Question** or formulate questions before you read.
3. **Recite** or read your questions, answers, and notes out loud.
4. **Review** or reread your notes.

Note-Taking Basics

- Listen attentively
- Have note-taking materials ready
- Skim through the lesson material
- Write down key words and ideas
- Anticipate what comes next
- Review notes soon after taking them

Employment-at-Will

Can you be fired from a job for no reason?

Most employees in the United States work in states that follow a rule called employment-at-will. **Employment-at-will means that an employer or employee can end an employment relationship at any time, for any reason or for no reason, with or without notice.** The doctrine is based on the principle that each party should be free to end employment at any time without penalty. Still, some employees fall outside of this rule. Some also benefit from certain **exceptions** that the courts have created recently.

Situations outside Employment-at-Will

Certain situations fall outside the rule of employment-at-will. These situations include unionized employees, employees with individual employment contracts, and protected classes of employees.

Unionized Employees A union is an organization of employees formed to promote the welfare of its members. Employers cannot hire or fire union members at will, because employees who are members of labor unions have specific procedures built into their employment agreements. Union members are guaranteed certain wages, conditions, and benefits, but they are not free to negotiate their own contracts.

Employees with Individual Employment Contracts Some employees, such as sports stars and entertainment figures, negotiate their own individual employment contracts.

Some businesses and educational institutions also establish contracts for certain classes for employees, such as senior officers in a company or faculty members at a college.

Employment contracts can benefit employees, but they can also prevent people from leaving a job when they want and working for whomever they want.

➡ **Exceptions to Employment-at-Will** Employment-at-will does not apply to entertainers, sports figures, and executives who negotiate their own individual employment contracts. *What other types of employees are not subject to employment-at-will?*

Vocabulary You can find vocabulary definitions in the **Key Terms** glossary and **Academic Vocabulary** glossary in the back of this book.

Chapter 15 Employment Law **327**

TEACH
Discussion Starter

Class Discussion
Ask students if they would prefer to have a contract when they get their first job or if they would prefer to be working at-will, which allows them to leave at any time. Encourage them to examine the advantages and disadvantages of both types of situations.

D Develop Concepts

Unionized Employees Help students distinguish between employees-at-will and unionized workers. Ask which group enjoys more protections. (unionized employees) Explain that union employees are protected by the contract negotiated by their union to cover their wages, benefits, and conditions of termination.

As You Read

Predict Ask students to consider this question in the context of employment-at-will. Remind them that at-will means there is no contract. (Individuals working in an at-will status may be fired for no reason. The rights for other employees depend on their individual employment contracts.)

▲ USING VISUALS

➡ **Situations outside Employment-at-Will Answer** Unionized employees and protected classes of employees.

Activity Pair students up for a role-play activity. Have one student imagine he or she is a sports figure, celebrity, or executive. The other student will act as a manager who is negotiating a contract with the first student. Have the students negotiate (a) salary, (b) vacation time, (c) reasons for being terminated, and (d) bonuses for performance achievement. Allow students to be inventive and creative, yet realistic.

TEACH *(cont.)*

D Develop Concepts

Exceptions to Employment-at-Will Have four students go up to the board one by one. Each volunteer will write down the name of one of the four exceptions to employment-at-will. Then ask the student to read the text describing each exception out loud. Have the student summarize the key characteristics of the exception.

✓ Reading Check

Discuss Public policy can be violated when the public at large is harmed. For example, firing bus drivers, air traffic controllers, and other necessary civil servants might be deemed to hurt the public.

Guided Practice

Implied Contract

Have a student summarize what implied contract means. Ask students to invent a situation that depicts how an employer might say, write, or do something that implies a contract exists with an employee. (Answers will vary, but students should include the fact that the court examines many aspects of the employment relationship— such as time on the job, salary, and responsibilities— not just the oral promises.)

328

Protected Classes of Employees Groups such as women, racial minorities, people with disabilities, and veterans are often referred to as protected classes. Protected classes of employees cannot be fired for a reason based on their race, color, creed, national origin, or gender. The law also protects workers from being fired based solely on their age.

Exceptions to Employment-at-Will

D Despite the protections noted above, many workers remain at-will employees in most situations. Ending employment relationships under employment-at-will can lead to injustice. As a result, many courts now challenge employment-at-will by ruling against the company or the firm which has discharged an employee. However, to challenge a firing in an at-will state, an employee must base his or her argument on one of the following grounds: promissory estoppel, implied contract, public policy tort, or implied covenant. Lawsuits that challenge employment-at-will are called wrongful discharge or unjust dismissal suits.

Promissory Estoppel Promissory estoppel bars an employer from taking back certain types of promises. To build a solid case on promissory estoppel, a terminated employee must show four elements:

W
- The employer made a promise that the employee reasonably expected to rely on.
- The employee actually relied on the promise and changed his or her position as a result.
- The employee would not have acted as he or she did, if the employer had not made the promise.
- The employee was harmed (usually in a financial way) by the employer's refusal to honor the promise.

If all of these elements exist, then the court may prevent the employer from denying responsibility for the loss suffered by the employee as a result of that reliance.

Implied Contract Another exception to employment-at-will is when an implied contract exists. **An implied contract is a contract that exists when an employer has said, written, or done something to lead an employee to reasonably believe that he or she is not an at-will employee.** When determining whether an employer has created an implied contract, the court can look at all of the facts involving the employment relationship, not just the oral promises made by the employer.

Public Policy Tort Public policy holds that no one should be allowed to do anything that harms the public. **Public policy tort is a legal theory that permits a discharged employee to bring a wrongful discharge lawsuit against a former employer based on the argument that the firing somehow hurts the public at large.** Many states now permit a fired employee to recover compensatory and punitive damages in public policy tort if he or she can prove that the firing violated public policy.

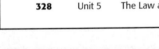

✓ Reading Check

Discuss How might firing an employee violate public policy?

W Writing Support

Promissory Estoppel Emphasize to students that four elements are required to prove promissory estoppel. Ask them to write a letter to a lawyer explaining that they were just wrongfully terminated from a job. In the letter, they must explain why they believe their firing was a wrongful discharge by citing four elements.

Implied Covenant **Implied covenant is a legal argument that holds that any employment relationship is based on an implied promise that the employer and the employee will be fair and honest with one another.** Unlike an implied contract, an implied covenant exists simply because the employment relationship exists. If a state has adopted the implied covenant rule, then both the employer and the employee have the duty to treat one another with honesty and fair play.

Unionized Employees

What laws protect you if you are a member of a labor union?

In the past, employees were at the will of their employers on an individual basis. During the Industrial Revolution, workers banded together into labor unions to demand better working conditions.

Global Law

Collective Bargaining in Poland

Poland is an ex-communist country in Central Europe. During the 1980s, there was labor turmoil in the country that lead to the establishment of Solidarity, an independent trade union. Solidarity eventually gained political force and caused a change in the Polish government. Following the fall of communism in Poland, many new laws were passed, including a law governing the resolution of collective bargaining disputes.

The law was passed on May 23, 1991, and then later amended after the passage of Poland's new constitution in 1997. Following are some important points of the law.

Article 1 Employees' collective disputes with an employer or employers can concern working conditions, wages, or social benefits.

Article 3 In a place of work in which more than one union organization is active, any of them can represent the employees' interests in the collective dispute.

In a place of work in which no trade union is active, a union organization that the employees ask to represent their collective interests can conduct a collective dispute in the name of the employees.

Article 7 A collective dispute exists from the date it is announced by the unit representing the employees' interests to the employer.

The employer has not less than three days to remedy the situation.

Article 10 If the employer does not adequately respond to the employees' demands, the issue goes into mediation.

Article 15 If mediation fails, the employees have the right to strike as a means of last resort.

Article 18 Participation in a strike is by choice.

Article 23 During a strike, employees are entitled to all benefits from their jobs, except wages.

> **Across Cultures: Lech Walesa**
>
> Lech Walesa was an instrumental leader in the Solidarity movement. In the 1970s and 1980s he worked for creating and maintaining rights for workers in Poland. Eventually, after Solidarity gained power in the Polish Congress, Lech Walesa was elected President of Poland.

Critical Thinking *Who benefits from collective bargaining agreements?*

Global Law

Collective Bargaining in Poland

Answer Employees benefit from collective bargaining, since these agreements are used mostly as a means of gaining greater benefits for the employees. However, the employer also benefits. By having collective bargaining agreements in place, employers are ensured of certain rights. For example, there is a long process before employees can go on strike. Most agreements require mediation by neutral third-party mediators. Provisions can be made to allow individuals holding certain positions to work during a strike. There are also guarantees that allow persons to continue working if they do not wish to strike.

TEACH (cont.)

Extending the Content

Unionized Employees

Have students research music and songs about union workers. Have them find out the history of the song, what era it was written in, by whom, and why.

Role Play
Divide the class into four groups, and ask each group to read one of the exceptions to employment-at-will covered on the previous page and this one: promissory estoppel, implied contract, public policy tort, and implied covenant. Then ask each group to make up a story, poem, or song that serves to teach the rest of the class about the nature of the exception they have read about.

ASSESS

Quiz

Ask students to answer the following questions:

1. What is employment-at-will? (Each party is free to end the employment relationship at any time without penalty.)

2. What types of people are not subject to employment-at-will? (sports stars, entertainment figures, faculty, executives, and unionized employees)

3. What is the name of a lawsuit that challenges employment-at-will? (wrongful discharge or unjust dismissal suit)

RETEACH

Guided Practice

History of Unions

Ask students to draw a time line on the board from 1929 to the present. Place dots on the timeline for 1932, 1935, 1947, and 1959. Have one student write next to each of these dates the name of the federal act that was passed in that year and a few key words about the act. Have the students place a plus sign or a minus sign next to each act, indicating if the act was pro-union or anti-union.

STUDY TO GO Have students go to the *Business and Personal Law* Online Learning Center through glencoe.com to download free Study-to-Go content to their cell phones or PDAs.

Review Key Terms

Encourage students to access the *Business and Personal Law* Online Learning Center through glencoe.com and use the electronic flashcards to review the key terms.

Collective Bargaining
Unionized employees negotiate their employment contracts with company lawyers in collective bargaining sessions. *What kinds of employment issues are worked out in these sessions?*

Governments felt unions were destructive to the economic system and banned most of them as illegal conspiracies. Following the Great Depression in 1929, however, the government began to recognize unions and allow them to negotiate their own contracts through collective bargaining. **Collective bargaining is a process in which union and management representatives get together to work out issues such as wages, working conditions, and hiring and firing policies.**

The Norris-LaGuardia Act (1932)

This act is one of the first federal laws in support of employees joining unions. It outlaws yellow dog contracts, which are contracts workers are forced to sign in which they agree not to join a union as a condition of employment. The act also bars the federal courts from issuing orders preventing labor strikes. Strikes are organized work stoppages.

The Wagner Act (1935)

This Wagner Act requires employers to negotiate wages, hours, and conditions of employment with unions. It created the National Labor Relations Board (NLRB) to hear complaints about unfair labor practices. However, the courts have ruled that, despite the act, executives still have the ability to control decisions that are not considered true conditions of employment such as plant closures.

▲ USING VISUALS

Collective Bargaining **Answer** Collective bargaining sessions often work out issues on wages, working conditions, and hiring and firing policies.

Activity Divide the class into groups, one representing a hypothetical union and another representing management. Give them an issue to debate (e.g., workplace safety, wages, vacation time, etc.) and allow each side five to ten minutes to state its case. Then ask them to point out the advantages and disadvantages of having workers advocate their case as a union instead of individually.

The Taft-Hartley Act (1947)

As the unions grew more powerful in the 1930s and 1940s, this act amended the Wagner Act. Officially known as the Labor-Management Relations Act, it requires unions to give a 60-day notice before calling a strike. It prohibits strikes that endanger the nation's health or safety, such as air traffic controllers, and allows the president to go to court to stop a strike for 80 days. The act also prohibits labor unions from featherbedding, or requiring employers to hire more employees to a job than are actually needed.

The Landrum-Griffin Act (1959)

The Landrum-Griffin Act also amended the Wagner Act and is aimed at halting **corruption** in unions. Unions must have a constitution and bylaws which they must register with the Secretary of Labor. They must also submit yearly reports on their financial condition, including sources of revenue and loans to union members. Unions must also have a members' bill of rights.

Forming or Dissolving a Union

Employees today may still create unions. The usual process is to contact one of the large national unions, such as the AFL/CIO. The organizers must then try to **solicit** workers within the company. At least 30 percent of the workers must agree to contact the National Labor Relationshions Board (NLRB) to organize a full vote to form a union. In a secret ballot, a majority of the workers must approve the union. The NLRB will then certify it as an official union which the employer must recognize. A similar process must be followed if employees want to dissolve an existing labor union.

After You Read

Summarize What are the situations outside employment-at-will?

SECTION 15.1 ASSESSMENT

Self Check

1. What is employment-at-will?

2. What are the exceptions to employment-at-will?

3. What is collective bargaining?

Academic Connection

Social Studies The history of labor unions can be traced back to Medieval Europe, when artisans and craftsmen formed guilds to protect their interests, set working standards, and help each other get jobs. The modern labor movement begins with the Industrial Revolution in the late 18th and early 19th centuries, when thousands of people went to work in factories that offered extremely poor pay and working conditions. Workers organized into unions to demand conditions such as fair pay and working hours.

Go on the Internet or to the library and do some research on the history of labor. Create a time line showing some of the milestones in labor history.

Critical Thinking

Pros and Cons Is it better to be an employee-at-will or a member of a labor union? What are the advantages and disadvantages of each?

 Go to **glencoe.com** to check your answers.

glencoe.com

Chapter 15   Employment Law   **331**

 15.1 SECTION

RETEACH (cont.)

After You Read

Summarize Employees who are outside employment-at-will include unionized employees, employees with individual employment contracts, and protected classes of employees.

ASSESS

Self-Assessment

Have students go to the *Business and Personal Law* Online Learning Center through **glencoe.com** to take the Section 15.1 Practice Test.

CLOSE

Culminating Activity

Unions

Explain that the AFL-CIO is a federation of autonomous trade unions from every state. Have students research the organization to identify how many members they have and a brief history of the organization. (Answers will vary; about 9 million.)

SECTION 15.1 ASSESSMENT

Self Check

1. employment situations where parties to employment may end the relationship at any time without penalty

2. promissory estoppel, implied contract, public policy tort, and implied covenant

3. Union and management work out issues such as wages, conditions, and hiring and firing policies.

Academic Connection

Social Studies
Answers and milestones will vary.

Critical Thinking

Pros and Cons
At-will employment provides less protection to the employee, while union membership requires payment of dues.

 Activity correlated to the Social Studies standard on page 326

FOCUS

 Bell Ringer Activity

Ask students if they think government regulation of employment conditions is necessary. Lead students to understand that regulations foster fairness and protect employees. Explain that this section will cover employment issues like safety, health, privacy, and equal opportunity.

Preteaching

Key Terms
Read the definitions and ask students to create a sentence using each term.

Academic Vocabulary

Explain that developing vocabulary is key to academic success. An efficient method to develop vocabulary is to study how words are formed.

- **voluntary** Adjective, from the Latin *voluntas* (free will). Means done out of free will.

- **random** Adjective, from the old French *randir* (to run). Means lacking method.

- **waiver** Noun, from the Anglo-Norman *weyver* (to abandon). Means an intentional relinquishment of a right.

Activity Ask students to give a noun, an adjective, or an adverb form that comes from each word.

 Connects to academic content

What You'll Learn

- ◆ Explain how the law protects employee health and safety.
- ◆ Describe the laws that guarantee fair wages and benefits.
- ◆ Identify the laws that prohibit different forms of discrimination.
- ◆ Define disparate treatment and disparate impact.

Why It's Important

Understanding employment law will help you to protect your rights to safety, privacy, and fair pay as a worker.

Academic Standards

Reading and completing the activities in this section will help you practice the following academic standards:

Social Studies (NCSS 6) Study how people create and change structures of power, authority, and governance.

English Language Arts (NCTE 4) Adjust the use of spoken, written, and visual language to communicate effectively with a variety of audiences and for different purposes.

SECTION 15.2 Employee Rights

Reading Guide

 Before You Read

Connect Maybe you have family members who had to leave a job because they were laid off, injured, or retired. If so, were they entitled to any benefits?

Focus on Ideas

Once you have a basic understanding of the rights and benefits that are due to workers on the job today, you will be better equipped to deal with problems in the workplace.

Take Notes

Create a graph like the one shown and use it to take notes as you read this section. Go to **glencoe.com** to find graphic organizers and tips on how to improve your note-taking skills.

Laws Protecting Employees

Health and Safety	Wages and Benefits	Privacy	Equal Opportunity

 Key Terms

You will learn these legal words and expressions in this chapter. You can also find these terms in *Black's Law Dictionary* or in an online legal dictionary.

- Occupational Safety and Health Administration (OSHA)
- equal pay rule
- pension plan
- Social Security
- unemployment compensation
- workers' compensation
- discrimination
- disparate treatment
- disparate impact

 Academic Vocabulary

You will find these words in your readings and in your tests. Look them up in a dictionary and familiarize yourself with them.

- voluntary
- random
- waiver

R Reading Strategy

Read for Knowledge

1. **Survey** or preread the chapter.
2. **Question** or formulate questions before you read.
3. **Recite** or read your questions, answers, and notes out loud.
4. **Review** or reread your notes.

Note-Taking Basics

- Listen attentively
- Have note-taking materials ready
- Skim through the lesson material
- Write down key words and ideas
- Anticipate what comes next
- Review notes soon after taking them

Health and Safety

What laws protect your health and safety on the job?

In the beginning of the Industrial Revolution, employers had little regard for their workers' safety and quality of life. Since then, the government has passed numerous laws to regulate employment conditions and to protect employees. Employee rights can be divided into four areas:

- right to health and safety protections
- right to fair wages and benefits
- right to privacy
- right to equal opportunity in the workplace

Two major federal government acts protect the health and safety of workers.

The Occupational Safety and Health Act

This act set up the Occupational Safety and Health Administration (OSHA), the federal government agency that regulates health and safety standards for companies in the United States. To make sure employers follow the rules, OSHA does the following:

- inspects workplaces at random
- investigates written employee complaints, workplace deaths, and disasters
- protects employees from being fired for filing complaints
- levies fines for rule violations

The Environmental Policy Act

In 1969, Congress passed the National Environmental Policy Act, which established the Environmental Protection Agency (EPA). The purpose of the EPA is to set up a national policy for fighting pollution, and to protect the environment and human health from exposure to hazardous chemicals and waste. The EPA encourages **voluntary** compliance by businesses. It also supports the efforts of state and local governments to carry out enforcement actions in their own territory. When such efforts do not work, the EPA can act against companies that pollute the environment.

Fair Wages and Benefits

What wages and benefits are you guaranteed when you work?

The government has long been concerned about the conditions under which employees perform their jobs. The government responded

As You Read

Predict What kind of assistance can you get if you lose your job?

Vocabulary You can find vocabulary definitions in the **Key Terms** glossary and Academic Vocabulary glossary in the back of this book.

Employee Benefits
Employee benefits include Social Security and disability insurance, but can also include health and life insurance. *What other kinds of benefits may be available to employees?*

TEACH (cont.)

D Develop Concepts

Fair Wages and Benefits
Instruct students that the government protects fair benefits outside of work via five major acts. Name the acts and ask students to infer what each act governs. (Employment Retirement Income Security Act prevents the abuse and misuse of employee pension plans. Family and Medical Leave allows workers who have just given birth or have ill family members to attend to them. Social Security Act provides income for those who retire, for those with disabilities, or to family members after the death of a worker. The Unemployment Tax Act provides temporary income for people out of work. Individual states' Workers' Compensation acts help workers who have been injured on the job or who have a job-related disability or disease.)

W Writing Support

Fair Labor Standards Act
Ask students to write a letter to a friend telling the person about the new job they just started in a restaurant. The letter explains that in the past month, the students worked many hours of overtime: 42 hours in week 1, 47 hours in week 2, 40 hours in week 3, and 49 hours in week 4 at $8.00 per hour. Ask students to calculate how much money they will earn in their first-month paycheck and explain it in a letter to their friend. (overtime hours = $12/hour; week 1 = $344 + week 2 = $404 + week 3 = $320 + week 4 = $428; Total = $1,496 for the month)

334

to many of the hardships suffered by workers during the Great Depression by passing several laws to regulate wages, hours, and benefits.

The Fair Labor Standards Act

The Fair Labor Standards Act, also known as the Wage and Hour Law, requires certain employers, such as hospitals, retail businesses, restaurants, and schools, to pay their workers a minimum hourly wage and time-and-a-half for all work over 40 hours per week. The Fair Labor Standards Act also regulates the employment of minors. The act covers employees who produce goods for interstate commerce. Professional employees, administrators, and executives are not covered by this act.

Equal Pay Act

The Equal Pay Act is an amendment to the Fair Labor Standards Act. It established the equal pay rule. **The equal pay rule is a standard that states that employers working in interstate commerce must pay women the same rate of pay as men**

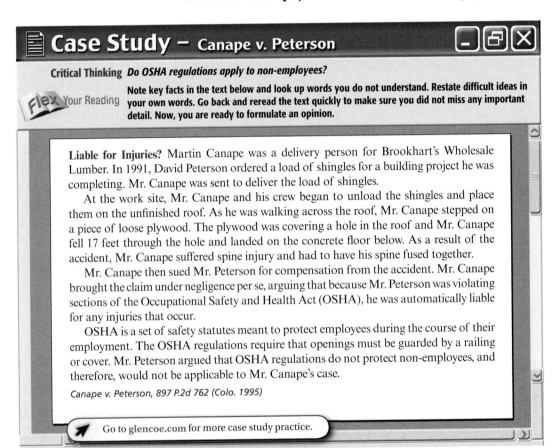

📄 Case Study – Canape v. Peterson

Critical Thinking *Do OSHA regulations apply to non-employees?*

Flex Your Reading Note key facts in the text below and look up words you do not understand. Restate difficult ideas in your own words. Go back and reread the text quickly to make sure you did not miss any important detail. Now, you are ready to formulate an opinion.

Liable for Injuries? Martin Canape was a delivery person for Brookhart's Wholesale Lumber. In 1991, David Peterson ordered a load of shingles for a building project he was completing. Mr. Canape was sent to deliver the load of shingles.

At the work site, Mr. Canape and his crew began to unload the shingles and place them on the unfinished roof. As he was walking across the roof, Mr. Canape stepped on a piece of loose plywood. The plywood was covering a hole in the roof and Mr. Canape fell 17 feet through the hole and landed on the concrete floor below. As a result of the accident, Mr. Canape suffered spine injury and had to have his spine fused together.

Mr. Canape then sued Mr. Peterson for compensation from the accident. Mr. Canape brought the claim under negligence per se, arguing that because Mr. Peterson was violating sections of the Occupational Safety and Health Act (OSHA), he was automatically liable for any injuries that occur.

OSHA is a set of safety statutes meant to protect employees during the course of their employment. The OSHA regulations require that openings must be guarded by a railing or cover. Mr. Peterson argued that OSHA regulations do not protect non-employees, and therefore, would not be applicable to Mr. Canape's case.

Canape v. Peterson, 897 P.2d 762 (Colo. 1995)

Go to glencoe.com for more case study practice.

 glencoe.com

📄 Case Study

Canape v. Petersen

Answer OSHA regulations do not apply to nonemployees. The Colorado Supreme Court held that Mr. Canape could not avail himself of the OSHA regulations because Mr. Canape was not in the employ of Mr. Peterson. Rather, he was an employee of Brookhart's and was only at the work site delivering on behalf of his employer. Under OSHA, Mr. Peterson has a responsibility only to his own employees, not to visitors at the site.

holding the same type of job. The equal pay rule covers hourly workers, executives, administrators, professional employees, and outside salespeople who receive a salary and/or a commission.

The Employment Retirement Income Security Act

The Employment Retirement Income Security Act (ERISA) prevents the abuse of employee pension plans. **A pension plan is a program established by an employer or a union to provide income to employees after they retire.** Pensions are typically based on an employee's salary and length of service. ERISA came about because some employers failed to invest the employee retirement funds wisely or used the money for their own business expenses. The act thus requires employers to place employee pension contributions in a trust fund outside of the employer's control. It also imposes a duty of good faith on pension fund managers. Employees must receive regular reports about their retirement benefits.

The Family and Medical Leave Act

Under the Family and Medical Leave Act, an employee of a company with at least 50 employees is entitled to 12 weeks of unpaid leave during any 12-month period to care for a new child or a relative with a serious medical condition. The employee is entitled to return to his or her previous job or an equivalent job with the same pay and benefits. To be eligible, the employee must have at least one year of service with the company.

The Social Security Act

Social Security is a government program that provides continuing income to workers and their dependents when their earnings stop or are reduced because of retirement, disability, or death. The Social Security Act and its amendments set up a social insurance program funded by contributions from both employers and employees. People become eligible to receive Social Security benefits by working for a certain time period or by being a dependent of a person who meets that requirement.

Unemployment Compensation

Unemployment compensation is a system of government payments to people who are out of work and looking for a job. The program is funded by having employers pay payroll taxes or insurance premiums. Under the Federal Unemployment Tax Act, each state operates its own system, subject to conditions imposed by the federal government. Each state determines the tax rate employers must pay and the amount an unemployed worker can receive. Unemployed workers must apply at state employment offices. They may be disqualified if they refuse to accept a suitable job, if their unemployment is due to a labor strike, if they were discharged for misconduct, or if they voluntarily quit a job without good cause.

Chapter 15   Employment Law   **335**

TEACH (cont.)

C Critical Thinking

Equal Pay Act Ask students why they think the Equal Pay Act covers only employers working in interstate commerce. (The act is a federal act and thus can only cover workers in interstate commerce whose jobs extend beyond their own state. However, many states have laws similar to the Equal Pay Act that cover employees working for companies whose business is conducted only within the state.)

Extending the Content

Laws Regulating Employment Conditions

Have students choose to research one of the acts in this section. Students may use the Internet, your school's media center, or your local library to find out under whose administration the law was enacted and what conditions led to its enactment. Invite students to give an oral presentation of their findings to the class.

Extending the Content

Social Security

Have students interview someone who receives Social Security benefits. Have students find out at what age the person was eligible for Social Security, whether the person feels the benefits are sufficient to live on, and other information that the person is willing to share. Students can report their findings back to the class.

TEACH *(cont.)*

D Develop Concepts

Privacy Rights Open a discussion with students about privacy. Ask them to comment on areas in their lives in which privacy is important. (Answers might include personal relationships, e-mail, or lifestyle.) Explain that government employees have the right to know what their employment file contains via the Federal Privacy Act.

C Critical Thinking

Workers' Compensation Tell students that some individuals have attempted to abuse the Workers' Compensation system by claiming to have an injury so that they may receive benefits. Ask students to debate how the system can prevent people from abusing workers' compensation. (Answers will vary, but suggestions may include making sure the person receives a legitimate medical checkup that confirms the injury.)

Extending the Content

Drug Use Tests

Ask students if they have ever been asked to take a drug-use test for employment. Have students explain what procedures were used and if any paperwork was required in order to complete the test.

336

Research Title VII
Title VII of the Civil Rights Act is a federal law that prohibits discrimination in the workplace. Log on to **glencoe.com** to begin your WebQuest project. Look up what this law specifically covers.

List and explain each section in your WebQuest folder.

Workers' Compensation

Workers' compensation is an insurance program that provides income for workers who are injured on the job or develop a disability or disease as a result of their job. Loss of income due to accidents, illness, or death on the job became a serious problem with the introduction of machines to industry. Faced with this situation, several state legislatures passed laws in the early 1900s creating workers' compensation programs. By 1959 all 50 states had programs in place.

Workers' compensation laws vary by state. In many states, employers pay into a state's workers' compensation fund through payroll taxes. In Texas, workers' compensation law was first enacted in 1913, and the Texas Workers' Compensation Program evolved over time to address a variety of workplace needs. The Texas Workers' Compensation Act of 1989 was adopted to consolidate and strengthen workplace health and safety programs, improve benefits and benefits delivery, assist in resolving claim disputes, ensure compliance with workers compensation laws, and develop medical fee and treatment guidelines to help control medical costs. Texas has also established the Texas Workforce Commission (TWC), the state agency that provides workforce development services to employers and job seekers in Texas. Employers are offered recruiting, retention, training, and outplacement services, as well as labor market statistics. Job seekers are provided with access to job search tools, training programs, and career development information, among other job-related resources. For a general review of basic employee rights, see **Figure 15.1.**

Employee Privacy Rights

Do you have a right to privacy in the workplace?

Three areas of privacy law have become important in recent years:
- guaranteeing privacy for governmental employees
- testing employees for drug use
- using polygraph (lie detector) tests in the hiring and firing of employees

The Federal Privacy Act

The Federal Privacy Act protects the privacy of government workers, but not workers in the private sector. It gives Government employees the right to know what is in their employment files, to restrict access to their files, and to fix any mistake they might find in their files.

The Drug-Free Workplace Act

The Drug-Free Workplace Act, which applies to companies that have contracts with the federal government, aims to create a drug-free work environment. Drug testing is not required, but if a drug test is given improperly, it can violate the Fourth Amendment to the United States Constitution, which prohibits unreasonable

 glencoe.com

Research Title VII Answer Title VII of the Civil Rights Act outlaws discrimination in employment in any business on the basis of race, color, religion, sex, or national origin.

Figure 15.1 Employee Rights

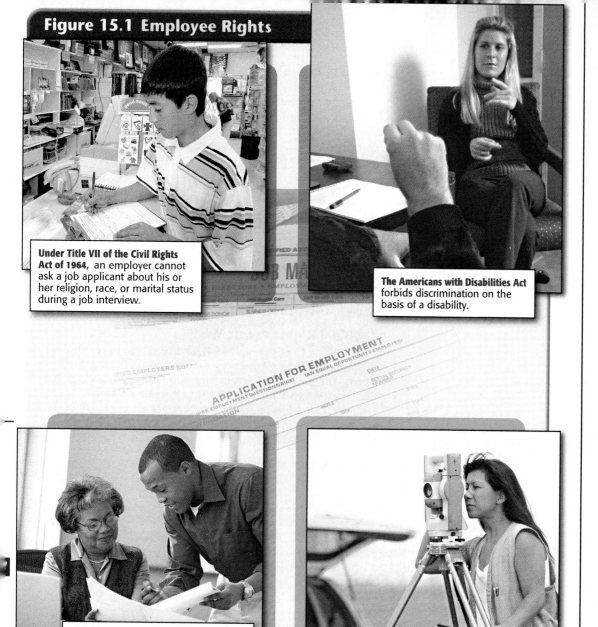

Under Title VII of the Civil Rights Act of 1964, an employer cannot ask a job applicant about his or her religion, race, or marital status during a job interview.

The Americans with Disabilities Act forbids discrimination on the basis of a disability.

The Age Discrimination in Employment Act prohibits an employer from discriminating against any person aged 40 or older in hiring, firing, promotion, or other aspects of employment.

The Equal Pay Act requires employers to pay women the same rate of pay as men for doing the same type of job.

The federal government has passed laws guaranteeing employees certain rights. *Can employers make employees take a polygraph test?*

Chapter 15   Employment Law   **337**

TEACH (cont.)

W Writing Support

Employment Discrimination Tell students there was a time when employers could legally discriminate on the basis of gender, race, religion, or national origin. However, social attitudes changed over time and resulted in dramatic changes to the law. Ask students to write a one- to two-page report that relates social attitudes to changes in the laws regulating employment discrimination.

Extending the Content

Affirmative Action

Ask students to research companies in your area and view the affirmative action policy that the company provides job applicants. Have them present their findings in class, comparing the language used in various policies.

Guided Practice

Disabilities

Explain that the Americans with Disabilities Act defines a disability as any impairment that substantially limits one or more of the major life activities. Ask students whether a person with a vision impairment could file a suit against a company if he or she was not hired for a job because it required driving at night. (If the person's vision could be corrected, there might be a basis for a lawsuit. Otherwise, there would be a valid reason for not hiring the person.)

▲ USING VISUALS

➡ Figure 15.1 Employee Rights Answer Usually not. Exceptions include those businesses whose employees are involved in security or in the handling of controlled substances. Also, private investigation firms may use polygraph tests with the permission of the subject.

Activity Ask students to pair up and to act out a public service commercial that illustrates one of the types of discrimination identified on this page. The students should reenact a job applicant interviewing with a manager who asks inappropriate questions about the person's status in an illegal way.

TEACH (cont.)

W Writing Support

Polygraph Machines Ask students to use the Internet to research how polygraph machines work and if they are reliable in detecting lies. Ask them to find pictures of such machines and find out how they developed technologically over the years. Have them research the application of the machines in today's world and ask them to write a report detailing what factors might influence the accuracy of a lie detector test.

Role Play

Remind students about unemployment compensation, a system of government payments to people out of work and looking for a job. Ask students if they agree that the government should provide assistance to certain unemployed persons. Have students with opposing views argue for their position in front of the class and take a vote to see if your class agrees or disagrees with laws providing unemployment compensation.

---

search and seizure. Some states have passed statutes that regulate drug testing in the private sector.

The Employee Polygraph Protection Act

W The Employee Polygraph Protection Act bars employers from using lie detector tests for the screening of employment applicants. It also prohibits the **random** testing of employees. There are, however, several exceptions. It does not apply to businesses involved in security or the handling of controlled substances. Drug firms and private investigation companies are also permitted to use polygraph tests.

Equal Employment Opportunity

What can you do if you think you have been discriminated against?

Since the 1960s, the federal government has passed six major acts to ensure fairness and ethical behavior in employment and to prevent discrimination. **Discrimination is the unequal treatment of individuals based on sex, age, race, nationality, or religion.**

The Civil Rights Act of 1964

Title VII of the Civil Rights Act of 1964 prohibits discrimination in employment based on race, color, religion, sex, or national origin. The attempt to recruit, hire, and promote workers based on these characteristics is referred to as affirmative action.

Under Title VII, a job interviewer cannot ask applicants questions about their religion, race, age, or marital status. Employees who believe they have been discriminated against can file a complaint

EEOC The EEOC has a Web site that offers job information and resources for teenagers. *What kinds of resources are available on the site?*

▲ USING VISUALS

EEOC Answer The Youth at Work portion of the EEOC Web site gives information on employee rights, how to file a complaint, summaries of real EEOC cases, free outreach events, and partnership relationships. The Web site speaks to the responsibilities that teens have as employees. Guidelines for employee behavior include refraining from discriminatory actions, reporting discrimination, and requesting workplace changes if necessary.

with the Equal Employment Opportunity Commission (EEOC) or seek a private remedy in court. The EEOC can seek a court injunction or sue the employer for damages.

Disparate Treatment **Disparate treatment is when an employer intentionally discriminates against an individual or a group of individuals belonging to a protected class.** For instance, an employer who holds a general policy against hiring female engineers or male nurses would be practicing this type of discrimination.

A defense employers can use against the charge of disparate treatment is a *bona fide* occupational qualification, or BFOQ. A *bona fide* occupational qualification is a job requirement that might seem discriminatory but which is actually a good faith requirement to perform a particular job. For example, requiring that applicants for a job modeling women's clothing be female is a *bona fide* occupational qualification. The BFOQ defense can never be used to justify discrimination based on race.

Disparate Impact **Disparate impact is when an employer has an employment policy that appears neutral on the surface but has an unfair impact on members of a protected class.** For example, an employer who requires applicants to be over six feet tall is discriminating by disparate impact. The height requirement seems neutral on the surface, but has an unfair impact on women.

A defense against disparate impact is business necessity. Business necessity is a job requirement based on actual skills needed by an employee to perform a specific job. For example, it is acceptable for a hospital to require that all applicants for a job as a surgeon have a medical degree.

The Civil Rights Act of 1991

The Civil Rights Act of 1991 was enacted by Congress to strengthen the doctrine of disparate impact. The law requires employers to prove business necessity in disparate impact cases. It requires employers to prove that the qualifications for hiring or promoting employees are directly related to the specific job involved in a court case. It also allows plaintiffs who have been discriminated against to recover not only back pay owed to them, but compensatory and punitive damages.

The Pregnancy Discrimination Act

The Pregnancy Discrimination Act makes it unlawful to discriminate against a woman because of pregnancy or childbirth. An employer cannot create an employee benefits package that discriminates against women who are pregnant.

The Immigration Reform Act

The Immigration Reform Act makes employers responsible for verifying the identity and employment eligibility of all employees. It applies to U.S. citizens, permanent residents, and nonimmigrant visa holders.

glencoe.com

Reading Check

Explain *Why did the government think it was necessary to create protected classes of workers?*

Legal Talk

Bona fide: *adj* Latin for *good faith.*

Quid pro quo: *n* Latin for *something for something.*

Vocabulary Builder Many European languages are romance languages, or languages based on the Roman language of Latin. In Latin, *bonus* means good and *fides* mean faith. In class, name words in other languages you know that mean good or faith.

Look It Up! Check definitions in *Black's Law Dictionary* or an online glossary. For direct links, go to glencoe.com to find more vocabulary resources.

RETEACH

S Skills Practice

List Ask students to list the five characteristics on which companies may not discriminate against job applicants. (race, color, religion, sex, or national origin) **L1**

Explain Have students specify what job applicants can do if they believe that discrimination occurred in the hiring process in which they were involved. (Report it to the Equal Employment Opportunity Commission or seek a private remedy in court by bringing a lawsuit against the company.) **L2**

Classify Ask students to write a paragraph that distinguishes between disparate treatment and disparate impact. For each one, students must classify what defense arguments are valid for each type of discrimination. (Disparate treatment is discrimination against a protected class. Only bona fide job qualifications are allowed as a defense. Disparate impact is discrimination that appears neutral but has a discriminatory impact on a protected class. Only business necessity is allowable as a defense.) **L3**

Business ETHICS

Contract Negotiations

You are an attorney for a nationwide chain of weight-loss clinics for men. Your company provides counseling to men and encourages them to eat in a healthier manner and to exercise regularly. Clients visit your clinics weekly where they are weighed and undergo personal counseling for 30 minutes. After performing a random survey of 1,000 men, you determine that men are more comfortable with male workers and counselors in your clinics, and that more men would become clients if they were assured that a male would assist them in their weight loss. Right now your company has approximately 45% female workers.

Critical Thinking: *Can you replace the women with men?*

All job applicants must present original documents and, if hired, they must sign an employment eligibility verification form in front of a supervisor or human resources officer.

The Age Discrimination in Employment Act

The Age Discrimination in Employment Act (ADEA) applies only to employment agencies, employers with 20 or more employees, and labor unions with more than 25 members. The act forbids discriminating against any person aged 40 or older in hiring, firing, or other employment decisions. The law does not apply if age is a true job qualification, such as modeling children's clothing. The ADEA was amended by Congress in 1990 to forbid discrimination against older employees with regard to their retirement and pension plans. The amendment, known as the Older Workers' Benefit Protection Plan Act (OWBPPA), gives workers a legal way to remedy a situation in which they have been cheated or coerced into surrendering their ADEA rights by signing a **waiver**.

Americans with Disabilities Act

The Americans with Disabilities Act of 1990 (ADA) forbids discrimination on the basis of a disability if the disabled individual can do the essential functions of a job. Employers cannot discriminate against those with disabilities when screening or hiring, granting promotions, offering pay raises, or offering on-the-job-training opportunities. Both direct and indirect forms of discrimination are outlawed. Indirect discrimination occurs when an employer makes a hiring decision based on a qualification that is not related to job performance but has the effect of eliminating disabled individuals.

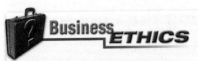

Business ETHICS

Contract Negotiations

Answer In order to replace the women, your company must prove that hiring men is a bona fide occupational qualification. This is a very strict requirement. It is likely that a court would not allow your clinics to discriminate based on client preference. Your company must prove that it is almost impossible to perform its business without the discrimination. If your business is doing well with a workforce that is 45 percent female, it is unlikely you could prove that you need to hire men only.

Sexual Harassment

There are also laws covering sexual harassment in the workplace. Sexual harassment can occur either through a quid pro quo activity or through the creation of a hostile working environment. Quid pro quo sexual discrimination occurs when one worker demands sexual favors from another worker in exchange for something employment related, such as a raise or a promotion. A hostile working environment exists when a pattern of severe and pervasive sexually demeaning behavior has altered the workplace, making it a distressing, humiliating, or hostile place. Such demeaning behavior could include sexually explicit comments, jokes, photographs, cartoons, posters, or gestures.

International Employment Law

What rights do you have when you work in another country?

Most U.S. employment laws do not apply to employment in other countries, even if you work for an American company overseas. For example, minimum wage laws will be different. Protections against discrimination may not exist in other countries. Some countries, however, have better pension and compensation programs, and more legal guarantees of job security. In Europe, for example, it can be extremely difficult to fire a employee.

After You Read

Summarize What wage and benefit rights are held by workers?

SECTION 15.2 ASSESSMENT

Self Check

1. What four areas can employment conditions be divided into?

2. For what reasons can you be disqualified from receiving unemployment compensation?

3. What are the objectives of the Civil Rights Act?

Academic Connection

English Language Arts
Businesses that violate the law are subject to fines, lawsuits, and additional government regulations.

To avoid such problems, many companies have created their own code of ethics to set standards of conduct for both employers and employees in the workplace. Assume the classroom is a business, with the teacher as employer and students as employees. Get together in a group with other students and write a code of ethics for the classroom. Issues can range from classroom conditions to the behavior of students and teacher. For assistance, go online and look up the code of ethics for a well-know company such as Ben and Jerry's or Microsoft.

Critical Thinking

Meet the New Boss
Suppose you learn that your friend, June (aged 42), was passed up for a promotion where you work in favor of a younger (aged 27) and much less qualified male candidate who also happens to be the boss's nephew. Do you have any advice to give June under these circumstances? Explain.

 Go to **glencoe.com** to check your answers.

RETEACH (cont.)

After You Read

Summarize fair labor standards; equal pay; employment retirement income; family and medical leave; social security; unemployment compensation; and workers' compensation

ASSESS

Self-Assessment

Have students go to the *Business and Personal Law* Online Learning Center through **glencoe.com** to take the Section 15.2 Practice Test.

CLOSE

Culminating Activity

Flashcards

Have pairs of students prepare a set of flashcards with the names of federal laws regulating employment on one side and the protections they provide on the other side. Have students quiz each other using the flashcards to ensure a basic understanding of each regulation.

SECTION 15.2 ASSESSMENT

Self Check

1. health and safety; fair wages and benefits; privacy; equal opportunity in the workplace

2. refusal to accept a suitable job; unemployment due to labor strike; discharged for misconduct; voluntarily quitting a job without good cause

3. to prevent discrimination by strengthening the doctrine of disparate impact

Academic Connection

English Language Arts
Codes of ethics will vary.

Critical Thinking
Answers should include mention of the Age Discrimination in Employment Act.

 Activity correlated to the English Language Arts standard on page 332

Chapter 15 Review and Assessment

Summary by Sections

Ask students to read the summaries one key point at a time. Then, ask them to work in groups to create two examples to illustrate each key point.

Vocabulary Builder

Cooperative Learning

1. Have students work in groups to prepare their sentences. Ask the groups to exchange their sentences and assess each other's sentences.

Vocabulary Development

- Ask students to use a dictionary or to go online to look up the etymology of each key term listed.
- Then, ask students to list several words derived from the same root or origin. For example, *contract* has the same root as *contractual* or *contractually*.

Summary

Section 15.1 Employment Agreements

- According to the doctrine of employment-at-will, employers and employees are free to end the employment relationship at any time without penalty.
- Situations that fall outside employment-at-will include unionized employees, employees with individual employment contracts, and protected classes of employees.
- Wrongful discharge exceptions to employment-at-will include implied contract, promissory estoppel, and public policy tort.
- Implied covenant is a legal argument that holds that any employment relationship is based on an implied promise that the employer and the employee will be fair and honest with one another.
- Legislation that regulates union activities includes the Norris-LaGuardia Act, the Wagner Act, the Taft-Hartley Act, and the Landrum-Griffin Act.

Section 15.2 Employee Rights

- Legislation that regulates employment conditions includes the Occupational Safety and Health Act, the Fair Labor Standards Act, the Equal Pay Act, and the Immigration Reform and Control Act.
- Worker benefits include Social Security, unemployment compensation, workers' compensation, and pension protection.
- Legislation that regulates employee rights includes Title VII of the Civil Rights Act, the Americans with Disabilities Act, the Age Discrimination in Employment Act, and the Family and Medical Leave Act.
- Disparate treatment is when an employer intentionally discriminates against an individual or a group.
- Disparate impact is when an employer has an employment policy that appears neutral on the surface but has an unfair impact on the members of one or more of the protected classes.

Vocabulary Builder

1 On a sheet of paper, use each of these terms in a sentence.

Key Terms

- employment-at-will
- union
- implied contract
- public policy tort
- implied covenant
- collective bargaining
- Occupational Safety and Health Administration (OSHA)
- equal pay rule
- pension plan
- Social Security
- unemployment compensation
- workers' compensation
- discrimination
- disparate treatment
- disparate impact

Academic Vocabulary

- exception
- corruption
- solicit
- voluntary
- random
- waiver

 Go to **glencoe.com** to play a game and improve your legal vocabulary.

Study Skills for Success

Prepare Your Students for Studying

Tell students that they can improve their ability to understand and remember material from their courses by learning and practicing study skills. Remind students to:

- **Get motivated!** Motivation must come from within. To motivate yourself, think of ways in which what you learn now will fit into your long-term personal and professional goals.
- **Get organized!** Make studying part of your daily routine, not something you do at the last minute.
- **Concentrate!** Study in an environment that is as free of distractions as possible.

342

Key Points Review

Answer the following questions. Refer to the chapter for additional reinforcement.

❷ What is the general rule of employment that guides hiring and firing in the U.S. today?

❸ What types of employees can negotiate their own individual employment contracts?

❹ What are the major provisions of the Wagner Act?

❺ What classes of employees are protected by the Civil Rights Act?

❻ What law bans discrimination based on age?

❼ What requirements were instituted by the Fair Labor Standards Act?

❽ What is the equal pay rule?

❾ What is the difference between disparate treatment and disparate impact?

Standardized Test Practice

❿ Read the following information about the Occupational Safety and Health Act and complete questions 1 and 2.

The Occupational Safety and Health Act of 1970 assigns OSHA two functions: setting standards and conducting inspections to ensure that employers provide safe and healthful workplaces. OSHA standards may require that employers adopt certain practices, means, methods, or processes reasonably necessary and appropriate to protect workers on the job. Employers must become familiar with the applicable standards and eliminate hazards.

Compliance may include ensuring that employees have been provided with, have been effectively trained on, and use personal protective equipment when required for safety or health. Where specific standards do not exist, employers must comply with the Act's "general duty" clause [Section 5(a)(1)], which requires each employer to "furnish . . . a place of employment which is free from recognized hazards that are causing or are likely to cause death or serious physical harm to his employees."

1. The Occupational Safety and Health Act of 1970 requires employers:

Ⓐ to furnish employees with information about their jobs

Ⓑ to ensure employees are provided and trained to use protective equipment

Ⓒ give general employee training sessions to keep trends and policies current

Ⓓ fire any employees who do not comply with OSHA regulations

2. OSHA ensures employer compliance by:

Ⓐ providing posters, training, and informational sessions for employers and employees

Ⓑ having three regulatory functions to set standards and oversee guidelines of employers

Ⓒ requiring a place of employment free from recognized hazards that could harm employees

Ⓓ providing safety equipment and training to employees to meet regulations

Test-Taking Strategies Rely on your first impression. The first answer that comes to mind is often correct.

Chapter 15   Employment Law   **343**

Standardized Test Practice

10. B and C

Strategies for Standardized Test Prep Success

Whether your students have a standardized test coming up in a few days or a few weeks, these last-minute test-prep tips and strategies will help them relax and do their best.

- **Test Format** Help students become familiar with the format of the test by practicing with test items that imitate the actual test items as closely as possible.

- **Test Timing** Have your students take timed practice tests so that they become comfortable with the length, design, and timing of the actual test.

---

15 Chapter
Review and Assessment

Key Points Review

2. Civil Rights Act of 1964

3. sports stars, entertainment figures, faculty members, senior officers of a company

4. requires employers to negotiate wages, hours, and conditions of employment with unions

5. employees who are members of the protected classes based on race, color, religion, sex, or national origin

6. Age Discrimination in Employment Act

7. Certain employers must pay workers a minimum hourly wage and time-and-a-half for any hours over 40 per week

8. dictates that employers in interstate commerce pay women the same rate of pay as men for doing the same job

9. Disparate treatment is when an employer intentionally discriminates against members of a class. Disparate impact is when an employer has an employment policy that unfairly impacts members of a protected class.

Review and Assessment

Apply and Debate

Students should use chapter content to arrive at conclusions. The legal resolutions are listed below:

11. Probably not. The company promised her a job in the Boston store, and she got one there. When it made the promise to Rose, the company could not have known that the Boston store would close two years later.

12. No. The company had a strict policy regarding use of company computers, regardless of the type of personal activity.

13. No. Women can design men's fitness centers and men can design women's. The gender of an architect is not a bona fide job qualification.

14. No. Franco did not follow specific instructions given to him by his boss.

15. Possibly. Ashley may be able to make a case that the company used her age in the promotion decision rather than her job qualifications.

Apply and Debate

C Read the following scenarios. Get together with other students in pairs or groups of three and take a position on each scenario. Debate your position in class with students taking the opposite position or prepare a written argument justifying your position.

11 Promises, Promises

Rose's company sent her to London to open a new store. They promised her a position as manager of their Boston store if she spent two years in London. When Rose moved to Boston after two years, the company was having financial problems. They closed the Boston store within three weeks of her arrival and Rose was terminated.

You Debate *Can Rose sue for wrongful discharge based on the promise made to her?*

12 Personal vs. Company Time

Johnson Manufacturing had a strict company policy forbidding personnel to use office computers for personal business. They dismissed Eliot Menson, a 3-year employee, after discovering that he used his computer to trade stocks during his lunch hour.

You Debate *Was Eliot wrongfully terminated? What if Eliot were writing a novel?*

13 Men's Fitness Center

Archer & Bower Architects received a contract to design two fitness centers—a men's and a women's—in a new housing tract. The company insists that it must hire a male architect to work on the men's center and a female to work on the women's center.

You Debate *Can the company make a case for bona fide job qualifications?*

14 Roofer Accident

Franco works as a roofer. His employer normally supplies safety harnesses to all roofers. One day, Franco and his co-worker Mario could find only one harness in the truck. The boss asked Franco to wait on the ground until one was obtained. Mario needed help, so Franco went up on the roof. He slipped and fell, breaking his leg.

You Debate *Can Franco sue his company for negligence in addition to workers' comp?*

15 Young and Hip

Ashley, age 44, an advertising executive with 12 years experience, applied to become Senior Director at her firm's new office in Seattle. The job was given to a flashy 33-year old woman who had seven years experience. The firm claimed their clients wanted someone "young and hip."

You Debate *Should Ashley sue for age discrimination?*

C Critical Thinking

Age Discrimination Ella Campbell, a 58-year-old janitorial worker at Bell High School, was fired and replaced by a 42-year-old worker. Ella filed suit against the school district, alleging age discrimination. The district argued that it could not be held liable for the violation because the replacement was also within the protected class of workers age 40 and over.

Debate Practice

- Is the school district right? (No. The objective of the law is to protect older workers from discrimination based on age. The fact that the new worker was younger than Ella is what matters here.)

- Can Ella sue the school district? (Assuming there was no other reason for the termination, Ella can sue the school district for age discrimination.)

Review and Assessment

←?→ Ethics Application

17. Yes. Kim has a careless attitude toward workplace safety. The forklift can be a dangerous workplace tool, and Kim is endangering not only herself, but also others who work with her. Serena should report Kim's actions to her supervisor. OSHA requires workplaces to be free from safety hazards, and Kim's actions would be considered a hazard that should be addressed by management.

Internet Application

18. According to OSHA requirements, emergency action plans must provide procedures for reporting a fire or other emergency; emergency evacuation; employees in critical plant operations; employees performing rescue or medical duties; and other important information.

📖 Reading Strategy

Reading Connection

American Bar Association Resources

Go to the *Business and Personal Law* Online Learning Center through glencoe.com to find links for further readings that relate to this chapter. Ask students to read, review, and summarize the documents to use as reference material for their Unit Thematic Project on pages 348–349.

📄 Case Study Practice– Bearley v. Friendly Ice Cream Corp. ⬁▢✕

16 Fair Offer? Dorothy Bearley worked 22 hours a week as a bookkeeper for Friendly Ice Cream Corporation (Friendly's) in Dunmore, PA, and 18 hours a week for the Friendly's district that covered Dunmore. This amounted to full-time employment. She also worked a few hours a week as a hostess in the Dunmore restaurant. On July 5, 2000, Ms. Bearley informed her boss that she needed to undergo toe surgery. Her boss granted her medical leave, but informed her that while she was gone, Friendly's bookkeeping functions were going to be automated.

Upon returning to work in August, Ms. Bearley discovered that much of her job had been automated and her bookkeeping hours reduced. Friendly's offered Ms. Bearley 22 hours bookkeeping, 13 hours food preparation, and three hours hostessing. Ms. Bearley rejected the offer and sued Friendly's, claiming it had violated the Family Medical Leave Act by not reinstating her to a position equal to her previous one.

Source: Bearley v. Friendly Ice Cream Corp., 322 F.Supp.2d 563 (M.D. Pa. 2004)

Practice Was Friendly's offer acceptable under the law?

17 Ethics
←?→ Application _____

Safety Standards Serena works in the stockroom of a sports clothing company. Her co-worker, Kim, has decided to take the forklift for a ride. Serena knows that heat, noise, and intoxication can lead to work-related accidents, but is not sure Kim is violating safety standards.

◆ Does Kim have a careless attitude toward workplace safety? Should Serena report Kim to their supervisor?

18 Internet
Application _____

Emergency Preparedness OSHA health and safety standards call for employers to create written employee emergency action plans. Sarah's supervisor tells her the company needs to update its emergency action plan and asks Sarah to research OSHA's requirements.

Go to **glencoe.com** to access the Web site sponsored by the U.S. Department of Labor and research OSHA standards for emergency action plans. Prepare a table that lists the minimum elements of an emergency action plan.

📖 Reading Connection

Outside Reading Go to **glencoe.com** for a list of outside reading suggestions about employment law.

📄 Case Study Practice

16. Yes. The court ruled that under the Family Medical Leave Act, the employer must offer the employee the same or substantially equivalent position when the employee returns to work. However, if the job changes while the employee is on leave, the employer is only obligated to offer the employee the same offer it would have extended to the employee had the employee continued to work. Because Ms. Bearley's job would have changed even if she had not gone on leave, the offer Friendly's gave Ms. Bearley upon her return to work was sufficient under the law.

UNIT 5 Careers in Law

Judith Silver
CEO, CoolLawyer.com Legal Forms

What do you do at work?

"I look at the online marketplace to identify what makes CoolLawyer.com unique compared to other legal forms companies, figure out how to best sell my product, and understand my customer base. I also spend time doing search engine marketing, writing articles that are posted on the Web to help my search engine standing (to reach more customers), monitoring my marketing efforts and updating them, and conducting interviews for publicity to enhance my Web site."

Introduce Career Planning

Ask students to discuss what they believe are some of the key values of the entrepreneurial spirit. How does harnessing these skills and talents lead people into new adventures?

Career Decisions

Self-Assessment Checklist

Use this checklist to help students determine their career path:

✓ Think about things you are good at

✓ Write down your interests

✓ Think about the lifestyle you want

✓ Write down your aptitudes and abilities

✓ Consider your personality

✓ Determine your learning style

✓ List some careers that might match these characteristics

Résumé Builder

Answer Many entrepreneurs feel that on-the-job training is the most important kind of education available. They are eager to learn from their successes and mistakes.

What skills are most important to you?

"The most important is the ability to follow through and solve problems in the way I believe to be best, regardless of what others might say is the most important thing in being a successful entrepreneur. This doesn't mean you don't ask and listen to advice from others, but ultimately, you are the key to understanding your business and you are your business."

What training do you recommend?

"Get as much experience as possible in regards to problem solving in the area in which you want to work. I understand my business and other aspects of my career well because I have handled every aspect of the business at one time or another. It's important to learn a position and a career from the ground level and up. Learning from others is just never the same as learning from your own hands-on experience."

What is your key to success?

"There are so many—persistence, creativity, curiosity, common sense. This profession requires that you constantly learn new technology and gain business information to move your business forward. It's amazing what you can learn from simple things like talking to customers and helping them. Often you'll discover entirely new lines of business or ways that you never thought of to improve your business."

Résumé Builder

Academic Skills
- Manage numerous sets of information at one time
- Ability to shift focus while staying on task

Education and Training

A bachelor's degree in business administration, finance, and marketing, plus the following high school and college courses:

- Business, contracts, and consumer law
- English language arts (rhetoric and composition)
- E-commerce
- International business
- Marketing
- Technology/media arts
- U.S. government
- Social Studies

Critical Thinking

Why is technology essential for small business owners? What are some software programs entrepreneurs might use to manage their companies?

Go to **glencoe.com** to find legal careers resources.

Research Technology

Specialized technology is available for a variety of law-related tasks. For example, LexisNexis and Westlaw are two competing electronic databases that attorneys and other legal professionals use to conduct research. These services give users access to online legal information, including the text of court decisions and legislation, the content of public records, and many legal articles.

Activity Ask students to access the American Bar Association's Web site through glencoe.com and read about technology uses in legal professions.

Expository Writing Practice

The Price of a Dream Marcus meets Jackie, a talent agent for Hackman & Broad Agents, who tells him he could be a model. Jackie says he could probably make $1,000 an hour. A few days later, Marcus pays her a $500 consultation fee to discuss his career and the agency's offerings. At this point, Marcus still has not signed a contract. Marcus also needs to pay an additional $1,500 for a portfolio of photographs to show prospective clients. A few weeks later, Jackie calls to tell Marcus his portfolio is ready for pick-up, but that unfortunately the agency has closed due to bankruptcy.

Assignments

Research Research employee rights in the modeling and talent industry.

Write Consider the situation above and write an expository essay about laws that protect employees. Describe how and why Marcus should have investigated the talent agency before acting on a verbal agreement. Include a list of warning signs of a non-reputable talent manager or agent, and the factors for choosing the right representative.

Writing Tips Authors organize their writing in a specific way for a specific purpose. These patterns of organization are called text structures. When writing an expository essay, it is important to address these common type of text structures:

✓ Comparison and contrast shows how things are the same and different.

✓ Cause and effect shows how events are related.

✓ Problem and solution describes a problem and offers solutions.

✓ Chronological order presents events in time order.

Essay Test Strategies Preview the test question by slowly reading through all its part and pieces. In the directions, underline the questions that your essay needs to answer. In the paper's margin, create a rough outline of the information you want to be sure to include in the essay. Use the outline as a checklist while working your way through the writing.

Go to **glencoe.com** to find more writing resources.

 glencoe.com

The Writing Connection

W Writing Support

Objectives

Write a brief expository essay outlining employee rights in the modeling and talent industry.

Essay Rubric

Evaluate the students' writing according to the following criteria:

- The essay presents a consistent point of view and sound organization. **(6 points)**

- The essay uses statement of fact. **(6 points)**

- The essay demonstrates the understanding of purpose and audience. **(5 points)**

- The essay includes textual examples and illustrations for effect. **(4 points)**

- Syntax, grammar, and spelling are error-free. **(4 points)**

Total: 25 points

U Universal Access

English Language Learners

Defining Exposition

Have students work in groups and discuss the Writing Tips before finalizing their essays to make sure they are in line with the expectations.

Culminating Activity

Ask students to work in groups to give each other feedback on their first drafts.

Assignments

Discuss with students the following elements found in expository writing:

- content
- thesis
- organization
- development
- unity and coherence
- tone
- word choice

Supply students with a sample of an expository essay. Ask them to mark up the essay, indicating the placement of each element. They should discuss how each part is important and relates to the whole essay.

Thematic Project

FOCUS

🔔 Bell Ringer Activity

Bring to class the classified section of the newspaper to allow students to conduct a job search. Also provide sample job application forms to show the students the kind of information needed to complete one.

TEACH

Workshop Overview

The objective of this workshop is to prepare an employment guide of federal and state employment laws.

Language Arts

Ask students to write a cover letter to the hiring manager for their dream job. Remind students to keep the tone formal and professional. The first paragraph indicates the position of interest and source of job posting. The second paragraph summarizes education and work experience tailored to match the vacancy. Use the third paragraph to sell personal attributes which match the job requirements. Use a standard closing for the letter.

Employment Guide

For this project, you will use what you have learned to prepare an employment guide of federal and state employment laws to add to your portfolio. This project is to be done individually.

Here is a checklist of skills that you will need to complete this project. Your teacher will consider these skills when evaluating your work.

Evaluation Rubric

Academic Skills		
1. Online and library research	1.	10 points
2. Reading for information	2.	10 points
3. Note-taking	3.	5 points
4. Estimation and computation of facts/figures you discover	4.	10 points
5. English composition to summarize findings	5.	15 points
Legal Skills		
6. Researching employment laws	6.	15 points
7. Knowledge of federal versus state labor laws	7.	15 points
8. Analysis of essential legislative acts governing employers and employees	8.	15 points
9. Use of technology	9.	5 points
		Total 100 Points

For more resources and for grading rubrics, go to **glencoe.com**.

Step 1: Preparation

❶ Write a proposal for the area of employment law you plan to research.

❷ Use all you have learned in this unit, at the library, or on the Internet as tools.

❸ Complete this project in a format acceptable for portfolio addition.

 glencoe.com

Time Management Rubric

Have students evaluate their usage of time by rating the skills below on a scale of "poor" to "apprentice" to "proficient."

- Sets research goals in time to cull the needed materials and sources.
- Prioritizes assignments.

- Concentrates on one item at a time.
- Asks for advice when needed.
- Sets deadlines.
- Completes assignments on time.

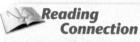
Step 2: Procedure

❶ **Review** the text in this unit and make a list of the laws that relate to your area of interest, such as discrimination or unions. Go to **glencoe.com** to find additional help and resources.

❷ **List** all the employment terms you might include in your document that pertain to your area of research. Here are a few sample questions you might want to answer: What are the federal requirements in hiring workers? What laws protect workers from unsafe labor practices? How are these laws enforced?

❸ **Write** an informational guide about the legal terms and documents that an employer and employee must abide by for employment placement. Use the Internet to research and download labor forms (e.g., work permit) and other important documents. Make enough copies so your classmates can review and annotate your guide.

❹ **Describe** an advertisement for an employment opportunity. Present your guide and see if your classmates can use it as a primer to apply for the job.

Step 3: Create an Analysis Report

As a class, compare the employment guides presented. Compare and contrast the information presented in each and look for common themes or areas covered. See if any of the guides stand out and if so what makes the information presented easier to understand. After comparing the guides, answer the following questions:

❶ How many and what areas of laws were presented?

❷ Did the guides presented include all the necessary information needed to apply for a job?

❸ If not, what should have been added to make the information easier to use?

❹ How was your guide similar to and different from the other guides presented?

Community Connection

Select a business you are interested in learning more about. Look up statistics on employment opportunities, salary range, and future expectations for that business. How do these statistics affect your chosen career path? Summarize your findings for the class. Go to **glencoe.com** to find resources.

Competitive Event Prep

Equal Employment

Situation Your aunt (event judge) owns a maid service called Maid for You. She has owned the service, which specializes in house cleaning, for over ten years. During the entire company history all of the cleaners have been female. Your aunt recently advertised for new cleaners to fill vacancies. For the first time, a well-qualified man has applied for a position. Your aunt wonders if her clients will accept a man as a cleaner. She is unsure about how to handle the situation and asks you for your advice.

Activity You are to explain to your aunt the legal aspects of equal employment legislation and the impact it could have on her business.

 For more Competitive Event preparation, performance tips, and evaluation rubrics, go to **glencoe.com**.

TEACH (cont.)

Extending the Content

Cases of Interest

Ask students to use the Internet to research how federal agencies discipline businesses for not adhering to an employment law. They should share their findings.

Reading Connection

American Bar Association Resources

Ask students to go back to their ABA readings, notes, and summaries. Direct them to apply any relevant ABA content to review and revise their outline and first draft.

ASSESS

Evaluation

Make sure students review the evaluation rubric. They should distinguish between federal and state labor laws, and be clear on which prevail in cases of conflict.

CLOSE

Culminating Activity

Cooperative Learning

Ask students to determine if this activity has shed any light on the labor laws that might influence them or a family member.

R Reading Strategy

Reading Source Documents

Ask students to summarize the work hours, minimum wage, and overtime wage requirements of the Fair Labor Standards Act and indicate which jobs are not covered by it. Additionally, ask students to describe the requirements of the Family Medical Leave Act and indicate which employers are exempt from it.

C Critical Thinking

Debating

Ask students to debate the benefits and disadvantages of unions and of collective bargaining for workers.

349

FOCUS

Why It's Important

- The Supreme Court held that retaliation is an actionable cause under Title IX.

- Retaliation can occur not only against persons bringing sex discrimination claims for themselves, but also against people who bring sex discrimination claims on behalf of third parties.

TEACH

Preteaching

Your Reading

This text is a long excerpt from a key case where U.S. anti-discrimination law was applied.

Preread Skim the text, look at headings and the first few sentences of every section.

C Critical Thinking

Making Inferences Ask students to explain how discrimination can harm all Americans, not just those who are its targets. Remind students that the Thirteenth, Fourteenth, and Fifteenth Amendments as well as numerous laws were intended to guarantee equal opportunities and equal protection, but they were not enforced for decades and so had little value. This discussion offers an opportunity to reinforce the relationship among the three branches of government.

350

Jackson v. Birmingham Board of Education
U.S. Supreme Court 544 U.S. 167 ____ (2005)

Read Critically As you read the case, ask yourself the following questions:

R
1. Who did Mr. Jackson file a sex discrimination claim for?
2. Under what law did Mr. Jackson bring his claim?
3. Why did the Eleventh Circuit rule against Mr. Jackson?
4. What did the U.S. Supreme Court hold about retaliation?

Assignment When you are done, write a short summary of the situation. Include the court's decision and a couple of sentences about why or how the court reached its decision.

Facts **New Coaching Job** Roderick Jackson was an employee of the Birmingham Alabama School District for more than 10 years. He was hired in 1993 to be a physical education teacher and girls' basketball coach. In 1999, Mr. Jackson transferred within the district to Ensley High School. When he started, he discovered that the girls' teams at Ensley were not receiving equal funding and equal access to the athletic equipment and facilities. Because of the inequalities, Mr. Jackson discovered he was unable to do his job as the girls' basketball team's coach. **Sex Discrimination Complaint** In December of 2000, Mr. Jackson began to complain to his supervisors about the unequal treatment of the girls' basketball team. However, his supervisors did not respond to his claims and the school district failed to remedy the situation. Instead, Mr. Jackson began to receive negative work evaluations and ultimately was removed as the girls' basketball coach in May 2001.

Mr. Jackson was retained as a teacher, but was no longer a coach and did not receive the supplemental pay he did as a coach. **Lawsuit Commencement** After the Birmingham School District terminated Mr. Jackson's coaching duties, he filed a lawsuit in U.S. District Court against the school district. Mr. Jackson alleged that the Birmingham School District had violated Title IX of the Education Amendments by retaliating against him for protesting the discrimination against the girls' basketball team.

Opinion **U.S. Eleventh Circuit Court of Appeal Proceedings** The U.S. Court of Appeals for the Eleventh Circuit held that Title IX does not include a provision where Mr. Jackson could bring a claim for retaliation, since there is no private cause of retaliation available under Title IX. The Court also held that even if Title IX prohibited retaliation, Mr. Jackson would not be entitled to relief because he is

C

350   Unit 5   The Law and the Workplace

? Landmark Case Questions

R Reading Strategy

Answers

1. the girls' basketball team that he coached

2. Title IX of the Education Amendments

3. There was no private cause of action for retaliation under Title IX, because Mr. Jackson was not the actual victim.

4. Retaliation is an actionable private cause of action under Title IX.

not within the class of persons protected by the statute, nor is he an actual victim of sex discrimination himself.

Title IX Title IX was passed in 1972 as part of the Education Amendments. It states as follows:

20 U.S.C. §1681 (Title IX)
(a) Prohibition against discrimination; exceptions
No person in the United States shall, on the basis of sex, be excluded from participation in, be denied the benefits of, or be subjected to discrimination under any education program or activity receiving Federal financial assistance.
(c) "Educational institution" defined

An educational institution means any public or private preschool, elementary, or secondary school, or any institution of vocational, professional, or higher education, except that in an educational institution composed of more than one school, college, or department which are administratively separate units, such term means each such school, college, or department.

In 1979, in Cannon v. University of Chicago, the Supreme Court held that Title IX includes a private right of action. Private citizens have the right to bring a claim against the offending party, to enforce the prohibition on intentional sex discrimination. Later, in 1992, in Franklin v. Gwinnett County Public Schools, the Supreme Court held private parties can seek monetary damages for intentional violations of Title IX. In all the cases, the Court relied on the text of Title IX, which except for a few narrow exceptions prohibits discrimination on the basis of sex.

Retaliation The court then looked at retaliation. Like private causes of action, Title IX does not speak directly to the issue of retaliation. In previous cases, the Supreme Court has held that retaliation is, by definition, an intentional act. It is also a form of discrimination, since the complaining person is subjected to differential treatment. Further, retaliation is discrimination on the basis of

sex when it is an intentional response to a sex discrimination complaint.

School District's Argument The Birmingham School Board argued that if Congress wished to include retaliation in Title IX, then it would have included it as it did in the Civil Rights Acts. However, the causes of action under the Civil Rights Acts are explicit, whereas the courts have inferred all the causes of action under Title IX. Under Title IX Congress prohibited all forms of discrimination in education and the courts have, therefore, allowed that broad prohibition to apply to a broad number of actions. Discrimination is a term that covers a wide range of intentional unequal treatment and the Court will ensure that the action is not allowed in the educational system by allowing a broad number of causes of action.

Holding **The Court's Decision** The Supreme Court held that retaliation is an actionable cause under Title IX. Further, retaliation can occur not only against persons bringing sex discrimination claims for themselves, but also for people who bring sex discrimination claims on behalf of third parties. The actions of the Birmingham School District could amount to retaliation and Mr. Jackson is permitted to bring his cause of action before a jury to make that determination.

TRIAL PREP

The National High School Mock Trial Association organizes competitions at the local, regional, and national levels where teams of high school or college students prepare and argue fictional legal cases before practicing attorneys and judges. Mock Trial team members are each assigned a role as either an attorney or witness. Each team must develop a courtroom strategy, legal arguments, and a presentation style.

Go to **glencoe.com** to find guided activities about case strategy and presentation.

Winning the Case

Title IX

One of the reasons the Eleventh Circuit Court of Appeals ruled against Mr. Jackson was that he was not in the class of persons protected by Title IX. Title IX was passed to prevent sex discrimination in the educational arena. It mandates that males and females must be treated equally. In reality, the actual victims would be the girls' basketball team, not Mr. Jackson. Ask students whether third parties should be able to bring actions under Title IX. Remind them that normally parents or guardians must bring lawsuits on behalf of minors and that the members of a high school team are probably minors.

ASSESS

S Skills Practice

Write the following excerpt from the Fourteenth Amendment on the board: *"No State shall…deny to any person within its jurisdiction the equal protection of the laws."* Ask students if treating people equally means treating them the same. Then what is discrimination? What are some examples of discrimination that are not necessarily negative or unfair? (Discrimination means distinguishing between two or more things based on a set of criteria. Discrimination is problematic when it becomes unfair and is thus illegal.)

CLOSE

Understand the Decision

In this decision, the Supreme Court ruled that retaliation is a cause of action within Title IX, even though that cause of action is not specifically delineated within the statute. Title IX is a broad law that prohibits all discriminatory behavior on the basis of sex, without specifically stating what actions are prohibited. Should laws be written so that they are as specific as possible? (It is easier for people to evade a law that is overly specific.)

UNIT 6 *Starting a Business*

Unit Objectives

Chapter	Section	Objectives
Chapter 16	**16.1**	• **Describe** how to form and run a sole proprietorship. • **List** the advantages and disadvantages of a sole proprietorship. • **Explain** the rights and responsibilities of partners. • **Identify** the different types of partners. • **Explain** how a partnership can be terminated.
	16.2	• **Characterize** corporations. • **Explain** the different types of corporations. • **Discuss** the steps involved in forming a corporation. • **Explain** what a limited liability company is. • **List** the steps in forming a limited liability company.
Chapter 17	**17.1**	• **Distinguish** the roles of corporate directors and corporate officers. • **List** the rights shareholders have. • **Explain** the business judgment rule. • **Explain** the fairness rule. • **Describe** the liability of corporate directors and officers.
	17.2	• **Describe** the different types of corporate stock. • **Distinguish** between a merger, a consolidation, and a conglomerate. • **Explain** asset acquisition and stock acquisition. • **Identify** the ways a corporation can be terminated.
Chapter 18	**18.1**	• **Explain** the source of federal power in the regulation of business. • **Identify** the laws that regulate the sale of securities. • **Distinguish** between the laws that regulate antitrust activity. • **Describe** what laws regulate corporate takeovers.
	18.2	• **Describe** the laws that regulate the environment. • **Identify** the federal and state agencies that regulate the environment. • **Identify** the federal and state agencies that are responsible for regulating energy. • **Describe** the impact of international law on energy regulation and conservation.
Chapter 19	**19.1**	• **Explain** the nature of a cybercrime. • **List** different types of cybercrimes. • **Describe** the nature of a cybertort. • **Distinguish** between cyberdefamation and cyberinvasion of privacy.
	19.2	• **Explain** intellectual property and copyright for digital products. • **Explain** the importance of trademarks. • **Identify** the characteristics of a patentable invention. • **Recognize** two unsettled issues in e-commerce law. • **Explain** new laws regarding digital signatures and documents.

Understanding Brackets, Letters, and Ability Levels in the Teacher Wraparound Edition

Brackets Brackets on the reduced student edition page correspond to teaching strategies and activities in the Teacher Wraparound Edition. As you teach the lesson, the brackets show you exactly where to use the teaching strategies and activities.

Letters The letters on the reduced student edition page identify the type of strategy or activity. See the key below to learn about the different types of strategies and activities.

Ability Levels Teaching strategies that appear throughout the chapters have been identified by one of three codes to give you an idea of their suitability for students of varying learning styles and abilities.

Resources Key program resources are listed in each chapter. Icons indicate the format of resources.

KEY TO LETTERS

R **Reading Strategy** activities help you teach reading skills and vocabulary.

C **Critical Thinking** strategies help students apply and extend what they have learned.

S **Skills Practice** strategies help students practice historical analysis and geographical skills.

W **Writing Support** activities provide writing opportunities to help students comprehend the text.

D **Develop Concepts** activities use various strategies to help teachers gauge and plan for students' concept development.

U **Universal Access** activities provide differentiated instruction for English language learners, and suggestions for teaching various types of learners.

NCLB **No Child Left Behind** activities help students practice and improve their abilities in academic subjects.

KEY TO ABILITY LEVELS

L1 strategies should be within the ability range of all students. Often full class participation is required.

L2 strategies are for average to above-average students or for small groups. Some teacher direction is necessary.

L3 strategies are designed for students able and willing to work independently. Minimal teacher direction is necessary.

KEY TO RESOURCE ICONS

📁 Print Material

💿 CD/DVD

🖱 Internet

Teacher Wraparound Edition

Student Activity Workbook with Academic Integration Teacher Annotated Edition

For the Unit:
Lesson Plans
National and State Standards Correlations

For the Chapters:
Lessons Plans
Note-Taking Graphic Organizers
Chapter Outlines
Chapter Summaries
Enrichment Activities Masters

Supplemental Cases
Internet Connection Student Activities Masters
Blackline Masters for Student Edition Figures and
    Supplemental Figures
Ethics and Business Law Activities
Competitive Events Test-Taking Prep
Reproducible Chapter Tests

 Link to the ***Business and Personal Law*** Online **Learning Center** with Podcasts through glencoe.com.

Real-World Applications

Demonstrate Case Resolutions

Learning Objective

- Identify the powers and duties of partners (p. 360).
- Explain the concept of stock acquisition (p. 388).
- Understand the laws that regulate anti-trust activity (p. 399).
- Describe antitrust violations as they relate to doing business with Internet companies (p. 423).

- Describe how a partnership can be terminated (p. 375).
- Understand the duties and responsibilities of shareholders (p. 393).
- Identify when a developer or corporation may be exempt from environmental laws (p. 411).
- Explain the concept of jurisdiction as it relates to a company doing business over the Internet (p. 429).

- Understand the roles of corporate directors and corporate officers (pp. 434–435).

Apply Business Law Concepts

Learning Objective

- Understand different types of corporations (p. 354).
- Recognize the role of corporate directors and officers (p. 376).
- Describe the laws that regulate the environment (p. 394).
- Describe cybercrime (p. 412).

- Differentiate between the two business organizational structures in Brazil (p. 370).
- Identify the steps a South African company must use in order to incorporate (p. 380).
- Explain the environmental protection laws in Cambodia (p. 404).
- Describe the Internet privacy laws in Taiwan (p. 424).

- Explain the types of corporate stock (p. 385).
- Explain the nature of a cybercrime (p. 415).

- Describe how a partnership can be terminated (p. 375).
- Explain the fairness rule as it relates to non-profit corporations (p. 393).

- Understand laws that regulate the environment (p. 411).
- Explain copyright laws for digital products (p. 429).
- Explain how a partnership can be terminated (p. 363).
- Understand the laws that regulate the environment (p. 406).

Teach Financial Literacy

Learning Objective

- Understand types of corporate stock (p. 353).

Bring Project-Based Learning into the Law Classroom

Protecting Social and Environmental Concerns

- **Introduce Concepts**
  The environment and the health of the public are protected by laws which impose safe business practices on companies.

- **Explore Concepts**
  Read the Thematic Project Preview and the WebQuest activity (p. 353).

  Ask students to think of the information they need to gather on environmental laws and business practices as they study Chapters 16, 17, 18, and 19.

- **Apply Concepts**
  Research federal, state, and international environmental laws, outline the responsibilities of companies toward the environment and society, and present views and findings (pp. 432 and 433).

Extend Content

Reading Connection

Using American Bar Association (ABA) Resources

- Direct students to pages 375, 393, 411, and 429 in the Student Edition.
- Ask them to use glencoe.com to find links to ABA resource documents.
- Students should browse and select one document for each chapter.
- See pages 375, 393, 411, 429, and 435 in this edition for specific instructions.

Reading and Writing Support

Feature or Activity	Topic	Reading Strategy	Writing Strategy
STANDARD &POOR'S	Listing of stocks on a stock market	Reading a primary source document	
Thematic Project Preview	Protecting social and environmental concerns		Researching and taking notes
BusinessWeek	Readings about family-owned business (Ch. 16), corporate governance (Ch. 17), environmental law (Ch. 18), and cybercrime (Ch. 19)	Reading for detail Developing flexibility in reading speed	
Section Reading Guide	Before-reading activities and tools	Connect students' lives with content Focus on the main idea	Using a graphic organizer to take notes
As You Read	During-reading tool	Predict content Determine what students already know	
Reading Check	During-reading tool	Self-check understanding of content	
After You Read	After-reading tool	Summarize section content	Writing and organizing a list of key concepts
Standardized Test Practice	Microenterprise development (Ch. 16) Buying a franchise (Ch. 17) Energy law (Ch. 18) International cybercrime (Ch. 19)	Reading a primary source document Practicing critical reading skills	
Reading Connection	American Bar Association online resources	Reading a primary source document Extending and applying content Reading for knowledge	Taking notes Summarizing
The Writing Connection	Personal essay		Creating outlines, topic sentences, editing
Unit Thematic Project	Protecting social and environmental concerns	Using resources notes to support writing effort	Creating outlines, writing drafts, editing
Landmark Case	Corporate Opportunity Doctrine case	Developing critical reading skills	Summarizing

UNIT 6

Unit Overview

Main Idea

Unit 6 explores the various forms of business, what it takes to manage a corporation, and the laws that regulate corporations, as well as electronic commerce.

⏱ 00:00 OUT OF TIME?

If class time is too short to cover the chapters thoroughly, have students:

- Write down the vocabulary terms and their definitions.
- Read What You'll Learn and Why It's Important at the beginning of each section.
- Go to the *Business and Personal Law* Online Learning Center at **glencoe.com** and download the free Study-to-Go content to their cell phones or PDAs.

▶ **USING VISUALS ....**

Your Own Boss *Answer*
The three main forms of business ownership are sole proprietorships, partnerships, and corporations.

UNIT 6

Starting a Business

In This Unit You Will Find:

Chapter 16
Forms of Business

Chapter 17
Operating a Corporation

Chapter 18
Business and Regulations

Chapter 19
Cyberlaw and E-Commerce

• • • • • • • • • • • • • • • • •

Be Your Own Boss An alternative to going to work for someone else is starting your own business. *What are the three main forms of business ownership?*

Unit Thematic Project Preview

W Writing Support

The National Environmental Policy Act (NEPA) along with a handful of other enactments was created around 1970 to protect the environment from public harm to ecosystems.

Critical Thinking Describe how the government manages energy, land use, and natural resources while still respecting the interests of businesses in those areas.

Thematic Project Preview

Protecting Social and Environmental Concerns

As you read this unit, use this checklist to prepare for the unit project:

✓ List the environmental laws the government requires businesses to obey.

✓ Differentiate between safe and unsafe business practices as they relate to environmental laws.

✓ Explain how laws protect the environment and society in general.

✓ Determine the impact environmental laws have on business and society.

Legal Portfolio When you complete the Unit Thematic project, you will have a guide of environmental protection law for your portfolio.

Web Quest

W

Entrepreneurship

Owning and operating your own business can be very exciting, and there are lots of federal agencies that can help to get you started. Log on to **glencoe.com** to find federal agencies that offer guidance to starting or buying a new business. Then, continue working on your WebQuest as you study Unit 6.

Find Unit 6 study tools such as **Graphic Organizers, Academic Skills Review,** and **Practice Tests** at **glencoe.com**.

Ask

STANDARD &POOR'S   **Get Listed on a Stock Market**

Q: How do shares of a company get traded on the New York Stock Exchange?

A: Suppose you run a successful company and want to start selling shares on the New York Stock Exchange (NYSE). The first thing you need to do is hire an investment banker to arrange an initial public offering (IPO), which is a company's first sale of stock to the public. After the government approves the sale, the stock is made available to investors. Then, the stock can be traded on a stock market. For your company's stock to be traded or listed on the NYSE, you must apply with the NYSE, which will review your company to determine if it meets certain requirements (such as having a minimum number of shareholders, a minimum market value, follows basic reporting procedures, has a board of directors, and has in place appropriate corporate governance rules). The NYSE's listing application and requirements are available online.

R **Language Arts/Reading** Standard & Poor's is one of the world's main providers of credit ratings and financial-market indices. Go to **glencoe.com** and read more about the stock market and how it works.

 glencoe.com

Unit 6   Starting a Business   **353**

Ask

STANDARD &POOR'S

R Reading Strategy

Language Arts/Reading Direct students to explore S&P's resources on the stock market.

Math Activity Two Inc. sold 850,000 shares of stock at $18.53 per share. The investment banker's commission was 4 percent of the value of the stock. The other expenses were 0.5 percent of the value of the stock. What net proceeds did Two Inc. receive? What is the selling expense per share?
($15,041,728; $0.834)

KWL Chart Organize students into small groups. Have each group select one of the chapters in Unit 6 to review. Encourage students to identify at least ten points of interest they can list in a KWL chart. After completing the unit, revisit the chart and reassess their knowledge of each chapter by asking them what they have learned.

Building Law Background

Ask students these questions to activate prior knowledge:

Chapter 16
Discuss local businesses that are owned by one person. How are these different from other businesses that provide the same good or service? (Answers will vary depending on location. Students might state that a single business owner operates on a smaller scale than a corporation.)

Chapter 17
What is the difference between a sole proprietorship and a partnership? (A sole proprietorship is a business that is owned by one person; a partnership is created when two or more parties combine their money, efforts, and skills for the purpose of carrying on a business.)

Chapter 18
Who owns a corporation? (Corporate shareholders are the owners of a corporation.)

Chapter 19
Who creates and interprets the laws that regulate the corporate takeover process? (Congress, state legislatures, and the courts)

Plan Your Lesson Section by Section

NBEA	**NATIONAL BUSINESS LAW STANDARDS**
Section 16.1	• **Outline** the legal procedures for forming and running a sole proprietorship. • **Describe** legislation that affects partnerships (e.g., Uniform Partnership Act and Revised Uniform Partnership Act). • **Explain** the property rights involved in partnerships (e.g., tenancy in partnership and sharing of profits). • **Discuss** other partnership rights (e.g., right to manage, right to reimburse, right to inspect the books, and right to an account). • **Distinguish** between a limited partnership and a general partnership. • **Describe** how the Revised Uniform Limited Partnership Act affects limited partnerships. • **Explain** the rights and duties of limited partners and general partners in a limited partnership. • **Explain** the distribution of assets after the dissolution of a limited partnership. • **Identify** how a partnership may be dissolved by the acts of the partners, operation of the law, and order of the court. • **Determine,** after a dissolution, whether a partnership would continue or terminate through a winding up. • **Explain** the winding up of partnership affairs and distribution of partnership assets after dissolution. • **Differentiate** between other partnership-type business organizations (e.g., joint ventures, limited partnership associations, and registered partnerships having limited liability).
Section 16.2	• **Differentiate** between types of corporations (e.g., profit, nonprofit, domestic, foreign, and alien corporations). • **Explain** the steps involved in forming a corporation. • **Define** a limited liability company. • **Explain** the steps in forming a limited liability company. • **Explain** the circumstances under which courts may disregard the corporate entity and "pierce the corporate veil." • **Explain** the advantages and disadvantages of doing business as a limited liability company. • **Explain** the nature of management responsibilities in a limited liability company. • **Describe** the effects of the tax code on limited liability companies.

NCLB	**ACADEMIC STANDARDS**	**Activity/Feature**
English Language Arts: NCTE 3 Apply a wide range of strategies to comprehend, interpret, evaluate, and appreciate texts.		*BusinessWeek* News, Case Study, Case Study Practice, Section 16.1 Assessment
Mathematics: NCTM NOS 2a Judge the effects of such operations as multiplication, division, and computing powers and roots on the magnitude of quantities.		Section 16.2 Assessment
English Language Arts: NCTE 10 Students whose first language is not English make use of their first language to develop competency in the English language arts and to develop understanding of content across the curriculum.		Key Terms, Academic Vocabulary, Legal Talk, Vocabulary Builder
Social Studies: NCSS 7 Study how people organize for the production, distribution, and consumption of goods and services.		Case Study, Cyberlaw
Social Studies: NCSS 5 Study interactions among individuals, groups, and institutions.		Global Law

Connect Your Business Law Classroom to the World of Work

This chart shows the 21st Century Skills, foundation skills, and workplace competencies that students develop as they work in this chapter.

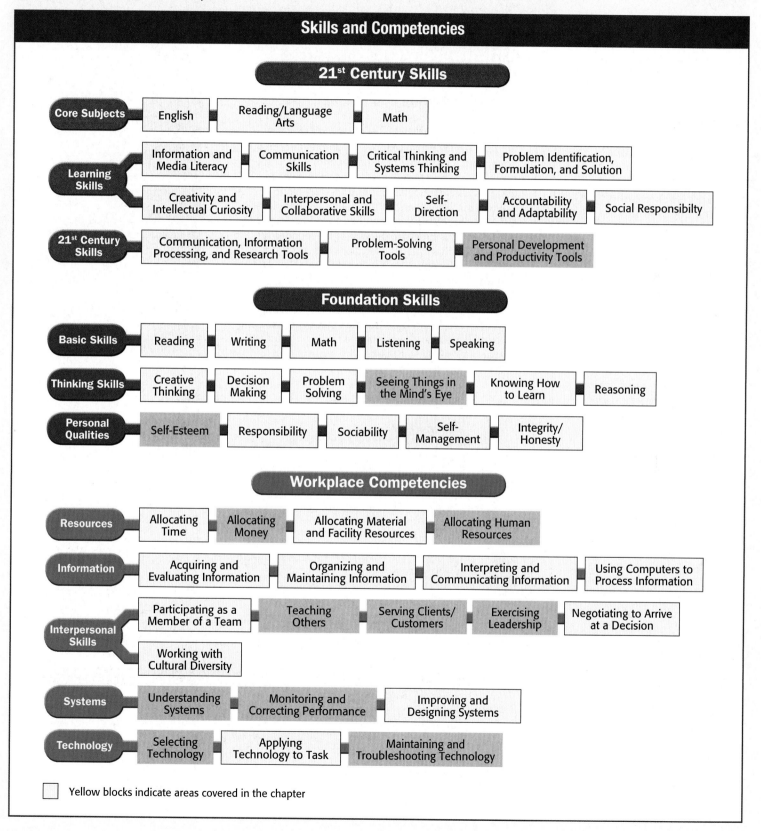

Skills and Competencies

21st Century Skills

Core Subjects: English | Reading/Language Arts | Math

Learning Skills: Information and Media Literacy | Communication Skills | Critical Thinking and Systems Thinking | Problem Identification, Formulation, and Solution | Creativity and Intellectual Curiosity | Interpersonal and Collaborative Skills | Self-Direction | Accountability and Adaptability | Social Responsibilty

21st Century Skills: Communication, Information Processing, and Research Tools | Problem-Solving Tools | Personal Development and Productivity Tools

Foundation Skills

Basic Skills: Reading | Writing | Math | Listening | Speaking

Thinking Skills: Creative Thinking | Decision Making | Problem Solving | Seeing Things in the Mind's Eye | Knowing How to Learn | Reasoning

Personal Qualities: Self-Esteem | Responsibility | Sociability | Self-Management | Integrity/Honesty

Workplace Competencies

Resources: Allocating Time | Allocating Money | Allocating Material and Facility Resources | Allocating Human Resources

Information: Acquiring and Evaluating Information | Organizing and Maintaining Information | Interpreting and Communicating Information | Using Computers to Process Information

Interpersonal Skills: Participating as a Member of a Team | Teaching Others | Serving Clients/Customers | Exercising Leadership | Negotiating to Arrive at a Decision | Working with Cultural Diversity

Systems: Understanding Systems | Monitoring and Correcting Performance | Improving and Designing Systems

Technology: Selecting Technology | Applying Technology to Task | Maintaining and Troubleshooting Technology

Yellow blocks indicate areas covered in the chapter

Introduce the Chapter

Forms of Business

Chapter 16 introduces the major forms of business ownership: sole proprietorship, partnership, corporations, and limited liability companies. Students learn about the advantages and disadvantages of each and how to form and terminate them.

Building Background

Write the main forms of business on the board in columns. Ask students to tell you all they know about each form of business, and write their descriptions on the board in the appropriate column. Have students copy the information and compare it to their knowledge when they finish the chapter.

BusinessWeek News

Explain to students that this article is about a privately held corporation owned by a family. Ask students to list the people named in the article and make a chart showing the relationships between them. Help students understand that the article discusses a family feud occurring within the company's board of directors. Explain that a corporate board is the governing body of a corporation.

R **Reading Strategy**

Your Reading

Tell students that an efficient way to preview a chapter is to read the bulleted items under the heading "What You'll Learn" at the beginning of each section.

354

A Sizzling Family Food Fight

By Ronald Grover

Quintessential California drive-in chain In-N-Out Burger has built a cult-like following among fast-food gourmands for its juicy grilled patties and "secret" menu items. But the beef these days at the family-owned, 200-plus restaurant outfit isn't its trademark Double-Doubles but allegations that the chain's 23-year-old heir, Lynsi Martinez, and others are plotting to force out her 86-year-old grandmother, the wife of the founder. It's a soap opera that includes allegations of fraud and a backroom power play. Matriarch Ester Snyder is alleged in court documents to have told ex-employee Richard Boyd that they "only want me dead."

The saga is playing out in a state court in Los Angeles where Boyd, a former In-N-Out real estate vice-president and board member, claims Martinez and her stepsister's husband, Vice-President Mark Taylor, maneuvered to oust Boyd and take over the chain.

Flex Your Reading

Efficient critical reading involves being flexible with speed and comprehension. There are several ways of reading critically, and you need to fit a reading style to your needs and to the material.

Go to **glencoe.com** for Flex Your Reading activities, more information on reading strategies for this chapter, and guided practice in reading about family-owned businesses and partnerships.

Classroom Resources

- Student Edition
- Teacher Wraparound Edition
- Student Activity Workbook with Academic Integration (SE/TAE)
- TeacherWorks™ Plus! CD
- *ExamView*® Assessment Suite CD
- *Presentation Plus!* CD

- National Mock Trial Championship DVD
- Online Learning Center with Podcasts at glencoe.com
- Study-to-Go™ at glencoe.com
- Online Student Edition
- Interactive Student Edition

Paying Your Dues Running a business comes with responsibilities. *Who pays the taxes, and who is liable for debts in a partnership?*

(355)

Practice the Concept

Forms of Business
Have students decide whether they would like to work as a sole proprietor, in a partnership, or in a corporation as an employee. Go around the room and give each student a chance to explain his or her choice.

Key Terms Explain to students the word *corporation* comes from the Latin word *corpus*, meaning body. A corporation is a body of people who have come together to conduct business. Emphasize that a corporation is a separate legal entity. As such, it pays taxes and can be sued just like an individual. Have students bring the business section of the newspaper to class and look for articles about corporations.

Legal Basics Tell students that all types of businesses must adhere to city, county, and state laws. This usually means registering the business with one or more of those governments, obtaining a reseller's permit, and paying for a business license and taxes.

▲ USING VISUALS

Paying Your Dues Answer Explain that partnerships do not pay taxes independently, as a corporation does. Instead, partnership income is passed through to all the partners. Each partner includes his or her share of the partnership profits in his or her own income tax filing. Thus each partner effectively pays a share of the partnership taxes based on his or her own income tax bracket. If a partner cannot pay his or her share of the debts, the other partners are completely liable for the debts.

FOCUS

Bell Ringer Activity

Ask students to name some of the businesses in their community that they visit frequently. Ask if they know whether these businesses are owned by a single owner, partners, or a corporation.

Preteaching

Key Terms

Read the definitions and ask students to create a sentence using each term.

Academic Vocabulary

Explain that developing vocabulary is key to academic success. An efficient method to develop vocabulary is to study how words are formed.

- **perpetual** Adjective, from the Latin *perpetuus, per-* + *petere* (to go toward). Means continuous.

- **dormant** Adjective, from the Latin *dormire* (to sleep). Means inactive.

- **incompetence** Noun, from the Latin *in-* (not) + *competens* (skill). Means not qualified, not effective.

Activity Ask students to give a noun, a verb, an adjective, or an adverb form that comes from each word.

NCLB Connects to academic content

What You'll Learn

- ◆ Describe how to form and run a sole proprietorship.
- ◆ List the advantages and disadvantages of a sole proprietorship.
- ◆ Explain the rights and responsibilities of partners.
- ◆ Identify the different types of partners.
- ◆ Explain how a partnership can be terminated.

Why It's Important

Knowing the differences between sole proprietorships and partnerships will help you decide which form of business is best for you.

Academic Standards

Reading and completing the activities in this section will help you practice the following academic standards:

Social Studies (NCSS 7) Study how people organize for the production, distribution, and consumption of goods and services.

English Language Arts (NCTE 3) Apply a wide range of strategies to comprehend, interpret, evaluate, and appreciate texts.

Reading Guide

Before You Read

Connect Have you ever tried to start your own business on the Internet or at school?

Focus on Ideas

Sole proprietorships and partnerships both have advantages and disadvantages.

Take Notes

Create a graph like the one shown and use it to take notes as you read this section. Go to **glencoe.com** to find graphic organizers and tips on how to improve your note-taking skills.

	Sole Proprietorships	Partnerships
Advantages	_____	_____
Disadvantages	_____	_____

Key Terms

You will learn these legal words and expressions in this chapter. You can also find these terms in *Black's Law Dictionary* or in an online legal dictionary.

- sole proprietorship
- unlimited liability
- partnership
- joint liability
- dissolution
- dissociation
- limited partnership
- limited liability partnership (LLP)

Academic Vocabulary

You will find these words in your readings and in your tests. Look them up in a dictionary and familiarize yourself with them.

- perpetual
- dormant
- incompetence

glencoe.com

R Reading Strategy

Read for Knowledge

1. **Survey** or preread the chapter.
2. **Question** or formulate questions before you read.
3. **Recite** or read your questions, answers, and notes out loud.
4. **Review** or reread your notes.

Note-Taking Basics

- Listen attentively
- Have note-taking materials ready
- Skim through the lesson material
- Write down key words and ideas
- Anticipate what comes next
- Review notes soon after taking them

Sole Proprietorships

If you start a babysitting service, what kind of business is it?

A sole proprietorship is a form of business that is owned and operated by one person. A sole proprietorship is the most common way to do business. It is also the easiest type of business to form. Common sole proprietorships are repair shops, small retail stores, and service organizations.

Advantages of a Sole Proprietorship

Sole proprietorships offer specific advantages. These advantages include ease of creation, total control, retention of profits, and one-time taxation of profits.

Ease of Formation There are only a few requirements to meet in forming a sole proprietorship. Some businesses, such as restaurants and motels, must get licenses to operate legally. Other businesses, such as barbers or plumbers, must have occupational licenses and liability insurance. Zoning ordinances which forbid the operation of businesses in residential neighborhoods can restrict the location of a sole proprietorship. If an owner plans to hire employees, he or she must obtain an employer identification number (EIN) from the Internal Revenue Service for tax purposes.

Total Control and Retention of Profits In a sole proprietorship, the owner has complete control of the business and makes all of the decisions. The proprietor also gets to keep all of the profits from the business. Proprietors, however, must still pay taxes on the profits that they make.

One-Time Taxation of Profits Sole proprietorships do not pay taxes as a business. The sole proprietor pays taxes based on his or her income. A full-time sole proprietor will pay income

 Family Business Many sole proprietorships are family-owned businesses passed down from one generation to the next. *About what percentage of businesses in the U.S. are sole proprietorships?*

TEACH

Discussion Starter

Class Discussion
Ask students to imagine they are about to open a business of their own. Have them discuss what type of business they might open, how many employees they would need, and what kinds of challenges they expect. (licenses, insurance, training, taxes)

D Develop Concepts

Sole Proprietorships
Explain that a sole proprietorship is owned and operated by one person. Ask students whether they think a sole proprietorship can hire employees. (yes) Stress that the term *sole proprietorship* refers to the business form, but it does not mean that the owner must work alone.

As You Read

Predict Ask students to guess how partners in a partnership handle taxes. (Partners pay the taxes individually, as the partnership income is passed through to them on a prorated share.)

As You Read
Predict Who pays taxes in a business partnership?

▲ USING VISUALS

Family Business **Answer** Approximately 70 percent of businesses in the United States are sole proprietorships.

Activity Explain to students that the abbreviation DBA means "doing business as." Some states also use the terms "fictitious business name," "trade name," or "assumed name." Bring in newspapers that contain DBA business announcements. Let students find the announcements and read them aloud to the class. Many DBA announcements are for sole proprietorships. Ask students to prepare a summary of how many businesses of each form are mentioned.

TEACH (cont.)

D Develop Concepts

Unlimited Liability Ask students to imagine that they have owned and operated a public relations firm for the last two years. It is structured as a sole proprietorship. The business is experiencing financial losses, and students must consider filing bankruptcy. Ask students how they think this will affect their personal credit rating. (The sole proprietor is responsible for all the financial losses incurred by the business. The bankruptcy will place all personal assets of the owner at risk and probably damage the sole proprietor's personal credit rating.)

R Reading Strategy

Advantages and Disadvantages of the Sole Proprietorship Ask students to set up two columns on a sheet of paper. Use the labels "Advantages" and "Disadvantages" at the top of each column. Have students write the advantages and disadvantages of the sole proprietorship form in the appropriate column. Emphasize that this is an effective note-taking strategy when contrasting two ideas.

---

taxes on all profits made in a year. If the business is a part-time venture, those profits plus all other income made by the sole proprietor are taxed.

Disadvantages of a Sole Proprietorship

Sole proprietorships have several disadvantages. These disadvantages include limited capital, unlimited liability, and limited lifetime.

Limited Capital An obvious shortcoming of a sole proprietorship is the fact that the business owner has limited access to capital. All money used to finance the business must come from the proprietor's savings or income, or from loans obtained by the proprietor.

Unlimited Liability Perhaps the biggest disadvantage of a sole proprietorship is unlimited liability. **Unlimited liability is a legal duty placed on a business owner that requires the owner to be responsible for all losses experienced by the business.** Even the personal property of a sole proprietor may be used to satisfy the debts of the business.

Limited Lifetime Unlike a corporation, which has **perpetual** existence, a sole proprietorship lasts only as long as the proprietor. When the proprietor dies or chooses to sell or close the business, the business ceases to exist.

Vocabulary You can find vocabulary definitions in the **Key Terms** glossary and **Academic Vocabulary** glossary in the back of this book.

General Partnerships

How can you start a business with some friends?

Partnership law is in a developmental stage. A new law called the Revised Uniform Partnership Act (RUPA) has been adopted by many states. However, many states still operate under the traditional Uniform Partnership Act (UPA). This chapter will discuss both laws and point out where the two acts are the same and where they differ. You will need to find out which partnership act your state follows.

Elements of a Partnership

A partnership, according to the RUPA, is an association of two or more persons to carry on as co-owners of a business for profit. This definition differs slightly from the definition in UPA, but both emphasize two essential elements:

- A partnership must involve at least two persons.
- A partnership must carry on a business for profit.

Advantages and Disadvantages of a Partnership

Partnerships have several advantages over sole proprietorships. More capital and credit is usually available to a partnership. The burden of all the work does not fall on one person. A partner does not have sole responsibility for any losses suffered.

A disadvantage to a partnership is that the partners must share the profits. Also, because all partners have a voice in running the

---

Extending the Content

Business Logos

Have students think about starting a business. In addition to naming the business, they will want to create a logo that will be used for signs and business cards. Encourage them to draw their own logo, or to work with an artistic student to describe the design they desire.

Guided Practice

Sole Proprietorships

Ask for volunteers to contact the clerk of your community's city hall to find out what the local laws are concerning starting a new business. Have students report their findings to the class.

business, bickering can cause problems. The biggest disadvantage is that the partners share in the liability. Each partner is responsible for the other partners' actions taken within the scope of the partnership. Partners share in two types of liability.

Contract Liability Partners have joint liability when a contract is made for the partnership. **Joint liability is liability shared by two or more people.** Every partner must be included in a breach of contract case against the partnership.

Tort Liability In a tort case against the partnership, partners have joint and several liability. Joint and several liability means that a tort case can be brought against all of the partners, one of the partners, or any combination of the partners. The partners named in the tort case must pay if they lose in court. If one partner settles the case on his or her own behalf, the rest of the partners are not released from the lawsuit. However, the partner who is actually responsible for the tort may be forced to pay the other partners back.

Forming a General Partnership

A general partnership can be formed in one of two ways: by agreement and by proof of existence.

Partnership by Agreement Forming a general partnership by agreement requires the valid assent of all parties. Such an agreement is usually express and may be written or oral. However, under the Statute of Frauds, if a partnership is to last more than a year, it must be in writing. A partnership formed to sell, buy, or lease real property must also be in writing. The partnership agreement is called the Articles of Partnership.

A partnership that is set to last for a certain period of time or to do a certain job is a term partnership. Partners cannot leave a term partnership until the time has passed or the job is done. A partnership at will means that the partners are free to leave the partnership any time that they want to. No liability follows a partner who leaves such a partnership.

Partnership by Proof of Existence A partnership can also be formed by the way two or more people conduct business together, regardless of what they label the business. For example, if two or more people share the profits of a business venture, it is likely that a partnership exists. This is called a partnership by proof of existence. Both the RUPA and the UPA provide a list of characteristics to show whether a partnership actually exists.

Partnerships An advantage a partnership has over a sole proprietorship is the burden of all the work does not fall on one person. *What is the main disadvantage of a partnership?*

Chapter 16   Forms of Business   **359**

TEACH (cont.)

C Critical Thinking

Liability Ask students to think about what solutions partners may create since they hold liability for each other's actions. (Answers will vary, but students may suggest that partners agree that all or most decisions are to be made jointly.)

D Develop Concepts

Contract Liability Explain to students that partners have liability for the actions of the other partners. Tell students to imagine that a partnership has a contract to provide music for a citywide festival but fails to deliver. Ask students whether they think liability for the breach must be shared by all the partners in the partnership, or whether liability could be assigned to just one partner. (must be shared) Remind students that partners have joint liability when a contract is involved.

Extending the Content

Being a Partner
Ask students to describe their experiences with a group or team. Have them discuss the challenges faced when working with other people and what advantages the arrangement brings. Ask students if they believe a partnership form of business would suit their personality and why or why not.

TEACH (cont.)

Guided Practice

Types of Partners

List the following types of partners who may be involved in a partnership: general, secret, silent, dormant, and limited. Have five students act out being one of the five types of partners. Each student will give a brief presentation of one type of partner, indicating its key characteristic and whether that type has liability. (general—active role, unlimited liability; secret—connection kept secret, unlimited liability; silent—no active role, unlimited liability; dormant—no active part, connection with the firm secret, unlimited liability; limited—no active part, liability extends only to investment amount)

Extending the Content

Famous Partnerships

Have students research a famous business that began as a partnership. Examples include Ben & Jerry's, Hewlett-Packard, Apple Computer, and Proctor & Gamble. Have them write a report that describes the history of the business, the products or services it offers, and information on the founders.

Types of Partners

The law recognizes five types of partners who may be involved in a partnership: general, secret, silent, dormant, and limited. They differ according to how active a role they play in the partnership, whether their role is known to the public, and the amount of liability they have.

General Partner A general partner plays an active role in the management of the partnership and is known to the public. Every partnership must have at least one general partner. A general partner has unlimited liability.

Secret Partner A secret partner is a general partner who has an active role in the management of the partnership, but whose connection with the partnership is kept a secret. A secret partner has unlimited liability.

Silent Partner A silent partner does not play an active role, but is known to the public. A silent partner has unlimited liability.

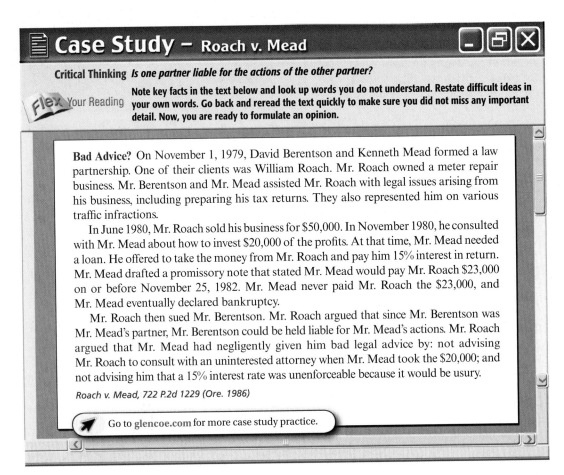

📄 Case Study – Roach v. Mead

Critical Thinking *Is one partner liable for the actions of the other partner?*

Flex Your Reading Note key facts in the text below and look up words you do not understand. Restate difficult ideas in your own words. Go back and reread the text quickly to make sure you did not miss any important detail. Now, you are ready to formulate an opinion.

Bad Advice? On November 1, 1979, David Berentson and Kenneth Mead formed a law partnership. One of their clients was William Roach. Mr. Roach owned a meter repair business. Mr. Berentson and Mr. Mead assisted Mr. Roach with legal issues arising from his business, including preparing his tax returns. They also represented him on various traffic infractions.

In June 1980, Mr. Roach sold his business for $50,000. In November 1980, he consulted with Mr. Mead about how to invest $20,000 of the profits. At that time, Mr. Mead needed a loan. He offered to take the money from Mr. Roach and pay him 15% interest in return. Mr. Mead drafted a promissory note that stated Mr. Mead would pay Mr. Roach $23,000 on or before November 25, 1982. Mr. Mead never paid Mr. Roach the $23,000, and Mr. Mead eventually declared bankruptcy.

Mr. Roach then sued Mr. Berentson. Mr. Roach argued that since Mr. Berentson was Mr. Mead's partner, Mr. Berentson could be held liable for Mr. Mead's actions. Mr. Roach argued that Mr. Mead had negligently given him bad legal advice by: not advising Mr. Roach to consult with an uninterested attorney when Mr. Mead took the $20,000; and not advising him that a 15% interest rate was unenforceable because it would be usury.

Roach v. Mead, 722 P.2d 1229 (Ore. 1986)

✈ Go to **glencoe.com** for more case study practice.

glencoe.com

📄 Case Study

Roach v. Mead

Answer Yes. The Oregon Supreme Court held that under the Oregon version of the Uniform Partnership Act, every partner is an agent of the partnership. Thus, each partner can bind the partnership and the other partners through his or her actions. Of course, the actions of the partner must be related to the partnership. In this case, Mr. Mead was giving advice that Mr. Roach normally received from the partnership, even if it was not entirely legal in nature. The fact that the partnership had prepared Mr. Roach's tax returns meant that the partnership was providing more than strictly legal advice.

Dormant Partner A **dormant** partner is a general partner who takes no active part in the management of the firm and whose connection with the firm is kept secret. A dormant partner, however, still has unlimited liability.

Limited Partner A limited partner is one whose liability does not extend beyond his or her investment. Limited partnerships are discussed later in this section.

Partnership Rights

Partners share certain rights. These rights include the right to use the property, the right to manage the firm, and the right to share in the profits.

Property Rights of the Partners It is important to distinguish between property that belongs to the partnership and property that belongs to individual partners. Property contributed directly to the partnership when the partnership is created is partnership property.

The UPA and the RUPA differ on the right to use property. According to the RUPA: "A partner is not co-owner of partnership property and has no interest in partnership property which can be transferred either voluntarily or involuntarily." Partners are permitted to use partnership property, but the right to use the property is limited to partnership purposes. In contrast, the UPA states that partners are co-owners of all real and personal property included in the partnership. This co-ownership of property, called tenancy in partnership by the UPA, creates certain limitations. For example, a partner cannot personally transfer ownership of property. Also, the property cannot be taken by a partner's personal creditors.

Right to Manage the Firm Unless otherwise stated in the partnership agreement, each partner has an equal voice in managing the firm. Each partner can bind the partnership on any matter within the scope of its business affairs. In a disagreement, the decision of the majority is final. If there is an even number of partners and the vote is split, no decision can be made. If a deadlock persists, the partners might consider ending their partnership.

Right to Share in the Profits Unless otherwise stated in the partnership agreement, partners share equally in the profits, regardless of their initial capital contribution or the time devoted by each partner to the business. This right can be assigned to others. Partners also have a right to reimbursement for any money they personally spend on behalf of the partnership.

Enforcement Rights Under the UPA, partners had three enforcement rights: the right to inspect the firm's books; the right to an account; and the right to dissolve the partnership. The RUPA added a fourth right: a partner has the right to sue a partner or the partnership itself to enforce his or her rights as stated in the partnership agreement or in the RUPA.

S

Chapter 16   Forms of Business   **361**

Reading Check

Analyze What is the difference between limited and unlimited liability?

16.1 SECTION

TEACH (cont.)

S Skills Practice

List Ask students to list the rights of partners. (property, management, share of profits, enforcement) **L1**

Explain Have students explain how the management right operates in a partnership and what partners do if they cannot agree. (Each partner has an equal voice and the right to bind the partnership. If they disagree, majority vote wins. If there is an even number of members and the vote is split, no decision can be made.) **L2**

Classify Ask students to write a paragraph that contrasts the property rights of partners under the RUPA versus the UPA. (Under the RUPA, a partner is not a co-owner of property but has the right to use it only for partnership purposes. The partnership effectively owns the property. Under the UPA, a partner is a co-owner of all partnership property, but cannot transfer or sell it.) **L3**

Reading Check

Analyze Limited liability extends only to the partner's investment in the partnership. Unlimited liability has no limit.

Extending the Content

Types of Partners

Point out to students that a partnership may have more than two partners and may conduct many sorts of operations. As a class, consider some types of partnerships that may have several partners. For example, several doctors may work together in one office and be partners. (accountants, attorneys, architects, dentists)

TEACH (cont.)

D Develop Concepts

Partners' Duties Tell students that if a partner refuses to accept the decision of the other partners, the duty of obedience has been ignored. Ask students what consequences might result. (Answers will vary, but consequences might include the majority of partners voting to expel the dissenting partner, or possibly declaring dissociation if the state follows the RUPA.)

Guided Practice

Partnership Duties

Remind students that the duties of partners are loyalty, obedience, and due care. Ask students to discuss why these three duties are vital to the preservation of a partnership. (Answers will vary, but should emphasize that partners have a fiduciary relationship that creates the duty of loyalty. Having an agreement creates the duty of obedience. Finally, joint liability creates the duty of due care.)

362

Partnership Duties

The RUPA states that partners have three duties: loyalty, obedience, and due care.

The Duty of Loyalty Loyalty is always the first duty because a partnership is a fiduciary relationship, or a relationship based on trust. The RUPA emphasizes loyalty more strongly than the UPA did. According to the RUPA, each partner must:

- tell the partnership about property, profits, or benefits that any partner receives for using partnership property
- avoid dealing with individuals who have any interest that somehow hurts the partnership
- avoid competing with the partnership

A partner does keep the right to look after his or her own interests before the partnership is actually formed.

The Duty of Obedience Once the partners have written the articles of partnership, the partners have the duty to obey those articles. The partners must follow the decisions made by the partners. If a partner disobeys the articles of partnership or partnership decisions, then that partner will be liable for any loss that results.

The Duty of Due Care The duty of due care means that a partner must work to the best of his or her ability, based on his or her talents, education, and experience, when that partner is working on partnership business.

Terminating a Partnership

A partnership may end in a number of ways. A partner may die, go bankrupt, become incapacitated, be expelled by the other partners, or simply wish to leave a partnership. Partners can leave a partnership any time they want to. However, they do not always have the legal right to do so. Whether a partner has the right to leave may depend on whether the partnership is a term partnership or a partnership at will. If the partner does not have the right, he or she may have to pay damages to the other partners.

Dissolution of a Partnership A **dissolution is when a partnership (or any legal entity) breaks up.** Dissolution is not the same as the termination of the business. Dissolution occurs at the moment one partner ceases to be associated with the firm. There are three ways dissolution can happen:

- **By the acts of the partners.** This arises when one partner decides to leave and the other partners agree; when the original agreement had a set time period or goal that has been reached; or when the majority of partners vote to expel a partner.
- **By operation of law.** This arises in cases of bankruptcy or death of a partner.

U Universal Access

English Language Learners Students for whom English is a second language may have trouble distinguishing words with related meanings. For example, learning objectives may require students to identify, explain, or discuss. Inform students that identifying usually involves listing by category, explaining requires giving reasons in a complete form, and discussing requires giving pros and cons.

- **By a court order.** This arises when partners obtain a court order to end the partnership because of misconduct, **incompetence**, or incapacity of a partner.

C

Winding up a Partnership The dissolution of a partnership does not cause it to end immediately. The partnership must close down its business operations, called a winding up. During the winding up period, the business does not continue. The partners perform an accounting of the old firm's affairs, sell the partnership property, pay creditors, and divide what remains of the profits.

D

Dissociation of a Partnership Dissolution does not necessarily end a partnership. Other partners may want to continue the business. If so, a new agreement must be drawn up regarding the conduct of a new firm. There must be an accounting of the old firm's affairs and new financial arrangements must be made regarding the new firm. Public notice must be given to relieve retiring partners from liability for any new debts.

Under the UPA, a partnership ends automatically any time a partner leaves the partnership. The RUPA changed the law by adding a way for a partnership to continue even after a partner leaves, called a dissociation. **A dissociation, according to the RUPA, is when a partner is no longer associated with the firm.** A dissociation allows the business to continue doing business with the remaining partners or with a new partner.

Courdy v. Paycom Billing Services, Inc.
2006 WL 847212 (Cal. Ct. App. 2006)

On July 1, 1997, Edward Courdy and Paycom Billing Services, Inc. (Paycom) entered into a general partnership called Internet Commerce Solutions (ICS). According to the written partnership agreement, the purpose of the partnership was "to engage in the business of Internet Commerce." ICS provided check processing for Internet merchants by taking check information from the merchants and relaying that information to banks. After experiencing problems with the online check processing, Paycom decided to end the partnership. It gave notice on August 12, 1998, that it wished to dissolve the partnership. Six days later, Paycom then notified ICS's clients that it would be providing a new check-processing service plus a credit-card processing service. Courdy sued Paycom on a number of counts, including fraud, arguing that Paycom stole Internet Commerce from ICS when it dissolved the partnership.

Ruling and Resolution
The California Court of Appeals held that the partnership was at will; that is, it could be dissolved at any time. Courdy did not have a right to any damages from profits gained by Paycom from former ICS clients.

Critical Thinking Are partnerships at will a good thing?

Courdy v. Paycom Billing Services, Inc.
Answer At-will partnerships are a lot like at-will employees. Parties may recognize both positive and negative aspects of the at-will situation. If a party is unsatisfied with a partnership, that partner can dissolve the partnership without needing to prove cause. However, as this case demonstrates, at-will partnerships lend themselves to opportunities where one partner leaves and takes the partnership's clients, potentially escaping liability. If a partner is worried about this happening, it is recommended that a written partnership agreement include clauses to prevent this from happening.

TEACH *(cont.)*

C Critical Thinking

Terminating a Partnership
Emphasize that dissolution of partnership is not the same thing as termination of a business. Tell students that if one partner decides to leave and the other partners agree, the partnership is dissolved. Ask students to think of other reasons a partnership might break up, or be dissolved. (bankruptcy, misconduct, incompetence, or incapacity of a partner)

D Develop Concepts

Winding Up a Partnership
Ask students how quickly they think a partnership can be dissolved. (time varies, but can be quite lengthy; partners need to sell property, pay creditors, divide remaining profits)

Guided Practice

Dissociation
Ask students what they think it means to dissociate oneself from a practice or event. (Answers will vary, but students may convey an understanding that dissociation means to separate or remove oneself from a practice or event.) Expand the idea by explaining that when a partner no longer wishes to be associated with the partnership, a dissociation allows the business to continue with the remaining partners or a new partner.

Quiz

Ask students to answer the following questions:

1. What are the three advantages of a sole proprietorship? (ease of formation, total control, one-time taxation of profits)

2. What are the two essential elements of a partnership? (involve at least two persons; carry on a business for profit)

3. How is a limited partner different from all the other types of partners? (has limited liability, while the others have unlimited liability)

RETEACH

Guided Practice

Proof of Existence

Explain to students that extended behaviors and ways of conducting business can constitute the appearance of a partnership, therefore forming one by "proof of existence." Ask students to imagine that Matt began sharing his profits from an auto repair business with Jennifer because of the referrals that she sent his way. Matt shared profits with Jennifer for 13 months. Lead a class discussion on what might happen if Matt suddenly stopped sharing the profits. Has a partnership been formed? Is Jennifer entitled to share profits if she is still actively sending referrals to Matt?

Limited Partnerships Limited partners have no right to manage a partnership, but have only limited liability if the partnership is sued or goes bankrupt. *What happens to a limited partner who gets involved in running a partnership?*

Other Types of Partnerships

The business world constantly adjusts to the changing needs of the marketplace. As a result, several types of partnerships that differ from general partnerships are now legally recognized.

Limited Partnerships Limited partnerships are controlled by provisions of the Revised Uniform Limited Partnership Act (RULPA). **A limited partnership is a partnership formed by two or more persons, with one or more general partners and one or more limited partners.** The general partners of a limited partnership have the same types of duties as a general partner in a general partnership. Limited partners are investors who have no right to manage the partnership.

Limited partnerships must meet stricter formalities than general partnerships. The names of the limited partners cannot appear in the partnership name. The partners must file a certificate of limited partnership with the appropriate state or county office. The business name must indicate that it is a limited partnership. This is to warn third parties that some partners have only limited liability.

In terms of liability, the limited partnership falls between the general partnership, in which all owners have unlimited liability, and the corporation, in which all owners have limited liability. When a limited partnership ends, the assets are first distributed to creditors of the firm, and then to the partners.

Registered Limited Liability Partnerships **A limited liability partnership (LLP) is a registered partnership in which each partner is not liable for the acts of the other partners.** Partners can escape joint and several liability for the torts, wrongful acts, negligence, or misconduct of other partners by registering with the appropriate state office. The registration statement usually includes the following information:

▲ USING VISUALS

Limited Partnerships Answer If a limited partner becomes involved in the daily operations of a partnership, he or she may lose the protection of limited liability. It is the general partners who have the duties of operation of the partnership. Limited partners are investors who have no right to manage the partnership. In exchange for that limited participation, they have limited liability for the debts of the partnership. Creditors of the company are informed that certain partners have only limited liability in the certificate of limited partnership that is filed with the appropriate state or county office.

- the name of the partnership
- the purpose of the partnership
- the number of partners in the partnership
- a statement of the intent to form an LLP
- the address of the partnership's main place of business
- the name and address of a statutory agent for service of process

All the partners, or at least the partners holding a majority interest in the partnership, must file the statement. The registration statement must be updated annually. LLPs are taxed in the same way as general partnerships.

Partnership-Type Business Organizations

Other partnership-type business organizations include limited partnership associations and joint ventures.

Limited Partnership Associations A limited partnership association is like a corporation in that it is considered an entity having an existence all its own. The participants own shares in the association and can convey their shares to another individual as long as the other participants vote to accept the new individual. The participants can lose only the amount of their initial investment. Not every state has made statutory provisions for limited partnership associations.

Joint Ventures A joint venture is a business enterprise in which two or more participants combine in order to complete a single task. There is no ongoing relationship in a joint venture, unlike a partnership.

After You Read

Summarize What are the different types of partners?

After You Read

Summarize general, secret, silent, dormant, and limited

ASSESS

Self-Assessment

Have students go to the *Business and Personal Law* Online Learning Center through **glencoe.com** to take the Section 16.1 Practice Test.

CLOSE

Culminating Activity

Who Is a Partner?
Offer the following scenario to students: Jon and Carla own and operate a partnership, for which Jon's wife, Teresa, keeps the books. Jon has given Teresa the power to transact business on behalf of the partnership. Was he correct in doing so? (No. Teresa is not a partner, and is not authorized to make decisions or contract for the business.)

SECTION **16.1** ASSESSMENT

Self Check

1. What is a sole proprietorship?
2. What is a partnership?
3. What is a limited partnership?

Academic Connection

English Language Arts Get together with three other members of the class to form a partnership. Decide what kind of business you want to go into, what kind of

partnership to create, and how much each partner will invest. Then decide how the duties of managing the business might be divided, what kind of partner each person will be, and how the profits will be split. For example, one partner might want to be a secret partner and another a dormant partner. One partner might want to focus on running the day-to-day operations of the business and the other focus on bringing in

business. Write up a brief partnership agreement laying out what you decide.

Critical Thinking

Extent of Liability
Suppose you are running a sole proprietorship in a building that you have just purchased. The floor collapses and injures several customers. Will your losses be limited to the amount of money in your company's business accounts?

 Go to **glencoe.com** to check your answers.

SECTION **16.1** ASSESSMENT

Self Check

1. form of business owned and operated by one person
2. association of two or more persons to carry on as co-owners of a business for profit

3. a partnership having one or more general partners and one or more limited partners

Academic Connection

English Language Arts
Partnership agreements will vary.

Critical Thinking

No. A sole proprietor has unlimited liability, so the owner's personal property may also be at risk.

 Activity correlated to the English Language Arts standard on page 356

FOCUS

Bell Ringer Activity

Pass out a variety of magazines and newspapers to the class. Ask students to clip advertisements, articles, and logos for major corporations that are familiar to them. Arrange the clippings on a bulletin board and use these as real-world examples as you discuss the topics of the chapter.

Preteaching

Key Terms
Read the definitions and ask students to create a sentence using each term.

Academic Vocabulary
Explain that developing vocabulary is key to academic success. An efficient method to develop vocabulary is to study how words are formed.

- **domestic** Adjective, from the Latin *domus* (house). Means internal to a country.
- **process** Noun, from the Latin *processus* (to advance). Means a series of actions to obtain a result.
- **similar** Adjective, from the Latin *similis* (like). Means alike but not identical.

Activity Ask students to give a noun, a verb, an adjective, or an adverb form that comes from each word.

Connects to academic content

What You'll Learn

- ◆ Characterize corporations.
- ◆ Explain the different types of corporations.
- ◆ Discuss the steps involved in forming a corporation.
- ◆ Explain what a limited liability company is.
- ◆ List the steps in forming a limited liability company.

Why It's Important

Knowing how to form a corporation or limited liability company will help you if you want to expand your business.

Academic Standards

Reading and completing the activities in this section will help you practice the following academic standards:

Math (NCTM NOS 2a) Judge the effects of such operations as multiplication, division, and computing powers and roots on the magnitudes of quantities.

Social Studies (NCSS 5) Study interactions among individuals, groups, and institutions.

Reading Guide

Before You Read

Connect How many different corporations can you name?

Focus on Ideas
A corporation is treated by law as a person.

Take Notes
Create a graph like the one shown and use it to take notes as you read this section. Go to **glencoe.com** to find graphic organizers and tips on how to improve your note-taking skills.

Key Terms
You will learn these legal words and expressions in this chapter. You can also find these terms in *Black's Law Dictionary* or in an online legal dictionary.

- corporation
- share
- shareholder
- articles of incorporation
- certificate of incorporation
- limited liability company (LLC)
- expropriation

Academic Vocabulary
You will find these words in your readings and in your tests. Look them up in a dictionary and familiarize yourself with them.

- domestic
- process
- similar

 glencoe.com

R Reading Strategy

Read for Knowledge

1. **Survey** or preread the chapter.
2. **Question** or formulate questions before you read.
3. **Recite** or read your questions, answers, and notes out loud.
4. **Review** or reread your notes.

Note-Taking Basics
- Listen attentively
- Have note-taking materials ready
- Skim through the lesson material
- Write down key words and ideas
- Anticipate what comes next
- Review notes soon after taking them

Corporations

Are all corporations giant multi-national companies?

A corporation is an entity with the legal authority to act as a single person, distinct from its owners. Unlike a sole proprietorship or partnership, a corporation is treated by law as if it is an individual person. It can make contracts, buy and sell goods, sue, and be sued.

All corporations have the same basic form. Ownership of a corporation is divided into shares. **A share is a single unit of ownership of a corporation. A shareholder is an individual who owns shares of a corporation.** Each shareholder has one vote for each share of stock that he or she owns in the corporation. Shareholders elect a board of directors who run the corporation.

Advantages and Disadvantages of a Corporation

Corporations have several advantages. A corporation can obtain a great deal of capital by selling shares, while general partnerships and sole proprietorships cannot. Each shareholder's liability is limited to the amount of money he or she paid for shares in the corporation. Corporations also have perpetual existence. This means that a corporation continues to exist after the founders, shareholders, managers, and directors are gone.

Corporations also have disadvantages. First, a corporation's income may be taxed more than once: the corporation is taxed on the profits it makes, and then the shareholders are taxed on the dividends (share of the profits) they receive. This is called double taxation. Second, corporations face numerous government regulations and are looked at very closely. Finally, the original founders of the corporation can lose control and ownership of the corporation to the shareholders or the board of directors.

Types of Corporations

Not all corporations are large. In fact, about 40 percent of all corporations have fewer that five employees. Corporations may be classified as public or private corporations, stock or nonstock corporations, and domestic, foreign, or alien corporations (see **Figure 16.1** on page 368).

Public Corporations Public corporations include incorporated political units, such as towns, villages, cities, and school districts. These entities often incorporate to obtain the protections of this form of business organization, such as limited liability.

Private Corporations Private corporations are owned by private individuals and may be for profit or nonprofit. For profit corporations are organized for the purpose of making money. A for profit corporation may be either a C corporation or an S corporation. A C corporation is a standard corporation and the type subject to double taxation: the corporation is taxed on its income and the shareholders are taxed on their dividends.

 glencoe.com

Chapter 16   Forms of Business   **367**

TEACH

Discussion Starter

Class Discussion

Ask students to predict how corporations might differ from sole proprietorships and partnerships. Pose questions on the legal structure, taxation, and ownership of corporations compared to other business forms.

As You Read

Predict What are the disadvantages of a corporation?

As You Read

Predict To help students answer this question, have them imagine the operations, accounting, and taxation of a large corporation such as Microsoft. (founders lose control to directors and stockholders, income is taxed more than once, face many government regulations)

 Legal Talk

De jure: *adj* Latin for as a matter of law.
De facto: *adj* Latin for as a matter of fact.

Vocabulary Builder In class, list as many words as you can think of in two minutes that come from the Latin root *jure*. Then, compare your list with the rest of the class.

Look It Up! Check definitions in *Black's Law Dictionary* or an online glossary. For direct links, go to **glencoe.com** to find more vocabulary resources.

Legal Talk

(judge, jury, judicial, adjudicate, justice, injustice, jurisprudence, injury)

Ask students to practice their academic and legal vocabulary with the electronic flashcards available at the *Business and Personal Law* Online Learning Center through glencoe.com.

Extending the Content

Corporate Stock

Ask students to raise their hands if they or members of their family own stock in a corporation. Ask students why they think people buy stock. (to profit from selling them at a higher price, to save for retirement with anticipation of increased value, or to receive income from dividends)

TEACH *(cont.)*

D Develop Concepts

Corporate Entity Remind students that a corporation is an artificial entity. Ask them why it is important that a corporation have a unique identity. (Answers will vary, but students may suggest that this form allows the government to tax the corporation rather than the stockholders. It allows for a separate legal liability as well.)

U Universal Access

Visual/Spatial Learners Explain to students that corporations can be classified as either private or public. Private corporations may operate for profit or as a nonprofit company. Draw two circles on the board to illustrate the categories of public and private corporations. Then, intersect the private corporation circle, representing the idea that a private corporation may be nonprofit or for profit.

W Writing Support

Prevalence of Corporations Divide students into three groups. Have one group draft a letter to your secretary of state's office to find out how many new corporations are organized each year in your state. Have the other two groups draft similar letters to other states. Compare responses and discuss reasons for differences.

368

Figure 16.1 Types of Corporations

D **Private** Most corporations are privately held corporations. They are organized to make a profit and are usually owned by a small group of private individuals.

U **Public** A public corporation is a corporation created by the federal, state, or local government for governmental purposes, or a large private corporation that sells its stock to the general public.

W **Nonprofit** A nonprofit corporation, such as Habitat for Humanity, is formed for educational, religious, charitable, or social purposes. Membership is acquired by agreement, rather than by acquisition of stock, and no stockholder may share in the profits.

There are different types of corporations, but they all have the same form. *What is the difference between a domestic and a foreign corporation?*

368   Unit 6   Starting a Business

▲ USING VISUALS

➜ **Figure 16.1 Types of Corporations** Answer A corporation is considered domestic in the state in which it is incorporated and foreign in all other states.

Activity Have students use the Internet, your school's media center, or your local library to find news articles about local corporations near you. Ask students to summarize the articles and then share them with the class.

An S corporation is a special type of corporation that avoids double taxation. With an S corporation, the corporation itself does not pay income tax and the shareholders pay tax on their share of the income as if they were partners. However, an S corporation has limitations on the number of shareholders it can have.

Nonprofit corporations are formed for educational, religious, charitable, or social purposes. A nonprofit corporation in which membership is acquired by agreement, rather than by the sale and acquisition of stock, is called a nonstock corporation.

Domestic, Foreign, and Alien Corporations A corporation is considered a **domestic** corporation in the state in which it is incorporated. In any other state in which it operates, a corporation is considered a foreign corporation. An alien corporation is one that is incorporated in another country but does business in this country.

Forming a Corporation

Creating a corporation requires extensive paperwork according to each state's laws. Corporations can choose any state to incorporate in, even if they do not do business in that state. Despite differences, in the requirements of different states, there are many common procedures to the incorporation **process**.

Corporate Promoters A corporate promoter is someone who organizes the new corporation. The promoter may help assemble investors, lease office and warehouse space, purchase supplies and equipment, and hire employees. Promoters are personally liable for the contracts they make in the name of the corporation.

Choosing a Corporate Name The name of a corporation must include the word *corporation*, *incorporated*, or *company*, or the abbreviation for one of these words. A corporation cannot use the name of another corporation, foreign or domestic. In some states, the name cannot be **similar** to another business name in use.

Articles of Incorporation **The articles of incorporation is a legal document filed with the state to establish a corporation.** It describes the corporation's organization, powers, and authority. This can sometimes be done online. There may be a requirement to have a minimum amount of capital, such as $500 to $1,000. After the application is filed and fees are paid to the office of the secretary of state, the company will receive a certificate of incorporation. **A certificate of incorporation is a corporation's official authorization to do business in a state.** In some states, the certificate is called a charter.

Structure of the Corporation The shareholders of a new corporation elect a board of directors. The board elects a chairman and the top officers of the corporation. The officers manage the company and carry out the board's policies and decisions. Officers can be members of the board, or they may be hired employees.

Vocabulary You can find vocabulary definitions in the **Key Terms** glossary and **Academic Vocabulary** glossary in the back of this book.

16.2 SECTION

TEACH (cont.)

D Develop Concepts

Forming a Corporation
Ask students to recall the steps for forming a sole proprietorship. Then review with them the four steps for forming a corporation: promoters, corporate name, articles of incorporation, and structure. Ask students to speculate on the types of problems that might surface during this process. (promoter gives up or runs out of money, business name already taken, application to incorporate denied, lost or incomplete paperwork, problems appointing a board of directors)

Reading Check

Discuss The corporate name must include the word corporation, incorporated, or company. It cannot be similar to another corporate name, domestic or foreign.

Extending the Content

Incorporation
Obtain an application for incorporation from your secretary of state's office. Discuss with students the kinds of information required on the application and help them fill it out as if they are preparing to incorporate a business.

ASSESS

Quiz

Ask students to answer the following questions:

1. What does "perpetual existence" refer to? (The corporation continues to exist after the founders, shareholders, managers, and directors are gone.)

2. What is the difference between a C corporation and an S corporation? (The C corporation is subject to double taxation; the S corporation is not.)

3. What is the difference between a domestic and a foreign corporation? (A corporation is domestic in the state in which it incorporates. It is foreign in the other states in which it operates.)

4. What is a corporate promoter? (someone who organizes the new corporation)

RETEACH

Guided Practice

S Corporations

Present the class with the following scenario: Kate, a small business owner, complains to you that she is being taxed twice: her corporation and herself as an individual owner. Ask your class: "Is there a type of business entity that you could recommend to Kate that would avoid double taxation?" (Yes. A sub-chapter S corporation would allow Kate to only be taxed at the individual owner's level.)

Review Key Terms

Encourage students to access the *Business and Personal Law* Online Learning Center through glencoe.com and use the electronic flashcards to review the key terms.

STUDY TO GO Have students go to the *Business and Personal Law* Online Learning Center through glencoe.com to download free Study-to-Go content to their cell phones or PDAs.

Global Law

Brazilian Corporations

In 2002, the country of Brazil updated its corporation laws by passing the New Civil Code, Law 10.406. Under that system, there are many different business organizational structures. However, there are two main forms that make up the majority of businesses.

Limitadas

A *sociedade por quotas de responsabilidade limitada (limitada)* is similar to a limited liability company, limited partnership, or closely-held company in the United States. By law, a *limitada* must have at least two partners. Partners can be either individuals or legal entities.

The articles of association for a *limitada* must state the *limitada's* name and for what period of time the business has been created. It must also state the company's main activities and the location of its main place of business.

Finally, the *limitada* can be managed by all the partners, some of the partners, or by only one partner. The only requirement is that power to run the company must be in the hands of at least one legal resident of Brazil.

Sociedade anônima

The *sociedade anônima* is like a joint-stock company or corporation in the United States. Like a *limitada,* the *sociedade anônima* requires no less than two partners. However, there are additional requirements to forming one.

For example, all the documents relating to the formation of a *sociedade anônima* must be filed at the commercial registry. It must then be published in the *Official Gazette* and in a second major newspaper in the region where the company will be located.

Finally, shareholders of stock in *sociedade anônimas* have the following rights: the right to the company's profits; the right to distribution of the company's assets, if the company is dissolved; and the right to oversee the company's management.

> **Across Cultures: Ethanol Fuel**
>
> As the rest of the world is struggling to get enough oil for its energy needs, Brazil has shifted its focus from petroleum to ethanol. At least 20% of Brazilian cars run on pure ethanol, which is produced in Brazil from sugar cane. Many countries are looking to follow Brazil's lead in the future.

Critical Thinking: *Is publishing the documents for forming a new corporation in a newspaper a good idea?*

Incorporation Problems

If the incorporation process has been completed, the corporation legally exists and it is known as a *de jure* corporation. However, sometimes mistakes or problems interrupt the incorporation process. Although the corporation does not legally exist, some states will still recognize it as a *de facto* corporation as long as the incorporators made a good faith attempt to incorporate.

Piercing the Corporate Veil

The corporate entity can be seen as a veil protecting the shareholders from liability. Under some circumstances, however, the court will "pierce the corporate veil" and hold shareholders personally liable. This happens when a corporation is formed to avoid paying debt or is run like a sole proprietorship. The court will also hold shareholders liable if they use corporate assets for their own purposes or commit fraud in the corporation's name.

Global Law

Brazilian Corporations

Answer Answers will vary. The benefit to the notice is that individuals or other businesses would be aware that another company is being established. The Brazilian system is different from that used in the United States, which requires no notice. However, the publication is similar to the legal notices published today in American newspapers.

Activity Have students use the Internet or a local library to research the types of corporations that are allowed in Canada, Britain, Australia, or other English-speaking countries. Ask students to make an oral report to the class on how corporations must be established in such a country.

Limited Liability Companies

Are there any other ways you could set up your own company?

A **limited liability company (LLC) is an entity with the legal authority to act as a single person, distinct from its owners, and combines the best features of a partnership and a corporation.** Like a corporation, it offers limited liability to its owners. Like the partners in a partnership, the owners of an LLC escape double taxation.

The first step in forming an LLC is to draw up the articles of organization. The LLC must have a statutory agent within the state where it is organized. Filing fees must also be paid.

The dissolution of an LLC is similar to a partnership and can occur for any of the same reasons. It must also be followed by a winding up to put the LLC officially out of business. However, a winding up need not follow a dissolution if the remaining members want to continue the LLC.

Doing Business Internationally

What do you think you would need to do to create a company abroad?

Different countries have different tax codes and different laws regarding establishing a business. For example, many countries have favorable corporate tax laws designed to attract corporations there. On the other hand, the LLC form of business does not exist in most countries. Businesses in other countries are also subject to expropriation. **Expropriation is when a government seizes a privately-owned business to be used for a public purpose.**

After You Read

Summarize What are the different types of corporations?

After You Read

Summarize public, private, profit, nonprofit

ASSESS

Self-Assessment

Have students go to the *Business and Personal Law* Online Learning Center through glencoe.com to take the Section 16.2 Practice Test.

CLOSE

Culminating Activity

Forming an S Corporation

Tell students to imagine that Mr. Chang wanted to set up a for-profit corporation that would protect him from personal liability, yet allow him to raise funds from a stock offering. He seeks to avoid double taxation. What type of corporation might he choose? (S corporation) What restriction would he face? (limited number of stockholders allowed)

SECTION 16.2 ASSESSMENT

Self Check

1. What is a corporation?

2. What is the difference between a public and a private corporation?

3. What is a limited liability company?

Academic Connection

Mathematics The Miller Metal Products Corporation manufactures hand-held can openers. It plans to manufacture

750,000 can openers to be sold at $0.44 each. The fixed costs to make them are $142,570. The variable costs to make them are $0.19 each. How many can openers must Miller Metal Products sell to break even?

THEORY **Number and Operations:** To find the break-even point in units, use the following formula:

Total Fixed Costs ÷ (Selling Price per Unit − Variable Costs per Unit)

 For more math practice, go to the Math Appendix.

Critical Thinking

Changing Form Why might a sole proprietorship or a partnership want to incorporate?

 Go to **glencoe.com** to check your answers.

SECTION 16.2 ASSESSMENT

Self Check

1. legal entity formed by law; distinct from its owners

2. public corporations—formed by towns, cities, or other public organizations; private corporations—privately owned, may be for profit or nonprofit

3. hybrid form of business that merges corporate protection of limited liability with single taxation of a partnership

Academic Connection

Mathematics
570,280 units

Critical Thinking

may seek to gain the limited liability of corporations, gain access to more capital, or increase exposure

 Activity correlated to the Mathematics standard on page 366

Summary by Sections

Ask students to read the summaries one key point at a time. Then, ask them to work in groups to create two examples to illustrate each key point.

Vocabulary Builder

Cooperative Learning

1. Have students work in groups to prepare their sentences. Ask the groups to exchange their sentences and assess each other's sentences.

Vocabulary Development

- Ask students to use a dictionary or to go online to look up the etymology of each key term listed.
- Then, ask students to list several words derived from the same root or origin. For example, *contract* has the same root as *contractual* or *contractually*.

Summary

Section 16.1 Sole Proprietorships and Partnerships

- ◆ A sole proprietorship is a form of business that is owned and operated by one person.
- ◆ A partnership is an association of two or more persons to carry on as co-owners of a business for profit.
- ◆ General partnerships can be formed by agreement or by proof of existence.
- ◆ There are five types of partners: general, secret, silent, dormant, and limited.
- ◆ Partners have three duties: to be loyal to the firm; to be obedient to the arrangements made by the partnership agreement; and to act with due care in carrying out the business of the firm.
- ◆ Partnerships can end through dissociation and dissolution.

Section 16.2 Corporations and Limited Liability Companies

- ◆ A corporation is an entity with the legal authority to act as a single person, distinct from its owners.
- ◆ A shareholder is an individual who owns shares of a corporation.
- ◆ A share is a single unit of ownership of a corporation.
- ◆ Corporations may be classified as public or private corporations, stock or nonstock corporations, and domestic, foreign, or alien corporations.
- ◆ A limited liability company (LLC) is an entity with the legal authority to act as a single person, distinct from its owners, and combines the best features of a partnership and a corporation.

Vocabulary Builder

❶ On a sheet of paper, use each of these terms in a sentence.

Key Terms

- sole proprietorship
- unlimited liability
- partnership
- joint liability
- dissolution

- dissociation
- limited partnership
- limited liability partnership (LLP)
- corporation
- share

- shareholder
- articles of incorporation
- certificate of incorporation
- limited liability company (LLC)
- expropriation

Academic Vocabulary

- perpetual
- dormant

- incompetence
- domestic

- process
- similar

 Go to **glencoe.com** to play a game and improve your legal vocabulary.

Study Skills for Success

Prepare Your Students for Studying

Tell students that they can improve their ability to understand and remember material from their courses by learning and practicing study skills. Remind students to:

- **Get motivated!** Motivation must come from within. To motivate yourself, think of ways in which what you learn now will fit into your long-term personal and professional goals.
- **Get organized!** Make studying part of your daily routine, not something you do at the last minute.
- **Concentrate!** Study in an environment that is as free of distractions as possible.

Key Points Review

Answer the following questions. Refer to the chapter for additional reinforcement.

2 What are the advantages and disadvantages of a sole proprietorship?

3 What is unlimited liability?

4 What are the advantages of forming a partnership?

5 What is the difference between a term partnership and a partnership at will?

6 What are the advantages of a corporation?

7 What are the steps in the formation of a corporation?

8 What are the articles of incorporation?

9 What is needed to form an LLC?

Standardized Test Practice

10 Read the following information about the concept of micro-enterprise development and complete questions 1 and 2.

The concept of micro-enterprise development has its roots in the recognition of a previously untapped market—skilled or motivated individuals who could provide desired services to the public but lacked access to traditional forms of credit and, in many cases, business and financial expertise. The micro-enterprise theory is simple. Loan these individuals small amounts of money for business start-up costs, make the loan terms affordable, and give them business training and support. This formula has proven to be a success.

Today the term micro-enterprise is commonly used to describe a business with up to five employees, which requires $25,000 or less in start-up capital, and does not have access to the traditional commercial banking sector. Many aspiring micro-entrepreneurs have little formal business training and varying levels of education. Training and technical assistance can often be the biggest factor in the success of a new business.

1. Which statement best describes what a micro-enterprise is?

A a group of individuals who invest in small business concepts

B business counselors who work with entrepreneurs to start companies

C technical assistants who guide entrepreneurs with technology problems

D small businesses with few employees that need minimal start-up capital

2. Often the biggest factor to the success of a micro-enterprise is the

A ability to have an endless supply of funds

B ability to offer training and technical assistance

C ability to have new entrepreneurs be self-sufficient

D ability to provide raw materials and employees

 Test-Taking Strategies Notes that are complete and well organized, with key terms defined and highlighted, will make reviewing for a test easier.

---

16 Chapter

Review and Assessment

Key Points Review

2. advantages: ease of creation, total control, retention of profits, and one-time taxation of profits; disadvantages: limited capital, unlimited liability, and limited lifetime

3. The owner is personally responsible for all losses experienced by the business.

4. more capital and credit, distribution of work, and less responsibility

5. term partnership: established to last for a certain period of time; partnership at will: partners are free to leave at any time

6. ability to raise capital; shareholders' liability is limited; perpetual existence

7. find promoter, choose a name, prepare articles of incorporation and file them, pay fees, elect board of directors and officers

8. document that describes a corporation's organization, powers, and authority

9. articles of organization, a statutory agent, and payment of filing fees

---

Standardized Test Practice

10. D and B

 Strategies for Standardized Test Prep Success

Whether your students have a standardized test coming up in a few days or a few weeks, these last-minute test-prep tips and strategies will help them relax and do their best.

• **Test Format** Help students become familiar with the format of the test by practicing with test items that imitate the actual test items as closely as possible.

• **Test Timing** Have your students take timed practice tests so that they become comfortable with the length, design, and timing of the actual test.

Chapter 16

Review and Assessment

 Apply and Debate

Students should use chapter content to arrive at conclusions. The legal resolutions are listed below:

11. No. It is likely that Ruth is infringing on Mark's registered business name. The fact that his store is not open is not relevant.

12. No. Even though Ming did not agree, he remained in the partnership rather than resign. He is still involved in the suit.

13. Yes. Tasha receives profits from the business and participates in its management. Due to the proof of existence doctrine, she will probably be considered part of the partnership.

14. While verbal communications are difficult to prove, Luca's lawyer might be able to make such a case as long as Luca had something somewhere in writing.

15. Yes. It is legal to incorporate, as long as you follow all necessary procedures.

 Apply and Debate

Read the following scenarios. Get together with other students in pairs or groups of three and take a position on each scenario. Debate your position in class with students taking the opposite position or prepare a written argument justifying your position.

11 Who Owns a Name

Mark registered the business name Crazy Cookies, but did not open his bakery right away. When Ruth later opened Crazy Cool Cookies, Mark sued her for infringing on his registered business name.

You Debate Should Ruth be allowed to use the business name? Why or why not?

12 Disagreeing Partner

Ming was one of four general partners in a business. The other partners voted to terminate a contract. Ming disagreed, fearing they might be sued. They were.

You Debate If you were one of the other partners, would you excuse Ming from being held liable in the lawsuit as partnership law requires since he had disagreed?

13 Widow Partner

Tasha's husband was a partner in a store. When he died, the other partners continued to pay Tasha for his share of the profits. Tasha eventually decided to go into the store everyday to help. One day, a patron tripped in the store and sued.

You Debate If you were the lawyer for the suing patron, would you make a case that Tasha is also one of the partners?

14 Lost Letter

Luca filed to incorporate his company. He was told that the charter was in the mail. He began his business. Later, when he was sued for an accident, he learned that the state had never mailed the incorporation charter and he was not protected.

You Debate If you were the lawyer for Luca, would you defend him by saying that he was told that his business was incorporated?

15 Putting on a Corporate Veil

Your sole proprietorship company has debts of $200,000 but only $27,000 in cash. You consider incorporating to protect yourself, in case your creditors sue you for failure to pay.

You Debate Is it legal and valid to incorporate to get the protections under law, even though you know you may not be able to pay your debts?

C Critical Thinking

Corporate Veil Martin Grumman started a small publishing company as a sole proprietor. Last year, he incorporated and appointed himself and his wife to be on the board of directors. However, he has not conducted annual meetings, and his wife has no say in the company. This year he published a book that claims a local politician accepted bribes. The politician sues Martin for libel and defamation of character.

Debate Practice

- Is Martin's corporation valid? (Probably not. Although he paid the fees and has the articles of incorporation, he is still running the business as a sole proprietor.)

- Can the politician pierce the corporate veil to sue Martin personally? (Probably. If the politician can show that Martin's corporation was a sham, he can hold Martin personally liable.)

Case Study Practice– Hurwitz v. Padden

16 When Does a Partnership End? In September 1991, Thomas Hurwitz and Michael Padden formed a two-person law firm. They failed to enter into a written partnership agreement, but orally agreed to share all firm proceeds on a 50-50 basis. They also agreed to split all costs and fees on a 50-50 basis. In January 1993, Mr. Hurwitz and Mr. Padden changed their firm from a partnership to a limited liability company. On February 15, 1996, Mr. Padden notified Mr. Hurwitz that he wanted to dissolve the firm effective March 1, 1996. The two men resolved all the business issues involving their relationship except for a batch of attorneys' fees from several of the firm's cases, which Mr. Padden worked on after he gave notice of termination. Mr. Padden argued that since he worked on the cases after dissolution began, he was entitled to additional fees. Mr. Hurwitz argued that during dissolution, fees are split the same as they were prior to dissolution.

Source: Hurwitz v. Padden, 581 N.W.2d 359 (Minn. Ct. App. 1998)

Practice How should the fees be split?

17 Ethics
←?→ Application

Conflict of Interest? Moesha Allen is co-owner of a small restaurant in a partnership at will. She is planning on leaving the partnership and opening her own restaurant in a couple of months. Her favorite customers keep asking her about her plans for the future.

◆ Is Moesha entitled to tell her customers about her new restaurant or will it appear as if she is trying to steal customers?

18 Internet
Application

Read about Forming a Partnership Layla and Denyce both operate small gift shops in nearby shopping centers. They decide they might as well open one big gift shop by combining their resources and assets while lowering their monthly overhead costs.

 Go to **glencoe.com** to access the Web site sponsored by QuickForms to see how to write up a partnership agreement. With a partner, discuss how you would handle creating a partnership agreement that Layla and Denyce could use for their gift shop.

Reading Connection
Outside Reading Go to **glencoe.com** for a list of outside reading suggestions about forming a business.

R

Review and Assessment

←?→ Ethics Application

17. Moesha is still a partner in the current restaurant and thus has a duty of obedience to the partnership. Rather than giving any appearance of trying to steal customers, it would be better for her to leave the current partnership, which she can easily do at any time because it is at-will.

Internet Application

18. Some of the items to be discussed when setting up a partnership are: name of partnership; itemized contributions of cash or property; allocations of profits and losses; partners' authority and decision making; management duties; admitting new partners; withdrawal or death of partner; resolving disputes.

R Reading Strategy

Reading Connection

American Bar Association Resources

Go to the *Business and Personal Law* Online Learning Center through glencoe.com to find links for further readings that relate to this chapter. Ask students to read, review, and summarize the documents. Advise students to keep their reviews and summaries to use as reference material for their Unit Thematic Project on pages 432–433.

Case Study Practice

16. The Minnesota Court of Appeals held that since the dissolution of an LLC is the same as the dissolution of a partnership, the UPA should govern. Absent the existence of a contract to the contrary, under the UPA no partner is entitled to additional pay for doing a job that he or she would have done prior to the dissolution. Even if Mr. Padden had been the only one to work on the cases prior to dissolution, he and Mr. Hurwitz would have split the fees earned from those cases evenly. Therefore, the additional fees should be divided evenly.

Plan Your Lesson Section by Section

NBEA	NATIONAL BUSINESS LAW STANDARDS
Section 17.1	• **Describe** the functions of the board of directors and officers of a corporation with regard to control of corporate affairs. • **Identify** shareholder rights (e.g., right to receive dividends, right to vote, right to inspect the books) and preemptive rights. • **Explain** the nature of the shareholders' liability. • **Describe** when promoters, directors, and officers are liable to the corporation, shareholders, and third persons.
Section 17.2	• **Differentiate** between common and preferred stock. • **Differentiate** between types of corporate expansion (e.g., mergers, consolidations, and conglomerates). • **Describe** the ways corporate existence may be terminated.

NCLB	ACADEMIC STANDARDS	Activity/Feature
	English Language Arts: NCTE 3 Apply a wide range of strategies to comprehend, interpret, evaluate, and appreciate texts.	*BusinessWeek* News, Case Study, Case Study Practice
	English Language Arts: NCTE 9 Develop an understanding of and respect for diversity in language use, patterns, and dialects across cultures, ethnic groups, geographic regions, and social roles.	Global Law
	English Language Arts: NCTE 6 Apply knowledge of language structure, language conventions, media techniques, figurative language, and genre to create, critique, and discuss print and non-print texts.	Legal Talk, ad copy, Key Terms, and Academic Vocabulary
	English Language Arts: NCTE 7 Conduct research on issues and interests by generating ideas and questions, and by posing problems.	Section 17.1 Assessment
	Mathematics: NCTM CS 12 Communicate mathematical thinking coherently and clearly to peers, teachers, and others.	Section 17.2 Assessment
	English Language Arts: NCTE 10 Students whose first language is not English make use of their first language to develop competency in the English language arts and to develop understanding of content across the curriculum.	Key Terms, Academic Vocabulary, Legal Talk, Vocabulary Builder
	English Language Arts: NCTE 1 Read a wide range of print and non-print texts to build an understanding of texts; to acquire new information; to respond to the needs and demands of society and the workplace; and for personal fulfillment.	Global Law
	Social Studies: NCSS 5 Study interactions among individuals, groups, and institutions.	Global Law
	Social Studies: NCSS 6 Study how people create and change structures of power, authority, and governance.	Case Study

Connect Your Business Law Classroom to the World of Work

This chart shows the 21st Century Skills, foundation skills, and workplace competencies that students develop as they work in this chapter.

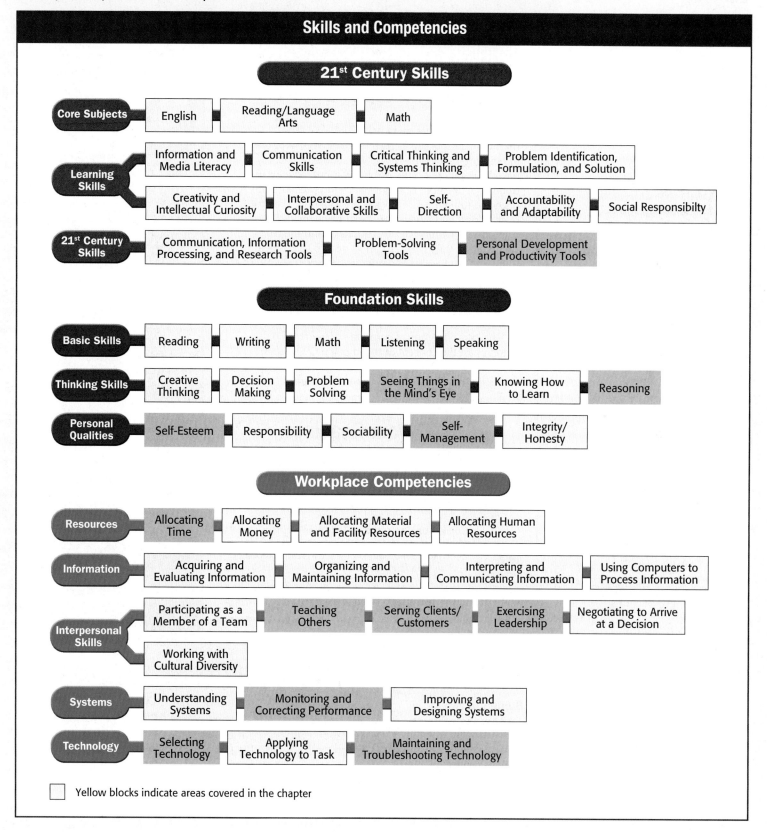

Skills and Competencies

21st Century Skills

Core Subjects
- English
- Reading/Language Arts
- Math

Learning Skills
- Information and Media Literacy
- Communication Skills
- Critical Thinking and Systems Thinking
- Problem Identification, Formulation, and Solution
- Creativity and Intellectual Curiosity
- Interpersonal and Collaborative Skills
- Self-Direction
- Accountability and Adaptability
- Social Responsibilty

21st Century Skills
- Communication, Information Processing, and Research Tools
- Problem-Solving Tools
- Personal Development and Productivity Tools

Foundation Skills

Basic Skills
- Reading
- Writing
- Math
- Listening
- Speaking

Thinking Skills
- Creative Thinking
- Decision Making
- Problem Solving
- Seeing Things in the Mind's Eye
- Knowing How to Learn
- Reasoning

Personal Qualities
- Self-Esteem
- Responsibility
- Sociability
- Self-Management
- Integrity/Honesty

Workplace Competencies

Resources
- Allocating Time
- Allocating Money
- Allocating Material and Facility Resources
- Allocating Human Resources

Information
- Acquiring and Evaluating Information
- Organizing and Maintaining Information
- Interpreting and Communicating Information
- Using Computers to Process Information

Interpersonal Skills
- Participating as a Member of a Team
- Teaching Others
- Serving Clients/Customers
- Exercising Leadership
- Negotiating to Arrive at a Decision
- Working with Cultural Diversity

Systems
- Understanding Systems
- Monitoring and Correcting Performance
- Improving and Designing Systems

Technology
- Selecting Technology
- Applying Technology to Task
- Maintaining and Troubleshooting Technology

Yellow blocks indicate areas covered in the chapter

Introduce the Chapter

Operating a Corporation
In Chapter 17, students will examine the responsibilities, liabilities, and duties of corporate officers and directors. The processes of mergers and acquisitions, consolidations, and stock and asset acquisitions are described.

Building Background
Tell students that CEOs come from various backgrounds. Managing a corporation requires strong leadership skills with a capacity for risk. Successful CEOs surround themselves with a team of advisors and managers who bring the right knowledge and talent to the company.

BusinessWeek News

Tell students that this article reports on the difficulty experienced when Nike's founder tries to step down and appoint his or her successor. This scenario highlights how difficult it is for new CEOs to replace a charismatic corporate founder whose personality and ego are closely tied to his or her company.

R Reading Strategy

Your Reading

Tell students that they can use various reading styles to accommodate their purpose for reading. If they are searching for a particular piece of information, suggest that they scan through the material until they locate a relevant word or phrase.

BusinessWeek News

A Short History of Unpassed Torches
By Jena McGregor

There was an eerie sense of déjà vu about the management shakeup at Nike Inc. this week. Not only has the edgy shoemaker failed at earlier attempts to pass the baton, but business history is littered with the troubled successions of charismatic entrepreneurs and once and future kings. For visionary founders, the years of emotional investment, the inextricable melding of their own identity with the business, and the distancing from their creation can all pile up to create a transition that has classic corporate melodrama written all over it. "It's like Shakespeare or Greek tragedy or the Bible," says Jeffrey A. Sonnenfeld, senior associate dean at the Yale School of Management. "It's just such a predictable script."

R "The core challenge of corporate governance is getting past the concept of the imperial CEO," says Ric Marshall, chief analyst at The Corporate Library, a research firm specializing in governance issues.

 Flex Your Reading

Efficient critical reading involves being flexible with speed and comprehension. There are several ways of reading critically, and you need to fit a reading style to your needs and to the material.

Go to **glencoe.com** for Flex Your Reading activities, more information on reading strategies for this chapter, and guided practice in reading about how corporations operate.

Classroom Resources

- Student Edition
- Teacher Wraparound Edition
- Student Activity Workbook with Academic Integration (SE/TAE)
- TeacherWorks™ Plus! CD
- *ExamView®* Assessment Suite CD
- *Presentation Plus!* CD

- National Mock Trial Championship DVD
- Online Learning Center with Podcasts at glencoe.com
- Study-to-Go™ at glencoe.com
- Online Student Edition
- Interactive Student Edition

Stock Exchange Shares in U.S. and global companies are publicly traded in marketplaces called stock exchanges. *What is the most famous stock exchange in the United States?*

377

▲ USING VISUALS

Stock Exchange Answer The New York Stock Exchange (NYSE) is the most famous stock exchange in the United States. It trades the largest dollar volume in the country. The NYSE trading floor is located at 11 Wall Street in Manhattan, and trading is carried out in five rooms. Exchange members who are present to buy and sell stock on behalf of investors gather around the appropriate post where a specialist broker acts as an auctioneer in an open outcry auction market environment.

Practice the Concept

Stock Ownership and Corporate Governance
Explain that all stocks are not created equal. Stock prices increase and decrease for a variety of reasons. The decisions that corporate directors and officers make as they manage the company can be a critical component in stock appreciation or depreciation. Tell students that decisions to discontinue a product line or expand into a new market have been known to make or break a company.

Key Terms Explain to students that directors or officers of a corporation who possess inside information must either refrain from acting on it or reveal it publicly before acting on it. Otherwise they are committing *insider trading.* Examples of insider trading may include buying or selling stocks just before a major development occurs that will affect their price, or passing valuable information to an outsider who trades in the corporation's stock and subsequently rewards the insider.

Legal Basics Explain that owning stock in a corporation carries with it the potential for sizable profit. For example, Nike stock sold at $49.36 in October of 2001. In September of 2006, shares were selling for $89.17. The stock had appreciated by 82 percent. On the flip side, if a corporation's stock price dives, the investment decreases as well.

SECTION 17.1

FOCUS

 Bell Ringer Activity

Bring in photos of Ted Turner, Bill Gates, Steve Jobs, and Mary Kay. Ask students if they can name these people and explain why they are famous. Lead a class discussion about what personal qualities it might take to be a corporate director or president.

Preteaching

Key Terms

Read the definitions and ask students to create a sentence using each term.

Academic Vocabulary

Explain that developing vocabulary is key to academic success. An efficient method to develop vocabulary is to study how words are formed.

- **proportionate** Adjective, from the Latin *pro* (for) + *portio* (part). Means in relation to the whole.

- **preemptive** Adjective, from the Latin *praeemer*, *pre* + *emere* (to buy). Means having seized the initiative.

- **exploit** Verb, from the Latin *explicare* (to unfold). Means to turn to one's own use.

Activity Ask students to give a noun, an adjective, or an adverb form that comes from each word.

N C L B Connects to academic content

SECTION 17.1 Managing a Corporation

What You'll Learn

- ◆ Distinguish the roles of corporate directors and corporate officers.
- ◆ List the rights shareholders have.
- ◆ Explain the business judgment rule.
- ◆ Explain the fairness rule.
- ◆ Describe the liability of corporate directors and officers.

Why It's Important

If you ever manage or buy stock in a corporation, you need to know how a corporation is run and what rights shareholders have.

Academic Standards

Reading and completing the activities in this section will help you practice the following academic standards:

N C L B

Social Studies (NCSS 5) Study interactions among individuals, groups, and institutions.

English Language Arts (NCTE 7) Conduct research on issues and interests by generating ideas and questions, and by posing problems.

Reading Guide

 Before You Read

Connect You have probably heard of corporations such as Bank of America, Microsoft, and Coca-Cola. Who do you think actually owns these companies?

Focus on Ideas

Owners of stock in a corporation have certain rights.

Take Notes

Create a graph like the one shown and use it to take notes as you read this section. Go to glencoe.com to find graphic organizers and tips on how to improve your note-taking skills.

R

Key Terms

You will learn these legal words and expressions in this chapter. You can also find these terms in *Black's Law Dictionary* or in an online legal dictionary.

- corporate director
- corporate officer
- direct suit
- derivative suit
- insider trading

Academic Vocabulary

You will find these words in your readings and in your tests. Look them up in a dictionary and familiarize yourself with them.

- proportionate
- preemptive
- exploit

glencoe.com

 Reading Strategy

Read for Knowledge

1. **Survey** or preread the chapter.
2. **Question** or formulate questions before you read.
3. **Recite** or read your questions, answers, and notes out loud.
4. **Review** or reread your notes.

Note-Taking Basics

- Listen attentively
- Have note-taking materials ready
- Skim through the lesson material
- Write down key words and ideas
- Anticipate what comes next
- Review notes soon after taking them

Corporate Management

What is the difference between a corporate director and a corporate officer?

In a sole proprietorship or a partnership, power is concentrated in the hands of a few individuals. In a corporation, power is scattered among many individuals and institutions that make up the directors, corporate officers, and shareholders. Some key figures can also play more than one role. For example, directors can be officers and shareholders of the corporation.

Corporate Directors

Corporate directors are people elected by the shareholders to make broad policy decisions in the running of a corporation. Generally, directors do not have to meet any legal qualifications unless the corporation's certificate of incorporation or its bylaws specify. For example, the bylaws might require that a director be a shareholder or a state resident. Directors usually serve for a set number of years and must be reelected by the shareholders. Directors are subject to the duty of due care and the duty of loyalty to the corporation.

Corporate Officers

Corporate officers are people chosen by the directors to run the day-to-day affairs of a corporation. The officers include a president, several vice-presidents, a secretary, a treasurer, and assistant officers. Officers are agents of the corporation. This means that the rules of agency law apply. Like directors, officers are subject to the duties of loyalty and due care.

Corporate Shareholders

Corporate shareholders, or simply shareholders, are the owners of a corporation based on the number of shares they hold. Shareholders are also called investors, but in fact they are both the investors in and owners of a corporation. Shareholders are often individual people, but partnerships, labor union retirement funds, and other corporations can also be shareholders in a corporation.

The Rights of Shareholders

What rights do shareholders of a corporation have?

Owners of stock in a corporation acquire certain rights. These include the right to:

- receive a stock certificate
- receive dividends
- examine the corporate books and records
- transfer all shares
- maintain a proportionate share of stock
- exercise a vote for each share of stock owned
- sue

As You Read

Predict Do shareholders have any say in the management of a corporation?

Legal Talk

Dividend: *n* Portion of a corporation's profits paid to shareholders.

Proxy: *n* Person authorized to vote on behalf of shareholders.

Vocabulary Builder List five synonyms for *dividend* and five synonyms for *proxy*. If you need help, you can find synonyms in a printed or online thesaurus.

Look It Up! Check definitions in *Black's Law Dictionary* or an online glossary. For direct links, go to **glencoe.com** to find more vocabulary resources.

TEACH

Discussion Starter

Class Discussion

Tell students to imagine that they are corporate directors for a large hotel chain. Have them describe some of the ways they would manage their corporation on issues such as labor, public relations, and financial matters. Use this discussion to introduce the topics of corporate officers and shareholders.

As You Read

Predict Inform students that shareholders own stock in the corporation and have certain rights. Ask students whether they would want a say in a business in which they were part owners. (Shareholders have voting rights and therefore can exercise their power on management by examining corporate records and by using their voting power to impact decisions by the directors.)

 Legal Talk

(dividend: allowance, allotment, bonus, reward, surplus; proxy: representative, advocate, substitute, assignee, equivalent)

Ask students to practice their academic and legal vocabulary with the electronic flashcards available at the *Business and Personal Law* Online Learning Center through glencoe.com.

Extending the Content

Corporate Management

Have students interview a manager in the human resources department of a corporation (large or small) in your area to find out how that corporation is organized. Students should find out who the chairperson of the board of directors is, how many directors are on the board, and the titles and duties of the officers that are appointed by the board. Students should also find out the type of business this corporation is involved in and its corporate mission. Have students report their findings to the class. Suggest that students create a chart for their reports showing the chain of command. Divide students into groups and have them discuss the similarities, if any, in management structure among the companies they found. Ask students to infer associations between management structure and business type.

TEACH (cont.)

D Develop Concepts

Dividends Explain that shareholders in a corporation invest so that they will enjoy some form of financial return on their investment. Dividends are profits distributed to shareholders. Ask students whether they think directors must pay dividends to shareholders if the corporation makes a profit. (No. Directors may decide to retain the profit and use it for other purposes, such as expansion or purchases of new equipment.)

C Critical Thinking

Right to Examine Corporate Books Tell students that a shareholder has the right to review the books and records of a company in which he or she owns stock. Ask students why they think stockholders are given this right. (Answers will vary, but may include the desire on the part of the shareholder to ensure that the corporation is being run ethically and follows appropriate rules of accounting.) Tell students about corporate scandals involving companies such as Enron and WorldCom. In light of the numerous lawsuits against corporations for financial misdeeds, the right to examine corporate books is especially important.

380

Global Law

Businesses in South Africa

All companies in South Africa are governed by the Companies Act, which is based on the English system of company law. There are specific rules and regulations to follow for forming a business. The Act is governed by the Companies and Intellectual Property Registration Office (CIPRO).

Steps to Incorporation

There are three steps for a company to follow before it can be incorporated in South Africa.

1. The company must reserve a company name.
2. The company must file a memorandum and articles of association.
3. The company must provide a written consent of auditors to act for the company.

The first and third steps are straightforward. The second step, however, requires a few more steps.

Memorandum and Articles of Association

The memorandum and articles of association must include the following:

1. the name of the company
2. the primary purpose and business of the company
3. the number of shares and the amount of capital invested in the company

In addition to registering with CIPRO, new companies usually must register with other government offices, such as tax and unemployment offices. Finally, the number of shareholders needed depends on the type of company. A private company needs only one shareholder and a director, who may be the same person. In contrast, a public company must have at least seven shareholders and at least two directors.

> **Across Cultures: Three Capital Cities**
> South Africa has three capital cities. Pretoria is the administrative capital, where the president and his cabinet reside. Cape Town is the legislative capital, where the National Assembly meets. Bloemfontein is the judicial capital, where the Constitutional Court sits.

Critical Thinking: *What is a reason for requiring at least seven shareholders and two directors for a public company?*

Right to Receive a Stock Certificate

A stock certificate proves that the shareholder owns part of the corporation. The right to receive this document is an essential shareholder's right.

Right to Receive Dividends

D Dividends are profits distributed to shareholders. When a corporation has made a profit, the board of directors may declare a dividend. Dividends must be distributed proportionately among shareholders. A dividend can be in the form of shares or cash.

Directors do not automatically have to declare a dividend when the corporation has made a profit. They may instead decide to keep the profit for the benefit of the corporation.

Right to Examine Corporate Books and Records

C The law requires a corporation to keep records of its business affairs, including a list of shareholders, an accounting of all transactions, and the minutes of all directors' meetings. Shareholders have a statutory right to see these records.

Global Law

Businesses in South Africa

Answer Answers will vary. Diversity in the business world is usually viewed as a good thing. By requiring at least seven shareholders, the law presumes that power will not be concentrated in too few hands. Further, multiple directors prevent one person from maintaining absolute control over the company. Students should remember that these regulations are for public companies, or companies that are going to have their shares traded on a public market. Therefore, diversity may help ensure that investment funds are safer than if they were invested in a company where one person controls everything.

Right to Transfer All Shares

Shareholders have the right to transfer or sell their shares. The person who sells or transfers stock is the transferor, and the person who receives it is the transferee.

Right to Maintain a Proportionate Share of Stocks

Shareholders have the right to purchase a **proportionate** share of every new stock issue before it is offered to the public. This right is called the shareholder's **preemptive** right. The purpose of this right is to prevent directors from taking control of the corporation by issuing more shares and buying them all themselves. However, this right can be limited or denied by the corporation's certificate of incorporation, by its bylaws or regulations, or by state law.

Right to Vote for Each Share of a Stock Owned

Shareholders have voting powers as part owners. They can, therefore, be involved in a corporation's management. The incorporation statutes of most states require that a meeting of shareholders be held annually to elect the board of directors and conduct other necessary business. Such meetings typically follow parliamentary procedure. Shareholders may vote on issues put up for a vote at the meeting. However, only holders of stock called common stock have full voting rights.

Shareholders who disagree with the decisions of the board of directors may be able to get more voting power than their own shares entitle them to have. One method is called proxy voting. A proxy vote is the right to vote on behalf of other shareholders. Proxy voting arises when shareholders who believe in one position solicit other shareholders and obtain their permission to vote for them. The shareholders may then win the majority votes they need to defeat the board on an issue.

Right to Sue

There are three types of lawsuits shareholders can bring: direct suits, class action suits, and derivative suits. **A direct suit is a lawsuit a shareholder can bring against a corporation for denying his or her rights as a shareholder.** Shareholders may also bring a class action lawsuit against a corporation on behalf of all shareholders in their position. **A derivative suit is a lawsuit a shareholder can bring on behalf of the corporation to correct an injury to the corporation.**

Vocabulary You can find vocabulary definitions in the **Key Terms** glossary and **Academic Vocabulary** glossary in the back of this book.

Company Records Shareholders have a statutory right to see all company records. *What kind of lawsuit could a shareholder bring if the company refuses to show its records?*

▲ USING VISUALS

Company Records **Answer** If a corporation refuses to show its records to a shareholder, the shareholder could file a direct suit. A direct suit is a lawsuit a shareholder can bring against a corporation for denying his or her rights as a shareholder. The right to examine corporate books and records is a common right of shareholders. The accounting records for the publicly traded corporation must be prepared in a certain manner to meet SEC requirements.

TEACH (cont.)

D Develop Concepts

Proportionate Share of Stocks Tell students that some people prefer to maintain their standing as shareholders, or keep a proportionate share of stock ownership. Explain that corporations often offer more stock, called a stock issue, from time to time. Ask students how the current stockholders can keep their proportionate share of stock when new stock is issued. (Current stockholders often have a preemptive right to purchase newly issued shares.)

Guided Practice

Derivative Suits

Remind students that shareholders can bring three types of suits against a corporation: a direct suit, a class action suit, and a derivative suit. Ask them to explain why the law makes it more difficult to initiate a derivative suit than a direct suit. (Answers should convey an understanding that a derivative suit is brought on behalf of the corporation, and the shareholder must prove that the corporation has suffered an injury. The direct suit is brought against a corporation for denying a shareholder's rights.)

W Writing Support

Class Action Suits Have students research corporations that have been sued in class action suits. Ask them to write a report on the issues involved in one of these suits.

TEACH (cont.)

✓ Reading Check

Discuss The rule is too easy because it is very subjective in its assessment of what good faith and prudent judgment would be; or the rule is appropriate since directors may make mistakes, but they should only be held responsible for fraud or gross negligence.

ASSESS

Independent Practice

Dividends

Give students the following scenario: Thunder Productions, Inc., issued financial statements for 2007 reflecting a substantial profit. The board of directors did not declare dividends for the year. The stockholders filed suit against the corporation, stating that the corporation must declare and pay dividends if the business earns a profit. Are the stockholders right? (No. Corporations do not have to declare dividends when they make a profit.)

RETEACH

 STUDY TO GO Have students go to the *Business and Personal Law* Online Learning Center through glencoe.com to download free Study-to-Go content to their cell phones or PDAs.

➡ **Insider Trading** It is illegal for corporate directors or officers to buy or sell stock based on inside information about a company not available to the public. *What kinds of outsiders could also be involved in insider trading?*

Liability of Directors and Officers

If you make a bad decision as the director of a corporation, can you be sued?

To test the decisions of corporate directors and officers, the courts have developed two standards: the business judgment rule and the fairness rule.

The Business Judgment Rule

The business judgment rule presumes that the decisions of corporate directors and officers are legal, made in good faith, with due care, and in the best interests of the corporation. However, a court will find against directors or officers if a decision involved fraud, lack of good faith, abuse of discretion, a conflict of interest, negligence, or illegality. The rule focuses not on whether a particular decision was the right decision but on how the decision was made. For example, a director who enters a deal with another corporation without doing any research could be considered negligent.

Directors and officers are not obligated to guarantee that the corporation makes a profit. If the corporation suffers a loss from a transaction the board authorized, the directors are not liable to the shareholders unless they violate the business judgment rule. Some states hold directors and officers liable only if they are grossly negligent in carrying out their duties, and some have even passed anti-liability statutes that limit the liability of directors.

✓ Reading Check

Discuss *Is the business judgment rule too easy on corporate directors and officers?*

The Fairness Rule

Directors and officers have a duty of loyalty to their corporation. They must not **exploit** their positions for personal gain at the expense of the corporation. Their main goal must be to act in the

▲ USING VISUALS

➡ **Insider Trading Answer** Insider trading may include spouses, family members, friends, or agents of corporate insiders who are given inside information used to make stock trades. Remind students of the Martha Stewart case, in which she was accused of insider trading and lying to federal investigators. After she was given information from a friend about ImClone's cancer drug, Stewart sold 3,928 shares, avoiding a loss of $45,673. She pleaded guilty to lying to federal investigators in 2004, and accepted a five-month prison sentence. Under the settlement, Stewart, without admitting guilt, agreed to pay a maximum penalty of about $195,000.

best interests of the corporation. They must not deliberately hurt the corporation. A director's or an officer's duty of loyalty may be questioned if he or she has a personal interest in a business decision. According to the fairness rule, if a manager profits in some way by a decision, the decision must be fair to the corporation.

Insider Trading One way directors or officers might exploit their position for personal gain is insider trading. **Insider trading is when a corporate director or officer buys or sells shares in a corporation based on firsthand information about the corporation that is not available to the public.** Insider trading gives an unfair advantage to people in a position of trust within a corporation. It also applies to passing valuable information to outsiders so they can profit from it. Under the insider trading rules, directors or officers who possess inside information must either refrain from acting on it or reveal it publicly before acting on it. Insider trading is legally considered a felony crime under the rules of the Securities and Exchange Commission (SEC).

Corporate Opportunity Doctrine The corporate opportunity doctrine is an extension of the duty of loyalty. According to this doctrine, directors and officers cannot take advantage of a business opportunity for themselves if they know that the corporation would want to take that opportunity for itself. The directors must first present the opportunity to the corporation. If the corporation turns it down, then the directors or officers can take the opportunity for themselves.

The only exception to this rule is if the director or officer knows that the corporation is financially incapable of taking the opportunity, despite its interest.

After You Read

Summarize Under the business judgment rule, for what reasons might a court find against a director for a bad decision?

SECTION 17.1 ASSESSMENT

Self Check

1. What are the differences between corporate directors and corporate officers?

2. What are the rights held by corporate shareholders?

3. What are the two standards courts have developed to test the decisions of corporate directors and officers?

Academic Connection

English Language Arts
At one time, insider trading was considered an acceptable business practice. People assumed that the directors, officers, and their friends would profit from their access to information about the company. Today, it is considered illegal and unethical. Research events such as the Great Depression that lead up to making insider trading illegal. Write a brief essay explaining how insider trading harms investors, companies, and the economy in general.

Critical Thinking

Insider Trading What are different ways a corporate director could engage in insider trading?

 Go to **glencoe.com** to check your answers.

RETEACH (cont.)

After You Read

Summarize a decision involved fraud, lack of good faith, abuse of discretion, a conflict of interest, negligence, or illegality

ASSESS

Self-Assessment

Have students go to the *Business and Personal Law* Online Learning Center through **glencoe.com** to take the Section 17.1 Practice Test.

CLOSE

Culminating Activity

Business Rules

Ask students to identify the business rules involved in the following situation: An officer of a corporation wants to launch a new line of products even though the company is experiencing a cash shortage. The officer plans to launch the products on his own if the corporation fails to seize the opportunity. (fairness rule and corporate opportunity doctrine)

SECTION 17.1 ASSESSMENT

Self Check

1. Directors: elected by shareholders; make broad policy decisions. Officers: chosen by directors; run day-to-day affairs.

2. the right to receive a stock certificate and dividends, examine the corporate books, transfer all shares, maintain a proportionate share of stock, exercise a vote for each share of stock owned, and sue

3. business judgment rule, fairness rule

Academic Connection

English Language Arts
Reports will vary.

Critical Thinking

use of restricted information to trade directly, passing information to an outsider who trades on the information, passing on information for a fee or personal benefit

 Activity correlated to the English Language Arts standard on page 378

383

FOCUS

Bell Ringer Activity

Ask students if they do business with a store that has changed names or ownership. Have students describe any changes in products or operations as a result of the change. Use this discussion to introduce the ideas of mergers and acquisitions.

Preteaching

Key Terms

Read the definitions and ask the students to create a sentence using each term.

Academic Vocabulary

Explain that developing vocabulary is key to academic success. An efficient method to develop vocabulary is to study how words are formed.

- **subscription** Noun, from the Latin *subscriptionem* (written underneath). Means a formal agreement to buy.

- **significant** Adjective, from the Latin *significantia* (force, energy). Means meaningful.

- **unanimous** Adjective, from the Latin *unanimus* (of one mind). Means in full agreement.

Activity Ask students to give a noun, an adjective, or an adverb form that comes from each word.

NCLB Connects to academic content

What You'll Learn

- ◆ Describe the different types of corporate stock.
- ◆ Distinguish between a merger, a consolidation, and a conglomerate.
- ◆ Explain asset acquisition and stock acquisition.
- ◆ Identify the ways a corporation can be terminated.

Why It's Important

Knowing the laws that regulate corporate financing, expansion, and dissolution will prepare you for any dealings you might have with a corporation in the future.

Academic Standards

Reading and completing the activities in this section will help you practice the following academic standards:

NCLB

Math (NCTM CS1 2) Communicate mathematical thinking coherently and clearly to peers, teachers, and others.

Social Studies (NCSS 6) Study how people create and change structures of power, authority, and governance.

Reading Guide

Before You Read

Connect Many of the corporations you come into contact with regularly are franchises. What are some franchises you can name?

Focus on Ideas

Corporations raise money by selling stocks and bonds.

Take Notes
Create a graph like the one shown and use it to take notes as you read this section. Go to glencoe.com to find graphic organizers and tips on how to improve your note-taking skills.

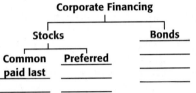

Corporate Financing — Stocks (Common paid last / Preferred) — Bonds

R

Key Terms

You will learn these legal words and expressions in this chapter. You can also find these terms in *Black's Law Dictionary* or in an online legal dictionary.

- merger
- consolidation
- conglomerate
- asset acquisition
- stock acquisition
- franchise

Academic Vocabulary

You will find these words in your readings and in your tests. Look them up in a dictionary and familiarize yourself with them.

- subscription
- significant
- unanimous

glencoe.com

 Reading Strategy

Read for Knowledge

1. **Survey** or preread the chapter.
2. **Question** or formulate questions before you read.
3. **Recite** or read your questions, answers, and notes out loud.
4. **Review** or reread your notes.

Note-Taking Basics

- Listen attentively
- Have note-taking materials ready
- Skim through the lesson material
- Write down key words and ideas
- Anticipate what comes next
- Review notes soon after taking them

Corporate Financing

How do you get money to finance a corporation?

Corporations need financing to pay for their business activities, such as research, product development, office space, marketing, and advertising. Corporations can finance their activities by raising money through the sale of stocks or borrowing money through the sale of bonds.

Corporate Stocks

Corporations raise money by selling stock. Shares of stock represent a shareholder's interest or investment in a corporation.

All stock is originally sold by the corporation. At the time a corporation is organized, the promoters seek **subscriptions** from investors. These stock subscriptions are contracts to buy stock once the corporation is authorized by the state to sell stock to the public. The subscribers do not become stockholders until the organization is completed and stock certificates are issued to them. The corporation may continue to sell shares after its incorporation is complete.

Purchasers of stock may buy the stock from the corporation or from current owners who want to sell their shares. They may buy stock personally or through agents called brokers. A broker fills the purchaser's order in one of two ways. The broker may buy the stock on a stock exchange, which is a public auction in which stocks are bought and sold. The largest and best-known stock exchange is the New York Stock Exchange (NYSE). The broker may also purchase stocks over the counter, meaning outside the organized exchanges. Many stock trades today are done online, using a brokerage house that has a Web site where the public can place buy and sell orders.

As You Read

Predict Why do corporations sell stocks and bonds?

Vocabulary You can find vocabulary definitions in the **Key Terms** glossary and the **Academic Vocabulary** glossary in the back of this book.

Business ETHICS

Executive Pay

As President and CEO, Paul Krocker guided his company stock price from $3.23 to $81.00 per share. Now, Big Blue Technology wants to hire him away. They offer him $50 million dollars per year. He accepts and begins by cutting some jobs and reducing salaries by 25 percent, which help to make Big Blue more profitable. The share price of Big Blue shoots up 35 percent in one month.

Critical Thinking *Is it ethical for an executive to earn a huge salary while the employees lose jobs or salaries, but the stock price increases to the benefit of thousands of shareholders?*

TEACH

Discussion Starter

Class Discussion
Explain that the growth of business can be accomplished by joining with another business. The closing or dissolution of a business may also take several forms. Ask students if they have heard of ways a company may expand or dissolve. Tell students that this section will cover various ways that businesses can join together and break apart.

C Critical Thinking

Subscriptions Have students offer their opinions as to why a company secures subscriptions prior to its incorporation. Be sure that students understand the definition of a subscription as it relates to stocks. (contracts to buy stock once the corporation is authorized by the state to do so; company is assured of financing when it is organized)

 As You Read

Predict Correlate the idea of a corporation's stocks and bonds issue to a student who might sell part ownership in his or her bicycle to a friend for extra cash. (A corporation issues stocks and bonds to raise cash.)

Business ETHICS

Executive Pay

Answer Answers will vary. Some individuals may believe that CEOs are paid too much for the services they provide, while others believe that a good CEO can have a positive effect on the company's performance and, therefore, high compensation is needed to attract the best talent. A CEO is often forced to make difficult decisions, such as layoffs, for the overall good of the company. Ethically, the CEO might decide to divert some of his or her earnings to the retention of employees, but this would be a purely personal decision and would not be required by the board of directors.

385

TEACH (cont.)

Reading Check

Analyze Because when people buy bonds it is as if they are lending money to a corporation.

Types of Stock There are two types of corporate stock: common stock and preferred stock. Common stock is the basic form of corporate ownership. All public corporations issue common stock. Holders of common stock have voting rights in a corporation. As a group, they elect the corporation's board of directors. Common stock sometimes pays dividends to the shareholders based on how the corporation performs. Holders of common stock are the last shareholders to be paid.

The second type of stock a corporation issues is preferred stock. Holders of preferred stock cannot vote. However, they do have the right to receive a fixed dividend. Holders of preferred stock are the first shareholders to be paid.

Corporate Bonds

A corporation may also finance its activities through bonds. Bonds are notes issued for money that the corporation borrows. When a company makes bonds available, it is called a bond issue. Unlike stocks, bonds earn interest and must be repaid in the future. If a company files for bankruptcy, bondholders are paid before shareholders.

Corporate Expansion

How can you increase the size of a corporation?

A corporation might want to expand by acquiring new land, new manufacturing plants, new sales outlets, or entering new fields of business. A corporation can expand by buying or investing in another corporation through a merger or consolidation, by acquiring the assets or stock of another company, or by opening new franchises (see **Figure 17.1**).

Merger and Consolidation

A merger is when two companies join together, with one company keeping its corporate identity and the other company losing its corporate identity. A consolidation is when two or more companies join together to form a new corporation. There is no **significant** difference between a merger and a consolidation, and the terms are often used interchangeably. Most of the time, the term merger is used to describe both scenarios. The boards of directors and shareholders of the corporations being merged must give their approval.

In some cases, companies merge or consolidate to form a conglomerate. **A conglomerate is a corporation that owns many different types of companies.** These companies do business in a variety of separate marketplaces, such as clothing, food, and entertainment. General Electric, for example, owns financial services, plastics companies, and theme parks.

Asset Acquisition

An asset acquisition is when one corporation agrees to purchase the assets, such as property, buildings, and

Reading Check

Analyze Why do bonds pay interest but stocks do not?

D
S

C

Figure 17.1 Ben & Jerry's

In 2000, Ben & Jerry's was acquired by the corporate giant Unilever, which sells 400 different brands of home, personal care, and food products worldwide.

Ben & Jerry's started out as a small partnership formed by Ben Cohen and Jerry Greenfield in 1978. When demand for its innovative line of ice cream soared, Ben & Jerry's became a public corporation.

As part of the agreement with Unilever, Ben & Jerry's was able to retain its corporate identity, with its own board of directors, while increasing its global sales and the value of its stock.

Not all mergers are bad for a smaller company taken over by a larger company. *What kind of corporation is Unilever?*

▲ USING VISUALS

Figure 17.1 Ben & Jerry's Answer Unilever is a conglomerate with businesses in health and beauty, foods, and household products.

Activity Ask students to research one conglomerate of interest to them. Have them prepare a report in which they list the businesses or brands that the company owns and outline the chronology of the company's growth. Encourage students to create a visual time line using brand logos or product advertisements. Ask volunteers to share their reports with the class.

17.2 SECTION

TEACH (cont.)

Independent Practice

Advantages to a Merger

Outline the following situation to students: Rasor Tech is a small information technology company that owns several innovative patents but has minimal cash to develop the ideas. The company is taken over by Microsoft and loses its corporate identity. Ask students to identify the advantages to Rasor Tech in this scenario. (Answers will vary, but may include a new infusion of capital to develop and market products based on patents, and ability to produce on a larger scale.)

Extending the Content

Takeovers

Point out that there are many colorful terms that deal with takeovers in the business world. List the following terms on the board and ask students to research their meanings:

- white knight (company that makes a friendly takeover offer to a target company that is being faced with a hostile takeover from a third party)

- poison pill (actions taken by a target company to prevent a hostile takeover bid from occurring)

ASSESS

Quiz

Ask students to answer the following questions:

1. What are two types of corporate stock? (common stock and preferred stock)

2. For what types of purposes might a corporation issue stock? (raise funds for expansions, advertising, operations, product research and development, capital investments)

3. What is a merger? (Two companies joining together, with one company keeping its corporate identity and the other company losing its corporate identity.)

RETEACH

Guided Practice

Types of Expansion

Remind students that corporations may expand using different techniques such as merger and consolidation, asset acquisition, and stock acquisition. Have students brainstorm the efforts involved in a merger for the suitor company. (Answers will vary, but mergers involve financing issues, voting by both boards of directors and shareholders, legal paperwork, and organization of the new combined entities.)

Case Study – Unocal Corporation v. Mesa Petroleum Company

Critical Thinking *Who do you think should win this case and why?*

Flex Your Reading Note key facts in the text below and look up words you do not understand. Restate difficult ideas in your own words. Go back and reread the text quickly to make sure you did not miss any important detail. Now, you are ready to formulate an opinion.

Interests of the Company Mesa was the owner of about 13 percent of the stock of Unocal. Mesa made a tender offer to buy an additional 37 percent of the stock of Unocal at $54 per share. The eight outside directors and six inside directors of Unocal fought this takeover bid. They offered a deal to Unocal shareholders in which the corporation itself would repurchase its own shares at $72 per share. This offer, however, was not open to Mesa. In reaction to this tactic, Mesa filed suit. In the suit, Mesa argued that the repurchase deal was unfair and represented an attempt by the board of directors to keep themselves in power.

Unocal Corporation v. Mesa Petroleum Company, 493 A.2d 946 (Delaware)

Go to glencoe.com for more case study practice.

equipment, of a second corporation. A corporation will buy the assets of another corporation rather than the corporation itself to avoid taking on the debts and liabilities of the other corporation. The shareholders and directors of the corporation selling the assets must approve the transaction.

Stock Acquisition

A stock acquisition is when an individual or a corporation buys enough shares of stock in another corporation to take over control of it. A stock acquisition often begins when a prospective buyer makes a tender offer. A tender offer is an offer to buy a specific number of shares at a specific price.

Tender offers are often referred to as takeover bids. The party making the offer is called the suitor. The corporation the suitor wants to take over is called the target. The suitor does not need to buy all the stock of the target. The suitor only needs to buy enough stock to control the election of directors.

Franchises

A franchise is a license a company grants to a business or individual for the right to use its name and sell its products or services. The business buying the franchise benefits from the trade name and expertise of the parent company. The corporation benefits by expanding its business without spending money or building new stores itself. McDonald's, Blockbuster, and Holiday Inn are well-known franchises.

 glencoe.com

Case Study

Unocal Corporation v. Mesa Petroleum Company

Answer Answers will vary. The court decided in favor of the Unocal directors. The court applied the business judgment rule because most of the directors were not profiting from the new stock offer. As long as the directors were acting in the best interests of the corporation and did not simply want to keep themselves in office, they could make this type of decision.

Dissolution of a Corporation
Can shareholders end a corporation?

As with partnerships and LLCs, the end of a corporate entity is referred to as a dissolution. The dissolution of a corporation can come about in two ways: voluntarily or involuntarily.

Voluntary Dissolution

A corporation can end voluntarily through a **unanimous** vote of its shareholders. The directors can vote for its end, provided they get the support of two-thirds of the shareholders. After the decision to end the corporation has been made, a statement of intent to dissolve must be filed with the secretary of state's office. The dissolution must be reported to the government, to creditors, and to the public.

Involuntary Dissolution

An involuntary dissolution occurs when the government itself terminates a corporation. If a corporation was formed by fraud, conducted business illegally, or exceeded its authority, the secretary of state can ask the state attorney general to bring a *quo warranto* action against it. If such an action is taken, the corporation could lose its charter and would no longer be authorized to do business in the state. Grounds for bringing such an action also include failure by the corporation to file annual reports, or pay franchise taxes.

A shareholder can also seek the involuntary dissolution of a corporation. However, the shareholder must have appropriate grounds to do this. Such grounds include evidence of fraud, waste of corporate assets, and that a dissolution is necessary to protect the shareholders' rights.

After You Read

Summarize List the ways a corporation can expand its business.

SECTION 17.2 ASSESSMENT

Self Check

1. What are the differences between stocks and bonds?

2. What is a tender offer, and what else is it called?

3. On what grounds might the government bring an action to dissolve a corporation?

Academic Connection

Mathematics You bought 80 shares of Netmark Associates stock at $24 per share last year. The company had a good year and paid all of its stockholders annual dividends of $0.72 per share. How much is your total annual dividend?

THEORY **Number and Operations:** To calculate the dividend, multiply the annual dividend per share times the number of shares.

 For more math practice, go to the Math Appendix.

Critical Thinking

Online Trading Buying and selling stock over the Internet has become a common way of playing the stock market. Why can this be risky for small investors?

Go to **glencoe.com** to check your answers.

 glencoe.com

RETEACH (cont.)

After You Read

Summarize merger and consolidation, asset acquisition, stock acquisition, and franchising

ASSESS

Self-Assessment

Have students go to the *Business and Personal Law* Online Learning Center through glencoe.com to take the Section 17.2 Practice Test.

CLOSE

Culminating Activity

Dissolution of a Corporation

Tell students that on March 30, 2007, shareholders of the HOW Corporation voted unanimously to end the corporation. Can this action dissolve the corporation? Why or why not? *(Yes. A unanimous vote is required to end a corporation.)*

SECTION 17.2 ASSESSMENT

Self Check

1. Stocks represent a shareholder's investment in a corporation; bonds are notes issued for money borrowed by the corporation.

2. offer to buy a specific number of shares at a specific price, also called a takeover bid

3. corporation repeatedly conducts business illegally; fails to file annual reports, pay franchise taxes, or maintain a statutory agent for service of process; exceeds its authority, or is formed fraudulently

Academic Connection

Mathematics
$57.60

Critical Thinking

Traders may impulsively buy or sell stock without the proper education or knowledge of the consequences.

 Activity correlated to the Mathematics standard on page 384

Chapter 17 Review and Assessment

Summary by Sections

Ask students to read the summaries one key point at a time. Then, ask them to work in groups to create two examples to illustrate each key point.

Vocabulary Builder

Cooperative Learning

1. Have students work in groups to prepare their sentences. Ask the groups to exchange their sentences and assess each other's sentences.

Vocabulary Development

- Ask students to use a dictionary or to go online to look up the etymology of each key term listed.

- Then, ask students to list several words derived from the same root or origin. For example, *contract* has the same root as *contractual* or *contractually*.

Summary

Section 17.1 Managing a Corporation

- Corporate directors are elected by shareholders to make broad policy decisions. Corporate officers are chosen by the directors to run the day-to-day affairs of a corporation. Corporate shareholders are the owners of a corporation based on the number of shares they hold.

- Shareholders rights include: (1) to receive a stock certificate; (2) to receive dividends; (3) to examine the corporate books and records; (4) to transfer all shares; (5) to maintain a proportionate share of stock; (6) to exercise a vote for each share of stock owned; and (7) to sue.

- The courts hold corporate directors and officers to two standards: the business judgment rule and the fairness rule.

Section 17.2 Financing, Expanding, and Dissolving a Corporation

- Corporations raise money by selling stocks or bonds.

- The public can purchase stock personally or through a stock broker.

- The two types of stocks corporations sell are common stock and preferred stock.

- Bonds are notes issued to those who lend money to the corporation. Bonds earn interest.

- A corporation can expand through a merger, a consolidation, an asset acquisition, a stock acquisition, or by opening new franchises.

- A corporation can be dissolved either voluntarily by the directors or shareholders, or involuntarily by the government.

 Vocabulary Builder

1 On a sheet of paper, use each of these terms in a sentence.

Key Terms

- corporate director
- corporate officer
- direct suit
- derivative suit
- insider trading
- merger
- consolidation
- conglomerate
- asset acquisition
- stock acquisition
- franchise

Academic Vocabulary

- proportionate
- preemptive
- exploit
- subscription
- significant
- unanimous

Go to **glencoe.com** to play a game and improve your legal vocabulary.

 Study Skills for Success

Prepare Your Students for Studying

Tell students that they can improve their ability to understand and remember material from their courses by learning and practicing study skills. Remind students to:

- **Get motivated!** Motivation must come from within. To motivate yourself, think of ways in which what you learn now will fit into your long-term personal and professional goals.

- **Get organized!** Make studying part of your daily routine, not something you do at the last minute.

- **Concentrate!** Study in an environment that is as free of distractions as possible.

Key Points Review

Answer the following questions. Refer to the chapter for additional reinforcement.

❷ What are the two duties corporate directors and officers owe a corporation?

❸ What is the difference between a direct suit and a derivative suit?

❹ What is insider trading?

❺ What is the corporate opportunity doctrine?

❻ What are the differences between common and preferred stock?

❼ What are corporate bonds and how are they different from corporate stocks?

❽ What are the differences between a merger, an asset acquisition, and a stock acquisition?

❾ What are the ways a corporation can be dissolved voluntary?

Standardized Test Practice

❿ Read the excerpt below about buying a franchise and complete questions 1 and 2.

Anyone who thinks about buying an existing business should know the phrase *caveat emptor*, which is Latin for let the buyer beware. It is in the seller's best interest to paint the prettiest possible picture of the business. It is in the prospective buyer's best interest to investigate the accuracy of the seller's statements. This means asking both technical and social questions.

Technical questions usually require the help of professionals such as accountants or lawyers. Are the financial records accurate? Are the legal requirements of the business in order? Was the business sued in the past?

Asking social questions means talking to the present owner, the employees, and the customers. Why is the owner selling? What is the business's reputation? How does the company compare to its competition? All of these questions need to be answered before deciding to purchase an existing business.

1. What does *caveat emptor* mean?

Ⓐ Let the seller beware.
Ⓑ Let the buyer beware.
Ⓒ Ask questions.
Ⓓ The truth is out there.

2. Which is an example of a technical question?

Ⓐ Why is the owner selling?
Ⓑ What is the business's reputation?
Ⓒ Was the business sued in the past?
Ⓓ How does the company compare to its competition?

 Test-Taking Strategies Choose a good seat to take the test. To avoid distractions, do not sit near a door or near friends.

Standardized Test Practice

10. B and C

 Strategies for Standardized Test Prep Success

Whether your students have a standardized test coming up in a few days or a few weeks, these last-minute test-prep tips and strategies will help them relax and do their best.

- **Test Format** Help students become familiar with the format of the test by practicing with test items that imitate the actual test items as closely as possible.

- **Test Timing** Have your students take timed practice tests so that they become comfortable with the length, design, and timing of the actual test.

---

2. loyalty and due care

3. Direct: shareholder against a corporation for denying shareholders' rights. Derivative: shareholder on behalf of the corporation to correct an injury to the corporation.

4. illegal use of inside information to buy or sell stock before information is made publicly available

5. Directors and officers must present an opportunity to the corporation before rejecting it.

6. Common stock has voting rights and may receive dividends; preferred stock is entitled to receive fixed dividends and is first in line to receive them.

7. Bonds are notes issued for money that the corporation borrows. Unlike stocks, bonds earn interest and must be repaid in the future.

8. Merger: one corporation absorbs another. Asset acquisition: one corporation agrees to purchase the assets or property of another. Stock acquisition: an individual or a corporation purchases enough shares of stock in a corporation to control it.

9. unanimous vote of shareholders, or by directors if two-thirds of shareholders support it

Review and Assessment

 Apply and Debate

Students should use chapter content to arrive at conclusions. The legal resolutions are listed below:

11. Yes. Cyrus has delivered inside information to his aunt, and she has profited from a stock transaction based on that information.

12. Maybe. Executive managers should avoid even the appearance of a conflict of interest. The relationship between Lakefront's chairman and the owner of Green Paddle makes the transaction questionable.

13. No. While moving the trucks may have been the safest thing to do, the officers likely acted in good faith.

14. Probably not. Complications in the research process is something that could not have been foreseen. Company officers were not grossly negligent in this case.

15. Positions will vary. Corporate mergers may not benefit all involved. The community may benefit from the new store as a whole, but individuals may be negatively impacted.

 Apply and Debate

Read the following scenarios. Get together with other students in pairs or groups of three and take a position on each scenario. Debate your position in class with students taking the opposite position or prepare a written argument justifying your position.

11 Insider Trading

Cyrus is an executive assistant at GenCom. His boss asks him to type a press release announcing that Gencom will soon merge with Billcom. That night, he discusses the merger with his aunt, who is a business journalist. She then buys 1,000 shares of GenCom, and, after the news is released, makes $20,000 in stock price gains.

You Debate Did Cyrus engage in insider trading by discussing the merger?

12 Conflict of Interest?

Lakefront Craft, Inc. manufactures boats. To expand the company, the board of directors decided to purchase Paddle Canoes, Inc. for $3.5 million. Lakefront's stock price rose with this news. A reporter later discovered that a cousin of Lakefront's chairperson was the owner of Paddle Canoes, and made $1 million on the sale.

You Debate Is there a conflict of interest in this situation?

13 Hurricane Loss

Scott, a shareholder, brought suit against Big Trucking, Inc. when the company lost $2 million because the senior executives failed to move 200 trucks out of the path of a hurricane that was forecast. The trucks and their contents were destroyed.

You Debate Are executives responsible for losses arising out of natural disasters?

14 Missed Market

Jackson was a shareholder in Life Pharmaceuticals, Inc. The company announced its plans to launch a new cancer drug. Jackson's stock soared. After the company delayed the drug's release due to complications in the research, his stock dropped. Jackson sued the company for mismanagement.

You Debate Are stockholders right to sue for product delays?

15 Merger Pros and Cons

Linda often shops at PayDown. When PayDown was bought out by a chain called High Quality Clothing, Inc., Linda was joyful because it carries nicer merchandise. Later, she learned her friend Sharon lost her job at PayDown.

You Debate Is it important for a community to have better stores even though it may create job losses for some people?

C Critical Thinking

Hostile Takeover? Ted Holmes, an investor, offered to purchase TellTale, Inc. but the board of directors rejected his offer. The next day, Holmes placed an ad in *The Financial Times* and offered to buy shares of TellTale at $35 per share while its current market price was at $29. TellTale asked one of its major shareholders not to sell to prevent the "hostile takeover."

Debate Practice

- Is Holmes's strategy to purchase the company's stock legal? (Yes. Ted Holmes approached the company with an offer, then placed an ad, called a tender offer.)

- Is the plea to TellTale's existing shareholders a legal way to combat the takeover bid? (Yes. Companies may also invite a friendly third party to purchase a valuable asset of the corporation to make it a less attractive target.)

📄 Case Study Practice – Hoschett v. TSI International Software, Ltd.

⑯ Shareholders' Meeting TSI International Software, Ltd. (TSI) was incorporated in the state of Delaware in 1993, but its headquarters is in Wilton, Connecticut. The company is a privately-held corporation. Less than 40 stockholders hold all the shares in the corporation. Fred Hoschett owns 1,200 shares of common stock, which is much less than 1% of all the stock. Since its incorporation, TSI has never had an annual meeting to elect its directors. Mr. Hoschett, as a shareholder, sued the corporation to make it hold an annual meeting. Under the Delaware Code, a Delaware corporation must have an annual meeting to elect directors, unless the by-laws of the corporation say otherwise. TSI argued that on November 16, 1995, the company received written consent from a majority of shareholders who chose five individuals as directors of TSI. Since a majority of shareholders had provided written consent, TSI argued that an annual meeting was unnecessary.

Source: Hoschett v. TSI International Software, Ltd., 683 A.2d 43 (Del. Ct. Chan. 1996)

Practice Does TSI have to hold an annual meeting?

⑰ Ethics ←?→ Application

Nonprofit Monica Edwards and Javier Perez formed a political watchdog group as a nonprofit corporation. Because of political changes, income from donations and membership dues soared in the first year. Monica and Javier gave themselves huge bonuses and took lavish, fact-finding trips because, as a nonprofit corporation, there was no need to show a profit.

◆ Are Monica and Javier entitled to do this? Why or why not?

⑱ Internet Application

Find out about Stocks Your aunt and uncle give you 100 shares of ComTech stock for your birthday. You follow the stock and notice that after one week it has increased in value by $2.00, and the next week it has gone down by $1.37. You want to understand what makes a company's stock price go up and down. Why does it fluctuate?

Go to **glencoe.com** to find out where you can learn about the stock market, how stocks are traded, and why stock prices fluctuate.

Reading Connection

Outside Reading Go to **glencoe.com** for a list of outside reading suggestions about corporate management.

 glencoe.com

📄 Case Study Practice

16. Yes. The Delaware Court of Chancery held that the Delaware General Corporation Law specifically requires an annual meeting, unless the corporation has provided for an alternative in its bylaws. Although there are provisions in the Delaware Code that allow for written appointment of officers when a majority consent in writing, that is only a temporary fix and does not preclude a corporation from holding an annual meeting. The purpose of the annual meeting is more than just the election of officers. It is also a time for discussing business relevant to the running of the corporation.

Review and Assessment

←?→ Ethics Application

17. Students may argue that Monica and Javier are within their rights to take the extra income. Point out that nonprofit does not necessarily mean low budget, and that many charitable organizations pay their directors large salaries. By taking the extra profits themselves, though, Monica and Javier may lose goodwill with their members.

💻 Internet Application

18. Answers will vary. Factors influencing stock price fluctuation include bad or good press on the company, and supply and demand of a company's stock.

R Reading Strategy

Reading Connection

American Bar Association Resources

Go to the *Business and Personal Law* Online Learning Center through **glencoe.com** to find links for further readings that relate to this chapter. Ask students to read, review, and summarize the documents. Advise students to keep their reviews and summaries to use as reference material for their Unit Thematic Project on pages 432–433.

Plan Your Lesson Section by Section

NBEA	NATIONAL BUSINESS LAW STANDARDS
Section 18.1	• **Identify** federal, state, territory, and province statutes that regulate corporations. • **Explain** the circumstances under which courts may disregard the corporate entity and "pierce the corporate veil." • **Differentiate** between the rules of the International Law Commission, the U.N. Commission on International Trade Law, and the World Trade Organization.
Section 18.2	• **Describe** the various federal statutes (e.g., National Environmental Policy Act, Clean Air Act, Clean Water Act, and Toxic Substance Control Act) that impact the environment. • **Describe** the various state statutes that impact the environment. • **Describe** the various federal agencies (e.g., Department of Energy, Energy Regulatory Commission, and Nuclear Regulatory Commission) that impact energy regulation and conservation. • **Describe** the various international initiatives that influence environmental regulations. • **Describe** the various state statutes that impact energy regulations and conservation.

NCLB	ACADEMIC STANDARDS	Activity/Feature
English Language Arts: NCTE 3 Apply a wide range of strategies to comprehend, interpret, evaluate, and appreciate texts.		*BusinessWeek* News, Case Study, Case Study Practice
English Language Arts: NCTE 9 Develop an understanding of and respect for diversity in language use, patterns, and dialects across cultures, ethnic groups, geographic regions, and social roles.		Global Law
English Language Arts: NCTE 6 Apply knowledge of language structure, language conventions, media techniques, figurative language, and genre to create, critique, and discuss print and non-print texts.		Legal Talk, ad copy, Key Terms, and Academic Vocabulary
English Language Arts: NCTE 11 Participate as knowledgeable, reflective, creative, and critical members of a variety of literacy communities.		Section 18.1 Assessment
Social Studies: NCSS 3 Study people, places, and the environment.		Section 18.2 Assessment
English Language Arts: NCTE 10 Students whose first language is not English make use of their first language to develop competency in the English language arts and to develop understanding of content across the curriculum.		Key Terms, Academic Vocabulary, Legal Talk, Vocabulary Builder
English Language Arts: NCTE 1 Read a wide range of print and non-print texts to build an understanding of texts; to acquire new information; to respond to the needs and demands of society and the workplace; and for personal fulfillment.		Global Law, Cyberlaw

Connect Your Business Law Classroom to the World of Work

This chart shows the 21st Century Skills, foundation skills, and workplace competencies that students develop as they work in this chapter.

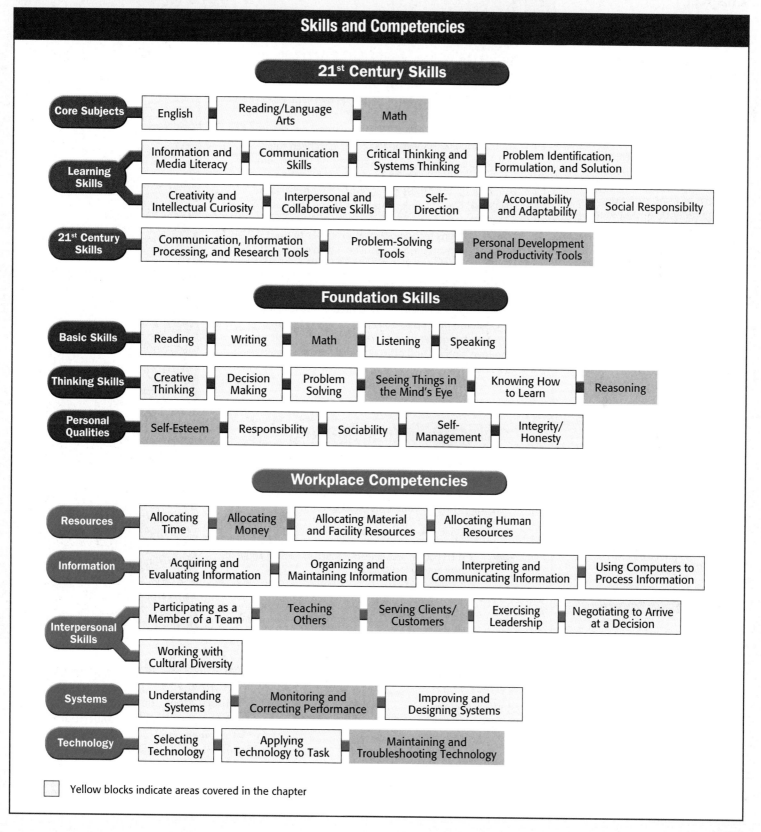

Skills and Competencies

21st Century Skills

- **Core Subjects:** English | Reading/Language Arts | Math
- **Learning Skills:** Information and Media Literacy | Communication Skills | Critical Thinking and Systems Thinking | Problem Identification, Formulation, and Solution | Creativity and Intellectual Curiosity | Interpersonal and Collaborative Skills | Self-Direction | Accountability and Adaptability | Social Responsibilty
- **21st Century Skills:** Communication, Information Processing, and Research Tools | Problem-Solving Tools | Personal Development and Productivity Tools

Foundation Skills

- **Basic Skills:** Reading | Writing | Math | Listening | Speaking
- **Thinking Skills:** Creative Thinking | Decision Making | Problem Solving | Seeing Things in the Mind's Eye | Knowing How to Learn | Reasoning
- **Personal Qualities:** Self-Esteem | Responsibility | Sociability | Self-Management | Integrity/Honesty

Workplace Competencies

- **Resources:** Allocating Time | Allocating Money | Allocating Material and Facility Resources | Allocating Human Resources
- **Information:** Acquiring and Evaluating Information | Organizing and Maintaining Information | Interpreting and Communicating Information | Using Computers to Process Information
- **Interpersonal Skills:** Participating as a Member of a Team | Teaching Others | Serving Clients/Customers | Exercising Leadership | Negotiating to Arrive at a Decision | Working with Cultural Diversity
- **Systems:** Understanding Systems | Monitoring and Correcting Performance | Improving and Designing Systems
- **Technology:** Selecting Technology | Applying Technology to Task | Maintaining and Troubleshooting Technology

☐ Yellow blocks indicate areas covered in the chapter

Introduce the Chapter

Business and Regulations
In this chapter, students are given an overview of the origins and purposes of securities regulation, antitrust law, and environmental law.

Building Background
Ask students if they have ever dreamed of owning stock in a company such as Sara Lee. Tell them to imagine that Sara Lee recently engaged in unfair business practices and also ignored environmental protection regulations at one of its manufacturing plants. Ask students to imagine how they would react to this news as a stockholder.

BusinessWeek News

Tell students that in 2006 the Environmental Protection Agency (EPA) mandated that diesel engines use special catalytic converters in the exhaust system. This means there must also be a switch to "ultra-low-sulfur diesel (ULSD)" fuel. When the conversion to ULSD is complete, diesels will be nearly indistinguishable from gasoline engines for environmental purposes.

R Reading Strategy

 Your Reading

Have students review the headings in the chapter, and write a summary of how they think the information in this chapter will help them in their daily lives.

BusinessWeek News

Diesel Gets Cleaner and Greener
By Gail Edmondson

For years diesel engines have been the rage in Europe. They're powerful, use relatively cheap fuel, and can propel a car 40 miles on a single gallon. But they've never really caught on in the U.S., where memories of the 1970s-era soot-belching diesel cars still linger. Now, DaimlerChrysler is trying to clear away that old image. The company has engineered a new emissions technology that promises to make diesel as clean-burning as gasoline. Daimler also has just announced plans to unveil its clean-diesel exhaust system in the U.S. in the latest Mercedes E-class sedans.

Mercedes clean-diesel cars will cost less than an equivalent hybrid while offering greater power and acceleration, plus up to 40% better mileage over conventional gas engines. That's a lure for Americans who love big cars and off-road vehicles. And diesels can go 500 miles without a fill-up.

 Flex Your Reading

Efficient critical reading involves being flexible with speed and comprehension. There are several ways of reading critically, and you need to fit a reading style to your needs and to the material.

Go to **glencoe.com** for Flex Your Reading activities, more information on reading strategies for this chapter, and guided practice in reading about new energy technology.

Classroom Resources

- Student Edition
- Teacher Wraparound Edition
- Student Activity Workbook with Academic Integration (SE/TAE)
- TeacherWorks™ Plus! CD
- ExamView® Assessment Suite CD
- Presentation Plus! CD

- National Mock Trial Championship DVD
- Online Learning Center with Podcasts at glencoe.com
- Study-to-Go™ at glencoe.com
- Online Student Edition
- Interactive Student Edition

Environmental Impact The federal government has passed laws to conserve energy and protect the environment. *Which government agency was created to deal with pollution and toxic waste?*

(395)

Practice the Concept

Regulating Corporations
Explain that corporations are not free to operate any way they choose. Governmental regulation extends into various areas of a corporation's existence. Ask students to list the ways in which a corporation might be regulated. (Answers will vary, but students may list product safety, manufacturing processes and their impact on the environment, selling stock to the public, and business practices.) Stress to students that when a company such as Daimler manufactures its Mercedes, it is required to adhere to numerous government regulations.

Key Terms Write the names of several agencies mentioned in the chapter on the board, such as the Environmental Protection Agency and the Nuclear Regulatory Commission. Point out that the names of these agencies contain terms such as *protection* and *regulatory*. Tell students that these agencies exist to protect the environment and regulate certain practices by businesses or individuals.

The Fine Print Tell students that the sticker on the window of a new car often includes an estimate of fuel economy. Warn students that they should read the fine print on the sticker as well. Actual mileage may vary depending on issues such as the mechanical condition of the car and road conditions.

▲ USING VISUALS

Environmental Impact Answer The Environmental Protection Agency was created to establish a national policy to combat pollution. The agency can make regulatory policies and laws that deal with water, air, solid waste, toxic substances, and noise pollution. The EPA performs research tasks and supports programs that make sure pollution standards are met. If businesses do not comply with regulations, the EPA will bring action against them.

FOCUS

SECTION 18.1 **Corporate Regulations**

Bell Ringer Activity

Ask students if they can recall recent events that involved U.S. businesses and government regulation of the activities of the business. (antitrust violations, mergers, discrimination cases)

Preteaching

Key Terms

Read the definitions and ask students to create a sentence using each term.

Academic Vocabulary

Explain that developing vocabulary is key to academic success. An efficient method to develop vocabulary is to study how words are formed.

- **commerce** Noun, from the Latin *commercium* (trade). Means the exchange of goods and services.

- **administer** Verb, from the Latin *administrare* (to assist). Means to manage.

- **certify** Verb, from the Latin *certificare* (to make certain). Means to attest.

Activity Ask students to give a noun, an adjective, or an adverb form that comes from each word.

 Connects to academic content

What You'll Learn

- ◆ Explain the source of federal power in the regulation of business.
- ◆ Identify the laws that regulate the sale of securities.
- ◆ Distinguish between the laws that regulate antitrust activity.
- ◆ Describe what laws regulate corporate takeovers.

Why It's Important

Once you understand the background for governmental regulations, you will appreciate why the government plays a regulatory role to ensure competition and fairness.

Academic Standards

Reading and completing the activities in this section will help you practice the following academic standards:

NCLB

English Language Arts (NCTE 11) Participate as knowledgeable, reflective, creative, and critical members of a variety of literacy communities.

Social Studies (NCSS 6) Study how people create and change structures of power, authority, and governance.

SECTION 18.1 Corporate Regulations

Reading Guide

 Before You Read

Connect If you have ever been someplace where you could only buy goods at one store, you are familiar with a monopoly. Name an instance where you experienced a monopoly.

Focus on Ideas

The federal government regulates corporations to make sure they do business fairly.

Take Notes	Antitrust Laws	
Create a graph like the one shown and use it to take notes as you read this section. Go to glencoe.com to find graphic organizers and tips on how to improve your note-taking skills.	**Act**	**Purpose**
	Sherman Antitrust Act	

Key Terms

You will learn these legal words and expressions in this chapter. You can also find these terms in *Black's Law Dictionary* or in an online legal dictionary.

- Commerce Clause
- security
- registration statement
- prospectus
- monopoly

Academic Vocabulary

You will find these words in your readings and in your tests. Look them up in a dictionary and familiarize yourself with them.

- commerce
- administer
- certify

 glencoe.com

R Reading Strategy

Read for Knowledge

1. **Survey** or preread the chapter.
2. **Question** or formulate questions before you read.
3. **Recite** or read your questions, answers, and notes out loud.
4. **Review** or reread your notes.

Note-Taking Basics

- Listen attentively
- Have note-taking materials ready
- Skim through the lesson material
- Write down key words and ideas
- Anticipate what comes next
- Review notes soon after taking them

Business and the Constitution

What gives the federal government the right to regulate businesses?

The federal government gets its power to regulate business from the Commerce Clause of the United States Constitution. **The Commerce Clause is a statement in Article I of the Constitution giving Congress the power to regulate commerce among the states.** Over the last two hundred years, the U.S. Supreme Court has enlarged the government's power to regulate business. Now the federal government can regulate any business activity that affects interstate **commerce**, even one that occurs completely within the borders of a single state.

The individual states also have laws to regulate commerce. However, all state laws must abide by the Constitution. For example, the U.S. Supreme Court has ruled that a state violates the Commerce Clause when it creates a law that treats in-state and out-of-state businesses differently when the different treatment hurts the out-of-state business.

There are three major areas in which governments regulate commerce:

- securities (sale of stocks)
- antitrust (unfair competition)
- corporate takeovers

Securities Regulation

In October 1929 the stock market collapsed in what became known as the Great Crash or the Crash of '29. The crash led to a severe worldwide economic depression. Experts identified the sale of worthless securities as a major cause of the collapse. **A security is a monetary investment that seeks to make a profit solely because of another's efforts.** Corporate stocks, interests in savings and loans, interests in racehorses or sports teams, and even the sale of coins are types of securities.

The Securities Act of 1933 To prevent another stock market crash, Congress passed the Securities Act of 1933. The Securities Act is designed to protect investors by making sure they can learn about the securities they buy. It also provides a way to uncover fraud and unfair practices.

The Securities and Exchange Commission The Securities Exchange Act of 1934 created the Securities and Exchange Commission (SEC). The SEC is an independent federal agency set up to **administer** federal securities law. It consists of five commissioners appointed by the President. The SEC also employs lawyers, accountants, and securities analysts who oversee the sale of securities and the brokers, dealers, and bankers who sell them.

The Registration Requirement One way the SEC ensures that investors know what they are buying is through the registration

As You Read

Predict For what reasons do you think the government tries to regulate certain aspects of business?

Vocabulary You can find vocabulary definitions in the **Key Terms** glossary and **Academic Vocabulary** glossary in the back of this book.

TEACH

Discussion Starter

Class Discussion
Bring a company stock prospectus to class. Read excerpts from the document so that students understand that it is a detailed description of a stock offering. Ask students why they think the government requires a company to publish a prospectus. (to inform potential investors about the shares offered)

D Develop Concepts

Securities Explain that a security is a type of investment instrument that represents financial value. Ask students if they can identify several forms of securities. (corporate stocks, interest in savings and loans, interest in sports teams, sale of coins)

As You Read

Predict To help students answer this question, have them name any instances they can recall when consumers or investors were harmed financially. Lead the discussion to the ways government regulation can prevent this harm. (protects investors from fraud or unfair practices by corporations, bankers, brokers)

Independent Practice

The Stock Market Crash

Have students research the stock market crash of 1929 and perform the following activities:

- Write a paragraph describing what happened. **L1**

- Write a one-page report explaining the relationship of the crash to the Great Depression. **L2**

- Write a one-page report describing the steps President Roosevelt took to ease America's economic problems. **L3**

TEACH (cont.)

D Develop Concepts

Sarbanes-Oxley Act Ask students whether they know reasons why the Sarbanes-Oxley Act was enacted in 2002. (result of the Enron collapse and other high-profile cases in which companies and their CEOs were accused of fraud and financial misrepresentations) Explain that the Sarbanes-Oxley Act is intended to help restore trust in the financial reporting process.

C Critical Thinking

Monopolies Explain that a monopoly is a business situation in which one person, company, or group of companies controls the market for a product or service. Ask students why a monopoly is not good for the economy or for consumers. (hinders competition, blocks fair pricing)

 Reading Check

Analyze The Williams Act requires a suitor who offers to acquire more than 5 percent of a target's stock to file a statement with the SEC indicating where the money is coming from, why the suitor is purchasing the stock, and how much of the target the suitor owns.

Antitrust In 1911 the Supreme Court ruled that Standard Oil had violated the Sherman Antitrust Act by using devious means to drive its competition out of business. *What did the Supreme Court make Standard Oil do?*

Reading Check

Analyze *How does the Williams Act control takeover bids to ensure fairness to shareholders?*

requirement. This requires companies to file a registration statement and a prospectus with the SEC before they offer securities for sale. **The registration statement is a general description of the securities and of the company making the offer. The prospectus is a document that contains a detailed explanation of the stock offering for potential investors.** These documents further prevent the sale of fraudulent securities. A firm caught selling securities without SEC approval can be punished with fines or imprisonment.

Sarbanes-Oxley Act Following a series of corporate failures in the 1990s, Congress passed the Sarbanes-Oxley Act. The Act requires all chief executive officers (CEOs) and chief financial officers (CFOs) to **certify** periodic company reports filed with the SEC. It prohibits most corporate loans to directors and executive officers. The law also places an affirmative duty on the board of directors to make certain that their company is conforming to all legal requirements.

Antitrust Law

In the nineteenth century a popular way for someone to gain control of several companies was to form a trust. In a trust, the voting power of the stock for all the companies was given to one person, or trustee. Today, this type of trust is usually called a monopoly. **A monopoly is a business situation in which one person, company, or group of companies controls the market for a product or service.** Antitrust laws were created to prevent monopolies.

The Sherman Antitrust Act In 1890 Congress passed the Sherman Antitrust Act, which made monopolies illegal. However, a Supreme Court ruling that said contracts or combinations were illegal only if they formed an "unreasonable restraint of trade" undermined the Sherman Act.

The Clayton Antitrust Act In 1914 Congress passed the Clayton Antitrust Act. The Clayton Act makes specific business practices illegal. For example, a business cannot sell goods to one company for less than the price it charges another company if it harms competition. It also makes it illegal to sell goods on the condition that a buyer cannot buy products from a competitor.

USING VISUALS

Antitrust Answer The U.S. Supreme Court required Standard Oil to split up. Standard Oil separated into 34 companies, each with its own distinct board of directors. ExxonMobil, Chevron, ConocoPhillips, and Amoco are a few of those new companies. Before the split up of Standard Oil, the company controlled 88 percent of the refined oil flows in the United States.

Activity Ask students to use the Internet or library to research the history of Standard Oil and create a basic time line of the milestones in the company's development and breakup.

The Federal Trade Commission Act Congress passed the Federal Trade Commission Act in 1914 to protect businesses from the wrongful acts of other businesses. It allows the courts to determine unfair methods of competition. The act also created the Federal Trade Commission (FTC). The FTC prevents businesses from violating the Federal Trade Commission Act.

The Robinson-Patman Act The Robinson-Patman Act is an amendment to the Clayton Act. It says companies cannot sell goods at lower prices to large purchasers without offering the same discount to smaller purchasers. It also outlaws unfair behavior, such as setting up a delivery schedule that helps one seller but hurts another.

Regulation of Corporate Takeovers

Starting in the 1980s, many large corporations took over smaller corporations in what became known as merger mania. The deals were often valued in the billions of dollars and created huge conglomerates and multinational corporations. As a result, Congress, state legislatures, and the courts became involved in regulating the corporate takeover process.

Federal Regulation The Williams Act strictly controls takeover bids. Under this act, when a suitor offers to acquire more than five percent of a target's stock, the suitor must file a statement with the SEC indicating where the money for the takeover is coming from, why the suitor is purchasing the stock, and how much of the target the suitor owns. The goal is to make certain shareholders know the qualifications and the intentions of the suitor.

State Regulation State legislatures have passed anti-liability statutes to protect corporate directors whose companies are

Legal Talk

Prospectus: *n* Latin for *view, outlook.*

Monopoly: *n* From Greek *mono* = one + *polein* = seller: one seller.

Vocabulary Builder The prefix *mono* means one in Greek. List and define five words that begin with this prefix in terms of its meaning. For example, *monochrome* means one color.

Look It Up! Check definitions in *Black's Law Dictionary* or an online glossary. For direct links, go to **glencoe.com** to find more vocabulary resources.

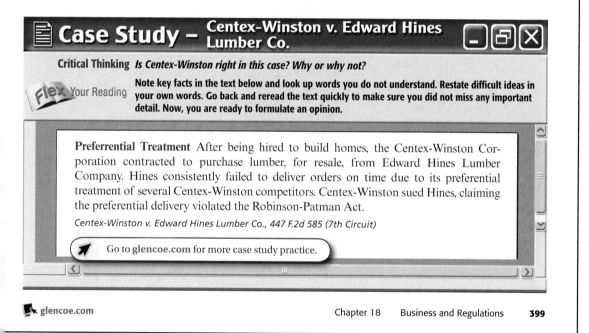

Case Study – Centex-Winston v. Edward Hines Lumber Co.

Critical Thinking *Is Centex-Winston right in this case? Why or why not?*

Flex Your Reading Note key facts in the text below and look up words you do not understand. Restate difficult ideas in your own words. Go back and reread the text quickly to make sure you did not miss any important detail. Now, you are ready to formulate an opinion.

Preferential Treatment After being hired to build homes, the Centex-Winston Corporation contracted to purchase lumber, for resale, from Edward Hines Lumber Company. Hines consistently failed to deliver orders on time due to its preferential treatment of several Centex-Winston competitors. Centex-Winston sued Hines, claiming the preferential delivery violated the Robinson-Patman Act.

Centex-Winston v. Edward Hines Lumber Co., 447 F.2d 585 (7th Circuit)

Go to **glencoe.com** for more case study practice.

glencoe.com

Case Study

Centex-Winston v. Edward Hines Lumber Co.

Answer Yes. The court identified the purpose of the Robinson-Patman Act as prevention of special favors granted by a seller to one or more purchasers at the expense of competitors. Robinson-Patman provisions relate not only to price, but also to services and facilities involved in the sale of goods. Remind students that the Robinson-Patman Act also prohibits companies from selling goods at lower prices to large purchasers without offering the same discount to smaller purchasers.

TEACH (cont.)

Legal Talk

(monogamy, having only one mate; monobasic, containing a single atom; monophonic, recording using one channel)

Ask students to practice their academic and legal vocabulary with the electronic flashcards available at the *Business and Personal Law* Online Learning Center through **glencoe.com**.

ASSESS

Independent Practice

Government Regulation

Present the following scenario to students: Match Industries agrees to sell lumber to Swift Cabinetry Company on the condition that Swift agrees not to buy products from Match's competitor. Ask students whether this agreement is legal. Why or why not? (No. The agreement violates the Clayton Antitrust Act.)

RETEACH

Review Key Terms

Encourage students to access the *Business and Personal Law* Online Learning Center through **glencoe.com** and use the electronic flashcards to review the key terms.

RETEACH (cont.)

After You Read

Summarize Sherman Antitrust Act, Clayton Antitrust Act, Robinson-Patman Act

ASSESS

Self-Assessment

Have students go to the *Business and Personal Law* Online Learning Center through glencoe.com to take the Section 18.1 Practice Test.

CLOSE

Culminating Activity

Commerce

Ask students to name the three main areas in which government regulates commerce. Have them describe one example of an illegal event in each area. (securities—company misrepresents an offering of its stock; antitrust—one company controls a majority of an industry; corporate takeover—no notice to SEC when a company tries to take over more than 5 percent of another)

---

involved in takeovers. Several state legislatures have also enacted anti-takeover statutes to discourage suitors from targeting companies within their states.

Judicial Scrutiny Sometimes, a corporation's directors and officers who successfully resist a takeover bid are sued by dissatisfied shareholders who may complain that the suitor's takeover would have been more profitable for them. In such lawsuits, the courts must evaluate the decisions made by the corporation's directors and officers. One question courts must ask is whether the business judgment rule should apply. Recall that the business judgment rule (Chapter 17) presumes a director acts with due care. However, the business judgment rule does not apply if the director acts illegally or if there is a conflict of interest.

Operating a Business Internationally

Several organizations regulate international business dealings. The International Law Commission (ILC) is an agency within the United Nations responsible for the codification of international law dealing with relations among countries. The U.N. Commission on International Trade Law (UNCITL) codifies a set of international laws that regulate international trade among private businesses. The World Trade Organization (WTO) is not a U.N. agency, but a separate international organization that drafts rules dealing with trade among member nations. The WTO tries to limit or remove trade barriers. The rules drafted by all three organizations are enacted in the United States through the treaty process, and if Congress approves the rules, they become valid laws on par with Federal statutes.

After You Read

Summarize List the three major acts passed by Congress to help regulate unfair business practices.

SECTION 18.1 ASSESSMENT

Self Check

1. What is the federal government's authority to regulate business based on?

2. What are securities and what are some examples of them?

3. What is a monopoly?

Academic Connection

English Language Arts
Economist Alan Greenspan argues that the very existence of antitrust laws discourages businessmen from some activities that might be socially useful out of fear that their business actions will be determined illegal and dismantled by government. In his essay entitled "Antitrust," Greenspan says: "No one will ever know what new products, processes, machines, and cost-saving mergers failed to come into existence, killed by the Sherman Act before they were born. No one can ever compute the price that all of us have paid for that Act which, by inducing less effective use of capital, has kept our standard of living lower than would otherwise have been possible."

Write a one-to-two-page essay explaining why you agree or disagree with Alan Greenspan.

Critical Thinking

Monopoly Why is it a bad thing if one company controls the entire market for a particular product?

 Go to **glencoe.com** to check your answers.

SECTION 18.1 ASSESSMENT

Self Check

1. Commerce Clause in Article I of the United States Constitution

2. monetary investments that seek to make a profit solely because of another's efforts; corporate stocks, interests in savings and loans

3. business situation in which one person, company, or group of companies controls the market for a product or service

Academic Connection

English Language Arts
Answers will vary, but should focus on the advantages and disadvantages of antitrust laws.

Critical Thinking

Competition is diminished or eliminated; quality suffers; prices are inflated.

 Activity correlated to the English Language Arts standard on page 396

Environmental Laws

Reading Guide

 Before You Read

Connect Have you ever noticed days when the sky is brown with smog? Name some of the sources that you think might be responsible for the smog.

Focus on Ideas

To ensure a higher quality of life for its citizens, federal and state governments have passed laws to protect the environment and conserve energy.

Take Notes

Create a graph like the one shown and use it to take notes as you read this section. Go to **glencoe.com** to find graphic organizers and tips on how to improve your note-taking skills.

 Key Terms

You will learn these legal words and expressions in this chapter. You can also find these terms in *Black's Law Dictionary* or in an online legal dictionary.

- Environmental Protection Agency (EPA)
- Federal Energy Regulatory Commission (FERC)
- Nuclear Regulatory Commission (NRC)

 Academic Vocabulary

You will find these words in your readings and in your tests. Look them up in a dictionary and familiarize yourself with them.

- comply
- emissions
- proactive

What You'll Learn

- ◆ Describe the laws that regulate the environment.
- ◆ Identify the federal and state agencies that regulate the environment.
- ◆ Identify the federal and state agencies that are responsible for regulating energy.
- ◆ Describe the impact of international law on energy regulation and conservation.

Why It's Important

If you ever go into business, you need to know that there are environmental and energy laws you have to obey.

Academic Standards

Reading and completing the activities in this section will help you practice the following academic standards:

Social Studies (NCSS 3) Study people, places, and environments.

English Language Arts (NCTE 7) Conduct research on issues and interests by generating ideas and questions, and by posing problems.

N C L B

FOCUS

Bell Ringer Activity

Bring in a bunch of fresh grapes from the grocery store. Ask students whether government has any involvement in the way grapes are grown or harvested. Use this discussion to introduce the idea of environmental laws.

Preteaching

Key Terms

Read the definitions and ask students to create a sentence using each term.

Academic Vocabulary

Explain that developing vocabulary is key to academic success. An efficient method to develop vocabulary is to study how words are formed.

- **comply** Verb, from the Latin *complere* (fill up). Means to act in accordance with.
- **emissions** Noun, from the Latin *emittere* (to send out). Means things that are discharged.
- **proactive** Adjective, from the Latin *pro-* (before) + *activus* (doing). Means acting in advance.

Activity Ask students to give a noun, an adjective, or an adverb form that comes from each word.

 N C L B Connects to academic content

R Reading Strategy

Read for Knowledge

1. **Survey** or preread the chapter.
2. **Question** or formulate questions before you read.
3. **Recite** or read your questions, answers, and notes out loud.
4. **Review** or reread your notes.

Note-Taking Basics

- Listen attentively
- Have note-taking materials ready
- Skim through the lesson material
- Write down key words and ideas
- Anticipate what comes next
- Review notes soon after taking them

TEACH

Discussion Starter

Class Discussion

Ask students to identify some of the environmental issues that affect our planet. (Answers may include global warming, climate change, ozone depletion, recycling, hazardous waste, acid rain, air and water pollution, oil spills, endangered species, energy conservation, ecosystems, pesticides, and sun protection.) Tell students that this section will cover the government measures taken to protect the environment and the agencies that enforce them.

D Develop Concepts

Environmental Protection Agency Tell students that the primary purpose of the EPA is apparent from its name. Have students give examples of the kinds of situations, areas, and cases that the EPA deals with. (solid waste, water, air, noise pollution, toxic substances) Ask students what course of action the EPA might take if a company is intentionally or unintentionally polluting. (close down operations, require company to pay fine)

As You Read

Predict Ask students to consider during which period in U.S. history people became concerned about the environment and why. (after the damage caused by industrialization was apparent during the mid-twentieth century)

402

As You Read

Predict When were the first environmental laws created?

Vocabulary You can find vocabulary definitions in the **Key Terms** glossary and Academic Vocabulary glossary in the back of this book.

Environmental Protection

What does the federal government do to make sure our air and water are not polluted?

In the nineteenth century, the rapid rise of industrialism led to an increase in factory-produced waste which polluted the land, air, and water. The only environmental laws that existed were based on common law, such as nuisance claims. For example, if a farmer had a feed lot that was a nuisance to its neighbors, the matter could be taken to court. By the mid-twentieth century, as the damage caused by industrialization to the environment and human health became apparent, the government recognized the need to pass laws specifically designed to protect the environment (see **Figure 18.1**).

The Environmental Protection Agency

In 1969 Congress passed the National Environmental Policy Act, which established the Environmental Protection Agency. **The Environmental Protection Agency (EPA) is the federal agency responsible for protecting the environment.** It is an independent agency that is a part of the executive branch. The EPA was set up to establish a national policy to combat pollution.

Regulatory Responsibilities The EPA can make regulations involving environmental policies, including laws that deal with air, water, solid waste, toxic substances, and noise pollution. Such regulations must be written in clear and unambiguous language to give fair notice of the regulations to individuals and institutions affected by them.

Research, Administrative, and Support Responsibilities The EPA can do research, create and administer pollution control guidelines, and support programs designed to make sure that pollution standards are met. The agency can also administer grants to help eliminate pollution under state-run programs.

Enforcement The EPA prefers that businesses voluntarily **comply** with its standards. However, if businesses do not comply, the EPA can bring action against them for polluting the environment, even if the pollution is unintentional.

Current Legislation Congress has continued to increase the EPA's power to deal with new environmental challenges. For instance, the EPA was given the authority to deal with major oil spills using funds provided under the Oil Pollution Act. This allowed the EPA to compel oil storage plants to be built and to fund the development of strategies for dealing with oil-related accidents.

The Clean Air Act

There are actually several Clean Air Acts, each of which was an attempt to improve upon the preceding act. The first clean air act, the Air Pollution Control Act, was passed by Congress in 1955 to provide funds for research into the problems of air pollution. It also recognized that air pollution was a national problem.

Extending the Content

Compliance Issues

Ask students to locate one story about a compliance violation on the EPA Web site and prepare a written summary to share with the class. Be sure students include the date and nature of the violation, and how the case was investigated and settled. Suggest that students comment on the potential or actual dangers caused by the violation.

Figure 18.1 Environmental Regulations

The Environmental Protection Agency was created by the federal government in response to the growing public demand for cleaner water, air, and land. The EPA's tasks include repairing the damage already done to the environment, creating guidelines for controlling pollution, and promoting the use of more environmentally friendly sources of green energy, such as wind and solar power.

The purpose of the Clean Water Act is to protect the nation's waterways, wetlands, and drinking water. One of the biggest environmental problems is the illegal or negligent dumping of waste materials into lakes and rivers by mining operations.

The Clean Air Act identified automobile emissions as a major source of air pollution and created emission standards for motor vehicles. It also regulates the level of pollutants that can be emitted by factories and even common household items such as house paints. Corporate officers who knowingly violate the Clean Air Act are subject to criminal penalties, including imprisonment.

Before laws such as the National Environmental Policy Act were passed, the federal government was not equipped to deal with pollutants that harm human health and the environment. *What are some of the problems businesses have with environmental laws?*

▲ USING VISUALS

Figure 18.1 Environmental Regulations **Answer** The costs of upgrading factories or equipment, disposing of waste, or cleaning up accidental spills can be too high for some companies and drive them out of business. U.S. companies subject to environmental regulation often find it difficult to compete with companies based in other countries where lax environmental regulations prevail.

TEACH (cont.)

C Critical Thinking

Clean Water Act Tell students to imagine that Travis Mining Company uses chemical agents to separate sediments in its mining process. The company claims that the waste materials it dumps into a local river are not toxic. Ask students what role the EPA might play in this situation. (test waste for toxicity and pollutant levels, require a company to change its waste dumping, or assess a penalty)

Guided Practice

Preservation of the Environment

Have students list the most disturbing environmental issues that they believe the United States faces. (Answers will vary, but may include ozone layer depletion, water pollution, solid waste disposal, air quality.) Ask them to identify ways in which individuals can help moderate these problems. (recycling efforts, alternative fuels, reduce driving, purchase alternative fuel vehicles)

Extending the Content

Green Energy

Have students use the Internet or local library to research the meaning of "green" energy. Ask them to provide examples of advances in this field. (Green energy is clean, efficient, renewable, and secure energy. Examples of green energy include hydrogen, biodiesel, ethanol, wind, solar, hydropower.)

TEACH (cont.)

Guided Practice

Clean Air Act

Ask students to identify ways in which the Clean Air Act affects their lives. (Cars must be inspected periodically for emissions controls; some cities have air pollution alerts; pollution affects asthma and other health issues.) Stress that the Clean Air Act was amended in 1977 to establish more practical guidelines.

W Writing Support

Clean Air Act Programs
Have students research the Clean Air Act and write a one-page report on the environmental issues addressed by it. (Answers may include interstate and international air pollution, smog and other air pollutants, cleaner fuels, cleaner vehicles, acid rain, ozone layer, and consumer products that cause damage to the ozone layer.)

C Critical Thinking

Clean Water Act Ask students to name some of the kinds of activities and facilities that the Clean Water Act governs. (discharge of waste into lakes and rivers; sewage plants; managing polluted runoff water from farms, industrial plants, urban storm sewer systems) Remind students that the Clean Water Act gave the EPA the authority to implement pollution-control programs such as setting wastewater standards for industry.

Global Law

Environmental Law in Cambodia

In 1992, the country of Cambodia created a new constitution. Since that time, a system of laws has been created to provide for peaceful resolutions. This system is not too different from the one in the United States and consists of five levels of laws:

1 The Constitution

2 Laws passed by the National Assembly

3 Decrees issued by the Council of Ministers

4 Implementing legislation enacted by the Ministries

5 Decree Laws, or laws passed before the 1992 Constitution

Constitutional Environmental Protections

Cambodia passed a series of laws to permanently protect the environment. Article 59 of the Constitution states:

The State shall protect the environment and balance of abundant natural resources and establish a precise plan of management of land, water, air, wind, geology, ecologic system, mines, energy, petrol and gas, rocks and sand, gems, forests and forestrial products, wildlife, fish and aquatic resources.

In November 1996, the Cambodian National Assembly passed the Law on Environmental Protection and Natural Resource Management. This law's goals are:

- Reduce and control pollution
- Establish the Environmental Impact Assessment system
- Ensure the sustainable use of resources
- Make the public aware and eager to participate
- Stop activities that are detrimental to the environment

Across Cultures: Civil War
In the 1970s and 1980s, the economy of Cambodia was destroyed by civil war. In the 1990s, however, the economy began to recover as Cambodia began to export rice, rubber, and timber.

Critical Thinking *Should the United States amend the Constitution to provide for environmental protections?*

The Clean Air Act of 1963 The Clean Air Act of 1963 was the first statute passed by Congress to use the words *clean air*. The act set aside funds that state and local programs could use to fight air pollution. The act also identified automobiles as a major source of air pollution and set automobile **emissions** standards.

The Clean Air Acts of 1970 and 1977 The Clean Air Act of 1970 set up the National Ambient Air Quality Standards to further improve air quality. Unfortunately, the standards were difficult, if not impossible, to meet. As a result, the act was amended once again in 1977 to establish more practical guidelines.

The Clean Water Act

The Clean Water Act is also known as the Federal Water Pollution Control Act. It was passed by Congress to guard against water pollution in the United States. The act set up guidelines for dealing with the risks involved in dumping pollutants into the nation's waterways. The act also provides money to help cities develop sewage treatment plants. The act encourages state and national cooperation in the effort to clean up the waterways.

404   Unit 6   Starting a Business

Global Law

Environmental Law in Cambodia

Answer Answers will vary. While amendments to the U.S. Constitution can be made, the process is lengthy. However, this does not mean that an amendment is not feasible. Currently, a number of state and federal laws exist that seek to protect the environment.

The Toxic Substance Control Act

The Toxic Substance Control Act authorizes the EPA to police the production, use, and importation of industrial chemicals. The act gives the EPA the power to order the assessment of certain chemical agents and to outlaw the development of harmful chemical substances. Under the act, the EPA has authority over the production and use of existing chemical agents and over the introduction and use of newly developed chemical substances.

State Legislation and Regulation

The EPA encourages state and local governments to enforce actions in their own regions. Many states have passed their own state laws and standards to deal with environmental concerns. Massachusetts, for example, has established its own Department of Environmental Protection, which enforces air and water quality standards within the state. California has passed vehicle emissions standards that are stricter than the federal standards.

International Influences on Environmental Regulation

Environmental concerns are among the most serious problems facing the global community today. In response to these problems, the nations of the world have held a variety of international conferences over the last two decades. Some of these conferences have produced protocols or procedures for dealing with these concerns. For instance, a United Nations conference held in Kyoto, Japan produced a set of protocols for the gradual reduction of greenhouse gases such as carbon dioxide. Many countries have passed the Kyoto Protocols into law; however, the United States has not.

Reading Check

Discuss Can environmental laws be too strict?

 Solar Energy The government offers tax breaks to individuals and businesses who install solar panels. *What are some of the advantages and disadvantages of using solar energy?*

TEACH (cont.)

D Develop Concepts

Greenhouse Gases Ask students if they can explain the impact of greenhouse gases on the environment. (Greenhouse gases allow sunlight to freely enter the atmosphere, trapping a heat-causing "greenhouse" effect.) Explain that burning fossil fuels such as petroleum, coal, or natural gas causes emission of carbon dioxide, a greenhouse gas. Tell students that many countries have passed the Kyoto Protocols— a set of protocols for the gradual reduction of greenhouse gases—into law.

Extending the Content

State Environmental Protection Laws

Tell students that many states have enacted their own environmental protection laws. Then ask them to use the local library or the Internet to find your state's agency that deals with environmental issues. Have students report on one or two conservation programs that the state sponsors.

Reading Check

Discuss Businesses may object to the cost and inconvenience of compliance with environmental standards; however, citizens may agree with protecting their air and water at any cost.

▲ USING VISUALS

Solar Energy Answer The primary advantage to the use of solar energy is that it is free and produces no waste or pollution. In remote places where there is no electricity, solar power is a good alternative. The primary disadvantage to solar energy is that it is expensive initially to install solar power equipment. Of course, the solar panels cannot work at night and they can be unreliable unless located in a very sunny climate.

ASSESS

Quiz

Have students answer the following questions:

1. What law authorizes the EPA to police the production, use, and importation of industrial chemicals? (Toxic Substance Control Act)

2. Which act was passed by Congress to deal with problems associated with dumping pollutants into waterways? (Clean Water Act)

3. What are two responsibilities of the EPA? (regulation of environmental policies; research; enforcement; administration)

RETEACH

Guided Practice

Polluting the Environment

Write the following actions on the board, then ask students to call out the legislation that regulates the activity.

- dumping pollutants into a lake (Clean Water Act)

- leaving open cans of paint on the curb (Clean Air Act)

- water runoff from oil-change garage (Clean Water Act)

STUDY TO GO Have students go to the *Business and Personal Law* Online Learning Center through glencoe.com to download free Study-to-Go content to their cell phones or PDAs.

CYBERLAW

Qwest Communications Corp. v. The City of Berkeley

146 F.Supp.2d 1081 (N.D. Cal. 2001)

Qwest Communications Corp. (Qwest) is a telecommunications company authorized to do business in the state of California. The California Public Utilities Commission granted Qwest the power to do public projects using public rights-of-way. In December 1999, Qwest was contracted to provide faster telecommunications, including higher-speed Internet, to the Lawrence Berkeley National Laboratory. To complete the project, Qwest needed to lay new fiber optic cable in the City of Berkeley's right-of-way. The City of Berkeley refused to let Qwest use the right-of-way. Qwest sued to use the right-of-way. Among the reasons Berkeley refused permission was that Qwest had to be certified under the California Environmental Quality Act to create the 4,300-foot trench needed for the cable.

Ruling and Resolution

The Federal District Court in California held that under the California Environmental Quality Act, construction projects must receive certification. A project is defined as any activity that causes direct physical change in the environment. However, the court was not persuaded that a single 4,300-foot trench could be considered a project under the law.

Critical Thinking How detailed should environmental regulations be?

Energy Regulation and Conservation

Why do we need laws to regulate energy?

Up until the early 1970s, Americans were accustomed to a seemingly endless supply of cheap gasoline. Then, in 1973, the oil-producing countries of the Mideast cut off the supply of oil to many nations in the West, including the U.S., creating a major gas shortage. As a result of the 1973 oil crisis, the U.S. government recognized the need to conserve and regulate its energy resources.

Federal Agencies

In 1977, the federal government created the Department of Energy (DOE). Although it was created in 1977, the roots of the DOE go back to World War II and the Manhattan Project, which developed the first nuclear weapons. To control this new form of energy, the government created the Atomic Energy Commission (AEC), the forerunner of the DOE.

The DOE has a dual function. First, the DOE develops and implements a national policy on energy resources. Second, the DOE has responsibility for the nation's nuclear energy program.

The Federal Energy Regulatory Commission The Federal Energy Regulatory Commission (FERC), which is part of the DOE, regulates electricity and natural gas. FERC controls the wholesale price of natural gas and electricity sold for use in interstate (between states) commerce and the interstate transportation of electricity and natural gas. Intrastate (within a state) prices are regulated by state utility agencies. FERC is also responsible for regulating oil pipeline rates.

CYBERLAW

Qwest Communications Corp. v. The City of Berkeley

Answer Answers will vary. The level of detail needed in law and regulation is a difficult task. The more detailed the regulation is, the less flexibility there is for changing situations. For example, if a regulation lists 50 specific prohibited activities, and there is an activity that is not one of those 50 but is equally harmful, that action may not be considered illegal. However, if regulations are too broad, people may be unable to determine which activities are prohibited.

The Nuclear Regulatory Commission The Nuclear Regulatory Commission (NRC), which is also part of the DOE, regulates nuclear energy. It regulates the licensing, constructing, and opening of nuclear power plants. The NRC also handles the possession, use, transportation, and disposal of nuclear material.

State Agencies

Every state in the United States now has an energy office to deal with energy-related concerns. Although the names of these agencies differ, the functions are the same. These functions are to improve energy regulation, to promote energy-efficient technologies, and to reduce the cost of energy development and production. Some states are more **proactive** than others in promoting and financing the development of alternative energy sources, such as solar power, wind power, and hydropower.

International Influences on Energy Regulation

The International Energy Agency (IEA) is the main worldwide group established to research energy conservation. The IEA is made up of 26 nations, including the United States. Originally, the IEA focused on planning for unanticipated oil shortages. Today, it has expanded its scope to include wide-ranging energy issues, including the development of alternate forms of energy and the creation of strategies for dealing with shifts in the Earth's climate.

After You Read

Summarize List the federal acts that deal with clean air and clean water.

SECTION **18.2** ASSESSMENT

Self Check

1. What federal agency is responsible for combating pollution?

2. What was the Federal Energy Regulatory Commission (FERC) created to do?

3. What are the goals of the International Energy Agency (IEA)?

Academic Connection

Social Studies The Resource Conservation and Recovery Act of 1976 (RCRA) gave the EPA the authority to control hazardous waste from cradle to grave. This includes the generation, transportation, treatment, storage, and disposal of hazardous waste. The RCRA also set forth a framework for the management of non-hazardous wastes. The RCRA was amended in 1986 to enable the EPA to address environmental problems that could result from underground tanks storing petroleum and other hazardous substances. The RCRA focuses only on active and future facilities and does not address abandoned or historical sites. Read about the Resource Conservation and Recovery Act. Then write an environmental act proposal to address a current environmental issue you are interested in.

Critical Thinking

A Matter of Jurisdiction What is the difference between interstate commerce and intrastate commerce and why is the distinction important?

> Go to **glencoe.com** to check your answers.

 After You Read

Summarize Clean Air Acts of 1963, 1970, 1977; Clean Water Act; Toxic Substance Control Act

ASSESS

Self-Assessment

Have students go to the *Business and Personal Law* Online Learning Center through glencoe.com to take the Section 18.2 Practice Test.

CLOSE

Culminating Activity

Environmental Concerns

Ask students to comment on the reasons they think individuals or businesses do not pay attention to the needs of the environment. (Businesses may object to cost of disposing of waste or controlling pollution. Individuals often do not take the time to conserve or recycle.)

SECTION **18.2** ASSESSMENT

Self Check

1. Environmental Protection Agency

2. regulate energy industry; control the wholesale price of natural gas and electricity sold for use in interstate commerce; regulate interstate transport of electricity and natural gas

3. development of alternate forms of energy and strategies for dealing with shifts in the earth's climate; planning for oil shortages

Academic Connection

Social Studies
Answers will vary but should focus on environmental consequences and measures to be taken to control the issue.

Critical Thinking

Interstate commerce crosses state lines (federal jurisdiction), and intrastate commerce occurs solely within one state (state laws apply).

 Activity correlated to the Social Studies standard on page 401

Summary by Sections

Ask students to read the summaries one key point at a time. Then, ask them to work in groups to create two examples to illustrate each key point.

Vocabulary Builder

Cooperative Learning

1. Have students work in groups to prepare their sentences. Ask the groups to exchange their sentences and assess each other's sentences.

Vocabulary Development

- Ask students to use a dictionary or to go online to look up the etymology of each key term listed.
- Then, ask students to list several words derived from the same root or origin. For example, *contract* has the same root as *contractual* or *contractually*.

Chapter 18 Review and Assessment

Summary

Section 18.1 Corporate Regulations

- ◆ The federal government gets its power to regulate business from the Commerce Clause of the United States Constitution, which gives Congress the power to regulate commerce among the states.
- ◆ Congress passed the Securities Act of 1933 and the Securities Exchange Act of 1934 to protect investors in securities from fraud and unfair practices.
- ◆ Congress has passed a series of antitrust laws to prevent monopolies from controlling the market for a product or service.
- ◆ Congress, state legislatures, and the courts have created various laws to regulate the corporate takeover process.

Section 18.2 Environmental Laws

- ◆ Federal laws passed to protect the environment include the National Environmental Policy Act, the Clean Air Act, the Clean Water Act, and the Toxic Substance Control Act.
- ◆ Many states have created their own state laws and standards to deal with environmental concerns.
- ◆ The Department of Energy (DOE), the Federal Energy Regulatory Commission (FERC), and the Nuclear Regulatory Commission (NRC) were created to develop an energy policy and regulate the energy industry.
- ◆ Every state in the U.S. has an energy office to deal with energy-related concerns, such as improving energy regulation, promoting energy efficient technologies, and reducing the cost of energy development and production.

Vocabulary Builder

❶ On a sheet of paper, use each of these terms in a sentence.

Key Terms

- Commerce Clause
- security
- registration statement
- prospectus

- monopoly
- Environmental Protection Agency (EPA)
- Federal Energy Regulatory Commission (FERC)

- Nuclear Regulatory Commission (NRC)

Academic Vocabulary

- commerce
- administer

- certify
- comply

- emissions
- proactive

Go to **glencoe.com** to play a game and improve your legal vocabulary.

Study Skills for Success

Prepare Your Students for Studying

Tell students that they can improve their ability to understand and remember material from their courses by learning and practicing study skills. Remind students to:

- **Get motivated!** Motivation must come from within. To motivate yourself, think of ways in which what you learn now will fit into your long-term personal and professional goals.
- **Get organized!** Make studying part of your daily routine, not something you do at the last minute.
- **Concentrate!** Study in an environment that is as free of distractions as possible.

Key Points Review

Answer the following questions. Refer to the chapter for additional reinforcement.

2 What is the function of the Securities and Exchange Commission (SEC)?

3 Why were antitrust laws created?

4 What was the Federal Trade Commission Act designed to do?

5 What is the goal of the Williams Act?

6 Why did Congress pass the National Environmental Policy Act?

7 What does the Toxic Substance Control Act do?

8 What is the role of the Department of Energy?

9 What is the difference between the Federal Energy Regulatory Commission (FERC) and the Nuclear Regulatory Commission (NRC)?

Standardized Test Practice

10 Read the following excerpt about energy law and complete problems 1 and 2.

Within the framework of energy laws, governments establish their policies, rules and regulations concerning ownership, exploitation, development, and use of energy resources within the boundaries of their jurisdiction. Some countries have comprehensive energy laws which regulate resource exploration, development, production, transport, purchase, and distribution of energy for one or more than one energy carrier. Other countries have issued separate laws for each type of fuel governing resource ownership, exploration rights, and trade regulations as well as supply and pricing rules. In most countries, energy supply systems, and electricity supply in particular, remain in the domain of the public sector. Due to the strategic and economic importance of energy, private sector activity in this field also remains highly regulated. However, conventional energy laws typically focus on the development and management of the energy resource and supply side, and do not normally provide specific guidelines concerning energy use or demand management.

1. In most countries, who controls the energy supply systems?

Ⓐ government agencies

Ⓑ public and private sectors

Ⓒ private corporations

Ⓓ the public sector

2. Conventional energy laws typically focus on

Ⓐ energy use

Ⓑ development and management of the energy resource

Ⓒ demand management

Ⓓ resource ownership

Test-Taking Strategies Always pace yourself when taking a test and avoid spending too much time on a single passage or question.

Key Points Review

2. to administer federal securities law and regulate the sale of securities and the brokers, dealers, and bankers who sell them

3. to prevent monopolies

4. to protect businesses from the wrongful acts of other businesses

5. to make certain shareholders know the qualifications and the intentions of the suitor in a takeover bid

6. to establish a national program to fight pollution and clean up the environment

7. authorizes the EPA to police the production, use, and importation of industrial chemicals

8. developing and implementing a coherent national policy on energy resources of the United States; overseeing the nation's nuclear energy program

9. FERC regulates natural gas and electricity, and the NRC regulates nuclear energy.

Standardized Test Practice

10. D and B

 Strategies for Standardized Test Prep Success

Whether your students have a standardized test coming up in a few days or a few weeks, these last-minute test-prep tips and strategies will help them relax and do their best.

• **Test Format** Help students become familiar with the format of the test by practicing with test items that imitate the actual test items as closely as possible.

• **Test Timing** Have your students take timed practice tests so that they become comfortable with the length, design, and timing of the actual test.

Review and Assessment

 Apply and Debate

Students should use chapter content to arrive at conclusions. The legal resolutions are listed below:

11. Normally, countries have a right to use natural resources in their country. It is doubtful that Country B has any recourse against Country A.

12. Probably. Although the directors have the right to decline a takeover bid, the shareholders can seek judicial review of the decision. The court would decide if the board chairman can take shelter under the business judgment rule.

13. No. The fact that the chairman had taken lavish trips to Italy and bought property there does not prove that he had acted solely in self-interest with regard to the original purchase.

14. Probably. The Robinson-Patman Act prohibits such behavior. If Rich's Models can show that the delayed delivery schedule hurt its business, then it should bring a suit.

15. A private citizen has no authority to require Mr. Heeley to cease his practice. Unless federal, or Vermont, environmental regulators find that the store is violating pollution laws, Mr. Heeley is under no obligation to discontinue the use of the stove.

410

Apply and Debate

Read the following scenarios. Get together with other students in pairs or groups of three and take a position on each scenario. Debate your position in class with students taking the opposite position or prepare a written argument justifying your position.

⑪ Downstream Pollution

Country A has a river running through it which flows into Country B. A lumber mill in Country A that makes plywood for needed housing is located on the river. When pollutants from the mill end up in Country B, they demand that it be closed down.

You Debate — *Do you think that Country B has a right to ask Country A to close the lumber mill that supplies jobs and housing materials to the people in its country?*

⑫ Family History

The Jeffersons have owned a manufacturing company for over 100 years. They incorporated it in 2003. Now Merkson Industries is attempting a hostile takeover. But the board chairman, a descendant of the founder, refuses to sell.

You Debate — *Do shareholders have a right to insist that the company be sold?*

⑬ Assessing a Primary Motive

After purchasing Italian eyewear company Ugo, Cambria Eye Glasses, Inc. lost money for years. The shareholders sued when they learned that Cambria's chairman had taken 12 lavish trips to Italy in two years and purchased a villa there.

You Debate — *Does the evidence prove that the chairman acted solely in self-interest?*

⑭ Model Airplanes

Allied, Inc. manufactures model airplanes. Whenever their best customer, Flying Toys, calls to order 1,000 models, Allied ships them in 24 hours. But whenever Rich's Models places its usual 500 model order, Allied says it takes two weeks to ship.

You Debate — *Could Rich's Models sue Allied for infringing on the Robinson-Patman Act guaranteeing them equal service?*

⑮ Grocery Store Fireplace

Dick Heeley has owned a cozy grocery store in Vermont for ten years. In the winter, hundreds of neighbors come in to sit by the wood-burning stove to chat. One day, a town resident complains to Dick that the stove pollutes the air. She insists that he halt its usage.

You Debate — *Should the owner stop using the wood-burning stove?*

C Critical Thinking

Securities The directors of the Mount Vernon Research Corporation sold tracts of land in its diamond mines under a series of land contracts. Each purchaser would be entitled to a return on his or her investment based on the year-end profits and in proportion to the number of land contracts that he or she owned.

Debate Practice

- Would the SEC consider each of these contracts a security? Explain. (Yes. The Securities Act defines a security as a money investment that looks for profit solely because of another's efforts.)

- What documentation would the SEC require from the corporation? (registration statement; audited financial statements; certification by the CEO and CFO of financial reports)

Case Study Practice– Community Group v. City of San Diego

16 **Exempt from Environmental Laws?** Developers in San Diego wanted to construct a 14-unit residential building with an underground parking garage. The site of the project was a 10,247-square-foot vacant lot. Across the street is Balboa Park, an 1,100-acre urban park that contains theaters, museums, restaurants, and other public facilities.

In January 2004, the City of San Diego issued a building permit for the parking garage. Banker's Hill, Hillcrest, Park West Community Preservation Group (Community Group) filed a petition to stop the construction project. The Community Group argued that the developers had not obtained an environmental review as required under California Environmental Quality Act (CEQA). Under CEQA, developers can be exempt from CEQA, if the project qualifies as urban in-fill. Urban in-fill is defined as an area that: is surrounded by urban structures; has no value to endangered species; would not result in significant traffic or noise; and would be adequately serviced by already installed utilities.

Source: Banker's Hill, Hillcrest, Park West Community Preservation Group v. City of San Diego, 2006 WL 1216918 (Cal. Ct. App. 2006)

Practice Can the City exempt the project from CEQA?

17 Ethics ←?→ Application

Who Is Responsible? Margaret works for a furniture refinishing company. She notices that the chemicals used in the process are rinsed into the floor drains, which flow into the city's sewer system. She tells her boss he should dispose of the chemicals in a safe manner. He tells her that it is too costly, and the chemicals are not that dangerous.

◆ Does Margaret have an ethical duty to report the problem to the Environmental Protection Agency, or is it the responsibility of her boss or the company?

18 Internet Application

Find out about the Clean Air Act Five factories in your town have gigantic smokestacks and are clearly polluting the air. You and your friends want to find out what you can do about this.

Go to **glencoe.com** and research the Clean Air Act of 1970 and its amendments to find out what businesses are required to do. Research the steps that a community can take to encourage or force businesses to clean up their emissions.

>
> **Reading Connection**
> **Outside Reading** Go to **glencoe.com** for a list of outside reading suggestions about environmental laws.

Review and Assessment

←?→ Ethics Application

17. Answers will vary, but students should be encouraged to view the problem as one that both Margaret and her company are responsible for. She could report the problem anonymously if she fears that she will lose her job.

Internet Application

18. Students should find that the Clean Air Act of 1970 provides emission standards for all hazardous pollutants. If a facility discharges more than the standard, it will be required to modify its practices. Citizens can schedule meetings with the companies to voice their concerns and to ask for modifications or testing. The Clean Air Act includes a provision for citizen enforcement.

R Reading Strategy

> **Reading Connection**
>
> **American Bar Association Resources**
>
> Go to the *Business and Personal Law* Online Learning Center through glencoe.com to find links for further readings that relate to this chapter. Ask students to read, review, and summarize the documents. Advise students to keep their reviews and summaries to use as reference material for their Unit Thematic Project on pages 432–433.

Case Study Practice

16. Yes. The CEQA gives discretion to cities in California to determine whether projects are exempt from its requirements. For a development to be exempt, there cannot be a reasonable probability that the development would have significant impact on the environment. In this situation, the presence of Balboa Park does not mean the project is not surrounded by urban uses. The lot is currently vacant and not a habitat to any endangered species. There will only be 14 units, so traffic should not be seriously impacted.

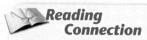

Plan Your Lesson Section by Section

NBEA	NATIONAL BUSINESS LAW STANDARDS
Section 19.1	• **Define** the key terms involved in computer law. • **Define** different types of business crime (e.g., arson, forgery, and embezzlement). • **Distinguish** between a tort and a crime.
Section 19.2	• **Discuss** the issue of taxation and e-commerce • **Describe** the Uniform Computer Information Transactions Act (UCITA), the Uniform Electronic Transactions Act, the Electronic Signatures in Global and National Commerce Act, and the Millennium Digital Commerce Act. • **Define** intellectual property and list types of intellectual property. • **Discuss** the impact of the laws of different countries on contractual transactions.

NCLB	ACADEMIC STANDARDS	Activity/Feature
English Language Arts: NCTE 3 Apply a wide range of strategies to comprehend, interpret, evaluate, and appreciate texts.		*BusinessWeek* News, Case Study, Case Study Practice
English Language Arts: NCTE 9 Develop an understanding of and respect for diversity in language use, patterns, and dialects across cultures, ethnic groups, geographic regions, and social roles.		Global Law
English Language Arts: NCTE 6 Apply knowledge of language structure, language conventions, media techniques, figurative language, and genre to create, critique, and discuss print and non-print texts.		Legal Talk, ad copy, Key Terms, and Academic Vocabulary
Social Studies: NCSS 9 Study global connections and interdependence.		Section 19.1 Assessment
Mathematics: NCTM NOS 2 Understand meanings of operations and how they relate to one another.		Section 19.2 Assessment
English Language Arts: NCTE 10 Students whose first language is not English make use of their first language to develop competency in the English language arts and to develop understanding of content across the curriculum.		Key Terms, Academic Vocabulary, Legal Talk, Vocabulary Builder
English Language Arts: NCTE 1 Read a wide range of print and non-print texts to build an understanding of texts; to acquire new information; to respond to the needs and demands of society and the workplace; and for personal fulfillment.		Global Law
English Language Arts: NCTE 8 Use a variety of technological and information resources to gather and synthesize information and to create and communicate knowledge.		Business Ethics
Social Studies: NCSS 8 Study relationships among science, technology, and society.		Global Law

Connect Your Business Law Classroom to the World of Work

This chart shows the 21st Century Skills, foundation skills, and workplace competencies that students develop as they work in this chapter.

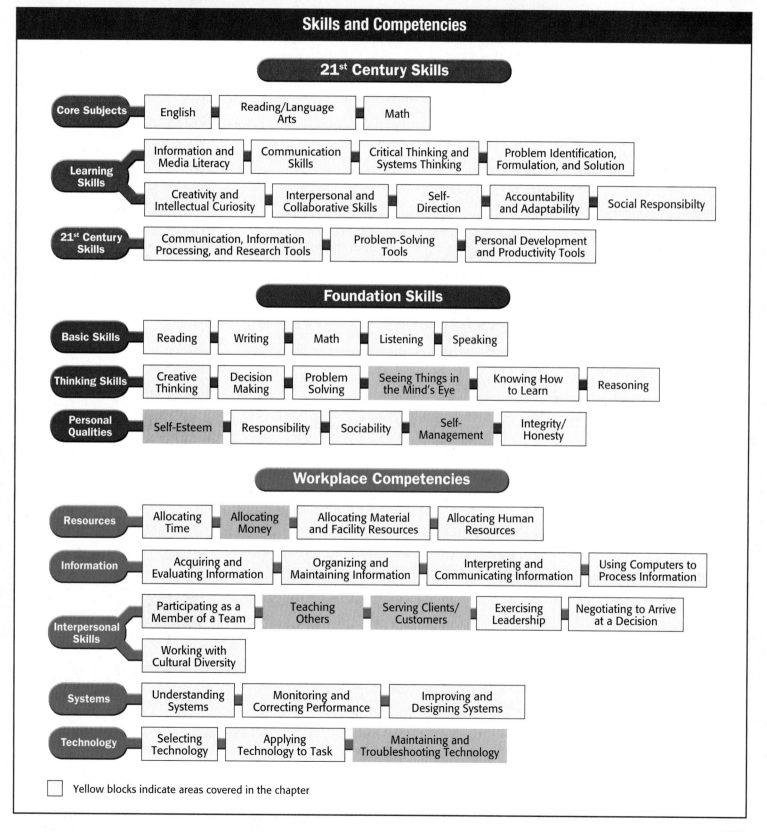

Skills and Competencies

21st Century Skills

Core Subjects
English | Reading/Language Arts | Math

Learning Skills
Information and Media Literacy | Communication Skills | Critical Thinking and Systems Thinking | Problem Identification, Formulation, and Solution

Creativity and Intellectual Curiosity | Interpersonal and Collaborative Skills | Self-Direction | Accountability and Adaptability | Social Responsibilty

21st Century Skills
Communication, Information Processing, and Research Tools | Problem-Solving Tools | Personal Development and Productivity Tools

Foundation Skills

Basic Skills
Reading | Writing | Math | Listening | Speaking

Thinking Skills
Creative Thinking | Decision Making | Problem Solving | Seeing Things in the Mind's Eye | Knowing How to Learn | Reasoning

Personal Qualities
Self-Esteem | Responsibility | Sociability | Self-Management | Integrity/Honesty

Workplace Competencies

Resources
Allocating Time | Allocating Money | Allocating Material and Facility Resources | Allocating Human Resources

Information
Acquiring and Evaluating Information | Organizing and Maintaining Information | Interpreting and Communicating Information | Using Computers to Process Information

Interpersonal Skills
Participating as a Member of a Team | Teaching Others | Serving Clients/Customers | Exercising Leadership | Negotiating to Arrive at a Decision

Working with Cultural Diversity

Systems
Understanding Systems | Monitoring and Correcting Performance | Improving and Designing Systems

Technology
Selecting Technology | Applying Technology to Task | Maintaining and Troubleshooting Technology

Yellow blocks indicate areas covered in the chapter

CHAPTER

19 Cyberlaw and E-Commerce

Introduce the Chapter

Cyberlaw and E-Commerce
Chapter 19 introduces students to the fields of cyberlaw and e-commerce law. Students will learn about how the government protects against computer-related crimes, as well as how new laws reflect the intersection of computers, commerce, and intellectual property.

Building Background
Write these three terms on the board: *cybercrime, e-commerce,* and *intellectual property.* Ask students to tell you all they know about each word.

BusinessWeek News

Ask students if they have ever heard of e-gold. Explain that some Internet companies buy and sell e-gold as a way to standardize cash payments to avoid having to convert currencies, such as dollars to euros or pounds. Explain that this article focuses on how some e-gold companies are now suspected of laundering illegally earned money. Criminals deposit stolen cash or drug money in one country, send it to a partner as e-gold, then withdraw it as cash in another country.

R **Reading Strategy**

Flex Your Reading

Tell students that this chapter covers several new areas of law. Ask students to skim the chapter looking for words that may be recent additions to the field of law.

412

BusinessWeek News

E-Gold: Losing More Shine
By Brian Grow

Gold & Silver Reserve's tangle with the U.S. government is deepening. The company operates a bullion-backed "digital currency" unit called e-gold that U.S. law enforcement officials say has become a popular payment system for online criminals. On December 16, agents from the U.S. Secret Service and FBI raided Gold & Silver Reserve's offices in Melbourne, Fla., and took copies of documents and computer files. Now the U.S. Justice Department is demanding that the company forfeit more than $800,000 in two of its bank accounts. The funds were seized on December 15 by the Secret Service, which declined to comment, citing ongoing investigations being conducted with the FBI.

Law enforcement officials worry that digital currency is becoming the money-laundering machine of choice for cybercriminals. At least a dozen such services allow users to deposit and transfer funds. Eight, including e-gold, claim to be backed by actual bullion.

Flex Your Reading

Efficient critical reading involves being flexible with speed and comprehension. There are several ways of reading critically, and you need to fit a reading style to your needs and to the material.

Go to **glencoe.com** for Flex Your Reading activities, more information on reading strategies for this chapter, and guided practice in reading about e-commerce and cybercrime.

📖 *Classroom Resources*

- 📖 Student Edition
- 📖 Teacher Wraparound Edition
- 📁 Student Activity Workbook with Academic Integration (SE/TAE)
- 💿 TeacherWorks™ Plus! CD
- 💿 *ExamView® Assessment Suite* CD
- 💿 *Presentation Plus!* CD

- 💿 National Mock Trial Championship DVD
- 💿 Online Learning Center with Podcasts at glencoe.com
- 💿 Study-to-Go™ at glencoe.com
- 💿 Online Student Edition
- 💿 Interactive Student Edition

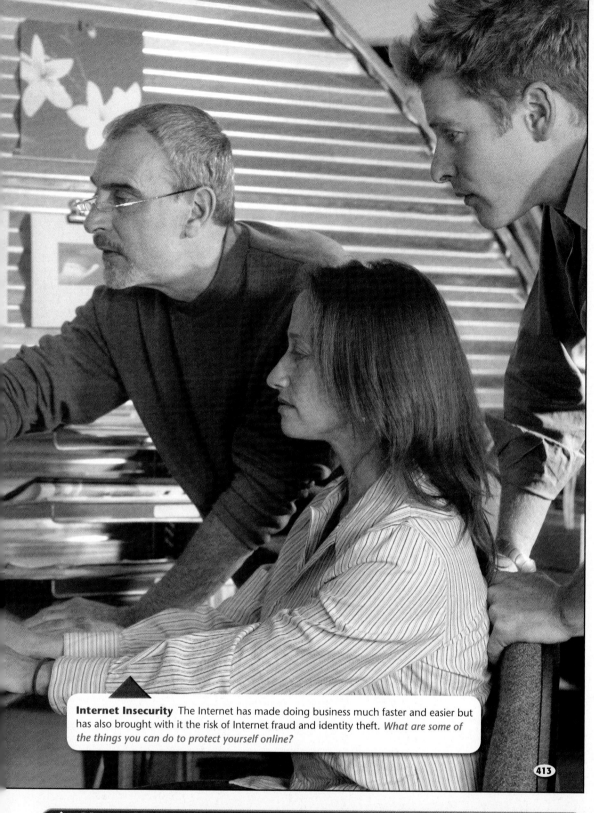

Internet Insecurity The Internet has made doing business much faster and easier but has also brought with it the risk of Internet fraud and identity theft. *What are some of the things you can do to protect yourself online?*

413

Practice the Concept

Protecting Yourself on the Internet
Ask students if they have ever heard about crimes perpetrated using the Internet. Go around the room and give every student a chance to discuss an incident he or she is familiar with. Encourage students to categorize the various incidents they know about such as identity theft, credit card theft, piracy, or others.

Key Terms Tell students that this chapter discusses many types of *cybercrime*, meaning crime committed using computers over the Internet. Inform them that the terminology for each type of crime always begins with the prefix *cyber-*. They must therefore be able to read and distinguish between many types of crimes that, at first, sound the same. Suggest they use note cards to keep track of the various cybercrimes explained in the text.

The Fine Print Ask students if they have ever signed up for a service on the Internet for which they had to agree to a contract by checking the box "I accept." Ask them if they have ever actually read the fine print in such contracts. Give an example by pointing out that many music-downloading sites require the user to agree not to distribute the music to another party.

▲ Using Visuals

Internet Insecurity **Answer** Ways to protect online users include the use of firewalls and anti-virus software. Users should never give out personal information, reply to e-mails with free offers, or go to unknown Web sites to buy goods. Computer users should be sure that they protect their passwords and are careful about opening files sent by e-mail. Discuss the fact that the Internet is an open network that allows anyone with enough skills to pry into other computers.

FOCUS

Bell Ringer Activity

Ask students if any of them know how the Internet works. Explain that the Internet is an unprotected network that allows users to gain access to millions of other computers, including Web sites and databases. Use this to open a discussion about the pros and cons of using the Internet.

Preteaching

Key Terms

Read the definitions and ask students to create a sentence using each term.

Academic Vocabulary

Explain that developing vocabulary is key to academic success. An efficient method to develop vocabulary is to study how words are formed.

- **simulate** Verb, from the Latin *similis* (likeness). Means to imitate.

- **infrastructure** Noun, from the Latin *infra* (below) + *struere* (to construct). Means underlying base or foundation.

- **sabotage** Noun, from the French *saboter* (to walk noisily). Means destruction of property.

Activity Ask students to give a noun, a verb, an adjective, or an adverb form that comes from each word.

 Connects to academic content

What You'll Learn

- ◆ Explain the nature of a cybercrime.
- ◆ List different types of cybercrimes.
- ◆ Describe the nature of a cybertort.
- ◆ Distinguish between cyberdefamation and cyberinvasion of privacy.

Why It's Important

Learning how the law deals with computer-related crimes and torts will help you keep up with new technology.

Academic Standards

Reading and completing the activities in this section will help you practice the following academic standards:

Social Studies (NCSS 9) Study global connections and interdependence.

 English Language Arts (NCTE 8) Use a variety of technological and information resources to gather and synthesize information and to create and communicate knowledge.

Reading Guide

Before You Read

Connect If you have ever received an e-mail with a virus in it, you know what cybercrime is. What are some cybercrimes that you have experienced?

Focus on Ideas

Technology has created new areas of law to prosecute criminals who use computers to commit crimes.

Take Notes

Create a graph like the one shown and use it to take notes as you read this section. Go to glencoe.com to find graphic organizers and tips on how to improve your note-taking skills.

```
                                    ┌─── Types of
                                    │    Cybercrimes—
                    Cyberlaw ───────┤
                                    │
                                    └─── Types of
                                         Cybertorts—
```

Key Terms

You will learn these legal words and expressions in this chapter. You can also find these terms in *Black's Law Dictionary* or in an online legal dictionary.

- cyberlaw
- cybercrime
- cybertrespass
- cyberspoofing
- cyberpiracy
- cyberblackmail
- identity theft
- cybervandalism
- cybertort
- cyberdefamation
- cyberinvasion of privacy

Academic Vocabulary

You will find these words in your readings and in your tests. Look them up in a dictionary and familiarize yourself with them.

- simulate
- infrastructure
- sabotage

 glencoe.com

Reading Strategy

Read for Knowledge

1. **Survey** or preread the chapter.
2. **Question** or formulate questions before you read.
3. **Recite** or read your questions, answers, and notes out loud.
4. **Review** or reread your notes.

Note-Taking Basics

- Listen attentively
- Have note-taking materials ready
- Skim through the lesson material
- Write down key words and ideas
- Anticipate what comes next
- Review notes soon after taking them

The Development of Cyberlaw

Are there laws that control your use of a computer?

The interaction of the law and the world of computers is so new that new words have had to be invented. The field is now called cyberlaw. **Cyberlaw is the area of the law which concerns computers and computer-related crimes.** Some people also call it computer law, electronic law, or e-law. Cyberlaw merges concepts, doctrines, and principles from many legal fields—criminal law, tort law, intellectual property law, and contract law—and puts them into the context of computers. Cyberlaw is intended to deal with cybercrimes. **A cybercrime is any criminal activity associated with a computer.** Legal experts at the federal and state levels have developed two approaches for creating cyberlaws to deal with the new area of cybercrime.

D

The Cybertrespass Approach

Some states have dealt with the problem of covering cybercrimes by adding cybertrespass statutes to the traditional criminal code. **Cybertrespass, or computer trespass, is any illegal activity already in the criminal code committed by using a computer.** Under the cybertrespass approach, states do not define each individual cybercrime.

Rewriting of Criminal Code

Some state legislatures have dealt with cybercrime by writing individual statutes for every crime that can possibly be committed by using a computer. This approach is difficult because every new statute must be individually created. Some state legislators prefer this approach because criminal law statutes must be very specific

As You Read

Predict How does the government keep our laws current with new technology that is used to commit crimes?

Czech Investments

As a recent immigrant to the United States from the Czech Republic, you are trying to start a new life as a business owner. Back in the Czech Republic, you owned and operated a successful stock brokerage firm. Since moving to the U.S., you have realized that many people are interested in investing in Czech companies. The easiest thing for you to do is to set up an Internet investment company that would link American investors with the Czech stock market. U.S. law limits promoting stock for sale on the Internet, but Czech law does not. You want to send mass e-mails out to a lot of people promoting your new service.

Critical Thinking: *What kinds of issues should you be concerned about in using the Internet to link American investors with the Czech stock market?*

TEACH

Discussion Starter

Class Discussion

Ask students what they would do if they purchased a product on the Internet, the seller never delivered the product, and then the Web site disappeared. (contact the bank or credit card company to cancel the transaction; cancel the credit card to prevent future misuse)

D Develop Concepts

Cyberlaw While the term *cyberlaw* may seem like something from a science fiction movie, the expansion of the Internet and the widespread use of computers make this concept a reality. Ask students to name movies that have dealt with the concept of cyberlaw or cybercrime. (*Firewall* with Harrison Ford, *War Games* with Matthew Broderick)

As You Read

Predict Direct students to read the section of content titled "The Development of Cyberlaw." (cybertrespass approach, which considers any criminal activity with a computer to be a crime; rewriting the criminal code statute by statute to address computer-related crimes)

Czech Investments **Answer** Although you may not be committing any illegal acts, you should proceed with caution. The Internet provides a medium that is susceptible to fraud, so you have to make sure you are not opening up either American investors or the Czech stock market to fraud. Check with U.S. government agencies, both federal and state, to make sure you are not violating regulations. Also check with the Czech stock market to make sure your company is legal and to find out if you can conduct business without having a presence in the Czech Republic.

TEACH (cont.)

D Develop Concepts

Cybercrimes Tell students that this section covers seven cybercrimes. Cybercrime is a crime committed on the Internet using the computer as either a tool or a target. All cybercrimes involve both the computer and the person behind it as victims. It is difficult to classify cybercrimes because they evolve daily, and occasionally there is no clear distinction if the person or the computer is the victim. Ask seven students to read one of the sections under "Cybercrimes" and come to the front of the class to present a summary of the crime.

Legal Talk

(extend, exhaust, exhume; transportation, translate, transition)

Ask students to practice their academic and legal vocabulary with the electronic flashcards available at the *Business and Personal Law* Online Learning Center through glencoe.com.

Reading Check

Differentiate
Cyberpiracy uses a computer to steal data in digital format. Cyberspoofing uses a computer to create a false identity in order to commit fraud.

416

Legal Talk

Trespass: *v* Unlawful act committed against a person or person's property. From Latin *trans* = beyond + *passer* = pass.

Extort: *v* To obtain from a person by force. From Latin *ex* = out + *tort* = twist: to twist out.

Vocabulary Builder List and define three words each that begin with the prefix *ex* and the prefix *trans*.

Look It Up! Check definitions in *Black's Law Dictionary* or an online glossary. For direct links, go to **glencoe.com** to find more vocabulary resources.

Vocabulary You can find vocabulary definitions in the **Key Terms** glossary and **Academic Vocabulary** glossary in the back of this book.

Reading Check

Differentiate *What is the difference between cyberpiracy and cyberspoofing?*

---

in detailing an outlawed behavior. Otherwise, when the statute is used to prosecute a cyberdefendant, the court might decide that the statute is void because it is too vague.

Cybercrimes
What kinds of crimes can be committed using computers?

Cybercrimes include both crimes directed at people using a computer and crimes directed at other computers.

Cyberspoofing

Cyberspoofing is a crime in which a cybercriminal falsely adopts the identity of another computer user or creates a false identity on a computer Web site in order to commit fraud. One of the most common types of cyberspoofing is called *phishing*. This involves creating a phony Web site that **simulates** a real bank, credit card agency, or retail store. The criminals then broadcast false e-mails in the name of the business with a link to the phony Web site. They attempt to lure people into believing the Web site is real and attempt to obtain from the victims their private information such as credit card and bank account numbers, personal ID numbers (PINs), and passwords.

Cyberspoofers also use online auction sites, such as eBay, to deceive legitimate buyers. They pretend to have goods for sale that they do not actually have. After the consumers purchase the goods, the criminals pocket the money and do not deliver any goods.

Cyberpiracy

Cyberpiracy is a crime that involves using a computer to steal computer data stored in a digital format. Cyberpiracy often involves the theft of intellectual property, such as downloading software programs or transmitting them to others without payment or permission. To combat this, Congress passed the Digital Millennium Copyright Act (DMCA). The DMCA makes it illegal to pirate copyrighted computer programs using methods that bypass software copyright protection systems. The penalties for violating the DMCA are very severe, reaching as high as ten years in prison for second time offenders. The DMCA also allows individual plaintiffs to bring civil lawsuits against cyberpirates who violate its provisions.

Cyberblackmail

Cyberblackmail, sometimes called cyberextortion, is the use of information unlawfully obtained by computer to pressure a victim into granting a payoff to the blackmailer. Generally, the criminal threatens to reveal some sort of illegal or embarrassing conduct gathered about the person. Computer users who spend time in chat rooms are especially vulnerable to this type of crime. The cyberblackmailer often befriends a person, learns damaging information, then uses it to extort money from the victim.

glencoe.com

W Writing Support

Cyberpiracy Tell students to imagine they own a music company that sells CDs on a Web site. Ask students to write the text that will be placed on their Web site warning users not to pirate their music. Have them explain why it is illegal to pirate music.

Extending the Content

Cyberspoofing on Auction Web Sites

Ask students if they purchase items on eBay or other auction Web sites. Involve them in a discussion of the risks of buying from fraudulent sellers or sellers who are selling illegal merchandise such as stolen items or fake goods. Ask students to create policies that would protect them from cyberspoofing.

Identity Theft

Identity theft is using a computer to steal financial, employment, educational, medical, and personal data. Identity thieves attempt to obtain credit card numbers, financial data, passwords, PINs, Social Security numbers, and access codes. They then use the data to empty bank accounts, run up credit card bills, steal cash, and generally disrupt the target's personal life. It is important to be aware of all activity on your accounts to prevent identity theft because once your identity is stolen it can take years to fix the problem.

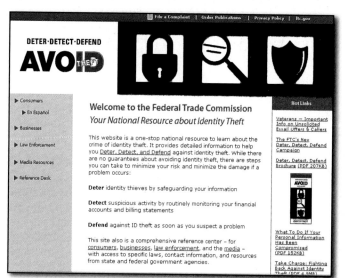

DETER · DETECT · DEFEND

AVO**ID** THEFT

⊞ File a Complaint | Order Publications | Privacy Policy | ftc.gov

▶ Consumers
▶ En Español
▶ Businesses
▶ Law Enforcement
▶ Media Resources
▶ Reference Desk

Welcome to the Federal Trade Commission
Your National Resource about Identity Theft

This website is a one-stop national resource to learn about the crime of identity theft. It provides detailed information to help you Deter, Detect, and Defend against identity theft. While there are no guarantees about avoiding identity theft, there are steps you can take to minimize your risk and minimize the damage if a problem occurs:

Deter identity thieves by safeguarding your information

Detect suspicious activity by routinely monitoring your financial accounts and billing statements

Defend against ID theft as soon as you suspect a problem

This site also is a comprehensive reference center – for consumers, businesses, law enforcement, and the media – with access to specific laws, contact information, and resources from state and federal government agencies.

Hot Links

Veterans — Important Info on Unsolicited Email Offers & Callers

The FTC's New Deter, Detect, Defend Campaign

Deter, Detect, Defend Brochure (PDF 207KB)

What To Do If Your Personal Information Has Been Compromised (PDF 152KB)

Take Charge: Fighting Back Against Identity Theft (PDF 4.9MB)

Cyberterrorism

Cyberterrorism is committed when someone operating a computer disrupts part of the national electronic **infrastructure**. This includes power grids, the air traffic control system, and the national defense system, among others. It also includes disrupting corporate computer systems, such as banks, brokerages, and telecommunications.

Cybervandalism

Cybervandalism is disrupting, damaging, or destroying a Web site or computer network. Cybervandals, also called hackers, might attack a business or government computer system as an act of **sabotage** or revenge. Although many people commit cybervandalism as a prank, to gain attention, or to show off, cybervandalism is still a crime and cybervandals are criminals.

Cybergerm Warfare

Cybergerm warfare involves transmitting computer viruses to people to destroy their computer system or files. Like cybervandals, perpetrators transmit viruses as a prank or to show off, but others use viruses intentionally to commit crimes, such as cyberterrorism or cybervandalism. Firewalls and anti-virus software can block many viruses.

Cybertorts

What is the difference between a tort and a cybertort?

A tort is a private wrong committed by one person against another. **A cybertort is the invasion, theft, falsification, misuse, or deletion of data stored in a computer to commit a tort.** The two most common cybertorts are cyberdefamation and cyberinvasion of privacy.

🔓 **Cybercrime** The advent of computer technology and the Internet created new ways of communicating and doing business. Unfortunately, it also created new opportunities for criminals. *What crimes have computers and the Internet made it much easier to commit?*

TEACH (cont.)

Extending the Content

Cybergerm Warfare
Ask if any students are familiar with virus protection software. Ask volunteers to explain to the class how computer firewalls and virus scanning software work, or how they can protect computer users against cybergerm warfare. Have students call out ways to avoid getting computer viruses.

ASSESS

Quiz
Ask students to answer the following questions:

1. What crime involves using a computer to obtain a payoff? (cyberblackmail)
2. What crime involves disrupting infrastructure? (cyberterrorism)
3. What crime involves using a computer to steal financial, employment, or personal information? (identity theft)

RETEACH

Guided Practice

Cyberspoofing
Ask students to indicate how they can recognize when they are being cyberspoofed. (Phishing e-mails often do not address users by name, have misspelled words, pressure users by saying their account will be closed if they do not update their password, or send them to a Web site whose URL address is suspect.)

▲ USING VISUALS

➡ **Cybercrime** **Answer** The widespread use of computers and the Internet has made many crimes easier to commit. Most prevalent is identity theft, whereby a thief gains access to personal records and uses that information to commit crimes, purchase products, or steal cash. Vandalism, terrorism, blackmail, and piracy are also now more easily accomplished using technology and the Internet.

Activity Ask for volunteers to pick one of the cybercrimes discussed in this section. Have each student research the crime and learn methods that can be used to protect individuals against that crime. Volunteers should report their findings to the class.

RETEACH (cont.)

 After You Read

Summarize
cyberspoofing,
cyberterrorism,
cybervandalism, and
cybergerm warfare

ASSESS

Self-Assessment

Have students go to the *Business and Personal Law* Online Learning Center through glencoe.com to take the Section 19.1 Practice Test.

CLOSE

Culminating Activity

Identify Theft

Ask students to imagine what can happen to someone whose identity has been stolen. Ask them to name as many repercussions as they can identify. (loss of credit or cash, opening unauthorized accounts in their name, not paying for goods purchased under their name)

Cyberdefamation

Cyberdefamation is the communication via computer or other electronic device of false data that damages a person's reputation. Cyberdefamation may involve sending out e-mails or text messages that contain false information about a company that ruins its name in the public. Congress recently passed the Communications Decency Act (CDA) that protects Internet Service Providers (ISPs) from being held liable for any cyberdefamation performed by users on these services.

Cyberinvasion of Privacy

Cyberinvasion of privacy is an unwelcome intrusion into the private matters of an individual carried out or sustained by a computer. Cyberinvasion of privacy often involves employees who, because of their jobs, work closely with confidential files, such as medical records, financial records, scholastic records, and employment records.

The government has passed several laws to protect the privacy of individuals and their computer records. The Fair Credit Reporting Act protects records kept by credit bureaus. The law says that credit bureaus must tell people about their files and must send corrections to anyone who might have been misled by false reports. The Right to Financial Privacy Act states that financial institutions cannot open customer records to a government official without the customer's permission, unless there is a court order. The Electronic Communications Privacy Act restricts the unauthorized access of e-mail and instant messaging. However, employers can monitor the e-mail transmissions of employees if the employees consent to it.

After You Read

Summarize List the four types of crimes in which the computer is the victim.

SECTION 19.1 ASSESSMENT

Self Check

1. What is a cybercrime?
2. What is a cybertort?
3. What is the difference between cyberdefamation and cyberinvasion of privacy?

Academic Connection

English Language Arts
You are a small business owner who conducts business internationally via the Internet. You are concerned that this may expose your computer system to cybervandalism and cybergerm warfare. To combat this, you wish to upgrade your anti-virus software. Research three brands of anti-virus software, such as Norton and EZAntivirus. Create a chart comparing and contrasting the various features offered by each brand and determine which product best suits your needs. Write a brief report stating your reasons for choosing this software application.

Critical Thinking

Cyberterrorism
Since 9/11 the federal government has become much more involved in combating the threat of cyberterrorism. What are some of the concerns about what cyberterrorists could do?

 Go to **glencoe.com** to check your answers.

glencoe.com

SECTION 19.1 ASSESSMENT

Self Check

1. any criminal activity associated with a computer
2. use of a computer to commit a tort
3. Cyberdefamation: communication via computer of false data that damages a person's reputation. Cyberinvasion: using a computer to intrude into someone's personal matters.

Academic Connection

English Language Arts
Answers will vary, but should focus on computer security and protection.

Critical Thinking

Cyberterrorism
Answer Cyberterrorists could break into military, financial, or power networks to disrupt the nation's infrastructure from anywhere in the world.

 Activity correlated to the English Language Arts standard on page 414

Internet Transactions

Reading Guide

Before You Read

Connect What are some of the problems with doing business over the Internet you do not usually have doing business face-to-face, by phone, or by mail?

Focus on Ideas

The government has been very careful to balance the rights of the Internet buyer with those of the Internet seller.

Take Notes

Create a graph like the one shown and use it to take notes as you read this section. Go to **glencoe.com** to find graphic organizers and tips on how to improve your note-taking skills.

Issues in E-Commerce

Jurisdiction   Intellectual Property

 ### Key Terms

You will learn these legal words and expressions in this chapter. You can also find these terms in *Black's Law Dictionary* or in an online legal dictionary.

- e-commerce
- digital signature
- domain name

Academic Vocabulary

You will find these words in your readings and in your tests. Look them up in a dictionary and familiarize yourself with them.

- tangible
- broadcast
- duplicate

What You'll Learn

- ◆ Explain intellectual property and copyright for digital products.
- ◆ Explain the importance of trademarks.
- ◆ Identify the characteristics of a patentable invention.
- ◆ Recognize two unsettled issues in e-commerce law.
- ◆ Explain new laws regarding digital signatures and documents.

Why It's Important

Knowing the laws that affect e-commerce will help you whenever you download music or movies, or buy goods on the Internet.

Academic Standards

Reading and completing the activities in this section will help you practice the following academic standards:

Math (NCTM NOS 2) Understand meanings of operations and how they relate to one another.

Social Studies (NCSS 8) Study relationships among science, technology, and society.

R Reading Strategy

Read for Knowledge

1. **Survey** or preread the chapter.
2. **Question** or formulate questions before you read.
3. **Recite** or read your questions, answers, and notes out loud.
4. **Review** or reread your notes.

Note-Taking Basics

- Listen attentively
- Have note-taking materials ready
- Skim through the lesson material
- Write down key words and ideas
- Anticipate what comes next
- Review notes soon after taking them

FOCUS

 Bell Ringer Activity

Ask students to identify the sales tax rate in your county or state. Then ask them what should happen when a seller located in another state with a different tax rate sells goods to them. Have students consider what solutions are used today to resolve this jurisdictional problem.

Preteaching

Key Terms

Read the definitions and ask students to create a sentence using each term.

Academic Vocabulary

Explain that developing vocabulary is key to academic success. An efficient method to develop vocabulary is to study how words are formed.

- **tangible** Adjective, from the Latin *tangere* (to touch). Means possible to touch.
- **broadcast** Verb, from the Middle English *brood* (wide) + the Norse *kasten* (to cast). Means to transmit over a wide area.
- **duplicate** Verb, from the Latin *duplicare* (to double). Means to make a copy of.

Activity Ask students to give a noun, a verb, an adjective, or an adverb form that comes from each word.

NCLB Connects to academic content

TEACH

Discussion Starter

Class Discussion
Explain to students that a decade ago, businesses did not realize how popular e-commerce would become. Now, most major retailers have both "clicks" and "bricks," meaning Internet sites and traditional "bricks-and-mortar" stores, for their customers. Ask students if they believe online shopping will have outgrown in-store shopping by the time they are out of school.

D Develop Concepts

Authentication Issues
Remind students that one of the most important legal conventions is having witnessed signatures on a contract that verify the identity of the parties and bind them. Before reading this section, ask students how they think e-commerce deals with this issue. Then discuss the section to review the E-sign Act.

As You Read

Predict Inform students that software is considered intellectual property. Ask students to pay close attention to the section on "Copyrights." (Software programs can be copyrighted.)

As You Read
Predict Can a software program be copyrighted just like a book or song?

E-Commerce and Computer Law
The world of e-commerce has quickly evolved in the last ten years. Log on to **glencoe.com** to see what types of regulations are being created to protect consumers.

List and explain three regulations you find in your WebQuest folder to share with your class.

E-Commerce Laws
How does e-commerce save you time?

E-commerce, short for electronic commerce, is the process of conducting business using electronic means, especially the Internet. E-commerce includes purchasing products by using electronic credit or debit cards, extracting money from a checking account at the local ATM, and transferring funds electronically between financial institutions. These new electronic forms of business have raised jurisdictional issues, taxation issues, and authentication problems, as well as intellectual property rights issues (see **Figure 19.1**).

Jurisdictional Issues
Doing business over the Internet raises the question of which state has jurisdiction in a case when the user or buyer does not reside in the same state as the seller. The courts have recognized two principles on this matter:

- Just because a Web site can be accessed in a state does not, by itself, give jurisdiction to that state.
- A state may gain jurisdiction over an e-commerce transaction when a Web site allows users to purchase merchandise on that site. The merchandiser Amazon.com is an example. In such cases, the state in which the buyer resides has jurisdiction, even though the physical home of the seller is another state.

Tax Issues
The jurisdictional issue above is important because it plays a role in determining which state has the right to tax Internet sites that sell goods. The courts have ruled that sellers who do not have a store, office, or wholesale shop within a state cannot be taxed by that state. However, the buyer may be taxed at the buyer's location, such as a sales tax. At this time, Internet sales are governed by the Internet Tax Freedom Act, which has delayed a decision on how to standardize Internet-use taxes until 2008.

Authentication Issues and the E-Sign Act
One difficulty with buying and selling on the Internet is making certain that the buyer and the seller really are who they claim to be. This is referred to as authentication. To manage this problem, Congress passed the E-sign Act, a short name for the Electronic Signatures in Global and National Commerce Act. This act ensures that any cybercontract is considered as legal as a paper equivalent if the parties have agreed to use digital signatures. **A digital signature is an encoded message that appears at the end of a contract created online.** The signature can be verified by a confidential password, by a special smart card, or by electronic equipment that can identify a person by scanning his or her fingerprints or retina.

 glencoe.com

Research Tip Access the *Business and Personal Law* Online Learning Center through glencoe.com and print a couple of examples of the resources available. Make sure students understand how to use them in their research project.

Extending the Content

Consumer Protection
The Organisation for Economic Cooperation and Development (OECD), which has 29 country-members including the United States, has signed on to new guidelines for the protection of e-commerce consumers. These guidelines are posted on the Federal Trade Commission for the Consumer Web site.

Figure 19.1 Issues in Cyberlaw

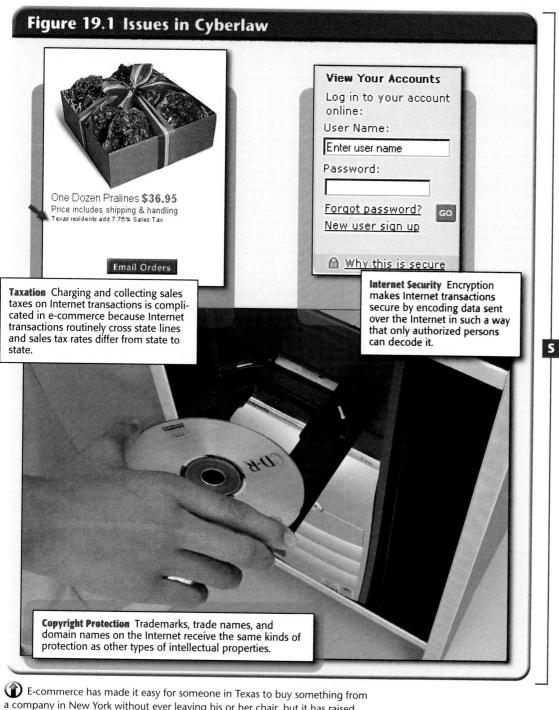

One Dozen Pralines $36.95
Price includes shipping & handling
Texas residents add 7.75% Sales Tax

Email Orders

View Your Accounts
Log in to your account online:
User Name:
Enter user name
Password:

Forgot password?   GO
New user sign up

🔒 Why this is secure

Taxation Charging and collecting sales taxes on Internet transactions is complicated in e-commerce because Internet transactions routinely cross state lines and sales tax rates differ from state to state.

Internet Security Encryption makes Internet transactions secure by encoding data sent over the Internet in such a way that only authorized persons can decode it.

Copyright Protection Trademarks, trade names, and domain names on the Internet receive the same kinds of protection as other types of intellectual properties.

E-commerce has made it easy for someone in Texas to buy something from a company in New York without ever leaving his or her chair, but it has raised questions regarding issues such as jurisdiction, security, and taxation. *What does a cybercontract require to be considered completely legal?*

Chapter 19   Cyberlaw and E-Commerce   **421**

19.2 SECTION

TEACH (cont.)

S Skills Practice

List Ask students to list three main issues that e-commerce has raised. (jurisdiction, taxation, and authentication) **L1**

Explain Have students explain the two conclusions that the courts have drawn in regard to jurisdictional issues. (Just because a Web site can be accessed in a given state, does not give that state jurisdiction over the Web site if it is not located in that state. If a Web site allows users to purchase goods, the state in which purchasers reside has jurisdiction over transactions involving those purchases.) **L2**

Classify Ask students to write a paragraph that distinguishes between a copyright and a trademark. (Copyrights protect literary, scientific, and artistic works from being copied. Trademarks protect an image, logo, symbol, or slogan for a company or product.) **L3**

Extending the Content

Differing Tax Rates
Tell students that they are about to open an Internet store. They must tax buyers who live in various states. Ask students to research the state tax rates in all 50 states. Tell them to disregard local taxes.

▲ USING VISUALS

➡️ **Figure 19.1 Issues in Cyberlaw** Answer In order to be valid, a cybercontract has the same requirements as a paper contract, including signatures; however, in this case, a digital signature is acceptable.

Activity Ask if any students know what encryption is and how it works. (Explain that encryption is a process of altering electronic data so they cannot be read by someone who does not have the same code as the one used to encrypt the message.) Next, ask students to do research on 64-bit or 128-bit encryption. (64-bit encryption means that 64 digits can be used to code each letter or character of the alphabet or a number. The more bits, the harder the message is to decrypt.)

SECTION 19.2

TEACH (cont.)

W Writing Support

Copyrights Ask students to write a brief essay discussing reasons why an author or artist's work must be protected by a copyright. Have students read their essays to the class. To demonstrate how to copyright work, tell students to write "Copyright © 200X by [name]" at the bottom of their papers. Inform them that this provides them protection against having someone copy their work and claim it as their own.

C Critical Thinking

Copyrights Ask students to theorize why copyrights extend only 70 years after the author's life. (author should be protected during his or her lifetime; extending the copyright 70 years grants the author's heirs protection for the work; beyond 70 years, the government believes that the public has a right to the work)

✓ Reading Check

Analyze Answers will vary. Sample answers include a Web search to locate work, and hiring private agencies to scour the Web looking for copies of a work.

✓ Reading Check

Analyze *How can an author or songwriter keep track of whether people are illegally copying their works on the Internet?*

Vocabulary You can find vocabulary definitions in the **Key Terms** glossary and **Academic Vocabulary** glossary in the back of this book.

⊕ Electronic Copying Federal laws have given computer programs the same copyright protection as literary works and made it illegal to make electronic duplicates of them. *What exceptions are there to the law?*

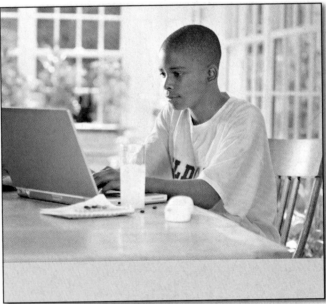

Cyberlaw and Intellectual Property

Is there any way to protect intellectual property on the Internet?

Another new legal area is cyberprotection law. This involves laws that protect people and businesses that create or invent any of the following:

- products that can be distributed digitally using computers, such as music and movies
- new computer products and inventions, such as hardware devices
- products that use or work with computers, such as software

New cyberprotection laws have been created in three areas: copyrights, trademarks, and patents. These types of laws allow writers, artists, inventors, and businesses to protect their ideas, products, and trade names from having other people imitate, copy, use, or sell them without permission and/or payment.

Copyrights

A copyright is a legal protection that has been available in the United States for literary, artistic, and scientific works since 1790. Under the federal Copyright Act, the originator of a work in a "fixed **tangible** medium of expression" is granted the exclusive authority to publish, reproduce, and sell his or her work. The Computer Software Copyright Act of 1980 added computer software programs to the types of work to which copyright protection can be extended.

Copyrighting a work is done by registering it at the Copyright Office in Washington, D.C., although a formal registration is no longer required to obtain protection. As soon as a work exists in tangible form, the owner is protected. A copyright extends for the creator's life plus 70 years. If the originator is a corporation, the copyright lasts 120 years from when it was first written or 95 years from its first publication. After the copyright period is over, the work goes into the public domain where it may be copied by others.

Another new area of copyright law concerns the **broadcast** of artistic works over the Internet. Millions of computer users can get free access to a protected literary or artistic work if just one person illegally publishes it on a Web site. As a result, Congress passed the No Electronic Theft Act (NET Act) in 1997. This statute provides prison terms and fines for anyone

▲ USING VISUALS

➜ Electronic Copying Answer The law permits making a single duplicate of copyrighted works on the Internet as long as there are legitimate reasons for making the copy, such as for educational purposes, and the maker does not make a profit from it. Libraries and archives may duplicate works for preservation and make limited copies for library users.

Activity Ask students to research criminal liability for copyright infringement. (If there is willful infringement for profit or financial gain, or the value of the work exceeds $1,000, the court can sentence the infringer to one year in jail plus fines. If the value of the work exceeds $2,500, the infringer can be sentenced to five years plus fines.)

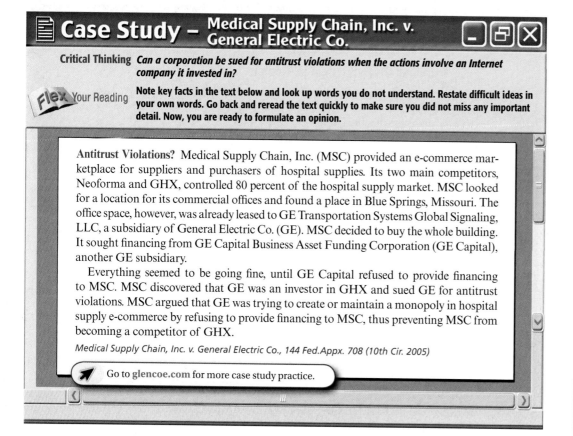

Case Study – Medical Supply Chain, Inc. v. General Electric Co.

Critical Thinking *Can a corporation be sued for antitrust violations when the actions involve an Internet company it invested in?*

Flex Your Reading Note key facts in the text below and look up words you do not understand. Restate difficult ideas in your own words. Go back and reread the text quickly to make sure you did not miss any important detail. Now, you are ready to formulate an opinion.

Antitrust Violations? Medical Supply Chain, Inc. (MSC) provided an e-commerce marketplace for suppliers and purchasers of hospital supplies. Its two main competitors, Neoforma and GHX, controlled 80 percent of the hospital supply market. MSC looked for a location for its commercial offices and found a place in Blue Springs, Missouri. The office space, however, was already leased to GE Transportation Systems Global Signaling, LLC, a subsidiary of General Electric Co. (GE). MSC decided to buy the whole building. It sought financing from GE Capital Business Asset Funding Corporation (GE Capital), another GE subsidiary.

Everything seemed to be going fine, until GE Capital refused to provide financing to MSC. MSC discovered that GE was an investor in GHX and sued GE for antitrust violations. MSC argued that GE was trying to create or maintain a monopoly in hospital supply e-commerce by refusing to provide financing to MSC, thus preventing MSC from becoming a competitor of GHX.

Medical Supply Chain, Inc. v. General Electric Co., 144 Fed.Appx. 708 (10th Cir. 2005)

➤ Go to **glencoe.com** for more case study practice.

---

who creates an electronic **duplicate** of a copyrighted work for commercial profit or private financial gain. The Digital Millennium Copyright Act (DMCA) also outlaws pirated copies of software made by disabling the internal protection system of the software.

Trademarks and Domain Names

A trademark is a distinctive name, word, symbol, image or slogan used by a business to identify and distinguish its goods from products sold by others. Trademarks are registered with the United States Patent and Trademark Office in Washington, D.C. Many hardware and software companies trademark their name and the name of their products.

A domain name is the Internet address of a business. Domain name disputes arise when one party has registered a domain name that uses a famous person's name, a trademark, or a trade name that is registered by another user. In some cases, cybersquatters register a person's name, a trademark, or a trade name as a domain name with no intent to actually use it. Instead, the cybersquatter holds on to the name until the real holder of the name, the trademark, or the trade name appears to claim the name.

C

glencoe.com

Case Study

Medical Supply Chain, Inc., v. General Electric Co.

Answer No. The Tenth Circuit Court of Appeals held that MSC could not sue GE directly. Although GE may have invested in GHX, it was only one of many investors. Further, it was not GE's parent corporation that had invested in GHX, but rather a subsidiary of GE. In order for a party to be guilty of antitrust monopoly statutes, that party must have the opportunity to conspire with another party to control the flow of trade. In this situation, GHX and Neoforma control 80 percent of the e-commerce hospital supply market. However, there was no proof that GE had any control over GHX or that GHX was conspiring with Neoforma.

TEACH (cont.)

C Critical Thinking

Trademarks Ask students to speculate on why the law allows companies to protect their names, logos, and slogans. (Answers may include that branding promotes the identity of a company and prevents others with similar branding from profiting on well-recognized and successful companies.)

ASSESS

Independent Practice

Jurisdiction
Outline the following scenario for students. RightWay Productions, based in Florida, offers advertising services to clients all over the United States. Joe's Hardware store in Austin, Texas, asks RightWay to produce a commercial for the store. Joe's Hardware and RightWay subsequently have a dispute on the scope and delivery of the commercial. Joe's Hardware files a lawsuit in Texas. RightWay Productions contends that the suit must be filed in a Florida court. Ask students who is correct. (Joe's Hardware; the state of the buyer gains jurisdiction over an e-commerce transaction)

RETEACH

Review Key Terms

Encourage students to access the *Business and Personal Law* Online Learning Center through glencoe.com and use the electronic flashcards to review the key terms.

RETEACH (cont.)

Independent Practice

Trademarks and Patents

Ask students to explain the difference between a trademark and a patent. (A trademark protects a logo, slogan, symbol or image. A patent protects an invention.)

C Critical Thinking

Patents Ask students to think about why two companies can come up with very similar products but both can receive a patent on their inventions. (The patent covers only the actual design of the invention, not the concept. Two companies can produce vacuum cleaners, but as long as they are designed differently, each can have a patent.)

Extending the Content

Patents

Have students visit the Web site of the U.S. Patent Office and write a brief report indicating what steps must be followed to register a patent.

STUDY TO GO Have students go to the *Business and Personal Law* Online Learning Center through glencoe.com to download free Study-to-Go content to their cell phones or PDAs.

Global Law

Internet Privacy Laws in Taiwan

In 1995, the Taiwanese legislature passed the Computer-Processed Personal Data Protection Law 1995. This law covers the privacy of information collected over the Internet.

Who the Law Covers

The law only applies to the public sector and some industries within the private sector. The private sector categories only include:

- credit information organizations
- hospitals
- schools
- telecommunications businesses
- bank and financial institutions
- securities businesses
- insurance companies
- mass communications

Government Regulation

The law provides regulations for the transmission of private information from Taiwan to other locations in the world. There are four reasons the government can block a transmission:

1 to protect Taiwan's national interest

2 where an international treaty or agreement prohibits the transfer

3 where the receiving country lacks sufficient laws or regulation to protect personal information

4 the indirect transmission of information to a third country to get around Taiwan's laws

> **Across Cultures: Convenience Store Culture**
>
> Taiwan boasts more convenience stores per person than any other country. There are over 8,000 convenience stores in Taiwan. Because they are so prevalent, the stores provide a number of services, such as collection of parking fees, utility bills, and credit card payments. Eighty percent of Taiwan's urban population visits a convenience store weekly.

Critical Thinking *How much should the government do to control private information sent over the Internet?*

The cybersquatter then asks for an enormous amount of money to sell the name back to the real owner.

To deal with this tactic, Congress passed the Anticybersquatting Consumer Protection Act. The object of the act is to provide a shield for the real owners of trademarks and trade names.

Patents

A patent is a property right that inventors can acquire to protect their right to make, use, and sell their inventions for a number of years as set by law. In order for an invention to be patentable, it must meet three requirements. The invention must fit within the statute as "patentable subject matter." The invention must consist of some nonobvious, new, and useful feature. The application designed for the invention must be so specific that, from its detail, the invention could be reproduced by experts in the field.

For many years, lawmakers debated whether stand-alone computer programs were patentable. Once lawmakers determined that software programs are indeed a process, or a means of doing something, they agreed that they qualify as patentable subject matter. Another software programmer must invent a different way to do the same thing as the one who owns the patent.

Global Law

Internet Privacy Laws in Taiwan

Answer Answers will vary. There are many different ways for governments to deal with privacy issues on the Internet. Governments' positions range from not having any legal protections to having a highly regimented system where information can only be shared if the right to share it has been specifically granted in advance. The government must balance its duties to protect the public and national security with the preservation of an individual's right to privacy. Because of the sheer size of the Internet, it would be impossible to completely regulate any system, whether that system is broad or narrow.

The patent application process requires documenting in detail the plans, structure, and operation of the invention. The document is then filed at the United States Patent and Trademark Office. If approved, the inventor is given a number that must be placed on the invention along with the word *patent* or the abbreviation *pat.*

Cybercontract Law
What is the difference between a contract and a cybercontract?

Cybercontract law deals with the buying and selling of computers and computer programs. One area of cybercontracts involves the sale of custom-programmed software. For example, a company might hire a programmer to come to its business to develop a new program. The legal issue in this matter is the question of who owns the source code, which is the actual code behind the software.

The Uniform Computer Information Transactions Act

The Uniform Computer Information Transactions Act (UCITA) governs the law for cybercontracts such as software agreements and licenses, software formulation contracts, and software maintenance contracts. Once the parties to a cybercontract have entered an agreement using electronic means, the agreement will be just as binding as a similar one negotiated outside of the Web. The UCITA is a default statute, which means that the parties can use it to resolve any issues not covered by their own contracts.

After You Read

Summarize List three issues of law that e-commerce has raised.

SECTION 19.2 ASSESSMENT

Self Check

1. What kinds of products and property do cyber-protection laws cover?

2. What is a domain name dispute?

3. What is the purpose of the No Electronic Theft Act?

Academic Connection

Mathematics Appleton Wholesale Grocers, Inc. plans to construct a new building at a cost of $875,000 to house the new computer installation.

Appleton hires an architect, a systems analyst, and a computer programmer. The architect charges seven percent of the total cost of the building. The system analyst charges a flat fee of $6,000. The computer programmer charges $30 an hour and works 150 hours. What is the total cost of the professional services?

THEORY **Number and Operations:** To calculate the total cost of professional services, find the sum of consultants' fees using the formula:

(Cost of Building × 7%) + Systems Analyst Fee + (Computer Programmer Rate × Total Hours)

 For more math practice, go to the Math Appendix.

Critical Thinking

The Future of Cyberlaw
What are some of the legal challenges you can imagine facing lawmakers in the future?

 Go to **glencoe.com** to check your answers.

SECTION 19.2 ASSESSMENT

Self Check

1. intellectual property distributable using computers, new computer products and inventions, and products that use or work with computers

2. a dispute arising when one party has registered a domain name that uses a famous person's name, or a trademark or a trade name registered by another user

3. provides prison terms and fines for anyone who creates an electronic duplicate of a copyrighted work for profit or gain

Academic Connection
Mathematics
$71,750

Critical Thinking
Answers will vary, but may include that it is difficult to write laws for all cybercrimes because they evolve daily.

 Activity correlated to the Mathematics standard on page 419

After You Read

Summarize jurisdiction, taxation, and authentication issues

ASSESS

Self-Assessment

Have students go to the *Business and Personal Law* Online Learning Center through glencoe.com to take the Section 19.2 Practice Test.

CLOSE

Culminating Activity

Copyrights, Trademarks, and Patents

Divide the class into three groups. Tell one group to create a poem or song for the class. Tell the second group to create a logo or slogan. Ask the third group to invent a product for the classroom. Allow students to be creative in the allotted time period. Then ask each group to present their creation and tell the class what they must do to protect it.

Summary by Sections

Ask students to read the summaries one key point at a time. Then, ask them to work in groups to create two examples to illustrate each key point.

Vocabulary Builder

Cooperative Learning

1. Have students work in groups to prepare their sentences. Ask the groups to exchange their sentences and assess each other's sentences.

Vocabulary Development

- Ask students to use a dictionary or to go online to look up the etymology of each key term listed.
- Then, ask students to list several words derived from the same root or origin. For example, *contract* has the same root as *contractual* or *contractually*.

Summary

Section 19.1 Cyberlaw and Cybercrime

- Cyberlaw is the area of the law which concerns computers and computer-related crimes.
- A cybercrime is any criminal activity associated with a computer.
- Some states have dealt with cybercrimes by adding cybertrespass statutes to the traditional criminal code.
- Some states have dealt with cybercrimes by writing individual statutes for every crime that can be committed by using a computer.
- Cybercrimes include cyberblackmail, cyberspoofing, cyberpiracy, cyberterrorism, identity theft, cybervandalism, and cybergerm warfare.
- Cybertorts include cyberdefamation and cyberinvasion of privacy.

Section 19.2 Cyberlaw and E-Commerce

- E-commerce is the process of conducting business using electronic means, especially the Internet.
- E-commerce has raised jurisdictional issues, taxation issues, and authentication problems.
- Cyberprotection laws protect intellectual property that can be distributed using computers, new computer products and inventions, and products that use or work with computers.
- No Electronic Theft Act provides prison terms and fines for anyone who creates an electronic duplicate of a copyrighted work for commercial profit or private financial gain.
- The Uniform Computer Information Transactions Act (UCITA) governs software agreements and licenses, software formulation contracts, and software maintenance contracts.

Vocabulary Builder

1 On a sheet of paper, use each of these terms in a sentence.

Key Terms

- cyberlaw
- cybercrime
- cybertrespass
- cyberspoofing
- cyberpiracy
- cyberblackmail
- identity theft
- cybervandalism
- cybertort
- cyberdefamation
- cyberinvasion of privacy
- e-commerce
- digital signature
- domain name

Academic Vocabulary

- simulate
- infrastructure
- sabotage
- tangible
- broadcast
- duplicate

Go to **glencoe.com** to play a game and improve your legal vocabulary.

Study Skills for Success

Prepare Your Students for Studying

Tell students that they can improve their ability to understand and remember material from their courses by learning and practicing study skills. Remind students to:

- **Get motivated!** Motivation must come from within. To motivate yourself, think of ways in which what you learn now will fit into your long-term personal and professional goals.
- **Get organized!** Make studying part of your daily routine, not something you do at the last minute.
- **Concentrate!** Study in an environment that is as free of distractions as possible.

Key Points Review

Answer the following questions. Refer to the chapter for additional reinforcement.

2 What two approaches have states used to cover cybercrimes?

3 What is cyberspoofing?

4 How do identity thieves work?

5 What is a cybertort?

6 What are the two principles courts use to decide jurisdiction in e-commerce sales?

7 What is a digital signature and how can it be verified?

8 What did the Computer Software Copyright Act of 1980 do?

9 What is the purpose of the Anticybersquatting Consumer Protection Act?

Standardized Test Practice

10 Read the following excerpt about efforts to combat cybercrime internationally and complete questions 1 and 2.

In May 2006, representatives of the Group of Eight (G8) industrialized nations, including France, Japan, and the U.S., met in Paris and agreed to boost cooperation to fight cybercrime. Participants there confirmed their support of the France-based Council of Europe's efforts to finalize a Convention on Cybercrime, which will be the first international treaty to deal with the different forms of criminal activity in cyberspace. The treaty would require countries to approve and enforce laws regarding interception of data, interference with computer systems, fraud, and forgery via the Internet. It also requires them to provide national law enforcement with the authority to carry out computer searches and seizures of computer data. "Everyone realizes that we are at a point where business is in transition, technology is in transition, and there is a legal transition as well," says Randy Picker, a law professor at the University of Chicago. "The reality is, the legal clock is a lot slower than the business or technology clock."

1. The first international treaty to deal with cybercrime will allow:

A the G8 to represent the world in technology
B laws to meet the needs of technology
C methods to deal with cyberspace crimes
D ability to search and seize computer data

2. The treaty would require countries to approve and enforce laws regarding:

A fraud, forgery, interception of computer data, and overuse of the Internet
B forgery, interception of data, fraud, and computer system interference
C search and seizures, computer data, fraud, forgery, and cyberspace
D cybercrime, technology, forgery, fraud, and computer system interference

Test-Taking Strategies Do not cram the night before a test. Plan to get a full eight hours of sleep.

Key Points Review

2. merging traditional criminal code with computer misuse; writing individual statutes for every computer crime

3. criminal falsely adopts the identity of another computer user or creates a false identity to commit fraud

4. gain access to a target's credit card numbers, financial data, passwords, PINs, Social Security number, access codes, or debit card information

5. invasion, theft, falsification, misuse, or deletion of the data stored in a computer to commit a tort

6. Because a Web site can be accessed in a state does not give jurisdiction to that state. A state may gain jurisdiction over an e-commerce transaction if a Web site allows users to purchase merchandise.

7. coded message at the end of an electronic contract; verified by password, smart card, or electronic identification of a person's retina or fingerprint

8. made computer software copyrighted works

9. provides shield for real owners of trademarks and trade names

Standardized Test Practice

10. C and B

Strategies for Standardized Test Prep Success

Whether your students have a standardized test coming up in a few days or a few weeks, these last-minute test-prep tips and strategies will help them relax and do their best.

- **Test Format** Help students become familiar with the format of the test by practicing with test items that imitate the actual test items as closely as possible.

- **Test Timing** Have your students take timed practice tests so that they become comfortable with the length, design, and timing of the actual test.

Review and Assessment

 Apply and Debate

Students should use chapter content to arrive at conclusions. The legal resolutions are listed below:

11. Security companies can benefit from a hacker's knowledge, but it is not guaranteed that a hacker would land a good job. Penalties for hackers are quite stiff.

12. Tina will need to be careful that any photo she is using is not copyrighted by the site she obtained it from.

13. The law is clear that Internet-based companies only have to charge sales tax in states where that company has a business presence.

14. Under UCITA, the programmer's ownership rights would depend upon traditional contract interpretation. If the contract is specific as to what programs need to be created, then any extra programming would belong to the programmer. However, if it is a broad contract, then a court may award ownership to the hiring company.

15. The court should probably rule in favor of Alison as there is no way of verifying that Alison did, in fact, send the e-mail. It is suspicious when a company receives an e-mail with order and credit card information without any security or password protection.

428

 Apply and Debate

Read the following scenarios. Get together with other students in pairs or groups of three and take a position on each scenario. Debate your position in class with students taking the opposite position or prepare a written argument justifying your position.

⑪ Computer Hacker Dilemma

A computer hacker, Raoul, broke into computer systems at several businesses for fun. He did not do any damage, but he was caught and put on probation. After a year, he was hired to work at a computer security firm helping to stop hackers.

You Debate — *Does it send the wrong message to computer hackers that they can get good jobs after committing crimes?*

⑫ Web Site with Music

Tina is a candle maker and sells her candles on a Web site. The site also contains photos of famous celebrities and the caption: "These stars would love my candles." Tina found the photos on the Internet.

You Debate — *Is it fair that Tina uses photos of famous people to help sell her products?*

⑬ Online Purchase Fairness

To avoid paying sales tax, Jack buys his big purchases online from sellers located outside his state. Jack's friend's TV store loses sales because it must charge sales tax.

You Debate — *Is it fair that some Internet-based companies are able to avoid charging sales tax when local stores must charge it?*

⑭ A Smart Programmer

Nick is a programmer. A company hired him to develop software that translates Web sites into French. While doing this, he also figured out how to translate the Web sites into Italian, German, and Russian. Nick claims he owns the extra programs.

You Debate — *Do you think programmers own the rights to software program they create that go beyond what they were hired to do?*

⑮ Fake Internet Order?

Juicy Oranges, Inc. received an e-mail from Alison Adams providing her credit card number and ordering five crates of oranges, worth $272. When the shipment was delivered, Alison claimed she never sent the e-mail and refused to pay.

You Debate — *If you were the judge in this case, would you rule in favor of Alison or Juicy Oranges, Inc.?*

C Critical Thinking

Patent Dispute TrueView, Inc., sells their patented software to Internet merchants, which shows their products in 3D. Close-Up Merchandisers is selling similar software, while their patent is pending. TrueView is now suing Close-Up for patent infringement.

Debate Practice

- Can TrueView sue Close-Up? (Yes, if they believe their patent has been infringed.)

- Does Close-Up have a right to invent software similar to patented ones? (Yes, as long as they do not use the same technology that True-View has patented. Patents must be specific to a technology.)

Case Study Practice – See, Inc. v. Imago Eyewear Party, Ltd.

16 Does the Court Have Jurisdiction? See, Inc. is an American corporation that sells eyewear over the Internet on their Web site, seeeyewear.com, which it registered as a domain name in 1998. See, Inc. owns federal trademarks on SEE and SEE SELECTIVE EYEWEAR ELEMENTS. See, Inc. has also filed for a trademark on SEE EYEWEAR.

The Defendant, Imago Eyewear Party, Ltd., is an Australian company that also sells eyewear over the Internet. Imago uses the Web site "seeyewear.com" to sell its products. This Web site domain name was registered in 2002. Image has filed for a United States trademark on SEEYEWEAR. See, Inc. sued Imago Eyewear in Michigan Federal Court. See, Inc. claimed that Imago, by using the Web site seeyewear.com, had violated Federal trademark law and Michigan's unfair trade practices statutes.

Imago argued that there is no jurisdiction for See, Inc. to sue in Michigan. Imago argued that See, Inc. is an Australian corporation and that, although Michigan residents can access its Web site on the Internet, no Michigan resident has every contacted See, Inc. via its Web site. Therefore, a U.S. Court does not have jurisdiction to hear this case.

Source: See, Inc. v. Imago Eyewear Party, Ltd., 167 Fed.Appx. 518 (6th Cir. 2006)

Practice Can See, Inc. sue Imago Eyewear in Michigan?

17 Ethics ←?→ Application _____

Is It Ever Okay to Copy CDs? Five students from your school who graduated two years ago are in a band. They just cut a CD and began selling it. You love the music and buy a copy. Your two closest friends also love the music and ask you to make copies of the CD for them.

◆ Is it ethical for you to copy this CD and give it to other people? Explain your position.

18 Internet Application _____

Copyrighting Your Novel You have decided to write a novel. You learn that it is now easy to publish a book on your own, but you want to protect your copyright. You plan to sell both a print edition of the book and also an electronic book (e-book) that you will sell from your Web site.

 Go to **glencoe.com** to research copyright law. Find out what you must do as an author to copyright your book and protect it in both print form and on the Internet.

 Reading Connection
Outside Reading Go to **glencoe.com** for a list of outside reading suggestions about cyberlaw and e-commerce.

 glencoe.com

Case Study Practice

16. No. The Sixth Circuit Court of Appeals held that while the Internet provides a means for Michigan residents to access Imago's international Web site, the evidence indicates that they do not. The court determined that a party cannot simply argue that the Internet provides potential access. Instead, they must prove that people are actually accessing it to prove infringement. Because Imago sells in Australia, New Zealand, Singapore, and the Netherlands, its Web site does not overlap with See's American customer base. This was an important case about how the Internet promotes international competition.

17. No. It is not ethical to make copies of CDs, even for friends. In general, the law accepts that a person may make a personal copy of a CD to use in another location, but copying CDs to sell or even to give to other people is considered piracy. An exception might be if the band authorized making copies to help promote their album.

Internet Application

18. Authors have copyright protection from the moment of the fixed creation of their work. However, registering your copyright with the U.S. Copyright Office in Washington, D.C., adds further legal protection in the event of an infringement.

R Reading Strategy

Reading Connection

American Bar Association Resources

Go to the *Business and Personal Law* Online Learning Center through **glencoe.com** to find links for further readings that relate to this chapter. Ask students to read, review, and summarize the documents. Advise students to keep their reviews and summaries to use as reference material for their Unit Thematic Project on pages 432–433.

UNIT 6

Careers in Law

Introduce Career Planning

Bell Ringer Activity

A consultant is a sole proprietor who needs to know all the laws pertaining to his or her business. Ask students why this is important.

Career Decisions

Self-Assessment Checklist

Use this checklist to help students determine their career path:

✓ Think about things you are good at
✓ Write down your interests
✓ Think about the lifestyle you want
✓ Write down your aptitudes and abilities
✓ Consider your personality
✓ Determine your learning style
✓ List some careers that might match these characteristics

Résumé Builder

Answer Answers may address quality performance in school and in the workplace. Managing time efficiently, meeting deadlines, and expressing an interest in increased responsibility can lead to promotion, an increase in number of clients, and other career achievements.

Patrick A. McNutt
Antitrust Consultant

What do you do at work?

"My job as a strategic antitrust consultant involves the preparation of advices for private clients, liaison with lawyers, and representations before competition agencies. On a larger scale it has involved the implementation of competition in a jurisdiction, drafting the legislation, and recruitment of staff. My work also involves quite a bit of travel, lecturing, and participating as a speaker at international conferences."

What skills are most important to you?

"The skills set includes an ability to communicate effectively, an ability to understand the client's problem from the client's perspective, and an ability to work in teams or alone depending on the nature of the assignment. Up-to-date knowledge of the law is taken for granted."

What kind of training do you recommend?

"I would recommend a primary degree in law and economics with an elective in antitrust economics and competition law. Early in one's career, one could work as a paralegal in a law firm or join an economic consultancy firm in order to gain experience. Alternatively, one could gain experience as a case handler, either as a lawyer or economist with a national competition agency, and then move later in your career to the private sector as a consultant."

What is your key to success?

"It is important to showcase a combination of hard work and dedication to the job without necessarily sacrificing a personal life. The key to this is developing good time management skills. Prioritizing and meeting deadlines reflects well on your professional image. Listening to clients and understanding the issue at hand from their idiosyncratic perspective also aid in the steps needed to move a successful professional relationship forward."

Résumé Builder

Academic Skills

- Above average analytical skills
- Good speaking, listening, and negotiating skills

Education and Training

Obtain a bachelor's degree in business administration, law, and economics as well as augment these with specifics in the industry of interest. The following high school and college courses will help develop the necessary background knowledge:

- Business Management
- Business law courses
- Communication
- English Language Arts (rhetoric and composition)
- Introduction to Business
- U.S. Government
- Social Studies

Critical Thinking

How can quality performance and time management skills impact your career?

 Go to **glencoe.com** to find legal careers resources.

 glencoe.com

Research Technology

Specialized technology is available for a variety of law-related tasks. For example, LexisNexis and Westlaw are two competing electronic databases that attorneys and other legal professionals use to conduct research. These services give users access to online legal information, including the text of court decisions and legislation, the content of public records, and many legal articles.

Activity Ask students to access the American Bar Association's Web site through glencoe.com and read about technology uses in legal professions.

Personal Essay Practice

The Particulars of a Dream Four college graduates come up with the dream of starting their own cultural magazine on music, literature, and art. They envision running the magazine full time and drawing salaries as the owners and editors of the magazine. One of the friends, a business major, brings up the real-world details of accomplishing their dream. They should form their business as a 501(c)(3) nonprofit corporation. They could then hold fundraisers, write grant proposals, and seek out funding from businesses, the government, and other sources. First, they will need to find out how to propose a budget, create an accounting system, and write a grant.

Assignments

Research Find out what it takes to form a nonprofit corporation in your state. Be sure to examine the federal laws as well as state laws.

Write Consider the situation above and write a personal essay about the nonprofit company you would want to start.

Writing Tips Before you start writing your personal essay, remember that it should:

✓ represent the writer's point of view
✓ reflect the writer's life and interests

✓ share a life lesson with the reader or talk about a relevant past experience

Discuss the specific details of how to start a nonprofit, and explain why you think there is a need in the marketplace for your idea. What makes you so passionate about your idea? Why would individuals, corporations, or organizations want to invest in your idea?

Essay Test Strategies CollegeBoard, a not-for-profit membership association, recommends the following tips on essay writing: read the entire assignment before writing; do not oversimplify; and support your idea with facts and figures.

Go to **glencoe.com** to find more writing resources.

 glencoe.com

The Writing Connection

W Writing Support

Objectives

Write a brief personal essay discussing a new and worthwhile nonprofit business.

Essay Rubric

Evaluate the students' writing according to the following criteria:

- The essay presents a variety of sentence lengths and structures. **(6 points)**
- The essay incorporates financial information. **(6 points)**
- The essay shows thoughtfulness. **(5 points)**
- The introduction captures the reader's attention. **(4 points)**
- Syntax, grammar, and spelling are error-free. **(4 points)**

Total: 25 points

U Universal Access

Intrapersonal Learning

Intrapersonal learners enjoy working alone and keeping personal journals. Ask students to try out this form of learning by journaling their thoughts and feelings before crafting their essay.

Culminating Activity

Ask students to work in groups to give each other feedback on their first drafts.

Assignments

Students should craft their personal essays by writing them to the general public. Essays should be engaging, explore the reasons for wanting to open the nonprofit organization, and assert arguments for why it is needed.

Encourage them to analyze their position during their pre-writing stage. They need to think about a collection of anecdotes before settling on the ones that best illustrate the essay's purpose and position.

FOCUS

Bell Ringer Activity

Have students think of new businesses that have opened in the community within the past five years. Did citizens raise any concerns regarding issues that might affect the environment? Ask students if they know who opened these businesses and whether or not they are still operating.

TEACH

Workshop Overview

The objective of this workshop is to prepare an informational guide on an environmental law affecting society as well as business.

Science

Organize students into small groups. Have each group select an environmental issue of importance to the local community. They should evaluate the community's response to the issue and then write an editorial supporting the community efforts and suggesting constructive ways to resolve the environmental issue. After reviewing the editorial, encourage groups to submit their reports to the local newspaper's op-ed editor for possible publication.

UNIT 6 Thematic Project

Protecting Social and Environmental Concerns

For this project, you will use what you have learned to prepare an informational guide on an environmental law affecting society at large, as well as business. You can work on this project alone or with a partner.

Here is a checklist of the skills that you will need to complete this project. Your teacher will consider these skills when evaluating your work.

Evaluation Rubric

Academic Skills		
1. Online and library research	1.	10 points
2. Reading for information	2.	10 points
3. Note-taking	3.	5 points
4. Estimation and computation of facts/figures you discover	4.	10 points
5. English composition to summarize findings	5.	15 points
Legal Skills		
6. Researching laws that protect the environment	6.	15 points
7. Knowledge of federal laws that set precedent for businesses	7.	15 points
8. Analysis of essential legislative acts governing businesses	8.	15 points
9. Use of technology	9.	5 points
		Total 100 Points

 For more resources and for grading rubrics, go to **glencoe.com**.

Step 1: Preparation

1. Write a proposal for an area of environmental protection law you plan to research.
2. Use all you have learned in this unit and library or Internet resources as tools.
3. Complete this project in a format that is actceptable for adding to your portfolio.

 glencoe.com

Time Management Rubric

Have students evaluate their usage of time by rating the skills below on a scale of "poor" to "apprentice" to "proficient."

- Creates a personal schedule (including class time, eating time, hours at work, homework, and any other regular commitments).
- Keeps a calendar to organize deadlines and important dates.

- Prioritizes a list of tasks.
- Concentrates on high-priority tasks.
- Tackles one action item at a time.
- Keeps agreement with self to get something done—lessens the feeling of being overwhelmed.

Step 2: Procedure

❶ Review the text in this unit and make a list of the environmental protection laws that pertain to your specific area of interest, such as air pollution, oil spills, global warming, disposing of nuclear waste, etc. Go to **glencoe.com** to find additional help and resources.

❷ List all the legal terms you come across in your research. What laws protect the public and regulate business? How are these laws enforced?

❸ Write an informational guide about the legal terms and documents that a business owner would need to know about the law you chose. Use the Internet to research and download important documents. Make enough copies so your classmates can review and annotate your guide.

❹ Describe a real-world situation in which a business violated the laws in your area of interest. Explain the impact of the violation not only on the business, but on the public and on the environment as well. Present your guide and conclusion to your classmates.

Step 3: Create an Analysis Report

As a class, compare and contrast the information presented in each guide. See if any of the guides stand out, and if so what makes the information presented most interesting. After comparing the guides, answer the following questions:

❶ How many and what areas of environmental laws were presented?

❷ Did the guides presented include all the necessary information needed to understand the importance of federal environmental legislation?

❸ If not, what should have been added to make the information easier to use?

❹ How was your guide similar to and different from the other guides presented?

Community Connection

Research current environmental laws that are being debated by politicians, businesses, and environmental organizations either on a local, national, or international level. Decide who has the most to win and who has the most to lose if the law is passed. Go to **glencoe.com** to find resources.

Competitive Event Prep

New Business Venture

Situation: Assume the role of a high school business law student. A college student friend is a landscaping major who is planning to open a new landscaping and lawn service business. Your friend is concerned about the type of business ownership that should be established. Your friend has cared for lawns on a casual basis without a formally established business. This new venture will require the purchase of equipment and hiring help.

Activity: You must explain the different types of business ownership to your friend, with an emphasis on the pros and cons of each.

 For more Competitive Event preparation, performance tips, and evaluation rubrics, go to **glencoe.com**.

 glencoe.com

TEACH (cont.)

Extending the Content

Environmental Activists

Ask students to research organizations and businesses that focus on environmental issues. Ask students to present their research results.

Reading Connection

American Bar Association Resources

Ask students to go back to their ABA readings, notes, and summaries. Direct them to apply any relevant ABA content to review and revise their outline and first draft.

ASSESS

Evaluation

Make sure students review the evaluation rubric. Ask students to find a case in which a business, person, or organization was indicted for harming the environment.

CLOSE

Culminating Activity

Cooperative Learning

Pair students up and have them examine each other's informational guides. Each should write down lingering questions they still have after reading it.

S Skills Practice
Asking Questions

Encourage students to imagine that they are reporters attending a press conference on an environmental issue of their choice. Ask them to write a news story on the press conference, detailing the major issues raised and summarizing the discussions that ensued.

U Universal Access
Visual-Spatial Learning

A word map shows relationships between words and concepts. A commonly used map has a central bubble containing a key word or idea, with bubbles surrounding it. Place a word or concept from the unit in the center of a word map on the board. Then have students fill in the surrounding bubbles.

433

Broz v. Cellular Information Systems, Inc.
Delaware Supreme Court 673 A.2d 148 (1996)

R **Read Critically** As you read this case, ask yourself the following questions:

1. What companies did Mr. Broz have a responsibility to?
2. Why did CIS sue Mr. Broz?
3. What legal doctrine applies to his case?
4. What did the Delaware Supreme Court hold with regard to Mr. Broz?

Assignment Write a short summary of the situation. Include the court's decision and a couple of sentences about why or how the court reached its decision.

Facts **Board Member** Robert Broz was the president and sole stockholder of RFB Cellular, Inc. (RFBC), a Delaware corporation that provided cellular phone service. Mr. Broz was also a member of the board of directors of Cellular Information Systems, Inc. (CIS), a publicly-held Delaware corporation that was a competitor of RFBC. **License Availability** Among the service areas it covered, RFBC had a license for service in the Michigan-4 area. In 1994, a license for service in the Michigan-2 area became available. This area was right next to Michigan-4. The owner of the Michigan-2 license, Mackinac Cellular Corp. (Mackinac) contacted Mr. Broz about selling the license to RFBC. Mackinac did not contact CIS to see whether it was interested in the license because CIS had just emerged from bankruptcy. At the same time, PriCellular, Inc. expressed an interest in buying the license from Mackinac. RFBC won a bidding war and bought the license.

CIS Financial Struggles At the time Mr. Broz was interested in buying the Michigan-2 license, CIS was going through financial problems. In fact, CIS was negotiating with PriCellular, Inc. for PriCellular to buy CIS. However, PriCellular was having trouble financing the purchase, and it took several months before it was able finally to do so. PriCellular finalized the purchase nine days after RFBC bought the Michigan-2 license. **Lawsuit Commencement** After RFBC bought the license and PriCellular bought CIS, CIS sued Mr. Broz and RFBC. CIS argued that Mr. Broz should have notified the board of CIS about the availability of the Michigan-2 license to see if CIS was interested in buying the license. CIS argued that the actions of Mr. Broz constituted an "impermissible usurpation of a corporation opportunity" belonging to CIS.

Opinion **Delaware Court of Chancery Proceedings** The Delaware Court of Chancery held that the actions

? Landmark Case Questions

of Mr. Broz did constitute a usurpation of a corporate opportunity that belonged to CIS. The Court found that CIS could have required Mr. Broz to abstain from the purchase out of deference to the CIS board, and that if Mr. Broz had notified the CIS board, the board could have notified PriCellular about the pending purchase.

Corporate Opportunity Doctrine In making its decision, the Delaware Supreme Court first had to define the law that applied. The Court had previously defined the corporate opportunity doctrine in the case *Guth v. Loft, Inc.* as follows:

A corporate officer or director may not take a business opportunity for his/her own if:

(1) the corporation is financially able to exploit the opportunity;

(2) the opportunity is within the corporation's line of business;

(3) the corporation has an interest or expectancy in the opportunity; and

(4) by taking the opportunity for his own, the corporate fiduciary will thereby be placed in a position inimical to his duties to the corporation.

A director or officer may take a corporate opportunity if:

(1) the opportunity is presented to the director or officer in his individual and not his corporate capacity;

(2) the opportunity is not essential to the corporation;

(3) the corporation holds no interest or expectancy in the opportunity; and

(4) the director or officer has not wrongfully employed the resources of the corporation in pursuing or exploiting the opportunity.

Applying the Corporate Opportunity Doctrine Under the doctrine, CIS must have been in a financial position to buy the license from Mackinac to keep Mr. Broz from pursuing the opportunity to do so himself. The testimony of board members was that CIS was emerging from bankruptcy and was not in a position to buy any additional licenses. Further, PriCellular had not yet

bought CIS, so even if PriCellular had the money it could not be considered by the court.

In addition, CIS must have an interest or expectancy in the opportunity. By the time CIS had emerged from bankruptcy, it no longer held cellular phone licenses in the area. The testimony of board members in court was that CIS's business plan after bankruptcy did not include getting any additional licenses.

Finally, CIS argued that, in applying the doctrine, it was an implicit requirement that Mr. Broz, as a board member, must present the opportunity to the full board of CIS so that the board can officially discuss the opportunity for its own benefit.

Holding **The Delaware Supreme Court** held that the Delaware Court of Chancery had improperly applied the corporate opportunity doctrine. The Supreme Court found that CIS was in no position to acquire or expect the license. The Court further held that board members are not required to present an opportunity to a full board, if such a presentation would result in the board's rejection of the offer, as was the case in this situation.

TRIAL PREP

The National High School Mock Trial Association organizes competitions at the local, regional, and national levels where teams of high school or college students prepare and argue fictional legal cases before practicing attorneys and judges. Mock Trial team members are each assigned a role as either an attorney or witness. Each team must develop a courtroom strategy, legal arguments, and a presentation style.

Go to **glencoe.com** to find guided activities about case strategy and presentation.

Winning the Case

Corporate Opportunity Doctrine

This case turns on the application of the corporate opportunity doctrine. The doctrine was created to prevent officers from taking advantage of a potential business opportunity for themselves without first presenting the offer to the corporation of which they are an officer. This is to ensure that officers are fulfilling their fiduciary responsibilities to the company. Ask: If CIS had not just emerged from bankruptcy, might the outcome have been different?

As students read the case, they may encounter text or information that they do not understand. Point out to students they need to adjust their reading strategies to increase their comprehension. Read a section of the case aloud. As you read, ask content questions to check students' understanding.

CLOSE

Understand the Decision

Why was this case litigated in Delaware and not in Michigan, where the parties were located, and why is that important? (This case was litigated in Delaware because CIS was incorporated in Delaware. Although that means the ruling will only apply to cases litigated in Delaware, it is still an important ruling. Due to the state being perceived as "corporation-friendly," Delaware is the state of choice for incorporating many large, multi-state corporations. As such, Delaware's state code and case law have become very important when it comes to determining and litigating corporate matters. Many states' courts look to Delaware's jurisprudence when making decisions on novel corporate matters.)

Unit Objectives

Chapter	Section	Objectives
Chapter 20	**20.1**	• **Name** the rights and duties involved in marriage. • **Describe** the different types of marriages. • **Explain** the types of marriages that are prohibited by law. • **List** the requirements of a legal marriage.
	20.2	• **Describe** the differences between an annulment, a legal separation, and a divorce. • **Identify** the common grounds for divorce. • **Explain** the issues involved in a divorce settlement.
Chapter 21	**21.1**	• **Explain** the meaning and purpose of insurance. • **Describe** the different types of property insurance. • **Distinguish** between types of life insurance. • **Identify** the different types of health insurance.
	21.2	• **Identify** the major types of retirement plans. • **Name** the formal requirements of a will. • **Describe** how to revoke or change a will. • **Identify** the different types of trusts.

Understanding Brackets, Letters, and Ability Levels in the Teacher Wraparound Edition

Brackets Brackets on the reduced student edition page correspond to teaching strategies and activities in the Teacher Wraparound Edition. As you teach the lesson, the brackets show you exactly where to use the teaching strategies and activities.

Letters The letters on the reduced student edition page identify the type of strategy or activity. See the key below to learn about the different types of strategies and activities.

Ability Levels Teaching strategies that appear throughout the chapters have been identified by one of three codes to give you an idea of their suitability for students of varying learning styles and abilities.

Resources Key program resources are listed in each chapter. Icons indicate the format of resources.

KEY TO LETTERS

R **Reading Strategy** activities help you teach reading skills and vocabulary.

C **Critical Thinking** strategies help students apply and extend what they have learned.

S **Skills Practice** strategies help students practice historical analysis and geographical skills.

W **Writing Support** activities provide writing opportunities to help students comprehend the text.

D **Develop Concepts** activities use various strategies to help teachers gauge and plan for students' concept development.

U **Universal Access** activities provide differentiated instruction for English language learners, and suggestions for teaching various types of learners.

NCLB **No Child Left Behind** activities help students practice and improve their abilities in academic subjects.

KEY TO ABILITY LEVELS

L1 strategies should be within the ability range of all students. Often full class participation is required.

L2 strategies are for average to above-average students or for small groups. Some teacher direction is necessary.

L3 strategies are designed for students able and willing to work independently. Minimal teacher direction is necessary.

KEY TO RESOURCE ICONS

📁 Print Material

💿 CD/DVD

🖱 Internet

TeacherWorks™
All-In-One Planner and Resource Center

Teacher Wraparound Edition

Student Activity Workbook with Academic Integration
Teacher Annotated Edition

For the Unit:
Lesson Plans
National and State Standards Correlations

For the Chapters:
Lessons Plans
Note-Taking Graphic Organizers
Chapter Outlines
Chapter Summaries
Enrichment Activities Masters

Supplemental Cases
Internet Connection Student Activities Masters
Blackline Masters for Student Edition Figures and
  Supplemental Figures
Ethics and Business Law Activities
Competitive Events Test-Taking Prep
Reproducible Chapter Tests

 Link to the ***Business and Personal Law* Online Learning Center** with Podcasts through glencoe.com.

Real-World Applications

Demonstrate Case Resolutions

Learning Objective

- Explain the law as it relates to divorce and alimony (p. 450).
- Describe the requirements necessary for a valid will (p. 467).

- Describe the differences between divorce and annulment (p. 455).
- Understand property insurance as it relates to automobiles (p. 475).

- Understand wills and trusts (pp. 480–481).

Apply Business Law Concepts

Learning Objective

- Understand love and marriage (p. 438).
- Explain estate planning and the various types of trusts (p. 456).

- Discuss marriage laws in Kenya (p. 442).
- Explain automobile insurance in Russia (p. 459).

- Understand health insurance (p. 463).

- Identify the requirements of a legal marriage (p. 455).
- Understand the purpose of health insurance (p. 475).

- Understand the requirements of a legal marriage (p. 441).

Teach Financial Literacy

Learning Objective

- Understand the advantages and disadvantages of credit cards (p. 437).

Bring Project-Based Learning into the Law Classroom

Health Insurance Legislation

- **Introduce Concepts**
  The health care system is changing as deregulation and competition impact health care services and pricing.

- **Explore Concepts**
  Read the Thematic Project Preview and the WebQuest activity (p. 437)

  Ask students to think of the issues and federal policies that affect health care as they study Chapters 20 and 21.

- **Apply Concepts**
  Research federal policies, deregulation, and competitive trends in health care, and draft a guide based on these findings (pp. 477 and 478).

Extend Content

Using American Bar Association (ABA) Resources

- Direct students to pages 455 and 475 in the Student Edition.
- Ask them to use glencoe.com to find links to ABA resource documents.
- Students should browse and select one document for each chapter.
- See pages 455, 475, and 481 in this edition for specific instructions.

Reading and Writing Support

Feature or Activity	Topic	Reading Strategy	Writing Strategy
STANDARD &POOR'S	Student credit cards	Reading a primary source document	
Thematic Project Preview	Health insurance legislation		Researching and taking notes
BusinessWeek	Love and marriage (Ch. 20) Estate planning (Ch. 21)	Reading for detail Developing flexibility in reading speed	
Section Reading Guide	Before-reading activities and tools	Connect students' lives with content Focus on the main idea	Using a graphic organizer to take notes
As You Read	During-reading tool	Predict content Determine what students already know	
Reading Check	During-reading tool	Self-check understanding of content	
After You Read	After-reading tool	Summarize section content	Writing and organizing a list of key concepts
Standardized Test Practice	Marriage law (Ch. 20) Indemnification and insurance (Ch. 21)	Reading a primary source document Practicing critical reading skills	
Reading Connection	American Bar Association online resources	Reading a primary source document Extending and applying content Reading for knowledge Developing critical reading skills. Developing flexibility of reading speed	Taking notes Summarizing
The Writing Connection	Personal essay		Creating outlines, topic sentences, editing
Unit Thematic Project	Health insurance legislation	Using resources notes to support writing effort	Creating outlines, writing drafts, editing
Landmark Case	Corporate Opportunity Doctrine case	Developing critical reading skills	Summarizing

Family Law

Unit Overview

Main) Idea

Unit 7 prepares students for some of the many changes they might experience once on their own. They will learn about the responsibilities of forming a family unit, settling a divorce, purchasing insurance, and planning their estate.

00:00 OUT OF TIME?

If class time is too short to cover the chapters thoroughly, have students:

- Write down the vocabulary terms and their definitions.
- Read What You'll Learn and Why It's Important at the beginning of each section.
- Go to the *Business and Personal Law* Online Learning Center at glencoe.com and to download the free Study-to-Go content to their cell phones or PDAs.

▶ **USING VISUALS ....**

Looking Ahead Answer
Answers include getting married and having children, owning and maintaining a home, obtaining health insurance, and planning for retirement.

In This Unit You Will Find:

Chapter 20
Marriage and Divorce

Chapter 21
Insurance and Estate Planning

· · · · · · · · · · · · · · · ·

Looking Ahead Once you finish your education, you may look forward to traveling, getting a good job, or buying a home. *What are some of the aspects of life that require long-term planning?*

436

Unit Thematic Project Preview

W Writing Support

The Center on Budget and Policy Priorities stated that Americans with job-based health insurance coverage has significantly increased and stands at about 60 percent.

Critical Thinking What are some of the reasons employers are no longer providing health insurance to their employees? (Answers will vary, but might include that health care costs are too high for employers to afford, leaving employees responsible for finding their own coverage. Given this, low- to middle-income families are less likely to have health insurance due to the cost. The *New York Times* reported that health care costs are rising at twice the rate of inflation.)

Thematic Project Preview

Health Insurance Legislation

As you read this unit, use this checklist to prepare for the unit project:

- ✓ List the laws and the legislation governing health care.
- ✓ Compare advantages and disadvantages of a health care legislation policy.
- ✓ Explain why a particular aspect of health care has been contentious.
- ✓ Determine the outcome of an issue in the health care debate.

Legal Portfolio When you complete the Unit Thematic project, you will have a guide to the politics of health care law for your portfolio.

Find Unit 7 study tools such as Graphic Organizers, Academic Skills Review, and Practice Tests at **glencoe.com**.

WebQuest

Protecting Your Future
Log on to **glencoe.com** to explore various laws and contracts to protect your assets and standard of living. List your findings in your WebQuest folder to share with your class.

5-minute Launch

KWL Chart Have students make a list of what they know about marriage and divorce laws. Next, have them skim through the unit and find the key words associated with those topics that are both familiar and unfamiliar. Discuss the lists and create a KWL chart with their responses. Remind students that they can often determine the meaning of a word they do not know by using context—the words and sentences that surround an unfamiliar word. They should also look for examples that illustrate the word.

Building Law Background

Ask students these questions to activate prior knowledge:

Chapter 20
Why is marriage a business and personal law topic?
(Marriage is a civil contract.)

Chapter 21
What is the purpose of having insurance? (to protect against the financial repercussions of problems that arise in life)

Ask

STANDARD &POOR'S   Manage Your Finances

Q: I notice that there are now credit cards for students. Should I get one?

A: Credit cards can be more convenient to carry than cash and they can be useful in an emergency. If you use them wisely, they can help you build a strong credit rating that will make it easier to get a car or home loan later. However, you should not accept just any credit card offer. Shop around first and read the fine print on the applications. Look for cards that have low interest rates and no annual fees. Do not be fooled by cards with low introductory rates that go way up after a few months. Do not use a credit card to borrow cash: the interest rates for cash are much higher than they are for store purchases. If you cannot pay off the card every month, pay as much as you can. Credit card balances continue to accumulate interest charges. If you only make the minimum monthly payment, it can take years to pay off the card and cost thousand of dollars in interest.

R **Language Arts/Reading** Standard & Poor's is one of the world's main providers of credit ratings and financial-market indices. Go to **glencoe.com** and read more about managing your finances.

 glencoe.com

Ask

STANDARD &POOR'S

R Reading Strategy

Language Arts/Reading Direct students to explore S&P's resources on the use of credit.

Math Activity Anthony Bucca has a $1,000 balance on his credit card with a 15 percent interest rate. He only pays the minimum amount of $25 each month. How long will it take to pay off the debt in full? How much interest will he have paid?
(Almost 11 years to pay off, with a total interest of $757.98.)

Plan Your Lesson Section by Section

NBEA	NATIONAL BUSINESS LAW STANDARDS
Section 20.1	• **Identify** the issues and concerns that might be included in a prenuptial agreement. • **Distinguish** between common law and ceremonial marriages. • **Identify** the types of marriages that are prohibited by law.
Section 20.2	• **Explain** the law of domestic relations as it relates to child custody. • **Outline** the law of domestic relations as it relates to child support. • **Describe** the law as it relates to the distribution of property in a divorce.

NCLB	ACADEMIC STANDARDS	Activity/Feature
English Language Arts: NCTE 3 Apply a wide range of strategies to comprehend, interpret, evaluate, and appreciate texts.		*BusinessWeek* News, Case Study, Case Study Practice
English Language Arts: NCTE 9 Develop an understanding of and respect for diversity in language use, patterns, and dialects across cultures, ethnic groups, geographic regions, and social roles.		Global Law
English Language Arts: NCTE 6 Apply knowledge of language structure, language conventions, media techniques, figurative language, and genre to create, critique, and discuss print and non-print texts.		Legal Talk, ad copy, Key Terms, and Academic Vocabulary
English Language Arts: NCTE 12 Use spoken, written, and visual language to accomplish your own purposes.		Section 20.1 Assessment
Mathematics: NCTM CS2 3 Recognize and apply mathematics in contexts outside of mathematics.		Section 20.2 Assessment
English Language Arts: NCTE 10 Students whose first language is not English make use of their first language to develop competency in the English language arts and to develop understanding of content across the curriculum.		Key Terms, Academic Vocabulary, Legal Talk, Vocabulary Builder
English Language Arts: NCTE 1 Read a wide range of print and non-print texts to build an understanding of texts; to acquire new information; to respond to the needs and demands of society and the workplace; and for personal fulfillment.		Global Law, Cyberlaw
Social Studies: NCSS 10 Study the ideals, principles, and practices of citizenship in a democratic republic.		Global Law
Social Studies: NCSS 4 Study individual development and identity.		Case Study

Connect Your Business Law Classroom to the World of Work

This chart shows the 21st Century Skills, foundation skills, and workplace competencies that students develop as they work in this chapter.

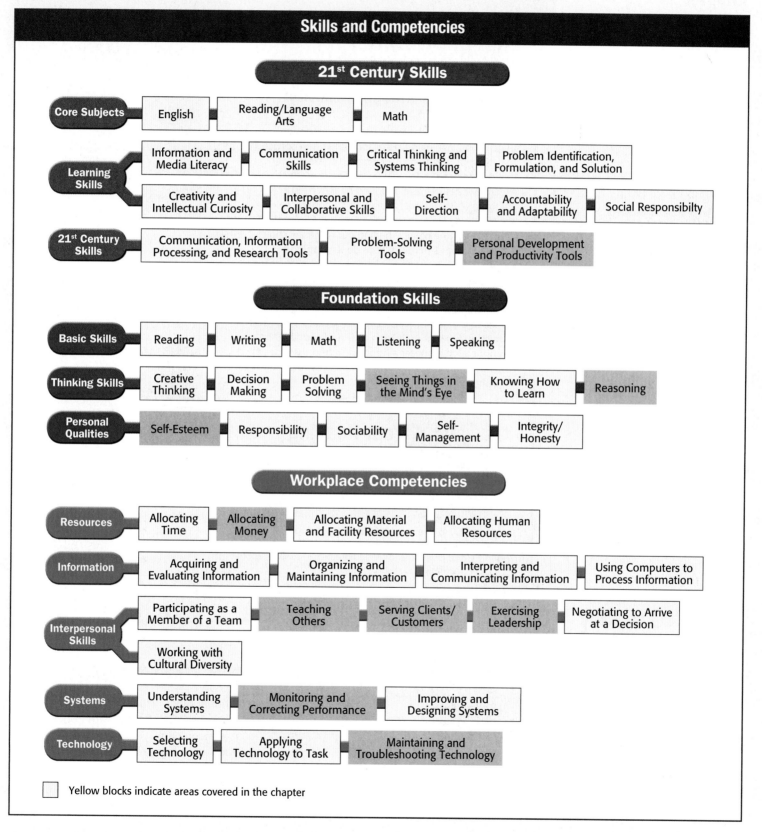

Skills and Competencies

21st Century Skills

Core Subjects
- English
- Reading/Language Arts
- Math

Learning Skills
- Information and Media Literacy
- Communication Skills
- Critical Thinking and Systems Thinking
- Problem Identification, Formulation, and Solution
- Creativity and Intellectual Curiosity
- Interpersonal and Collaborative Skills
- Self-Direction
- Accountability and Adaptability
- Social Responsibilty

21st Century Skills
- Communication, Information Processing, and Research Tools
- Problem-Solving Tools
- Personal Development and Productivity Tools

Foundation Skills

Basic Skills
- Reading
- Writing
- Math
- Listening
- Speaking

Thinking Skills
- Creative Thinking
- Decision Making
- Problem Solving
- Seeing Things in the Mind's Eye
- Knowing How to Learn
- Reasoning

Personal Qualities
- Self-Esteem
- Responsibility
- Sociability
- Self-Management
- Integrity/Honesty

Workplace Competencies

Resources
- Allocating Time
- Allocating Money
- Allocating Material and Facility Resources
- Allocating Human Resources

Information
- Acquiring and Evaluating Information
- Organizing and Maintaining Information
- Interpreting and Communicating Information
- Using Computers to Process Information

Interpersonal Skills
- Participating as a Member of a Team
- Teaching Others
- Serving Clients/Customers
- Exercising Leadership
- Negotiating to Arrive at a Decision
- Working with Cultural Diversity

Systems
- Understanding Systems
- Monitoring and Correcting Performance
- Improving and Designing Systems

Technology
- Selecting Technology
- Applying Technology to Task
- Maintaining and Troubleshooting Technology

Yellow blocks indicate areas covered in the chapter

CHAPTER

20 Marriage and Divorce

Introduce the Chapter

Marriage and Divorce
Chapter 20 explains the rights, requirements, and duties involved in a marriage contract. It also identifies different types of marriage and explains the ways marriage may come to an end. Students will learn how the divorce settlement deals with property division, child custody and support, and alimony.

Building Background
Ask students to name some high-profile weddings that have been featured in the news recently. Have them report on any details they recall about the couple and the wedding itself.

BusinessWeek News

Tell students that approximately 22 million Americans subscribe to online dating sites. The industry earns about $500 million a year. With that much revenue at stake, sites such as Chemistry.com carefully draft their legal agreements for members. The contract between the site and the member addresses issues such as limitations of liability, assumption of risk, and dispute resolution.

R Reading Strategy

 Your Reading

Tell students that an effective way to read is to search actively for the answer to a self-written question. Ask students to write one or two questions that they think this chapter will answer. As they read, have them search for the answer.

438

BusinessWeek News

Better Loving Through Chemistry?

By Catherine Arnst

On October 11, the largest online dating site, Match.com, launched Chemistry.com, a new service that attempts to use neuroscience to come up with the ideal match for its subscribers. The centerpiece is a lengthy questionnaire designed by Helen Fisher, an anthropologist at Rutgers University whose recent book, *Why We Love: The Nature and Chemistry of Romantic Love,* lays out the biology behind our romantic choices.

So how does Chemistry.com do its magic? By studying brain scans and behavioral studies, Fisher theorizes that the type of person who can ring your bell is hard-wired into your neurons. Embedded in each of our brains is a "love map," she says, that guides our choice of a mate. Chemistry.com's questions are meant to decipher that map. It then runs each profile through a proprietary computer algorithm to find that special someone who will light up your neurons. And you thought romance was in the stars.

 Flex Your Reading

Efficient critical reading involves being flexible with speed and comprehension. There are several ways of reading critically, and you need to fit a reading style to your needs and to the material.

Go to **glencoe.com** for Flex Your Reading activities, more information on reading strategies for this chapter, and guided practice in reading about marriage and divorce laws.

Classroom Resources

- Student Edition
- Teacher Wraparound Edition
- Student Activity Workbook with Academic Integration (SE/TAE)
- TeacherWorks™ Plus! CD
- *ExamView® Assessment Suite* CD
- *Presentation Plus!* CD

- National Mock Trial Championship DVD
- Online Learning Center with Podcasts at glencoe.com
- Study-to-Go™ at glencoe.com
- Online Student Edition
- Interactive Student Edition

Age of Consent A marriage is a personal relationship, but it is also a civil contract. *How old do you have to be to get married without parental consent?*

439

▲ USING VISUALS

Age of Consent **Answer** In every state except Mississippi and Nebraska, the age of consent is 18. Individuals younger than 18 can marry only with the consent of a parent, guardian, or judge. Tell students that the law establishes these age limits in an attempt to prevent minors from entering into unsuitable or coerced marriages.

Activity Have students use the Internet or your library to find out what other requirements exist in your state for individuals who want to marry. (Requirements may include blood tests, physical exams, waiting periods.)

Practice the Concept

Marriage and Divorce
Tell students that the median age for a man's first marriage is 27 and for a woman's it is 25. Emphasize that 20 years ago, the median ages for first marriages were 25 and 22, respectively. Ask students why they think the median age is rising. (Answers may include decreased pressure from family to marry, and more people pursuing educational or career goals.) Approximately 59 percent of the U.S. population is married. On the other hand, about 12 percent of the population is divorced. Ask students to suggest reasons why people want to marry. (Answers may include love, companionship, family, and spiritual beliefs.)

Key Terms Tell students that the events of marriage and divorce involve contracts. As such, contractual obligations carry rights and responsibilities, many of which are described in the language of a contract. For example, a divorce decree may stipulate *physical custody* of children (where the child will live). Terms such as *community property state* will have a bearing on how assets are divided between parties to a divorce.

Legal Basics Explain that a marriage changes the legal status of both parties, as does divorce. Tell students that the new legal status in both instances brings new rights and responsibilities.

FOCUS

Bell Ringer Activity

Ask students if they know the origin of the custom of using a ring as an engagement and marriage token. (circle of the ring represents eternity, a symbol that the agreement to marry will continue forever)

Preteaching

Key Terms

Read the definitions and ask students to create a sentence using each term.

Academic Vocabulary

Explain that developing vocabulary is key to academic success. An efficient method to develop vocabulary is to study how words are formed.

- **spouses** Noun, from the Latin *sponsus* (bridegroom). Means husband and wife.

- **status** Noun, from the Latin *status* (position). Means official rank or standing.

- **ceremony** Noun, from the Latin *cærimonia* (reverent rite). Means a formal act.

Activity Ask students to give a noun, a verb, an adjective, or an adverb form that comes from each word.

NCLB Connects to academic content

SECTION 20.1 Marriage Laws

What You'll Learn

- ◆ Name the rights and duties involved in marriage.
- ◆ Describe the different types of marriages.
- ◆ Explain the types of marriages that are prohibited by law.
- ◆ List the requirements of a legal marriage.

Why It's Important

If you ever get married, you need to know what the rights, responsibilities, and requirements of marriage are.

Academic Standards

Reading and completing the activities in this section will help you practice the following academic standards:

NCLB

English Language Arts (NCTE 12) Use spoken, written, and visual language to accomplish your own purposes.

Social Studies (NCSS 10) Study the ideals, principles, and practices of citizenship in a democratic republic.

Reading Guide

Before You Read

Connect A wedding is the final step in a long process. What are some decisions a couple should make before they marry to avoid problems in the future?

Focus on Ideas

Marriage is a legal contract that binds the parties to specific legal rights and obligations.

Take Notes	**Marriage Rights and Duties**	
Create a graph like the one shown and use it to take notes as you read this section. Go to glencoe.com to find graphic organizers and tips on how to improve your note-taking skills.	**Rights**	**Duties**
	Support	_____
	_____	_____
	_____	_____
	_____	_____
	_____	_____

Key Terms

You will learn these legal words and expressions in this chapter. You can also find these terms in *Black's Law Dictionary* or in an online legal dictionary.

- marriage
- prenuptial agreement
- common-law marriage
- bigamy
- polygamy
- consanguinity
- affinity

Academic Vocabulary

You will find these words in your readings and in your tests. Look them up in a dictionary and familiarize yourself with them.

- spouses
- status
- ceremony

440   Unit 7   Family Law

 glencoe.com

R

 Reading Strategy

Read for Knowledge

1. **Survey** or preread the chapter.
2. **Question** or formulate questions before you read.
3. **Recite** or read your questions, answers, and notes out loud.
4. **Review** or reread your notes.

Note-Taking Basics

- Listen attentively
- Have note-taking materials ready
- Skim through the lesson material
- Write down key words and ideas
- Anticipate what comes next
- Review notes soon after taking them

Understanding Marriage Law

What is legally considered a marriage?

Marriage is considered the basis of the family unit and vital to the preservation of traditional values and culture. **Marriage is defined by most states and the federal government as the legal union of one man and one woman as husband and wife.**

The Marriage Contract

Is an engagement ring a kind of contract?

Marriage is not just a personal relationship between two people. It is also a contract. The engagement represents the offer and acceptance of the contract. The consideration is the promise to give up one's right to remain single. During engagement, the marriage contract is in its executory stage. It is is fully executed when the wedding occurs.

In some states, a man is entitled to the return of the engagement ring when an engagement is called off. The legal theory holds that the ring is a contingent gift, dependent upon carrying out the marriage. In other states, the courts have allowed a woman to keep the ring if the man ended the engagement.

D

Prenuptial Agreements

Before marrying, soon-to-be **spouses** sometimes create a prenuptial, or premarital agreement. **A prenuptial agreement is a written and signed legal contract couples make before getting married dealing with property and support issues.**

As You Read

Predict Does every state have the same laws about marriage?

Vocabulary You can find vocabulary definitions in the **Key Terms** glossary and **Academic Vocabulary** glossary in the back of this book.

CYBERLAW

Ureneck v. Cui
798 N.E.2d 305 (Mass. App. Ct. 2003)

Joseph Ureneck runs Rainbow International Marriage Service, Inc. (Rainbow), a Massachusetts company, from a hotel in Beijing, China. Rainbow maintained a Web site that was marketed as "a personal and convenient way to meet your marriage partner." Clients paid Rainbow a fee of $700 to put their profiles on the Internet. If a match led to a marriage, clients agreed to pay Rainbow a second fee of $7,500 within 60 days of getting married. On May 20, 1995, Ping Cui paid her registration fee, and her profile was placed on the Web site. On November 28, 1997, John Choma met Ms. Cui on the Web site. On May 18, 1998, Ms. Cui sent a letter to Rainbow, stating she was unemployed and could not pay the $7,500 fee if she found love, and requesting that her profile be removed from the Web site. Ms. Cui and Mr. Choma were married in Massachusetts on April 24, 1999. Ms. Cui did not pay the $7,500 fee, so Rainbow sued for breach of contract.

Ruling and Resolution

The Massachusetts Appeals Court held that marriage brokerage contracts, where a third party is paid to negotiate or procure a marriage, are void as a matter of public policy in Massachusetts. Therefore, Rainbow could not sue for breach of contract because the contract was void.

Critical Thinking Should marriage brokerage contracts be legal?

CYBERLAW

Ureneck v. Cui

Answer Answers will vary. The rationale used by the Massachusetts Appeals Court was that of preventing the exploitation of innocent parties in a marriage. The court cited an old case from 1810 that said marriage brokerage contracts, although "not fraudulent on either party, are yet void, because they are a... public mischief, as they have a tendency to cause matrimony to be contracted on mistaken principles." Paying someone to negotiate a marriage, even with precautions in place, provides no guarantees that the third party is looking to create purely love-based marriages.

TEACH
Discussion Starter

Class Discussion
Ask students whether they think they will choose to marry at some point in their lives or not. Explain that the laws governing marriage are important to everyone because these relationships can affect children, property, and other contracts.

D **Develop Concepts**

Marriage Contracts Explain that a marriage represents a contract. Ask students what consideration is given in this contract. (promise to give up one's rights to remain single) Tell students that the contract is fully executed once the wedding occurs. If one party fails to go through with the wedding, a breach of contract suit was once possible. Now, this is no longer possible in most states.

As You Read

Predict Tell students that the definition of marriage is important when answering this question. (No. Most states define marriage as the union of one man and one woman. Some states now recognize civil unions, in which same-sex couples have the same rights as married couples.)

TEACH *(cont.)*

D Develop Concepts

Prenuptial Agreements

Tell students to imagine that Randy Keller wants his fiancée to sign a prenuptial agreement. Ask students what the advantages of a prenuptial agreement are. (protects the assets of each party and the division of property upon separation, divorce, or death) Explain that the agreement becomes effective upon marriage.

Extending the Content

Prenuptial Agreements

Have students use the Internet or local library to research the laws in your state concerning prenuptial agreements. Have them report their findings to the class and bring a sample of an agreement if possible.

C Critical Thinking

Marriage Rights Versus Single Rights To help students understand the change in legal status upon marriage, ask them to compare the rights they believe a single person has with the rights of a married person. (Single rights may include freedom to date and use property and money for oneself; married duties include supporting spouse and sharing expenses.)

442

D This agreement lists the assets of each party, the rights each party has to control their property, and the division of property upon separation, divorce, and death. This formal agreement becomes effective upon marriage.

Marriage Rights and Obligations

Marriage changes a couple's legal **status**. The law gives them new rights and obligations as a married couple. This is not true for people who live together without being married. Marriage includes the right to:

C
- support by your spouse when necessary
- inheritance from your deceased spouse
- property if the marriage ends
- compensation to continue your standard of living if the marriage ends
- file a joint income tax return

Global Law

Marriage Laws in Kenya

The Kenyan Constitution recognizes five systems of marriage and grants all systems equal importance under the law. The five systems are: Customary Law, Islamic Law, Hindu Law, Christian Law, and Civil Law. The Christian Law and Civil Law systems are identical when it comes to marriage laws.

Civil & Christian Law:
- Civil law is based on the English legal and Christian belief systems.
- Marriages must be monogamous.
- Both the man and the woman must be at least 18 years of age.

Muslim Law:
- Muslim law is based on the Islamic faith and teachings of the Koran.
- In Muslim law a man may have as many as four wives at any given time.
- There is no minimum age for marriage; rather a party can marry once puberty is reached. However, a guardian can give permission for a prepubescent child to marry.

Hindu Law:
- Hindu law is based on the Hindu faith.
- Marriages are monogamous under Hindu law.
- The groom must be at least 18 years of age, while the bride need only be 16. If the bride is 16 to 18 years old, then permission must be granted by a guardian or by a court of justice.

Customary Law:
- Customary law is based on the traditional Kenyan tribal law.
- Under customary law, a man may have as many wives as he wishes.
- Like Muslim law, minimum age to marry is linked to reaching puberty.

> **Across Cultures: The Kenyan National Motto**
> The national motto of Kenya is *harambee*, which in Swahili means to pull together. Volunteers nationwide have taken that motto to heart and built numerous schools and hospital clinics throughout the country, and pooled money to send Kenyan children to study abroad.

Critical Thinking *Should different religious and ethnic groups be allowed to follow their own laws, even though their members are citizens of a particular country?*

Global Law

Marriage Laws in Kenya

Answer Answers will vary. Students may argue that each group has a common goal and can effectively govern itself. In the United States, for example, the Native American tribes are considered sovereign nations and can pass and enforce their own sets of laws. One could also argue, however, that there should be one governing law for all groups within a larger country. If there are different laws for different groups of people—for example, one couple is married under customary law, while their neighbors are married under Hindu law—it could be confusing and unfair.

The primary obligation of marriage is the duty of the spouses to be faithful to each other. This duty cannot be surrendered, even by agreement. In addition, all people, married or not, are obligated to refrain from causing bodily harm to those with whom they live. The law does not tolerate the physical abuse of spouses or children. Doing so is a criminal offense, punishable by imprisonment and the loss of the custody of one's children. In addition, all parents have the duty to support their children.

Types of Marriage

If two people simply claim they are married, are they legally married?

Each state has its own laws regulating the types of marriage it will recognize.

Common-Law Marriage

In the English common law system, people did not need a formal **ceremony** to be married. They could simply agree that they were married in a common-law marriage. **A common-law marriage is an informal type of marriage created by the parties themselves.** Today, 11 states and the District of Columbia still allow common-law marriages. In the remaining 39 states, only ceremonial marriage is recognized. However, under the U.S. Constitution's Full Faith and Credit clause, every state must treat as valid common-law marriages that originated in other states. States that continue to allow common-law marriage require that the parties agree, by words in the present tense, that they are husband and wife. There is no such thing as a common-law divorce.

Ceremonial Marriage

In early colonial times, a marriage ceremony had to be performed by a cleric or magistrate in a specific manner. Today, most states still require some kind of ceremony to formalize the marriage, but no particular form need be followed. However, the parties must declare that they are married in the presence of a person authorized by state law to conduct marriages.

Proxy Marriage

The Uniform Marriage and Divorce Act allows a proxy marriage. A proxy marriage occurs when one or both of the parties cannot be present for the wedding ceremony. Instead, an agent acts on behalf of the absent party.

Covenant Marriage

The covenant marriage, adopted in Arkansas, Arizona, and Louisiana, is an attempt to reduce divorce and protect children. The parties must have counseling before the wedding and during the marriage to solve conflicts. In most cases, the couple can divorce only after a period of separation.

Legal Talk

Bigamy: *n* The state of being married to two people at the same time. From Latin *bi* = two + Greek *gamos* = marriage.

Polygamy: *n* The state of being married to multiple people at the same time. From Greek *poly* = many + *gamos* = marriage.

Vocabulary Builder The Greek root *poly* means *many*. List and define five words that contain this root word.

Look It Up! Check definitions in *Black's Law Dictionary* or an online glossary. For direct links, go to glencoe.com to find more vocabulary resources.

20.1 SECTION

TEACH (cont.)

C Critical Thinking

Common-Law Marriage
Tell students that common-law marriage is an informal type of marriage created by the parties themselves. Ask students why they think most states consider this form of marriage contrary to public policy. (requires no formal commitment)

Reading Check

Enumerate Marriage rights include the right to support from your spouse when necessary, inheritance from your deceased spouse, property if the marriage ends, compensation to continue your standard of living if the marriage ends, and to file a joint income tax return.

Legal Talk

(polymorphic, polyunsaturated, polyester, polyphonic, polygon)

Ask students to practice their academic and legal vocabulary with the electronic flashcards available at the *Business and Personal Law* Online Learning Center through glencoe.com.

Extending the Content

Marriage Ceremonies

Marriage ceremonies can range from the ultra-formal religious event to a quick exchange of vows at the county clerk's office. Ask students to use the Internet, magazines, or books to make a list of the types of ceremonies available to couples today. Also have them identify the persons who are authorized to conduct marriages in your state.

443

Reading Check

Enumerate List the marriage rights that spouses are entitled to receive from each other.

444

Making Wedding Plans
Preparing for marriage includes meeting certain legal requirements, such as obtaining a marriage license. *Where can you obtain a marriage license?*

Marriages Performed Internationally

If Americans get married abroad, those marriages are usually recognized in the United States as valid, as long as the marriages are legal in those foreign countries. Similarly, most marriages in the United States are recognized in other countries.

Prohibited Marriages

Is it illegal for first cousins to marry?

Certain types of marriages are prohibited in every state of the country, while others are prohibited in just some states.

Bigamy and Polygamy

Bigamy and polygamy are crimes under the laws of every state in this country. **Bigamy is the illegal act of having two spouses at the same time. Polygamy is the illegal act of having more than two spouses at the same time.** Thus, any marriage that occurs while one party is already married is void in every state. Any children born of a man and woman whose marriage is void are considered illegitimate. In some states, if one of the parties married without knowing the other party was already married, the second marriage becomes valid upon the death or divorce of the partner to the first marriage.

Marriage between Relatives

Some states have statutes that prohibit marriage between persons related by consanguinity or by affinity. **Consanguinity means related by blood. Affinity means related by marriage.** For example, many states prohibit the marriage of first cousins. Almost half the states do not have a law against marriages between persons related by affinity, such as the brother of one spouse marrying the sister of the other spouse.

Requirements of a Legal Marriage

Why do you have to go through a waiting period before you get married?

Depending on the state, there are various requirements that must be followed in order for a marriage to be legal.

Age Requirement

In nearly every state except Mississippi and Nebraska, you can marry at age 18. Teens younger than 18 can marry only with the consent of a parent or guardian. Laws requiring parental permission are intended to prevent minors from entering into unsuitable or coerced marriages.

444 Unit 7 Family Law

▲ USING VISUALS

Making Wedding Plans Answer In most states, a marriage license is obtained at the county or city clerk's office. In some states, such as Hawaii, there are marriage license agents who can prepare the license. Proof of age and a license fee are required. Once issued, the license is not completed until the marriage is performed by a recognized official and signed.

However, marriage age differs around the world. Some countries allow children to be married as young as age 13.

Marriage License

You must get a marriage license before you can get married. This is a certificate issued by a government office giving permission to marry. Once issued, the license becomes effective after any waiting period required by state law. The license will expire if the couple does not marry during the prescribed time period. A common-law marriage does not require a license.

Waiting Period

Most states require a waiting period to give the couple time to reconsider their decision. Also, a waiting period may allow evidence of fraud, force, or jest to be uncovered. Moreover, the delay gives interested parties, such as the parents, an opportunity to object on other grounds.

Blood Test/Physical Examination

Some states require a blood test before a marriage license is issued. Such tests screen prospective spouses for AIDS, venereal disease, sickle cell anemia, rubella (German measles), and infectious tuberculosis.

Use of Names

After marriage, the parties may use any name provided they do not commit fraud. A wife does not have to adopt her husband's surname. Today, many married women continue to use their maiden name, or they hyphenate their name with their husband's surname.

After You Read

Summarize List the requirements the parties must fulfill in a legal marriage.

SECTION 20.1 ASSESSMENT

Self Check

1. What is the primary obligation of marriage?

2. What types of marriages are prohibited by law?

3. What is required in most states for a marriage to be legal?

Academic Connection

English Language Arts
More and more couples are signing prenuptial marriage agreements before they marry. A prenuptial marriage agreement is a contract that spells out how a couple will handle the financial aspects of their marriage. Although not very romantic, having this honest financial discussion before a wedding can be a very positive experience. Review samples of prenuptial agreements available on the Internet and use them as a guide to write your own. In class, compare your agreement with other students' agreements and discuss what you would and would not change.

Critical Thinking Activity

Surnames Although it is traditional when people get married for the wife to take the husband's surname (last name), many women today choose to keep their own surname. Why do you think this is?

 Go to **glencoe.com** to check your answers.

RETEACH (cont.)

After You Read

Summarize age, marriage license, waiting period, and blood test/ physical examination

ASSESS

Self-Assessment

Have students go to the *Business and Personal Law* Online Learning Center through glencoe.com to take the Section 20.1 Practice Test.

CLOSE

Culminating Activity

Types of Marriage
Ask students to determine the types of marriage demonstrated below.

1. Mark has been called to service in the army and sends an agent on his behalf to his wedding to Jennifer. (proxy)

2. Kevin and Jane agree to undergo counseling before their wedding and during the marriage. (covenant)

SECTION 20.1 ASSESSMENT

Self Check

1. the duty of the spouses to be faithful to each other

2. marriages by one person to two or more other people at the same time, and, in some states, marriages between people related by blood and marriages between people related by marriage

3. a marriage license, a waiting period, and a minimum age of 18

Academic Connection

English Language Arts
Answers will vary.

Critical Thinking

Answers may include legal, financial, and personal considerations due to the changing status of women in society.

 Activity correlated to the English Language Arts standard on page 440

FOCUS

🔔 Bell Ringer Activity

Ask students to brainstorm reasons that might cause couples to seek a divorce. (adultery, job stress, incompatibility, money problems) Explain that the probability of a marriage ending in divorce is 44 to 56 percent.

Preteaching

Key Terms

Read the definitions and ask students to create a sentence using each term.

Academic Vocabulary

Explain that developing vocabulary is key to academic success. An efficient method to develop vocabulary is to study how words are formed.

- **persistent** Adjective, from the Latin *persistere* (continue steadfastly). Means repeated.
- **reconciliation** Noun, from the Latin *reconcilare* (to bring back together). Means the act of reconciling.
- **capacity** Noun, from the Latin *capacitas* (able to hold). Means the ability to receive or contain.

Activity Ask students to give a noun, a verb, an adjective, or an adverb form that comes from each word.

Connects to academic content

What You'll Learn

- ◆ Describe the differences between an annulment, a legal separation, and a divorce.
- ◆ Identify the common grounds for divorce.
- ◆ Explain the issues involved in a divorce settlement.

Why It's Important

Before you ever consider getting a divorce, you need to know what the legal grounds and consequences of divorce are.

Academic Standards

Reading and completing the activities in this section will help you practice the following academic standards:

Math (NCTM CS2 3) Recognize and apply mathematics in contexts outside of mathematics.

Social Studies (NCSS 4) Study individual development and identity.

Divorce and Its Legal Consequences

Reading Guide

Before You Read

Connect Almost one-half of all marriages end in divorce today. Can you think of ways to help reduce the divorce rate?

Focus on Ideas

In a divorce, issues of alimony, child support and custody, and division of property must be legally settled.

Take Notes

Create a graph like the one shown and use it to take notes as you read this section. Go to **glencoe.com** to find graphic organizers and tips on how to improve your note-taking skills.

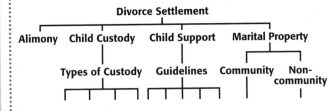

📖 Key Terms

You will learn these legal words and expressions in this chapter. You can also find these terms in *Black's Law Dictionary* or in an online legal dictionary.

- annulment
- divorce
- adultery
- no-fault divorce
- alimony

📖 Academic Vocabulary

You will find these words in your readings and in your tests. Look them up in a dictionary and familiarize yourself with them.

- persistent
- reconciliation
- capacity

glencoe.com

ℝ Reading Strategy

Read for Knowledge

1. **Survey** or preread the chapter.
2. **Question** or formulate questions before you read.
3. **Recite** or read your questions, answers, and notes out loud.
4. **Review** or reread your notes.

Note-Taking Basics

- Listen attentively
- Have note-taking materials ready
- Skim through the lesson material
- Write down key words and ideas
- Anticipate what comes next
- Review notes soon after taking them

How Marriages End

Is divorce the only way a marriage can end?

A marriage comes to an end in one of three ways: the death of a spouse, annulment, or divorce. Couples can also become legally separated, without a divorce or annulment. Annulment and divorce are subject to specific state laws.

Annulment

An annulment is a declaration by the court that a marriage was never valid. To have a marriage annulled, the parties must go before a probate court judge and prove certain grounds. Proof varies from state to state, but two common grounds the courts accept are duress and fraud. Duress is when someone is forced to marry against his or her will. Examples of fraud include being below the state's legal age to marry, secretly intending never to have children, or concealing pregnancy by someone other than the husband.

Legal Separation

A legal separation, also called a limited divorce or a separation from bed and board, is a court judgment ending the right to cohabitation. In making a separation judgment, the court will temporarily decide the issues of child custody and support. The two people remain married until there is a final divorce, which does not need to follow immediately.

Divorce

A divorce (called dissolution of marriage in some states) is a declaration by the court that a valid marriage has come to an end. The procedure for obtaining a divorce varies from state to state. The process may be contested by the parties, or they may agree to the divorce.

Grounds for Divorce

Do you have to prove anything in court to get a divorce?

States differ on the grounds they accept for divorce. The most common grounds are explained below.

Adultery

Adultery is when one spouse has sexual relations with someone outside of the marriage. It is a crime in some states, in addition to being grounds for divorce. Because of its private nature, criminal adultery is difficult to prove beyond a reasonable doubt. Without solid proof, the injured spouse must show convincing circumstantial evidence that the other spouse had the opportunity to commit adultery and the inclination to do so.

As You Read

Predict Is an annulment of a marriage the same as a divorce?

TEACH

Discussion Starter

Class Discussion

Ask students to think of ideas that might cause married couples to seek a divorce. Explain that this section will address the various reasons for divorcing and the legal consequences that arise from a divorce.

D Develop Concepts

Divorce Have students scan newspapers, magazines, and the Internet for news stories dealing with divorce. In class, present each case they find and have them identify the reasons for each divorce.

As You Read

Predict While students may not understand the specific reasons for the difference, they may know that there is a difference between a divorce and an annulment. (No. Annulment: marriage was never valid; divorce: end to a legal marriage.)

U Universal Access

Divorce and the Family Some students in your class may have parents who are divorced or in the process of divorcing. It is important to present the subject matter of the chapter in a manner that will not embarrass or offend these students. You may wish to discuss with them privately whether they would like to share their experiences and feelings with the class.

TEACH (cont.)

Guided Practice

Divorce Settlement

Explain to students that when a marriage ends, the parties must resolve issues surrounding property, custody of children, alimony, and child support. The resolution of these issues is often complicated and emotional. Ask students what they believe happens with the assets that the couple gained during the marriage. (In non-community property states, assets are divided according to how much each spouse contributed. In community property states, assets are divided equally.)

 Writing Support

Alimony Explain that the word *alimony* comes from Latin and means "sustenance," or "nourishment." Alimony is an allowance for support and maintenance made to a divorced person by a former spouse. Ask students to write a one-page essay about the kinds of factors they think might justify the payment of alimony to an ex-spouse. Have them include the kinds of factors that might be considered when determining the amount of alimony.

Reading Check

Analyze *Why do the states ask couples to live apart for a while before allowing the divorce to occur?*

Vocabulary You can find vocabulary definitions in the **Key Terms** glossary and **Academic Vocabulary** glossary in the back of this book.

Cruelty

To prove cruelty, a spouse must show that there was personal violence that endangered his or her life or health. Usually, more than one act of violence is required. Sometimes, a spouse can claim cruelty due to mental suffering, not physical violence.

Other Grounds

Other grounds include desertion, alcohol or drug addition, and nonsupport. Desertion is the unjustified separation of one spouse from the other with the intent of not returning. The length of separation to qualify as desertion is one year in most states. Alcohol or drug addition must be confirmed, **persistent**, voluntary, and excessive. Divorce can be based on nonsupport if one spouse can show that the other had the ability to provide economic support but willfully failed to do so. Husbands, as well as wives, may claim nonsupport as grounds for divorce. Many states allow a divorce if one spouse is convicted of a felony or imprisoned for a certain number of years after the marriage occurs.

No-Fault Divorce

Almost all states now have a no-fault divorce law. **A no-fault divorce is a divorce granted without either party having to prove the other party guilty of misconduct.** The parties simply agree that they have a personality conflict so deep that there is no chance for **reconciliation**. Many states require that the spouses live apart for a period of time before the divorce is finalized. Some states have reconciliation bureaus that attempt to save the marriages through counseling.

Divorce Settlement

How do courts decide who gets custody of the children?

The parties in a divorce must come to a legal settlement regarding the issues of alimony, child custody and support, and distribution of property (see **Figure 20.1**).

Alimony

W **Alimony is an allowance for support paid to one person by the former spouse in a divorce.** In an at-fault divorce, the spouse who is found to have been at fault will not be awarded alimony. In determining alimony, each person's age, income, and financial resources are considered. Their obligations and number of dependents are taken into account. Also examined are each spouse's future earning **capacity** and separate property owned. Software is often used to make alimony calculations today.

Child Custody and Support

Parents are considered to be joint guardians of any offspring born during their marriage. Upon divorce, each parent has an equal right to custody of the children. Most states divide custody into two parts:

Reading Check

Analyze Students may infer that living apart for a period of time gives the couple opportunity to consider whether they want the divorce or not.

Extending the Content

Child Support

The Uniform Interstate Family Support Act (UIFSA) allows support orders of one state to be enforced in every state. Ask students if they agree that states should cooperate to

enforce child support. (Opinions will vary. Some students may argue that "deadbeat" parents would move to other states without enforcement across state lines.) Ask students to research the penalties for nonpayment of child support in your state.

Figure 20.1 Divorce Settlement

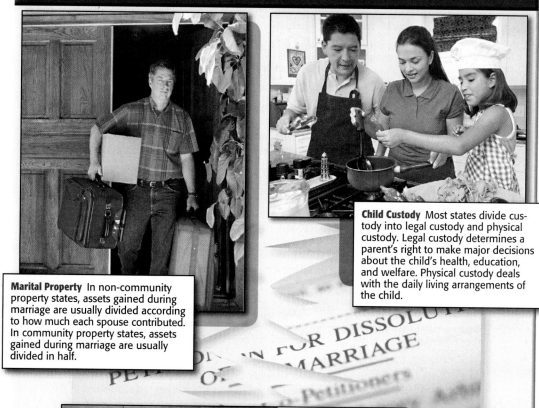

Marital Property In non-community property states, assets gained during marriage are usually divided according to how much each spouse contributed. In community property states, assets gained during marriage are usually divided in half.

Child Custody Most states divide custody into legal custody and physical custody. Legal custody determines a parent's right to make major decisions about the child's health, education, and welfare. Physical custody deals with the daily living arrangements of the child.

Alimony and Child Support The amount a spouse receives in alimony is based on factors such as the income, earning capacity, financial resources, health, and age of the spouses. Child support is usually paid by the noncustodial parent to the custodial parent and must cover a child's basic needs.

C

Federal regulations require every state to adopt child support guidelines. *What information do you think should be in a mathematical formula to determine parents' support obligations?*

Chapter 20   Marriage and Divorce   **449**

TEACH (cont.)
Guided Practice
Grounds for Divorce
Write the following grounds for divorce on the board:

- cruelty
- adultery
- desertion
- alcohol or drug addiction
- nonsupport

Have students define some of the less obvious grounds. (desertion: unjustified separation of one spouse from the other with the intent of not returning; nonsupport: one party refuses the other financial support)

C Critical Thinking

Alimony Ask students why alimony cannot be awarded to the individual found to be at fault in an at-fault divorce. (Answers may include the idea that to cause a divorce and then expect support is unreasonable.) Tell students that if alimony is awarded, software or online calculators can be used to calculate the amount.

▲ USING VISUALS

➡ Figure 20.1 Divorce Settlement Answer Remind students that child support is usually paid by the noncustodial parent to the custodial parent and should be sufficient to cover each child's basic needs. Information that the court uses to determine support payments includes each parent's separate income, state and local taxes, alimony payments, medical insurance payments, Social Security and pension payments, number of children requiring support, and child care expenses.

ASSESS

Quiz

Ask students to answer the following questions:

1. What is the difference between custody of children and support of children? (Custody means being a guardian; support means providing money.)

2. What is the difference between alimony and child support? (alimony: financial support for the former spouse; child support: financial support for the children)

3. What is a no-fault divorce? (Neither party has to prove that the other party was guilty of misconduct.)

RETEACH

 Writing Support

Custody Remind students that most states divide custody into legal custody and physical custody. Have them write a brief explanation of both types of custody. (legal custody: parents' rights to deal with decisions on child's health, education, and welfare; physical custody: which parent the child will live with)

Review Key Terms

Encourage students to access the *Business and Personal Law* Online Learning Center through glencoe.com and use the electronic flashcards to review the key terms.

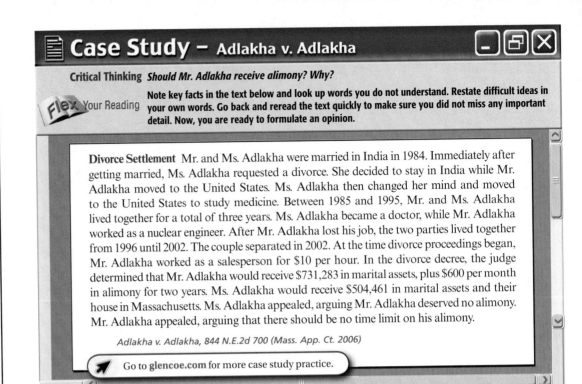

Case Study – Adlakha v. Adlakha

Critical Thinking *Should Mr. Adlakha receive alimony? Why?*

Flex Your Reading — Note key facts in the text below and look up words you do not understand. Restate difficult ideas in your own words. Go back and reread the text quickly to make sure you did not miss any important detail. Now, you are ready to formulate an opinion.

Divorce Settlement Mr. and Ms. Adlakha were married in India in 1984. Immediately after getting married, Ms. Adlakha requested a divorce. She decided to stay in India while Mr. Adlakha moved to the United States. Ms. Adlakha then changed her mind and moved to the United States to study medicine. Between 1985 and 1995, Mr. and Ms. Adlakha lived together for a total of three years. Ms. Adlakha became a doctor, while Mr. Adlakha worked as a nuclear engineer. After Mr. Adlakha lost his job, the two parties lived together from 1996 until 2002. The couple separated in 2002. At the time divorce proceedings began, Mr. Adlakha worked as a salesperson for $10 per hour. In the divorce decree, the judge determined that Mr. Adlakha would receive $731,283 in marital assets, plus $600 per month in alimony for two years. Ms. Adlakha would receive $504,461 in marital assets and their house in Massachusetts. Ms. Adlakha appealed, arguing Mr. Adlakha deserved no alimony. Mr. Adlakha appealed, arguing that there should be no time limit on his alimony.

Adlakha v. Adlakha, 844 N.E.2d 700 (Mass. App. Ct. 2006)

Go to **glencoe.com** for more case study practice.

- **Legal custody** deals with a parent's right to make major decisions about the child's health, education, and welfare.
- **Physical custody** deals with which parent the child will live with.

Courts can declare sole or joint custody. Sole custody gives all parental rights, duties, and powers to one parent. The children live with that parent and the noncustodial parent has visitation rights. In contrast, joint custody gives both parents rights and duties. Children may live with each parent at different times. In awarding custody, the court attempts to determine the best interests of the child. Some states favor awarding custody to the primary caretaker, that is, the parent who spent the most time caring for the child. Many states give great weight to the child's personal wishes.

Child Support Guidelines Child support is a basic obligation of every parent. This obligation exists regardless of which parent has custody. Federal regulations require every state to adopt child support guidelines, following these principles:

- Both parents should share responsibility for child support in proportion to their income.
- The financial needs of each parent should be considered, but each parent must contribute more than zero.
- Child support must cover a child's basic needs and ensure that the child shares in a parent's standard of living.

 glencoe.com

Case Study

Adlakha v. Adlakha

Answer Yes. The Massachusetts Appeals Court held that Mr. Adlakha had a valid claim for alimony. However, the court further held that an arbitrary time limitation on the alimony needed further explanation. In this situation, Ms. Adlakha's medical practice had led the couple to maintain a "very high" standard of living, and the court decided that Mr. Adlakha was entitled to maintain a high standard of living after the couple divorced, although not necessarily as high as his ex-wife's. During the early part of the couple's relationship, Mr. Adlakha was making considerably more than Ms. Adlakha, so each person was providing for the other at various times.

- Each child has an equal right to share in a parent's income, the income of a current spouse, and other dependents.
- Each child is entitled to support, even if the parents were not married at the time of the child's birth.

Enforcement of Child Support Child support is enforced using a legal order obtained from a judge or from an administrative hearing officer. If a parent moves out of state, the support order must be enforced in any other state. Support orders can be registered in different states so that parents who do not pay can be found. Out-of-state employers can withhold support payments from an employee's paycheck. Federal and state income tax refunds can be garnished to pay for support. Liens can be placed on out-of-state real estate. Passports may also be denied to enforce child support orders.

Marital Property

State law and judges determine property distribution. Some states are non-community property states. In these states, the assets and earnings gained during marriage are divided proportionately. For example, the higher wage earner might take two-thirds of the assets while the lower wage earner receives only one-third. In contrast, in community property states, each spouse is entitled to a one-half interest in property acquired during the marriage. This applies regardless of which spouse purchased the property or if only one spouse worked. There are exceptions in community property states for property a spouse owned before marriage or received as a gift.

After You Read

Summarize What are the issues that a divorce settlement must cover?

SECTION 20.2 ASSESSMENT

Self Check

1. What are the two common grounds for annulment?

2. What are the most common grounds for divorce?

3. Explain the difference between sole custody and joint custody.

Academic Connection

Mathematics Jay and Kay were married for six years when they got a divorce. They have two children, ages 2 and 4. After taking into account the finances of Jay and Kay, and granting Kay primary custody of the children, the court ordered Jay to pay 10% of his net income to Kay in alimony for one-half the length of the marriage, and 15% of his net income to Kay for child support until the children are 18. Jay's net income is $40,000 per year. How much does Jay pay in combined alimony and child support the first four years?

 THEORY **Number and Operations: Using Multiple Operations** Calculate the amount for alimony and for child support by multiplying the net income times the percentage for each. Then multiply the amount for each by the number of years. Keep in mind that Jay pays alimony only for half the length of the marriage.

 For more math practice, go to the Math Appendix.

Critical Thinking

No-Fault Divorce Why do you think most states have a no-fault divorce law?

Go to **glencoe.com** to check your answers.

ASSESS

Self-Assessment

Have students go to the *Business and Personal Law* Online Learning Center through **glencoe.com** to take the Section 20.2 Practice Test.

CLOSE

Culminating Activity

Marital Property
Tell students that Randy and Donna are divorcing in a community property state. Randy has worked outside the home the entire marriage while Donna has been a stay-at-home mom. The value of the assets they acquired during marriage is $926,000. How should the assets be divided? (In a community property state, assets acquired during the marriage are divided equally.)

SECTION 20.2 ASSESSMENT

Self Check

1. duress and fraud

2. adultery, cruelty, desertion, alcohol or drug addition, and nonsupport

3. Sole custody gives all parental rights, duties, and powers to one parent. Joint custody divides rights, duties, and powers between parents.

Academic Connection
Mathematics
Alimony: $12,000
Child Support: $36,000

Critical Thinking
Most states today recognize the need to allow divorces even though the parties do not commit cruelty, adultery, desertion, or other traditional grounds for divorce.

NCLB Activity correlated to the Mathematics standard on page 446

Summary by Sections

Ask students to read the summaries one key point at a time. Then, ask them to work in groups to create two examples to illustrate each key point.

Vocabulary Builder

Cooperative Learning

1. Have students work in groups to prepare their sentences. Ask the groups to exchange their sentences and assess each other's sentences.

Vocabulary Development

- Ask students to use a dictionary or to go online to look up the etymology of each key term listed.
- Then, ask students to list several words derived from the same root or origin. For example, *contract* has the same root as *contractual* or *contractually*.

Summary

Section 20.1 Marriage Laws

- Most states and the federal government define marriage as the union of one man and one woman.
- Marriage changes a couple's legal status and gives them new rights and obligations as a married couple.
- The primary obligation of marriage is the duty of the spouses to be faithful to each other.
- Types of marriage include common-law marriage, ceremonial marriage, proxy marriage, and covenant marriage.
- Prohibited marriages include bigamy and polygamy, and marriage between relatives.
- For a marriage to be legal requires a marriage license, a waiting period, a blood test, and a minimum age of 18 in most states.

Section 20.2 Divorce and Its Legal Consequences

- A marriage comes to an end in one of three ways: the death of a spouse, annulment, or divorce.
- An annulment is a declaration by the court that the marriage was never effective and was void from the beginning.
- A divorce is a declaration by the court that a valid marriage has come to an end.
- Common grounds for divorce include adultery, cruelty, desertion, alcohol or drug addition, and nonsupport.
- Almost all states have a no-fault divorce law.
- The parties in a divorce must come to a legal settlement regarding the issues of alimony, child custody and support, and distribution of property.

Vocabulary Builder

1 On a sheet of paper, use each of these terms in a sentence.

Key Terms

- marriage
- prenuptial agreement
- common-law marriage
- bigamy
- polygamy
- consanguinity
- affinity
- annulment
- divorce
- adultery
- no-fault divorce
- alimony

Academic Vocabulary

- spouse
- status
- ceremony
- persistent
- reconciliation
- capacity

Go to **glencoe.com** to play a game and improve your legal vocabulary.

Study Skills for Success

Prepare Your Students for Studying

Tell students that they can improve their ability to understand and remember material from their courses by learning and practicing study skills. Remind students to:

- **Get motivated!** Motivation must come from within. To motivate yourself, think of ways in which what you learn now will fit into your long-term personal and professional goals.
- **Get organized!** Make studying part of your daily routine, not something you do at the last minute.
- **Concentrate!** Study in an environment that is as free of distractions as possible.

20 **Chapter**

Review and Assessment

Key Points Review

Answer the following questions. Refer to the chapter for additional reinforcement.

2 When does the marriage contract actually come into existence? Explain your answer.

3 What is a prenuptial agreement?

4 List five rights that are given by law to people when they marry.

5 What is a common-law marriage and how widely recognized is it?

6 What is the difference between an annulment and divorce?

7 What is a no-fault divorce?

8 What is the difference between legal custody and physical custody of a child?

9 How is marital property divided in community and noncommunity property states?

Standardized Test Practice

10 Read the following legal excerpt regarding marriage and the rights afforded through a legalized marriage, and then complete questions 1 and 2.

Marriage is the legal union of two people in which a ceremony is performed. Non-religious ceremonies, called civil ceremonies, must be performed by a judge, justice of the peace, or court clerk who has legal authority to perform marriages, or by a person given temporary authority by a judge or court clerk to conduct a marriage ceremony. Religious ceremonies must be conducted by a clergy member (priest, minister, or rabbi). Native American weddings may be performed by a tribal chief or by another official, as designated by the tribe. Federal laws regarding marriage and divorce are listed in the Uniform Marriage and Divorce Act. When you are married, your responsibilities and rights toward your spouse concerning property and support are defined by the laws of the state in which you live.

1. Marriage can best be defined as:

Ⓐ the legal union of two people in which a ceremony has been performed

Ⓑ two people agreeing to be married and sharing all their assets and debts

Ⓒ a legal agreement between two people that is witnessed to be married

Ⓓ the legal union of two people that is not witnessed or no ceremony is performed

2. Marriage responsibilities and rights between the spouses are defined by the:

Ⓐ Uniform Marriage and Divorce Act

Ⓑ state in which the couple resides

Ⓒ spouses in their prenuptial agreement

Ⓓ adopted customs and practices of society

 Test-Taking Strategies As you prepare to answer a question, first identify the verbs or words in the question that give you direction.

Key Points Review

2. upon engagement, with an offer and acceptance

3. written and signed legal contract made prior to marriage dealing with property and support issues should the marriage fail

4. right to (1) support from one's spouse when necessary, (2) inheritance from one's deceased spouse, (3) property if the marriage ends, (4) compensation to continue one's standard of living if the marriage ends, (5) file a joint tax return

5. informal type of marriage created by the parties themselves; recognized in 11 states and D.C.

6. Annulment: court declares that a marriage was never valid. Divorce: court declares that a valid marriage has ended.

7. granted without either party having to prove the other party guilty of misconduct

8. Legal custody: parents' right to make major decisions regarding the child. Physical custody: which parent the child will live with.

9. Non-community property states: marital assets are divided proportionately to each spouse's contribution during the marriage. Community property states: each spouse receives one half of the marital assets.

Standardized Test Practice

10. A and B

 Strategies for Standardized Test Prep Success

Whether your students have a standardized test coming up in a few days or a few weeks, these last-minute test-prep tips and strategies will help them relax and do their best.

• **Test Format** Help students become familiar with the format of the test by practicing with test items that imitate the actual test items as closely as possible.

• **Test Timing** Have your students take timed practice tests so that they become comfortable with the length, design, and timing of the actual test.

Review and Assessment

Apply and Debate

Students should use chapter content to arrive at conclusions. The legal resolutions are listed below:

11. **Probably not.** Although it was Rick's actions that led Betty to call off the wedding, it was still Betty who actually called off the wedding.

12. **Maybe.** A valid premarital agreement is a binding contract, meaning Darnell is entitled to the money. However, because it is a contract, Reta can try to void the contract through a fraud claim.

13. **Probably not.** In states that recognize community property, a legal separation will usually prevent any claims for the right to property acquired after the separation.

14. **A court will have to make this determination.** Parents come to court on an equal footing to present their case. The court considers many things, including who primarily cared for the children, what the wishes of the children are, family stability issues, and monetary issues, including child support.

15. **The key word is *irreconcilable*.** The couple has already decided they cannot be reconciled and a judge will usually grant the divorce without asking many questions.

454

Apply and Debate

C Read the following scenarios. Get together with other students in pairs or groups of three and take a position on each scenario. Debate your position in class with students taking the opposite position or prepare a written argument justifying your position.

11 Broken Engagement and the Ring

Despite Betty's warning him that she would break off their engagement, Rick took a ten-day fishing trip with his buddies. When Betty broke off the engagement, Rick asked for his ring back, but Betty refused, saying he caused the breakup.

You Debate *Assume the couple lives in a state that allows the woman to keep the ring if the man breaks off the engagement. Is Betty entitled to keep the ring?*

12 Premarital Agreement Difficulties

Reta, a wealthy heiress, fell in love with Darnell. Their premarital agreement allowed him nothing if he divorced her before 24 months, but after that he would be entitled to $1 million. Darnell asked for a divorce 25 months after the wedding.

You Debate *Do you think Darnell is entitled to the $1 million?*

13 A Long Separation

Dan and Vicki were married for 12 years. Due to incompatibility, they obtained a legal separation but never divorced. Ten years later, Vicki wanted the divorce and felt entitled to half of the assets Dan acquired after the separation.

You Debate *Assume the couple lives in a community property state. Do you think that Vicki is right to ask for one-half of Dan's assets?*

14 Who Takes the Children?

Luana and Dang have two sons and live in Texas. They are divorcing. Luana wants to move to Idaho to live with her parents. Dang, a wealthy executive who often travels, wants the sons with him. He is remarrying with a woman who will care for the boys.

You Debate *Which parent do you think should get custody of the sons?*

15 Dogs, Cats, and Divorce

Selma has acquired six dogs and eight cats since she and Sam got married. Sam now wants a divorce on grounds of irreconcilable differences. He cannot stand living with so many animals.

You Debate *If you were the judge in this case, would you suggest the couple seek counseling or would you agree to let them divorce?*

C Critical Thinking

Divorce Settlement Jana and Paul are divorcing and have a dispute over the custody of their two children. Jana is the primary income earner for the family. Paul works part-time from home. Paul wants to keep the house that was in his name before they married but is now titled in both their names. Paul and Jana live in a community property state.

Debate Practice

- Can Paul keep the house? (No. In community property states, assets are to be divided equally.)

- Who will most likely receive physical custody of the children? (Answers will vary. Paul has more time to spend with the children since he works part-time, but Jana can provide a stable and secure environment.)

Case Study Practice– Lukich v. Lukich

16 Divorce or Annulment? In March 1985, George and Phyllis Lukich were married. They lived together as a married couple for 19 years. On August 21, 2002, Ms. Lukich filed for legal separation and an award of alimony, alleging that Mr. Lukich was physically cruel and adulterous. Prior to a decree of divorce, Mr. Lukich began to suspect that Ms. Lukich had never legally divorced her first husband, Charles Havron, whom she had married in 1973. The South Carolina authorities were able to provide a copy of the marriage certificate issued for Ms. Lukich and Mr. Havron. However, there was no evidence that they ever received a divorce decree. On September 25, 2003, Mr. Lukich filed for an annulment of his marriage to Ms. Lukich on the grounds that Ms. Lukich was a bigamist. Prior to a hearing on Mr. Lukich's motion, on October 21, 2003, Ms. Lukich filed for an annulment of her marriage to Mr. Havron on the grounds that they were married while they were intoxicated and that they had never actually lived together after they were married. Ms. Lukich was granted her annulment against Mr. Havron on October 31, 2003, so in the eyes of the law, Ms. Lukich was never married to Mr. Havron.

Source: Lukich v. Lukich, 627 S.E.2d 754 (S.C. Ct. App. 2006)

Practice Can Mr. Lukich still get an annulment of his marriage to Ms. Lukich?

17 Ethics ←?→ Application

Green Card Marriage Rodney, an American, met Zuzana, a woman from Slovakia, in college. After graduating, Zuzana asked Rodney to help her become a permanent resident of the United States by marrying her. Rodney likes her, but is not sure he loves her. He knows that a fraudulent marriage is illegal, but that it is also difficult to prove. He wants to help his friend. The marriage would only be for two or three years.

◆ Do you think it is ethical for Rodney to marry Zuzana to help her gain U.S. citizenship?

18 Internet Application

Find out about Divorce Laws After twelve years of marriage, Marcus and Sharon have decided to divorce. Since they do not have children, only their assets have to be divided.

 Log on to **glencoe.com** to access the Web site sponsored by FindLaw and find out the steps for filing for divorce, the time line for their steps, and these rights. Assume the couple lives in the same state as you.

 Reading Connection

Outside Reading Go to **glencoe.com** for a list of reading suggestions about marriage laws.

 glencoe.com

Review and Assessment

←?→ Ethics Application

17. Students may consider the difficulty of obtaining permanent residency in the United States and the fact that Zuzana is college educated and would probably be a responsible taxpayer. However, students may also discuss the lack of love in the marriage and the treatment of the marriage as a (fraudulent) business deal. Finally, students may consider the purpose of U.S. immigration laws and the need for people to go through the proper channels.

Internet Application

18. Responses will vary depending on the state of residence. Students should perform adequate research and cover issues such as child custody, support, and waiting periods.

R Reading Strategy

 Reading Connection

American Bar Association Resources

Go to the *Business and Personal Law* Online Learning Center through **glencoe.com** to find links for further readings that relate to this chapter. Ask students to read, review, and summarize the documents. Advise students to keep their reviews and summaries to use as reference material for their Unit Thematic Project on pages 478–479.

Case Study Practice

16. Yes. The South Carolina Court of Appeals found that Ms. Lukich could not use the annulment of her first marriage as a defense against an annulment of her second marriage. The court found that the public policy behind the bigamy law in South Carolina overrides the public policy supporting the finality of judgments. Although the annulment of Ms. Lukich's first marriage is final, public policy dictates that it is not so final that it can be a defense against bigamy.

Plan Your Lesson Section by Section

NBEA	NATIONAL BUSINESS LAW STANDARDS
Section 21.1	• **Compare** and contrast the different types of property insurance (e.g., automobile, homeowner's, and marine). • **Compare** and contrast the different types of life insurance (e.g., ordinary, limited payment, endowment, and term). • **Define** insurance and differentiate between requirements for an insurable interest for property insurance and those needed for life insurance. • **Explain** some of the differences in health insurance coverages.
Section 21.2	• **Define** testamentary capacity and testamentary intent. • **Identify** the requirements necessary for a valid will. • **Distinguish** between signing, attesting, and publishing a will. • **Explain** how a will may be modified or revoked. • **Distinguish** between the protection given to spouses and to children under the law of wills. • **Explain** what happens to a decedent's estate when a person dies without a will. • **Identify** the key characteristics of trusts. • **Explain** the advantages and disadvantages of establishing a trust. • **Differentiate** between the various types of trusts (e.g., charitable, private, spendthrift, revocable, and irrevocable trusts).

NCLB	ACADEMIC STANDARDS	Activity/Feature
English Language Arts: NCTE 3 Apply a wide range of strategies to comprehend, interpret, evaluate, and appreciate texts.		*BusinessWeek* News, Case Study, Case Study Practice
English Language Arts: NCTE 9 Develop an understanding of and respect for diversity in language use, patterns, and dialects across cultures, ethnic groups, geographic regions, and social roles.		Global Law
English Language Arts: NCTE 6 Apply knowledge of language structure, language conventions, media techniques, figurative language, and genre to create, critique, and discuss print and non-print texts.		Legal Talk, ad copy, Key Terms, and Academic Vocabulary
Social Studies: NCSS 1 Study culture and cultural diversity		Section 21.1 Assessment
Mathematics: NCTM CS2 3 Recognize and apply mathematics in contexts outside of mathematics.		Section 21.2 Assessment
English Language Arts: NCTE 4 Adjust the use of spoken, written, and visual language to communicate effectively with a variety of audiences and for different purposes.		Vocabulary Builder, Apply and Debate
English Language Arts: NCTE 7 Conduct research on issues and interests by generating ideas and questions, and by posing problems.		WebQuest

Connect Your Business Law Classroom to the World of Work

This chart shows the 21st Century Skills, foundation skills, and workplace competencies that students develop as they work in this chapter.

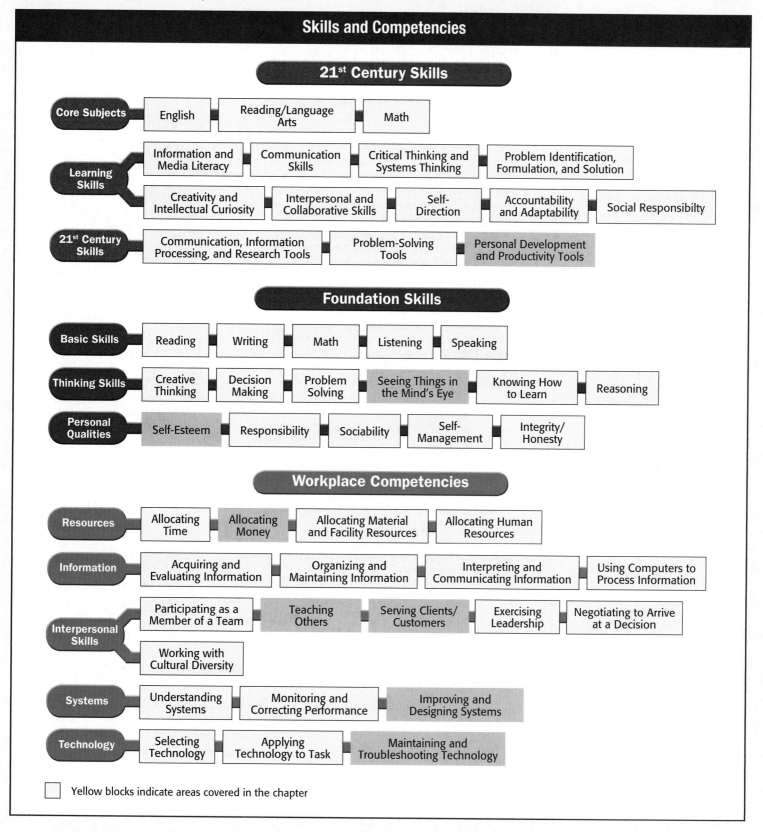

Skills and Competencies

21st Century Skills

Core Subjects
- English
- Reading/Language Arts
- Math

Learning Skills
- Information and Media Literacy
- Communication Skills
- Critical Thinking and Systems Thinking
- Problem Identification, Formulation, and Solution
- Creativity and Intellectual Curiosity
- Interpersonal and Collaborative Skills
- Self-Direction
- Accountability and Adaptability
- Social Responsibilty

21st Century Skills
- Communication, Information Processing, and Research Tools
- Problem-Solving Tools
- Personal Development and Productivity Tools

Foundation Skills

Basic Skills
- Reading
- Writing
- Math
- Listening
- Speaking

Thinking Skills
- Creative Thinking
- Decision Making
- Problem Solving
- Seeing Things in the Mind's Eye
- Knowing How to Learn
- Reasoning

Personal Qualities
- Self-Esteem
- Responsibility
- Sociability
- Self-Management
- Integrity/Honesty

Workplace Competencies

Resources
- Allocating Time
- Allocating Money
- Allocating Material and Facility Resources
- Allocating Human Resources

Information
- Acquiring and Evaluating Information
- Organizing and Maintaining Information
- Interpreting and Communicating Information
- Using Computers to Process Information

Interpersonal Skills
- Participating as a Member of a Team
- Teaching Others
- Serving Clients/Customers
- Exercising Leadership
- Negotiating to Arrive at a Decision
- Working with Cultural Diversity

Systems
- Understanding Systems
- Monitoring and Correcting Performance
- Improving and Designing Systems

Technology
- Selecting Technology
- Applying Technology to Task
- Maintaining and Troubleshooting Technology

☐ Yellow blocks indicate areas covered in the chapter

CHAPTER

21 Insurance and Estate Planning

Introduce the Chapter

Insurance and Estate Planning

Insurance protects individuals and businesses against losses involving property, life, and health. In this chapter, students will study how insurance products work. They will also learn about planning for retirement and creating a will.

Building Background

Ask students if they have ever wondered whether they might inherit money from a rich relative. Have they considered how much money they will need to have when they retire? What safeguards will they have in place to protect themselves against catastrophic financial losses during their lives?

BusinessWeek News

Explain that a trust is a legal device used by an individual to hold property for the benefit of another person or persons. This allows the deceased person's heirs to avoid the probate process when the person dies. Explain that when an estate is in a trust, it is not on public record, so that privacy of the estate is retained.

R Reading Strategy

Your Reading

Encourage students to write down any questions they have as soon as they finish reading. This will allow them to focus on the points that need review immediately.

BusinessWeek News

Interest Rates and Your Estate

By Anne Tergesen

As everyone knows, the ups and downs of interest rates can have a significant impact on the price of your home, the value of your investments, and what you pay for loans. But rates can also play a big role in estate planning. Indeed, when it comes to many popular types of trusts and other estate-planning techniques, even small moves in interest rates can make a big difference in what you'll be able to pass along to your heirs— or what you'll have to fork over to Uncle Sam. "It's simply a question of knowing which technique works better depending on the interest rate," says Blanche Lark Christerson, a managing director at Deutsche Bank Private Wealth Management. Of course, when shopping for a trust, your decisions should hinge not just on interest rates but also on factors such as the kind of assets you wish to transfer to heirs, the degree of control you'd like to maintain over your wealth, and whether you want to leave something to charity.

Flex Your Reading

Efficient critical reading involves being flexible with speed and comprehension. There are several ways of reading critically, and you need to fit a reading style to your needs and to the material.

Go to **glencoe.com** for Flex Your Reading activities, more information on reading strategies for this chapter, and guided practice in reading about estate planning.

Classroom Resources

- Student Edition
- Teacher Wraparound Edition
- Student Activity Workbook with Academic Integration (SE/TAE)
- TeacherWorks™ Plus! CD
- *ExamView®* Assessment Suite CD
- *Presentation Plus!* CD

- National Mock Trial Championship DVD
- Online Learning Center with Podcasts at glencoe.com
- Study-to-Go™ at glencoe.com
- Online Student Edition
- Interactive Student Edition

Uninsured Many people do not have any kind of health insurance. *What can you do if you get injured unexpectedly and do not have health insurance?*

457

◢ USING VISUALS

Uninsured **Answer** Public health programs such as Medicare and Medicaid can help individuals who are injured and have no health insurance. Medicare is a health insurance program for people over the age of 65, or for people with disabilities under the age of 65. Medicaid is a program designed to assist people with low incomes. Medicaid benefits vary from state to state, but must include hospital services, vaccinations, prenatal care, pediatric service and screenings, and laboratory services. Communities often offer free health clinics for low-income individuals who are underinsured or uninsured.

Practice the Concept

Insurance
Tell students that two out of five adults polled reported having serious problems paying for health insurance for their own or a family member's health care in the past two years. Approximately 16 percent of the population has no health insurance. Explain that the cost of insurance coverage is one that is commonly debated in political arenas. The benefits of having health insurance are clear. It can cover routine visits to the doctor, but it can also cover major medical events such as cancer or injuries from a car accident. Other types of insurance protect the policyholders from losses on property.

Key Terms Stress to students that a health insurance policy or a car insurance policy will contain many terms that are important. Tell students that exclusions are conditions or events that a policy does not cover. Pay attention to key words such as *reasonable* and *customary* and *medically necessary* since these are subjective terms open to interpretation.

Legal Basics Emphasize that many financial advisors view insurance as a key part of a successful financial plan. In addition to saving for retirement and setting up an estate, failure to protect your assets and health can ruin an otherwise good plan.

457

FOCUS

Bell Ringer Activity

Ask students to raise their hands if they have cell phones. Then ask what would happen if the phones were lost or damaged. (Cell phone companies provide insurance coverage for the replacement of lost or damaged equipment.)

Preteaching

Key Terms
Read the definitions and ask students to create a sentence using each term.

Academic Vocabulary
Explain that developing vocabulary is key to academic success. An efficient method to develop vocabulary is to study how words are formed.

- **comprehensive**
  Adjective, from the Latin *comprehensivus* (containing much). Means of large scope.

- **endowment** Noun, from the Latin *dotare* (bestow) + *-ment* (action). Means the act of granting.

- **routine** Noun, from the French *route* (usual action). Means a regular procedure.

Activity Ask students to give a noun, a verb, an adjective, or an adverb form that comes from each word.

 Connects to academic content

458

What You'll Learn

- ◆ Explain the meaning and purpose of insurance.
- ◆ Describe the different types of property insurance.
- ◆ Distinguish between types of life insurance.
- ◆ Identify the different types of health insurance.

Why It's Important

Knowing the different types of insurance that are available will help you protect your property and your health.

Academic Standards

Reading and completing the activities in this section will help you practice the following academic standards:

Social Studies (NCSS 1) Study culture and cultural diversity.

English Language Arts (NCTE 4) Adjust the use of spoken, written, and visual language to communicate effectively with a variety of audiences and for different purposes.

Reading Guide

Before You Read

Connect If you drive, you probably have car insurance. What other kinds of insurance are there?

Focus on Ideas

People and businesses buy insurance to protect themselves against the loss of their property, income, health, or life.

Take Notes

Create a graph like the one shown and use it to take notes as you read this section. Go to **glencoe.com** to find graphic organizers and tips on how to improve your note-taking skills.

Key Terms

You will learn these legal words and expressions in this chapter. You can also find these terms in *Black's Law Dictionary* or in an online legal dictionary.

- insurance
- premium
- beneficiary
- insurable interest
- straight life insurance
- term life insurance

Academic Vocabulary

You will find these words in your readings and in your tests. Look them up in a dictionary and familiarize yourself with them.

- comprehensive
- endowment
- routine

glencoe.com

R

R Reading Strategy

Read for Knowledge

1. **Survey** or preread the chapter.
2. **Question** or formulate questions before you read.
3. **Recite** or read your questions, answers, and notes out loud.
4. **Review** or reread your notes.

Note-Taking Basics

- Listen attentively
- Have note-taking materials ready
- Skim through the lesson material
- Write down key words and ideas
- Anticipate what comes next
- Review notes soon after taking them

What Is Insurance?

Can you insure your iPod?

Insurance is an agreement in which one party (the insurer) compensates another party (the insured) for any losses. The purpose of insurance is to protect individuals and businesses against losses by spreading the risks of loss among a large number of people. Every state has its own set of laws that governs the various types of insurance offered in that state.

As You Read

Predict How is insurance a type of contract?

Insurance Basics

An insurance policy is the written contract between a person or business buying insurance and an insurance company. The buyer of the insurance policy is called the policyholder. **The premium is the amount of money an insured pays for insurance coverage.** The proceeds are payments by insurance companies for losses covered by a policy. **The beneficiary is the person named in a life insurance policy to receive the proceeds.**

To acquire an insurance policy, an insurable interest in the person or property insured is required. **An insurable interest is the financial interest (or its possible loss) that a policyholder has in the insured person or property.** For life insurance, the insurable interest must exist at the time you buy the insurance. For property insurance, the insurable interest must exist at the time of loss.

D

Global Law

Russian Automobile Insurance

In 2003, the Russian legislature passed the OSAGO law, requiring all drivers to have liability insurance. Russian car owners must pay a minimum of 1,980 rubles per year (about $75). However, factors such as car model, location, and driver's experience can push the sum up to 3,760 rubles (about $140) or more.

Since the law was passed, there have been many complaints. From 2003 to 2005, the insurance companies received 89.6 billion rubles in premiums, but only paid out 26.3 billion rubles in claims, meaning they made 63.6 billion rubles in profits.

Another complaint is that to receive an insurance settlement, persons involved in an accident must have a police report. However, the police do not often respond quickly to an accident, causing

drivers to get frustrated and leave the scene rather than wait to make a police report.

Finally, there is an active black market for fake insurance certificates. People buy the black market certificates to get out of paying for the OSAGO insurance. When one person is in an accident with someone who has a black market certificate, there is no coverage by the OSAGO insurance company.

> **Across Cultures: Business Etiquette in Russia**
>
> There are things you should keep in mind when doing business in Russia. In Russia, meetings begin on time and negotiations can be lengthy. The exchange of business cards is very important. Have one side translated into Russian.

Critical Thinking *Should the government require everyone to buy car insurance?*

Global Law

Russian Automobile Insurance

Answer Answers will vary. Insurance is a pooling mechanism so that costs of accidents or injuries are distributed among the purchasers. Automobile insurance is one type of insurance required by the government in the United States. There are minimum limits on the amount of coverage drivers must have. There are arguments, though, that the government should not mandate insurance coverage and that it should be an individual decision. For many the cost of insurance is prohibitive.

21.1 SECTION

TEACH

Discussion Starter

Class Discussion

Ask students to consider what property they own and whether these items are insured. Have them consider what would happen if they lost this property and whether they could afford to replace it.

D Develop Concepts

Insurance Ask students to explain in their own words the purpose of insurance. (Explanations should include an understanding that the insurance company agrees to compensate the insured for any losses.) Discuss how insurance is like a savings account that covers catastrophic losses. Explain that the *insured* is the person whose property is insured. The *insurer* is the insurance company.

As You Read

Predict Explain to students that an insurance policy is a contract between a person and an insurance company. (The policyholder gives consideration [insurance premium] to an insurance company in return for the insurer providing benefits to a beneficiary upon events occurring in the future.)

SECTION 21.1

TEACH *(cont.)*

D Develop Concepts

Property Insurance Tell students that an insurance company may require specific evidence of the existence and worth of certain valuable items. Ask students why they think it is important for people to have a written inventory of their personal property and what other kinds of proof might be helpful. (Answers should indicate that written inventory lists provide documentation in the case of loss of what existed prior to the loss. Receipts that show the value of property would also be helpful.)

Independent Practice

Liability Insurance

Ask students to describe a situation in which liability insurance comes into play. (You cause injury or damage to another person or property; your liability insurance covers the losses.)

Guided Practice

Types of Automobile Insurance

Write the following injuries and damages on the board. Ask students to identify which type of insurance would cover such a damage or injury.

- A hailstorm damages the roof and hood of your car (comprehensive insurance)

- You are in a car accident and damage to your vehicle is $5,000 (collision insurance)

460

Property Insurance
Does homeowner's insurance cover your losses due to flooding?

Property insurance is a contract that covers damage or destruction of property. Buyers can purchase property insurance on such items as cars, homes, boats, and personal items. A special type of property insurance is a floater policy. It insures property that constantly changes value or location, such as a bicycle or an iPod.

Liability insurance covers claims for damages or injuries made against a policyholder. For example, if you hit another car while driving and injure the occupants, your liability insurance pays for the injuries. Vehicle, homeowner's, and renter's insurance policies usually cover both physical property and liability. Businesses can buy insurance to protect against commercial liability.

Automobile Insurance

Most states legally require drivers to carry liability insurance to cover any physical injuries or property damage they might cause. There are other types of insurance drivers should also carry.

Collision insurance covers damage to your vehicle if it is in an accident, regardless of who was at fault. **Comprehensive** insurance covers damage to your vehicle from sources other than collision, such as fire, theft, flood, and vandalism. Uninsured motorist insurance provides protection when the insured's auto is in an accident caused by a driver who has no insurance.

Vocabulary You can find vocabulary definitions in the **Key Terms** glossary and **Academic Vocabulary** glossary in the back of this book.

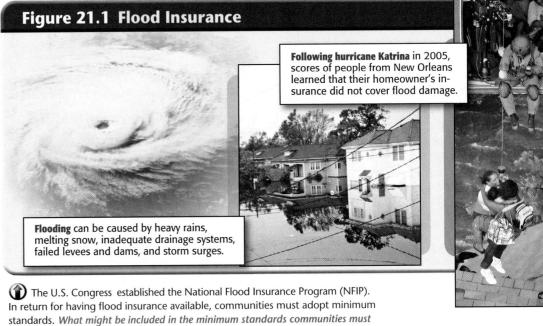

Figure 21.1 Flood Insurance

Following hurricane Katrina in 2005, scores of people from New Orleans learned that their homeowner's insurance did not cover flood damage.

Flooding can be caused by heavy rains, melting snow, inadequate drainage systems, failed levees and dams, and storm surges.

The U.S. Congress established the National Flood Insurance Program (NFIP). In return for having flood insurance available, communities must adopt minimum standards. *What might be included in the minimum standards communities must adopt to obtain flood insurance?*

460 Unit 7 Family Law

USING VISUALS

Figure 21.1 Flood Insurance Answer Minimum standards might include the prohibition of building in flood-prone areas; placing buildings on pilings or higher ground; requiring more open space for water to flow; and keeping dams and levees in good condition.

Activity Ask students to research the approximate losses caused by Hurricane Katrina. Have students discuss how they think these losses will be compensated and the kinds of rebuilding efforts that will be required along the Mississippi and Louisiana coasts. (Estimates of loss range from $30 to $35 billion; losses will be compensated through FEMA funding, private loans, and insurance.)

Many states settle auto accident claims under no-fault insurance law. Regardless of who causes an accident, all drivers involved collect any money due from their own insurance company, rather than going to court to determine responsibility.

Homeowner's and Renter's Insurance

Homeowner's insurance protects against losses of both real and personal property related to home ownership. These include fire, windstorm, vandalism, burglary, and injuries suffered by others while on the property. Homeowner's policies also cover personal property anywhere in the world. Mortgage lenders usually require anyone with a mortgage to carry homeowner's insurance so their investment in the home is covered if something happens. Renter's insurance protects renters against loss of personal property and liability for a visitor's personal injury.

Flood Insurance

Homeowner's policies ordinarily do not cover flood damage, and special flood insurance must be obtained (see **Figure 21.1**). Almost all flood insurance is backed by the National Flood Insurance Program (NFIP) established by Congress. Communities that agree to manage flood hazard areas can participate in the NFIP. Communities that do not agree cannot receive flood insurance. Banks that are federally regulated or insured require flood insurance on property located in Special Flood Hazard Areas (SFHAs).

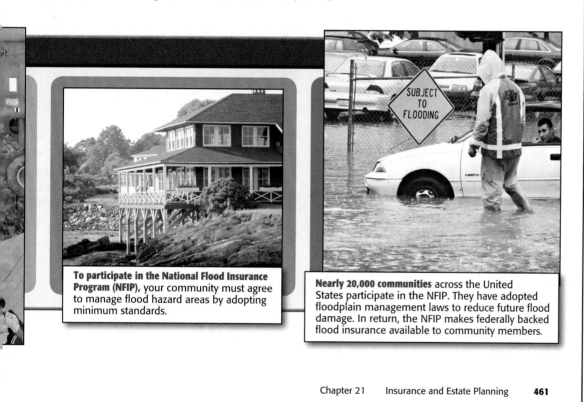

To participate in the National Flood Insurance Program (NFIP), your community must agree to manage flood hazard areas by adopting minimum standards.

Nearly 20,000 communities across the United States participate in the NFIP. They have adopted floodplain management laws to reduce future flood damage. In return, the NFIP makes federally backed flood insurance available to community members.

Independent Practice

Homeowner's or Renter's Insurance

Have students ask their parents if they have homeowner's or renter's insurance and, if so, to explain the coverages provided by the insurance policy. Ask what kinds of events or perils the policy will not cover. Have students write a brief report on their findings. Remind students that a landlord's policy on his or her building will not cover the renter's personal belongings and property.

TEACH (cont.)

C Critical Thinking

Homeowner's Insurance Remind students that homeowner's insurance protects against losses of the structure and personal property. Ask why mortgage lenders require borrowers to carry homeowner's insurance. (Investment in the home [lien] is protected in the event of loss.)

Extending the Content

Coinsurance Clause

Coinsurance is a provision in an insurance policy that limits your recovery for a loss if the property is not insured for its full replacement value. For example, if your insurance policy has an 80 percent coinsurance clause, your house must be insured for 80 percent of its replacement value to receive full reimbursement for a loss. If it would cost $100,000 to replace your house, and you had insured it for $60,000, the insurance company would pay only three fourths of any loss: $60,000 ÷ ($100,000 × 80%) = $60,000 ÷ $80,000 = 3/4. If a fire causes $40,000 worth of damage to your house, you can recover $30,000 from the insurance company ($40,000 × 3/4).

U Universal Access

Language Impaired Ask volunteers to summarize orally the main points of each topic to help students with reading disabilities. Encourage oral discussion and questions.

461

TEACH (cont.)

D Develop Concepts

Life Insurance Explain that life insurance is a contract that provides compensation for losses due to a person's death. The cost of insurance is based on risk of death for the insured. Ask students when the cost of life insurance is lowest. (Because risk of death is low for young people, it is least expensive when the insured is young.)

Extending the Content

Life Insurance

Have students further research the types of life insurance discussed in this section and write a one-page report. Ask several students to read their reports to the class.

Guided Practice

Goods in Transit

Ask students how they think goods in transit on ocean barges or trains are insured. (Ocean marine insurance covers goods shipped at sea. Inland marine insurance covers goods moved by trains, trucks, and airplanes.)

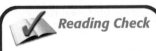
Reading Check

Enumerate (automobile, homeowner's and renter's, flood, fire, and marine insurance)

Reading Check
Enumerate *List five types of property insurance.*

Fire Insurance

Many businesses purchase fire insurance to cover losses resulting directly from a fire, and damages resulting from smoke and from water used to put out the fire. Damages caused by soot, smoke, water, or heat from a nearby burning building may also be covered.

Marine Insurance

Marine insurance is one of the oldest forms of insurance and dates back to old Venetian traders who sailed the Mediterranean Sea. It covers property that is transported and the means of transportation. Today, ocean marine insurance covers goods shipped at sea. Inland marine insurance covers goods moved by trains, trucks, and airplanes.

Life Insurance

What is the least expensive kind of life insurance you can buy?

Life insurance is an insurance contract that provides compensation for losses due to a person's death. Because the cost of insurance is based on risk, it is less expensive to buy life insurance when you are young because the death rate for young people is low so they are considered low risk.

Life Insurance Term insurance is the least expensive kind of life insurance. *Why do the premiums for term insurance increase at the end of each term?*

Straight Life Insurance

Straight life insurance, also called ordinary life or whole life, is life insurance that requires the payment of premiums until the face value is reached or the insured is deceased. The face value is the amount of protection stated in the policy. Straight life insurance also builds up a cash and loan value, which is an amount you can cash the policy in for or borrow on.

Term Life Insurance

Term life insurance is life insurance issued for a particular period, usually five or ten years. It is the least expensive kind of life insurance because it has no cash or loan value. Premiums for term insurance increase at the end of each term because the insured is older and is considered a greater risk. **D**

Other Types of Life Insurance

Limited-payment life insurance allows you to stop paying premiums after a stated length of time, usually 20 or 30 years. The beneficiary

---

▲ USING VISUALS

➡ **Life Insurance Answer** The premiums for term insurance increase because the insured is older and is considered a greater risk. Tell students that when a life insurance company reviews an application for a life insurance policy, the company considers the age, health, life expectancy, and gender of the applicant to determine the premium he or she will pay.

Business ETHICS

Health Insurance Benefits

You are the chief executive of a nine-person architecture company in a small town. Under your state's labor laws, companies with 15 or more employees must provide health insurance to their employees. At this time, your company has made the decision not to offer health insurance. However, due to an increase in home building in your area, your company could make much more money if you hired five more architects. You know that you will attract better applicants if you can offer them health benefits.

Critical Thinking: *Should you offer health insurance?*

21.1 SECTION

ASSESS

Quiz
Have students fill in the appropriate term.

1. _____ insurance protects you from financial loss if real or personal property is destroyed. (Property)

2. _____ life insurance is life insurance that requires the payment of premiums until the face value is reached or the insured is deceased. (Straight)

RETEACH

Guided Practice

Insurance Basics

Write the following phrases on the board and ask students to identify the term that the phrase describes:

- amount of money an insured pays for insurance coverage (premium)
- person named in an insurance policy to receive proceeds (beneficiary)
- written contract between an insurance buyer and an insurance company (insurance policy)

---

receives the amount of the policy upon the death of the insured, even if it occurs before the payment period is over.

Endowment insurance is insurance that provides protection for a stated time period and pays the proceeds either when the period is up or at death, whichever occurs first. Endowment policies are typically written for periods of ten, 20, or 30 years.

An annuity is a guaranteed retirement income that is purchased by paying either a lump-sum premium or by making periodic payments to an insurer. You may choose to receive a reduced income for a certain fixed number of years, with a beneficiary receiving whatever remains in the annuity when you die. You may choose to receive full payments as long as you live, but should you die before using up the annuity, your heirs receive nothing.

Health Insurance

What can you do if you cannot afford health insurance?

Two major categories of health insurance are basic and major medical. Major medical coverage typically pays only for long-term hospitalization and the cost of catastrophic illness. It does not cover **routine** medical care and prescriptions. In contrast, basic health insurance includes additional coverage, such as inpatient and out-patient hospital care, physician care, surgery, and prescription drugs.

Individual and Group Insurance

Many people get their health insurance through a group insurance plan where they work. Insurance companies can offer lower premiums to large groups because more people are sharing the expense of medical care. Employers often pay part of the premium and employees pay the remainder. People who work for themselves or for a company that does not offer health insurance may purchase their own individual health insurance. Individual insurance is more expensive than group insurance.

Chapter 21   Insurance and Estate Planning   **463**

Business ETHICS

Health Insurance Benefits   Answer You are under no legal obligation to provide health insurance to your employees. However, as with any business decision, you must weigh legal obligations against ethical and business considerations. If the company could attract better people by offering health insurance, the increased income could outweigh the increased costs of health insurance. Further, offering employees health insurance, given the high costs of health care, may increase their morale and their loyalty to the company.

STUDY TO GO Have students go to the *Business and Personal Law* Online Learning Center through **glencoe.com** to download free Study-to-Go content to their cell phones or PDAs.

RETEACH (cont.)

After You Read

Summarize Group policies are less expensive and are often offered through employers or unions. Individual policies are policies purchased by individuals and are more expensive.

ASSESS

Self-Assessment

Have students go to the *Business and Personal Law* Online Learning Center through glencoe.com to take the Section 21.1 Practice Test.

CLOSE

Culminating Activity

Insurance Policies

Have students make a list of the types of insurance policies they think they will need over the next five years. Ask them to include a description and value of their property and what kind of policy will cover each property. (may include auto coverage, homeowner's or renter's insurance, life insurance)

After You Read

Summarize What is the difference between a group health policy and an individual health insurance policy?

Two of the most common types of health insurance plans today are HMOs and PPOs. A Health Maintenance Organization (HMO) is a health care organization that contracts with doctors to provide services for its members. Members pay monthly premiums and must choose from a list of doctors provided by the HMO. A Preferred Provider Organization (PPO) is a group of doctors or hospitals that provide care for employees at reduced rates. PPOs are usually sponsored as part of an employer's group health plan.

Government Health Care Plans

Medicare is a federally funded health insurance program for people who are covered by Social Security. Medicare has two parts. Part A helps pay for inpatient hospital care. Part B pays for 80 percent of doctors' visits and certain other medical services. Many people buy an additional policy, called Medigap insurance, to cover the 20 percent not covered by Medicare. Another government health insurance program is called Medicaid. Medicaid is a health care plan for low-income people, administered by each state government and funded by both state and federal funds. Most states also offer health care plans to cover children from low-income families.

Disability Insurance

Disability insurance pays benefits if the policyholder cannot work because of a disability. Many employers purchase disability insurance for their employees. A long-term disability plan pays if a person cannot perform normal job duties for a year or longer. A short-term disability plan pays for a few months of being disabled.

SECTION 21.1 ASSESSMENT

Self Check

1. What is the purpose of insurance?
2. What is the difference between a policyholder and a beneficiary?
3. What is the difference between straight life insurance and term life insurance?

NCLB

Academic Connection

Social Studies For every type of risk there is some form of insurance coverage. For exampale, Fred Astaire, the famous dancer, had his legs insured for $650,000. Employers can buy insurance for employees who quit if they win the lottery. You can even buy alien abduction insurance. One company offers insurance not only for alien abductions, but for injury caused by an asteroid or a piece of a falling satellite.

Go to the library or on the Internet and research unusual insurance policies and claims, past and present. Share your findings with the class.

Critical Thinking

Life Insurance Why do you think you cannot take out insurance on anyone you want?

 Go to **glencoe.com** to check your answers.

glencoe.com

SECTION 21.1 ASSESSMENT

Self Check

1. to protect individuals and businesses against losses by spreading the risks of loss over a large number of people

2. Policyholder buys insurance; beneficiary named in policy receives benefits in the event of a loss.

3. Straight life: requires payment of premiums throughout the insured's life and pays its face value to the beneficiary. Term: issued for a particular period, usually five or ten years.

Academic Connection

Social Studies
Answers will vary.

Critical Thinking

You could collect on insurance for someone you had no insurable interest in, such as a complete stranger.

NCLB Activities correlated to the Social Studies standard on page 458

Estate Planning

Reading Guide

Before You Read

Connect Has anyone in your family ever inherited anything?

Focus on Ideas

It is never too early to plan for retirement.

Take Notes

Create a graph like the one shown and use it to take notes as you read this section. Go to glencoe.com to find graphic organizers and tips on how to improve your note-taking skills.

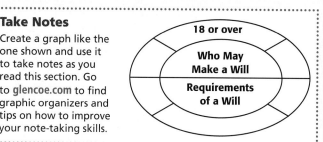

18 or over

Who May Make a Will

Requirements of a Will

Key Terms

You will learn these legal words and expressions in this chapter. You can also find these terms in *Black's Law Dictionary* or in an online legal dictionary.

- will
- testator/testatrix
- testamentary intent
- testamentary capacity
- intestate
- probate
- executor/executrix
- trust
- trustee

Academic Vocabulary

You will find these words in your readings and in your tests. Look them up in a dictionary and familiarize yourself with them.

- supplement
- elective
- directive

What You'll Learn

- Identify the main types of retirement plans.
- Name the formal requirements of a will.
- Describe how to revoke or change a will.
- Identify the different types of trusts.

Why It's Important

Knowing about retirement plan, wills, and trusts will help you plan for the future.

Academic Standards

Reading and completing the activities in this section will help you practice the following academic standards:

English Language Arts (NCTE 7) Conduct research on issues and interests by generating ideas and questions, and by posing problems.

Math (NCTM CS2 3) Recognize and apply mathematics in contexts outside of mathematics.

NCLB

glencoe.com

FOCUS

Bell Ringer Activity

Ask students if they have ever thought about how they will spend their retirement years. Then ask if they know how a person plans for retirement or makes a will. (Answers may include saving money, buying property, investing in stocks or bonds, and hiring an attorney to draft a will.)

Preteaching

Key Terms

Read the definitions and ask students to create a sentence using each term.

Academic Vocabulary

Explain that developing vocabulary is key to academic success. An efficient method to develop vocabulary is to study how words are formed.

- **supplement** Verb, from the Latin *supplementum* (something added). Means to add to.
- **elective** Adjective, from the Latin *eligere* (to select). Means chosen.
- **directive** Noun, from the Latin *dirigere* (to give direction). Means an instruction.

Activity Ask students to give a noun, a verb, an adjective, or an adverb form that comes from each word.

NCLB Connects to academic content

R Reading Strategy

Read for Knowledge

1. **Survey** or preread the chapter.
2. **Question** or formulate questions before you read.
3. **Recite** or read your questions, answers, and notes out loud.
4. **Review** or reread your notes.

Note-Taking Basics

- Listen attentively
- Have note-taking materials ready
- Skim through the lesson material
- Write down key words and ideas
- Anticipate what comes next
- Review notes soon after taking them

TEACH

Discussion Starter

Class Discussion
Explain to students that planning for retirement provides for the financial independence of people when they can no longer work to earn money. Ask students what might happen if a person did not plan for his or her retirement.

Develop Concepts

Identify Ask students to name the pension plan provided to workers by the U.S. government. (Social Security) **L1**

List Have students list other retirement plans that individuals might have to provide money for their retirement years. (company-sponsored pension plans such as an SEP or profit-sharing; individual IRAs, Roth IRAs, Keogh plan for self-employed persons) **L2**

Analyze Have students consider the obstacles that individuals encounter when trying to save for retirement. (high current expenses, low income, procrastination) **L3**

U Universal Access

Kinesthetic Learners Have students take turns role-playing human resources workers describing pension plans to workers. They should describe the private pension plans using charts and other visual aids to contrast the varieties.

466

As You Read

Predict Is it too early to begin planning your retirement if you are only 18?

Web Quest

Planning for Retirement
Planning for your retirement seems like a long way off. The sooner you begin saving for your retirement, however, the easier it will be to maintain an income. Log on to **glencoe.com** to research the main types of retirement plans and the benefits each offers you.

Create a table in your WebQuest folder to compare the plans with your class.

466   Unit 7   Family Law

 As You Read

Predict Remind students that to have the kind of retirement years you dream about, you must save a substantial sum of money. (No. Individuals often begin saving money as soon as they start a job.)

Protecting your Assets
Why should you care about estate planning?

Estate planning is the process of assuring that a person's assets remain intact to protect the family before and after death. Estate planning includes contributing to one's retirement income as well as using certain legal instruments such as wills and trusts. Large estates can benefit from estate planning, but the process can be financially useful to others, regardless of income. Estate planning does have costs, such as attorney fees for creating wills and trusts. However, individuals can save money by doing their own research on each aspect of estate planning.

Retirement Income

D
U

It is important to start a retirement plan as early as you can. This is because the earlier you start a plan, the more valuable it will be later. Social Security is the principal pension plan offered to workers by the U.S. government. Some employers offer pension plans through their companies. An Individual Retirement Account (IRA) is an individual's own personal pension plan. Roth IRA's are attractive because distributions are not required while you are alive. Also, your savings can grow and be taken out tax free. A simplified employee plan (SEP) is an IRA funded by an employer. A Keogh plan is for self-employed people and their employees.

Wills
Do children who are left out of a parent's will have any recourse?

A will is a document that is signed during your lifetime that provides for the distribution of your property upon death. Each state has its own requirements for making a will.

Testate means to die with a will. **A testator (male) or a testatrix (female) is a person who dies with a will.** A gift of personal property made by will is called a bequest or legacy. A gift of real property made by will is called a devise in most states. A beneficiary is someone who receives property by will. They are also known in most states as legatees if they receive personal property, or as devisees if they receive real property under a will. An heir refers to one who inherits property under a will or from someone dying without a will.

Who May Make a Will?

Any person who has reached the age of 18 and has both testamentary intent and testamentary capacity may create a will. **Testamentary intent is the intention that the document is meant to be a last will and testament. Testamentary capacity is the mental ability (being of sound mind) to create a will.** Sound mind is defined as having sufficient mental capacity to do the following:

 glencoe.com

Web Quest

Research Tip Access the *Business and Personal Law* Online Learning Center through **glencoe.com** and print a couple of examples of the resources available. Make sure students understand how to use them in their research project.

- Understand the nature and extent of your property
- Know who would be the natural persons to inherit your property, even though you may leave your property to anyone you choose
- Know that you are making a will
- Be free from delusions that might influence the dispensation of your property

Formal Requirements of a Will

A will must conform exactly to the law of the state where it is made. A will legally made in one state must be recognized in most every other state. However, a few states require that an out-of-state will meet their own state requirements as well.

To be valid, a will must be published, attested, and signed. Published means that it must be written and declare on its face that the will is a true expression of the testator or testatrix's intent. Oral (nuncupative) wills of personal property are allowed for soldiers and mariners. Attested means that the will must be witnessed by the number of people required by the state, usually two.

C

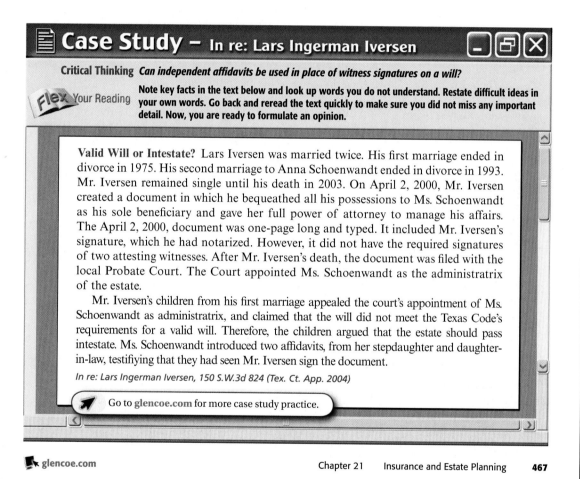

Case Study – In re: Lars Ingerman Iversen

Critical Thinking *Can independent affidavits be used in place of witness signatures on a will?*

Flex Your Reading Note key facts in the text below and look up words you do not understand. Restate difficult ideas in your own words. Go back and reread the text quickly to make sure you did not miss any important detail. Now, you are ready to formulate an opinion.

Valid Will or Intestate? Lars Iversen was married twice. His first marriage ended in divorce in 1975. His second marriage to Anna Schoenwandt ended in divorce in 1993. Mr. Iversen remained single until his death in 2003. On April 2, 2000, Mr. Iversen created a document in which he bequeathed all his possessions to Ms. Schoenwandt as his sole beneficiary and gave her full power of attorney to manage his affairs. The April 2, 2000, document was one-page long and typed. It included Mr. Iversen's signature, which he had notarized. However, it did not have the required signatures of two attesting witnesses. After Mr. Iversen's death, the document was filed with the local Probate Court. The Court appointed Ms. Schoenwandt as the administratrix of the estate.

Mr. Iversen's children from his first marriage appealed the court's appointment of Ms. Schoenwandt as administratrix, and claimed that the will did not meet the Texas Code's requirements for a valid will. Therefore, the children argued that the estate should pass intestate. Ms. Schoenwandt introduced two affidavits, from her stepdaughter and daughter-in-law, testifiying that they had seen Mr. Iversen sign the document.

In re: Lars Ingerman Iversen, 150 S.W.3d 824 (Tex. Ct. App. 2004)

Go to **glencoe.com** for more case study practice.

glencoe.com

Case Study

In re: Lars Ingerman Iversen

Answer No. The Texas Court of Appeals held that the two affidavits by Ms. Schoenwandt's stepdaughter and daughter-in-law were not equivalent to attesting witness signatures on a purported will. The will must be attested by two signatures (the notary's signature on the affidavits would count for one signature). The signatures of the witnesses must either be on the document itself or on an attached affidavit, which the deceased also signed. The two affidavits submitted by Ms. Schoenwandt were not attached to the document, nor did they include the signature of Mr. Iversen. Therefore, Mr. Iversen was considered to have died intestate.

TEACH *(cont.)*

C Critical Thinking

Time to Make a Will Point out that the purpose of a will is to ensure preferred distribution of assets upon one's death. Ask students at what time in a person's life they think a will should be made. (Answers should convey that the age will differ for different people depending on job situations, marital status, financial status, and whether or not they have children.)

Guided Practice

Creating a Will

Have students imagine that they have been asked to make a will. Have them describe requirements that they think would make the document legal and binding. (conform to state law; published, attested, and signed)

Extending the Content

Wills

Have students interview an adult family member or close personal friend about wills. Suggest that they ask such questions as: (1) Do you have a will? (2) Why or why not? (3) When did you make the will? (4) Did you consult an attorney? (5) Who were the witnesses? (6) Have you ever changed the will? Make sure students and the interviewee understand that the interview is for the student's benefit, and that no personal information will be shared with the class.

TEACH (cont.)

C Critical Thinking

Omitted Children Explain to students that a parent who wishes to omit his or her child from a will must state that wish in the will. Otherwise the omitted child may try to prove that he or she was mistakenly left out. Ask students how much a child who was actually left out of the will might receive of a parent's estate. (the same share that he or she would have received if the parent had died without a will)

Guided Practice

Intestate

Ask students what they think are the disadvantages to dying intestate. Also ask whether there are advantages. (Answers will vary, but students should recognize that to die intestate means you do not get to determine specifically who gets what from your estate.)

Reading Check

Analyze States heavily regulate the laws about wills because, in many cases, substantial property is being divided, and many parties are usually involved—each with their own interests in the property at stake.

Reading Check

Analyze Why would the states heavily regulate the laws about wills?

Vocabulary You can find vocabulary definitions in the **Key Terms** glossary and **Academic Vocabulary** glossary in the back of this book.

Family Protection State laws have been made to protect surviving family members when a spouse dies. *What does the homestead exemption do?*

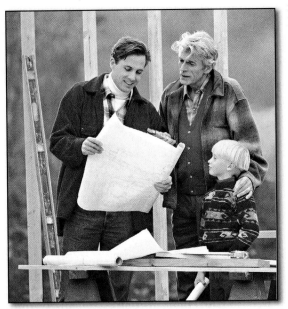

468   Unit 7   Family Law

The signature on a will can be any mark (even an X) as long as it is intended to be a signature. If a testator cannot write, someone else can sign in the testator's presence with the testator's consent. In many states, a holographic will—a will written entirely in the handwriting of the testator—is valid without witnesses.

Revoking or Changing a Will

States have different rules about changing a will, but in general, a will may be revoked by (a) burning, tearing, canceling, or obliterating it with intent to revoke it; (b) making a new will; or (c) marrying after the will was created. A divorce usually revokes gifts made under a will to a former spouse. A codicil is a formal document used to **supplement** or change an existing will. It must be signed and witnessed just like a will to be valid.

Family and Spouse Protections

State laws contain provisions designed to protect surviving family members. One protection is the homestead exemption, which puts the family home beyond the reach of creditors up to a certain limit. Some states have a property exemption, which allows certain property to remain beyond the reach of creditors. In Indiana, the surviving spouse is entitled to $25,000 (in money or personal property) from the estate, regardless of what the will provides. If there is no surviving spouse, the decedent's minor children equally share the $25,000. After the $25,000 has been distributed, the estate is then probated according to the will or statute.

A surviving spouse who does not like the provisions of a deceased spouse's may petition to take a different portion of the estate set by state statute. This is known as a spouse's **elective** or forced share.

Children who can prove that they were mistakenly left out of a parent's will also have certain protections in most states. Forgotten children may receive the same share that they would have received if their parent had died without a will. Adopted children are treated, in most states, as though they were the naturally born children of their adoptive parents. However, if a will specifically states that a child has been intentionally omitted from a parent's will, the will must be followed.

C

Intestate Succession

Intestate means to be without a will. Dying without a will can have serious consequences. The people you want to inherit your estate may not be able to do so. You cannot identify the person responsible for distributing your property. The beneficiaries may have to pay higher legal costs and taxes.

▲ USING VISUALS

Family Protection Answer The homestead exemption puts a family home beyond the reach of creditors up to a certain limit. Tell students that homestead exemption laws typically have three primary features: (1) prevent forced sale of a home to meet demands of creditors; (2) provide shelter for the surviving spouse; (3) provide an exemption from property taxes that can be applied to a home. A homestead, for these purposes, is defined as a person's primary residence. No other exemption may be claimed on any other property anywhere.

Figure 21.2 Intestate Succession*

If you are survived by:	Your estate is distributed:
1. Spouse and child(ren)	One half to spouse, one half to children
2. Spouse, no children, but next of kin (including parents, siblings, niece, nephew, aunt, uncle, cousin, etc.)	Where the estate is less than $200,000, all to spouse. If the estate is larger than $200,000, the first $200,000 plus one half of everything in excess of $200,000 to spouse. The remainder to next of kin in this order: parents(s), siblings, nieces and nephews, grandparents, uncles and aunts, cousins.
3. Spouse, no child, no next of kin	All to spouse
4. No spouse, one or more children	All to children
5. No spouse, no child, but next of kin	All to next of kin, in the order described above in 2.
6. No spouse, no child, no next of kin	All "escheats" to the state, that is, all turned over to the state because there are no heirs or beneficiaries.

*Massachusetts Law of Descent and Distribution Law of Intestate Succession (G.L. c. 190 §1)

 Each state has its own law of intestate succession. *What does such a law determine?*

Without a will, the deceased's personal property is distributed according to the laws of the deceased's home state. If there is real property, it passes according to the laws of the state in which it is located. The distribution of property is done according to relationship to the deceased. A surviving spouse is usually entitled to one-third or one-half of the estate. The balance is divided equally among any children. If a child has died since the will was written, then his or her children share that portion. If those people have died, the line of succession continues through the decedent's parents, if living, and if not, to brothers and sisters, and then to cousins. If a decedent has no living blood relatives, the property is said to escheat, meaning that the state owns it. **Figure 21.2** shows Massachusetts's laws of intestate succession.

Probate and Estate Settlement

Probate is the process of validating and executing a will. A probate court supervises the process. Its first job is to validate the will. If no one opposes it, the settlement is usually simple. Sometimes heirs may contest the will if they were left out or disagree with the division of assets. When this happens, they must prove either that the will does not conform to state law, that the testate was not of sound mind, or that someone exerted undue influence. Some people intentionally include a clause in their will that bars a contesting heir from inheriting anything.

The executor (male) or executrix (female) is the person designated in the will to carry out its terms. If no one is named, if the person named refuses the position, or if there is no will, the court will appoint an executor to carry out the will.

D

Legal Talk

Devise: *n* The act of giving real property by will. From Latin *dividere* = divide.

Codicil: *n* An addition to or modification of a will. From Latin *codicillus* = a short writing.

Vocabulary Builder The words *devise* and *divide* are derived from the Latin prefix *dis* which means *apart.* List and define five words that begin with this prefix.

Look It Up! Check definitions in *Black's Law Dictionary* or an online glossary. For direct links, go to glencoe.com to find more vocabulary resources.

 glencoe.com

TEACH (cont.)

D Develop Concepts

Probate Explain that when a person dies, the will should be validated and executed. This process is called probate. Ask students what kinds of things might happen during the probate process. (Answers will vary. Discuss the ideas that a family member might contest the will, the will might not conform to state rules or be properly signed, someone might have influenced the deceased when he or she made the will, or the person may not have been of sound mind at the time he or she made the will.) Point out that some people intentionally include a clause in their will that prevents a contesting heir from inheriting anything.

Legal Talk

(disturb: to interrupt; disbelief: refusal to believe something as true; dislike: regard with aversion; disown: deny ownership of something; disbar: expel from legal profession)

Ask students to practice their academic and legal vocabulary with the electronic flashcards available at the *Business and Personal Law* Online Learning Center through glencoe.com.

▲ USING VISUALS

⟹ Figure 21.2 Intestate Succession Answer Intestate laws determine how the assets of a person who dies intestate will be distributed. Intestate laws identify the order of distribution depending on the kinds and relationship of survivors. For example, in many states, if a person dies intestate with a spouse and three children, half of the estate will go to the spouse and the other half will be divided three ways by the children. If a person dies with no spouse, children, or next of kin, all assets of the deceased are turned over to the state.

ASSESS

Intestate Succession
Give students the following scenario: Paula Cantrell died without a will. Her husband, Kenneth, had passed away years earlier, and they had no children. Paula's sister, Dawn, is alive and her brother, Frank, is deceased. Frank had three children, all of whom are still living. Both of Paula's parents are dead, but she still has one living uncle, Mike. Mike has two sons, both living. After Paula's debts and taxes are paid, there is $1,000,000. Ask students to determine who inherits from Paula if you follow the general guidelines given in the text. (Dawn and Frank's three children)

RETEACH

Role Play
Have four students act out the drafting of a will. Ask one student to play the role of Kevin Nance, a man who is married with four children. He also has two living brothers, who each have one child. Ask two students to play the roles of witnesses. The fourth student will act as the attorney. Encourage students to use proper terminology when discussing the elements of the will.

470

🕐 **The Importance of Making a Will** Not making a will can have serious consequences. *What happens to a person's property if there are no blood relatives?*

That person is called an administrator or administratrix. The responsibilities of the executor or administrator are to inventory the assets, pay any debts and taxes, and distribute any remaining assets as stated in the will or by state law.

Power of Attorney

Another aspect of estate planning involves creating one or more powers of attorney. A power of attorney grants power to a representative to legally act on your behalf. The person giving power of attorney is the grantor. The person receiving the power of attorney is the attorney-in-fact.

A special power of attorney gives authority over a specific item, such as managing the grantor's real property. A general power of attorney gives authority over all matters. A durable power of attorney gives authority to the attorney-in-fact while the grantor is incompetent and can be either specific or general. Elderly people often grant durable general power of attorney to a younger loved one in case the grantor becomes incapacitated and cannot take care of their personal business. A power of attorney must be completed following a state's specific laws. It must be witnessed, notarized, and recorded in a local government's recording office.

Medical Directives Many people also create a medical **directive**. A medical directive is a special power of attorney that deals solely with medical care. Medical directives allow the appointed attorney-in-fact, rather than a court, to make decisions with regard to grantor's medical care in the event the person becomes incompetent.

Living Will

A living will is a special power of attorney document that directs whether your life should be prolonged by artificial means if you become incapacitated with no reasonable expectation of recovery. Because technology may allow people to stay alive for a long time, individuals create living wills giving their representative the authority to make health care decisions according to the directives in the living will.

Trust

Why might property bequeathed to a minor be held in trust?

A trust is a legal device by which property is held by one person for the benefit of another. The settler is the person who sets up a trust. **A trustee is a person who holds title to the property for another's benefit.** The beneficiary is the person for whose benefit the property is held in trust.

▲ USING VISUALS

➡️ **The Importance of Making a Will** **Answer** If a person has no blood relatives or spouse and dies without a will, the person's property becomes the property of the state. In this case, the property is said to *escheat*, meaning that the state owns it.
Activity Tell students that it is entirely possible to draft your own will without the help of an attorney. Ask students to describe an advantage and disadvantage to a do-it-yourself will. (advantage—low cost alternative; disadvantage—complexity may lead to errors)

Trusts are a tool in estate planning that help people provide for their children. They also avoid the time and cost of probate, and save on taxes. The legal fees of creating a trust can be costly, which is a disadvantage.

Types of Trusts

Several types of trusts can be established. A private trust is one involving individual settlers and beneficiaries. Most familial trusts are of this type.

A testamentary trust is a trust created by a will. It comes into existence only upon the death of the testator.

A living trust is a trust that comes into existence while the settler is alive. It may be revocable, which means that the settler can take it back or change it while still alive. It may also be irrevocable, which means that the settler cannot change it. Such trusts save money on taxes.

Another type of trust is a spendthrift trust. It protects the settler's assets from being spent recklessly by the beneficiary. There is also a charitable trust, which is established to fund a charitable purpose upon death. It allows the trustee to decide how much will be given to each beneficiary rather than the settler doing so.

Rights and Duties of Parties

Trustees are obligated by law to use a high degree of care in investing the trust funds. They cannot take extraordinary risks or commingle (mix) their own property with the trust property. The beneficiaries are entitled to periodic accountings from the trustee. Beneficiaries also have the right to be notified when a will is probated.

After You Read

Summarize List the types of trusts a person can establish.

SECTION 21.2 ASSESSMENT

Self Check

1. Who may make a will?
2. How may a will be revoked?
3. Define the role of a trustee.

Academic Connection

Mathematics The federal government collects an estate tax on the value of a person's property at the time of the person's death.

As of 2006, the estate tax is 48 percent of everything over $2 million. As of 2009, the estate tax is 48 percent of everything over $3.5 million. What is the estate tax in 2006 on an estate worth $7 million? What is the estate tax for the same estate in 2009?

THEORY **Number and Operations:** To calculate the amount for each year, subtract the amount that is not taxed and multiply the remainder by 48 percent.

 For more math practice, go to the Math Appendix.

Critical Thinking

Holographic Will Why do you think a holographic will is valid without witnesses in many states?

 Go to **glencoe.com** to check your answers.

After You Read

Summarize private, testamentary, living, spendthrift, charitable

ASSESS

Self-Assessment

Have students go to the *Business and Personal Law* Online Learning Center through **glencoe.com** to take the Section 21.2 Practice Test.

CLOSE

Culminating Activity

Lack of a Will

Ask your students to share thoughts regarding a person who dies intestate. Have them comment on whether this makes it easier or harder on the surviving family. Ask them to offer reasons why a person would intentionally not make a will. (Answers will vary, but students may suggest that the individual may want to avoid the topic of his or her death and may not want to offend anyone by the distribution of assets.)

SECTION 21.2 ASSESSMENT

Self Check

1. any person 18 years of age or older with both testamentary capacity and intent

2. by burning, tearing, canceling, or obliterating the document with the intent of revoking it; by executing a new will; and by changing marital status

3. a person who holds title to the property for another's benefit and should exercise a high degree of care in investing the trust funds

Academic Connection

Mathematics
2006: $2.4 million
2009: $1.68 million

Critical Thinking

Intent is exhibited by the act of handwriting and the handwriting itself.

 Activities correlated to Mathematics standard on page 465

Review and Assessment

Summary by Sections

Ask students to read the summaries one key point at a time. Then, ask them to work in groups to create two examples to illustrate each key point.

Vocabulary Builder

Cooperative Learning

1. Have students work in groups to prepare their sentences. Ask the groups to exchange their sentences and assess each other's sentences.

Vocabulary Development

- Ask students to use a dictionary or to go online to look up the etymology of each key term listed.

- Then, ask students to list several words derived from the same root or origin. For example, *contract* has the same root as *contractual* or *contractually*.

Chapter 21 Review and Assessment

Summary

Section 21.1 Insurance

- Insurance is an agreement in which one party (the insurer) compensates another party (the insured) for any losses.
- Property insurance is a contract that covers damage or destruction of property.
- Liability insurance covers claims for damages or injuries made against a policyholder.
- Types of property insurance include homeowner's, renter's, fire, flood, and marine insurance, as well as vehicle and business insurance.
- Principal types of life insurance are straight life insurance, term life insurance, limited-payment life insurance, and endowment insurance.
- Types of health insurance include individual health insurance, group health insurance, government health plans, and disability insurance.

Section 21.2 Estate Planning

- Estate planning is the process of assuring that a person's assets remain intact to protect the family before and after death.
- Main types of retirement income are Social Security, pension plans employers offer through their companies, Individual Retirement Accounts (IRAs), and Keogh plans.
- A will is a document that provides for the distribution of a person's property upon death.
- Probate is the process of validating and executing a will. Intestate means to be without a will.
- A trust is a legal device by which property is held by one person for the benefit of another.
- Types of trusts include testamentary trusts, living trusts, spendthrift trusts, and charitable trusts.
- Beneficiaries have a right to periodic accountings from a trustee, and the right to be notified when a will is probated.

Vocabulary Builder

1 On a sheet of paper, use each of these terms in a sentence.

Key Terms

- insurance
- premium
- beneficiary
- insurable interest
- straight life insurance

- term life insurance
- will
- testator/testatrix
- testamentary intent
- testamentary capacity

- intestate
- probate
- executor/executrix
- trust
- trustee

Academic Vocabulary

- comprehensive
- endowment

- routine
- supplement

- elective
- directive

Go to **glencoe.com** to play a game and improve your legal vocabulary.

 ## Study Skills for Success

Prepare Your Students for Studying

Tell students that they can improve their ability to understand and remember material from their courses by learning and practicing study skills. Remind students to:

- **Get motivated!** Motivation must come from within. To motivate yourself, think of ways in which what you learn now will fit into your long-term personal and professional goals.
- **Get organized!** Make studying part of your daily routine, not something you do at the last minute.
- **Concentrate!** Study in an environment that is as free of distractions as possible.

Key Points Review

Answer the following questions. Refer to the chapter for additional reinforcement.

2 What is an insurable interest?

3 What are the differences between homeowner's and renter's insurance?

4 Describe the principal types of life insurance.

5 What types of government health care plans are available?

6 What are the requirements for a valid will?

7 What are the responsibilities of an executor or administrator in the settlement of an estate?

8 What is required to contest a will?

9 What happens to a decedent's estate when a person dies without a will, or intestate?

Standardized Test Practice

10 Read the following excerpt about indemnification and insurance and complete questions 1 and 2.

An entity seeking to transfer risk (an individual, corporation, or association of any type) becomes the insured party once risk is assumed by an insurer, the insuring party, by means of a contract, defined as an insurance policy. This legal contract sets out terms and conditions specifying the amount of coverage (compensation) to be rendered to the insured, by the insurer upon assumption of risk, in the event of a loss, and all the specific perils covered against (indemnified), for the term of the contract.

When insured parties experience a loss for a specified peril, the coverage entitles the policyholder to make a claim against the insurer for the amount of loss as specified by the policy contract. The fee paid by the insured to the insurer for assuming the risk is called the premium. Insurance premiums from many clients are used to fund accounts set aside for later payment of claims—in theory for a relatively few claimants—and for overhead costs. So long as an insurer maintains adequate funds set aside for anticipated losses, the remaining margin becomes their profit.

1. In reading the above passage, "indemnified" could best be defined as

A transferring personal risk to another party

B taking an assumption of risk in an activity

C protecting against damage, loss, or injury

D receiving compensation for an injury

2. The purpose of insurance is to

A get money from an insurance company when you have a loss

B spread the losses over a greater number of people

C set aside an adequate amount of funds for losses

D be profitable by anticipating losses before they occur

Test-Taking Strategies While taking a test, if other students finish before you, stay focused on the test in front of you.

Chapter 21   Insurance and Estate Planning   **473**

Chapter **21**

Review and Assessment

Key Points Review

2. financial interest a policyholder has in the insured person or property

3. Homeowner's: protects against losses of both real and personal property. Renter's: protects renters against loss of personal property and liability for a visitor's personal injury.

4. Straight life: requires payment of premiums for life and builds up cash and loan value. Term life: issued for a particular period; no cash or loan value. Limited-payment life: payment of premiums stops after a stated length of time. Endowment: protection for a stated time.

5. Medicare for Social Security recipients; Medicaid for low-income people; state-funded health care plans for children from low-income families.

6. written, published, signed, and witnessed

7. gathers the estate assets, pays the debts and taxes, and distributes the remainder of the assets according to the terms of the will or state law

8. prove that the will does not conform to state law, lack of testator's sound mind, or the presence of undue influence

9. The decedent's estate is distributed according to the appropriate law of intestate distribution.

Standardized Test Practice

10. C and B

⚠ Strategies for Standardized Test Prep Success

Whether your students have a standardized test coming up in a few days or a few weeks, these last-minute test-prep tips and strategies will help them relax and do their best.

- **Test Format** Help students become familiar with the format of the test by practicing with test items that imitate the actual test items as closely as possible.

- **Test Timing** Have your students take timed practice tests so that they become comfortable with the length, design, and timing of the actual test.

Apply and Debate

Students should use chapter content to arrive at conclusions. The legal resolutions are listed below:

11. The law requires drivers to carry car insurance. Frank will be in greater financial harm if he gets in an accident and does not have insurance. He could also face criminal penalties.

12. Yes. Any will should be given credibility until proven otherwise. Most people who get (re)married after writing a will wish to leave their current spouse with something.

13. A living will is a binding contract stating the wishes of an incapacitated individual. It is clear what Lisette wanted to happen in this situation.

14. If Jackson's father specifically omitted Jackson from the will, then Jackson has no legal recourse for receiving an equitable share of his father's estate. Jackson can appeal directly to his siblings for an equitable share. He should consider, though, whether it is worth doing as it could cause strife within the family.

15. Maybe. A revocable trust can be changed at any time by the settler. The judge should take into consideration the lawyer's claims, especially since Jamal desired to make an equitable change for his children.

474

Apply and Debate

C Read the following scenarios. Get together with other students in pairs or groups of three and take a position on each scenario. Debate your position in class with students taking the opposite position or prepare a written argument justifying your position.

11 Car Insurance Dilemma

Frank's state requires all drivers to have car insurance, which he pays monthly. This month Frank is short on cash and plans to wait until his next paycheck to pay.

You Debate   *Should Frank drive without insurance, or find another ride?*

12 Holographic Wills

When Lillian died, her estate was valued at over $2 million, which she left to her children from her first marriage. However, her second husband of five years produced a holographic will that was authentic and in her handwriting. This will gave him $1 million, but it did not say "voiding all previous wills."

You Debate   *Should the judge give any credibility to the second husband's holographic will?*

13 Medical Quandary

Lisette created a living will authorizing her son, Arthur, to tell doctors not to resuscitate her if she suffered a severe stroke. Unfortunately, this is what happened. Now Lisette's sister insists that Arthur cannot implement his mother's wishes.

You Debate   *Should Arthur listen to his mother's sister or should he do as his mother's living will ordered him to do?*

14 Family in Dispute

Jackson and his father simply did not get along. When he was 21, Jackson moved to another state. When his father passed away three years later, he left Jackson's three siblings $100,000 each, but nothing for Jackson.

You Debate   *Should Jackson ask his siblings to share the estate more fairly?*

15 Revocable Trust Change of Mind

Jamal set up a revocable trust giving 75 percent of his estate to one child and 25 percent to the other. He later decided to make it equal. Jamal called his attorney and told him, but died on the way to the lawyer's office. The children are now battling it out in court.

You Debate   *Should the judge acknowledge that Jamal had changed his mind?*

C Critical Thinking

Revoking a Will Keisha Brant became angry with her son and tore up the original copy of her will, which had included a generous bequest to him. She made a new will, leaving him $1. After her death, the son tried to have the will set aside in favor of the previous will, a copy of which was found among Brant's papers. Her daughter was not mentioned in either will.

Debate Practice

- Can the son have the new will set aside? (No. The old will was properly revoked.)

- How will the daughter be viewed in terms of the will? (If the daughter can prove that she was mistakenly left out of the will, she will receive the same share as if Keisha had died intestate.)

Case Study Practice – Mr. Padgett v. Georgia Farm Bureau Mutual Insurance Company

16 Ambiguous Terms Mr. Caravella was injured by a vehicle driven by Mr. Walker. Mr. Padgett was a passenger in the vehicle driven by Mr. Walker. The vehicle was insured by Georgia Farm Bureau Mutual Insurance Co. (Farm Bureau).

Mr. Caravella sued Mr. Walker. He also sued Mr. Padgett on the grounds that he negligently entrusted Mr. Walker with the vehicle. Farm Bureau filed a lawsuit to determine whether it was obligated to defend Mr. Padgett.

The insurance policy defined an "insured" party as "any person using" the insured vehicle. Farm Bureau argued that Mr. Padgett was not "using" the vehicle and, therefore, was not covered. Mr. Padgett argued that in other parts of the insurance contract it states that the driver of the vehicle is the one who "operates" it, and that if Farm Bureau meant only the driver was insured, it should have said "operating."

Source: Mr. Padgett v. Georgia Farm Bureau Mutual Insurance Company, 625 S.E.2d 76 (Ga. Ct. App. 2005)

Practice Is Mr. Padgett insured under the Farm Bureau contract?

17 Ethics ←?→ Application

Car Dents and Accidents On Saturday, you dented your car fender by hitting a telephone pole while backing up without looking. A week later, someone hit the back of your car and damaged the area next to the dent you dented yourself.

◆ Should you tell the insurance company that all the damage was caused at the same time so the insurer will pay to fix all dents?

18 Internet Application

Find out about Health Insurance Your friend Michelle's family is in a tough position because her parents both recently lost their jobs due to the downsizing of a large company in your city. Right now, Michelle does not have any health insurance, but would like to see a doctor for the sore foot she developed after ice skating with you.

Go to **glencoe.com** to research health insurance programs available in your state for minors whose parents cannot afford or do not have coverage. Prepare an informational pamphlet of where people can go for help.

Reading Connection
Outside Reading Go to **glencoe.com** for a list of reading suggestions about insurance.

Review and Assessment

←?→ Ethics Application

17. Answers will vary, but lead your students to understand that it is not ethical to claim that both dents occurred at the same time. Some students may feel that as long as the insurer is fixing one dent, they might as well fix the other right next to it. Explain to students that false claims on insurance policies cause premiums to increase for all purchasers of insurance.

Internet Application

18. Responses will vary from state to state, but students should demonstrate adequate research of availability of state programs or insurance for people who do not have coverage.

R Reading Strategy

Reading Connection

American Bar Association Resources

Go to the *Business and Personal Law* Online Learning Center through glencoe.com to find links for further readings that relate to this chapter. Ask students to read, review, and summarize the documents. Advise students to keep their reviews and summaries to use as reference material for their Unit Thematic Project on pages 478–479.

Case Study Practice

16. Yes. The Georgia Court of Appeals held that under Georgia law, "where a term of a policy of insurance is susceptible to two or more constructions, even when such multiple constructions are all logical and reasonable, such term is ambiguous and will be strictly construed against the insurer as the drafter and in favor of the insured." Therefore, the contract must be construed against Farm Bureau, and Mr. Padgett would be insured under the policy.

Careers in Law

Introduce Career Planning

Bell Ringer Activity

Ask students to discuss how they filter helpful from unhelpful information on the Internet. How do they refine their searches to find the information they need? How can they assess the legitimacy of a Web page?

Career Decisions

Self-Assessment Checklist

Use this checklist to help students determine their career path:

✓ Think about things you are good at
✓ Write down your interests
✓ Think about the lifestyle you want
✓ Write down your aptitudes and abilities
✓ Consider your personality
✓ Determine your learning style
✓ List some careers that might match these characteristics

Résumé Builder

Answer Students' answers will vary but may mention the ability to quickly sift through large amounts of data to find the most credible and useful information for the task at hand.

476

Phyllis Lile-King
Attorney, Donaldson & Black, P.A.

What do you do at work?
❝When a potential client contacts me, my first step is to gather information. Usually, this is as simple as listening to the person and asking questions that will help me assess whether the complaint is something that is legally cognizable. Because I work on several cases at one time, in any given week, I am reviewing psychosocial records in one case, attending a deposition of a treating physician in another case, traveling to the morgue to examine pill bottles on another case, and talking to potential clients every day. I'll also be answering written discovery, researching case law for another case, and thinking about strategy and liability issues on another case. The typical life of a lawsuit from the initial call to a jury verdict is three years.❞

What skills are most important to you?
❝The most important skills I think a lawyer should have are organizational skills, analytical skills, logic/reasoning skills, the ability to write clearly, persuasively and succinctly, and persuasion/storytelling skills.❞

What kind of training do you recommend?
❝I recommend the study of math, which helps one think analytically. A good analytical mind will usually translate to an ability to write analytically. I also recommend the study of philosophy, because I believe it expands and challenges one's mind to be creative and consider the policy underpinnings of the law, which are useful in the practice. I also recommend applying to and attending the best law school to which you can be admitted.❞

What is your key to success?
❝I'm a bootstraps kind of thinker, and I believe that most entitlements of birth (who you are) and genetics (how high your IQ is) can be overcome or at least usually equalized with hard work and perseverance. What often makes or breaks my cases are the degree of my investigation and research. My goal is to prepare more fully than my opponent. The lawyer who knows the most about the case usually has the advantage.❞

Résumé Builder

Academic Skills
• Above average reading and writing
• Analytical approach to thinking and problem solving
• Good speaking and debating skills

Education and Training
Obtain a bachelor's degree in business, English, philosophy, or math. The following high school and college courses will help develop the necessary background knowledge:
• Business, contracts, and consumer law
• Economics
• Mathematics for business
• Philosophy
• Science (chemistry, biology, physics)
• Social Studies
• U.S. Government

Critical Thinking
Why are critical thinking skills so important in the information age?

 Go to **glencoe.com** to find legal careers resources.

 glencoe.com

Research Technology

Specialized technology is available for a variety of law-related tasks. For example, LexisNexis and Westlaw are two competing electronic databases that attorneys and other legal professionals use to conduct research. These services give users access to online legal information, including the text of court decisions and legislation, the content of public records, and many legal articles.

Activity Ask students to access the American Bar Association's Web site through glencoe.com and read about technology uses in legal professions.

A Secret Account Kiki and Wayne have been renting an apartment together since they got married six years ago. Both came into the marriage with some debt from school loans and car payments. After they married, they opened joint bank accounts. Both are computer consultants, worked 60 to 70 hours a week, and pay the bills together. Their goal in working so many hours is to save up and buy a house. When it came time to actually purchase the house, however, the financial loan documents revealed to Wayne that Kiki had a separate savings account worth $30,000 she had kept secret. This financial infidelity created a huge conflict in their marriage.

Assignments

Research Research money problems in marriages and find out if it is a leading cause of divorce.

Write Consider the situation above and write a personal essay about the role money plays in marriages or other personal relationships.

Writing Tips Before you write your personal essay, ask yourself the following questions to help you make it more meaningful to you:

✓ What in your research did you respond to personally?

✓ What are you own thoughts and opinions on the subject?

✓ Can you relate the subject to any personal experiences?

✓ Did you come across any information that you found personally useful or surprising?

✓ Did anything you read change any preconceptions you might have had on the subject?

Essay Test Strategies When you are preparing to write an essay, you can often figure out the meanings of unfamiliar words by looking at their context—the other words and sentences that surround them. Look for clues such as a synonym or an explanation of the unfamiliar word in the sentence, a reference to what the word is or is not like, a topic associated with the word, and a description or action associated with the word.

 Go to **glencoe.com** to find more writing resources.

Assignments

Most state courts uphold marriages even if the couple failed to observe a technicality (e.g., they did not get blood tests). Nevertheless, couples should strictly comply with all local requirements. Have students speculate on the age at which most people get married. During the past 30 years, the average age at which people marry has risen in the United States. At the same time, a larger number of American children are being born out of wedlock. Ask students to develop hypotheses to explain these trends.

The Writing Connection

W Writing Support

Objectives

Write a brief personal essay discussing the role of financial matters in a marriage.

Essay Rubric

Evaluate the students' writing according to the following criteria:

- The essay presents a variety of sentence lengths and structures. **(6 points)**
- The essay incorporates financial information. **(6 points)**
- The essay shows thoughtfulness. **(5 points)**
- The introduction captures the reader's attention. **(4 points)**
- Syntax, grammar, and spelling are error-free. **(4 points)**

Total: 25 points

C Critical Thinking

Synthesize

Divide the class into groups of three or four and have each group create a marriage application containing questions they believe are most important. Then compare the questions posed by various groups. Ask students to explain their reasons for each question.

Culminating Activity

Ask students to work in groups to give each other feedback on their first drafts.

UNIT 7

Thematic Project

Health Insurance Legislation

For this project, you will use what you have learned to prepare an informational guide on health insurance legislation. You can work on this project alone or with a partner.

Here is a checklist of the skills that you will need to complete this project, and that your teacher will consider when evaluating your work.

Evaluation Rubric

Academic Skills		
1. Online and library research	**1.**	10 points
2. Reading for information	**2.**	10 points
3. Note-taking	**3.**	5 points
4. Estimation and computation of facts/figures you discover	**4.**	10 points
5. English composition to summarize findings	**5.**	15 points
Legal Skills		
6. Researching health care legislation and/or health policy	**6.**	15 points
7. Contrasting the public interest and the economic theories	**7.**	15 points
8. Analysis of an aspect of the health care system	**8.**	15 points
9. Use of technology	**9.**	5 points
		Total 100 Points

 For more resources and for grading rubrics, go to **glencoe.com**.

Step 1: Preparation

❶ Write a proposal for the area of health care legislation you plan to research.

❷ Use all you have learned in this unit, at the library, or on the Internet as tools.

❸ Complete this project in a format acceptable for portfolio addition.

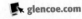 glencoe.com

---

Thematic Project

 Bell Ringer Activity

Ask students to recall news stories or magazine articles dealing with a famous person's marriage or divorce. Were there any legal issues raised in those cases?

TEACH

Workshop Overview

The objective of this workshop is to prepare an informational guide on health insurance legislation.

Language Arts

The large amount of printed materials converted to data and placed online now increases the glut of material that has to be reviewed in order to find the right source documents. Students need to learn how to evaluate information by asking themselves these questions while reading: Is the author qualified to write on this subject? Is the point of view biased? Are there other points of view not expressed in the article? Are opinions backed by facts, statistics, and examples? Have them apply these questions while sifting through documents to compile their informational guides.

 Time Management Rubric

Have students evaluate their usage of time by rating the skills below on a scale of "poor" to "apprentice" to "proficient."

- Organization (materials, files, data)
- Leadership (self-disciplined, motivated)
- Attention to detail (conscientious, efficient)
- Communication (technique, effectiveness)
- Problem solving (identifies, investigates, devises, evaluates)
- Critical thinking (defines, concludes, examines, constructs, supports, assesses)

Step 2: Procedure

❶ Review the text in this unit and make a list of the aspects of the health care system you chose, such as deregulation of the health care industry, federal support of medical research, insurance policy legislation, or Medicare. Go to **glencoe.com** to find additional help and resources.

❷ List all the various terminology, key issues, and historical turning points that are crucial to creating an outline and understanding the story of your particular area of research.

❸ Write an informational guide about the area you chose, including the parties involved and why it is being debated. Use the Internet to research and download forms, charts, or other important documents. Make enough copies so your classmates can review and annotate your guide.

❹ Describe a real-world federal policy or health care company that is the basis for your area of interest in the politics of health care. Present your guide and conclusion to your classmates.

Step 3: Create an Analysis Report

As a class, compare and contrast the information presented in each guide and look for common themes or areas covered. See if any of the guides stand out and if so what makes the information presented most interesting and surprising. After comparing the guides, answer the following questions:

❶ How many and what areas of health care legislation were presented?

❷ Did the guides presented include all the necessary information needed to understand the controversial issues with the politics of health care legislation?

❸ If not, what should have been added to make the information easier to use?

❹ How was your guide similar to and different from the other guides presented?

Community Connection

Research volunteer activities and work-based learning experiences in your school or community, such as career and technology education student organizations. Choose one and determine its benefits and service requirements. Prepare a brief report. Go to **glencoe.com** to find resources.

Competitive Event Prep

Planning for the Future

Situation: Assume the role of apartment dweller. You share your apartment with two friends. All three of you have signed the apartment lease. You just had a visit from your landlord. One of your roommates has failed to pay his/her share of the rent for three months. The landlord is threatening to begin eviction procedures against all of you because the entire amount of rent has not been paid.

Activity: You must explain to your roommates that since all three of you signed the lease, all three of you share responsibility for the rent and the consequences for not paying the rent, even though only one of you failed to pay.

For more Competitive Event preparation, performance tips, and evaluation rubrics, go to **glencoe.com**.

 glencoe.com

TEACH (cont.)

Extending the Content

Health Benefits for Married Couples

Explain to students that when married couples combine their health insurance coverage under one plan, the employer has to spend more money per person; hence, premiums go up.

Reading Connection

American Bar Association Resources

Ask students to go back to their ABA readings, notes, and summaries. Direct them to apply any relevant ABA content to review and revise their outline and first draft.

ASSESS

Evaluation

Make sure students review the evaluation rubric. Have them discuss why a particular issue interested them most.

CLOSE

Culminating Activity

Cooperative Learning

Have students learn about the needs of a local charity. Then develop a plan of action to help.

Skills Practice

Interpret

Ask interested students to research the impact obesity has had on the American economy over the last twenty years. Have students create either a table or a chart showing the growth of obesity and its impact on the health care system. They should consult the World Health Organization for the latest statistics on this issue.

Taking a Position

Have students make journal entries about American dependence on superior health care coverage. How does health care coverage in a capitalist society compare to that in a socialist society? Instruct students to write a persuasive essay on which they feel is better.

FOCUS

Why It's Important

- The Supreme Court held that although the probate exception is a valid exception to federal jurisdiction, the probate exception did not apply to this case.

- The Court held that the California federal courts had proper jurisdiction.

TEACH

Preteaching

Your Reading

This text is a long excerpt from a key case where U.S. probate law was applied.

Preread Skim the text, look at headings and the first few sentences of every section.

R Reading Strategy

Understanding Vocabulary Remind students about the difference between synonyms and antonyms. Tell students that they can easily remember this difference if they imagine that the "s" in synonym could stand for "same." As students read the section and encounter words that are unfamiliar, have them use a thesaurus to identify an appropriate synonym and antonym based on the words' context. Have students write a sentence for each word they identify in this way.

480

Marshall v. Marshall
U.S. Supreme Court 126 S.Ct. 1735 (2006)

Read Critically As you read this case, ask yourself the following questions:

R

1. What did J. Howard's estate plan provide?
2. In what court did Anna Nicole's case begin?
3. What exclusion were the courts applying to this case?
4. What did the U.S. Supreme Court hold with regard to Anna Nicole's case?

Assignment When you are done, write a short summary of the situation. Include the court's decision and a couple of sentences about why or how the court reached its decision.

Facts **The Relationship** Vickie Lynn Marshall, also known as Anna Nicole Smith (Anna Nicole), met J. Howard Marshall II (J. Howard) in October 1991. The two dated for more than two years and were eventually married on June 27, 1994. J. Howard died a little more than a year later on August 4, 1995. Although J. Howard showered Anna Nicole with a number of gifts and a significant amount of money during their courtship and marriage, J. Howard did not include anything for her in his will.

J. Howard Marshall's Will While J. Howard was alive, he created an estate plan for his vast fortune. The plan consisted of a living trust and a pourover will. As such, a significant portion of his estate was placed in a trust, listing himself as the beneficiary while he was alive. Per the instructions in his will, when J. Howard died, the remaining portion of his estate that was not already in the trust was transferred into the trust. The trust's beneficiary was then changed from J.

Howard to his son, E. Pierce Marshall (Pierce). After his death, Pierce submitted J. Howard's will into probate in the Probate Court of Harris County, Texas.

Anna Nicole's Troubles In January 1996, after Pierce had begun probate proceedings in Texas, Anna Nicole filed for bankruptcy in the United States Bankruptcy Court for the Central District of California. Among the debts Anna Nicole sought to discharge was a debt to Pierce. Pierce then filed a proof of claim in the bankruptcy court, arguing that Anna Nicole's debt was not dischargeable because she had defamed Pierce shortly after J. Howard's death, by telling the press that Pierce had engaged in forgery and fraud to gain control of his father's estate. Under bankruptcy law, debt is not dischargeable if it arises from "willful and malicious injury by the debtor."

Anna Nicole asserted a defense of truth, arguing that her statements to the press could not be defamation since they were all true statements. Further, Anna Nicole filed a counterclaim, alleging Pierce had tortiously

480 Unit 7 Family Law

? Landmark Case Questions

R Reading Strategy

Answers

1. A living trust with J. Howard as beneficiary and a "pourover" will. Upon death, any property not in the trust would be deposited into the trust, with Pierce as the new beneficiary.

2. U.S. Bankruptcy Court, Central District of California

3. probate exception

4. The probate exception does not apply to this case; therefore, federal court has jurisdiction.

interfered with a gift she expected from J. Howard's estate. Anna Nicole further alleged that Pierce had interfered by imprisoning J. Howard against his wishes, surrounding J. Howard with bodyguards to prevent contact between J. Howard and Anna Nicole, making misrepresentations to J. Howard, and by transferring property against J. Howard's wishes.

Court's Findings After a trial, the Bankruptcy Court entered judgment in favor of Anna Nicole, finding that Pierce had tortiously interfered with Anna Nicole's expected gift from J. Howard. The Court awarded Anna Nicole $449 million in compensatory damages and $25 million in punitive damages. Pierce then appealed to the U.S. District Court for the Central District of California, which upheld the finding of the Bankruptcy Court, but changed the award to $44.3 million in compensatory damages and $44.3 million in punitive damages. Pierce appealed again, this time to the Ninth Circuit Court of Appeals.

Opinion Ninth Circuit Court of Appeals Proceedings

The Ninth Circuit Court of Appeals set aside the judgments entered by the lower courts. In its holding, the Ninth Circuit found that although Anna Nicole's claim did not "involve the administration of an estate, the probate of a will, or any other purely probate matter," the probate exception bars federal jurisdiction in Anna Nicole's case and any determinations on her case must be made by the Probate Court in Harris County, Texas, rather than a federal court in California because the matter arises out of a probate being conducted in Texas.

The Probate Exception The probate exception is a recognized exception to federal jurisdiction, in which the federal courts will defer diversity jurisdiction it would normally have under the Constitution in probate matters to the state courts. The exception dates back to The Judiciary Act of 1789, which stated federal courts had diversity jurisdiction over "all suits of a civil nature at common law or in equity."

Under the current understanding of the probate exception, federal courts reserve

jurisdiction to the state probate courts the probate or annulment of a will and the administration of a decedent's estate. The exception also precludes the federal courts from trying to dispose of property that is currently under the custody of a state's probate court. However, it does not bar federal courts from adjudicating matters outside those confines regardless of whether those matters may be tenuously connected to a probate matter.

Holding The Court's Decision

The United States Supreme Court held that although the probate exception is still a valid exception to federal jurisdiction, the probate exception does not apply to this case. Anna Nicole's claim of tortious interference is against Pierce, personally, and not against the estate of her late husband in probate, or an annulment of J. Howard's will. The Court further found that Anna Nicole did not seek to attack any property that was part of the probate proceedings—her claim was strictly against Pierce. Therefore, the Court held that the California Federal Courts had proper jurisdiction. The Court remanded the case back to the Ninth Circuit to determine whether the factual findings were proper now that the Supreme Court had held jurisdiction was proper.

TRIAL PREP

The National High School Mock Trial Association organizes competitions at the local, regional, and national levels where teams of high school or college students prepare and argue fictional legal cases before practicing attorneys and judges. Mock Trial team members are each assigned a role as either an attorney or witness. Each team must develop a courtroom strategy, legal arguments, and a presentation style.

 Go to **glencoe.com** to find guided activities about case strategy and presentation.

Go to **glencoe.com** to find guided activities about case strategy and presentation.

ASSESS

Role Play
Ask students to find details of married life during a historical period. They should research the validity of marriage laws and discuss how each was handled: marriage, spousal abuse, infertility, infidelity, and so on. Encourage them to draft contracts based on the laws they find. Then, they can act out the scenes.

CLOSE

Understand the Decision

The Supreme Court held that jurisdiction over probate matters is still held by the state courts. Why do the state courts have exclusive jurisdiction over probate matters? (In 1789, the Judiciary Act gave federal courts diversity jurisdiction over "all suits of a civil nature at common law or in equity." Since federal courts only had jurisdiction over common law or equity matters, probate was not included in federal jurisdiction and was left to the state courts' jurisdiction.)

Winning the Case

Dischargeable Debt

In this case, Anna Nicole initiated litigation in federal bankruptcy court by trying to discharge debt she owed to Pierce. However, Pierce argued that the debt was not dischargeable because it arose from "willful and malicious injury by the debtor." Pierce argued that Anna Nicole had defamed him shortly after his father's death. The jury found for Anna Nicole, but what about the following cases? A man drank 11 beers and crashed into a building, then tried to discharge the debt owed as a result of necessary repairs having been made to the building. A woman tried to discharge a debt owed to lawyers who had unsuccessfully defended her against embezzlement charges. Neither obligation is dischargeable.

Number and Operations

▶ *Understand numbers, ways of representing numbers, relationships among numbers, and number systems*

Fraction, Decimal, and Percent

A percent is a ratio that compares a number to 100. To write a percent as a fraction, drop the percent sign, and use the number as the numerator in a fraction with a denominator of 100. Simplify, if possible. For example, $76\% = \frac{76}{100}$, or $\frac{19}{25}$. To write a fraction as a percent, convert it to an equivalent fraction with a denominator of 100. For example, $\frac{3}{4} = \frac{75}{100}$, or 75%. A fraction can be expressed as a percent by first converting the fraction to a decimal (divide the numerator by the denominator) and then converting the decimal to a percent by moving the decimal point two places to the right.

Comparing Numbers on a Number Line

In order to compare and understand the relationship between real numbers in various forms, it is helpful to use a number line. The zero point on a number line is called the origin; the points to the left of the origin are negative, and those to the right are positive. The number line below shows how numbers in percent, decimal, fraction, and integer form can be compared.

$$-\frac{1}{2} \quad 0.25 \quad 75\% \quad 2.5$$

$$\begin{array}{ccccccc} & & & & & & \\ -3 & -2 & -1 & 0 & 1 & 2 & 3 \end{array}$$

Percents Greater Than 100 and Less Than 1

Percents greater than 100% represent values greater than 1. For example, if the weight of an object is 250% of another, it is 2.5, or $2\frac{1}{2}$, times the weight.

Percents less than 1 represent values less than $\frac{1}{100}$. In other words, 0.1% is one tenth of one percent, which can also be represented in decimal form as 0.001, or in fraction form as $\frac{1}{1,000}$. Similarly, 0.01% is one hundredth of one percent, 0.0001, or $\frac{1}{10,000}$.

Ratio, Rate, and Proportion

A ratio is a comparison of two numbers using division. If a basketball player makes 8 out of 10 free throws, the ratio is written as 8 to 10, 8:10, or $\frac{8}{10}$. Ratios are usually written in simplest form. In simplest form, the ratio "8 out of 10" is 4 to 5, 4:5, or $\frac{4}{5}$. A rate is a ratio of two measurements having different kinds of units—cups per gallon, or miles per hour, for example. When a rate is simplified so that it has a denominator of 1, it is called a unit rate. An example of a unit rate is 9 miles per hour. A proportion is an equation stating that two ratios are equal. $\frac{3}{18} = \frac{13}{78}$ is an example of a proportion. The cross products of a proportion are also equal. $\frac{3}{18} = \frac{13}{78}$ and $3 \times 78 = 18 \times 13$.

Representing Large and Small Numbers

In order to represent large and small numbers, it is important to understand the number system. Our number system is based on 10, and the value of each place is 10 times the value of the place to its right.

The value of a digit is the product of a digit and its place value. For instance, in the number 6,400, the 6 has a value of six thousands and the 4 has a value of four hundreds. A place value chart can help you read numbers. In the chart, each group of three digits is called a period. Commas separate the periods: the ones period, the thousands period, the millions period, and so on. Values to the right of the ones period are decimals. By understanding place value you can write very large numbers like 5 billion and more, and very small numbers that are less than 1.

Scientific Notation

When dealing with very large numbers like 1,500,000, or very small numbers like 0.000015, it is helpful to keep track of their value by writing the numbers in scientific notation. Powers of 10 with positive exponents are used with a decimal between 1 and 10 to express large numbers. The exponent represents the number of places the decimal point is moved to the right. So, 528,000 is written in scientific notation as 5.28×10^5. Powers of 10 with negative exponents are used with a decimal between 1 and 10 to express small numbers. The exponent represents the number of places the decimal point is moved to the left. The number 0.00047 is expressed as 4.7×10^{-4}.

Factor, Multiple, and Prime Factorization

Two or more numbers that are multiplied to form a product are called factors. Divisibility rules can be used to determine whether 2, 3, 4, 5, 6, 8, 9, or 10 are factors of a given number. Multiples are the products of a given number and various integers. For example, 8 is a multiple of 4 because $4 \times 2 = 8$. A prime number is a whole number that has exactly two factors: 1 and itself. A composite number is a whole number that has more than two factors. Zero and 1 are neither prime nor composite. A composite number can be expressed as the product of its prime factors. The prime factorization of 40 is $2 \times 2 \times 2 \times 5$, or $2^3 \times 5$. The numbers 2 and 5 are prime numbers.

Integers

A negative number is a number less than zero. Negative numbers like –8, positive numbers like +6, and zero are members of the set of integers. Integers can be represented as points on a number line. A set of integers can be written {..., –3, –2, –1, 0, 1, 2, 3, ...} where "..." means "continues indefinitely."

Real, Rational, and Irrational Numbers

The real number system is made up of the sets of rational and irrational numbers. Rational numbers are numbers that can be written in the form a/b where a and b are integers and $b \neq 0$. Examples are 0.45, $\frac{1}{2}$, and $\sqrt{36}$. Irrational numbers are non-repeating, non-terminating decimals. Examples are $\sqrt{71}$, π, and 0.020020002....

Complex and Imaginary Numbers

A complex number is a mathematical expression with a real number element and an imaginary number element. Imaginary numbers are multiples of i, the "imaginary" square root of –1. Complex numbers are represented by $a + bi$, where a and b are real numbers and i represents the imaginary element.

When a quadratic equation does not have a real number solution, the solution can be represented by a complex number. Complex numbers can be added, subtracted, multiplied, and divided.

Vectors and Matrices
A matrix is a set of numbers or elements arranged in rows and columns to form a rectangle. The number of rows is represented by m and the number of columns is represented by n. To describe the number of rows and columns in a matrix, list the number of rows first using the format $m \times n$. Matrix A below is a 3×3 matrix because it has 3 rows and 3 columns. To name an element of a matrix, the letter i is used to denote the row and j is used to denote the column, and the element is labeled in the form $a_{i,j}$. In matrix A below, $a_{3,2}$ is 4.

$$\text{Matrix A} = \begin{pmatrix} 1 & 3 & 5 \\ 0 & 6 & 8 \\ 3 & 4 & 5 \end{pmatrix}$$

A vector is a matrix with only one column or row of elements. A transposed column vector, or a column vector turned on its side, is a row vector. In the example below, row vector b' is the transpose of column vector b.

$$b = \begin{pmatrix} 1 \\ 2 \\ 3 \\ 4 \end{pmatrix}$$

$$b' = \begin{pmatrix} 1 & 2 & 3 & 4 \end{pmatrix}$$

▶ *Understand meanings of operations and how they relate to one another*

Properties of Addition and Multiplication
Properties are statements that are true for any numbers. For example, $3 + 8$ is the same as $8 + 3$ because each expression equals 11. This illustrates the Commutative Property of Addition. Likewise, $3 \times 8 = 8 \times 3$ illustrates the Commutative Property of Multiplication.

When evaluating expressions, it is often helpful to group or associate the numbers. The Associative Property says that the way in which numbers are grouped when added or multiplied does not change the sum or product. The following properties are also true:

- **Additive Identity Property:** When 0 is added to any number, the sum is the number.

- **Multiplicative Identity Property:** When any number is multiplied by 1, the product is the number.

- **Multiplicative Property of Zero:** When any number is multiplied by 0, the product is 0.

Rational Numbers
A number that can be written as a fraction is called a rational number. Terminating and repeating decimals are rational numbers because both can be written as fractions. Decimals that are neither terminating nor repeating are called irrational numbers because they cannot be written as fractions. Terminating decimals can be converted to fractions by placing the number (without the decimal point) in the numerator. Count the number of places to the right of the decimal point, and in the denominator, place a 1 followed by a number of zeros equal to the number of

places that you counted. The fraction can then be reduced to simplest form.

Writing a Fraction as a Decimal

Any fraction $\frac{a}{b}$, where $b \neq 0$, can be written as a decimal by dividing the numerator by the denominator. So, $\frac{a}{b} = a \div b$. If the division ends, or terminates, when the remainder is zero, the decimal is a terminating decimal. Not all fractions can be written as terminating decimals. Some have a repeating decimal. A bar indicates that the decimal repeats forever. For example, the fraction $\frac{4}{9}$ can be converted to a repeating decimal, $0.\overline{4}$

Adding and Subtracting Like Fractions

Fractions with the same denominator are called like fractions. To add like fractions, add the numerators and write the sum over the denominator. To add mixed numbers with like fractions, add the whole numbers and fractions separately, adding the numerators of the fractions, then simplifying if necessary. The rule for subtracting fractions with like denominators is similar to the rule for adding. The numerators can be subtracted and the difference written over the denominator. Mixed numbers are written as improper fractions before subtracting. These same rules apply to adding or subtracting like algebraic fractions.

Adding and Subtracting Unlike Fractions

Fractions with different denominators are called unlike fractions. The least common multiple of the denominators is used to rename the fractions with a common denominator. After a common denominator is found, the numerators can then be added or subtracted. To add mixed numbers with unlike fractions, rename the mixed numbers as improper fractions. Then find a common denominator, add the numerators, and simplify the answer.

Multiplying Rational Numbers

To multiply fractions, multiply the numerators and multiply the denominators. If the numerators and denominators have common factors, they can be simplified before multiplication. If the fractions have different signs, then the product will be negative. Mixed numbers can be multiplied in the same manner, after first renaming them as improper fractions. A fraction that contains one or more variables in the numerator or denominator is called an algebraic fraction. Algebraic fractions may be multiplied using the same method described above.

Dividing Rational Numbers

To divide a number by a rational number (a fraction, for example), multiply the first number by the multiplicative inverse of the second. Two numbers whose product is 1 are called multiplicative inverses, or reciprocals. $\frac{7}{4} \times \frac{4}{7} = 1$. When dividing by a mixed number, first rename it as an improper fraction, and then multiply by its multiplicative inverse. This process of multiplying by a number's reciprocal can also be used when dividing algebraic fractions.

Adding Integers

To add integers with the same sign, add their absolute values. The sum then takes the same sign as the addends. The equation $-5 + (-2) = -7$ is an example of adding two integers with the same sign. To add integers with different signs, subtract their absolute values. The sum takes the same sign as the addend with the greater absolute value.

Subtracting Integers

The rules for adding integers are extended to the subtraction of integers. To subtract an integer, add its additive inverse. For example, to find the difference $2 - 5$, add the additive inverse of 5 to 2: $2 + (-5) = -3$. The rule for subtracting integers can be used to solve real-world problems and to evaluate algebraic expressions.

Additive Inverse Property

Two numbers with the same absolute value but different signs are called opposites. For example, -4 and 4 are opposites. An integer and its opposite are also called additive inverses. The Additive Inverse Property says that the sum of any number and its additive inverse is zero. The Commutative, Associative, and Identity Properties also apply to integers. These properties help when adding more than two integers.

Absolute Value

In mathematics, when two integers on a number line are on opposite sides of zero, and they are the same distance from zero, they have the same absolute value. The symbol for absolute value is two vertical bars on either side of the number. For example, $|-5| = 5$.

Multiplying Integers

Since multiplication is repeated addition, $3(-7)$ means that -7 is used as an addend 3 times. By the Commutative Property of Multiplication, $3(-7) = -7(3)$. The product of two integers with different signs is always negative. The product of two integers with the same sign is always positive.

Dividing Integers

The quotient of two integers can be found by dividing the numbers using their absolute values. The quotient of two integers with the same sign is positive, and the quotient of two integers with a different sign is negative. $-12 \div (-4) = 3$ and $12 \div (-4) = -3$. The division of integers is used in statistics to find the average, or mean, of a set of data. When finding the mean of a set of numbers, find the sum of the numbers, and then divide by the number in the set.

Adding and Multiplying Vectors and Matrices

In order to add two matrices together, they must have the same number of rows and columns. In matrix addition, the corresponding elements are added to each other. In other words $(a + b)_{ij} = a_{ij} + b_{ij}$. For example,

$$\begin{pmatrix} 1 & 2 \\ 2 & 1 \end{pmatrix} + \begin{pmatrix} 3 & 6 \\ 0 & 1 \end{pmatrix} = \begin{pmatrix} 1+3 & 2+6 \\ 2+0 & 1+1 \end{pmatrix} = \begin{pmatrix} 4 & 8 \\ 2 & 2 \end{pmatrix}$$

Matrix multiplication requires that the number of elements in each row in the first matrix is equal to the number of elements in each column in the second. The elements of the first row of the first matrix are multiplied by the corresponding elements of the first column of the second matrix and then added together to get the first element of the product matrix. To get the second element, the elements in the first row of the first matrix are multiplied by the corresponding elements in the second column of the second matrix, then added, and so on, until every row of the first matrix is multiplied by every column of the second. See the example below.

$$\begin{pmatrix} 1 & 2 \\ 3 & 4 \end{pmatrix} \times \begin{pmatrix} 3 & 6 \\ 0 & 1 \end{pmatrix} = \begin{pmatrix} (1\times3)+(2\times0) & (1\times6)+(2\times1) \\ (3\times3)+(4\times0) & (3\times6)+(4\times1) \end{pmatrix} = \begin{pmatrix} 3 & 8 \\ 9 & 22 \end{pmatrix}$$

Vector addition and multiplication are performed in the same way, but there is only one column and one row.

Permutations and Combinations

Permutations and combinations are used to determine the number of possible outcomes in different situations. An arrangement, listing, or pattern in which order is important is called a permutation. The symbol $P(6, 3)$ represents the number of permutations of 6 things taken 3 at a time. For $P(6, 3)$, there are $6 \times 5 \times 4$ or 120 possible outcomes. An arrangement or listing where order is not important is called a combination. The symbol $C(10, 5)$ represents the number of combinations of 10 things taken 5 at a time. For $C(10, 5)$, there are $(10 \times 9 \times 8 \times 7 \times 6) \div (5 \times 4 \times 3 \times 2 \times 1)$ or 252 possible outcomes.

Powers and Exponents

An expression such as $3 \times 3 \times 3 \times 3$ can be written as a power. A power has two parts, a base and an exponent. $3 \times 3 \times 3 \times 3 = 3^4$. The base is the number that is multiplied (3). The exponent tells how many times the base is used as a factor (4 times). Numbers and variables can be written using exponents. For example, $8 \times 8 \times 8 \times m \times m \times m \times m \times m$ can be expressed $8^3 m^5$. Exponents also can be used with place value to express numbers in expanded form. Using this method, 1,462 can be written as $(1 \times 10^3) + (4 \times 10^2) + (6 \times 10^1) + (2 \times 10^0)$.

Squares and Square Roots

The square root of a number is one of two equal factors of a number. Every positive number has both a positive and a negative square root. For example, since $8 \times 8 = 64$, 8 is a square root of 64. Since $(-8) \times (-8) = 64$, -8 is also a square root of 64. The notation $\sqrt{}$ indicates the positive square root, $-\sqrt{}$ indicates the negative square root, and $\pm\sqrt{}$ indicates both square roots.

For example, $\sqrt{81} = 9$, $-\sqrt{49} = -7$, and $\pm\sqrt{4} = \pm 2$. The square root of a negative number is an imaginary number because any two factors of a negative number must have different signs, and are therefore not equivalent.

Logarithm

A logarithm is the inverse of exponentiation. The logarithm of a number x in base b is equal to the number n. Therefore, $b^n = x$ and $\log_b x = n$. For example, $\log_4(64) = 3$ because $4^3 = 64$. The most commonly used bases for logarithms are 10, the common logarithm; 2, the binary logarithm; and the constant e, the natural logarithm (also called $ln(x)$ instead of $\log_e(x)$). Below is a list of some of the rules of logarithms that are important to understand if you are going to use them.

$$\log_b(xy) = \log_b(x) + \log_b(y)$$
$$\log_b(x/y) = \log_b(x) - \log_b(y)$$
$$\log_b(1/x) = -\log_b(x)$$
$$\log_b(x)y = y\log_b(x)$$

▶ **Compute fluently and make reasonable estimates**

Estimation by Rounding

When rounding numbers, look at the digit to the right of the place to which you are rounding. If the digit is 5 or greater, round up. If it is less than 5, round down. For example, to round 65,137 to the nearest hundred, look at the number in the tens place. Since 3 is less than 5, round down to 65,100. To round the same number to the nearest ten thousandth, look at the number in the thousandths place. Since it is 5, round up to 70,000.

Finding Equivalent Ratios

Equivalent ratios have the same meaning. Just like finding equivalent fractions, to find an equivalent ratio, multiply or divide both sides by the same number. For example, you can multiply 7 by both sides of the ratio 6:8 to get 42:56. Instead, you can also divide both sides of the same ratio by 2 to get 3:4. Find the simplest form of a ratio by dividing to find equivalent ratios until you can't go any further without going into decimals. So, 160:240 in simplest form is 2:3. To write a ratio in the form 1:n, divide both sides by the left-hand number. In other words, to change 8:20 to 1:n, divide both sides by 8 to get 1:2.5.

Front-End Estimation

Front-end estimation can be used to quickly estimate sums and differences before adding or subtracting. To use this technique, add or subtract just the digits of the two highest place values, and replace the other place values with zero. This will give you an estimation of the solution of a problem. For example, 93,471 − 22,825 can be changed to 93,000 − 22,000 or 71,000. This estimate can be compared to your final answer to judge its correctness.

Judging Reasonableness

When solving an equation, it is important to check your work by considering how reasonable your answer is. For example, consider the equation $9\frac{3}{4} \times 4\frac{1}{3}$. Since $9\frac{3}{4}$ is between 9 and 10 and $4\frac{1}{3}$ is between 4 and 5, only values that are between 9×4 or 36 and 10×5 or 50 will be reasonable. You can also use front-end estimation, or you can round and estimate a reasonable answer. In the equation 73×25, you can round and solve to estimate a reasonable answer to be near 70×30 or 2,100.

Algebra

▶ Understand patterns, relations, and functions

Relation

A relation is a generalization comparing sets of ordered pairs for an equation or inequality such as $x = y + 1$ or $x > y$. The first values in each pair, the x values, form the domain. The second values in each pair, the y values, form the range.

Function

A function is a special relation in which each member of the domain is paired with exactly one member in the range. Functions may be represented using ordered pairs, tables, or graphs. One way to determine whether a relation is a function is to use the vertical line test. Using an object to represent a vertical line, move the object from left to right across the graph. If, for each value of x in the domain, the object passes through no more than one point on the graph, then the graph represents a function.

Linear and Nonlinear Functions

Linear functions have graphs that are straight lines. These graphs represent constant rates of change. In other words, the slope between any two pairs of points on the graph is the same. Nonlinear functions do not have constant rates of change. The slope changes along these graphs. Therefore, the graphs of nonlinear functions are *not* straight lines. Graphs of curves represent nonlinear functions. The equation for a linear function can be written in the form $y = mx + b$, where m represents the constant rate of change, or the slope. Therefore, you can determine whether a function is linear by looking at the equation. For example, the equation $y = \frac{3}{x}$ is nonlinear because x is in the denominator and the equation cannot be written in the form $y = mx + b$. A nonlinear function does not increase or decrease at a constant rate. You can check this by using a table and finding the increase or decrease in y for each regular increase in x. For example, if for each increase in x by 2, y does not increase or decrease the same amount each time, the function is nonlinear.

Linear Equations in Two Variables

In a linear equation with two variables, such as $y = x - 3$, the variables appear in separate terms and neither variable contains an exponent other than 1. The graphs of all linear equations are straight lines. All points on a line are solutions of the equation that is graphed.

Quadratic and Cubic Functions

A quadratic function is a polynomial equation of the second degree, generally expressed as $ax^2 + bx + c = 0$, where a, b, and c are real numbers and a is not equal to zero. Similarly, a cubic function is a polynomial equation of the third degree, usually expressed as $ax^3 + bx^2 + cx + d = 0$. Quadratic functions can be graphed using an equation or a table of values. For example, to graph $y = 3x^2 + 1$, substitute the values -1, -0.5, 0, 0.5, and 1 for x to yield the point coordinates $(-1, 4)$, $(-0.5, 1.75)$, $(0, 1)$, $(0.5, 1.75)$, and $(1, 4)$. Plot these points on a coordinate grid and connect the points in the form of a parabola. Cubic functions also can be graphed by making a table of values. The points of a cubic function from a curve. There is one point at which the curve changes from opening upward to opening downward, or vice versa, called the point of inflection.

Slope

Slope is the ratio of the rise, or vertical change, to the run, or horizontal change of a line: slope = rise/run.

Slope (m) is the same for any two points on a straight line and can be found by using the coordinates of any two points on the line:

$$m = \frac{y_2 - y_1}{x_2 - x_1}, \text{ where } x_2 \neq x_1.$$

Asymptotes

An asymptote is a straight line that a curve approaches but never actually meets or crosses. Theoretically, the asymptote meets the curve at infinity. For example, in the function $f(x) = \frac{1}{x}$, two asymptotes are being approached: the line $y = 0$ and $x = 0$. See the graph of the function below.

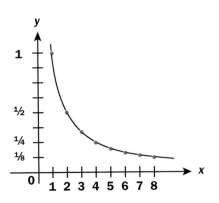

▶ Represent and analyze mathematical situations and structures using algebraic symbols

Variables and Expressions

Algebra is a language of symbols. A variable is a placeholder for a changing value. Any letter, such as x, can be used as a variable. Expressions such as $x + 2$ and $4x$ are algebraic expressions because they represent sums and/or products of variables and numbers. Usually, mathematicians avoid the use of i and e for variables because they have other mathematical meanings ($i = \sqrt{-1}$ and e is used with natural logarithms). To evaluate an algebraic expression, replace the variable or variables with known

values, and then solve using order of operations. Translate verbal phrases into algebraic expressions by first defining a variable: choose a variable and a quantity for the variable to represent. In this way, algebraic expressions can be used to represent real-world situations.

Constant and Coefficient

A constant is a fixed value unlike a variable, which can change. Constants are usually represented by numbers, but they can also be represented by symbols. For example, π is a symbolic representation of the value 3.1415.... A coefficient is a constant by which a variable or other object is multiplied. For example, in the expression $7x^2 + 5x + 9$, the coefficient of x^2 is 7 and the coefficient of x is 5. The number 9 is a constant and not a coefficient.

Monomial and Polynomial

A monomial is a number, a variable, or a product of numbers and/or variables such as 3×4. An algebraic expression that contains one or more monomials is called a polynomial. In a polynomial, there are no terms with variables in the denominator and no terms with variables under a radical sign. Polynomials can be classified by the number of terms contained in the expression. Therefore, a polynomial with two terms is called a binomial ($z^2 - 1$), and a polynomial with three terms is called a trinomial ($2y^3 + 4y^2 - y$). Polynomials also can be classified by their degrees. The degree of a monomial is the sum of the exponents of its variables. The degree of a nonzero constant such as 6 or 10 is 0. The constant 0 has no degree. For example, the monomial $4b^5c^2$ had a degree of 7. The degree of a polynomial is the same as that of the term with the greatest degree. For example, the polynomial $3x^4 - 2y^3 + 4y^2 - y$ has a degree of 4.

Equation

An equation is a mathematical sentence that states that two expressions are equal. The two expressions in an equation are always separated by an equal sign. When solving for a variable in an equation, you must perform the same operations on both sides of the equation in order for the mathematical sentence to remain true.

Solving Equations with Variables

To solve equations with variables on both sides, use the Addition or Subtraction Property of Equality to write an equivalent equation with the variables on the same side. For example, to solve $5x - 8 = 3x$, subtract $3x$ from each side to get $2x - 8 = 0$. Then add 8 to each side to get $2x = 8$. Finally, divide each side by 2 to find that $x = 4$.

Solving Equations with Grouping Symbols

Equations often contain grouping symbols such as parentheses or brackets. The first step in solving these equations is to use the Distributive Property to remove the grouping symbols. For example $5(x + 2) = 25$ can be changed to $5x + 10 = 25$, and then solved to find that $x = 3$.

Some equations have no solution. That is, there is no value of the variable that results in a true sentence. For such an equation, the solution set is called the null or empty set, and is represented by the symbol $\varnothing$ or $\{\}$. Other equations may have every number as the solution. An equation that is true for every value of the variable is called the identity.

Inequality

A mathematical sentence that contains the symbols $<$ (less than), $>$ (greater than), $\leq$ (less than or equal to), or $\geq$ (greater than or equal to) is called an inequality. For example, the statement that it is legal to drive 55 miles per hour or slower on a stretch of the highway can be shown by the sentence $s \leq 55$. Inequalities with variables are called open sentences. When a variable is replaced with a number, the inequality may be true or false.

Solving Inequalities

Solving an inequality means finding values for the variable that make the inequality true. Just as with equations, when you add or subtract the same number from each side of an inequality, the inequality remains true. For example, if you add 5 to each side of the inequality $3x < 6$, the resulting inequality $3x + 5 < 11$ is also true. Adding or subtracting the same number from each side of an inequality does not affect the inequality sign. When multiplying or dividing each side of an inequality by the same positive number, the inequality remains true. In such cases, the inequality symbol does not change. When multiplying or dividing each side of an inequality by a negative number, the inequality symbol must be reversed. For example, when dividing each side of the inequality $-4x \geq -8$ by -2, the inequality sign must be changed to $\leq$ for the resulting inequality, $2x \leq 4$, to be true. Since the solutions to an inequality include all rational numbers satisfying it, inequalities have an infinite number of solutions.

Representing Inequalities on a Number Line

The solutions of inequalities can be graphed on a number line. For example, if the solution of an inequality is $x < 5$, start an arrow at 5 on the number line, and continue the arrow to the left to show all values less than 5 as the solution. Put an open circle at 5 to show that the point 5 is *not* included in the graph.

Use a closed circle when graphing solutions that are greater than or equal to, or less than or equal to, a number.

Order of Operations

Solving a problem may involve using more than one operation. The answer can depend on the order in which you do the operations. To make sure that there is just one answer to a series of computations, mathematicians have agreed upon an order in which to do the operations. First simplify within the parentheses, and then evaluate any exponents. Then multiply and divide from left to right, and finally add and subtract from left to right.

Parametric Equations

Given an equation with more than one unknown, a statistician can draw conclusions about those unknown quantities through the use of parameters, independent variables that the statistician already knows something about. For example, you can find the velocity of an object if you make some assumptions about distance and time parameters.

Recursive Equations

In recursive equations, every value is determined by the previous value. You must first plug an initial value into the equation to get the first value, and then you can use the first value to determine the next one, and so on. For example, in order to determine what the population of pigeons will be in New York City in three years, you can use an equation with the birth, death, immigration, and emigration rates of the birds. Input the current population size into the equation to determine next year's population size, then repeat until you have calculated the value for which you are looking.

▶ *Use mathematical models to represent and understand quantitative relationships*

Solving Systems of Equations

Two or more equations together are called a system of equations. A system of equations can have one solution, no solution, or infinitely many solutions. One method for solving a system of equations is to graph the equations on the same coordinate plane. The coordinates of the point where the graphs intersect is the solution. In other words, the solution of a system is the ordered pair that is a solution of all equations. A more accurate way to solve a system of two equations is by using a method called substitution. Write both equations in terms of y. Replace y in the first equation with the right side of the second equation. Check the solution by graphing. You can solve a system of three equations using matrix algebra.

Graphing Inequalities

To graph an inequality, first graph the related equation, which is the boundary. All points in the shaded region are solutions of the inequality. If an inequality contains the symbol $\leq$ or $\geq$, then use a solid line to indicate that the boundary is included in the graph. If an inequality contains the symbol $<$ or $>$, then use a dashed line to indicate that the boundary is not included in the graph.

► *Analyze change in various contexts*

Rate of Change

A change in one quantity with respect to another quantity is called the rate of change. Rates of change can be described using slope:

$$\text{slope} = \frac{\text{change in } y}{\text{change in } x}.$$

You can find rates of change from an equation, a table, or a graph. A special type of linear equation that describes rate of change is called a direct variation. The graph of a direct variation always passes through the origin and represents a proportional situation. In the equation $y = kx$, k is called the constant of variation. It is the slope, or rate of change. As x increases in value, y increases or decreases at a constant rate k, or y varies directly with x. Another way to say this is that y is directly proportional to x. The direct variation $y = kx$ also can be written as $k = \frac{y}{x}$. In this form, you can see that the ratio of y to x is the same for any corresponding values of y and x.

Slope-Intercept Form

Equations written as $y = mx + b$, where m is the slope and b is the y-intercept, are linear equations in slope-intercept form. For example, the graph of $y = 5x - 6$ is a line that has a slope of 5 and crosses the y-axis at $(0, -6)$. Sometimes you must first write an equation in slope-intercept form before finding the slope and y-intercept. For example, the equation $2x + 3y = 15$ can be expressed in slope-intercept form by subtracting $2x$ from each side and then dividing by 3: $y = -\frac{2}{3}x + 5$, revealing a slope of $-\frac{2}{3}$ and a y-intercept of 5. You can use the slope-intercept form of an equation to graph a line easily. Graph the y-intercept and use the slope to find another point on the line, then connect the two points with a line.

Geometry

▶ *Analyze characteristics and properties of two- and three-dimensional geometric shapes and develop mathematical arguments about geometric relationships*

Angles

Two rays that have the same endpoint form an angle. The common endpoint is called the vertex, and the two rays that make up the angle are called the sides of the angle. The most common unit of measure for angles is the degree. Protractors can be used to measure angles or to draw an angle of a given measure. Angles can be classified by their degree measure. Acute angles have measures less than 90° but greater than 0°. Obtuse angles have measures greater than 90° but less than 180°. Right angles have measures of 90°.

Triangles

A triangle is a figure formed by three line segments that intersect only at their endpoints. The sum of the measures of the angles of a triangle is 180°. Triangles can be classified by their angles. An acute triangle contains all acute angles. An obtuse triangle has one obtuse angle. A right triangle has one right angle. Triangles can also be classified by their sides. A scalene triangle has no congruent sides. An isosceles triangle has at least two congruent sides. In an equilateral triangle all sides are congruent.

Quadrilaterals

A quadrilateral is a closed figure with four sides and four vertices. The segments of a quadrilateral intersect only at their endpoints. Quadrilaterals can be separated into two triangles.

Since the sum of the interior angles of all triangles totals 180°, the measures of the interior angles of a quadrilateral equal 360°. Quadrilaterals are classified according to their characteristics, and include trapezoids, parallelograms, rectangles, squares, and rhombuses.

Two-Dimensional Figures

A two-dimensional figure exists within a plane and has only the dimensions of length and width. Examples of two-dimensional figures include circles and polygons. Polygons are figures that have three or more angles, including triangles, quadrilaterals, pentagons, hexagons, and many more. The sum of the angles of any polygon totals at least 180° (triangle), and each additional side adds 180° to the measure of the first three angles. The sum of the angles of a quadrilateral, for example, is 360°. The sum of the angles of a pentagon is 540°.

Three-Dimensional Figures

A plane is a two-dimensional flat surface that extends in all directions. Intersecting planes can form the edges and vertices of three-dimensional figures or solids. A polyhedron is a solid with flat surfaces that are polygons. Polyhedrons are composed of faces, edges, and vertices and are differentiated by their shape and by their number of bases. Skew lines are lines that lie in different planes. They are neither intersecting nor parallel.

Congruence

Figures that have the same size and shape are congruent. The parts of congruent triangles that match are called corresponding parts. Congruence statements are used to identify corresponding parts of congruent triangles.

When writing a congruence statement, the letters must be written so that corresponding vertices appear in the same order. Corresponding parts can be used to find the measures of angles and sides in a figure that is congruent to a figure with known measures.

Similarity

If two figures have the same shape but not the same size they are called similar figures. For example, the triangles below are similar, so angles A, B, and C have the same measurements as angles D, E, and F, respectively. However, segments AB, BC, and CA do not have the same measurements as segments DE, EF, and FD, but the measures of the sides are proportional.

For example, $\dfrac{\overline{AB}}{\overline{DE}} = \dfrac{\overline{BC}}{\overline{EF}} = \dfrac{\overline{CA}}{\overline{FD}}$.

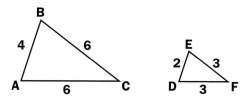

Solid figures are considered to be similar if they have the same shape and their corresponding linear measures are proportional. As with two-dimensional figures, they can be tested for similarity by comparing corresponding measures. If the compared ratios are proportional, then the figures are similar solids. Missing measures of similar solids can also be determined by using proportions.

The Pythagorean Theorem

In a right angle, the sides that are adjacent to the right angle are called legs. The side opposite the right angle is the hypotenuse.

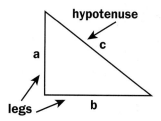

The Pythagorean Theorem describes the relationship between the lengths of the legs a and b and the hypotenuse c. It states that if a triangle is a right triangle, then the square of the length of the hypotenuse is equal to the sum of the squares of the lengths of the legs. In symbols, $c^2 = a^2 + b^2$.

Sine, Cosine, and Tangent Ratios

Trigonometry is the study of the properties of triangles. A trigonometric ratio is a ratio of the lengths of two sides of a right triangle. The most common trigonometric ratios are the sine, cosine, and tangent ratios. These ratios are abbreviated as *sin*, *cos*, and *tan*, respectively.

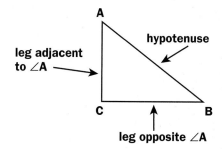

If $\angle A$ is an acute angle of a right triangle, then

$$sin \angle A = \frac{\text{measure of leg opposite } \angle A}{\text{measure of hypotenuse}},$$

$$cos \angle A = \frac{\text{measure of leg adjacent to } \angle A}{\text{measure of leg opposite } \angle A}, \text{ and}$$

$$tan \angle A = \frac{\text{measure of hypotenuse}}{\text{measure of leg adjacent to } \angle A}.$$

▶ Specify locations and describe spatial relationships using coordinate geometry and other representational systems

Polygons

A polygon is a simple, closed figure formed by three or more line segments. The line segments meet only at their endpoints. The points of intersection are called vertices, and the line segments are called sides. Polygons are classified by the number of sides they have. The diagonals of a polygon divide the polygon into triangles. The number of triangles formed is two less than the number of sides. To find the sum of the measures of the interior angles of any polygon, multiply the number of triangles within the polygon by 180. That is, if n equals the number of sides, then $(n - 2)$ 180 gives the sum of the measures of the polygon's interior angles.

Cartesian Coordinates

In the Cartesian coordinate system, the y-axis extends above and below the origin and the x-axis extends to the right and left of the origin, which is the point at which the x- and y-axes intersect. Numbers below and to the left of the origin are negative. A point graphed on the coordinate grid is said to have an x-coordinate and a y-coordinate.

For example, the point $(1,-2)$ has as its x-coordinate the number 1, and has as its y-coordinate the number -2. This point is graphed by locating the position on the grid that is 1 unit to the right of the origin and 2 units below the origin.

The x-axis and the y-axis separate the coordinate plane into four regions, called quadrants. The axes and points located on the axes themselves are not located in any of the quadrants. The quadrants are labeled I to IV, starting in the upper right and proceeding counterclockwise. In quadrant I, both coordinates are positive. In quadrant II, the x-coordinate is negative and the y-coordinate is positive. In quadrant III, both coordinates are negative. In quadrant IV, the x-coordinate is positive and the y-coordinate is negative. A coordinate graph can be used to show algebraic relationships among numbers.

▶ Apply transformations and use symmetry to analyze mathematical situations

Similar Triangles and Indirect Measurement

Triangles that have the same shape but not necessarily the same dimensions are called similar triangles. Similar triangles have corresponding angles and corresponding sides. Arcs are used to show congruent angles. If two triangles are similar, then the corresponding angles have the same measure, and the corresponding sides are proportional. Therefore, to determine the measures of the sides of similar triangles when some measures are known, proportions can be used.

Transformations

A transformation is a movement of a geometric figure. There are several types of transformations. In a translation, also called a slide, a figure is slid from one position to another without turning it. Every point of the original figure is moved the same distance and in the same direction. In a reflection, also called a flip, a figure is flipped over a line to form a mirror image. Every point of the original figure has a corresponding point on the other side of the line of symmetry. In a rotation, also called a turn, a figure is turned around a fixed point. A figure may be rotated 90° clockwise, 90° counterclockwise, or 180°. A dilation transforms each line to a parallel line whose length is a fixed multiple of the length of the original line to create a similar figure that will be either larger or smaller.

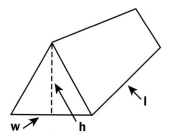

► *Use visualizations, spatial reasoning, and geometric modeling to solve problems*

Two-Dimensional Representations of Three-Dimensional Objects

Three-dimensional objects can be represented in a two-dimensional drawing in order to more easily determine properties such as surface area and volume. When you look at the rectangular prism below, you can see the orientation of its three dimensions, length, width, and height. Using the drawing and the formulas for surface area and volume, you can easily calculate these properties.

Another way to represent a three-dimensional object in a two-dimensional plane is by using a net, which is the unfolded representation. Imagine cutting the vertices of a box until it is flat then drawing an outline of it. That's a net. Most objects have more than one net, but any one can be measured to determine surface area. Below is a cube and one of its nets.

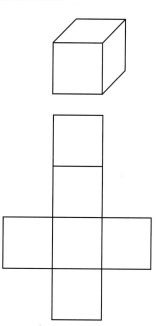

Measurement

▶ Understand measurable attributes of objects and the units, systems, and processes of measurement

Customary System

The customary system is the system of weights and measures used in the United States. The main units of weight are ounces, pounds (1 equal to 16 ounces), and tons (1 equal to 2,000 pounds). Length is typically measured in inches, feet (1 equal to 12 inches), yards (1 equal to 3 feet), and miles (1 equal to 5,280 feet), while area is measured in square feet and acres (1 equal to 43,560 square feet). Liquid is measured in cups, pints (1 equal to 2 cups), quarts (1 equal to 2 pints), and gallons (1 equal to 4 quarts). Finally, temperature is measured in degrees Fahrenheit.

Metric System

The metric system is a decimal system of weights and measurements in which the prefixes of the words for the units of measure indicate the relationships between the different measurements. In this system, the main units of weight, or mass, are grams and kilograms. Length is measured in millimeters, centimeters, meters, and kilometers, and the units of area are square millimeters, centimeters, meters, and kilometers. Liquid is typically measured in milliliters and liters, while temperature is in degrees Celsius.

Selecting Units of Measure

When measuring something, it is important to select the appropriate type and size of unit. For example, in the United States it would be appropriate when describing someone's height to use feet and inches. These units of height or length are good to use because they are in the customary system, and they are of appropriate size. In the customary system, use inches, feet, and miles for lengths and perimeters; square inches, feet, and miles for area and surface area; and cups, pints, quarts, gallons or cubic inches and feet (and less commonly miles) for volume. In the metric system use millimeters, centimeters, meters, and kilometers for lengths and perimeters; square units millimeters, centimeters, meters, and kilometers for area and surface area; and milliliters and liters for volume. Always use degrees to measure angles.

▶ Apply appropriate techniques, tools, and formulas to determine measurements

Precision and Significant Digits

The precision of measurement is the exactness to which a measurement is made. Precision depends on the smallest unit of measure being used, or the precision unit. One way to record a measure is to estimate to the nearest precision unit. A more precise method is to include all of the digits that are actually measured, plus one estimated digit. The digits recorded, called significant digits, indicate the precision of the measurement. There are special rules for determining significant digits. If a number contains a decimal point, the number of significant digits is found by counting from left to right, starting with the first nonzero digit. If the number does not contain a decimal point, the number of significant digits is found by counting the digits from left to right, starting with the first digit and ending with the last nonzero digit.

Surface Area

The amount of material needed to cover the surface of a figure is called the surface area. It can be calculated by finding the area of each face and adding them together. To find the surface area of a rectangular prism, for example, the formula $S = 2lw + 2lh + 2wh$ applies. A cylinder, on the other hand, may be unrolled to reveal two circles and a rectangle. Its surface area can be determined by finding the area of the two circles, $2\pi r^2$, and adding it to the area of the rectangle, $2\pi rh$ (the length of the rectangle is the circumference of one of the circles), or $S = 2\pi r^2 + 2\pi rh$. The surface area of a pyramid is measured in a slightly different way because the sides of a pyramid are triangles that intersect at the vertex. These sides are called lateral faces and the height of each is called the slant height. The sum of their areas is the lateral area of a pyramid. The surface area of a square pyramid is the lateral area $\frac{1}{2}bh$ (area of a lateral face) times 4 (number of lateral faces), plus the area of the base. The surface area of a cone is the area of its circular base (πr^2) plus its lateral area (πrl, where l is the slant height).

Volume

Volume is the measure of space occupied by a solid region. To find the volume of a prism, the area of the base is multiplied by the measure of the height, $V = bh$. A solid containing several prisms can be broken down into its component prisms.

Then the volume of each component can be found and the volumes added. The volume of a cylinder can be determined by finding the area of its circular base, πr^2, and then multiplying by the height of the cylinder. A pyramid has one-third the volume of a prism with the same base and height. To find the volume of a pyramid, multiply the area of the base by the pyramid's height, and then divide by 3. Simply stated, the formula for the volume of a pyramid is $V = \frac{1}{3}bh$. A cone is a three-dimensional figure with one circular base and a curved surface connecting the base and the vertex. The volume of a cone is one-third the volume of a cylinder with the same base area and height. Like a pyramid, the formula for the volume of a cone is $V = \frac{1}{3}bh$. More specifically, the formula is $V = \frac{1}{3}\pi r^2 h$.

Upper and Lower Bounds

Upper and lower bounds have to do with the accuracy of a measurement. When a measurement is given, the degree of accuracy is also stated to tell you what the upper and lower bounds of the measurement are. The upper bound is the largest possible value that a measurement could have had before being rounded down, and the lower bound is the lowest possible value it could have had before being rounded up.

Data Analysis and Probability

► *Formulate questions that can be addressed with data and collect, organize, and display relevant data to answer them*

Histograms

A histogram displays numerical data that have been organized into equal intervals using bars that have the same width and no space between them. While a histogram does not give exact data points, its shape shows the distribution of the data. Histograms also can be used to compare data.

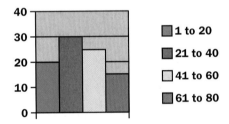

- 1 to 20
- 21 to 40
- 41 to 60
- 61 to 80

Box-and-Whisker Plot

A box-and-whisker plot displays the measures of central tendency and variation. A box is drawn around the quartile values, and whiskers extend from each quartile to the extreme data points. To make a box plot for a set of data, draw a number line that covers the range of data. Find the median, the extremes, and the upper and lower quartiles. Mark these points on the number line with bullets, then draw a box and the whiskers. The length of a whisker or box shows whether the values of the data in that part are concentrated or spread out.

Scatter Plots

A scatter plot is a graph that shows the relationship between two sets of data. In a scatter plot, two sets of data are graphed as ordered pairs on a coordinate system. Two sets of data can have a positive correlation (as *x* increases, *y* increases), a negative correlation (as *x* increases, *y* decreases), or no correlation (no obvious pattern is shown). Scatter plots can be used to spot trends, draw conclusions, and make predictions about data.

Perfect Positive Correlation

Randomization

The idea of randomization is a very important principle of statistics and the design of experiments. Data must be selected randomly to prevent bias from influencing the results. For example, you want to know the average income of people in your town but you can only use a sample of 100 individuals to make determinations about everyone. If you select 100 individuals who are all doctors, you will have a biased sample. However, if you chose a random sample of 100 people out of the phone book, you are much more likely to accurately represent average income in the town.

Statistics and Parameters

Statistics is a science that involves collecting, analyzing, and presenting data. The data can be collected in various ways—

through a census or by making physical measurements, for example. The data can then be analyzed by creating summary statistics, which have to do with the distribution of the data sample, including the mean, range, and standard error. They can also be illustrated in tables and graphs, like box-plots, scatter plots, and histograms. The presentation of the data typically involves describing the strength or validity of the data and what they show. For example, an analysis of ancestry of people in a city might tell you something about immigration patterns, unless the data set is very small or biased in some way, in which case it is not likely to be very accurate or useful.

Categorical and Measurement Data

When analyzing data, it is important to understand if the data is qualitative or quantitative. Categorical data is qualitative and measurement, or numerical, data is quantitative. Categorical data describes a quality of something and can be placed into different categories. For example, if you are analyzing the number of students in different grades in a school, each grade is a category. On the other hand, measurement data is continuous, like height, weight, or any other measurable variable. Measurement data can be converted into categorical data if you decide to group the data. Using height as an example, you can group the continuous data set into categories like under 5 feet, 5 feet to 5 feet 5 inches, over 5 feet five inches to 6 feet, and so on.

Univariate and Bivariate Data

In data analysis, a researcher can analyze one variable at a time or look at how multiple variables behave together. Univariate data involves only one variable—height in humans, for example.

You can measure the height in a population of people then plot the results in a histogram to look at how height is distributed in humans. To summarize univariate data, you can use statistics like the mean, mode, median, range, and standard deviation, which is a measure of variation. When looking at more than one variable at once, you use multivariate data. Bivariate data involves two variables. For example, you can look at height and age in humans together by gathering information on both variables from individuals in a population. You can then plot both variables in a scatter plot, look at how the variables behave in relation to each other, and create an equation that represents the relationship, also called a regression. These equations could help answer questions such as, for example, does height increase with age in humans?

▶ Select and use appropriate statistical methods to analyze data

Measures of Central Tendency

When you have a list of numerical data, it is often helpful to use one or more numbers to represent the whole set. These numbers are called measures of central tendency. Three measures of central tendency are mean, median, and mode. The mean is the sum of the data divided by the number of items in the data set. The median is the middle number of the ordered data (or the mean of the two middle numbers). The mode is the number or numbers that occur most often. These measures of central tendency allow data to be analyzed and better understood.

Measures of Spread

In statistics, measures of spread or variation are used to describe how data are distributed. The range of a set of data is the difference between the greatest and the least values of the data set. The quartiles are the values that divide the data into four equal parts. The median of data separates the set in half. Similarly, the median of the lower half of a set of data is the lower quartile. The median of the upper half of a set of data is the upper quartile. The interquartile range is the difference between the upper quartile and the lower quartile.

Line of Best Fit

When real-life data are collected, the points graphed usually do not form a straight line, but they may approximate a linear relationship. A line of best fit is a line that lies very close to most of the data points. It can be used to predict data. You also can use the equation of the best-fit line to make predictions.

Stem and Leaf Plots

In a stem and leaf plot, numerical data are listed in ascending or descending order. The greatest place value of the data is used for the stems. The next greatest place value forms the leaves. For example, if the least number in a set of data is 8 and the greatest number is 95, draw a vertical line and write the stems from 0 to 9 to the left of the line. Write the leaves from to the right of the line, with the corresponding stem. Next, rearrange the leaves so they are ordered from least to greatest. Then include a key or explanation, such as 1|3 = 13. Notice that the stem-and-leaf plot below is like a histogram turned on its side.

```
0|8
1|3 6
2|5 6 9
3|0 2 7 8
4|0 1 4 7 9
5|1 4 5 8
6|1 3 7
7|5 8
8|2 6
9|5
```
Key: **1|3 = 13**

▶ Develop and evaluate inferences and predictions that are based on data

Sampling Distribution

The sampling distribution of a population is the distribution that would result if you could take an infinite number of samples from the population, average each, and then average the averages. The more normal the distribution of the population, that is, how closely the distribution follows a bell curve, the more likely the sampling distribution will also follow a normal distribution. Furthermore, the larger the sample, the more likely it will accurately represent the entire population. For instance, you are more likely to gain more representative results from a population of 1,000 with a sample of 100 than with a sample of 2.

Validity

In statistics, validity refers to acquiring results that accurately reflect that which is being measured. In other words, it is important when performing statistical analyses, to ensure that the data are valid in that the sample being analyzed represents the population to the best extent possible. Randomization of data and using appropriate sample sizes are two important aspects of making valid inferences about a population.

▶ Understand and apply basic concepts of probability

Complementary, Mutually Exclusive Events

To understand probability theory, it is important to know if two events are mutually exclusive, or complementary: the occurrence of one event automatically implies the non-occurrence of the other. That is, two complementary events cannot both occur. If you roll a pair of dice, the event of rolling 6 and rolling doubles have an outcome in common (3, 3), so they are not mutually exclusive. If you roll (3, 3), you also roll doubles. However, the events of rolling a 9 and rolling doubles are mutually exclusive because they have no outcomes in common. If you roll a 9, you will not also roll doubles.

Independent and Dependent Events

Determining the probability of a series of events requires that you know whether the events are independent or dependent. An independent event has no influence on the occurrence of subsequent events, whereas, a dependent event does influence subsequent events. The chances that a woman's first child will be a girl are $\frac{1}{2}$, and the chances that her second child will be a girl are also $\frac{1}{2}$ because the two events are independent of each other. However, if there are 7 red marbles in a bag of 15 marbles, the chances that the first marble you pick will be red are $\frac{7}{15}$ and if you indeed pick a red marble and remove it, you have reduced the chances of picking another red marble to $\frac{6}{14}$.

Sample Space

The sample space is the group of all possible outcomes for an event. For example, if you are tossing a single six-sided die, the sample space is {1, 2, 3, 4, 5, 6}. Similarly, you can determine the sample space for the possible outcomes of two events. If you are going to toss a coin twice, the sample space is {(heads, heads), (heads, tails), (tails, heads), (tails, tails)}.

Computing the Probability of a Compound Event

If two events are independent, the outcome of one event does not influence the outcome of the second. For example, if a bag contains 2 blue and 3 red marbles, then the probability of selecting a blue marble, replacing it, and then selecting a red marble is $P(A) \times P(B) = \frac{2}{5} \times \frac{3}{5}$ or $\frac{6}{25}$.

If two events are dependent, the outcome of one event affects the outcome of the second. For example, if a bag contains 2 blue and 3 red marbles, then the probability of selecting a blue and then a red marble without replacing the first marble is $P(A) \times P(B$ following $A) = \frac{2}{5} \times \frac{3}{4}$ or $\frac{3}{10}$. Two events that cannot happen at the same time are mutually exclusive. For example, when you roll two number cubes, you cannot roll a sum that is both 5 and even. So, $P(A$ or $B) = \frac{4}{36} + \frac{18}{36}$ or $\frac{11}{18}$.

The Constitution of the United States

PREAMBLE

We the People of the United States, in Order to form a more perfect Union, establish Justice, insure domestic Tranquility, provide for the common defence, promote the general Welfare, and secure the Blessings of Liberty to ourselves and our Posterity, do ordain and establish this Constitution for the United States of America.

* Text of the Constitution printed in gray and crossed out indicates that it has been amended and is no longer in effect.

ARTICLE I

Section 1 ■ All legislative Powers herein granted shall be vested in a Congress of the United States, which shall consist of a Senate and House of Representatives.

Section 2 ■ The House of Representatives shall be composed of Members chosen every second Year by the People of the several States, and the Electors in each State shall have the Qualifications requisite for Electors of the most numerous Branch of the State Legislature.

No Person shall be a Representative who shall not have attained to the Age of twenty five Years, and been seven Years a Citizen of the United States, and who shall not, when elected, be an Inhabitant of that State in which he shall be chosen.

*Representatives and direct Taxes shall be apportioned among the several States which may be included within this Union, according to their respective Numbers, which shall be determined by adding to the whole Number of free Persons, including those bound to Service for a Term of Years, and excluding Indians not taxed, three fifths of all other Persons. The actual Enumeration shall be made within three Years after the first Meeting of the Congress of the United States, and within every subsequent Term of ten Years, in such Manner as they shall by Law direct. The Number of Representatives shall not exceed one for every thirty Thou-sand, but each State shall have at Least one Representative; and until such enumeration shall be made, the State of New Hampshire shall be entitled to chuse three, Massa-chusetts eight, Rhode-Island and Provi-dence Plantations one, Connecticut five, New-York six, New Jersey four, Pennsylvania eight, Delaware one, Maryland six, Virginia ten, North Carolina five, South Carolina five, and Georgia three.

When vacancies happen in the Representation from any State, the Executive Authority thereof shall issue Writs of Election to fill such Vacancies.

The House of Representatives shall chuse their Speaker and other Officers; and shall have the sole Power of Impeachment.

Section 3 ■ The Senate of the United States shall be composed of two Senators from each State, chosen by the Legislature thereof, for six Years; and each Senator shall have one Vote.

Immediately after they shall be assembled in Consequence of the first Election, they shall be divided as equally as may be into three Classes. The Seats of the Senators of the first Class shall be vacated at the Expiration of the second Year, of the second Class at the Expiration of the fourth Year, and of the third Class at the Expiration of the sixth Year, so that one third may be chosen every second Year;

and if Vacancies happen by Resignation, or otherwise, during the Recess of the Legislature of any State, the Executive thereof may make temporary Appointments until the next Meeting of the Legislature, which shall then fill such Vacancies.

No Person shall be a Senator who shall not have attained to the Age of thirty Years, and been nine Years a Citizen of the United States, and who shall not, when elected, be an Inhabitant of that State for which he shall be chosen.

The Vice President of the United States shall be President of the Senate, but shall have no Vote, unless they be equally divided.

The Senate shall chuse their other Officers, and also a President pro tempore, in the Absence of the Vice President, or when he shall exercise the Office of President of the United States.

The Senate shall have the sole Power to try all Impeachments. When sitting for that Purpose, they shall be on Oath or Affirmation. When the President of the United

States is tried, the Chief Justice shall preside: And no Person shall be convicted without the Concurrence of two thirds of the Members present.

Judgment in Cases of Impeachment shall not extend further than to removal from Office, and disqualification to hold and enjoy any Office of honor, Trust or Profit under the United States: but the Party convicted shall nevertheless be liable and subject to Indictment, Trial, Judgment and Punishment, according to Law.

Section 4 ■ The Times, Places and Manner of holding Elections for Senators and Representatives, shall be prescribed in each State by the Legislature thereof; but the Congress may at any time by Law make or alter such Regulations, except as to the Places of chusing Senators.

The Congress shall assemble at least once in every Year, and such Meeting shall be on the first Monday in December, unless they shall by Law appoint a different Day.

Section 5 ■ Each House shall be the Judge of the Elections, Returns and Qualifications of its own Members, and a Majority of each shall constitute a Quorum to do Business; but a smaller Number may adjourn from day to day, and may be authorized to compel the Attendance of absent Members, in such Manner, and under such Penalties as each House may provide.

Each House may determine the Rules of its Proceedings, punish its Members for disorderly Behaviour, and, with the Concurrence of two thirds, expel a Member.

Each House shall keep a Journal of its Proceedings, and from time to time publish the same, excepting such Parts as may in their Judgment require Secrecy; and the Yeas and Nays of the Members of either House on any question shall, at the Desire of one fifth of those Present, be entered on the Journal.

Neither House, during the Session of Congress, shall, without the Consent of the other, adjourn for more than three days, nor to any other Place than that in which the two Houses shall be sitting.

Section 6 ■ The Senators and Representatives shall receive a Compensation for their Services, to be ascertained by Law, and paid out of the Treasury of the United States. They shall in all Cases, except Treason, Felony and Breach of the Peace, be privileged from Arrest during their Attendance at the Session of their respective Houses, and in going to and returning from the same; and for any Speech or Debate in either House, they shall not be questioned in any other Place.

No Senator or Representative shall, during the Time for which he was elected, be appointed to any civil Office under the Authority of the United States, which shall have been created, or the Emoluments whereof shall have been encreased during such time; and no Person holding any Office under the United States, shall be a Member of either House during his Continuance in Office.

Section 7 ■ All Bills for raising Revenue shall originate in the House of Representatives; but the Senate may propose or concur with Amendments as on other Bills.

Every Bill which shall have passed the House of Representatives and the Senate, shall, before it become a Law, be presented to the President of the United States; If he approve he shall sign it, but if not he shall return it, with his Objections to that House in which it shall have originated, who shall enter the Objections at large on their Journal, and proceed to reconsider it.

If after such Reconsideration two thirds of that House shall agree to pass the Bill, it shall be sent, together with the Objections, to the other House, by which it shall likewise be reconsidered, and if approved by two thirds of that House, it shall become a Law. But in all such Cases the Votes of both Houses shall be determined by yeas and Nays, and the Names of the Persons voting for and against the Bill shall be entered on the Journal of each House respectively. If any Bill shall not be returned by the President within ten Days (Sundays excepted) after it shall have been presented to him, the Same shall be a Law, in like Manner as if he had signed it, unless the Congress by their Adjournment prevent its Return, in which Case it shall not be a Law.

Every Order, Resolution, or Vote to which the Concurrence of the Senate and House of Representatives may be necessary (except on a question of Adjournment) shall be presented to the President of the United States; and before the Same shall take Effect, shall be approved by him, or being disapproved by him, shall be repassed by two thirds of the Senate and House of Representatives, according to the Rules and Limitations prescribed in the Case of a Bill.

Section 8 ■ The Congress shall have Power To lay and collect Taxes, Duties, Imposts and Excises, to pay the Debts and provide for the common Defence and general Welfare of the United States; but all Duties, Imposts and Excises shall be uniform throughout the United States;

To borrow Money on the credit of the United States;

To regulate Commerce with foreign Nations, and among the several States, and with the Indian Tribes;

To establish an uniform Rule of Naturalization, and uniform Laws on the subject of Bankruptcies throughout the United States;

To coin Money, regulate the Value thereof, and of foreign Coin, and fix the Standard of Weights and Measures;

To provide for the Punishment of counterfeiting the Securities and current Coin of the United States;

To establish Post Offices and post Roads;

To promote the Progress of Science and useful Arts, by securing for limited Times to Authors and Inventors the exclusive Right to their respective Writings and Discoveries;

To constitute Tribunals inferior to the supreme Court;

To define and punish Piracies and Felonies committed on the high Seas, and Offences against the Law of Nations;

To declare War, grant Letters of Marque and Reprisal, and make Rules concerning Captures on Land and Water;

To raise and support Armies, but no Appropriation of Money to that Use shall be for a longer Term than two Years;

To provide and maintain a Navy;

To make Rules for the Government and Regulation of the land and naval Forces;

To provide for calling forth the Militia to execute the Laws of the Union, suppress Insurrections and repel Invasions;

To provide for organizing, arming, and disciplining, the Militia, and for governing such Part of them as may be employed in the Service of the United States, reserving to the States respectively, the Appointment of the Officers, and the Authority of training the Militia according to the discipline prescribed by Congress;

To exercise exclusive Legislation in all Cases whatsoever, over such District (not exceeding ten Miles square) as may, by Cession of particular States, and the Acceptance of Congress, become the Seat of the Government of the United States, and to exercise like Authority over all Places purchased by the Consent of the Legislature of the State in which the Same shall be, for the Erection of Forts, Magazines, Arsenals, dock-Yards, and other needful Buildings; And

To make all Laws which shall be necessary and proper for carrying into Execution the foregoing Powers, and all other Powers vested by this Constitution in the Government of the United States, or in any Department or Officer thereof.

Section 9 ∎ The Migration or Importation of such Persons as any of the States now existing shall think proper to admit, shall not be prohibited by the Congress prior to the Year one thousand eight hundred and eight, but a Tax or duty may be imposed on such Importation, not exceeding ten dollars for each Person.

The Privilege of the Writ of Habeas Corpus shall not be suspended, unless when in Cases of Rebellion or Invasion the public Safety may require it.

No Bill of Attainder or ex post facto Law shall be passed.

No Capitation, or other direct, Tax shall be laid, unless in Proportion to the Census or Enumeration herein before directed to be taken.

No Tax or Duty shall be laid on Articles exported from any State.

No Preference shall be given by any Regulation of Commerce or Revenue to the Ports of one State over those of another: nor shall Vessels bound to, or from, one State, be obliged to enter, clear, or pay Duties in another.

No Money shall be drawn from the Treasury, but in Consequence of Appropriations made by Law; and a regular Statement and Account of the Receipts and Expenditures of all public Money shall be published from time to time.

No Title of Nobility shall be granted by the United States: And no Person holding any Office of Profit or Trust under them, shall, without the Consent of the Congress, accept of any present, Emolument, Office, or Title, of any kind whatever, from any King, Prince, or foreign State.

Section 10 ∎ No State shall enter into any Treaty, Alliance, or Confederation; grant Letters of Marque and Reprisal; coin Money; emit Bills of Credit; make any Thing but gold and silver Coin a Tender in Payment of Debts; pass any Bill of Attainder, ex post facto Law, or Law impairing the Obligation of Contracts, or grant any Title of Nobility.

No State shall, without the Consent of the Congress, lay any Imposts or Duties on Imports or Exports, except what may be absolutely necessary for executing it's inspection Laws: and the net Produce of all Duties and Imposts, laid by any State on Imports or Exports, shall be for the Use of the Treasury of the United States; and all such Laws shall be subject to the Revision and Controul of the Congress.

No State shall, without the Consent of Congress, lay any Duty of Tonnage, keep Troops, or Ships of War in time of Peace, enter into any Agreement or Compact with another State, or with a foreign Power, or engage in War, unless actually invaded, or in such imminent Danger as will not admit of delay.

Article II

Section 1 ∎ The executive Power shall be vested in a President of the United States of America. He shall hold his Office during the Term of four Years, and, together with the Vice President, chosen for the same Term, be elected, as follows

Each State shall appoint, in such Manner as the Legislature thereof may direct, a Number of Electors, equal to the whole Number of Senators and Representatives to which the State may be entitled in the Congress: but no Senator or Representative, or Person holding an Office of Trust or Profit under the United States, shall be appointed an Elector.

The Electors shall meet in their respective States, and vote by Ballot for two Persons, of whom one at least shall not be an Inhabitant of the same State with themselves. And they shall make a List of all the Persons voted for, and of the Number of Votes for each; which List they shall sign and certify, and transmit sealed to the Seat of the Government of the United States, directed to the President of the Senate. The President of the Senate shall, in the Presence of the Senate and House of Representatives, open all the Certificates, and the Votes shall then be counted. The Person having the greatest Number of Votes shall be the President, if such Number be a Majority of the whole Number of Electors appointed; and if there be more than one who have such Majority, and have an equal Number of Votes then the House of Representatives shall immediately chuse by Ballot one of them for Presi-dent; and if no Person have a Majority, then from the five highest on the List the said House shall in like Manner chuse the President.But in chusing the President, the Votes shall be taken by States, the Representation from each State having one Vote; A quorum for this Purpose shall consist of a Member or Members from two thirds of the States, and a Majority of all the States shall be necessary to a Choice.In every Case, after the Choice of the President, the Person having the greatest Number of Votes of the Electors shall be the Vice Pres-ident. But if there should remain two or more who have equal Votes, the Senate shall chuse from them by Ballot the Vice President.

The Congress may determine the Time of chusing the Electors, and the Day on which they shall give their Votes; which Day shall be the same throughout the United States.

No Person except a natural born Citizen, or a Citizen of the United States, at the time of the Adoption of this Constitution, shall be eligible to the Office of President; neither shall any Person be eligible to that Office who shall not have attained to the Age of thirty five Years, and been fourteen Years a Resident within the United States.

In Case of the Removal of the President from Office, or of his Death, Resignation, or Inability to discharge the Powers and Duties of the saidOffice, the Same shall devolve on the Vice President, and the Congress may by Law provide for the Case of Removal, Death, Resignation or Inability, both of the President and Vice President, declaring what Officer shall then act as President, and such Officer shall act accordingly, until the Disability be removed, or a President shall be elected.

The President shall, at stated Times, receive for his Services, a Compensation, which shall neither be encreased nor diminished during the Period for which he shall have been elected, and he shall not receive within that Period any other Emolument from the United States, or any of them.

Before he enter on the Execution of his Office, he shall take the following Oath or Affirmation: "I do solemnly swear (or affirm) that I will faithfully execute the Office of President of the United States, and will to the best of my Ability, preserve, protect and defend the Constitution of the United States."

Section 2 ▪ The President shall be Commander in Chief of the Army and Navy of the United States, and of the Militia of the several States, when called into the actual Service of the United States; he may require the Opinion, in writing, of the principal Officer in each of the executive Departments, upon any Subject relating to the Duties of their respective Offices, and he shall have Power to grant Reprieves and Pardons for Offences against the United States, except in Cases of Impeachment.

He shall have Power, by and with the Advice and Consent of the Senate, to make Treaties, provided two thirds of the Senators present concur; and he shall nominate, and by and with the Advice and Consent of the Senate, shall appoint Ambassadors, other public Ministers and Consuls, Judges of the supreme Court, and all other Officers of the United States, whose Appointments are not herein otherwise provided for, and which shall be established by Law: but the Congress may by Law vest the Appointment of such inferior Officers, as they think proper, in the President alone, in the Courts of Law, or in the Heads of Departments. The President shall have Power to fill up all Vacancies that may happen during the Recess of the Senate, by granting Commissions which shall expire at the End of their next Session.

Section 3 ■ He shall from time to time give to the Congress Information of the State of the Union, and recommend to their Consideration such Measures as he shall judge necessary and expedient; he may, on extraordinary Occasions, convene both Houses, or either of them, and in Case of Disagreement between them, with Respect to the Time of Adjournment, he may adjourn them to such Time as he shall think proper; he shall receive Ambassadors and other public Ministers; he shall take Care that the Laws be faithfully executed, and shall Commission all the Officers of the United States.

Section 4 ■ The President, Vice President and all civil Officers of the United States, shall be removed from Office on Impeachment for, and Conviction of, Treason, Bribery, or other high Crimes and Misdemeanors.

ARTICLE III

Section 1 ■ The judicial Power of the United States, shall be vested in one supreme Court, and in such inferior Courts as the Congress may from time to time ordain and establish. The Judges, both of the supreme and inferior Courts, shall hold their Offices during good Behaviour, and shall, at stated Times, receive for their Services, a Compensation, which shall not be diminished during their Continuance in Office.

Section 2 ■ The judicial Power shall extend to all Cases, in Law and Equity, arising under this Constitution, the Laws of the United States, and Treaties made, or which shall be made, under their Authority; to all Cases affecting Ambassadors, other public Ministers and Consuls; to all Cases of admiralty and maritime Jurisdiction;—to Controversies to which the United States shall be a Party;—to Controversies between two or more States; between a State and Citizens of another State;—between Citizens of different States, between Citizens of the same State claiming Lands under Grants of different States, and between a State, or the Citizens thereof, and foreign States, Citizens or Subjects.

In all Cases affecting Ambassadors, other public Ministers and Consuls, and those in which a State shall be Party, the supreme Court shall have original Jurisdiction. In all the other Cases before mentioned, the supreme Court shall have appellate Jurisdiction, both as to Law and Fact, with such Exceptions, and under such Regulations as the Congress shall make.

The Trial of all Crimes, except in Cases of Impeachment, shall be by Jury; and such Trial shall be held in the State where the said Crimes shall have been committed; but when not committed within any State, the Trial shall be at such Place or Places as the Congress may by Law have directed.

Section 3 ■ Treason against the United States, shall consist only in levying War against them, or in adhering to their Enemies, giving them Aid and Comfort. No Person shall be convicted of Treason unless on the Testimony of two Witnesses to the same overt Act, or on Confession in open Court.

The Congress shall have Power to declare the Punishment of Treason, but no Attainder of Treason shall work Corruption of

Blood, or Forfeiture except during the Life of the Person attainted.

ARTICLE IV

Section 1 ■ Full Faith and Credit shall be given in each State to the public Acts, Records, and judicial Proceedings of every other State. And the Congress may by general Laws prescribe the Manner in which such Acts, Records and Proceedings shall be proved, and the Effect thereof.

Section 2 ■ The Citizens of each State shall be entitled to all Privileges and Immunities of Citizens in the several States.

A Person charged in any State with Treason, Felony, or other Crime, who shall flee from Justice, and be found in another State, shall on Demand of the executive Authority of the State from which he fled, be delivered up, to be removed to the State having Jurisdiction of the Crime.

~~No Person held to Service or Labour in one State, under the Laws thereof, escaping into another, shall, in Consequence of any Law or Regulation therein, be discharged from such Service or Labour, but shall be delivered up on Claim of the Party to whom such Service or Labour may be due.~~

Section 3 ■ New States may be admitted by the Congress into this Union; but no new State shall be formed or erected within the Jurisdiction of any other State; nor any State be formed by the Junction of two or more States, or Parts of States, without the Consent of the Legislatures of the States concerned as well as of the Congress.

Clause 2: The Congress shall have Power to dispose of and make all needful Rules and Regulations respecting the Territory or other Property belonging to the United States; and nothing in this Constitution shall be so construed as to Prejudice any Claims of the United States, or of any particular State.

Section 4 ■ The United States shall guarantee to every State in this Union a Republican Form of Government, and shall protect each of them against Invasion; and on Application of the Legislature, or of the Executive (when the Legislature cannot be convened) against domestic Violence.

ARTICLE V

The Congress, whenever two thirds of both Houses shall deem it necessary, shall propose Amendments to this Constitution, or, on the Application of the Legislatures of two thirds of the several States, shall call a Convention for proposing Amendments, which, in either Case, shall be valid to all Intents and Purposes, as Part of this Constitution, when ratified by the Legislatures of three fourths of the several States, or by Conventions in three fourths thereof, as the one or the other Mode of Ratification may be proposed by the Congress; Provided that no Amendment which may be made prior to the Year One thousand eight hundred and eight shall in any Manner affect the first and fourth Clauses in the Ninth Section of the first Article; and that no State, without its Consent, shall be deprived of its equal Suffrage in the Senate.

ARTICLE VI

All Debts contracted and Engagements entered into, before the Adoption of this Constitution, shall be as valid against the United States under this Constitution, as under the Confederation.

This Constitution, and the Laws of the United States which shall be made in Pursuance thereof; and all Treaties made, or which shall be made, under the Authority of the United States, shall be the supreme Law of the Land; and the Judges in every State shall be bound thereby, any Thing in the Constitution or Laws of any State to the Contrary notwithstanding.

The Senators and Representatives before mentioned, and the Members of the several State Legislatures, and all executive and judicial Officers, both of the United States and of the several States, shall be bound by Oath or Affirmation, to support this Constitution; but no religious Test shall ever be required as a Qualification to any Office or public Trust under the United States.

ARTICLE VII

The Ratification of the Conventions of nine States, shall be sufficient for the Establishment of this Constitution between the States so ratifying the Same.

Done in Convention by the Unanimous Consent of the States present the Seventeenth Day of September in the Year of our Lord one thousand seven hundred and Eighty seven and of the Independence of the United States of America the Twelfth In witness whereof We have hereunto subscribed our Names,

> G. O. Washington—Presidt.
> and deputy from Virginia

> [Signed also by
> the deputies of twelve States.]

AMENDMENT I

Congress shall make no law respecting an establishment of religion, or prohibiting the free exercise thereof; or abridging the freedom of speech, or of the press; or the right of the people peaceably to assemble, and to petition the Government for a redress of grievances.

AMENDMENT II

A well regulated Militia, being necessary to the security of a free State, the right of the people to keep and bear Arms, shall not be infringed.

AMENDMENT III

No Soldier shall, in time of peace be quartered in any house, without the consent of the Owner, nor in time of war, but in a manner to be prescribed by law.

AMENDMENT IV

The right of the people to be secure in their persons, houses, papers, and effects, against unreasonable searches and seizures, shall not be violated, and no Warrants shall issue, but upon probable cause, supported by Oath or affirmation, and particularly describing the place to be searched, and the persons or things to be seized.

AMENDMENT V

No person shall be held to answer for a capital, or otherwise infamous crime, unless on a presentment or indictment of a Grand Jury, except in cases arising in the land or naval forces, or in the Militia, when in actual service in time of War or public danger; nor shall any person be subject for the same offence to be twice put in jeopardy of life or limb; nor shall be compelled in any criminal case to be a witness against himself, nor be deprived of life, liberty, or property, without due process of law; nor shall private property be taken for public use, without just compensation.

AMENDMENT VI

In all criminal prosecutions, the accused shall enjoy the right to a speedy and public trial, by an impartial jury of the State and district wherein the crime shall have been committed, which district shall have been previously ascertained by law, and to be informed of the nature and cause of the accusation; to be confronted with the witnesses against him; to have compulsory process for obtaining witnesses in his favor, and to have the Assistance of Counsel for his defence.

AMENDMENT VII

In suits at common law, where the value in controversy shall exceed twenty dollars, the right of trial by jury shall be preserved, and no fact tried by a jury, shall be otherwise reexamined in any Court of the United States, than according to the rules of the common law.

AMENDMENT VIII

Excessive bail shall not be required, nor excessive fines imposed, nor cruel and unusual punishments inflicted.

AMENDMENT IX

The enumeration in the Constitution, of certain rights, shall not be construed to deny or disparage others retained by the people.

AMENDMENT X

The powers not delegated to the United States by the Constitution, nor prohibited by it to the States, are reserved to the States respectively, or to the people.

AMENDMENT XI

The Judicial power of the United States shall not be construed to extend to any suit in law or equity, commenced or prosecuted against one of the United States by Citizens of another State, or by Citizens or Subjects of any Foreign State.

AMENDMENT XII

The Electors shall meet in their respective states and vote by ballot for President and Vice-President, one of whom, at least, shall not be an inhabitant of the same state with themselves; they shall name in their ballots the person voted for as President, and in distinct ballots the person voted for as Vice-President, and they shall make distinct lists of all persons voted for as President, and of all persons voted for as Vice-President, and of the number of votes for each, which lists they shall sign and certify, and transmit sealed to the seat of the government of the United States, directed to the President of the Senate; the President of the Senate shall, in the presence of the Senate and House of Representatives, open all the certificates and the votes shall then be counted; The person having the greatest number of votes for President, shall be the President, if such number be a majority of the whole number of Electors appointed; and if no person have such majority, then from the persons having the highest numbers not exceeding three on the list of those voted for as President, the House of Representatives shall choose immediately, by ballot, the President. But in choosing the President, the votes shall be taken by states, the representation from each state having one vote; a quorum for this purpose shall consist of a member or members from two-thirds of the states, and a majority of all the states shall be necessary to a choice.

And if the House of Representatives shall not choose a President whenever the right of choice shall devolve upon them, before the fourth day of March next following, then the Vice-President shall act as President, as in case of the death or other constitutional disability of the President.

The person having the greatest number of votes as Vice-President, shall be the Vice-President, if such number be a majority of the whole number of Electors appointed, and if no person have a majority, then from the two highest numbers on the list, the Senate shall choose the Vice-President; a quorum for the purpose shall consist of two-thirds of the whole number of Senators, and a majority of the whole number shall be necessary to a choice. But no person constitutionally ineligible to the office of President shall be eligible to that of Vice-President of the United States.

AMENDMENT XIII

Section 1 ■ Neither slavery nor involuntary servitude, except as a punishment for crime whereof the party shall have been duly convicted, shall exist within the United States, or any place subject to their jurisdiction.

Section 2 ■ Congress shall have power to enforce this article by appropriate legislation.

AMENDMENT XIV

Section 1 ■ All persons born or naturalized in the United States, and subject to the jurisdiction thereof, are citizens of the United States and of the State wherein they reside. No State shall make or enforce any law which shall abridge the privileges or immunities of citizens of the United States; nor shall any State deprive any person of life, liberty, or property, without due process of law; nor deny to any person within its jurisdiction the equal protection of the laws.

Section 2 ■ Representatives shall be apportioned among the several States according to their respective numbers, counting the whole number of persons in each State, excluding Indians not taxed. But when the right to vote at any election for the choice of electors for President and Vice-President of the United States, Representatives in Congress, the Executive and Judicial officers of a State, or the members of the Legislature thereof, is denied to any of the male inhabitants of such State, being twenty-one years of age, and citizens of the United States, or in any way abridged, except for participation in rebellion, or other crime, the basis of representation therein shall be reduced in the proportion which the number of such male citizens shall bear to the whole number of male citizens twenty-one years of age in such State.

Section 3 ■ No person shall be a Senator or Representative in Congress, or elector of President and Vice-President, or hold any office, civil or military, under the United States, or under any State, who, having previously taken an oath, as a member of Congress, or as an officer of the United States, or as a member of any State legislature, or as an executive or judicial officer of any State, to support the Constitution of the United States, shall have engaged in insurrection or rebellion against the same, or given aid or comfort to the enemies thereof. But Congress may by a vote of two-thirds of each House, remove such disability.

Section 4 ■ The validity of the public debt of the United States, authorized by law, including debts incurred for payment of pensions and bounties for services in suppressing insurrection or rebellion, shall not be questioned. But neither the United States nor any State shall assume or pay any debt or obligation incurred in aid of insurrection or rebellion against the United States, or any claim for the loss or emancipation of any slave; but all such debts, obligations and claims shall be held illegal and void.

Section 5 ■ The Congress shall have the power to enforce, by appropriate legislation, the provisions of this article.

AMENDMENT XV

Section 1 ■ The right of citizens of the United States to vote shall not be denied or abridged by the United States or by any State on account of race, color, or previous condition of servitude.

Section 2 ■ The Congress shall have the power to enforce this article by appropriate legislation.

AMENDMENT XVI

The Congress shall have power to lay and collect taxes on incomes, from whatever source derived, without apportionment among the several States, and without regard to any census or enumeration.

AMENDMENT XVII

The Senate of the United States shall be composed of two Senators from each State, elected by the people thereof, for six years; and each Senator shall have one vote. The electors in each State shall have the qualifications requisite for electors of the most numerous branch of the State legislatures.

When vacancies happen in the representation of any State in the Senate, the executive authority of such State shall issue writs of election to fill such vacancies: *Provided*, That the legislature of any State may empower the executive thereof to make temporary appointments until the people fill the vacancies by election as the legislature may direct.

This amendment shall not be so construed as to affect the election or term of any Senator chosen before it becomes valid as part of the Constitution.

AMENDMENT XVIII

Section 1 ▪ After one year from the ratification of this article the manufacture, sale, or transportation of intoxicating liquors within, the importation thereof into, or the exportation thereof from the United States and all territory subject to the jurisdiction thereof for beverage purposes is hereby prohibited.

Section 2 ▪ The Congress and the several States shall have concurrent power to enforce this article by appropriate legislation.

Section 3 ▪ This article shall be inoperative unless it shall have been ratified as an amend-ment to the Constitution by the legislatures of the several States, as provided in the Constitu-tion, within seven years from the date of the submission hereof to the States by the Congress.

AMENDMENT XIX

The right of citizens of the United States to vote shall not be denied or abridged by the United States or by any State on account of sex. Congress shall have power to enforce this article by appropriate legislation.

AMENDMENT XX

Section 1 ▪ The terms of the President and the Vice President shall end at noon on the 20th day of January, and the terms of Senators and Representatives at noon on the 3d day of January, of the years in which such terms would have ended if this article had not been ratified; and the terms of their successors shall then begin.

Section 2 ▪ The Congress shall assemble at least once in every year, and such meeting shall begin at noon on the 3d day of January, unless they shall by law appoint a different day.

Section 3 ▪ If, at the time fixed for the beginning of the term of the President, the President elect shall have died, the Vice President elect shall become President. If a President shall not have been chosen before the time fixed for the beginning of his term, or if the President elect shall have failed to qualify, then the Vice President elect shall act as President until a President shall have qualified; and the Congress may by law provide for the case wherein neither a President elect nor a Vice President shall have qualified, declaring who shall then act as President, or the manner in which one who is to act shall be selected, and such person shall act accordingly until a President or Vice President shall have qualified.

Section 4 ▪ The Congress may by law provide for the case of the death of any of the persons from whom the House of Representatives may choose a President whenever the right of choice shall have devolved upon them, and for the case of the death of any of the persons from whom the Senate may choose a Vice President whenever the right of choice shall have devolved upon them.

Section 5 ■ Sections 1 and 2 shall take effect on the 15th day of October following the ratification of this article.

Section 6 ■ This article shall be inoperative unless it shall have been ratified as an amendment to the Constitution by the legislatures of three-fourths of the several States within seven years from the date of its submission.

AMENDMENT XXI

Section 1 ■ The eighteenth article of amendment to the Constitution of the United States is hereby repealed.

Section 2 ■ The transportation or importation into any State, Territory, or Possession of the United States for delivery or use therein of intoxicating liquors, in violation of the laws thereof, is hereby prohibited.

Section 3 ■ This article shall be inoperative unless it shall have been ratified as an amendment to the Constitution by conventions in the several States, as provided in the Constitution, within seven years from the date of the submission hereof to the States by the Congress.

AMENDMENT XXII

Section 1 ■ No person shall be elected to the office of the President more than twice, and no person who has held the office of President, or acted as President, for more than two years of a term to which some other person was elected President shall be elected to the office of President more than once. But this Article shall not apply to any person holding the office of President when this Article was proposed by Congress, and shall not prevent any person who may be holding the office of President, or acting as President, during the term within which this Article becomes operative from holding the office of President or acting as President during the remainder of such term.

Section 2 ■ This article shall be inoperative unless it shall have been ratified as an amendment to the Constitution by the legislatures of three-fourths of the several States within seven years from the date of its submission to the States by the Congress.

AMENDMENT XXIII

Section 1 ■ The District constituting the seat of Government of the United States shall appoint in such manner as Congress may direct:

A number of electors of President and Vice President equal to the whole number of Senators and Representatives in Congress to which the District would be entitled if it were a State, but in no event more than the least populous State; they shall be in addition to those appointed by the States, but they shall be considered, for the purposes of the election of President and Vice President, to be electors appointed by a State; and they shall meet in the District and perform such duties as provided by the twelfth article of amendment.

Section 2 ■ The Congress shall have power to enforce this article by appropriate legislation.

AMENDMENT XXIV

Section 1 ■ The right of citizens of the United States to vote in any primary or other election for President or Vice President, for electors for President or Vice President, or for Senator or Representative in Congress, shall not be denied or abridged by the United States or any State by reason of failure to pay poll tax or other tax.

Section 2 ■ The Congress shall have power to enforce this article by appropriate legislation.

AMENDMENT XXV

Section 1 ■ In case of the removal of the President from office or of his death or resignation, the Vice President shall become President.

Section 2 ■ Whenever there is a vacancy in the office of the Vice President, the President shall nominate a Vice President who shall take office upon confirmation by a majority vote of both Houses of Congress.

Section 3 ■ Whenever the President transmits to the President pro tempore of the Senate and the Speaker of the House of Representatives his written declaration that he is unable to discharge the powers and duties of his office, and until he transmits to them a written declaration to the contrary, such powers and duties shall be discharged by the Vice President as Acting President.

Section 4 ■ Whenever the Vice President and a majority of either the principal officers of the executive departments or of such other body as Congress may by law provide, transmit to the President pro tempore of the Senate and the Speaker of the House of Representatives their written declaration that the President is unable to discharge the powers and duties of his office, the Vice President shall immediately assume the powers and duties of the office as Acting President.

Thereafter, when the President transmits to the President pro tempore of the Senate and the Speaker of the House of Representatives his written declaration that no inability exists, he shall resume the powers and duties of his office unless the Vice President and a majority of either the principal officers of the executive department or of such other body as Congress may by law provide, transmit within four days to the President pro tempore of the Senate and the Speaker of the House of Representatives their written declaration that the President is unable to discharge the powers and duties of his office. Thereupon Congress shall decide the issue, assembling within forty-eight hours for that purpose if not in session. If the Congress, within twenty-one days after receipt of the latter written declaration, or, if Congress is not in session, within twenty-one days after Congress is required to assemble, determines by two-thirds vote of both Houses that the President is unable to discharge the powers and duties of his office, the Vice President shall continue to discharge the same as Acting President; otherwise, the President shall resume the powers and duties of his office.

AMENDMENT XXVI

Section 1 ■ The right of citizens of the United States, who are eighteen years of age or older, to vote shall not be denied or abridged by the United States or by any State on account of age.

Section 2 ■ The Congress shall have power to enforce this article by appropriate legislation.

AMENDMENT XXVII

No law, varying the compensation for the services of the Senators and Representatives, shall take effect, until an election of representatives shall have intervened.

The Declaration of Independence

IN CONGRESS, JULY 4, 1776. THE UNANIMOUS DECLARATION OF THE THIRTEEN UNITED STATES OF AMERICA.

When in the Course of human events, it becomes necessary for one people to dissolve the political bands which have connected them with another, and to assume among the powers of the earth, the separate and equal station to which the Laws of Nature and of Nature's God entitle them, a decent Respect to the Opinions of Mankind requires that they should declare the causes which impel them to the separation.

We hold these truths to be self-evident, that all men are created equal, that they are endowed by their Creator with certain unalienable Rights, that among these are Life, Liberty and the Pursuit of Happiness. That to secure these rights, Governments are instituted among Men, deriving their just powers from the consent of the governed, that whenever any Form of Government becomes destructive of these Ends, it is the Right of the People to alter or to abolish it, and to institute new Government, laying its foundation on such principles, and organizing its Powers in such form, as to them shall seem most likely to effect their Safety and Happiness. Prudence, indeed, will dictate that Governments long established should not be changed for light and transient causes; and accordingly all experience hath shewn, that mankind are more disposed to suffer, while evils are sufferable, than to right themselves by abolishing the forms to which they are accustomed. But when a long train of abuses and usurpations, pursuing invariably the same Object, evinces a design to reduce them under absolute Despotism, it is their right, it is their duty, to throw off such Government, and to provide new Guards for their future security. Such has been the patient Sufferance of these Colonies; and such is now the necessity which constrains them to alter their former Systems of Government. The history of the present King of Great Britain is a history of repeated injuries and usurpations, all having in direct object the Establishment of an absolute Tyranny over these States. To prove this, let Facts be submitted to a candid world.

He has refused his Assent to Laws, the most wholesome and necessary for the public good.

He has forbidden his Governors to pass Laws of immediate and pressing importance, unless suspended in their operation till his Assent should be obtained; and when so suspended, he has utterly neglected to attend to them.

He has refused to pass other Laws for the accommodation of large districts of people, unless those people would relinquish the right of Representation in the Legislature, a right inestimable to them, and formidable to tyrants only.

He has called together legislative bodies at places unusual, uncomfortable, and distant from the depository of their public Records, for the sole purpose of fatiguing them into compliance with his measures.

He has dissolved Representative Houses repeatedly, for opposing with manly firmness his invasions on the rights of the people.

He has refused for a long time, after such dissolutions, to cause others to be elected; whereby the Legislative powers, incapable of the Annihilation, have returned to the People at large for their exercise; the State remaining in the mean time exposed to all the dangers of invasion from without, and the convulsions within.

He has endeavoured to prevent the population of these States; for that purpose obstructing the Laws for Naturalization of Foreigners; refusing to pass others to encourage their migrations hither, and raising the conditions of new Appropriations of Lands.

He has obstructed the Administration of Justice, by refusing his Assent to Laws for establishing Judiciary powers.

He has made Judges dependent on his Will alone, for the Tenure of their offices, and the amount and payment of their salaries.

He has erected a multitude of New Offices, and sent hither swarms of Officers to harrass our people, and eat out their substance.

He has kept among us, in times of peace, Standing Armies, without the Consent of our Legislatures.

He has affected to render the Military independent of and superior to the Civil power.

He has combined with others to subject us to a jurisdiction foreign to our constitution, and unacknowledged by our laws; giving his Assent to their Acts of pretended Legislation:

For quartering large bodies of armed troops among us:

For protecting them, by a mock Trial, from punishment for any Murders which they should commit on the Inhabitants of these States:

For cutting off our Trade with all parts of the world:

For imposing Taxes on us without our Consent:

For depriving us, in many Cases, of the benefits of Trial by Jury:

For transporting us beyond Seas to be tried for pretended Offences:

For abolishing the free System of English Laws in a neighbouring Province, establishing therein an Arbitrary government, and enlarging its Boundaries so as to render it at once an example and fit instrument for introducing the same absolute rules into these Colonies:

For taking away our Charters, abolishing our most valuable Laws, and altering fundamentally the Forms of our Governments:

For suspending our own Legislatures, and declaring themselves invested with power to legislate for us in all cases whatsoever.

He has abdicated Government here, by declaring us out of his Protection and waging War against us.

He has plundered our Seas, ravaged our Coasts, burnt our towns, and destroyed the lives of our people.

He is at this time transporting large Armies of foreign Mercenaries to compleat the works of death, desolation, and tyranny, already begun with circumstances of Cruelty and perfidy scarcely paralleled in the most barbarous ages, and totally unworthy the Head of a civilized nation.

He has constrained our fellow Citizens taken Captive on the high Seas to bear Arms against their Country, to become the executioners of their friends and Brethren, or to fall themselves by their Hands.

He has excited domestic insurrections amongst us, and has endeavoured to bring on the inhabitants of our frontiers, the merciless Indian Savages, whose known rule of warfare, is an undistinguished destruction, of all ages, sexes and conditions.

In every stage of these Oppressions we have Petitioned for Redress in the most humble terms: Our repeated Petitions have been answered only by repeated injury. A Prince, whose character is thus marked by every act which may define a Tyrant, is unfit to be the ruler of a free people.

Nor have We been wanting in attentions to our British brethren. We have warned them from time to time of attempts by their legislature to extend an unwarrantable jurisdiction over us. We have reminded them of the circumstances of our emigration and settlement here. We have appealed to their native justice and magnanimity, and we have conjured them by the ties of our common kindred to disavow these usurpations, which, would inevitably interrupt our connections and correspondence. They too have been deaf to the voice of justice and of consanguinity. We must, therefore, acquiesce in the necessity, which denounces our Separation, and hold them, as we hold the rest of mankind, Enemies in War, in Peace, Friends.

We, therefore, the Representatives of the united States of America, in General Congress, Assembled, appealing to the Supreme Judge of the world for the rectitude of our intentions, do, in the Name, and by Authority of the good People of these Colonies, solemnly publish and declare, That these United Colonies are, and of Right ought to be, Free and Independent States; that they are absolved from all Allegiance to the British Crown, and that all political connection between them and the State of Great Britain, is and ought to be totally dissolved; and that as Free and Independent States, they have full Power to levy War, conclude Peace, contract Alliances, establish Commerce, and to do all other Acts and Things which Independent States may of right do. And for the support of this Declaration, with a firm reliance on the protection of divine Providence, we mutually pledge to each other our Lives, our Fortunes, and our sacred Honor.

Signed by Order and in Behalf of the Congress,
JOHN HANCOCK, PRESIDENT.

Attest. CHARLES THOMSON, Secretary.

Philadelphia: Printed by JOHN DUNLAP.

Key Terms Glossary

acceptance The second party's unqualified willingness to go along with the first party's proposal

accord and satisfaction A legal way to settle contractual disputes by which one party agrees to accept less than the amount due as full payment

actual authority The real power a principal gives to an agent

actual notice A formal notice given directly to a party, usually using certified mail with a receipt

adhesion contract A take-it-or-leave-it offer made by a party who holds most of the power in a bargaining session

administrative law The body of rules created by government agencies

adultery When one spouse has sexual relations with someone outside of marriage

affinity Related by marriage

agency A type of working relationship in which one person represents another person in a business transaction with a third party

agency by estoppel When the principal's actions lead the third party to believe that the agent is working for the principal

agent The person who has been authorized to do the work

agent's agent An agent who is appointed by another agent without the principal's authority to do so

alimony An allowance for support paid to one person by the former spouse in a divorce

Alternative dispute resolution Parties try to resolve disagreements outside of the usual court system, by mediation, arbitration, conciliation, and negotiation

annual percentage rate (APR) The true interest rate of the loan

annulment A declaration by the court that a marriage was never valid

apparent authority Authority that a third party believes an agent has while acting on behalf of the principal

appellate court The U.S. courts of appeals in the federal system; hears appeals and reviews cases from the lower courts

arraignment A formal hearing during which the defendant is read the indictment or information and is asked to plead guilty or not guilty

arrest Occurs when a person is legally deprived of his or her freedom

articles of incorporation A legal document filed with the state to establish a corporation

assault Attempt to commit a battery

asset acquisition When one corporation agrees to purchase the assets, such as property, buildings, and equipment, of a second corporation

assignment The transfer of a right under contract

assumption of risk A defense against negligence that is raised when the plaintiff knew of the risk and still took the chance of being injured

bail Money or other property that is left with the court to assure that a person who has been arrested, but released, will return to trial

bailment The transfer of possession and control of personal property to another with the intent that the same property will be returned later

bankruptcy The legal process by which a debtor can make a fresh start through the sale of assets to pay off creditors

battery The unlawful touching of another person

beneficiary The person named in an insurance policy to receive the proceeds of the policy

bigamy The illegal act of having two spouses at the same time

bilateral contract A contract that contains two promises: one party promises to do something in exchange for the other's promise to do something else

bill of sale Formal evidence of ownership

breach of contract When one party to a contract fails to perform the duties spelled out by the contract

burglary Breaking and entering a house or other structure to commit a felony

capacity The legal ability to enter into a contract

carrier A business that transports persons, goods, or both

certificate of incorporation A corporation's official authorization to do business in a state

Chapter 11 bankruptcy A type of bankruptcy that allows businesses to reorganize their financial affairs and still remain in business

Chapter 12 bankruptcy A form of bankruptcy that lets family farmers, and fishing businesses, create a plan for debt repayment that allows them to keep their operations running

Chapter 13 bankruptcy A form of bankruptcy that permits individual debtors to reorganize their debts and develop payment plans

Chapter 7 bankruptcy A type of bankruptcy that allows individual debtors to discharge all their debts and make a fresh start; ordinary bankruptcy

class action suit A lawsuit shareholders with a common claim can bring as a group against a corporation

collateral The property that is offered as a security interest

collective bargaining A process in which union and management representatives get together to work out issues such as wages, working conditions, and hiring and firing policies

Commerce Clause A statement in Article I of the Constitution giving Congress the power to regular commerce among the states

common carrier A carrier that is compensated for providing transportation to the general public

common law A set of laws made by the courts that provide a series of consistent rules that later courts must follow

common-law marriage An informal type of marriage created by the parties themselves

comparative negligence A defense against negligence which is raised when the carelessness of each party is compared to the carelessness of the other party

compensation Fair payment for the job performed

conglomerate A corporation that owns many different types of companies

consanguinity Related by blood

consideration The exchange of benefits and detriments by the parties to a contract

consolidation When two or more companies join together to form a new corporation

constitution A country's formal document that spells out the principles by which its government operates

Consumer Credit Protection Act A federal law that requires creditors to inform consumers of the costs and terms of credit; Truth in Lending Act

contract Any agreement enforceable by law

contributory negligence A defense against negligence when the defendant can show the victim did something to help cause his or her own injuries

copyright A right granted to an author, composer, photographer, or artist to publish and sell an artistic or literary work

corporate director A person elected by shareholders to make broad policy decisions in the running of a corporation

corporate officer A person chosen by the directors to run the day-to-day affairs of a corporation

corporation An entity with a legal authority to act as a single person distinct from its owners

counteroffer A response to an offer in which the terms of the original offer are changed

credit An arrangement in which one may receive cash, goods, or services now and pay in the future

creditor The party who sells the goods on credit or lends the money

crime An offense committed against the public good, or society

cyberblackmail The use of information unlawfully obtained by computer to pressure a victim into granting a payoff to the blackmailer

cybercrime Any criminal activity associated with a computer

cyberdefamation The communication via computer or other electronic device of false data that damages a person's reputation

cyberinvasion of privacy An unwelcome intrusion into the private matters of an individual carried out or sustained by a computer

cyberlaw The area of law that concerns computer and computer-related crimes

cyberpiracy A crime that involves using a computer to steal computer data stored in a digital formal

cyberspoofing A crime in which a cybercriminal falsely adopts the identity of another computer user or creates a false identity on a computer Web site in order to commit fraud

cybertort The invasion, theft, falsification, misuse, or deletion of data stored in a computer

cybertrespass Any illegal activity already in the criminal code committed by using a computer

cybervandalism Disrupting, damaging, or destroying a Web site or computer network

damages Payment recovered in court by a person who has suffered an injury

debtor The party who buys the goods on credit or borrows money

deed A written instrument that transfers title of ownership of property

default A failure in making timely payments on a loan

defendant A person who is accused of a crime

delegation Transferring of a duty under a contract

derivative suit A lawsuit a shareholder can bring on behalf of the corporation to correct an injury to the corporation

detention hearing A court session during which the judge tries to learn whether there are good reasons to keep an accused juvenile in custody

digital signature An encoded message that appears at the end of a contract created online

direct suit A lawsuit a shareholder can bring against a corporation for denying his or her rights as a shareholder

disaffirm To show the intent not to live up to a contract

discharge by agreement The act of ending contracts by mutual agreement

discrimination The unequal treatment of individuals based on sex, age, race, nationality, or religion

disparate impact When an employer has an employment policy that appears neutral on its surface, but has an unfair impact on members of a protected class

disparate treatment When an employer intentionally discriminates against an individual or a group of individuals belonging to a protected class

dissociation When a partner is no longer associated with a firm

dissolution The breakup of a partnership or any legal entity

divorce A declaration by the court that a valid marriage has come to an end; sometimes called dissolution of marriage

domain name The Internet address of a business

double representation When an agent works simultaneously for two competing principals

draft An order to a third party to pay money

drawee The person to whom an order is given to pay money in a draft

drawer The person who orders money to be paid in a draft

duress The act of destroying somebody's free will by force, threat of force, or bodily harm

easement An irrevocable right to the limited use of another's land

e-commerce (Electronic commerce) The process of conducting business using electronic means, especially the Internet

electronic fund transfer (EFT) A computerized system for transferring funds electronically rather than by writing checks

emancipation Freeing someone from the control of another; especially a parent's relinquishing authority and control over a minor child

eminent domain The right of the government to take private land for a public purpose

employment-at-will Based on the principle that each party should be free to end the employment relationship at any time without penalty

Environmental Protection Agency (EPA) The federal agency responsible for protecting the environment

Equal Credit Opportunity Act (ECOA) Makes it illegal for banks and businesses to discriminate against credit applicants on the basis of their gender, race, marital status, national origin, religion, age, or because they get public assistance income

equal pay rule A standard that states that employers working in interstate commerce must pay women the same rate of pay as men holding the same type of job

estate The interest or right that a person has in real property

ethics The rules used to determine the difference between right and wrong

eviction Occurs when a landlord deprives a tenant of the possession of the premises

executor/executrix The person named to carry out the terms of a will (executor—male; executrix—female)

express authority Comes from the orders, commands, or instructions a principal explicitly gives an agent

express contract A contract statement that may be oral or written

express warranty An oral or written statement, promise, or other representation about the quality of a product

expropriation When a government seizes a privately-owned business to be used for a public service

Fair Credit Billing Act Requires creditors to correct billing errors brought to their attention

Fair Credit Reporting Act A federal law that grants people the right to know what is contained in their credit reports

Fair Debt Collection Practices Act (FDCPA) Prohibits certain practices by debt collectors

Federal Energy Regulatory Commission (FERC) Part of the Department of Energy, this agency regulates electricity and natural gas

felony A major crime

fiduciary relationship A relationship based on trust

finance charge The cost of the loan in dollars and cents

firm offer A merchant's written promise to hold an offer open for the sale or lease of goods.

fixtures Items of personal property attached in such a way that they become real property

forbearance The act of not doing what you have the right to do

forgery The fraudulent making or material alteration of a writing

franchise A license a company grants to a business or individual for the right to use its name and sell its products or services

fraud A deliberate deception intended to secure an unfair and unlawful gain

full warranty An assurance that a defective product will be repaired or replaced without charge within a reasonable time

garnishment The legal procedure through which a worker's earnings are withheld for payment of a debt

general agent An agent who has authority to perform any act within the scope of a business

genuine agreement An agreement that is true and genuine: a valid offer is met by a valid acceptance

gratuitous bailment A bailment for the sole benefit of the bailor

holder A person who possesses a negotiable instrument payable to "the order of" the person holding it or to "bearer"

holder in due course A holder who takes an instrument for value, in good faith, and without notice that the instrument is defective

identity theft Using a computer to steal financial, employment, educational, medical, and personal data

implied authority Additional authority that allows an agent to perform reasonable acts necessary to carry out the express authority

implied contract A contract that comes about from the actions of the parties; a contract that exists when an employer has said, written, or done something to lead an employee to reasonably believe that he or she is not an at-will employee

implied covenant A legal argument that holds that any employment relationship is based on an implied promise that the employer and employee will be fair and honest with one another

implied warranty A guarantee of quality imposed by law

impossibility of performance When one of three situations prevent the performance of a service contract: a death or illness that prevents the performance of a personal service contract; the destruction of the exact subject matter, or the means for performance; and illegality

indemnification Payment for losses suffered by an agent because of a principal's instructions

independent contractor A person who works for a proprietor to perform a particular task using his or her own tools and deciding the best way to do the job

indorsement The act of placing one's signature on an instrument, usually on the back, to transfer it to another

infraction A minor offense that is usually punishable with a fine and not with jail time

injunction A court order that prevents a party from performing a specific act

insider trading When a corporate director or officer buys or sells shares in a corporation based on firsthand information about the corporation that is not available to the public

insurable interest A legal interest in the protection of property from injury, loss, or destruction

insurable interest The financial interest a policyholder has in the person or property that is insured and would suffer from the loss of

insurance An agreement in which one party (the insurer) compensates another party (the insured) for any losses

intellectual property An original work fixed in a tangible medium of expression

intentional tort Actions that hurt, embarrass, or scare other people

interest A fee charged by creditors for lending money or extending credit

intestate To be without a will

invitations to negotiate Invitations to deal, trade, or make an offer

involuntary bankruptcy When creditors begin the proceeding instead of the debtor

joint liability Liability shared by two or more people

jurisdiction A court's power to hear a case and make a judgment

justice Treating people fairly and equally

larceny The unlawful taking of someone's personal property with the intent to keep the property away from that person

law A system of rules of conduct established by a country's government to maintain stability and justice according to the values that are relevant to that country

lease The contract between a tenant and a landlord

lessee The tenant in a lease

lessor The landlord in a lease

license A temporary, revocable right to the limited use of another's land

lien A legal claim against another person's property as a security for a debt or loan to ensure it will be paid

Key Terms Glossary

Key Terms Glossary

limited liability company (LLC) An entity with the legal authority to act as a single person distinct from its owners and combines the best features of a partnership and a corporation

limited liability partnership A registered partnership in which each partner is not liable for the acts of the other partners

limited partnership A partnership formed by two or more persons, with one or more general partners and one or more limited partners

limited warranty Any written warranty that does not meet the requirements of a full warranty

majority The status of reaching the age of adulthood, 18 in most states

manslaughter Voluntary or involuntary killing of another person without intending to do so

maker The person who promises to pay money in a note

marriage Defined by most states and the federal government as the legal union of one man and one woman as husband and wife

merger When two companies join together, with one company keeping its corporate identity and the other company losing its corporate identity

minor A person who has not yet reached the age of adulthood

mirror image rule The terms stated in the acceptance must exactly mirror or match the terms of the offer

misdemeanor A less-serious crime

monopoly A business situation in which one person, company, or group of companies controls the market for a product or service

morality The values that govern a group's ideas about right and wrong

murder The intentional killing of another person

mutual benefit bailment A bailment in which both the bailor and bailee receive benefits

negligence A tort that results when one person carelessly injures another

negotiable instrument A written document giving legal rights that may be passed to others by endorsement or delivery; commercial paper

negotiation The transfer of an agreement in such a way that the transferee becomes a holder

no-fault divorce A divorce granted without either party having to prove the other party guilty of misconduct

nondelegable duty A duty that cannot be delegated, or transferred, to another party

note A written promise to pay money; promissory note

notice by publication Notice usually given by publishing a notice in a local newspaper

Nuclear Regulatory Commission (NRC) Part of the Department of Energy, this agency regulates nuclear energy

Occupational Safety and Health Administration (OSHA) The federal government agency that regulates health and safety standards for companies in the United States

offer A proposal by one party to another intended to create a legally binding agreement

partnership An association of two or more persons to carry on as co-owners of a business for profit

patent A grant giving an inventor the exclusive right to make, use, or sell an invention for a period set by Congress

payee The person to whom the promise is made in a note

pension plan A program established by an employer or a union to provide income to employees after they retire

personal property Everything, other than real property, that can be owned

plaintiff The party that accuses a person of a crime

polygamy The illegal act of having more than two spouses at the same time

power of attorney Any writing granting someone authority to act as an agent

premium The amount of money an insured pays for insurance coverage

prenuptial agreement A written and signed legal contract couples make before getting married dealing with property and support issues

principal The person who authorizes someone to represent his or her interests

probate The process of validating and executing a will

promissory estoppel The principle that a promise made without consideration may nonetheless be enforced to prevent injustice

prosecutor The government official who brings the case against the defendant

prospectus A document that contains a detailed explanation of the stock offering for potential investors

proximate cause When the link between negligent conduct and injury is strong enough to be recognized by the law

public policy A legal principle that holds that nobody should be allowed to do something that harms the public

public policy tort A legal theory that permits a discharged employee to bring a wrongful discharge lawsuit against a former employer based on the argument that the firing somehow hurts the public at large

punitive damages Money payments for damages that go beyond what the innocent party actually lost and that are designed to punish the wrongdoer

ratification The act of agreeing to go along with a contract that could have been avoided

real property The ground and everything permanently attached to it

registration statement A general description of the securities and of the company making the offer

reimbursement Payment for money spent by an agent on behalf of a principal

rejection A refusal of an offer by the offeree that brings the offer to an end

remedy A legal means of enforcing a right or correcting a wrong

repossession When a creditor reclaims property on which it has a lien if the debtor does not make payment

respondeat superior A legal doctrine that holds that the master is responsible for the torts of his or her servants

revocation The taking back of an offer by the offeror

Key Terms Glossary

risk of loss The responsibility for loss or damage to goods

robbery The wrongful taking of someone's property by threatening or using violence

secured loan A loan which is backed up by property that the creditor can take if the loan is not repaid

security A monetary investment that seeks to make a profit solely because another's efforts

security interest A creditor's right to use collateral to recover a debt

self-dealing When agents make deals that benefit themselves rather than their principal

share A single unit of ownership in a corporation

shareholder An individual who owns shares of a corporation

Social Security A government program that provides continuing income to workers and their dependents when their earnings stop or are reduced because of retirement, disability, or death

sole proprietorship A form of business that is owned and operated by one person

special agent An agent whose authority is restricted to accomplishing only a specific job or purpose; limited agent

special bailment A bailment for the sole benefit of the bailee

statute A law passed by a government body that has been made for the purpose of creating laws

Statute of Frauds A state law that requires that certain contracts be in writing so that there is evidence that the contract exists and that it has certain definitive terms

statute of limitations Establishes a time limit for suing in a civil case, based on the date when the breach occurred or was discovered

stock acquisition When an individual or a corporation buys enough shares of stock in another corporation to take over control of it

straight life insurance Life insurance that requires the payment of premiums until the face value is reached or the insured is deceased; also called ordinary life or whole life

strict liability A legal doctrine that says some activities are so dangerous that liability will always follow any injury that results from those activities

subagent An agent lawfully appointed by another agent

sublease The transfer of part of the term of a lease, but not the remainder of it, to someone else

substantial performance A situation in which a party has, in good faith, completed the major requirements of a contract, leaving only a few minor details unfinished

tenancy An interest in the real estate they lease; leasehold estate

tender An offer to do what you have agreed to do under a contract

term insurance Life insurance issued for a particular period, usually five or ten years

testamentary capacity The mental ability (being of sound mind) to create a will

testamentary intent The intention that the document is meant to be a last will and testament

testator/testatrix A person who dies with a will (testator—male; testatrix—female)

third party The person with whom the agent does business on behalf of the principal

title The right of ownership to goods

tort A private wrong committed by one person against another

tortfeasor A person who commits a tort

trust A legal device by which property is held by one person for the benefit of another

trustee A person who holds title to the property for another's benefit

unconscionable contract An agreement in which the consideration is so out of line with the actual value of the subject matter and so unfair that shocks the court's conscience

undue influence An action or series of overly persuasive actions that make inappropriate use of one person's position of power over another person to create an agreement that is very favorable to the person with all the power

unemployment compensation A system of government payments to people who are out of work and looking for a job

Uniform Commercial Code (UCC) A collection of laws that governs various types of business transactions

unilateral contract A contract that contains a promise by only one person to do something, if and when the other party performs some act

union An organization of employees formed to promote the welfare of its members

unlimited liability A legal duty placed on a business owner that requires the owner to be responsible for all losses experienced by the business

usury law A law restricting the amount of interest that can be charged

vandalism Willful or malicious damage to property

voidable title A title that may be canceled if the injured party chooses to do so

voluntary bankruptcy When a debtor files for bankruptcy to eliminate or reduce the burden of debt

warranty A guarantee, usually by a seller to a buyer, that a product will perform as promised

warranty of fitness for a particular purpose An implied warranty that goods will be fit for a specific use

warranty of merchantability An implied warranty that goods are fit for the ordinary purpose for which the goods are sold

will A document that is signed during your lifetime that provides for the distribution of your property upon death

workers' compensation An insurance program that provides income for workers who are injured on the job or develop a disability or disease as a result of their job

Academic Terms Glossary

A

acquired Gained possession of

adhere To carry out a plan, or an operation without deviation; to stick to

administer To manage or direct

advantage Benefit, profit, or gain

affected Influenced by

alternative A situation presenting a choice between two mutually exclusive possibilities

apparent Appearing as such, seeming

assets Property, tangible and intangible, including cash, inventories, and property rights

assign To transfer to another

assume To take on; adopt

assumption Something taken for granted or accepted as true without proof

B

benefit Something that promotes well-being; a useful aid

broadcast To send out or communicate, especially by radio, television, or the Internet

C

capacity Ability to perform or produce

ceremony A formal act performed as prescribed by ritual or custom

certify To confirm formally as true or genuine

commerce The exchange or buying and selling of goods on a large scale

compensate To make up for a loss

comply To act in accordance with another's command or request

comprehensive Covering completely or broadly

conduct To direct, manage, control, or carry out

confidential Communicated or entrusted in secret

consent To give approval

contain To have as component parts; include or comprise

contempt Open disrespect or willful disobedience of a court or legislative body

cooperation The act of working together toward a common end or purpose

corruption Impairment of integrity, morals, and honesty; promoting wrong by improper or illegal means

D

definite Unquestionable; certain; precise

determine To decide or settle conclusively or definitely

directive An order or instruction, especially one issued by a central authority

discharge To set aside; annul

disclose To make known

dispensing Distributing; dealing out in portions

distress Anxiety or mental suffering

domestic Relating to home or household, or to a specific state or country

dominant Exercising the most influence or control

dormant Inactive

download Transfer data from a computer to another device

duplicate Identically copied from an original

effective In force; in effect

elective A choice; an option

emission A substance that is discharged

empathy Understanding, being sensitive to

endowment The act of furnishing with an income

exaggerate To enlarge beyond the truth; overstate

exceed To go beyond the limits of; surpass

exception Something omitted, excluded, or neglected

exclude To prevent from being included, considered, or accepted; reject

exclusive Not divided or shared with others

expire To come to an end; terminate

exploit To make use of unfairly for one's own advantage

extent The degree to which something is stretched out

foreseeable To see or know beforehand

genuine Actually possessing the apparent attribute or character; authentic

gratuitous Given or received without cost or obligation; free.

impersonate To assume the character or appearance of, especially fraudulently

impose To force; to establish as compulsory; to apply by authority

impulse An impelling force; an urge that prompts an unpremeditated act or feeling

incidental Of a minor, casual, or subordinate nature

incompetence Lack of physical or intellectual ability or qualifications

indicating Serving as a sign, symptom, or token of; signifying

informal Appropriate to ordinary, casual, or familiar use

infrastructure The basic facilities, services, and installations needed for the functioning of a community, society, or a system such as the national electronic system

intent The purpose to commit a wrongful act; meaning; significance

involved Connected by participation or association

irrevocable Impossible to take back

jeopardy Exposure to loss or injury

loyal Faithful to a person, ideal, custom, cause, or duty

malicious Deliberately harmful; spiteful

mediator One who intervenes between conflicting parties to bring about an agreement

motive A need or desire that causes a person to act

mutual Possessed in common; having the same relationship

objective Uninfluenced by emotions or personal prejudices; factual

obligation Something one is bound to legally or morally

option The act of choosing; choice

permissible Allowable

permission Formal consent

perpetual Instituted to or continue for an unlimited time

persistent Existing or remaining in the same state for an indefinitely long time; enduring

petition A formal written application requesting a court for a specific judicial action

preemptive Undertaken or initiated to deter or prevent an anticipated situation or occurrence

prevalent Generally or widely accepted, practiced, or favored; widespread

proactive Controlling a situation by causing something to happen rather than waiting to respond to it after it happens

process A series of actions, changes, or functions bringing about a result

proportionate Properly related in size, degree, or other measurable characteristics; corresponding

provision A measure or requirement made beforehand

random Having no specific pattern, purpose, or objective

reasonable Moderate, fair, rational

reconcile To make compatible or consistent; to balance, as a bank statement

reconciliation Reestablishment of a relationship

register To set down in writing; record; enter in a record

require To impose an obligation on; compel

revoke To void or annul by recalling, withdrawing, or reversing

routine Habitual; regular

sabotage Destruction of property or obstruction of normal operations

schedule A plan for performing work or achieving an objective, specifying the order and allotted time for each part

signature A distinctive mark, characteristic indicating identity

significant Having or likely to have a major effect; important

similar Having the same or some of the same characteristics

simulate To have or take on the appearance, form, or sound of; imitate

solicit To seek to obtain by persuasion, entreaty, or formal application

specify To state in detail or as a condition

spouse A marriage partner; a husband or wife

standard A model, measure, or criterion

status The legal character or condition of a person or thing

subscription The completion of a legal instrument (such as a contract or deed) by signing it so that it becomes legally binding and enforceable

subsidize Supported materially or financially

substitute Something that takes the place of another; a replacement; a copy

supplement Something added to complete a thing, make up for a deficiency, or extend or strengthen the whole.

tangible That which can be valued monetarily or touched; real

unanimous Having the agreement of all

unauthorized Not having official permission or approval

unconditional Without conditions or limitations; absolute

uniform Conforming to one principle, standard, or rule; consistent

usury Charging more than the maximum legal interest rate

vacate To make legally void

voluntary Done or undertaken of one's own free will

waiver Intentional relinquishment of a right, claim, or privilege

Academic Terms Glossary

Case Index

Index

Index

Index

Index

N

O

Index

Index

Index

Index

Credits

DATE DUE

GAYLORD			PRINTED IN U.S.A.